P-VII
Basic sources of data
- New data, collected by the researcher for the express purpose at hand
- Available data (as they may be relevant to the research problem)

→ 5

P-VIII
Method of gathering data
- Observation
- Questioning
- Combined observation and questioning
- Other

→ 4

P-IX
Number of properties used in research
- One
- A few
- Many

→ 2, 7, 8

P-X
Method of handling single properties
- Unsystematic description
- Measurement (of variables)

→ 2, 3, 7, 9

P-XI
Method of handling relationships among properties
- Unsystematic description
- Systematic analysis

→ 2, 3, 8, 11

P-XII
Treatment of system properties as
- Unitary
- Collective

→ 4, 7, 8, 9, 10, 12

SOCIOLOGICAL RESEARCH
I. A Case Approach

SOCIOLOGICAL RESEARCH *consists of two volumes: I. A Case Approach. II. Exercises and Manual. The two volumes constitute an integrated program of study, which has been developed in association with:*

JOHN W. RILEY, JR.
RICHARD M. COHN
MARY E. MOORE
MARILYN E. JOHNSON
SARANE S. BOOCOCK
ANNE FONER

SOCIOLOGICAL RESEARCH

I A CASE APPROACH

Matilda White Riley
Rutgers University

Under the General Editorship of
ROBERT K. MERTON
Columbia University

Harcourt, Brace & World, Inc. *New York and Burlingame*

Contents

UNIT ONE
INTRODUCTION TO SOCIOLOGICAL RESEARCH

The Research Process: Empirical Methods · The Research Design · The Conceptual Model · The Research Objective · The Research Findings · Methods of Interpretation   *The Use of Conceptual Models:* Model of a Two-Person Group · Conceptual Model and Theory · Nature of a Social System Model · A Small Group Example · Levels of the Social System · Some Implications for Research · Exploration vs. Hypothesis-Testing · Use of the Model in Research   *Empirical Research Methods:* The Design · The Data · The Specific Procedures · The Principles of Design · Some Alternatives of Research Design · The Research Case · The Time Factor · The Researcher's Control · Assembling the Data · Handling the Data · The Design as a Whole · Criteria for Selection · Design and Conceptual Model · Design and Research Findings · Feasibility   *Methods of Interpretation:* Two Directions of the Process · From Data to Model · From Model to Data · The Interplay Between Data and Model   *How To Use This Book*

UNIT TWO
DESCRIPTIVE CASE STUDIES

Commentary

Malinowski and Trobriand Society: Gathering the Data · Handling the Data · Malinowski's Conceptual Model · Nature of the Social System ·

Some System Properties   *Whyte and the Corner Gang:* Design Decisions · Whyte's Conceptual Model · Nature of the Social System · System Boundaries and Equilibrium · Role as a Connecting Link   *Some Methodological Implications:* Exploratory Research and the Social System Model · Some Advantages of Descriptive Case Studies · Some Limitations of Descriptive Case Studies, and Ways of Offsetting Them · Limitations Imposed by the Researcher's Taking a Role **(P-VIII)** · Manipulating the Role of Participant Observer · Limitations Imposed by Description **(P-X** and **P-XI)** · A Modified Descriptive Approach · Limitations Imposed by the Single Case **(P-II)** · Some Uses of a Sample of a Single Case · Composite Character of the Research Design

Le Play and the Study of the Family: Gathering the Data **(P-VIII)** · Le Play's Use of Measurement **(P-X)** · Use of Data on the Occupational Characteristics of the Workman · Use of Budgetary Data · The Explanatory Supplements · Measurement and Description Combined · Le Play's Use of Many Cases **(P-II)**   *Bales and Small Group Research:* Gathering the Data **(P-VIII)** · Systematic Control of the Action Under Study **(P-VI)** · Bales' Use of Measurement **(P-X)** · Bales' Use of Tables · The Use of Percentages · The Who-to-Whom Matrix · Marginal Information About Total Roles · Cell Information About Dyads · A Mathematical Model · Another Mathematical Model · Graphs and Charts · Bales' Use of Many Cases **(P-II)**   *Some Methodological Implications:* Some Advantages of the Methods Used · The Selective Focus Prescribed by Measurement

Cottrell's Use of Intensive Interviews: Role and System as Research Cases · Intensive Interviews with Both Husband and Wife · Handling Data on Several Members of a Group · An Example of the Difficulties · A Possible Fallacy · Some Potentialities of Collective Measures   *Lundberg and Lawsing and the Sociometric Approach:* The Gathering of Sociometric Data · The Sociogram · Advantages and Limitations of the Sociogram · The Sociometric Matrix · The Role as the Research Case · Collective vs. Unitary Role Measures · Problems of Identification in Collective Measures · The Dyad as the Research Case · The Group as the Research Case · Special Character of the Two-Person Group · Advantages and Limitations of the Sociometric Matrix   *Merton's Study of Influentials:* A Developing Conceptual Model · The Serendipity Component of Research · Procedure for Designating Influentials · A Matrix Based on Statistically Grouped Individuals · The Latent Structure of Orientations   *Some Methodological Implications:* Difference in Focus of Observation and Questioning · Direct Focus · Indirect Focus · Some Pros and Cons of Observation and Questioning · Observation Without Participation · Participant Observation · Questioning of Separate Individuals · Sequences of Questioning and Observation · Other Sources of Information · Questioning the Several Group Members · The Self-Administered Questionnaire · Value of Questioning Group Members

Thomas and Znaniecki and the Use of Letters: Nature and Handling of Data · Some Limitations · Some Advantages   *Zelditch and the Reanalysis of Cross-Cultural Studies:* Use of Existing Cross-Cultural Studies · Some Advantages of Cross-Cultural Analysis · Total Society as Research Case · Limitations of Secondary Analysis · Hypothesis-Testing · Analysis of Deviant Cases · Differing System References   *Sorokin's Study of Long-Term Trends:* Nature of the Data · Available Data and the Study of Historical Trends   *Available vs. New Data:* Forms of Available Data · A General Rule · Combined Use of New and Available Data · Advantages · Disadvantages

Commentary   328

Some Examples of Coding: Zelditch's Coding Procedure · The Place of
Coding in the Research Sequence · Coding Parent-Child Relationships ·
Difficulties of Abstraction · Finding a Standard · The Code as a Link
Between Concept and Data   *Massing's Use of Composite Measures:*
Procedure for Composite Measurement · Content Analysis · Bales' Use
of Composite Measures · Composite vs. Simple Measures   *Bogue's
Use of Collective Measures:* Procedure for Collective Measurement ·
Mathematical Characteristics of Collective Measures · Some Assumptions
Underlying Collective Measures · Individuals vs. Families as the Consti-
tuent Case   *Weber and the Multidimensional Measure:* The Ideal Type
· The Property-Space · A Property-Space for Classifying Religions ·
A Property-Space for Classifying Deviance · The Typology as a Reduc-
tion of the Property-Space   *Some Methodological Implications:* Meas-
urement Rules · Measurement Models · Tests of the Measurement Model

UNIT EIGHT
RELATIONSHIPS AMONG VARIABLES   354

Commentary   402

Strodtbeck and the Testing of Two-Variable Models: Control of Variables
Through Sampling · A Test of Validity · Use of a Statistical Test ·
Testing the Association Between Two Variables · Conceptions of the
Relationship · Use of Mathematical Models in Studying Relationships ·
Another Statistical Test   *Stouffer's Simultaneous Analysis of Several
Explanatory Variables:* Control of Variables Through Cross-Tabulation ·
The Mobility Analysis · The Tolerance Analysis   *Lazarsfeld's Use of
Multivariate Analysis:* Specification of the Relationship · The Relative
"Strength" of Two Relationships · Difficulties of Interpretation   *Durk-
heim's Early Contribution to Multivariate Analysis:* Durkheim's Use
of the Suicide Rate · Tests of Theoretically Derived Hypotheses ·
Elimination of an Extraneous Factor · Test of Religion as an Ex-
planatory Variable · A Difficulty in Analyzing Collective Measures ·
Marriage as an Explanatory Variable · A Four-Variable Analysis · The
Relative "Strength" of Two Relationships—Another Example   *Some
Methodological Implications:* Some Empirical Procedures · Use of Correlations To Describe Populations · Implications for Study of the Case

Commentary 548

Ogburn and Thomas and the Trend Study: Form of the Analysis · Advantages of Such Trend Studies · Control of Confounding Factors · Standardization · Identification of Parts of the System   *Panel Study of Individual Voting Behavior:* Nature of Panel Analysis · Use of the Case in Panel Analysis · Use of Properties in Panel Analysis · A Combined Approach · Samples for Panel Analysis   *Panel Study of Friendship as Social Process:* Lazarsfeld's Scheme for Analysis · Possible Elaborations and Predictions · Use of Mathematical Models · The Problem of Role Identification   *A Combined Approach in the Drug Diffusion Study:* Theoretically Based Trend Models · Identification of Dyads and Roles   *Use of Computers To Simulate Behavior:* Hare's Simulation of Small Group Predictions   *Some Methodological Implications*

UNIT ELEVEN
EXPERIMENTAL DESIGN 570

Commentary 612

The Cambridge-Somerville Youth Study and the Classical Experimental Design: Outline of the Design · Function of a Control Sample · Types of Interim Factors · Offsetting of the Effects of Interim Factors · The Selection of Equivalent Samples · Matching or Stratification · Randomization · The Estimation of Chance Error · Problems of Interpretation · Problems of Empirical Procedure · Conceptual Problems   *Sherif and the Manipulation of Experimental Conditions:* Sherif's Explanatory Variables · Manipulating the Experimental Conditions · One Modification of the Experimental Design   *The Hawthorne Studies and Problems of Control Effect:* Time Periods in a Single-Sample Design · Control Effects · The Log   *Chapin and the Problem of Equivalent Samples:* Problems of the Nonrandom Sample · Utility of the Ex Post Facto Design · Premature Rigor of Design   *Some Implications for Sociological Research:* Elaborations of the Classical Design · Nonexperimental Designs as Modified Experiments · Generalizing from Experimental Findings · Representativeness of the Equivalent Sample Design · Other Restrictions on Generalization · Statistical Tests of Hypotheses · Two Uses of Statistical Tests · Ethical Problems · Theory and Experimental Design · The Importance of Flexibility · The Importance of Planned Design

UNIT TWELVE
SPECIAL PROBLEMS OF SOCIOLOGICAL ANALYSIS

644

Commentary

700

Some Possible Fallacies: From Model to Method · Aggregative Fallacies · Atomistic Fallacies · From Method to Facts · Psychologistic Fallacies · Sociologistic Fallacies · The Data for Social System Analysis   *Davis and Golden and Group Analysis:* Form of the Group Analysis · Nature of the Data · Utility of the Group Analysis · The Combining of Groups · Ambiguity of Collective Measures   *Faris and Dunham and Structural Analysis:* The Initial Group Analysis · Segmental Comparisons · Nature of the Data · Durkheim and Within-Group Analysis · Nature of the Data · Two Forms of Structural Analysis   *James Davis and Contextual Analysis:* An Individual Analysis · Introduction of the Contextual Variable · The Contextual Analysis · Nature of the Data · Comparison with a Structural Analysis · Segmental Comparisons · Within-Group Analysis   *The Analysis of Dyadic Networks:* The Contextual Analysis · Nature of the Data · Supplementary Structural Analysis · Use of Data Based on Dyads   *A Social System Analysis:* Limitations of the Group Analysis · An Example · A Social System Scheme for Two-Person Groups · Some Advantages of Social System Analysis · A Simpler Example · A Complete Tabulation of the Data   *Some Methodological Implications:* Problems of Handling Larger Groups · Extensions of Partial Analyses · Importance of These Problems

FINAL PROGRAM
DESIGNING A STUDY

740

Introduction

Through the years, textbooks have managed to earn a dubious reputation for being dull and plodding, especially when they deal with the methods of inquiry employed in an academic discipline. The reader of *Sociological Research* may therefore find himself a bit puzzled as he experiences a distinct sense of intellectual excitement in working his way through it. Having had the benefit of studying the book in detail, I can give one version of the principal reasons for its being both profoundly instructive and seriously interesting.

The first thing to notice about the book is its systematic character. It presents a program for instructing students in the discriminating use of a wide range of methods now available for collecting sociological data, for analyzing them, and for interpreting them. Each Unit builds upon the Units that have gone before. The program schools the student in the use of procedures which are in turn related to other procedures that enter into the design of an investigation. In this way, the program does much to ensure that the student will progressively see the connections between these diverse procedures, thus avoiding that common fault of considering the components of research discrete and unrelated.

The substance and organization of the program also ensure that the student will acquire a practiced competence in actually using the various methods of sociological inquiry, for he is required throughout to use, not merely to describe or talk about, these methods. In this sense, the program calls for activity rather than passivity on the part of the student. He must try out each procedure in order to learn how to conduct sociological research rather than only to talk learnedly about how it should be conducted. (Evidently the author of this book accepts the important distinction made by William James between direct "acquaintance with" and "knowledge about" matters of skill and learning.) As he goes through his paces, the student finds himself taking a certain pleasure in the craftsmanlike competence with which he is able to handle the difficulties that turn up in actual investigation. He learns how to learn, both from his own accumulating experience in sociological research and from the vicarious experience reported in the many case studies incorporated in the book. Indeed, the orderly step-by-step organization of this program of instruction seems expressly designed to satisfy what Pavlov once described as the indispensable requirement of disciplined knowledge, the need of schooling oneself to "severe gradualness in the accumulation of knowledge. Learn the ABC of science before you try to ascend to its summit. Never begin the subsequent without mastering the preceding . . . [and yet] do not become the archivists of facts. Try to penetrate to the secret of their occurrence, search persistently for the laws which govern them."

As the reader will soon see for himself, the book pivots on the basic idea that empirical research in sociology, as in other disciplines, calls for a series of decisions, of choices among alternative steps needed to collect pertinent data and to analyze them. A repertoire of methods is supplied for each stage of inquiry. The advantage of serially programing these stages is that the student becomes adept at using each of the alternatives from which he will select, in any given investigation, those methods best suited to the problem in hand. By providing a practiced versatility in the use of various research methods, qualitative as well as quantitative, this program helps the student to choose those methods most appropriate for dealing with the theoretical problem, thus helping him to avoid that familiar kind of "trained incapacity" which tempts researchers who are drilled in a limited range of methods to adapt the problem to the methods they happen to know best.

Focused on the conception that research inevitably involves a series of choices among alternative methods, this program avoids the notion of recipes for sociological research. Any such idea is remote from the complex decisions that enter into an investigation worth making. A range of alternatives from which appropriate choices can be made is outlined in a compact paradigm which, set out in Unit 1, is put to use throughout the book, and should help the student to learn to respond with discrimination to the many separate occasions for decision that make up the design for a sociological investigation. The program is arranged to require him to check his tentative decisions against indicated criteria, helping him to learn by reinforcing correct decisions and extinguishing mistaken ones. The student thus learns what to do and how to do it; he also learns what not to do, an integral part of learning what to do.

Still another feature of this program of instruction is its consistent linking up of sociological theory, conceptual models, and methods of empirical investigation. It does not merely advocate theoretically oriented research, but teaches the student how to achieve that widely advertised objective. From the beginning of the program to the end, he is taught how to get at concepts and hypotheses through empirical inquiry. He learns the art of sociological fact-finding, as well as that more subtle art of finding those facts that truly bear upon the combination of concepts set out in a sociological model, or the propositions that make up a sociological theory. What is no less basic, he learns how to arrange and interpret these theoretically pertinent facts once he has them in hand. Throughout the program, he is encouraged to work toward the outermost limits of his "trained capacity" and to become aware of those limits.

The great variety of case studies incorporated in this volume together with the pedagogically useful field and laboratory exercises in the companion volume make this a self-contained program of instruction in methods of investigation.

Guided by the text, the student gains practice in examining published research with a methodologically sensitive eye. More than he might have thought possible, he comes to see and to understand what goes on in these reported investigations and so lays the foundations for subsequent learning from the research literature.

By the time the reader has completed this tight-knit program of instruction, he will not be surprised to discover that the author and her associates took pains to try it out in practice, not once or twice but many times, with all manner of students, ranging from undergraduates at every level to students in their early years of graduate training. Internal evidence attests that the program has been successively—and, I must add, successfully—revised on the basis of an extended teaching experience with it.

In a word, this introduction to the principles and practice of sociological research excites our interest by providing the stuff of authentic education. It makes use of a new format of instruction not for the sake of novelty, but in order to guide the student to a practiced skill in the use of these methods. Once he has faithfully worked through the program developed in this volume and the companion volume of exercises, he will have acquired skill in the principal methods of sociological inquiry, will have learned the grounds for choosing among them in designing a particular investigation, and will have discovered how to translate complex theoretical ideas into appropriate operations of empirical research. Having reached this plane of competence, he will have understandable cause for a degree of intellectual pleasure.

ROBERT K. MERTON

Columbia University
June 15, 1963

Preface

Sociological research today faces unprecedented opportunities. In this era of complex organizations, lonely crowds, and rapid change, experts in research method are increasingly needed both in the development of the basic sociological science and in the expanding fields of sociological application.

Yet these opportunities constitute a challenge. Personnel competent to train the oncoming generation of social researchers are scarce. The materials for methodological training are at once complex and fragmentary. There is no over-arching set of rules for *sociological* research; instead there are many procedures specifically designed for survey research or demographic analysis, for example, or for small group studies or computer simulation of social behavior. All these diverse procedures—often overlapping, sometimes borrowed from other fields, themselves rapidly developing and changing—must be coordinated. Above all, they must be critically reviewed and adapted to the peculiarly sociological objectives of studying groups and societies as social systems, and of understanding individuals as they play roles in such systems.

If the demand for sociological researchers is to be met, a special program of study is needed. Such a program should acquaint the student with the range of available methods. It should familiarize him with specific techniques, and train him in the often tedious routines of using them. More important, it should teach him to identify and to grapple with underlying assumptions—to select only those methods which fit the theory under study. It should stimulate him to modify old tools, or even to invent new ones, as his conceptual scheme and his research objective may require.

To meet the need for such a special program of study, *Sociological Research* has been designed and tested in two universities over several years. This is not a traditional textbook. It aims to teach by example and practice rather than by abstract precept. It brings together the necessary resources from library and laboratory, and is organized in two volumes that constitute an integrated program of study—one volume to be read, studied, and discussed; the other to be used concomitantly as an exercise book and a reference manual. The program of study has five distinctive features:

1. It asks the student to analyze as case examples of research a wide variety of *sociological studies*, in which particular theories have actually been examined by particular research methods and techniques. It thus focuses the attention of students on the design of inquiry as a rounded whole, rather than

fragmenting the design by dealing with each research step separately and requiring student or instructor to consolidate the steps. Experience shows that such a case approach helps the student to comprehend the several aspects of method, the fitting together of these aspects in the total design, and the correspondence between design and sociological objectives and interpretations.

2. The program gives the student firsthand experience with selected research procedures through *field and laboratory exercises*. The exercises, together with the accompanying *manual,* constitute procedural extensions of the case study analyses, indicating how the various techniques of data-gathering and processing —and of sampling, statistical analysis, and statistical-testing—fit into the research process as a whole. (The book does not duplicate the materials typically taught in statistics courses, but indicates the relevance of simple statistical and mathematical models for sociological research, and affords a working knowledge of the basic principles.) No special equipment is required for most exercises. (For the two exercises that give practice with the I.B.M. counter-sorter, there are alternative exercises that demonstrate comparable manual procedures. Decks of I.B.M. cards for the former may be obtained, at a nominal charge to cover shipping costs, from the Sociology Research Laboratory, Rutgers University, New Brunswick, New Jersey.) Each exercise is followed, wherever appropriate, with suggested answers and checklists to enable students—working either independently or in small groups—to teach themselves through self-correction and review.

3. The program is organized in twelve major Units, which first deal with some of the simpler designs, then move on to the more complicated ones, and culminate in the student's planning of a study of his own. Each Unit contains an extensive *commentary*. The commentary rests upon the student's prior reading of specified case studies and his completion of given exercises. It affords a framework within which he is encouraged to synthesize these diverse materials and to focus upon major methodological problems. Each commentary ends with a set of questions for study, class discussion, and review, which stimulate further independent consideration of such problems. Thus the commentary attempts— not to formulate a complete set of methodological principles—but to act as a catalyst toward such formulation.

4. A major aid for organizing the program is the *Paradigm: Some Alternatives of Sociological Research Design* (printed on the front endpaper of Volume I). This lists the basic decisions a researcher makes in planning a study. The student uses it as a scheme for locating his accumulating information about various research methods, their advantages, and their limitations. The subject index (which appears at the end of both volumes) cross-references the methodological points which, treated within the context of actual use, recur in several different parts of the book.

5. A final distinction of the program is its *flexibility* as a teaching device. It is addressed to both undergraduate and graduate students in sociology. The

instructor will find it so designed that undergraduates with no previous training in research can take hold of the fundamentals and grasp a wide array of procedures which they can then put to use. More advanced students are given a thorough and synthesized review of the fundamentals and become aware of many of the special problems actually encountered in social research; they are thus encouraged to adopt methods best suited to the investigation of distinctive sociological problems, rather than turning, almost by rote, to a standardized set of methods.

The suggested program of study, as outlined in the introductions to the twelve Units, has been shown through experience to be adaptable for either a full-year or a single-semester course (which omits certain of the more advanced Units, such as 6, 9, 10, 11, and 12). For both schedules—the full-year or the one-semester course—it is recommended that Unit 1 be read at the beginning as as introduction, and as a summary at the end after the individual project design has been completed. It is recommended also that the exercises be started in advance of the Units to which they belong in order to help students to learn research by doing it and by thinking about it with reference to concrete problems. Within such an over-all framework, individual teachers may want to vary the case studies, to eliminate some exercises and develop others to fit specific class needs, to build upon research projects of their own, or to substitute their own commentary.

Acknowledgments

Sociological Research rests upon the joint efforts of a team of scholars. The program of study has been devised and tested over a period of years in courses taught at Rutgers University and New York University by the author and by her husband and esteemed colleague, John W. Riley, Jr. (formerly Chairman of the Department of Sociology at Rutgers, now Director of Social Research at the Equitable Life Assurance Society of the United States). Richard Cohn, Professor of Mathematics at Rutgers, guided the development of the mathematical and statistical aspects of the program and the treatment of simple probability models as integral parts of the research process. Important contributions were made by Mary E. Moore (now a psychologist in the Department of Psychiatry at the University of Pennsylvania School of Medicine). Assistance in the final drafting of the manuscript was provided by Marilyn E. Johnson (Rutgers), who also prepared the subject index; by Sarane S. Boocock (now of The Johns Hopkins University); and by Anne Foner (New York University). In addition, special contributions to the early development of the manuscript were made by Winston White (now of Marplan); and numerous ideas and improvements were contributed to Volume II by Charles Estus, Coralie Farlee, Frank Fasick, Robert Guerrin, Robert Krauss, Arthur Liebman, June Wells, and Louis

Wilker. The translation of the Le Play study was prepared by Pearl J. Lieff and edited by Paul W. Massing (Rutgers).

The following sociologists were kind enough to read earlier versions of portions of the manuscript and to make valuable suggestions: Robert F. Bales, James S. Coleman, Leonard S. Cottrell, Jr., James A. Davis, Kingsley Davis, Robert E. L. Faris, Uriel G. Foa, Elihu Katz, Paul W. Massing, Talcott Parsons, Frederick F. Stephan, Fred L. Strodtbeck, Jackson Toby, and Morris Zelditch, Jr.

Many others have helped in the successive revisions of the manuscript and the arduous process of committing it to print. Mildred G. Aurelius kept track of the many editorial changes, and prepared the bibliographical references and the name index. The manuscript was produced, under the competent direction of Emily Hahn, by Eileen Dockery, Carol Hackenfort, Marion Erhart, and Margaret Mula. Gail Lenzi, Edward Mednick, and Arlyne Pozner supplied technical help in proofing and checking.

Although much of this assistance came from friends and colleagues who contributed generously of their time, funds from various sources have also helped to make this book possible. A gift from the General Electric Foundation allowed the production and testing of certain parts of Volume II. And a number of methodological principles reported in the book reflect studies conducted in the Rutgers Sociology Laboratory which were supported from research grant M-926 from the National Institute of Mental Health of the National Institutes of Health, Public Health Service; from grant G-5554 from the National Science Foundation; and from a series of grants from the Rutgers Research Council.

To all these persons and agencies the author expresses her profound appreciation. Her final indebtedness is to Robert K. Merton, superb sociologist and long-time friend, who contributed incisive criticism and provocative suggestion.

M . W . R .

SOCIOLOGICAL RESEARCH
I. A Case Approach

UNIT ONE

INTRODUCTION TO SOCIOLOGICAL RESEARCH

Sociological research *assembles, organizes,* and *interprets* facts that help to explain human society. In this book, we shall examine the methods actually used in a variety of studies as concrete examples of sociological research. These studies seek answers to many kinds of questions about social behavior and man's relationship to man. They use many different empirical methods of assembling and organizing facts, and various ways of interpreting them. They deal with widely diversified sociological facts—about individuals in role conflict; about networks of influence in a community; about the economic, religious, or scientific aspects of a single complex society; or about the varied values or occupational structures of many total societies.

Different as these studies are, the scientific importance of each depends, as you will see, upon its ability to contribute new facts to the growing body of sociological knowledge, to test accepted sociological ideas and theories, or to suggest new ones.

The Research Process

It will help us in our major task of analyzing the methods of sociological research if we first locate them in the basic research process which seems to underlie all these varied studies. In brief, we can distinguish two main phases in this process, as suggested in Figure 1-A. In the *empirical phase,* the researcher is led by his sociological ideas and theories to certain facts (his research findings). In the *interpretative phase,* he compares these facts with his initial theories and tries to understand their larger significance. Each of these phases has its own

Figure **1-A**   *Diagram of the research process*

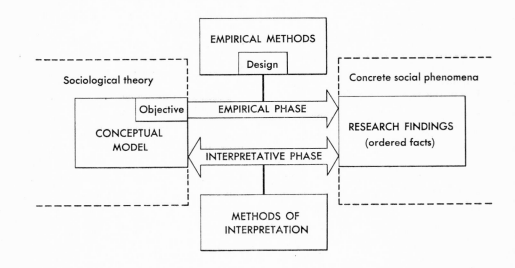

methods, or rules of procedure. The combined methods enable the investigator to bring together for comparison specific facts from the real world of concrete social phenomena, on the one hand, and corresponding ideas and propositions from sociological theory, on the other. Let us outline this process before going on to consider it in further detail.

EMPIRICAL METHODS

We shall devote major attention in this book to the empirical phase, describing and evaluating the empirical methods of research—the rules the investigator follows in seeking new facts and discovering the connections among them.

Sociological investigators today employ many special empirical methods rather than a single unified method. Some conduct controlled experiments in the laboratory; others question cross-section samples of individuals about their opinions and attitudes; still others trace the web of interpersonal attitudes in complex organizations. Some observe and describe small group interaction, while others analyze the volume and density of human populations and the changing rates of marriages, births, and deaths. Some classify and quantify the content of mass communication; others make cross-cultural comparisons of role prescriptions and social structures. Some are concerned with using electronic computers to simulate human behavior, others with allowing for chance errors in statistical inferences from experimental findings.

The Research Design. In each inquiry, the investigator selects—from the common reservoir of these and many other available methods—a particular set of methods that he will follow in obtaining his research findings. We refer to this set of selected methods as the research design.

In making the broad plans for his research design, and in choosing the specific technical procedures he will use to carry it out, he decides how he will select certain facts (his data), how he will classify these facts, how he will seek to uncover the order or pattern in which they actually occur. He may decide as part of his design, for example, to gather new data rather than use available materials; to use a large rather than a small sample of cases; and to use such specific procedures as interviewing with a structured questionnaire and simple random sampling.

THE CONCEPTUAL MODEL

But the research process does not take place entirely at the empirical level, that is, it does not rely exclusively upon observation or experiment. It is more than a set of empirical procedures that yield specific findings. Whether he is aware of it or not, the researcher does not simply "look at all the facts," classifying them or finding correlations among them. His way of selecting certain facts and searching for order among them is guided by some prior notions or theories about the nature of the social phenomena under study.

A researcher may approach the problem of success or failure in marriage, for example, with an image of marriage as the re-enactment of childhood roles. This leads him to abstract relevant facts from the full complexity of phenomena and to report them in special ways. His methods and his findings might be different if his conceptions were different—if, for example, he thought of marriage as the juxtaposition of two sets of personality traits. Another researcher, in studying the diffusion of a message through a community, may proceed on the notion that diffusion occurs mainly through interaction in which citizens talk to one another, rather than simply through mass communication to all citizens directly. Here again the researcher's conception may affect the manner in which he gathers, classifies, and analyzes the data and the character of his findings.

In short, the research process starts with a conceptual model, or an organizing image, of the phenomena to be investigated. That is, it starts with a set of ideas—whether vague hunches or clearly formulated propositions—about the nature of these phenomena. It is this conceptual model, as we shall see, that determines *what questions are to be answered* by the research, and *how* empirical procedures are to be used as tools in finding answers to these questions.

The Research Objective.   The researcher usually states the questions to be answered by the research in the form of a research objective. That is, he states the purposes for which he will gather and analyze the data. The objective may be very general or very specific. It sometimes leads to exploration and sometimes to the testing of hypotheses. It is usually stated rather succinctly, as, for example, to discover uniformities in social interaction, to explore the process of disruption of small groups, to study the conditions determining political behavior, to test the hypothesis that the spouse who talks most will be most likely to win in family arguments, or to observe quantitative fluctuations in the influence of the main systems of values. Each study typically states one or more major objective as well as numerous minor objectives governing specific portions of the research.

Such concisely stated objectives are only part of the larger set of underlying ideas, assumptions, and definitions in the conceptual model. Thus we think of the objective as a few ideas selected from the model that specify the purpose of the investigation.

THE RESEARCH FINDINGS

Guided by the conceptual model and the objective, the researcher then applies the empirical methods he has selected in order to obtain the research findings. These findings consist of sets of facts drawn from the multitude of phenomena in the real world. Protestants are found to be more likely to commit suicide than Catholics, for example; status hierarchies are observed in certain corner gangs; urbanization is seen to vary concomitantly with industrialization at certain periods of time; experimentally treated delinquents show lower recidivism rates than the untreated control sample; and the like.

Thus the findings obtained by empirical methods are reports of empirical regularities—recurring processes, patterns, and structures—in the data.

METHODS OF INTERPRETATION

The researcher rarely concludes the research process with such specific factual findings, for he wants to interpret them. Accordingly, having started with theory, he completes the circle in the interpretative phase by bringing the findings back into the conceptual model, setting the new facts into the context of his ideas.

Here, the methods that he uses—logical reasoning, mathematics, creative imagination—are often, as you will see, hard to define. There is often no straightforward execution of a clear-cut plan, but a working back and forth between theory and data. What the researcher tries to do is to interpret the particular facts he has uncovered by relating them to the more general principles and theories of his conceptual model. In order to explain the finding of a statistical correlation between religion and suicide, for example, he may build a new concept into his model—the notion of the differing degrees of integration characterizing the institutional arrangements of Protestants as compared with Catholics—the differing strength, that is, of the bonds holding individuals to their fellows and to life itself. He uses this new concept to explain the observed empirical regularity in terms of a more general theoretical principle.

Thus a final step in the research process is to interpret the empirical data by incorporating them into the conceptual model. Indeed (although particular studies often have methodological or applied objectives) the major aim of scientific research is to supplement or test the ideas with which the research began—to extend, revise, specify, confirm, or discard the conceptual model.

In this book, we shall see how each piece of sociological research proceeds through these empirical and interpretative phases in the interplay between theory and fact. Let us now prepare for the detailed analyses in the Units to come by considering, first, the *conceptual model* as it affects what facts will be assembled, and how they will be assembled and interpreted; second, the *empirical methods* for assembling these facts and organizing them into specific research findings; and third, the *interpretative methods* for explaining the findings in terms of the conceptual model.

The Use of Conceptual Models

A conceptual model, as used in sociological research, is the researcher's image of the phenomena in the real world that he wants to study.

As a sociologist, he typically wants to study certain aspects of the behavior of human beings in collectivities. His model generally consists of ideas—more or less clearly formulated—about (1) these human beings in collectivities (his *case*), (2) these aspects of behavior (the *properties*), and (3) the ways these aspects fit together and affect each other (the *relationships* among properties). Thus one set of ideas in the model describes the collectivity or part of a collectivity he will use as the case or point of reference for his investigation. This may be a particular type of small group (characterized by sustained interaction); a larger society (whose members share common values although they do not all interact directly with one another); the subgroups into which the collectivity is divided; or the individuals who play roles as members of the group. A second set of ideas in the model refers to certain properties of the case—such as the integration of the group, the attitudes of group members toward one another, the norms which group members generally accept, and so forth. The third set of ideas postulates certain relationships among these properties, as, for example, that increasing social interaction among the members of a group makes for a growing differentiation in their roles. (These abstract distinctions among case, properties, and relationships among properties will be useful when we begin to apply the model in research. See Table 1-A below.)

Many conceptual models are employed in the studies you will be analyzing in this book (although the researcher does not always state his model explicitly). These models are extremely varied. This is partly because the studies focus on different phenomena—one focuses on certain properties of one type of group or society, another on different properties of a different type of case. The models also differ because sociologists, even when they study similar phenomena, do not always agree upon terminology and definitions of concepts. They have not yet developed a single body of definitions and principles from which to build their models.

At the same time, these varied models do have many basic elements in common. And these common elements are important to us in this book—not because as researchers we are interested in the content of particular models—but because we must consider how, in general, conceptual models may be used in sociological research, and because we must evaluate research designs and interpretative procedures in terms of their appropriateness for the kinds of models most commonly used. In this Unit, then, we shall mention some of the ideas and assumptions common in sociological models—provisionally (and sometimes arbitrarily) using terms that we shall need later in translating concepts into empirical operations. You will find that such ideas and assumptions will take on clearer meaning as you encounter them repeatedly in this book.

MODEL OF A TWO-PERSON GROUP

Let us start with some small group examples. A number of the studies and exercises in this book investigate relationships among various properties of two-person groups—married couples, for example, or pairs of friends. It will be helpful, therefore, to define in advance some general ideas that might be contained in the model of so small a collectivity (see, *e.g.,* Parsons *et al.,* 1951).

In a model of a friendship pair, for example, we may think of two actors, *A* and *B,* as interacting with one another as members of the *AB* group. Each is motivated toward certain goals, and has certain attitudes and feelings (orientations) toward the other. Thus *A* may aim to achieve certain personal satisfactions from friendship with *B,* and may like *B* (hold toward him positive cathectic orientations or emotional attitudes). *A* and *B* share certain beliefs about the actual state of affairs and certain values about what is desirable. These common values are built into (institutionalized in) the norms of the *AB* group, and indicate how each partner is ordinarily supposed to act, think, and feel toward the other. Thus interaction among friends may be affected by the norm of reciprocity, for example, by the extent to which *A* and *B* assume that each gesture of friendship is to be returned in kind.

It is important to note that the sociologist, when he constructs the conceptual model, focuses on the *social* aspects of such groups. When he uses the model in research, to be sure, he must deal with concrete groups in which the social aspect does not exist apart from other aspects—i.e., apart from the biological aspects of *A* and *B* as organisms of a particular age and sex, *e.g.,* of a certain skin color, or with certain sexual drives; or apart from the psychological aspects of *A* and *B* as personalities with certain individual capacities, traits of dominance or submission, and so on. As a sociologist, the researcher wants to abstract from the total situation those social properties of special interest to him. Thus his conceptual model deals with individuals, not as rounded wholes, but as they enter into typical or expected behavior in social roles; and with their motives as mechanisms through which the social system functions. Or it deals with values as these define the ideal patterns (norms) governing group behavior.

CONCEPTUAL MODEL AND THEORY

The foregoing example of a two-person group suggests how a model may be built. Ideally, its definitions and assumptions are drawn, in large part, from sociological theory. To be sure, the researcher rounds out his model with any first-hand knowledge he may have of the particular groups to be studied, or any hunches of his own that seem to merit further investigation. But he builds the model, insofar as possible, not from such *ad hoc* fragments, but from the available general theories that seem germane and from appropriate portions of the larger body of sociological knowledge.

When we talk about sociological theory here, we mean not only the sociologist's particular way of thinking about what is going on—his interest, as Kingsley Davis puts it, in "the interpretation of phenomena in terms of their interconnections with societies as going concerns" (Kingsley Davis, 1959, p. 760). We mean not only the common-sense ideas and distinctions employed in everyday discussions of social questions which are still (and perhaps always should be—see Conant, p. 136; Nagel, 1961, Chapter 14) widely employed in sociological theory. More than this, we mean sociological theory as scientific theory—the accumulating body of sociological facts as these are continually being classified, organized, and analyzed in their relations to one another and used as the basis for general propositions and explanatory principles. Despite the present inadequacies of scientific sociological theory in this sense (see, *e.g.,* Shils, 1961; Bierstedt, pp. 23–24), sociological research promises to become increasingly fruitful as it makes use of those theories which are so far available.

Although sociological theory as a whole may not be his domain, the sociological researcher should, then, utilize a *portion* of *theory*—his conceptual model—as an integral part of his research. He should, in advance of any empirical investigation, put together not only the specific related findings of previous studies, but also all formal statements in the sociological literature of relevant general concepts and principles.

NATURE OF A SOCIAL SYSTEM MODEL

One very general idea pervading the models used by many sociologists is that of the collectivity as a social system whose parts and properties are interdependent —an idea we shall find useful in this book in describing various conceptual models and locating them in the research process. Social systems are, of course, only one kind of system: there are biological, physiological, chemical, psychological, cultural, and ecological systems as well. Systemic modes of thinking have much in common, irrespective of the particular kind of system under examination.

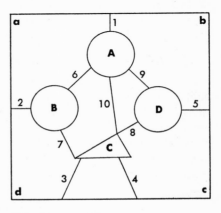

Figure **1-B**   *Henderson's diagram of a system* [a]

[a] Henderson, p. 14.

Lawrence J. Henderson, the late Harvard physiologist, illustrates a system model by a simple mechanical example (see Figure 1-B, and Henderson, pp. 13–14). He says about the figure:

> The four rigid bodies, *A, B, C,* and *D,* are fastened to a framework ... by the elastic bands 1, 2, 3, 4, and 5. *A, B, C,* and *D* are joined one to another by the elastic bands 6, 7, 8, 9, and 10. . . .

> Now imagine the point of attachment of 5 on the frame to be moving toward b, all other points of attachment remaining unchanged. What will happen? Consider *A*. There will be action on *A* by the path 5, 9, by the path 5, 8, 10, and by the path 5, 8, 7, 6. But in each case these actions do not cease at *A*, just as they do not previously cease at *D*. The first, for example, continues along the path 10, 8, and so back to 5.

Thus a definition to keep in mind for later use in our discussions of method is that a system is (1) made up of identifiable *parts,* which are (2) mutually *interde-*

pendent so that each part influences all the others and is in turn influenced by them; and (3) together the several parts form the *system as a whole.*

A Small Group Example. In order to see how this system idea affects the sociologist's image of the empirical groups he plans to study, let us translate the Henderson scheme into a sociological example. Several small group studies in this book use a conceptual model (as suggested in Figure 1-C) in which the bodies *A, B, C,* and *D* in Henderson's drawing may be taken to correspond to the roles of group members as the parts of the system (regarded as the case). The frame then becomes the boundary that sets off the *ABCD* group from its environment, and the rubber bands become the actions and attitudes the members direct

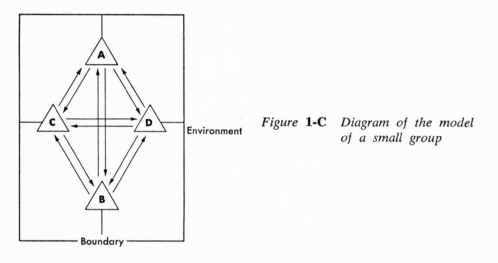

Figure **1-C** *Diagram of the model of a small group*

toward one another and toward other persons and objects in their environment. The roles the individuals play as members of the group are identifiable, so that each has a distinguishable pattern of actions and attitudes (the properties); in the crew of a fishing canoe, for instance, *A* might be the master, *B* the steersman, *C* the watcher for fish, and *D* the caster of nets. And as the group members interact with one another and develop mutual feelings and attitudes, their roles become interdependent, fitting together to form the system of the group as a whole. Thus, a disturbance from outside the system that affects *D* (such as an illness in *D*'s family that prevents him from joining the fishing expedition) would affect each of the other roles and, in turn, react upon the role of *D* himself.

The sociologist often fills in further details of such a model, as you will see later, perhaps describing such properties as how the members interact, how the several roles are integrated and the equilibrium of the group maintained, how each actor adapts to the other members, and how the system adapts to the environment outside the boundary of the group itself. All such properties are bound together in a network of interrelationships—like Henderson's rubber bands.

Levels of the Social System.   In this example we have defined the case at two levels, treating the role as the constituent part of the system and the small group as the higher-level system. But different models define the social system and its social-structural parts at many different levels. Thus the dyadic relationships between pairs of individuals in Figure 1-C might be taken as the parts of the small group as the system. Or, since *A* interacts with *B, C,* and *D* respectively, *A*'s several dyadic relationships might be treated as the parts of *A*'s total group role as the system. Or Figure 1-C might be viewed as a community system within which families are the interdependent parts, or as a country (system) within which regional populations are the parts. A more complex model of the political structure of a state, for instance, might be defined at three levels—consisting of individual voters who make up county subsystems, while the counties in turn fit together into the higher-level system of the state.

The various levels at which social system models may be defined have distinctive meanings for an understanding of social systems in general, and will present different problems when we come to translate the models into empirical operations. You will notice, for example, that the individual—with his characteristics, motivations, and orientations as a person—enters directly into the role, but individuals do not enter directly into the levels of the subgroup, group, or larger society. Thus, certain properties of roles, such as the feelings and attitudes of the individual members, are replaced at the collectivity levels by other types of properties, such as the integration or division of labor that characterizes the collectivity.

Some Implications for Research.   Such examples begin to suggest certain distinctive characteristics of social system models that have pronounced effects, as we shall see, on the methods of sociological research to be considered in this book. The underlying system model requires that the group, for example, be treated neither as a talking and thinking entity in itself, nor as a mere aggregate of discrete individuals whose opinions and attitudes can be simply added together to represent a "mass society." The systemic relationships between parts and whole require special research methods for dealing simultaneously at one level with the identifiable parts, and at a higher level with the inclusive larger system.

The essential interdependence among the parts of any system means, *e.g.,* that a system cannot be analyzed in terms of a simple notion of cause and effect. Many earlier "reductionist" sociological theories tried to explain social phenomena as "caused by" the physical environment, for instance, or by economic factors. That is, a single factor was thought to determine the others in a simple chain of cause and effect. But in the system model, each part is thought to influence each other part, and in turn to be influenced by each. As Henderson says: "If we try to think of all this as cause and effect we must inevitably reach a state of confusion." Ideally, the familiar cause-and-effect analysis must be replaced by other kinds of analysis that will somehow take into account the way in which all the parts interact with and affect one another.

Ultimately, the sociological researcher may solve many of these methodological problems by developing models in which all the key ideas are clearly defined and measurable so that their presumed interrelations can be empirically tested. The Henderson model suggests how a system may sometimes be reduced to a small number of variables, each variable measured quantitatively (Henderson introduces spring balances into the rubber bands), and mathematics used to analyze, as Henderson puts it, "the simultaneous variations of mutually dependent variables" (Henderson, p. 13). Although few sociological models have been handled completely by mathematics in this way (see the analysis of Homans' model by Simon, 1952, for example), we shall later note briefly how electronic computers can aid in the simultaneous analysis of many interrelated variables. We shall also see how certain rather complex—but highly specific—models are sometimes handled in research by the method of detailed qualitative description, as in an ethnographer's account of a particular primitive society.

With such exceptions, however, the researcher does not usually attempt to set forth in his model—and to handle simultaneously in his research—his full set of relevant ideas. Until his theories become more highly articulated and more closely aligned with the relevant facts, he typically works with a partial model— a model that merely outlines the structure of the system under study in order to locate a few fragmentary, but developing, ideas within it. (Compare the use of structural-functional models in sociological theory in, *e.g.*, Parsons, 1951, Chapter 1.)

Most of the studies you will examine in this book illustrate the use in research of models that are partial or generally vague or that select for attention only a portion of the ideas regarded as essential. Some partial models specify just a few selected properties of the system. Other models restrict the focus to a single level of the system. Thus one model may deal only with roles, for example, without fitting the roles together into the higher-level collectivity. Another model may treat the collectivity as a global entity without regard to its parts, as a country's changing prosperity might be related to its changing participation in wars and revolutions without any attempt to identify *which parts* of the society (subgroups or individuals in roles) contribute what acts or orientations to the over-all system pattern.

In using such partial models, the researcher is required, as you will see, to follow one general rule: he must keep in mind the model of the system as a whole. If he selects for attention only two properties of a social system, for example, treating one as the "cause" of the other, he must not disregard the implicit assumption of his model that there are several other properties—all of which are interdependent. Or, if he selects for attention only one level of the system, he must not overlook the other system levels to which it is bound. As long as the underlying idea of the full social system remains implicit in the model, the researcher will be prevented from attempting to reduce the system to one level. He will be protected from the fallacies of reifying either the individual role or the group by locating his analysis and his interpretation of a single selected level within the larger conceptual framework, which includes both the role of the individual actor and the encompassing group or society.

Thus, as you will see, the design of the research must find ways to control, or allow for, the other properties and other levels not selected for attention in the model. And the interpretation of the findings must take into consideration the ways in which the selected properties or levels under immediate study may fit together into the total system.

EXPLORATION VS. HYPOTHESIS-TESTING

A final point to be noted about the model concerns the general character of the research objectives it generates. Just as the model is a selection from theory, the objective is a further selection from the model (although the lines dividing theory, model, and objective are often indistinct). The objective states which elements in the model—which levels of which kinds of groups (cases), which properties, and which connections among properties—are to be investigated; but it is the model that defines, describes, and states the assumptions underlying these elements. Thus the objective can be no more clearly formulated than the set of ideas from which it is drawn, and the clarity of the relevant portion of the model will affect the main emphasis of the objective.

We can distinguish between two broad types of emphasis. On the one hand, the objective may be *exploratory*. If the researcher feels that his model is vague and incomplete, his main purpose may be to learn as much as he can about the properties of the system—about the process, for example, of interaction among the members. The researcher who works with an exploratory objective tries to find clues to what is going on in the system, or tries to gain insights that suggest hypotheses which will improve his model.

On the other hand, the objective may be to *test* certain *hypotheses* or predictions, based on the model, about what the research will find. A model might include the hypothesis that those members of small groups (cases) who interact with one another most intensively (one property) will be most apt to like one another (another property). The researcher might then design a study with the objective of testing this hypothesis, translating his model into research operations by using children's clubs as specimens of small groups, determining which members of these clubs talk and work together most often, and then analyzing the data to see whether in fact these interacting members are the ones who like each other.

Here the researcher hypothesizes in advance that certain properties or elements in the model are related in specified ways; then he is ready to test the hypothesis through research to see whether the conceptual model seems to fit the facts.

The objectives of this hypothesis-testing variety are more definitive than those of exploration. Any body of scientific knowledge rests ultimately upon the development and testing of mutually supporting hypotheses. Nevertheless, it is often difficult to formulate good hypotheses until a considerable amount of exploratory work has been carried out. Premature preoccupation with specific hypotheses may divert attention from the broad exploration of social systems in the round. Hence both types of objective are always important.

USE OF THE MODEL IN RESEARCH

In summary, then, you will see how each of the studies in this book rests— whether explicitly or not—on a conceptual model of a group or society and its properties. This model is clearly distinguishable from the concrete groups the researcher will study and from the observable acts and characteristics he will take as indicants of these concepts.

Each researcher properly makes use of the model at three different stages of the research process. First, he uses it in advance in selecting significant problems when gaps in the theory make exploration necessary, or when theoretical propositions require further testing, or—if he has a practical end in view—in defining applied research objectives within a broader framework. Second, he makes use of the model in selecting appropriate empirical methods for his research design. And third, after obtaining his empirical findings, he interprets them with reference to his larger conceptual scheme.

Thus the conceptual model is a heuristic device serving to guide the formulation and solution of sociological problems. It is a working model—a tentative way of construing a particular set of social phenomena. The researcher will review and revise it in the light of the evidence he obtains. Tolman describes the use of such a working model as "wholly pragmatic"; it can, he says, "be defended only insofar as it proves helpful in explaining and making understandable already observed behavior and insofar as it also suggests new behaviors to be looked for" (Tolman, p. 283).

As sociological theory and knowledge develop, and more and more models are tested through research, we can expect the models used by sociologists to become less fragmentary and tentative. Concepts will become more general, facilitating comparisons among different groups and societies, and enhancing the cumulative character of sociological research. And concepts will become better integrated with one another, so that each model will take on larger meaning as it fits into the emerging body of logically related propositions.

Empirical Research Methods

Once the sociological researcher has worked out a conceptual model (or accepted certain implicit assumptions) and chosen a specific objective, he approaches the empirical phase of his investigation. He now wants to test this model against reality, to find out to what extent his ideas are "right"—that is, to what extent concrete phenomena behave the way he thinks they will. He wants to acquire new knowledge about what is actually going on, so that he will be in a position to extend, or revise, the model. He is ready, then, to employ empirical research methods that will translate his ideas into appropriate operations.

In this Unit, which serves as a brief synopsis of the book and a guide to its use as a program of study, we shall merely outline the kinds of basic decisions the sociologist makes in designing a piece of research, and begin to suggest the bases upon which he makes such decisions.

THE DESIGN

The design of a study is the researcher's plan for assembling and organizing certain concrete facts (his data) by following certain specific rules and procedures.

The Data.   In deciding exactly what his data are to be—what kinds of facts he will examine—he is guided by the nature of the case and its properties as defined in his conceptual model. In order to move from the conceptual to the empirical plane (see Table 1-A), he decides what kinds of concrete *cases* from the real world (such as children's peer groups in a particular school, or the countries in nineteenth-century Europe) to use as specimens of the social system he has in mind. He also decides what kinds of concrete data he will gather to index the *properties* of each case, so that he can organize these data and observe their patterns and *relationships*.

Table **1-A**   *The translation of model into data*

Conceptual	Empirical
Conception of the CASE	Concrete CASES **(P-I)**
Conception of PROPERTIES	Concrete INDICANTS **(P-X)**
Postulated RELATIONSHIPS among properties	Observed RELATIONSHIPS **(P-XI)**

The researcher translates into research operations his idea of each property by selecting certain *empirical indicants* or manifestations of it. In an analogue from the physical sciences, temperature is an abstract idea of a property. As a concrete indicant of the temperature of a body of water (the case), for instance, we find the degree of expansion of a column of mercury in an enclosed tube (a thermometer). In effect, the relative amounts of the abstract quality, temperature, are inferred from the height of the mercury in the tube. Although the sociologist's measuring instruments may be typologies or Guttman scales rather than thermometers, he too must find sense data (such data as answers to questions, the talking and gesturing he observes in interaction, or the reports and documents he finds in the library) that he can use as indicants of the properties in which he is interested: the integration of the group, the group's adaptation to its environment, or the various actions, attitudes, and feelings of the individual group members.

The Specific Procedures. In designing a study, the researcher must also decide what particular set of procedures, techniques, or rules he will follow in selecting and analyzing these data. Here he chooses from a wide array of possibilities—from the details of how to construct a questionnaire or code raw data to how to run tabulations on an I.B.M. machine or compute averages. These are the operations he will perform in order to arrive at his research findings.

The Principles of Design. In making his selections of the data and of the specific procedures he will use, he is basically concerned, of course, with broader problems of empirical method. His design is like the architect's drawings, which consist of the larger plan of the building as well as the detailed specifications for its construction. The researcher must consider not just the technical details of how to construct his questionnaire and how to word specific questions, but whether the questionnaire itself is suitable for the purpose of the inquiry; he must consider not just how to run a particular tabulation, but what the logic of such tabulation is in terms of the problem at hand.

As methodologists, our major concern in this book will be with these more basic design problems. In our analyses of the selected studies, we shall seek the broad principles that underlie particular sets of procedures as applied to particular types of data for particular research objectives.

SOME ALTERNATIVES OF RESEARCH DESIGN

Since the great variety of possible research designs cannot be contained in any simple classificatory scheme, we shall think of design as the *series of basic choices* the researcher makes in planning the types of data to be assembled and organized and the types of procedures to be used in his study. Any given design is a selection from a list of alternatives. A checklist of some of the common choices confronting the researcher is provided in Table 1-B, *Paradigm: Some Alternatives of Sociological Research Design.* This Paradigm will be used as a kind of multidimensional scheme for classifying the research designs discussed throughout the book. It shows at a glance what basic possibilities exist. *You are asked to use this Paradigm as a practical working guide to empirical research methods.* Use it in your critical appraisal of the studies being analyzed, in considering the alternatives open to you in designing your own research, and finally, in determining the important criteria for selecting the most appropriate alternatives.

Table **1-B**   **Paradigm: Some Alternatives of Sociological Research Design**

P-I. *Nature of research case:*
>Individual in role (in a collectivity)
>Dyad or pair of interrrelated group members
>Subgroup
>Group, society
>Some combination of these

P-II. *Number of cases:*
>Single case
>Few selected cases
>Many selected cases

P-III. *Sociotemporal context:*
>Cases from a single society at a single period
>Cases from many societies and/or many periods

P-IV. *Primary basis for selecting cases (sampling):*
>Representational
>Analytical
>Both

P-V. *The time factor:*
>Static studies (covering a single point in time)
>Dynamic studies (covering process or change over time)

P-VI. *Extent of researcher's control over the system under study:*
>No control
>Unsystematic control
>Systematic control

P-VII. *Basic sources of data:*
>New data, collected by the researcher for the express purpose at hand
>Available data (as they may be relevant to the research problem)

P-VIII. *Method of gathering data:*
>Observation
>Questioning
>Combined observation and questioning
>Other

P-IX. *Number of properties used in research:*
>One
>A few
>Many

P-X. *Method of handling single properties:*
>Unsystematic description
>Measurement (of variables)

P-XI. *Method of handling relationships among properties:*
>Unsystematic description
>Systematic analysis

P-XII. *Treatment of system properties as:*
>Unitary
>Collective

You will find in using this Paradigm that, since the alternatives are stated as pure types that merely suggest the possible nature of the various decisions, any actual design will only roughly approximate these types. (Eventually, after you have finished this program of study and start using the Paradigm in your own research, you may want to revise it; for, like all such classifications, it is in many respects arbitrary, and other equally good or better arrangements could doubtless be made.)

Let us now describe in brief the various items in the Paradigm. They will be defined in detail as they apply in subsequent Units.

The Research Case. First, let us examine the alternatives facing the researcher as he makes his most important decision under Paradigm item I (hereafter referred to as **P-I**): what his research case is to be. He will obviously choose empirical cases to fit his idea of a social system as defined in his conceptual model, and to fit the level of that system on which his objective focuses. If his focus is on the level of the role, he might decide to study actual leaders of military companies, or women in a particular community who are mothers. That is, he would choose the individual-in-a-role as his research case. If his focus is on the dyad (the smallest relational unit in a social system), he might decide to study all possible pairs of members within given groups, or the paired relationships between certain children and each of their parents. If his focus is on subsystems within a larger system, his research case would be the subgroup (or subcollectivity)—such as a ward within a hospital, or a community within a country. If his focus is on the total system, he would use the total group or society as his research case: hospitals or countries, for example, or wards or communities no longer treated as subgroups.

Since the focus is very often on more than one level of the system, the case may be the collectivity made up of subcollectivities or of roles, *e.g.,* or it may be the role made up of dyadic relationships. Here the researcher must find means of working simultaneously with individual boys in the role of scout, for example, and with the more inclusive scout troop as it comprises these individual roles; or simultaneously with particular families as subgroups and with the larger community as it embraces these families.

The alternatives listed under **P-I** are to be used broadly to cover the variety of cases that are of major interest to the sociological researcher—ranging from social macrocosms to microcosms. From the point of view of research method, what we want to emphasize here is not the size or complexity of the collectivities to be studied, but the distinction between the level to be treated (following the model) as the more inclusive system, and the level to be treated as the constituent part. Thus, by a kind of shorthand, we often refer to the higher-level collectivity (small group or large, complex society) as the "group," irrespective of its size, and the subsystem, again irrespective of its size, as the "subgroup."

Obvious as it may appear that the choice of concrete cases for study should depend upon the conceptual model, sociological researchers, curiously enough, often run into various difficulties on precisely this point. They sometimes study the roles of individuals when their objective is to draw inferences about the collectivity, or they study groups (or aggregates of individuals) when their theoretical interest is actually in the individual personality. This leads them into possible fallacies or misleading conclusions, as when, for instance, they erroneously interpret a rise in unemployment in certain *communities* as a sudden drop in the employability or efficiency of *individual* workers. The proper system reference for interpreting this finding is, of course, not the individual, but the collectivity.

As a researcher, you must, therefore, be sure in advance whether the conceptual model requires that you use one or another level of the social system or several levels in conjunction whenever you draw a sample or gather data or use a given unit in analysis or state the implications of your findings.

P-II in the list of alternatives refers to the number of these cases which the researcher selects to examine. Often, in a "case study," the researcher decides to work intensively with just one or just a few cases, examining in detail the structure of a single society, for example, or the patterns of relationship in just a few married couples. Very often, however, he may go beyond the single case, or the few cases, to select many cases for study so as to isolate those properties that are common to many cases from those that are peculiar only to exceptional cases. The conceptual model is not ordinarily limited in itself, of course, to just one or a few cases. If the sociologist uses a model of the street-corner gang, for instance, he does not regard this model as applying to just one gang on one particular corner—but to all such gangs (the *universe* of gangs). Hence, he often wants to test his model on many gangs and to revise it when necessary so that it will fit gangs more generally.

P-III is concerned with the sociotemporal context from which the cases are chosen. Sometimes the cases are drawn from a single society at a single period of time, so that all the gangs studied occur in the United States today, for example, or all the fishing crews examined belong to a particular primitive society at the time of the investigation. Such restrictions on time and space are often necessary to the feasibility of the research operations, but they limit the generality of the findings. Alternatively, other studies draw their cases from more than one society or from various historical periods, so that the conceptual model can be tested more widely and comparisons can be made across sociocultural or temporal boundaries.

This raises the question of sampling **(P-IV)**—of deciding which cases to study out of the total universe of cases in which the researcher is interested (all the gangs, crews, schools, or communities, for example). Samples are often chosen by precise procedures that aim to represent the conceptual universe through the sample selected. A second important aim is to select a sample that will facilitate the analysis to be made of the data (by controlling the size of the sample, for example, or holding constant certain key variables). Although most samples combine these two bases for selection, the researcher often places primary emphasis on one or the other.

The Time Factor.   Since in most models the social system is conceived as undergoing a continual process of interaction and change, the researcher faces the alternatives **(P-V)** of limiting his investigation to a static analysis made at a single point in time, or of extending it to deal with the dynamics of interaction and change over time. A good deal of research on the social system consists of cross-section studies—studies of the system caught at a moment of time, as in a snapshot. Such static studies, which are often easier to conduct than dynamic studies, are useful in defining the state of the system—mapping the status structure of a bureaucracy, for instance, or locating the roles of women in the United States. Such descriptions of structure are important as the bench marks to which subsequent studies of process and change may be referred. Dynamic studies, on the other hand, are used to observe the processes of interaction that take place within the structure, or to record the basic structural changes that may occur when, for example, the introduction of new role definitions enhances the prestige of the working woman in the United States, or the development of strains in a marriage results in divorce as the final dissolution of the system.

The Researcher's Control.   Under **P-VI,** the investigator decides whether or not, as part of the research, to control or change the natural dynamic processes of the system under study. On the one hand, he may attempt to prevent his data-gathering operations or his measuring devices from changing the observed situation in any way. On the other hand, he may set out systematically to control the process (as the natural scientist often does) by making up the groups himself, by establishing a special setting (such as a laboratory) for the action he is observing, by manipulating an independent variable in order to discover its effect, and the like.

Sometimes he elects certain research procedures despite the fact that they will have undesired and unsystematic control effects on the processes of interest. Thus he may himself participate in the action he is studying (in order to gain a firsthand acquaintance) even though his presence will undoubtedly exert unsystematic control over this action. Or he may pre-test the attitudes of an audience before exposing them to a persuasive lecture (in order to provide a basis for measuring attitude change) even though the pre-test will exert an unwanted influence upon their reactions to the lecture by alerting them in advance.

Assembling the Data.   Items **P-VII** and **P-VIII** refer to decisions which the researcher makes regarding the sources of information about his cases. Under **P-VII,** he considers whether there are data already available in one form or another that will serve his purposes, or whether he must gather new data. New data can be gathered according to the researcher's own specifications in line with his particular objectives. Alternatively, many kinds of available materials—historical writings and documents, public records, and studies completed by other researchers, to name only a few—are widely used in sociology to provide information on many otherwise inaccessible matters.

The researcher using new material decides whether, under **P-VIII,** to gather the data by acting as a direct observer—i.e., by watching the interaction of a small group; or by questioning the group members themselves to learn their attitudes and perceptions; or by combining observation and questioning, as the participant observer may do, for example, when he lives with certain families or with certain primitive tribes. Even if the researcher decides to use already available materials, he will often want to assess the procedures by which they were originally gathered—*e.g.,* the questioning by which census records or police reports on suicides were obtained. Of course, many available materials used in research are obtained not by observation or questioning, but by other methods, since—like works of art, scientific inventions, or letters—these materials were not originally produced for research purposes at all.

Handling the Data.   The three Paradigm items, **P-IX, P-X,** and **P-XI,** all refer to the representation in research of social system *properties* (actions, value patterns, structural characteristics, etc.). Under item **P-IX,** the researcher decides how many of the properties from his model he will actually introduce into his research in line with his objective. Sometimes he decides to explore a single property, such as leadership, hierarchical structure, or the personality tendency toward universalism or particularism. By detailed study of a single property a great deal can often be learned about the correspondence between the concept as defined and the patterning of empirical facts. This often helps to elucidate the meaning of the concept, suggesting which ideas fit together in a property such as status, or showing that a property such as leadership may in fact consist of several separate dimensions.

More commonly, the sociological researcher is interested in more than one property, so that he may begin to uncover the principles through which properties are related to one another within the system (as hierarchical structure may be related to the pattern of interaction, for example). The more properties the researcher uses, the more rounded his picture of the system becomes, so that ideally he might like to deal with many (indeed all) of the relevant properties in the model. Yet, the more properties he uses, the more complex the handling of the interrelationships among them becomes. Thus, although the desire to understand the system may press for maximization of the number of properties used, the practical difficulties tend to restrict this number.

One way in which a researcher can manage to handle a whole complex of properties is by working in a purely discursive, descriptive fashion (called unsystematic description in **P-X** and **P-XI**). Qualitative descriptions often serve the important purpose of dealing with the social system in the round, since these studies are not limited by the rigorous requirements of measurement and analysis. Of course, they sacrifice in reliability what they achieve in comprehensiveness, for a high degree of reliability and comparability of observations requires the use of systematic procedures.

The alternative to describing **P-X,** the single property, is to specify or measure it. Measurement involves an explicit, organized plan for classifying (and often quantifying) the particular sense data at hand—the indicants—in terms of the general concept in the researcher's mind. This allows the concept to be used in the analysis as a variable. Just as the physicist arrived at the thermometer as a device for measuring temperature, the social scientist attempts to develop instruments (*e.g.,* various types of scales) that can measure such variables as deviance, system integration, or disposition to vote the Republican or Democratic ticket.

In parallel fashion, under **P-XI,** the alternative to unsystematic descriptive handling of relationships among properties is systematic analysis. Thus in a study of the connection between system integration and interaction (as properties of a group), the researcher may merely describe verbally a succession of specific examples and indicate the ways in which one property seems to affect the other; or he may attempt to specify systematically (using techniques of cross-tabulation and correlation) the degree to which—and the conditions under which—one property varies with the other.

A further decision must often be faced in measuring properties of a system **(P-XII)** when the sociological case is defined as a complex system made up of parts. The researcher frequently gathers his data about the constituent parts, and then decides to collect these data—to add them up or piece them together in some way—so as to refer to the higher-level system. If he questions individuals, for instance, about their satisfaction with the roles they play as parts of a group, he may then index the extent of satisfaction collectively for the group by counting the number of its individual members who express satisfaction. Or, by using income data about each of the families (constituent parts) of a country, he may obtain a collective measure of the economic well-being of the country (the more inclusive system) by taking the median income of all the families. Such measures of system properties are collective in that they combine the properties of the lower-level parts. Comparable unitary measures refer directly to the more inclusive system rather than working through the social-structural parts—as group satisfaction might be indexed by whether the group remains intact or disbands, or the economic well-being of a country by its gross agricultural and industrial product.

Collective measures, although widely used, raise a number of problems of research procedure and interpretation because each measure involves two system levels. It is often unclear, for instance, whether a collective measure reflects a group property, as it is assumed to do, or merely the aggregation of discrete individual properties. Or the researcher may want to go behind the collective measure to identify the parts and describe the nature of their relationship to the whole. He might want to know which kinds of individuals contribute to the satisfaction in different groups—whether, for example, satisfaction pervades the group more extensively if it is the high-status members who show marked satisfaction. Thus he may seek procedures that will show which parts of the system contribute to the total group pattern. Such questions of system levels and cross-level analyses involve some of the least well-formulated areas of sociological research. As we shall see, these are highly challenging problems because their solution will lead to a better understanding of the internal arrangements and processes of social systems.

THE DESIGN AS A WHOLE

These Paradigm items—referring to the case, the researcher's use of time, his control over the process under study, and the problems of assembling and handling the data—are not to be regarded as separate or independent of one another. Each item should be referred to the over-all design, which must be thought of as a whole. To a considerable extent, each decision hinges upon the others so that any change in the plan for one item will usually affect the decisions on other items as well. The various parts of the design must fit together, just as the design itself must be fitted to the underlying theory.

The decisions on the items need not be made in any particular sequence. The researcher does not always decide first upon the method of gathering data, for example, and then upon the method of handling single properties merely because **P-VIII** happens to appear earlier in the Paradigm than **P-X.** For each particular study, the researcher should plan the whole design carefully in advance before he starts the first steps of the research operations.

CRITERIA FOR SELECTION

As you work with this list of basic design decisions, you will see how, in each study, the researcher translates his conceptual model and his objectives into research operations, choosing specific procedures from the rapidly developing reservoir of available techniques. The design used in each study is tailor-made, and no single set of firm rules can be set down. No one design can be looked upon as either right or wrong, but must be judged in terms of its appropriateness for the given research situation.

We shall devote much attention, then, to defining and weighing the relative strengths and weaknesses of particular designs for particular purposes. From your own analyses too, you will gradually abstract some of the basic principles on which the broad design decisions should be made—the criteria of appropriateness for the selection of one or another set of alternatives from the Paradigm, or for the evaluation of any particular design.

Design and Conceptual Model.   We can distinguish at the outset three main sets of criteria—two of them suggested by the diagram of the research process in Figure 1-A. The first major set of criteria in working out the design is: Will this design fit my conceptual model? Is it appropriate in terms of the theory to be explored or to be tested? Will it lead to the search for the relevant facts?

Theory is, of course, essential to any research. A special demand is presently placed upon the research sociologist, however, to rely heavily upon the conceptual model because many of the available research tools were originally designed for use, not in sociology, but in other disciplines. Sampling techniques worked out by quality-control statisticians for industrial applications, for instance, or aptitude and attitude tests developed by psychologists for study of the individual rather than the social system are only examples of tools that cannot always be applied directly without regard to the conceptual framework of the research. Accordingly we, as sociological researchers, must make a special effort to translate our own theory into method, to adapt old methods and invent new ones for our special needs.

Design and Research Findings.   Just as the design must fit the model, it must also fit the facts. We shall see how the researcher may do "pilot" interviewing in advance of a study, for example, to find out how respondents actually think or talk about a topic of interest. We shall see how he selects methods of measurement and statistical analysis that will not obscure any of the relevant patterns that actually exist in the data. We shall examine a variety of "errors" that may prevent the research findings from reflecting accurately the phenomena of the real world (such as bias due to unsystematic control effect, errors of unreliability, chance errors, etc.). Each design may be assessed on the basis of the kinds of errors it seems to entail when applied to the particular empirical situation.

Feasibility.   In addition to these fundamental criteria of conceptual appropriateness and empirical validity, we should also mention the question of immediate feasibility: Is the design practical? Have suitable techniques been developed for carrying it out? Are adequate resources, time, facilities, and abilities available? This third set of criteria may affect not only certain design decisions, but may, on occasion, even cause the research objective to be modified or redefined so as to permit a feasible design to be developed.

Thus the design depends upon a delicate balance among the requirements set by the model, by the nature of the facts under study, and by the facilities and resources immediately available.

Methods of Interpretation

Just as each of the studies you will analyze uses empirical methods to arrive at its findings, it also employs procedures for interpreting the sociological significance of the findings by comparing them with the model. But these interpretative methods are not yet codified even to the extent that we can now classify and state general rules of empirical method. Indeed, some interpretative procedures presently used to suggest the wider meaning of the data may scarcely merit the term method at all. An important future task for us as students of sociological research is to begin to identify and formulate possible rules for feeding specific findings back into the growing body of sociological theory and knowledge.

There are various orders of questions the researcher may ask about his findings in terms of his conceptual model. He may ask, for example, how a particular fact relates to a more general theoretical principle, or whether a certain fact is caused by another set of facts, or how certain facts have consequences (functions or dysfunctions) for the system, or what the conditions are under which facts are associated in certain ways (see, *e.g.,* Braithwaite; Nagel, 1961, Chapter 2).

Ideally, a science asks and seeks answers to such questions in relation to a body of interrelated ideas and principles. Hempel uses the figure of a network of concepts, held together by definitions and hypotheses, which floats over the "plane of observation." The network is linked to specific places in the plane of observed data by strings, so that:

> From certain observational data, we may ascend, via an interpretive string, to some point in the theoretical network, thence proceed, via definitions and hypotheses, to other points, from which another interpretive string permits a descent to the plane of observation. (Hempel, p. 36.)

This metaphor suggests how each set of findings, rather than having its own isolated interpretation, ties one "interpretive string" to the whole web of theory. The data explained by one proposition are logically related to all the other ideas and propositions. And, as many findings are obtained from many studies, the several "interpretive strings" are all anchored to the common network.

Sociology does not yet approach such a scientific ideal, of course (see, *e.g.,* Parsons, 1961, pp. 31–33). It does not consist of precise concepts that match the empirical facts and are logically integrated with one another. But sociology can and does adapt to its own use many of the methods of interpretation utilized in the more highly developed sciences. You will find important clues to these methods scattered throughout the Studies and the Commentaries in this book.

TWO DIRECTIONS OF THE PROCESS

The process of interpretation—the bringing together of theory and findings —commonly works back and forth between the conceptual model and the data being analyzed (as indicated by the two-directional arrow in Figure 1-A). But we can also think of each of these directions separately. The researcher can go in one direction—from the model to the data—by providing an interpretation as part of the model in advance of the data-gathering. Or he can go the other way—from data to model—by adding new ideas to the model after he has completed the empirical phase of his research. (This difference, you will notice, is closely related to whether the research objective is to test hypotheses or to make explorations.)

From Data to Model. You will analyze a number of studies—and perform a number of exercises yourself—which use the research findings to suggest new ideas. As *exploratory research* uncovers empirical regularities, the investigator typically looks for clues to new ideas and hypotheses that might account for these findings.

The tools he uses in seeking such clues (although he rarely describes them fully) seem to include abstraction of relevant aspects of the data, generalization to wider situations, empathy or insight into social relationships and processes (see, *e.g.,* Shils, 1961), association of the phenomenon studied with analogous phenomena that are better understood, and various other devices, which we shall refer to as creative imagination. As Timasheff puts it:

> Theory cannot be derived from observations and generalizations merely by means of rigorous induction. The construction of a theory is a creative achievement. . . . There is always a jump beyond the evidence, a hunch, corresponding to the creative effort. (Timasheff, p. 10.)

When the interpretative process operates in this direction, starting with the facts, it is an explicit attempt to use research as the stimulus for new ideas and theories. It may, if the investigator is theoretically sophisticated and creatively endowed, result in theory-building. Its outcome should at the least be the amplification or specification in further detail of the conceptual model.

From Model to Data. You will also read several studies that approach interpretation the other way, by formulating and *testing hypotheses*. These studies specify in advance what the *expected findings* would be if the assumptions of the model were in accord with the facts. That is, they determine the *implications* of the model for the type of concrete situation to be investigated. For instance, an experiment based on the assumption that treatment X is more effective than treatment Y in reducing deviant attitudes may hypothesize in advance as an implication of the assumption that, under certain experimental conditions, persons treated with X will show less deviance on a particular test than persons treated with Y. Or a cross-cultural study based on a theory that husbands and wives play differentiated roles within the nuclear family may state as an expected finding that more than half of any sample of societies will be characterized by family role differentiation defined in a particular way.

Here, the researcher, whose imagination and knowledge of theory have previously gone into the construction of the model, now utilizes logical or mathematical reasoning to help him derive implications and expected findings. The actual findings of a great many studies are stated numerically as percentages, medians, or measures of correlation, *e.g.;* and we shall see several examples of the use of simple mathematical models to determine what the expected numerical findings would be if the assumptions and theories of the conceptual models are in accord with the facts. Such mathematical models become part of the conceptual model, serving as a precise language for formulating interrelated ideas and implications.

Once the implications of the conceptual model are worked out, the task of the researcher is to obtain and examine the actual findings to see whether, for the particular conditions under study and within the limits of chance error, they are consistent with the expected findings. The outcome of this approach, then, is to support or discard an hypothesis and its underlying assumptions. Interpretation of this sort is necessary to provide the evidence upon which theory rests.

THE INTERPLAY BETWEEN DATA AND MODEL

We can distinguish in the abstract between the two directions of the interpretative process; but the two are complementary, and both are essential to research. Although exploration may suggest new ideas and hypotheses, these must be tested under a variety of conditions before the investigator can, with any confidence, incorporate them into the model. The testing of a single hypothesis only leads to further testing, not only of the same hypothesis under different conditions, but of related hypotheses also. Since, as we have seen, the model of a social system consists of many interdependent parts, the finding that X seems to cause Y, for example, then raises many further questions about how Y is related to the other properties of the system which may, in turn, have their effect upon X.

While particular inquiries differ in their emphasis on exploration or hypothesis-testing as the main approach to interpretation, in practice both are usually interwoven in each single study and the researcher works back and forth between model and data. You will see how the participant observer, for example, starts by making exploration, obtains clues from his data to new ideas and hypotheses, then goes back to look for further data to test these hunches. Or, in a statistical analysis, you will see how the finding of a correlation between religion and the suicide rate (to take one instance) leads to integration as an explanatory concept, how this suggests the further hypothesis that suicide should also be associated with differing degrees of integration in the family, and how the data are then examined to test the new hypothesis. Or the researcher starting with an hypothesis rather than with data does not often stop with the finding of the predicted correlation (see Kendall and Lazarsfeld). He may seek new ideas that might specify or extend the findings, then return to the data to test his new ideas. Or he may find unexpected regularities in the data that suggest new hypotheses for further testing.

The development of sociology as a science will rest, of course, not upon the findings and interpretations of single, isolated pieces of research, but upon the accumulating ideas and facts from many related studies. Thus, the process of interpretation typically runs through a whole sequence of studies to see, for instance, how integration may be related more generally, not only to suicide, but also to transiency, alcoholism, mental illness, and many other forms of social deviance. Although sociological investigations still tend to be largely isolated rather than cumulative, scientific development requires a never ending sequence of studies to suggest new ideas followed by studies to test these ideas.

The process is summed up in a compact description that Conant cites from a chemistry textbook:

> Scientists collect their facts by carefully observing what is happening. They group them and try to interpret them in the light of other facts that are already known. Then a scientist sets up a theory or picture that will explain the newly discovered facts, and finally he tests out his theory by getting more data of a similar kind and comparing them with the facts he got through the earlier experiments. When his theory does not quite fit the facts, he must modify it and at the same time verify the facts by getting more data. (Quoted by Conant, p. 36.)

Conant quotes this summary as the basis for insisting that "well-ordered empirical inquiry is only one element in the advance of science; the other element is the use of new concepts, new conceptual schemes that serve as working hypotheses on a grand scale" (Conant, p. 46).

Thus, the challenge to the oncoming generation of sociological researchers is to find better means of combining the methods of empirical research with the methods of interpretation, of building existing sociological theory as working hypotheses into research, and using research to generate new theory and new hypotheses.

How To Use This Book

The suggested program of study in this book is intended to give you a working knowledge of these specific technical procedures and an imaginative understanding of these basic design principles that constitute empirical research method.

The field and laboratory Exercises and Manual, which accompany this volume, will give you actual experience with many *selected techniques and procedures.* The Exercises, though often involving work that may seem dull and routine, give you the "feel" of the procedures discussed in the Studies and the Commentaries; to those students already somewhat familiar with such procedures, they afford additional practice. The Exercises are arranged to require, first, the performance of each technique, and then later, as experience accumulates, the designing of the instruments themselves. The aim is to stimulate each student to think creatively about the possibilities of adapting familiar techniques, and even of developing new ones, for the rather special methodological problems of translating sociological theory into empirical operations.

The *basic questions of research design* in relation to sociological theory will be approached in this book through the analysis of studies as examples. You will be asked, in reading the various selected studies, to consider each in terms of its design. These are studies in which research methods have been used to solve actual sociological problems—in which conceptual model and research design have been brought together. Although many of them may already be familiar to you, you will now reread them in your capacity as methodologist, and will seek in them the underlying principles of sociological research. Ultimately, when you come to design your own research, you will be able to make critical use of some of these studies as models. By considering what Whyte did in a given situation, for example, or how Durkheim or Weber handled a given research objective, you will find clues and suggestions about what to do (or not to do) in designing a new study.

The Commentaries in Units 2 through 12—each to be read *after* you have independently analyzed the related studies and completed the exercises—will suggest to you the kinds of research problems to be considered and the types of general principles to be abstracted. These Units do not attempt to formulate all of these principles for you. Indeed, they are often in the nature of a three-sided conversation among the author of each study selection, the author of the Commentary, and you, the student of research method. The Questions for Review and Discussion at the end of each Unit will illustrate the kinds of organization you should, on your own, introduce into the diverse materials of the book. These are intended to stimulate you to further consideration of the design most appropriate for particular theoretical problems and research objectives.

SUGGESTED READINGS FOR UNIT ONE

Ackoff, Chapter 1; Berger *et al.;* Beshers; Bridgman; Cohen and Nagel, Chapters 10, 11, 20; Goode and Hatt, Chapters 2, 5, 6; Henderson; Lazarsfeld, 1959; Loomis, 1960, Essay 1; Meadows; Merton, 1957, Chapters 1, 2, 3; Nagel, 1961, Chapters 1, 2, 13, 14; Newcomb, 1953-a; Parsons, 1949-b, Essays 1 and 2; Selltiz *et al.,* Chapter 14; Stouffer, 1957; Zetterberg.

You may want to review the treatment of theory and research in one of the introductory textbooks in sociology such as: Bell; Bierstedt; Bredemeier and Stephenson; Broom and Selznick; Chinoy; Cuber; Davis, 1949; Freedman *et al.;* Arnold Green; Johnson; Paul Landis; Lundberg, Schrag, and Larsen; MacIver and Page; Mercer; Merrill; Ogburn and Nimkoff; Rose, 1956; Sutherland, Woodward, and Maxwell; Williams; Wilson and Kolb; Young and Mack.

NOTE: Full bibliographical references, arranged alphabetically by author, will be found at the end of Volume I.

UNIT TWO
DESCRIPTIVE CASE STUDIES

SUGGESTED PROGRAM OF STUDY

The objectives of this Unit are: (1) to introduce you to research procedures for conducting descriptive case studies, (2) to consider how conceptual models are used in the investigation of single social systems, and (3) to begin to evaluate the methodological implications of selecting certain alternatives of research design.

Exercises and Manual

Since exploratory, unstructured observation of social action is often used in the gathering of data, it is important to acquire first-hand experience with such techniques. **Exercise I-1** is designed to provide such experience. It will also enhance any skill you may already have acquired through previous field work. Start by completing this exercise, or its equivalent, as a basis for your subsequent evaluation of such procedures. Follow **Manual I-A.**

Studies

Read carefully, and take notes (you will need these for frequent future reference) on the two studies in the anthropological tradition by **Malinowski** and **Whyte.** Assuming the role of methodologist, you should consider for each of these studies the following questions: What are the research objectives? What conceptual model does the researcher have in mind? Which alternatives (following the Paradigm) does the researcher select in designing his study? What specific techniques does he choose—and why does he make each of these selections?

Commentary

Now read the Commentary, which considers the kinds of results obtained from these particular descriptive case studies and discusses some of the advantages and limitations of the methods used. Keep notes on your own questions, general observations, and cross references.

Questions for Review and Discussion

Organize your methodological thinking by preparing answers to the Questions for Review and Discussion at the end of this Unit. These will suggest the kinds of summaries you should now, on your own, begin to introduce into the diverse materials of this program of study, encouraging you to think independently about the problems of sociological research method.

BRONISLAW MALINOWSKI

Crime and Custom in Savage Society

I. The Automatic Submission to Custom and the Real Problem

When we come to inquire why rules of conduct, however hard, irksome, or unwelcome, are obeyed; what makes private life, economic cooperation, public events run so smoothly; of what, in short, consist the forces of law and order in savagery —the answer is not easy to give, and what anthropology has had to say about it is far from satisfactory. So long as it could be maintained that the 'savage' is really savage, that he follows what little law he has but fitfully and loosely, the problem did not exist. When the question became actual, when it became plain that hypertrophy of rules rather than lawlessness is characteristic of primitive life, scientific opinion veered round to the opposite point: the savage was made not only into a model of the law-abiding citizen, but it became an axiom that in submitting to all his tribal rules and fetters, he follows the natural trend of his spontaneous impulses; that in this way he glides, so to speak, along the line of least resistance.

The savage—so runs to-day's verdict of competent anthropologists—has a deep reverence for tradition and custom, an automatic submission to their biddings. He obeys them 'slavishly', 'unwittingly', 'spon-

Reprinted in part from Bronislaw Malinowski, *Crime and Custom in Savage Society,* New York: Harcourt, Brace & World, Inc., 1926, pp. 9–11, 14–23, 25–39, 120–21, 125–27, with permission of Humanities Press, Inc. and Routledge & Kegan Paul, Ltd.

taneously', through 'mental inertia', combined with the fear of public opinion or of supernatural punishment; or again through a 'pervading group-sentiment if not group-instinct'. Thus we find the following in a recent book: "The savage is far from being the free and unfettered creature of Rousseau's imagination. On the contrary, he is hemmed in on every side by the customs of his people, he is bound in the chains of immemorial tradition not merely in his social relations, but in his religion, his medicine, in his industry, his art: in short, every aspect of his life" (E. Sidney Hartland in *Primitive Law,* p. 138). With all this we might agree, except that it seems doubtful whether the "chains of tradition" are identical or even similar in art and in social relations, in industry, and in religion. But when, immediately, we are told that "these fetters are accepted by him (the savage) as a matter of course; he never seeks to break forth"—we must enter a protest. Is it not contrary to human nature to accept any constraint as a matter of course, and does man, whether civilized or savage, ever carry out unpleasant, burdensome, cruel regulations and taboos without being compelled to? And compelled by some force or motive which he cannot resist?

Yet this automatic acquiescence, this instinctive submission of every member of the tribe to its laws, is the fundamental axiom laid at the basis of the inquiry into primitive order and adherence to rule. . . .

It would be easy to multiply statements and to show that the dogma of the automatic submission to custom dominates the whole inquiry into primitive law. In all fairness, however, it must be stressed that any shortcomings in theory or observation are due to the real difficulties and pitfalls of which this subject is so full.

The extreme difficulty of the problem lies, I think, in the very complex and diffuse nature of the forces which constitute primitive law. Accustomed as we are to look for a definite machinery of enactment, administration, and enforcement of law, we cast round for something analogous in a savage community and, failing to find there any similar arrangements, we conclude that all law is obeyed by this mysterious propensity of the savage to obey it.

Anthropology seems here to be faced by a similar difficulty as the one overcome by Tylor in his "minimum definition of religion". By defining the forces of law in terms of central authority, codes, courts, and constables, we must come to the conclusion that law needs no enforcement in a primitive community and is followed spontaneously. That the savage does break the law sometimes, though rarely and occasionally, has been recorded by observers and taken into account by builders of anthropological theory, who have always maintained that criminal law is the only law of savages. But that his observance of the rules of law under the normal conditions, when it is followed and not defied, is at best partial, conditional, and subject to evasions; that it is not enforced by any wholesale motive like fear of punishment, or a general submission to all tradition, but by very complex psychological and social inducements—all this is a state of affairs which modern anthropology has so far completely overlooked. In the following account I shall try to establish it for one ethnographic province, north-west Melanesia, and I shall show reasons why observations of similar nature to those carried out by myself should be extended to other societies in order to give us some idea about their legal conditions.

We shall approach our facts with a very elastic and wide conception of the problem before us. In looking for 'law' and legal forces, we shall try merely to discover and analyse all the rules conceived and acted upon as binding obligations, to find out the nature of the binding forces, and to classify the rules according to the manner in which they are made valid. We shall see that by an inductive examination of facts, carried out without any preconceived idea or ready-made definition, we shall be enabled to arrive at a satisfactory classification of the norms and rules of a primitive community, at a clear distinction of primitive law from other forms of custom, and at a new, dynamic conception of the social organization of savages. Since the facts of primitive law described in this article have been recorded in Melanesia, the classical area of 'communism' and 'promiscuity', of 'group-sentiment', 'clan-solidarity', and 'spontaneous obedience', the conclusions we shall be able to draw —which will dispose of these catch-words and all they stand for—may be of special interest.

II. Melanesian Economics and the Theory of Primitive Communism

The Trobriand Archipelago, which is inhabited by the Melanesian community referred to, lies to the north-east of New Guinea and consists of a group of flat coral islands, surrounding a wide lagoon. The plains of the land are covered with fertile soil and the lagoon teems with fish, while both afford easy means of intercommunication to the inhabitants. Accordingly, the islands support a dense population mainly engaged in agriculture and fishing, but expert also in various arts and crafts and keen on trade and exchange.

Like all coral islanders, they spend a great deal of their time on the central lagoon. On a calm day it is alive with canoes carrying people or produce, or engaged in one of their manifold systems of fishing. A superficial acquaintance with these pursuits might leave one with an impression of arbitrary disorder, anarchy, complete lack of system. Patient and painstaking observations would soon reveal, however, not only that the natives have definite technical systems of catching fish and complex economic arrangements, but also that they have a close organization in their working teams, and a fixed division of social functions.

Thus, within each canoe it would be found that there is one man who is its rightful owner, while the rest act as a crew. All these men, who as a rule belong to the same sub-clan, are bound to each other and to their fellow-villagers by mutual obligations; when the whole community go out fishing, the owner cannot refuse his canoe. He must go out himself or let some one else do it instead. The crew are equally under an obligation to him. For reasons which will presently become clear, each man must fill his place and stand by his task. Each man also receives his fair share in the distribution of the catch as an equivalent of his service. Thus the ownership and use of the canoe consist of a series of definite obligations and duties uniting a group of people into a working team.

What makes the conditions even more complex is that the owners and the members of the crew are entitled to surrender their privileges to any one of their relatives and friends. This is often done, but always for a consideration, for a repayment. To an observer who does not grasp all the details, and does not follow all the intricacies of each transaction, such a state of affairs looks very much like communism: the canoe appears to be owned jointly by a group and used indiscriminately by the whole community.

Dr. Rivers in fact tells us that "one of the objects of Melanesian culture which is usually, if not always, the subject of common ownership is the canoe", and further on, in reference to this statement, he speaks about "the great extent to which communistic sentiments concerning property dominate the people of Melanesia" (*Social Organization,* pp. 106 and 107). In another work, the same writer speaks about "the socialistic or even communistic behaviour of such societies as those of Melanesia" (*Psychology and Politics,* pp. 86 and 87). Nothing could be more mistaken than such generalizations. There is a strict distinction and definition in the rights of every one and this makes ownership anything but communistic. We have in Melanesia a compound and complex system of holding property, which in no way partakes of the nature of 'socialism' or 'communism'. A modern joint-stock company might just as well be called a 'communistic enterprise'. As a matter of fact, any descriptions of a savage institution in terms such as 'communism', 'capitalism' or 'joint-stock company', borrowed from present-day economic conditions or political controversy, cannot but be misleading.

The only correct proceeding is to describe the legal state of affairs in terms of concrete fact. Thus, the ownership of a Trobriand fishing canoe is defined by the manner in which the object is made, used and regarded by the group of men who produced it and enjoy its possession. The master of the canoe, who acts at the same time as the head of the team and as the fishing magician of the canoe, has first of all to finance the building of a new craft, when the old one is worn out, and he has to maintain it in good repair, helped in this by the rest of his crew. In this they remain under mutual obligations to one another to appear each at his post, while every canoe is bound to come when a communal fishing has been arranged.

In using the craft, every joint owner has a right to a certain place in it and to certain duties, privileges, and benefits associated with it. He has his post in the canoe, he has his task to perform, and enjoys the corresponding title, either of 'master' or 'steersman', or 'keeper of the nets', or 'watcher for fish'. His position and title are determined by the combined action of rank, age, and personal ability. Each canoe also has its place in the fleet and its part to play in the manœuvres of joint fishing. Thus on a close inquiry we discover in this pursuit a definite system of division of functions and a rigid system of mutual obligations, into which a sense of duty and the recognition of the need of cooperation enter side by side with a realization of self-interest, privileges and benefits. Ownership, therefore, can be defined neither by such words as 'communism' nor 'individualism', nor by reference to 'joint-stock company' system or 'personal enterprise', but by the concrete facts and conditions of use. It is the sum of duties, privileges and mutualities which bind the joint owners to the object and to each other.

Thus, in connexion with the first object which attracted our attention—the native canoe—we are met by law, order, definite privileges and a well-developed system of obligations.

III. The Binding Force of Economic Obligations

To enter more deeply into the nature of these binding obligations, let us follow the fishermen to the shore. Let us see what happens with the division of the catch. In most cases only a small proportion of it remains with the villagers. As a rule we should find a number of people from some inland community waiting on the shore. They receive the bundles of fish from the fishermen and carry them home, often many miles away, running so as to arrive while it is still fresh. Here again we should find a system of mutual services and obligations based on a standing arrangement between two village communities. The inland village supplies the fishermen with vegetables: the coastal community repays with fish. This arrangement is primarily an economic one. It has also a ceremonial aspect, for the exchange has to be done according to an elaborate ritual. But there is also the legal side, a system of mutual obligations which forces the fisherman to repay whenever he has received a gift from his inland partner, and vice versa. Neither partner can refuse, neither may stint in his return gift, neither should delay.

What is the motive force behind these obligations? The coastal and inland villages respectively have to rely upon each other for the supply of food. On the coast the natives never have enough vegetable food, while inland the people are always in need of fish. Moreover, custom will have it that on the coast all the big ceremonial displays and distributions of food, which form an extremely important aspect of the public life of these natives, must be made with certain specially large and fine varieties of vegetable food, which grow only on the fertile plains inland.

There, on the other hand, the proper substance for a distribution and feast is fish. Thus to all other reasons of value of the respectively rarer food, there is added an artificially, culturally created dependence of the two districts upon one another. So that on the whole each community is very much in need of its partners. If at any time previously these have been guilty of neglect, however, they know that they will be in one way or another severely penalized. Each community has, therefore, a weapon for the enforcement of its rights: reciprocity.

This is not limited to the exchange of fish for vegetables. As a rule, two communities rely upon each other in other forms of trading and other mutual services as well. Thus every chain of reciprocity is made the more binding by being part and parcel of a whole system of mutualities.

IV. Reciprocity and Dual Organization

. . . I venture to foretell that wherever careful inquiry be made, symmetry of structure will be found in every savage society, as the indispensable basis of reciprocal obligations.

The sociological manner in which the relations of reciprocity are arranged, makes them yet more stringent. Between the two communities the exchanges are not carried out haphazard, any two individuals trading with each other at random. On the contrary, every man has his permanent partner in the exchange, and the two have to deal with each other. They are often relatives-in-law, or else sworn friends, or partners in the important system of ceremonial exchange called *kula*. Within each community again the individual partners are ranged into totemic sub-clans. So that the exchange establishes a system of sociological ties of an economic nature, often combined with other ties between individual and individual, kinship group and kinship group, village and village, district and district.

Going over the relations and transactions previously described, it is easy to see that the same principle of mutuality supplies the sanction for each rule. There is in every act a sociological dualism: two parties who exchange services and functions, each watching over the measure of fulfilment and the fairness of conduct of the other. The master of the canoe, whose interests and ambitions are bound up with his craft, looks after order in the internal transactions between the members of the crew and represents the latter externally. To him each member of the crew is bound at the time of construction and ever after, when co-operation is necessary. Reciprocally, the master has to give each man the ceremonial payment at the feast of construction; the master cannot refuse any one his place in the boat; and he has to see that each man receives his fair share of the catch. In this and in all the manifold activities of economic order, the social behaviour of the natives is based on a well-assessed give-and-take, always mentally ticked off and in the long run balanced. There is no wholesale discharge of duties or acceptance of privileges; no 'communistic' disregard of tally and earmark. The free and easy way in which all transactions are done, the good manners which pervade all and cover any hitches or maladjustments, make it difficult for the superficial observer to see the keen self-interest and watchful reckoning which runs right through. To one who knows the natives intimately, nothing is more patent than this. The same control which the master assumes within his canoe, is taken within the community by the headman who is, as a rule, also the hereditary magician.

V. Law, Self-Interest, and Social Ambition

It scarcely needs to be added that there are also other driving motives, besides the constraint of reciprocal obligations, which keep the fishermen to their task. The utility of the pursuit, the craving for the fresh, excellent diet, above all, perhaps, the attraction of what to the natives is an intensely fascinating sport—move them more obviously, more consciously even, and more effectively than what we have described as the legal obligation. But the social constraint, the regard for the effective rights and claims of others is always prominent in the mind of the natives as well as in their behaviour, once this is well understood. It is also indispensable to ensure the smooth working of their institutions. For in spite of all zest and attractions, there are on each occasion a few individuals, indisposed, moody, obsessed by some other interest—very often by an intrigue—who would like to escape from their obligation, if they could. Anyone who knows how extremely difficult, if not impossible, it is to organize a body of Melanesians for even a short and amusing pursuit requiring concerted action, and how well and readily they set to work in their customary enterprises, will realize the function and the need of compulsion, due to the native's conviction that another man has a claim on his work.

There is yet another force which makes the obligations still more binding. I have mentioned already the ceremonial aspect of the transactions. The gifts of food in the system of exchange described above must be offered according to strict formalities, in specially made measures of wood, carried and presented in a prescribed manner, in a ceremonial procession and with a blast of conch-shells. Now nothing has a greater sway over the Melanesian's mind than ambition and vanity associated with a display of food and wealth. In the giving of gifts, in the distribution of their surplus, they feel a manifestation of power, and an enhancement of personality. The Trobriander keeps his food in houses better made and more highly ornamented than his dwelling huts. Generosity is the highest virtue to him, and wealth the essential element of influence and rank. The association of a semi-commercial transaction with definite public ceremonies supplies another binding force of fulfilment through a special psychological mechanism: the desire for display, the ambition to appear munificent, the extreme esteem for wealth and for the accumulation of food.

We have thus gained some insight into the nature of the mental and social forces which make certain rules of conduct into binding law. Nor is the binding force superfluous. Whenever the native can evade his obligations without the loss of prestige, or without the prospective loss of gain, he does so, exactly as a civilized business man would do. When the 'automatic smoothness' in the run of obligations so often attributed to the Melanesian is studied more closely, it becomes clear that there are constant hitches in the transactions, that there is much grumbling and recrimination and seldom is a man completely satisfied with his partner. But, on the whole, he continues in the partnership and, on the whole, every one tries to fulfil his obligations, for he is impelled to do so partly through enlightened self-interest, partly in obedience to his social ambitions and sentiments. Take the real savage, keen on evading his duties, swaggering and boastful when he has fulfilled them, and compare him with the anthropologist's dummy who slavishly follows custom and automatically obeys every regulation. There is not the remotest resemblance between the teachings of anthropology on this subject and the reality of native life. We begin to see how the dogma of mechanical obedience to law would prevent the field-worker from seeing the really relevant facts of primitive legal organization. We understand now that the rules of law, the rules with a definite binding obligation, stand out from the mere rules of custom. We can see also that civil law, consisting of positive ordinances, is much more developed than the body of mere prohibitions, and that a study of purely criminal law among savages misses the most important phenomena of their legal life.

It is also obvious that the type of rules which we have been discussing, although they are unquestionably rules of binding law, have in no way the character of religious commandments, laid down absolutely, obeyed rigidly and integrally. The rules here described are essentially elastic and adjustable, leaving a considerable latitude within which their fulfilment is regarded as satisfactory. The bundles of fish, the measures of yams, or bunches of taro, can only be roughly assessed, and naturally the quantities exchanged vary according to whether the fishing season or the harvest is more abundant. All this is taken into account and only wilful stinginess, neglect, or laziness are regarded as a breach of contract. Since, again, largesse is a matter of honour and praise, the average native will strain all his resources to be lavish in his measure. He knows, moreover, that any excess in zeal and generosity is bound sooner or later to be rewarded.

We can see now that a narrow and rigid conception of the problem—a definition of 'law' as the machinery of carrying out justice in cases of trespass—would leave on one side all the phenomena to which we have referred. In all the facts described, the element or aspect of law, that is of effective social constraint, consists in the complex arrangements which make people keep to their obligations. Among them the most important is the manner in which many transactions are linked into chains of mutual services, every one of them having to be repaid at some later date. The public and ceremonial manner in which these transactions are usually carried out, combined with the great ambition and vanity of the Melanesian adds also to the safeguarding forces of law.

VI. The Rules of Law in Religious Acts

I have referred so far mainly to economic relations, for civil law is primarily concerned with ownership and wealth among savages as well as among ourselves. But we could find the legal aspect in any other domain of tribal life. Take for example the most characteristic acts of ceremonial life—the rites of mourning and sorrow for the dead. At first we perceive in them, naturally, their religious character: they are acts of piety towards the deceased, caused by fear or love or solicitude for the spirit of the departed. As the ritual and public display of emotion they are also part of the ceremonial life of the community.

Who, however, would suspect a legal side to such religious transactions? Yet in the Trobriands there is not one single mortuary act, not one ceremony, which is not considered to be an obligation of the performer towards some of the other survivors. The widow weeps and wails in ceremonial sorrow, in religious piety and fear—but also because the strength of her grief affords direct satisfaction to the deceased man's brothers and maternal relatives. It is the matrilineal group of kindred who, according to the native theory of kinship and mourning, are the people really bereaved. The wife, though she lived with her husband, though she should grieve at his death, though often she really and sincerely does so, remains but a stranger by the rules of matrilineal kinship. It is her duty towards the surviving members of her husband's clan, accordingly, to display her grief, to keep a long period of mourning and to carry the jawbone of her husband for some years after his death. Nor is this obligation without reciprocity. At the first big ceremonial distribution, some three days after her husband's death, she will receive from his kinsmen a ritual payment, and a substantial one, for her tears; and at later ceremonial feasts she is given more payments for the subsequent services of mourning. It should also be kept in mind that to the natives mourning is but a link in the life-long chain of reciprocities between husband and wife and between their respective families.

VII. The Law of Marriage

This brings us to the subject of marriage, extremely important for the understanding of native law. Marriage establishes not merely a bond between husband and wife, but it also imposes a standing relation of mutuality between the man and the wife's family, especially her brother. A woman and her brother are bound to each other by characteristic and highly important ties of kinship. In a Trobriand family a female must always remain under the special guardianship of one man—one of her brothers, or, if she has none, her nearest maternal kinsman. She has to obey him and to fulfil a number of duties, while he looks after her welfare and provides for her economically even after she is married.

The brother becomes the natural warden of her children, who therefore have to regard him and not their father as the legal head of the family. He in turn has to look after them, and to supply the household with a considerable proportion of its food. This is the more burdensome since marriage being patrilocal, the girl has moved away to her husband's community, so that every time at harvest there is a general economic *chassé-croisé* all over the district.

After the crops are taken out, the yams are classified and the pick of the crop from each garden is put into a conical heap. The main heap in each garden plot is always for the sister's household. The sole purpose of all the skill and labour devoted to this display of food is the satisfaction of the gardener's ambition. The whole community, nay, the whole district, will see the garden produce, comment upon it, criticize, or praise. A big heap proclaims, in the words of my informant: "Look what I have done for my sister and her family. I am a good gardener and my nearest relatives, my sister and her children, will never suffer for want of food." After a few days the heap is dismantled, the yams carried in baskets to the sister's village, where they are put up into exactly the same shape in front of the yam-house of the sister's husband; there again the members of the community will see the heap and admire it. This whole ceremonial side of the transaction has a binding force which we know already. The display, the comparisons, the public assessment impose a definite psychological constraint upon the giver—they satisfy and reward him, when successful work enables him to give a generous gift, and they penalize and humiliate him for inefficiency, stinginess, or bad luck.

Besides ambition, reciprocity prevails in this transaction as everywhere else; at times, indeed, it steps in almost upon the heels of an act of fulfilment. First of all the husband has to repay by definite periodical gifts every annual harvest contribution. Later on, when the children grow up, they will come directly under the authority of their maternal uncle; the boys will have to help him, to assist him in everything, to contribute a definite quota to all the payments he has to make. His sister's daughters do but little for him directly, but indirectly, in a matrilineal society, they provide him with his heirs and descendants of two generations below.

Thus placing the harvest offerings within their sociological context, and taking a long view of the relationship, we see that every one of its transactions is justified as a link in the chain of mutualities. Yet taking it isolated, torn out of its setting, each transaction appears nonsensical, intolerably burdensome and sociologically meaningless, also no doubt 'communistic'! What could be more economically absurd than this oblique distribution of garden produce, where every man works for his sister and has to rely in turn on his wife's brother, where more time and energy is apparently wasted on display, on show, on the shifting of the goods, than on real work? Yet a closer analysis shows that some of these apparently unnecessary actions are powerful economic incentives, that others supply the legal binding force, while others, again, are the direct result of native kinship ideas. It is also clear that we can understand the legal aspect of such relations only if we look upon them integrally without over-emphasizing any one link in the chain of reciprocal duties.

VIII. The Principle of Give and Take Pervading Tribal Life

In the foregoing we have seen a series of pictures from native life, illustrating the legal aspect of the marriage relationship, of co-operation in a fishing team, of

food barter between inland and coastal villages, of certain ceremonial duties of mourning. These examples were adduced with some detail, in order to bring out clearly the concrete working of what appears to me to be the real mechanism of law, social and psychological constraint, the actual forces, motives and reasons which make men keep to their obligations. If space permitted it would be easy to bring these isolated instances into a coherent picture and to show that in all social relations and in all the various domains of tribal life, exactly the same legal mechanism can be traced, that it places the *binding obligations* in a special category and sets them apart from other types of customary rules. . . .

[Excerpts From the Concluding Remarks]

[About the "hearsay method"] . . . When the native is asked what he would do in such and such a case, he answers what he *should* do; he lays down the pattern of best possible conduct. When he acts as informant to a field-anthropologist, it costs him nothing to retail the Ideal of the law. His sentiments, his propensities, his bias, his self-indulgences as well as tolerance of others' lapses, he reserves for his behavior in real life. And even then, though he acts thus, he would be unwilling to admit often even to himself, that he ever acts below the standard of law. The other side, the natural, impulsive code of conduct, the evasions, the compromises and non-legal usages are revealed only to the field-worker, who observes native life directly, registers facts, lives at such close quarters with his 'material' as to understand not only their language and their statements, but also the hidden motives of behaviour, and the hardly ever formulated spontaneous line of conduct. . . .

But it is worth while to realize once more that throughout our discussion we found the real problem not in bald enumeration of rules, but in the ways and means by which these are carried out. Most instructive we found the study of the life situations which call for a given rule, the manner in which this is handled by the people concerned, the reaction of the community at large, the consequences of fulfilment or neglect. All this, which could be called the cultural-context of a primitive system of rules is equally important, if not more so, than the mere recital of a fictitious native *corpus juris* codified into the ethnographer's notebook as the result of question and answer, in the hearsay method of field-work.

With this we are demanding a new line of anthropological field-work: the study by direct observation of the rules of custom as they function in actual life. Such study reveals that the commandments of law and custom are always organically connected and not isolated; that their very nature consists in the many tentacles which they throw out into the context of social life; that they only exist in the chain of social transactions in which they are but a link. I maintain that the staccato manner in which most accounts of tribal life are given is the result of imperfect information, and that it is in fact incompatible with the general character of human life and the exigencies of social organization. A native tribe bound by a code of disconnected inorganic customs would fall to pieces under our very eyes.

We can only plead for the speedy and complete disappearance from the records of field-work of the piecemeal items of information, of customs, beliefs, and rules of conduct floating in the air, or rather leading a flat existence on paper with the third-dimension, that of life, completely lacking. With this the theoretical arguments of Anthropology will be able to drop the lengthy litanies of threaded statement, which makes us anthropologists feel silly, and the savage look ridiculous. I mean by this the long enumerations of bald statement such as, for example, "Among the Brobdignacians when a man meets his mother-in-law, the two abuse each other and each retires with a black eye"; "When a Brodiag encounters a Polar bear he runs away and sometimes the bear follows"; "in old Caledonia when a native accidentally finds a whiskey bottle by the road-side he empties it at one gulp, after which he proceeds immediately to look for another"—and so forth. (I am quoting from memory so the statements may be only approximate, though they sound plausible.)

It is easy, however, to poke fun at the litany-method, but it is the field-worker who is really responsible. There is hardly any record in which the majority of statements are given as they occur in actuality and not as they should or are said to occur. Many of the earlier accounts were written to startle, to amuse, to be facetious at the expense of the savage, till the tables were turned and it is more easy now to be facetious at the anthropologist's expense. To the old recorders what mattered really was the queerness of the custom, not its reality. The modern anthropologist, working through an interpreter by the question and answer method can again collect only opinions, generalizations, and bald statements. He gives us no reality, for he has never seen it. The touch of ridicule which hangs about most writings of anthropology is due to the artificial flavour of a statement torn out of its life-context. The true problem is not to study how human life submits to rules—it simply does not; the real problem is how the rules become adapted to life.

As regards our theoretical gains the analysis of Trobriand law has given us a clear view of the forces of cohesion in a primitive society, based on solidarity within the group as well as on the appreciation of personal interest. The opposition of primitive 'group-sentiment', 'joint personality' and 'clan absorption' to civilized individualism and pursuit of selfish ends appear[s] to us altogether artificial and futile. No society, however primitive or civilized, can be based on a figment or on a pathological growth on human nature.

WILLIAM FOOTE WHYTE
Street Corner Society: The Social Structure of an Italian Slum

Preface

This book is a report upon a three-and-a-half-year study of "Cornerville." My aim was to gain an intimate view of Cornerville life. My first problem, therefore, was to establish myself as a participant in the society so that I would have a position from which to observe. I began by going to live in Cornerville, finding a room with an Italian family. Since the mother and father of the family spoke no English, I began studying Italian. Conversations with them and practice with the Linguaphone enabled me to learn enough to talk fairly fluently with the older generation. As I became largely concerned with the second-generation men, who conducted their activities in English, Italian was not essential to me; but the fact that I made the effort to learn the language was important, since it gave the impression that I had a sincere and sympathetic interest in Cornerville people.

Staying with an Italian family gave me a view of family life and also provided important contacts with the community.

Reprinted in part from William Foote Whyte, *Street Corner Society: The Social Structure of an Italian Slum,* Chicago: University of Chicago Press, 1943, pp. v–xi, 255–76, with permission of The University of Chicago Press.

Through the family I met a cousin of State Senator George Ravello's secretary. Through the cousin I met the secretary, and through the secretary I met Ravello. In this way I was able to establish myself in the politician's office at a time when he was running for Congress. He had no opposition from within Cornerville in this campaign, which made it possible for me to work for him without losing standing with other local groups. During the campaign I did various odd jobs which were of no particular significance for the organization but which gave me an excuse for being around when things were happening. It was in this way that I found most of my material on politics.

I made my first contacts with the "corner boys" known as the Nortons through the Norton Street Settlement House. I subsequently learned that too close identification with the settlement would prevent me from becoming intimate with the rank and file of the people, but at this time I was fortunate in meeting corner boys who, while they had some contact with the settlement, also had a recognized position outside of it. Through the Nortons I came to know the college men of the Italian Community Club.

After I had lived eighteen months with the Italian family, I married, and my wife and I moved into a flat on Shelby Street. This opened for me a new field of contacts. One evening I went with the son of my Italian family to a banquet in honor of the local police lieutenant. There were three main groups of people present: policemen, politicians, and racketeers. My companion had met Tony Cataldo, a prominent local racketeer, and Tony had seen me around his district. We became acquainted in this way, and shortly thereafter Tony invited my wife and me to dinner at his house. We spent a number of evenings with the Cataldos and also came to know other members of the family. In order to study the influence of the racketeer upon a specific group of people, I joined the Cornerville Social and Athletic Club. Since the organization was located on Shelby Street, my contacts made it quite natural for me to join.

It was not enough simply to make the acquaintance of various groups of people. The sort of information that I sought required that I establish intimate social relations, and that presented special problems. Since illegal activities are prevalent in Cornerville, every newcomer is under suspicion. So that I would not be taken for a "G-man," I had to have some way of explaining my presence. I began by telling people that I was studying the history of Cornerville since the beginning of the Italian immigration, but I used this story only a few times. I found that in each group I met there was one man who directed the activities of his fellows and whose word carried authority. Without his support, I was excluded from the group; with his support, I was accepted. Since he had to take the responsibility of vouching for me, I made a practice of talking with him quite frankly about the questions in which I was interested. When his friends questioned him, he knew much more about me than they did, and he was therefore in a position to reassure them. In the course of my stay in Cornerville, several of these men came to have a very

clear and detailed idea of the nature of my research, and this knowledge made it possible for them to help me by observing and discussing with me the sort of situations in which I was interested.

When I became accepted into a group, it was no longer necessary for me to explain what I was doing. Being accepted meant that I was a "good fellow" and that meant that whatever I was doing was all right. It became generally understood that I was writing a book about the old Italian customs in Cornerville, and occasionally I was asked, "How is your book coming?" I always replied that I was making progress but that there was still a lot for me to learn. No further answer was necessary, although I tried to give the impression that I was prepared to tell much more about my work than my questioner wanted to know.

The first few weeks of my association with any group brought in little information of value. Although my right to associate with the men was unquestioned, they could not feel at ease in my presence until they had become familiar with me. Therefore, I put in a great deal of time simply hanging around with them and participating in their various activities. I bowled, played baseball and softball, shot a little pool, played cards, and ate and drank with my Cornerville friends. This active participation gave me something in common with them so that we had other things to talk about besides the weather. It broke down the social barriers and made it possible for me to be taken into the intimate life of the group.

My aim was to be a friend to the people whom I was with, and I tried to act as a friend was supposed to act in that society. My friends helped me with my work, and I helped my friends as individuals in whatever way I could. I found it even more important to my social position to ask them to help me. I made it a rule that I should try to avoid influencing the actions of the group. I wanted to observe what the men did under ordinary circumstances; I did not want to lead them into different activities. I violated this rule several times and did so particularly flagrantly during the political crisis in the Cornerville S. and A. Club, but on the whole I held to it. Of course, my presence changed the situation for the group. I tried to minimize that change because it was much easier for me to study group activities if I could assume that my own influence had not been a significant factor in bringing about the actions I observed. Above all, I avoided making moral admonitions. I did not tell people that they were behaving improperly or suggest to them the way in which they should act. I was there to learn about Cornerville life, not to pass judgment upon it.

I was not immediately interested in broad generalizations upon the nature of Cornerville life. It seemed to me that any sound generalizations must be based upon detailed knowledge of social relations. Therefore, I concentrated my attention upon the interaction of individuals in their groups. I was concerned not only with the "important events," because at the outset I had no basis for determining what was important except my own preconceived notions. I tried to keep my eyes and ears open to everything that went on between people in my presence. Frequently, I asked people to explain to me what had happened. Most of my interviewing was conducted informally while I was participating in group activities. I found that what people told me helped to explain what had happened and that what I observed helped to explain what people told me, so that it was helpful to observe and interview at the same time. In order to fill in the background in the history of the individual and of the group and to

take up things which could best be discussed in private, I invited men to come separately and talk with me at my home. Much of the background of the Nortons and the Italian Community Club was gathered in this way.

It is customary for the sociologist to study the slum district in terms of "social disorganization" and to neglect to see that an area such as Cornerville has a complex and well-established organization of its own. I was interested in that organization. I found that in every group there was a hierarchical structure of social relations binding the individuals to one another and that the groups were also related hierarchically to one another. Where the group was formally organized into a political club, this was immediately apparent, but for informal groups it was no less true. While the relations in such groups were not formally prescribed, they could be clearly observed in the interactions of individuals. To determine the relative standing of members of the group, I paid particular attention to the origination of action. When the group or several of its members engaged in some common activity, I wanted to know who suggested what was to be done and whose agreement was necessary before the action could be carried out. Observation of this sort provided the basis for the charts of hierarchical organization which are presented in the stories of the Nortons and the Cornerville S. and A. Club and for the discussion of "The Gang and the Individual" in my conclusions.

The study of the Cornerville S. and A. Club presented some special problems. Since at times there were as many as fifty members, it was necessary to study the club through observing the groupings into which the men naturally divided themselves. Every afternoon or evening when I went into the club I looked around to see which members were grouped together, playing cards, listening to the radio, or talking. When the men were moving around, I could not retain all the movements; but, when they settled down, I counted the men present and fixed in my mind the spatial position of each individual in relation to the others. When I went home, I mapped the spatial positions of the members and indicated which ones were participating together. These maps showed quite clearly the main division between the two cliques and the subdivisions within each clique.

The events to be described will provide the evidence for assigning positions to the most prominent members of the Cornerville S. and A. Club. The relative positions of the minor members were discovered by observing which men took the initiative in group action when one of the top men was not present. The evidence for fixing the positions of all minor members is too detailed to be included in a book of this nature.

My observations of interactions and of spatial positions would have been of no use to me if I had not made a permanent record of them. When I went to political rallies and campaign committee meetings, I was able to take notes on the spot; but on all other occasions I had to rely upon my memory until I could write in private. When I recorded conversations, I tried to put down in so far as possible the exact words that were said. Frequently, the phrase used carries a meaning which escapes any paraphrase, and therefore I felt that it was important to try for verbatim recordings. This is a skill which develops with practice. At first I found that I could remember only a few phrases used and give an impressionistic picture of the rest of the conversation; but, as I went on, I was able to record in greater and greater detail, so that I feel confident that the quo-

tations I cite represent substantially what was actually said. I had the same experience in mapping spatial positions.

The stories of the Nortons and of the Cornerville S. and A. Club provide a body of information upon corner gangs, but they constitute only the smallest fraction of the total number of such groups to be found in Cornerville. So that I might be able to generalize upon the nature of the corner gang, I solicited the aid of several corner-boy leaders who discussed with me their own experiences and became interested in making the same sort of detailed observations that are found in my corner-boy stories. . . .

The corner boys do not explicitly recognize the structure of the gang, but it is implicit in all their actions. When, toward the end of my study, I discussed these matters with my informants, I made them conscious of the nature of their unreflective behavior. To that extent I changed the situation; the men talked to me about things that they had never formulated before. This did not mean that they were enabled to act more effectively. Doc, my chief informant, once told me:

> You've slowed me up plenty since you've been down here. Now when I do something, I have to think what Bill Whyte would want to know about it and how I can explain it. . . . Before I used to do these things by instinct.

This awareness, however, contributed toward building up a systematic picture of the corner gang. . . .

I. The Gang and the Individual

The corner-gang structure arises out of the habitual association of the members over a long period of time. The nuclei of most gangs can be traced back to early boyhood, when living close together provided the first opportunities for social contacts. School years modified the original pattern somewhat, but I know of no corner gangs which arose through classroom or school-playground association. The gangs grew up on the corner and remained there with remarkable persistence from early boyhood until the members reached their late twenties or early thirties. In the course of years some groups were broken up by the movement of families away from Cornerville, and the remaining members merged with gangs on near-by corners; but frequently movement out of the district does not take the corner boy away from his corner. On any evening on almost any corner one finds corner boys who have come in from other parts of the city or from suburbs to be with their old friends. The residence of the corner boy may also change within the district, but nearly always he retains his allegiance to his original corner.

Home plays a very small role in the group activities of the corner boy. Except when he eats, sleeps, or is sick, he is rarely at home, and his friends always go to his corner first when they want to find him. Even the corner boy's name indicates the dominant importance of the gang in his activities. It is possible to associate with a group of men for months and never discover the family names of more than a few of them. Most are known by nicknames attached to them by the group. Furthermore, it is easy to overlook the distinction between married and single men. The married man regularly sets aside one evening a week to take out his wife. There are other occasions when they go out together and entertain together, and some corner boys devote more attention to their wives than others, but, married or single, the corner boy can be found on his corner almost every night of the week.

His social activities away from the corner are organized with similar regularity. Many corner gangs set aside the same night each week for some special activity, such as bowling. With the Nortons this habit was so strong that it persisted for some of the members long after the original group had broken up.

Most groups have a regular evening meeting-place aside from the corner. Nearly every night at about the same time the gang gathers for "coffee-and" in its favorite cafeteria or for beer in the corner tavern. When some other activity occupies the evening, the boys meet at the cafeteria or tavern before returning to the corner or going home. Positions at the tables are fixed by custom. Night after night each group gathers around the same tables. The right to these positions is recognized by other Cornerville groups. When strangers are found at the accustomed places, the necessity of finding other chairs is a matter of some annoyance, especially if no near-by location is available. However, most groups gather after nine in the evening when few are present except the regular customers who are familiar with the established procedure.

The life of the corner boy proceeds along regular and narrowly circumscribed channels. As Doc said to me:

> Fellows around here don't know what to do except within a radius of about three hundred yards. That's the truth, Bill. They come home from work, hang on the corner, go up to eat, back on the corner, up a show, and they come back to hang on the corner. If they're not on the corner, it's likely the boys there will know where you can find them. Most of them stick to one corner. It's only rarely that a fellow will change his corner.

The stable composition of the group and the lack of social assurance on the part of its members contribute toward producing a very high rate of social interaction within the group. The group structure is a product of these interactions.

Out of such interaction there arises a system of mutual obligations which is fundamental to group cohesion. If the men are to carry on their activities as a unit, there are many occasions when they must do favors for one another. The code of the corner boy requires him to help his friends when he can and to refrain from doing anything to harm them. When life in the group runs smoothly, the obligations binding members to one another are not explicitly recognized. Once Doc asked me to do something for him, and I said that he had done so much for me that I welcomed the chance to reciprocate. He objected: "I don't want it that way. I want you to do this for me because you're my friend. That's all."

It is only when the relationship breaks down that the underlying obligations are brought to light. While Alec and Frank were friends, I never heard either one of them discuss the services he was performing for the other, but when they had a falling-out over the group activities with the Aphrodite Club, each man complained to Doc that the other was not acting as he should in view of the services that had been done him. In other words, actions which were performed explicitly for the sake of friendship were revealed as being part of a system of mutual obligations.

Not all the corner boys live up to their obligations equally well, and this factor partly accounts for the differentiation in status among them. The man with a low status may violate his obligations without much change in his position. His fellows know that he has failed to discharge certain obligations in the past, and his position reflects his past performances. On the other hand, the leader is depended upon by all the members to meet his personal obligations. He cannot fail to do so without causing confusion and endangering his position.

The relationship of status to the system of mutual obligations is most clearly revealed when one observes the use of money. . . .

The leader spends more money on his followers than they on him. The farther down in the structure one looks, the fewer are the financial relations which tend to obligate the leader to a follower. This does not mean that the leader has more money than others or even that he necessarily spends more—though he must always be a free spender. It means that the financial relations must be explained in social terms. Unconsciously, and in some cases consciously, the leader refrains from putting himself under obligations to those with low status in the group.

The leader is the focal point for the organization of his group. In his absence, the members of the gang are divided into a number of small groups. There is no common activity or general conversation. When the leader appears, the situation changes strikingly. The small units form into one large group. The conversation becomes general, and unified action frequently follows. The leader becomes the central point in the discussion. A follower starts to say something, pauses when he notices that the leader is not listening, and begins again when he has the leader's attention. When the leader leaves the group, unity gives way to the divisions that existed before his appearance.

The members do not feel that the gang is really gathered until the leader appears. They recognize an obligation to wait for him before beginning any group activity, and when he is present they expect him to make their decisions. One night when the Nortons had a bowling match, Long John had no money to put up as his side bet, and he agreed that Chick Morelli should bowl in his place. After the match Danny said to Doc, "You should never have put Chick in there."

Doc replied with some annoyance, "Listen, Danny, you yourself suggested that Chick should bowl instead of Long John."

Danny said, "I know, but you shouldn't have let it go."

The leader is the man who acts when the situation requires action. He is more resourceful than his followers. Past events have shown that his ideas were right. In this sense "right" simply means satisfactory to the members. He is the most independent in judgment. While his followers are undecided as to a course of action or upon the character of a newcomer, the leader makes up his mind.

When he gives his word to one of his boys, he keeps it. The followers look to him for advice and encouragement, and he receives more of their confidences than any other man. Consequently, he knows more about what is going on in the group than anyone else. Whenever there is a quarrel among the boys, he hears of it almost as soon as it happens. Each party to the quarrel may appeal to him to work out a solution; and, even when the men do not want to compose their differences, each one takes his side of the story to the leader at the first opportunity. A man's standing depends partly upon the leader's belief that he has been conducting himself properly.

The leader is respected for his fair-mindedness. Whereas there may be hard feelings among some of the followers, the leader cannot bear a grudge against any man in the group. He has close friends (men who stand next to him in position), and he is indifferent to some of the members; but, if he is to retain his reputation for impartiality, he cannot allow personal animus to override his judgment.

The leader need not be the best base-ball player, bowler, or fighter, but he must have some skill in whatever pursuits are of particular interest to the group. It is natural for him to promote activities in which he excels and to discourage those in which he is not skilful; and, in so far as he is thus able to influence the group, his competent performance is a natural consequence of his position. At the same time his performance supports his position.

The leader is better known and more respected outside his group than are any of his followers. His capacity for social movement is greater. One of the most important functions he performs is that of relating his group to other groups in the district. Whether the relationship is one of conflict, competition, or cooperation, he is expected to represent the interests of his fellows. The politician and the racketeer must deal with the leader in order to win the support of his followers. The leader's reputation outside the group tends to support his standing within the group, and his position in the group supports his reputation among outsiders.

The leader does not deal with his followers as an undifferentiated group. Doc explained:

> On any corner you would find not only a leader but probably a couple of lieutenants. They could be leaders themselves, but they let the man lead them. You would say, "They let him lead because they like the way he does things." Sure, but he leans upon them for his authority. Many times you find fellows on a corner that stay in the background until some situation comes up, and then they will take over and call the shots. Things like that can change fast sometimes. . . .

This discussion should not give the impression that the leader is the only man who proposes a course of action. Other men frequently have ideas, but their suggestions must go through the proper channels if they are to go into effect.

In one meeting of the Cornerville S. and A., Dodo, who held a bottom ranking, proposed that he be allowed to handle the sale of beer in the clubrooms in return for 75 per cent of the profits. Tony spoke in favor of Dodo's suggestion but proposed giving him a somewhat smaller percentage. Dodo agreed. Then Carlo proposed to have Dodo handle the beer in quite a different way, and Tony agreed. Tony made the motion, and it was carried unanimously. In this case Dodo's proposal was carried through, after substantial modifications, upon the actions of Tony and Carlo. . . .

The actions of the leader can be characterized in terms of the origination of action in pair and set events. A pair event is one which takes place between two people. A set event is one in which one man originates action for two or more others. The leader frequently originates action for the group without waiting for the suggestions of his followers. A follower may originate action for the leader in a pair event, but he does not originate action for the leader and other followers at the same time—that is, he does not originate action in a set event which includes the leader. Of course, when the leader is not present, parts of the group are mobilized when men lower in the structure originate action in set events. It is through observation of such set events when the top men are not present that it is possible to determine the relative positions of the men who are neither leaders nor lieutenants.

Each member of the corner gang has his own position in the gang structure. Although the positions may remain unchanged over long periods of time, they should not be conceived in static terms. To have a position means that the individual has a customary way of interacting with other members of the group. When the pattern of interactions changes, the positions change. The positions of the members are interdependent, and one position cannot change without causing some adjustments in the other positions. Since the group is organized around the men with the top positions, some of the men with low standing may change positions or drop out without upsetting the balance of the group. For example, when Lou Danaro and Fred Mackey stopped participating in the activities of the Nortons, those activities continued to be organized in much the same manner as before, but when Doc and Danny dropped out, the Nortons disintegrated, and the patterns of interaction had to be reorganized along different lines.

One may generalize upon these processes in terms of group equilibrium. The group may be said to be in equilibrium when the interactions of its members fall into the customary pattern through which group activities are and have been organized. The pattern of interactions may undergo certain modifications without upsetting the group equilibrium, but abrupt and drastic changes destroy the equilibrium.

The actions of the individual member may also be conceived in terms of equilibrium. Each individual has his own characteristic way of interacting with other individuals. This is probably fixed within wide limits by his native endowment, but it develops and takes its individual form through the experiences of the individual in interacting with others throughout the course of his life. Twentieth-century American life demands a high degree of flexibility of action from the individual, and the normal person learns to adjust within certain limits to changes in the frequency and type of his interactions with others. This flexibility can be developed only through experiencing a wide variety of situations which require adjustment to different patterns of interaction. The more limited the individual's experience, the more rigid his manner of interacting, and the more difficult his adjustment when changes are forced upon him.

This conclusion has important implications for the understanding of the problems of the corner boy. As we have seen, gang activities proceed from day to day in a remarkably fixed pattern. The members come together every day and interact with a very high frequency. Whether he is at the top and originates action for the group in set events, is in the middle and follows the origination of the leader and originates for those below him, or is at the bottom of the group and always follows in set events, the individual member has a way of interaction which remains stable and fixed through continual group activity over a long period of time. His mental well-being requires continuance of his way of interacting. He needs the customary channels for his activity, and, when they are lacking, he is disturbed. . . .

A man with a low position in the group is less flexible in his adjustments than the leader, who customarily deals with groups outside of his own. . . . However, no matter what the corner boy's position, he suffers when the manner of his interaction must undergo drastic changes. This is clearly illustrated in the case of . . . Doc's dizzy spells. . . .

Doc's dizzy spells came upon him when he was unemployed and had no spending money. He considered his unemployment the cause of his difficulties, and, in a sense, it was, but in order to understand the case it is necessary to inquire into the changes which unemployment necessitated in the activity of the individual. While no one enjoys being unemployed and without money, there are many Cornerville men who could adjust themselves to that situation without serious difficulties. Why was Doc so different? To say that he was a particularly sensitive person simply gives a name to the phenomenon and provides no answer. The observation of interactions provides the answer. Doc was accustomed to a high frequency of interaction with the members of his group and to frequent contacts with members of other groups. While he sometimes directly originated action in set events for the group, it was customary for one of the other members to originate action for him in a pair event, and then he would originate action in a set event. That is, someone would suggest a course of action, and then Doc would get the boys together and organize group activity. The events of Doc's political campaign indicate that this pattern had broken down. Mike was continually telling Doc what to do about the campaign, and I was telling him what to do about seeing Mr. Smith and others to get a job. While we originated action for him with increasing frequency, he was not able to originate action in set events. Lacking money, he could not participate in group activities without accepting the support of others and letting them determine his course of action. Therefore, on many occasions he avoided associating with his friends—that is, his frequency of interaction was drastically reduced. At a time when he should have been going out to make contacts with other groups, he was unable to act according to the political pattern even with the groups that he knew, and he saw less and less of those outside his circle of closest friends. When he was alone, he did not get dizzy, but, when he was with a group of people and was unable to act in his customary manner, he fell prey to the dizzy spells.

When Doc began his recreation-center job, the spells disappeared. He was once again able to originate action, first for the boys in his center, but also for his own corner boys. Since he now had money, he could again associate with his friends and could also broaden his contacts. When the job and the money ran out, the manner of interaction to which Doc was adjusted was once more upset. He was unemployed from the time that the center closed in the winter of 1939–40 until he got a W.P.A. job in the spring of 1941. The dizzy spells came back, and shortly before he got his job he had what his friends called a nervous breakdown. A doctor who had an excellent reputation in Eastern City examined him and was unable to find any organic causes to account for his condition. When I visited Cornerville in May, 1941, he was once again beginning to overcome the dizzy spells. He discussed his difficulties with me:

> . . . I have thought it all over, and I know I only have these spells when I'm batted out. I'm sorry you didn't know me when I was really active around here. I was a different man then. I was always taking the girls out. I lent plenty of money. I spent my money. I was always thinking of things to do and places to go.

Doc showed that he was well aware of the nature of his difficulties, but understanding was not enough to cure him. He needed an opportunity to act in the manner to which he had grown accustomed. When that was lacking, he was socially maladjusted. If he had been a man with low standing in the group and had customarily been dependent upon others to originate action for him in set events, the dependence which resulted from having no money would have fitted in with the pattern of his behavior in the group. Since he had held the leading position among his corner boys, there was an unavoidable conflict between the behavior required by that position and the behavior necessitated by his penniless condition.

The type of explanation suggested to account for the difficulties of . . . Doc has the advantage that it rests upon the objective study of actions. A man's attitudes cannot be observed but instead must be inferred from his behavior. Since actions are directly subject to observation and may be recorded like other scientific data, it seems wise to try to understand man through studying his actions. This approach not only provides information upon the nature of informal group relations but it also offers a framework for the understanding of the individual's adjustment to his society.

II. The Social Structure

The story of Cornerville has been told in terms of its organization, for that is the way Cornerville appears to the people who live and act there. They conceive society as a closely knit hierarchical organization in which people's positions and obligations to one another are defined and recognized. This view includes not only the world of Cornerville but also the world of the supernatural. The picture becomes clear when one observes the way in which people symbolically represent their world to themselves. . . .

The *Festa* [annual festival of the patron saint] was a religious and social ceremonial and a sort of carnival at the same time. It was an elaborate affair entailing an expense up to $2,500 and receipts of a comparable amount.

I talked with members of the committees of various *Festas* to get an explanation of what it meant to them. One of my informants expressed it in this way:

> . . . Some ignorant people think that the saint can perform miracles. That is

not true. The saint can only ask God to perform the miracles. God is a God of Mercy. If the sinner prays to the saint, the saint stands in right with God, and God takes pity upon the sinner and forgives him his sins. That is the spiritual world. It is the same way in the material world except that here we are dealing with material things. If you drive a car, and the policeman stops you for speeding and gives you a ticket, you don't wait till you go before the judge. You go to the sergeant, the lieutenant, or the captain—some person of influence—and perhaps the captain knows your brother or some friend of yours. Out of friendship he will forgive you for what you did and let you go. If the captain won't listen to you, you talk to the sergeant or the lieutenant, and he will speak to the captain for you.

. . . It is true that the *Festas* are largely activities of the older generation, but nevertheless the view of society that they represent is fundamentally the same as that of the younger generation. According to Cornerville people, society is made up of big people and little people—with intermediaries serving to bridge the gaps between them. The masses of Cornerville people are little people. They cannot approach the big people directly but must have an intermediary to intercede for them. They gain this intercession by establishing connections with the intermediary, by performing services for him, and thus making him obligated to them. The intermediary performs the same functions for the big man. The interactions of big shots, intermediaries, and little guys build up a hierarchy of personal relations based upon a system of reciprocal obligations.

Corner gangs such as the Nortons and the cliques of the Cornerville Social and Athletic Club fit in at the bottom of the hierarchy, although certain social distinctions are made between them. Corner-boy leaders like Doc, Dom Romano, and Carlo Tedesco served as intermediaries, representing the interests of their followers to the higher-ups. Chick and his college boys ranked above the corner boys, but they stood at the bottom of another hierarchy, which was controlled from outside the district. There are, of course, wide differences in rank between big shots. Viewed from the street corner of Shelby Street, Tony Cataldo was a big shot, and the relations of the corner-boy followers to him were regulated by their leaders. On the other hand, he served as an intermediary, dealing with big shots for the corner boys and trying to control the corner boys for the big shots. T. S., the racket boss, and George Ravello, the state senator, were the biggest men in Cornerville. T. S. handled those below him through his immediate subordinates. While Ravello refused to allow any formal distinctions to come between himself and the corner boys, the man at the bottom fared better when he approached the politician through an intermediary who had a connection than when he tried to bridge the gap alone.

The corner gang, the racket and police organizations, the political organization, and now the social structure have all been described and analyzed in terms of a hierarchy of personal relations based upon a system of reciprocal obligations. These are the fundamental elements out of which all Cornerville institutions are constructed.

III. The Problem of Cornerville

The trouble with the slum district, some say, is that it is a disorganized community. In the case of Cornerville such a diagnosis is extremely misleading. Of course, there are conflicts within Cornerville. Corner boys and college boys have different standards of behavior and do not understand each other. There is a clash between generations, and, as one generation succeeds another, the society is in a state of flux—but even that flux is organized.

Cornerville's problem is not lack of organization but failure of its own social organization to mesh with the structure of the society around it. This accounts for the development of the local political and racket organizations and also for the loyalty people bear toward their race and toward Italy. This becomes apparent when one examines the channels through which the Cornerville man may gain advancement and recognition in his own district or in the society at large.

Our society places a high value upon social mobility. According to tradition, the workingman starts in at the bottom and by means of intelligence and hard work climbs the ladder of success. It is difficult for the Cornerville man to get onto the ladder, even on the bottom rung. His district has become popularly known as a disordered and lawless community. He is an Italian, and the Italians are looked upon by upper-class people as among the least desirable of the immigrant peoples. This attitude has been accentuated by the war. Even if the man can get a grip on the bottom rung, he finds the same factors prejudicing his advancement. Consequently, one does not find Italian names among the leading officers of the old established business of Eastern City. The Italians have had to build up their own business hierarchies, and, when the prosperity of the twenties came to an end, it became increasingly difficult for the newcomer to advance in this way.

To get ahead, the Cornerville man must move either in the world of business and Republican politics or in the world of Democratic politics and the rackets. He cannot move in both worlds at once; they are so far apart that there is hardly any connection between them. If he advances in the first world, he is recognized by society at large as a successful man, but he is recognized in Cornerville only as an alien to the district. If he advances in the second world, he achieves recognition in Cornerville but becomes a social outcast to respectable people elsewhere. The entire course of the corner boy's training in the social life of his district prepares him for a career in the rackets or in Democratic politics. If he moves in the other direction, he must take pains to break away from most of the ties that hold him to Cornerville. In effect, the society at large puts a premium on disloyalty to Cornerville and penalizes those who are best adjusted to the life of the district. At the same time the society holds out attractive rewards in terms of money and material possessions to the "successful" man. For most Cornerville people these rewards are available only through advancement in the world of rackets and politics.

Similarly, society rewards those who can slough off all characteristics that are regarded as distinctively Italian and penalizes those who are not fully Americanized. Some ask, "Why can't those people stop being Italians and become Americans like the rest of us?" The answer is that they are blocked in two ways: by their own organized society and by the outside world. Cornerville people want to be good American citizens. I have never heard such moving expressions of love for this country as I have heard in Cornerville. Nevertheless, an organized way of life cannot be changed overnight. As the study of the corner gang shows, people become dependent upon certain routines of action. If they broke away abruptly from these routines, they would feel themselves disloyal and would be left helpless, without support. And, if a man wants to forget that he is an Italian, the society around him does not let him forget it. He is marked as an inferior person—like all other Italians. To bolster his own self-respect he must tell himself and tell others that the Italians are a great people, that their culture is second to none, and that their great men are unsurpassed. It is in this connection that Mussolini became important to Cornerville people. Chick Morelli expressed a very common sentiment when he addressed these words to his Italian Community Club:

> Whatever you fellows may think of Mussolini, you've got to admit one thing. He has done more to get respect for the Italian people than anybody else. The Italians get a lot more respect now than when I started going to school. And you can thank Mussolini for that.

It is a question whether Mussolini actually did cause native Americans to have more respect for Italians (before the war). However, in so far as Cornerville people felt that Mussolini had won them more respect, their own self-respect was increased. This was an important support to the morale of the people.

If the racket-political structure and the symbolic attachment to Italy are aspects of a fundamental lack of adjustment between Cornerville and the larger American society, then it is evident that they cannot be changed by preaching. The adjustment must be made in terms of actions. Cornerville people will fit in better with the society around them when they gain more opportunities to participate in that society. This involves providing them greater economic opportunity and also

giving them greater responsibility to guide their own destinies. The general economic situation of the Cornerville population is a subject so large that brief comments would be worse than useless.

One example, the Cornerville House recreation-center project, will suggest the possibilities in encouraging local responsibility. The center project constituted one of the rare attempts made by social workers to deal with Cornerville society in its own terms. It was aimed to reach the corner gangs as they were then constituted. The lesson which came out of the project was that it is possible to deal with the corner boys by recognizing their leaders and giving them responsibility for action.

The social workers frequently talk about leaders and leadership, but those words have a special meaning for them. "Leader" is simply a synonym for group worker. One of the main purposes of the group worker is to develop leadership among the people with whom he deals. As a matter of fact, every group, formal or informal, which has been associated together for any period of time, has developed its own leadership, but this is seldom recognized by the social workers. They do not see it because they are not looking for it. They do not think of what leadership is; instead they think of what it should be. To outsiders, the leading men of the community are the respectable business and professional men—people who have attained middle-class standing. These men, who have been moving up and out of Cornerville, actually have little local influence. The community cannot be moved through such "leaders." Not until outsiders are prepared to recognize some of the same men that Cornerville people recognize as leaders will they be able to deal with the actual social structure and bring about significant changes in Cornerville life. . . .

COMMENTARY
DESCRIPTIVE CASE STUDIES

Let us begin our examination of research method by considering the two research reports from the literature of cultural anthropology which you have read as illustrations of one important approach to the study of social systems. Both Malinowski, in studying Trobriand society, and Whyte, in investigating a street-corner gang, select *one case* or a small number of cases (see **P-II** of the Paradigm of design alternatives), collect a wide variety of data about *many properties* of each case **(P-IX)** by the special method of *participant observation* **(P-VIII),** and handle and report the data in a largely *descriptive* fashion **(P-X and P-XI).** Thus these studies represent one of the many possible complex combinations of specific design decisions under the Paradigm. We shall start by examining this particular complex, and then begin to assess some of the specific alternatives of which it is composed.

It is significant that, in making their decisions, both researchers have an *exploratory* objective. Rather than aiming to test a limited set of specific hypotheses, Malinowski and Whyte present in advance only the outlines of a conceptual model, and then utilize their research findings primarily to fill in the specific details.

We, as methodologists, are concerned with these findings, not in their substantive aspects, but as the products of particular methods. Since we are interested in learning how to study social systems and their properties, we must also be concerned with assessing the kinds of results obtainable by various research designs. And because it is hardly fruitful to consider the methodological aspects of a piece of research apart from its theoretical framework, the present discussion suggests how each study selection may be evaluated in terms of the closeness of fit between sociological theory and research method.

Malinowski and Trobriand Society

Malinowski starts with a loosely formulated objective, stating that he wishes "to discover and analyze all the rules conceived and acted upon as binding obligations" in primitive societies. He does, to be sure, inevitably make certain basic assumptions, particularly about the nature of law enforcement in primitive societies, postulating that primitive man is motivated by "very complex psychological and social inducements," rather than by the automatic, "spontaneous" obedience to the norms and rules assumed by many anthropologists at the time. Although primitive man's law may manifest itself in forms different from the "central authority, codes, courts, and constables" characteristic of modern cultures, it does not follow from this that he obeys them automatically through some mysterious "group sentiment."

Thus Malinowski designates the broad conception he wishes to discard, and alludes to what we shall later call a null hypothesis, which is to be rejected, if possible, after examination of the data. Yet his alternative conceptual formulations are "very elastic and wide." He presents no specific research hypotheses of his own, asserting instead that he plans to work inductively from the facts, "without any preconceived idea or ready-made definition." We shall accordingly classify his research objective as coming closer to exploration than to hypothesis-testing; it is aimed at further specification of a model deliberately left vague at the outset.

The conceptual model which Malinowski translates into research operations deals with norms and rules as *properties* of primitive society as the *case*. Scattered throughout his account are numerous clues to the method he uses, clues sufficient to allow us to classify his design under certain items of the Paradigm—the first step toward our later evaluation of these items. As his concrete research case **(P-I)** he selects Trobriand society, concentrating attention upon this as a single case **(P-II)**. He sets out to amass a wide variety of information about this single unit, to study many relevant properties of the system **(P-IX)**. In short, given the exploratory nature of his objective, Malinowski chooses to conduct an intensive case study.

GATHERING THE DATA

Accordingly, Malinowski decides **(P-VIII)** to use a special combination of observing and questioning which is often called participant observation. He spends a long time with the group, "lives at . . . close quarters with his 'material,' " and gets to know the natives "intimately." As you have noted in your own reading, this procedure for gathering data enables him to extract clues, for example, to the manner in which Trobrianders handle a particular law in a particular system, and to the "reaction of the community at large" and the "consequences of fulfillment or neglect." Although he mentions the testimony of "informants," indicating that he *questioned* the natives about their norms and their activities, he also depends heavily upon "patient and painstaking *observation*," calling for "direct observation of the rules of custom as they function in actual life." He points out that the researcher cannot rely solely on what people say, but must combine observation with questioning. The "hearsay method" may reveal the ideal pattern of behavior as sanctioned by the community as a whole, but it may not disclose the extent to which actual behavior departs from this ideal. Hence he feels that the researcher must check what he is told with what he sees.

By employing this combination of intensive observation and questioning of the members of the group, Malinowski hopes also to avoid "piecemeal items of information, of customs, beliefs" and to avoid leaving the "rules of conduct floating in the air, or rather leading a flat existence on paper with the third-dimension, that of life, completely lacking." His recommended technique implies that the investigator immerse himself in the system under analysis. For example, in discussing the obligations surrounding procurement and distribution of food, he invites the reader to join him in observing the activity of fishing: "To enter more deeply into the nature of these binding obligations, *let us follow the fishermen* to the shore. *Let us see what happens* with the division of the catch." (Italics added.)

HANDLING THE DATA

As we continue to classify Malinowski's design decisions—in order subsequently to evaluate them—we note that still another distinctive feature of his procedure is its essentially discursive, *descriptive* method **(P-X)** of handling each of the properties of the social system. Malinowski seems, first, to describe what he observes, and then to make generalizations from these observations about many sociologically central underlying concepts such as mutual obligations, division of functions, sense of duty, realization of self-interest, and the like. That is, he isolates and gives names to a good many properties of the system, dealing with each in terms of his data. To be sure, he is not concerned with organizing the data systematically in terms of such concepts. The concepts are not explicitly defined or measured. Malinowski's report contains no scheme for classifying the kinds of obligations, for example, or for measuring the degree of obligation occurring in any given situation. He uses imagination and insight in dealing with system properties, but does not state exactly *how* he deals with them. His design is descriptive: it is not based on any form of systematic measurement.

Similarly, in handling relationships among properties **(P-XI)** he does not use an explicit, organized plan for determining how the categories are related to one another. Here again, his approach is qualitative and descriptive. He does not attempt to measure the degree to which one property varies with another; nor does he attempt to test statistically any specific hypotheses about the interrelationships of variables. Note that this descriptive handling of the data need not imply that Malinowski is unconcerned with the relationships among variables; as our discussion will show, Malinowski's model is based upon a conception of the interrelationship of system properties and parts. Nor would it be impossible by another research approach to handle just such relationships systematically and quantitatively. The point is that in this exploratory study the researcher is more concerned with locating and describing the relevant variables, and suggesting how they are related to each other, than with organizing his materials in more systematic form.

MALINOWSKI'S CONCEPTUAL MODEL

This study—like the one by Whyte—seems methodologically important exactly because it produces a detailed description of an actual social system. Although Malinowski does not refer explicitly to a system model, his findings are, in fact, consistent with such a model; and the study suggests, by way of example, how research may be used to arrive at a conceptual model of a social system. Let us now examine some of these findings, and then ask how they are obtained.

Nature of the Social System.   Trobriand society as a whole is described as bound together by a *system of mutual obligations.* For instance, Malinowski tells us that "the coastal and inland villages respectively have to rely upon each other for the supply of food." One has fish, the other has vegetables. The villages, which are economically interdependent, are also bound together by a complex network of kinship obligations and ceremonial exchanges, and "every chain of reciprocity is made the more binding by being part and parcel of a whole system of mutualities," with each community having "a weapon for the enforcement of its rights: reciprocity." Thinking of the villages as the parts of a society held together by these relational bonds enables us to see how the system model introduced in Unit 1 can be applied to a whole society.

Along the same lines, his description of the fishing fleet suggests that this fleet may be regarded as an occupational system existing within the larger society. Actually, three system levels are involved here: the *fleet,* which is composed of *canoes,* each of which is, in turn, composed of men playing *roles.* Since fishing is a joint venture, each canoe constitutes an integral element of the fleet. Thus each canoe has "its part to play in the manœuvres of joint fishing," and "every canoe is bound to come when a communal fishing has been arranged."

Within the canoe itself, each member of the crew, who is at the same time a joint owner, "has a right to a certain place in it and to certain duties, privileges, and benefits associated with it." That is, each has a role to perform in fishing;

each has defined responsibilities in the building and repair of the canoe; and each is rewarded by his share of the catch and by the approval of the others for having met his obligations.

Since the canoe is a small and yet complete system, we can easily see how it corresponds to the rubber band contraption described by Henderson in Figure 1-B above. The triangles in Henderson's diagram might represent the roles of crew members, and the connecting rubber bands the system of mutual obligations. (We might even think of the frame of the canoe, corresponding to Henderson's frame, as a purely symbolic representation of the social boundary that separates this system from its environment.) Illness on the part of a crew member and his resulting inability to perform his role effectively would disturb the equilibrium of the system. A severe disturbance, such as the absence of a member, might result in at least a temporary breakdown of the system altogether. Ordinarily, however, a substitute is provided for the absent member, so that all the roles are occupied even though the particular role incumbents may have changed.

Some System Properties. Malinowski's method enables him to deal specifically with a number of generally important social system properties. In the first place, he uncovers the property of *differentiation of functions* within the system. Catching fish, for example, is only made possible by each member's fulfilling the special duties of his role, each role making a specific contribution to the joint enterprise. There is a steersman, a net-tender, a lookout, and a master who (in the special role of leader) coordinates this activity and settles disputes, who is responsible for keeping the canoe in good working condition, and who also represents the crew in the larger community. Thus the data accumulated by Malinowski point to a division of labor within each system and subsystem of Trobriand society.

Malinowski also tries to ascertain how such a system of roles is maintained, another question of general significance in the study of social systems. Although he rejects the idea that Trobrianders perform their roles from any "automatic" or "instinctive" submission to custom, his data do suggest other types of inducements. On the one hand, he reports that personal desires motivate the fishermen to perform their appointed tasks, and he mentions the "utility of the pursuit, the craving for the fresh, excellent diet" and "the fascinating sport." Such *individual motivations* are reinforced, on the other hand, by the social system mechanisms of *role expectations* and *sanctions*.

In describing these social system mechanisms, Malinowski speaks of the "constraint of reciprocal obligations" that serves to keep the system going, claiming that "the social constraint, the regard for the effective rights and claims of others is always prominent in the mind of the natives as well as in their behaviour" (although such social inducements may be less apparent than the more direct personal ones both to the observer and to the native himself). The "mutual obligations" and the "regard for the rights of others" imply that each group member *expects* his own behavior, and that of the other members, to conform to the norms and values which are commonly accepted (*institutionalized*) within the system (or, as Malinowski says, "well understood"). Social constraint can be observed in the form of *sanctions*—the tendency to reward members for conforming to these values and fulfilling their role obligations and, conversely, to disapprove and punish deviance. Malinowski finds in Trobriand society a "sanction for each rule." He says, "There is in every act a sociological dualism: two parties who exchange services and functions, each watching over the measure of fulfillment and the fairness of conduct of the other." The native knows that failure to comply with his obligations will have serious consequences or sanctions. If he does not deliver his fish, he will not get his yams, or he will not participate in the ceremonial display of food and wealth which flatters his vanity and fulfills his ambitions. (Malinowski makes it plain, however, that not all the natives necessarily observe these role expectations rigidly. The rules are essentially "elastic and adjustable," and many a native will "evade his obligations" as long as he can get away with it. Thus the institutionalized values allow for a certain slippage, and sanctions are invoked only within certain limits.)

Malinowski sums up the social system in a remarkably compact statement, which, although referring specifically to the canoe, may be applied to all Trobriand society:

> Thus on a close inquiry we discover . . . a definite system of division of functions and a rigid system of mutual obligations, into which a sense of duty and the recognition of the need of cooperation enter side by side with a realization of self-interest, privileges, and benefits.

Thus Malinowski's research report deals with certain crucial aspects of any social system—aspects for which we shall often be seeking research indicators. It is generally true that social systems are built up of distinctive and connected roles; that role expectations and sanctions operate to maintain these roles; and that failures on the part of some role incumbents introduce strains on the system to which adjustments tend to be made. But these general characteristics take specific forms in concrete systems. And the exploratory investigator watches the details of the particular social system as they emerge, following each clue to the further observations suggested by the model.

Whyte and the Corner Gang

Whyte's research objective, like Malinowski's, is mainly exploratory. He states that "My aim was to gain an intimate view of Cornerville life," and further explains that "I was not immediately interested in broad generalizations upon the nature of Cornerville. It seemed to me that any sound generalizations must be based upon detailed knowledge of social relations."

Also like Malinowski, Whyte apparently wishes to "disprove" a theory—in this instance, the belief that a slum district is characterized by "social disorganization." Contrary to this belief, Whyte expects to find that "an area such as Cornerville has a complex and well-established organization of its own," although he apparently did not specify the nature of this organization prior to his research other than to note that it rests upon the "interaction of individuals in their groups." He thus began his study with a conceptual model that was little more than a skeleton, intending to fill in the structural details during the course of his research.

DESIGN DECISIONS

Let us also classify Whyte's design decisions according to our Paradigm, so that we shall be in a better position to judge their general methodological implications. Whyte, too, uses an intensive, descriptive case approach in order to obtain clues to the organization of this Boston slum area. As he puts it, "I was concerned not only with the 'important events,' because at the outset I had no basis for determining what was important except my own preconceived notions. I tried to keep my eyes and ears open to everything that went on between people in my presence."

Under **P-I,** his research case is clearly the group. While in the most general sense the empirical research case is Cornerville as a social system (parallel to the primitive Melanesian society studied by Malinowski), Whyte actually focuses major attention upon one particular part of the system—the gang—a subsystem found within the larger structure of the whole community, as Malinowski focused at times on the canoe as a small but complete social system within Trobriand society. (Whyte concentrates upon not one but a few such gangs as cases—**P-II.**) This decision to focus on one part of the social system of interest is often made by the investigator seeking a *strategic research site* (see Merton, 1959, p. xxvi ff.). Study of a part is strategic when it illuminates some of the more general characteristics and workings of the larger social system; the part represents, in miniature, the role structure and social processes which are often more difficult to detect (especially by a single participant observer) in the larger system.

Under **P-VIII,** Whyte's method of collecting data about the gang is also that of participant observation. In trying to understand the nature of the group's interaction, he found that "what people told me helped to explain what had happened and that what I observed helped to explain what people told me, so that it was helpful to observe and interview at the same time." In order to obtain data of sufficient depth to meet his research objective, Whyte lived in Cornerville for three and a half years, boarding for a time with an Italian family and learning the Italian language so as to gain access to otherwise inaccessible material and to show "sincere and sympathetic interest." He participated in the everyday activities of the community—joining clubs, taking part in team bowling matches, escorting local girls to dances, becoming a campaign worker for a local politician, and the like. Although the members of the group seem never to have lost their awareness of him as an "outsider" who was writing a book about their community, he did succeed in becoming a very active member of the social system he wished to study.

Whyte's methods of handling properties and their interrelationships **(P-X, P-XI)** are largely descriptive, enabling him to deal with many properties **(P-IX)**, and affording a vivid and detailed picture of the hierarchical organization of the gang and its position in the community structure. He does, however, also employ two essentially systematic devices. Through "positional mapping," Whyte sets down "the spatial positions of the members of a . . . club and indicate[s] which ones were participating together," thus delineating the clique structure both within and among gangs. Through the analysis of "set events" (in which "one man originates action for two or more others") and "pair events" (which take place between just two people), Whyte tells how he determines the hierarchical positions of the gang leader and his several followers (see also Whyte, 1941, pp. 647–64). These two devices suggest how some of the data from exploratory case studies may be handled systematically. They also point the way to procedures, to be illustrated in later studies, which are based upon a fully organized plan of measurement. Yet, the rich detail of Whyte's findings rest, not so much upon these rather special devices, as upon the broad, descriptive approach.

WHYTE'S CONCEPTUAL MODEL

This study, essentially a specific description of a concrete community and a few selected subsystems within it, again demonstrates how the descriptive case approach can be used to explore the nature of a social system.

Nature of the Social System. Cornerville as a community is perceived as a hierarchical structure in which the corner gangs, along with rackets, police, and political organizations, all fit into place, with intermediaries operating between lower and upper parts of the hierarchy. As a smaller unit within the community, the corner gang itself is described "in terms of a hierarchy of personal relations based upon a system of reciprocal obligations."

In analyzing the social interaction within the gang, Whyte develops a working model that seems basically similar to Malinowski's. The following passage—describing the mutual obligations in which the common values of the corner boys are institutionalized as a *code*—might easily be applied to the relationships Malinowski found among the islanders:

> The group structure is a product of . . . interactions. Out of such interaction there arises a system of *mutual obligations* which is fundamental to group cohesion. If the men are to carry on their activities as a unit, there are many occasions when they must do favors for one another. The *code* of the corner

boy requires him to help his friends when he can and to refrain from doing anything to harm them. (Italics added.)

As a matter of fact, every role structure can be conceived as involving patterns of reciprocal obligations. The field observer who is alerted to this conception will take pains to identify the particular sets of reciprocal obligations at work in the system he is observing.

System Boundaries and Equilibrium.   Whyte's analysis of the gang throws light on the nature of the boundaries that set the social system off from its environment, and on the major problem of how the system maintains itself within these boundaries. Although the system may be analyzed as a separate entity, it must also be understood as a network of complicated relationships and interchanges with other systems. The Nortons had to relate across the gang boundaries not only to other gangs like themselves, but also to social workers and school and occupational groups; they had to fit into the larger system of the community as a whole.

Within this complex setting of the whole community, the gang finds means of survival within its own boundaries (see Loomis, 1960, pp. 31–32). Whyte explains this in terms of group equilibrium as follows:

> Each member of the corner gang has his own position in the gang structure. Although the positions may remain unchanged over long periods of time, they should not be conceived in static terms. To have a position means that the individual has a customary way of interacting with other members of the group [the concept of role again]. When the pattern of interaction changes, the positions change. The positions of the members are interdependent, and one position cannot change without causing some adjustments in the other positions. ... One may generalize upon these processes in terms of *group equilibrium*. The group may be said to be in equilibrium when the interactions of its members fall into the customary pattern through which group activities are and have been organized. The pattern of interactions may undergo certain modifications without upsetting the group equilibrium, but abrupt and drastic changes destroy the equilibrium. (Italics added.)

As this passage indicates, equilibrium does not imply that the system is static, but rather that it is able to maintain itself against internal and external pressures. The corner gang is in a constant process of change as the group members find and lose jobs, spend money or borrow it from each other, win or lose at bowling, and so on. Role positions shift, patterns of action become modified, new values are institutionalized. The system changes, in fact, without necessarily returning to the same conditions that existed before the change took place. But the group continues in existence as long as it maintains its basic identity (as "the Nortons," for example) and as long as the group boundaries distinguishing it from other groups are discernible. According to the very definition of the system, it is only when this dynamic balance is seriously disturbed, when the system can no longer retain this identity within discernible boundaries, that the system deteriorates or disappears altogether.

Equilibrium is maintained here, as among the Trobrianders, by various mechanisms. The complex hierarchical structure of the gang, with its binding sets of mutual obligations, the role expectations and institutionalized values comprising the corner boy's code, all operate as *control mechanisms* serving to maintain equilibrium or to restore it when it has been disturbed. Although Whyte does not discuss control mechanisms as such, he does call attention to the "adjustments in other positions" that come into play when changes or disturbances occur in one part of the system. In analogous fashion, physiologists study the equilibrating mechanisms of the living organism—the biological processes that allow the body to adjust to injuries or disease.

A difficulty in understanding the nature of the equilibrium within a given empirical social system is presented by its latent character. Frequently the equilibrium is not readily visible until it has been disturbed in some way. Thus the code uncovered by this research is not a set of explicitly defined and recognized rules and responsibilities, for, as Whyte explains:

> When life in the group runs smoothly, the obligations binding members to one another are not explicitly recognized. . . . It is only when the relationship breaks down that the underlying obligations are brought to light . . . [It is only then that] actions which were performed explicitly for the sake of friendship were revealed as being part of a system of mutual obligations.

The methodological principle is that a *slight disturbance* in a system is sometimes necessary to reveal the workings of the system. This is the principle of the Henderson model in Unit 1 (see also Henderson, pp. 46–47). It is the same principle Walter Cannon used when he interfered slightly with the circulation of the blood in order to discover how the circulatory system works. Sociologists often want to investigate the various control mechanisms which serve to maintain or restore social equilibrium, and Whyte's work suggests one approach to the definition and detailed description of such mechanisms.

Role as a Connecting Link. An important part of the social system studied in Whyte's analysis is the role of the individual member—in particular, the role of the leader. Whyte looks at the leader—not, as the psychologist might, in terms of his personality—but in terms of his role in the social system. Whyte describes him as the "focal point for the organization of his group . . . the man who acts when the situation requires action" and who is "respected for his fairmindedness." Whyte's emphasis then is on the leader's role in the group, on the pattern of his action in the group.

Although Whyte, like Malinowski, is concerned with the role as part of the social system, other researchers may be more interested in role as part of the personality system. The role as the research case **(P-I)** may be conceived as part of either system. The researcher who deals with the social system (the corner gang or the fishing crew) will focus on the leadership role in relation to other roles in the group, and his model will be that of a social system (see Figure 2-A). For example, he might compare several groups to see whether their leaders tend to interact in similar fashion with other group members. If, however, the researcher's concern is with the personality of individuals, he will treat the leader's role, not as part of the social system, but as part of the personality system. He may, for instance, compare personality characteristics of several leaders to discover any similarities. Here he will need a model of the personality system, in which the particular individual plays this leadership role and also plays parts in various other social systems (his family, his church, and so on).

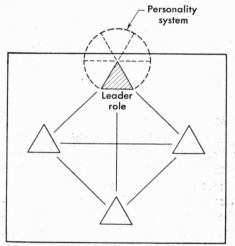

Figure **2-A** *Role as a link between social system and personality*

Since role is a component of both systems, it is conceived as a link between the two, making it possible to analyze the articulation of the personality system with the social system. Whyte, in his analysis of the situation of Doc's unemployment, conceives of the role as such a link. Doc has a role in the gang—as part of the social system; but he has also incorporated this role into his individual system of roles—as an aspect of his personality. If this role is altered by a disturbance in the equilibrium of the social system, then the dynamics of his personality system are changed. In this instance, as it happens, Doc develops dizzy spells which Whyte postulates may be related to a coincident restriction on his ability to initiate action within the gang. Thus, a change in a role may have an effect on both the personality and the social system; and the investigator who focuses on roles gains insights into both.

Some Methodological Implications

We have just seen how certain kinds of results can be obtained from a special combination of specific design decisions: the descriptive treatment of data **(P-X** and **P-XI)** collected by participant observation **(P-VIII)** about many relevant properties **(P-IX)** of a single social system **(P-II).** We have pointed out how the research *method* affects the nature of the data obtained, and suggested how some of the *conceptual elements* introduced in Unit 1 may be utilized in designing and conducting a study, and how, in turn, the interpretative phase of the research may add to and clarify the conceptual model. (See also, for example, such sociological community studies as those by Lynd and Lynd or Hollingshead.)

Let us now begin to consider some of the methodological implications of these studies—implications we will look at again as we analyze other related studies. What in general can we learn from the two descriptive case studies by Malinowski and Whyte? How can their particular methods yield findings that will feed back into sociological theory?

EXPLORATORY RESEARCH AND THE SOCIAL SYSTEM MODEL

We have classified these studies, in general, as exploratory in objective rather than hypothesis-testing. Exploratory studies are not to be confused, however, with raw empiricism, with fact-gathering that is unrelated to sociological theory. To be sure, both of these researchers assert that they are working inductively from "all the facts." Yet (as you have already seen from Exercise I-1), no observer can ever perceive and report *all* the "raw data." The well-trained investigator generally realizes that he is forced to select from the universe of phenomena, and so makes an effort to become aware of the bases for his selection. This selection tends to reflect the theory he has in mind, the kinds of assumptions which are implicit, if not explicit, in the original conceptual model.

Malinowski and Whyte undoubtedly started, then, with some concepts in mind—notions of the group as a network of relationships that support and are supported by the interaction among its members—concepts which guided them in looking for particular kinds of data and in abstracting the relevant aspects of interaction from what they saw and heard. A different model might have led them to look for quite different data, even to arrive at different (though not necessarily contradictory) conclusions.

Interestingly enough, both researchers protest against what they feel are mistaken interpretations of the groups they are studying: Malinowski protests against the common conception of primitive man's "automatic submission to custom," and Whyte against the common conception of the slum district's "social disorganization." These are both notions that developed out of a given set of assumptions, and it may well be that their use of different assumptions enabled Malinowski and Whyte to challenge these earlier interpretations. *Without some implicit notion* of a social system they might have been unable to discover the existence of a social structure at variance with the previous research findings.

To be sure, exploration based on a loosely defined model seems to involve what Stouffer calls certain "random ratlike movements on the part of the researcher before he can even begin to define" his problem (Stouffer, 1962, p. 297), but this does not mean that he has no model. His model and the concepts it generates are merely not yet precise. He has to seek data and elaborate on them for what Merton calls the "recasting of theory" (Merton, 1957, pp. 108–11). To state specific hypotheses before the model is clearly formulated would focus too early upon selected aspects of the system—aspects that may prove, after all, not to be the critical ones. This would prematurely divert attention away from, and perhaps even seriously distort, the broader view. Hence exploratory designs are necessary when the model, like the explorer's crude map, is still an outline to be filled in.

SOME ADVANTAGES OF DESCRIPTIVE CASE STUDIES

The designs of Malinowski and Whyte seem eminently qualified for this exploratory purpose. Let us tentatively list some of the assets, reserving until later any attempt to formulate them or to determine which of them may be produced by which design decisions under the Paradigm.

In the first place, the method used in both of these studies provides a *wide range of detail*. Instead of concentrating on just one specific area and selecting a few aspects for consideration, the researcher gathers such a great variety of data that he is able to see the actors in their total life situation. The reader of Malinowski's report, for example, learns about the Trobriand native as a member of a fishing canoe, as part of a complex matrilineal family, as carrying out his obligations in religious rituals and economic exchanges. Malinowski makes the fishing excursions and other activities come to life so vividly that the reader himself feels like a participant. This wealth of detail gives an immediacy to the findings that would be difficult to duplicate by any other research method.

Second, many *latent patterns of behavior*—patterns the participants themselves are not completely aware of and so cannot report—may become apparent through this procedure. Malinowski deals with the "hidden motives of behavior, and the hardly ever formulated spontaneous line of conduct." He uncovers—though he is not always clear *how* he does so—a state of affairs which no native, however intelligent, can formulate. Whyte discovers through his observations that a hierarchy of status actually exists among the members of the gang and is implicit in all their actions, even though "the corner-boys do not explicitly recognize the structure of the gang." In such situations, when group members themselves are unaware (as they frequently are) of the social structure in which they participate, the researcher cannot simply find an informant or an "expert" who can tell him what is happening. He needs some special technique to disclose these latent social structures, these hidden patterns of interactions and interrelationships. Psychologists have developed the *projective* test for studying latent attitudes and personality characteristics of the individual which are difficult to tap through direct questioning. And in some sense, the descriptive case study appears to be one parallel technique for uncovering latent aspects of the social system by piecing together a wide variety of relevant details and insights.

Third, and closely related to the other two assets of the descriptive case method, the observer is actually present throughout the selected interaction under study, and thus can grasp the *processes and patterns of behavior as a whole.* He does not try to recreate them, as an interviewer might have to do, by assembling information and assessing the consequences *after* they have happened. By spending entire afternoons and evenings at the headquarters of the Cornerville Social and Athletic Club, for instance, Whyte was able to follow an action process through its entire cycle, thus obtaining a rounded view of the patterns of interaction among the members.

The success of these studies is in large part attributable, then, to the combination of such assets—to the detailed, probing, rounded grasp of the system as a whole. In a sense, the method is an approximate application, through the use of purely descriptive data, of the rather complete approach (described in Unit 1), which translates into research the entire conceptual model, in contrast to the more usual (but second-best) partial approach, which only attempts to deal with a few isolated system properties. Malinowski and Whyte succeed in studying *many* of the relevant properties **(P-IX).** Claiming to work inductively from all of the facts, and they would hardly exclude from attention any property that appears theoretically important as the research develops. Then, after examining the relevant properties, they also succeed in *fitting these properties together.* Each phenomenon is studied within its social context—not, as Malinowski puts it, "isolated, torn out of its setting." Thus the focus is on the system as a functioning whole, on the organization of the several parts and properties of which it is composed.

SOME LIMITATIONS AND WAYS OF OFFSETTING THEM

In contrast to such assets, this type of research design also has a number of limitations. We shall examine, under each of three Paradigm headings, certain difficulties encountered by Malinowski and Whyte that tend to interfere with the accuracy of results—to produce *errors.* We shall also begin to consider certain means of offsetting these difficulties. Later on, as our methodological analyses accumulate, the difficulties will appear as particular kinds of errors, as instances of the failure to secure validity or reliability or generality of findings. Our attempts to prevent such failures will begin to provide the basis for subsequent evaluation of the full set of design alternatives.

Limitations Imposed by the Researcher's Taking a Role (**P-VIII**). These studies are subject to two types of error—control effect and biased-viewpoint effect—because Malinowski and Whyte, combining observation and questioning in the special form of participant observation they use, assume a role in the very system under scrutiny, and live "at close quarters" with the group in order to "gain an intimate view."

Control effect is a change in the action the researcher wants to study which, although it is not systematically built into the research design, is brought about by some aspect of the research process itself (as discussed in Units 4 and 11). This is a potential source of error in participant observation because the addition of a new member—like any change in a system—may affect the entire structure of interdependent parts (as indicated in Henderson's model, Figure 1-B). Especially in small social systems, introducing not only another person but also another role—that of observer—can affect markedly the relationships among the other members. Thus the researcher, often unintentionally and even unwittingly, controls, or changes to some extent, the action he is observing. Although Whyte made a conscious effort to avoid influencing the actions of the group, the effect of his presence is shown in Doc's comment to him: "You've slowed me up plenty since you've been down here. Now when I do something, I have to think what Bill Whyte would want to know about it. . . ." (Similarly, the physicist, in measuring the temperature of a liquid, may change its temperature somewhat by the act of introducing into it a thermometer that may itself be initially warmer or cooler.)

The difficulty with control effect in participant observation, and in many other research designs, is that it is *unsystematic* (**P-VI**) in contrast to the *systematic* controls which the experimenter, for example, builds into his research design when he interferes slightly with the action in order to measure the effects (Unit 11). The participant observer rarely attempts to measure the unsystematic control effects. Yet, as a sophisticated researcher, he will recognize the danger in advance, making every effort to minimize the changes he himself may introduce, and to allow for such changes in interpreting his data.

In addition to the control effect (which changes the action under study), there may also be a *biased-viewpoint effect*—a potential limitation affecting the observer's perception of this action. The observer, by virtue of the very fact that he plays a role in the group, tends thereby to impose certain restrictions upon his own understanding of the situation. His viewpoint may be biased in various ways. As long as he plays only one role, he perceives only those aspects of the system apparent from this role. As he forms alliances with certain members, he cuts himself off from the channels of information available through others. Since the leader of the gang and the lower-level followers obviously perceive the group differently, Whyte, if he had taken only Doc's opinions, would not have fully understood the opinions and orientations of the other men; his conception of the corner gang would consequently have been inaccurate and biased. (Sometimes the only feasible way to reduce the bias is to play more than one role, as Whyte managed to do so well.) Moreover, once the researcher becomes a full-fledged member of the group, familiarity may lead him to take certain phenomena for granted. He may lose his sensitivity to the possibility of latent patterns and merely adopt the attitudes and stereotypes of his informants. Or he may jump to conclusions, accepting too hastily an overly "neat" image of the action under study so that he unconsciously forecloses the possibility of further revision. To the extent that his familiarity with the group dulls the researcher's sharpness of observation, his results lose their objectivity.

Manipulating the Role of Participant Observer. In making participant observations **(P-VIII),** the researcher can govern to a certain extent the control effect and the biased-viewpoint effect by the way he establishes his presence in the field (as your experiences with Exercise I-1 undoubtedly begin to suggest). He may openly let his subjects know they are being observed, as both Malinowski and Whyte did, and as Whyte himself strongly recommends (Whyte, 1951, pp. 493–513). Or he may enter the system incognito, assuming some plausible role that the field affords (such as taking a job). Although the incognito approach often raises serious ethical questions, it may reduce the control effect more than would be possible if the observer makes his presence as a researcher known. If the role he takes is already an integral part of the system, his presence in that role is less likely to affect the rest of the system. Not knowing that they are being observed, the members of the group will probably be more spontaneous in their actions.

On the other hand, the covert observer may find complete immersion in the system, and the subsequent likelihood of a biased viewpoint, more difficult to avoid. Limited to his specified role, he may be cut off from valuable channels of information, unable to solicit information not normally accessible to his role without arousing suspicion. He cannot combine questioning with direct observation **(P-VIII)** as Malinowski and Whyte did. Moreover, since his project is being carried on *sub rosa,* he will not be able to stimulate interest in it (as Whyte did so effectively), and his subjects will be less likely to volunteer information that might be relevant to the research.

Occasionally, several observers are employed, some openly identified as sociological researchers, others not so identified, in order to avoid some of the difficulties. In general, however, control effect and biased-viewpoint effect, even though they may be manipulated somewhat by the type of entry, cannot be entirely eliminated in participant observation. Both need to be taken into consideration in planning and in evaluating the results of research that utilizes this method (see Manual I-A).

Limitations Imposed by Description **(P-X** *and* **P-XI).** Regardless of whether the researcher takes a role in the system under study, a second limitation arises whenever the procedure rests on unsystematic description rather than on measurement. Because the procedure is *not standardized,* the researcher himself cannot always employ it consistently (although long practice in a particular descriptive procedure may lead to a degree of standardization). Because the procedure is *not* entirely *open to inspection,* the reader cannot be sure just how each piece of evidence was secured. Thus it is possible that all sorts of errors may have been introduced in the course of observing, recording, and interpreting the data. These potential errors are not fully explicated or assessed; that is, one cannot determine how reliable the evidence is.

Reliability is often considered in the methodological literature in terms of independent study of the same social phenomenon by two or more researchers using the same (or comparable) methods. In this sense, reliability is defined as the extent to which the two obtain the same results. Clearly, the descriptive approach used by Malinowski and Whyte cannot state its procedures explicitly enough to enable others to conduct similar investigations in exactly the same way. (Whyte himself, in an appendix to *Street Corner Society,* says, "To some extent my approach must be unique to myself, to the particular situation, and to the state of knowledge existing when I began research." Whyte, 1955, p. 280.) It would therefore be difficult to compare the results of the Malinowski or Whyte studies with those of other researchers who might attempt a replication in either the same or other social systems. Suppose, for example, that a researcher wanted to test the generality of Whyte's findings by examining corner gangs in other cities. And suppose that his data produced results quite different from Whyte's. He could not be sure that his findings really contradicted Whyte's, because he could not be sure that his method was the same. The apparent differences might be due entirely to differences of method. That is, the two sets of gangs might in fact be fairly similar, yet appear different to different researchers who operate in a purely descriptive manner. Thus, participant observation, if it is to remain highly flexible and to exploit every fresh opportunity, cannot also attain the incompatible goal of maximum reliability.

A Modified Descriptive Approach. A degree of reliability may often be introduced into exploratory studies, however, by supplementing description with certain more systematic procedures **(P-X** and **P-XI).** Whyte's techniques of positional mapping and analysis of set events are not essentially descriptive, but are relatively standardized and open to inspection. Similarly, no exploratory study need remain altogether qualitative and impressionistic. Quite the contrary: the investigator making a descriptive case study in sociology should always remain alerted to the possibility of taking one sector in his initial observations and working out a limited but analytically informative systematic analysis, just as Whyte has done in this instance.

Limitations Imposed by the Single Case **(P-II).** In the third place, the researcher who devotes his full attention to the holistic analysis of a single system will encounter limitations on the *generality of his findings.* Just as generalization is restricted by the fact that the findings of descriptive studies cannot be precisely evaluated or replicated (see Lewis; Mack; Rose, 1953), it is also restricted by the researcher's focus (under **P-II**) on just one, or just a few, cases. He can hardly expect to represent accurately by a single case the many other unstudied cases of possible interest. The case study method does not determine whether other primitive societies, or other corner gangs, are similar to the ones under study, or whether these are atypical examples in which the researcher has described purely idiosyncratic properties. The primary research objective of such studies is not to generalize, but to provide fresh insights into the nature of a particular system, to suggest new ideas that might later be subjected to rigorous testing on larger samples of cases.

Some Uses of a Sample of One. Interestingly enough, however, the evidence from both of these studies suggests that skillful selection and analysis of even one social system may sometimes provide more generally useful information than might at first appear. For one thing, in studying any single *complex* social system, such as that of a local community, one typically finds several or many instances of similar subsystems—many families, or many gangs, for example. Both Trobriand society and Cornerville were complex enough so that the same pattern could be observed repeatedly in the various subsystems. Malinowski traces a consistent pattern of mutual obligations through a wide variety of institutions and organizations (fishing teams, marriage relationships, food exchanges, ceremonial mournings). Whyte finds the same hierarchical structure repeating itself in "every group" in the Boston slum district. Exactly because Whyte wants, as he says, to generalize beyond the single case, he studies qualitatively an aggregate of subsystems, dealing with five different gangs, and eliciting reports on other gangs from their leaders. Despite such consistency of patterns of actions and orientations throughout the structure of a single social system, it is dangerous to conclude that such patterns necessarily characterize other systems as well, for these may be merely reflections of the cultural integration of a single system as distinct from other systems.

Even more suggestive is the fact that, in each study, the case was selected as an *extreme example* of a particular model—in accord here with the researcher's stated intention to negate, if possible, an accepted theoretical position. Thus, Whyte studies the proverbially "disorganized area," and yet establishes the point that organization exists. Malinowski chooses to study that primitive society believed to be the "classical area of communism" and of "spontaneous obedience." His ability to reject the "spontaneity" assumption even here supports his generalization that, "wherever careful inquiry be made, symmetry of structure will be found in every savage society, as the indispensable basis of reciprocal obligations." Here Malinowski follows the logic of a fortiori reasoning: namely that his finding is all the more conclusive since, if it holds for the unlikely case under observation, it is almost certain to hold for more likely cases. In similar fashion, any specific hypothesis may be tested with a single case by selecting as that case one regarded as *least* likely to be compatible with the conceptual model.

COMPOSITE CHARACTER OF THE RESEARCH DESIGN

Although we have discussed these studies as if they used a single method, this method clearly breaks down into several separate design decisions. Other studies, by varying one or more of the design decisions, may offset some of the limitations and problems of the method used here. Many cases may be employed **(P-II)** rather than just one, as in Stouffer's study of community leaders discussed in Unit 6. Intensive interviews may be substituted for participant observation **(P-VIII)** in order to reduce control effects and certain biased-viewpoint effects (see the Cottrell study in Unit 4, for example). Systematic measurement may replace descriptive procedures **(P-X** and **P-XI)**—sometimes even in analyzing a single case (see Stouffer, 1962, pp. 253–60).

A crucial question is whether such modifications will reduce the effectiveness of the composite procedure we have been examining—a procedure at once detailed, descriptive, qualitative, and intuitive. The procedure, as we have seen, can be highly effective, especially for exploratory research, in developing a remarkably full understanding of the social system under study. How, then, can such a basically useful method be strengthened? How can it be modified so as to maintain the full understanding it provides while avoiding some of its major disadvantages? Much of our further analysis of other studies will attempt to find answers to such questions.

SUGGESTED READINGS FOR UNIT TWO

Becker; Dean, 1954; Furfey, Chapter 13; Goode and Hatt, Chapter 10 and pp. 330–40; Hughes; Daniel Katz, 1953; Madge, Chapter 7; Selltiz *et al.,* Chapter 3; Stouffer, 1962, Chapter 12; Whyte, 1951.

QUESTIONS FOR REVIEW AND DISCUSSION

Review the following methodological terms as used in this Unit:

biased-viewpoint effect
case study
control effect
descriptive analysis
generality of findings
participant observation
positional mapping
reliability
set and pair events

1. What are the chief advantages of the method of data-gathering which you used in Exercise I-1? What are the chief disadvantages and limitations of the method? Can you think of any ways of offsetting such limitations? When would you be most likely to use this particular method?

2. How would you compare Malinowski's procedure with Whyte's in terms of the degree of reliability obtained? (Define what you mean by reliability in making this comparison.)

3. How would you evaluate Whyte's techniques for establishing himself in a group as a participant observer, taking a role, explaining his presence, selecting group members to contact, and developing relationships with these members? What are the effects of such techniques on the action under study?

4. Imagine that you wish to study the social system of a large department store.

a. Discuss the suitability of the de-scriptive case study approach for this particular objective.

b. Would you become a participant observer? Why or why not? What kinds of roles might you assume? Why not simply ask the members of the system about the social structure they partici-pate in, combining their answers in some way to get the "true" over-all pic-ture?

c. How might you attempt to focus on the subsystems within the store (*e.g.,* particular departments)? Would you be likely to use Whyte's technique of positional mapping? His technique of studying pair events and set events? Why or why not?

d. What kinds of events might oc-cur which would allow you to study the equilibrating mechanisms of the sys-tem? Are there any which you as an investigator might consider introduc-ing?

e. What kinds of data would you record in attempting to study the kinds of role relationships, the systems of mu-tual expectations and obligations, in which Malinowski and Whyte were in-terested?

5. From your analysis of Malinowski's study, what do you take to be the con-ception of a social system with which he started his research—before actually do-ing any field work? What do you imagine was Whyte's initial conception?

6. Imagine that Whyte, instead of Ma-linowski, is observing the fishing expedi-tion. In what ways do you think his

method of observation and the resulting data would be different? In what ways similar?

7. What are the methodological implications of using two observers, as in Exercise I-1, rather than a single observer, as in the studies by Malinowski and Whyte?

8. Describe the methods used by Malinowski and by Whyte in interpreting the findings. Compare these with your own use of interpretation in Exercise I-1.

UNIT THREE
STUDIES BASED ON
MEASUREMENT

SUGGESTED PROGRAM OF STUDY

Unit 3 examines two pieces of research that attempt to measure their concepts according to some organized plan **(P-X)**, rather than to report their findings in an unsystematic, descriptive fashion. Since measurement involves systematic handling and analysis of the data, this Unit also constitutes an introduction to various ways of presenting the findings in tables or graphs.

Exercises and Manual

It is important, as the first step in Unit 3, that you review the use and computation of percentages—an elementary but very useful technique for handling properties that are measured and used as variables. **Exercise III-2,** together with the answers to it, and **Manual III-B,** provide such a review. Even though you may have had considerable experience in the use of percentages, several of the problems in this exercise illustrate some less familiar sociological uses of such simple calculations.

Studies

In making your methodological analyses of the studies by **Le Play** (and the Le Play monograph by Zimmerman and Frampton) and by **Bales,** consider the research objective, the underlying conceptual model, and the selections—and reasons for selection—of the particular designs and procedures.

Commentary

The Commentary to Unit 3 discusses some of the systematic procedures developed by Le Play and his followers, and scrutinizes the types of statistical tables and graphs in which Bales reports his findings. After careful study of this Commentary, you should take notes on the main points, making cross references to the Paradigm, the Studies, and the Manual.

Questions for Review and Discussion

Answer the Questions for Review and Discussion at the end of this Unit. Although these questions only partially cover the subject matter to which you have so far been exposed, they do suggest how to approach the cumulative methodological materials as they are presented.

FRÉDÉRIC LE PLAY
The European Workers

Preface

Since 1789, France has had ten different governments. Each of these has been established, then overthrown by violence. A state of instability and distress such as this is without parallel. . . .

I vowed to dedicate my life to the reestablishment of social peace [1] in my country. I never forgot this vow, and I am giving to the public the results of work begun a half-century ago. . . .

To rediscover the secret of governments which offer men happiness founded in peace . . . I developed a scientific procedure: . . . a method which gave me the opportunity to know personally all the nuances of peace and discord, of well-being and suffering which are characteristic of contemporary European societies. The goal of this present volume is to describe and justify this method. . . .

Everywhere societies are blessed where each individual has his "daily bread," and practices the "moral law." In making comparative studies of four types of societies, I learned how a society could acquire, keep, lose, and then rediscover these two basic values of humanity.

Among "simple and happy" peoples [2] . . . daily bread is plentifully produced by easy and attractive work done under the

direction of the head of the family. . . . The moral law is taught and its practice imposed upon all members of the community. . . . The father expresses his authority in the name of God: he is both pontiff and king. . . . This type of government . . . maintains peace and stability without any change. . . .

"Complex and happy" peoples occupy an important place in history. . . . The society is made up of many families, but each relatively weak. . . . The daily bread is provided . . . by wearisome and sometimes distasteful work. . . . In this type of social organization [3] families are very unequally provided for. Burdened, like their children, under the weight of manual labor, most heads of families have neither the knowledge nor the leisure time to teach the moral law and assure social harmony. In these two functions they are replaced by two public bodies which rule in the name of religion and government. . . .

In my travels I have never seen, nor has history ever pointed out, any people which has been able, beyond certain limits, to reconcile accumulation by conquest with maintenance of peace. Sooner or later, public power violates local customs . . . and oppresses the people, who, stripped of their former benefits, sometimes deprived of their daily bread, corrupted by bad example, fail in the duty to obey. By their revolt, they substitute dissension for peace and plunge the nation into an abyss of misery. This is the

Translated for this volume by Pearl J. Lieff, edited by Paul W. Massing, from Frédéric Le Play, *Les Ouvriers Européens*, Paris: Alfred Mame et Fils, 1879, *I*, pp. vii–xii, 12–14, 208–39.

[1] *Paix.*   [2] *Races.*

[3] *Organisation.*

change which is characteristic of "complex and distressed" peoples: it is this change which has been in effect in France since the splendors of the reign of Louis XIV.

This decline did not always result in ruin. Since the Middle Ages great nations, reacting against this evil, have created "complex and reformed" peoples. Such was the condition in France under Charles V, Louis XII, and Louis XIII; such was the happy situation of England around 1830; and such is still that in Sweden. These nations, in order to effect their reforms, utilized the means pointed out by the sages from Socrates to Montesquieu . . . namely the return to those local and national customs of flourishing periods. . . .

The method of observation of *The European Workers* has carefully traced the paths leading to reform; and henceforth those devoted to the truth will not be led astray. . . .

F. LE PLAY
Paris, July 1, 1879

Societies, Social Science and Methodology

In 1827, when I was leaving École Polytechnique, I saw the beginning of those social ills which today have become so dangerous; and like my eminent confrères, I at first dreamed of a means to remedy these. Since then, discouraged by various influences, my friends abandoned these projects. . . . I alone persisted . . . and, after a half-century of strenuous work, I am presenting my conclusions. The contrast between our results cannot be attributed to any superiority which I possess—rather it is explained by the differences in the methods which we have applied in our work. . . . My friends were convinced that the ills mentioned above could not be cured other than by the invention of a new social system. . . . I agreed that a reliable scientific procedure was necessary in order to cure those ills whose seriousness we all recognized; but I inferred that this science—like our natural sciences—must be founded not upon concepts established *a priori,* but upon facts systematically observed and upon inferences derived from rigorous reasoning. . . . I made, quite simply, a valuable discovery: in order to cure social ills, there is nothing to invent . . . [and] once I began to see this, I was quite surprised to learn that I could have found this truth demonstrated on each page of history. . . .

In all types of regimes, we may find the lasting indexes of happiness, peace, and stability in studying the sages who presided over the families, workshops, neighborhoods, cities or nations. . . . To understand the various types of social orders which exist we must carefully report upon the practices and precepts of those who were the true masters in each place, or in each epoch. . . .

To understand social science thoroughly, we are not obliged to decipher manuscripts and resort to the historians. In our field trips we can collect various data, and then fit them together with the help of our own reasoning powers.

The knowledge of happy peoples is only half the science. The reign of suffering began as early as that of happiness. The question of reform, which so justly preoccupies our contemporaries, has presented itself in every period, and we may find the solution of it in the facts of our time as well as in those of the past.

As to the mysterious problem raised by the eternal cycles of prosperity and suffering in societies, the method of observation resolves it as clearly as do the facts of history. . . .

The Method Used in Preparing Monographs on Workers' Families

According to common usage I call *workers* those individuals who work with their hands to make the products which satisfy the customary needs of societies. These individuals play an outstanding part in creating the means for essential subsistence. But these needs, as I have shown, show great differences depending upon the places, the peoples, and the times. From this it follows that the material and moral organization of the working population and the nature of the work it performs constitutes one of the characteristic traits of a social order.[4]

Among the most simple peoples, all families are engaged in producing for direct consumption. To a very great degree, the family is the exact model of the society. In order to understand such a social order, it is sufficient to observe the means and the way of life of the family as the typical producer. By the very nature of things, the worker is the customary object of this method of observation.

Among peoples which have achieved a higher degree of complexity, the working population still comprises the greatest majority of producers and consumers. The minority is represented by two groups, whose significance is quite unequal.

The first group, relatively numerous, consists of the ruling group, that is to say, the landowners, capitalists, and leaders of all types who provide means of production to certain categories of workers and direct them in technical operations. They also provide moral leadership and guidance which extend to the workshop those paternal functions performed in the home by the head of the family for his own children. This system of authority has always played a most important role in the most famous social orders....

[4] *Constitution des sociétés.*

The second group invariably consists of only a few individuals in the most stable systems: it is made up of families and sometimes only individuals who do not belong to the previously mentioned categories but who devote themselves completely to the liberal arts. Even in areas where devotion to the arts is especially strong, however, we may still acquire a good understanding of the prevailing social order by limiting our observations to that part of the population which is concerned with manual labor. In any case, it is necessary that this method of observation point out, with all necessary details, the relationships between the workman and the owner, and, if they exist, the relationships between him and the doctor, teacher, priest, judicial authorities, the armed forces, public officials of all kinds, and members of other liberal professions.

At first sight one could doubt that the study of a society spread over a vast area could be reduced to a systematic observation of a small number of families engaged in the principal types of manual labor. Man's nature shows infinite diversity. Children from the same marriage . . . often show opposing character traits. It seems, therefore, that there might be even more reason for expecting great differences among a number of families in the same environment and same profession. This assumption is not at all borne out by the facts. I am going to explain how good social orders can succeed in doing away with those inequalities which the diversity of human nature would produce.

Characteristics of Different Families Among Workers in Simple Social Groupings

The shepherds on the frontier of Europe and Asia present characteristics so identical that it is sufficient to observe methodically one family in order to know them all. The same is true for the semi-nomadic shepherds of the plains of the Atlas Mountains. . . . In these three regions the families maintain traditional uniformity and social peace through blood ties and customary neighborly relationships. Although, there, as elsewhere, the younger generation shows itself to be very receptive to new ideas and to change. . . .

Diversity Among Families of Workers in Complex Social Groupings

The need for peace and stability exists for complex peoples as well as simple, and it is satisfied by the same means. In both types of groupings, the society is made up of families, not of isolated and independent individuals. The problem of peace is always the same: to prevent individuals from giving in to those tendencies which will create discord. If this problem is resolved for families, it is also for the most part resolved for the total society; and the solution is the same for each of these social units, regardless of the degree of simplicity or complexity of the total society. . . .

The social problem does not change but the solutions to it are not identical. The solution must be modified in detail, if not in principle, as the number of families increases. Several factors work together to create major inequalities [among them]: not all families are engaged in the same type of work, . . . as is the case with herdsmen and coastal fishermen; the new occupations which develop do not contribute in the same degree to the moral order and consequently to peace and stability; finally within each occupation inequalities tend to arise in a territory which is densely settled and in a society which accumulates wealth. . . .

This growing division of labor and the complexity of social interaction always complicate the problem of peace and make the solution more difficult. Even in connection with paternal authority, which is one of the fundamental bases of the whole system,[5] conditions of well-being are lessened. It is clear, for example, that the tenant farmer, absorbed by his job, and subject along with his family to the dictates of several masters, does not afford the same type of security to the society as does the herdsman. . . . Primitive societies, in emerging from a simple to a complex social order, have always supplemented the loss of power of certain heads of families by means of two new institutions: they have always given to the church and to government the duty of rectifying these defects. . . . This solution has always been necessary; and, in the period when I began my work, I was fortunate enough to note among complex social groupings . . . a well-being similar to that existing in simple peoples. . . .

How by Observing Some Families the Criterion of Good and Bad Social Orders May Be Developed

In 1828, through my interest in social problems, I started on the path toward the solution—which I have pointed out in this work. . . . I was encouraged by my colleagues, who unselfishly were ready to share in my tiring endeavors. . . . At last after several years of sustained effort, my original conception of the observational method, which had been inspired only by reason and analogy, began to prove itself by the results. Although I had not yet reached any definite conclusions, it dawned on me that populations thought and acted differently in several important

[5] *Constitution.*

respects depending on whether they were satisfied or dissatisfied with their lot and that consequently, sooner or later, the method would yield to me the secret of well-being in a society. This is just what happened. The revolution of 1848 influenced me to make a new effort to draw, from twenty years of observations, the conclusions which my shocked colleagues rejected.... The following truths appeared to me indisputable.

Everywhere happiness consists in the satisfaction of two principal needs which are absolutely imposed by the very nature of man.... The first is the practice of moral law.... The second is the enjoyment of one's daily bread....

The method of writing monographs gives us ... the means to understand how these two needs are taken care of within the moral and material life of each family. It shows us the lasting qualities of the two fundamental elements of the basic system among flourishing peoples.... For a half-century, many of the observers mentioned in Volumes II to VI of *The European Workers,* and in Volumes I to V of *Workers of Two Worlds* frequently used this method in all regions of Europe and in many other countries of the world. They found in this work enough enlightenment to escape the yoke of contemporary innovations and return to an understanding of the great traditions of humanity.... The simplicity and usefulness of the method is attested to by the consistency and universality of findings obtained by a small number of monographs....

Peoples are made up of families, not of individuals: the observation technique, which would be vague, indefinite and inconclusive, if it were to extend in any given locality to individuals of different age and sex, becomes precise, definite, and conclusive as soon as it deals with families. It is in this obvious fact, based upon the social nature of man, that the practical effectiveness of family monographs rests.

How To Do Monographs

... The numerous details which are listed in the following chapters and which form the body of all the monographs, could only be acquired by long and painstaking investigation.... The observer must delve into every corner of the home; list furniture, dishes, linen, clothing; evaluate the real estate, available sums of money, domestic animals ... in general all the property of the family; estimate the food reserves, meals; follow in detail the work of the members outside as well as inside the home. The study of the domestic chores may present the observer with unending complications.... Still more delicate are those investigations which address themselves to the intellectual and moral life, religion, education, recreation, feelings about kinship and friendship, relationships with proprietors, associates, domestics and apprentices, and lastly to details of family history. Actually this last task is easier to accomplish than one would at first believe: because in general workers like to talk about memories of their childhood....

The observer must ask innumerable questions of the family he is studying, therefore causing them loss of time.... It may be presumed that a mass of questions may cause mental fatigue among people not accustomed to reflective thought and little able to coordinate their ideas.

Long experience has proven that these anticipated fears are groundless; at least the very nature of the work has always furnished the means to dispel them. Since the time of my first field trip, I have worked on 300 monographs, and have never failed to finish them to my complete satisfaction and to that of the family under observation. It has even often happened that my departure has been a cause for regret, sometimes even a sort of grief for all the members of the family. . . . Every intelligent observer understands the necessity of utilizing the following means to gain the good will of the family. Never ask a question brusquely or one which may appear to be insolent. Try to shorten . . . the preliminaries by getting the recommendation of some wisely chosen authority. Assure yourself of the confidence and the sympathy of the family by making them understand the goal of public service and the dedication which inspire the observer. Hold the attention of the subjects by telling them things which might interest them. Compensate them by allowances of money for the loss of their time which the questioning causes them. Discreetly praise the wisdom of the men, the charm of the women, the politeness of the children, and give well-chosen little gifts to all.

But all these elements of success are worthless or become even detrimental if they are not graced by the master virtue of the observer: respect for scientific endeavor. . . . In social science matters, observation applied to lasting facts offers guarantees of accuracy which do not exist in pure reasoning applied to the changeable conditions of private life or of politics. . . .

Guarantees of Accuracy Given by the Monographs

In this type of work as in all other scientific work, nothing can replace devotion to the truth which establishes the integrity of the scholar. . . . Guarantees of accuracy must be inherent in the method itself as much as possible. The family monographs fulfill this condition. For an outside observer the surest means of understanding the material and moral life of man is very similar to the techniques which chemists employ to disclose the secret nature of minerals. . . . Quantitative verification of the same kind is always at the disposal of the scholar who analyzes, systematically, the family as a social unit. . . .

Families, that is to say, those distinct social units which make up the whole of humanity, number in the millions. Each consists of several individuals. Each individual has his own life . . . each is endlessly altered by the stimuli with which the social institutions affect him. . . .

Indeed, as can be confirmed by studying the monographs published in *The European Workers,* all the acts which constitute the life of a family of workers result, more or less immediately, in income or expenditures. For it is in the nature of things that the money income of a family . . . be exactly equal to the sum of expenses and savings. Consequently, an observer can obtain complete knowledge of a family, when, having analyzed all the items contained in the two parts of the domestic budget, he finds exact agreement between the two totals.

This methodical principle seems on first sight to reduce social science to a study of the material elements of human life. In reality, it leads by the most direct route to the opposite result. Analysis of household budgets often produces startling evidence of this fact. Often in this respect a single figure tells more than a lengthy discourse. Thus, for example, it is not possible to doubt the degradation of a stevedore in the outskirts of Paris . . . who expends annually 185 fr. or twelve per cent of his income for drink but does not give a cent for the moral education of his five children between four and fourteen years of age.

The Two Research Guidelines on the Principal Conditions of Well-Being or Misfortune

... The material, intellectual, and moral life of the simplest family consists of innumerable details. In his research the observer should include as many as possible; but in the description he should neglect those details which do not serve the special purpose of the method, the work of social reform.... To reach safely the conclusions of his study he has two infallible guidelines, if he observes in all details the family situation concerning its understanding of the moral law, and enjoyment of its daily bread. He is always in a position to show that the family fares ill or flourishes according to whether these two main prerequisites for well-being or misfortune are present or not. These details appear very precisely in the figures which make up the gist of the monograph, that is to say, the household budget....

The Three Parts of the Monographic Model

In some respects the monographs give to the reader an understanding of the populations better than if he actually visited the places described.... This kind of usefulness increases with time; and in the future, our collections will offer to the reader a type of retrospective travel which the historians of our era will not supply.

This however is not the only purpose of these monographs; they should be consulted more often than read.... They are files of numerous facts in which scholars may seek information.... To aid in the comparison of places and individuals, I have reduced each monograph to an average of about fifty pages, keeping only the indispensable data. I have been able to attain this conciseness without deviating from my main goals. For this purpose I have always grouped the data into three parts:

1. The main subsection of the monograph, or the distinctive characteristics of the workman described;
2. The monograph proper, or the description of the family summarized in terms of the household budget;
3. The two supplements which explain the household budget simply and fully.

The Main Subsection of the Monograph

All workers are identified by common characteristics as has been pointed out in the earlier definition and hereby they can be distinguished from other social classes. However, they are far from being equal among themselves. In Europe, more than on the other continents they differ from each other in three main respects: the occupation that they have; the rank they hold in the work hierarchy of this occupation, the system of hiring which links them to their superiors in this hierarchy.

In describing the means of subsistence of populations, I compared the "social value" of different kinds of customary skills. I took as the criterion of superiority the relative aptitude which each of these skills shows in preserving the moral order for the families who employ it. Thus it is sufficient to list the occupation of the worker at the beginning of the main subsection of the monograph, so that the reader has a good method of placing the family he is studying in its correct position in a methodical classification of the population.

Workers in an occupation do not all achieve the same level. In rising progressively from a lower position to that which indicates the highest degree of comfort and respect, they can occupy six stations which usually follow each other in the order that I am going to describe. The specific nuances of each echelon vary according to the different regions in Europe: I herewith describe those which are most customary in the West.

Domestic Workers seldom have their own home: they are unmarried and attached to the household of their master. . . . In societies with simple customs the domestic has a lowly but secure position. . . . In complex Western societies the domestic has higher wages, but is rarely satisfied with his position and shows inclinations toward changing it.

Day Laborers are heads of families. In the simple societies of the Orient and in northern Europe they are always settled in houses they own. In the West they are more and more reduced to that abnormal situation which in this region is one of the principal causes of social antagonism and instability: they must content themselves with houses furnished by landlords. . . . The day laborers work exclusively for one or several employers. They are remunerated in part by subsidies based upon the needs of their families but chiefly by a money wage proportional to the number of days worked.

Contract Workers are heads of families working exclusively for others as do day laborers. However, they rank higher than day laborers because of two important characteristics. They enter into a contract with the employer . . . which obligates them to perform a given quantity of work for a given price. . . . In addition they acquire legitimate independence by becoming free to use their time according to their own convenience. They thereby take a first decisive step toward the condition of independence enjoyed by the master artisan who works for himself.

Tenant Workers take a further step toward independence. They use a furnished house rented from an owner belonging to another social class. This is always a lucrative arrangement. It brings two families together in a natural association. The owner is relatively well to do. He owns on his property means of production of which alone, he cannot make the best use. . . . The second is a family which does not have the capital necessary for efficient use of the property, but which possesses those moral qualities which are sufficient for success with the support of the owner. . . .

Worker-Owners occupy situations similar to those of the tenant workers but differ from them in owning outright the property which they occupy. This difference, even among those who occupy two pieces of property of equal importance, implies the social superiority of the owner over the tenant. The monographs on the two classes bring this superiority into relief with regard to material conditions, culture, and moral qualities. The owner does not have to deduct a rental from the fruits of his labor. He has sufficient discernment to avoid some of the dangers of failure and bad judgment; he does not need to have constant recourse to the good will of an owner as does the tenant. Finally, he resists vices stirred up by his sensual appetites and thus avoids the ambushes laid for him by the money lenders. The contrast that I have just pointed out demonstrates that we cannot suddenly transform tenants into independent owners.

Master Craftsmen, whether tenants or owners, are ranked above the preceding categories. . . . They work exclusively for their own benefit. . . . They are known by two special names in the two most customary occupations in the West: in agriculture they are called *farmers* and in the manufacturing industries of the cities and the rural areas, *artisans.* . . .

The ways of the worker's life are not totally defined by the mutual material interests between him and his master. The most important characteristic to be kept in mind is not the salary paid by the master to the domestic, to the day laborer or to the contract worker, no more than the debt owed by the tenant to the proprietor: it is the type and, above all, the duration of the relationship which binds the two parties. In general, this information is not specific to the worker being studied; it is characteristic of the society of which he is a part. In fact, it often allows us to anticipate whether the dominant characteristic of the social order is peace or unrest.

As the local population increases, there are three types of obligations which usually succeed each other. *Compulsory agreements* are common in countries where available soil is plentiful. . . . From what we know about the West in the Middle Ages and contemporary Russia, it can be inferred that the owner is more inclined than the worker to break the feudal bonds, when available soil becomes scarce.

Permanent voluntary agreements have succeeded the preceding type in the countries of the North and in the flourishing areas of the West in which peace and stability have been maintained. But since 1830 this second type of agreement has itself been increasingly replaced by the third type, that of *Short Term Agreements*. This last transformation occurs when respect for the moral law is undermined by the corruption of beliefs and mores. The shared values upon which rested the solidarity of owner and worker are rapidly crumbling; from then on it

becomes no longer possible to cooperate amiably in fixing wages or debt-payments. The discontinuance of the former relationship soon becomes inevitable. But since relationships between the two classes must continue and cannot be ignored, the previous state of social peace is little by little replaced by hostility. . . .

These discussions are enough to show how the description of a family is greatly simplified by mentioning the type of agreement in the main subsection, after having given information about the worker's occupation and the rank which he holds.

The Monograph Proper

The life of the workers is sometimes complicated in all its details, but it can always be summed up in two principal characteristics. Workers toil without reprieve to satisfy their subsistence needs; . . . and equally to develop some sort of balance between the struggle for their livelihood and the satisfaction of their needs. This daily and close correlation between these two elements of existence is hardly found among families who devote themselves to the free professions; it is often absent among those who have achieved the greatest amount of wealth; and at this social level it is altogether absent in corrupted social orders.

The rich . . . may actually be strangers to work. They often live far from the area where the source of their wealth is located. And even when they are not absentee owners, they are free to lead a life of leisure, and build for themselves an artificial existence, enjoying products from the various parts of the world. The description of a family based upon such foundations would bring little useful material to social science. It would give little information about the lives of other families of the same class. Finally it could suggest false impressions of the social order in countries where these families reside.

With rare exceptions the workers are in the opposite situation. They are settled in the places where they work. They cannot avoid taking part in local activities. They must be content with a most economical existence and they must secure locally the things which they do not themselves produce. For that reason, the workers, who constitute the most numerous part of the population, are the principal consumers of the products of the soil. Thus the description of a working family makes it possible to know most of the other families and mentions all the elements which are essential to the social order.

From what has been said, it follows that to have complete knowledge of a family, it is enough to report in full detail what it produces and what it consumes. By studying this information, we can become familiar not only with the material life, but also with the intellectual and moral life. As the monographs on *The European Workers* show, there is hardly a feeling or action worthy of mention in the life of the worker which does not leave its mark in the budget of income and expenses. . . .

The Two Supplements to the Household Budget

The method of the family monographs was developed as soon as I arranged all the details into a budget. I made it up of two lists placed opposite each other; and I made sure I had all the data by establishing the balance between the two totals of annual income and expenses. Summarized in the household budget of the

families under study, the monographs are able to furnish rigorously the basic principles of social science to the reader who has the time to extract them himself out of the figures, through sustained concentration. . . .

"Preliminary Observations" is placed before the budget to which it serves as an introduction. Subdivided into 13 paragraphs, it describes the kind of places, the occupational structure in the area, and above all the special characteristics of the family being studied. It then goes into the general features of income and expenditures, or in other words, the *means* and *mode* of existence. The twelfth paragraph gives a history of the family, pointing out the salutary traditions which have preserved awareness of the moral law, or those undesirable influences which have weakened or destroyed the practice of it. Finally, the last paragraph of the preliminary observations shows how the moral condition of the family, in combination with the customs and institutions of the country, create for it well-being or material discomfort. . . .

"Relevant Aspects of the Social Order" . . . does not belong to the main body of the monograph but is added as a final appendix. Here are pointed out those social phenomena in the face of which the worker is passive and the consequences of which, good or bad, cannot be attributed to him. . . . In complex, centralized social orders, the conditions imposed upon the worker by the restraints of the law, the acts of governments, the examples of the ruling classes, are very important: they cannot be related to the particular activities of the families who must submit to them; they must be included in the appendix as salient elements of the social order. . . .

Finally, it is needless to insist any longer that the often complicated life of a working family can be portrayed very simply through its household budget. In this respect, the many monographs in *The European Workers* give complete instruc- tion. A glance at a few of these mono- graphs will inform the reader much bet- ter than a lengthy dissertation could.

[The following monograph, *A Poverty-Stricken but Stable Ozark Highland Family* by **Carle C. Zimmerman and Merle E. Frampton,** adapts the Le Play method for studying the American family. It is one of a series for which Frampton collected the data during 1932–33, and is reprinted in part from *Family and Society,* New York: D. Van Nostrand Company, 1935, pp. 238–50, with permission of Carle C. Zimmerman.]

I. Introduction

This tenant family is probably the poorest in the region from an economic point of view, but its self-sufficiency and its solidarity have enabled it to maintain itself without recourse to public charity.

The farm is located two miles from Horseneck. Of the thirty acres share- rented, ten are in corn, nineteen in cot- ton, and one in garden and pasture. The farm home is located on a hill overlook- ing a narrow valley, at an elevation of about 750 feet above sea level. Three springs furnish the farm home with good drinking water and refrigeration. There are few trees on the land.

The soil is composed largely of dolo- mite and calcareous sandstone. It has been cropped for so many years without the necessary fertilizer that the yield is light, averaging less than half a bale of cotton or ten bushels of corn per acre.

The family purchases groceries, cloth- ing, furniture, and household equipment at Horseneck. Here also are found the bank, the high school, and the church. The family physician lives at Batesville, Arkansas. The railroad is at Lovetown, nine miles from the farm. The roads to the farm from Horseneck are dirt, good in dry weather, but impassable by car in wet weather. The roads from Horseneck to Batesville and Lovetown are gravel. Some of the family go to town once a week during the summer, but in winter only about twice a month.

II. The Family

The family at home consists of a hus- band and wife, five children, one daugh- ter-in-law, and three grandchildren. There are eleven members at home; three are away.

A. Living at home:
1. John, family head, age 60 years
2. Mary, homemaker and wife, age 56
3. Elbert, the second son, age 27
4. Ruth, the third daughter, age 22
5. Ray, the third son, age 19
6. Helen, the fourth daughter, age 15
7. Olin, the fourth son, age 13
8. The daughter-in-law, Elbert's wife, age 25; born in Horseneck
9. One grandson, age 5, Elbert's child
10. One granddaughter, age 3, Elbert's child

11. One granddaughter, age 1, Elbert's child
B. Away from home:
   1. Leta, the first child and the eldest daughter, age 36, married, living in Oklahoma on a farm, has five children.
   2. Rose, the second daughter, age 32, married, living in Texas, farming, three children.
   3. Ed, the first son, age 30, married, farming in Oklahoma, four children.

John, the head of the household, is a rather small man about five feet six inches tall. He is nearly blind and works little on the farm, having been more or less sickly since his early thirties.

Mary, his wife, is frail and has been ill constantly since her late twenties. In spite of this she does much of the work of the household.

Elbert, the second son, is married and has three children living in the household. He is in excellent health. He is the heir, and will be responsible for carrying on the family after the death of John.

His children, the boy five, and the girls three and one, are all healthy and have been free from the usual children's diseases.

Ray, the third son, drinks a great deal.

Ruth, the third daughter, is the most physically fit of all. She is married but not living with her husband. Ruth has had two illegitimate children, both of whom died in early infancy.

The other members of the family living at home are in excellent health and have no physical handicaps.

The oldest daughter, Leta, who resides away from home, is the mother of five children, all strong and healthy. The second daughter, Rose, is sickly, probably with tuberculosis. She is married and has three children. Edward, the oldest son, is married and has four children.

None of the members of the family have attended school. Even the children now of school age are not in school, and have never attended. The father of the family, and the daughters, Ruth and Helen, seem to be bordering on feeble-mindedness. The youngest son, Olin, seems brightest of all. The father thinks education ruins children. "Teach them at home is the best method." Schools cost too much, and have too many "big" ideas. Parents expect children to become self-supporting at fourteen to sixteen years of age.

John, who is illiterate, is a typical share-cropper of the poorest class. He has been on this farm for forty years. The family is considered "white trash" by the neighbors, and "poor whites" by the lowland people. He is a "little queer," but is well-liked and considered harmless. The family is always in debt at the close of each crop year.

The wife, Mary, also comes from a poor share-cropper's family. She is illiterate and is supposed to come from poor intellectual stock.

The boy, Ray, stole an overcoat at a basketball game during the fall of 1932, but the owner discovered him and made him return it. The community did not feel this a case for the courts. The older boys often get drunk and get into trouble with the "law," but nothing serious has happened thus far.

Leta, the oldest girl, married a shiftless mountaineer who moved to Flint, Michigan, for a few years of work. He has returned to the hills, owing to unemployment, and is a share-cropper. Other members of the family fear he will leave Leta and that the family will have to take care of her and the children.

Marriage is early in this family among both the men and women. John was married at the age of 22; Mary, his wife, at

18; Leta, their first daughter, at 18; Rose, their second daughter, at 17; Edward, their first son, at 19; Elbert, their second son, at 20; and Ruth, their third daughter, at 16. Elbert's wife was married at the age of 18.

III. The History and Religious Background of the Family

John was born in this township in 1874. He was the third son of seventeen children of Jim ————, a share-cropper whose parents migrated to these Ozark Hills from eastern Kentucky in 1840. His father left him not even a good name. The ancestry is Scotch-Irish from Pennsylvania. John's brothers, eight in all, settled at Lafferty's Creek about the time John settled at Horseneck. Five of these brothers are still living in the area. The sisters are married and all but two live near Horseneck. Two have migrated, one to Dallas, Texas, and the other to Tulsa, Oklahoma.

The parentage of Mary is very obscure. Her father, an Englishman, and her grandfather came from Virginia to the Ozark region in 1847. They were horse traders by profession. They left Virginia hurriedly and for unexplained reasons. Mary brought no money or worldly possessions as her dowry. She did, however, bring willing and capable hands which have enabled the family to exist through the present depression.

The present landlord set John and Mary up on this farm forty years ago. They had no money or stock when married. There have been periods of difficult times, but the family has never been without food. Nor has there been any great suffering. The members of the family enjoy life and seem content.

The family has little sympathy with many of the local religious communions. They attend the religious revivals which are held once or twice a year, and there they "get their religion" for the year. The members are superstitious and may be seen carrying out a regular family ritual for appeasing the "haunts." They like to sing hymns, and consequently attend the "meeting sings." Their favorite hymns are "The Old Rugged Cross," "Rock Mountain," "Rock of Ages," and "Shall We Gather at the River." The religious life of the children, so far as regular instruction is concerned, is meager. There is a Bible in the home but none of the adults read sufficiently well to use it. No Grace is said at table. The women profess to have an interest in religion, and talk a good deal about religious matters, but do not attend church, and contribute little or nothing to its upkeep.

They would not move to the city if they could. "It's cheaper and better here."

The family has some pride in itself. The children have been taught since early childhood to obey the community mores as these are interpreted by the family. The time spent about the evening hearth is devoted largely to gossip and talk about the crops. There is little formal instruction by the parents. Discussion often turns about the "furriner" and what he enjoys. The children are devoted to their parents and to their home. They visit frequently among themselves and find a good deal of happiness and pleasure in their family relationships. The family stands together as a unit, and if any member gets into trouble the whole family and all relatives stand behind the individual member. Elbert, the second son, will become head of the household and take over the tenure upon the death of his father, providing the owner will give his consent. Owing to the strength of local custom this consent may be expected.

The family as a whole spends little

time in trading or formal recreational activities. There are many family gatherings which are social affairs. The men pitch horseshoes and the women sew. The "religious meetings" are partly social and recreational. The boys play basketball frequently and two of the girls, Helen and Ruth, attend the 4H clubs. The youngest boy, Olin, plays a violin which he secured through a neighbor who taught him to play. For Highland families the social and religious life of this family seems unusually meager, but the members seem to be contented and happy.

IV. The Property

The property of the family consists of: *Values*

1. *The house*

The house, built in 1911, has one floor which is divided into two bedrooms, a kitchen, and a living room. There are no modern improvements nor outdoor toilet. Value at local reproduction prices is $150.00

2. *Farm buildings*

One barn, one hay-shed, one pig-pen.   Value $75.00.

3. *Farm land*

The family owns no land.

4. *Money*

The family has no savings. The only money which the family is able to secure is for extra work on roads or the sale of nuts or chickens to tourists. They have little cash and do their buying on credit established by their landlord.

5. *Stock*

One horse, two mules over two years of age, two milk cows, five pigs, twenty-five chickens, two bird dogs, and two hives of bees. $200.00

6. *Tools and equipment*

These include:

One plow	One harrow
One wagon	Two pitchforks
Two hoes	One anvil
One axe	One gun
One hammer	One rake
One hatchet	One sickle
Two shovels	One ladder
Two sets of harness	One saddle
One hand-saw	One large kettle
One drag	

(The landlord owns a half interest in the plow and the wagon)   50.00

7. *Household furnishings and personal property*   100.00

Total property owned by tenant   *$350.00*

Family debt owed to merchant and guaranteed by the owner of the farm   500.00

Gross debt owed after surplus from 1932–33 operations ($77.00) has been deducted   *$423.00*

V. The Work of the Members of the Household

The head of the household feeds and cares for the horse and mules, takes produce to market, cuts wood for home use, and works in the fields. The wife does the milking, feeds and cares for the poultry, takes care of the vegetable garden, and works in the fields. She also does the regular housework. She receives considerable help from the other women in the household. Elbert's wife, Ruth, and Helen do their share of the work. Elbert does most of the heavy field work and is helped by Ray and Olin. Olin cares for the pigs. Considering the size of the family and the amount of work to do, no member of the family should find his task burdensome.

They rise early and retire early. They all seem to have sufficient time on their hands, with little to do but sit and chew. The family begins work at 5 a.m. in the winter, and 4 a.m. in the summer. The tempo of the work is not rapid. They stop at 6 in the winter, and 8 in summer.

Little supplementary work was done by the family during the year of this study. Some years the older boys pick cotton for a few weeks, work on the roads, or go to Batesville and work in the mines for a short time, but this year very few supplementary occupations were found. Elbert did road work this year for wages amounting to $18.

VI. The Food and Food Habits

Seldom in the Highlands does one find a family whose table is so meager as is that of this family. The diet is composed largely of cornbread and pork. Some milk is consumed, and also chickens. The chief vegetables are potatoes (Irish and sweet), beets, turnips, onions, cabbage, beans, cucumbers, peas, tomatoes, and corn. Oatmeal, macaroni, and crackers are sometimes purchased. Honey from the hives is consumed. On special occasions, such as berry-pickings and "hawg-killin's" the family has a slightly different diet.

Three meals are eaten each day and all three of these meals are composed of practically the same food. Coffee is drunk with all meals. Breakfast is at about 6 a.m., lunch about noon, and dinner about 5 p.m. Pies, cakes, and sweets are rarely consumed. The parents have never seen nor tasted bananas, oranges, or grapefruit. Tobacco is generously consumed by all members of the household, men and women. All the male adults drink liquor which is made on the farm for home consumption only. The family spends about thirty minutes at each meal. Regular places are reserved for men and children. The women wait until the men have finished the meal.

VII. The House and Its Surroundings

The house is a small combination box and cabin type. In addition to the four rooms, there are two porches, one in front and one in back. The kitchen and the living room are heated in the winter by a large fireplace in the living room. Over this most of the meals are cooked. The kitchen has a kerosene cookstove, a table, and a cupboard which contains the few eating utensils. The living room has, besides the fireplace, one bed used by Elbert and his wife when no guests are present, two chairs, one table, one trunk, several small three-legged stools, and two pictures, one depicting the Arkansas Traveler, and the other a gentleman of the 18th century who is supposed to be a very important ancestor. No detailed information could be secured about this personage other than that he was famous for his good deeds in Scotland. The first bedroom is occupied by John and his wife, Mary. In addition to the bed there are two chairs, one dresser, one trunk, and a table. A straw tick in this room serves as a bed for Olin and one grandchild. The second bedroom has a bed, two chairs, a dresser, and two small ticks on the floor. Ray, age 19, sleeps on the porch in summer and in the hay barn in winter. When guests are housed Elbert goes to the hay barn and his wife sleeps with Ruth or Helen. A night spent in the household convinces one that over-crowding is not a serious problem even though personal privacy is not to be had.

On the back porch is a washstand, and towels are hung on nails driven into the house.

The kitchen utensils include one pot hanger, two andirons, one iron kettle, one copper kettle, one frying pan, four knives, four spoons, six forks, eight dinner plates, six china bowls, two drinking glasses, five tin cups, one jug, twenty-two lard buckets, one five-gallon kerosene can.

Lighting is by kerosene. There are two lamps for the house, and a lantern for the barn.

Laundry is done outdoors. Two flat-irons, a kettle, and an ironing board make up the laundry equipment.

The bedclothing consists of two cotton blankets, eight quilts, and one shawl (wool). There are no sheets. The straw ticks are made from sugar sacks sewed together. The two hand towels are also made from sugar sacks.

The walls of the house are covered with comic papers and magazine covers. The yard around the house is clean and bare of grass. There are a few roses growing around the house. The homestead is not well kept up.

VIII. The Clothing

The chief wearing apparel for men and boys is overalls. There are three caps, one hat, eight pairs of overalls, nine work shirts, two winter union suits, seven pairs of shoes, one pair of overshoes, and five handkerchiefs for four men and one child.

The four women and two girls have nine dresses, six pairs of cotton underclothes, three pairs of shoes, seven pairs of cotton stockings, and twelve handkerchiefs.

The clothing is exceedingly meager but they seem to have sufficient to meet their needs.

IX. The Family Budget for 1932–33

	Kind	*Money or* trade credit	*Total*
A. Income for the year			
1. Food produced and used at home			
Potatoes, 12 bu.	$9.00		$9.00
Sweet potatoes, 15 bu.	9.00		9.00
Beets, 2 bu.	2.00		2.00
Turnips, 5 bu.	2.50		2.50
Onions (dry), 3 bu.	1.00		1.00
Cabbage, 5 bu.	5.00		5.00

	Kind	Money or trade credit	Total
Onions (green), 1 bu.	2.00		2.00
Cucumbers, 1 bu.	1.00		1.00
Tomatoes, 10 bu.	5.00		5.00
String beans, 4 bu.	4.00		4.00
Peas, 5 bu.	2.00		2.00
Corn (sweet), 3 bu.	2.00		2.00
Blackberries, 4 bu.	3.00		3.00
Milk, 2,144 qts.	107.00		107.00
Chickens, 150 lbs.	12.00		12.00
Pork, 400 lbs.	20.00		20.00
Sorghum, 20 gals.	10.00		10.00
Honey, 3 gals.	1.20		1.20
Whiskey, 8 gals.	4.00		4.00
2. Rent of house	30.00		30.00
3. Fuel	25.00		25.00
4. Money or trade credits			
Sale of 7 bales cotton at $25		175.00	175.00
Sale of 25 lbs. chicken at $.07		1.75	1.75
Road work of Elbert		18.00	18.00
Total income	*$256.70*	*$194.75*	*$451.45*

B. Expenses for the year
   1. Food purchased for home consumption

	Kind	Money or trade credit	Total
Oatmeal, 40 boxes		4.00	4.00
Macaroni, 10 boxes		1.00	1.00
Crackers, 20 boxes		2.00	2.00
Lard, 20 buckets		15.00	15.00
Sugar, 150 lbs.		7.50	7.50
Coffee, 52 lbs.		4.50	4.50
Salt, pepper, 23 boxes		1.50	1.50
Baking powder, 25 boxes		2.00	2.00
Lye, 10 boxes		1.00	1.00
Blueing, 4 bottles		.40	.40
Matches, 30 boxes		.90	.90
Tacks, 1 box		.05	.05
2. Food produced for home consumption	201.70		201.70
3. Clothing purchased		49.50	49.50
4. Rent and fuel	55.00	3.00	58.00
5. All other expenses			
Doctor and medicine		8.00	8.00
Fork for hay		1.00	1.00
Postage		.15	.15
Personal taxes		2.25	2.25

	Kind	Money or trade credit	Total
Candy, gum, taxes		2.00	2.00
Tobacco		12.00	12.00
Total expenses	*$256.70*	*$117.75*	*$374.45*

C. Summary of income and expenses for the year

	Kind	Money or trade credit	Total
Income	256.70	194.75	451.45
Expense	256.70	117.75	374.45
Profit from operations, applied to reduce the debt of the family at the store		*$77.00*	*$77.00*

Any surplus over and above the amount of living expenses at the store is used to pay off the old debts, or to get credit on the next year. The landlord agreed to be responsible for the tenants' bills up to $150 for 1932–33, and the surplus was used to reduce the $500 debt to $423. Cotton production was checked at the gin and all grocery accounts were checked at the store. The tenants have almost no cash during the year, and depend almost entirely upon the income derived from the crop and the produce from their garden to furnish them with the basic needs of living.

X. Summary and Analysis

This family is simple and self-sufficing, not prosperous but making a living by raising most of its food. Mobility is low. Collective enterprises are few in number, and the members are extremely familistic in sentiment. They contribute virtually nothing to the agricultural surplus and are not a burden on the relief funds of county, state, and federal agencies. They have a few cultural contacts with the urban or rural worlds. The family is, on the whole, living in relative peace and stability and in partial isolation. It represents a low type tenant family of the Ozark Highlands.

The most important factors in the physical and moral well-being of this tenant family are its geographic and psychosocial isolation. Isolated as the family is, there is no special urge for its members to attempt to follow the standard of living of the lowlands or urban areas; such an attempt would wreck the moral as well as the economic structure of the family. They are content with what they have, and though their material goods are few, their wants are also few. Like their more successful Highland neighbors, they have moral and religious beliefs which strongly encourage habits of work, obedience to parents, early marriage, strict sex regulations, and strong familistic tendencies. The family hearth takes the place of the school room, and educates the children after its own fashion. Unlike their successful Highland neighbors, they are not blessed with much intelligence, and the ability to save and plan is lacking.

Briefly, this Highland family, at the bottom of the social pyramid, having poor native intelligence (the family, it will be remembered, is dependent upon a Highland owner whose father helped Elbert's father, and who feels an obligation to Elbert), and meager capital equipment, is able to exist, is semi-self-sufficing, and is content. The heir is already named, so that the family organization is the same as that of the other families described. Judging this family on the basis of its standards of living and its general mental ability, it would be on the relief rolls in any urban or commercialized agricultural area. The position of the family is, however, quite the opposite. It is socially prosperous although not economically prosperous. The chief reason for the success of this family, poorly equipped as it is, lies in the social organization of which it is a part. In the first place, the moral and religious sentiments of the community develop strong familistic ties which bind the families of the community in close relationship. In the second place, the social constitution guarantees a real interest of the "owner-patron" (in this case he owns land, house, and most of the equipment) in the tenant, his welfare, his family and his happiness. This "per-manent-voluntary" relationship makes it possible for this family to exist, while if one were to transplant this same family to another area under a system of "monetary engagements" it would in a very short time be on the charity rolls. In the third place, this family receives certain "subventions" or voluntary arrangements which provide the family with various necessities. The food, clothing, and sundry accounts at the store, guaranteed by the landlord, the road work arranged for them through the landlord, the payment of services in kind, the use of capital goods, and the carrying of debts without interest, are types of "subventions" granted by the social organization, making it possible for this family to exist and be socially prosperous although it is economically un-prosperous. Thus we find in the social organization the chief elements which make this family relatively successful in spite of its many handicaps.

ROBERT F. BALES
Some Uniformities of Behavior in Small Social Systems

I. Introduction

There is a growing emphasis in several of the social sciences on the microscopic study of social interaction in small face-to-face groups. Children at play, classroom and discussion groups, committees, planning groups, work groups, therapy groups, and many others are being studied

Reprinted in part by permission from Guy E. Swanson, Theodore M. Newcomb, and Eugene L. Hartley (eds.), *Readings in Social Psychology* (rev. ed.), New York: Holt, Rinehart and Winston, Inc., 1952, pp. 146–59.

by direct observation. This work requires standardized methods of observing, analyzing, and comparing the behavior which goes on in widely different sorts of groups under different sorts of conditions.

For several years at the Laboratory of Social Relations at Harvard a number of researchers have been engaged in the development of a method for the recording and analysis of social interaction. Up to the present time we have observed a variety of different kinds of groups, including some from other cultures, but our main experience has been with what could be called decision-making or problem-solving conferences of persons, ranging from two to ten, of our own culture. We are interested in the kinds of differences which appear under different experimental conditions. But our major interest has been in the understanding of certain approximate uniformities of interaction which seem to appear in spite of rather wide differences in experimental conditions. The uniformities reported below are all related to the fact that any particular piece of social behavior is always a part of a larger organized system of actions and reactions of more than one person. This inclusion in a system of interdependent activities affects the present character of each act and its probability of repeated occurrence.

A Standard Diagnostic Task

One of our basic assumptions is that there are certain conditions which are present to an important degree not only in special kinds of groups doing special kinds of problems, but which are more or less inherent in the nature of the process of interaction or communication itself, whenever or wherever it takes place. In aggregates of cases where the special conditions associated with individual cases are varied enough to approximate randomness, one would expect the effects of those interaction system tendencies that are due to inherent conditions to become apparent. We have used averages of large numbers of cases to help us form hypotheses as to what such tendencies of interaction systems might be, and have then tried to set up conditions in the laboratory, in the form of a certain type of task, of personnel, etc., which will produce actual results like our averages.

Gradually we have evolved a laboratory task for groups which does tend to produce typical results in this sense. In this task the subjects are asked to consider themselves as members of a staff who have been requested by their superior to meet and consider the facts of a case, a human-relations tangle of some sort in his organization. The staff committee is asked to advise him as to why the people involved in the case are behaving as they do and what he should do about it. Each subject is given a summary of the case material. After each has read his summary, the typed copies of the case are collected by the experimenter. The manner of presentation is such that the subjects are made uncertain as to whether or not they possess exactly the same facts but are assured that each does possess an accurate, though perhaps incomplete, factual summary.

It should be noted that this particular concrete task has certain abstract characteristics which are important in eliciting a range of diversified behavior. It emphasizes certain *communication problems* (or conditions) which are present to some degree in all social interaction. The communication problems of *orientation, evaluation,* and *control* are each to a major degree unsolved at the beginning of the meeting and can typically be solved to some partly satisfactory degree for the members of the group during the period they are under observation. More specifically:

a. With regard to *orientation,* members of the group have some degree of ignorance and uncertainty about the relevant facts, but, individually, possess facts relevant to decision. Their problem of arriving at a common cognitive orientation or definition of the situation must be solved, if at all, through interaction.

b. With regard to problems of *evaluation,* the members of the group will ordinarily possess somewhat different values or interests, and the task is such that it typically involves several different values and interests as criteria by which the facts of the situation and the proposed course of action are to be judged. Again, the problem of arriving at common value-judgments necessary to cooperative action can only be solved through interaction.

c. With regard to problems of *control* —that is, attempts of the members directly to influence each other's actions and to arrive at a way of controlling or influencing their common environment— the acceptance of the task sets up, in most instances, a moderately strong pressure for group decision, with the expectation that the excellence of the decision can and will be evaluated by each of them as well as by the experimenter, and, in this way, affect their status. The members typically face a number of possible alternative decisions or solutions, with uncertain degrees of potential frustration or satisfaction associated with various choices.

It is likely that these problems of orientation, evaluation, and control, with emphasis varying according to particular circumstances, are characteristic of a wide range of social interaction. They have much the same form and emphasis in a great many group conferences, work groups, committees, and the like that we find in our experimental groups. When group problems or tasks lack or greatly minimize any of these three abstract characteristics, we speak of them as being "truncated." When they are all present, and appreciably so, we speak of the problem as "full-fledged." All the uniformities to be described are apparently most characteristic of interaction in newly formed (initially leaderless) small groups, engaged in a "full-fledged" task. This raises such *problems of organization* as those of

determining the number of leaders there shall be, the parts or roles each member shall play in the process, and the status or prestige order.

Whether or not the members are explicitly aware of these problems of communication and organization, the necessity of some way of coping with them is inherent in the experimental conditions which have been set up, and this necessity will affect the character and course of the members' interactions. The members and their overt activities can be said to constitute a *social system*. This conception implies that the group cannot steadily move toward making decisions unless *all* the problems rising from both of these sources are solved. It also implies that the members' attempts to solve some of the problems will tend to make unsuitable the solutions they have already obtained on certain others.

But group members do not have *problems of communication* unless they have reasons to communicate. Faced with a "full-fledged" task, members of newly formed small groups are confronted with two major conditions requiring them to talk to each other. The first condition is that they want to perform the task. The second condition follows from the first: to perform the task, the experimenter requires them to reach a joint decision; and to do this they must find some way of forming and maintaining a social-emotional organization.

As people try to handle these interdependent problems or conditions of communication and group organization (which tend to change and evolve with each new act as it emerges), the overt focus of their activity tends to "circulate" among members and to "oscillate" from one problem to another, converging (in successful groups) toward some sort of "satisfactory" final body of mutually consistent solutions. Thus the interaction tends to go through both minor and major "phases" in which attempts to adjust to one kind of problem create certain other disturbances, attempts to readjust to these disturbances, in turn, create further disturbances, attempts to readjust in turn to these second-order disturbances, and so on. The idea of an interdependent system of members and their overt activities tending to reach or maintain some sort of appropriate and mutually consistent solutions to their problems is the basic concept that appears to lead to an understanding of a whole series of persistent uniformities in social interaction which hold over a fairly wide range of minor differences in social setting.

We shall discuss the way three types of uniformities of interaction arise in this process: first, uniformities pertaining to the "Profile"—the way in which qualitatively different sorts of acts tend to reach a sort of balance with each other; second, those found in the "Matrix"—the way in which the different members of the group tend to reach a sort of balance with regard to the relative amounts and qualities of activities they initiate and receive; third, uniformities seen in the "Phase Movement"—the way in which the members' activities are typically distributed through time in such a way as to produce a balance of work on problems of orientation, evaluation, and control. In each of these three ways of looking at the interaction process we should anticipate some kind of "give and take" which tends toward the solution of all major communication and organization problems facing the group in such a way as to maintain, or constantly regain, the members' ability to work together. Let us first, however, describe the method for observing interaction to obtain the data we need. A concrete example may help.

Description of the Method

A special room is available in which groups can meet and be observed from an observation room through a set of large one-way mirrors. Let us imagine we are observing a group of five persons who are meeting to come to a decision about a point of policy in a project they are doing together. What does the observer do, according to the present method?

The heart of the method is a way of categorizing behavior at the time it occurs, act by act. The data are analyzed later to obtain summary measures descriptive of the group process, from which inferences can then be made as to the nature of underlying factors influencing the process. The set of categories as it actually appears on the observation form is shown in Figure 1. The outer brackets and labels do not appear on the observation form, but, rather, show how each category is related to the problems of communication and organization which all such groups are theoretically supposed to encounter. The set of categories is held to form a logically exhaustive classification system. Every act that occurs is classified into one of the twelve categories. All of the categories are positively defined—that is, none of them is treated as a residual or wastebasket category for "leftovers." With competent observers and hard training, correlations between observers ranging from .75 to .95 can be obtained.

Let us turn now to a concrete example. We will suppose that this particular meeting is very orderly and will describe it in terms of a series of three phases. Each of the major problems of operation that groups typically face has been made into an implicit "agenda item."

Figure **1** *Set of categories used for direct observations of the interaction process*

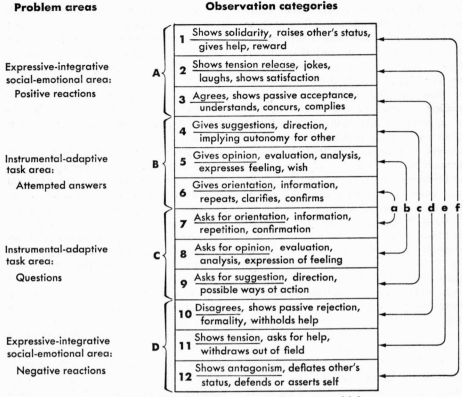

Problem areas   **Observation categories**

A subclassification of system problems to which
each pair of categories is most relevant:

a. Problems of orientation   d. Problems of decision
b. Problems of evaluation   e. Problems of tension-management
c. Problems of control   f. Problems of integration

Phase 1. Emphasis on Problems of Orientation: (*deciding what the situation is like*). The chairman brings the meeting up to date with a few remarks. He says, "At the end of our last meeting we decided that we would have to consider our budget before laying out plans in greater detail."

The interaction observer looks over the set of twelve categories and decides that this remark is most relevant to the problem of orientation and, specifically, that it takes the form of an "attempted answer" to this problem, and so he classifies it in Category 6. The observer has already decided that he will designate the chairman by the number 1, and each person around the table in turn by the numbers 2, 3, 4, and 5. The group as a whole will be designated by the symbol 0. This remark was made by the chairman and was apparently addressed to the group as a whole, so the observer writes down the symbols 1-0 in one of the spaces following Category 6 on the observation form. In this one operation, the observer has thus isolated a unit of speech or process which he considers a proper unit for classification, has classified it according to its quality, identified the member who performed the act, and the person or persons to whom it was directed.

As the chairman finishes his remark, Member 2 asks the chairman, "Has anybody gone over our expenditures to date?" The observer decides that this is a "question" indicating that a problem of orientation exists, and so should be classified in Category 7. He so records it by placing the symbols 2-1 in the space following Category 7.

The chairman replies, "I have here a report prepared by Miss Smith on the expenditures to date." The observer marks down the symbols 1-2 following Category 6, indicating an "attempted answer" to the previous question. As the chairman goes over the report the observer continues to score, getting a good many scores in Categories 6 and 7, but also occasional scores in other categories.

Phase 2. Emphasis on Problems of Evaluation: (*deciding what attitudes should be taken toward the situation*). As the chairman finishes reviewing the items on the report he may ask, "Have we been within bounds on our expenditures so far?" The observer puts down a score under Category 8.

Member 3 says, "It seems to me we have gone in pretty heavily for secretarial help." The observer puts down a score in Category 5.

Member 4 comes in with the remark, "Well I don't know. It seems to me. . . ." The observer puts down the symbols 4-3 in Category 10 to indicate the disagree-

ment, and continues with scores in Category 5 as Member 4 makes his argument. The discussion continues to revolve around the analysis of expenditures, with a good many scores falling in Category 5, but also in others, particularly Categories 10 and 3, and interspersed with a number in Categories 6 and 7 as opinions are explained and supported by reference to facts.

Phase 3. Emphasis on Problems of Control: (*deciding what to do about it*). Finally the chairman says, "Well . . . what do you think we should do about that piece of equipment?" The observer scores 1-0 in Category 9. Member 2 says, "I think we should get it." The observer scores 2-0 in Category 4. As Member 2 begins to support his suggestion, Member 3 breaks in with a counterargument, and the discussion begins to grow heated, with more disagreement. Presently the observer notices that Member 5, who has said little up to this point, sighs heavily and begins to examine his fingernails. The observer puts down a score under Category 11.

In the meantime, Member 3, the chronic objector, comes through with a remark directed at Member 2, "Well, I never did agree about hiring that deadhead secretary. All she's got is looks, but I guess that's enough for Joe." The others laugh at this. The observer scores the first and second remarks under Category 12 as showing antagonism, and scores the laugh which follows as tension release in Category 2.

At this point Member 5 comes in quietly to sum up the argument, and by the time he finishes several heads are nodding. The observer scores both the nods and the audible agreements in Category 3. Member 3, the chronic objector, who is also the chronic joker, comes in with a joke at this point, and the joking and laughing continue for a minute or two, each member extending the joke a little. The observer continues to score in Category 2 as long as the laughing continues. As the members pick up their things one of them says, "Well, I think we got through that in good shape. Old Bill certainly puts in the right word at the right time, doesn't he?" The observer marks down two scores for the speaker under Category 1, shows solidarity, and after a few more similar remarks the meeting breaks up.

The idea that groups go through certain stages or phases in the process of solving problems, or that problem-solving would somehow be more effective if some prescribed order were followed, has been current in the literature for some time. However, the distinction between predicting an empirical order of phases as they will actually take place under some specific set of conditions, and prescribing an ideal order in terms of value judgments has not always been clearly drawn. It has typically not been recognized that different types of conditions or problems may result empirically in different sorts of phase movement. We have found that there are, indeed, *certain* conditions which must be quite carefully specified, under which a group problem-solving process essentially like that sketched above does tend to appear. These conditions can be set up experimentally in the laboratory, and have already been described above as the standard diagnostic task around which our other generalizations all revolve.

Unfortunately, space does not permit the presentation of the evidence in detail. In general, the patterns described and illustrated can be understood to refer to approximate or average uniformities in aggregates of large numbers of cases under randomly varying external conditions, and in addition, they can be understood to hold more uniformly and in particular under the full-fledged conditions of the standard diagnostic task described above.

Profiles

One of the important characteristics of interaction is the distribution of total number of acts among the twelve categories listed in Figure 1. A distribution of this kind, expressed in percentage rates based on the total number of acts, is called a profile. An illustrative and typical comparison of group profiles of two five-man groups working on the standard diagnostic task is shown in Table 1.

Different kinds of groups operating under different kinds of conditions produce different types of profiles. In the present illustration the "successful" group attained a higher rate of suggestions and more often followed these with positive reactions, rather than with negative reactions and questions, than did the "unsuccessful" group.

The profiles produced by groups, however, are not completely and radically different from each other. The profile produced by the average of these two illustrative groups is more or less typical of averages of larger aggregates. "Attempted Answers"—that is, giving orientation, opinion, and suggestion—are nearly always more numerous than their cognate "Questions"—that is, asking for orientation, opinion, or suggestion. Similarly, "Positive Reactions"—that is, agreement, showing tension release, and solidarity—are usually more numerous than the "Negative Reactions" of showing disagreement, tension, and antagonism. Intuitively, one would feel that the process would surely be self-defeating and self-limiting if there were more questions than answers and more negative reactions than positive.

On the average, for the groups we have examined, the relative proportions of different kinds of interaction are about as they are in Table 1. Although the illustration makes no breakdown to show

Table **1** *Profiles of "satisfied" and "dissatisfied" groups on case discussion task*

Category	Satisfied [a]	Dissatisfied [b]	Average of the two	Average rates by sections
		Meeting profiles in percentage rates		
1. Shows solidarity	.7	.8	.7	
2. Shows tension release	7.9	6.8	7.3	25.0
3. Agrees	24.9	9.6	17.0	
4. Gives suggestion	8.2	3.6	5.9	
5. Gives opinion	26.7	30.5	28.7	56.7
6. Gives orientation	22.4	21.9	22.1	
7. Asks for orientation	1.7	5.7	3.8	
8. Asks for opinion	1.7	2.2	2.0	6.9
9. Asks for suggestion	.5	1.6	1.1	
10. Disagrees	4.0	12.4	8.3	
11. Shows tension	1.0	2.6	1.8	11.4
12. Shows antagonism	.3	2.2	1.3	
Raw score total	*719*	*767*	*1486*	*100.0*

[a] The highest of sixteen groups, identified as HR2-2. The members rated their own satisfaction with their solution after the meeting at an average of 10.4 on a scale running from 0 to a highest possible rating of 12.

[b] The lowest of sixteen groups, identified as HR3-3. Comparable satisfaction rating in this group was 2.6.

changes over time, note how the final balance among the proportions suggests that it might be the end result of a series of small sequences which consists of (1) an initial disturbance of a system (precipitated by the introjection of a new idea, or opinion, or suggestion into the group) followed by (2) a dwindling series of feedbacks and corrections as the disturbance is terminated, quenched, or assimilated by other parts or members of the system. "Attempted Answers," or, as one might call them for the moment, "Initial Acts," account for a little over half (or 57 percent) of the total activity, with "Positive and Negative Reactions" and "Questions" accounting for roughly the other half. One might say that quantitatively (as well as qualitatively, by definition) interaction is a process consisting of action followed by reaction. Sometimes a single positive reaction restores the "balance." At other times a longer sequence is necessary. Consider the rates in the following way. Looking at the reaction side alone, and assuming it to be 50 percent of the total, about half (or 25 percent) is "Positive" and presumably terminates the disturbance introduced by the initial action. This leaves a portion of about 25 percent which fails to terminate the disturbance. Of this nonterminating portion, about half (or 12 percent) consists of "Negative Reactions," which typically precipitate further "Attempted Answers," thus beginning a repetition of the cycle. Of the remaining hypothetical 13 percent or so, about half (or 7 percent) are "Questions," which also, typically, precipitate "Attempted Answers." If about 7 percent of "Attempted Answers" are in direct response to "Questions," these might well be called "Reactions," thus leaving the balance of "Initial acts" to "Reactions" about 50-50, as assumed above.

When tabulations are made of the frequency with which specific acts tend to lead to other types of specific acts the mechanisms by which the gross distribution of the profile arises become apparent. "Attempted Answers" tend to lead to "Positive Reactions" which in turn tend to return to more "Attempted Answers." When "Negative Reactions" appear, they tend to lead back to more "Attempted Answers." When "Questions" appear they tend to lead to "Attempted Answers." "Questions" seldom lead directly to either "Positive" or "Negative Reactions." These tendencies appear to be more or less inherent in interaction that is purposeful and goal-directed, if indeed it is "getting anywhere" and producing "satisfaction" even in a minimal way for the participants. The interesting differences between groups tend to be relatively minor variations on this general pattern, as in Table 1.

Who-to-Whom Matrix

Another important direction of analysis deals with the way in which participation is distributed between members. The total number of different possible combinations of who is speaking and to whom for a given time period is called a matrix. Table 2 shows a matrix containing all the interaction initiated by and directed toward the members of eighteen different six-man groups.

The pattern of distribution for particular groups is different in detail under different conditions. For example, groups with no designated leader generally tend to have more equal participation than groups with designated leaders of higher status. However, in spite of these differences, the distribution of total amounts each member tends to address to the group as a whole, as well as the amounts men in each rank tend to talk to men in each other rank position seem to be subject to system-influences, which tend to produce similarities from group to group, and some regular gradations by group size.

Table **2** *Aggregate matrix for eighteen sessions of six-man groups, all types of activity*

Rank of person originating act	To individuals of each rank						Total to individuals	To group as a whole	Total initiated
	1	2	3	4	5	6		0	
1		1,238	961	545	445	317	3,506	5,661	9,167
2	1,748		443	310	175	102	2,778	1,211	3,989
3	1,371	415		305	125	69	2,285	742	3,027
4	952	310	282		83	49	1,676	676	2,352
5	662	224	144	83		28	1,141	443	1,584
6	470	126	114	65	44		819	373	1,192
Total received	*5,203*	*2,313*	*1,944*	*1,308*	*872*	*565*	*12,205*	*9,106*	*21,311*

These generalizations may be illustrated in part by reference to Table 2. Although this is an aggregate matrix for eighteen different groups, each of which has been rank-ordered before adding, it is sufficiently like those of particular groups to serve as an illustration. If the personnel for a particular group are arrayed in rank order according to the total amount they speak we then find that they are spoken to in amounts proportionate to their rank order. In general, each man receives back about half as much as he initiates in total. It will be remembered from the data in the profile that something like half of all interaction is "reactive" in a qualitative sense. Each man spends a certain portion of his time reacting to the initial acts of others. This amount of time differs, however, according to the rank of the member.

Matrices have been constructed for particular categories of activity. The most frequent initiator of acts tends to give out more information and opinion to specific individuals than he receives, while, on the contrary, initiators with low frequencies give out more agreement, disagreement, and requests for information than they receive. The profiles of participants tend to change systematically as we proceed downward in rank. High-ranking men tend to have more "Initial Actions" (Section B) in their profiles, while low-ranking men have more "Reactions," both positive and negative. These qualitative differences are important for the social organization of the members. *Quantitative* differentiation in participation is accompanied by, or is symptomatic of, *qualitative differentiation of roles* of members.

If this is true one might expect quantity of participation to be related to the status hierarchy of the members. We typically find that the order produced by ranking individuals according to their total amounts of participation is the same as the order produced by their own ratings of each other as to "Productivity"—who has the best ideas and who does the most to guide the discussion effectively, as well as the order of "popularity" produced by their own ratings of whom they most like and dislike. Similar findings are reported by Norfleet and Bass with correlations of about .95 in each case. Strodtbeck finds, in addition, a fairly dependable connection between amount of activity initiated and probability of winning in contested decisions (which is a kind of measure of power or influence). The empirical correlation between status as the participants feel it and amounts of participation given out and received under the conditions described seems to be pretty well established. The explanation of this regularity apparently lies in understanding the values ascribed by the members to the qualitative differences in roles which are usually connected with quantity—not in the sheer quantity alone.

Size of group is obviously an important condition affecting the distribution of activities. From present indications it appears that the top man in groups larger than five or so tends to speak considerably more to the group as a whole than to specific individuals in the group, as in Table 2. All other members tend to speak more to specific individuals (and particularly to the top man) than to the group as a whole. Each man tends to speak to each other man in an amount which is a probability function of both his own rank on outwardly directed remarks, and the rank of the other on the receiving of communication. As groups increase in size, a larger and larger relative proportion of the activity tends to be addressed to the top man, and a smaller and smaller relative proportion to other members. In turn, as size increases, the top man tends to address more and more of his remarks to the group as a whole, and to exceed by larger amounts his proportionate share. The communication pattern tends to "centralize," in other words, around a leader through whom most of the communication flows.

The tendency toward centralization is illustrated in Figure 2, which shows the relation of men in each rank position as to total acts initiated, by groups of increasing size. The matrix for each individual session was put in rank order and then all matrices for groups of a given size were added together. The points plotted thus represent aggregate or average rates of activity for men in each rank position. (The groups included in this graph were all observed before the present standard task was evolved, and include a wide variety of types. Data gathered on the standard task are expected to show similar tendencies but probably smoother curves and smoother gradations

Figure **2** *Rank ordered series of total acts initiated, compared with harmonic distribution, for groups of sizes three to eight*

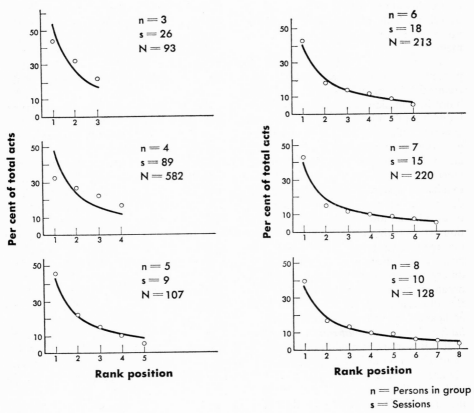

by size.) The points are plotted against a mathematically derived curve, the so-called "harmonic distribution," or "rank-size" curve for purposes of visual comparison. (This curve is of some general interest to social scientists, since it is often found to be a fair approximation of the distribution of factors such as income in large social systems.) In the present case the fit, although visually helpful, is not actually acceptable in a statistical sense. One of the reasons the fit is not good is precisely because of the tendency for communication to centralize and for a "leader" to appear. The points indicate that groups of size three and four tend to have a relatively "flatter" or more even distribution of amounts of participation between members, while the groups of larger size tend to show the rank 1 man with a higher amount of participation than the harmonic curve predicts. The prominence of rank 1 men in the larger groups is striking.

If the situation is one in which *inter-action* is expected by the participators, however, there would seem to be a ceiling on amount of participation for the top man somewhere around 50 percent, apparently connected with the general tendency for interaction under such expectations to come to a system-closure, such that each "action" of one member, as it were, tends to be countered with a "reaction" from some other. Even if the top man is initiating most of the action, he still has to expect that he will receive a "feedback of reactions," of both a positive and negative sort, that will tend to equal the amount of action he initiates. It may very well be that the expectation of "equality" which is so often present in groups of our culture, is based on an expectation of an over-all balance of action and reaction rather than of an equality of amounts of output of all members, which in practice is practically never found.

Phase Movement

Changes in quality of activity as groups move through time in attempting to solve problems may be called phase patterns. The pattern of phases differs in detail under different conditions. However, these changes in quality seem to be subject to system-influences which produce similarities from group to group. An increase of task-oriented activities in the early parts of a meeting—that is, "Questions" and "Attempted Answers,"—seems to constitute a disturbance of a system "equilibrium" which is later redressed by an increase in social-emotional activities—that is, both "Positive" and "Negative Reactions."

Part of our observations prior to the development of the standard diagnostic task were kept by time sequence. Each available meeting was divided into three equal parts, and the amount of each type of activity in each part of each meeting was determined. The meetings were divided into two kinds: those which were dealing with full-fledged problems (essentially problems of analysis and planning with the goal of group decision as described for the standard diagnostic task), and those dealing with more truncated or specialized types of problems. Those groups dealing with full-fledged problems tended to show a typical phase movement through the meeting: the process tended to move qualitatively from a *relative* emphasis on attempts to solve problems of *orientation* ("what is it") to attempts to solve problems of *evaluation* ("how do we feel about it") and subsequently to attempts to solve problems of *control* ("what shall we do about it"). Concurrent with these transitions, the relative frequencies of both *negative reactions* (disagreement, tension, and antagonism), and *positive reactions* (agreement, tension release, and showing solidarity), tend to increase. The reasons why both negative and positive reactions have to increase are given below. It should be remembered that they are both "reactive." Figure 3 presents the summary data for all twenty-two group sessions examined in the phase study.

The underlying theory as to why the phase movement just described is characteristic of full-fledged conditions is again the same "system-equilibrium" rationale depending on the "interdependence of problems" in systems of social interaction. Consider first those problems immediately concerned with the task. An individual may be cognitively oriented to a situation and speak of it to others in cognitive terms without committing himself (or the other when the other agrees), either to evaluation of it or an attempt to control it. But in speaking to the other in evaluative terms he attempts to commit both himself and the other to some assumed previous orientation, and further, if he suggests a way to control the situation by joint cooperative action, he assumes a successful solution has been obtained for problems of both orientation

and evaluation. When the problems of arriving at a common orientation and evaluation of the situation have not been substantially solved by the group members, attempts at control will meet with resistance on the part of the others and frustration on the part of the person attempting to exercise the control. Probably generally, unless there are contrary cultural, personality, or group organizational factors, the interacting persons tend to avoid or retreat from this frustration-producing type of interaction by "backtracking" toward orientation and evaluative analysis until the prior problems are solved.

In addition to their task problems, the members of any cooperating group have problems of their social and emotional relationships to solve and keep solved. Efforts to solve problems of orientation, evaluation, and control as involved in the task tend to lead to differentiation of the roles of the participants, both as to the functions they perform and their gross amounts of participation. Some major features of this differentiation have already been described in the presentation of findings about the matrix. Both qualitative and quantitative types of differentia-

*Figure **3**   Relative frequency of acts by type and phase based upon twenty-two sessions*

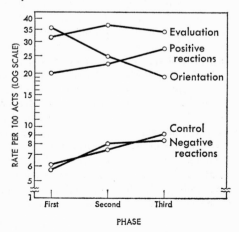

tion tend to carry status implications which may threaten or disturb the existing order or balance of status relations among members. Disagreement and an attempt to change existing ideas and values may be necessary in the effort to solve the task problem but may lead, nevertheless, to personalized anxieties or antagonisms and impair the basic solidarity of the group.

This impairment, or the threat of it, we may assume, tends to grow more marked as the group passes from emphasis on the less demanding and more easily resolved problems of cognitive orientation on to problems of evaluation, and still more acute as it passes on to its heaviest emphasis on problems of control. Thus, a series of disturbances in the social-emotional relationships of the members tends to be set in motion by pressures arising initially from attempts to meet the demands of the external task or outer situation. These social-emotional problems tend to be expressed in a kind of status struggle as they grow more acute—hence the increasing rate of negative reactions.

However, at the extreme end of the final period, assuming that the members' attempts at control over the outer situation and over each other are successful and a final decision is reached, the rates in Categories 1, 2, and 3 also rise to their peak. In other words, the successfully recovering group tends to confirm its agreement and to release in diffuse ways the tensions built up in its prior task efforts, repairing the damage done to its state of consensus and social integration.

We note joking and laughter so frequently at the end of meetings that they might almost be taken as a signal that the group has completed what it considers to be a task effort, and is ready for disbandment or a new problem. This last-minute activity completes a cycle of operations involving a successful solution both of the task problems and social-emotional problems confronting the group. The apparent incongruity of predicting a peak for both negative and positive reactions in the third phase is thus explained. Negative reactions tend to give way to positive reactions in the final part of the third phase. The arbitrary division of the meeting into three equal periods of time is too crude to show the final dropping off of negative reactions in the third phase as solution is reached.

Conclusion

It may be that average tendencies like those presented can be taken as representative of typical social-system effects under full-fledged conditions. In experimental designs, then, where a full-fledged problem is used as the basic testing situation, deviations from empirical norms might be used as evidences of the effects of known or experimentally introduced conditions. For example, the experimental introduction of persistent difficulties of communication or orientation by placing together in the same group persons of widely different value standards might upset the profile, matrix, and phase sequence expected on the basis of the internal tendencies of the interaction system alone. Conversely, in using the method for clinical analysis or training of particular groups, groups might be set up under full-fledged conditions, and the deviations from the empirical norms used as diagnostic indicators of otherwise unknown characteristics of the group or the members.

The uniformities of the profile, matrix, and phase movement are all interdependent. They are manifest evidence that interaction is not a random collection of acts, but constitutes the observable process of a social system.

COMMENTARY
STUDIES BASED ON MEASUREMENT

Le Play and Bales base their procedures on somewhat more clearly defined conceptual models than do Malinowski and Whyte, and their design decisions result in more systematic gathering and handling of the data. First, each sets forth an organized plan for collecting and classifying data as indicants **(P-X)**, i.e., each uses the data to *measure* properties and presents the findings according to a classificatory scheme. Second, their research rests, not upon a single case, but upon many cases **(P-II)**. As we examine these two studies, contrasting them with the descriptive study of a single case, we shall begin to understand the impact that these Paradigm decisions have upon the research design as a whole. We saw in Unit 2, for example, that the designs used by Malinowski and Whyte provide graphically vivid detail, but are limited in respect to (1) the *reliability* and (2) the *generality* of the findings. Let us now consider how Le Play and Bales deal with these problems—reserving until later our more detailed discussion of sampling (Unit 6) and of measurement (Units 7 and 9).

Le Play and the Study of the Family

Le Play's classic studies of the families of European workers constitute a remarkable early contribution to related sociological theory and method. Extending over five decades of nineteenth-century political, social, and economic upheaval, his research aimed "to rediscover the secret of governments which offer men a happiness founded in peace." With such an objective, it may seem strange that he chooses the families of workingmen as his research case. His reasons for doing so involve the fundamental assertion that a "society is made up of families, not of isolated and independent individuals." Moreover, "to a very great degree, the family is the exact model of the society." Le Play does not seem to mean here that the family as a social unit is an exact image of the macrocosm, but rather that the condition of the family will reflect, and be reflected by, the condition of the larger society. Thus in order to understand a social system, "it is sufficient to observe the means and the way of life of the family as the typical producer."

There remains the question of why workers' families are singled out for study. The answer lies in Le Play's explanation of the sources of social peace and stability. "Everywhere," he says, "happiness consists in the satisfaction of two principal needs which are absolutely imposed by the very nature of man." These are "the practice of moral law [and] enjoyment of one's daily bread . . . corresponding to the moral life and the material life of each family." The working population, which even in a complex society "comprises the greatest majority of producers and consumers," is most intimately bound up with fulfillment of these needs. Social discord is created when, deprived of the bases of well-being, the people "fail in the duty to obey . . . substitute dissension for peace and plunge the nation into an abyss of misery." Thus, "by the very nature of things, the worker is the customary object of this method of observation" and, conversely, the bases for existence of the rich and professional classes are such that study of them "would bring little useful material to social science."

Thus, Le Play was working with an elaborate theory. In translating his conceptual model into research, he sought a "scientific procedure . . . founded not upon concepts established *a priori,* but upon facts systematically observed and upon inferences derived from vigorous reasoning." To Le Play, the observational method provides "the surest means of understanding the material and moral life of man . . . similar to the techniques which chemists employ to disclose the secret nature of minerals."

Unlike Malinowski and Whyte, whose projects were not the work of a lifetime, Le Play was able to develop rather clear (if somewhat archaic) definitions of the elements in a conceptual model. He went through a long period of preliminary explorations and then decades of organized application of his method (with the assistance of various co-workers and local leaders). Moreover, he was able to perceive problems of research method, and to work out partial solutions to some of these problems, far in advance of the recent clarifications we shall see in various modern studies. His method is illustrated by the modern American monograph of Zimmerman and Frampton.

GATHERING THE DATA **(P-VIII)**

Le Play's data-gathering procedures are more systematic than those of Malinowski and Whyte. To be sure, he combines direct observation with questioning in a fashion similar to theirs, living with families (his main research case, **P-I**), learning their language, and coming to understand their work, their customs of food and dress, and the nature of their social relationships and their intellectual and moral life. (Modern, indeed, is his set of instructions for gaining the "good will" of the family!) And, too, he deals with each case in a fairly intensive and detailed manner. But we shall consider two important respects in which his procedure for data-gathering differs from theirs: First, corresponding to his more specific conceptual definitions of the properties to be studied, he is more systematic than they are in selecting data to use as indicants **(P-X)**. Second, he does not limit himself to one case or just a few **(P-II),** but deals with 300 cases, widely diversified by nationality and type of worker. These decisions have the effect of enhancing both the reliability and generality of his findings. Let us consider each decision in turn.

LE PLAY'S USE OF MEASUREMENT **(P-X)**

Although Le Play worked long before modern developments in the methodology of sociological measurement, he states an explicit and fairly standardized plan for the gathering and classification of data to be used as indicants. Measurement typically involves (as already suggested in Unit 1) the abstract idea of a case and its empirical counterpart **(P-I),** and the abstract idea of certain properties of this case and their concrete manifestations or indicants **(P-X)**. Le Play wants, in effect, to use his data as indicants of certain underlying properties of families, for, as he puts it, a major difficulty in the scientific analysis of human society stems from the fact that "the material, intellectual and moral life of the simplest family consists of innumerable details." The observer must find some way to "neglect those details which do not serve the special purpose of the method." Accordingly, he gathers and classifies the data on each family under three main headings: the characteristics of the workman, the budget or monograph proper, and the explanatory supplements. He then defines the exact kinds of material to be included as indicants under each heading. Let us consider the nature of these indicants and the conceptual elements to which they correspond.

Use of Data on the Occupational Characteristics of the Workman.   In the section on the worker, Le Play first includes data that indicate the worker's profession (such as mining or agriculture). Second, he makes systematic use (following his careful definitions) of data that indicate the worker's rank in the hierarchy of his profession (from servant worker and day laborer to owner worker and managerial worker). These two sets of data are ordinarily included in occupational classifications today, but Le Play also adds a third set of data (the modern counterpart of which is often overlooked in present-day research) that classifies the relationship of the worker to the heads of the hierarchy as "compulsory," "permanent-voluntary," or "temporary." Le Play stresses as highly important "the type and above all the duration of the relationship which binds [worker and employer]. In general, this information is not specific to the worker being studied; it is characteristic of the society of which he is a part." For instance, although the particular categories designated by Le Play may be no longer relevant, the student of a modern factory system may want to know whether the employer-employee relationships are stable or unstable, whether they are authoritarian or permissive, whether profit-sharing is involved, or whether the communication channels within the plant are clearly defined and open.

At the conceptual level, the *property* Le Play is investigating here is the relationship of the family system to its environment (much as Whyte deals with the relationship between the corner gang and the larger community). This relationship—that between a system and its environment—is a key concept in sociological theory and is often referred to today as *adaptation*. Le Play is investigating the adaptation of the family system and, further, conceives of it, not as a simple characteristic, but as multidimensional. We might say that Le Play defines adaptation here as having three dimensions: the worker's profession, his rank in the hierarchy of his profession, and his relationship to the heads of the hierarchy. (The distinction between a property and its dimensions is somewhat arbitrary, depending upon the definition of the concept.) It is the clear definition of some such conceptual dimensions that enables Le Play to penetrate beneath the "innumerable details" obtained in the course of the research and to specify which of the data are to be used as indicants in classifying each family, and which are to be ignored as of little importance. In this way, he can represent quite simply (that is, measure) the family's location in the larger social structure.

Notice also how skillfully Le Play shifts the *research case* here **(P-I).** His conceptual concern is with the whole family, which is composed of many individuals—"each individual has his own life . . . each is endlessly altered by the stimuli with which the social institutions affect him." Yet if he is to translate this concept into systematic research procedures, he must reduce it to manageable terms. He accomplishes this by focusing upon the single role of the worker which becomes, in effect, the connecting link between the family system and the larger economic system to which it belongs (see, *e.g.,* Loomis, 1960, p. 32 ff.). That is, although he leaves explicit formulation to later scholars, Le Play treats the head of the house as the family *representative* outside. (The role of *D* in Figure 3-A thus suggests a generally useful elaboration of our diagram of a small group in Figure 1-C above.)

This is not an arbitrary decision for Le Play; it merely illustrates again his ingenuity in translating theory into research. The head of the family, by virtue of the authority he exercises, occupies a crucial position in the maintenance of traditional customs and practices. The same is true of leaders in a larger society. Le Play is convinced that:

In all types of regimes, we may find the lasting indices of happiness, peace and stability in studying the sages who presided over the families, workshops, neighborhoods, cities or nations. . . . To understand the various types of social orders which exist we must carefully report upon the practices and precepts of those who were the true masters in each place, or in each epoch.

By thus selecting the representative role and disregarding the lesser roles of the other members in the family's adaptation to its environment (such as the mother's relationship to neighbors or the child's to the school), Le Play succeeds in the complex task of classifying each family within the larger social system.

Figure **3-A**   *Diagram of a small group showing the linkage role of the "representative"*

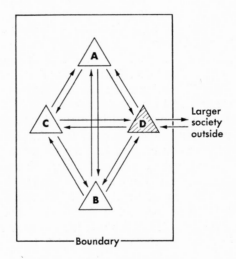

Thus Le Play demonstrates, to the benefit of future scholars, two means of selection or abstraction from complex phenomena in order to deal systematically with a general property such as the family's adaptation to its environment. First **(P-X),** he selects from the vast range of research materials and classifies them so that they will correspond to (index) the conceptual dimensions of the property. Second **(P-I),** he does not attempt to study the complex family system as a whole, but selects for study only one role—that of the family's representative outside. Thus, as he puts it, "the description of a family is greatly simplified," facilitating both delineation of the property under study and classification of the research cases according to that property.

Use of Budgetary Data. The *budget* is another systematically organized set of data that Le Play provides in each monograph and uses as an indicant of the abstract properties of a social system. The details of the budget are of interest to

Le Play, not for their own sake, but because they reflect "all the acts which constitute the life of a family of workers." Since Le Play regards production and consumption as the basic elements of life, any given family's solution of the problem of establishing equilibrium between the two reveals a great deal about their social, intellectual, and moral life. In his words, for example, the budget reveals clearly "the degradation of a stevedore in the outskirts of Paris who expends annually 185 fr. or twelve percent of his income for drink but does not give a cent for the moral education of his five children between four and fourteen years of age."

Le Play's budget suggests a means of indexing another central, yet complex, social system property—the *integration* or solidarity of the family system, including the maintenance of societal values and norms. Although many sociologists may feel that the budget does not represent closely enough the sociologically important aspects of integration, they must admire it as a rare illustration —even today—of an indicant which is not only objective but also representative of the *collective* actions of the group members. The various family members participate separately and jointly in activities which determine the balance between the securing of necessary resources and the satisfaction of needs; and Le Play succeeds in developing a simple enough set of data (the budget) to be used systematically as an indicant of this delicate equilibrium—an equilibrium which is a property of the family system as a whole.

Although basically crude, the budget as well as the occupational classification are prototypes of measuring instruments; they clearly differ from the unorganized materials used in the method of description discussed in Unit 2. Le Play deals with the "files of numerous facts" by arranging the (fifty pages of) "indispensable data" about each family under the main headings of the classificatory scheme to "aid in the comparison of places and individuals." Although, to be sure, he does not treat his properties as variables in the modern manner of a Bales, his procedure is systematic enough to solve to a certain extent the problems of reliability that faced both Malinowski and Whyte. Not only are the monographs themselves *open to inspection* by the reader, but the method is sufficiently *standardized* to be replicated by Le Play himself and by a number of other researchers sometimes referred to as the "Le Play school." The one example included in the present selection, Zimmerman and Frampton's monograph on the Ozark Highland family during the depression of the 1930's, shows how Le Play's theory and methods may be adapted to apply to other societies and cultures.

The Explanatory Supplements. When the researcher specifies the selection of certain data for use as indicants, he places definite limitations on the research design. If he decides to measure the property of family integration solely by means of income and expenditure as reflected in the family budget, for example, he will exclude any potentially relevant material that is not contained in the budget. The result may be oversimplification or premature closure. Once the classification scheme is set, the scope of the analysis is restricted, perhaps drastically limiting opportunity for new insights that may subsequently arise. Le Play is aware of this problem, for he adds two descriptive sections. One section, "Preliminary Observations," includes an interpretation of the geographical surroundings, the "special characteristics," the particular budget, and the "moral condition" of the family. The other, "Relevant Aspects of the Social Order," comments on the external conditions affecting the family. These supplements are largely unsystematic and descriptive **(P-X)**. Although their subject matter is fairly clearly prescribed, there is in these largely descriptive sections far more leeway for the insights and interpretations of the researcher than in the occupational classification or the budget.

MEASUREMENT AND DESCRIPTION COMBINED

Through such devices, Le Play seems to take advantage of both ways of handling properties **(P-X)**. On the one hand, he uses systematic procedures that afford a considerable degree of precision in measurement. On the other, his explanatory supplements, though less precise than categorization or measurement, are nevertheless more flexible, making room for the unexpected or "serendipitous" finding.

Such a combined procedure is useful to the sociological researcher who, having tentatively specified his conceptual model, is still uncertain about this specification. The combined procedure may sometimes prove valuable (as we shall see later in Unit 11) even in highly systematic, hypothesis-testing designs where the original hypotheses did not, after all, fully account for the situation under study. Thus the early efforts of Le Play suggest one important way to achieve the desirable balance of research that is reliable but that, at the same time, avoids too narrow a view.

LE PLAY'S USE OF MANY CASES **(P-II)**

If Le Play reduces errors of unreliability by measuring the properties of each single case **(P-X)**, he also begins to avoid the restrictions on *generality* imposed by the study of single cases (as in Unit 2). Since reliability does not in itself contribute to sociology as a science unless the findings also have a degree of generality, Le Play devotes himself to the examination of many different kinds of families in "all regions of Europe and in many other countries of the world." Building upon his background as a mining engineer, he discovers that, although "families, . . . those distinct social units which make up the whole of humanity, number in the millions," nevertheless the methods of studying society by observation are similar to those which chemists use in the study of minerals. Thus, he maintains, investigation of only 300 families—very few in comparison to these millions—enables him to comprehend "a society spread over a vast area."

This use of a *sample* of widely varied cases leads him toward a crude test of his conception that satisfied and dissatisfied populations differ in essentials of social structure. As you know from your examination of the study, he reports consistent differences between strong and weak structures in the peace, harmony, and happiness of the people—stressing the coincidence between social solidarity and material, intellectual, and moral well-being. And it is his method of comparing scores of families that allows him to discern such consistencies, such socially structured uniformities underlying the apparently infinite diversity of man's nature. It is, he asserts, in this "consistency and universality of findings" that the simplicity and therefore the practical utility of the method consists.

Thus, long before the development of modern sampling methods, Le Play designed a sample of families (**P-IV**) that not only allowed him to generalize beyond the idiosyncrasies of the single case, but also facilitated his analysis and enabled him to make comparisons between the suffering and the prospering types of families. To be sure, modern representational methods (described in Unit 6) might well have allowed him to generalize more accurately, but even today it is difficult to design truly representative samples of families *in general,* apart from particularities of time and place.

Bales and Small Group Research

In contrast to the early and necessarily limited efforts of Le Play, a sophisticated contemporary example of the systematic handling of properties as variables is afforded by the Bales study. Bales and his colleagues at the Harvard Laboratory of Social Relations have developed (and trained many students in) a special method of "interaction process analysis" for observing, analyzing, and comparing behavior in various small groups—especially groups devoted to decision-making or problem-solving. Starting with the theory that "any particular piece of social behavior is always a part of a larger organized system of actions and reactions of more than one person," Bales assumes that "certain conditions" and "certain approximate uniformities of interaction" are "more or less inherent in the nature of the process of interaction or communication itself."

His conceptual model then defines a number of *properties* of the interaction of any group, such as the positive or negative direction, the instrumental or expressive character, and the focus on any of six system problems of communication and organization. He explicitly defines each of these rather complex properties, and within each he further defines various categories into which the property is divided. Parsons and Bales have shown how this conceptual model is related to the larger body of theoretical work carried on by Parsons and his collaborators at Harvard (see Parsons and Bales, 1953). The Bales study, therefore, exemplifies a fruitful parallel development of theoretical analysis and research design.

GATHERING THE DATA (P-VIII)

The Bales procedure for data-collection is strikingly different from the participant observation employed by Malinowski, Whyte, and Le Play. One difference lies in Bales' major reliance upon direct observation, rather than upon the combined observation and questioning used in the anthropological studies. (Although

Bales does use some supplementary questioning, you will find it instructive to consider what kinds of data that can be obtained by questioning are not available through direct observation.) Another contrast is that the researcher, Bales, has little interaction with the members of the group (his research case under **P-I**). Once the standard task has been assigned to the group, the data are gathered by unseen observers behind a one-way glass. Since these observers avoid active participation in the system under study, they reduce the danger of unsystematic control effects. They also make an effort to minimize biased-viewpoint effects. Indeed, special safeguards are built into the data-collection procedure to ensure equivalent treatment of all group members. For example, the actors are seated around the table in such a way that the observers can watch the facial expressions of every member.

SYSTEMATIC CONTROL OF THE ACTION UNDER STUDY **(P-VI)**

The Bales procedure does involve a special kind of *systematic control* by the investigator over the action to be studied. First, he controls the selection of *actors*. He brings together aggregates of unrelated individuals who are removed from their ordinary group relations, and watches how they form new social systems, instead of utilizing natural groups such as families or corner gangs. Second, he controls the *goal* of the interaction by giving the group a problem to solve. Third, he controls the *environment* within which the interaction occurs by taking the actors from their natural settings and bringing them into the laboratory. In contrast to participant observation, Bales exerts this control intentionally and according to a specified plan. And his work demonstrates how such controls may heighten the opportunity of discovering the uniformities in the system processes (see also Swanson).

Although Bales does not exploit the full potentialities of systematic controls as used in experimental designs (Unit 11), his concluding remarks do mention possible experimentation. "Persistent difficulties of communication or orientation" could be experimentally introduced by placing together in the same group persons of widely differing value standards, he suggests; and the effects could then be studied by observing deviations from "the profile, matrix, and phase sequence expected on the basis of the internal tendencies of the interaction system alone."

BALES' USE OF MEASUREMENT **(P-X)**

In order to measure each property of interaction, Bales specifies exactly what kinds of data are to be gathered for use as indicants—that is, which of the acts observed in the laboratory are to be classified in which categories as reflecting each property. Such a set of categories, with specifications of the ways in which indicants are to be classified, is called a *code*. The Bales code, now rather widely used in sociology, is described in his section called Description of the Method, and appears down the side of his Table 1 (see also Bales, 1950, Appendix). The analogue in the Le Play study consists of the several headings for each monograph and the rules for inclusions under each.

Two points about the Bales code deserve special attention, since they illustrate important general principles of codes. First, the categories are mutually exclusive, that is, every act can and must be classified in one, and only one, category (and there is no miscellaneous or "wastebasket" category). Second, observers are given detailed training on how to classify each act, so that one observer's classification will accord closely with that of another observer and thus ensure a high degree of reliability (see Borgatta and Bales).

BALES' USE OF TABLES

Of course, the systematic measurement and use of properties as variables requires not only the defining and gathering of the appropriate data as indicants; it includes also the systematic handling of the data once they have been collected and classified. According to Le Play, the purpose of systematization is to allow comparison; he accomplishes this by standardizing the monograph on each family and reducing it to some fifty pages. Nevertheless, the student of these monographs who wants a general analysis of all the families is still required to read a great deal. Therefore, because the modern researcher often wants to carry the analysis further than Le Play did—to see how *many* families are similar or different in certain respects, for instance—he must not only classify the cases in terms of their properties but also count the cases. Bales, for example, after categorizing behavior act by act, then analyzes the data "to obtain summary measures descriptive of the group process, from which inferences can then be made as to the nature of underlying factors influencing the process." Thus he arrives at sets of figures that can be presented in the form of tables or graphs, rather than in the expositional form used by Le Play.

The researcher uses his code both to collect relevant data and then to pigeonhole them so that they can be counted and presented to the reader in numerical form. In this sense, the same logic usually underlies the tables or graphs and the collection of data since both are derived from the same conceptual model. Practically speaking, the researcher who plans to gather data for measuring properties as variables should consider in advance in what tabular form he will present his findings. Since Bales offers some particularly useful examples of the forms in which systematic data may be organized and presented, let us now consider the general nature of such tables.

THE USE OF PERCENTAGES

Percentages are widely used in sociological research because they facilitate comparison. In his Table 1, which represents the total distribution of group acts, Bales employs percentages as a device to help the reader determine the main points of the findings. For example, by simply comparing the 24.9 per cent with the 9.6 per cent in the third row of that table, you can quickly establish that there is a tendency for satisfied groups to show relatively more agreement than dissatisfied groups.

Elementary and familiar as percentages may be, a number of rather basic questions often arise in connection with their use, as illustrated in Exercise III-2. When is it appropriate to use percentages in a particular table, instead of absolute numbers or other statistical expressions, such as averages or standard deviations? If percentages are used, in what direction should they be computed? What is the proper base?

In Bales' Table 1, for example, you will note that the bases refer, not to total individual *actors,* but to the numbers of *acts* (719 and 767 respectively) performed by each type of group. Thus the percentages are taken to mean here: If we suppose that each type of group performed 100 acts (that is, an equal number of acts—the 100 is simply a convenient number), how do the groups compare in the way they distribute these acts among the several categories? As the percentage exercise has reminded you, percentages based on numbers of actors have a different meaning—and sometimes yield quite different results—from those based on numbers of acts. The key to reading a table of percentage comparisons lies in locating and defining the numbers used as the bases.

THE WHO-TO-WHOM MATRIX

Bales' Table 2 represents another type of table which is of particular interest to students of the social system. Here Bales is shifting his attention from the pattern (profile) of acts that characterizes the group as a whole, to the acts as indicants of the interrelationships among the group members. This form of presentation is called a *matrix*. The matrix, used in mathematics and in diverse fields of application, is often employed by sociologists to represent individuals in roles interacting with one another. We shall now suggest how it deals with several elements in a conceptual model of a social system. (Our Figure 3-B is a diagram of a six-member system comparable to the Bales matrix.)

The Bales matrix shows which members of the group talk to which other members. As Bales describes this table, each group member is given a key number, indicating his rank in the group as an initiator, or *subject,* of action. Then each group member is listed (by key number) down the side of the table as a subject. Each is again listed across the top of the table as a recipient, or *object,* of the action. If we read across a row (or horizontal line of figures) we can determine what any given subject does: for example, No. 1 directs 1,238 acts to No. 2; 961 to No. 3; and so on. Or, if we read down a column (or vertical line), we can see what any given object receives: for example, No. 1 receives 1,748 acts from No. 2; 1,371 from No. 3; and so on.

Marginal Information About Total Roles. There are two main types of information in the matrix. Let us consider first the *marginal* information— that is, the totals or sums of the respective rows and columns. For example, if we add all the figures in the row describing No. 1 as a subject, we obtain a total of all the acts which he initiated, a *subject total.* The addition, which is listed in the marginal column headed *total initiated,* shows that No. 1's subject total is 9,167 acts. In the same column we find the total number of acts initiated by each of the other persons. In this particular table, No. 1's subject role might be labeled "high initiator" or perhaps "leader," since his total is higher than any of the other totals.

Similarly, to obtain a total of all the acts received by a person, an *object total,* we simply add all the figures in the respective vertical column. The totals of the columns are listed in the margin across the bottom of the table, entitled *total received.* Using No. 1 as an example again, we see that he received a total of 5,203 acts.

Figure **3-B** *Diagram of a six-member group*

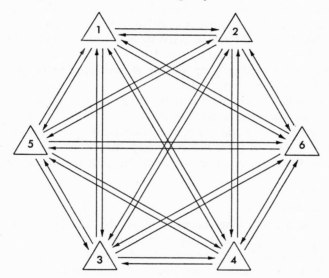

Thus, Bales describes the total role of each person in this group by the two figures: his subject total and his object total. He analyzes these marginals, reporting that if individuals as subjects are arrayed in rank order according to the amount of action they initiate, they receive action as objects in amounts proportional to this rank order.

Comparison of the matrix with the social system model in Figure 3-B makes clear that the marginals for No. 1, for instance, represent all the arrows which go out from No. 1 (as subject) to the other members of the group, as well as all the arrows coming in to No. 1 (as object) from all the other members of the group. In terms of the Paradigm, Bales' unit of research here **(P-I)** is the role as an aspect of the social system. Under **P-X,** he has systematically measured a property of each role (the disposition to act or to receive the action), using observed acts as indicants, entering them in the appropriate matrix, and then counting them in order to treat the property as a variable.

Cell Information About Dyads.   Bales is interested not only in the total roles played by the several group members but also in the dyadic subroles. He is interested in the interaction between any two members, illustrated in Figure 3-B by the pair of arrows connecting No. 1 and No. 6, for example, in contrast to No. 1's connections with all the group members taken together. Note that this implies a shift in the research case **(P-I)** from the *role* to the *dyad* (or pair)—or from one level of the social system to another. This information about pairs of individuals is given, not in the marginals, but in the boxes or cells of the matrix. Since many sociological tables deal with questions about dyadic relationships, let us now discuss the nature of this cell information.

If we look at the main body of Bales' Table 2, we find that the information about the relationship between No. 1 and No. 6 is contained in two places: in the lower left-hand cell (470 acts directed by No. 6 to No. 1), and in the upper right-hand cell (317 acts directed by No. 1 to No. 6). The complete data about any dyad can be assembled only by looking at both cells (corresponding to the two-directional arrows in Figure 3-B).

If we look at the matrix more closely we can recognize how these matching cells are arranged. The white space in the table suggests an imaginary line from the upper left corner of the matrix to the lower right, which divides the matrix diagonally in half. One of these halves corresponds to the other, so that, if the table were folded over on this line, the matching cells would fall on top of one another.

A MATHEMATICAL MODEL

Bales makes the following statement about the cells in this matrix: "Each man tends to speak to each other man in an amount which is a probability function of both his own rank on outwardly directed remarks, and the rank of the other on the receiving of communication." Let us examine this statement both as one type of analysis of cell information, and as an example of the use of a mathematical model—an important tool that the sociologist uses in interpreting his data.

Sociologists often use mathematical models as aids in testing their theories, i.e., in examining the fit between the conceptual model and the data obtained from research. We can think of the use of a mathematical model, as illustrated again in various applications in subsequent chapters, in three simple steps:

Step A

The sociologist sets up certain simple assumptions about what is going on, based on his conceptual model (or on observed regularities in empirical data).

Step B

The mathematician (or the mathematically trained sociologist) then translates these assumptions into mathematically manipulatable terms—i.e., a mathematical model. He determines from this model what the *expected findings* would be if the assumptions (from A) are a fairly accurate description of the true situation.

Step C

Finally, the sociologist compares the actual findings of his research with the expected findings (from B). The closeness of fit helps him to determine whether the original assumptions (from A) are correct.

Although Bales does not fully describe the mathematical model underlying his Table 2, his statement sets up certain simple sociological assumptions (Step A) to account for the information in the cells. Consider, for example, No. 2's action toward No. 3. Bales, in effect, assumes that this action is determined by No. 2's total subject role (his disposition to talk) and by No. 3's total object role (his tendency to elicit communication from others). Bales means that all that is needed in order to make predictions about the *dyadic* relationship—the amount that No. 2 will talk to No. 3—is the proper information about the *total roles* of No. 2 and No. 3. This prediction can be made without knowing anything else about the structure of the group or the interrelationships of the members.

In order to illustrate the principle of a mathematical test of Bales' assumptions, we shall substitute a fairly similar—but more explicit—statement based upon each individual's share of the total action, rather than upon his rank position. Using the example of the 2-to-3 cell, we might predict (Step B) that this cell's proportion of the total acts will be the product of No. 2's total initiating share of the acts times No. 3's total receiving share. We can now make the required computations by merely inspecting the figures. First, to determine No. 2's initiating share, we look at the subject marginals for No. 2 and find that he initiates about 4,000 (3,989) out of a total of about 20,000 (21,311) acts. That is, his subject share is 4,000 out of 20,000, or about $\frac{1}{5}$. Then, looking at the object marginal for No. 3, we can see that he receives about 2,000 (1,944) out of the 20,000. That is, his object share is roughly $\frac{1}{10}$. The product of these two shares —$\frac{1}{5}$ multiplied by $\frac{1}{10}$—is $\frac{1}{50}$. According to our assumptions, then, No. 2 will direct to No. 3 $\frac{1}{50}$ of the total (approximately 20,000) acts, or 400 acts. Thus our very crude prediction based on these simple assumptions of the model would be that the *expected number* of acts in this cell should be somewhere around 400.

Finally (Step C), we check whether the expected number corresponds to what was actually found in the research. The number in Table 2 is 443, which appears fairly close to the expected 400.

Bales makes somewhat similar computations for each of the cells in the matrix, finding throughout a good agreement between what he actually observes and what he could expect if his very simple assumptions account for what is going on. In other words, his data fit his mathematical model fairly well. This fit provides some assurance that the dyadic subroles are in fact a simple function of the total subject and object roles of the individuals, and thus supports his sociological assumptions (Step A). (For a discussion of the related work of Joseph Keller and Frederick Stephan, see Coleman, 1960, pp. 62–64.)

Of course, one can think of other types of situations in which the data would not fit this model. Imagine a formal organization in which the channels require that No. 1 talk mostly to No. 2, No. 2 to No. 3, and so on. In that case, a much larger figure would be found in the 2-to-3 cell than would be expected from the Bales assumptions. The Bales assumptions would not account for such a situation, since something more is operating here than just the individual's disposition to act and to receive action. Here there is also a *structuring* within the group. In such an instance, this particular mathematical model would not fit the data (Step C), and the discrepancy would thus help to uncover the inadequacy of the assumptions for the designated type of situation. The failure of the model would alert the investigator to the need for different or additional assumptions, perhaps leading to the development of a new model.

ANOTHER MATHEMATICAL MODEL

Bales' study provides another example of the use of a mathematical model, but here the expected findings do *not* quite fit the actual data (Step C). Bales wants to account for the differing degrees to which individuals contribute to the action when the groups are of varying size. Here (Step A) Bales does not seem to start with any *theoretically derived* assumptions about the character of the roles or of the interaction; he merely seeks a model to fit his data—one that will represent, and thus help him to interpret, the observed regularities in simple mathematical form. His assumption, which is based on these observed regularities, is that (for a group of a given size) the individual's contribution to the group action is inversely proportional to the numerical rank of his initiating score. The curves in Bales' Figure 2 show what the mathematician would expect to find (Step B) provided this assumption alone accounts for the real situation.

Then (Step C), Bales compares the actual findings (indicated by the dots in his Figure 2) with these expected findings. Actually, he regards the fit as rather poor (although he does not attempt to develop any statistical test to determine whether the discrepancies might be merely due to chance). In the larger groups, the leader has a larger share than expected (No. 1's dot falls above the expected point on the curve), while in the smaller groups he has a smaller share (his dot falls below the curve). In this instance, the empirically based assumption (Step A) does not seem to account adequately for what is going on.

To provide a possible after-the-fact explanation, Bales refers back to the tendency for the leader to take care of most of the initiating action. Such initiating action cannot constitute more than about 50 per cent of the total, however, since actions tend to be countered with reactions; thus, he suggests, "there would seem to be a ceiling on amount of participation for the top man somewhere around 50 percent." Because the model shows that Bales' initial assumption does not, in this instance, fit the actual situation, he now develops an additional new assumption (which in turn might later be tested).

The examples we have just discussed suggest the potential value of mathematical models in the interpretative phase of sociological research whenever the conceptual model is simple enough and precise enough to be translated into mathematical terms. If the data seem to fit the mathematical model, the researcher has a provisional basis for regarding the assumptions as correct. But if the data do not fit the model, he can recognize some inadequacy in the original assumptions, and revise his assumptions or seek additional hypotheses that may account more fully for the phenomena under study. (Mathematical models may be even more useful, though this is not illustrated by the Bales selection, when it is possible to draw from a system of mutually supporting hypotheses mathematical conclusions that could not be obtained from any of the hypotheses individually. Then the whole set of related ideas may be tested by checking these conclusions against the data.)

GRAPHS AND CHARTS

Let us now look at a final example of Bales' systematic handling of his materials. His Figure 3 illustrates the use of graphic presentation of numerical data that are too complex to be readily comprehended from a table. Figure 3 is of further interest because it illustrates the translation into research of the dynamic character of his conceptual model, of its emphasis on process **(P-V)**. This particular graph is drawn to a logarithmic scale in order to facilitate comparison between two changes that differ in orders of magnitude. The logarithmic principle will become clear if you sketch into the Bales figure (using two of the time periods) two imaginary changes: a change *a* which goes from 10 at the first time period to 20 at the second; and a change *b* which goes from 20 at the first time period to 40 at the second. Ordinary graphing, of course, would show the *b* curve as going up more steeply than the *a*; that is, it would indicate the greater absolute increase for *b* (20) than for *a* (10). But logarithmic graphing takes into account the fact that *b* starts at a higher point than *a,* and it further indicates the same percentage increase for both *a* and *b*. Thus the lines which you plot into Figure 3 will run parallel to one another, indicating that both increase at similar rates. The advantages of such presentation, in which complex relationships in the data may be seen at a glance, seem clear.

BALES' USE OF MANY CASES **(P-II)**

Like Le Play, Bales employs many cases (he does not tell exactly how many) rather than single cases for intensive analysis. Just as Le Play uses his multiple cases to determine the "consistency and universality of findings," so Bales wants to repeat his observations on enough small groups to uncover those "interaction system tendencies that are due to inherent conditions." One of his procedures is to use "averages of large numbers of cases," putting together the findings from different groups so that "the special conditions associated with individual cases are varied enough to approximate randomness." For example, his Table 2 is based upon the aggregated data from eighteen six-man groups, from which emerges the pattern of relationship between initiating rank in group and reception of action. His Figure 2 again aggregates many groups, classifying them by size. By using such composites of cases, Bales hopes that the various idiosyncratic elements of single groups will tend to counteract one another so that the basic pattern will stand out.

It is clear that Bales obtains findings of greater generality from many groups than from a single group, since different groups behave somewhat differently even when subjected to similar laboratory conditions. Yet it is difficult to determine how far Bales may be justified in generalizing. He does not attempt to follow sampling procedures aimed at representing the indefinitely large number of laboratory groups that might be assembled in the United States, for example, or in the world. Moreover, the extent to which he can generalize about situations *outside* of the laboratory is restricted by the particular groups he chooses as his sample. He is ultimately concerned with the interaction process itself, "wherever or whenever it takes place," and he does mention observing "a wide variety of different kinds of groups, including some from other cultures," and under "rather wide differences in experimental condition." Nevertheless, the tests he actually reports here are based primarily on groups of volunteers brought together in the laboratory and typically assigned to a standard task. He does not attempt to answer such provocative questions as whether or not the characteristics of Balesian interaction are the same for ordinary groups going about their own affairs outside the laboratory. Such problems of sample representativeness will be discussed in Unit 6.

Some Methodological Implications

Thus Le Play and in particular Bales differ from Malinowski and Whyte in their decisions on two of the basic methodological issues, **P-X** and **P-II**. These differences relate to the conceptual models and objectives involved. The models used by Le Play and Bales are simpler and clearer. For, if Malinowski and Whyte deal with a social system in the round and define it only after the data are in hand, Le Play and Bales reduce the case and its properties to a few elements that can be translated into measurement operations. The objectives used by Le Play and Bales are less clearly exploratory. For, if Malinowski and Whyte explore the very nature of the system and its properties, Le Play and Bales explore only the relationships among properties they have defined in advance. (That all four studies are, though in varying degrees, exploratory rather than hypothesis-testing is suggested by Bales' use of mathematical models. Even though he uses precise procedures, his apparent purpose is primarily to summarize in convenient form certain regularities *after* they have been observed in the findings —rather than to make advance predictions derived from sociological theory with the aid of the simpler mathematical language.)

Let us now consider what preliminary methodological understandings of design items **P-X** and **P-II** may be gleaned from a specific comparison of the Le Play and Bales studies with the studies by Malinowski and Whyte.

SOME ADVANTAGES OF THE METHODS USED

We have seen how the studies based on measurement and multiple cases succeed in avoiding certain limitations of the descriptive case studies—or, to state this positively, how they achieve certain distinctive advantages. First, under **P-X,** whereas the decision to handle properties qualitatively and descriptively may restrict the *reliability* of the findings, the alternative decision to measure the properties certainly tends to offset such restrictions. Not only does Bales explicitly demonstrate the reliability of his coding procedure (that two coders will independently classify the same interactions fairly similarly), but Le Play and Bales each standardized his method to a point where a whole "school" of followers has been able to employ it. Second, under **P-II,** whereas the decision to focus attention on just one (or just a few) cases restricts the applicability of the findings, the alternative use of many cases by Le Play, Bales, and their respective followers suggests how such findings may be *generalized*. Just as Le Play's method has been adapted by his followers and widely applied (see Sorokin, 1928, Chapter 2), Bales' method has been extended to varied types of small social systems both inside and outside the laboratory. (See the study of Strodtbeck in Unit 8 and, for a full description, Hare, 1962.) Thus the systematic character of each method allows widespread replications that test the conceptual model under varied conditions, and allow the research results to become cumulative and more and more generally applicable.

THE SELECTIVE FOCUS PRESCRIBED BY MEASUREMENT

Compared to the assets of these more systematic studies, what are the drawbacks of these design decisions? What of the flexibility of the descriptive case study, its ability to amass details and to suggest new insights and formulations? Here Le Play, and still more obviously Bales, must sacrifice certain advantages. Indeed, the more systematic the measurement the more rigid the requirements it sets for making selections (and consequent exclusions) from the total complex of data at hand. These selections may apply (as Unit 1 states) both to the data chosen as indicants of properties **(P-X)** and to the levels of the social system **(P-I)** upon which attention is focused. Of course, the data for any study always constitute a selection from the real world, but the range of data permissible may be more or less restricted, and the rules governing the selection more or less rigid. In contrast to the flexibility of selection in the descriptive study, Le Play and Bales each state specific requirements, as we have seen.

Le Play, whose conceptual focus is on the society, selects the family, as it is built into and reflects the larger system, as his research *case*. Even within the family he sometimes focuses selectively upon a single role—although he develops the important device of selecting, not just any role, but the role of the family's representative. In studying the *properties* of the family, he does not attempt to record and use the many details of family life, but chooses only certain budgetary and occupational information defined by his code as appropriate indicants.

Bales' selection procedure is somewhat more elaborate. He starts by controlling the interaction systematically, i.e., by directing it along certain lines germane to his model and inhibiting communications irrelevant to the system tendencies of research interest. Then, by applying his code, he governs the selection of data to be used as indicants of *properties.* Although, unlike Le Play, Bales classifies *every* act within the observation period, he too abstracts from these acts only those aspects that index the properties under study. As Bales' code has been applied to jury deliberations, for example, it does not measure the specific content of discussions about the trial or of the arguments pro and con. (See Strodtbeck, James, and Hawkins; Strodtbeck and Mann.) In his use of the small group as his research *case,* Bales skillfully avoids too limited a focus by shifting the social system level to deal sometimes with the total group as it distributes its collective acts, sometimes with the total role, sometimes with the dyadic relationship, and sometimes with these roles and relationships as they fit together within the matrix of the group as a system **(P-X).**

Interestingly enough, this selective focus prescribed by measurement, although it may restrict the flexibility and variety discussed in Unit 2, does not seem to reduce the important potential for tapping latent system patterns of which the participants themselves are unaware. On the contrary, the actors in the small task group almost certainly do not comprehend the problem-solving phases or the action-reaction equilibrium discovered by Bales; nor are family members able to formulate for Le Play the function performed by the mores in maintaining solidarity and preventing suffering.

In sum, the studies by Le Play and Bales illustrate the general character of research based on measurement—on the systematic, as opposed to the unsystematic and descriptive, handling of data. Certain comparative advantages of the systematic procedure (as ordinarily applied to many cases) have been suggested, and will be seen in greater detail in the varied uses of measurement discussed in later Units. Yet the measurement of properties also has disadvantages which make it unsuitable for certain studies—especially those where the elements in the conceptual model and their definitions are not clear in advance. Here again, then, the choice of design in any given study should depend upon both the methodological implications of the alternative decisions and the nature of the conceptual model and the research objective.

SUGGESTED READINGS FOR UNIT THREE

Bales, 1950; Hagood and Price, Chapter 5; Heyns and Lippitt, 1954; Heyns and Zander, 1953; Madge, Chapter 12; Parsons and Bales, 1953; Selltiz *et al.,* Chapter 6; Sorokin, 1928, Chapter 2; Zeisel, Chapter 1.

QUESTIONS FOR REVIEW AND DISCUSSION

Review the following methodological terms as used in this Unit:

code
graphic presentation
interaction process analysis
interaction profile
mathematical model
measurement
representative role
tabular presentation
who-to-whom matrix

1. Le Play studies differences between societies characterized by "happiness" or "distress"; Bales, between "satisfied" and "dissatisfied" groups. How would you state the similarities and the differences in the methods by which the two researchers confront these related problems?

2. How does the study of the Ozark Highland family by Zimmerman and Frampton illustrate the importance of Le Play's emphasis on the family's relationship to the larger social system?

3. Bales contrives a special laboratory setting for small group interaction, instead of observing interaction as it occurs "naturally" in the field. How would you say that such contrived interactions correspond to the "real life" processes of interest to the researcher?

4. How would you modify the methods of observation you used in Exercise I-1 in order to observe and record interaction according to a more highly structured procedure? What advantages would

result from these changes? What disadvantages?

5. Suppose that you wanted to study a number of small corner gangs, altering Whyte's design in the following ways: (1) using straight observation rather than participant observation; and (2) coding your observations in the Bales categories. How would your findings differ in character from those obtained by Whyte? Would any kinds of information be lost which Whyte secured?

6. Referring to Bales' Table 2, how might you test the assumption that 4's tendency to speak to 5 is a function of both 4's own share of total actions initiated and 5's own share of total actions received?

7. Can you figure out what computations Bales uses to derive the harmonic curves in his Figure 2?

8. Suppose you were to undertake a study of adaptation and integration in American families today in the manner of Le Play.

   a. What dimensions of these properties would you select as defining the properties?

   b. What kinds of indicants might you select as aptly reflecting the dimensions you have chosen?

   c. For what reasons might your selections differ from those used by Le Play?

   d. Would you in your study retain the device of the explanatory supplements? Why or why not?

UNIT FOUR

QUESTIONING COMPARED WITH OBSERVATION

SUGGESTED PROGRAM OF STUDY

This Unit deals with the method of gathering data by questioning the group members themselves **(P-VIII),** and compares this method and the nature of the data obtained with the method of direct observation of interaction studied in the two previous Units.

Exercises and Manual

Since questioning is one of the major ways of obtaining data in sociological research, two exercises are recommended—at least one of which (Exercise I-2) should be completed now as background for your analysis of the studies in this Unit. **Exercise 1-2** on exploratory interviewing will give experience with the interviewer-interviewee relationship and develop your skill in eliciting detailed responses and capturing nuances of meaning. **Exercise I-3** places you in the more formal and standardized role of the interviewer using a structured questionnaire. The data from both of these exercises are to be used in later exercises on problems of coding, analysis, and interpretation.

Study and follow carefully the notes on Questioning in **Manual I-B (1), (2),** and **(3).** You may want to read this entire Section I-B at this time, although you will need more experience before you actually design a questionnaire yourself or attempt to interview the collective members of a group as described in I-B(4) and (5).

Studies

Examine the research methods used in the studies by **Cottrell; Lundberg** and **Lawsing;** and **Merton.** Note that data are obtained by questioning the several group members, and the data are then used to index collective properties of groups or roles.

Commentary

Read the Commentary, which discusses the kinds of data obtainable by questioning the members of a group and the ways of handling such data, and which suggests some bases upon which the researcher might decide to gather data either by questioning or observing.

Questions for Review and Discussion

Consider the Questions for Review and Discussion. You should now begin to abstract for your own use some of the general principles of research design, and to formulate the advantages and limitations of various combinations of alternatives.

LEONARD S. COTTRELL, JR.
Roles and Marital Adjustment

In this paper we are interested in marriage as a problem of adjustment of rôles that people tend to play, these rôles being conceived of as results of the past experiences of the marriage partners. We shall go a step farther in defining our problem and limit it to a study of marriage as an adjustment between rôles that have developed in the childhood and adolescent family experiences of husband and wife. This limitation is not made for convenience merely. Such a concentration of attention is due to the fact that so many of our case studies, both of well-adjusted and of poorly adjusted marriages, picture people who seem to be seeking to re-enact in their marriage, relational systems or situations which obtained in their parental families. These efforts are sometimes conscious and sometimes unconscious.

It is not necessary for the task in hand to enter a discussion of what is meant by personality. For the purposes of this paper the following definitions will hold:

1. Personality, or the most significant part of it, is the organization of the rôles the person plays in group life. This definition connotes two aspects of the phenomenon we term personality. One is the aspect of traits or characteristics belonging to a person—one might say the content of personality. For example, we say a person is lovable, affectionate, spite-

ful, rebellious, enthusiastic. These terms indicate attitudes and relationships. The second is the integrative aspect. For example we think of stable and unstable, rigid and flexible persons, persons who are the same or nearly so in all situations and persons who are chameleon-like in their variability. These terms indicate the texture of the fabric or structure of the personality. In many, though not all, personalities there is a predominant or central rôle that tends to be most characteristic of the person, while other rôles, while present, are organized in subordinate relationships.

2. The rôle is the organization of habits and attitudes of the individual appropriate to a given position in a system of social relationships. For example, when we say that a given person plays a child rôle, we may mean that his habitual modes of response in a situation and his attitude toward others as well as toward himself are such that he fits into a position of dependence on and of the expectation of solicitous, protecting, guiding, and controlling movements from the environmental situation.

There are certain points concerning the concept of the rôle which, though recognized by those who developed and refined the concept, need for our purposes added emphasis.

First, in our use of the concept rôle we

Reprinted in part from *Publications of the American Sociological Society*, 1933, *27*, pp. 107–15, with permission of the American Sociological Association and the author.

are prone to think of certain character-istic responses or tendencies to respond which the person makes or tends to make to persons or situations. Frequently we fail to recognize clearly enough what might be called expectations entertained by the subject as to actions or responses which are to come from other persons. The writer recognizes that it is impossible to separate these two things since in reality they are aspects of the same thing. There is no conception of one's rôle, con-scious or unconscious, without reference to what action is expected of the situa-tion of which the rôle is a part. It is well, however, to emphasize the expectancy as-pect, particularly in using the notion in the study of marriage situations. A num-ber of our cases of marital difficulty seem capable of analysis in terms of the in-ability of one mate to fit into the expected response pattern called for by the other.

A second point to be called to mind is that in marriage the partners do not play single rôles with respect to one another, although a single rôle may be most char-acteristic of a given person in his mar-riage relations. Cases seem to indicate a multiplicity of rôles. For example, a wife may play a much depended upon mother-rôle, a hated sister-rôle, and a loved brother-rôle at different times for her hus-band. The husband may in turn be for his wife her distantly respected father, her hated younger brother, and her loved older sister. The startling ambivalence fre-quently displayed by married persons for one another may not be true ambivalence in the strict Freudian sense. It may ac-tually be the result of corresponding at-titudes for different rôle patterns derived from early family relations. Thus a hus-band may call out affectionate as well as hostile responses from his wife by play-ing rôles of members of her family who earlier called out the different responses. Of course it is not at all necessary nor

even likely that either husband or wife will be aware that he is playing such rôles.

A third point to be mentioned is that rôles may be stereotyped and unique. The stereotyped rôles, for example, of hus-band and father, wife and mother, are defined in the folkways and mores of so-ciety. But within these definitions by a given culture there are individual patterns of rôles that are determined by the pecul-iar social experience of the individual. Thus an adult may continue to play an infantile rôle as a result, let us say, of his having been the youngest child in a family that has coddled him a great deal.

A fourth point which needs emphasis is that, frequently, we might say usually, many of the rôles that persons play are unconscious. If all of the rôles a married pair play for one another are not uncon-scious, the most significant ones are fre-quently so.

We shall not here attempt an exegesis of the conception of the unconscious. It is sufficient for our purposes to realize that, if we analyze any act or series of actions, we find that there are phases of the act which can be said to be unknown to the actor, and are, moreover, not sub-ject to his unaided conscious scrutiny and reflection. The conscious phase of the act in which the individual has defined for himself or has defined for him his objects and purposes and motives is one phase only. There are preliminary to and con-comitant with his acts, goals, motives, etc., of which he is unconscious. Ex-amples might be taken from the cases cited by Mr. H. D. Lasswell in his *Psychopathology and Politics* in which the conscious political activity directed against a present order turns out to be a displacement of drives and hostilities of the child with respect to its parent or sibling. Of these more primary and ele-mentary motives the person is not aware and accepts his own definitions of goals and reasons as the only ones present in the action. Our contention here is that the same kind of unconscious character can be attributed to much of marital activity.

There may be some objection to thinking of rôles as unconscious. We do not hold that all rôles are unconscious. Some seem to be completely unconscious; some only partially so. We are not wedded to a word. If the term "rôle" is to be used only for conscious action patterns and relationships, then we must give another name to these unconscious patterns and relationships that exist in fact.

The narrowed angle of approach represented in this paper, namely, the study of marriage as an adjustment of rôles, may be indicated by laying down certain propositions.

First, marriage adjustment may be regarded as a process in which marriage partners attempt to re-enact certain relational systems or situations which obtained in their own earlier family groups. Or, in other words, marriage partners tend to play the habitual rôles they evolved in their childhood and adolescence.

Second, the kinds of rôles that marriage partners bring to the marriage will determine the nature of their marriage relationship and the degree of adjustment that they will achieve.

Third, that maladjusted marriages may be regarded as results of the failure of marriage situation to provide the system of relationships called for by the rôles which the marriage partners bring to the marriage.

Now the writer is quite aware that these propositions leave out of account a great many important factors—cultural, economic, etc.—and there is no effort to deny that such factors are of importance. Let it be emphatically affirmed that these propositions are laid down in an effort

to make a logical delimitation of the problem. However, there is considerable justification for the opinion that the unique rôle patterns are the chief determinants of the success or failure of marriages in which the persons come from similar cultural backgrounds. And it should not be forgotten that the greater number of marriages are contracted by persons of reasonably similar cultural backgrounds.

Let us consider the case of Mr. and Mrs. A. who have been married about a year.

Mr. A. (aged 24) is the youngest of a family of seven. When asked to tell about his childhood, he launches into a rather enthusiastic account of his happy and satisfactory family life. From his story one gathers that his mother was a powerful and aggressive personality, the chief center, drive, and control factor in the family. She ran the father's affairs, planned the children's vocational and, social activities, maneuvered the daughters' marriages, and tried to maneuver the sons' marriages. Mr. A. boasts of her iron will. He is proud of her determined look, and tells how her spirit never sagged. He tells how she faced death with the same unshaken will and determination never to admit defeat.

The father is described as a pleasant, reliable, steady, quiet, and meek person who seemed to figure merely as an unimportant though kindly fixture in the household. He worked steadily, turned his earnings over to his wife, never seriously opposed her, and after her death, agreeably allowed his daughters to place him in an old people's home.

The three sisters are described as being very much like the mother, particularly the two older ones. These two have married husbands to whom they play pretty much the same rôle which their mother played toward her husband. The youngest sister, whom we shall call Martha, is two years older than Mr. A. Although not quite so Amazonian as her sisters, she is fairly aggressive, active, and adequate in meeting situations. She has played a decidedly mothering rôle to Mr. A., especially since the death of their mother when Mr. A. was about fifteen years old. He says of Martha in an interview, "We have always been very close together. She has comforted me and consoled me in my troubles. I have confided in her and she has shielded me. She used to advise me and tell me what to do." . . .

In speaking of all the sisters he says: "I was always proud to go places with my sisters. They were lively and popular and I was proud of them. I could walk around and enjoy myself and they could take care of themselves." (This was said in comparing his sisters with his wife, who depends too much on him, he says, for pleasant times at social gatherings.)

Mr. A. does not feel that there was much conflict in his home. Things seemed to be secure and to run smoothly under the orderly supervision of the mother. He feels that the home life was happy. He says: "There was always something going on at my home. My mother and sisters were always doing interesting things, having people over and having jolly times that I like to remember. They didn't sit around like she does (alluding to his wife) and wait for something to happen. My father is quiet and never participated much in what was going on, but he enjoyed watching and listening to other people. I am like my father. I liked to watch and listen, and, if I felt like it, put in a word or do something. I hate to feel I *have* to talk or take the initiative." (This remark also was made with reference to his wife's irritating dependence upon him.)

Mr. A.'s two brothers are interesting. The older brother, who is also the oldest child, is called the black sheep. His relations with the mother and with the sister next to him were particularly hostile. He rebelled and left home early. The next brother is the middle child. He was the mother's favorite. He was and still is a dependable, quiet, kindly, non-aggressive person. The children say he is the mainstay of the family. Mr. A. describes him as a kind of parent to the younger children.

[Mr. A.] was punished very little. A typical instance is revealing. His mother and brother scolded him and threatened to punish him for not practicing his music. They told him he should be willing to practice for them if they paid for his lessons. Mr. A.'s comment is interesting: "I remember I was very angry that they should expect anything from me just because they paid for the lessons. I hated to feel obligated." (This represents an attitude characteristic of Mr. A.—that of expecting the environment to minister unto him with no obligation or responsibilities on his part.)

One gets the impression from Mr. A.'s conversation that he was an extremely dependent, much indulged, and coddled child; that he resented any responsibility or expectation or demand from him on the part of the environment; and that he felt insecure in situations where he was thrown on his own initiative. He tended to assume a passive rôle, expecting the environment to furnish aggressive support, backing, and leadership. On several occasions he made what he describes as attempts to win his independence by leaving home. He usually went under the tutelage of a decisive and aggressive boy friend who told him he ought to learn to stand on his own feet. On each occasion when he faced a shortage of jobs or money he felt forced to retreat home. After a few attempts he was ashamed to go home and would retreat to the family of the girl he finally married. He said: "I just can't bear feeling all alone in a strange place with no money and no home I can go to."

Mr. A. met his wife shortly before his mother's death. He says: "I was timid and bashful, but she was pleasant and talked to me and I felt comfortable with her." Soon after Mr. A.'s mother died the girl's family moved to another city. A. wept the night before her departure and said: "First I lose my mother; then I lose you." (The girl had the same first name as Mr. A.'s mother.) He told her he loved her at that time, but felt that he had said more than he meant; and the next day he contrived to arrive at the railroad station too late to see her off. Largely through the girl's efforts, a correspondence was kept up between the two. Later, after some of his unsuccessful forays into the world of affairs, he would seek the shelter of the girl's home. She would be very sympathetic about his trials and tribulations and she readily accepted his alibis for failure and excused him to himself. When she consoled him on his retreats from unsuccessful attempts to make good in the world (which, by the way, he expected to do in short order) he would tell her that she was just like his sister. . . .

Before we discuss further the relations between Mr. A. and his wife, it is necessary to describe briefly Mrs. A.'s family. The families of both Mr. and Mrs. A. represent the same cultural and economic levels; if there is any difference, it is slight and in favor of Mr. A.'s family.

Mrs. A. (aged 23) describes her father as a successful merchant until a few years ago, when he developed an interest in gambling and taking extended vacations. He had never saved money but his business kept the family in good circumstances. For some time now, however, he had been very improvident and irrespon-

sible. He has obtained good positions, but has given them up for very trivial reasons. Mrs. A. says she used to admire and respect her father, but since he has allowed the family to come upon evil days she has lost respect for him and feels very resentful toward him. The father accuses the mother of being responsible for the condition of the family. He says: "You should have taken the money from me and not allowed me to gamble." And "You should have made me attend to our business." Mrs. A. feels that her father has acted as something of a spoiled child toward his wife.

The mother is described as patient, long suffering, submissive. Mrs. A. feels that she is close to her mother because, as she says, "I am very much like my mother and can understand her." She has always taken sides with her mother in family arguments, which seems to align the father and older brother against the mother and Mrs. A. These arguments turn out to be tongue lashings from the father and older brother, with the mother and daughter passively resisting. . . .

There are three children in the family, an oldest son, Mrs. A., and her younger brother. Mrs. A. speaks bitterly of the intense hatred she bears her older brother, who appears from her description to be a very domineering, overbearing, egocentric person. But she follows her statements of hostility toward him with the admission that she secretly admires his aggressiveness and capabilities and envies his assertiveness. She has wished all her life that he would love her. When on rare occasions he would be kind to her or give her a birthday gift, she would feel much encouraged and hope for better relations. She would experience great disappointment when he would resume his usual tactics.

The son's hostilities toward his mother and sister seem to date from early childhood. Mrs. A. has fought back somewhat, but she usually cries, feels blue, and suffers inwardly. She still dreams of having bitter fights with him but in these dreams her rôle is one of defending herself against his attacks. Occasionally she will dream of a more aggressive rôle in which she vehemently commands her brother to get out of the house. She says that one reason she liked Mr. A. was that he seemed to be the opposite of her brother in every way.

Mrs. A. is fond of her younger brother and feels that they were quite close as children, though their relationship is not so close now.

Mrs. A.'s conversation gives one the impression of a person with some hostile drives, who, nevertheless, tends to assume a passive rôle in all situations. She tends to wait for something to happen, for others to make suggestions and to take the initiative. Her lack of decisive self-assertion is a characteristic which drives her husband, so he says, to distraction.

With this all too meager account of the backgrounds of our subjects, let us turn again to their relationship with one another.

Mr. A. became more and more frightened and restless as it became clearer to him that the natural and expected result of his relationship to Mrs. A. was marriage. He made some attempts to extricate himself by protesting to her that they were in no position to marry and by leaving her home. Quoting from an interview with him: "I wanted to be away to be free to work out my problems alone, but I felt myself dragged deeper and deeper." Early attempts to leave and get a job resulted in failure and an inevitable return to the girl, who was always ready with her sympathy and mothering solicitude. Her family was hospitable; but what worried Mr. A. was that they assumed his frequent returnings for prolonged visits

to mean that he was intent on marriage. The father finally became more urgent and tried to encourage the diffident young man by letting him know that what he needed to settle him down was marriage.

These urgings and expectations on the part of the family plus the pleadings of the girl, plus his own inability to do without some sympathetic reassuring, proved too much for him. Finally, he says, he shut his eyes and jumped. We do not have time to give his description of his mental anguish as he walked the streets for two days trying to make up his mind. "Then," he says, "with superhuman effort I forced myself to go to the courthouse and say 'I want a marriage license.'"

After the marriage Mr. A. began to have many fears and forebodings. He was afraid Mrs. A.'s mother or father would die and he would have to help take care of Mrs. A.'s younger brother. He feared that he had wrecked his chances to realize his best self and should get out of the marriage. He began to find Mrs. A. ugly; and this, he said, outraged his aesthetic sensibilities. But the main theme throughout his interviews is: "My wife is a drag on me. She depends too much on me. Instead of feeling myself being pulled forward, I feel like she is pulling me backward. Why can't she be like my sisters? She is weak and casts a gloom over my spirit that I can't shake off. I must go away so I can feel free again and be on my own."

He did break away once to go to his sister for comfort and solace. He said: "While I was there I was happy again unless I thought of my plight. My sister said 'all you need is the comfort of your home' and she was right. While I was with her I felt all right."

The wife complained that she didn't feel secure with her husband. She wished that he could be like other men who seem to know what they want to do and how to go about it, who seem to take charge of things and forge ahead and not appear so helpless. She resented the fact that, although her husband was out of work and she was supporting him, he seemed to take that for granted as his due. Moreover, he showed great irritation toward her if she came home tired and, as he puts it, "sagging and weak looking." He says: "I simply can't stand that sagging, droopy look."

Their sexual adjustment is interesting when seen on this background. Neither knew how to proceed and their first attempts at intercourse were clumsy and unsuccessful. The husband's history shows considerable curiosity during childhood, and avoidance and fear in adolescent encounters. Even after receiving coaching from a physician and becoming somewhat adept in sexual technique, he is still described by his wife as clumsy and diffident in his approaches. He himself reveals a certain resentment and resistance to assuming the rôle of aggressor in relation with his wife. He has to assume a rôle in the sexual situation that runs contrary to his desires.

In both husband and wife there are evidences of strong repressions of sexual drives. These specifically sexual attitudes are undoubtedly a part of the situation, but they may also be thought of as parts of the basic rôle patterns, particularly in the case of the husband.

This represents the barest outline of some of the high spots in the case, but if we could present all of our materials they would hardly do more than amplify the picture which must be evident from even such a scant description.

The central problem in this case is a problem of basic rôles, which are apparently the result of the early family relationships.

The husband is looking for a solicitous, protecting, aggressive, decisive, parent en-vironment which the wife, who expects something of the same sort of environment, cannot supply. She was able to furnish sympathy and to that extent supplied the rôle of mother and sister in the husband's family. But she is not equipped to supply the more positive and aggressive part of the rôles that these people represented in Mr. A.'s personality development.

Neither of them is quite fully aware of what the basis for their trouble is. The husband thinks his marriage is a mistake, that he is not cut out for marriage, that his artistic temperament needs complete freedom to realize itself. The wife thinks the husband is sulky, inconsiderate, selfish, and jealous of her interest in her family. They both think that relief of the financial tension would be a partial solution.

Those who take the psychoanalytic approach would probably classify the man as a homosexual type, and interpret the difficulties on that basis. If we recognize that for the male the category "homosexual" applies to general psycho-sexual traits of passivity rather than to certain specific sexual attitudes, merely, then the classification is probably valid. But it should be pointed out that the classification is not fully descriptive of the rôle pattern Mr. A. represents. He is not only passive but has an infantile dependent attitude or rôle which is not necessarily characteristic of the homosexual.

The case might also be interpreted as a result of guilt feelings which arise when Mr. A. engages in sexual activity with a person who stands as a substitute for his sister Martha. Sexual impulses with reference to his sister must have been heavily repressed and, when they are allowed expression on a love object that stands for her, they give rise to strong guilt feelings from which Mr. A. seeks to escape by terminating the marriage. Even here, however, we get into a usage of the notion of rôles. But it is apparent that this specifically sexual explanation leaves out of account too much of Mr. A.'s general pattern of response to all types of situations.

The writer would suggest that, at the present stage of the game, it seems preferable to use concretely descriptive categories of rôle types. It may turn out later that some such set of master categories as those now used in the psychoanalytic field will apply. But their application

should be made when empirical evidence justifies such usage.

Turning to a different approach, it should be pointed out that analysis of marital problems in terms of the usual categories of economic, cultural, response, temperamental, health, and other tensions is rather sterile unless such analysis is done with the insight that rôle analysis supplies. Any and all of the usual tensions may and do appear in a given case, but frequently they are meaningless unless seen in reference to the basic problem of rôles.

GEORGE A. LUNDBERG
MARGARET LAWSING
The Sociography of Some Community Relations

I.

The explanation of social groupings and their behavior as groups is generally regarded as the basic problem of sociology. Accordingly, any comprehensive social theory must provide a logically consistent description of this phenomenon. All systematic thinkers on the subject have recognized this need and they have usually advanced, therefore, some generalized principle, such as gregarious instincts, consciousness of kind, class consciousness, etc. The main difficulty with these theories has been that they have posited within the individual or the group some mechanism, itself unexplained or only implicitly accounted for, by which the observed behavior was to be explained.

Reprinted in part from *American Sociological Review*, 1937, *2*, pp. 318–35, with permission of the American Sociological Association and the author.

plained. This approach is in striking contrast to that which physical science has found so useful, namely, that the behavior of any particle or aggregate is to be explained mainly in terms of the structure of the field within which it operates. The swing toward this position in sociology is evidenced by the increasing emphasis upon the situation (of which the individual or the group under consideration is always a part) rather than upon the individual characteristics of the behaving entity.

Geographers and ecologists have given one type of recognition to the situational interpretation of social behavior. At first these studies emphasized chiefly the purely geographic, structural, and spatial relationships of the community. The mapping and charting of these features admittedly provided a useful framework within which to interpret many aspects of community behavior. . . .

The next step after mere mapping in

the process of describing the community was to convert behavior itself into symbolic indexes which can in turn be represented in geometric, isometric, isotypical, or gradient terms. Thus birth, death, disease, and delinquency rates or any other behavior phenomena can be computed for local areas and the relationship of such phenomena to these regions can be shown by lines representing gradients or other geometric devices. A line on the same map representing the declining delinquency rate from the center of the city toward the periphery, denotes a phenomenon just as actual, observable and meaningful as a line representing the main street. . . . Both types of lines represent both a structural and a functional phenomenon. At present, many of these behavior phenomena have not yet been metricized. Until they are reduced to metric units we may deal with them by topological constructs, which may be an intermediate step toward metrical statement. The correlation of these various indexes when worked out for *all* the relevant aspects of community behavior would represent all the description and explanation of the life of a community which science can attain. For this description, multiplied and generalized, would say in a more precise and verifiable fashion all that is factually valid in all the wordy and obscure treatises we now have on the community. . . .

Next below the formal, official, or latent organization of the whole community is a network of so-called private groups —families, religious bodies, clubs, fraternities, etc. These have a considerable degree of formal organization and permanence, but are usually thought of as relatively selective and "voluntary" instead of inclusive and automatic in their membership. Also, they are more limited and specialized in the type of interests which give

rise to them. This level of community organization is usually regarded as less "tangible" than the formal political organization of the whole community. The feeling that these informal groupings are less tangible is due to the relative absence of objective and systematic information about them and the relatively unstable and shifting nature of most of them. Attempts to study and chart this level of community structure are, however, becoming increasingly objective. This is notably true of studies of family structure, function and behavior.

Finally, there is underlying these private and more or less "voluntary" social groupings the tremendously intricate and elementary network of informal social nuclei which we describe in such terms as affinities, friendships, love affairs, cliques, gangs, etc. These are at present the least tangible social units because of their informal, transitory, private and frequently secret character, as well as their occasionally illicit and sometimes illegal nature. These groupings are not structurally enshrined in any of the objective forms usually accompanying other forms of social organization such as written constitutions, buildings, and other "material" paraphernalia, and they are charged with no formal functions by the larger community. Yet the basic nature of these nuclei and their profound influence in determining especially the functioning of the more formal structures has always been recognized. The influence of these alignments is what we rely upon "insiders," "dopesters," and gossips to convey to us, since objective and official accounts of the behavior of the generally recognized social groups contain no mention of these underlying influences. Yet it is admitted that the generally recognized behavior of a community can in a given case be adequately explained only if these basic alignments are understood. Behind all present objective explanations of community behavior, therefore, there is always an aura of data, at present largely in the form of gossip, because of its subjective form, which we all feel constitutes the "real" explanation of what takes place. In the same way, the clever leader knows that the success of any program must take into consideration the cultural, psychological, emotional, and other clique alignments, especially of "key" people, the existence of which may not be consciously recognized by the people concerned, and certainly not admitted by them. Failure to take these alignments into consideration is generally recognized as a tactical blunder, lack of tact, diplomacy, etc. The objective study of these elementary social nuclei is, therefore, quite basic both to understanding and intelligent control of the community. . . .

The present paper is mainly concerned with the problem of representing more objectively some of these community nuclei which are at present considered the subtler and more intangible facts of community structure, and which have hitherto, therefore, been left chiefly to literary and philosophic exploitation. Such terms as subtlety, complexity, and intangibility should be recognized as being not inherent characteristics of data but merely words describing the degree of our adjustment to certain aspects of phenomena, i.e., the stage of development of our techniques of dealing with them. If we take this view, then the principal task of science, today as in the past, is undoubtedly to objectify the subtle and intangible and so to make possible verification of the type generally recognized in science.

The basic assumption of ecologists and others who have attempted to chart the community is that the structures which they depict represent the channels along which flows the energy or force which we must postulate as behind all activity. This assumption also meets the common objection to the ecologist's technique, that it does not portray the dynamic interactions which are the essence of social activity. Just as the trend of development has been from mapping geographic features to the spatial representation of group behaviors of the more obvious (i.e., formally recorded) type, so the next step is to develop techniques of representing in their significant relationships the subtler (i.e., as yet imperfectly understood) energy currents or forces that animate and define a community. These patterns are here regarded as existing in social space as well as in geographic space. It has become highly conventional and useful to represent the latter by charts, maps, and other geometric devices. The adequate representation of relationships in social space may likewise be greatly facilitated by a kind of sociography or psychological geography. We proceed now to review some attempts at more objective and intensive analysis of these "subtle," elementary societary phenomena.

II.

An important step forward in detailed and objective studies of social groupings has been taken by Moreno in undertaking to chart the attraction-repulsion patterns of an entire institutional community. Moreno asked all the members of the State Training School for Girls at Hudson, New York, to indicate their choices, in order from one to five, of the members of the community with whom each would like to occupy the same house. The choices were confidential and it was definitely understood that they would become the basis for a reassignment to different houses. This is a closed community with a population of between five and six hundred. The girls live in sixteen cottages each with a housemother. Tabulation of the choices of desired housemate, including housemothers, revealed an intricate set of sociological nuclei of five principal types. (1) The most elementary and definite nucleus was the mutual first choice of two or more individuals among themselves. This might be represented by figures of couples, triangles, squares, circles, or figures of more intricate dimensions. (2) Then there were the patterns most simply represented by chains of a nonmutual character, as, for example, when A chooses B, B chooses C, and C chooses A. Such chains might, of course, consist of any number of individuals. (3) A third type of configuration resulted from a clustering of a large number of choices around a single individual, to some of which this "star" may respond by mutual choice, to others by indifference, and to others by repulsion. (This information regarding indifference and repulsion was secured through separate private interviews.) (4) A fourth type of nucleation, of great practical significance, was the phenomenon of the powerful as contrasted with the popular individual, and the phenomenon of indirect influence. Thus, an individual may be the object of a large number of choices by people relatively isolated from the rest of the community. The center of such a cluster of choices may be very popular with his immediate group but may not have very much influence in the community because of the limited contacts of his admirers. On the other hand, an individual chosen by only a few may wield a powerful indirect influence by virtue of the extensive connections of the few popular persons for whom he is a center of attraction. Thus, Moreno cites one case, herself chosen by only four individuals, all of whose attraction she reciprocates. But

these four are in their turn chosen by nearly one hundred individuals. This seems to be the sociological position of the "power behind the throne" and the "dark horse" who wields the real power through the personalities of popular nominal leaders. As Moreno has pointed out, "the distribution of power in large groups depends upon the intricate distribution of emotional currents. An individual who is in control and can steer the course of one of these currents can wield an immense potential influence out of all proportion to his immediate following." Finally, (5) there is the isolated individual, chosen by nobody, although he may choose some other persons. Such individuals are almost certain to be maladjusted and to cause maladjustment in any group with which they have to live. Sometimes, to be sure, such individuals, not chosen by anyone as housemates, may, however, be chosen as desirable work companions, so that isolation is always with reference to a criterion. The completely isolated individual would be one who was not chosen by anyone as an associate in any of the activities or relations of a community. Such an individual could not be very sensitive to the behavior standards of the community because he is cut off from the currents which constitute the pressures by which these standards become operative on the individual, and hence he would almost certainly be a social problem.

Now the individuals attracted to another individual regarded as a nucleus together with the individuals to which this nucleus is attracted, any or all of which attractions may or may not be mutual, may be regarded as a social atom with reference to any social interest, i.e. any adjustment need. Thus, each individual, provided he is not socially isolated, is the nucleus of one or more social atoms according to the number of relationships in which he is the center of attraction. He may at the same time be the nucleus of one or more atoms and part of the electronic system of other atoms. These atomic structures may therefore overlap in a tremendous intricacy of interrelationship, each individual being at the same time part of numerous diverse structures, but in various degrees of completeness or intensity.

As was to be expected, Moreno found that a knowledge of the societal energy patterns of his community enabled him to explain events which occurred, such as a series of runaways, and, what is more important, it also enabled him to organize the community so as to relieve tensions and cause the virtual disappearance of certain types of maladjustment. He also suggests the applicability of these methods in the social as well as in the physical planning of other than institutional communities, for example, such as those projected by the Resettlement Administration. In this connection the question at once arises: How possible is it to carry on in an uncontrolled, open, and ordinary community such studies as Moreno and others have carried on with conspicuously successful results in schools and among other institutional groups? In short, can the informal and private affinities and nucleations of an ordinary community be discovered and charted with any degree of accuracy, and if so, what does this elementary and basic societary structure reveal?

As a first attempt to answer this question we undertook a complete house-to-house canvass of a small Vermont village.[1] Ninety-four per cent of the families gave the desired information, the wife being most frequently the source of the information secured. The bulk of the interview consisted of (1) scoring the liv-

[1] Population about 1,000; area about one square mile. . . .

ing room according to the Chapin scale,[2] designed to measure socio-economic status, (2) securing certain additional information regarding occupation, family size, general housing conditions, and kinds of reading matter. This information is not relevant to the present report and will therefore not be analyzed at this time. (3) In the course of the interview, or at its conclusion, the person interviewed was asked to name her most intimate friends in the community, after having been assured that this, in common with other information secured, would be kept strictly confidential.

It is recognized, of course, that the results secured and analyzed in part below are merely verbal testimony of friendship groupings voluntarily contributed by the persons interviewed.[3] Under these conditions we would be likely to miss (1) illicit friendships, love affairs, and other attachments not approved by the community or otherwise embarrassing to the reporting individual. This would include all so-called subconscious attachments, if any. (2) The friendship patterns reported would not be complete for the whole community because other members of the family than the housewife would be members of other groups which we did not attempt to chart. This is perhaps more true of the children than of the father in a community of this kind, and less true of either than it would be in a large urban community. (3) We did not attempt to secure the negative or repulsion patterns for fear of compromising the success of

[2] [See Chapin study in Unit 11 below.]
[3] Corroboration of the verbal testimony was attempted through interviews with certain local people after the main field work had been completed, and also through a study of the social columns of the local newspaper. While the groupings thus revealed are less complete than those secured through the interviews, they corroborate, as far as they go, the interview results.

the whole study. The results secured, however, may be said to represent a highly reliable account of the friendship nuclei of the housewives of this village *as they were willing to have the investigator know these relationships* in the fall of 1936. As such, the purely verbal nature of the behavior studied is significant from some points of view, even if we make no assumption whatever as to its correlation with other friendship behavior. (4) Finally, it is recognized that the results secured represent only the general friendship patterns as regards perhaps primarily recreational or prestige association, i.e., "social" in the limited sense of the "visiting" type of association. One's friends are usually chosen with reference to special types of association. Thus, Moreno, for example, found that girls would sometimes choose different companions for work associates than for housemates. We secured in this study perhaps primarily the "social" type of patterns.[4] These are, however, very spontaneous and basic forms of social nucleation. They represent, perhaps, the individual's own estimate of his social status.

[4] The term "friendship," like most other sociological terms, is too general and vague a category to allow conclusions as to just what relationships it covers in a given case. In the present study, the person interviewed was asked to name confidentially her best friends in the community. The aim was to secure the names spontaneously volunteered in response to what appeared to be a casual inquiry at the end of an interview dealing entirely with other matters. If further interpretation was requested, the interviewer explained that what was desired was the names of people with whom "social" visiting for other than business or professional reasons most frequently took place. The problem of the interpretation of this verbal behavior in terms of other behavior remains, of course. But this is true of all behavior. It takes on meaning in proportion as it is related to some larger pattern, and verbal behavior is not in this respect unique.

The primary objective of this study has not been so much to arrive at reliable facts and generalizations about this particular community as to suggest an approach to certain subtle social phenomena. We are, for example, not concerned over the accuracy of the Chapin scale as a measure of socio-economic status. We used it merely as an illustration of how scales of *any kind* measuring perhaps a great variety of family and personality variables could be profitably used in the interpretation of social groupings.

Of 256 persons successfully interviewed, only 3 cases of completely isolated persons were found. (Twenty-nine others admitted no friends in the village, but mentioned friends in the adjoining area. Thirteen of these 29 were also mentioned as friends by others in the village.) All of these three isolated cases were older people without relatives, some of them with organic defects, such as deafness. They were very eager for contacts and urged the interviewers to come back for further visiting.

Forty-six persons gave only one other person as their friend, and in 13 of these cases the choice was mutual. Only one of these pairs (men) was exclusive in the sense that neither member made any other choices, though both were chosen by several others. (See Figure 2, M 1 and M 19.) All of the other 12 pairs were women. More complicated forms of triangles (e.g., Figure 2, S 10, W 10 and W 16) and other patterns of the various types classified above wait upon further analysis. These groupings are not commonly themselves isolated but have one or more ties with other similar groups.

At the opposite extreme from the isolated persons stands the "star" or the person who is the object of a large concentration of choices. The most conspicuous of these cases, with her satellites, is depicted in Figure 1 (M 31). She is the

Figure **1**   *"Friendship" constellation in a village* [a]

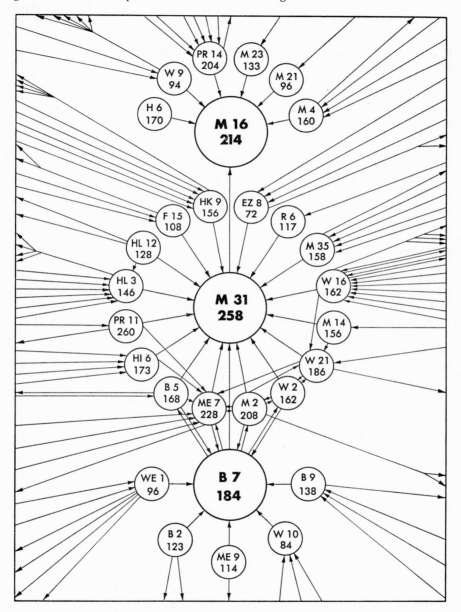

[a] Each person is represented by a circle. The letter and the first number in the circle is the code symbol of the person. The second number is that person's score of socio-economic status on the Chapin scale. Each arrow represents a choice made or received according to to the direction of the arrow. Mutual choices are represented by double-headed arrows.

"lady bountiful" of the village—a widow of about 60 years, old and reputable family, wealthy, and generous in her donations to all village undertakings, from uniforms for the fire department to the major charities. Her donations are apparently the chief basis for her prestige. This person was mentioned as a friend by 17 people, most of them with heavy social ramifications of their own. Yet the "star" herself mentioned only one person (a physician and politician, not among the 17 satellites) as her friend. The intricacy of the interrelationships among the satellites as shown in the lower part of the constellation indicates a very definite clique of high social potential (i.e., number and mutuality of choices). Two mutual triangles converge upon B 7 (a banker's wife) who has in addition a group of five satellites whose choices she does not reciprocate. These satellites are recipients of a total of 21 choices by persons outside of the constellation here depicted. The satellites of the main star, M 31, receive from the outside a total of 46 designations as friends. The magnetic power of M 31 in the community as well as the high interaction among her satellites depicted in the lower part of Figure 1 indicates a societal structure which would have to be considered in the description and explanation of a great many aspects of this community's behavior.

In Figure 2 we have a relationship suggesting the survival of the ancient connections between the barber's trade and the physician's profession. A physician (M 1) and a barber (M 19) indicate each other as friends and mention no others. The physician, however, is the recipient of eight direct choices from his satellites who in turn receive a total of 26 choices from other people in the community. The barber likewise receives six direct choices from his satellites, who are together recipients of 26 choices from others. When we consider all of the major characters in

the constellation from the point of view of the number of times they are chosen as friends directly and indirectly (by one remove) we find a constantly decreasing volume of incoming social currents as we proceed from the center of the diagram toward the periphery, as follows:

Table **1**

Person	Number of choices received		
	Direct	*Indirect*	*Total*
M 1	8	26	34
M 19	6	26	32
B 12	6	15	21
W 16	4	8	12
S 10	3	8	11
W 10	2	4	6

Thus the central mutual pair (M 1, M 19) receives a total of 66 choices; the other mutual pair (B 12, W 16) receives a total of 33; the mutual triangle (W 16, S 10, W 10) totals only 29 such choices.

Only 4 of the 23 individuals represented in Figure 2 are also represented in Figure 1. While they are connected in various ways along the periphery they represent two well-defined social constellations with a total of 46 individuals, representing about a sixth of the total families in the village.

If none of the people represented in Figures 1 and 2 chose any friends outside of the individuals represented in each figure respectively (i.e., if there were no arrows pointing toward the boundary of the figure) each group could be said to be highly nucleated, self-sufficient, independent, clannish, etc., by which is meant a high degree of social cohesion and (if many mutual choices appear) interaction between the members of the constellation. Actually, however, a great many of the individuals represented in these charts also mentioned friends outside of the circles here charted. If we consider these out-

Figure **2**   *"Friendship" constellation centering on a physician (M 1) and a barber (M 19)* [a]

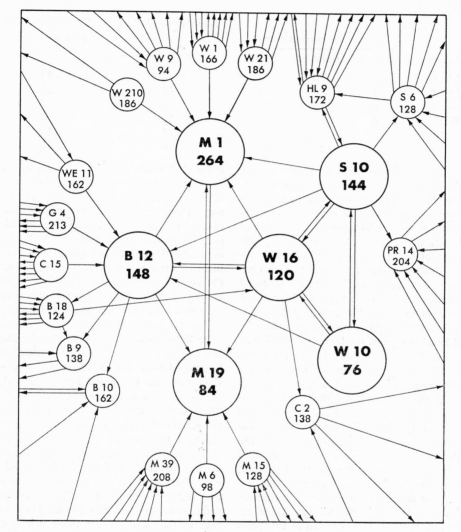

[a] (For meaning of symbols see Figure 1.)

going stimuli in the form of choices made rather than choices received as in Table 1, we get [from Figure 2 the result shown in the following table]:

Table **2**

Person	Number of choices made			Number of choices received (direct and indirect)	Choices received minus choices made
	Direct	Indirect	Total		
M 1	1	0	1	34	33
M 19	1	0	1	32	31
B 12	6	13	19	21	2
W 16	6	13	19	12	7
S 10	7	18	25	11	14
W 10	3	17	20	6	14

The surplus of choices received over the choices made (incoming over outgoing stimuli) may be regarded as a sort of index of the degree of cohesion or nucleation of any social segment. If the social bonds of a number of individuals with each other are no greater than with individuals outside of the aggregation considered (i.e., if choices received equal choices made, in the present illustration) there is no reason for regarding the population studied as nucleated or otherwise defined as against the larger population of which they are a part. If, on the other hand, there is a surplus of incoming over outgoing choices of friends, we may regard the population within which such surplus obtains as centered or nucleated around the individuals upon which the greatest surplus of incoming choices are directed. The situations depicted in both of the accompanying charts represent, therefore, highly nucleated constellations as contrasted with a random selection of individuals within the village. More extensive tests of the operation of this principle need to be made and are under way. In the meantime, we tentatively suggest as a measure of social cohesion, interaction, or degree of social nucleation in a group of individuals, the following generalized statement: Social cohesion varies with the preponderance of stimuli coming into and exchanged between the individuals in a group over the stimuli directed outside the group; i.e., incoming stimuli plus interaction (mutuals) equals degree of nucleation. The adequate measurement of these social currents is therefore the central problem. The technique here employed represents, of course, only one type of interstimulation or social bond.

The fragmentary data reviewed above raise the question as to what may be the basis, or bases, of any social nucleation in a population such as is here under consideration. In the cases here reviewed, socio-economic status, professional or political status were clearly present. To test the general hypothesis as to whether people tend to name as friends persons of higher socio-economic status than themselves, we compared the choices made with the scores of the persons choosing and being chosen on the Chapin living-room scale. A glance at Figure 1 shows that in the cases of the three principal "stars," all except one (27 out of 28) of the persons naming these "stars" as friends have a lower socio-economic score than the "star" chosen. The choices are seven to one in the direction of higher

Table **3**

Socio-economic score	Number of cases	Average number of choices per chooser	Percentage of choices made in direction of higher scores than those of choosers	Standard errors (per cent)
0–49	13	2.4	97	
50–74	26	2.1	75	8.5
75–99	51	2.3	81	5.5
100–124	54	1.9	66	6.5
125–149	50	2.7	50	7.1
150–174	36	2.0	36	8.0
175–199	13	1.5	50	
200–and up	13	2.0	15	

socio-economic scores among the satellites. Excluding mutuals (which cancel each other) there are in fact only three choices in the entire chart (of 29) in the direction of lower socio-economic status and one of these (Pr 11) represents too slight a difference to be significant. Including the mutuals, the proportions are 35 to 9. Figure 2 reveals the same tendency but in a less striking manner.

As was to be expected, the tendency to choose friends of higher socio-economic status varies with the socio-economic level of the chooser, as shown in Table 3.

These results are of course in part due to the fact that the person at the very bottom of the socio-economic scale would necessarily choose friends of higher status, and the person at the very top would necessarily choose friends of lower status. This principle would tend to operate in all groups to the extent that the limits are approached.[5] To correct this tendency

[5] This does not mean, of course, that all the differences noted in Table 3 are necessarily to be explained by the operation of this principle of pure chance. It is reasonable that the groups of lower socio-economic status should be deliberately more concerned to associate themselves with persons of higher status, as is indicated in the behavior of the median group as noted in these pages.

and to discover the inclination to choose friends with higher socio-economic status when the total numbers from which choices may be made is about even above and below the chooser, we studied separately the median group with scores ranging from 93 to 143, i.e., 25 points immediately above and 25 points immediately below the median (118). This group, consisting of more than one-third of all persons in the study and located in the middle of the socio-economic distribution, directed 60% of their choices of friends in the direction of higher socio-

The average number of choices made does not vary significantly with socio-economic status, but the average number of choices received varies uniformly and directly with socio-economic score. Some of the percentages in Table 3 are, of course, based on too few cases to be significant. The Standard Errors given are computed by Yule's formula $\sigma p = \sqrt{pq/n}$. (*An Introduction to the Theory of Statistics*, p. 262). . . . [In Table 3, the Standard Error of 8.5 for scores 50–74, *e.g.*, means that, if many samples of the same size as this (26) were drawn in the same way, then the percentages of upward-directed choices would in most of the samples range between 66.5 and 83.5. (That is, the 75 found in the present sample would tend to vary upward or downward within the limits set by the Standard Error of ±8.5.) See Exercise V-1.]

economic status. There is a tendency for choices to cluster in the classes nearest to that of the chooser, but skewed in this median group toward the side of rising scores.

Space does not permit a more complete analysis at this time of the personalities, occupations, family relationships, and other factors which influence or determine the constellations noted, or of others in the remainder of the population. The complete pattern for the village and its full interpretation will be published later. In the meantime it may be pointed out that the type of analysis attempted above with respect to the relationship of socio-economic status to social groupings could be extended to include any or all other factors as well, especially when adequate scales for the measurement of these factors have been constructed. If comprehensively carried out such analyses should yield generally valid conclusions regarding the bases of social nucleation in different cultures.

III. Conclusion

This paper considers the community (1) from the spatial point of view, merely as a certain kind of segment of the social universe. (2) From the dynamic point of view, the community is regarded as a system of energy operating within a field of force, in time. Energy is defined, as in any science, as *that which* produces observable manifestations of interaction. The field of force, as in any science, is merely that segment of the universe which for given purposes of study, with the sensory and symbolic apparatus we command at present, we find it convenient or relevant to define as the situation in which we are interested. Similarities and differences (of charactistics or positions), attractions and repulsions (imbalances of whatever sort) within this total system determine the vigor and the direction of the flow of this energy. These differences may be of any kind—social-spatial (status), temporal (e.g., age), sexual, economic, esthetic, temperamental, developmental, or any other. The imbalances may vary in degree from intensest hate to the vaguest dislike, and from fervid love to a vague and even subconscious affinity. Their character, degree, intensity, size (or any other measure), direction, and duration determine the resulting societal configurations in a community, and hence at any given moment, the organization and social functioning of the community. For this energy flow *constitutes* both the behavior and the structure of the community, as of all other observable phenomena. . . .

In approaching the community as here outlined, we do not propose to ignore any significant observation of community life which previous students, whether ancient or modern, have made. We merely propose to translate these observations into a set of concepts and symbols which lend themselves to a representation of their true position in a complex so intricate as to be impossible to represent adequately in the language of folklore.

ROBERT K. MERTON

Patterns of Influence: A Study of Interpersonal Influence and of Communications Behavior in a Local Community

I. Introduction

This is an exploratory study focused upon the place of mass communications in patterns of interpersonal influence. Based primarily upon interviews with eighty-six men and women drawn from diverse social and economic strata in "Rovere," a town of 11,000 on the Eastern seaboard, it is essentially a case study rather than a statistical analysis [1] of influence patterns. The initial substantive aim of this pilot study was fourfold: (1) to identify types of people regarded as variously "influential" by their fellows; (2) to relate patterns of communications behavior to their roles as influential persons; (3) to gain clues to the chief avenues through which they came to acquire influence; and (4) to set out hypotheses for more systematic study of the workings of interpersonal influence in the local community.

The body of this report is devoted to

Reprinted in part with permission of the publisher from Paul F. Lazarsfeld and Frank N. Stanton (eds.), *Communications Research 1948–1949,* copyright 1949 by Harper & Row, Publishers, Incorporated, pp. 189–91, 193–95, 197–203, 208–11, 214.

[1] Although figures summarizing our case-study materials are cited from time to time, these are merely heuristic, not demonstrative, in character. They serve only to indicate the sources of interpretive hypotheses which await detailed, systematic inquiry.

an analysis of basically different types of influential persons: types which we shall call the "local" and the "cosmopolitan." But before turning to these substantive materials, there may be some interest in glancing briefly at two procedural and methodological detours encountered on the way. The first detour was taken when an applied research in sociology, originally devoted to a delimited practical problem, gave rise to theoretic constructs which unexpectedly emerged in the process of investigation. Although the pilot study was in the beginning undertaken to learn the functions served by a national newsmagazine for various types of readers—a problem in the sociology of mass communications—it was soon reoriented as a result of initial impressions and findings. For it appeared that the magazine was utilized in markedly different ways by people who exercised varying degrees of interpersonal influence in their community. In rapidly retracing our steps over the second detour, we shall meet the obstacle which required us to devise alternative schemes for analyzing the same qualitative data. The plain fact is that our initial analysis was quite unproductive. With the emergence of the concepts of local and cosmopolitan influentials, however, the "same" qualitative data led to productive results which have since lent themselves to elaboration. After this brief procedural review of these two phases of our qualitative analysis, we shall be better prepared to assess the substantive account of local and cosmopolitan influentials.

II. Conversion of an Applied Into a Theoretic Research

The practical problem which gave rise to this inquiry was clear enough. The research department of a national newsmagazine sought to learn how one could locate the areas of personal influence in a community. Further, what were the characteristics, including magazine readership, of these influential persons? Was this magazine reaching the "key" persons in networks of personal relations? And however this might be, what patterns of use of this magazine were made by influential people in comparison with rank-and-file readers?

As the practical problem was formulated, it at once led to a focus on evolving *methods of identifying* persons with varying degrees of interpersonal influence. Obviously, one could not determine whether readers of this newsmagazine were or were not disproportionately comprised of "influentials," unless procedures for locating and identifying influentials were at hand. Furthermore, the very fact that a research was initiated to deal with this problem indicated that some plausible indices of influence were considered inadequate by the client. Such seeming indices of influence as occupation, income, property-ownership, and organizational affiliations of readers were available in the files of the newsmagazine or were readily obtainable through a canvass of readers. A research directed toward evolving more effective indices of influence was thus premised on the hypothesis that although people of high "social status" *may* exert relatively great interpersonal influence, social status is not an adequate index. Some individuals of high status apparently wield little interpersonal influence, and some of low-status have considerable interpersonal influence. New qualitative investigation was needed to evolve more direct indices of interpersonal influence.

But, as is not infrequently the case, it was assumed that the problem had been adequately stated at the outset. Do the readers of this magazine disproportionately comprise people of influence and, in any case, do influentials put the magazine to different uses than do rank-and-file readers? Actually, this was a *premature specification* of the problem, as we realized only after the pilot study had been under way for some time. For, as we discovered, it is not so much a matter of identifying *influentials* (and the use they make of newsmagazines) but of detecting types of *influentials* (and the associated differences in their orientation toward newsmagazines as agencies of information concerning the larger society rather than their own local community).

The major shift in this study, as we shall see, occurred with the recognition that the *practical problem had been overspecified* in its initial formulation. This overspecification for a time diverted our attention from salient alternatives of investigation. Only when the initial problem had been reformulated, only when the search for means of identifying influentials was converted into a search for types of influentials likely to differ in their communications behavior, did the research prove productive both in its applied and in its theoretic dimensions. Only then did data, not previously assimilable by our interpretive scheme, "fall into place." Only then were we able to account for diverse and previously unconnected observational data through a limited number of concepts and propositions.

As we shall see in the central part of this report, it was only after the restatement of the problem that we were in a position to advance toward both the applied and the theoretic objectives of the inquiry.

III. Two Phases of a Qualitative Analysis of Influentials

Following upon the reformulation of the problem, we were concerned with devising procedures, however crude, for enabling informants to single out people (apart from their immediate family) who exerted significant "influence" upon them in the course of social interaction. We were not concerned with influence exercised indirectly through political, market, and other administrative decisions which affect large numbers of people. In prolonged interviews, informants were led to mention people to whom they turned for help or advice regarding various types of personal decisions (decisions ranging from choice of a job or educational plans for self and children to selections of books, plays or furniture). Informants were invited, further, to indicate those persons who, so far as they knew, were generally sought out for advice in these several spheres. Such tentative identifications of individuals exercising interpersonal influence were of course linked with reasons advanced by informants for singling out these individuals rather than others.

In the course of these interviews, our eighty-six informants came to mention a total of 379 people who, in one respect or another, were said to have exerted influence upon them in a concrete situation involving decisions. Some people turned up repeatedly in this canvass. (There were 1043 "mentions" referring to 379 persons, some of whom were referred to on thirty or more occasions.) Of the 379, fifty-seven, or 15 per cent, were mentioned four or more times and this was provisionally taken as our working criterion of "influentiality." As we shall presently see, this wholly tentative and arbitrary criterion enabled us to identify cases

in which we could examine the operation of interpersonal influence. Thirty of these influential people were subsequently interviewed with regard to their own evaluation and image of their influence, evaluations of the influence exercised by others upon them, situations in which they exerted influence, their communications behavior, and the like. All this comprised the data for analysis.

This is not the place to report in detail the first, rather unproductive, phase of our analysis of the communications behavior of influentials. But by briefly considering how and why this gave rise to an alternative kind of analysis something may be gained toward a *codification* of methods of qualitative analysis.[2] Just enough will be said to indicate how the data exerted pressure upon the research worker for successively so modifying his concepts that, with the recasting of the data in terms of the new concepts, there emerged a set of suggestive uniformities in place of the previously untidy aggregation of facts.

[2] This part of our report, then, is a bid to the sociological fraternity for the practice of incorporating in publications a detailed account of the ways in which qualitative analyses *actually* developed. Only when a considerable body of such reports are available will it be possible to *codify* methods of qualitative analysis with something of the clarity with which quantitative methods have been articulated. The present report suffers from the deletion of concrete materials illustrating the successive shifts in the categories of analysis; the few details reported here are drawn from a more extensive monograph on file in the Bureau of Applied Social Research. However, this may be sufficient to emphasize the need for increasingly detailed accounts of qualitative analyses in sociology which report not only the *final product* but also the sequential steps taken to obtain this product. In the view of the Bureau, this codification is devoutly to be desired both for the *collection* and the *analysis* of qualitative sociological data.

In what we now know to be the relatively sterile Phase I of our analysis, we not only distinguished the influentials from the rank-and-file, but went on to distinguish influentials according to their dynamic position in the local influence-structure. Thus, distinctions were drawn between the currently influential (occupying a supposedly stable position), the potentially influential (the rising star—still upward mobile), the waning influential (passed the zenith—now downward mobile), and the dormant influential (possessing the *objective* attributes of the influential but not exploiting these for the exercise of influence). The noninfluentials were in turn divided into the rank-and-file (with a limited range of social contacts in which they are typically the recipients rather than the dispensers of advice) and the isolates (largely shut off from social contacts).

This classification proved to be logically impeccable, empirically applicable, and virtually sterile. To be sure, our data could readily be arranged in these categories. But this resulted in few clear-cut uniformities of communications behavior or other patterns of behavior. In short, the distinctions were valid but relatively fruitless for our purposes. But since, as L. J. Henderson once remarked, "almost any classification is better than none," this did lead to some scattered clues concerning the functions of newsmagazines and other communications for those occupying various positions in the influence-structure. Thus, we found that some influentials characteristically use the newsmagazine not so much for self-clarification as for the clarification of others who look to them for guidance and orientation. It also seemed clear that the functions of the newsmagazine differ greatly for the rank-and-file and the influential reader. For the one, it serves a private, personal function; for the other, a public

function. For the rank-and-file reader, the information found in the newsmagazine is a *commodity for personal consumption,* extending his *own* conception of the world of public events; whereas for the influential, it is a *commodity for exchange,* to be traded for further increments of prestige, by enabling him to act as an interpreter of national and international affairs. It aids him in being an opinion-leader.

But at best, this first classification resulted in a welter of discrete impressions not closely related one to the others. It did not enable us to account for the diverse behaviors of influentials. Somewhat more than half of the influentials read newsmagazines, for example, but our classification gave no systematic clue as to why the others did not. The sterility of Phase I of our analysis *motivated the search* for new working concepts, but it was a series of observations incidentally turned up in the course of this analysis which directed attention to the *actual concepts* with which we came to operate.

Above all else, one strategic *fact* shaped Phase II of the analysis. The interviews with influentials had been centered on their relations with*in* the town. Yet, in response to the same set of queries, some influentials spoke wholly in terms of the local situation in Rovere, whereas others managed to incorporate frequent references to matters far beyond the reaches of Rovere. A question concerning the impact of the war upon the Rovere economy would elicit in the one instance a response dealing exclusively with problems within the town and in the other, to remarks about the national economy or international trade. It was this characteristic patterning of response within a peculiarly local or a more extended frame of reference—a patterning which could, perhaps, have been anticipated but which was not—that led to the conception of two major types of influentials: the "local" and the "cosmopolitan."

Whereas the first classification had dealt with phases in the cycle of personal influence, the second was in terms of influentials' *orientation* toward local and larger social structures. The one centered on position within the influence-structure; the other on the grounds for influence and the ways in which this influence was exercised.

With the emergence of the concepts of local and cosmopolitan influentials, a number of new uniformities at once came to light. The "same" materials took on quite new implications as they were re-examined and re-analyzed in terms of these concepts. Facts which found no pertinent place in the first analysis became not only relevant but critical in the second. Thus the varying types of career-patterns of influentials—whether these developed largely within Rovere or were furthered in Rovere after having been initiated elsewhere—came to be an integral part of the second analysis whereas they had been "interesting" but unincorporated data in the first. Such seemingly diverse matters as geographic mobility, participation in networks of personal relations and in voluntary organizations, the translation of influence-potentials into influence-operations, patterns of communications behavior—all these were found to be expressions of these major orientations toward the local community: orientations ranging from virtually exclusive concern with the local area to a central concern with the great world outside.

In this prelude to the main body of the report, then, we have noted two matters of procedural and methodological interest. We have seen, first, that an applied social research, originally focused upon a severely limited objective, gave rise to a more extended inquiry bearing upon a sociological theory of patterns of inter-

personal influence. And, second, we have briefly reviewed the circumstances pressing for a modification of qualitative concepts, with the consequent rearrangement of discrete facts into coherent patterns and uniformities. With this brief introduction, we are prepared for the substantive account of two basically different types of influentials and their respective patterns of communications behavior.

IV. Types of Influentials: The Local and the Cosmopolitan

The terms "local" and "cosmopolitan" do not refer, of course, to the regions in which interpersonal influence is exercised. Both types of influentials are effective almost exclusively within the local community. Rovere has few residents who command a following outside that community.

The chief criterion for distinguishing the two is found in their *orientation* toward Rovere. The localite largely confines his interests to this community. Rovere is essentially his world. Devoting little thought or energy to the Great Society, he is preoccupied with local problems, to the virtual exclusion of the national and international scene. He is, strictly speaking, parochial.

Contrariwise with the cosmopolitan type. He has some interest in Rovere and must of course maintain a minimum of relations within the community since he, too, exerts influence there. But he is also oriented significantly to the world outside Rovere, and regards himself as an integral part of that world. He resides in Rovere but lives in the Great Society. If the local type is parochial, the cosmopolitan is ecumenical.

Of the thirty influentials interviewed at

length, fourteen were independently assessed by three analysts [3] as "cosmopolitan" on the basis of case-materials exhibiting their orientation toward the Rovere community, and sixteen, as "local."

These orientations found characteristic expression in a variety of contexts. For example, influentials were launched upon a statement of their outlook by the quasi-projective question: "Do you worry much about the news?" (This was the autumn of 1943, when "the news" was, for most, equivalent to news about the war.) The responses, typically quite lengthy, readily lent themselves to classification in terms of the chief foci of interest of the influentials. One set of comments was focused on problems of a national and international order. They expressed concern with the difficulties which would attend the emergence of a stable postwar world; they talked at length about the problems of building an international organization to secure the peace; and the like. The second set of comments referred to the war news almost wholly in terms of what it implied for interviewees personally or for their associates in Rovere. They seized upon a question about "the news" as an occasion for reviewing the immediate flow of problems which the war had introduced into the town.

Classifying influentials into these two categories, we find that twelve of the fourteen [4] cosmopolitans typically replied

within the framework of international and national problems, whereas only four of the sixteen locals spoke in this vein. Each type of influential singled out distinctively different elements from the flow of events. A vaguely formulated question enabled each to project their basic orientations into their replies.

All other differences between the local and cosmopolitan influentials seem to stem from their difference in basic orientation. . . .[5] From the group-profiles [of the two types] we see . . . the tendency of local influentials to be devoted to localism: they are more likely to have lived in Rovere for a long period, are profoundly interested in meeting many townspeople, do not wish to move from the town, are more likely to be interested in local politics, *etc.* Such items, which suggest great disparity between the two types of influentials, are our main concern in the following sections. There we will find that the difference in basic orientation is bound up with a variety of other differences: (1) in the structures of social relations in which each type is implicated; (2) in the roads they have traveled to their present positions in the influence-structure; (3) in the utilization of their present status for the exercise of interpersonal influence; and (4) in their communications behavior. . . .

---

[3] This complete coincidence of assessments is scarcely to be expected in a larger sample. But the cosmopolitan and local syndromes were so clearly defined for this handful of cases, that there was little doubt concerning the "diagnoses." A full-fledged investigation would evolve more formal criteria, along the lines implied in the following discussion, and would, accordingly, evolve an intermediate type which approaches neither the local nor the cosmopolitan pole.

[4] It should be repeated that the figures cited at this point, as throughout the study, should not be taken as representative of a

parent population. They are cited only to illustrate the heuristic purpose they served in suggesting clues to the operation of diverse patterns of interpersonal influence. As is so often the fact with quantitative summaries of case-studies, these figures do not confirm interpretations, but merely suggest interpretations. The tentative interpretations in turn provide a point of departure for designing quantitative studies based upon adequate samples.

[5] Nothing is said here of the objective *determinants* of these differences in orientation. To ascertain these determinants is an additional and distinctly important task, not essayed in the present study.

SOCIABILITY: NETWORKS OF PERSONAL RELATIONS

In the course of the interview, influentials were given an occasion to voice their attitudes toward "knowing many people" in the community. Attitudes differed sharply between the two types. Thirteen of the sixteen local influentials in contrast to four of the fourteen cosmopolitans expressed marked interest in establishing frequent contacts with many people.

This difference becomes more instructive when examined in qualitative terms. The local influential is typically concerned with knowing *as many* people as possible. He is a "quantitativist" in the sphere of social contacts. Numbers count. In the words of an influential police officer (who thus echoes the sentiments of another "local," the Mayor):

> I have lots of friends in Rovere, if I do say so myself. I like to know everybody. If I stand on a corner, I can speak to 500 people in two hours. Knowing people helps when a promotion comes up, for instance. Everybody mentions you for the job. Influential people who know you talk to other people. . . .

This typical attitude fits into what we know of the local type of influential. What is more, it suggests that the career-function of personal contacts and personal relations is recognized by the local influentials themselves. Nor is this concern with personal contact merely a consequence of the occupations of local influentials. Businessmen, professionals, and local government officials among them all join in the same paeans on the desirability of many and varied contacts. . . .

The cosmopolitan influentials, on the other hand, have notably little interest in meeting *as many* people as possible.[6] They are more selective in their choice of friends and acquaintances. They typically stress the importance of confining themselves to friends with whom "they can really talk," with whom they can "exchange ideas." If the local influentials are quantitativists, the cosmopolitans are "qualitativists" in this regard. It is not *how many* people they know but the *kind of people* they know that counts.[7]

The contrast with the prevailing attitudes of local influentials is brought out in these remarks by cosmopolitan influentials:

> I don't care to know people unless there is something to the person.

> I am not interested in quantity. I like to know about other people; it broadens your own education. I enjoy meeting people with knowledge and standing. Masses of humanity I don't go into. I like to meet people of equal mentality, learning and experience.

Just as with the local influentials, so here the basic attitude cuts across occupational and educational lines. Professional men among the cosmopolitans, for example, do not emphasize the importance of a wide and extensive acquaintanceship, if one is to build up a practice. . . .

[6] This was interestingly confirmed in the following fashion. Our informants were confronted with a random list of names of Rovere residents and were asked to identify each. Local influentials recognized more names than any other group of informants, and cosmopolitans, in turn, knew more persons than the non-influential informants.

[7] In this pilot study, we have confined ourselves to the expression of attitudes toward personal contacts and relations. A detailed inquiry would examine the quantum and quality of *actual* personal relations characteristic of the local and cosmopolitan influentials.

In a later section of this study, we shall see that these diverse orientations of locals and cosmopolitans toward personal relations can be interpreted as a function of their distinctive modes of achieving influence. At the moment, it is sufficient to note that locals seek to enter into manifold networks of personal relations, whereas the cosmopolitans *on the same status level,* explicitly limit the range of these relations. . . .

AVENUES TO INTERPERSONAL
INFLUENCE

The foregoing differences in attachment to Rovere, sociability, and organizational behavior help direct us to the different avenues to influence traveled by the locals and the cosmopolitans. And in mapping these avenues we shall fill in the background needed to interpret the differences in communications behavior characteristic of the two types of influentials.

The locals have largely grown up in and with the town. For the most part, they have gone to school there, leaving only temporarily for their college and professional studies. They held their first jobs in Rovere and earned their first dollars from Rovere people. When they came to work out their career-pattern, Rovere was obviously the place in which to do so. It was the only town with which they were thoroughly familiar, in which they knew the ins and outs of politics, business, and social life. It was the only community which they knew and, equally important, which knew them. Here they had developed numerous personal relationships.

And this leads to the decisive attribute of the local influentials' path to success: far more than with the cosmopolitans, *their influence rests on an elaborate network of personal relationships*. In a for-

mula which at once simplifies and highlights the essential fact, we can say: *the influence of local influentials rests not so much on what they know but on whom they know. . . .*

With the cosmopolitan influential, all this changes. Typically a newcomer to the community, he does not and cannot utilize personal ties as his chief claim to attention. He usually comes into the town fully equipped with the prestige and skills associated with his business or profession and his "worldly" experience. He begins his climb in the prestige-structure at a relatively high level. It is the prestige of his previous achievements and previously acquired skills which make him eligible for a place in the local influence-structure. Personal relations are much more the product than the instrumentality of his influence.

These differences in the location of career-patterns have some interesting consequences for the problems confronting the two types of influentials. First of all, there is some evidence, though far from conclusive, that the rise of the locals to influentiality is slow compared with that of the cosmopolitans. Dr. A, a minister, cosmopolitan, and reader of newsmagazines, remarked upon the ease with which he had made his mark locally:

> The advantage of being a minister is that *you don't have to* prove yourself. You are immediately accepted and received in all homes, including the best ones. [Italics added.]

However sanguine this observation may be, it reflects the essential point that the newcomer who has "arrived" in the outside world, sooner takes his place among those with some measure of influence in the local community. In contrast, the local influentials *do* "have to prove" themselves. Thus, the local bank president who required some forty years to rise from his job as messenger boy, speaks feelingly of the slow, long road on which "I worked my way up."

The age-composition of the local and cosmopolitan influentials is also a straw in the wind with regard to the rate of rise to influence. All but two of the sixteen locals are over forty-five years of age, whereas fewer than two-thirds of the cosmopolitans are in this older age group.

Not only may the rate of ascent to influence be slower for the local than for the cosmopolitan, but the ascent involves some special difficulties centered about the local's personal relations. It appears that these relations may hinder as well as help the local boy to "make good." He must overcome the obstacle of being intimately known to the community when he was "just a kid." He must somehow enable others to recognize his consistent change in status. Most importantly, people to whom he was once subordinate must be brought to the point of now recognizing him as, in some sense, superordinate. . . . The problem of ascent in the influence-structure for the home-town individual may be precisely located in sociological terms: change of status within a group, particularly if it is fairly rapid, calls for the revamping of attitudes toward and the remaking of relations with the mobile individual. The pre-existent structure of personal relations for a time thus restrains the ascent of the local influential. Only when he has broken through these established conceptions of him, will others accept the reversal of roles entailed in the rise of the local man to influence. . . .

The cosmopolitan does not face the necessity for breaking down local preconceptions of himself. . . . As we have seen, his credentials are found in the pres-

tige and authority of his attainments elsewhere. He thus manifests less interest in a wide range of personal contacts for two reasons. First, his influence stems from prestige rather than from reciprocities with others in the community. Secondly, the problem of disengaging himself from obsolete images of him as "a boy" does not exist for him, and consequently does not focus his attention upon personal relations as it does for the local influential.

The separate roads to influence traveled by the locals and cosmopolitans thus help account for their diverging orientations toward the local community, with all that these orientations entail.

SOCIAL STATUS IN ACTION: INTERPERSONAL INFLUENCE

At this point, it may occur to the reader that the distinction between the local and cosmopolitan influentials is merely a reflection of differences in education or occupation. This does not appear to be the case.

It is true that the cosmopolitans among our interviewees have received more formal education than the locals. All but one of the cosmopolitans as compared with half of the locals are at least graduates of high school. It is also true that half of the locals are in "big business," as gauged by Rovere standards, whereas only two of the fourteen cosmopolitans fall in this group; and furthermore, that half of the cosmopolitan influentials are professional people as compared with fewer than a third of the locals.

But these differences in occupational or educational status do not appear to determine the diverse types of influentials. When we compare the behavior and orientations of professionals among the locals and cosmopolitans, their characteristic differences persist, even though they have the same types of occupation and have received the same type of education. Educational and occupational differences may *contribute* to the differences between the two types of influentials but they are not the *source* of these differences. Even as a professional, the local influential is more of a businessman and politician in his behavior and outlook than is the cosmopolitan. He utilizes personal relationships as an avenue to influence conspicuously more than does his cosmopolitan counterpart. In short, *it is the pattern of utilizing social status and not the formal contours of the status itself which is decisive.*

While occupational status may be a major support for the cosmopolitan's rise to influence, it is merely an adjunct for the local. Whereas all five of the local professionals actively pursue local politics, the cosmopolitan professionals practically ignore organized political activity in Rovere. (Their offices tend to be honorary appointments.) Far from occupation serving to explain the differences between them, it appears that the same occupation has a different role in interpersonal influence according to whether it is pursued by a local or a cosmopolitan. This bears out our earlier impression that "objective attributes" (education, occupation, etc.) do not suffice as indices of people exercising interpersonal influence.

The influential businessman, who among our small number of interviewees is found almost exclusively among the locals, typically utilizes his personal relations to enhance his influence. It is altogether likely that a larger sample would include businessmen who are cosmopolitan influentials and whose behavior differs significantly in this respect. Thus, Mr. H., regarded as exerting great influence in Rovere, illustrates the cosmopolitan big-

business type. He arrived in Rovere as a top executive in a local manufacturing plant. He has established few personal ties. But he is sought out for advice precisely because he has "been around" and has the aura of a man familiar with the outside world of affairs. His influence rests upon an imputed expertness rather than upon sympathetic understanding of others.

This adds another dimension to the distinction between the two types of influential. It appears that the cosmopolitan influential has a following because *he knows;* the local influential, because *he understands.* The one is sought out for his specialized skills and experience; the other, for his intimate appreciation of intangible but affectively significant details. The two patterns are reflected in prevalent conceptions of the difference between "the extremely competent but impersonal medical specialist" and the "old family doctor." Or again, it is not unlike the difference between the "impersonal social welfare worker" and the "friendly precinct captain." It is not merely that the local political captain provides food-baskets and jobs, legal and extra-legal advice, that he sets to rights minor scrapes with the law, helps the bright poor boy to a political scholarship in a local college, looks after the bereaved —that he helps in a whole series of crises when a fellow needs a friend, and, above all, a friend who "knows the score" and can do something about it. It is not merely that he provides aid which gives him interpersonal influence. It is *the manner in which the aid is provided.* After all, specialized agencies do exist for dispensing this assistance. Welfare agencies, settlement houses, legal aid clinics, hospital clinics, public relief departments— these and many other organizations are available. But in contrast to the professional techniques of the welfare worker which often represent in the mind of the recipient the cold, bureaucratic dispensation of limited aid following upon detailed investigation are the unprofessional techniques of the precinct captain who asks no questions, exacts no compliance with legal rules of eligibility and does not "snoop" into private affairs. The precinct captain is a prototype of the "local" influential.

Interpersonal influence stemming from specialized expertness typically involves some social distance between the advice-giver and the advice-seeker, whereas influence stemming from sympathetic understanding typically entails close personal relations. The first is the pattern of the cosmopolitan influential; the second, of the local influential. Thus, the operation of these patterns of influence gives a clue to the distinctive orientations of the two types of influential.

Against this background of analysis it is now possible to consider more fully the utilization of mass communications by the local and the cosmopolitan influential.

V. The Communications Behavior of Influentials

It appears that communications behavior is part and parcel of the routines of life and basic orientations characteristic of the two types of influentials. Their selections of magazines, newspapers, and radio programs at once reflect and reinforce the basic orientations. Although the *motives* for their selection of materials from the vast flow of mass communications may vary widely, the psychological and social *functions* fulfilled by the selection are fairly limited. Since the local and cosmopolitan make distinctly different demands of their social environment, they utilize mass communications for distinctly different results. . . .

VI. Patterns of Reciprocal Evaluations: Who Regards Whom as Influential?

To this point, we have been examining the influentials: their diverse modes of exerting interpersonal influence, their avenues to positions of influence, their communications behavior. But, after all, we consider these persons as "influential" only because they are so reported by our informants.[8] What can we learn about patterns of interpersonal influence by looking at patterns of reciprocal evaluations? What can we learn by looking at the relations between the mentionee and the mentioner, between those who emerge as variously influential and those whose judgments have defined them as influential?

THE INFLUENTIAL AND THE INFLUENCED

Although one often speaks of "men of influence," it is clear that this phrase is an elliptical way of saying: "men who exert influence upon a certain number of other people in certain situations. . . ." Interpersonal influence implies an asymmetrical *relation* between people. Influence is not an abstract attribute of a person, it is a process implicating two or more people. Accordingly, in an analysis

[8] It should be repeated that interpersonal influence is here regarded as not simply a matter of evaluation, but as a matter of fact. Whether the *judgments* of informants and *objective observation* would lead to the same results must remain an open question. This exploratory study has utilized informants' reports in order to locate certain types of problems with respect to interpersonal influence; a full-fledged inquiry would utilize observation as well as interviews to ascertain the actual degree of interpersonal influence and the spheres in which this is exercised.

of these patterns, we must not *only* look at the man who is influential, but also at the people who are influenced by him. Otherwise put, we have much to learn by exploring the question: who is influential for whom?

This general question at once divides into a series of more specific questions. Who are influential for people variously located in the influence-structure? Are people more often subject to influence by those above them in the influence-structure or by people in their own stratum of influence?

When the Rovere informants are divided into "top influentials" (those mentioned by 15 per cent or more of our informants), the "middle influentials" (mentioned by 5 to 14 per cent), and the "rank-and-file" (mentioned by fewer than 5 per cent), and when we relate these to their identifications of people who exert influence upon them, several clear impressions emerge. First, there is an impressive agreement on every level of the influence-structure concerning the people who belong at the top of the structure. Very largely, it is the *same* people who are reported as influential, irrespective of the position in the influence-structure of those who are doing the judging. From two-thirds to three-quarters of mentions by the three strata are concentrated on the top 15 per cent of influentials.

However, differences among the several strata in the influence structure do occur. Informants in each influence-stratum report a larger proportion of people in their own stratum as influential for them than do informants in the other strata. More concretely: the top influentials are more likely to mention others among the top influentials than are middle influentials or rank-and-file informants; the middle influentials are more likely to mention other middle influentials than are either the top influentials or the

rank-and-file; and the rank-and-file more often mention people in this stratum than do the other informants. One thus gains the impression that although relatively few people—the top influentials—exert influence upon people on all levels of the influence-structure, there occurs a secondary tendency for people to be otherwise most influenced by their peers in that structure. If this proves to be generally true, it is a most important fact concerning the operation of interpersonal influence.

The striking concentration of interpersonal influence may divert our attention from the entire distribution of influence. This could easily lead to mistaken inferences. Despite this concentration, it appears likely that *a greater number of personal decisions in a community may be the result of advice by the many people ranking low in the influence-structure than by the few ranked at the top.* For although the top influentials *individually* have a large measure of interpersonal influence, they are likely to be so few in number that they *collectively* have a minor share of the total amount of interpersonal influence in the community. And correlatively, although *each person* among the middle-influentials and the rank-and-file has relatively little influence, they may *collectively* account for the greater share of interpersonal influence, since these strata include the great bulk of people in the community. . . . Our Rovere inquiry is sufficient to formulate, though not, of course, to confirm the central point: a few individuals at the top may have a large *individual* quantum of influence, but the *total* amount of influence of this comparatively small group may be less than that exercised by the large numbers of people found toward the lower ranges of the influence-structure.

Our pilot study has thus far yielded two major impressions concerning the structure of influence which await further inquiry: (1) people in each influence stratum are more likely to be influenced by their peers in this structure than are people in the other strata and (2) despite the great concentration of interpersonal influence among a relatively few individuals, the bulk of such influence is widely dispersed among the large number of people in the lower reaches of that structure.

A third impression deserving further inquiry is suggestive of the pattern through which interpersonal influence percolates down through the influence-structure. From the Rovere data, it appears that this structure involves a "chain of influence," with the links in the chain constituted by persons in adjacent strata of influence. People in each influence-stratum are more likely to regard as influential people who are in the stratum immediately above their own than are informants in other strata, either above or further below. Thus rank-and-file informants looking upward toward their adjacent stratum (the middle influentials) more often mention these people as influential than do the top influentials, and middle influentials, in turn, more often mention the top influentials than do the rank-and-file. This suggests that some opinions and advice originated (or derived from mass communications) by the top influentials may be passed on progressively down the line. Other opinions, originating at lower levels in the structure, may be successively transmitted through adjacent successively lower strata. Our limited materials provide only a straw in the wind. In a full-scale inquiry dealing with several strata of influentials, this impression of a pattern of the percolation of interpersonal influence could be put to a decisive test.

We have thus far considered these patterns solely in terms of the position of the influenced and the influencer in the local influence-structure. Manifestly, it would be rewarding to examine the same patterns from the standpoint of the location of people in other social systems. The generic problem can be stated briefly enough: to what extent and in which situations does interpersonal influence operate largely *within* one's own social group or stratum or category (age, sex, class, power-stratum, prestige-stratum, etc.) and when does it operate largely *between* groups, strata, or social categories? . . .

SPHERES OF INFLUENCE: MONOMORPHIC AND POLYMORPHIC

A final suggestion is needed for future studies into the interpersonal influence-structure of a community. This preliminary inquiry strongly suggests . . . that formal criteria such as education, income, participation in voluntary organizations, number of references in the local newspaper and the like, do not provide adequate indicators of those individuals who exert a significant measure of interpersonal influence. Systematic interviewing supplemented by direct observation are required. Otherwise put, location within various social hierarchies of wealth, power, and "class" does not predetermine location within a local structure of interpersonal influence.

COMMENTARY
QUESTIONING COMPARED WITH
OBSERVATION

In the studies in the foregoing Units (and in Exercise I-1), the researcher directly *observes* the interaction of the group members, but in many sociological studies, he removes the individual members from the interactive situation in order to *question* each one privately. The studies and exercises in the present Unit (and a variety of subsequent study selections by Stouffer, Lazarsfeld, James Davis, and others) exemplify the peculiarly sociological uses of questioning to study individuals—not *as* individuals—but as they play roles in groups, or as individual roles combine to constitute a group.

Of course, the distinction between observation and questioning as data-gathering procedures is not clear-cut. All science rests upon observation in its broadest sense—upon data which are accessible to the researcher through his senses. But in a more limited sense, we can distinguish **(P-VIII)**, on the one hand, between the data obtained by watching the group, listening to it, and noting its physical characteristics and its collective products, and, on the other hand, the data obtained by questioning—that is, the respondent's written answers, or his oral reports as recorded by the interviewer. The distinction comes into sharp focus when we compare certain pure forms of the two procedures as used by sociologists: observation as applied directly to interaction, and private questioning of the several individual group members in turn.

As much as these two procedures differ in technical details, they parallel and supplement one another in the data they obtain. Although either may be used to study the social system, at various levels, as the research case, the two deal with different, though interrelated, sets of basic *properties* of such a case. If data from observation refer directly to *interaction,* to the "overt activities" of the members of the system (as Bales says), the answers to questions represent directly the *orientations* of the members—their feelings, attitudes, perceptions, and evaluations—about the group, for example, about their own roles in it, or about the interaction as they themselves observe it. Answers to questions, although they do not always report interaction as the observer might perceive it, have the peculiar merit of reflecting directly the subjective states of the actors, the underlying dispositions to act. When skillfully used as a sociological tool, questioning frequently reveals dormant aspects of the system which are not acted out while the observer watches, and which may also be concealed from the other group members. Thus questioning reveals the *structure of orientations*—the subjective patterns of attitudes, feelings, mutual expectations, and interpersonal relationships among the members—that underlie the overt interaction, but are not always accessible to observation.

Before questioning can provide maximum insight into the subjective structure of the group, however, two challenging problems must be solved. First, how can the well-established techniques—as you have learned them from Manual I-B and practiced them in Exercises I-2 and I-3—for questioning *discrete* individuals be extended to cover *several* members of the same social system? And second, since questioning typically starts with the individual, how can data about individuals be *fitted together* into *collective data* **(P-XII)** from which inferences may be drawn about the group? We shall now consider several attempts to meet these two problems. At the end of our discussion we shall compare *questioning* and *direct observation* as methods of gathering data about social systems.

Cottrell's Use of Intensive Interviews

Cottrell's study of the roles and marital adjustment of Mr. and Mrs. A. is an illustration of the use of questioning to study individual roles and their adjustment within the two-person system. Let us start—as we always must—by defining the conceptual model and objective as a basis for evaluating the method.

In your reading of the study you will have noticed how carefully Cottrell (following the seminal theories of George Herbert Mead) states his conceptual model in advance. He makes the basic assumption that the individual incorporates within his personality the various roles he learns throughout his life—both his own and those of the other persons with whom he interacts. Cottrell reports this study as an illustration of the propositions that, for the individual, marriage is a re-enactment of childhood roles; and for the group, that "maladjusted marriages may be regarded as results of the failure of [the] marriage situation to provide the system of relationships called for by the roles which the marriage partners bring to the marriage."

ROLE AND SYSTEM AS RESEARCH CASES

Cottrell's discussion illustrates again (as in the Whyte study analyzed in Unit 2) the use in research of the role as the basic unit both of the personality and of the social system **(P-I).** Starting with the personality of Mr. A., Cottrell's first objective is to ask, in effect: How does Mr. A. organize his role in relation to Mrs. A. with all his other earlier roles? A diagram of the roles incorporated in his personality might divide a circle into a number of triangles, of which his

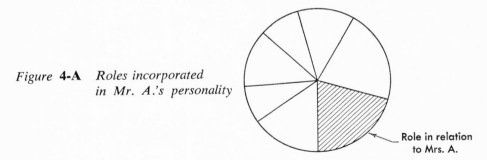

Figure **4-A**   *Roles incorporated
in Mr. A.'s personality*

Role in relation
to Mrs. A.

role relationship to Mrs. A. is the shaded one (see Figure 4-A). (Further subdivisions might be used to suggest the various types of role content, such as the "submissive" role or the "comforting sister" role, and a more detailed diagram might show the relative importance of the various roles and how they interpenetrate one another.) In a similar manner, Cottrell then deals with Mrs. A.'s marital role as it reflects the other roles organized within her personality.

But Cottrell's study of the two personalities is merely preparatory to his study of the marital pair as a research case. Once he has discovered what each individual brings to the marriage and what he hopes for in return, Cottrell then turns his attention to the two-person social system. He wants to study the relationship between the roles of two different individuals, each with his (or her) distinctive personality. The model now involves two levels: role and married pair (see Figure 4-B). Here the research objective is to discover: How does Mr. A.'s role mesh with Mrs. A.'s role? How do their personalities, as incorporated in these roles, fit together? To what extent does each succeed in meeting the role expectations of the other?

Mrs. A.'s role in
relation to Mr. A.

Mr. A.'s role in
relation to Mrs. A.

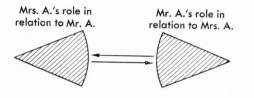

Figure **4-B**   *Mr. and Mrs. A.'s*
role relationship

INTENSIVE INTERVIEWS WITH BOTH HUSBAND AND WIFE

In translating these objectives into research operations, Cottrell faces both of the problems we stated at the beginning: (1) He must gather data, not from just one, but from each of the group members. And (2) when these data are in hand for the individuals singly, he must fit them together to refer to the group (the married pair).

He gathers most of the data from each individual, much as you did in Exercise I-2, by intensive interview. The full details of the questioning procedure are not included in the present study, since they are reported by Cottrell and his co-worker, Ernest Burgess, in their larger study, *Predicting Success or Failure in Marriage.* Describing how they collected detailed information on 100 married couples (of which Mr. and Mrs. A. were one), Burgess and Cottrell explain that "the procedure in the case studies was to get as full a picture as possible of the subject's important relational patterns in his family experience, and to see how far these patterns obtained in his marriage or had any relation to the patterns which did characterize his marriage." That these were thorough studies is suggested by the fact that some of the subjects were interviewed "as many as 20 to 30 times" (Burgess and Cottrell, 1939, p. 177).

The intensive, detailed interview approach—following the rules set forth in Manual I-B—is clearly appropriate for such a study of delicate topics, in which people are deeply involved emotionally, and of which they often have little understanding. The Cottrell study illustrates how this approach can yield rich details about many aspects of the roles of the marital partners.

The procedure used in this study differs from yours in Exercise I-2 in one important respect, however. You obtained only one point of view by interviewing only the offspring in each family; Cottrell and Burgess, on the other hand, interviewed (either in their own homes or in the interviewer's office) *both* the husband and wife—usually separately—see Manual I-B(4). Their work demonstrates the feasibility of such multiple-member questioning, and presents one situation in which our *first* problem can be solved. Further, their work illustrates the great advantages of the method by reporting the many insights gained in treating the marital relationship, not from just one, but from both points of view. Only by studying both partners could Cottrell discover which aspects of the two roles fitted together and which failed to fit. The clear research finding that the role relationship of Mr. A. and Mrs. A. lacked complementarity (because each was looking for something which the other could not supply) could not have been obtained by interviewing only one or the other of them. (See also the studies of complementary needs, Winch, Chapter 15.)

HANDLING DATA ON SEVERAL MEMBERS OF A GROUP

Whenever the student of the group uses this important procedure of multiple-member questioning, he is confronted with the *second* problem: having obtained answers from each group member separately, he must now fit the answers together into *collective data* (**P-XII**) from which he can make inferences about the group as a whole. Thus Cottrell faces the problem of putting together the statements of both Mr. A. and Mrs. A. so as to obtain an over-all picture of the married pair. He is able to meet this problem successfully because of his special study design. He does not attempt here to *measure* role properties, but handles the data in a purely qualitative, descriptive fashion (**P-X** and **P-XI**). Moreover, his analysis is based on a *single* group (**P-II**)—and a small, two-person group at that. But how would he attempt to handle the mountains of data obtained from all 100 Burgess-Cottrell interviews?

An Example of the Difficulties. We shall be concerned throughout this book with various answers to this question—with ways and means of retaining the distinct advantages of the Cottrell approach, while at the same time seeking systematic procedures for handling large numbers of cases. We can indicate some of the difficulties now by anticipating an example you will investigate thoroughly later (in Exercise III-6). In this simplified fictitious example (the content of which is borrowed from an actual study by Jacobson, 1952), we imagine 100 married couples and 100 divorced couples. Each spouse, questioned separately, is asked to accept or reject each of a series of statements regarding equality of marital roles. Examples of these statements are:

> The husband should help with the housework.
> If a husband runs around, so may the wife.
> It's all right for the wife to earn as much as her husband.

A score, which measures the degree to which his answers reflect an equalitarian attitude, is then assigned to each individual. (Low scores indicate an antiequalitarian, and high scores an equalitarian, position.)

Let us now think of two possible ways of analyzing the resultant data, one of which will mislead the student of the group into a possible fallacy. Imagine a set of just a few individuals who have answered this questionnaire and who have been scored in this way. (A form for classifying such individuals is shown in Table 4-A.) In these imaginary data, there is one divorced male with a score of 25, another one with a score of 50, and so on; and, because we want to illustrate a principle, there is also one divorced female with a score of 25, one with a score of 50, and so on. How, then, may such data be used to compare the equalitarian attitudes of divorced couples with those of married couples? Some investigators might perhaps proceed by first finding the average score for divorced males, and then comparing this with the average score for married males. As you can see right away, any such analysis as this will result in the finding that there is no difference between the divorced individuals and the married individuals.

Table **4-A**   *An analysis based on individuals*

Individuals' scores	Divorced		Married	
	Individual males	Individual females	Individual males	Individual females
25	1	1	1	1
50	1	1	1	1
75	1	1	1	1
100	1	1	1	1

Apart from the possibly puzzling substantive result (if one were to predict that there *is* a difference in attitudes between divorced and married individuals), such an analysis seems unsatisfactory. Some important information appears to be lost. We do not know, for example, whether the divorced male with an individual score of 25 is the spouse (or ex-spouse) of the female with the similar score of 25, or whether he was married to one of the females with a score different from his own. The analysis in Table 4-A is based on *individuals,* but Jacobson is interested in the *couple* as his point of reference.

Let us consider, then, how these same fictitious data in Table 4-A might be rearranged in an analysis based on couples—in effect, by "marrying" the individuals, i.e., putting each husband together with his own wife (or ex-wife), and then deriving a score for the pair. Jacobson does this by substracting the husband's score from the wife's, showing how much more (or less) equalitarian the wife is than the husband in each couple. One extreme example of the possible pairing of these individuals will clarify the point. In Table 4-B, as it turns out in this example, the divorced male with an individual score of 25 was married to the divorced female with an individual score of 75 (as the arrow indicates); their pair score then is +50. Similarly, each of the divorced individuals (in our example) was formerly married to a spouse with a score different from his own. Each of the married individuals, however, turns out to have a spouse with a score identical to his own. If we assume that the pair scores come out in such a fashion for the total sample of 200 couples, these pair scores in Table 4-B certainly reveal a finding which was completely obscured in the individual data shown in Table 4-A. From the pair scores it appears that all the divorced couples have high (positive or negative) ratings, indicating that the former husband and wife disagree with each other; whereas, among the married couples, husband and wife show no disagreement at all.

Table **4-B**   *An analysis based on couples*

| Individuals' scores | Divorced | | | Married | | |
	Individual males	Individual females	Pair score	Individual males	Individual females	Pair score
25	1	1	(−50)	1 ⟶ 1		0
50	1	1	(−50)	1 ⟶ 1		0
75	1	1	(+50)	1 ⟶ 1		0
100	1	1	(+50)	1 ⟶ 1		0

A Possible Fallacy.   The point of this example is, of course, that the research case **(P-I)** must correspond to the conceptual model; any such differences between married and divorced couples in the real situation would not be noticed by the researcher if he used only the individual scores. The researcher who hopes to uncover the facts about the structuring of orientations—the agreements and disagreements—within the role system of groups must find appropriate ways of fitting together the data for individual members. The example, though highly simplified, begins to suggest the nature of the differences between an analysis of data on separate individuals and a reanalysis of the same data now combined to reflect the relationships of the individual attitudes within the groups. In this reanalysis, we often combine the individual data into a collective measure **(P-XII)**, such as Jacobson's score for each couple.

The difficulties of developing such collective measures are especially acute when the materials about each individual are diffuse (as from intensive interviews, for example) so that many indicants have to be combined into some kind of score or scale (as discussed in Unit 9). Thus even in some recent large-scale studies of marital couples, for instance, the researcher may be so preoccupied with organizing the diffuse individual data that he fails to prepare any collective measures. Burgess and Cottrell, whose early predictive scores for individuals were far ahead of their time in use of such highly systematic procedures as multiple-factor analysis, made little attempt at systematic large-scale analysis based on couples. In such studies, people like Mr. A. and Mrs. A. are not treated as a married pair at all. Husbands are studied, as individuals, to determine which ones will be more successful in marriage; wives are then studied separately for the same purpose. The researcher does not use the data to ask what would seem to be an essential question in such a study: How successful will this husband be if he is married to this wife? To the extent that marital success or failure does depend upon the couple, the sociological researcher who fails to use the couple as the research case runs the risk, as in the example of our Tables 4-A and 4-B, of drawing misleading inferences—of committing what we shall later call an *atomistic fallacy.*

Some Potentialities of Collective Measures.   Despite such difficulties, you can begin to appreciate the special approach open to the sociologist in studying the structure of orientations: he first questions every member of the group separately, and then studies how the several points of view fit together. Perhaps husband and wife have quite different goals and hopes for their marriage, but have not communicated these to one another—perhaps they are not fully aware of their own goals, nor of the absence of harmonious integration. By comparing and combining the two sets of answers obtained by individual questioning of the marriage partners, the researcher may be able to uncover such discrepancies even before they become manifest in the system at all.

Lundberg and Lawsing and the Sociometric Approach

If Cottrell's research procedure can reflect in rich detail the structure of orientations in a social system, it is nevertheless restricted to unsystematic description of a very small group. Another procedure, which deals systematically with a considerably larger group, is presented in the Lundberg and Lawsing investigation of a small Vermont community. These investigators regard this community as consisting not only of organizations and private groups such as families or clubs, but also of the "tremendously intricate and elementary network of informal social nuclei which we describe in such terms as affinities, friendships, love affairs, cliques, gangs, etc." Their research objective is to discover and chart some of these community nuclei "which have hitherto . . . been left chiefly to literary and philosophic exploitation." They want "to objectify the subtle and intangible and so to make possible verification of the type generally recognized in science."

THE GATHERING OF SOCIOMETRIC DATA

The researchers use a sociometric approach here which has an immediate applicability to studies of the subjective elements of a social system. It provides a means of measuring interpersonal orientations so as to represent the structure of group relationships when groups consist of three or more members. Sociometry began as the more or less personal philosophy of J. L. Moreno, who drew attention to "tele"—the cathectic orientations or tendencies for members of a group to attract or repel one another.

Moreno and his immediate followers (of whom Lundberg is one) worked out various useful and ingenious procedures for studying tele-relationships. Basically, their procedures—which you will see extended and applied to varied situations in later studies in this book—start by questioning each member of a group about each other member. Each is asked to choose those others with whom he would like to interact, and to indicate those others with whom he would prefer not to interact. In order to make these choices as realistic as possible, the questions are phrased in terms of some specific criterion; school children might be asked, for example, "Whom would you like to sit beside?"

Lundberg and Lawsing modify these standard data-gathering techniques in several ways. For one thing, they do not question all of the residents of the community—perhaps because of the field problems entailed—but talk instead with only one member of each household (usually the housewife). This modification introduces certain difficulties into the subsequent handling of the data, as we shall see, since information about some of the links in the relational networks is consequently missing. They further modify the standard procedure when they ask, "Who *are* your most intimate friends in the community?"—for they are in effect asking not "Whom would you choose?" but "Whom have you already chosen?" This form of question elicits a report of actual relationships rather than preferred ones. Thus, the sociometric questionnaire may be adapted in various ways, but always retains an interpersonal focus.

Lundberg and Lawsing also add other questions about the individual respondent (about his occupation, for example), thus covering, as Cottrell did, the individual's direct reports on his own role as well as on his relationships to others. Finally, they add the Chapin scale as a measure of each individual's socioeconomic status in the community, a measure based not on questioning, but on the researcher's observations of the living-room equipment, i.e., of the products of family activity. (Compare Le Play's budget.) Such additional information will be useful later in the analysis for tying the patterns of interpersonal orientations to the occupational and socioeconomic structures of the community.

THE SOCIOGRAM

Let us now consider how the answers to the sociometric choice questions in particular are used systematically as indicants of the underlying structure of interpersonal relationships. As in all research, both the conceptual model and the data-collection procedure affect the forms in which the data are analyzed and presented. A number of systematic procedures have been developed by the sociometrists for handling their data. The simple answers to the sociometric questions consist merely of lists of names of persons chosen, and, by themselves, do not immediately serve the research purpose of indexing the group structure. The answers must first be fitted together in some way—transformed into collective data. As Lundberg and Lawsing put it, their observations must be translated "into a set of concepts and symbols which lend themselves to a representation of their true position in a complex so intricate as to be impossible to represent adequately in the language of folklore." The sociometrists' procedures for accomplishing this constitute a major contribution to sociological research method. One of these procedures, as illustrated in the Lundberg-Lawsing study, results in the *sociogram* (or *sociograph*)—a map of social space, corresponding to the geographical mapping of delinquency rates or disease rates by the ecologist (see Unit 12).

Lundberg and Lawsing's Figure 1, for example, is a map or picture of one portion of the network of friendship relationships in the Vermont village. You will notice that this picture is fairly similar to Henderson's rubber-band model of a social system. (The main difference is that the sociogram shows arrows only when a choice is made—when one person names another as his friend—whereas the arrows in the conceptual models of Unit 1 are drawn to show all the possible relationships, whether actual or potential.)

If we look at Lundberg and Lawsing's Figure 1 we can readily see that there are three clusters of group members around three central individuals. One of these clusters (the one around M 31) is much larger than the other two. Upon closer study, we observe various other interesting points: All the arrows binding M 31 to the others are directed *to* M 31, with the exception of one. That is, in her cluster, all except one person name her as a friend although she does not in turn name them. Her single choice is one man, M 16, who is himself the center of another group of satellites. Thus, M 31 appears from the picture to be a sort of queen, or "sociometric star"—with M 16 as a possible power-behind-the-throne.

Advantages and Limitations of the Sociogram. The sociogram has the virtue of picturing clearly and informatively the structure of the *group* and the positions of the various *individual roles* in that structure. By raising only one or a few crucial questions about interpersonal relationships, and by organizing the data in a single diagram, the sociometrist can view the social system literally at a glance. The sociogram also shows graphically the pattern of *dyadic relationships* within a social system, i.e., how each individual is related to every other individual in the group. Lundberg and Lawsing's Figure 1 makes plain, for example, that B 7 likes M 31 (the "sociometric star") but that M 31 does not in return name B 7 as a friend; the relationship is not reciprocal. B 7 and M 2, on the other hand, have a reciprocal relationship, each naming the other. (In this particular study, part of the structural information is missing, since only 256 of the 1,000 inhabitants were actually questioned. Thus an apparently unreciprocated dyadic relationship, for example, might merely mean that the person chosen did not himself have an opportunity to name his friends in turn. This shows the importance for problems such as these of exhaustive questioning of all the members of the system.)

The sociogram presents this collective information in a special form that symbolizes the structure of orientations graphically. It locates the roles within the structure, traces the patterns of dyadic bonds, and shows who contributes what to the collective pattern. As in Henderson's diagram, the interdependent parts of the system are clearly *identified*.

A sociogram has very definite limitations, however. For one thing, its use is practical only when the group is fairly small. For larger groups, the picture becomes a welter of criss-crossing lines. Lundberg and Lawsing, who work here with a relatively large group (256 individuals), come out with two very clear pictures. But they show only part of the data and do not portray how their Figures 1 and 2 fit together. (Again they encounter special difficulties here since not all inhabitants were questioned.) In general, despite a number of procedural rules which have been developed (see Proctor and Loomis), a great deal of trial and error, drawing and redrawing, are often necessary to uncover even the simplest structures. (You will readily see the difficulties if you try to construct a sociogram yourself, starting with the choice of one person by another and successively adding choices. If you work with a sizable group, the resulting picture may grow large enough to cover an entire floor. Use of rubber bands on a pegboard sometimes proves simpler than pencil drawings.)

Another limitation of the sociogram is that it is usually practicable for studying simultaneously only one or possibly two criteria of choice or *items*. Suppose, for instance, that Lundberg and Lawsing had wanted to ask not only "Who are your friends?" but also "Whom do you admire?" "Who influences you?" and "How would you describe the various people in your community?" How might they have represented all these different items in the same picture? They might use a different colored pencil, or a tissue overlay for each item. But the resulting picture often becomes too complicated to be easily comprehensible. It would be impossible to graph in this way the intricate detail of the Cottrell data, for example.

THE SOCIOMETRIC MATRIX

An alternative procedure developed by sociometrists for handling their data, and one which overcomes some of these limitations of the sociogram, is the *sociometric matrix*. Conceptually similar to the sociogram, it differs mainly in the ease with which certain types of data can be handled. Though not used in the study by Lundberg and Lawsing, one type of sociometric matrix might be constructed from their data by first listing each of the 256 individual residents down the side as the choosers—or subjects—and then again across the top as the chosen—or objects. (A second type of matrix that we shall discuss might first group the individuals statistically according to a given role characteristic.) Imaginary choices for the first four residents might appear as in Table 4-C, where a plus sign indicates that one person chooses another; a minus sign, that he does not. Thus, No. 1 names No. 2, No. 3, and No. 4 as his friends; No. 2 names only No. 4; and so on.

You will see at once that this form of representation is very similar to that used by Bales in Unit 3. In other words, the sociometric matrix and Bales' interaction matrix are both special uses of a general presentation procedure, which we have called the "who-to-whom" matrix. In other words, two studies which are strikingly different in design produce data which are strikingly similar in form. Bales uses observation in order to abstract directly from the acts—the overt behaviors—which the members of a group perform toward one another. Lundberg and Lawsing use questioning in order to abstract directly from the orientations—the feelings, definitions, or attitudes—which the members of a group hold toward one another. Yet, if Lundberg and Lawsing were to question the same subjects that Bales observes, the two sets of data might be set side by side in exactly comparable matrices. This points to a basic principle for us to examine later in this Unit: although questioning and observation are quite different as methods of gathering data, they concentrate upon inextricably interrelated aspects of a social system, i.e., interactions and the latent structure of orientations.

Table **4-C** *A sociometric matrix based on individuals*

| | Objects | | | | Subject |
Subjects	NO. 1	NO. 2	NO. 3	NO. 4	totals
No. 1		+	+	+	3
No. 2	—		—	+	1
No. 3	—	+		+	2
No. 4	—	—	+		1
Object totals	0	2	2	3	

THE ROLE AS THE RESEARCH CASE

Further consideration of the who-to-whom matrix as used by Lundberg and Lawsing will help us to appreciate its special value in research on the social system. Not only does the researcher use it to arrange his data in such form that he can see how the parts of the system fit together, but he also uses it to generate several types of collective measures—each referring to a different level of the system. Let us first review its relevance for study of the individual role, and then examine its further applicability to the study of the dyadic relationship and of the group as a whole.

When the research focus is on the roles of the several group members, we use the marginal information as collective measures of the subject roles and the object roles. Treating the four residents shown in Table 4-C as if they were the whole community (just to simplify the example), we obtain the total number of friends each subject says he has by adding across each row. In this example, then, No. 1 has a subject score of 3, No. 2 has a score of 1, and so on. If we regard this score as a measure of friendliness, we can conclude that No. 1 is the most friendly, and No. 2 and No. 4 the least friendly (Zeisel, pp. 110–14). Then, by adding down each column, we obtain the number of times each object is chosen as a friend, or the individual's object score. Since No. 4 receives the most "votes," we might consider him the most popular; No. 1, with no votes at all, seems to be the least popular. By using both subject and object measures, we might say, for example, that No. 1 is the most "friendly" but the least "popular."

Here the marginal information describes the individual's role in relation to the group as a whole, just as in the Bales matrix, although the role properties being measured here (friendliness, popularity) are the feelings and attitudes the individual directs to, or elicits from, the other members, rather than the actions he initiates or receives.

Lundberg and Lawsing show how such role information can be used in research by classifying persons as objects in their Table 1, for example, according to the number of sociometric choices received. (It is interesting to note that since these researchers work from the sociogram in their Figure 1, rather than from a sociometric matrix, they can elaborate further the place of each object in the structure by showing also how many *indirect* choices he receives. See their Table 1.)

Collective vs. Unitary Role Measures.   This derivation of role information from the matrix marginals illustrates further the nature of a collective measure (obtained by combining information about the parts of a system in order to describe the system itself) in contrast to a unitary measure (based on data that refer directly to the system). We have seen how, in a study of married couples, information about the roles of husband and wife (as parts of the system) may be collected (combined) to refer to the *group*. Here we move to another level of the social system, and combine information about several dyadic relationships (as parts) to refer to the *role*. In Table 4-C, for example, the measure of No. 3's popularity as an object collects information from all the cells in the appropriate column. The measure of No. 3's friendliness as a subject is also collective—obtained by combining all the cells in the appropriate row. Both these collective role measures pull together No. 3's dyadic relationships to the several other members of the group.

Such a collective role measure is quite different from a unitary role measure, which is often obtained by questioning or observing the one individual without reference to his particular dyadic relationships. To secure a unitary measure of No. 3's friendliness, for instance, we might ask him directly how friendly he is; his own estimate of his role in the group might be substantively at variance with the collective measure built up from his many specific sociometric choices. Methodologically, the collective measure is the more complicated of the two since the researcher must decide how to put together for each role a whole set of dyadic relationships; he must decide, that is, whether merely to count the number of friends the individual has, as in this example, or to follow some more elaborate procedure that might take into account the status of each friend or the strength of each friendship bond.

PROBLEMS OF IDENTIFICATION IN COLLECTIVE MEASURES

Despite the great importance of many types of collective measures in studies of the social system, certain perplexing general problems arise in connection with their use. To pursue the present example, let us consider what happens when we add the number of friends No. 3 has. By merely collecting or aggregating them as "two friends" or as a "friendliness" score of two, we derive a new measure, but we also lose some information: we lose any identification of *who* his friends are. The marginal figure in itself does not convey the fact that No. 3's friends are No. 2 and No. 4. Although such a loss of information may not always be crucial, the identification of these friends may often be extremely valuable to the research objective. For example, the researcher may be interested in the fact that No. 3 associates with fairly popular people, instead of with unpopular people like No. 1 (with his popularity score of 0).

This loss of *identification* of the parts combined into the collective measure is a characteristic limitation of many such measures—a limitation that will concern us often in this book. We have already seen in the sociogram one of the possible ways of overcoming it.

THE DYAD AS THE RESEARCH CASE

In other instances, the research is not focused on the role but on the dyadic relationships between pairs of group members. Here the collective information is taken (again as in the Bales study) from the two relevant cells, rather than from the marginals, of the matrix. Thus Table 4-C shows for the No. 1–No. 4 dyad, for example, a one-sided dyadic relationship, with No. 1's liking unreciprocated by No. 4; No. 3 and No. 4, on the other hand, do reciprocate each other's liking.

The nature of the substantive findings obtained from study of dyadic relationships is illustrated in the Lundberg and Lawsing analysis of the proposition that individuals tend to choose friends in higher socioeconomic status levels than themselves. In their Table 3, all the dyads (or "choices") are first classified according to the socioeconomic score of the chooser (or subject); then each dyad is again classified according to whether the object's socioeconomic score is higher or lower than the subject's. Thus, each dyad is classified in terms of role information about both of the dyadic partners. The method is one whereby, as Lundberg and Lawsing say, "A great variety of family and personality variables could be profitably used in the interpretation of social groupings." Here the study moves from the plane of describing patterns of interpersonal relationship to the plane of interpreting such patterns in terms of the roles of individuals within the socio-economic structure of the community. (The form of the matrix typically used to facilitate such analysis of the relationship between dyadic data and individual role data will be illustrated in connection with the Merton study below.)

THE GROUP AS THE RESEARCH CASE

The Lundberg-Lawsing study of a Vermont community illustrates systematic use of collective data to study only a single large group. But the same procedures may be extended to the higher-level measurement of collective properties of the group as a whole, thus making it possible to compare and analyze many groups. Data from a series of who-to-whom matrices may be collected to refer to the whole community as the research case by combining either the role information or the dyadic information. Suppose that Lundberg and Lawsing had studied several communities and prepared for each a matrix similar in form to Table 4-C. By collecting the role information (the object marginals) which show how "popular" each individual is, for example, the researcher might give each community a score indicating the proportion of its members who are popular. Then he could compare community scores to discover why communities differ in popularity. Such a community score would refer to the group as a whole by aggregating the role measures. Although here again certain information about the individual roles has been sacrificed, the new score measures the *role structure of the group.*

Alternatively, the *dyadic* information (from the matrix cells) may be combined to provide a collective measure of the *dyadic structure of the group.* A common sociometric procedure, for example, is to base a group score on the proportion of choices which are reciprocated. Or a researcher may measure "cohesion"—as Lundberg and Lawsing suggest in discussing the cliques within the community—by comparing the number of choices of objects who are inside, rather than outside, the group (see, *e.g.,* Festinger, Schachter, and Back, Chapters 11, 13).

Special Character of the Two-Person Group.   Comparison of such matrix analyses of groups of three or more members with the foregoing husband-wife analysis indicates the special character of the two-person group (see Simmel, p. 122 ff.), both substantively and in its methodological implications. The role structure of the two-person group can be studied, just as it was in the larger group, by collecting *role* information, but *dyadic* information obviously cannot be collected for the two-person group that consists of only a single dyad. Similarly, there can be no collective—but only unitary—role measures for each member of the two-person group.

ADVANTAGES AND LIMITATIONS OF THE SOCIOMETRIC MATRIX

To study systematically the interrelationships of persons in groups, the researcher can use, as we have seen, two sociometric devices: the sociogram and the matrix. With the help of these devices, he will be able to combine data about many individuals so as to represent the group and reveal the underlying structure of relationships.

The sociometric matrix serves to present formally the full information on one item, or criterion, of sociometric choice. It spreads all the data before the researcher for his scrutiny. Unlike the sociogram, it is appropriate for groups of varied size, even for those composed of several hundred members. It facilitates the development of many types of collective measures which, as selections from the full matrix, focus upon one or another level of the system.

Its chief limitation is apparent from a comparison of the findings of the Lundberg-Lawsing and the Cottrell studies: it is not in itself equipped to handle several criteria of sociometric choice or diffuse, multidimensional information about interpersonal relationships. It fits more closely the Lundberg-Lawsing problem of discovering which group members are connected by interpersonal bonds than it does the Cottrell problem of describing the shades and nuances in these bonds. Since the sociometrists often learn only one thing about each dyad— whether a given person chooses a given other person—they can handle such data simply by placing a + or a − (or some kind of score) in each cell of a matrix. But if the researchers obtain, for example, three pieces of information, they would have to make three entries in each cell, thereby creating difficulties in handling and comprehending the data. With many more than three pieces of information (as in the Cottrell study) they can continue to use matrix analysis only by reducing the complexity of the data (employing various procedures for such reduction which we shall consider in Unit 9).

Merton's Study of Influentials

Merton's exploratory study of influence structure (which began as a study of "the place of mass communications in the patterns of interpersonal influence") exemplifies a two-stage use of questioning. He uses questioning, first, to locate individuals who occupy roles of "influentiality"; and, second, to interview these influentials about their image of their own influence and their mass communications behavior.

A DEVELOPING CONCEPTUAL MODEL

The research report, a remarkably realistic picture of the difficulties typically encountered—though seldom acknowledged—in exploratory studies, shows how the conceptual model itself may be clarified in the course of the research. The original attempt—which proved sterile—was to relate newsmagazine readership and other communications behavior to the roles of individuals classified, on the one hand, as the rank and file, and, on the other hand, as influentials according to their "dynamic position in the local influence structure." Since this classification yielded "few clear-cut uniformities," however, a new conceptual model was sought which would account for the diverse behaviors of influentials. The key to the conceptualization finally used lay in the observations—which were "incidentally turned up"—that some influentials were interested almost exclusively in the local community whereas others were oriented more to the world outside the community. Merton could then distinguish between two basic types of influentials, allowing the "consequent rearrangement of discrete facts into coherent patterns and uniformities."

The Serendipity Component of Research.   This experience illustrates Merton's principle of the serendipity pattern (Merton, 1957, p. 103)—the principle that the unanticipated finding can be adapted to extend a theory or to originate a new hypothesis. In this pilot study, which was avowedly searching for hypotheses, the investigator was able to benefit from the serendipitous clue, to avoid the dangers of premature specification, and to bring the conceptual categories into line with the data. More generally, the experience suggests the value of sufficient flexibility in any research design—even in the systematic testing of hypotheses—to allow exploitation of the possible serendipitous finding.

PROCEDURE FOR DESIGNATING INFLUENTIALS

In developing his conceptual model, Merton studies the interpersonal structure of the community in order to locate the roles of influentials within it, since he feels that simple role measures (such as occupation or income) are not adequate means of discriminating among influentials. Adapting the sociometric approach, he starts with eighty-six respondents (since this is a pilot study he does not attempt to uncover the full pattern of community relationships) who were led, in "prolonged interviews," to "mention people to whom they turned for help or advice regarding various types of personal decisions." Thus Merton begins by asking *many* group members what is, in effect, a *single* sociometric question— "Whose advice do you follow?" Like Lundberg and Lawsing, he combines all the answers to this question, counting the number of "votes" received by various individuals as objects—classifying individual object roles as in the marginals of a matrix. Those receiving sufficient votes (four or more) are designated as influentials; and thirty influentials are then questioned intensively in the second stage of the research.

A Matrix Based on Statistically Grouped Individuals.   Merton is not content merely to collect role information in this way. He also wants to *identify* those subjects who name the various classes of objects, and thus to investigate the interesting problem of who is influential for whom. A different type of matrix underlies such an analysis, which is based not on single individuals as in Table 4-C above, but on individuals statistically grouped together according to a given role characteristic—in this instance, as either "top influentials," "middle influentials," or "rank-and-file."

Since, in this report, Merton does not show the matrix actually employed, our Table 4-D, taken from another piece of research, suggests the nature of this type of analysis. High school students were asked to name the others in their grade with whom they discuss a number of specified topics. Before the dyadic communications scores (based on the number of topics on which a given subject would talk with a given object) were arranged in the matrix, the individual students themselves were grouped statistically according to a given role characteristic—in this example, their social status in the school grade. The percentaging in one direction to allow for differing numbers of subjects distributing communications, and again in the other direction to allow for the differing numbers of objects having a chance to receive communications, illustrates the use of Rule 4 in Manual III-B. (See also the comparable matrix analysis in Exercise III-2, Problem 6.)

Table **4-D**   *A sociometric matrix based on statistically grouped individuals* [a]

(*extent of dyadic communication by the statuses of both partners*)

Status of subject		Status of object					
		LOW					HIGH
		0	1	2	3	4	5
LOW	0	.07	.26	.22	.26	.41	.49
	1	.11	.26	.26	.34	.47	.60
	2	.07	.20	.38	.42	.54	.69
	3	.07	.18	.36	.62	.76	.81
	4	.05	.19	.33	.52	.81	.88
HIGH	5	.04	.16	.25	.39	.66	1.36

[a] The figures shown in the cells are indexes of the number of dyads reporting communication on at least one topic. The raw data in the rows were divided by the percentage of *objects* in the several status categories; the resultant figures in the columns were again divided by these same percentages to allow for the status distributions of the *subjects*. (Riley, Cohn, Toby, and Riley, 1954, p. 721.)

You will find it instructive to interpret Table 4-D (making comparisons both *across* within each row, and *down* within each column), and then to compare your interpretation with Merton's discussion of his own findings on "The Influential and the Influenced."

The Latent Structure of Orientations.   The data in Table 4-D illustrate again the exciting possibilities of uncovering latent structures of orientations by questioning the several group members and fitting their answers together. For example, the index of reported communication from status 1 (low) individuals to status 5 (high) individuals, is .60; the index of communication from status 5 to status 1 is only .16. These figures mean that if one member of a pair is high status and the other low, the low-status person is fairly likely to name the high as somebody he talks to, although the high-status person is fairly unlikely to name him in return. We can see now that mere *observation* of this particular pair would tell us only whether or not they talk to each other. *Questioning,* on the other hand, provides us with reports—partially conflicting—which indicate that these two individuals perceive and evaluate their relationship quite differently. Perhaps the relationship is very important to the low-status member, whereas the high-status member has so many friends that he forgets to mention this particular friend at all.

Such disparities, which reflect lack of complementarity or potential strains in the system, may sometimes be uncovered through *questioning* before they are ever manifested in the interactions accessible to *observation.* In this sense, questioning the several group members seems to be uniquely suitable for uncovering interpersonal orientations.

Some Methodological Implications

Before summing up what we have learned from these studies about the relevance of questioning for research on social systems, let us assess the differences and the parallelism between questioning and direct observation as possible alternative methods of gathering new data **(P-VIII).**

DIFFERENCE IN FOCUS OF OBSERVATION AND QUESTIONING

Researchers sometimes feel—mistakenly, we believe—that they can obtain a true picture of a social phenomenon *only* if they observe it with their own eyes. To be sure, observation and questioning often give different results; but this occurs, not because one method is more valid than the other, but because the two focus, as we have already noted, on different sets of social system properties. Data from observation reflect the network of actions and reactions among group members—the objective properties of the system. Data from questioning reflect the subjective network of orientations and interpersonal relationships—the underlying ideas and feelings of the members, their dispositions to act toward the others and to define and evaluate these others in various ways.

Direct Focus. Although this difference between the two methods is one of emphasis, we can understand its importance by comparing the direct focuses of the methods used by Bales and Cottrell. Bales, as an observer, focuses on who says what to whom. If No. 1 expresses agreement with No. 2, Bales observes this. Yet Bales has no direct way of knowing what attitudes underlie this verbal agreement. No. 1 may agree, or he may secretly disagree, thinking to himself, "That fellow is all wrong, but it's useless to disagree with him. I'd better be quiet and let him think I agree." Bales cannot know such secret attitudes, nor is he immediately interested in knowing them; his major focus is upon action, not orientation.

On the other hand, Cottrell, as a questioner, studies how Mr. and Mrs. A. feel about each other, how each defines the other, what each hopes from their marriage, and the like. (As questioners in Exercise I-2, you studied how an offspring felt about his parents, how he defined them, what his hopes and fears were, how his parents felt about him, and so on.) The fact that the respondents' underlying thoughts and feelings are often at variance with their overt behavior does not concern Cottrell, for his immediate focus is on underlying orientation, not on interaction.

In this sense, each approach is especially valid for one set of system properties, as diagramed in Figure 4-C, but often misses information about the other set of properties which is directly available only through the other approach.

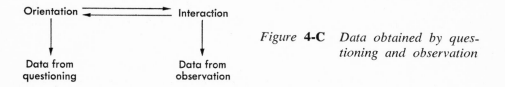

Figure **4-C**   *Data obtained by questioning and observation*

Indirect Focus.   Yet the two types of data—from questioning and from observation—differ only in their direct focuses. *Indirectly,* they are inextricably bound together, because action and orientation, though distinct types of properties, are by no means entirely separate from one another. Orientations, defined as dispositions to act, are at any given moment being partially acted out (although generally a certain part of the orientations remains latent or concealed). Conversely, these orientations tend themselves to *reflect* this interaction. What No. 2 *thinks* of No. 1, for example, is greatly influenced by what No. 1 has *done* to No. 2. Thus, each actor's orientations—his definitions and expectations of the other actors—are constantly being tested and revised in the light of what these others actually do. The arrows in Figure 4-C that indicate this interdependence between orientations and interactions suggest how neither can be fully understood without the other. Orientations may be indirectly reflected in data from observation, and interactions indirectly reflected in data from questioning.

Bales, for example, after observing No. 2's actions, may go on to make indirect inferences about No. 2's orientations. If he observes No. 2 talking and agreeing a great deal with No. 3, he might then draw the indirect inference that

No. 2 has a high regard for No. 3. Thus, observation indirectly reveals orientations. Although in some instances such inferences will be wrong—No. 2 may be successfully concealing feelings of hostility for No. 3—they are drawn with great frequency on the assumption that much of the time they will be correct.

In a similar fashion, questioning is often used to elicit reports from respondents, not about their orientations, but about their actions. Useful as such data may often be, however, they are always an *indirect* report of the action, described by the actor as he perceives and evaluates it. Thus, his report may be quite different from that of the outside observer who watches the interaction, because the interaction has been screened through the orientations of the reporting actor.

SOME PROS AND CONS OF OBSERVATION AND QUESTIONING

Apart from this basic difference in focus, questioning and observing as methods of data-gathering may be used either alone or in various combinations to gather data of varying scope, content, and accuracy. We can begin to evaluate the possibilities and limitations by reviewing briefly a series of typical procedures.

In making evaluations, one important criterion is to ask how accurately the method seems to describe the facts. As we saw in Unit 2, there are two major types of possible error in data-gathering: a *biased viewpoint,* or failure of the researcher to perceive the facts correctly, and an unwanted and unsystematic *control* over the system under study, so that the research itself has the effect of changing the facts.

Observation Without Participation. One widely used procedure is the direct observation of interaction in which the observer himself does not participate. The observer in Exercise I-1, for example, may watch a group of three children playing in a park while the actors are entirely unaware of the ongoing research. (The major method employed by Bales is a modification of this procedure: the observers are behind a one-way glass and, because they cannot communicate with the actors, even by exchanging glances, the actors may soon forget that they are being watched.)

The method of observation without any participation has obvious *advantages,* as you know from your own field experience and from the Bales study. It can uncover patterns of action (as in Bales' profiles and phase movements) and structures of roles (as in Bales' matrix) that the participants themselves do not fully comprehend. It minimizes any control effect over the action being studied, and avoids the biased viewpoint that comes from immersion in the group —although the observer's position outside the group often limits his perceptions, restricting his view of facial expressions, for example, and his full grasp of conversation.

There are definite *restrictions,* however, on the content of research based on direct observation. In the first place, strict and methodical observation seems suitable only for *fairly small* groups, although an observer (or better, several observers) can effectively record impressions of the "social atmosphere" of somewhat larger assemblages (such as crowds, meetings, audiences). In the second place, cultural taboos prevent observation of *private* interaction, such as the intimate communications between marital partners or the deliberations of juries. The method is applicable to action taking place only *in the present*. It obviously cannot be used to refer to periods prior to the inception of the research; and to extend observation into the future in order to trace a gradual development of some social system property over time requires a considerable investment of research time. Even if it were permissible to observe Mr. and Mrs. A. throughout their married life—and this might not be long enough, given Cottrell's hypothesis—to append a sociologist-observer to the couple would be an absurdly impractical procedure.

Participant Observation.   When the researcher participates in the action he is observing, he may obtain extensive information, as Malinowski, Whyte, and Le Play were able to do. As we have seen, however, a degree of control effect, and a possible biased-viewpoint effect, are likely to result.

Questioning of Separate Individuals.   Techniques for questioning individuals have been highly developed for use in personality tests, the census, public opinion polls, attitude studies, and the like. You have gained an acquaintance with some of these techniques from your study of Manual I-B. Let us now define the nature of questioning as a general research procedure before returning to the questioning of the several members of a group used as a special method in the studies in this Unit.

Questioning, because of its potentially wider range of content, can overcome many of the restrictions placed upon the direct observation of interaction. But it too is subject to certain possible errors. An interview—and to a lesser extent the self-administration of a questionnaire—always establishes a new and temporary social system.

The respondent, typically separated from the group under study, now plays a new role in relation to the questioner. The nature of this role relationship may affect not only the interviewer's perceptions of, and testimony about, the respondent's answers—but the answers themselves. If the respondent thinks the interviewer expects him to make certain responses, he may adjust his answers to meet such expectations (see, *e.g.,* Merton, 1947). Both types of possible distortion—the response bias of the person being questioned and the selective perception of the questioner—combine to bias the researcher's view of the respondent's true orientations. This is akin to the biased-viewpoint effect we have noted in participant observation, though in the interview it is often called "interviewer bias."

Various devices have been developed for reducing such a biased-viewpoint effect (Manual I-B, and Hyman *et al.,* 1954, *passim*). In the main, these devices seek to reduce the social interactive character of the interview relationship and to neutralize the questioner's role. As in Exercise I-2, the questioner attempts, for example, to avoid the communication of normative expectations about what the respondent ought to say by expressing neither approval nor disapproval of the answers given.

The questioner who attempts to neutralize his own role in such fashion is, in one sense, similar to the observer who attempts to minimize his participation in the interaction he is studying: both are trying to avoid biased-viewpoint effect. But in another sense, there is a marked difference: the questioner does not—except under special conditions that we shall discuss—intrude upon the interaction he wants to study. When you interviewed respondents about their past role relationships to their parents, for instance, you yourself did not enter into those relationships. Thus the questioner does not—under the usual conditions—face the danger of control effect.

It is sometimes possible to turn into a positive advantage the interactive character of the questioner-respondent relationship, instead of trying to neutralize it. The researcher may use the new interactive system to simulate a real situation in which the interviewer acts out one of the roles. If Exercise I-2 were conducted with children, for example, the questioner might learn much about a child by playing the role of one of his parents. Or market researchers may make door-step interviews that simulate the buyer-seller relationship in a store when a new product is introduced (see Franzen and Teilhet). Although it is impossible to draw any exact line between such role-playing and the method of participant observation, this device has important, and largely unexplored, possibilities (see, *e.g.,* Stanton, Back, and Litwak).

Sequences of Questioning and Observation. There are many other special conditions under which questioning and observation may be used, each of which modifies the research advantages and the types of possible errors.

In some designs, for example, respondents are questioned repeatedly, as in panel analysis (Unit 10) or experiments (Unit 11). This allows the investigator to study changes in orientation and attitudes over time. But even though questioning that occurs *after* the action under study cannot affect the interaction process itself, repeated questioning that occurs *during* the process does tend to produce undesirable control effects. Here the investigator seeks means of offsetting, or measuring, such effects.

In another combination, the researcher may ask questions after the observations are completed. For example, you have seen how Bales supplements his observation data by asking the group members to evaluate one another after the interaction sessions are at an end. This is a good combination for many purposes because it avoids the control effect on the action under study; it cannot, of course, study the orientations themselves during the interaction process since the questions ask for an ex post facto reconstruction.

OTHER SOURCES OF INFORMATION

Observation need not be focused directly upon the interaction itself. The method may be extended to cover all observable properties of the group or of the group members (*e.g.,* the size of the group or the sex and approximate age of the members); the artifacts or products of action (the furnishings of the living room, the records of delinquent behavior); or recorded interactions (the series of letters which constitute family interaction, the war propaganda materials which constitute the political interactions between opposing states). Examples of the use of artifacts, documents, and other available materials will be discussed in Unit 5.

QUESTIONING THE SEVERAL GROUP MEMBERS

Now that we have seen a few of the advantages and disadvantages of questioning, observation, and some of their possible combinations, let us consider once again the special use of questioning to study social systems. In each of the studies we examined, the essentials of this method consist, first, of questioning many (or all) of the group members individually, and, second, combining these data (using a map, a matrix, or a simple description) to refer to the role, the dyad, or the larger system of the group.

What special problems are entailed when the techniques of questioning separate individuals are applied to multiple group members? There is clearly a danger of control effect if one member, who has already been questioned, discusses the matter with another member who has not yet been questioned. The researcher may offset this effect by one of the following devices: by using several interviewers in order to question all the group members simultaneously; in a two-member group, such as a husband and wife, by conducting one interview immediately after the other without allowing any interim interaction between the two members; or by administering a written questionnaire to all the members at the same time.

Another possible solution, following Le Play, is to interview the incumbent of a representative role in the system. But this is not a solution for those frequent research situations where there is no single individual in the role of representative. The relationship between Mr. and Mrs. A. could not have been learned from a single spouse as an "expert," nor could the structure of the Vermont community have been revealed by a single "informant."

The Self-Administered Questionnaire.   One form of questioning to which we shall pay considerable attention is the self-administered questionnaire—especially because it lends itself to simultaneous questioning of the members of a social system without any concomitant interaction among these members.

This method, which does not require an interviewer because the respondent reads the questions himself and fills out his own answers, takes various forms. Sometimes an administrator is present to guide the respondents in answering the questions, and sometimes not. Sometimes the respondents form a "captive audience," such as a school class or an army unit, in which everybody is required to reply—in contrast to the self-selected set of respondents who themselves decide to reply to a mail questionnaire.

The self-administered form has a number of *advantages* other than its suitability for questioning many members simultaneously. First, it is relatively inexpensive since many cases may frequently be collected at one time without the cost of interviewing. Second, it affords a simple means of continual reporting over time, as in diary-keeping. Third, it gives the respondent a sense of privacy. Although there is, of course, always a degree of interaction between a respondent and the questioner who ultimately reads his responses, the respondent will often report more freely because no interviewer is present. Thus the biased-viewpoint effect is reduced.

Like all research procedures, the self-administered questionnaire has *disadvantages*. Unless the respondents are "captive," there are problems of nonresponse. Complete returns from a mail questionnaire may range as low as 10 per cent or less. Self-selection is likely to produce a bias, since those who are especially interested in the topic, even fanatical about it in one direction or the other, are often the most likely to reply. Another disadvantage of this method is that in most cases there is no one (except possibly a busy administrator) to interpret and explain matters to the respondent, or to assess his emotional reactions. There is no real possibility for probing, as there is in an interactive interview situation, although some respondents will often write long and revealing essays in answer to open questions.

Value of Questioning Group Members.   We shall continue in later Units to explore the ways in which such devices enable the sociologist to draw inferences about a social system from the combined answers of several members of the same system. Skillful use of observation can lead to an understanding of patterns of interaction not apparent to the actors themselves. But skillful use of questioning can delve still deeper to an understanding of the structures of orientation—the unrecognized strains in marital relationships, or the lack of reciprocity in friendship relations—that are not yet manifest in the interaction.

SUGGESTED READINGS FOR UNIT FOUR

Cannell and Kahn, 1953; Coleman, 1961-b; Furfey, pp. 321–33; Goode and Hatt, Chapters 11–13; Hyman *et al.*, 1954; Kahn and Cannell; Kornhauser and Sheatsley, 1959; Lazarsfeld, 1944; Lindzey and Borgatta; Maccoby and Maccoby; Merton, Fiske, and Kendall, 1956; Parten, Chapters, 6, 10, 11, 12; Riesman and Glazer; Selltiz *et al.*, Chapters 7, 8; Stinchcombe; Weiss and Jacobsen; Young, Chapters 8, 9.

QUESTIONS FOR REVIEW AND DISCUSSION

Review the following methodological terms as used in this Unit:
collective measure
focus on orientations
identification of parts of the system
intensive interview
self-administered questionnaire
self-selection of respondents
serendipity component of research
sociogram
sociometric matrix
sociometry

1. Cottrell formulates three "propositions" which reflect his approach to marriage as "an adjustment of roles." With these propositions in mind, consider how you might systematize and tabulate the data in such a way that the nature of the dyadic relationship is not concealed. What advantages might there be to such systematization in this particular study?

Consider the kinds of information which might be lost by such an approach.

2. Suppose that you wanted to code the data obtained in the interviews in Exercise I-2. Would you expect to find the Bales categories useful? Consider how you might go about developing a different set of categories which might be more appropriate for such data.

3. Imagine that, in Exercise I-2, you wished to interview the parents as well as the offspring. What additional sociologically relevant information might you obtain?

4. In interviewing several members of the same group (as in Question 3), consider the possible advantages and difficulties of:

a. Using several interviewers to question all the group members simultaneously;

b. Conducting one interview imme-

diately after the other without allowing interaction between the group members;

c. Conducting a "group" interview,
in which the several members are simultaneously questioned and allowed
to interact.

5. What does the following sociogram show? Suppose you wanted to add
a third criterion of choice (or rejection),

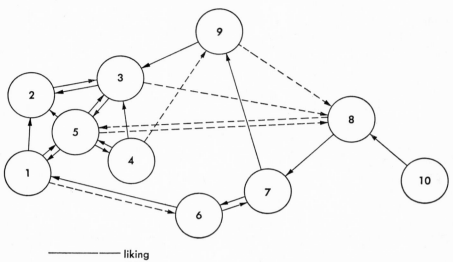

——————— liking
— — — — — — disliking

* (Adapted from Proctor and Loomis, p. 565.)

how would you indicate this in the sociogram?

6. Both the sociogram and Whyte's
techniques of positional mapping and
analysis of set events are aimed at revealing the structure of the group. Consider
the differences between them. Are they
essentially similar devices, or do they
point up a basic distinction in methods
of gathering data?

7. Contrast the role of observer with
that of interviewer. What are the special
advantages and difficulties of each in establishing the kind of relationship with
the people under study that will yield the
data sought?

8. What does the following who-to-
whom matrix show? What aspects of the
social system may be studied by using the
marginal data? The cell data? By comparing several matrices for a series of
groups?

*Number of Hours Each Subject Would
Like To Spend With Each Object*

| Group Member | Group Member as Object | | | | Subject |
as Subject	A	B	C	D	Totals
A	x	0	4	5	
B	1	x	0	0	
C	2	2	x	5	
D	0	0	4	x	

Object Totals

9. Show how Merton's findings on
patterns of "reciprocal evaluation" might
be set up in the form of a matrix,
as in Table 4-D. How might Lundberg

and Lawsing have used such a matrix for their analysis of dyads by status (as in their Table 3)?

10. Merton suggests the direction a "full-fledged" inquiry into patterns of influence should take. Do you agree with this plan? If so, how would you proceed to gather data both by observation and by questioning? How would you use the two sets of data?

11. How did Merton secure reliability in the classification of leaders as locals or cosmopolitans?

12. Lundberg and Lawsing analyze a single community; Cottrell describes a single dyad. Discuss what each accomplishes by focusing on a single case (a) in terms of the particular research objective and (b) in the extent to which the findings may be generalized.

UNIT FIVE
USES OF AVAILABLE DATA

SUGGESTED PROGRAM OF STUDY

Unit 5 deals with research based on material already at hand, rather than on data newly gathered by the researcher himself to meet his immediate objective **(P-VII).**

Exercises and Manual

Start by completing **Exercise I-5,** which will give you some practice in selecting and using existing materials for your own particular research aims. **Manual I-C** will give you an idea of the wide variety of sources (*e.g.,* in libraries and local institutions and agencies) from which the sociologist draws "ready-made" data (either in raw form or already systematically organized).

Studies

Analyze the methods used in the studies by **Thomas** and **Znaniecki, Zelditch,** and **Sorokin.** Consider the different research problems for which available data may be suitable, and the possible connections between the use of available data and the decisions made under each of the other items in the Paradigm.

Commentary

Read the Commentary, which begins to suggest how, and under what conditions, a researcher may decide to use available data.

Questions for Review and Discussion

Finally, consider the Questions for Review and Discussion. Think of each study as a rounded whole, and make comparisons with the designs of the studies you have previously analyzed. Record all general rules that seem to apply to locating and handling available materials in contrast with new materials which you might gather by questioning or observing the interaction directly.

WILLIAM I. THOMAS
FLORIAN ZNANIECKI

The Polish Peasant in Europe and America

from Volume I

... Our object-matter is one class of a modern society in the whole concrete complexity of its life. The selection of the Polish peasant society, motivated at first by somewhat incidental reasons, such as the intensity of the Polish immigration and the facility of getting materials concerning the Polish peasant, has proved during the investigation to be a fortunate one. The Polish peasant finds himself now in a period of transition from the old forms of social organization that had been in force, with only insignificant changes, for many centuries, to a modern form of life. He has preserved enough of the old attitudes to make their sociological reconstruction possible, and he is sufficiently advanced upon the new way to make a study of the development of modern attitudes particularly fruitful. ... The whole mechanism of social creation is therefore here particularly transparent and easy to understand, and in general the role of human attitudes in social life becomes much more evident than in a society not living under the same strain, but able to rely to a large extent upon the inherited formal organization for the preservation of its culture and unity.

We use in this work the inductive

Reprinted in part from William I. Thomas and Florian Znaniecki, *The Polish Peasant in Europe and America,* Chicago: University of Chicago Press, *I,* 1918, pp. 74–77, 87, 89–90, 303–05, and *II,* pp. 296–97, 303–08, 406–07, 409–10, 413–15, 421–22, 424–32.

method in a form which gives the least possible place for any arbitrary statements. The basis of the work is concrete materials, and only in the selection of these materials some necessary discrimination has been used. But even here we have tried to proceed in the most cautious way possible. The private letters constituting the first two volumes have needed relatively little selection, particularly as they are arranged in family series. Our task has been limited to the exclusion of such letters from among the whole collection as contained nothing but a repetition of situations and attitudes more completely represented in the materials which we publish here. ...

The analysis of the attitudes and characters given in notes to particular letters and in introductions to particular series contains nothing not essentially contained in the materials themselves; its task is only to isolate single attitudes, to show their analogies and dependences, and to interpret them in relation to the social background upon which they appear. Our acquaintance with the Polish society simply helps us in noting data and relations which would perhaps not be noticed so easily by one not immediately acquainted with the life of the group.

Finally, the synthesis constituting the introductions to particular volumes is also based upon the materials, with a few exceptions where it was thought necessary to draw some data from Polish ethnological publications or systematic studies. The sources are always quoted.

The general character of the work is

mainly that of a systematization and classification of attitudes and values prevailing in a concrete group. Every attitude and every value ... can be really understood only in connection with the whole social life of which it is an element, and therefore this method is the only one that gives us a full and systematic acquaintance with all the complexity of social life. But it is evident that this monograph must be followed by many others if we want our acquaintance with social reality to be complete.... Naturally the value of every monograph will increase with the development of the work, for not only will the method continually improve, but every social group will help to understand every other....

THE PEASANT FAMILY

The Polish peasant family, in the primary and larger sense of the word, is a social group including all the blood- and law-relatives up to a certain variable limit —usually the fourth degree. The family in the narrower sense, including only the married pair with their children, may be termed the "marriage-group." These two conceptions, family-group and marriage-group, are indispensable to an understanding of the familial life....

The family is thus a very complex group, with limits only approximately determined and with very various kinds and degrees of relationship between its members. But the fundamental familial connection is one and irreducible; it cannot be converted into any other type of group-relationship nor reduced to a personal relation between otherwise isolated individuals. It may be termed *familial solidarity,* and it manifests itself both in assistance rendered to, and in control exerted over, any member of the group by any other member representing the group as a whole. It is totally different from territorial, religious, economic, or national

solidarity, though evidently these are additional bonds promoting familial solidarity, and we shall see presently that any dissolution of them certainly exerts a dissolving influence upon the family. And again, the familial solidarity and the degree of assistance and of control involved should not depend upon the personal character of the members, but only upon the kind and degree of their relationship; the familial relation between two members admits no gradation, as does love or friendship....

Form and Function of the Peasant Letter

The Polish peasant, as the present collection shows, writes many and long letters. This is particularly striking, since the business of writing or even of reading letters is at best very difficult for him. It requires a rather painful effort of reflection and sacrifice of time. Letter-writing is for him a social duty of a ceremonial character, and the traditional, fixed form of peasant letters is a sign of their social function.

All the peasant letters can be considered as variations of one fundamental type, whose form results from its function and remains always essentially the same, even if it eventually degenerates. We call this type the "bowing letter."

The bowing letter is normally written by or to a member of the family who is absent for a certain time. Its function is to manifest the persistence of familial solidarity in spite of the separation. Such an expression became necessary only when members of the family began to leave their native locality; as long as the family stayed in the same community, the solidarity was implicitly and permanently assumed. The whole group manifested its unity at periodical and extraordinary meetings, but no single member in particular was obliged to manifest his own familial feelings more than other members, unless on some extraordinary occasions, e.g., at the time of his or her marriage. But the individual who leaves his family finds himself in a distinctive situation as compared with that of other members, and the bowing letter is the product of this situation. There is nothing corresponding to it in personal, immediate familial relations.

In accordance with its function, the bowing letter has an exactly determined composition. It begins with the religious greeting: "Praised be Jesus Christus," to which the reader is supposed to answer, "In centuries of centuries, Amen." The greeting has both a magical and a moral significance. Magically it averts evil, morally it shows that the writer and the reader are members of the same religious community, and from the standpoint of the moral-religious system every community is religious. A common subordination to God may also be otherwise expressed throughout the entire letter, but the greeting is the most indispensable expression. There follows the information that the writer, with God's help, is in good health and is succeeding, and wishes the same for the reader and the rest of the family. We know that health (struggle against death) and living constitute the reason [for] natural and human solidarity (only spiritual solidarity aims at power). Finally come greetings, "bows," for all the members of the family, or from all the members of the family if the letter is written to the absent member. The enumeration should be complete, embracing at least all the members who still live in the same locality, if the family is already scattered, as often happens today.

These elements remain in every letter, even when the function of the letter becomes more complicated; every letter, in other words, whatever else it may be, is a bowing letter, a manifestation of solidarity. Various elements may be schematized; the words "bows for the whole family" may, for example, be substituted for the long enumeration, but the principle remains unchanged in all the familial letters.

The bowing letter is the only one which has an original function. The functions of all the other types of familial letters are vicarious; the letter merely takes the place of a personal, immediate communication. It has to perform these vicarious functions when the absence of the member of the family becomes so long that it is impossible to wait for his arrival....

from Volume II

Correspondence Between Husbands and Wives

... the common problem in all the series of letters is that of the constitution of what may be termed a "natural" family, i.e., a family based, not upon social traditional attitudes, but only upon the actual relations between its members, and therefore practically limited to a married couple with their children; it is the family as elementary social group of the classical sociological theory. It proves here to be the result of a relatively late social evolution. As the older form of familial unity, in which the family embraced relatives up to the fourth or fifth degree (without very clearly determined limits), decomposes under the influence of new conditions, its parts enter into the composition of different territorial, professional, sometimes national and religious groups, and thus their former connection is loosened. Simultaneously an evolution goes on within each of these parts—each elementary group of married couple + children; the reciprocal relations of its members undergo a change. This may perhaps be best expressed in the following way: As long as the familial group was constituted by all the relatives on the sides of both husband and wife, the fundamental conjugal norm was that of "respect," because the married pair was not an isolated couple related only as individuals, but in them and through them their respective families were united, and the dignity of these families was involved in the conjugal relation. When this large family is dissociated, the fundamental conjugal norm becomes that of love and reciprocal confidence, because the relation is a purely personal one. In the larger family the children were not merely children of the given couple, but in a sense belonged to the family as a whole, and the parents, particularly the father, represented the total group with regard to them, and was to some extent responsible for them before the group. Hence the relation between parents and children was one of authority and obedience, and bore at the same time a certain impersonal character, precisely because it lacked exclusiveness, for the children as members of the larger group had a quality which put them partly outside of the smaller group. The isolation of the latter brought new forms of interior life; the parents' authority and the children's obedience became personal, not social, attitudes, and the individualization called for a new norm—that of reciprocal personal affection.

The Polish peasant is now on the way from the older form of familial life to the new one, and we find in the present volume the two forms mixed in various proportions. But since in the new form individual factors play a much more important part than in the old one, the strength and harmony of familial life begin to depend in a much larger measure upon such factors as character, intellectual development, sentimental refinement, etc. Thus we find examples of a stronger or weaker connection between the members of the new marriage-group, of a more or less perfect harmony in the life of this group, of its more or less solidary behavior with regard to the external world, etc.

In arranging the materials we place first those in which the marriage-group is shown as being merely a part of the family, and later those in which the "natural family" is definitely constituted. . . .

Kukiełka Series

The familial character of marriage viewed from the husband's side is depicted in the letters of this series. It is difficult to establish whether in this case the relation is really closer than in that of the Pawlaks.[1] At any rate the letters show much more eagerness to keep the familial solidarity and manifest greater claims on familial affection than those of Pawlak's wife, and it seems that Kukiełka's wife is also less interested in the questions of familial solidarity than her husband. If we compare these facts with the situations found in other series (for example, the Markiewicz series), where the wife evidently does not share her husband's familial attitude, and with other cases where the wife seems rather passive and the husband even writes all the familial letters (Stelmach, Cugowski), a general conclusion seems to present itself: As it is primarily the man, not the woman, who represents and understands the group standpoint, in marriage-groups based upon the familial organization the conjugal affection is maintained much more through the husband than the wife. The attitude of the latter is always personal, and she is

[1] [References are to other sets of correspondence between members of family-groups.]

never satisfied with being treated by her husband merely as a member of the group with certain functions to perform, and not as an individual. Therefore, after a shorter or longer time, she turns her affection toward her children and becomes often almost indifferent toward her husband, because in the case of the children her individualistic affection finds an easier response. This enables her afterward to assume the rôle of a mediator between her husband and her children when the latter develop an individualistic attitude. (Cf. Osiński series.) Meanwhile the husband shows the same unchanging kind and degree of attachment as prescribed by the organization of the family. Of course the sexual factor must exert a powerful if unconscious influence upon the conjugal relation, but it is not consciously allowed to interfere with the social and moral side of this relation.

The respective rôles of husband and wife change, as we shall see, as soon as marriage becomes an individual matter.

There is no contradiction between the lack of familial solidarity in the married woman and the solidarity which an unmarried girl shows toward her parents, brothers, sisters, and relatives. The unmarried girl has no particular familial function to perform and hence her personal affection to individual members of the family can still easily fit into the familial organization.

506–09, Jan Kukiełka, in America, to His Wife, in Poland

August 9, 1911

506

[A page and a half of the usual greetings, wishes, and generalities about health.] Now I inform you, dearest little wife, about what you ask, whether Mańka shall go to Warsaw, although she is the daughter of a farmer. Well, I answer you that she is not to go, because I do not allow this.[2] Now, as to our son An-

[2] Going to Warsaw means going to serve as a housemaid. The father forbids it as contrary to the peculiar dignity of a farmer as against a landless peasant. We find the same aversion to any hired work for wives. This aversion is weakened, without disappearing, when the child or the wife has to go, not to a Polish estate or city, but abroad—to Germany or to America. Sending children to hired work in the country is not suitable for a farmer who has some 10 morgs of land, while only rich farmers, owning 20 to 30 morgs, consider it below their dignity to send their children to Germany. Evidently the reason [for] this difference is that the work abroad has some characters of novelty which make the application of traditional inhibitions to it less natural and immediate. Further, the inhibition is not so strong with regard to boys as to girls, not so strong with regard to girls as to wives, and in the process of industrial evolution the first has almost disappeared. But it seems still to be instinctively held with regard to the oldest son or, more exactly, to the son who is to take his father's farm. It is certainly neither by mere sentiment nor by rational calculation that the son who is destined to take the farm is more unwillingly allowed to go to hired work than other sons. The aversion to hired work certainly goes back to the time when the work away from the familial farm was mainly servage work; but this is hardly sufficient by itself to explain the facts. We must take into consideration the distinction, pointed out elsewhere, between farm-income and income from hired labor, the latter being additional and destined primarily to cover such expenses as in the peasant's economy are relatively new, while the farm-income is the essential basis of living of the whole family. All these facts are explained if we remember that economic organization is determined by familial organization. The essentially familial property is the hereditary farm, and against this the money earned outside represents the more individual form of property. Wages, being a relatively recent phenomenon, cannot be as completely subordinated to the familial standpoint as land and land-income, even if their subordination is manifested by the demand that earned money be turned over to the family. Therefore, hired work is felt as particularly un-

toni, with him it's going very badly, and in this way, that he does not keep his work, and is without a cent at all, and if anybody says anything to him, he does not listen at all, but is ready to fight. What can be done with such a boy? You can understand, dearest little wife, that it would be quite unsuitable for me to give him money, because you know yourself that I must think of you all, and it would be too much if I had still to have difficulties with him or to be concerned with his difficulties. When I sometimes predicted to him [the bad consequences of his behavior] he took pains not to meet me at all. What more can I do? I inform you however that he is in good health; that is all that I can tell you, dearest little wife.[3] I inform you also, dearest little wife, that I will send you about 100 roubles after some days. So don't answer this letter, because after some days another will come, and then you will answer both. Now I want to say this also, my dear little wife, that I am very much pleased with your doing good farming for me, and keeping the boars, sows, and pigs, and with your having harvested the crops. I am very much pleased with this letter, dearest little wife.[4] Now I inform

you about my work. I work in a brick-factory and earn very good money, that is, $2.70 for 13 hours. The work is very heavy, but I don't mind it; let it be heavy, but may it last without interruption. The brick-factories are going all right during the summer but in winter they stop, and I am afraid of it. But let it be as our Lord God sends it. When that day comes, some way will be found. Now I have nothing more to write, only I may add that in America there have been enormous fevers, for some days thousands.... [End of the letter missing.]

[Jan Kukiełka]

January 6, 1912
507

[Two pages of greetings, wishes, reproaches, and justifications about writing or not writing letters.] Now, dearest little wife, as to what you write about sending a ship-ticket for [our daughter] Mańka, it is so: As to the ship-ticket, it does not matter much, but I mind most this: If I take Mańka, what will you do there, dearest little wife? You know yourself that she is of great help to you. That is one thing. And secondly I mind that the girl will be very sad and will suffer misery. Here in America it is not the same as in our country. What if she does come to me? She cannot remain with me, but must go into service, and in the service it is necessary to learn the English language, and even to learn washing and cooking. Then there will be misery and weeping, because somebody speaks and

---

suitable for those whose connection with the main familial group is particularly close, while a certain relaxation of the inhibition is natural for the members who will sooner or later establish a new branch of the family.

[3] Particularly rapid emancipation of the boy. The father's authority is not sufficient when not supported by the whole family-group and community.

[4] The farm-work done by the wife is presented here as meritorious and as if it were done for the husband and deserved his particular gratitude. This attitude seems contrary to the familial principle, according to which there is no division of property between husband and wife because there is no private property. Kulielka is also evidently conservative and it is improbable that he would occupy an individualistic standpoint.

The explanation is connected with the situation outlined in the first note on this letter. The husband's emigration and the hired work he is doing, even if necessitated by the situation, are still formally a departure from his familial duty, which would oblige him to remain on the farm. The wife by doing his work performs his duty and is therefore entitled to gratitude. Their arrangement is personal even if its object—farm-work—is familial.

you can only look at him. If you want it exceedingly I will send [the ticket], but then don't blame me. Now I inform you also, dearest little wife, that after this letter I will send you some roubles, so wait some days before you answer.

The loving father of our children,[5]
[Jan Kukiełka]

December 30, 1913
508

... And now, dear wife and daughters, write to me, when do you think it best for me to return home? On Easter or at some other time? And now I greet you, dear wife and daughters, and I greet my dear sisters Katarzyna, Rozalia, Maryanna, with their husbands and children. And now I greet the whole household of father-in-law, father and mother and brothers-in-law. And now, dear wife I inform you [send you this] through the Mrozys [who are returning], and I send you 4 roubles for your expenses. Buy for yourself, Rózia, a white waist and for Nastusia and Jagusia shawls that you may have them for summer when I come home. And now dear wife, tell my sister Rozalia Figlisz not to allow her daughter Marysia to marry Bzdziuch, because no good will come of it. As the father, so is the son, as the tree, so is the wedge. And then it is a near family, and therefore God will not bless such a marriage, because there are enough people in the world.[6] If she does not believe my words let her be persuaded by the example of those who married their relatives. As a good brother, I admonish Sister Rozalia, let her not do it, what she intends to do. [More greetings for the whole family.]

Your husband,
Jan Kukiełka

[5] Curious expression of the familial attitude.
[6] God does not need an increase in population badly enough to bless with children a marriage of this kind.

Gut bai [goodbye]. It means *do widzenia.* [More wishes of divine blessing for the whole family.] I will ask you only, don't ever quarrel with sister Maryanna, don't abuse her, don't let the children laugh at her, God forbid you this! But on the contrary, as a good mother, you ought more than once to buy either bread or sugar or [illegible word] and to give them to herself and her children, and God will be satisfied with your life and will bless you.[7] [More greetings.]

February 15 [1914]
509

[Letter from husband Jan to his wife Rozalia.] In the first words of my letter I speak to you, dear wife, with those words that are pleasant to you: "Praised be Jesus Christus" and I hope that you will answer me, "For centuries of centuries. Amen."

And now I inform you, dear wife, that I received your letter on February 13, for which may God reward you, that you wrote me about your dear health and success.[8] And now I inform you, dear wife, that that letter did not please me at all, because I asked you to write me when I should come, and you did not answer me, as if you were not my own wife but a cook or some other hired woman. And now I inform you, that you wrote twice for me to send you my photograph, you gave me no peace. To tell the truth, I did not even wish it, but when you wrote once and then once more, I was obliged to send you the photograph. But it was expensive for me alone, so I asked my companion, and this cost us cheaper. My companion

[7] The whole letter is a notable expression of familial solidarity.
[8] The beginning is particularly formal, preparatory to the scolding which is to follow. His masculine vanity is particularly offended by the lack of respect shown in connection with the photograph, especially as the wife of the other man behaved better in this respect.

sent one at once to our country, and they answered him and thanked him very much, but when I sent it I did not even get an answer. Such is the gratitude I got. I had thought that I left a good wife at home, but I was disappointed; the husband is far away. I wrote letters as to a wife, but I did not receive any good answers for them. When I was a little boy with my parents I was glad and happy, I had whatever I wished, and now I have a wife who does not even write to me about my daughters. Such is the reward for one's goodness.

And now, dear wife, you write me that Józef, your brother, writes about those few roubles, asking for them. So I write you, dear wife, you may write to him that I will send him those few roubles, but only when I am at home. Now I will not send money home because I need it for my journey, and what is left I will give back. And now you write, that you have no milk. Do you think that I have it? You have rye for bread, 10 korcy, and I must buy bread; you have a house, and I must pay rent, 7 roubles a month, and so my work goes on. And now, dear wife, you write that you have a fat pig [ready] to be killed, so I advise you, if they pay you well, you can sell him, if pigs are dear; but if they are cheap, don't sell. [End missing.]

[Jan Kukiełka]

Jabłkowski Series

In the present case we have the only example of a perfectly solidary and harmonious "natural family," as the result of an evolution which has substituted individual bonds between the members of a marriage-group for traditional social bonds between the members of the "large family."

We see also an important social consequence of this evolution—the particularly marked isolation of the marriage-group from the rest of the community, even from the relatives who in the old organization would be the most important members of the group, namely, the parents of the man and the woman and the brothers and sisters. On the one hand, the marriage-group, perfectly solidary within itself, acts in economic and social matters toward the rest of the community as toward strangers, sometimes even with a marked hostility; on the other hand, any action from outside is received as affecting the marriage-group as a whole. In this respect the reactions to external influences tending to disaggregate the group —gossip, efforts to compel the husband or the wife to act in economic matters in a personal way—are significant. These influences themselves, the more or less unfriendly acts of neighbors, acquaintances, relatives, which Jabłkowska attributes to "jealousy," are perhaps better understood if we take into consideration the very natural hostile attitude of the social environment toward so isolated and impenetrable a familial group. The old type of family, at least in Poland, has no place for such an isolation. Under these conditions it is obvious that when for any reason the marriage-group tends to separate itself sharply from the family-group the latter not only shows a sharp resentment, but the smaller group is by the fact of the resentment thrown more and more back upon itself, until its isolation is greater than that of the modern family.

Another interesting point in this connection is the important part played by the woman in the constitution of the new family. This role is complicated, as is the situation of the woman itself. In the old group the woman's position in the family was in one respect more secure than in the new one, because she was backed by her group. But, on the other hand, the woman's relation to her husband and children always tended to be as exclusive and personal as possible; she always occupied the standpoint of particular individuals, not that of the group as a whole. And thus the new group appears from this point of view as a realization of a certain tendency of the woman—the tendency to substitute a few subjective personal relations for the many objective social relations. In all the cases in which the new group is or tends to be constituted, the woman seems to be the principal factor of its unity and isolation. But as she has not the help of any social traditions her success depends upon her personality.

The whole evolution in the Jabłkowski case seems relatively recent, for the older generation has preserved much of the traditional peasant attitude. Probably the Jabłkowskis are the children of peasants, who settled in the city.

630–48, To Konstanty Jabłkowski, in America, From His Wife and Children, in Poland.[9]

February 17, 1914

631

Most beloved Father: I thank you very nicely for the scrap upon which you wrote a few words for me. Dear father, you tell me to learn to be an ironmoulder. But I won't learn to be an ironmoulder, for it is a hard specialty. One earns a few roubles more, but he must work like an ox. And here if a moulder is kept anywhere, he is, but if they throw him away he cannot find work, but must work as a simple laborer. Thus it happened with Hojnacki. You write me that any peasant can do the work which I do. But you don't know yet what work it is. Myka wanted to work at the light and said that he had worked at the light in the cement-factory, but they refused to admit him for they were afraid he would

[9] [Several of the letters are omitted.]

spoil something. . . . I learned for almost half a year in helping an electro-technician, and as he liked me he explained to me everything . . . so that now if I got a plan, I could install the light myself, and I can decompose and recompose a dynamo machine. . . . And if the factory stops I can do locksmith's work. . . . I earn now almost 25 roubles, and later I shall have almost 35 roubles, or even more. Now, dear father, don't trouble about me. I shall find my way and even help you.[10] Now, dear father, I need a suit for Easter, for this one which I have is quite spoilt . . . and I need also shoes, for these which I have are torn. . . . Besides this, dear father, send me some neckties . . . and if they reach me I shall beg you to send me perhaps 2 stiff shirts, for I have only one such . . . and it is not enough. I must take it to the laundry too often. . . .

Jan Jabłkowski

February 21, 1914

632

Most beloved and dearest Husband: I received your letter . . . written on February 8. . . . As to lending money, you may be calm, for I am not so silly as to lend money or to warrant for anybody. You know that I am not very eager to do such things. I won't lend to my brother either, for I know how eager he is in paying back. . . .[11] Now you ask about my overcoat. It is a little worn on the

[10] We have here the new attitude toward work—appreciation of skill and efficiency. . . .

[11] A sign of the degree to which the old solidarity is dissolved. In peasant life money should be lent, not only to so near a relative, but to any member of the community, and the question of his paying the debt would hardly be raised as self-evident. So the solidarity between members of the family is here weaker than the traditional solidarity between members of the community.

front side, about the pockets and sleeves, but it does not look so bad yet. You write me, dear husband, to buy a fur collar, but now I don't want to buy any, for spring is near. Since I did not buy in the beginning of the winter I won't buy now, for immediately some persons would be found ready to say that I did not buy it for winter, only for summer.... And I shall put this whole 100 roubles into the savings-bank; I won't divide it. As to the debts, I owe 8 roubles to my father, which I lacked to live, for I have not worked for almost a month and Janek's salary does not suffice for our household, because I spend now on everything one rouble a day. Yes, my dear husband. So I took 7 roubles for living and 1 rouble for your mother, together 8 roubles. I have not yet paid these 2 roubles to your mother which I owed her, but I gave her this 1 rouble, for she was at the wedding of your foster-daughter. Tomaszewski came to invite me and mother to that wedding, but what was the need to them of my going there.[12] And now, dear husband, I owe still 10 roubles to Gelblum [Jewish shopkeeper] on the booklet [in which goods taken on credit are inscribed]. So I write you, dear husband, that I shall put these 100 roubles into the bank and I won't pay these debts.[13] Father does not need money much so I will pay him 1 rouble on my pay day and 1 rouble on Janek's pay day and thus I shall pay it back gradually. And from Gelblum I won't take now on the booklet, but as far as possible for cash, until you send me money for the children's clothing; then perhaps a few roubles will remain from the clothing, and these I shall pay to Gelblum. For the children need clothes

---

[12] Another attitude which would be quite incomprehensible in a peasant group.
[13] In order not to destroy the round number. A vestige of the qualitative character of economic quantities.

absolutely. Janek must have another suit for going out, and Oleś has only one which has been repaired already and he has nothing to put on when he goes to church. Now, as to the Jałozos [husband's sister and brother-in-law], I shall write you what a *bryndza* [literally sheep-cheese, slang for "bad condition," "misery" or "disorderly life"] there is now, only in another letter, for now I am not particularly healthy. I have toothache and my arm pains me.... Goodbye, my dear Kostuś, for I long very much without you. I kiss you heartily innumerable times.

Your wife,
Marcyanna Jabłkowska

Now I kiss you once more strongly. Now, dear husband, Oleś was a little angry, because you did not send kisses for him in your letter.

March 17, 1914
634

Most beloved Husband: [Letters received and written; description of her sickness.] Now I tell you, I was so worried when I lay in bed, you have no idea, and it is impossible to describe, because you were not at home. For it seemed to me that if you said to me even a single word I should be healthier. Moreover, letters are now so late from you; they don't arrive normally.... Now, dear husband, as to the good heart, whether I have a good heart toward you or not, I tell you only this, that as I love God and want my soul's salvation after my death, I always love you and always have a good and constant heart toward you. Yes, my dear husband. And I would never write any testy things in my letters, but yourself, dear husband, you lead [incite] me to do it. And I shall write you, my dear, a few words from a good heart. My dear, when you learn anything about me and it does not please you, you ought to write me at once, "so and so, my dear (or however else, in your manner), and I hear that you have been where I don't wish you to go." For I even acknowledge that you are right when you write that it is not a fit company for me, and I regretted myself that I was there and I said to myself that I will never more go anywhere. And you write me about it after a year, as if you had waited for something more to make a conviction against me. Yes, my dear husband, I shall never be angry with you, even if you write me something like this in every letter and if you make any remarks to me, for you have the right and you ought to make remarks to me without any fear, if you are displeased with anything, and I shall listen to you at any time. Yes, my dearest husband.

[Calculation of income and expenses.] My dear husband, once more I make this remark, for you write precisely that you did not intend to answer my letter. It was very bad of you to think so, and to have written only after listening to the advice of *Kum* Wierzba. My dear husband, I write to you with a good intention, without any wrath, and it seems to me that you will agree with me. Answer me whether I don't write the truth, my dear husband, that you ought to answer without hesitation every letter, good or bad ... and that you ought to accept everything from me, whether it is written good or bad [praise or blame], and I must also accept from you good and bad writing. We must listen to each other in order that it may be well, until we are united with each other, for I wish our life to be happy as long as we live upon the world. And don't listen to any Hams whatever they may tell you against me, or to any apes, whatever they may write you in their letters about me. And if anything comes to your ears about me, write me at once and I will listen to you and won't be an-

gry at all if you make any remark to me. For I don't listen to anybody except you. For if we listen to everything that people bark with their tongues, we should be well off! If I wrote to you everything that I hear from women who have their husbands in America! For if their husbands are of a bad conduct, they think and say at once that all are the same. But I don't listen to anybody except you for you have ever written me not to listen. Yes, dear husband. [Usual ending.]

Marcyanna

My most beloved and dearest Father: I am healthy and I wish you the same with my whole heart. And now, dear father, you write that you won't come until the next year. But, dear father, don't think this; it won't be so. For mother says that she will not stop working until you come. And do you know, father, that mother is sick, but goes to work nevertheless. And I beg you, father, very much, earn for journey and come, for I am very much worried. When Sunday comes, mother does not go anywhere, and I have not even 1 companion and must play alone, so I am very much worried. I have nothing more to write, I kiss you innumerable times, your hands and lips. Goodbye.

Marysia J.

March 28, 1914
640

Dearest and most beloved Husband: [Easter wishes; money received and spent.] Now, dear husband, I write you a few words about Lucek [husband's brother] and his wife, for I was with them just now. Lucek began to abuse us, saying that we lacked confidence in them and were afraid to lend them some money. He was offended with you for not having written the letter to him, but having sent it in my letter, for I gave them this letter without the envelope, because I did not notice the inscription, "To be forwarded to Lucek" and tore the envelope. I did not give them the envelope therefore, but said that the letter was inclosed in mine. And why should we turn our heads [trouble ourselves] about the Luceks? We have enough of our own troubles. We should never come to an end with them. Lucek began at once to worry me, asking me to lend him 100 roubles nevertheless, even without your knowing it. I said that I positively would not lend without your knowing it. Lucek began to laugh at me, saying that I was afraid of you. And I said: "Yes, it is true, I am afraid. My husband wrote me that he confided everything to me but on the condition that I would not lend money to anybody, either of my family or of his own. I write to my husband about every rouble which I spend. I must listen to my husband and nobody else." I had to find an excuse for he worried me about this loan. He said that he will write a letter to you some day, but I don't know what about. He said that we shall still beg his favor some day. Is he our father or what else? Stupid Lucek! . . .

Marcyanna Jabłkowska

June 7, 1914
643

Dearest and most beloved Husband: [Letters delayed.] I write you a few words precisely about this christening in Adam's house. I am not satisfied with it at all, for I grudge these 6 roubles which we have spent, for each rouble is awfully necessary to me. But it was impossible to act otherwise for there would be more talking than all this is worth. For if he had said to Janek that it was a christening we should not have gone at all. But I cannot say that they have treated us badly—God forbid! They behaved very politely, for the christening was on Sunday, and on

Monday *poprawiny* and we returned rather late on both evenings, about midnight, and he brought us home in a cab both times. I was there and Janek and Mania, while Oleś . . . was in the country with his companion. [Describes with whom and how long he stayed; why she permitted him to go, etc.] And these Majewskis [Adam's friends] admired [wondered] that I am still so young and have such big and handsome and good children. And they wondered that Janek was going out with me; they said that another boy would not be willing. [Money-matters; choice of career for Oleś.]

Now, dear husband, I write you a few words, that Golasiowa has asked my pardon, for she was in Czestochowa [on a pilgrimage], and after this she came to me and began to cry and to beg my pardon, and she wanted to kiss my hand, but I did not allow her, and we kissed each other in the face. And she asked me to beg your pardon, that you might not be angry with her. Now I inform you, dear husband, what a misfortune befell Brzozowksi. . . . He went also to America and his wife died here . . . and 4 small children remained. People wrote for him to come. Only don't be impressed with it, my dear husband, for we are in good health, thanks to God. If I am a little unwell, never mind, for I am not very sick either; I walk, I work, perhaps gradually this sickness will pass. I write you on a separate scrap what is the matter with me. [The scrap was probably destroyed by the sender of the letters.] And if I write you that she is dead, why, you don't need to grieve about anybody else except yourself and your family. So don't mind it much. I write you this news that you may know, for I am also curious when you write me anything like this. Now, dear husband, I write you about this sickness of mine, since what time I have not felt well. My dear husband [it has been] since you wrote me disagreeable letters about this whole trouble. When Wierzba's wife told us nothing, and you were in such a wrath against me unjustly. Only don't be angry with me again for mentioning this, for I don't remember it any more [I have forgiven]. But when you ask me since what time I have been unwell, I write you the positive truth. If you had not asked me I would not have written at all. So it was, my dear husband, that I cried very much and could not eat and could not sleep, only grieved that you had so little confidence in me and listened to gossip. And I worked more than ever. [Describes her work; writes what the factory-doctor prescribed.] And the doctor told me that if I don't feel better, I must go to a specialist for women's diseases, and I should go and should not grudge the money, but, to tell the truth, dear husband, I am ashamed. . . .

[Marcyanna]

June 17, 1914
644

Dearest and most beloved Husband: [Two pages describing receipt of a letter in a torn envelope and asking him not to send such thick letters because the post-officials think they contain money. Three pages itemizing expenditures, etc.] I write you a few words about Mania. Write a sheet to her and admonish her to be more polite and not to fight with Janek, for when he makes any remark to her and pushes her a little, she begins at once to cry awfully and jumps at him. Once he told her not to eat in the courtyard, for I worked at night, and she went into the courtyard with a pot [of food]. She did not listen, and he struck her a little on the face. She came immediately to me to the factory, weeping, and said that Janek had beaten her on the face. I got angry,

went home and asked who was guilty. They told me so and so. Thus she had merited to be struck a little. I got angry and said that by the love of God I would write to you. And I must write because I have said so. Now write her not to cry thus about any trifle, for I tell you, dear husband, that she is such a weeper that it is awful. She cries about anything. When I have worked over night, I am unwilling to go anywhere, I lay down and tell her, "Mania, don't go anywhere into the field alone." Then she begins to weep at once saying that she is worried, and sometimes she listens, sometimes not, and does not tell me where she is going. And I am afraid, for now different accidents happen; I read in the paper what is going on in the world. Therefore I don't allow her to go alone into the field. But she says: "When the boys go out you are not angry." And I say: "It is permitted to the boys, for they are boys, and you are a girl, you ought not to walk alone." So, my dear husband, admonish her always, perhaps then she will sooner listen, for this crying of hers angers me awfully. More than once I got so angry that I had to strike her, but I should prefer to have her listen to me when I tell her anything, rather than to beat her, for it is not a pleasure to beat a child. . . .

Now, dear husband, I write you about Oleś, that he finished his school and received a very good certificate . . . nothing but fives and two fours [5 is the highest mark]. He received a book as reward for having learned well. This book costs perhaps 2 roubles, but unhappily it is Russian. When he was leaving the teacher kissed him on the head and said that he would try perhaps to get a job for him. And Oleś came home and said: "Well, mother, give me a few copecks for having passed the examination." And he was so glad that he had passed it! I kissed him and gave him only 15 copecks, for I had little money, but he was glad even thus, went at once and hired a bicycle and took a ride. And you, dear husband, when you send money, set aside a rouble or a half for him, for his having passed the examination; then he will be glad. . . . He wants to go to the country for a week. I permit him; let him rest a little. [Relates how she tried to get a job for him at once.] Now, dear husband, I write you a few words about *Kum* Wierzba and this pig. You ought to have known yourself that you are not in your own home but with strangers, and that this does not pay; for you write that it did not pay. Nowadays nobody is ever to be believed. When I hear [read] what you write I say [to myself] that I did not expect anything like this from Wierzba—that you would not come to an understanding. But such are the times today. Describe to me everything you had between yourselves [the whole quarrel]. But I would beg you, dear husband, not to quarrel. Let him manage his own pocket and not profit from you. And don't ever hasten to such common undertakings. Yes, my dear husband. But it is always more pleasant to have somebody to talk with. Manage things as your reason advises you, that it may be well. Don't have any common undertakings and don't quarrel with each other. . . . Now, dear husband, as to Syroka, don't fear that I tell anything there. I only listen to what she tells me and I laugh, for she says that those two [women] are very angry because you send 100 roubles every two months, and they write to their husbands, and these are angry that you send so much, for their wives write them that you send money and they do not. Petruniowa has only 100 roubles. Syroka said it herself, for I don't ask. . . .

Marcyanna Jabłkowska

July 5, 1914
646

Dearest and most beloved Husband:
. . . I received from you money, 110 roubles . . . only I am very anxious why I have got no letter. . . . The porter went to the country for a few days, and the doorkeeper who took his place may have opened and read it from curiosity. . . . For some people lie in wait for these letters like dogs, because they can learn nothing from me. Other men who are in America don't send so much money, so they are curious why you send so often. Parzuch has sent only 200 roubles, a watch and a pin during a year. . . . Now, dear husband, I inform you what I did with this money for I have no letter and I don't know your decision. . . . I asked you for 120, but evidently you could not; nothing can be done. . . . I put 100 roubles into the bank, and we have there already 800. . . .

Oleś is still working in the factory. . . . I shall write you when he gets some other job. Only I beg you, dear husband, write Oleś a few words and tell him to listen to me, for when he goes to the town and I tell him to be back at such a time for dinner, he does not listen; twice already he has not been in time for dinner. And he smokes cigarettes secretly. He kept company with Lutek. I abused him, and he got a little away from Lutek, but now again he walks [associates] with Stadolak. I am not satisfied with it, for the boy is not orderly; I don't need to explain much, but [the fact is that] he is not orderly and everything pleases him. Therefore I don't want Oleś to walk with him. [Oleś] had a good companion, but he is now with his father in the country. [News about poultry; 2 pages about her health.] So I must go to a specialist for women's diseases, but for me it is a great shame, for, as you know, up to the present I have never known such a doctor, and it makes a terrible impression upon me. Stanislawowa was sick and went to such a doctor, and she told me that there is a sofa and he orders to lie down and puts his hand inside, for he must inspect. . . . But you know me [and you understand] that it is for me fearful and disgusting. . . .[14]

Marcyanna Jabłkowska

July 22, 1914
647

Dearest and most beloved Husband: [Letter received; thanks for a prayer-book; health.] As to my not going to work, don't write me anything about it and don't stir up Janek still more, for even now I must dispute with him. He does not want me to work, he says that he is ashamed that I am working. He has talked so for a year. And more than once he gets angry, particularly if I am sick. Now also he has talked much when he read this letter saying that you don't allow me to go to work. I did not want him to read this letter and I hid it in a drawer, but he found it. And they all began to clamor: "Mother won't work any more, father writes well; enough of this work." And Janek said: "Father writes you not to work, and you don't listen." And he talked much, and said that if I work he won't give me all his money, only 4 roubles [on each pay day]. But he has said so more than once, and still I work and he gives me his money. So I write you thus, dear husband. I should like myself not to work any more, for you know that people often abuse those women who work in the factory. Even now more than one tell [bad things] about Parzuchowa and Piotrowska, because they are so hot

tempered. And people say: "Jabłkowska alone is an orderly [good] woman, and it is a pity for her to work here with them." But I should like to help you still to put these 1,000 roubles aside, as you desire yourself. So if I work for some time still it is some help for you, because I have fuel and a few roubles for living, and the expense is big, for everybody wants to dress and to eat well, and here everything is expensive. Yes, my dear husband. You see, we still lack 200 roubles. So I will work for some time still, we shall put it aside sooner. And I should like you to come back at last, for I am tired already with all this. I don't promise you to work for a long time, only till you come back. Yes, my dear husband. Now you write me not to go to work and not to do anything [at home], for there are people to do the work for me. Well, bad is my "ladyship" now. When you come, then I shall be a lady [do no housework]. But now grandmothers want to be ladies. Well, my mother may be excused sometimes, for she is right when she complains that [your mother] does not want to help her to do anything in the kitchen.[15] When we drink tea in the evening your mother takes her own pot and washes it, but leaves the glasses from which I and the children drank. And it is always so. I don't say anything until you come back; let all this go on, for it is near than farther [nearer to the end than to the beginning]. And she always holds up her nose saying that she gave her money here, that she is not here from pity. If there is sometimes something worse at dinner, they all know how to be squeamish—the children, particularly Janek and Oleś, and your mother also lets her nose fall. I don't wonder at

---

[14] The attitude of the peasant woman on this point is even more extreme. Not only is the idea of medical inspection revolting, but she would not venture to write of it to her husband.

[15] Both the grandmothers are kept in the home, the wife's in return for doing the housework, and the husband's in return for money lent. The latter, therefore, does not feel obliged to help with the work.

the children . . . but your mother wants to be a lady. Now she does not know herself how to walk [she is so proud]. If you were at home you would laugh. And she always reproaches us about this money, saying that we have risen to our feet for her money. And she says that she ought to have interest on these 300 roubles. And she does not like to be with us; she wants only to have those 300 roubles back, and she does not know herself how to tear this money away. For once she said that Tomaszewski wanted her to lend him 300 roubles and promised her to take her to his home. Then again she said that Antek wants to borrow this money and will give a big interest. But I say so: I won't lend until you come back, and then it will be as you do. And she is tired of staying with us, she wants to go to Józef. She was always calling on Kasia, until once they almost fought about this money. For she [your mother] said that she had lost her money. And she [Kasia] said: "Where do you have your money? Why have you given me nothing?" And so always. Once she began to reproach me about this money, and I told her to be silent, when you come, you will give her these 300 roubles back and let her go wherever she will be better off. And she said: "What does it matter if I have 300 roubles? And where is my interest?" And she said that you went to America on her money, and that money makes money.[16] And thus, dear husband. But she has got calmer since I told her that you will pay her back and now she says nothing, only that if she doesn't stay with us she will go to Józef.

[16] She gets her living instead of interest and this is three or four times as much as the money would bring in cash. But the mother retains the attitude of the peasant, with whom the lending of money is not considered as a purely economic investment but as a personal help to be subjectively appreciated.

Only I beg you very much, don't be angry, for I write to you as to my husband, for I have nobody to talk to. [Four pages about Oleś' apprenticeship in a jeweler's shop.]

Marcyanna Jabłkowska

August 28, 1914
648

Dearest and most beloved Husband: . . . I thank you once more [for the letters] for I don't know what will be our further destiny. Perhaps because of this trouble [war] it will be difficult to get even a letter. But nothing can be done, we must comply with God's will, we must bear steadfastly everything. Pray to God that He may keep us all in good health, and you, my dear husband, remember about your health and be steadfast, don't grieve about us. Why, we are not alone, whatever happens to everybody else here will happen also to us. And I write you once more and beg you, dear husband, don't grieve, that you may not fall sick, for you know very well that I want to see you, and the children want it also. Yes, my dear husband, pray only to the Holiest Mother to care for us and to defend us, and don't grieve so, dear husband. For when I received the postcard with your last farewell, I fell upon my knees before the image of God's Mother and, crying, I prayed to God and to God's Mother to guard you from any misfortune, as well as our children and our parents. And you see that up to the present God keeps us in His care and in health, so He won't leave us further on. Dear husband, be steadfast and work happily with God, and care for yourself and don't forget us. . . . And I beg you, dear husband, don't send any money at all . . . although I wrote you in my preceding letter for money. . . . Now I receive a few roubles from the bank every week. . . . I have taken already 40 roubles. Yes, dear husband, there is no work, and living must be bought. . . . If we had no money in the bank, we should perhaps die from hunger, for it would be impossible even to borrow. . . . Our bad enemies rejoiced [thinking] that when there is no work and I take the money from the bank they would come surely and rob me of the money. But I went to the cashier and asked him what to do, whether I should take money from the bank. But he reprimanded me and said, God forbid me to take money, for some misfortune might befall me. He said that the money in the bank will never be lost. . . . So I write you, dear husband, don't grieve about our money, for not we alone have those few hundred roubles. People from the high sphere have thousands and they don't get it all, only a few roubles at once. . . . So don't send me any money, put it into the bank, don't keep it with you, so that somebody may not take it. And keep the bank book carefully. Care for your labor's fruit, dear husband, for you work

hard. . . . Don't be angry with me, dear husband, for not sending you any money-accounts, but I have not a calm head. . . . And if sometimes letters don't reach you and you have no news from us, I beg you for God's sake, don't grieve, only pray to God for patience and health, and I must be patient here also with our children. . . . Goodbye, my dear and beloved husband. Be calm about us, I beg you very much, dear husband. Don't lose your courage, comply with God's will, and I and our children we must also comply with God's will, since we have lived to see such things.[17] I kiss you and I press you in my embrace, and I kiss your face, the dearest one for me. And once more I kiss you heartily, my dear husband.

> Your wife, always well-wishing
> and loving you,
> Marcyanna Jabłkowska

[17] Compare the fortitude of this letter with that in Starkiewicz series, No. 525, Kluch series, No. 532, and Porzycki series, No. 627.

MORRIS ZELDITCH, JR.
Role Differentiation in the Nuclear Family: A Comparative Study

The Generic Significance of Nuclear Family Structure

The nuclear family in our society has a particular pattern of roles which we

Reprinted in part with permission of the publisher from Talcott Parsons and Robert F. Bales, *Family, Socialization and Interaction Process*, copyright 1955 by The Free Press, a corporation, pp. 308–10, 312–20, 327–36, 338–40, 341–42.

now suggest has a *generic* significance. There is, in other words, an underlying structural uniformity which gives a baseline for the analysis of the range of variation usually noted.

A statement of this sort, of course, can be only hypothetical at this point. It is the purpose of this paper, however, to indicate that it is not *only* hypothetical. On what basis can we argue that this uniformity occurs? . . . We argue, for instance, that it is essentially fruitful to consider the nuclear family as a special case of a small group, and that the mode of differentiation observed in small groups has a generic significance which extends to any of its special cases. . . .

More generally, a nuclear family is a social system, and the peculiar attributes which distinguish it from other systems (its particular age-sex structure and primary function, for instance) should be examined *within* this more general context. All groups are subject to certain imposed *conditions* of existence; not that all groups exist, but that all groups that *do* exist meet these conditions. If we assume the existence of a nuclear family, therefore, we must inquire into the conditions of its existence. And certain of these conditions are common to all groups, appearing in such diverse forms as Bales's experimental groups and the family pattern of peasant Ireland.

Directions of Differentiation in the Nuclear Family

Among the conditions of a system's existence is at least a certain degree of differentiation along lines imposed by the orbits of the system's movement. Consider first the general pattern of differentiation which in broad outline appears from the experimental small group. There is a tendency for a *task leader* and a *sociometric star* to appear. Although there is some problem in clearly isolating the complex factors defining the task leader he seems to be associated with certain *behaviors* (in general terms, "task" behaviors; more specifically in giving suggestions, directions, opinions), and certain *attitudes* (involving, apparently, an inhibition of emotions and the ability to accept hostile reactions from others in the process of pressing a point, etc.).

There are also, of course, reciprocal behaviors and attitudes on the part of other system-members towards the task leader. The sociometric star, although the term originally derives from attitudes taken toward ego by alters, also tends to show a certain pattern of behaviors and attitudes; namely, the *expression* of emotions, supportive behavior to others, the desire to please and be liked, and a more generalized liking for other members. The star may, of course, express negative reactions as well as positive supports; typically these are significant in releasing negative reactions (often through humor) of the group as a whole, reducing, in consequence, the general tension level. (The difference between a "leader," here, and one who fails to become a leader may very well lie, in part, in the capacity to express reactions felt by the group as a *whole*.)

From a general theoretical point of view this is *not* a fortuitous pattern of differentiation; it defines, in fact, the two basic conditions of the existence of a social system. In order to clarify and illustrate what we mean by this, we may take the nuclear family as a specific case; . . .

A considerable refinement is involved in the further differentiation of the structure of *roles* in the system. . . .

Why after all, are *two* parents necessary? For one thing, to be a stable focus of integration, the integrative-expressive "leader" can't be off on adaptive-instrumental errands all the time. For another, a stable, secure attitude of members depends, it can be assumed, on a *clear* structure being given to the situation so that an *uncertain* responsibility for emotional warmth, for instance, raises significant problems for the stability of the system. And an uncertain managerial responsibility, an unclear definition of authority for decisions and for getting things done, is also clearly a threat to the stability of the system.

We can say, then, that the system must differentiate behaviors and attitudes in order to continue to exist as a system; and that a further condition of stability is also that some specialization occur in responsibility for the attitudes and behaviors involved.

Age and Sex in the Nuclear Family

We actually want to examine two things in this paper. One is related to the generic significance of a certain pattern of differentiation. The relevant role-system, however, is indeterminate with respect to allocation when taken at this level. It is necessary to consider the nuclear family as a type of group peculiarly structured around age-sex differences in order to arrive at a hypothesis concerning who plays the instrumental and expressive roles.

Now any system, it should be noticed first, has a problem often considered peculiar to families, that is the processing of new recruits. While the "barbarian invasion" may be considered of special significance for the family, and thus to impose special conditions on its existence, the problem is in fact generic to all systems. Thus the family resembles other groups in this respect as well as in the more general terms discussed so far. What differs, and the difference is of crucial structural significance, is the age-sex matrix of the family, and with it the situational reference points for the allocation of *facilities* in the performance of roles. At the grossest level of analysis, for instance, the father is stronger than the son, so that he, rather than the son,

is allocated to leadership roles in instrumental activities. . . .

At least one fundamental feature of the external situation of social systems—here a feature of the physiological organism—is a crucial reference point for differentiation in the family. This lies in the division of organisms into lactating and nonlactating classes. Only in our own society (so far as I know, that is) have we managed to invent successful bottle-feeding, and this is undoubtedly of importance for our social structure. In other societies necessarily—and in our own for structural reasons which have *not* disappeared with the advent of the bottle—the initial core relation of a family with children is the mother-child attachment. And it follows from the principles of learning that the gradient of generalization should establish "mother" as the focus of gratification in a diffuse sense, as the source of "security" and "comfort." She is the focus of warmth and stability. Thus, because of her special initial relation to the child, "mother" is the more 'likely expressive focus of the system as a whole.

The allocation of the instrumental leadership to the husband-father rests on two aspects of this role. The role involves, first, a manipulation of the external environment, and consequently a good deal of physical mobility. The concentration of the mother on the child precludes a *primacy* of her attention in this direction although she always performs *some* instrumental tasks. In addition to the managerial aspects of the role there are certain discipline and control functions of the father role. . . .

We may summarize the hypothesis we have stated then, in this way. Because the nuclear family is a special case of the more general class of social systems, and because it must meet certain conditions of existence common to all social systems, we suggest that:

1. If the nuclear family constitutes a social system stable over time, it will differentiate roles such that instrumental leadership and expressive leadership of the system are discriminated.

Because the nuclear family, on the other hand, has certain peculiar features not common to all systems, we are further able to state a certain hypothesis about the *allocation* of these roles to system-members. This peculiar feature is the age-sex matrix of the nuclear family and the differential distribution of facilities for the performance of the fundamental roles. We suggest that:

2. If the nuclear family consists in a defined "normal" complement of the male adult, female adult and their immediate children, the male adult will play the role of instrumental leader and the female adult will play the role of expressive leader.

Choosing a Sample

Two courses are open in making some sort of test of the hypotheses that have been stated. A careful and refined analysis of a few societies, made from the best of the ethnographic reports available, is from many points of view the best approach to take. There is some point, however, in sacrificing both a great deal of information and the more refined aspects of analysis, for a simple replication of cases. In this paper, at any rate, the second approach is taken.

Having made this initial decision, an attempt was made to take a random sample of some sort. This is a particularly difficult procedure with cross-cultural studies. In the first place, the universe one would *like* to use actually falls into two strata, all those societies reported by ethnographers and all those societies not reported. Societies belonging to the second of these strata are immediately excluded, and there is no basis of judging with what confidence inferences can be made from available reports to the entire universe of cases.

The effective universe on which the propositions can be tested, then, is reduced to available reports. In this, as in any case of sampling, significant bias can enter simply by a failure to make an adequate *listing* of the universe from which the sample is chosen. The list for the sample used here was compiled from several sources. G. P. Murdock's bibliography, R. H. Lowie's bibliography, and some additional materials available in the Widener and Peabody Museum libraries at Harvard were the chief listing sources. It is doubtful, of course, that this produced a complete listing.

From this list, nevertheless, about 75 "societies" were selected for examination. From these 75 cases a final sample was chosen according to the following rules:

1. The sample should be random, or failing this, systematic bias should be minimized.
2. Sample units should be independent; i.e., the duplication of cases should be minimized. Because two groups have different names does not mean they are independent cases.
3. If information is incomplete, this will be proper grounds for exclusion from the sample. Information is incomplete where there is insufficient evidence *either for or against* the hypothesis tested.

In the final sample of 56 cases perfect randomness may have failed for two reasons: first, the differential availability of monographs; and, second, the operation of the rule for exclusion. Certain societies were omitted merely because they were more difficult to gather material on than others. These societies failed to get into the list of 75 in the first place. Conversely, certain societies were included in the list of 75 simply because they were readily available. Although these factors, in a certain sense, destroy the original design of the sample, there is no reason to suppose that the bias is systematic; i.e., that only negative cases were excluded, or that more than a proportionate share of negative cases were excluded.

Perfect independence is difficult to achieve because of the problems involved in drawing the lines between cases. This is a serious difficulty, since, having sacrificed refinement, the soundness of the test more or less rests on the numbers involved, and these numbers should not be spurious. Generally, if Murdock included both of two questioned cases in his sample, they were treated as independent; but Murdock's sample is itself open to question on this ground. A check was made with other sources; nevertheless judgments are difficult to make. In at least one case of possible duplication both cases were kept because both were negative (Cheyenne and Arapaho).

The cases excluded because of insufficient information were generally patrilineal societies, with strong authority vested in the males, but no clear picture of the role of the "mother." Certain matrilineal societies, in relatively brief reports, show a similar "bias" in reporting; strong authority vested in males of the matrilineage is reported without clear evidence of the role of the "mothers" and "sisters"; or in some cases the role of the females of the matrilineage is discussed, but not in their own nuclear family, violating the boundaries of the specific universe for the test. Thus no clear rating could be made.

It should be noted, finally, that it was taken as a policy decision of some importance, for this paper, that all ethnographic reports would be accepted as accurate. This is not "epistemological realism," it is merely that to question one is to question all. It is for this reason, in fact, that a crude analysis depending for its significance primarily on replication was made at all.

Designation Rules for the Rating of the Cases

Unfortunately, perhaps, the character of the indices used was determined by fortuitous circumstances of the test. The fact that the test was made on already digested material observed by many different investigators using widely varying categories makes a number of indirect indices inevitable, and certain ambiguities unavoidable. The most important operations, of course, should specify the direct designation rules for instrumental and expressive leadership; this is in terms of the patterns of *action* of the role-incumbents. But these can only be interpreted from the *statements* of the ethnographer. It is necessary, therefore, to set up the rules for designation in terms of the statements which will satisfy the theoretical categories involved. These basic categories involve, first, direct responsibility for the solution of group tasks, for the skills and information prerequisite to the role in its adaptive aspects, and for the authority required to make binding managerial decisions; and associated with this "managerial" complex the primary responsibility for discipline and "training" of children. Second, they include responsibility for maintenance of solidarity and management of tensions, for the skills prerequisite to this role, and associated with this "integrative-expressive" complex, the primary responsibility for "care" and emotional support of children.

Ego, therefore, will be considered *instrumental* leader of the nuclear family if the ethnographer's report offers statements of the form:

1. Ego is boss-manager of the farm; leader of the hunt, etc. Ego is the final court of appeals, final judge and executor of punishment, discipline, and control over the children of the family.

Ego will be considered *expressive* leader of the nuclear family if the ethnographer's report offers statements of the form:

2. Ego is the mediator, conciliator, of the family; ego soothes over disputes, resolves hostilities in the family. Ego is affectionate, solicitous, warm, emotional to the children of the family; ego is the "comforter," the "consoler," is relatively indulgent, relatively unpunishing.

The actual performance of the role, however, is often difficult to obtain. It is necessary, therefore, to admit certain indices which are related to the hypotheses by propositions not proved within the test-system itself.

The first set of indirect indices is based on the attitude of *alter* if ego plays the instrumental or expressive roles. If, for instance, ego plays an instrumental role, alter will (it is assumed) displace part of the antagonisms of the action process on ego. In order to preserve the family from disruption, however, alter will (it is assumed) be expected to restrain expression of antagonism, and instead will show "respect." This will be accompanied by a feeling of constraint, reserve, or some form of psychological distance between ego and alter. Or alternatively, one may phrase this as an element of "neutrality" (an inhibition of emotions) in the relation of ego and alter.

Ego will be considered as instrumental leader of the nuclear family, therefore, if the ethnographer's report offers statements of the form:

3. Alter shows respect to ego; the relations of ego and alter are constrained, reserved; alter on occasions indicates hostility toward ego.

If, on the other hand, ego plays an expressive role, alter will be more at ease in ego's presence, show attachment, "love," or in general ego will be the "sociometric star" of the family. Alternatively, one may phrase this as an element of "affectivity" in the relation of ego and alter.

Ego, therefore, will be considered *expressive* leader of the nuclear family if the ethnographer's report offers statements of the form:

4. Alter is at ease in ego's presence, emotionally attached to ego, is close and warm in relation to ego.

A second form of indirect index rests on the phenomenon of classificatory "extension" of kinship behavior. On the principle of the solidarity of siblings (which is, of course, not a "law," but one possible structural focus of kin systems) the attitudes to, and behavior of, father's siblings and of mother's siblings constitute extensions of the attitude toward, and behavior of, father and mother. Obviously, where the principle is *not* a structural feature of the system, e.g., in the bilateral case, the index cannot be used. Similarly in matrilineal systems, where mother's brother *is* differentiated in role from mother, the extension index again cannot be used.

Terminological equation is normally taken to indicate classificatory extension of behavior and attitudes; that is, if mother's brother is called "male-mother" the content of the two roles will be assumed equivalent, and similarly if father's sister is called "female-father." If, however, other evidence is available that this type of kinship equation is made, the same assumption of extension will be allowed.

Ego, therefore, will be considered *instrumental* leader of the nuclear family if the ethnographer's report offers statements of the form:

5. Ego's siblings are equated in status and role with ego, and play an instrumental role with respect to ego's children; e.g., father's sister is treated with respect, and is called "female-father."

Similarly, ego will be considered *expressive* leader of the nuclear family if the ethnographer's report offers statements of the form:

6. Ego's siblings are equated in status and role with ego and play an expressive role with respect to ego's children; e.g., mother's sister is terminologically a "mother" and is warm, indulgent, close. Or mother's brother is termed "male-mother" and is warm, indulgent, etc.

A General Test for Differentiation

The testing of the hypotheses is broken into two parts. At this point we wish only to test for the general *presence* of differentiation, and for the *directions* of this differentiation. But nothing is implied about the allocation of roles to concrete persons in the family. From the present point of view it makes no difference if a newborn baby is the instrumental leader and his elder sister the expressive leader, the theorems involved will still hold. The first theorem may be stated as follows:

1. If the nuclear family constitutes a social system stable over time, it will differentiate roles such that instrumental leadership and expressive leadership of the system are discriminated.

If we call those cases which are differentiated in the specified directions "*D*," and those negative for differentiation "*not-D*" the following results are indicated: [1]

D	Not-*D*
46	10

While these numbers appear reasonably significant, something of interest might be discovered from an analysis of negative cases. We would, certainly, be interested to discover if any systematic principle explains the negative cases. . . .

[In the passages omitted, Zelditch starts to examine all of these 10 societies which do not fit his hypothesis of role-differentiation within the nuclear family. Part of his analysis of one of these "negative" cases appears below.]

Malinowski and the Matrilineal Case

. . . The kinship structure of the Trobriand Islands is matrilineal; that is, when a child is born he is assigned to membership in a corporate group to which his

---

[1] If we assume the sample taken approaches randomness within the limitations of the universe and expect, by the null hypothesis, a chance variation, this difference is significant by a chi square test at better than the 1 per cent level.

mother belongs, and to which his father does not belong. This group is formed on the basis of actual or presumed descent in the female line. It is characteristic of such systems that, where the solidarity with the larger kinship grouping takes precedence over the solidarity of the nuclear family—where, that is, the obligations to members of the matrilineage are presumed to override obligations to members of the nuclear family—some member of the matrilineage has significant rights in authority over the members of the nuclear family. This is ordinarily formulated in the role of the "mother's brother." Entailed in this authority, of course, are also significant responsibilities.

In the Trobriands a significant part of a male's productive activity goes *not* to the maintenance of the nuclear family of which, by definition, he is a member, but rather to the nuclear family of his *sister*. In other words the role entails certain obligations of instrumental support, *not* to the system formed of himself, his wife, and his children, but to members of a "stronger" solidary group. . . . The male also assumes the functions of discipline and control over his *sister's* son. With his own child, "father" is a friend and companion. What authority he holds lies in the sentiment-system the child organizes about this affectionate relationship. . . .

What Malinowski suggests, therefore . . . is that there is an entire *class* of cases which do not fit the hypothesis we have stated; and that furthermore it is a variation in descent grouping which explains these cases.

If this is true, a number of propositions follow. First a significant proportion of our negative cases, Malinowski implies, can be accounted for by the operation of one basic principle. And it is true that half of the negative cases are matrilineal cases.

We might expect also, however, that if we were to partition out all matrilineal cases from our sample the number of proportionate negative cases for Malinowski's hypothesis should be at least no greater than the number of proportionate negative cases for our own hypothesis. (This merely states that we expect all matrilineal cases to show *both* father and mother expressive, but allow a certain "slippage" by comparing this sub-sample with the main sample.)

We may use the same designations, reverse what we take as a positive case, and examine the results for matrilineal cases alone.

Not-*D*	*D*
5	14

It is clear that Malinowski's hypothesis does not hold. We must now, however, follow the problem further and ask, just what explains the failure of Malinowski's hypothesis to hold.

The Husband-Father in Matrilineal Systems

The problem of the matrilineal case arises not so much from a failure of our differentiation hypothesis to hold for the nuclear family, but from a problem in the relations of nuclear families to the groups in which they are incorporated. Where the solidarity of the matrilineal descent group takes precedence over the solidarity of the nuclear family a problem arises which makes the matrilineal system particularly difficult to interpret. It is essential to note first that mother and father do not simply exchange roles (as we shall indicate when we test for allocation). The nuclear family in the matrilineage, that is, is not simply a mirror image of the nuclear family in a patrilineage. Mother does not take an instrumental role, *either* in matrilineal or patrilineal systems. The problem, rather, is who shall have greater authority and greater responsibility for the mother and children, the father as a member of the nuclear family or the mother's brother representing the matrilineage. . . . The basic point is that the problem is one of the relation of the *nuclear family as a system* to the *matrilineage as a system;* so that there is not so much a problem of differentiation in the stated directions within the first system, but rather of the relation of two levels of system reference. . . .

A breakdown of the instrumental role into "provision" and "socialization" functions is particularly illuminating at this point. For the case of the Trobriands is almost . . . unique. . . . Of 19 matrilineal cases *only* in the Trobriands does the husband-father "provide" regularly for his *sister's* family; even there this is not entirely the case. In other words, in *both* the matrilineal case and the supposedly more patripotestal patrilineal case, the husband-father is generally held responsible for the support of his *own* wife and children.

A further breakdown of the relative instrumental authority of father and mother's brother in the socialization context is also revealing. . . .

The crux of this pattern is a relation between *two systems,* the household group and the descent group; it is *not* a question of who, *in the nuclear family,* will play the instrumental role. The mother's brother holds the position of authority in the descent group, but the father controls the domestic household. The relative distribution of instrumental responsibilities of the two from case to case may be expected to vary with the relative degree of incorporation of each in the household group on the one hand, the matrilineage on the other. . . .

The mother's brother, however, is not a constituent member of the nuclear family. And the father generally, *relative to the wife-mother,* plays a distinctly instrumental role in almost all cases. Where the nuclear family is subordinate to the matrilineage, the father is, clearly, subordinate in authority over his wife and children to the mother's brother as representative of the matrilineage. And the more significant the role of the mother's brother as an authority figure, the more the father is freed from any restraint and inhibition in his relation to his own children. But relative to his wife, and *more* significantly to the degree that the mother's brother is *less* significant, the father plays the role both of provider for the family and of authority in socialization.

The Allocation of Roles in the Nuclear Family

Although a great deal has been said about the role of mother and father in the discussion of matrilineal systems, in point of fact only the *presence* of differentiation, and not the allocation of roles to system members, was at stake up to this point. It could quite easily have turned out that mother took the instrumental role, on the basis of her position as a representative of the matrilineage, and the hypothesis being tested would still have held. . . .

The "matriarch" of a matrilineal system, however, is *not* primarily an instrumental figure. In most matrilineal societies women have high status; and in many they have great influence. We may compare, however, the "Virgin Mary" in patrilineal imagery, and the "behind the scenes" influence of the woman who "really runs things" or "really holds the family together" in the "patripotestal" case. One is as likely to find an "old matriarch" in the one case as in the other. In both matrilineal and patrilineal societies, the "influence" of women seems to rest on their role as integrative focus of the family rather than on instrumental control. . . . A test for the instrumental leadership of mother in matrilineal cases, independent of the test for mother's brother or father, indicates the following, where "*E*" designates expressive leadership and "*I*" instrumental leadership in the nuclear family:

E	*I*
19	0

Clearly, the effect of focus on mother's descent group does *not* reverse the allocation of roles in the nuclear family. The entire problem of interpreting the allocation of instrumental leadership in matrilineal societies, therefore, rests in the relation of father and mother's brother, as we have already shown; and the crux of *this* problem is the relation of two systems (the nuclear family and the descent group) to each other and their relative solidarity.

If we are to look for cases which are negative for the allocation of roles according to the hypothesis we have stated, it is apparent that we must investigate not the matrilineal, but the patrilineal, bilateral, and dual descent cases in the remaining portion of our sample. Any new negative cases that might be added will be found in this portion of the sample, since, in effect, we have already treated allocation in the matrilineal case.

The sample includes 37 patrilineal, bilateral, and dual descent cases. In patrilineal societies we would expect that the father would take the instrumental role, *either* on the basis of the hypothesis we first stated, or on the basis of his role as representative of the descent group to which both he and his children belong. . . . The father should, we expect, play the role of instrumental leader in the nuclear family simply because of the character of the nuclear family as a system. Clearly, we assume that the mother plays the role of expressive leader on grounds already stated. If we use the designations "*A*" and "not-*A*", the "patripotestal" sample divides as follows:

A	Not-*A*
29	8

[Here Zelditch examines the eight cases which do not fit his hypothesis of role allocation.]

Summary and Conclusions

While rather significant conclusions can be drawn, the crudeness of the method of verifying them makes them rather difficult to evaluate. This should be carefully considered in accepting the conclusions of the tests. In at least half of the cases, for instance, if "respect" and "affection" do not in fact indicate instrumental and expressive leadership (i.e., as defined in terms of actions of ego), then the hypotheses cannot be legitimately considered "proved" *or* "disproved." This chance was taken on the grounds that, having sacrificed the method of intensive analysis in the original conditions of the design, extensive replication was necessary. This demands numbers; and the number of monographs which provide evidence on the basis of direct designation rules is limited. Differences in rating might also be considered; although it may fairly be said for the differentiation hypothesis, at least, that the number of negative cases could have been increased by the equivocal cases finally judged positive and the hypothesis would still have held. The chief equivocal cases were the Lozi and the American middle-class family, which some raters might have treated as negative.

We may, as a matter of fact, consider the American middle-class case in reviewing the definitions we have given to instrumental and expressive leadership. From certain points of view the American middle-class family approaches most clearly to equal allocation (or "no allocation") of instrumental and expressive activities. The universalistic value schema (in which women are "just as good as" men) coupled with the general attitude toward the explicit expression of authority ("I'm agin it") apparently constitutes the limiting case of no differentiation at all. Underlying this broad value-schema, however, a rather clear differentiation occurs.

In the distribution of instrumental tasks, the American family maintains a more flexible pattern than most societies. Father helps mother with the dishes. He sets the table. He makes formula for the baby. Mother can supplement the income of the family by working outside. Nevertheless, the American male, by definition, *must* "provide" for his family. He is *responsible* for the support of his wife and children. His primary area of performance is the occupational role, in which his status fundamentally inheres; and his *primary* function in the family is to supply an "income," to be the "breadwinner." There is simply something wrong with the American adult male who doesn't have a "job." American women, on the other hand, tend to hold jobs *before* they are married and to quit when "the day" comes; or to continue in jobs of a lower status than their husbands. And not only is the mother the focus of emotional support for the American middle-class child, but much more exclusively so than in most societies (as Margaret Mead has pointed out in her treatment of adolescent problems). The cult of the warm, giving "Mom" stands in contrast to the "capable," "competent," "go-getting" male. The more expressive type of male, as a matter of fact, is regarded as "effeminate," and has too much fat on the inner side of his thigh.

The distribution of authority is legitimized on a different basis in the "democratic" family than in the so-called "traditional" one; but the father is "supposed" to remain the primary executive member. The image of the "henpecked" husband makes sense only on this premise. His "commands" are validated on the basis of "good judgment," rather than *general* obedience due a person in authority. But when the mother's efforts at "disciplining" fail, she traditionally tells the errant child, "Wait till daddy gets home."

In generalizing this pattern of instrumental leadership focused on the achievement of tasks and expressive leadership focused on emotionally supportive behaviors, the most difficult problem of interpretation lies in clearly distinguishing the nuclear family from the descent groups which in some cases took precedence as solidarities over them. . . .

On the whole, therefore, when the nuclear family can be clearly distinguished from incorporating solidarities, it differentiates in the direction expected and allocates the relevant roles to the persons expected. And the problems which are raised in interpreting the data do not arise so much from whether or not this is true, but rather from what effect the precedence of obligations to corporate descent groups may have. This becomes, stated in a general form, a problem of the relative authority of the husband-father compared to that of some person in the superordinate descent group; where this descent group is matrilineal, the problem is one of the relative authority of father vs. mother's brother. The effect on patrilineal systems is to confine the difficulties in this relationship *within* the corporate descent group; and eventually the husband-father achieves a role of dominance in the descent group as well as the nuclear family. The effect in matrilineal systems is different, since the father can never become a member of the matrilineage. He must validate his position through his contribution to the everyday life of the household group, and his position is much less stable. In a great many cases, nevertheless, he *does* become the significant instrumental figure in the household group; and *always,* relative to *mother,* this is the case. From the point of view of his legal status in the system, he is at the same time freed from certain obligations to his own family and denied certain rights in control of his own family; from the point of view of the general conditions for the existence of social systems as systems, however, he *must* accept some of these obligations and be allowed certain of these rights.

PITIRIM A. SOROKIN
Fluctuation of Ideational, Idealistic, and Sensate Systems of Truth and Knowledge

I. Ideational, Idealistic, and Sensate Systems of Truth

From Art we pass now to the next fundamental "compartment" of culture— to its *System of Truth and Knowledge.* This system, in integrated or unintegrated form, is embodied in what is loosely styled *Religious, Philosophical, and Scientific Thought* of a given culture.

In the study of the categories of Truth and Knowledge, we shall employ a method similar to that used in the study

Reprinted from Pitirim A. Sorokin, *Social and Cultural Dynamics,* New York: American Book Company, *II,* 1937, pp. 3–7, 12–24, 27, 31–36, 38–39, 41–51, 53–55, 60. (Some revisions and abridgements were made by the author for the one-volume edition published by Porter Sargent, 1957.) Reprinted with permission of the Bedminster Press.

of the forms of art in Volume One. What are the main systems of truth and knowledge? Are the categories Ideational, Idealistic, and Sensate applicable to truth generally? If they are, what are the meanings of Ideational, Idealistic, and Sensate systems of truth and knowledge? What are the important characteristics of each of these systems of truth? Are such systems actually given in the historically existing cultures? Do they fluctuate in their domination in the life history of culture generally and of the cultures studied here specifically? If so, which have been the periods in the history of the Graeco-Roman and the Western cultures when each of these systems of truth dominated? How does the fluctuation of the system of truth reflect upon hundreds of various general and special theories? . . .

We should expect that in predominantly Ideational culture the dominant system of truth must be mainly "revelation" (the religious or magical system of truth) in a supersensory and even super-logical way "revealed," "granted," "inspired" by superempirical agency or power or source, be it personal or impersonal. Based upon the revealed truth of God, absolute, perfect, and omniscient, the truth is also believed to be absolutely certain in its validity.

In a Sensate society and culture the Sensate system of truth based upon the testimony of the organs of senses has to be dominant. Since for the bearers of a Sensate mentality and culture there is no reality behind and except the sensory reality of Becoming; and since this sensory reality is "signaled" to us through our organs of senses, through what we see, touch, hear, etc., these senses must become the main and almost the only judges of what is true and what is false. If we see or hear a given empirical phenomenon in exactly the same way in which it is described by a given theory, the theory is valid and "scientific." If the testimony of these organs contradicts it, the theory is wrong and "unscientific."

If now we consider the Idealistic mentality and culture, its underlying system of truth must be one between the supersensory revelation and sensory evidence; one in which both these systems are organically united. The system of truth which meets these requirements is the truth of human reason and logic, the *idealistically rationalistic system of truth of the medieval Scholastics* of the twelfth to the fourteenth centuries. In that system the main judge is human reason and logic itself with its own laws of the true and false. This judge, however, is not reluctant to hear the testimony of the organs of senses and is willing to use their information to transform it and to sanction it as true, and is also not reluctant to accept the truth of revelation when it appears to be reasonable and reconcilable with the logical laws of the human mind

which itself, in a sense, has a vein of divine nature.

The other "Mixed" mentalities and cultures require also a combination of truth of faith and of truth of senses, but the mixture is not necessarily a consistent synthesis, since these "mixed" mentalities are not integrated internally. The truth of faith and of senses may coexist mechanically, undigested and unintegrated. Finally, in the *passive and cynical forms of Sensate mentality,* the *system of skepticism, incapable of believing in any system of truth,* is by deduction the one most consistent with such a mentality and culture. Likewise, for the *Ideationalists of despair* the most consistent system of truth must be one "of a desperate will to believe" by those who, like Apostle Thomas, wish to but cannot believe without great difficulty.

From the very nature of each of these main systems of truth and knowledge several further characteristics follow. Their subject matter as well as the method of verification of any statement about the subject matter has to be profoundly different in each of these systems. . . .

Since Science and its system of truth are to be supreme in the Sensate and secondary in the Ideational society, it can be expected that Ideational cultures and periods are to be marked by fewer important scientific discoveries; and since the mentality of Ideational culture is turned away from the world of senses toward the ultimate reality of everlasting Being, it is neither interested in an investigation of this empirical world nor in making various scientific (that is empirico-Sensate) discoveries concerning it.

In Sensate periods the situation must be reversed for the same reasons. Sensate mentality turns to the Sensate reality and is eager to study it, and either does not recognize any other reality or is not interested in it. For these reasons it is to be expected that such periods and cultures are to be marked by comparatively greater progress in science, scientific discoveries, and technological inventions in the field of the natural and technological sciences. . . .

It can also be expected that even within the scientific system of truth of senses the main topics which would be worked out in Sensate and Ideational cultures would also considerably differ. The "scientists" of Ideational cultures are likely to concentrate their attention on one group of Sensate phenomena as the most important, while scientists of Sensate culture may find these problems unimportant and may concentrate on another class of phenomena having little interest for the scientists of Ideational culture.

The above expectations and inferences mean, if they are valid, that even such primordial values as truth and knowledge, so far as their content, criteria, and evidences are concerned, in sociocultural actuality (but not in Plato's world of ideas) depend greatly upon the type of culture of which they are a part. In other words, what appears to be true and what is not, what appears to be scientific and what is not, what is a valid criterion of truth and what is not, are, in the statistico-mathematical language, in a considerable degree a "function" of the sociocultural variable. If this be found valid, then the sociologist should have his say also in the problems of epistemology and logic, in so far as there is a place—and a large one—for what the Germans call *Wissenssoziologie*. Adequately understood, it composes one of the most important parts of sociology of culture.

Let us turn now to an empirical verification of these deductions. If the cultures studied are logically integrated, it will be found that these deductions are corroborated by the empirical data. . . .

II. Fluctuation of the Main Systems of Truth: Empiricism, Religious and Idealistic Rationalism, Mysticism, Skepticism, Fideism . . .

1. METHODOLOGICAL AND EXPLANATORY PRELIMINARIES

We plan to study now the quantitative fluctuations of the comparative influence and acceptability of the main systems of truth during some twenty-five hundred years. . . . The purpose of the study of this fluctuation is not to discuss the truth or error of the main systems of truth, nor is it to take sides concerning them. My objective is very different. Assuming the position of a perfectly impartial observer, and taking the systems involved as the factual datum, I am going to inquire whether in the life history of the Graeco-Roman and Western cultures the comparative influence and popularity of each of these systems of truth have been constant or variable in the mentality of the *leading thinkers* in the field. If variable, has there been in the course of time a linear trend of continuous increase in the influence and acceptance of one of these systems at the expense of the others, or has such a trend been absent? If such a trend exists, then what is its nature or, to use favorite terms of the nineteenth century, what has been its line of "progress" or its "historical tendency"? Has its direction been one of greater and better truth of faith, of reason, or of senses? If there be no such linear trend, then how have the rise and fall of these currents fluctuated? Have there been definite "cycles" and "periodicities" in these fluctuations, or only nonperiodic "ups and downs" of each of these currents, without any uniform tempo and rhythm? If the same themes recur, but each time with new variations, then is it possible to indicate with reasonable accuracy at which periods from about 580 B.C. to A.D. 1920 each of these systems of truth rose and declined, and to what extent? Finally, if the preceding questions are answered, what are the reasons (or the "causes" and "factors") [for] such fluctuations?

2. RESERVATIONS AND QUALIFICATIONS

A. The fluctuations of the influence of the truth of faith, of reason, and of senses are studied only within the Graeco-Roman and Western cultures, from about 580 B.C. up to A.D. 1920.

B. The study roughly estimates the increase and decrease of the comparative acceptability and influence of each of these currents of thought, as they are represented, first, by the *number* of their partisans among the majority of prominent thinkers in the field, in each twenty-year period, and in each one-hundred-year period from 580 B.C. to A.D. 1920; second, by the comparative "weight" or influence of these partisans in each of these periods.

Practically all the names of the great thinkers in the field of this problem were selected. For the last three or four centuries, when the number of scholars increased greatly, only the names of the most prominent philosophers and scientists who contributed to the problem were included. But the samples are so large that in all probability they are representative for these centuries. In this way Table 1 ... and Figure 1 are based upon material far larger than any study of this problem hitherto made.

Respectively, two sets of data were computed. First, for each period, was computed the number of partisans to each of these currents among the total number of thinkers in the field, in that period, whose names are preserved in the annals of history. Turned into percentages, these numbers indicate the main changes in the comparative strength of each current from period to period, as manifested by changes in the number and percentage of its partisans. Second, for each period, data are given concerning the *comparative weight or influence* of each current in each period among the same group of thinkers; whereas, from the point of view of the number of partisans in each period, each of the thinkers is assigned the same value of influence, namely, one. In the "weight" data each of them is assigned different values of influence on a scale of one to twelve. Those thinkers who, like Plato, Aristotle, Plotinus, St. Augustine, St. Thomas Aquinas, or Kant, obviously exerted much greater influence than many others, are given the highest weight of influence, namely twelve. Those whose influence seems to have been noticeable (or their names would not be preserved in the annals of history), but seemingly the smallest in comparison with the influence of the other thinkers, are given the value of one. The rest of the thinkers are assigned values intermediary between one and twelve proportionately to their appraised influence.

The assignment of these values to each thinker is a difficult but not an impossible problem, if it does not pretend to be more than roughly accurate, and if several conditions are present.

Guided by these considerations, and following the above conditions, Professors N. O. Lossky and I. I. Lapshin and I have assigned the appropriate value to each of the contributors (in their influence) in the following way.

As objective criteria of the comparative influence of each of the philosophers—the following data were selected:

a. The number of special monographs devoted to a philosopher.

b. The approximate frequency with which the philosopher's name has been mentioned, not only in the works of his contemporaries but also in those of the subsequent thinkers in this field.

c. Whether he was a founder of a school of philosophic thought.

d. Whether his name is mentioned even in the most elementary texts of history, epistemology, and theory of knowledge.

e. The number of his avowed disciples and followers among the thinkers in the field.

f. Whether his works have been translated into foreign languages.

g. Whether his works have been republished again and again in spite of the length of time that had elapsed since his death.

h. Whether he was a creator of an original and complete system of philosophy and epistemology.

From the above criteria one can see that almost all the relevant data have been considered. On the basis of these criteria the following number of units of influence and the corresponding scale of grades were constructed: We started with the number of special monographs devoted to the thinker and distributed them into twelve classes, from zero to 2560 and more monographic studies. Beginning with five the number doubles in each subsequent class. In the second row the value of influence assigned increases by one unit, giving a scale of values from one to twelve. Then the number of monographic studies has been corrected by other considerations mentioned previously. Weighting all these carefully, we assigned to each thinker in the field the value between one and twelve which appeared to be most adequate. In this way the elemental subjectivity in assigning the influence value to the thinkers has been reduced as much as it is humanly possible. . . .

The weight of all the partisans of a given current in each period is summed up; from these figures percentages are computed which indicate roughly the main changes in the increase and decrease of the influence of each current from period to period.

Number of monographs on a philosopher	Units of value given
0	1
1	2
5	3
10	4
20	5
40	6
80	7
160	8
320	9
640	10
1280	11
2560 and more	12

rent from period to period. This is the rough but systematic method used to estimate the movement of each of the currents of thought, in the course of time, as embodied in Table 1 . . . and Figure 1.

As stated before, these results from the points of view of both number and weight cannot pretend to reflect the changes in the mentality of the whole population from period to period. But it is probable that, in both cases, they indicate, at least roughly, the main changes in the mentality of the leading thinkers. In so far as the totality of the leading thinkers in a given field of a given period embodies the mentality of a given culture in that field, *upon its highest, or leading, or logically integrated level, the above results possibly reflect the main changes of the respective mentality of the Graeco-Roman and the European cultures upon this level in each of the specified periods.*

The reasonableness of our scale is attested, among other things, by the fact that the curves constructed upon a basis of weight and the curves constructed upon the basis of number, in which an equal value of one is given to each thinker, agree in their essential movements. This means that, all in all, the scale conforms to the principle that the greater the influence of a thinker in any given period, the greater is the proportion of thinkers who followed the same stream of thought, and vice versa.

The empirical system of truth is the system of the natural sciences; if one grows, the other must grow; if one declines, the other must decline. These curves are based upon radically different items and sources: one upon the *number of the discoveries and inventions in the natural sciences* computed from Darmstaedter's work; the other upon the systematic registration of all the known or all the important known thinkers who are mentioned in the histories of philosophy, epistemology, logic, and science. The items and the sources were entirely different and the computations were made by different persons who were not aware of the work of the other computers. (Professors Lossky and Lapshin had no knowledge of my study, and Dr. Merton, who made the computation of the scientific discoveries, was unaware not only of my study but also of the computations made by Professors Lossky and Lapshin.) Under the circumstances, the agreement between the curve of the scientific discoveries and inventions . . . and the curve of the fluctuations of the influence of the system of truth of senses . . . is particularly strong evidence that the results obtained in both cases are neither incidental nor misleading.

Not to mention other considerations, the preceding statements explain why we selected the above procedure and scale. In any case the reader now knows the scale or the "measuring stick" being used. In a sense it is arbitrary, but even the geometry of Euclid or that of Lobachevski; the mechanics of Newton, or those of Ein-stein; the Roman or the Arabic system of numbers; the computation of weeks, months, years, or the altitude, latitude, and longitude of a certain place—all are arbitrary because the fundamental assumptions, or the frame of reference, upon which these geometries, mechanics, arithmetics, time reckonings, or geographical locations are based are also arbitrary. This is true in any field of human knowledge. The arbitrariness per se does not invalidate the study, if the fundamental principles are not unsound, if they help to organize the material, and if, out of several possible arbitrary principles, the one accepted appears to be as satisfactory as any other, under the circumstances.

If it be maintained, especially by the historians, that no quantitative appraisal is possible in this field, and therefore any scale is inadmissible, the answer is simple: *Medice cura te ipsum.* The point is that there is scarcely any historical work, whether in this or in any other field, where, explicitly or implicitly, quantitative judgments are not given in verbal form. What historians of ideas, human thought, science, religion, art styles, political systems or economic processes do not use quantitative expressions like the following: "The period was marked by an *increase* of riots, revolts, and disorders," "The period was marked by a *decline* of idealism and religion," "Kant was one of the *greatest* philosophers," "It was the epoch of the *rise and triumph* of materialism, nominalism, the Gothic style, or socialistic doctrine," and so on? Statements like these, in many forms, are met in practically all historical works. They are but a variety of quantitative statements aimed to measure a comparative influence, popularity, magnitude, value, size, frequency; or an increase or decrease, growth or decline, rise or fall, of this or that cultural phenomenon. It is scarcely necessary to add that such statements are quite unavoidable in most sociocultural, humanitarian, and historical studies.

The usual statements of historians and social scientists are quantitative and also *verbal quantitative*. The procedure used here is *numerical quantitative*. The first makes quantitative statements but in an indefinite verbal form without the use of figures or numerical indicators. The second describes the quantitative changes with the help of figures. Which method is preferable, verbal or numerically quantitative? That is the question.

In the first place, the numerical method proposed is much more concise and economical.

In the second place, verbal quantitativism has a very limited number of gradations: "bad," "worse," "the worst"; "good," "better," "the best"; "big," "bigger," "the biggest"; and so on. The reason is that language has normally only from three to six comparative terms. With such limited gradations verbal quantitativists cannot describe any curve of movement of a social process in its numerous increases and decreases, "ups" and "downs"; or any series of quantitative values far more numerous than six.

In the third place, the method proposed makes clear to any reader its foundation, its bases, and its measuring stick. The yardstick used is uniform for all the periods compared, and these periods are all systematically taken and studied from this same standpoint. This claim can hardly be made for "increase," "decrease," and their equivalents used in most quantitative verbal judgments, where the bases, the nature of the measuring stick and its application remain unknown, or are often the result of intuitive guesswork.

Thus, while it is contended that Table 1, . . . constructed upon the above basis,

reflect[s] roughly the changes in the mentality of the leading thinkers in the field from period to period, and give[s] an idea of the comparative rise and decline of the influence of each system of truth, it is not maintained that the figures *measure* these changes exactly. They are aimed not so much to measure as to indicate the main periods of triumph and of greatest decline in the influence of each current. For minor, short-time fluctuations the figures and curves may be inadequate; but in all probability the major ups and downs in the curves of each current of thought reflect the change in the "high-level mentality" fairly accurately.

Table 1 . . . [has] several other defects besides. For the earliest periods there are known too few names upon which to base conclusions of a general character. For many of these periods probably not all the names of the prominent thinkers are preserved, and furthermore it is probable that several of the known names were overlooked inadvertently. For the most recent periods a somewhat arbitrary selection of names had to be made owing to their enormous number; therefore, only those professors who have proved to be eminent and prominent have been included. There are several other defects well known to the investigators, which, for reasons of economy of space, cannot be enumerated here. In spite of these inadequacies it is hoped, however, that the results obtained are valid in their essentials.

3. EMPIRICISM, RATIONALISM, MYSTICISM, SKEPTICISM, FIDEISM, CRITICISM

Let us now turn to our main task, *i.e.,* a study of the fluctuation of the main systems of truth in the life history of the Graeco-Roman and the Western cultures. The nature of the relevant material requires a slight modification of the three systems of truth. Instead of a direct study of the rise and decline of the truth of faith, of reason, and of senses, we shall follow the fluctuation of the influence of the six main epistemological currents in the mentality of the Graeco-Roman and European cultures; empiricism, religious or ideational rationalism and idealistic rationalism, mysticism, skepticism, fideism, and criticism. *Of these, ideational or religious rationalism, mysticism, and fideism incorporate mainly the truth of faith; the idealistic rationalism, mainly the truth of reason; empiricism, mainly the truth of senses.* Skepticism is a purely negative system of "cynical" and "passive" Sen-

sate mentality; criticism a specific mixture of skepticism, empiricism, and rationalism. The last two are important symptoms of specific cultural conditions and are discussed below. Following the fluctuation of the influence of these currents of thought from 580 B.C. to A.D. 1920, we shall obtain the fluctuation of influence of the three main systems of truth, translated into the above epistemological currents. . . .

Since we are mainly interested in the problem of fluctuation in the three systems of truth—of faith, of reason, and of senses—Table 1 . . . and Figure 1, given in the terms of these six systems of

Table 1 *Indicators of fluctuation of influence in main systems of truth by century periods*

(*on the basis of different values given from 1 to 12*)

PERIOD	EMPIRICISM		RATION-ALISM		MYSTICISM		CRITICISM		SKEPTICISM		FIDEISM		TOTAL	
	No.	Per cent	No.	Per cent	No.	Per cent	No.	Per cent	No.	Per cent	No.	Per cent	No.	Per cent
600–500 B.C.	6	19.4	25	80.6	0	0	0	0	0	0	0	0	31	100
500–400	23	19.2	61	50.8	0	0	0	0	36	30.0	0	0	120	100
400–300	31	14.6	89	42.0	17	8.0	0	0	54	25.4	21	10.0	212	100
300–200	34	21.7	34	21.7	1	0.6	0	0	28	17.8	60	38.2	157	100
200–100	11	19.6	16	28.6	1	1.8	0	0	12	21.4	16	28.6	56	100
100–0	26	24.3	26	24.3	7	6.5	0	0	7	6.5	41	38.4	107	100
0–100 A.D.	2	2.3	13	14.6	27	30.3	0	0	0	0	47	52.8	89	100
100–200	13	6.7	45	23.0	90	46.0	0	0	16	8.0	32	16.3	196	100
200–300	33	24.8	17	12.8	76	57.1	0	0	6	4.5	1	0.8	133	100
300–400	19	15.2	43	34.4	63	50.4	0	0	0	0	0	0	125	100
400–500	11	11.7	42	44.7	41	43.6	0	0	0	0	0	0	94	100
500–600	1	1.6	45	72.6	16	25.8	0	0	0	0	0	0	62	100
600–700	0	0	13	65.0	7	35.0	0	0	0	0	0	0	20	100
700–800	0	0	13	100	0	0	0	0	0	0	0	0	13	100
800–900	0	0	21	67.7	10	32.3	0	0	0	0	0	0	31	100
900–1000	0	0	6	75.0	2	25.0	0	0	0	0	0	0	8	100
1000–1100	3	7.7	17	43.6	11	28.2	0	0	0	0	8	20.5	39	100
1100–1200	13	14.3	38	41.8	37	40.7	0	0	0	0	3	3.2	91	100
1200–1300	21	12.8	117	71.4	26	15.8	0	0	0	0	0	0	164	100
1300–1400	28	17.2	83	51.3	40	24.7	0	0	7	4.3	4	2.5	162	100
1400–1500	3	7.2	15	35.7	20	47.6	0	0	0	0	4	9.5	42	100
1500–1600	24	15.8	44	29.0	51	33.6	0	0	21	13.8	12	7.8	152	100
1600–1700	132	29.6	179	40.1	104	23.3	0	0	21	4.7	10	2.3	446	100
1700–1800	260	37.5	212	30.6	131	18.9	41	6.0	29	4.0	20	3.0	693	100
1800–1900	644	42.6	320	21.1	261	17.2	156	10.3	42	2.8	90	6.0	1513	100

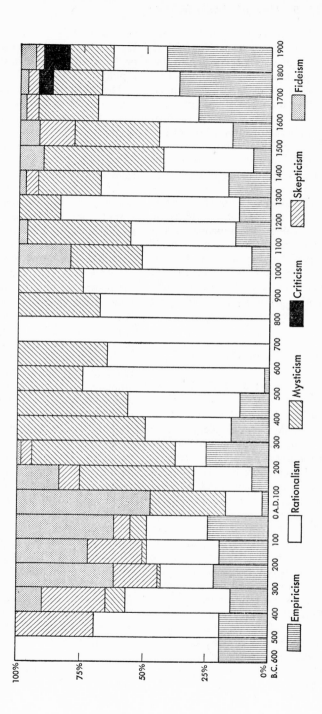

Figure 1   Fluctuation of the influence in systems of truth by century periods

231

truth and knowledge, have to be translated into the terms of the truth of faith, of reason, and of senses according to the previous explanation or "legend." The results of the study of the fluctuation of the comparative influence of each of these epistemological currents during twenty-five hundred years are summed up in the table . . . and the figure [above]. . . .

[Table 1 gives the numerical indicators of the comparative influence of each current by periods of one hundred years from 600 B.C. to A.D. 1900. The table is constructed on the "weighted" basis of the different values of influence of the thinkers enumerated on the scale from one to twelve. Another table, which analyzes the data from 580 B.C. to A.D. 1920, is here omitted. Figure 1 presents the information from Table 1 in graphic form.]

III. Main Results of the Study

The figures suggest the following conclusions.

A. *Trendless Fluctuation instead of Linear Trend.* A mere glance at Table 1 . . . and Figure 1 is sufficient to indicate that within the period of some twenty-five hundred years there has been no continuous linear trend of any kind. None of the main systems has tended steadily to increase or decrease or remain constant throughout all the period, but each system has fluctuated, now rising in its influence, now declining, or remaining for a time comparatively constant. The popular and almost commonly accepted opinion that there exists a linear trend in this field, and that the linear trend consists in a progressive increase of the empirical truth of senses at the expense of a progressively declining truth of faith (religious rationalism, mysticism, and fideism) or the truth of reason (idealistic

rationalism) is contradicted by the data. During the last five centuries empiricism or the truth of senses has been rising very rapidly.

The creative recurrent conception of sociocultural processes and likewise my contention that there have been different systems of truth which have fluctuated without leading to the "final" predominance of any one of them are well corroborated by the data.

B. *No Spencerian Evolution.* There was no perpetual Spencerian "evolution" from the less differentiated and integrated to the more differentiated and integrated status.

C. *Fluctuation of the Truth of Senses (Empiricism).* Turning to the table and the figure, we note the following fluctuations of the truth of senses in so far as it is embodied in empiricism. . . .

[Analysis of the data by twenty-year periods shows that] . . . the truth of faith, represented by the ideational or religious rationalism, until about 460 B.C. amounted in our system of indicators to about 90 per cent of all the systems of truth. It was only after 460 B.C. that the truth of senses (empiricism) began notably to rise and grow with minor fluctuations. It remained comparatively strong until 20 B.C., when it weakened again, and was low up to about A.D. 160, when it flared up again and stayed comparatively high until about A.D. 480. After that date it sharply declined and after A.D. 540 disappeared from the "highway" of the thought, being submerged by the rising truth of faith of Christianity. It remained hidden until about 1100, roughly some six centuries, then emerged again and began, with minor fluctuations, to climb; and in the twelfth, thirteenth, and the fourteenth centuries again attained considerable influence, notable but not dominant, somewhat approaching its influence in the fifth and the fourth centuries B.C. in Greece. In the fifteenth century, for some sixty years it disappeared again (1400–1460), then re-emerged and rose rapidly, and with minor fluctuations grew steadily up to the present time, reaching in the nineteenth century the extraordinary and unique indicator of 42 per cent (for the whole century) and for the twentieth century a still higher indicator of some 53 per cent! For the last four centuries we have thus had a rising tide of the truth of senses, the contemporary scientific truth. This extraordinary domination of this system of truth at the present time explains why we are inclined to identify truth generally with the truth of senses, why other truths appear to us as "superstitions," why we believe that from now on the truth of senses is destined to grow further and further until it will eliminate forever all the other systems of truth. Such a mentality is but natural for this period.

D. *Movements of Truth of Senses and of Discoveries and Inventions in the Natural and Technological Sciences.* Previously it was mentioned that an additional criterion of the approximate validity of the quantitative indicators of the absolute and relative changes in the expansion and contraction of the systems of truth in the course of time is the essential agreement of the curve of the discoveries in the natural sciences and technological inventions with the curve of empiricism. Let us place the data and the curves of both movements side by side in order to verify this statement. The century indicators for both movements are shown in Table 2.

Although the data on empiricism and the scientific discoveries are not comparable because, on the one hand, we have the number of the discoveries, on the other, the percentage of the influence of empiricism among all the systems of truth or

the weighted indicator of its representatives, nevertheless the three series are somewhat instructive. They show naturally many minor divergencies from century to century, and yet, when the most essential long-time waves of the discoveries and of the percentage of the influence of empiricism are taken, their remarkable agreement cannot fail to be noticed. Beginning with the twelfth century both grow from century to century. Through the period from the sixth to the twelfth century A.D. both are practically on zero line. In Greece both are comparatively high in the period from the sixth to the second century B.C.

E. *Fluctuation of the Truth of Faith. Ideational Rationalism, Mysticism, and Fideism.* The truth of faith is represented by religious or ideational rationalism, by mysticism, and by fideism. The latter two are esoteric and desperate forms of the truth of faith, while religious rationalism is the expression of a mentality free from any doubt or questioning of the truth of faith.

Understood, then, as an ensemble of religious rationalism, mysticism, and fideism, the truth of faith has had, within the period studied, the following periods of domination over the other two systems of truth.

a. Before the fifth century B.C. in Greece, by one-hundred-year periods, religious rationalism was given a value of 80.6 per cent, and a value of 71 to 90.9 per cent in the indicators by twenty-year periods. The whole field of the systems of truth was held by religious rationalism and by a minor stream of empiricism.

b. The period from the beginning of our era to the end of the fifth century A.D., when these three currents of the truth of faith give the indicators: 97.7 per cent for the first century; 85.3 per cent for the second; 70.7 per cent for the third; 84.8 per cent for the fourth; 88.3

Table **2**

Number of scientific discoveries and inventions				Indicators of empiricism	
				Weight (absolute figures)	Percentage of the influence of empiricism among all systems of truth
Century					
	GREECE	ROME	GREECE AND ROME	GREECE	GREECE
8 B.C.	6	0	6	0	0
7	3	2	5	?	?
6	26	5	31	6	19.4
5	39	1	40	23	19.2
4	52	5	57	31	14.6
3	42	3	45	34	21.7
2	14	3	17	11	19.6
				GREECE AND ROME	GREECE AND ROME
1	12	20	32	26	24.3
1 A.D.	25	35	60	2	2.3
2	5	13	18	13	6.7
3	0	6	6	33	24.8
4	1	15	16	19	15.2
5	0	4	4	11	11.7
6	3	1	4	1	1.6
			WESTERN CHRISTIAN EUROPE	WESTERN CHRISTIAN EUROPE	
7			4	0	0
8			4	0	0
9			6	0	0
10			7	0	0
11			8	3	7.7
12			12	13	14.3
13			53	21	12.8
14			65	28	17.2
15			127	3	7.2
16			429	24	14.8
17			691	132	29.6
18			1574	260	37.5
19			8527	644	42.6

per cent for the fifth. But qualitatively this period was very different from that before the fifth century B.C. because mysticism and fideism were most powerful and dominated the truth of faith. This means it was not a period of a serene faith, untroubled by doubt, but it was a period of a desperate "will to believe" assailed and attacked by empiricism and skepticism.

c. The centuries from the sixth to the twelfth. These centuries were periods of monopolistic domination of the truth of faith over the truth of senses and the truth of reason. The truth of faith occupied 100 per cent of the field.

d. The fifteenth century. All the three systems of truth of faith were given a total value of 92.8 per cent. Here again the main currents of the truth of faith are represented mainly by the desperate forms of mysticism and fideism, but not by religious rationalism.

It impresses us as being the last desperate effort of the truth of faith to maintain its influence before its inexorable decline for several subsequent centuries up to the present time. This decline is shown in Table 1 . . . by the indicators of hundred-year . . . periods. Beginning with the sixteenth century the truth of faith in all its forms declined more and more, giving the dominant position to other systems of truth, particularly to that of truth of senses.

The following periods of the minor upward movements of each of these two currents of the truth of faith can be noted.

For Mysticism: (1) At the debut of mysticism, about the middle of the fourth century B.C. (Plato after 385, Xenocrates, and others.) (2) Around the beginning of the Christian era (Philo, Thrasyllus, and others). (3) With slight oscillations it rose from the second to the end of the fourth centuries . . . ; remained generally high throughout the fifth, sixth, and seventh centuries; and then disappeared, being merged into religious rationalism. It appeared again in the ninth and reached a high point in the twelfth century (Erigena, Maximus, Confessor, and others). (4) In the thirteenth it was low. It rose again in the fourteenth and reached its climax in the fifteenth century. In the sixteenth century it stayed high, though much lower than in the fifteenth. (5) There were slight crescendos from 1660 to 1720 and from 1780 to 1840. Since 1840 it has steadily declined up to recent times.

Fideism's highs have been: 280–240 B.C.; the first century B.C.; the first and second centuries A.D.; from the third to the eleventh centuries it was submerged, emerged for a brief period, disappeared

again until the fourteenth century. Since that time, however, it has continually existed but as a current of even less importance than skepticism. Immediately after the French and other revolutions at the end of the eighteenth century it jumped up temporarily, but it soon receded and has remained at this low level up to the present time.

[F. Inverse Movement of Truth of Faith and Atheism. Omitted.]

G. *Fluctuation of the Truth of Reason. Idealistic Rationalism.* In the sense of the harmonious synthesis of the truth of reason, of faith, and of senses, with the truth of independent reason dominant (if not *de jure* then *de facto*), there were, so far, only two periods when this system of truth of Scholastic intellectualism was dominant. The first of these periods was about the fifth and the fourth centuries B.C. in Greece, and the second period was from the end of the twelfth to the second part of the fourteenth century with the thirteenth century as the climax. The rationalism of these periods (qualitatively not separated in Table 1 . . . from the religious rationalism) was idealistic rationalism. . . .

H. *Pulsation of Skepticism and Criticism.* Skepticism, as a denial of possibility of any truth, emerged rather late in the history of the Greek mentality (about the middle of the fifth century B.C.). The late appearance of this stream of thought as well as its comparatively lesser power is comprehensible. . . .

By examining its trends it can be observed that skepticism emerges usually when the truth of faith declines and when truth of reason and especially truth of senses begin to grow. In this sense it is a satellite of the first phases of growth of empiricism because of its relativistic and agnostic tendencies. However, when empiricism triumphs, skepticism retreats, although it does not disappear as it does in the periods when truth of faith dominates.

It can be observed, also, that the periods of a flaring up of skepticism have usually been those either immediately preceding or coinciding with the periods in which great social upheavals and calamities occurred: the Peloponnesian War and subsequent calamities; the great civil wars in Rome of the first and the second triumvirates; the Black Plague; the emergence of Christianity; the Reformation; the religious wars of the Reformation and of the League; and the great French Revolution.

The third fact to be noted is that as soon as skepticism rises its emergence or rise is almost immediately followed by emergence and rise of fideism as a desperate reaction against it.

Finally, *criticism* (in a specific sense a critical philosophy) is a special rivulet which emerged at the end of the eighteenth century mainly through the works of Hume and Kant. It appeared comparatively strong at once.... From the figures one can see that its movements are almost opposite to that of skepticism. This suggests that in a sense it is a diluted form of it and fulfills in a much milder way the functions of skepticism which in a pure form cannot function under the given psychosocial conditions.

I. *Total Mental Spectrum of the Main Periods.* We shall now concentrate on the total mentality of the main parts of the period under investigation. The following inferences are warranted by the character of the "mental spectrum" of these parts.

a. The total spectrum of mentality (in the field studied) of Greece before the fifth century B.C. appeared to be predominantly Ideational. The system of the religious rationalism was overwhelmingly dominant, and empiricism only as a minor force was present; neither skepticism, mysticism, fideism, criticism, nor even idealistic rationalism existed. It was

the period of certitude in the Greek mentality, the age of the certitude of faith; the age of calm serenity and untroubled simplicity.

b. The fifth century, especially its second part and also the first two-thirds of the fourth century B.C. were marked by the domination of the *idealistic rationalism* or the *truth of reason....*

c. In the subsequent centuries—the third, the second, and the first B.C.—the tide of empiricism grew and became as strong as rationalism. Rationalism of both types greatly declined and the negative and desperate forms of truth flourished. The above correlations indicated a rising tide of the Sensate culture and a decline of the Ideational and the Idealistic cultures in their strong and balanced forms; and a growth of the esoteric, exotic, and desperate mentality in the field; or a great mental disturbance, disorganization, and upheaval. Subsequent centuries—from the first B.C. to the third A.D.—were stamped by the entrance of the Romans in the field. In the first and second centuries A.D. Christianity with its thinkers appeared. The spectrum of the mentality in the field of truth in these centuries is very interesting and peculiar....

The total indicators of Table 1 ... for these two centuries thus represent a mixture of ... two widely different mentalities of the Pagan thought with a very dissimilar Christian truth of faith. The Pagan thought was thrown out of balance by the tragic circumstances of the preceding period and somewhat lost its faith in the truth of the senses as well as in that of independent reason and turned, instead, either to cynicism and skepticism or to fideism, as the artificial will to believe, and to mysticism, as the desperate truth of faith. The Christian thought broke completely with the truth of senses and turned to a belief in the truth of the Gospel, in revelation, and in mystical experience, slightly supported by the truth of logic in so far as it did not contradict the creed and could be used for its purpose. Here, then, was a great shattering of the empirical and idealistically rationalistic systems of truth which were dominant before.

d. When the indicators of the spectrum of mentality of the next two centuries—the third and the fourth—are examined, the first impression is that the mental balance shattered previously has been somewhat regained; skepticism and fideism practically disappeared; among the Pagans empiricism had a revival (even a few Christian thinkers shared it); rationalism grew also, mainly among the Christian thinkers; but mysticism gained especially great influence with the Pagan as well as with the Christian contributors.

e. We are at the end of the empirico-rationalistic system of truth and at the beginning of the domination of the truth of faith, with the truth of reason assuming a subsidiary role. Within one century or a little more this became clear; empiricism declined and disappeared. The truth of faith became dominant and clothed itself in the solid and confident form of the religious rationalism; as such it was stabilized and from that time needed no extreme and desperate forms, like fideism or esoteric mysticism. We are ushered into the age of faith which questioned nothing in the Gospel and in God's truth. We are in the age of a new great ideationalism of the Middle Ages, in the monopolistic domination of the truth of faith with its "handmaid" human reason (not questioning but only justifying and serving faith). The indicators show that such a situation continued for about six centuries.

This is certainly an Ideational age, not only on the basis of the dominant truth of faith, of the dominant Ideational art, but also upon the basis of data given sub-

sequently. If at any period in the history of the Western mentality the philosophers and the people as a whole felt that they were in the possession of truth, the whole truth, the nothing but truth, it was in these centuries. There was no skepticism, no questioning, no doubt, no relativity, no hesitation, no reservation.

f. Then in the eleventh century empiricism reappeared after many centuries. Weak at the beginning, it doubled its strength in the twelfth century, especially at its end, and stabilized itself in the thirteenth and fourteenth centuries. Thus in these centuries the monopolistic domination of the truth of faith with its subordinate, the truth of reason, was ended. The mental spectrum changed; it became a harmonious blending of empiricism and of mysticism with the dominant truth of independent rationalism different from religious rationalism of the previous period.

The harmonious blending of the truths of faith, of senses (empiricism), and of reason gave the idealistic rationalism of the great Scholastics of the twelfth and the thirteenth centuries the dominant position in that period. . . . It was the European replica of the Greek Idealistic mentality of the fifth and fourth centuries B.C.

In the second part of the fourteenth and in the fifteenth centuries the Idealistic system was shattered and a desperate and esoteric kind of mysticism prevailed. Its wave swept over Western society. During the second part of the sixteenth century, and especially in the seventeenth, however, mysticism subsided, and empiricism gained in strength, which with very slight fluctuations has persisted up to the present time. The system of faith, as well as rationalism, and the truth of reason also lost ground and the truth of senses became triumphant. At the end of the nineteenth and in the twentieth century (at least up to the prewar time) its influence has grown to unprecedented heights. Verily we are living in the age of scientism! This means our culture is Sensate culture par excellence! As a result, the other systems of truth have been constantly degraded to a lower level of sterile speculation, fantastic and unscientific and unverified purely logical derivations—in regard to the truth of reason; and to mere superstition and ignorance so far as the truth of faith is concerned. Discord between these systems of truth marks this period. Scientific truth leads the offensive in an effort to exterminate entirely the other systems of truth, and they in turn are fighting for their existence. . . .

J. *Principle of Limit and of Self-regulation of Sociocultural Processes.* If the closest rivals among these systems are selected and studied for three separate periods, and also for the entire period, the total sums of the indicators of each of the rival currents are shown in Table 3.

No arithmetical and mechanical balances are sought in this or in any other social process; nevertheless, considering the fact that the length of the total period studied is about twenty-five hundred years, and that all these indices have been made without any idea of an arithmetical balance, one must confess that the sums of the indices for fideism-skepticism and empiricism-rationalism are strikingly close. It suggests that in the sociocultural life and sociomental processes there seems to be present some factor which, in the long run, does not permit any single or extreme current to absorb all the other

systems for any length of time and thus to narrow the richness and many-colored completeness of truth.

These figures give a concrete idea of the principle of immanent self-regulation of sociocultural processes. . . .

For the whole period considered the total sums of the indicators for each of these currents and the respective systems of truth are as follows:

Fideism	369
Skepticism	279
Mysticism	1039
Criticism	197
Empiricism	1338
Rationalism	1534
Truth of faith	1650
Truth of reason	1292
Truth of senses	1338
Skepticism and criticism	476

These figures show that in the cultures studied the religious and the idealistic rationalism has been so far the most powerful system of truth. Then next in importance was empiricism, then mysticism, then fideism, then skepticism and criticism. Interpreted in another way, in reference to the system of truth, the total sums of the indicators of power of all the systems of truth are fairly close, giving a slight edge to the truth of faith. This demonstrates once more the principle of immanent self-regulation of sociocultural processes and their autonomous tendency to balance one another, sometimes quantitatively, sometimes qualitatively, sometimes quantitatively and qualitatively. The

Table **3**   *Sums of the indicators of sociocultural processes*

Periods	Fideism	Skepticism	Empiricism	Rationalism
580 B.C. to A.D. 100	185	137	133	264
100 to 1500	52	29	145	515
1500 to 1900	132	113	1060	755
Total	*369*	*279*	*1338*	*1534*

data suggest, also, that possibly each form of truth has its own important function in the psychosocial life of mankind and is equally necessary. . . .

Thus, the material presented seems to support well the hypothetical propositions with which this part of the work was concerned. We have observed: (1) that the systems of truth have been fluctuating; (2) that empirical truth has been only one of these systems and by no means the most influential; (3) that the empirical system of truth and the movement of the scientific discoveries go hand in hand, as is to be expected; (4) that the subject matter of the study of each of these systems and the method of verification are such as have been deductively characterized above; (5) that when we know which of these systems is dominant in a given period we can, with a reasonable degree of certainty, foresee what will be the dominant mentality of the period in relation to the progress of scientific discoveries, to the subjects and problems which will be studied mainly, and to the method of testing the validity of the theories presented; (6) that the dominant systems of truth correspond to the respective forms of the dominant type of the culture: truth of faith to the Ideational, truth of reason to the Idealistic, and truth of senses to the Sensate cultures, providing that, after further study of the cultural forms of the period studied, the Greek culture before the fifth century is found to be predominantly Ideational; that of the fifth and the fourth centuries predominantly Idealistic; that of the subsequent centuries predominantly Sensate or, from the beginning of the Christian era to the end of the fourth century, transitional; that the culture from the fifth to the twelfth centuries will be found predominantly Ideational again; the culture from the twelfth to the fourteenth centuries predominantly Idealistic; and the culture from the sixteenth to the twentieth centuries predominantly Sensate. Subsequent study of the other main compartments of the Graeco-Roman and Western cultures within the period considered will show whether these expectations are corroborated.

COMMENTARY

USES OF AVAILABLE DATA

Units 2, 3, and 4 have presented studies for which the researcher gathered his own data to accommodate his particular research objective. Indeed the student often assumes, in thinking about study design, that the researcher must either go into the field himself to observe interaction directly, or question individuals at first-hand. But a moment's thought reveals that sociological research also rests heavily upon data that already exist in one form or another. The studies in this Unit are examples in which the researcher makes the fundamental decision, under **P-VII,** to use available materials, rather than to collect new ones.

This choice does not usually mean that he can then safely ignore the implications of the Paradigm decisions that affect the collection of new data. For, although the investigator using data assembled for some earlier research cannot himself make the decisions about the procedures for gathering data **(P-VIII)** or about the extent of control over the system under study **(P-VI),** he must take into account the decisions which were made previously when the data were originally assembled.

An impressive array of available materials lend themselves to the study of many social system problems, as you know from Manual I-C. The researcher may make use of letters or television transcripts, historical documents or journalistic accounts, tribal artifacts or works of art. He may analyze the records of corporations, police courts, or the U.S. Bureau of the Census. He may re-examine within the framework of his own conceptual model and research objective the already completed studies of other scholars. As all these and diverse other materials accumulate, it may well be that increasing numbers of researchers will find that the data they need have already been gathered.

In the present Unit you have been focusing on three studies as examples of the ingenious selection and handling of very different kinds of existing data. These examples only begin to suggest the scope and nature of data from this important source. A fuller understanding of the types of available data and procedures for their use will rest upon your study of additional examples in later Units. Massing's content analysis of newspapers and other mass media materials, Weber's classification of historical writings and documents, and the analyses of public records by Durkheim, Faris and Dunham, Bogue, Davis and Golden, or Ogburn and Thomas provide useful examples.

Thomas and Znaniecki and the Use of Letters

The exchanges of letters in Polish families from which a member had emigrated to the United States comprise a major portion of the monumental work, *The Polish Peasant in Europe and America*. These letters reflect the changing relationships within peasant primary groups as communities and families are disrupted by the long absence of an important member, as well as by the changing social organization of one rural segment of western Europe. Thomas and Znaniecki are able to study the "role of human attitudes in social life" by examining families living within a society under "strain." They study a system by focusing upon this society at a time when its value contexts are shifting so that individuals must reorder their attitudes.

NATURE AND HANDLING OF DATA

An unusual feature of this particular work is the actual publication of the raw data in their original form—a device that enables the reader to see just how the materials were organized to support the authors' interpretations. Thomas and Znaniecki seem to have published nearly all of the letters they secured, though they do not state exactly how many, or upon what bases, any exclusions were made (see Madge, pp. 55–62, 73–75, for a discussion of this point). They do report, however, that "the private letters constituting the first two volumes have needed relatively little selection," and that they omitted only those letters which "contained nothing but a repetition of situations and attitudes more completely represented in the materials which we publish here."

The point of general methodological interest is that, whenever a series of letters is complete, it constitutes the total interaction between the Polish émigrés and their families. The research case **(P-I)** is the family which is composed of widely separated members. Through the letters the researchers have caught the interaction process, just as if Bales were to record on a motion-picture film and a sound track everything that goes on in his small groups.

The purely descriptive analysis (**P-X** and **P-XI**) and interpretation are separated from the presentation of data (just as you separated interpretations from data when you made unstructured observations in Exercise I-1). The interpretation is contained in the introductions to particular volumes (more than 200 pages introduces the letters in the first volume), in the footnotes to the letters, which clarify certain words and phrases or interpret attitudes and actions described in the letters, and in the introductions to the volumes and to the several sets of letters. The introductions to the letters range from very brief notes to lengthy and detailed case histories of the family, including information on family background, description of the community or geographical area in which the family lived, discussion of contemporary events which affected the family, and some interpretation of individuals' personalities based on clues in the letters. This analysis and interpretation varies from one series of letters to another, and is generally rather loose and intuitive, comparable to the method of Le Play's explanatory supplements. It is substantially aided by the additional data contributed from Znaniecki's close acquaintance with Polish society (see Angell, 1945; Blumer).

The work shows, then, how available data may sometimes be used to study interaction by the descriptive case study method that yields rich details and varied insights (as in Unit 2).

To be sure, the use of letters as data does not require such unsystematic handling. Thomas and Znaniecki might have rearranged their materials according to some standardized formula, as Le Play did with the characteristics of the worker and the budget when he too set out to observe the effects of Western industrialization on family life. Indeed, since the raw data are published, another researcher might now reanalyze the letters, using systematically defined categories, such as Bales' code or Parsons' pattern variables. (See, *e.g.,* the systematic content analysis of letters in Sussman.)

SOME LIMITATIONS

Although ideally the exchange of letters would represent the entire communication process between the husband-father (or some other member of the family in America) and the rest of the family in Poland, in fact the researchers typically obtained only one side of the epistolary exchange. In all such instances, then, their data refer only to selected members of each group (family) and cover only part of the interaction. These gaps illustrate an important potential limitation in the use of available data generally: not having been assembled for the purposes of the investigation, the data may be fragmentary or incomplete, thus depriving the researcher of valuable information.

Another limitation is that such privately owned and spontaneously produced materials may be rare or difficult to obtain. Owners of letters, diaries, or other personal documents may sometimes object to their use for research purposes (the letters in *The Polish Peasant* were obtained through an advertisement which offered payment for each letter). Moreover, situations producing appropriate materials may be rare. The continuing exchange of letters, for example, seems to depend upon long-term or frequent separation of the members, as well as upon a custom of detailed letter-writing. Nevertheless, there are no doubt many instances in which similar data are available for further research, as, for instance, when servicemen are separated from their families.

SOME ADVANTAGES

This study shows how available data can be used as the basis for research on interaction—and on the very type of continuing private interaction that is usually inaccessible to direct observation (as we have seen in Unit 4). When the members of a group are separated, the researcher may not be able to assemble them for observation. Or when the interaction is continued over long periods of time, he may not have the resources for observation. Or most important, the nature of the interaction may be so private that it admits of no observation at all. Nor is it likely that these difficulties could readily be overcome by the use of questioning, for the letters yield information of such complex and subtle nature that even the most skilled interviewer would have difficulty in obtaining an equivalent understanding of the constantly changing private lives of these Polish families.

In contrasting the use of letters with the methods of observation and questioning, let us emphasize again that the data used here were not produced originally for purposes of research. The letters *are* the interaction—in a form even more genuine than the interaction artificially induced in the laboratory. Thus these data are free from the potential errors that so often beset the observer or the questioner (Unit 4)—the errors of control effect, and (when the letters are in their complete and original form) the errors of biased-viewpoint effect. The preconceptions of the investigator cannot affect what the group members actually write to one another, nor is there any opportunity for selective reporting by a researcher.

Besides letters, there are other types of available data which offer comparably vivid and complete information about interaction under different conditions. Full transcriptions of court proceedings or committee meetings are often of sociological interest. Suggestive accounts (though often less accurate as factual reports) appear in newspaper stories, diplomatic memoirs, or personal diaries. Closely related, though we do not regard them as available data, are the life histories commissioned by the investigator for his research, such as the detailed autobiography of a Polish peasant prepared for Thomas and Znaniecki. Such accounts that are written at the instigation of the investigator are subject to the response bias and biased-viewpoint effect of self-administered questionnaires. (See, *e.g.,* Abel, 1947; Stouffer, 1930.) Similarly, medical, psychoanalytic, or social-work case records, often obtainable in anonymous form, may serve as "expert" records of complex human relationships and processes, affording insights not open to the lay investigator who himself attempts to gather such technical material.

Zelditch and the Reanalysis of Cross-Cultural Studies

In contrast to the use Thomas and Znaniecki make of their materials in descriptive analysis of data from a single cultural grouping, Zelditch systematically tests a carefully defined hypothesis, utilizing available cross-cultural data for many societies. As part of the family analysis developed by Parsons, Bales, and their Harvard collaborators, this study by Zelditch illustrates a number of design principles. Note especially the detail in which he specifies the conceptual model before seeking appropriate empirical indicants. He starts with the finding from small group research that task groups tend to develop two types of leaders—an instrumental leader, who directs the group in meeting its goals, and an expressive leader, who attends to the social-emotional problems. Zelditch then postulates that this role differentiation occurs in other types of groups also, so that in the family, for example, in no matter what society, there is typically an instrumental leader (the husband) and an expressive leader (the wife). He states this in the form of two hypotheses of role differentiation and role allocation which are to be tested:

1. If the nuclear family constitutes a social system stable over time, it will differentiate roles such that instrumental leadership and expressive leadership of the system are discriminated.
2. If the nuclear family consists in a defined "normal" complement of the male adult, female adult, and their immediate children, the male adult will play the role of instrumental leader and the female will play the role of expressive leader.

USE OF EXISTING CROSS-CULTURAL STUDIES

Obviously, such universal hypotheses require testing in a wide variety of societies, past as well as present. To meet this requirement, Zelditch uses a procedure of *secondary analysis*—that is, he reanalyzes the findings of studies already completed by other researchers (for other applications of secondary analysis, see, for example, Hyman 1953 and 1959; Lipset and Bendix, 1959). In this particular investigation, Zelditch utilizes findings about different total societies at different periods of time. He compiles a list of all societies for which ethnographers had reported relevant data (we shall discuss the sample in Unit 6), and then reanalyzes these reports.

Some Advantages of Cross-Cultural Analysis.   This cross-cultural approach **(P-III)** enables Zelditch, much as it did Le Play, to generalize about the family. If Zelditch had attempted to generalize from a single society, however—from the Trobriand family, for instance, or from the modern United States family—his inferences would have been culture-bound. Indeed, had he used either of these examples alone, he might have been misled into a rejection of his general hypothesis, as his discussion suggests. To avoid such pitfalls, he compared many societies at various periods of time.

Such a sweeping design was feasible in this instance, and could be carried out relatively quickly and inexpensively, because Zelditch could work in a library and take advantage of previously conducted research. Had the collection of new data been necessary, the researcher would have been totally unable to command the financing, time, and array of anthropological skills needed to study so many different societies. Thus, we can see from this example how the use of available materials may contribute greatly to the sociotemporal scope of a study without any commensurate increase in the costs.

Similar savings of time and expense are possible in studies for which suitable data are already indexed in the Human Relations Area File. Started at Yale as the Cross-Cultural Survey under the leadership of George P. Murdock (whose bibliography was utilized in the Zelditch study) this file is now housed at several universities. It covers a large number of human societies, and consists of excerpts from scholarly and scientific works, selected, classified, coded, and evaluated by specialists, and available in its complete form to researchers and students. The materials are organized by societies and further broken down by major categories (such as language, ideas about nature and man, socialization, kin groups) and by subtopics within categories. By consulting the index, a researcher might locate information on many subjects of possible interest—on the socialization of adolescents, for example, or on the division of labor—in all cultures for which data have been collected and processed by the File (see Murdock).

Public-opinion studies, which are accumulating in many different countries, also lend themselves increasingly to sociological reanalysis and cross-cultural comparison (see, *e.g.,* Rogoff; Inkeles and Rossi).

Total Society as Research Case. Although the family is the focus of conceptual concern in the Zelditch study, the cases **(P-I)** actually drawn into the sample and analyzed in the tables are whole societies. Each society is classified, from the reports, in terms of its predominant family structure. (Contrast Zelditch's use of the whole society in order to study the family with the use of the family by Le Play and, to a certain extent, by Thomas and Znaniecki, in order to study the larger society.) This important possibility of dealing with many total societies as the cases is facilitated by the method of secondary analysis.

LIMITATIONS OF SECONDARY ANALYSIS

The use of completed studies may involve a serious limitation, however, since these materials consist of *summary* reports rather than the unprocessed data. Zelditch was interested, according to his model, in families as the parts of each society, and in the role incumbents within each family. But, instead of being able to study families and roles directly, he was obliged to interpret the generalizations of the ethnographers. As he himself puts it, "The fact that the test was made on already digested material observed by many different investigators using widely varying categories makes a number of indirect indices inevitable, and certain ambiguities unavoidable."

The information in available reports may not occur in the exact form desired by the researcher, and may thus fail to fit the conceptual model. Still worse, many of the reports lack the necessary information altogether. Zelditch admits that in drawing his sample "certain societies were omitted merely because they were more difficult to gather material on than others," while other societies were included "simply because [data about them] were readily available." His experience shows the kinds of special precautions the sociologist must take—if he is to benefit from the obvious advantages of secondary analysis—to understand the implications and biases of already completed studies.

HYPOTHESIS-TESTING

The Zelditch study illustrates two other important principles of analysis, the testing of hypotheses and the analysis of deviant cases. Neither of these is, of course, in any way peculiar to research based on available data.

Starting with data which, in their raw form, are just as diffuse and unsystematic as the letters in *The Polish Peasant,* Zelditch proceeds systematically to classify each society, to count the number of societies in which his hypotheses are supported, and then to draw inferences about family structure in general. As a basis for later consideration of more complicated analyses, let us now specify the logic which seems to underlie his procedure.

As we noted in discussing methods of interpretation in Unit 1, researchers who want to test hypotheses specify in advance the implications of their conceptual model for the type of concrete situation to be investigated (see *e.g.,* Cohen and Nagel, p. 204). They often make use of mathematical language to determine what the expected numerical findings would be if their assumptions are in accord with the facts. The Zelditch study furnishes a very elementary example of this use of a mathematical model as a more precise statement of part of the conceptual model—following much the same basic steps taken by Bales (Unit 3) in using mathematical models for exploratory objectives:

Step A

In one of his analyses, Zelditch states his sociological assumptions as a *research hypothesis* of role differentiation within the family.

Step B

His research hypothesis is then translated into a statement which, although very simple, is nevertheless subject to mathematical manipulation and illustrates the purpose of a mathematical model. His statement might be that, out of all possible societies, more than half (since Zelditch does not predict an exact proportion) will show differentiation; that is, the probability of differentiation for any given society (*P*) is greater than one-half—$P > \frac{1}{2}$. Using this model, the *expected number* of differentiated societies may be predicted to be more than 28 out of the sample of 56, if the research hypothesis is correct.

(In practice, the mathematical model typically reverses the research hypothesis, stating a *null hypothesis*—often an assumption of no difference—which the researcher hopes to reject. The null hypothesis here would be that only half of the societies or less will show differentiation—$P \leq \frac{1}{2}$—with an expected frequency in the sample of 28 or less. A finding of considerably more than 28 would then be used to reject the null hypothesis under Step C.)

Step C

Zelditch compares his actual finding of 46 differentiated societies with this expected finding (under the research hypothesis) of more than 28. Because 46 is more than 28, he decides that the data are consistent with his expected finding, and hence may be accounted for by his theory of role differentiation (Step A).

Of course, even when the findings are consistent with the model (or inconsistent with the null hypothesis), there is a possibility that they may be accounted for by factors other than those contained in the theory. One possible source is *variation due to chance* which may arise whenever the findings are based on a sample of some larger conceptual universe of cases. The researcher may accordingly wish to take a fourth step in order to answer the question: Might the finding of the research (Step C) arise purely by chance? That is, if other similar samples were studied, would the same finding turn up repeatedly? Zelditch, whose conceptual universe seems to include all possible societies whenever and wherever they exist, takes this fourth step:

Step D

He uses a *statistical test* in order to make the appropriate allowance for chance variation. Although we shall not examine the procedures for such tests until later (Exercise V-3), it is important to understand their place in the research process.

ANALYSIS OF DEVIANT CASES

After testing his hypothesis by comparison with the actual findings and by statistical test (Step C in conjunction with Step D), Zelditch notes that there are, nevertheless, ten societies in which the differentiation does not immediately appear. He therefore decides to undertake a careful study of these ten "negative" or "deviant" cases (see Kendall and Wolf). He wants to discover whether there is an additional principle which might account for such deviation—a principle which would suggest either a reformulation of the hypothesis, or a more refined test of it. To demonstrate the rather intricate procedure actually employed, let us use a simplified illustration of the two basic steps in deviant case analysis. In the first step, the researcher scrutinizes each deviant case in detail for any additional clues to relevant factors not previously considered. In the second step, he tests this deviant case finding on the sample as a whole to see whether it holds generally true.

Zelditch, scrutinizing Trobriand society as a negative case (first step), finds that Malinowski's report affords a clue which may account for the lack of role differentiation. Malinowski stresses the matrilineal kinship structure of the Trobriand Islands, suggesting that it is the mother's brother who plays the instrumental role, leaving the father only the expressive functions of providing love and companionship.

Following this lead, Zelditch takes the second step in deviant case analysis. He begins by stating Malinowski's implied hypothesis that, in all matrilineal societies, *both* father and mother play expressive roles—at least, that they are more likely to do so in matrilineal than in other societies. Then he tests this hypothesis against all the matrilineal societies in his sample. As it turns out, Malinowski's hypothesis does not hold; the proportion of deviant cases it yielded—14 out of 19 matrilineal societies—is considerably greater than the proportion of deviant cases—10 out of 56—already found by Zelditch in testing his own differentiation hypothesis for societies in general. (Zelditch terms the deviant cases "negative," meaning that they do not fit the particular hypothesis under consideration.)

Abandoning this lead, then, Zelditch begins his investigation of the matrilineal groupings, painstakingly seeking clues to explain departures from the usual pattern, working back and forth between clues from single cases and the possible implications when these are tested on the sample as a whole. His final conclusion is that "the father generally, *relative to the wife-mother,* plays a distinctly instrumental role in almost all cases." That is, although the roles of both wife-mother and husband-father in a particular society may be expressive according to some absolute definition, nevertheless the father's role is *relatively* instrumental. Zelditch thus concludes his analysis with a reformulation of his original hypothesis, which enables him to account more generally for the role structure of the nuclear family.

In similar fashion, any analysis of deviant cases (those not accounted for by the hypothesis or by the general finding) may serve to uncover additional factors not previously considered. While such analysis is certainly not restricted to studies based on available data, Zelditch was greatly assisted by having sufficient detailed materials already at hand so that he could at once carry through both the first and second steps without gathering original materials. In the next Unit, we shall examine a study by Kahl that illustrates the more usual situation in which the researcher, even in order to scrutinize a few deviant cases (that is, to accomplish the first step), is obliged to go back into the field to collect new data.

Differing System References.   The Zelditch analysis of deviant cases also underscores another basic principle in interpreting any set of data: the data must be examined with reference to the relevant part (or level) of the conceptual model under study. In this particular study, Zelditch learns from his data that the system levels were inadequately specified at the outset. In order to understand the man's role in the nuclear family system, he was obliged, instead of focusing on the nuclear family alone, to consider also the man's role in the larger system of the extended family or descent grouping. (A similar model of two interlocking levels of the family system is used by Thomas and Znaniecki.) The crux of the pattern which Zelditch uncovers is, as he says, "a relation between *two systems*, the household group and the descent group" with the father's instrumental activities depending partly on this relation. The researcher often has difficulty in maintaining the appropriate system reference—in matching his research case **(P-I)** and his conceptual model—exactly because of the social system complexities illustrated in the Zelditch analysis.

Sorokin's Study of Long-Term Trends

Sorokin's *Social and Cultural Dynamics* demonstrates the vast possibilities of using a wide range of existing materials in research. Treating the whole system of Western Europe as his case, he deals with social and cultural change over a period of some 2,500 years. He applies what he terms the "logico-meaningful method" of ordering sociocultural phenomena—"the appropriate unification of the fragments into a whole according to their logical significance or their logical cobelonging" (*Social and Cultural Dynamics*, Vol. I, pp. 22–32). The task of the investigator utilizing such a method, he says, is to find the "central meaning or idea" which "permeates all the components, [and] gives sense and significance to each of them." Sorokin identifies three such basic principles or categories of meaning by which sociocultural systems may be logically integrated (although these may not be found empirically in any sort of pure form). Designating these concepts respectively as Ideational, Sensate, and Idealistic, he applies them to numerous components of the Western social and cultural world—to art, science, law, wars and revolutions, economic conditions, and so on—using data that range from many thousands of works of art to all the historical figures mentioned in the *Encyclopædia Britannica*.

The excerpt from his opus focuses on trends of thought—religious, philosophical, scientific. The immediate objective of this portion of the investigation is "to study the quantitative fluctuation of the comparative influence and acceptability of the main systems of truth."

NATURE OF THE DATA

Although we shall not consider the details of measurement until later (Units 7 and 9), we can see from the Sorokin study how it is possible to use the intellectual achievements of the past as the data for a systematic and quantitative analysis of historical trends. Working without benefit of modern sampling, Sorokin undertakes the sizable task of dealing with "practically all" the great thinkers in the field. He first relates each thinker to one of "the six main epistemological currents in the mentality of the Graeco-Roman and European cultures"— later translating these into the Ideational-Sensate-Idealistic categories for classifying societies and cultures in general. Then he assigns to each thinker a numerical weight from 1 to 12 as a rough measure of the thinker's "influence" on other thinkers; these weights are based on "the number of special monographs devoted to the thinker" as this was "corrected" by certain other considerations. Sorokin's Table 1 and Figure 1 show total scores (by hundred-year periods) composed of the *number* of thinkers espousing each current of thought, as these are then *weighted* by their influence. Thus Sorokin measures "roughly . . . the increase and decrease of the comparative acceptability and influence of each of these currents of thought"—producing massive statistics that reflect changes in underlying values. (Unless the reader checks the weights assigned to individual thinkers in an appendix, however, he cannot determine from any one aggregated score whether it represents a few thinkers who were very influential, or many thinkers with little influence. See Riley and Moore, 1963.)

Sorokin is using these data to measure meaning in two different connections. First, in classifying thinkers in relation to the main systems of truth, he states that he is "assuming the position of a perfectly impartial observer, and taking the systems involved as a factual datum." When he measures the influence of these thinkers on their partisans, however, he is approaching meaning in a different way, using data which reflect, not so much the objective view of the researcher, as the subjective states of the persons to whom the meaning is transmitted.

Sorokin wants to know whether these scores actually measure the particular concepts of meaning and influence he has defined. Consequently, he cites a number of tests to demonstrate that they do. Most interesting is his comparison (shown in his Table 2) between the curves for empiricism, as one system of Sensate truth, and the curves showing the number of discoveries and inventions in the natural sciences. The latter, though obtained by a different procedure (and presented in another part of the book) show "remarkable agreement" with the former, providing "particularly strong evidence that the results obtained in both cases are neither incidental nor misleading." This example illustrates the point that even in the use of available materials validity may often be assessed by comparing sets of materials obtained from differing sources. (The often confusing distinction between *validity*—and the *reliability* discussed in Unit 2—has been stated succinctly by Stouffer, who says, "By reliability is meant: Does the index measure something consistently? By validity is meant: Granted that the index measures something consistently, is it really describing what we think it is describing?" Stouffer, 1962, p. 265.)

AVAILABLE DATA AND THE STUDY OF HISTORICAL TRENDS

Sorokin thus provides a model, not only for research on values and meanings, but, above all, for the study of trends extending far back into the past. Bales, as we have seen, collects new data in order to study dynamic processes in the present, and is thus able to specify the short-term phases of problem-solving in small groups. But only through use of available data is Sorokin able to plot the epochal alternations between Ideational and Sensate cultures, hence to postulate the governing principle of the "immanent self-regulation" of broad sociocultural change. In general, a study of the past, or, more specifically, a study of social change (an area which, incidentally, many sociologists regard as unduly neglected), must rely almost exclusively on available data.

Available vs. New Data

FORMS OF AVAILABLE DATA

These three studies begin to suggest the diverse forms in which data may be available, and the procedures for handling and interpretation required by each form.

Sometimes the sociological researcher starts with data which were not originally produced for research purposes at all, as Sorokin or Thomas and Znaniecki did. In other instances, he uses for his own objectives research data initially compiled by another researcher, as Zelditch used ethnographic reports, or as you might undertake to analyze interviews previously completed by a Cottrell. The problems entailed by these two types of materials clearly differ. The biases and limitations of any data not produced for research purposes— such as the Polish peasant letters, or family case records—are quite different from the possible errors interjected by a researcher, whether this be an interviewer or an anthropologist describing his perceptions of a primitive society.

The sociologist may also choose between verbal and nonverbal data. Numerous techniques have been developed for analyzing verbal materials (novels, sermons, magazines, diaries, letters, documents, or case records from various fields) so as to discover underlying values or attitudes, social organization, or patterns of social behavior. Such data may be handled unsystematically and descriptively, as in *The Polish Peasant;* or arranged systematically in typologies, as Max Weber does, or classified and quantified in various ways. One systematic procedure, "content analysis" (see Berelson, 1952 and 1954), breaks down verbal content into small units of meaning, classifies these units, and handles them quantitatively. (We shall examine the details of this procedure as used in the Massing study in Unit 7.) Somewhat less commonly used in sociology are the rich sources of nonverbal materials (works of art, pieces of music, clothing, dwellings, household equipment, and various artifacts). Sorokin, for one, has extended his analysis to utilize such indicants, which also form a major basis for the sociology of art, music, and knowledge.

Available data may also be found at any of the several stages of research processing (as outlined in Manual I-C). At one extreme are "raw" data that have not yet been coded, tabulated, or analyzed, such as the letters used by Thomas and Znaniecki. In other instances, the data may already have been partially processed. They may be coded and punched and ready to be tabulated, such as the data from the One-in-a-Thousand Population Census Sample, or from the data bank at the Roper Public Opinion Research Center. Other data may already be tabulated, but not yet fully analyzed or interpreted, such as the statistical records of suicide used by Durkheim (Unit 8), the U.S. Census data on family income used by Bogue (Unit 7), or the storehouse of official world population statistics used by Davis and Golden (Unit 12). At the opposite extreme from raw data are the findings from completed studies that can be reanalyzed or reinterpreted through secondary analysis, as Zelditch demonstrates.

A GENERAL RULE

Although data may be available in widely diversified forms and stages, one general rule applies to their use: in his analysis, the researcher must try to reconstruct the process by which the data were originally assembled by somebody else.

The researcher who handles data he himself has collected already knows this process. Since he himself made the decisions (under **P-VI** and **P-VIII** *e.g.*), and selected and employed certain specific techniques, he has weighed the full implications of these procedures for the research problem at hand. He is aware of the restrictions and possible biases of his materials and can evaluate their validity as indicants of the concepts which he has defined. Consequently, he can adapt his analysis and his interpretation to the nature of the new data themselves.

Such adaptation is equally important, of course, when the researcher did *not* gather the data. He must attempt to determine, insofar as possible, the conditions under which these data were produced, what specific methodological and technical decisions may have been made by the previous researcher, and the consequent impact on the nature of the data now to be taken over for his own use. To be sure, to make such important assessments of available data may often be difficult, and sometimes impossible.

COMBINED USE OF NEW AND AVAILABLE DATA

One important type of study design combines both available and new materials as major bases of the research, working back and forth between the two (see, *e.g.*, John Riley, 1962; Riley, Johnson, and Boocock). Of course, it is always good practice to make the utmost use of existing background information, whether the stuff of which the study is built is new or available. But, in addition, a widely useful design starts with available materials as background for defining the conceptual model and the objective, then gathers and analyzes new data, and finally makes further recourse to existing materials to help interpret and develop the larger theoretical implications of the new research.

ADVANTAGES

In summary, perhaps the most obvious advantage of using available data is the greater efficiency—the time, labor, and expense that can often be saved when the researcher can go directly to the heart of his analysis, bypassing preliminary field work and even the early phases of data-processing. Certainly, for reasons of efficiency, if for no other reason, in planning your own research you will want to seek possible sources of suitable available data before deciding to collect new materials.

Such sources may be especially valuable when massive data are required, beyond the scope of a single new study. The vast fund at the Bureau of the Census, for example, could not be reproduced by an individual researcher collecting his own data; yet, for study of a given problem, they frequently afford a wide range of potentially relevant variables, and a high degree of refinement in the measurement of each variable. Use of data of this scope becomes increasingly feasible as materials of sociological interest are systematically accumulated, and as the development of new electronic equipment facilitates storage and processing of data.

Probably the most important advantage of available data is that they afford the only means of studying certain kinds of problems. Past events can no longer be observed directly by the researcher, nor can they be reached through questioning beyond the recollection of respondents living today. Thus, the important analysis of historical situations or of long-term trends—of social change itself—depends upon the prior existence of relevant materials. Similarly, study of cross-cultural phenomena from remote places may require data which would be inaccessible to new research. Data in technical fields which are beyond the competence of the research analyst may have been originally assembled in usable form by an "expert," such as a medical doctor or an ethnographer. Sometimes, as in *The Polish Peasant,* existing materials may provide insights in depth into intimate personal relationships, and, sometimes, as in Sorokin's analysis, they may widen the sociologist's focus to include macroscopic social systems.

DISADVANTAGES

Against such impressive assets must be set certain basic restrictions on the utilization of available sources. Because the data were not originally assembled for present purposes, they are often incomplete or in a form in which they are not readily usable. Thus, as we have seen, Zelditch had to omit many societies from his sample for lack of information about them; or Thomas and Znaniecki were obliged to make inferences from data when they often lacked one whole side of the family correspondence. Such incompleteness may mean that the data lack representativeness, as Zelditch feared when he was unable to determine whether his sample reflected societies in general. Another disadvantage may be lack of reliability, which frequently is quite difficult to establish. Historical records, for instance, cannot be checked (unless several different accounts are available for comparison) since one can no longer either observe the events reported, or question the participants.

Finally, the data that come to the researcher in a form he does not fully understand may not fit present definitions of the concepts under scrutiny; they may lack correspondence with the conceptual model. Systematic measures developed from *The Polish Peasant* letters, for example, might fail to describe what the analyst thinks they are describing—especially if the analyst is unfamiliar with Polish life.

Such disadvantages limit the usefulness of available materials. Indeed, the researcher may finally have to reject given data because he cannot adequately assess their limitations, nor find suitable means of compensating for them. Frequently, of course, there are no data at all that are relevant to the problem under study.

Despite such limitations, the great variety of available data constitutes a highly valuable resource for the researcher. If anything, the sociologist has not made enough use of them and has given too little attention to the possible methods for their use. Through creative analysis of well-chosen materials from existing stores the researcher should be able to widen the scope of the problems investigated, formulate new study objectives more clearly, and interpret new materials within a broader framework of scientific understanding. The important *caveat* is to consider carefully the process by which the data were originally produced, spelling out and, insofar as possible, offsetting any limitations and biases, and recasting the data in a form suitable for the new problem at hand.

SUGGESTED READINGS FOR UNIT FIVE

Angell and Freedman, 1953; Berelson, 1952 and 1954; Furfey, Chapter 19; Goode and Hatt, Chapter 9; Hagood and Price, Chapter 3; Madge, Chapter 3; Murdock, 1949, especially Preface and Chapters 1 and 2; Selltiz *et al.*, Chapter 9; Whiting, 1954, Pauline Young, 1949, Chapters 6, 10.

QUESTIONS FOR REVIEW AND DISCUSSION

Review the following methodological terms as used in this Unit:

analysis of deviant cases
available data
cross-cultural studies
hypothesis-testing
nonverbal data
null hypothesis
"processed" materials
"raw" materials
research hypothesis
secondary analysis
system reference
validity

1. Suppose that, instead of questioning the citizens of Rovere, Merton had attempted to locate the community's "influentials" by using data already available. What kinds of sources might provide suitable materials? Given the nature of Merton's research objective, consider the feasibility of such an approach, and the advantages and disadvantages which should be weighed.

2. Imagine that you wish to test the hypothesis that, in the United States, the underlying ideology of children's literature has increasingly departed from a once predominant individualism. Consider how you might use available data to test such an hypothesis. What difficulties might you encounter in locating and making measurements from such data?

3. How would you evaluate the handling of interpretative analysis, as distinct from the presentation of data, in *The Polish Peasant?*

4. Using the Parsons code, as given in Exercise II-1, code the mother-daughter relationship as described in letter 644 in *The Polish Peasant.* Or code the series of letters for one of the families, using the Bales code. Are these codes appropriate tools for handling these epistolary materials systematically?

5. Using the categories "instrumental" and "expressive," how would you categorize (or "code") each of the following acts at a family breakfast table:

Mother tells daughter to pour coffee into cups.
Father praises daughter for assisting her mother.
Daughter spills coffee on tablecloth.
Daughter expresses anxiety at her mistake.
Mother reassures daughter.
Daughter laughs, shows relief.

6. How does Sorokin attempt to avoid subjectivity in assigning weights to each thinker according to his influence on his partisans?

7. What inferences might be made about the woman's role in the family from a knowledge that she is or is not gainfully employed? In answering the question, consider carefully the different social system references involved, as discussed in the analysis by Zelditch.

8. The Zelditch study employs cross-cultural comparisons. What advantage does this have over comparisons made within a single culture **(P-III)?** Illustrate from the findings of the Zelditch study. Would you classify the Sorokin study in the same way on **P-III?**

9. Contrast Sorokin's selection and use of historical materials with intensive unsystematic sociological analysis of historical data.

UNIT SIX
SOME SAMPLING METHODS

Unit 6 considers procedures by which researchers select samples from the total population of cases in which they are interested. In designing a sample, the basic decisions are how many cases to select **(P-II)**, and whether to select these to represent the population as accurately as possible *and/or* to facilitate plans for the analysis of the data **(P-IV)**.

Exercises and Manual

First complete **Exercise V-I** which, together with **Manual V-A,** explains and illustrates some procedures of probability sampling and the use of data obtained from such samples. Since representational samples typically use mathematical principles of probability, **Exercise V-2** and the elementary definitions and rules of probability in **Manual V-B** provide an introduction to the application of probability to sampling. The principles of probability you learn here will also be used repeatedly throughout the book as the basis for several mathematical models and for statistical testing.

Studies

Review the details of **Zelditch's** random sampling procedure (Unit 5). Then study in detail the samples reported by **Stouffer** and by **Kahl.** Consider in each instance the sampling objective, steps in the methods used, reasons for choosing these methods, and difficulties encountered. Take special note of the methodological points developed by Stouffer, and regard these as an addition to the procedures set forth in the Manual.

Commentary

The Commentary, which as usual assumes familiarity with the materials in the indicated exercises, manual notes, and studies, will help you to organize the various technical and applied aspects of sampling. A working knowledge is necessary for the planning of your own research, and for assessing the sample data obtained by others.

Questions for Review and Discussion

Use the Questions for Review and Discussion to review your understanding of the various terms used in sampling, to examine the place of the sample design within the design of the study as a whole, and to formulate as fully as you can the principles affecting decisions under **P-II** and **P-IV.**

SAMUEL A. STOUFFER

Communism, Conformity, and Civil Liberties

What This Book Is About

This is a report to the American people on the findings of a survey which was unique in its scope and in some of its methods.

More than 6000 men and women, in all parts of the country and in all walks of life, confided their thoughts in an interview which was as impartial as fallible ingenuity was able to devise. Over 500 skilled interviewers from two national research agencies did the field work.

The survey examines in some depth the reactions of Americans to two dangers.

One, from the Communist conspiracy outside and inside the country. Two, from those who in thwarting the conspiracy would sacrifice some of the very liberties which the enemy would destroy.

This inquiry, made in the summer of 1954, was concerned not with transient opinions but with deeper latent attitudes or dispositions. Some types of reactions to the Communist threat are not new and will be encountered in years to come. . . .

The question is: *How can the sober second thought of the people be maintained in a state of readiness to resist external and internal threats to our heritage of liberties?* . . .

We hope that [the] findings, along with knowledge from other sources, can aid

From Samuel A. Stouffer, *Communism, Conformity, and Civil Liberties,* copyright © 1955 by Samuel A. Stouffer, pp. 13–21, 22–24, 49–55, 89–91, 93–94, 237–39, 241, 242, 243, 244, 246–47, 270–73. Reprinted in part with permission of Doubleday and Company, Inc.

responsible citizens—in our government; in our newspaper offices and broadcasting studios; in our schools, churches, and other organizations within the local community—as they plan better for the task ahead. Following are some of the questions considered:

Who are the people most likely to have given the sober second thought to the problems with which we are concerned?

What about the attitudes of responsible civic leaders as compared with the rank and file within a community?

Is the American public in a state of pathological fear?

Are we raising a new generation which will be more sensitive or less sensitive than its elders to threats to freedom? What is the impact of our educational system, which provides more schooling to more youth than in any other nation in history?

Do attitudes differ in different regions of the country? In cities as compared with rural areas? Among men as compared with women? What roles does religion play?

How are the images about Communists which people carry in their heads related to willingness to deprive other nonconformists, who are not necessarily Communists, of civil rights?

How important are agencies of mass communication likely to be in evoking more thoughtful reflection on the issues of Communism and civil liberties? How well do the people know the views of leaders they respect? What can be accomplished by responsible citizens in their local communities?

These are some of the topics which

this study has investigated. Not with an eye on the opinions about any particular public figure or on issues which may be ephemeral. Rather on basic underlying sentiments which do not change abruptly or fluctuate with the day's headlines. . . .

Who Were Interviewed in This Survey

The survey . . . is basically a public opinion poll and was conducted in the field not by just one but by two . . . public opinion research organizations. One was the American Institute of Public Opinion —the Gallup Poll. The other was the National Opinion Research Center, a non-profit organization with headquarters at the University of Chicago. Each agency used its own staff of sampling experts to draw independently what was intended to constitute a representative cross-section of the American population. . . . The greatest advantage of utilizing two agencies was that each was able to carry out a very large assignment within a reasonable time without adding inexperienced interviewers to its staff. Quality was the first consideration. . . .

The type of sampling method used was costly and time-consuming. . . . In simplest outline, the probability method, as employed in the present survey, consists of the following steps:

1. From a list of all the counties and metropolitan areas in the United States, a sample is drawn at random. These selected counties and metropolitan areas are called "primary sampling units."
2. Within each primary sampling unit, urban blocks and rural segments are selected, also strictly at random.
3. Within each selected block or seg-

ment, interviewers list systematically every dwelling unit. Among these dwelling units a sample of X is selected, also strictly at random.
4. Within each of the selected dwelling units all adults are enumerated, and *one* in each dwelling is selected for the interview. This one is selected according to a fixed rule which leaves the interviewer no flexibility in making substitutions.
5. Once the individual adult within the household is designated as the sample person, the interviewer is required to make repeated calls until he finds him or her at home and available for interview. This is the most time-consuming and costly part of the procedure.
6. No substitutions are permitted, and every effort is made to track down absentees, even assigning them to interviewers in other parts of the country if away on vacation. Some refusals are inevitable but are kept to a minimum by the resourcefulness of the trained interviewers. If that resourcefulness is unavailing, letters and even telegrams from the home office of the agency often overcome the remaining resistance. A careful analysis of the "fish that got away" appears in Appendix A, with the conclusion that bias thus occasioned could not be appreciably large. . . .

The probability method eliminates any possible bias of the interviewer in the selection of respondents. For example, those who respond readily without urging, or who live in more accessible places, or who are at home at the time of call may be so different in some respects relevant to the study that a bias is introduced. The probability method also has important advantages from the mathematical standpoint of calculating margins of error attributable to chance alone.

The probability method has disadvantages also. One is its cost, which can be two to five times as high as the quota method. An interviewer may have to spend the aggregate of a day's time on a succession of efforts to make contact with a single respondent. The other is its slowness. If a study must be completed in a few days, the quota method, or some modification of it, seems to be the only answer. But to stretch out the field work on a survey over a period of several weeks, as is necessary with a large probability sample, is to run the risk that some important happening in the news may change opinions in the middle of the survey. . . .

For further details on sampling, the reader is referred to Appendix A of this volume.

The aggregate number of cases obtained on the national cross-sections by the two agencies was 4933. . . . The agreement between the two cross-sections was quite close and most gratifying. . . .

But this combined cross-section of 4933 cases is only a part of the study. A unique feature of the survey lay in obtaining an additional special sample of 1500 selected local community leaders, entirely independent of the national cross-section. In this book the special sample of community leaders is always tabulated separately, never pooled with the cross-section.

Unlike the respondents in the cross-section, the community leaders were of necessity arbitrarily selected. But extreme care was taken to preclude interviewer bias in their selection. The steps in the sampling process were as follows:

1. From each of the cities of 10,000 to 150,000 in the sample, an arbitrary list of 14 occupational roles was drawn up. The same list was used in each city. It included the mayor, the president of the Chamber of Commerce, the chairman of the Community Chest, the president of a predesignated large labor-union local in the city, the chairmen of the Republican and Democratic county central committees, the commander of the largest American Legion post in the city, the regent of the D.A.R., the president of the local women's club, the chairmen of the school board and the library board, the president of the local council of the Parent-Teachers' Association (or if there was no such council, of the largest P.T.A. in the city), the president of the bar association, the publisher of the locally owned newspaper of largest circulation.

2. The list, it will be seen, was so drawn up that interviewer bias in selection was precluded, since one person only could fit a given description in a given community. Each interviewer prepared a list of the names and addresses of the 14 in his city, and to each of the 14 a letter was sent, signed by the head of the polling agency responsible for that city. (For this operation, each of the two polling organizations took full responsibility for half of the cities.) The letter, which spoke of the national importance of the survey without indicating the subject matter, was designed to pave the way for personal appointments at the least inconvenience to the respondents, many of whom are very busy people.

3. The selected community leaders were interviewed with questionnaires identical with those used in the national cross-section.

While the national cross-section can be defended as representative of all classes of the population, it must be stated here emphatically that the sample of leaders is not intended to be and is not a representative sample of community leaders in America. There is no objective definition of what constitutes a community leader and, even if there were, the cost of procuring a large and exhaustive sample would be prohibitive.

What, then, does the sample of leaders represent?

First, it represents only people in the cities of 10,000 to 150,000; people in rural communities, smaller cities, and larger metropolitan centers are by definition excluded.

Second, it represents only arbitrarily selected leaders. Strictly speaking, an average based on all such leaders combined is not susceptible of clear interpretation. What we can say, however, is the following: The mayors, for example, are a representative sample of all mayors in cities of 10,000 to 150,000. By "representative" we mean that if we had been able to interview all such mayors in all American cities of this size the result would differ from those in our sample only by a relatively small chance error, which is mathematically calculable. Similarly with each of the other incumbents of position as defined. And this can provide very important, interpretable knowledge.

But why 14? This is not a magic number but is simply the maximum which the budget of time and money permitted in a given city. And why these particular 14? There is no right or wrong answer to this question. Each leadership role was chosen either because, as in the case of the president of the Community Chest, for example, he was likely to be a generally respected figure; or because, as in the case of the president of the Chamber of Commerce or the bar association or the largest labor-union local, he was likely, on the average, to be influential among certain segments of the population; or because, as in the case of heads of patriotic organizations or in the case of various elected or appointed officials, the specific nature of their responsibility made their views especially relevant.

It would be easy to construct a list

twice as long or longer. . . . On the whole, in so far as the sample of leaders is biased, there are fewer rather than more leaders who would automatically be expected to have liberal attitudes.

For purposes of comparison with the views of each of the 14 selected types of leaders, a special sub-sample of the national cross-section has been segregated for exactly the same cities as those used for the sample of leaders. This sub-sample should be representative of the total population of all such cities, in the same sense as the mayors are representative of all mayors in cities of 10,000 to 150,000.

So much for the samples. We see that they introduce features some of which are rare and some of which are new in national surveys of this type.

What Kinds of Questions Were Asked?

The questionnaire used . . . is somewhat unconventional, by customary opinion-survey practice, in two main respects.

First, *it relied more heavily than many surveys on what are called free-answer or open-ended questions.* Much care was taken not to introduce specific check-list questions until the respondent had had a chance to talk generally about a subject. For example, the first twenty minutes or so of the interview were devoted to a general discussion of whatever things the respondent had most on his or her mind, without any hint as to the ultimate purpose of the survey. This was facilitated only by such leading questions by the interviewer as the following:

Everybody of course has some things he worries about, more or less. Would you say you worry more now than you used to, or not as much?

What kinds of things do you worry most about?

Are there other problems you worry or are concerned about, especially political or world problems?

We are interested in what kind of things people talk about. Offhand, what problems do you remember discussing with your friends in the last week or so?

(Unless volunteered above) Were there other things? For example, did you talk about any dangers facing people in the United States?

The questionnaire then led into a series of check-list questions on war and civil liberties, with no direct question on attitudes toward the internal Communist threat until nearly half of the interview was completed. Here, again, open-ended questions were introduced to get the flavor of opinions in the respondent's own language, which the interviewer was instructed to take down as nearly as possible verbatim. . . .

The approach is not too dissimilar to what would be used by an expert newspaper reporter. It provides invaluable data on the depth and intensity of opinions which may be later ascertained systematically by more conventional check-list questions. It evokes a given opinion within a larger context of the general attitudes of the individual. And it does not put into a person's head ideas that may not have been there before.

There are disadvantages as well. One is the sheer time it takes to conduct such an interview. [From one hour to more than three hours, averaging about an hour and a quarter, was required.] Another is dependency on the objectivity and accuracy of the interviewer in recording the salient remarks when, as is often the case, he or she cannot set down every word. A third is the monumental task of summarizing systematically such qualitative data from thousands of interviews, and the further dangers of bias or subjectivity in preparing such summaries.

Therefore, there is an important place for simple check-list questions to which there is a prescribed set of answer categories. Such questions were used in considerable numbers.

The second respect in which the questionnaire used on this survey represented some departures from current practice was in the planned use of *a series of questions to summarize a given opinion rather than in reliance upon a single question.* One would not think of offering a single word to a person to spell as a test of his spelling ability, nor a single little problem in arithmetic as a test of his ability to multiply or divide. Often one can come closer to ascertaining an opinion by a single question than to measuring ability by a single test item. But experience has shown that a test or a scale of opinions based on a series of related questions is usually much more stable than a single item and also makes possible an internal test for validity. Do the various answers a person gives hang together in some systematic, consistent way? If they do, and if they satisfy certain fairly rigorous technical requirements, we can say they constitute *a scale of measurement.* . . .

A Note to Enthusiasts and Skeptics

The limitations of studies like the present one are not always properly appreciated. There are some people who are disposed to seize a little too uncritically upon a reported number, like the percentage of people reported as giving a particular response to a question. There are others, perhaps reacting against too zealous enthusiasts, who retreat into agnosticism about all such figures.

It is a fact that no number reported in this study is exact. This is also the case with numbers reported in official statistics like the United States Census. No one really knows the actual population of New York City within plus or minus 100,000 or more. But this does not mean that Census figures are useless. One learns to take them for what they are—approximations. And normally they are closer approximations than somebody's guess.

Numbers in the present study are, of course, even less adequate approximations to unknown and unknowable "true national figures" than are most Census data. For they are based on a sample which, though larger than is customary and obtained with meticulous care, is still only a sample.

Even if the people whose opinions we report constitute a truly random sample of the population, we would expect the percentages in several such random samples to differ. The laws by which they would differ are well known—in fact, they constitute the basis of the science of mathematical statistics. Some of our percentages, calculated on the entire national cross-section, would fluctuate by chance only slightly. Others, based on sub-samples with much fewer cases, could have a theoretical variation of as much as 15 or 20 percentage points 5% of the time. In Appendix D we have sought to provide a compact rule-of-thumb guide. . . . Therefore, we have sought to be careful not to stress the importance or implications of findings which theoretically could have occurred fairly often by chance alone.

In addition to instability attributable to chance, there are other sources of error which could happen even in a total enumeration of a population, as in the Census. For example, even slight variations in the wording of a question

can produce variations in response. . . .

When we report that one class of persons has different attitudes from another class of persons—say, women as compared with men—our best test is the *consistency* with which we find this result in different parts of the country, or in different ages, or in different educational groups. . . . Consistency of a repeated finding is not a sure guarantee, because of some possible systematic error, but it adds considerably to our confidence. . . .

Introducing a Scale of Willingness to Tolerate Nonconformists

We will want to ask: In the cross-sections of the population, who are relatively the most tolerant toward nonconformists and who are least tolerant? City people or rural people? Easterners, Midwesterners, or Southerners? Older or younger? Men or women? Educated or the less educated? Etc. For sheer economy of presentation as well as for question reliability, we need a single index or scale which will summarize an individual's relative degree of tolerance.

Fortunately, we have such a scale. One of the most important findings . . . is the remarkable consistency in *patterns* of response. The community leaders, on almost all questions, are more willing to respect the rights of the nonconformist than are the rank and file. This is true on questions which 75% favor, or on which people split 50-50, or on questions which only 25% favor. It is true with respect to the rights of Socialists, atheists, suspected Communists who swear to their innocence, or admitted Communists. Further cross-tabulations show that, if a man or woman is one of only 25% who would be tolerant on a given item, he tends to be tolerant on most other items to which a still larger proportion give "tolerant" answers. And vice versa. If a person is one of a minority who would be severe on a Socialist, he tends to be one of a still larger group who would be tough on an atheist or admitted Communist. Not all questions are consistent, in this sense, with other questions, but most of them are.

These facts make a scale possible. Out of the questions here reported, 15 were selected to constitute that scale. . . .

For simplicity of presentation, the scale scores have been recombined into three still broader rank groups with the following labels:

Relatively more tolerant. Constituting about a third of the national cross-section, these people give *tolerant* types of an-swers on more of the 15 questions than other people.

Relatively less tolerant. Constituting about a fifth of the national cross-section, these people give *intolerant* types of an-swers on more of the 15 questions than other people.

In-between. Between these two group-ings are the rest of the population.

Figure 1 uses this scale to make a sum-mary comparison. . . .

Now, a word as how *not* to read this figure. It does *not* say that 66% of the community leaders are tolerant as com-pared with 31% of the national cross-section. Or that only 5% are intolerant as compared with 19% of the cross-section. The scale does not measure tol-erance in any absolute sense.

Figure 1   *Community leaders are relatively more tolerant than the rank and file on scale of tolerance of nonconformists*

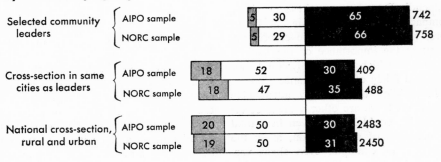

Percentage distribution of scale scores

What does Figure 1 say? It says (1) that we decided on a score on our tolerance scale high enough so that 31% of the national cross-section got that score or a higher one. We call these people our "more tolerant" group. Having set that score, we found that 66% of the community leaders got that score or a higher one. Similarly, (2) that we decided on a score that was low enough so that 19% of the national cross-section got that score or a lower one. We call that group our "less tolerant" group. Having set that score, we found that only 5% of community leaders got that score or a lower one. . . .

Table 1 . . . shows that each of the 14 selected categories of community leaders contains a larger proportion of individuals who are classed as "more tolerant" on the scale than are contained in the cross-section in the same cities or in the national cross-section. This result holds without exception even if we base our

Table **1** *Scale of willingness to tolerate nonconformists*

(*types of community leaders compared with cross-sections*)

	Percentage "relatively more tolerant" on scale [a]		
	AIPO sample	NORC sample	Combined samples
Public officials			
Mayors	59	62	60
Presidents, school board	66	59	62
Presidents, library board	82	75	79
Political party chairmen			
Republican county central committee	60	80	70
Democratic county central committee	70	58	64
Industrial leaders			
Presidents, chamber of commerce	77	54	65
Presidents, labor union	61	63	62
Heads of special patriotic groups			
Commanders, American Legion	45	47	46
Regents, D.A.R.	38	56	48
Others			
Chairmen, community chest	77	87	82
Presidents, bar association	75	79	77
Newspaper publishers	85	83	84
Presidents, women's clubs	46	53	49
Presidents, parent-teachers' association	68	68	68
Average of community leaders	65	66	66
Cross-section of same cities as leaders	30	35	32
National cross-section, rural and urban	30	31	31

[a] [The bases for all of Stouffer's percentages are shown in the original source.]

findings on the samples from each survey agency taken separately.

There is considerable range among the different types of leaders. But a further caution must be exercised in making such comparisons. Even the combined sample for any particular category of leader is small and therefore subject to considerable chance variation. For example, the comparative percentages in Table 1 for presidents of the Chamber of Commerce and for labor unions are 65 and 62, respectively. But in the AIPO sample the difference is in one direction; in the NORC sample the difference is reversed. Moreover ... we require differences between two categories of leaders to be at least 14% to be significant. [Numbers on which these percentages are based, shown elsewhere in the book, range around 50 and are all lower than 100. See Appendix D for required allowance of at least 14%.] We do see in Table 1 that the commanders of the American Legion are significantly less likely to be at the tolerant end of the scale than most of the other community leaders. Similarly, the regents of the D.A.R. and the presidents of the women's clubs. On the other hand, the presidents of the library board, the chairmen of the Community Chest, the presidents of the bar associations, and the newspaper publishers are significantly more tolerant on this scale than several others on the list. ...

Again let it be pointed out, this scale does not measure ... tolerance *in general*. It deals only with attitudes toward certain types of nonconformists or deviants. It does not deal with attitudes toward extreme right-wing agitators, toward people who attack minority groups, toward faddists or cultists, in general, nor, of course, toward a wide variety of criminals. For purposes of this study, the tolerance of nonconformity or suspected nonconformity is *solely* within the broad context of the Communist threat. ...

A Note on the Time Span of the Study as Related to These Attitudes

It was pointed out in Chapter One that this study went into the field in mid-May 1954, while the Army-McCarthy hearings were still in progress. About a third of the respondents were interviewed in May, about half in the first two weeks of June, and the remainder during the rest of June and July.

There were not many unusually dramatic events during this period. But, in any case, one would not expect the kind of latent tendencies reported here to shift markedly with ups and downs in the news over a period of a few weeks or even of several months.

There is evidence consistent with the probability of little change. The date of all but 51 of the interviews in the cross-section was reported on the questionnaires. The following table compares the tolerance scores of the national cross-section by time of interview:

Time of interview	Relatively less tolerant	In-between	Relatively more tolerant	Total	Number of cases
May 15–31	18	51	31	100	1476
June 1–15	19	51	30	100	2391
June 16–30	22	47	31	100	533
July 1–31	19	52	29	100	482

The differences in scores by time periods are clearly not significant. In general, the characteristics by education, etc., of those interviewed late were about the same as the characteristics of those interviewed early. We cannot, of course, say that some people's attitudes did not change during this period. But if there were changes, those in the direction of more tolerance were almost exactly balanced by other changes in the direction of less tolerance.

How Tolerant Is the New Generation?

First let us ask: *Are those who are classed as relatively "more tolerant" on our scale ... likelier to be the younger people or the older people?*

The answer is clear. It is the younger people: [See Table 2.]

This result may not be surprising to many readers, but the answers to the following questions are by no means obvious:

Does this mean that a young man of 30 is likely to be less tolerant when he becomes 60 than he is today? Or does it mean that a young man at 30 is likely to be more tolerant when he becomes 60 than his father is today?

In other words, do these figures reflect mere age change within a static culture, or do they reflect some basic trends in our culture which are working toward increasing tolerance?

From one standpoint, such questions are unanswerable. . . .

But if we are willing to imagine that the external incentives for intolerance remain constant, we may get some insight which will show us in what direction the *underlying tendencies* with respect to tolerance are headed.

Before undertaking our analysis let us seek one additional tabulation from our data. This is with respect to schooling: [See Table 3.] These data, like the pre-

Table **2**   *Percentage distribution of scores on scale of tolerance, by age*

	Less tolerant	In-between	More tolerant	Total	Number of cases
21 to 29	10	43	47	100	528
30 to 39	11	46	43	100	682
40 to 49	15	48	37	100	615
50 to 59	18	51	31	100	426
60 and over	21	61	18	100	517

Table **3**   *Percentage distribution of scores on scale of tolerance, by education*

	Less tolerant	In-between	More tolerant	Total	Number of cases
College graduates	5	29	66	100	308
Some college	9	38	53	100	319
High school graduates	12	46	42	100	768
Some high school	17	54	29	100	576
Grade school	22	62	16	100	792

vious data by age, are for those in our national cross-section who are more interested in the Communist threat and how it is being combated. They show decisively that the more the schooling, the more the tolerance.

Few findings of this study are more important. It will now be placed in juxtaposition with the earlier finding—the younger the person, the more tolerant.

The Younger Generation Has More Schooling. What Does This Fact Portend?

There is one very crucial fact which could support the prediction that as the younger generation ages it will still be more tolerant than its elders—given more or less the same external conditions. This fact is *the greater schooling which the younger generation has received.*

Consequently, if education, *independent of age,* makes for tolerance, the present younger generation, when it reaches later years, should be more tolerant than its elders are today. . . .

The question that we now ask of our data is important: *Among older people, as well as among younger people, by separate age groups, are the better educated more tolerant toward nonconformists?* If so, then one cannot say that aging alone will account for a difference between generations.

Figure 2 shows that in *all* age groups the better educated tend to be more tolerant than the less educated. The picture is quite decisive until we reach age 60. Even among those 60 and over, those who have attended or graduated from college are more likely to be tolerant of

nonconformists than those who have not completed high school, though the differences are smaller. Some bars in Figure 2 are based on too few cases to be decisive, but the over-all pattern is unmistakable.

We can say with some confidence, then, that older people are less tolerant not merely because they are older. As the educational level of those entering the older generation goes up decade after decade, we should expect our oldsters to be *increasingly tolerant*—unless external conditions change drastically.

At the same time, if we examine Figure 2 carefully, we observe that there is *also* a consistent tendency for the upper educational groups to become less tolerant as they get older. The percentages classed as "more tolerant" among college graduates go down progressively on Figure 2 as age increases—77, 75, 64, 57, 31. A similar pattern in spite of lower percentages throughout exists for the "some college" group. The two high school groups and the grade school people show no very consistent tendency to become less tolerant with age, though all drop off somewhat in this respect by age 60. This does not in the least invalidate the conclusion in the preceding paragraph. We may still, in effect, predict that a person, on the average, is likely to be more tolerant than his own parents. To this we must add: Although he is likely to be more tolerant when he reaches 60 than were his own parents at 60, he may at the same time be less tolerant than he was in his own younger days.

In its implications for the future of the American scene, Figure 2 may have very considerable significance. Whatever may happen externally to stimulate greater or less tolerance, we now have a glimpse at the tendencies inherent in the changing structure of our population. . . .

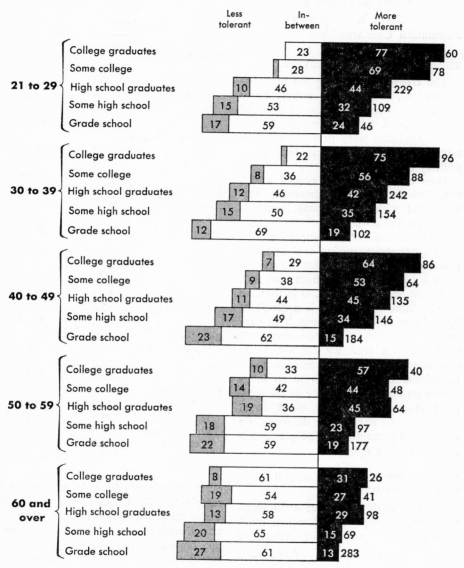

Percentage distribution on scale of
willingness to tolerate nonconformists

[a] Data for the "more interested" only.

**Appendix A. How the Samples
Were Selected and How Closely
They Conform With Known
Population Characteristics** [1]

THE NATIONAL CROSS-SECTION

The cross-section, using the probability method, sought to be representative of the American population 21 years of age and over, living in private households. Excluded were persons in hospitals, nursing homes, prisons, hotels, and military establishments.

How closely the final sample of respondents who completed interviews corresponded with the national figures is shown [in Table 4].

It will be seen that the sample is a quite satisfactory reconstruction of the population on these characteristics. There are some biases, but seldom more than 2%. The most serious, possibly, is in the case of education, where there is a deficit of 3.6% in grade school people. This may not be a sampling error, however, for it may reflect a tendency for people to overstate their schooling even more to an interviewer on a poll than to an interviewer on the Census. None of the sampling discrepancies above noted could have made an appreciable difference on the over-all percentages of people reporting a particular opinion. . . .

ANALYSIS OF THE "FISH WHICH WERE NOT CAUGHT"

For this study a total of 4939 interviews were completed, of which 4933 were usable for purposes of analysis. If

[1] For much of the substance of this appendix the author is indebted to Paul Sheatsley of the National Opinion Research Center and Paul Perry of the American Institute of Public Opinion.

Table **4** *Percentage distribution*

	U.S. adult civilian population (latest estimates from Census data)	Completed interviews in cross-section sample
By region		
East	27.6	25.6
Midwest	29.9	29.8
South	28.9	31.3
West	13.6	13.3
	100.0	*100.0*
By urban and rural		
Urban	64.0	66.0
Rural	36.0	34.0
	100.0	*100.0*
By sex		
Males	47.7	46.6
Females	52.3	53.4
	100.0	*100.0*
By age		
21–29	18.8	18.4
30–39	23.5	23.8
40–49	20.9	21.5
50–59	16.4	16.1
60 and older	20.4	20.2
	100.0	*100.0*
By color		
Negro	9.2	8.9
All others	90.8	91.1
	100.0	*100.0*
By education		
College	15.4	17.1
High school	43.5	45.4
Grade school or none	41.1	37.5
	100.0	*100.0*

every person specified in the original sample had been interviewed, the total would have been 5881. It is very important, therefore, to analyze the reasons for noncompletion. Actually, the completion rate is one of the best on record and was achieved by instructing every interviewer to make at least five attempts before giving up.

A breakdown of attempted interviews by the two agencies combined is as follows:

	Number	Per-centage
Completed interviews	4939	84.0
Not at home, no contact made	340	5.8
Too sick to be interviewed	64	1.1
Interviewer could not speak respondent's non-English language	52	0.9
Refused to be interviewed	415	7.0
Broke off interview	71	1.2
	5881	*100.0*

Even though it is reassuring that the completed interviews in the cross-section sample reproduced the population characteristics of the nation as closely as we have seen they did, we still must be concerned about the introduction of bias because of the "fish which were not caught."

By far the most important fact for our purposes is that only 1.2% broke off the interview after it began. If this number had been very large—say of the magnitude of 10%—we would have real grounds for worry. Why? Because these are the only people who could have failed to co-operate as a consequence of knowing what the questionnaire was driving at. Those who refused to be interviewed at all are a much less serious problem, since they could have had no idea about the contents of the study. Actually, even among the 1.2% who broke off the interview after it began, the majority of reasons were clearly unrelated to the content of the study. . . .

Not too much is known about the 5.8% who were not at home or not contacted. . . .

With respect to the refusal groups— the 7% who would not be interviewed and the 1.2% who broke off the interview after it began—some extraordinary pains were taken to discover whether the failure to get such cases would introduce a serious bias in our analysis. Our considered conclusion is that it would not.

Interviewers were instructed to record verbatim the respondent's stated reason for refusing to co-operate. Interviewers were then asked whether, in their view, this was the real reason he refused, and if not, what they considered to be the true reason. Special attention was given to the possibility of *fear*. The Communist issue directly could not have been a cause of fear among those who refused to be interviewed at all, since none knew that it would be discussed. Also, more than half of the breakoffs came before the subject of Communism was introduced. . . .

There were only seven cases in the entire survey where fear was explicitly expressed in the context of Communism, and only a dozen or so where the interviewer felt that this was an element in non-co-operation. . . .

Analysis of the demographic characteristics of the refusals shows that in the main they do not differ greatly from the population who were interviewed. . . .

The only respect with which those who refused appears to differ significantly from those who were interviewed is their place of residence, for refusal rates were markedly higher in the largest cities. In rural areas, for example, only 4% of the respondents refused to be interviewed, but in cities of more than 100,000 population the refusal rate was 13%. This phenomenon has been reported in many other surveys as well.

Any loss from a probability sample naturally introduces a possible bias. In general, however, it may be said that the loss rate in the current survey was of no different nature from nor any higher than the loss experienced in any survey inquiry, and that detailed analysis of the groups who contributed to the loss fails to reveal any special characteristics which would affect the over-all interpretation of the findings. . . .

The Sample of Local Community Leaders

. . . It is obvious . . . that no claims can be made that the present sample is representative of "leadership opinion" in the United States, or even that the 14 separate samples adequately reflect local opinion within each group. We have noted that the largest cities as well as the rural areas are generally not represented in these samples. Some of the leaders interviewed represent only one of several such leaders in the community. And there remains the problem of "weights." In our tabulations, every leader interviewed has been given equal weight, so that the views of the small-city newspaper publisher or school board chairman count just as much as the views of his opposite number in a larger city.

It will be best to evaluate the sample for exactly what it is: the opinions of local leaders of the specified types in a representative cross-section of more than 100 small and medium-sized cities. We cannot say that our sample of Chamber of Commerce heads, for example, represents "American business opinion" or even grass-roots Chamber of Commerce opinion. But we can say that the opinions of those we interviewed in this group accurately reflect the opinions of all leaders of the most influential business association in cities of the designated size.

And as such, their views—and the views of the 13 other leadership groups who were interviewed—command some attention and respect.

The rate of interview completion among the community-leader sample surpassed even that achieved among the regular population cross-section. . . .

The actual sample . . . totaled 1688,[2] yielding the following results:

	Number	Per- centage
Completed interviews	1533	90.9
Out of town, ill, unavailable	73	4.3
Never contacted	31	1.8
Refusal or breakoff	51	3.0
	1688	*100.0*

It will be noted that the refusal rate among the leaders was only about half that among the population cross-section. While the original refusal rate was considerably higher, every effort was made through personal letters, telephone calls, etc., to overcome the respondent's objection and to obtain his opinions. Considering the fact that these community leaders were in many cases extremely busy individuals, with many demands on their time, their willingness to contribute up to two hours of their time in replying to these questions is most gratifying. . . .

[2] In a few instances the same individual held more than one of the 14 leadership positions. Thus, a man might be the local newspaper publisher and also the chairman of the Community Chest. Since the leader sample was designed for separate analysis of each of the 14 groups, such individuals were counted twice and their interviews were duplicated. (If they refused to be interviewed, their refusal was counted twice.) The number of individuals in the total leader sample was therefore slightly less than the 1533 interviews which were tabulated.

Appendix D. How To Make an Allowance for Sampling Error in Looking at Differences Between Percentages [3]

This appendix is written to help the non-technical reader who wants some guidance as to when he should consider a difference between any two percentages significant and when he should not.

In some cases a difference of only 5% may be significant because the samples are large. In other cases a difference of 15% may not be significant because the samples are small. And in all instances we must keep in mind the possibility that questions which might seem to have the same content but which are worded differently can yield different results.

Throughout this report the emphasis has been put on the *pattern* of the percentages, not the actual amounts. If the questions had been phrased somewhat differently, most individual percentages would be shifted in the same direction by such a change, and if that is so, then the *patterns* would remain pretty much the same in spite of the shift produced by varying the precise meaning of the questions.

When we talk about any one percentage we must make some allowance for the effect of choosing a particular form of the question and we must not think of the reported percentage as being very accurate. An equally dependable survey made by similar methods at about the same time might well report percentages that are sometimes the same and sometimes as much as five, ten, or more points

[3] The author is indebted to Professor Frederick F. Stephan of Princeton University for preparing most of the substance of this appendix.

different from those that are reported here.

This is not true to the same extent of the *pattern* of percentages—that is, to the differences that are shown between the various percentages that are reported for groupings of people according to region, age, education, interest, tolerance scores, and other individual facts. Yet some allowance must be made for variations of the patterns too. Many minor things can happen to make the pattern shown by one survey a bit different from the patterns of other surveys of like kind and equal reliability. It is not easy to search for them and determine just how much allowance to make for each of these influences, but nevertheless it is possible to set up some simple recommendations that will help us to avoid two dangers of misinterpreting the information reported here:

1. taking seriously small differences that are mostly the result of chance in the sampling and minor variations of the survey work;
2. ignoring differences which may be indicative of important contrasts between two or more kinds of people.

We cannot escape these dangers altogether. Also, one of these dangers may be more serious than the other. Nevertheless, the following recommendations should strengthen the common sense we use in thinking about the patterns and at times correct our common sense when it errs:

1. When two or more percentages are identical, this is not evidence of almost perfect accuracy. Their agreement will usually be a combination of the effects of chance and rounding the figures to the nearest unit.
2. When two or more percentages dif-

fer, part of the difference may well be due again to chance and rounding as well as to various minor differences in the survey work for each group of people. The effects of chance in the sampling are less when the size of the groupings of people from which the percentages were calculated is larger. Hence our

allowance for these effects must take into account the size of the groups, usually shown in tables as the "number of cases." We can find out how much to allow—that is, how much of the difference we would do well to ignore—by looking up the appropriate figure in the following short table:

Comparison	Approximate size (number of cases)		Recommended allowance (percentage points)
(A) Average of community leaders	1500		4 to 6
with cross-section of their cities:	897		
(B) AIPO sample with NORC sample:			
National cross-section	2483,	2450	3 to 5
Cross-section of same cities as leaders	409,	488	6 to 10
Average of community leaders	742,	758	5 to 8
One type of community leader	50,	50	20 to 30
(C) Any grouping of people with another, in which the smaller group has a size appoximately equal to:			
		100	14 to 21
		150	12 to 18
		200	10 to 15
		400	7 to 10
		600	6 to 9
		800	5 to 8
		1000	4 to 6
		2000	3 to 5

The first and smaller allowance should be used when one is interested in several specific comparisons and then looks at the differences of percentages for these preselected comparisons. If the difference is not larger than the allowance, then it may be interesting and still worth considering as a weak clue, but it should not be taken seriously as pointing to an established fact. For example ... the AIPO and NORC samples differ for the national cross-section by 1 point on the percentage answering "Yes." This has little if any meaning, since it is smaller than the allowance of 3. On the other hand, the

leaders and the people in their cities differ by 16 percentage points in the proportions that answered "Yes," and this is much greater than the allowance of 4. Hence it is to be taken as substantial evidence of a difference between leaders and other people in their cities. How much difference? If we subtract the allowance from the difference, we find that it is very probably greater than 12 points. It may also be greater than 16 percentage points but not likely more than 20 percentage points.

The second and larger allowance is for use when one searches through the tables looking not at specific comparisons but at the larger differences which appear. In picking only these larger differences, one may be capitalizing on chance. If one looks at all possible comparisons, he is more likely to encounter these chance differences than if he looks at some limited set of comparisons. Thus, looking only for the larger differences may mislead us. It may lead us to take seriously patterns that will not reappear when another survey is taken or some other check is made on the validity of the patterns we select. Hence we must make a larger allowance to protect ourselves from this danger of misinterpretation of the reported percentages.

Again let us emphasize the fact that, even when no individual pair of percentages is significantly different, a pattern of such differences, most of them in the same direction, may be highly significant. . . . Individual pairs of percentages [may not] differ by enough to be significant in themselves. But when we have, say, 14 out of 17 matched comparisons showing differences *in the same direction,* we get a result which would happen by chance less than once in a hundred times, however small the individual differences. . . .

JOSEPH A. KAHL
Educational and Occupational Aspirations of "Common Man" Boys

This article is concerned with the ambitions of high school boys. It reports an interview study of 24 boys of the "common man" or "working" class. They all had enough intelligence to go to college and thereby get a good start toward the higher levels of occupational life, yet one-half of the boys chose not to strive for such success. Instead, they planned little or no schooling beyond high school and said they would be content with the lesser jobs that would likely be open to them. The aim of the study was to explore the social influences which helped to explain the choices of these boys, with particular focus on the question: why were 12 boys

Reprinted in part from Joseph A. Kahl, "Educational and Occupational Aspirations of 'Common Man' Boys," *Harvard Educational Review,* 1953, *23,* pp. 186, 187, 188–90, 192–94, 196, 197, 200–01, with permission of *Harvard Educational Review.*

striving to "better" themselves while 12 were not?

The study was part of a larger one called "The Mobility Project" under way at Harvard's Laboratory of Social Relations.[1] The sample of 24 for interview analysis was drawn from a larger sample of 3971 boys on whom questionnaire data were available. A brief discussion of the questionnaire data is necessary in order to establish a framework for the interview material.

I. The Questionnaire Study

It has long been known that occupational success is highly related to educational achievement. On the average, those

[1] The project is under the direction of Drs. Talcott Parsons, Samuel A. Stouffer, and Florence R. Kluckhohn.

with the most education get the best jobs (defined in terms of both income and prestige). Occupation, in turn, is at the center of the complex we call "social class." Thus if we learn more about the determinants of occupational placement, we learn more about social class placement. Yet the argument chases its tail, for we also know that social class of parents influences educational achievement of sons.

It seemed convenient to break into this circle of causation by studying large numbers of people who were readily available: boys in school. Their current educational plans would be predictors of their future occupational success. And their IQ scores plus their family class (status) backgrounds should divulge major determinants of their educational aspirations. Therefore a questionnaire was distributed to boys in public high schools in eight towns that are part of the Boston metropolitan area. (The omission of Catholic parochial schools was the major deficiency in the data.) All the boys in the sophomore and junior classes of those schools filled out a form, regardless of their curriculum. . . .

The IQ scores of the boys and the occupations of their fathers turned out to be of practically equal utility as predictors of the boys' educational ambitions. Most boys with high intelligence or from high status homes planned a college career, whereas most boys with low intelligence or from low status homes did not aspire to higher education. But IQ scores and social class level are known to be related; consequently, the data were arranged in the form of Table 1 to show the independent operation of these two factors. It indicates the percentage of boys who aim toward college in various IQ and status categories. At the extremes, the prediction was very good: boys from "major white collar" families who were among the top quintile of their classmates in intelligence strove for college 89 per cent of the time, whereas boys from "other labor and service" families who were among the bottom quintile of their classmates in intelligence strove for college only 9 per cent of the time. (623 cases where father's occupation or son's IQ were unknown have been eliminated from Table 1.)

Although prediction was good at the extremes, it was not good in the middle of the distribution. Of particular interest was the fact that if a boy had high intelligence and came from the most populous part of the status range—its lower middle section—one could not well predict his aspiration. Thus a boy from the top quintile of intelligence whose father was a

Table **1**   *Percentage of boys who expect to go to college, by IQ and father's occupation; 3,348 cases*

| | IQ quintile (boys) | | | | | |
| | LOW | | | | HIGH | *All* |
Father's occupation	*1*	*2*	*3*	*4*	*5*	*quintiles*
Major white collar	56	72	79	82	89	80
Middle white collar	28	36	47	53	76	52
Minor white collar	12	20	22	29	55	26
Skilled labor and service	4	15	19	22	40	19
Other labor and service	9	6	10	14	29	12
All occupations	*11*	*17*	*24*	*30*	*52*	*27*

minor white collar worker or a skilled laborer had almost a fifty-fifty chance of aiming at a college career.

It was found that the predicting variables could be used, though less adequately, for grammar school as well as high school accomplishment. Boys with high IQ scores usually had good marks starting with the first grade, but more especially boys with low IQ scores had poor marks. Social status was not an important factor in the earliest grades; it began to take effect around the 4th grade and had increasing effect as each year passed. By the time they chose from among the separate curricula in the 9th grade, boys from low status families both performed at and aspired to much lower levels than high status boys of equal intelligence, even though they had been similar in early school accomplishment.

II. The Interviews

The answers to the questionnaires raised an important problem: *what influences the aspirations of the boys in the lower middle levels of the status range whose environment gives them a wide choice?* Many of these boys have sufficient intelligence to aim high. They will not necessarily be isolated if they look up, for some of their friends do, yet it is not taken for granted by their families and neighbors that *all* boys should go to college. Therefore these boys must make a conscious and pointed decision at some stage of their careers.

In order to explore the decision-making of such boys, 24 of them were chosen for interview analysis. They fell into two groups: 12 boys were in the college preparatory course, had marks in the top half of their class, and definitely planned to go to a regular academic college after high school. The other 12 were not in the

college preparatory course and did not plan to go to college. All 24 had IQ scores in the top three deciles of their school; they had the intelligence to go to college if they chose to go. And all the boys had fathers who were petty white collar, skilled, or semi-skilled workers. The demographic variables of the larger study could not explain the differences in aspiration among these boys; the interviews were designed to begin where the statistics left off.

The interview material did disclose an additional factor which accounted for some of the remaining variation in aspiration: parental pressure, by which is meant a clear and overt attempt by either or both parents to influence their son to go to college. It was found that within a certain social class level to be defined and described below, namely, the "common man" group, some parents were satisfied with their own lot in life and did not attempt to push their sons up the status ladder, whereas other parents clearly encouraged their sons to strive for a "better" life. When the parents were rated on this factor on the basis of their interviews, its strong relationship with aspiration was clear. The results are shown in Table 2. . . .[2] The remainder of this article will summarize that part of the extensive case material which throws light on the relationship between parental pressure and son's aspiration.

[2] Some of the relationship between parental pressure and son's aspiration shown in Table 2 may be from contamination in the ratings: in most, though not all cases, I knew the aspiration of the son at the time I rated the pressure of his parents. . . . The Mobility Project is now working on a questionnaire for boys to measure their perceptions of pressure from their parents. Thus the interview study was not aimed at "proof"—it fulfilled its purpose of exploring a confusing questionnaire result and offering a new hypothesis which can be tested by further questionnaire data.

Table 2 Relation between parental pressure and son's aspirations; 24 boys

Son's aspiration	Parental pressure toward college	
	NO	YES
College	4	8
No college	11	1

The boys who were interviewed came from two industrial-residential suburbs of Boston with populations between 50,000 and 100,000. . . . The boys were interviewed during school hours in repeated sessions which totalled about 5 hours per boy. The parents were interviewed for an hour or two in their homes. The interviews did not follow a fixed schedule, but were focused on attitudes toward school and work; many were mechanically recorded.

III. The Common Man Class

The cases were chosen from the minor white collar, skilled and semi-skilled occupational groups. Preliminary interviews indicated that most of these families thought of themselves as belonging to a status level which I shall call the "common man" class. A few families in the sample as it was first chosen fell outside the common man class and they were eliminated in picking the final 24 for analysis.

Most parents spoke about a three class system with themselves in the middle. But they did not call themselves middle class; they used such phrases as "common man," "average sort," "ordinary folks," "working people." They saw a "lower class" beneath them—people who lived in slums, had rough manners and morals, and had tough kids who were a bad influence on their own children. And they

saw a group of "rich people," "business class" or "professionals" above them. . . .

Fifteen of the 24 families tended toward the view that the social scheme and their own place in it were morally proper and legitimate. They believed that people like themselves who were not overly bright or ambitious had, as a matter of course, a certain style of life which might be questioned in detail but not in substance. Some said this way of life was not only to be accepted but to be preferred, that the competitive game to rise higher was not worth the candle. These 15 families could be said to espouse the core value of "getting by."

Eight families felt that the general social scheme was not bad, but that they had not risen quite as high as they should have. And one man raised serious questions about the moral justice of the scheme itself—he had flirted with radicalism in his youth, but lacked the courage to stick to it in the face of social ostracism. These 9 families could be said to believe in the core value of "getting ahead."

The distinctions just made were based on the fathers' attitudes toward their own success in life. In a few instances the fathers were considerably more satisfied with their achievements than were their wives, but usually both spouses told the same story.

Let us first examine the attitudes of those who accepted the scheme of things and their own place within it—who believed in just "getting by." They were concerned with balancing the budget each week, with living for the moment in a smooth manner. They looked neither to the past nor the future. Father wanted a job which offered congenial workmates, an easy boss, a regular paycheck. Mother would work occasionally if current bills demanded it or if she enjoyed it—she generally had no strong principles for or against women working. The children were encouraged to enjoy themselves while they were young and before the burdens of life bound them to regular work—sometimes the school-age children were encouraged to work part-time to bring in a little extra money to the family purse, but the pressure was weak. The children were told to stay in high school because a diploma was pretty important in getting jobs nowadays, but they were allowed to pick their own curriculum according to taste. The value "doing what you like to do" was applied to schoolwork, to part-time jobs, and to career aspirations. Rarely was the possibility of a college education seriously considered: "we can't afford such things," or "we aren't very bright in school." Indeed, their perception of college and the kind of jobs college-trained people held were exceedingly vague; they understood that such people were professionals and made a lot of money, but they did not know any such people socially and had no concrete images of what such a life might be. In sum, they felt that common people like themselves were lucky to have a regular job, that the sons would be as the fathers, that such was life and why think about it.

By contrast, the parents who believed in "getting ahead" were more sensitive to social hierarchies and thought more about the subject than those who were satisfied with their lot. They used the middle class as a reference group that was close enough to have meaning, though far enough away to be different. They kept thinking: "there, but for a few small difficulties, go I." The difficulty they usually referred to was lack of education. These people spoke with monotonous regularity about their handicap of poor education. Sometimes they blamed themselves for not taking advantage of their opportunities when young; they said that they did

not realize when they still had time how important it was to get advanced training. Others merely shrugged their shoulders with the comment that they came from large families without much money; everyone had to go to work.

Often fathers pointed to the men immediately above themselves in the work hierarchy: machinists to mechanical engineers, carpenters to architects, clerks to office managers. Comparing themselves to those from whom they took orders, the fathers would say: "those fellows are better trained than I and can do things I can't do." Rarely did they complain that the people who got ahead were the sons of the bosses or people with good connections. Instead, they saw an occupational world stratified according to the basic principle of education, and education was something you got when you were young. These people felt vaguely guilty: they accepted the middle class value of getting ahead, they knew they had not gotten ahead, and thus they felt they were to some degree inadequate. They rationalized that it may not have been their fault that they had not received a good education, but nevertheless they felt themselves at least partial failures. Yet if they were blocked, their sons were not. Consequently, they encouraged their sons to take school seriously and to aim for college. By way of contrast, it is interesting to observe that two middle class fathers though admitting that education was important, denied it was crucial. They pointed to "self-made" men who got up because they were smart and worked hard, and they pointed to educated men who were loafers or stuffed with useless book-learning and were not successful in business. Thus it seems that a sense of failure seeks to excuse itself by an external factor like education, whereas a sense of success seeks to glorify itself by an internal factor like brains or "push."

IV. Boys' Attitudes Toward School and Work

. . . The boys, like the parents, can be divided into two groups: those who believed in "getting by" and those who believed in "getting ahead." This basic split was reflected in their more specific attitudes towards the details of schoolwork, after school recreation, and jobs. The boys who believed in just "getting by" generally were bored with school, anticipated some sort of common man job, and found peer group activity to be the most important thing in life. They were gayer than those who felt a driving ambition to do things and be successful. By contrast, the strivers who believed in "getting ahead" seemed to take schoolwork more seriously than recreational affairs. Each group noticed the difference in the behavior of the other. The non-strivers "didn't know how to have any fun." The strivers said that the non-strivers were "irresponsible; didn't know what was good for them. . . ."

The questionnaire study discussed at the beginning of this article indicated that IQ was the one factor which best accounted for marks received in early grammar school, though the correlation was not very high. It also indicated that social status of family became an important explanatory variable *after* grammar school. For common man boys, the interviews seem to have given some of the reasons why status became important only in the later years. It was in junior high that school became a problem to the boys: homework, the increased difficulties of the work in the college preparatory curriculum (and the much greater competition therein which followed from the selection procedures for entering it), and peer group pressures all combined to make it harder for a bright common man

boy to continue doing well in school—natural intelligence was no longer enough. In addition, he then began to worry about the availability of money for college—and college was the reason for doing well in high school. Some boys surmounted these difficulties and continued to do well. But this occurred because they had specific motivation that was strong enough to carry them over the hurdles—motivation which was more rare in the common man than the middle class. The interviews suggested that such motivation came from four directions:

1. If a boy had done well in the early years, *and* had built up a self-conception in which good school performance was vital, he would work hard to keep up his record. But an idea that school was vital occurred only when that early performance was truly exceptional, or if the importance of his standing to him was reinforced by one or more of the other factors listed below.

2. A boy would sacrifice other pleasures for homework when they weren't important to him. If a boy was not good at sports, if he did not have close and satisfying peer contacts, or if he had no hobby that was strongly rewarding as well as distracting, then the cost of homework was less and the balance more in its favor. In extreme cases frustrations in these alternative spheres motivated a boy to good school performance as compensation.

3. If a boy's family rewarded good school performance and punished poor performance, and the boy was not in rebellion against the family for emotional reasons, he was more likely to give up some play for homework.

4. If a boy had a rational conviction about the importance of schoolwork for his future career, he would strive to keep up his performance. But that conviction

never appeared unless the parents emphasized it.

There were no cases in which the boy found in schoolwork sufficient intellectual satisfactions to supply its own motivation. And there were no cases where a sympathetic and encouraging teacher had successfully stimulated a boy to high aspirations.

As a result of the four motivational factors in combination, each boy chose his curriculum and reacted to homework in his own way. Sometimes the balance of factors shifted after the first decision. About one-fifth of the boys moved down from one curriculum to a lower one; one boy moved up a step. These adjustments resulted from a difference between a boy's anticipation of what the college preparatory work would be like and his discovery of the facts.

The argument so far is that an intelligent common man boy was not college oriented in high school unless he had a very special reason for so being. Behind all the reasons stood one pre-eminent force: parental pressure.

Parents who believed in the value of "getting ahead" started to apply pressure from the beginning of the school career. They encouraged high marks, they paid attention to what was happening at school, they stressed that good performance was necessary for occupational success, they suggested various occupations that would be good for their sons. Their boys reached high school with a markedly different outlook from those who were not pushed. The strivers tended to have more specific occupational goals, they had educational aims to match, they worked harder in school, they thought more of the future, they were more sensitive to status distinctions, and they believed they could somehow manage to pay their way through college and reach the middle class. . . .

COMMENTARY
SOME SAMPLING METHODS

In the foregoing Units, we examined the nature of several types of research cases (P-I), and discussed various procedures for collecting and using data about the properties of such cases. Since study of the entire universe of cases (all the communities or primitive societies or workers' families of interest, for example) is seldom practical or even possible, the researcher characteristically studies only a selected sample of cases in order to draw inferences about the total universe (or the population). In designing any sample, then, he must decide how many cases to study (P-II), and upon what major bases (P-IV) to select these cases.

The importance of the *representational* basis for sample design is often taken for granted, since sociologists, like other scientists, typically want to generalize, from the concrete cases under study, to some larger universe of theoretical concern. To some degree, most sociological samples are designed as rough miniatures of a parent population.

Particular studies differ widely, however, depending upon their objectives, in the *relative* emphasis placed upon representativeness. At one extreme, the samples drawn by the United States Bureau of the Census—or those used in market research or public-opinion polling—are designed primarily so that inferences drawn from them will describe the larger population with a known degree of accuracy. Other types of samples may sacrifice a degree of representativeness either because the objective is purely exploratory, or because the universe of theoretical concern is too general to allow representational sampling, or because the requirements of the particular analysis are more compelling than the need for representativeness.

In addition to representativeness, the researcher in designing his sample also considers the *requirements of the analysis*. Although this basis for sample design is less clearly understood and less commonly discussed in textbook treatments of sampling, you will see how the character of the sample may be markedly affected by the plans for analyzing social processes and interrelationships of variables. Thus, a researcher may select only a few cases as his sample because he wants to examine them intensively, or many cases so that he can make extensive cross-tabulations. He may choose cases that he can observe under special conditions (as Bales does), or cases that he can subject to experimental manipulation. Or he may design the sample so that he can control (or hold constant) certain critical variables.

Ideally, the researcher uses both bases in designing his sample. In a study of boys' college plans, for instance, the sample may allow for analysis of the reasons behind the boys' decisions, and at the same time guarantee that the findings are a fair picture for boys in the United States today. Often, however, one basis outweighs the other in controlling the sample design. Thus the researcher may concentrate either on the representativeness of the sample (to estimate, for example, the proportion of boys going to college), or on the sampling requirements of the analysis (to determine the factors in their decisions).

The studies we shall discuss in this Unit illustrate varying degrees of emphasis upon one or the other—and occasionally both—bases for sampling design.

Zelditch and the Simple Random Sample

Let us start by examining the *representational* basis upon which a sample may be designed to approximate the universe of interest.

As our first example, we shall review the Zelditch study (from Unit 5) because it describes a realistic sociological application of probability sampling procedures—the procedures commonly preferred for most (though not all) attempts to draw representative samples. You have already learned (from Exercise V-1 and Manual V-A) some of the rules for specific types of probability sampling, including the simple random sample that Zelditch uses. You have begun to learn (from Exercise V-2 and Manual V-B) how these rules governing the research operations rest upon the principles of probability established by mathematicians and applied in many scientific fields. Our review of Zelditch will indicate the many practical difficulties involved—and some ways of handling these difficulties —when the researcher attempts to apply the operational rules and the abstract mathematical principles within the context of a sociological study.

We shall think of any probability sample design as starting with a definition of the conceptual universe, and then proceeding through three phases. (See Manual V-A and Table 6-A below.)

Table **6-A** *Sampling errors and other errors in a representational sample*

Research stages	Types of possible error	
Phase I: Designating (stratifying) the frame	Bias: failure to match conceptual universe	**Sampling errors**
Phase II: Drawing sample from frame	Chance error (measurable by statistical tests) Bias: failure in approximation of probability model	
Phase III: Covering the entire sample	Bias: researcher's substitutions, respondents' self-selection (*e.g.,* refusal, unavailability)	
Data-collection	Errors of observation and measurement (*e.g.,* control effect, biased-viewpoint effect)	**Non-sampling errors**
Coding, punching, tabulating	Errors in data-processing	
Analysis and interpretation	Errors of computation, weighting, interpreting	
Inferences about conceptual universe (as drawn from the research)		**Total errors**

DEFINING THE CONCEPTUAL UNIVERSE

The researcher specifies as part of his conceptual model, the total universe (or population) of cases to which his theory applies. The Zelditch study exemplifies the sociologically important instance in which the conceptual universe consists, not of individuals nor even of small groups, but of total societies as the cases. Zelditch believes that his hypothesis of family role differentiation within the society has "generic significance"; he wants to test the pertinence of this hypothesis to any society at any time. His conceptual universe, then, comprises all human societies over all time.

PHASE I. DESIGNATING THE SAMPLING FRAME

When the researcher moves from the conceptual level to the level of operations, his first step is to find an empirical universe (or population) of cases that corresponds as closely as possible to his conceptual universe. Ideally, he obtains a complete list (or map) of these empirical cases. From this list, called his *sampling frame,* he will (at Phase II) draw the sample of concrete cases **(P-I)** to be used in his research.

In practice, of course, the researcher usually has difficulty in obtaining an appropriate frame. Zelditch suggests the nature of these difficulties and the various types of compromises which must often be made. As he notes, "the universe one would *like* to use actually falls into two strata, all those societies reported by ethnographers and all those societies not reported." Since he is dependent upon the use of available materials, "societies belonging to the second of these strata are immediately excluded." He is also obliged to exclude other societies "because they were more difficult to gather material on than others." After all such exclusions, he ends up with a frame of seventy-five societies from which to draw his sample. The actual frame employed is thus a compromise with the ideal frame—but designated to correspond to his conceptual universe as closely as possible within the limits of the data available to him. (Of course, it would be hard to imagine any actual frame which corresponded exactly to this particular conceptual universe. Even if additional ethnographic reports were made to cover all existing societies, the reports would not conceivably cover these societies at all possible times and under all the possible conditions which might affect the family role structure.)

Zelditch's experience underscores an important general principle in regard to the matching of the sampling frame to the conceptual universe. Despite his efforts, the sampling frame is incomplete and may fail to match, in important respects, the universe he believes he is studying and to which he will refer his findings and interpretations. Whenever the desired list or sampling frame is incomplete, there is always a potential danger of "error" in the findings—error due to some *systematic bias* in the frame itself. As Zelditch says, it is always possible that, in line with the objective of discovering whether societies are positive or negative according to his hypothesis, "only negative cases were excluded, or that more than a proportionate share of negative cases were excluded." Although he sees no reason to suspect such a systematic bias, he cannot be sure that there is none, since he cannot inspect the cases that are missing from the frame. In short, as he points out, "there is no basis of judging with what confidence inferences can be made from [the sampling frame] to the entire universe of cases."

Thus the researcher must make every effort in Phase I of the procedure to discover and, insofar as possible, to eliminate or control the potential biases in the frame. Inadequacies in the frame may cast doubt upon the correspondence between any sample subsequently selected from it and the sociological universe about which inferences will be made.

PHASE II: SELECTING THE SAMPLE FROM THE FRAME

Once Zelditch has prepared the list of societies as his sampling frame, he must decide *how many* cases to use as his sample, and *how* to select them. In this particular study, he might have used *all* the cases in the frame since there are only seventy-five, and since the necessary materials are already available. He decides to draw a sample, however, apparently with the usual aims of avoiding labor (in coding the complex, detailed reports) and of devoting his full attention to the careful handling of the selected cases. He does not go to the other extreme of selecting a very small number of cases, and thus he foregoes the possibilities of refined and intensive analysis (as in the studies by Whyte or Merton). Instead, he chooses the middle road, selecting a substantial proportion of societies as "a simple replication of cases."

In deciding how to select these cases, Zelditch has the option of relying on his best judgment, or of following the procedures of probability sampling. Let us reconstruct his assessment of the situation. Hoping that bias has not seriously contaminated the sampling frame, Zelditch now wants to make his further selection from it without introducing (at Phase II) any possible further bias. He wants a sample which will represent the frame as closely as possible. How can he accomplish this? He might, perhaps, have used some judgment basis for designating some societies as "typical" in certain respects. But this would have required considerable preliminary study of the entire list. Moreover, since he has a definite hypothesis in mind, he fears he might be influenced—unintentionally, to be sure— to lean toward cases fitting his hypothesis, or over backward to avoid them. With such considerations in mind, he decides upon probability sampling, undoubtedly using a table of random numbers, selection by lot, or some other standard procedure (see Manual V-A).

Here again, the Zelditch study illustrates some general principles of controlling sampling error so as to achieve representativeness. At Phase I, there was the possibility of error due to systematic bias. At Phase II also (unless it is feasible to include *every* case from the sampling frame), errors of selection are likely to occur (see Table 6-A). On the one hand, if probability sampling is *not* used, there may be a *bias*. Thus, if the researcher decides to use his own best judgment and his knowledge of the research situation in order to secure representativeness, there is no built-in insurance against his unwittingly distorting the sample in drawing it from the frame. Such bias may be held to a minimum at this phase through strict adherence to probability sampling. On the other hand, when probability sampling *is* used, another type of error—*chance error*—is introduced, but chance error has the virtue of being measurable, as we shall see below.

PHASE III: COVERING THE ENTIRE SAMPLE

When the researcher uses probability sampling, he must meet a further procedural requirement: to cover in the research *all* the cases selected from the frame. If he omits any substantial proportion of the cases, some further selective principle is introduced and the rules of probability no longer apply. Thus, an additional source of bias may be met at this phase.

The many practical difficulties often encountered in trying to cover the entire sample are suggested in the Zelditch study by the way some of the selected societies had to be excluded when the information on them turned out, after all, to be incomplete. Zelditch has no way to meet the Phase III sampling requirement that even these cases be covered. He does, however, attempt to minimize systematic bias by defining (his rule 3) information as "incomplete where there is insufficient evidence *either for or against* the hypothesis tested."

Each of the three sampling phases, then, deals in its own fashion with the problems of possible sampling error (as distinct from the various possible errors in other parts of the research design; see Table 6-A). The researcher seeks a sampling frame to match his conceptual universe (Phase I), makes his selection from the frame (Phase II) by the procedures most appropriate for the problem at hand (usually—but not always—probability procedures), and, finally, attempts (Phase III) to include in his research all (or nearly all) the cases selected. By controlling sampling errors in all these ways, he hopes to find a representative sample, that is, a sample which corresponds as closely as possible to the conceptual universe defined in his model.

Some Principles of Probability Sampling

Since the sociologist who uses probability sampling relies upon tools he borrows from the fields of mathematics and statistics, we shall interrupt our discussion of the studies themselves to outline the rationale for the application of these tools to sociological research.

The rules for probability sampling (as set forth in Manual V-A, for example) are so designed that the selection of cases from the frame at Phase II depends upon chance alone—not upon the investigator's judgment, which may sometimes (as Zelditch feared) introduce bias. Probability samples (such as the simple random samples, area samples, or systematic samples described in the Manual) are defined as samples that give each case (and set of cases) in the frame a *known,* but not necessarily equal chance of being selected. The simple random sample is the special procedure in which each case (and set of cases) does have an *equal* chance of being selected. When the rules are followed, the sample obtained is said to support inferences about the population whose accuracy and precision can be estimated (in terms of probability). Or conversely, although the sampling findings are subject to chance error, this error can be measured.

A number of these ideas need explaining. Let us, accordingly, examine the connections between the procedures and characteristics of probability samples and the principles of probability you have begun to learn through Exercise V-2. (For a more advanced treatment of the theory of probability, see Nagel, 1955.)

THE PROBABILITY DISTRIBUTION

Probability sampling rests upon a notion that we shall describe and then illustrate through a familiar example. We imagine that very large numbers of similar samples (all the same size) are drawn successively in a specified manner from a given empirical population (frame). We also imagine that the population parameter of interest is known or assumed. (A *parameter* is a proportion, mean, or other number which describes the population. In contrast, a *statistic* describes a sample, and may be used to estimate the corresponding parameter.) The results (or statistics) obtained from all these samples will differ from sample to sample, as you saw in your own statistical experiments in Exercise V-2. These differences are the result of *chance variation* (also called sampling variability, fluctuations due to chance, variability due to chance).

Yet, these chance variations show certain definite regularities. Such a regular distribution of the results of sampling from a given population is called a *probability distribution for samples* (or a sampling distribution). This probability distribution can be estimated either by statistical experiments in which, for instance, pennies are tossed, dice rolled, or cards drawn from a deck; or by mathematical computations which parallel such experiments.

This probability distribution serves as a statistical model against which the statistician compares and evaluates the findings of any actual single sample that he uses in estimating the true population parameter.

An Example. A simple example will clarify this notion of a probability distribution, and also point out how it is possible (1) to make inferences from the findings of probability samples about the parameters of interest and (2) to make allowance for chance errors in these inferences.

Imagine that Zelditch has, after all, been able to construct the ideal sampling frame—that he has a complete list of all societies in his conceptual universe. Suppose, too, that his research hypothesis is true and that three-fourths of the societies in the frame are characterized by differentiation in the husband-wife roles, so that the population parameter is 75 per cent *D*. If he now proceeds to draw a simple random sample consisting of just three societies, what are the chances that his sample will indicate the true situation in the population (specifically, that more than half the societies in the sample will show differentiation)?

You already know from Exercise V-2 how to make such computations, and (by applying Definition 3 and Rule 2 in Manual V-B) you might compute the probabilities for each of the possible outcomes as follows (with the probability of $D = 3/4$ and of $N = 1/4$):

Possible outcomes	Probability
DDD	27/64
DDN	9/64 ⎫
DND	9/64 ⎬ 27/64
NDD	9/64 ⎭
DNN	3/64 ⎫
NDN	3/64 ⎬ 9/64
NND	3/64 ⎭
NNN	1/64

Thus the probability of obtaining more D's than N's in the sample is—the correct result—54/64.

If you draw a bar graph for all of these "theoretical" probabilities (as in Problem 3e of Exercise V-2), you can see the shape of the probability distribution. (A bar graph showing the results from a large number of actual random samples will tend to have this same shape.) We can say, then, that a given sample of this size, drawn at random from this population, will have a probability of 54/64 of containing more D's than N's, thus representing the population correctly. True, likelihood of *chance error* (that is, error due to chance variation) is still considerable. But the statistical model shows how much chance error there is likely to be, indicating in what proportion of such samples the finding would not represent the population accurately. The probability of a misleading finding in the above example is 10/64.

In illustrating the nature and use of a probability distribution, we have used this example of a very small sample because the exact probabilities can easily be computed. In larger probability samples (such as Zelditch's simple random sample or the complex samples used by Stouffer or the United States Census) the probability distribution serves in the same way as a statistical model—although other methods are used for estimating the distribution (some of these methods will be illustrated in the later Exercise V-3). The researcher uses these larger probability distributions to locate any particular sample finding relative to the findings of all possible samples of the given size, or to determine the probability of obtaining a finding higher (or lower) than his sample finding.

ALLOWING FOR CHANCE ERROR

Our example has shown the extent to which a particular probability sample tends to resemble, or to fail to resemble, the population from which it is drawn. But in this example, we assumed foreknowledge of the true proportion (of D's) in the population. In practice, we do not know this proportion—if we did, there would be no need of taking a sample at all. Nevertheless, probability distributions computed for various assumed population proportions enable the statistician to calculate, as Stouffer puts it, the "margins of error attributable to chance alone."

Statisticians commonly employ (in the statistics of inference) two main types of procedures for "measuring" in this way the chance error in probability samples: the setting of *confidence limits* around estimated parameters, and the *statistical testing* of hypotheses. You have seen from Exercise V-1 how the United States Census of Population, for example, allows for error in stating the estimates based on sample findings. If, *e.g.,* 24.5 per cent of the sample are found to have a certain characteristic, the Census states the chances as 19 out of 20 ($p = .05$) that the true proportion of the population having this characteristic falls somewhere between 24.1 per cent and 24.9 per cent. Here the probability distribution is used as a means of setting limits within which we can know, with a certain degree of confidence, that the true parameter lies.

Statistical tests of hypotheses, at present the procedure more widely used in sociology, employ probability distributions in a different way. The place of such tests in the research process has already been illustrated in Step D of Zelditch's use of a mathematical model (Unit 5), and we shall discuss their nature and use in further detail in Unit 11 and Exercise V-3.

ASSETS OF PROBABILITY SAMPLING

In sum, then, the principles of probability, as developed by mathematicians and statisticians, may be applied to sociological sampling to yield a highly precise —not at all a haphazard—procedure which has at least two assets. First, a probability sample, if it is large enough, will come close to representing the sampling frame from which it is drawn. (Of course, even a carefully drawn probability sample may yield inaccurate estimates unless the research is in all other respects properly designed and executed, and unless the sampling frame itself corresponds to the conceptual universe; see Table 6-A.) Thus representativeness in a sample does not depend upon the researcher's knowing the population in the frame well enough to attempt selection of "typical" cases on the basis of judgment. He need not run the risk of allowing his own special knowledge of—and interest in—the situation to bias his selection. Chance alone, if allowed to operate according to the rules of probability sampling, will take care of the problem of representativeness. Second, probability sampling allows the use of statistical tests which give the researcher some idea of how confident he can be that the findings from his sample are not distorted by chance error.

SAMPLE SIZE AND SAMPLING ERRORS

An important characteristic of probability sampling is that as the sample size increases, chance variation decreases; that is, the likelihood of drawing a misleading sample because of chance error is reduced (although in any probability sample, there is always some chance error). Thus greater precision in a probability sample may be achieved by increasing the sample size. Indeed, the size is often planned to fit the level of representativeness required by the research objective.

It is important to note, however, that—whether or not probability sampling is used—*bias is not affected by the sample size*. Large samples are no more successful than small samples in (1) overcoming distortion in the designation of the frame (at Phase I), for example, or (2) offsetting the tendency of interviewers (if left to their own devices) to select only certain types of respondents (at Phase II), or (3) counteracting (at Phase III) the greater readiness of certain respondents to reply (if respondents are allowed to select themselves). When such selections affect variables relevant to the analysis, sample bias may produce serious error in the results—regardless of sample size. Thus, the *Literary Digest* poll of 1936, in its forecast of the presidential election, was in error by 20 percentage points (and thereby failed to predict the winner), although 10,000,000 ballots were mailed. There would seem to have been two sources of bias in the sample design which could not be offset by the extremely large sample size: (1) the frame was constructed of *Literary Digest* and telephone subscribers, a portion of the electorate presumably having relatively higher income; and (2), since the respondents were allowed to select themselves in deciding whether to return the mail ballot, only 20 per cent, presumably the better-educated, more interested portion of the electorate, complied. The problem of self-selection is similarly reflected in the Kinsey sample, which was composed entirely of volunteers. Here too the representativeness of the sample may be doubted, despite its large size (see Cochran, Mosteller, and Tukey).

STRATIFIED SAMPLING

One further basic principle of probability sampling—useful for nonprobability samples also—is not illustrated in the Zelditch study, but is foreshadowed by Le Play's astute (if exaggerated) remark that "simple people"—such as shepherds and their families on the frontier of Europe and Asia—"present characteristics so identical that it is sufficient to observe methodically one family in order to know them all," whereas among workers in complex social groupings the problem is more complicated. If the conceptual universe is homogeneous in regard to the properties under study, a small sample will suffice to represent it; conversely, for a heterogeneous universe, a larger sample is required to reduce chance error. A useful device (in Phase I) is to stratify the sampling frame in respect to some characteristic(s) believed to be associated with the phenomenon under study. In stratified sampling, the frame is divided into cells, or strata, each of which is homogeneous in respect to such associated characteristics. Zelditch might, for example, have divided his sampling frame into the two strata of matrilineal and patrilineal societies. Then (Phase II) the researcher makes his selection, as usual, from each of the strata.

Accordingly, stratified sampling may increase the representativeness of a probability sample of any given size by ensuring that sufficient cases will be drawn from every single stratum. That is, stratification increases the efficiency of a sample. As one example, imagine drawing a sample of individuals from a large business organization. It is known in advance that the top management consists of only a few individuals, that the second echelon is also relatively small in size, but that the several classes of workers are relatively populous. A sample drawn at random from the organization as a whole might happen to include nobody at all from top management since there are altogether so few in this stratum. Yet the researcher feels that, for proper representation, individuals from the highest level should be included. By stratifying the individuals in advance, the researcher gains assurance that each of the echelons will be represented in the sample. Stratified sampling, then, combines the advantages of probability procedures with the researcher's own knowledge about which strata are important, how these may be identified, and how the population is divided among them.

Stratification is also useful in judgment samples (*e.g.,* in improving the quota samples in which the field investigator is instructed to make his own selections of cases from designated strata), and in samples designed to meet certain requirements of the analysis, which we shall discuss later in the Unit. Let us return to the studies for further illustrations of stratification and of the other principles outlined.

Stouffer's Use of Area Sampling

The study of *Communism, Conformity, and Civil Liberties* provides an additional illustration of probability sampling to achieve *representativeness;* it also exemplifies how plans for the subsequent *analysis* of the data may affect the sample design in certain respects. Thus, under **P-IV,** this sample is selected with both these aims in view. The details of the sampling procedure are set forth by Stouffer in the study selection, and serve to supplement the notes on simpler procedures in Manual V-A.

Although we shall deal in this Commentary only with matters of sample design, the study incorporates important general methodological features that you will want to consider. It demonstrates that extensive studies using representative samples—though perhaps popularly associated with the Census or with opinion polls—are not necessarily limited to short, highly structured questionnaires: they may effectively employ detailed, intensive interviews. Moreover, the study affords an interesting instance of the development and use of attitude scales that rest upon the consistency of the individual's answers to a set of related questions.

Directed and analyzed by Samuel Stouffer, guided by a committee of experts, executed in the field by two polling organizations, this survey aims to describe the attitudes of the American public on a vital issue. The conceptual model deals with individuals as citizens, and with civic leaders as compared with the "rank and file." Unlike a poll taken to gauge the opinions of a finite population (*e.g.,* voting intentions of adults in the United States in a given month before an election), the conceptual universe of citizens, though clearly defined as consisting of American adults, is not restricted to the particular time of the research. The attitudes under study are regarded, not as "transient opinions" which fluctuate with the day's headlines, but as "deeper latent" dispositions to be encountered among Americans in the past as well as in the years to come.

SAMPLING PHASES

Thus a major problem of sampling, as in most theoretically focused research, centers in Phase I: How can the conceptual universe which is not time-bound be matched by an empirical and necessarily finite sampling frame? Stouffer's practical solution is to use the current population of adults in the United States as the best available sampling frame corresponding to "all possible citizens" (with tests to demonstrate the relative stability of latent attitudes at least during the period of data collection). The frame of leaders, as Stouffer points out, is even more arbitrarily defined as consisting of fourteen specific types of leaders in each of the cities selected for study.

Stouffer, the master craftsman and lucid reporter, describes exactly how and to what degree representativeness is achieved in selecting the sample from the frame (Phase II), thereby affording a prototype for all such samples. "By 'representativeness' we mean," he says, "that if we had been able to interview all such [individuals] . . . the result would differ from those in our sample by only a relatively small chance error, which is mathematically calculable."

The area sampling procedure used here in making these selections from the frame is more complex than simple random sampling, but adapts the same basic principles of probability. It is this general type of area procedure which, originally developed by the United States government for demographic surveys, allows for supplementation of the United States decennial Census (which attempts to cover every household and every person in the country) with many interim reports (based on samples of a few thousand). The sample Census is often as accurate as the full Census. The unique feature of the method is its ingenious device for preparing the sampling frame. Since in the United States no up-to-date lists of all citizens are either available or readily usable for the country at large, each individual is associated with the dwelling unit in which he lives and with the area in which this dwelling unit is located. Thus the initial frame consists, not of individuals, but of areas, and the sampling progresses, as Stouffer describes it, through a series of stages, drawing first areas, then dwelling units, and finally the individuals themselves. (Frederick F. Stephan, one of the originators of area sampling, reports in a private communication that some of his early ideas developed out of an analogy to the types of sampling used in forestry.)

Stouffer next recounts the very considerable effort expended in Phase III to cover most of the cases selected. Repeated call-backs on respondents not easily found at home, persuasive telegrams from the central research office, and other devices attempt to minimize the tendency for certain types of respondents to "select themselves out" of the sample. And the interviewer himself is not allowed to make any further selections or substitutions. As it turned out, a considerable portion of the cross-section sample (16 per cent) was not finally covered in the study—a proportion sufficient to raise some doubts as to whether the actual sample was selected mainly by chance alone. Interestingly enough, the losses from the sample of leaders (pursued even more assiduously than the sample of citizens) were considerably lower—only 9 per cent.

STOUFFER'S HANDLING OF SAMPLING ERRORS

Stouffer's efforts to locate and assess the sources of potential bias merit careful study as a model. He is able to check certain findings of the cross-section study, for instance, against the current estimates from Census data, reporting a generally satisfactory similarity. Moreover, he makes a detailed analysis of the demographic characteristics and reasons for refusal of those 16 per cent of the original cross section who refused to be interviewed, broke off the interview after it began, or were for some other reason not covered in Phase III. Again, the reassuring outcome is that "the loss fails to reveal any special characteristics which would affect the over-all interpretation of the findings" (see Gaudet and Wilson, 1940).

A related procedure for handling the possible bias of nonresponse is to include in the sample only those respondents found at home at the first call, but to weight their answers according to their estimate of the proportion of days they are ordinarily at home at the time of the interview. Or, in studies based on mail questionnaires or other data-collection procedures in which respondents are self-selected, successive "waves" of follow-ups are sent out to the nonrespondents, and the answers of those replying readily are compared with those replying only after repeated prodding—or with those on the list who never reply at all (see *e.g.,* Wallace; Suchman and McCandless; Clausen and Ford). These comparisons may indicate at least the existence, and the general direction, of the bias of nonresponse—tending to show the differentials for the lazy or the busy—though not for the stubborn and hostile.

Other aspects of Stouffer's handling of errors which deserve special note as you review your analysis of the study are:

1. The conduct of the *field work by two different agencies* working independently, so that each set of data serves as a replication of the other (as in Stouffer's Figure 1 and his Table 1). The general consistency found between the two sets provides a kind of reliability check, suggesting that the respondents (as selected and questioned by the two agencies) tended to be similar. (Such a replication does not, of course, rule out the possibility that both samples may contain the same bias—a possibility which was examined by the other procedures noted above.)

2. *The allowance for chance error* (see the illuminating Appendix D, largely

prepared by Frederick F. Stephan) in approximating the "unknown and unknowable 'true national figures.'" Statistical tests are used here to set margins of error around the percentage differences found between types of respondents. These margins show how much allowance to make in interpreting the findings for possible chance error in the sampling.

3. The careful *scrutiny of patterns of consistency* among the percentages, rather than reliance upon the answers to any single question alone. Stouffer explains how the researcher may lack confidence in an isolated finding that may be due to sampling variability, but knows that a whole set of mutually conflicting findings are far less likely to be produced by chance alone.

4. *Recognition of nonsampling errors* (see Table 6-A) that also affect the accuracy of inferences from the sample about the universe—errors due, for example, to possible variations in response that may be produced by slight changes in the wording of a question.

SAMPLE DESIGN FOR ANALYSIS

In addition to devoting effort, time, and expense to these representational aims of this study, Stouffer also takes pains to design a sample that will support a particular plan for analysis. His research objectives are not merely to measure the incidence within the American public of certain attitudes—such as the extent of fear, or of tolerance toward nonconformity—but to determine what kinds of people hold these attitudes. Thus his sample must be large enough, and varied enough, to permit him to compare a large number of individuals according to their residence, their education, their age, their religious views, and the like. The nature of the statistical analysis for which the sample is designed is suggested in Stouffer's skillful examination of age and education as they may affect tolerance of nonconformists. Here Stouffer analyzes the sample (see his Figure 2) within each of twenty-five different age-and-education categories (following procedures we shall discuss in Unit 8). His sample must contain enough cases in each of the cells to enable him to hold the margin of chance error within manageable limits while he examines the differences in tolerance of nonconformists.

The proposed analysis may, accordingly, affect the size of the sample and the way it is stratified. Indeed, the researcher sometimes oversamples so as to have sufficient cases for his analysis in certain of the cells which are relatively small in the population being sampled (as you saw in Problem 4a of Exercise V-1).

The Harvard Mobility Project and Samples Designed for Analysis

There are a variety of ways in which the particular plan for analysis of a given study may govern the sample design. Comparison of the Stouffer studies on tolerance and nonconformity with the Harvard Mobility Project (in which Stouffer guided the planning of a number of different samples) will suggest how quite different sample designs are developed by the same person to meet different analytical requirements. In contrast to the area sample for the study of nonconformity, which emphasized *both* the representational and the analytical aims, the emphasis in the Mobility Project is primarily on the requirements of the analysis.

Unfortunately, Stouffer himself never completed the report on this study, but he mentions the sampling problems in various papers (Stouffer, 1962, pp. 225–31, 297). Kahl actually describes the sample for the major portion of the study as well as for the special investigation which he himself conducted (under the direction of Stouffer, Talcott Parsons, and Florence Kluckhohn).

Concerned with an exploration of the factors affecting the placement of an individual in the status structure of the larger society, the Harvard researchers focus upon high school boys as their research case **(P-I)**—sometimes including the parents of each boy as well. The corresponding conceptual universe is not clearly apparent—it might be "all boys in the United States today," or "all possible young people in a social structure such as ours." In any event, their primary sampling aim is not to represent such a universe, but to facilitate a certain kind of analysis—an analysis which will explain why some boys aspire to a college education while others do not. In order to explain this, the researchers examine family background, values, abilities, and other influences which may account for the differing ambitions of individual boys. What kind of sample, then, must they design in order to meet their objective? Three different approaches were successively tried.

A FEW CASES FOR INTENSIVE ANALYSIS

Stouffer describes (Stouffer, 1962, p. 297), as a first approach, a preliminary sample of fifty boys whose school records were tabulated and who, together with their parents, were interviewed at length. All of the boys were in the ninth grade of one junior high school. The researchers were obviously interested less in gaining a representative sample than in obtaining a sample that would be both easy to reach (a sample selected on the basis of convenience is sometimes called a "chunk") and small enough to permit intensive analysis.

Such loosely defined small samples are frequently useful in exploratory studies. As Stouffer says, they "may be productive of hypotheses, even if not proof" (Stouffer, 1962, p. 231); we saw (in Unit 4) how Merton, for example, uses only thirty cases to delineate two categories of influentials—the cosmopolitans and the locals. But the Harvard researchers were interested in many more than two categories of boys because they wanted to examine a number of theories about potentially relevant factors in mobility. Stouffer, later criticizing this particular sample of only fifty for not allowing sufficient control of the relevant variables, thus wrote:

> We had all the interviews written up in detail, and we had enough data to fill a book—with rather interesting reading, too. But it was a very wasteful process

because there were just too many intriguing ideas. We took a couple of ideas which were deducible from current general theory and tried to make some simple fourfold tables [as in Kahl's Table 2]. It was obvious that, with a dozen variables uncontrolled, such tables meant little or nothing. (Stouffer, 1962, p. 297.)

This weakness of the intensive study of a few cases was subsequently offset in the two different approaches to sample design, as described by Kahl.

MANY CASES FOR STATISTICAL ANALYSIS

The Harvard group used as a second approach a procedure with which we are already familiar—they *increased the size* of the sample markedly. Small statistical studies are of limited value, as Stouffer says, when a number of variables are to be examined, because "you cannot subdivide the data into enough boxes [categories]" (Stouffer, 1962, p. 230). Stouffer illustrates the principle (using a related problem from the study) by imagining that there are as many as 1,000 boys of one type (such as the ambitious boys) and 1,000 boys of contrasting type (such as the nonambitious boys). Should the researcher wish to isolate and evaluate a number of factors which might account for this difference (*e.g.,* income, occupation, education, ethnic origin of parents; attitudes of parents toward school and discipline; number of siblings, order of birth; the neighborhood; the child's peer groups; etc.), Stouffer concludes that it would be extremely difficult to make such evaluations "with anything less than an extremely large sample." Even the suggested 1,000 of each type of boy would not be nearly enough for the proposed statistical study.

Actually, the Mobility Project uses a sample of almost 4,000 boys in order to support the kind of statistical analysis exemplified by Kahl's Table 1. From this table, you can see that both I.Q. (if you read the percentages across) and father's occupation (if you read down) tend to be associated with the boy's plans for going to college. You might interpret this association to mean that both have some influence on his plans. The sample is large enough to yield reliable percentages in the several cells of such a table. (Students previously familiar with statistical testing may want to look ahead to Manual V-C for the relationship between sample size and statistical significance.) Thus the plan for analysis here of cross-tabulating several variables requires a sample consisting, not only of a large number of boys (sample size), but also of a wide variety of boys within each of the several types to be distinguished (appropriate stratification and adequate sampling within each cell).

Degree of Representativeness. Given this analytical emphasis in the sample design, we may also speculate about the degree of representativeness attained here. At Phase I, as we noted earlier, they do not attempt to find an empirical population that will match a clearly defined universe. Had they wished to specify a finite universe, such as "all American boys living at the time of the research," a probability sample would have been feasible for making their selections at Phase

II. But representativeness is clearly not a major aim, and the researchers do not proceed in this way—undoubtedly because of the attendant inconvenience and expense. What they do, as Kahl reports it, is to deal with "large numbers of people who were readily available: boys in school." They use the sophomore and junior classes of eight Boston high schools (with the omission of Catholic parochial schools as the "major deficiency in the data"). The eight schools are chosen by nonprobability procedures on the basis of judgment and convenience.

Once the sample in the eight schools is designated, however, the researchers clearly want (at Phase III) to prevent any possible biases that might be associated with the mobility patterns of individual boys and their families. They ensure exhaustive coverage by requiring that self-administered forms be filled out by *all* the boys in the selected classes so that no self-selection by the respondents is possible.

Thus the sample may be said to represent all the boys attending high school classes of this particular kind at this time, although it would be difficult to define exactly the meaning of "this particular kind."

THE FOCUSED SAMPLE

The third Harvard sample, used by Kahl in his exploratory interviews, suggests an entirely different way of designing a sample to support analysis of the relevant variables. A focused sample is one of an important class of samples that allows the researcher to concentrate attention upon the variables of immediate research interest—the explanatory variables—by *controlling* (holding constant) certain other associated variables outside his present concern—the extraneous variables. (We shall consistently use this broad distinction between explanatory and extraneous variables, for which we are indebted to Kish, 1959.) This control of the extraneous variables is effected here, not through statistical analysis as in Kahl's Table 1, but directly through the sample itself.

We can formulate the character of a focused sample, and of the more general class of samples to which it belongs, by studying the clues afforded in Kahl's brief discussion. Again the research objective is to explore the differences between the ambitious boys (who plan to go to college) and the other boys (who do not plan to go). But now it is already known (from the major study) that certain factors tend to govern this college decision: I.Q. and father's occupation. Kahl does not want to study these extraneous variables further; but he does need to hold them constant in order to go on to discover other possibly relevant factors. So (1) he designs a sample composed of two equal subsamples, each of which contains one of the two types of boys he wants to compare—those expecting to go, and those not expecting to go, to college. And (2) he matches the two subsamples so that they will be approximately alike on these two extraneous variables. He can accomplish this matching by selecting cases from just one cell (or a few adjacent cells) from his Table 1. Actually, he chooses those cells near the lower right-hand corner of the table which contain boys who have enough intelligence to go to college but whose environment (in the lower-middle levels of the status range) "gives them a wide choice." His study demonstrates the utility of the design, since, through intensive interviewing and comparison of his matched subsamples, he discovers "an additional factor which accounted for some of the remaining variations in aspiration: parental pressure."

Thus one of the special features of the focused sample is the deliberate restriction of attention to just a *few critical cells* selected from a stratified sampling frame. Kahl's Table 1 affords, as we have seen, a complete frame of the boys in these particular high school classes, already stratified by the two extraneous variables, and further subdivided according to the explanatory variable of college plans. Kahl's focus upon a strategic selection from these cells seems an ideal approach for his exploratory purposes; he can now work effectively with only twenty-four boys—a very *small sample*—while *controlling important extraneous* variables that might otherwise confound his results. Thus the focused sample is a particular instance of the many widely used *matched* (or *equivalent*) *sample designs* that control the effects of extraneous variables. A matched sample for a more extensive study might be drawn, for example, from *all* the cells in Kahl's Table 1.

A second distinguishing feature of the focused sample is its ingenious handling of the *explanatory* variables. What it accomplishes is a control over the "effects" of the process under study (the college plans, in this example) so as to focus on the search for "causes" or reasons for these plans. It separates the subsamples in terms of that explanatory variable often called the "effect variable" or the "dependent variable." This is the converse of the designs used in experiments, which separate the subsamples in terms of a very different explanatory variable— the "causal" or "independent variable"—so as to focus on discovery of what the effects may be. (The sample designs used in experiments have additional elements, such as randomization of the effects of uncontrolled extraneous variables and manipulation of the independent variable, as discussed in Unit 11.)

Degree of Representativeness. Still another special feature of the focused sample is its potential representativeness. Since all the boys had already been classified within the cells of Kahl's Table 1, the sample design represents certain cells which are themselves clearly located within the over-all sampling frame. Kahl's sample refers only to boys of a certain status and a certain I.Q., but he knows just how many of these boys there are and just how their college plans relate to those of the much larger population of boys in all the categories of status and intelligence. If he wished to define the representational character of his findings within this larger population, he might use probability sampling within each of his chosen cells. The principle is important in evaluating the possibilities of a focused sample, although Kahl does not tell whether in practice he chose his sample at random; perhaps, for these exploratory purposes, he preferred to use whatever congenial families were most willing to be interviewed at length.

A Deviant Case Analysis.   Incidentally, the Kahl study might also be regarded as the first step in a deviant case analysis, as discussed in Unit 5. Kahl, in a sense, examines certain cells in his Table 1 which are deviant in that they are *not* predicted very closely by the two factors of I.Q. and father's occupation. By exploring these in detail, he seeks clues to other factors which may also affect college plans. Thus the study "fulfilled its purpose of exploring a confusing questionnaire result and offering a new hypothesis which can be treated by further questionnaire data" (the possible second step in deviant case analysis).

Some Methodological Implications

This discussion, which has outlined some of the basic elements in sampling, also points to a number of related problems in sociological sampling. We shall now examine some of these problems, and begin to formulate some of the general principles of sample design in sociological research.

SAMPLING WITHIN SOCIAL SYSTEMS

Certain problems sometimes arise in the sampling of groups as systems made up of parts. For one thing, the sampling may take place at more than one system *level*. Students of voting behavior may first select a sample of all communities in the country, and then select a sample of individual citizens within each community. Thus, after a researcher has drawn a sample of groups, he may still have to decide whether and how to sample *within* groups.

In designs where the research objective is to represent the universe (of individuals, roles, or subgroups) within each group, or to analyze selected portions of this universe, it is appropriate to draw a sample within each group—as in all sampling. For example, in a sample of communities (groups), the socioeconomic composition of each might be indexed by its proportion of white-collar workers (group members); for this purpose data would certainly not be required for *everybody* within each community—a within-group *sample* of the members would be sufficient. In somewhat similar fashion, Merton uses a sample of the members within a sample community in order to discover whether they tend to name certain influential individuals more frequently than other individuals.

Other designs do not sample within groups, however, but utilize *all* (or nearly all) of the members of each group (as in the study by Coleman, Katz, and Menzel to be discussed in Unit 10). The need for this is illustrated by the Lundberg and Lawsing finding of a "queen" in the community (Unit 4) who, though chosen by many, herself chose only one other person—the "power behind the throne." A larger study of a sample of communities that is conducted to learn more about the existence of such rare—yet possibly strategic—structural phenomena can ill afford to sample within the group. Here data must often be obtained from everybody in the community (rather than from a sample) in order to ensure coverage of the complete pattern of interpersonal bonds. Indeed, one of the shortcomings of the Lundberg and Lawsing study, as we have seen, is that it does *not* cover everybody within the sample community. This means that we cannot be sure, for example, whether certain relationships are unreciprocated, or whether the dyadic partners simply were not questioned at all.

These examples suggest that, when the research objective is to *uncover the underlying structure* of particular social systems, it may be necessary to examine all (or nearly all) the component parts of this structure, rather than a sample of them. Thus, although the principle is not entirely clear, within-group sampling of social systems may not always be appropriate (see Coleman, 1961-b).

SAMPLING OF EVENTS

Sampling commonly means selecting from a universe of *cases*. It is convenient to think in the abstract about cases apart from their properties—and to sample by first selecting cases and then studying their properties through selected indicants at selected times. In a more exact sense, however, because we do not deal at all time periods with *all* the phenomena—the events—that might be used as indicants of the properties, sampling means selecting from the universe of *events*. We must be aware that the selection of *indicants* and the selection of *time periods,* as well as the selection of cases, may affect—sometimes markedly—the representativeness of the sample findings, as Stouffer's concern with these matters indicates. In a study of mathematical ability, for instance, a probability sample of individuals might yield different results depending upon which questions were selected for the test from the total "population" of possible questions. Again, in a study of household laundry habits, it was found that housewives interviewed on Monday (the typical washday) responded quite differently from those interviewed on other days. Even though the sample of cases (households) had been chosen on a probability basis, the research findings on the phenomena under study would have been biased had not the interviewing been carefully spaced over the seven days of the week in order to sample time more accurately.

THE REPRESENTATIONAL BASIS FOR SAMPLING

Apart from such problems of sampling to reflect social structures, and sampling from all the relevant phenomena that characterize the cases under study, the central questions of this Unit concern the *bases* upon which the selection of cases is made. Many discussions of sampling deal only with the choice of one or another representational procedure (probability sampling vs. nonprobability or judgment sampling, for example); but our examination of the varied designs of several samples has shown that a prior and more basic decision **(P-IV)** is whether to stress both the requirements of representation and of the analysis, or to place primary emphasis on one or the other. Each basis has its own effect on the sampling procedure, as we have seen.

In assessing the representational basis for his sample, the researcher must answer two interrelated questions: (1) How much importance does he attach to securing a high—or a measurable—degree of representativeness in the findings?

And (2) what representational sampling procedures will he use? Let us start by summarizing what we have learned in answer to the second question, since the answer to the first question is often contingent upon it.

Representational Procedures. The sampling process that strives for representativeness consists, as we have seen, of the definition of the conceptual universe, followed by the three phases of designating the frame, selecting a sample from the frame, and attempting to cover the entire sample.

The procedure most widely used at Phase II for selecting a sample that will represent the frame is *probability sampling*. It has the advantages of (1) minimizing selection bias; and (2) enabling the researcher to estimate the margins of chance error, and to govern the size and design of the sample for the level of accuracy desired. Probability sampling is thus extremely useful for research situations in which an appropriate frame is available. It can produce excellent estimates of the parameters of a finite population at a given time—of the age distribution in the United States in 1960, e.g., or of the number of United States families owning washing machines toward the end of World War II, or of the relationship between age and conformity among American adults in a given year.

But probability sampling is not always the most desirable procedure for securing representativeness. If the investigator knows a great deal about the cases to be sampled, and if he can avoid bias in making his selections, his own *judgment* may—by avoiding chance error—yield the more accurate sample. (It is difficult to assess how accurate the judgment sample is, however, unless the findings can be checked against an outside source, since judgment sampling has no self-contained measure of sampling error.) Judgment samples are especially recommended when the sample is very small (Deming, p. 23, mentions six or less), since chance error increases as the sample size decreases. Thus, a Malinowski probably does better to use his best judgment and all relevant information in selecting a single case to represent an extreme example under the theory he wishes to disprove. Or a Whyte does well to use his judgment in selecting just a few gangs in order to discover how similar (or different) they may be.

It should be noted too that probability sampling sometimes (as in Stouffer's study of conformity) requires greater expenditures of time and money than a comparable judgment procedure. But this is not invariably true. Zelditch, for instance, may well have spent less time in drawing his random sample than he would have spent drawing a judgment sample of the same size.

Moreover, in many important instances of scientific—in contrast with applied—research, probability sampling may prove impractical or fail to represent the universe of theoretical concern. The sociologist often wants to study populations that are too general, or too vaguely defined, to correspond (at Phase I) to any available empirical population (or sampling frame). If Bales should wish to represent all small groups in any place and at any time, he would be hard pressed indeed to find a suitable frame from which to draw a probability sample. Or even when Zelditch attempts to draw a random sample of all societies, one might question the utility of the effort in view of the many difficulties. In such instances, probability procedures may be used to avoid the biases of selection (Phases II and III); but the population actually represented in the sample does not clearly coincide with the ideal population to which the researcher wants to refer his findings.

Varying Emphasis on Representation. Quite apart from the use of probability or nonprobability procedures, samples vary widely in the extent to which representational considerations govern the design. Here we can distinguish three types of samples: (1) Samples designed to represent the conceptual universe (as in the Stouffer study of conformity). (2) Samples that succeed, because of Phase I difficulties, in merely representing a frame which is of little theoretical concern. And (3) samples in which the effort and expense of representational sampling are avoided (in an exploratory study, such as Merton's, elaborate representational design is not needed to suggest "clues to the operation of diverse patterns of interpersonal influence").

To a certain extent, of course, all samples are representational. Every scientific researcher hopes to generalize from his sample. And every sample is drawn from some specifiable empirical population or frame (see McGinnis, p. 412), whether or not this population is of theoretical interest. Nevertheless, in any particular study, to represent the conceptual universe may be so time-consuming, or to represent the mere frame may be of so little consequence, that no diversion of attention or funds from other aspects of the research seems justified.

THE ANALYTICAL BASIS FOR SAMPLING

The researcher must also decide how to design the sample most effectively to facilitate his plans for analysis. There are, as we have seen, many ways in which the proposed analysis may influence the design of the sample, and a variety of sample designs are possible. The samples so far examined range in size from the single case chosen for intensive analysis of one type of system or process (used by Lundberg and Lawsing or Malinowski), to the few cases chosen for intensive analysis of one or two types of systems or processes (used by Whyte or Merton), to the many and highly stratified cases chosen for statistical analysis of complex systems or processes (used in the two large samples designed by Stouffer). The focused sample used by Kahl illustrates the further possibility of matched samples in which the variables are controlled directly through the sample selection—an especially fruitful possibility for the design of experiments.

Thus the requirements of the analysis may determine how large the sample is to be; and they may affect the stratification used in the sampling procedure, or the matching or focusing used to control key variables.

CONFLICTING BASES

There appear to be certain situations—especially in laboratory research and experimentation—where designing a sample for purposes of the analysis may interfere with the possibility of generalizing to the universe of interest. Suppose that a researcher is concerned with the interaction processes of small groups, and defines as his conceptual universe all formal and informal student groups of certain sizes in a particular men's college. He might conceivably prepare a list of such groups and use probability procedures to obtain a fairly representative sample. But what happens to this representativeness if, alternatively, in order to facilitate laboratory observation, he depends only upon student volunteers? Obviously, the kinds of students who submit readily to such observation may be different from those who do not. Or what happens when he himself constructs the groups artificially, forming new groups to facilitate his analysis of the processes of group development? Obviously, these artificial groups may be different from the naturally established groupings of interest to the researcher.

In such fashion, samples are occasionally so designed for analytical purposes as to jeopardize representation of the theoretically relevant universe (see Donald Campbell, Wold). More generally, the relative emphasis placed upon one or the other basis reflects the optimal allocation, for the particular objective, of the resources available for the research.

COMBINED BASES

Although the two sampling bases may sometimes tend, then, to be mutually exclusive, and out of practical considerations many samples are designed primarily on one basis or the other, the optimum design combines the two. Some samples designed for purposes of the analysis also attempt—where cost and inconvenience present no obstacles—to match some relevant population through representational sampling. Still other samples adhere closely to the principles of representational sampling, yet still succeed in supporting elaborate analyses of social processes and the interrelationships of several variables.

SUGGESTED READINGS FOR UNIT SIX

Blalock, 1960, Chapters 9, 22; Chein, 1959; College Entrance Examination Board, Chapters 4–6; Deming, 1950, Chapters 1 and 4; Goode and Hatt, Chapter 14; Hagood and Price, Chapters 17 and 18; Hansen, Hurwitz, and Madow; Kish, 1952 and 1953; McCarthy, 1951; Moser, Chapters 4–8; Mueller and Schuessler, Chapters 8, 11; Parten, Chapters 4, 7–9, 12, 16; Stephan and McCarthy; Stouffer, 1934; Tippett.

QUESTIONS FOR REVIEW AND DISCUSSION

Review the following methodological terms as used in this Unit:

Terms which define samples:
  analytical
  area
  "chunk"
  focused
  matched
  multi-stage
  probability
  random
  representational
  stratified
bias
bias of nonresponse
conceptual universe
sampling distribution
sampling frame
sampling phases
sampling within social structures
sampling variability, chance error
self-selection of respondents

1. What is Kahl's research case **(P-I)?**

2. How would you analyze the aims and designs of the samples used by Cottrell, Merton, and Malinowski in relation to the conceptual model and research objective of each study?

3. What procedures might have been used for offsetting some of the bias in the *Literary Digest* poll of 1936?

4. Suppose you were designing a study of the effects of age, income, and education on family purchases of proprietary (nonprescription) drugs. How might you design an appropriate and efficient sample? If you were to use mail questionnaires, what difficulties of possible bias might you face, and how would you attempt to minimize these?

5. How would you select a representative sample of teen-age gangs in a large city? Give consideration in your answer to (1) constructing an adequate sampling frame and (2) avoiding as much bias as possible.

6. Why is Zelditch concerned about possible duplications in the list of societies which he uses as a sampling frame?

7. Sorokin, in reporting the procedure for his study of great thinkers, says, "the samples are so large that in all probability they are representative." How would you evaluate this statement?

8. Under what conditions might it be appropriate to use:
  a. a simple random sample?
  b. a multi-stage rather than a single-stage sample?
  c. a stratified sample?
  d. a focused sample?

9. How does Stouffer obtain a sample of communities in order to study the activities of their leaders? Suppose you wanted to discover the extent of consensus among the attitudes of college faculty members. How would you design a representative sample of colleges?

10. Compare the methods of gathering data for Stouffer's study of nonconformity with the methods used by Kahl; with those used by Lundberg and Lawsing.

11. Compare the sample used by Le Play with that used by the Harvard Mobility Project.

12. How does Stouffer define his scale of willingness to tolerate nonconformists?

UNIT SEVEN
SOME PRINCIPLES
OF MEASUREMENT

SUGGESTED PROGRAM OF STUDY

Unit 7 is an introduction to the systematic measurement of properties as variables (P-X). It describes various procedures for using data as indicants of the properties (acts, attitudes, etc.) which the researcher has set forth in his conceptual model.

Exercises and Manual

Exercise II-1 and **II-2** will give you experience, following **Manual II-A,** with coding as one important means of using data to classify cases in terms of concepts of theoretical concern. In Exercise II-1 you will use general sociological concepts for coding the unstructured, detailed data from your interviews on family relationships (Exercise I-2). In Exercise II-2 you will develop your own code from the empirical data on work plans of young people (obtained in Exercise I-3).

Exercise III-1 and **Manual III-A** will give you an understanding of the mathematical characteristics of nominal, ordinal, and ratio measures. **Exercise III-3** and **Manual III-C** furnish a simple introduction to (or review of) the main statistical measures of central tendency and dispersion.

Studies

Review the coding methods reported in the earlier studies by **Bales** (Unit 3) and **Zelditch** (Unit 5). Then examine the nature of the measures employed by **Massing** and by **Bogue**. Notice carefully what **Weber** means by an ideal type, and how he develops a particular ideal type for use in research.

Commentary

The Commentary outlines the procedures used in these exercises and studies for locating cases on single dimensions that may be combined later to refer to the property as a whole. It distinguishes two different types of measures—composite measures that combine indicants reflecting different aspects of the property, and collective measures that combine indicants reflecting different parts (or roles) in the group.

Questions for Review and Discussion

Use the Questions for Review and Discussion as a means of defining the elements in the measurement process, the major types of measurement, and the principles of measurement you have now learned.

PAUL W. MASSING
The Image of the Voice of America as Drawn in Soviet Media

Summary

This study analyzes the changing characteristics with which the Voice of America has been described in Soviet media during several ... phases in U.S.–U.S.S.R. relations. It attempts to document the proposition that the varying images of the Voice were not arbitrarily drawn but that the propagandistic treatment of the Voice was at least partially reflective of general Soviet policy. It is suggested, consequently, that such analyses may furnish some insight into Soviet intentions.

The time periods selected were the years 1948, 1952 and 1953; in view of momentous events in 1953, this annual period was once more subdivided.

Objective

This study tests the hypothesis that the image of the Voice of America as drawn in Soviet media provides some tangible clues to the understanding of the nature and direction of Soviet propaganda strategy.

In contrast to most of the earlier analyses of Soviet references to the VOA, where the interest was focused upon the subject matter of the reference and the context in which it appeared, the objective of the present study is to reconstruct

An unclassified study, not previously published, prepared for the United States Information Agency by the Department of Sociology, Rutgers University, June, 1954.

the characteristics which Soviet media have attributed to the Voice at various times. ... The study thus examines the assumption that changes in the image of the Voice as seen in Soviet media reflect in some degree changes in the general tactics and strategy of Soviet propaganda in the struggle with the United States. What has previously appeared arbitrary and unsystematic in specific attacks on, or reactions to, the Voice may, if viewed and analyzed as an aspect of the larger Soviet strategy, reveal certain patterns of consistency and design. Such factors as U.S. information policy and, specifically, changes in the programming of the Voice are necessarily included in the general assumption that Soviet assessment of the cold war expressed itself in the references to VOA. But it is not the objective of this study to find in the references a measure of VOA's effectiveness.

Method

The first step in the investigation was to reconstruct the image of VOA as it was presented in a sample of Soviet sources [newspapers and radio] over several distinct periods of time. All direct statements about the Voice were catalogued, and sentence by sentence, broken down into their smallest "meaning units." Usually more than one of these units appeared in any sentence, and each was counted as often as it was repeated. Every codable unit of the sentence was given independent consideration, taken literally, regardless of logic or related meanings. The mere fact that the meaning unit was there, linked within the sentence structure with the expression "Voice of America," was the single criterion for inclusion. From these units a code was developed empirically. The coding was carried out by two researchers familiar with the material, working alone and then rechecking the work of the other.

The component parts of the image, amounting to almost 4,000 discrete units, were classified under 69 subcategories which in turn could be distributed among 8 gross categories. The 8 categories, arranged under three mutually exclusive headings, are given below with enough illustrative material to describe their content.

I. THE AIMS AND ACTIVITIES OF VOA

Here belong all statements concerning the powers behind the Voice, its organizational set-up and its activities.

1. THE VOA IS A MOUTHPIECE, a stooge, megaphone, agent, voice, vehicle, of: *government* or governmental officials or politicians; of *capitalism,* Wall Street, monopolists, ruling circles, bankers, the dollar; of *imperialism,* expansionism; of American *warmongers,* stranglers of peoples, war incendiaries, transoceanic gangsters; of *fascism,* Goebbels, Hitler; of *reaction,* the status quo, of antipeople's conspirators, reactionary labor leaders, of monarchy, pessimism, mysticism.

2. THE ORGANIZATION OF VOA includes references to: *expansion* of network and programming; the use of *émigrés* and traitors; operation with *other radios;* direction by *government and big business boards;* the *personnel* of VOA.

3. VOA's ACTIVITIES include: *espionage; diversionism,* terrorism; *subversion,* leads astray, sows distrust, foments hostility, incites; *psychological warfare,* a weapon of the cold war; *dictates* to others; *covers up crime,* diverts attention; *engages in propaganda,* is a propaganda machine; *influences,* inspires.

II. THE NATURE OF VOA's PERFORMANCE

Here belong all statements which characterize the Voice, describe the broad contents of its messages and the nature of its tactics.

4. VOA PROPAGATES (or falsely claims to propagate): the *American way of life,* democracy, rights of workers, freedom of the press, enlightenment of the workers, itself as the font of culture, the voice of paradise; *U.S. policy; war,* aggression, hatred; *lies and slander* against the USSR and the Satellites; *denials* of U.S. shortcomings and of Soviet and Satellite advancement. VOA *remains silent* about: how the "simple folk in the USA" live, the lack of real democracy, racial discrimination, diplomatically embarrassing subjects.

5. THE TACTICS OF VOA include: *deceit,* being insinuating, hypocritical, cynical, forgery, withholding the truth, crocodile tears; *argumentation,* pernicious dialectics, unfounded assertions, hazy statements, comparing, contrasting, philosophizing; *loud and zealous behavior,* cries, boasts, implores, roars, trumpets, makes the ether ring; *attacks,* threatens; *advertises,* uses themes; *gets angry.*

6. VOA IS CHARACTERIZED as: *corrupt,* base, foul, notorious, unashamed, venal; *poor in quality,* ridiculous, uncouth, nonsensical, a chatterbox, absurd, a laughing stock, pedantic, loudmouthed; a *liar,* (in general); *uneasy,* fearful, alarmed, cowardly, nervous, hysterical.

III. VOA'S ACCOMPLISHMENTS

Here belong all "documentary evidence" of VOA's failure and all statements in refutation of the Voice.

7. VOA's FAILURE is shown by: statements of *Americans themselves;* the *people* of the world, millions, everybody; *its reception* by the Soviets and Satellites; *statements of individuals.*

8. VOA IS REFUTED by: *"true facts"* about the U.S., and about the USSR; the *Americans themselves;* the *people of the world,* everybody; *the USSR* and the "true voice of Moscow;" *impartial witnesses,* scientists, the foreign press; the *VOA itself; foreign governments;* and by direct *argumentation.*

The image of VOA thus reconstructed is complete in that it is based not on a sample of references or of meaning units within the references but on the totality of direct statements about VOA which appeared in the sampled Soviet media over given time periods.

The Time Periods

The periods chosen for comparison are the years of 1948, 1952 and 1953. To test the hypothesis that changes in Soviet propaganda policies toward the U.S. are reflected in the changing characteristics attributed to the Voice, it would have been highly desirable to analyze the characteristics over time periods about equal in length and clearly identifiable as representing different phases in U.S.–U.S.S.R. relations: for instance, six months before and after the outbreak of the Korean war. The data at hand, however, restricted the choice of the sample periods. As a compromise between what was most desirable and what was available, the following time periods were selected: the

year 1948, representing an early stage in the cold war; the year 1952, characterized by consistently strained relations between the U.S. and the U.S.S.R.; and the year 1953, which stood under the sign of Stalin's death and the "peace offensive" of his successors but also of the East German uprisings of June 17.

The outstanding but politically contradictory events of 1953 suggested a further separation of the 1953 references into three subperiods: (1) "pre-Berlin," that is, January 1 to June 17; (2) the weeks immediately following the Berlin uprisings (actually from June 23, when Soviet propaganda began to link the Voice with the uprisings, to August 31, when these specific references petered out); and (3) the rest of the year. These smaller time units are discussed separately.

Home and Foreign Media

Finally, it seemed important to differentiate between the treatment of VOA in Soviet home media (press, journals, domestic broadcasts and domestic press transmissions) and foreign media (foreign broadcasts and foreign press transmissions). Did Soviet propaganda deal with VOA differently at home and abroad? Were there two Soviet images of VOA, one drawn for the benefit of the Soviet population, the other for foreign consumption? A differential treatment of the Voice would certainly be relevant for the evaluation of Soviet propaganda policy.

The foreign radio data available for 1948 did not contain any annotation as to repeated broadcasts and master broadcasts. Therefore, to maintain comparability, these repetitions were also excluded for the 1952 and 1953 materials; each Soviet radio text was counted only once—regardless of the number of repetitions it may have obtained. This furnished the following number of image units for final analysis:

	1948		1952		1953	
	Home	Foreign	Home	Foreign	Home	Foreign
References to VOA	44	86	102	63	47	24
Number of image units contained in the references	339	594	486	470	369	240

Actually, inclusion of the repeats and master broadcasts would have yielded a total of 196 foreign references for 1952 (instead of 63) and 1914 image units (instead of 470). For 1953, inclusion of repeats and master broadcasts would have meant 135 references (instead of 24) and 1359 image units (instead of 240) in the foreign media. Because of the large differences involved, a separate analysis was made for 1952 and 1953 in which all repeats were included. One general finding might be stated here: the image constructed from the total number of references including repeats is, with the exception of the post-Berlin period, surprisingly similar to that obtained when repeats are omitted.

General Findings

I. THE IMAGE OF VOA IN THREE SAMPLE YEARS

The image of the Voice of America presented in the Soviet media changed from 1948, an early stage in the cold war, to 1952, a period of consistently strained relations between the U.S. and the U.S.S.R. Further shifts took place in 1953, a year of momentous events behind the Iron Curtain.

The overall patterns can be seen from summary Table 1 which gives separately for home and foreign audiences the distribution of the main categories by which the Voice was characterized in the three years.

Table 1 shows several noticeable developments:

1. *In 1948* the bulk of ideas communicated about the Voice (approximately 60 per cent of all statement units) pertained to its alleged *nature*, as observable from its *performance*. The Voice was presented as the boastful and deceiving propagator of the American way of life, particularly its high standard of living, and as the slanderer of the U.S.S.R. and the Satellite countries bent upon playing up their shortcomings and denying their "advances."

The image of the Voice drawn for the benefit of Soviet home and foreign audiences seemed largely a means for discrediting the United States and what it stands for.

2. The emphasis on the overt nature of VOA's performance declined between 1948 and 1952 (from about 60 per cent to about 45 per cent). Instead, the picture drawn *in 1952* focused more strongly than before on the *basic aims and activities* of the Voice. The description of how the Voice operates changed to information as to the *"real"* identity of the Voice; image units pertaining to basic aims and activities rose from 27 per cent to 43 per cent for the home, and from 22 per cent to 35 per cent for the foreign audiences.

More specifically, comments about the

Table **1**   *Distribution, by per cent, of image characteristics in three sample years*

	1948		1952		1953	
	Home	*Foreign*	*Home*	*Foreign*	*Home*	*Foreign*
Aims and activities	27	22	43	35	48	33
Backers	15	11	15	14	10	6
Organization	7	6	14	10	15	13
Function	5	5	14	11	23	14
Nature of performance	59	61	42	47	32	44
What it propagates	25	34	17	22	10	23
Tactics	17	18	12	18	10	13
Traits	17	9	13	7	12	8
Accomplishments	14	17	15	18	20	23
Failure	7	4	9	8	5	5
Refuted	7	13	6	10	15	18
Total per cent	*100*	*100*	*100*	*100*	*100*	*100*
Number of image units [a]	339	594	486	470	369	240

[a] The percentages for image units in all categories as well as subcategories are based throughout the report upon the total image units for the home and for the foreign audiences respectively in the time periods analyzed.

organization of the Voice doubled. And while 1948 audiences, in this respect, had been told largely about Voice personnel, 1952 audiences were presented with the picture of a powerful organization which cooperates with and operates through other radio networks and is continuously expanding its own technical facilities and programming (as to hours and languages).

Comments about the basic function of the Voice more than doubled. It was described increasingly in 1952 as the propaganda tool of American imperialism and of Wall Street, bent no longer merely on promoting the American way of life but on propagating hatred, aggression and psychological warfare.

The image of the Voice presented at home and abroad was congruent with the general imputations of aggressive intentions on the part of American "imperialism."

3. The overall picture for *1953* blurs the marked changes that took place within significant periods of this year. Therefore we merely note here for later discussion the rise of two features.

There was a notable further increase in references to VOA's function, and added to the catalogue of VOA's functions in the months following the Berlin uprisings was a new quality: VOA was described as a terroristic agency. This feature replaced the previous "propaganda" or "psychological warfare" functions associated with the Voice.

The yearly total for 1953 also shows more comments about VOA's "accomplishments," that is, failure, than any of the previous sample years. Again, the peak of such comments occurred after the Berlin demonstrations when the Soviet media pointed to the Voice as a disturber of the peace, an accomplice in the "fascist provocation" that failed.

4. Finally, Table 1 shows that the image of VOA presented to the audi-

ences *at home and abroad* was not identical. The technique of "unmasking" the Voice, the behind-the-scene look into VOA's basic *aims and activities* was at all times more often employed at home.

Conversely, in talking to foreign listeners, Soviet propagandists always referred more often to the nature of VOA's propaganda content and emphasized its *refutation* by facts and witnesses, while to the home audience they stressed VOA's characterological features: it is a liar, corrupt, *etc.* (As can be seen from the table, "traits" are more often discussed for home audiences, "refutation" for audiences abroad.)

On the other hand, it should not be overlooked that the basic changes from 1948 to 1952 occurred in both home and foreign media and that within both years differences in emphasis according to the two target areas were less marked than were the changes over time. It was only in 1953 that the tendencies toward differential treatment as to home and foreign targets became pronounced.

II. THE VOICE IMAGE IN 1953

The image of VOA drawn at various periods in 1953 was so different that it deserves special attention.

The first period detailed in . . . Table 2 covers the first six months of the year including Stalin's death and his successors' "peace offensive," up to the Berlin uprisings. The second period (June 18 through August 31) comprises the immediate reaction to the Berlin events; the third covers the rest of the year (September through December).

1. In the first six months of the year, *until the Berlin riots,* the Soviet home audience received much the same story about the Voice as it had in 1952. The characterization of VOA for audiences abroad, however, underwent a change. There, mentions of VOA's overall aims, particularly its backers, declined somewhat in share of the total as against 1952 (from 35 per cent to 28 per cent) while allegations concerning its alleged lack of accomplishment rose from 18 to

Table **2** *Distribution, by per cent, of image characteristics in three periods of 1953*

	January–June 17		June 18–August 31		September 1–December 31	
	Home	*Foreign*	*Home*	*Foreign*	*Home*	*Foreign*
Aims and activities	47	28	52	39	41	26
Backers	20	5	5	7	9	10
Organization	16	13	15	11	14	13
Function	11	10	32	21	18	3
Nature of performance	41	44	23	38	42	67
What it propagates	5	21	8	24	19	27
Tactics	21	13	5	10	10	27
Traits	15	10	10	4	13	13
Accomplishments	12	28	25	23	17	7
Failure	7	11	2	1	6	
Refuted	5	17	23	22	11	7
Total per cent	*100*	*100*	*100*	*100*	*100*	*100*
Number of image units	81	106	177	104	111	30

28 per cent. The testimony of facts as well as people, Americans and people all over the world, was more often called upon to refute VOA and to prove that it is a failure. The 1952 image of a powerful, aggressive opponent was modified into one of a costly but useless disturber of the peace.

2. The Berlin riots drastically changed the picture. References in the two and one-half months following the riots soared, and this quantitative increase was accompanied by a marked shift in the image presented. Descriptions of the nature of VOA's performance dropped. Comments on the function of VOA gained sharply; both home and foreign audiences were told that VOA is a terroristic agency—a function which had hardly been mentioned before. And the home audience was now assured as often as foreign audiences that VOA is refuted by impartial witnesses and the true facts.

3. The concerted effort of "unmasking" VOA as an agency of esponiage, subversion and terrorism dwindled in the latter part of the year, more so in the foreign than in the home media. (Even including the repeat broadcasts, there were only 9 references to VOA between September and December 1953 as compared to 86 in the two months following the riots.) For the rest of the year, VOA was depicted for the home audience much in the same way as in the six months prior to Berlin, which, as stated before, was similar to the pattern of 1952. However, in the few references that occurred in the foreign media the comments pertained mostly to the category, VOA's Nature of Performance, emphasizing again that VOA is a deceitful, loud and boastful slanderer of the U.S.S.R. and the Satellites. This image resembled strongly that of 1948 with the exception that in 1948 VOA was more strongly accused of lying about American affairs whereas the late 1953 charges concentrated on VOA's alleged distortions of Soviet conditions and intentions. Also, in late 1953 the Soviet foreign media were more restrained in mentioning VOA's function or failure than they had been at any of the periods sampled.

DONALD J. BOGUE
Income and Population Composition

Income as a Measure of Economic Well-Being

Money income is a sensitive measure of economic well-being in today's technologically advanced nations. In such so-

Reprinted in part with permission of the publisher from Donald J. Bogue, *The Population of the United States,* copyright 1959 by The Free Press, a corporation, pp. 646, 647–51, 653–54, 669.

cieties it is roughly synonymous with "livelihood," because very few families or individuals are able to maintain economic self-sufficiency and because barter exchange has almost disappeared. Except for a certain amount of household consumption of the produce from farms and vegetable gardens, there is comparatively little production-for-own-use (self-sufficiency). Only a few arrangements involving barter or "payment in kind" persist within these modern societies, and almost all obligations are now discharged by means of money payments. The few exceptions (such as farmers who are given the use of a dwelling as part of the rent bargain, or restaurant workers who get meals as a part of their pay) only emphasize the comparative infrequency of moneyless exchange. This situation means that statistics concerning money income are an excellent measure of the level-of-living potential among the population, the only major exception being found in the rural-farm population—and even there a study of income distribution can provide much insight. . . .

Income Distribution

The economic well-being of the population cannot be measured exclusively in terms of the average income available per citizen. . . . The *distribution* of the income must also be discovered, by means of such questions as, "To what extent do a very few persons receive very large incomes and a great many persons receive very small incomes?" "What percentage of persons receive less than the per capita share . . . and how much less do how many persons receive?" Revolutionary changes have taken place recently in income distribution, as well as in the nation's general level of economic well-being.

Beginning in the mid-1940's, the Bureau of the Census began to collect statistics concerning the income received from all sources by families and individuals, and it is these data which provide detailed information about income distribution.[1] During the calendar year 1957, 7 out of every 10 persons who were 14 years of age and over (70.7 percent) received at least some money income. It may surprise the reader to learn that so

[1] . . . It is known that the incomes enumerated for persons and families are smaller

large a percentage of the population receives income. The percentage of persons who are fully dependent on others for a livelihood is much smaller than it used to be, primarily because such a large proportion of housewives are now employed, such a large percentage of young persons attending school are working part time, and such a large percentage of persons 65 years of age and over (both male and female) regularly receive pensions or other similar kinds of payments. The percentage of the population that is dependent decreased substantially between 1945 and 1957, the span of time concerning which data are available.

The median income for individuals in 1957 was $2,452, or $204 per month, and for families it was $4,971, or about $415 per month; however, the dispersion from these midpoints is very wide. The distribution of income among individuals and among families who did receive income is shown in Table 1.[2] There is a characteristic "income curve" describing the distribution of income among individuals, and it indicates that a large proportion of the population receive very

than the incomes actually received, and that they may be underreported by as much as 20 percent. Little is known about the origin or nature of this error, or about its effect on the validity of the data if such data are to be used as a basis for inferences concerning differences between groups of the population or changes over periods of time. These data can be defended only in the sense that the uniform and "logical" sequences they present are sufficiently consistent with general observation and theoretical expectations that their "face value" validity seems very high.

[2] *Note concerning units for which incomes are reported: persons, families, and unrelated individuals:* Since income is paid to persons, the most basic income statistics that can be collected are those referring to the total money income received by individuals over one-year periods. Such data are called "personal" or "individual" income statistics. However, for a very large percentage of the population the family, rather than the

Table **1**   *Percent distribution of money income among families and individuals, 1950 and 1957*

Total money income [a]	Income of families			Income of individuals		
	1957	*1950*	*Change, 1950 to 1957*	*1957*	*1950*	*Change, 1950 to 1957*
Total	100.0	100.0		100.0	100.0	
Under $500	3.0	4.0	11.0	16.2	16.0	0.2
$500 to $999	3.4	5.0	−1.6	12.3	11.3	1.0
1,000 to 1,499	4.0	5.2	−1.2	8.2	9.3	−1.1
1,500 to 1,999	4.5	5.8	−1.3	6.7	7.2	−0.5
2,000 to 2,499	5.2	6.3	−1.1	7.3	8.8	−1.5
2,500 to 2,999	4.4	7.5	−3.1	5.6	9.3	−3.7
3,000 to 3,499	5.7	7.5	−1.8	6.9	7.5	−0.6
3,500 to 3,999	6.1	9.4	−3.3	5.9	7.8	−2.0
4,000 to 4,499	7.3	8.1	−0.8	6.4	6.3	0.1
4,500 to 4,999	6.8	7.2	−0.4	4.9	4.4	0.5
5,000 to 5,999	14.5	10.6	3.9	8.3	4.8	3.5
6,000 to 6,999	10.3	7.7	2.6	9.0	6.5	2.5
7,000 to 9,999	16.3	9.9	6.4			
10,000 to 14,999	6.5					
15,000 to 24,999	1.4	5.8	2.6	2.4	0.7	1.7
25,000 and over	0.5					

[a] The data for 1950 have been adjusted for change in price level; the income classes are expressed in 1957 dollars.

modest incomes and a small proportion of the population receive very large incomes. Figure 1[A] illustrates this curve very roughly (it would emphasize the concentration which exists at the low income level if it were plotted in units of 100 dollars instead of 500 dollars). For centuries, economists have speculated as to why the income curve for individuals has its characteristic skewed shape, with such a large proportion of income recipients concentrated toward the lower end

person, is the unit of consumption and livelihood. Since one-half of all today's families have two or more earners, one can gain a much more accurate picture of the livelihood situation by assembling income data in terms of family units. Hence, income statistics tabulated for families are an important type of income formation. (Often these family statistics are cross-classified according to the socio-economic characteristics of the family head.) But many individuals do not live in families; they live alone in single-person households, as lodgers or tenants in private homes, hotels, and rooming houses, or as employees who live in the private household of the employer. If a tabulation of family incomes is prepared, an income tabulation must also be made for this residue of "unrelated individuals" or nonfamily persons.

Thus, there are two major kinds of income tabulations:
    Incomes of persons (income recipients)
    Incomes of families and of unrelated individuals (nonfamily persons) . . . .

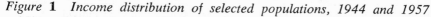

Figure **1** *Income distribution of selected populations, 1944 and 1957*

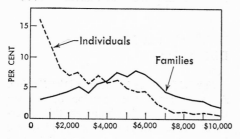

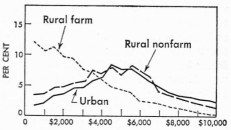

of the income scale. It is now rather generally agreed that a variety of factors interact to produce this distribution. Among these factors are:

a. *Differences in ability, intelligence, initiative, skill, health, and other characteristics that influence income-earning ability.* That great individual differences in productive ability exist among the population can be observed on every hand. There is no general agreement concerning the extent to which these differences arise from inherited limitations or capabilities and the extent to which they reflect the particular environment and experience of each individual. Whatever the origin of these differences, lack of productive capacity does curtail severely the earning power of some individuals, and extraordinary skill or talent does enable a few individuals to obtain larger than average incomes. It has often been pointed out, however, that differences in ability could not possibly be the only factor responsible for income differences, since differential abilities are known to be distributed among the population according to a "normal curve," rather than according to the kind of very skewed curve that is shown in Figure 1[A].

b. *Differences in the "market value" of various occupations.* Higher rates of pay are awarded to persons who perform certain essential activities that require

highly specialized training and for which applicants are scarce. Lower rates of pay are the general rule in less specialized occupations that require less skill and experience, and for which manpower can easily be recruited.

c. *Custom, tradition, and the "power structure" of the society.* The nation's economy may be regarded as a giant factory turning out a measurable quantity of those goods and services that are required for the satisfaction of the needs and desires of the population. The manner in which the product of this "factory" is divided, and the proportionate share awarded to each group of workers, is determined largely by custom and tradition, and by comparative "bargaining power." For example, specific laws governing the transmission of property from generation to generation through the custom of inheritance help to determine the extent to which individuals who have very modest ability but wealthy parents are able to enjoy large incomes, and the extent to which other individuals who have a great deal of innate ability but who inherit only poverty are prevented from acquiring the technical training necessary to develop their talents. Corporations and labor unions that are highly organized, and that hold a very strong position within the economy, are able to capture a larger share of the wealth produced than can individual workers or small businesses,

because the latter have less power to demand higher pay for their services. If it
were necessary to select one element as
the single factor underlying the recent
and current changes in the pattern of income distribution, the interplay of the
forces involved in this "power structure"
would have to be considered as one of the
leading contenders.

  d. *Labor turnover and part-time, part-
year employment.* Since some workers
are continuously entering and leaving the
labor force, they receive incomes for only
a part of the particular calendar year
concerning which statistics are collected.
Many others work only a few hours per
week, and receive small incomes for this
reason. Women workers and young workers who are attending school account for
much of the large concentration at the
low income level. Periods of unemployment also reduce the earnings of some
workers. Although these factors alone
cannot account for the shape of the income curve, they certainly increase the
number of persons earning small incomes.

  Studying income distribution in terms
of families rather than in terms of individuals produces a somewhat different
picture. Figure 1[A] shows that family
income distribution is not concentrated
at the lowest income levels, but takes the
shape of a long distribution with a small
hump in the middle. This difference between individual and family income distributions makes it evident that a large
percentage of the individuals who receive
exceptionally small incomes are members
of families, and are partially dependent
upon others for their livelihood. Hence,
if one wishes to gain a realistic picture of
the livelihood level of the population, the
income distributions for families and for
unrelated individuals will yield more in-

formation than will the income distributions for all persons as individuals. . . .

Differentials in Income Distribution

Sex Differences in Income Distribution.
A much smaller proportion of women
than of men receive incomes; this difference, of course, is due primarily to the
lower rates of labor force participation
among women. For example, the percentage of the total population 14 years of
age or over who received some income
during the calendar year of 1957 was as
follows:

	Both sexes	*Males*	*Females*
Total	70.7	91.5	52.4
Urban and rural nonfarm	71.5	92.0	53.9
Rural farm	65.0	88.1	40.8

Of those persons receiving income,
women received much smaller incomes
than men. Table 2 shows the income distribution in 1956 with respect to both
men and women, by urban and rural residence; it demonstrates that most of the
male income recipients are rather evenly
distributed over a range that includes incomes from $500 to $6,000, with a
smaller proportion having incomes larger
than $6,000, whereas the women recipi-
ents are highly concentrated at the lower
end of the scale. Less than one-half of the
women recipients received as much as
$1,200 per year, and only 7 percent re-
ceived more than $4,000. This sex differ-
ential is present in urban, rural-nonfarm,
and rural-farm areas. It is produced by a
variety of conditions, among which are
the lower rates of pay which women commonly receive (often for the kind of work

Table **2** *Income distribution of individuals by sex and urban-rural residence, 1956*

Income	Total, both sexes	Male				Female			
		Total	Urban	Rural non-farm	Rural farm	Total	Urban	Rural non-farm	Rural farm
Total	100.0	100.0	100.0	100.0	100.0	100.0	100.0	100.0	100.0
Less than $500	16.3	9.1	6.0	9.2	24.1	27.6	21.7	35.1	53.5
$500 to $999	12.5	8.1	6.6	8.2	15.4	19.3	19.3	20.1	17.7
1,000 to 1,499	8.0	6.2	5.4	5.6	11.4	10.6	11.2	10.0	8.1
1,500 to 1,999	6.8	5.5	4.7	5.5	9.7	8.7	9.4	7.8	5.8
2,000 to 2,499	7.4	6.4	5.9	6.7	8.1	9.0	10.0	7.6	5.2
2,500 to 2,999	6.1	5.7	5.6	5.6	7.0	6.7	7.4	5.4	4.6
3,000 to 3,499	7.0	7.4	7.7	7.8	5.2	6.5	7.7	4.5	2.0
3,500 to 3,999	6.3	7.4	7.9	7.6	4.6	4.5	5.2	3.4	1.1
4,000 to 4,499	6.8	9.2	10.5	9.3	3.1	3.0	3.5	2.2	1.4
4,500 to 4,999	4.6	6.7	7.7	6.2	3.0	1.3	1.6	1.1	0.3
5,000 to 5,999	7.8	11.9	13.3	12.8	3.2	1.5	1.8	1.4	0.1
6,000 to 6,999	4.0	6.2	7.2	5.9	2.0	0.5	0.6	0.6	0.1
7,000 to 9,999	4.1	6.5	7.4	6.3	2.0	0.4	0.5	0.5	
10,000 and over	2.3	3.6	3.1	3.3	1.3	0.2	0.2	0.5	
Median income	$2,432	$3,608	$4,010	$3,592	$1,461	$1,146	$1,402	$871	$468

performed by men at higher rates), more part-time work, more part-year employment, and the large numbers of widows who receive small pensions. . . .

Income Distribution and Urban and Rural Residence. The largest money incomes are found in urban areas, and the smallest in rural-farm areas. Inasmuch as a large share of the rural-farm population receives a certain amount of economic goods and services, in the form of housing and food, for which it does not pay money, the statistics concerning money income tend to understate the total rural-farm income. Even when a generous allowance is made for the value of housing and food, however, it is still obvious that the income of farm families is very low in comparison with that of urban and rural-nonfarm families. For example, the median income of families in 1956, . . .

by urban and rural residence, was as follows:

	All families
Total	$4,783
Urban	5,221
Rural nonfarm	4,619
Rural farm	2,371

The average rural-farm family receives only one-half as much money as the average United States family. It is doubtful whether the value of the food and rent that is produced or furnished on the farm accounts for more than a small fraction of this differential. Therefore, one seems forced to conclude that a disproportionately large number of the nation's "pockets of poverty" are found in rural-farm areas. Panel C of Figure 1 illustrates the differences in income distribution between urban, rural-nonfarm, and rural-farm populations. . . .

Conclusion

Additional materials concerning income are contained [elsewhere in the book]. . . . It is hoped that this brief exposition of income, supplemented by the materials presented in other chapters, makes it abundantly clear that income differences are one of the leading factors that help to explain differences in human behavior.

MAX WEBER
The Protestant Ethic and the Spirit of Capitalism

Introduction [1]

. . . The impulse to acquisition, pursuit of gain, of money, of the greatest possible amount of money, has in itself nothing to do with capitalism. This impulse exists and has existed among waiters, physicians, coachmen, artists, prostitutes, dishonest officials, soldiers, nobles, crusaders, gamblers, and beggars. One may say that it has been common to all sorts and conditions of men at all times and in all countries of the earth, wherever the objective possibility of it is or has been given. . . . Unlimited greed for gain is not in the least identical with capitalism, and is still less its spirit.

Reprinted in part from Max Weber, *The Protestant Ethic and the Spirit of Capitalism* (translated by Talcott Parsons from the German edition of 1920), New York: Charles Scribner's Sons, 1952, pp. 17, 19, 23, 24, 25, 26, 27, 47–48, 50, 51, 54, 55, 56, 57, 58, 59, 61, 62, 64, 74, 75, 79, 80, 89, 90, 91, 92, 97, 98, 153, 154, 155, 158, 159, 163, 170, 171, 172, 174, 180, 181, with permission of Charles Scribner's Sons, and George Allen & Unwin Ltd.

[1] [This was written by Weber for a series of essays, *Gesammelte Aufsätze zur Religionssoziologie,* of which the present study is the first, and others extend the methods to Confucianism, Taoism, Hinduism, Buddhism, and ancient Judaism.]

Capitalism *may* even be identical with the restraint, or at least a rational tempering, of this irrational impulse. But capitalism is identical with the pursuit of profit, and forever *renewed* profit, by means of continuous, rational, capitalistic enterprise. . . .

We will define a capitalistic economic action as one which rests on the expectation of profit by the utilization of opportunities for exchange, that is on (formally) peaceful chances of profit. . . . So far as the transactions are rational, calculation underlies every single action of the partners. . . . Now in this sense capitalism and capitalistic enterprises, even with a considerable rationalization of capitalistic calculation, have existed in all civilized countries of the earth, so far as economic documents permit us to judge. . . .

Hence in a universal history of culture the central problem for us is not, in the last analysis, even from a purely economic view-point, the development of capitalistic activity as such, differing in different cultures only in form: the adventurer type, or capitalism in trade, war, politics, or administration as sources of gain. It is rather the origin of this sober bourgeois capitalism with its rational organization of free labour. . . . Why did not the capitalistic interests [develop in the same form] in China or India? Why did not the scientific, the artistic, the political, or the economic development there enter upon that path of rationalization which is peculiar to the Occident? . . .

It is hence our first concern to work out and to explain genetically the special peculiarity of Occidental rationalism, and within this field that of the modern Occidental form. Every such attempt at explanation must, recognizing the fundamental importance of the economic factor, above all take account of the economic conditions. But at the same time the opposite correlation must not be left out of consideration. For though the development of economic rationalism is partly dependent on rational technique and law, it is at the same time determined by the ability and disposition of men to adopt certain types of practical rational conduct. When these types have been obstructed by spiritual obstacles, the development of rational economic conduct has also met serious inner resistance. The magical and religious forces, and the ethical ideas of duty based upon them, have in the past always been among the most important formative influences on conduct. In the studies collected here we shall be concerned with these forces. . . .

In this case we are dealing with the connection of the spirit of modern economic life with the rational ethics of ascetic Protestantism. Thus we treat here only one side of the causal chain. . . .

Chapter II: The Spirit of Capitalism

In the title of this study is used the somewhat pretentious phrase, the *spirit* of capitalism. What is to be understood by it? The attempt to give anything like a definition of it brings out certain difficulties which are in the very nature of this type of investigation.

If any object can be found to which this term can be applied with any understandable meaning, it can only be an historical individual, i.e. a complex of elements associated in historical reality which we unite into a conceptual whole from the standpoint of their cultural significance.

Such an historical concept, however, since it refers in its content to a phenomenon significant for its unique individuality . . . must be gradually put together out of the individual parts which are taken from historical reality to make it up. Thus the final and definitive concept cannot stand at the beginning of the investigation, but must come at the end. We must, in other words, work out in the course of the discussion, as its most important result, the best conceptual formulation of what we here understand by the spirit of capitalism, that is the best from the point of view which interests us here. This point of view (the one of which we shall speak later) is, further, by no means the only possible one from which the historical phenomena we are investigating can be analysed. Other standpoints would, for this as for every historical phenomenon, yield other characteristics as the essential ones. The result is that it is by no means necessary to understand by the spirit of capitalism only what it will come to mean to *us* for the purposes of our analysis. This is a necessary result of the nature of historical concepts which attempt for their methodological purposes not to grasp historical reality in abstract general formulae, but in concrete genetic sets of relations which are inevitably of a specifically unique and individual character.

Thus, if we try to determine the object, the analysis and historical explanation of which we are attempting, it cannot be in the form of a conceptual definition, but at least in the beginning only a provisional description of what is here meant by the spirit of capitalism. Such a description is, however, indispensable in order clearly to understand the object of the investigation. For this purpose we turn to a document of that spirit which contains what we are looking for in almost classical purity, and at the same time has the advantage of being free from all direct relationship to religion, being thus, for our purposes, free of preconceptions.

> For six pounds a year you may have the use of one hundred pounds, provided you are a man of known prudence and honesty.
> He that spends a groat a day idly, spends idly above six pounds a year, which is the price for the use of one hundred pounds.
> He that wastes idly a groat's worth of his time per day, one day with another, wastes the privilege of using one hundred pounds each day.
> He that idly loses five shillings' worth of time, loses five shillings, and might as prudently throw five shillings into the sea.
> He that loses five shillings, not only loses that sum, but all the advantage that might be made by turning it in dealing, which by the time that a young man becomes old, will amount to a considerable sum of money.

It is Benjamin Franklin who preaches to us in these sentences.... The peculiarity of this philosophy of avarice appears to be the ideal of the honest man of recognized credit, and above all the idea of a duty of the individual toward the increase of his capital, which is assumed as an end in itself.... It is not mere business astuteness, that sort of thing is common enough, it is an ethos. *This* is the quality which interests us....

[The] peculiar idea, so familiar to us to-day, but in reality so little a matter of course, of one's duty in a calling, is what is most characteristic of the social ethic of capitalistic culture, and is in a sense the fundamental basis of it. It is an obligation which the individual is supposed to feel and does feel towards the content of his professional activity, no matter in what it consists, in particular no matter whether it appears on the surface as a utilization of his personal powers, or only of his material possessions (as capital)....

In order that a manner of life so well adapted to the peculiarities of capitalism could be selected at all, i.e. should come to dominate others, it had to originate somewhere, and not in isolated individuals alone, but as a way of life common to whole groups of men. This origin is what really needs explanation. Concerning the doctrine of the more naïve historical materialism, that such ideas originate as a reflection or superstructure of economic situations, we shall speak more in detail below. At this point it will suffice for our purpose to call attention to the fact that without doubt, in the country of Benjamin Franklin's birth (Massachusetts), the spirit of capitalism (in the sense we have attached to it) was present before the capitalistic order.... In this case the causal relation is certainly the reverse of that suggested by the materialistic standpoint.

But the origin and history of such ideas is much more complex than the theorists of the superstructure suppose. The spirit of capitalism, in the sense in which we are using the term, had to fight its way to supremacy against a whole world of hostile forces....

At all periods of history, wherever it was possible, there has been ruthless acquisition, bound to no ethical norms whatever. . . .

And this fact has been treated either as ethically indifferent or as reprehensible, but unfortunately unavoidable. This has not only been the normal attitude of all ethical teachings, but, what is more important, also that expressed in the practical action of the average man of pre-capitalistic times. . . . Now just this attitude was one of the strongest inner obstacles which the adaptation of men to the conditions of an ordered bourgeois capitalistic economy has encountered everywhere.

The most important opponent with which the spirit of capitalism, in the sense of a definite standard of life claiming ethical sanction, has had to struggle, was that type of attitude and reaction to new situations which we may designate as traditionalism. . . .

A man, for instance, who at the rate of 1 mark per acre mowed $2\frac{1}{2}$ acres per day and earned $2\frac{1}{2}$ marks, when the rate was raised to 1·25 marks per acre mowed, not 3 acres, as he might easily have done, thus earning 3·75 marks, but only 2 acres, so that he could still earn the $2\frac{1}{2}$ marks to which he was accustomed. The opportunity of earning more was less attractive than that of working less. . . . Wherever modern capitalism has begun its work of increasing the productivity of human labour by increasing its intensity, it has encountered the immensely stubborn resistance of this leading trait of pre-capitalistic labour. . . .

For not only is a developed sense of responsibility absolutely indispensable, but in general also an attitude which, at least during working hours, is freed from continual calculations of how the customary wage may be earned with a max-

imum of comfort and a minimum of exertion. Labour must, on the contrary, be performed as if it were an absolute end in itself, a calling. But such an attitude is by no means a product of nature. It cannot be evoked by low wages or high ones alone, but can only be the product of a long and arduous process of education. To-day, capitalism, once in the saddle, can recruit its labouring force in all industrial countries with comparative ease. In the past this was in every case an extremely difficult problem. And even to-day it could probably not get along without the support of a powerful ally along the way, which, as we shall see below, was at hand at the time of its development. . . .

We provisionally use the expression spirit of (modern) capitalism to describe that attitude which seeks profit rationally and systematically in the manner which we have illustrated by the example of Benjamin Franklin. This, however, is justified by the historical fact that that attitude of mind has on the one hand found its most suitable expression in capitalistic enterprise, while on the other the enterprise has derived its most suitable motive force from the spirit of capitalism. . . .

Now, how could activity, which was at best ethically tolerated, turn into a calling in the sense of Benjamin Franklin? The fact to be explained historically is that in the most highly capitalistic centre of that time, in Florence of the fourteenth and fifteenth centuries, the money and capital market of all the great political Powers, this attitude was considered ethically unjustifiable, or at best to be tolerated. But in the backwoods small bourgeois circumstances of Pennsylvania in the eighteenth century, where business threatened for simple lack of money to fall back into barter, where there was hardly a sign of large enterprise, where only the earliest beginnings of banking were to be found, the same thing was considered the essence of moral conduct, even commanded in the name of duty. To speak here of a reflection of material conditions in the ideal superstructure would be patent nonsense. What was the background of ideas which could account for the sort of activity apparently directed toward profit alone as a calling toward which the individual feels himself to have an ethical obligation? For it was this idea which gave the way of life of the new entrepreneur its ethical foundation and justification. . . .

Chapter III: Luther's Conception of the Calling. Task of the Investigation

Now it is unmistakable that even in the German word *Beruf*, and perhaps still more clearly in the English *calling*, a religious conception, that of a task set by God, is at least suggested. . . .

The idea is new, a product of the Reformation. This may be assumed as generally known. It is true that certain suggestions of the positive valuation of routine activity in the world, which is contained in this conception of the calling, had already existed in the Middle Ages, and even in late Hellenistic antiquity. . . . But at least one thing was unquestionably new: the valuation of the fulfilment of duty in worldly affairs as the highest form which the moral activity of the individual could assume. This it was which inevitably gave every-day worldly activity a religious significance, and which first created the conception of a calling in this sense. The conception of the calling thus brings out that central dogma of all Protestant denominations which the Catholic division of ethical precepts into *praecepta* and *consilia* discards. The only way of living acceptably to God was not to surpass worldly morality in monastic asceticism, but solely through the fulfilment of the obligations imposed upon the individual by his position in the world. That was his calling. . . .

We thus take as our starting-point in the investigation of the relationship between the old Protestant ethic and the spirit of capitalism the works of Calvin, of Calvinism, and the other Puritan sects. But it is not to be understood that we expect to find any of the founders or representatives of these religious movements considering the promotion of what we have called the spirit of capitalism as in any sense the end of his life-work. We cannot well maintain that the pursuit of worldly goods, conceived as an end in itself, was to any of them of positive ethical value. . . . The salvation of the soul and that alone was the centre of their life and work. Their ethical ideals and the practical results of their doctrines were all based on that alone, and were the consequences of purely religious motives. We shall thus have to admit that the cultural consequences of the Reformation were to a great extent, perhaps in the particular aspects with which we are dealing predominantly, unforeseen and even unwished-for results of the labours of the reformers. They were often far removed from or even in contradiction to all that they themselves thought to attain.

The following study may thus perhaps in a modest way form a contribution to the understanding of the manner in which ideas become effective forces in history. . . . For we are merely attempting to clarify the part which religious forces have played in forming the developing web of our specifically worldly modern culture, in the complex interaction of innumerable different historical factors. We are thus inquiring only to what extent certain characteristic features of this culture can be imputed to the influence of the Reformation. . . .

We only wish to ascertain whether and to what extent religious forces have taken part in the qualitative formation and quantitative expansion of that spirit over the world. Furthermore, what concrete aspects of our capitalistic culture can be traced to them. In view of the tremendous confusion of interdependent influences between the material basis, the forms of social and political organization, and the ideas current in the time of the Reformation, we can only proceed by investigating whether and at what points certain correlations between forms of religious belief and practical ethics can be worked out. At the same time we shall as far as possible clarify the manner and the general *direction* in which, by virtue of those relationships, the religious movements have influenced the development of material culture. Only when this has been determined with reasonable accuracy can the attempt be made to estimate to what extent the historical development of modern culture can be attributed to those religious forces and to what extent to others.

Chapter IV: The Religious Foundations of Worldly Asceticism

. . . We are naturally not concerned with the question of what was theoretically and officially taught in the ethical compendia of the time, however much practical significance this may have had through the influence of Church dis-cipline, pastoral work, and preaching. We are interested rather in something entirely different: the influence of those psychological sanctions which, originating in religious belief and the practice of religion, gave a direction to practical conduct and held the individual to it. Now these sanctions were to a large extent derived from the peculiarities of the religious ideas behind them. The men of that day were occupied with abstract dogmas to an extent which itself can only be understood when we perceive the connection of these dogmas with practical religious interests. A few observations on dogma, which will seem to the non-theological reader as dull as they will [seem] hasty and superficial to the theologian, are indispensable. We can of course only proceed by presenting these religious ideas in the artificial simplicity of ideal types, as they could at best but seldom be found in history. For just because of the impossibility of drawing sharp boundaries in historical reality we can only hope to understand their specific importance from an investigation of them in their most consistent and logical forms. [In this chapter, Weber analyzes Protestant writings, showing how such doctrines as predestination and salvation served as incentives for the individual toward rational worldly activity.]

It is our next task to follow out the results of the Puritan idea of the calling in the business world, now that the above sketch has attempted to show its religious foundations. With all the differences of detail and emphasis which these different ascetic movements show in the aspects with which we have been concerned, much the same characteristics are present and important in all of them. But for our purposes the decisive point was, to recapitulate, the conception of the state of religious grace, common to all the denominations, as a status which marks off its possessor from the degradation of the flesh, from the world.

On the other hand, though the means by which it was attained differed for different doctrines, it could not be guaranteed by any magical sacraments, by relief in the confession, nor by individual good works. That was only possible by proof in a specific type of conduct unmistakably different from the way of life of the natural man. From that followed for the individual an incentive methodically to supervise his own state of grace in his own conduct, and thus to penetrate it with asceticism. But, as we have seen, this ascetic conduct meant a rational planning of the whole of one's life in accordance with God's will. And this asceticism was no longer an *opus supererogationis,* but something which could be required of everyone who would be certain of salvation. The religious life of the saints, as distinguished from the natural life, was—the most important point—no longer lived outside the world in monastic communities, but within the world and its institutions. This rationalization of conduct within this world, but for the sake of the world beyond, was the consequence of the concept of calling of ascetic Protestantism. . . .

Chapter V: Asceticism and the Spirit of Capitalism

In order to understand the connection between the fundamental religious ideas of ascetic Protestantism and its maxims for everyday economic conduct, it is necessary to examine with especial care such writings as have evidently been derived from ministerial practice. For in a time in which the beyond meant everything, when the social position of the Christian depended upon his admission to the communion, the clergyman, through his ministry, Church discipline, and preaching, exercised an influence . . . which we modern men are entirely unable to picture. In such a time the religious forces which express themselves through such channels are the decisive influences in the formation of national character.

For the purposes of this chapter, though by no means for all purposes, we can treat ascetic Protestantism as a single whole. But since that side of English Puritanism which was derived from Calvinism gives the most consistent religious basis for the idea of the calling, we shall, following our previous method, place one of its representatives at the centre of the discussion. Richard Baxter stands out above many other writers on Puritan ethics. . . . Baxter's principal work is dominated by the continually repeated, often almost passionate preaching of hard, continuous bodily or mental labour. . . . Labour came to be considered in itself the end of life, ordained as such by God. St. Paul's "He who will not work shall not eat" holds unconditionally for everyone. Unwillingness to work is symptomatic of the lack of grace. . . . Wealth is . . . bad ethically only in so far as it is a temptation to idleness and sinful enjoyment of life, and its acquisition is bad only when it is with the purpose of later living merrily and without care. But as a performance of duty in a calling it is not only morally permissible, but actually enjoined. . . .

This worldly Protestant asceticism . . . acted powerfully against the spontaneous enjoyment of possessions; it restricted consumption, especially of luxuries. On the other hand, it had the psychological effect of freeing the acquisition of goods from the inhibitions of traditionalistic ethics. It broke the bonds of the impulse of acquisition in that it not only legalized it, but (in the sense discussed) looked upon it as directly willed by God. The campaign against the temptations of the flesh, and the dependence on external things, was, as besides the Puritans the great Quaker apologist Barclay expressly says, not a struggle against the rational acquisition, but against the irrational use of wealth. . . . On the side of the production of private wealth, asceticism condemned both dishonesty and impulsive avarice. What was condemned as covetousness, Mammonism, etc., was the pursuit of riches for their own sake. For wealth in itself was a temptation. . . . When the limitation of consumption is combined with this release of acquisitive activity, the inevitable practical result is obvious: accumulation of capital through ascetic compulsion to save. . . .

As far as the influence of the Puritan outlook extended, under all circumstances—and this is, of course, much more important than the mere encouragement of capital accumulation—it favoured the development of a rational bourgeois economic life; it was the most important, and above all the only consistent influence in the development of that life. It stood at the cradle of the modern economic man. . . .

One of the fundamental elements of the spirit of modern capitalism, and not only of that but of all modern culture: rational conduct on the basis of the idea of the calling, was born—that is what this discussion has sought to demonstrate—from the spirit of Christian asceticism. One has only to re-read the passage from Franklin, quoted at the beginning of this essay, in order to see that the essential elements of the attitude which was there called the spirit of capitalism are the same as what we have just shown to be the content of the Puritan worldly asceticism, only without the religious basis, which by Franklin's time had died away. . . .

The Puritan wanted to work in a calling; we are forced to do so. For when asceticism was carried out of monastic cells into everyday life, and began to dominate worldly morality, it did its part in building the tremendous cosmos of the modern economic order. This order is now bound to the technical and economic conditions of machine production which to-day determine the lives of all the individuals who are born into this mechanism, not only those directly concerned with economic acquisition, with irresistible force. Perhaps it will so determine them until the last ton of fossilized coal is burnt. In Baxter's view the care for external goods should only lie on the shoulders of the "saint like a light cloak, which can be thrown aside at any moment." But fate decreed that the cloak should become an iron cage.

Since asceticism undertook to remodel the world and to work out its ideals in the world, material goods have gained an increasing and finally an inexorable power over the lives of men as at no previous period in history. To-day the spirit of religious asceticism—whether finally, who knows?—has escaped from the cage.

COMMENTARY
SOME PRINCIPLES OF MEASUREMENT

If sociological research is to test its developing theories of important interrelationships *among* variables, adequate procedures must first be worked out for measuring each *single* variable. Measurement—in contrast to the unsystematic descriptive handling of each property under **P-X**—is broadly defined here as the classification of cases, according to some rule, in terms of a given property of these cases. Thus men (cases) may be classified according to their height (property), couples according to their marital adjustment, groups according to their cohesion, voters according to their political predisposition, or group members according to their status.

In order to measure the property, to treat it as a variable, the researcher deals with *four basic elements* (see Unit 1, especially Table 1-A). The conceptual model contains definitions of the *case* (*e.g.,* individual in a role, social system) and its *properties* (*e.g.,* particular types of acts, orientations, characteristics, or products); correspondingly, the researcher selects for study certain *concrete cases* (*e.g.,* particular corner gangs or families), and certain *concrete indicants* (*e.g.,* answers to questions, observed acts) as manifestations of each property. Unlike the conceptual model, which is held in the mind, these indicants consist of observable sense data—overt behavior, artifacts, or answers to questions— from which the researcher infers how much, or what aspect, of the property belongs to each case.

Measurement requires, then, the selecting and combining of appropriate sense data (indicants) into various measures (ratings, scores, scales, indexes) that serve to translate concepts into operations. The more nearly these operations classify the case in terms of the property as defined in the conceptual model, the more valid the measure. The ideal, as Parsons puts it, "is to have theoretical categories of such a character that the empirical values of the variables concerned are the immediate products of our observational procedures" (Parsons, 1949-b, p. 5). In sociology today, however, this ideal is rarely met; few standard measuring devices comparable to the thermometer or the yardstick are available. Thus the sociologist must himself work out new measures for many concepts, and in doing so must grapple with the perplexing problems involved in the logic of measurement itself. He must scrutinize each measure carefully to see *whether* it reflects the concept adequately, and *how* he may use it appropriately in further analysis.

Figure **7-A** *Elements in measurement*

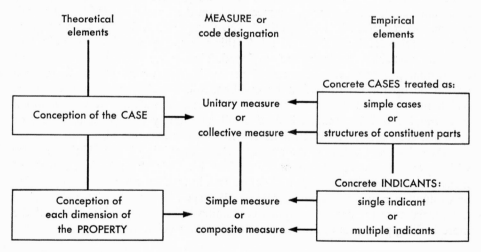

In measuring sociological variables, we shall often have to deal with two orders of complexity in the phenomena under study (see Figure 7-A). First the social system as a *case* must often be treated as a *structure* of constituent parts; and second, the *properties* of social systems are likely to consist of *patterns* of actions, orientations, or characteristics. To measure the former, the researcher may make use of *collective measures* (rather than unitary measures); for the latter, he may use *composite measures* (rather than simple measures).

In this Unit we shall see how each of these types of measures reflects the sociological property in a distinctive way, and how each follows its own procedure for selecting and combining indicants. Thus collective measures **(P-XII)**, as we have already used them in Unit 4, may put together data about individual husbands and wives to measure the structure of orientations for each couple, or data about individual citizens to index the configuration of influencer-influencee relationships for the community. Here the emphasis of the measurement procedure is on the social-structural base—on the arrangement of actors within the system. Composite measures, as we shall now begin to examine them, put together data to reflect the patterning of action and attitudes—the complex universalistic-particularistic character of a relationship or the expressive-instrumental quality of roles, for example.

Each measure—collective or unitary, composite or simple—consists not only of certain indicants taken to reflect the concepts under study, but also has certain *mathematical characteristics* that will affect the statistical operations appropriate for the subsequent analysis. When measurement consists of the assignment of *numbers* to cases to represent properties, the measures can be manipulated mathematically so as to yield new information about the cases under study. Yet, as Norman Campbell, the British physicist and philosopher of science, says, "[if such use of numbers] is really to mean anything, there must be some important resemblance between the property measured, on the one hand, and the numerals assigned to represent it, on the other" (N. Campbell, p. 1807). As you know from Exercise III-1 and Manual III-A, this resemblance varies markedly with the mathematical type of measure employed. Thus with *ratio measures* that have the formal properties of the numeral series, it makes sense to perform such arithmetic operations as adding or dividing. With *ordinal measures,* however, which merely reflect the rank order of the numeral series, and with *nominal measures* for which numbers, if used at all, are simply equivalent to names or symbols, such arithmetic operations are less clearly meaningful.

We shall now see how the studies we are examining in this Unit, together with several preceding studies and exercises, illustrate these basic elements of measurement (in Figure 7-A), and define certain problems involved in designing or evaluating any measuring instrument. We shall reserve for later discussion the special measurement procedures containing built-in tests (Unit 9) and the more baffling problems in the use of collective data (Unit 12).

Some Examples of Coding

Let us start with coding as one basic measurement procedure. Once the investigator has decided **(P-X)** to handle the data systematically, rather than leave them in descriptive form, he must now simplify them and abstract certain essentials from them. (Only then will he be ready to proceed to the later analysis of findings, to the comparison of cases, to the drawing of general inferences.)

He now wishes to bring data to bear (as indicants) upon certain general concepts (or properties).

In coding, as in measurement generally, the investigator utilizes his data as indicants for categorizing each of his sample cases. For example, an individual's answers to questions about his voting behavior may be used to code his political predisposition as Republican or Democratic. Or observation of his church attendance may be used to code his religious affiliation as Protestant, Catholic, or Jewish. His social status, or that of his family, may be coded as low, medium, or high, depending on the kind of living-room furniture observed in his home, or on the number of choices he elicits from other group members. Or a student's I.Q. may be coded as 120, or as belonging in the highest quintile of the school class, based on his answers to the questions in a test. Each of these code designations constitutes a *measure,* by which the investigator classifies the particular case relative to other cases in respect to the given property. (Note the similarity of such examples to the familiar procedure of determining the temperature of a liquid by observing the height of a bar of mercury in the thermometer. If the bar stands at 98°, for example, this figure is a measure—or a code designation— of this particular liquid in respect to the property, temperature.)

We shall now examine the nature of the coding procedure—first illustrated in our discussion of Le Play in Unit 3—through some actual examples of its use.

ZELDITCH'S CODING PROCEDURE

The Zelditch study showed specifically how the investigator requires a set of rules—a measuring instrument—for assigning to each case code designations which will indicate how much of (or which attributes of) the property it possesses. This instrument consists of (1) a *code,* or a set of code designations. Made up of numerals, symbols, or names of categories, the code lists all the points or intervals or categories marked off on each dimension of each property. (Properties are conceived as having one or more main *dimensions,* or aspects, as already illustrated in the coding Exercise II-1 and discussed later in this Unit.) The measuring instrument further contains (2) *coding instructions* which, on the one hand, define each dimension and its categories in terms of the conceptual model, and, on the other hand, specify the kinds of data to be taken as indicants under each category.

The Zelditch study describes in some detail the development and application of such a coding instrument to the previously digested data of ethnographic reports. Using the categories expressive leader and instrumental leader, Zelditch defines each in theoretical terms; he then states rules (with examples from his data) for designating the "pattern of action" of a husband (or wife) in a given society as belonging to one or the other category. His rules require use of information, not only about the role incumbent himself, but also about the attitudes of others which may indirectly reveal the character of his leadership. This study illustrates how the coding of interaction typically requires inferences from one role to another (or from observed behavior to underlying orientation, or from specific act to general characteristic). By coding the husband role and the wife role in each society according to his rules, Zelditch completes the task of measuring his central variable.

THE PLACE OF CODING IN THE RESEARCH SEQUENCE

The code is not always developed, as in the Zelditch study, after the data have been gathered. Bales, for example, sets up his code *in advance,* and then codes the interactions *as* he observes them. The questionnaire or observation schedule is frequently precoded to show checklists (or key numbers) for the set of code designations. Although such a practice saves time by reducing the mass of material assembled, it tends to set limits on the data to be collected, and hence on any later rearrangement of the coding categories.

The alternative procedure, developing and applying the code *after* the data are in hand, is, of course, essential when unstructured *available* data are used (as in Zelditch's secondary analysis of the reports of others, or in the content analysis exemplified by the Massing study). This procedure is also useful in *exploratory* studies, since it affords flexibility in the search for details as well as clues to possible hypotheses. One of its obvious disadvantages, however—as you may have experienced in the exercise in coding parent-child relationships (Exercise II-1)—is that the data gathered are often inadequate for the developing research objectives. If the hypotheses and coding categories are established in advance, much more consistently relevant information can certainly be gathered in the investigation.

CODING PARENT-CHILD RELATIONSHIPS

In order to supplement our analysis of the coding activities of other researchers that are not always fully reported in the studies, let us review your experience in Exercise II-1 as another example of certain principles of coding.

This exercise is based on the dyad as the research case **(P-I).** Thus you can see how the dyad—as well as the large or small group, or the individual—may be coded in terms of its properties. A distinctive feature of the dyad as the research case is that it is an interactive or relational unit. Hence, for example, you coded the universalistic or particularistic character of each dyad *twice* to represent the points of view of both partners (here the respondent and his parent). Each respondent in this study becomes the nexus of two dyadic relationships, as in Figure 7-B. You used one code sheet for each reciprocal dyad (just as reciprocal information for each dyadic pair may be punched into a single I.B.M. dyad card for use in further analysis, as described later in Manual II-D).

Figure **7-B**   *Dyads coded for each respondent, Exercise II-1*

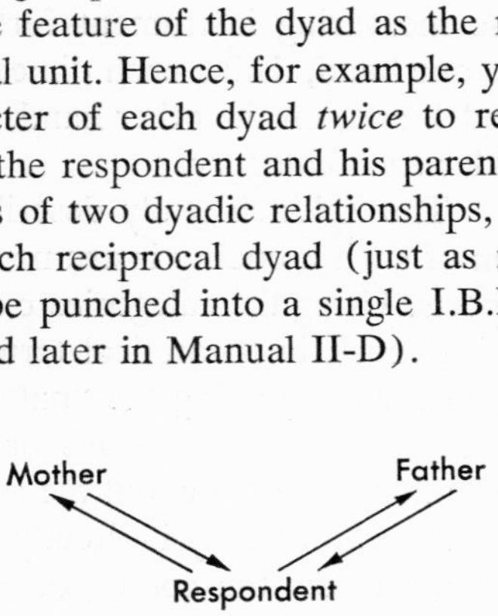

Exercise II-1 illustrates further how a basic code is designed, and later amplified, to meet the requirements of a particular study. The exercise requires a code—as do many sociological studies—which states the basic properties and dimensions of role relationships, and which can utilize the relevant detailed information about each dyad (from your earlier interview reports in Exercise I-2). Such a code aims at a balance between the many dimensions needed to retain the richness of the data, and the few dimensions needed to facilitate comparison and generalization. The basic code actually developed for the exercise arrives at such a balance by using a limited set of dimensions built upon the existing theory of Talcott Parsons—adapting his categories and his definitions of each dimension.

DIFFICULTIES OF ABSTRACTION

In using this theoretically based code, you encountered certain practical difficulties that are inherent in much social science coding. One difficulty arises because each of the dimensions in the basic code is very general in character, applicable indeed to orientations in all types of social roles. It is always difficult to find the general in the specific; it is a demanding task to search through complex, unstructured interview reports for all possible clues to the essential qualities of each relationship.

This task is particularly demanding since, in addition to perceptive exploration, the coder attempts to develop a degree of reliability in his inferences. Usually two coders can come to agree upon the meanings of the categories (and the kind of data belonging under each) only after the basic code has been considerably amplified and specified (compare the reliability of Bales' highly structured code in Unit 3). Categories must be defined—perhaps redefined—to fit the particular kind of data; many illustrations must be listed from the reports to explain each category. Some illustrations from Exercise II-1 might be, for instance:

> His only interest is in training me to contribute to family support. (Specific)
> As her son, I could get away with things that she didn't think other boys my age ought to do. (Particularistic)
> He didn't pay attention to what I did—just took it for granted that I was only a girl. (Quality)
> She was undemonstrative—never showed me how she felt. (Affectively-neutral)

Such careful definition and listing of examples is essential, not only in this particular exercise, but in any coding of unstructured materials in terms of general categories.

FINDING A STANDARD

Another difficulty in the use of a code often lies in finding a suitable standard or bench mark against which any given case may be compared. Exercise II-1 asks you to define a certain degree of specificity-diffuseness, for example, as typical of parent-child relationships in our society, and then to use this as a standard against which to judge each concrete case. To define such a standard may be difficult, but without it you would undoubtedly code most of the relationships in the same categories—under diffuse (or under affective, particularistic, quality), rather than discovering relative differences among them for use later in making comparisons. Of course, if this study were to be broadened to include many different kinds of relationships (teacher-student, employer-employee, doctor-patient, and so on), a common standard would have to be used for all in order to allow comparisons among them.

There are various ways of finding suitable standards. Often, as in Exercise II-1, the investigator defines the standard as part of his conceptual model. (See the discussion below of Weber's ideal type as a standard.) Sometimes, when he examines a large number of cases, the investigator determines the standard empirically—as a teacher may base examination grades on the set of scores obtained by a particular class, without reference to what good (or poor) performance *ought* to be. Another method is illustrated in the work of E. L. Thorndike, who, in measuring the quality of handwriting, attempted as early as 1910 to develop among the coders a common understanding of categories such as very bad, bad, good, etc. He was able to resolve some of the difficulty here by employing as standards actual specimens of handwriting which had first been ordered by handwriting "experts" serving as judges (E. L. Thorndike, p. 1).

THE CODE AS A LINK BETWEEN CONCEPT AND DATA

Experience with a theoretically based code, as in Exercise II-1, thus suggests how the code—or any measure—may be used to bring together concepts and the data used as indicants (see Figure 7-A). On the one hand, concepts (such as the Parsonian dimensions) taken from a larger theoretical scheme help the coder to see the broader implications of his *data,* to discover the more general meaning of the particular phenomena under study, to fit details and anecdotes from discursive interview reports into a pattern of deviance, for example, or into a pattern of affective and particularistic relationships. The concepts also point to the kinds of additional data which should be collected if further systematic research is to follow, guiding the researcher in the development of improved data-gathering instruments. Conversely, the objective of coding is, of course, to provide further understanding of *concepts* such as universalism-particularism, or affectivity-neutrality—to permit specification or redefinition of these concepts in the light of new empirical evidence. The empirical and interpretative phases of the research process involve a correlative translation of concepts into the data for measurement operations and, in turn, the use of measurement operations to clarify concepts (see also Unit 9).

Massing's Use of Composite Measures

Although coding often constitutes the entire measurement procedure, many measuring instruments require additional steps. A variety of procedures is possible, but we shall classify these variations for the present discussion under the major headings of collective measures or composite measures (used alone or in combination). In brief, the *procedures* for the two types are as follows: A *collective measure,* as you know from Manual III-A, breaks the *case* down into its social components (roles, for example, or dyads), codes each component separately, and then recombines them to yield the measure. A *composite measure,* in somewhat parallel fashion, breaks down the *property* into its parts or aspects, again codes each part, and then reassembles the parts to provide the measure (often called an index, score, or scale).

Let us first examine the composite measure that Massing uses in his study of changes in the characteristics attributed to the Voice of America by the Soviet media. Implied in his conceptual model is the notion of a mass communication process involving interchanges between (agencies of) two political systems in conflict. The Soviet state broadcasts to its audiences both at home and abroad an image of the Voice that is not only a response to the information policy of the United States (as one system), but also a reflection of the "general tactics and strategy" of the propaganda of the Soviet system. Inferences drawn from specific radio or newspaper allusions to the Voice suggest, for example, that in 1948 the Soviet policy was to discredit the United States and what it stands for, whereas in 1952 it was to impute aggressive intentions to American "imperialism."

PROCEDURE FOR COMPOSITE MEASUREMENT

The measurement problem then, stated in our terms, is to rate the Soviet state (the case) at each time period according to one aspect of its larger strategy (the property)—a strategy believed to have "certain patterns of consistency and design." The data to be used (as indicants) are the direct allusions, "the specific attacks on, or reactions to, the Voice," catalogued from a sample of Soviet sources.

Notice how Massing proceeds to make these measurements. He does not develop a *simple* over-all measure. That is, he does not attempt to code each article or radio program as a whole—much less to assess the total volume of Soviet output during a given period. Instead, he proceeds through the two steps required in *composite measurement.* First, taking all the relevant direct statements "sentence by sentence" he breaks each one down into its smallest "meaning units," and *codes each meaning unit* separately. He classifies each as it may refer to the aims and activities of the Voice, the nature of its performance, or its accomplishments—as well as to various subcategories. (Here the code is not taken from theory, but is developed empirically from the data themselves, much as you developed an empirically based code of factors in career choice in Exercise II-2.)

Second, Massing *counts* (or tabulates) the meaning units within each of the categories. His Table 1, for example, shows the counts or over-all patterns by which the Voice was characterized in each of the three years. It is these counts, as they combine the separate ratings of the many meaning units, that are used here as the *composite measures.*

Content Analysis. The type of composite measure used in the Massing study exemplifies a widely used procedure called content analysis which, though variously applied, is described by Berelson as "a research technique for the objective, systematic, and quantitative description of the manifest content of communication" (Berelson, 1954, p. 489). Many studies use this technique to quantify the body of meanings (content) communicated through verbal or other symbols in books, radio programs, speeches, and the like; and to draw "inferences from verbal material to its antecedent conditions" (Pool, 1959, p. 2). The essence of the technique lies in the frequency counts based on the standard units into which the particular content is subdivided; just as Massing divides each sentence into meaning units, other content analyses employ words, for example, or themes, or fictional or historical characters (see Berelson, 1952 and 1954; Merton, 1957, pp. 512–16).

Content analysis, then, is a special method of quantitative measurement of a special subject matter: communications content. More generally, of course, communications content can also be analyzed by other procedures that are not quantitative. Thomas and Znaniecki develop their ideas and hypotheses from unsystematic perusal of letters. Weber abstracts ideal types from nonquantitative research on the writings of a Benjamin Franklin or a Jonathan Edwards—and uses these ideal types in discursive, nonquantitative fashion to support his major comparative and evolutionary analyses of the meanings and values (the content) of religious or political movements (see, *e.g.,* Parsons, 1961, p. 241 ff.).

Moreover, beside the verbal mass communications for which content analysis is perhaps most commonly used (although Berelson includes all types of communication in his definition), various quantitative procedures are applicable to many other kinds of data that reflect meaning—such as the pieces of art on which Sorokin based part of his study of social and cultural dynamics, or the face-to-face communication that Bales observed in his laboratory.

BALES' USE OF COMPOSITE MEASURES

The measurement procedure that Bales uses in his study of group profiles (see Bales' Table 1, Unit 3) furnishes another example of a composite measure.

In classifying his cases (groups) according to various dimensions of interaction, Bales might well have observed an entire small group session and then assigned over-all ratings to indicate the extent to which solidarity was expressed, for example, or to which tension-management activities had occurred. That is, he might have chosen to use simple rather than composite measures (see, *e.g.,* Heyns and Zander, p. 386 ff.).

Instead, Bales breaks down the property (interaction) into its smallest parts (acts), and uses a procedure parallel to that in Massing's content analysis. He first categorizes behavior "act by act" (as showing agreement, *e.g.,* or asking for suggestion). Second, he counts the number of acts in each category, analyzing the data, as he puts it, "to obtain summary measures descriptive of the group process, from which inferences can then be made as to the nature of the underlying factors influencing the process." (See also Parsons and Bales, 1953, pp. 86–88, for discussion of acts as parts of the interaction process, in contradistinction to roles as parts of the social system.) He uses the resultant profile—the distribution of the total number of acts among the twelve categories of his code —to classify groups according to the extent that they show agreement, for example.

In this sense, Bales' Table 1, which compares the interactions of two types of groups through the percentage distributions of their total acts, is similar to Massing's Table 1, which compares Soviet mass communications at two different time periods through the percentage distribution of total meaning units. (Bales' procedure is somewhat more complicated, though, since it reflects also the collective action of the group members.) In sum, despite the many differences between these two studies in research objective and design, both develop composite scores to measure the amount of activity or communication within each category.

Incidentally, you can see here how the combining of indicants can change the mathematical character of a measure (as in Manual III-A in respect to collective measures). At the first step of the procedure, each act or meaning unit is coded on a nominal scale; but when all these codes are combined, the resultant composite measure is quantitative, and may be treated as an ordinal scale. Since such transpositions from one measurement level to another in the formation of complex measures affect the possibilities for subsequent analysis, we shall examine them in further detail presently when we come to collective measures.

COMPOSITE VS. SIMPLE MEASURES

Such a composite of many indicants clearly measures the property quite differently from a single indicant (a simple measure) of the property as a whole. In coding parent-child relationships (in Exercise II-1) you used *simple measures:* you gave each dyad an over-all rating on the dimension of activity-passivity, for example, by studying and assessing the full information—the entire set of indicants and clues—in the interview report. This procedure has the advantage of enabling you to judge each indicant within its wider context, so that you may give greater weight to those particular clues which seem the more important and discard others which seem irrelevant or inconsistent.

An alternative procedure in the exercise might have been to break down the interview report into its component incidents and details, and to develop *composite measures* by the procedure used by Massing or Bales: (1) coding each detail separately, and then (2) basing the rating upon the number of clues pointing to an active, as compared with the number pointing to a passive, relationship. Such composite measures might have been more precise, perhaps, since coding rules can be defined more specifically and coding decisions made more readily about each single indicant and clue in the interview report than about the complex report as a whole.

Whenever several indicants are to be combined into a composite measure, there arise further questions of how to select, assess, combine, and weight them. Are all clues to be treated as equal, for example, or do some deserve greater weight? Both Massing and Bales assume that all meaning units or acts are equally important in contributing to the measures. Moreover, they assume that each unit is to be coded individually, apart from its context. As Massing puts it, "Every codable unit of the sentence was given independent consideration, taken literally, regardless of logic or related meanings." In Unit 9, we shall scrutinize other methods of fitting indicants together into composite measures that answer such questions in various ways.

Bogue's Use of Collective Measures

Bogue's study of money income as a measure of the economic well-being of a technologically advanced nation—part of a compendious analysis of the demography of the United States—illustrates again as in Unit 4 the nature of the other main type of complex measure, the *collective* (as distinguished from the composite) measure. Bogue is concerned with describing present-day income distribution in the United States and a variety of factors believed to "interact to produce this distribution," *e.g.,* the distribution of individuals according to ability, the power structure of the society, and labor turnover. He develops measures of income distribution in order to use them to examine differences between men and women or between urban and rural segments of the population.

PROCEDURE FOR COLLECTIVE MEASUREMENT

Bogue's method of measuring income (like the method of Massing and Bales in preparing composite measures) is not accomplished in a single coding operation, but proceeds through a sequence of steps. Here, however, it is the case, rather than the property, which is broken down (into its constituent individual roles, subgroups, or dyads) and then recombined in the final measure. The typical steps in collective measurement (as you used them in Exercise III-1, and as they are outlined in Manual III-A) are as follows:

Procedure for Collective Measurement

1. Assign a constituent measure to each individual group member (or to each subgroup or dyad).
2. Collect these constituent measures for each group (or role).
3. Assign a collective measure to each group (or role) on the basis of Step 2.

Step 1 requires measuring a property of the parts of each case, while Steps 2 and 3 refer to the higher level structure or system of these parts. Since there are many variations on these basic steps, you should master the essential procedure now before we come later to some of the more intricate problems involved.

Bogue might have chosen to measure the economic well-being of the nation—his research case **(P-I)**—by a *unitary* rating for the country as a whole. He might have based this rating on the gross national output of coal and iron, the railroad freight ton mileage, or the like. He decides instead, however, to develop a *collective* measure, by first breaking the nation down into the constituent individual persons (or the families) questioned by United States Census enumerators. As the first measurement step, he assigns to each person a number (or code) corresponding to the size of his reported income. As the second step, he collects these individual measures for the nation, counting (or enumerating) the number of cases in each income category. As the third step, he arranges the proportions of individual cases along the scale of income, thereby obtaining a frequency distribution by income of all members of the society—as shown in his Table 1 and the curve in his Figure 1[A]. Thus, by first measuring each individual's income and then collecting these individual measures, he obtains a new measure (a frequency distribution in this instance) which no longer refers to the individual but to the group—much as the roles of husband and wife may be collected to measure the solidarity of given families, or dyads may be collected to measure the influentiality of individuals within a community. Bogue simplifies this collective measure by using the median of the distribution, thereby facilitating comparisons among different segments within the population.

MATHEMATICAL CHARACTERISTICS OF COLLECTIVE MEASURES

An interesting feature of the Bogue study is that it uses constituent individual measures (Step 1) which are quantitative—stated as numbers of dollars (unlike the nominal measures for individuals that are collected in Manual III-A). Let us see how the Bogue example highlights certain difficulties of interpreting quantitative measures of sociological variables.

The first question, which arises at Step 1, is whether the *individual* measure of income should be regarded here as a ratio, or merely an ordinal, measure. The answer is not clear-cut but depends upon the researcher's definition of the property. Certainly, if Bogue's interest were simply in the size of the income, the number of dollars would constitute a ratio measure; an individual with $10,000, for example, has twice as many dollars as one with $5,000. Yet Bogue's research interest is not in the size of the income as such, but in its standard-of-living potential. An additional $5,000 of income, because it would undoubtedly go into different kinds of expenditures from the initial $5,000, would not necessarily reflect a doubling of the individual's standard of living. Thus the numbers used in the individual measure seem only loosely related to the property at hand. The measure does not meet the criterion of a ratio (or interval) scale that equal intervals on the scale should mark off equal intervals of the property as defined in the conceptual model.

When individual measures are converted into collective measures at Steps 2 and 3, the mathematical character of the collective measure may turn out to be quite different from that of its constituent individual measures. In the Bogue study the constituent individual measure is the (ratio or ordinal) scale of dollar income; the collective measure, however, which is far more complex, is the distribution of individuals along this scale (the percentages of individuals at each point on the scale). This distribution has a shape, a central tendency, a dispersion, and other characteristics of a frequency distribution.

Bogue simplifies this collective measure so that he can compare different segments within the population. Various statistics are available for simplifying or *summarizing* such a frequency distribution based on the numerical scale of income (as described in Manual III-C, Measures of Central Tendency and Dispersion). If individual income had been treated as a ratio measure, then the average income of the United States as a whole might be described by the *mean*, and the spread of income through the population by the *standard deviation*. Alternatively, if individual income is regarded as an ordinal measure, an appropriate summary statistic is the *median*—as used by Bogue. Or the distribution might be dichotomized at a given point to show, for example, the *percentage* of individuals receiving incomes that are exceptionally small. The means of the different population segments would form a ratio measure for the segments (groups); whereas the medians or percentages would form an ordinal measure.

Bogue's Table 2 shows the use of median incomes for comparing population segments—men and women subclassified according to rural or urban residence. (Notice, however, that this is practical here only because dollar income is assumed to serve as a standard scale for all the different segments of the United States population. It might be more difficult to develop a standard measure of economic well-being based on money income for many different countries in such a way that medians would be comparable from one country to another.)

SOME ASSUMPTIONS UNDERLYING COLLECTIVE MEASURES

Just as Massing or Bales make certain assumptions in adding together units of properties, Bogue must also make assumptions in collecting individuals. By treating them all alike, he tacitly assumes that each individual makes the same contribution to the economic prosperity or depression of the collectivity. In other collective measures, however, the contributions of certain individuals might be regarded as relatively more important than others. In a measure of family status in the community based on the collective incomes of the members, for instance, the husband's income, if judged to be more important than the income of the wife or the offspring, might perhaps be weighted more heavily than that of the rest of the family.

INDIVIDUALS VS. FAMILIES AS THE CONSTITUENT CASE

Bogue prepares two sets of collective measures—one based on individual, the other on family, income. That is, he collects constituent individual measures, and he also collects constituent subgroup (family) measures (which are themselves collective). Let us now make a careful comparison between the two as Bogue presents them.

The two collective measures for the country as a whole yield quite different results, as the two curves in Bogue's Figure 1[A] show. The curve based on individuals is heavy at the low end of the income scale, whereas the "family income distribution is not concentrated at the lowest income levels, but takes the shape of a long distribution with a small hump in the middle." This points to an important general principle of sociological measurement, already suggested in Unit 4 in the discussion of marriage studies: the collective measure based on constituent individuals and the collective measure based on constituent smaller groups (subgroups) may give different results. Examination of one without the other—of only one of Bogue's curves, for instance—may obscure certain information important to the analysis.

A corollary to this principle is that, by utilizing *both* the subgroup as the constituent case and the individual as the constituent case, much may often be learned about the ways in which individuals fit together within these subgroups. Bogue's comparison between his two curves makes evident, as he says, "that a large percentage of the individuals who receive exceptionally small incomes are members of families, and are particularly dependent upon others for their livelihood." That is, because he knows the national distributions of both the individual data and the family data, he can make certain inferences about the arrangement of individuals within families.

Weber and the Multidimensional Measure

We have been discussing coding and measurement along single dimensions. Since many sociological concepts are defined as multidimensional, let us now turn—as an introduction to the more complicated process of multidimensional measurement—to Max Weber's monograph, *The Protestant Ethic and the Spirit of Capitalism*. This is one of a series of comparative studies that examine the economic implications of various religious ethics. Only in Western civilization does Weber find the particular sequence of ascetic Protestantism followed by rational bourgeois capitalism (see, *e.g.,* Parsons, 1949-a, Chapter 15). Postulating causal relationship between these two, he shows how the ethos of Protestantism laid the motivational groundwork for the spirit of capitalism, having "the psychological effect of freeing the acquisition of goods from the inhibitions of traditionalistic ethics." Thus, he examines a societal change in the institutionalization of values, then shows how this change may be understood through examination of "those psychological sanctions which, originating in religious belief and the practice of religion, gave a direction to practical conduct and held the individual to it."

It seems clear from such passages that Weber is using "psychological" data with an emphasis differing from that of the clinical psychologist. The psychologist focuses on the individual, asking why this personality (as compared with other personalities) behaves as he does; Weber focuses rather on Western society. We cannot understand social structure, he suggests, unless we understand the psychological processes of the group members within this structure (see Abel, 1948; Parsons, 1949-a, p. 635 ff.). Referring to this special sociological use of psychological data as *Verstehen* or *understanding* (a term which he also uses in a different context), Weber says "Statistical uniformities constitute understandable types of action . . . and thus constitute 'sociological generalization,' only when they can be regarded as manifestations of the understandable subjective meaning of a course of social action" (Weber, *Theory of Social and Economic Organization,* p. 100).

THE IDEAL TYPE

In demonstrating this relationship between the particular pattern or cluster of Protestant values and another pattern that he calls the spirit of modern capitalism, Weber tells us, though very briefly, how he goes about developing an ideal type: He apparently starts with a particular concrete case, "the historical individual," as "a complex of elements associated in historical reality which we unite into a conceptual whole from the standpoint of their cultural significance. Such an historical concept . . . must be gradually put together out of the individual parts which are taken from historical reality to make it up." His next step is to isolate the essential elements in such a concrete case and to oversimplify them, so that just these few elements stand out as an ideal type. He says, in developing the idea of the Protestant ethic, that "we can of course only proceed by presenting these religious ideas in the artificial simplicity of ideal types, as they could at best seldom be found in history. . . . We can only hope to understand their specific importance from an investigation of them in their most consistent and logical forms."

Thus Weber's ideal type is not an exact description of a concrete case. It may never exist in reality. At the theoretical level, it is a carefully defined set of related categories. At the research level, it is to be used as a kind of standard or model against which real cases can be compared, and found to be similar or different. Following Weber, many other social scientists have thought in terms of ideal types. In coding parent-child relationships (in Exercise II-1), for example, you compared concrete examples with an ideal type of parent-child relationship in our society (as affective, diffuse, and so on).

Two main aspects of the ideal type seem methodologically important. First, Weber does not think of the spirit of capitalism, for example, as a simple, unitary concept that can be described in terms of one idea; he thinks of it as a whole cluster of elements. He has carefully sorted out the main elements which seem to fit together, and he tells us what they are: the rational organization of labor, the rejection of traditionalism, the sober asceticism of the bourgeoisie, and so on. Second, he describes these elements in an idealized way. He does not think that historical reality ever was *exactly* like his ideal type (although the main elements may happen to appear in the writings of a single man, such as Benjamin Franklin). Neither does Weber maintain that the value pattern of the *average* ascetic Protestant in the seventeenth century was exactly like his ideal type. He maintains, only, that part of historical reality approximated this model. He also views the spirit of Protestantism, first, as a whole cluster of elements: asceticism, the pursuit of God in the calling, etc. And second, he looks upon this cluster, not as a full reflection of reality, but as an idealized selection from it.

THE PROPERTY-SPACE

Consider now the implications of such an ideal type for research. Subsequent research owes much to Weber's elaborate systems of ideal types, which deal with the orientations and values of religious movements and with many political and economic aspects of social structure. (See, for example, the recent and impressive literature on bureaucracy, as in Bendix, 1956, Peter Blau, 1956; Gouldner; and Selznick. See also the discussion of the relation between Weber's theory of bureaucracy and the property-space in Lazarsfeld, 1962.) Suppose that we as researchers compare a series of religions with the ideal type, the cluster of elements, called the Protestant ethic. We shall use the latter as a standard. Some ethics might match this standard rather closely, that is, fit this particular ideal type. But how do we classify those ethics that do not fit? Do we code all of them simply as misfits? Or is there some way to examine the respects in which they fail to fit?

One answer to such questions is provided by defining any given property in terms of *multiple* dimensions, rather than just one, and then translating these dimensions into a classification scheme called a *property-space*. (We are indebted to Paul Lazarsfeld and his colleagues for the principles by which the mathematical use of coordinates to locate points in a space may be applied to sociological measurement. See, *e.g.,* Barton, 1955.) A simple example of a property-space, to start with an analogy, would be the definition of standard of living as reflecting not dollar income alone, but also the education of the head of the house. Measurement in terms of such a two-dimensional concept would require double classification of each family: first, in regard to income, and second, in regard to education. Because both dimensions are defined as aspects of the same property—standard of living—we require a scheme for fitting the two separate measurements together, so as to handle both dimensions at once. Such a scheme appears in Figure 7-C. A family with a $10,000 income, for example, whose head went through college would be located at the single point x; in similar fashion, each of a sample of families would be located in single points in such a space.

Figure **7-C**   *A property-space for measuring standard of living using quantitative measures*

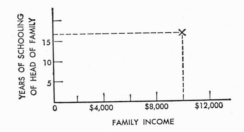

The principles of multidimensional measurement illustrated by this example hold that the property is defined in the conceptual model as complex and multidimensional, and that the measurement scheme for translating such a property into empirical operations must also be multidimensional. The property-space is such a scheme; it represents the dimensions of the concept in all their possible interrelationships—a "space" within which to measure the concept in respect to its several aspects or dimensions. Thus the property-space becomes a practical measuring tool for use with multidimensional properties.

The two dimensions in Figure 7-C happen to be based on quantitative measures; but the property-space can be used equally well with nominal or ordinal measures. Words like low, medium, or high income (or education) could be substituted for the numbers in Figure 7-C by dividing each dimension into two (or more) categories or elements. A property-space for use with nominal (or ordinal) measures that have only two elements for each dimension would appear as in Figure 7-D. In this space, each of the families would be classified in one of the cells rather than at a more exact point (as in the quantitative scheme in Figure 7-C).

What then is the meaning of such a space in relation to the ideal type? The space in Figure 7-D is divided into four cells: the high-income–high-education cell, the low-income–low-education cell, and so on. In other words, each cell represents a *cluster of elements,* of two elements in this example. Since a cluster of elements is involved in the notion of the ideal type, we can now locate the ideal type as the conceptual counterpart of one cell of such a property-space for measuring standard of living as a concept. The exciting idea that follows is that *each cell* suggests a different but related ideal type, so that the entire property-space corresponds to a complete set of logically related ideal types.

Figure **7-D** *A property-space for measuring standard of living using nominal (or ordinal) measures*

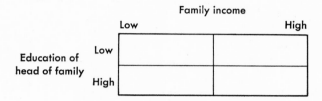

Let us state this same idea in another way: Underlying any single ideal type, it is often possible to delineate a whole system of interrelated ideal types—hence to extend and clarify the conceptual model. At the empirical level, then, whenever the researcher has a notion of an ideal type, he may derive from it a total property-space that he can use as a systematic procedure for classification or measurement.

A Property-Space for Classifying Religions. What is the general character of the property-space which seems to underlie Weber's study? Although each of his ideal types is a complex of many elements, let us use just two of these in considering the inherent logic. Think of the Protestant ethic, for instance, as consisting only of asceticism and emphasis on one's occupation as a calling. Now suppose that we are studying, as Weber actually set out to do, the religions of many societies—not merely the values underlying Protestantism—and that we want to classify each religion according to its ethical character (certainly a multi-dimensional property, although we shall deal for the moment with just two dimensions). For this purpose we need a classification scheme—a property-space. How may the larger scheme be derived from a single ideal type made up of the two elements of asceticism and emphasis on a calling?

This derivation is achieved by treating each element as a single category of an entire dimension and adding other related elements (or categories). Starting with asceticism as an element, we might extend a dimension from the ascetic pole to the opposite extreme of self-indulgence. Then any given religious ethic might be located at any point along such a dimension. To keep the example simple, let us merely dichotomize the dimension; that is, we classify any given religion as either characterized by asceticism or not. In the same way, the element of emphasis on a calling also implies the logical existence of other related elements. Here again the element may be extended to a whole dimension of varying degrees of emphasis on a calling, but for purposes of this example the categories are limited to emphasis on calling and no emphasis on calling. Thus, by using these two logically implied dimensions, we may derive a property-space as in Figure 7-E.

Figure **7-E**　*A simplified property-space for classifying religions*

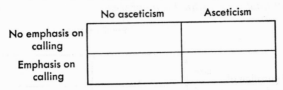

What have we accomplished here? We started with the ideal type of the Protestant ethic, which clearly belongs in the lower right-hand cell of Figure 7-E, but by extending the dimensions of this one cell, we obtained a property-space with three other cells. We derived, that is, at least three other ideal types, in addition to Weber's, which might logically belong in a complete classification of religious ethics.

Such derivation of the whole system of ideal types from a single ideal type—of the property-space from a cluster of elements—has a dual purpose. At the conceptual level, we have been forced to specify each element as one category in a dimension. We have been forced, that is, to define the underlying dimensions, their interrelationships, and the meanings of each possible ideal type in the cells of the underlying space. We have gone through a process that has helped to clarify the concept to be measured—in this instance, to clarify the possible ethical character of various religions (see Merton, 1957, pp. 114–17). Meanwhile, at the *empirical level,* we have developed a practical scheme for classifying a variety of ethics (although it may turn out on occasion that certain of the logically derived types do not exist, or do not make sense in actuality).

A Property-Space for Classifying Deviance.　Another way for a researcher to develop a property-space is to start with the large concept, rather than to extend the elements outward from the ideal type, a single cell. The researcher first isolates the basic dimensions of the concept—as we isolated income and education as dimensions of standard of living—and then fits these dimensions together to yield all the possible ideal types.

In effect, you used this procedure in handling two of the basic code dimensions (5 and 6) when you coded deviance in the parent-child relationship (Exercise II-1). Consider how Parsons conceives of the two dimensions of deviance used in this exercise, and how he fits them together into what we should now call a two-dimensional property-space. Parsons defines deviance, as the researcher must define any concept before he can measure it effectively, as a *motivated disturbance of the equilibrium of an interactive system*. Two people (such as a mother and daughter) are interacting, and something happens so that the daughter frustrates the expectations of the mother. Perhaps the mother handles this skillfully, and it all blows over. Or perhaps a regular pattern is established in which the daughter attempts to dominate the mother, the mother is afraid of losing the daughter's affection and becomes unduly submissive, and so on in a vicious circle. This is described as deviance, and the attitudes of the deviant members are described as "ambivalent" and "compulsive" (Parsons, 1951, Chapter 7).

To classify the forms in which such deviance may occur, Parsons starts by isolating the two dimensions or aspects of deviance used in our exercise. First, *A* must choose between holding on to *B*'s affection at any cost, or standing ready to alienate *B* in order to have his own way; Parsons labels these alternatives compulsive conformity and compulsive alienation. And second, whether he is conformist or alienative, *A* may be either active or passive in regard to his deviance: he may take the initiative, or he may let *B* take it.

Figure **7-F** *A property-space for classifying deviance* [a]

	Activity	Passivity
Compulsive conformity	Dominance	Submission
Compulsive alienation	Aggression toward object	Compulsive independence

[a] Adapted from Parsons, 1951, Chapter 7.

Next Parsons *fits* these two *dimensions together* in a scheme shown in Figure 7-F (parallel to the scheme derived by Merton in his "Social Structure and Anomie," (1957, pp. 131–60). Then Parsons gives a name to the ideal type in each of the cells. You will find that you can now carry your analysis from Exercise II-1 considerably farther by locating in one of the cells of Figure 7-F the dyadic relationships which you previously coded on each of the dimensions separately. Within the total scheme, each separate element will take on added meaning; each element is more useful when fitted together with the others.

Use of the property-space is not limited, of course, either to dichotomous variables or to two-dimensional schemes such as those in the foregoing examples. Many concepts are thought of as having three or four or even more dimensions. Actually, Parson's deviance scheme adds a third dimension—which distinguishes between another person and a norm as the primary focus of a person's deviance. This added dimension subdivides each column in Figure 7-F, producing eight cells, each one of which Parsons treats as a cluster of elements with its appropriate designation.

Some such schemes as these lie behind most research attempts to measure multidimensional concepts. The researcher is not always aware of the underlying scheme. If he does set out self-consciously to use such a scheme, however, he may often help his own cause by determining in advance what dimensions are relevant, or by avoiding the unintentional omission of some of the cells.

THE TYPOLOGY AS A REDUCTION OF THE PROPERTY-SPACE

The four pattern variables (see Parsons and Bales, 1953, pp. 80–83), which you also used in the coding Exercise II-1 as dimensions 1 through 4, are again viewed by Parsons as fitting together into a property-space of role structure. A property-space with four dimensions begins to be complicated, as Figure 7-G indicates. By adding two more dimensions to the space in Figure 7-F, we have expanded the four cells of the two-dimensional scheme into sixteen cells. In this way, each additional dimension used in defining and measuring a concept adds to the complexity of the measurement.

Figure **7-G**   *A property-space for classifying roles*

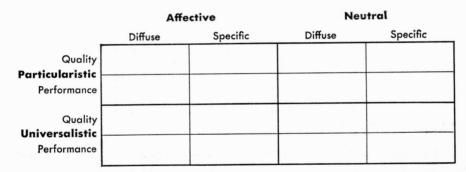

The full detail of such a complicated scheme is not always necessary, and there are various devices for simplifying or collapsing the scheme once it has been thought out. (We shall reserve for detailed discussion later the possibilities of using scores or Guttman scales to simplify the space when the emphasis is on the latent unity rather than on the several different dimensions of the concept.) One method of simplification is illustrated in the Zelditch study of instrumental and expressive roles. You will now notice that the upper left-hand cell in Figure 7-G represents the cluster of elements (the ideal type) called expressive, and the lower right-hand cell represents the instrumental complex, as defined by Parsons and used in the Zelditch study. Thus the Zelditch measurement procedure utilizes only the two extreme cells of a property-space like this, omitting the complexity of all the remaining cells.

A set of ideal types, such as expressive vs. instrumental roles, is often called a *typology.* Many typologies are, of course, familiar in sociology and often used in sociological research, such as Merton's cosmopolitan-local influentials, Sorokin's Sensate-Ideational cultures, Tönnies' *Gemeinschaft-Gesellschaft,* or Riesman's inner-directed, other-directed, and tradition-directed individuals. Such typologies may now be seen as just a few cells selected as especially interesting or useful from a total property-space. Yet a typology may often be better understood, and more effectively used in measurement, if it is viewed within the context of the total property-space.

Some Methodological Implications

This examination of various coding and measuring procedures has shown how indicants may be used to locate cases on single dimensions, which may be combined later to represent the property as a whole. The distinctions among the *property,* its component *dimensions,* and the *indicants* belonging to each dimension are defined by the researcher for each particular measurement problem. Moreover, we have seen how two different types of measures may be distinguished —composite measures, which combine indicants of several aspects (or units) of properties (acts or attitudes, for example); and collective measures, which combine indicants of several parts of the cases themselves (the social-structural base of the action or attitudes). Both types of measures combine indicants (or dimensions), but they have different meanings.

A number of general principles emerge from our examination. One fundamental point is that measurement is indirect. The researcher does not proceed directly from sense data to concept (see Guilford, p. 3). We make measurements every day without considering exactly what we are doing. We observe, for instance, the height of the bar of mercury in a thermometer, and infer from it that the liquid possesses a certain amount of the property temperature. Similarly, we measure an individual's standard of living by making inferences from his reported income, or the size or class composition of a small group by making inferences from its observed characteristics.

Durkheim stressed this point more than half a century ago. Noting that a particular concept (social solidarity) that he wishes to measure "does not lend itself to exact observation nor indeed to measurement," he says, "we must substitute for this internal fact which escapes us an external index which symbolizes it and study the former in the light of the latter" (*The Division of Labor in Society,* p. 64). Following this classic formulation, Merton defines an index or measure as a "sign of the conceptualized item," which "stands ideally in a one-to-one correlation with what it signifies" (Merton, 1957, p. 115).

MEASUREMENT RULES

Since measurement is indirect, it involves a set of rules (or a measuring instrument) for assigning to the cases being measured the numbers (or names) from which inferences are to be made. Even everyday measurements involve rules, though these are usually taken for granted; to measure a man's height, for example, the rules must state whether or not he is to wear shoes, and whether he is to stand erect or to lie down. In sociological measurement, the variables are often conceived as abstractions from a large number of observable acts (or responses) of many members of the group or society; hence it becomes essential to state precisely how, as Lazarsfeld puts it, "inferences from concrete observations to 'underlying' concepts are to be made" (Lazarsfeld, 1954, p. 354).

Thus the measurement rules specify (1) *what observable data* to use as indicants about *what concrete cases;* and (2) *how to use* these data—code them, combine or collect them in various ways—in order to classify each case in terms of the given property.

Each set of rules depends upon the conceptual definitions of the case and the property under study (see Figure 7-A above). Thus in regard to the *case,* the group, for example, may be *conceived,* for purposes of a given measurement, as either a *simple entity* (in respect to its geographical location, for example, or its community status), or as a *complex structure* of roles (within which each individual may have his characteristic voting intention, for example, or each family its characteristic income). Similarly the individual may be viewed at the conceptual level as a simple entity (in regard to sex, for example, or to the holding of given attitudes); or as a complex structure of role relationships (within which a particular individual relates in one way to his father, in another way to his mother, and in still a third way to his brother). Then, at the level of *operations,* the measurement rules prescribe what concrete cases are to be used to represent the conception; and whether—and if so how—data about constituent parts of the system are to be put together to yield a collective (rather than a unitary) measure. As we have seen, collective measures for a country may be based, for example, on constituent measures for individuals or for subgroups (families); or collective measures for a role may be based on constituent measures for dyads.

The conception of the *property* will also influence the character of the measurement rules. When the property is conceived as *unidimensional* (the extent to which the group shows agreement, for example, or the extent to which Soviet communication is concerned with the aims of the Voice of America), the definition of the property will affect what indicants are chosen, how many are chosen, and how they are used in the measure.

When the property is conceived as *multidimensional,* the rules become more complicated. If, to pursue the familiar illustration, the size of a man is regarded as a unidimensional property which varies directly with his height, the man may be measured once, with a linear rule. But if size is regarded as having two dimensions, height and weight, each man must be measured twice—with the yardstick and with the scales; a two-dimensional property-space is used for comparing several men with one another in respect to size. Here again the conception of the property affects the minimum number of indicants needed: for, although a *uni-*

dimensional property may sometimes be represented by one indicant and sometimes by many, a *multi*dimensional property will usually require *at least one* indicant for *each* dimension.

MEASUREMENT MODELS

Underlying any set of measurement rules (any measurement procedure) is the assumption that the sense data, or indicants, as the researcher selects and uses them, correspond in some way to the property defined in the conceptual model. The researcher assumes, either explicitly or implicitly, that a given set of observations may be taken, according to these rules, as a sign or symbol or measure of the concept. His assumptions about the correspondence between (1) his conception of the property and (2) the indicants (selected and combined according to the rules) is called a measurement model.

One type of assumption involved in any quantitative measure concerns the correspondence between the property and the *mathematical characteristics* of the numeral series, as we have discussed these. As the measurement rules become more complex—as indicants are weighted and combined, or group members are collected—the models underlying the resultant measures become more difficult to interpret. When constituent measures are put together in a *collective measure,* for example, the new measure refers, as we have seen, to a higher, more inclusive level of the research case. Consequently, the *definition* of the property sometimes changes; individual measures of neighborliness, for instance, may yield collective measures of quite a different property, cohesion. In addition, the procedure of collecting and summarizing constituent measures may change the *mathematical character* of the measure. (See the outline in Manual III-A, part 2.) Thus nominal measures (or any dichotomized measures) of constituent individuals as Republican or Democrat, for example, may result in a rank order of groups on an ordinal scale (according to the percentage of Republicans in each group). Or ordinal measures of the standard of living of individuals may, upon combination, produce another rank ordering of groups according to their medians. Such conversions from constituent to collective measures thus seem to involve a whole series of assumptions about the correspondence between the measure and the researcher's conception of the property—assumptions that should be carefully stated and weighed whenever a new measuring instrument is designed and used.

Tests of the Measurement Model.   The problematical character of many models for sociological measurement will doubtless be reduced as certain measures withstand the test of use. We no longer question the correspondence, for instance, between the property, temperature, and the measuring instrument, thermometer. The temperature-humidity index, on the other hand, is less readily taken for granted. It is less straightforward and less established in standard usage.

It may take considerable time for most sociological measures to become widely accepted. In the meantime, certain procedures contain inherent tests to determine whether the measurement model actually fits the observable data. These tests obviate the necessity of relying entirely upon the investigator's judgment for the selection of indicants and the determination of numerical values (or names) to be assigned. We shall consider in Unit 9 some measuring procedures with built-in tests of the relationships among *indicants*—after first examining, in Unit 8, procedures for studying relationships among the *properties* themselves.

SUGGESTED READINGS FOR UNIT SEVEN

Barton, 1955; Cartwright; Cohen and Nagel, Chapter 15; Goode and Hatt, Chapters 15, 16, 18, and pp. 313–30; Hagood and Price, Chapters 6–9; Kendall and Lazarsfeld, pp. 187–96; Lazarsfeld and Barton, 1955; Lazarsfeld and Menzel; Moroney, Chapters 4 and 5; Mueller and Schuessler, Chapters 2–7; Petersen, pp. 622–29; Selltiz *et al.*, Chapter 5, pp. 385–406; Siegel, pp. 21–30; Zeisel, Chapters 3, 5, and 6.

QUESTIONS FOR REVIEW AND DISCUSSION

Review the following methodological terms as used in this Unit:

    code
    coding instructions
    content analysis
    collective measure
    composite measure
    ideal type
    level of measurement (ratio, ordinal, nominal)
    measurement
    measurement model
    measurement rules
    measures of central tendency
    measures of dispersion
    multidimensional properties
    multiple indicants
    normal curve
    property-space
    typology

1. What collective properties might be derived for the family as a whole by using the data as coded in Exercise II-1? How would you design measures for each of these properties?

2. Bogue reports that incomes enumerated for persons and families are smaller than the incomes actually received. If you were to gather such data on income, what devices might you use to reduce this bias? How might this bias affect Bogue's collective measure of income distribution for the country as a

whole and for the several population segments that he compares?

3. State two reasons for using medians rather than means in Bogue's Table 2.

4. Contrast Bogue's collective measures with those used in Merton's study of influentials. Why is the who-to-whom matrix a useful device for Merton but not for Bogue?

5. Contrast the measurement models and the measuring procedures used by Massing and by Weber.

6. How would you define the measurement model (assumptions) underlying Sorokin's rules for measuring the influence and acceptability of the main currents of thought, as he states these rules in the study selection?

7. Kahl, in his report of interviews with parents of high school boys, distinguishes between emphasis on "getting by" and emphasis on "getting ahead."

a. Against what ideal type is this property implicitly measured by Kahl? Draw the property-space.

b. Consider the indicants you might select in developing a composite measure for this property and how you might define these in a set of coding instructions for use by interviewers.

c. How would you design a col-lective measure for this property, by which you might classify the family as a whole?

8. Suppose that you wish to study the relationship between adherence to the Protestant ethic and college achievement as measured by grades.

a. Describe how you might formulate an ideal type against which you could compare students according to their adherence to the Protestant ethic. Would you make use of any of the same elements that Weber used? Why or why not?

b. Show how you might derive a typology by extending the dimensions of your ideal type. Exactly how would you make use of such a typology in measurement?

9. As an exercise, try recoding the interview reports you coded in Exercise II-1, this time using the method of content analysis.

a. Before you start, define carefully what standard units to use in breaking down the content of the interview reports.

b. When you have completed the exercise, compare the uses and limitations of the two kinds of coding procedures.

UNIT EIGHT

RELATIONSHIPS AMONG VARIABLES

SUGGESTED PROGRAM OF STUDY

In this Unit, you will learn some empirical procedures for systematic analysis of relationships among variables **(P-XI),** and will see how research findings are interpreted at the conceptual level.

Exercises and Manual

Complete the sequence of **Exercises IV-1, IV-2,** and **IV-3,** which teach you to compute, and to interpret with reference to a conceptual model, the statistical relationships between two or more variables. Follow **Manual IV-A** and **IV-B** for the use of percentages and other measures of association that are suitable for use with nominal and ordinal measures.

You can obtain relevant practical experience by making your own cross-tabulations of actual data (by hand in **Exercise II-3** and/or by I.B.M. machine in **Exercise 11-4** following **Manual II-C**), applying the analytical tools you have learned, and reporting your findings.

Studies

Reread the analysis (Unit 6) in Stouffer's study of conformity and in the Harvard Mobility Project reported by Kahl. Then, in reading each of the new studies —by **Strodtbeck; Lazarsfeld, Berelson,** and **Gaudet;** and **Durkheim**—consider what variables are being analyzed, how the analysis is conducted, and what methods are used in interpreting the empirical findings. Note especially how the investigator often controls (holds constant) certain variables in order to focus attention on those of principal concern.

Commentary

In the Commentary, we shall pay special attention to the method of subgroup comparisons in which the investigator controls certain variables either through his sample design **(P-IV)** or through cross-tabulation. We shall also see how the plan for analysis and the interpretation of findings may be affected by the exploratory or hypothesis-testing emphasis of the research objective.

Questions for Review and Discussion

Use the Questions for Review and Discussion to help you to think of each study as a whole, so as to locate multivariate analysis within the total research process.

FRED L. STRODTBECK
Husband-Wife Interaction over Revealed Differences

In the course of a series of pilot studies of power, or influence, in small group situations the writer has developed a procedure, called the revealed difference technique, which has shown promise in a first application to husband-wife interaction. In the attempt to validate the results obtained by this technique, use has been made of similar groups in different cultures. The following paper is organized in a form to emphasize how this methodological innovation and the technique itself grew from successive sequences in which pilot findings led to further research operations.

Background

During 1948–49 the writer observed a series of groups engaged in decision-making. An effort was made to determine some of the correlates of differential ability to persuade others in accordance with the actor's desires. In one instance, four mathematics students were requested to recommend jointly the best of three possible solutions to particular problems. While these students were in the process of developing consensus they were asked to record privately the alternative they personally favored. Thus, the experimenter was provided with a continuous means of relating a type of private opinion to public behavior. The experimentation indicated that the ulti-

Reprinted in part from *American Sociological Review, 16,* 1951, pp. 468–73, with permission of the American Sociological Association and the author.

mate decision could be most accurately predicted by simply weighting the privately pre-determined opinion of each participant by the total time he had spoken during the experimental interaction. This finding was duplicated in various groups who worked at the task of jointly selecting the best move in a chess problem. . . .

We recognized that we had up to this time worked with *ad hoc* groups which had no group structure at the beginning of the observation period and no expectation of participating with one another at a later time. The problems they had considered were delimited and specific; the nature of their arguments and responses was highly structured. On the basis of this analysis, we were led to consider experimentation with groups whose members approached the opposite extreme of broad common interests, daily contact, and permanence—so-called primary groups.

Among the various types of primary groups that might profitably be studied, husband-wife dyads were selected because of the ease of replication of these units. Each couple was asked to pick three reference families with whom they were well acquainted. The husband and wife were then separated and requested to designate which of the three reference families most satisfactorily fulfilled a series of 26 conditions such as: Which family has the happiest children? Which family is the most religious? Which family is most ambitious? After both husband and wife had individually marked their choices they were requested to reconcile their differences and indicate a final "best" choice from the standpoint of their family. For the first ten couples studied, this pooling took place with the experimenter out of the room and under conditions such that the couple did not know they were being observed or having their voices recorded. Their lack of knowledge of the observation was ascertained after the session, at which time their permission to use the material in a scientific inquiry was obtained. The anticipated experimental difficulties—(a) producing "polite" interaction because of the intrusion of the experimenter, and (b) structuring the task to such a degree that the mode of interaction would be highly determined —were judged to have been satisfactorily avoided.

Omitting, for present purposes, a discussion of the content of the recorded protocols, it was found that women won 47 of the contested decisions and men, 36. In six of the eight cases in which there was a difference both in number of decisions-won and in talking-time, the spouse who talked most won the majority of the decisions. At this time there was no basis for appraising whether the women had won slightly more decisions because they had known more about the types of information under discussion, or whether the decision winning represented, as we had hoped, the operation of structured power relations in an area in which both participants were equally informed. The observed margin by which the women exceeded the men was not significant—a result which might have been much more valuable if we had predicted it in terms of independent knowledge of the equalitarian characteristics of the married veteran couples used in the sample. In short, further application was necessary to determine whether the technique was a valid method of indicating in any more general sense the balance of power between participants.

A field study was designed to throw further light on this problem. Three communities were selected which presumably differed in terms of the degree to which the wife was favored by the cultural phrasing of power. The communities were at the same time sufficiently small to increase greatly the probability that both spouses would be adequately, if not equally, informed concerning the behavior of the reference couples. The technique as described above was applied to ten couples from each of these cultures. It was proposed that the conformity of the experimental results with the a priori cultural expectations be taken as a crude measure of the validity with which the technique reflected power differences.

Description of Cultures

The cultures which were selected for study [as part of the larger Harvard Comparative Study of Values Project] are geographically adjacent communities in the Arizona–New Mexico area. Briefly described, the groups are Navaho Indians; dry farmers from Texas who have recently homesteaded in the area; and early settlers who utilize a dam operated under the supervision of the Mormon church.... For present purposes the communities will be designated Navaho, Texan, and Mormon. A brief recapitulation of power attributes of the culturally legitimized role of women in each culture is presented below.

The young Navaho man, who marries a girl from a moderately successful family, typically leaves his own family and resides with the girl's family and works under her father's direction until he has established himself as a responsible person. When this change of residence is made, the man leaves his sheep with his own family of orientation and his work activities result in little immediate increase in his own holdings. The children are considered a part of the wife's consanguine group, and marriages are generally unstable. Both men and women own sheep, but the women do the processing of wool into rugs and blankets. This assures the women a regular income throughout the year. The man has greater earning power when he performs wage work, but the wage work opportunities are scarce and seasonal. The man is considered the head of the household, but the relative economic independence of the wife and her close integration with her own consanguine group effectively limit his exercise of power. . . .

The Texan group is composed of migrants who came from Eastern Texas during the drought and depression of the early 1930's. With minor exceptions the households are farms on contiguous sections headed by persons who as young adults made the earlier move, or by their older children who have more recently married. . . . The ten couples who participated in this study were members of the ranking Presbyterian clique in the community.

The ten couples selected for study in the Mormon village were chosen from the most active participants in the affairs of the local church. Religious teachings which exercise a pervasive effect upon local social organization specifically stress the role of the husband as the head of the family. . . .

Corresponding prescriptions for the wife's role emphasize that she should above all else be a mother, for "motherhood is the noblest, most soul-satisfying of all earthly experiences." Mormonism has a this-worldly orientation, divine

grace is attained through effort, and the symbol of progress is the advancement the man makes in the priesthood and in extending his flocks and fields. The woman is not eligible for membership in the priesthood and her status is coupled with that of her husband both in her present life and in the next, by the regular Temple marriage. From the incomplete evidence now available, Mormon women of this community do not appear to have important land-holdings nor independent sources of income, and accounts of women's participation in church activities confirm the correspondence of women's current attitudes with the church writings quoted above. The historic emphasis by Brigham Young and others on woman's education and political participation was always hedged by the general reservation that motherhood should not be interfered with—the women of the community in question strongly emphasize this reservation.

In summary, the favored position of the Navaho woman in contrast to the Mormon woman was judged in terms of economic, religious, and kinship considerations to be quite unequivocal. Between Texan and Mormon women there is less difference, but in terms of holding church office and the present possession of productive land and semi-professional jobs, the women in the Texan community appear to be more favored than the Mormon women. On the basis of this analysis it was predicted that Navaho women would win the highest percentage of the decisions and the Mormon women the smallest.

Experimental Procedure

The area under study had no electrification, and since it was impractical to attempt to bring the subjects to an observation room, the field sessions of the experimental procedure were recorded by portable sound equipment powered from a truck. Although the subjects were separated from the experimenter and other persons, they knew that their voices were being recorded. The task was explained to the Navahos by an interpreter. An appropriate picture was presented for each question and underneath the illustration there were pockets representing the three reference couples. The Navaho would place his marker in the pocket which represented the couple of his choice. In those instances in which there had been a difference between the choice of the man and wife, the illustration was presented again to the two of them with their markers in separate pockets. They were requested to combine their markers in the position which best represented their joint opinion. Some questions were changed somewhat by translation into Navaho; for example, the question, "Which family is the most religious?" became "Which family follows the 'Navaho Way' best?" It was not felt that these changes would significantly modify the results here presented. These recordings were transcribed and, in the case of the Navaho, translated into English.

The written protocols were analyzed to determine the number of acts used by each participant and the distribution of these acts in terms of [Bales'] interaction process categories. This information plus knowledge of the number of decisions won by each participant provides the basis for the analysis presented below.

Findings

We present in Table 1 the sum of the decisions won by the husbands and wives in each of the three cultures. The appropriate null hypothesis is compounded of two elements: (a) the proposition that the Mormon wives win an equal or greater number of decisions than their husbands ($p = .007$); and (b) the proposition that Navaho husbands win an equal or greater number of decisions than their wives ($p = .16$). Since the combined probability associated with these two propositions is less than .01, we reject the null hypothesis and conclude that we were able to predict the balance of decision-winning from our study of the comparative social and cultural organization of the groups from which our sample was drawn.

Having to this limited degree established the validity of the technique, we are encouraged to inquire further into elements of behavior in the small group situation which are linked with decision-winning. Our earlier experience had indicated a very strong relationship between decision-winning, or leadership, and talking-time in *ad hoc* groups of four persons. In the present instance two-person primary groups are involved. From a broader study of the rank characteristics of participants in groups ranging in size from two to ten persons it is known that differentiation in speaking-time in two-person groups is relatively less than it is in larger groups, hence it is probable that the relation between speaking-time and decision-winning is less clearly defined in two-person than in larger groups. There was no compelling rationale for predicting the effects of the primary relationships upon "speaking and decision-winning." By combining the ten cases observed at Cambridge with

Table **1** *Decisions won, by spouse and culture*

Culture	Number of couples	Decisions won by Husband	Wife
Navaho	10	34	46
Texan	10	39	33
Mormon	10	42	29

the thirty cases from the field and eliminating the six cases in which the decisions were split evenly, we obtain the thirty-four cases compared in Table 2. The null hypothesis of independence between talking most and winning may be rejected at the .05 but not the .01 level.

Table **2**   *Decisions won and talking time for thirty-four married couples*

Spouse who talked most	Spouse who won most	
	Husband	Wife
Husband	14	5
Wife	5	10

To approach a more systematic description of the interaction characteristics of the spouse who talks most, we have selected the 24 cases in which there was a significant difference between the number of acts originated by the husband and the wife. We find that the most talking spouse tended more frequently to *ask questions,* carry out *opinion and analysis,* and make *rewarding remarks.* As Simmel suggested, in a dyad there can be no coalitions—the speaker does not have alternative audiences, so the "threat of withdrawal" is generally a more compelling adjustmental device in two-person than in larger groups. While we do not as yet have norms by group size for category usage on a common task, the unexpected finding in the present study that the most active participant is significantly high in question-asking gives us further insight into how withdrawal is anticipated and prevented. The finding that the frequency of opinion and analysis acts is higher for the most talking person is in agreement with Bales' notion that acts of this type have a central generative function which results in their being heavily represented in the profile of the most talking person in groups of any size.

The categories which discriminate the profile of the least talking participants are, in order of magnitude, the following: simple *acts of agreement, aggressive acts* designed to deflate the other actor's status, and simple *disagreements.* Taken together, these characteristics suggest the passive agreeing person who from time to time becomes frustrated and aggresses.

Concerning cultural differences in category usage, the Navahos gave *opinion, evaluation,* and *analysis* acts during the solution of their differences only one-half as frequently as the Mormon and the Texan group. As a result they required on the average fewer acts per decision (8 in contrast with 30 for the other groups) and the reasoning and persuasion in their protocols seemed extremely sketchy. They did not emphasize the arguments that might bear upon the issue, they tended to reiterate their choices and implore the other person to "go with them;" "go together," or simply consent. This is in marked contrast with the other couples who appeared to feel that they had to give a reasoned argument to show that they were logically convinced, even when they were giving in to the other person. It is a matter for further research to determine if other "traditional" people show a similar tendency to minimize analysis in social problem solving.

For the Texans it was a rational exercise, sometimes directly commented upon, to see that the decisions came out even. The standard deviation [of the differences] between spouses in decisions won was only 1.3. The Mormons were less concerned with equality, the comparable figure is 2.1, and among the Navaho there were marked differences between spouses, the standard deviation being 5.1. An analysis of the way in which couples tended to go from orientation acts to evaluative acts before making suggestions for a final disposition of the difference, the so-called phases in interaction, will be presented in a later paper.

Summary

The essence of the revealed difference technique here described consists of: (a) requesting subjects who have shared experiences to make individual evaluations of them; and then, (b) requesting the subjects to reconcile any differences in interpretations which may have occurred. It has been shown that the disposition of these reconciled decisions is related both to power elements in the larger social and cultural organization and amount of participation in the small group situation. It is believed that other couples as well as parent-child, foreman-worker, and similar relationships may be profitably studied with the technique, since it appears not only to reveal the balance of power, but also to produce a sample of interaction in which modes and techniques of influence can be studied by methods of content and process analysis.

PAUL F. LAZARSFELD
BERNARD BERELSON
HAZEL GAUDET
The People's Choice

I. Introduction

This is a report on modern American political behavior—specifically on the formation of votes during a presidential campaign. Every four years, the country stages a large-scale experiment in political propaganda and public opinion. The stimuli are comprised of everything the two parties do to elect their candidates. What the people do in the course of this campaign represents the reactions reviewed and analyzed in these pages.

We are interested here in all those conditions which determine the political behavior of people. Briefly, our problem is this: to discover how and why people decided to vote as they did. What were the major influences upon them during the campaign of 1940? We believe we know some of the answers; we are sure we do not know them all. Similar studies of a series of major elections, especially in comparison with one another, will confirm the valid findings of this report, correct its deficiencies, and in general clarify and complete existing knowledge of the determinants of political opinion in a modern democracy.

There are several ways to analyze elections. Until relatively recently, official vote records constituted the only available material on elections. They were useful for the study of the geographical distribution of the political temper of the people and not much else. Then a group of political scientists centering around the University of Chicago introduced what might be called the ecological analysis of voting. By examining vote records for small units of a city or state for which a considerable number of background (census) data were available, they were able to isolate to some extent the effects upon vote of such factors as religion and nationality and gross economic status. Although they worked under the handicap of dealing with voters in the large—e.g., not everyone living in a predominantly Irish district was an Irishman—nevertheless they increased our understanding of some major determinants of political decision.

Then came the public opinion polls and they advanced our knowledge by relating political opinion to the characteristics of the individual voter and by revealing vote intentions before the election itself. Thus they made much more precise the study of certain determinants of vote and, to some extent, they made possible the study of the development of vote during a political campaign.

But it was at this very point that further progress was needed. The full effect of a campaign cannot be investigated through a sequence of polls conducted with different people. They show only majority tendencies which are actually the residual result of various sorts of changes—to or from indecision and from one party to the other. They conceal minor changes which cancel out one another and even major changes if they are countered by opposing trends. And most of all, they do not show *who* is changing. They do not follow the vagaries of the individual voter along the path to his vote, to discover the rela-

tive effect of various influential factors upon his final vote.

In short, never before has the development of the person's vote been traced throughout a political campaign, from his pre-convention attitudes through his reactions to the barrage of propaganda which constitutes the campaign proper to his actual vote on Election Day. Only by such an investigation can we establish more closely the roles of the several influences upon vote (and other political attitudes), from both predispositions and stimuli. This study, designed to yield such answers, used the so-called panel technique as the next step forward in opinion research: *repeated interviewing of the same people.*

A NEW RESEARCH METHOD

Let us briefly examine the technical plan of the investigation; an outline of it is represented by the graphical scheme shown in Figure 1.

The survey was done in Erie County, Ohio, located on Lake Erie between Cleveland and Toledo. This county was chosen because it was small enough to permit close supervision of the interviewers, because it was relatively free from sectional peculiarities, because it was not dominated by any large urban center although it did furnish an opportunity to compare rural political opinion with opinion in a small urban center, and because for forty years—in every presidential election in the twentieth century—it had deviated very little from the national voting trends. Because of the diversity of American life, there is no such thing as a "typical American county." But it is not unlikely that Erie County was as representative of the northern and western sections of the country as any similarly small area could be. In any case, we were studying

Figure **1**　*The plan of the study*

Timetable	May	June	July	August	September	October	November
		Republican Convention	Democratic Convention			Election	
Interview number	1	2	3	4	5	6	7
Group interviewed	Total poll (3,000)	Main panel 600	Main panel 600	Main panel 600	Main panel 600	Main panel 600	Main panel 600
			Control A 600	Control B 600		Control C 600	

the *development* of votes and not their distribution.

In May, 1940, every fourth house in Erie County was visited by a member of the staff of from twelve to fifteen specially trained local interviewers, chiefly women. In this way, approximately 3,000 persons were chosen to represent as closely as possible the population of the county as a whole. This group—the poll—resembled the county in age, sex, residence, education, telephone and car ownership, and nativity.

From this poll, four groups of 600 persons each were selected by stratified sampling. Each group was closely matched to the others and constituted, in effect, a miniature sample of the whole poll and of the county itself.[1] Of these four groups of 600, three were re-

interviewed only once each—one in July, one in August, and one in October. They were used as "control groups" to test the effect that repeated interviewing might have on the panel.[2] At the same time they provided a larger sample (1,200 respondents) on a variety of important questions asked at the control points. The fourth group—the panel—was inter-

some who were temporarily unavailable because of illness or travel, and some who moved out of the county permanently or who died. Every effort to keep mortality at a minimum was made. In most cases of difficulty, the field supervisor personally attempted to regain the cooperation of the respondent. In many instances, respondents who were not successfully contacted on one interview were picked up again on the next wave of interviewing. In the panel group, missing cases on the seven interviews were kept down to 14 per cent, a figure which proved to be remarkably low in the experience of subsequent investigators. Analysis of the characteristics of the missing cases showed that the number lost was so small that their influence on the total trends was practically unnoticeable....

[1] All four groups approximated 600 at the outset. But in any questionnaire study involving repeated interviewing, the problem of "mortality" arises. That is, there are always a few instances in which it is impossible to contact some of the respondents on successive recalls. In this study, mortality arose from a few who refused to be reinterviewed,

[2] Proof that repeated interviewing did not affect the results will be presented in a separate paper.

viewed once each month from May to November.

Interviews were spaced about a month apart to fit best the natural course of campaign events. The first two interviews were made in May and June, prior to the Republican Convention—the original poll and the first recall on the panel members. The third interview came in July, between the two conventions, and the fourth in August, after both conventions. Two more calls were made between the conventions and Election Day, the second as close to the eve of the election as possible. The seventh and last interview was made in November, shortly after the election.

Thus, the 600 people of the panel were kept under continual observation from May until November, 1940. Whenever a person changed his vote intention in any way, from one interview to the next, detailed information was gathered on why he had changed. The respondents were also interviewed regularly on their exposure to campaign propaganda in all the media of communication—the press, radio, personal contacts, and others. In addition, the repeated interviews made it possible to secure voluminous information about each respondent's personal characteristics, social philosophy, political history, personality traits, relationships with other people, opinions on issues related to the election—in short, information on anything which might contribute to our knowledge of the formation of his political preferences.

... In summary, then, the panel was devised as a more effective method of getting at the important questions. What is the effect of social status upon vote? How are people influenced by the party conventions and the nominations? What role does formal propaganda play? How about the press and the radio? What of the influence of family and friends? Where do issues come in, and how? Why do some people settle their vote early and some late? In short, how do votes develop? Why do people vote as they do? By inference and by direct accounts of the respondents, we shall try to show what influences operated between May and November to determine the ballots cast on November 5, 1940.

Before pushing on to the findings themselves, let us summarize briefly the major contributions of the panel technique.

1. We can determine who the changers are during the campaign and can study their characteristics....

2. We can accumulate information pertaining to the whole campaign from one interview to the next. For example, we are able to distinguish people according to whether they were exposed to predominantly Republican or predominantly Democratic propaganda, on the basis of indices constructed from their answers at different times....

3. When a respondent changes his vote intention between two interviews, we catch his opinion in a process of flux. It obviously tells us little to ask a man who has voted Republican all his life why he favors the present Republican candidate. If, however, a respondent intended to vote Democratic last month and this month intends to vote Republican, the reasons for his change enable us to gauge the effectiveness of the propaganda and other influences to which he was subjected....

4. Repeated interviews also permit us to trace the effects of propaganda statistically. For example, we can study the people who are undecided at one interview but who have an opinion at the next. Anything such people did or thought at the time of the first inter-

view, then, precedes the time of their decision. By studying such data, we can infer what made the respondents decide as they did. This kind of information is quite different from that found in the usual public opinion surveys, which provide data related to opinion at the same point in time. There we cannot tell what is cause and what is effect, but the repeated interview technique allows us to establish a time sequence and therefore greatly facilitates causal analysis. . . .

III. Social Differences Between Republicans and Democrats

THE ROLE OF SOCIO-ECONOMIC STATUS

Before discussing the role which socio-economic status plays in the composition of the two major political parties, let us consider the index by which we measure this characteristic.

Public opinion research customarily makes use of interviewers' ratings of socio-economic status. For convenience let us refer to them as SES ratings. Interviewers are trained to assess the homes, possessions, appearance, and manner of speech of the respondents and to classify them into their proper stratum in the community according to a set quota. The people with the best homes, furniture, clothes, etc., i.e., the ones with the most money, would be classed as A's; and the people at the other extreme would be D's. In Erie County, the quota was approximated in the following distribution: A, 3%; B, 14%; C+, 33%; C−, 30%; and D, 20%.

There are a number of general considerations implied in such a classification which can only briefly be summarized here. The first question concerns the reliability of such a classification

procedure. Would two independent tests yield the same results? We have some evidence on this question. Experiments have shown that two sets of ratings, representing two independent appraisals of the same subjects by the same interviewers but spaced three weeks apart, have a correlation of .8. When the same subjects are observed by two different interviewers, the correlation goes down to .6 or .7. Although there is some variation, the ratings provide a fairly stable classification.

But do these ratings classify people so that the result corresponds to general experience? Again there is evidence to show that the SES ratings are closely related to the material possessions of the respondents. The higher the rating, the higher the average income, the average number of expensive household articles owned, and so on.

These SES ratings are closely related to the educational level of the subjects. Also, the higher ratings go to business and professional people, while the lower ones are given mainly to workers and manual laborers.

In short, special studies have shown that these qualitative ratings represent a sort of average of, or common factor to, the various status ratings for the different specific social groups with which people are associated. It is well known, for example, that in many communities a family name that dates from centuries back brings more prestige than does wealth. A respondent with money *and* family status is ranked higher by interviewers than one who qualifies on only one of these two points. And the latter person, in turn, would be placed ahead of someone who had neither money nor a time-honored name. The SES ratings can therefore be considered a measure of the number of qualifications each respondent has for a high rank on the socio-economic scale. In this sense, the SES ratings represent a general stratification index.

Now, to what extent did the SES levels differentiate party vote? To what extent did people on the various levels support the Republicans or the Democrats? The answer is that there were twice as many Republicans on the A level as on the D level (Figure 2). And with each step down the SES scale, the proportion of Republicans decreases and the proportion of Democrats correspondingly increases.

Such a general index, useful as it is in establishing general relationships, often obscures interesting nuances. For example, a sociologist interested in the concept of "class" might believe that such an index of socio-economic stratification befogs the issue more than it clarifies it. He might suggest that it is the objective and concrete position of the individual in the general system of business and production that really matters. For a statistical answer to this problem, a sub-classification of the respondents *within* the different SES levels is necessary. Although it is not the pur-

pose of this study to consider stratification systems in any great detail, an example or two of such sub-classifications will show that the *general* SES index does not obscure the more refined problems of social stratification, but rather aids in the study of them.

As a first basis for further classification (Figure 3), we can use the occupations of our respondents. On each SES level, the "upper" occupational groups —professionals, business men, clerical and commercial people—were more Republican than the "lower" groups (skilled mechanics, factory workers, and manual laborers).

However, once people are classified by the general SES index, the further classification by occupation does not refine the groups very greatly. In other words, people of the same general socio-economic status have about the same political attitudes regardless of their occupations. When the contribution of the general SES level is held constant, the influence of occupation itself upon vote is small indeed.

But perhaps the crucial factor is not so much a person's objective occupation

Figure **2** *Those high in socio-economic status (SES level) are more likely to vote Republican than Democratic.*

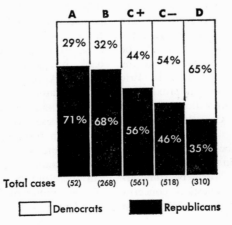

Total cases (52) (268) (561) (518) (310)

☐ Democrats   ■ Republicans

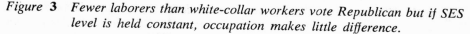

Figure **3** *Fewer laborers than white-collar workers vote Republican but if SES level is held constant, occupation makes little difference.*

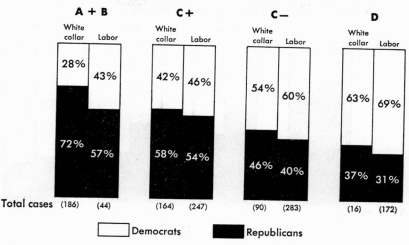

as his own opinion of his social status. A worker, for instance, may be or aspire to be a foreman and hence may identify himself with management. He may then feel that his personal welfare is linked to the welfare of business rather than labor. Perhaps a person's own "class" identification influences his vote more than his actual occupation. In order to study this possibility, the following question was asked in October and November: "To which of the following groups do you feel you belong?" For those who did not consider themselves in any of the groups, the following question was raised: "In which group are you most interested?" The answers which the respondents gave to these questions provided the data for our second sub-classification.

The identifications which people make in their own minds are more important in determining their vote than is their objective occupation (Figure 4). This is not surprising since we here introduce an attitudinal element closely related to other attitudinal factors which influence

vote. In fact, the addition of this element of identification considerably improves the predictability of political allegiance available from the classification by SES levels alone (Figure 2). There we found twice as many Republicans on the highest SES levels (A + B) as on the lowest. Now, with the people's own social identification included, the discrimination has increased to a ratio of almost three-to-one.

In short, the general SES index can be refined by combination with other social measures—particularly identification. As the social characterization of the respondent becomes more detailed a closer relationship to political affiliation can be established. The wealthier people, the people with more and better possessions, the people with business interests—these people were usually Republicans. The poorer people, the people whose homes and clothes were of lower quality, the self-acknowledged laboring class—they voted Democratic. Different social characteristics, different votes.

Figure **4** *Whereas actual occupation does little to refine the relationship be-*
tween SES level and vote, it makes more difference whether a voter
considers himself as belonging to "business" or "labor."

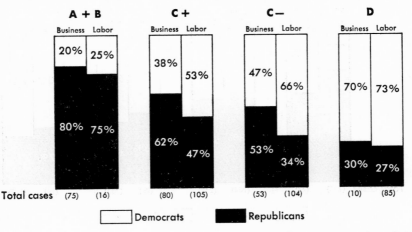

RELIGIOUS AFFILIATION AND AGE

In Erie County there was another factor which was no less important than SES level. That was religious affiliation.

Sixty percent of the Protestants and only 23% of the Catholics had Republican vote intentions in May. At first glance, this might appear to be a spurious result. As a group, Catholics are ordinarily lower in economic status than Protestants and hence this result may simply reflect SES levels. But it does not. On each SES level, religious affiliation plays an important role in determining political affiliation (Figure 5).

... The differences in the political inclinations of the two religious groups serves to introduce the relationship between age and vote preference. Legend has it that older people are more conservative in most things, including politics, both because they like to perpetuate their own idealized past and because they have more to conserve. By the same token, younger people are more liberal, more receptive to change. If one accepts the common stereotypes— that the Republican party is more "conservative" and the Democrats more "liberal"—then the legend seems to hold for Erie County in 1940.

In May, 50% of those below 45 years of age, but 55% of those over 45 intended to vote Republican. However, this result does not hold for the Protestants and Catholics separately (Figure 6). Only among the Protestants were the older people more Republican. Among the Catholics, the relationship was reversed: the older people were more Democratic. This refinement of the relationship between age and political preference probably has two explanations. First, the younger people, who are generally less church-influenced than their elders, show less influence of religion upon vote. Thus young Protestants are less Republican than old Protestants and young Catholics less Democratic than old Catholics. And secondly, the myth that age brings political conservatism—here shown to be incorrect —may apply in another sense. Like appetite, custom grows by what it feeds on.

Figure **5** *Religious affiliation splits vote sharply. This cannot be attributed to the fact that Catholics in this country are, on the average, lower in SES level than Protestants. The relationship between vote and religious affiliation holds true on each SES level.*

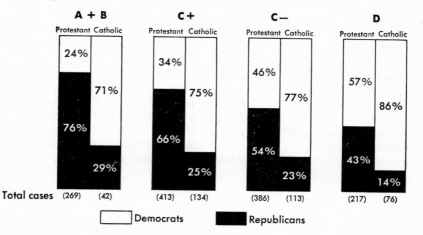

Figure **6** *Within each religious group the younger voters show tendencies of opposition. Younger Protestants vote less Republican than older Protestants, and younger Catholics less Democratic than older Catholics.*

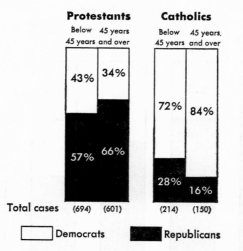

The religious factors which influence vote preference are intensified through the years so that they carry more weight for the elderly. They have a longer time to exercise their influence, to indoctri- nate the respondent, to affect him through the common elements. In other words, advancing age may not bring *political* conservatism but it does bring *social* conservatism.

AN INDEX OF POLITICAL
PREDISPOSITION

To this point, we have isolated two major influences upon vote: the SES level and religious affiliation. And, incidentally, we have seen that the political effect of age differs for Catholics and Protestants. A number of other factors were investigated, but only one proved statistically significant: there were 14% more Republican voters in the rural part of the county than in Sandusky, the one large industrialized town with a population of 25,000.

Other differences were less important.

Women were somewhat more inclined to favor the Republican party. The same was true for better-educated people, but education is so highly related to SES level that it is hard to say whether the influence of education alone would be distinguishable if a more refined economic classification were used. . . .

The greatest part of the predictive value of all these factors derives from three factors: SES level, religion, and residence. Of all rich Protestant farmers almost 75% voted Republican, whereas 90% of the Catholic laborers living in Sandusky voted Democratic.

In order to use these factors in a

Figure **7**   *High SES level, affiliation with the Protestant religion, and rural residence predispose a voter for the Republican party; the opposites of these factors make for Democratic predisposition. Summarized in an index of political predisposition (IPP), their effect is illustrated by the high correlation with vote intention.*

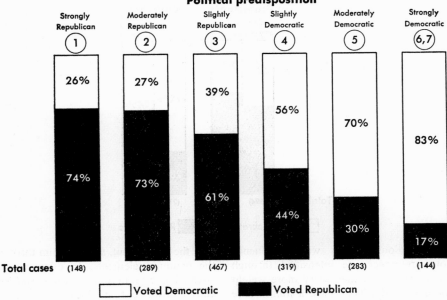

Political predisposition

simple way, we constructed an index of political predisposition (IPP) [3] so that the respondents could be classified on a

[3] [Note from Appendix] ... This index was formed by stratifying within each SES level for religion and residence. A wealthy Protestant farmer got an IPP score of 1, and this meant he had a strong Republican predisposition. A Catholic on the lowest SES level, living in the urban center of Erie County, was rated 7, and this meant he had a strong Democratic predisposition. The scoring procedure:

	Protestant		Catholic	
	Rural	Urban	Rural	Urban
A, B	1	2	3	4
C+	2	3	4	5
C−	3	4	5	6
D	4	5	6	7

Following is the distribution of the respondents in May according to this index:

Score	Frequency	
1	148	Predominantly
2	289	Republican
3	467	predispositions
4	319	Predominantly
5	283	Democratic
6	97	predispositions
7	47	

scale ranging from those with strong Republican predispositions at one extreme to those with strong Democratic predispositions at the other. While an index is, of course, [relatively crude] ... it does serve to distinguish easily among the votes of people with different combinations of personal characteristics (Figure 7). The proportion of Republicans falls off consistently and significantly from one extreme of political predispositions to the other. And thus a simple combination of three primary personal characteristics goes a long way in "explaining" political preferences. ...

VI. Time of Final Decision

... Interviews with the panel permitted us to distinguish three kinds of voters classified according to the time when they made their *final vote decision*—the decision which they followed throughout the rest of the campaign and in the voting booth. (Figure 8).

"*May Voters*": These pre-campaign

Figure **8** *People greatly interested in the election make their final vote decision earlier than less interested people.*

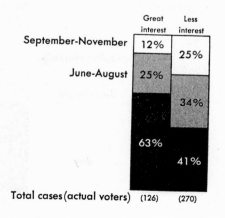

deciders knew in May, at our first interview, how they would vote, maintained their choice throughout the campaign, and actually voted for that choice in November. Their votes had been finally determined by May.

"*June-to-August Voters*": These people settled upon a candidate during the convention period (our August interview was the first interview after both conventions), maintained their choice throughout the rest of the campaign, and actually voted for that choice in November. Their votes were finally determined in June, July or August.

"*September-to-November Voters*": These people did not definitely make up their minds until the last few months of the campaign, some of them not until Election Day itself. Their votes were finally determined only in September, October or November.

What were the significant differences between these groups of people? Why did some people make up their minds before the campaign began, others during the first months of the campaign, and still others not until the end of the campaign?

The analysis in this chapter develops two major factors influencing the time of final decision. First, the people whose decision was delayed had *less interest* in the election. Second, those who made their choice in the late days of the campaign were people subject to *more cross-pressures*. By "cross-pressures" we mean the conflicts and inconsistencies among the factors which influence vote decision. Some of these factors in the environment of the voter may influence him toward the Republicans while others may operate in favor of the Democrats. In other words, cross-pressures upon the voter drive him in opposite directions.

INTEREST AND TIME OF DECISION

... The general tendency for late decision among the less interested held for both parties (Figure 9). But on each level of interest, the Democrats tended to decide later than the Republicans. ...

Figure **9**   *It is true for both parties: the higher the interest, the earlier the decision is likely to be made.*

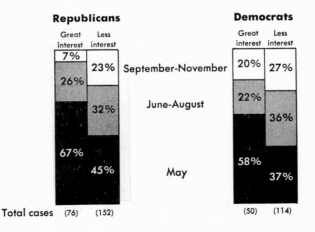

CROSS-PRESSURES AND TIME OF
DECISION

In Chapter III, we indicated that there
were a number of factors differentiating
Republican and Democratic voters. Each
of these factors could be considered a
"pressure" upon final vote decision. We
found the Protestant vote allied to the
Republicans and the Catholic vote more
strongly Democratic. We found that individuals on the higher SES levels tended
to vote Republican and their poorer
neighbors to vote Democratic. In other
words, a vote decision can be considered
the net effect of a variety of pressures.

Now what if these individual factors
work in opposite directions? Suppose an
individual is *both* prosperous and Catholic? How will he make up his mind?
Or suppose he belongs to the Protestant
faith and lives in a poor section of the
community? Which of the conflicting
influences will win out? People who are
subject to contradictory and opposing
influences of this kind are said to be under cross-pressures. . . .

THE EFFECT OF CROSS-PRESSURES

Whatever the source of the conflicting pressures, whether from social status
or class identification, from voting traditions or the attitudes of associates, the
consistent result was to delay the voter's
final decision. . . . The voters who were
subject to cross-pressures on their vote
decided later than the voters for whom
the various factors reinforced one another. And of all the cross-pressures
which we have identified, the single most
effective one in delaying vote decision
was the lack of complete agreement
within the family.

Why did people subject to cross-pressures delay their final decisions as to how
they should vote? In the first place, it
was difficult for them to make up their

minds simply because they had good reasons for voting for both candidates. . . .

In the second place, some of the people subject to cross-pressures delayed
their final vote decisions because they
were waiting for events to resolve the
conflicting pressures. In the case of conflicting personal characteristics, such res-
olution was hardly possible but in other
cases a reconciliation of conflicting interests might be anticipated. A person
might hope that during the campaign
he could convince other members of
his family, or even more, he might give
the family every chance to bring him
around to their way of thinking. And
the family often does just that. Or,
again, he might wait for events in the
campaign to provide him with a basis
for making up his mind. Although there
is a tendency toward consistency in attitudes, sometimes the contradiction was
not resolved and the voter actually went
to the polls with the cross-pressures still
in operation. . . .

INTEREST AND CROSS-PRESSURES

How are interest and cross-pressures
inter-related? Remembering that controversy often makes issues exciting, we
might expect that those for whom the
decision is difficult would become most
involved with and concerned about the
election. But that would leave out of
the reckoning a basic pattern of human
adjustment. When people desire and
shun a course of action in about equal
degree, they often do not decide for or
against it but rather change the subject or avoid the matter altogether. For
many clashes of interest, the easy way
to get out of the uncomfortable situation is simply to discount its importance
and to give up the conflict as not worth
the bother.

Thus, many voters subject to cross-
pressures tended to belittle the whole

affair. They escaped from any real conflict by losing interest in the election. They had no clear-cut stake in the victory of either candidate. Thus they were relatively indifferent as to who won, and the election became less important to them and less interesting. Those with no cross-pressures showed most interest in the election; even one cross-pressure meant a substantial increase in the proportion of voters who felt less interested in the election. And, as the number of cross-pressures increases, the degree of interest shows a steady decline (Figure 10).

Given that the two factors bear such an inverse relationship to one another, how do they work jointly to affect the time of final decision? Is one more important than the other?

Naturally, the people who made up their minds first were the people who *could* make them up with the least difficulty and who had the most incentive for doing so—i.e., the people with no or one cross-pressure in voting background and with great interest in the election (Figure 11). Fully three-fourths of them knew in May how they would vote in November, while only 7% of them waited until the last weeks of the campaign before settling their vote intention once and for all. At the other extreme were the people subject to two or more cross-pressures and without much interest in the election. Only one-fourth of them made a final decision as early as May and fully one-third waited until the last period of the campaign before finally making up their minds.

But what of the people with one of the factors favorable to an early decision and the other unfavorable, i.e., those with several cross-pressures and great interest and those with no or one cross-pressure and less interest? These middle-of-the-roaders do not differ from

each other in the time at which they made their final decision. In other words, when the two factors—interest and cross-pressures—work in opposing directions, they are about equal in strength. . . .

VIII. The Activation Effect

. . . Here we come to one of the main results of our study. For while people hesitate and meditate and imagine that they decide rationally on the better road to take, it would often have been possible to predict at the outset what they would decide to do in the end. Knowing a few of their personal characteristics, we can tell with fair certainty how they will finally vote: they join the fold to which they belong. What the campaign does is to activate their political predispositions.

Let us first explore the decisions made by those people whom we call the crystalizers, i.e., the respondents who at the first interview in May had not yet made up their minds for whom to vote but who decided later in the campaign. Their political predispositions are known from the IPP—the index established in Chapter III. The study of the people with well-established voting habits revealed that the three factors of SES level, religion and residence proved highly related to vote intention. We recall that if a person was Catholic, lived within the city of Sandusky, and belonged to the lower half of the SES scale, there was a strong likelihood that he would vote Democratic. The opposite of the same three factors identified the people with the strongest Republican predispositions: prosperous Protestant farmers.

Now suppose we apply this index to the crystallizers, who were undecided in May as to how they would vote but later made up their minds. About two-thirds

Figure **10** *As cross-pressures increase, the amount of interest in the election decreases.*

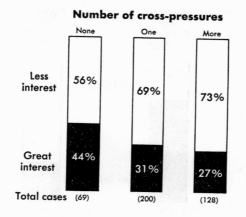

Figure **11** *Both cross-pressures and lack of interest delay the final vote decision. Their joint effect is especially strong. Separately, they show about equal strength.*

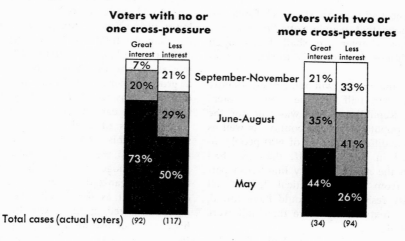

of those with Republican predispositions decided by October to vote Republican, and about three-fourths of those with Democratic predispositions decided for the Democrats (Figure 12). Thus from a simple three-factor index, we can predict with considerable consistency the outcome of deliberations which the deciders themselves cannot foresee. The explanation for this is clear. What the political campaign did, so to speak, was not to form new opinions but to raise old opinions over the thresholds of awareness and decision. Political campaigns are important primarily because they *activate* latent predispositions. . . .

Figure **12** *Predisposition, as measured by the IPP scale, permits us to predict subsequent vote decisions of people who originally are undecided.*

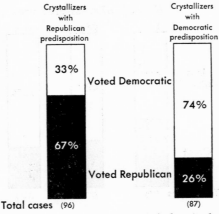

XV. The Political Homogeneity of Social Groups

Repeatedly in this study we found indications that people vote "in groups." In this chapter we shall focus upon the importance of this aspect of voting.

As the reader will remember, slightly more than half of Erie County voters were Republican. This was true for the total population of the county, as well as for the different groups of 600 people included in our study. If, then, we had taken the name of every hundredth person from an alphabetical list of all county residents, we would have found, again, that slightly more than half were Republicans.

But suppose now we had proceeded differently, had picked a score of Republicans at random, and had asked them to name as many friends, neighbors, and fellow workers as they could remember. If we then asked the people assembled on this list for whom they intended to vote, the proportion of Republicans would have been considerably higher than it was for the county

as a whole. And, conversely, if we had started with a score of Democrats and had asked them to name their associates in the different spheres of their lives, we would have found a considerably lower proportion of Republicans on this list than we found in the county.

This represents another formulation of our statement that voting is essentially a group experience. People who work or live or play together are likely to vote for the same candidates.

Two kinds of evidence may be provided for this general statement. On the one hand we can study directly the political homogeneity of such groups as fraternal organizations, churches, sports clubs as well as the family and similar institutionalized groups. On the other hand we can use an indirect approach. People who have certain characteristics in common are more likely to belong to the same groups. We know from general observation, for instance, that people tend to associate with others of their own age rather than with people considerably older or younger than themselves. If we find then that there are marked differences in voting between various age groups, we would have inferential evidence that people who have closer contacts with each other are more apt to vote alike.

SOCIAL STRATIFICATION AND POLITICAL HOMOGENEITY

... Thus, what we have said before can be reformulated in the following fashion: People who have similar ratings according to the index of political predispositions (IPP) are also likely to live in closer contact with each other. And the groups which they form are likely to be rather homogeneous in political outlook and behavior.

This tendency is accentuated during the course of the campaign.... To the extent that the campaign brings about changes in vote intention, then, these changes operate to increase the political homogeneity of social groups....

THE POLITICAL STRUCTURE OF THE FAMILY

The family is a group particularly suited to the purposes of our study, because here living conditions attain a maximum of similarity and because mutual contacts are more frequent than in other groupings....

Among husbands and wives, both of whom had decided to vote, only one pair in 22 disagreed. Among parents and children, one pair in 12 disagreed, the gap of a generation increasing differences in life and outlook. Agreement was least—as all the jokes emphasize —among "in-laws" living in the same household. One pair in five showed disagreement on party alignment.

The almost perfect agreement between husband and wife comes about as a result of male dominance in political situations. At one point of the study we asked each respondent whether he had discussed politics with someone else in recent weeks. Forty-five of the women stated that they had talked the election over with their husbands; but, of an equal number of randomly selected men, only four reported discussions with their wives. If these family discussions play as important a role for husbands as they do for wives, then we should get approximately the same number of reports on the interchange of political ideas from both sexes. But only the wives are aware of the political opinions of their husbands. Men do not feel that they are discussing politics with their wives; they feel they are telling them. And, as we can see from the following quotations, the wives are willing to be told:

> On previous interviews, I hadn't given it any thought, but it is close to election and I guess I will vote Democratic and *go along with my husband.*

> My husband has always been Republican. He says that if we vote for different parties there is no use in our voting. So *I think I will give in this year and vote* Republican....

It appears that not only the color of opinion, but the whole level of interest is contagious from one family member to another. Of the men who had a vote intention and great interest in the election, only 30% claimed that their wives did not intend to vote, or did not know for whom. For men with less interest, the figure is 52%.

If the relationships between father and daughter or between brother and sister are studied, we find a similar dominance of the male in political matters.

In addition, the political homogeneity of the family may extend over several generations. Our panel members were asked, "Do you consider that your family (parents, grandparents) have always been predominantly Democratic or predominantly Republican?" Fully three-fourths of the respondents with vote intentions in September followed the political lead of their families. Here are examples of two *first voters* who took over the family pattern at the very beginning of their voting careers:

> Probably will vote Democratic because *my grandfather will skin me if I don't.*

> If I can register I will vote Republican because *my family are all Republicans so therefore I would have to vote that way.*

These young voters, one a man and the other a woman, provide excellent illustrations of family influence. Neither had much interest in the election and neither paid much attention to the campaign. Both accepted family tradition for their first votes and both are likely to remain in line with that tradition. In the first case, there is even a hint that family sanctions are used to enforce the decision. Thus are party voters born.

Now, what of the exceptional cases in which disagreement does occur within the family? A number of respondents agreed with the young voter just quoted, that political conformity is the price of domestic peace. There was evidence of a good deal of tension in families which could not reach an agreement. . . .

It is reasonable to expect that with such pressure toward homogeneity, people with unhomogeneous family backgrounds will be more uncertain about their own political affiliations. Figure 13 compares the amount of shifting of political position by respondents from families with different degrees of homogeneity in vote intention.

Less than 3% of voters in families homogeneous in August changed their vote intention during the rest of the campaign. But if there were some relatives who were undecided (the second group in Figure 13) almost 10% of the respondents shifted between August and October. And in the small group of families in which there was definite disagreement, 29% of the respondents went

Figure **13**   *The less homogeneous the family is with respect to their votes, the more the members of the family tend to change their minds.*

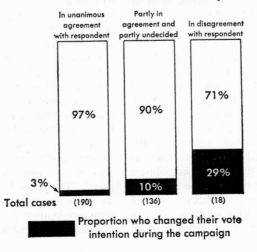

Political attitude of family

In unanimous agreement with respondent — 97% — 3% — Total cases (190)

Partly in agreement and partly undecided — 90% — 10% — (136)

In disagreement with respondent — 71% — 29% — (18)

Proportion who changed their vote intention during the campaign through at least one change in position.

And when the people in families not homogeneous in their vote intentions did change their minds, they changed toward the party favored by the rest of the family. Fully 81% of the members of Republican families who were originally undecided were pro-Republican in October; and 71% of those in Democratic families later came out for Roosevelt. Whatever the reason, whether honest conviction or family loyalty, the family molded their votes—and as a result the family became politically more homogeneous as the campaign wore on. . . .

VOTE DECISION AS A SOCIAL
EXPERIENCE

How may we explain the fact that social groups are politically homogeneous and that the campaign increases this homogeneity still more? There is, first, the fact that people who live together under similar external conditions are likely to develop similar needs and interests. They tend to see the world through the same colored glasses; they tend to apply to common experiences common interpretations. They will approve of a political candidate who has achieved success in their own walk of life; they will approve of programs which are couched in terms taken from their own occupations and adapted to the moral standards of the groups in which they have a common "belonging."

But this is only part of the picture. There may be many group members who are not really aware of the goals of their own group. And there may be many who, even if they were aware of these goals, would not be sufficiently interested in current events to tie the two together consciously. They acquiesce to the political temper of their group under the steady, personal influence of their

more politically active fellow citizens. Here again, we find the process of activation by which the predisposed attitudes of some are brought out by the influence of others. But, in addition, we see here the direct effectiveness of personal contacts. . . .

Dynamic Social Research [4]

Public opinion research is frequently misunderstood at the present time. From poll findings published in magazines and newspapers, laymen, and even colleagues in other social science fields, have gained the impression that such research is content to describe how people feel about a given issue at a particular time. Actually, the scope of this new discipline is much broader. Social scientists want to know the processes by which the various sectors of public opinion influence legislative action and other decision-making in government. Furthermore, we are eager to discover in what ways attitudes themselves are formed. *The People's Choice* focused its attention on this latter problem, the formation, change and development of public opinion. . . .

Now let us consider one phase of this dynamic analysis in order to discover its essential elements. The panel was interviewed for the sixth time during October and for the seventh and final time immediately after the election. Thus we know how these people intended to vote shortly before the election and for whom they actually voted. The results are [shown in Table 1].

[4] Reprinted in part from the preface to the second edition of Paul F. Lazarsfeld, Bernard Berelson, and Hazel Gaudet, *The People's Choice*, New York: Columbia University Press, 1948, pp. ix–xiv, with permission of Columbia University Press.

Table **1**   *Vote Intention in October*

Actual vote	Republican	Democrat	Don't know	Don't expect to vote	Total
Republican	215	7	4	6	232
Democrat	4	144	12	0	160
Didn't vote	10	16	6	59	91
Total persons	*229*	*167*	*22*	*65*	*483*

This simple table has a surprising number of implications. Let us assume for a moment that the interviews in October and November had been conducted with different people, rather than with the same people, as was actually the case. Then, the findings would have read as follows: in October 42 percent (167 out of 396) of those who had a vote intention meant to vote for the Democratic Party; in November 41 percent (160 out of 392) voted for it. This would have given the impression of great constancy in political attitudes. Actually, however, only the people in the major diagonal of the table remained unchanged: 418 out of 483 respondents did what they intended to do; 13 percent changed their minds one way or another.

This 13 percent represents the *turnover* which took place in the few weeks before the election. The concept of turnover is basic for analysis of opinion formation. If the turnover is large, it indicates that the opinion or behavior is unstable. We know that people feel uncertain and that propaganda may be effective, or that clarification and education are required.

If such dynamic research is conducted more frequently in the future, it may be possible to classify social events according to the following dimensions: What types of events show a small or large turnover as they develop? Does the turnover tend to become smaller as the events run their course? At what point is a minimum turnover reached and what is likely to increase it again? Under what conditions do we have a balanced turnover, as in this case, where the changes in various directions seem to cancel each other? When does turnover occur with a shift in "marginal distributions"?

Answers to such questions, however, would give only a rough picture of different social events. We can be more precise. Turnover is the result of changes which come about in the intentions, expectations and behavior of individual persons. Three broad questions can be raised in this connection:

(a) What kind of people are likely to shift?

(b) Under what influences do these shifts come about?

(c) In what directions are the shifts made?

Question (a) can be answered in a variety of ways. Let us concentrate here on the "crystallizers," those people who had no definite vote intention in October but who went to the polls in November. Long before they had reached a decision we could predict rather successfully what they would do: They would decide finally to vote in the same way as did people with similar social characteristics who had made up their minds earlier in the campaign. . . .

Such "external correlations" sometimes evoke expressions of disappointment. Turnover analysis, however, permits us to go "inside the situation." We can pick out a variety of psychological mediators which connect the social situation and the individual decision. In each interview, for example, respondents were asked who, in their opinion, would win the election. Even among those who had not yet formed a vote intention, there were many individuals with a definite expectation. And, significantly enough, the expectations expressed by the undecided were not haphazard ones, but instead were usually those prevailing in their own social environments. Following the process one step further, it turned out that expectations foreshadowed final decision: many people voted for the candidate they had previously picked as the winner. Thus these expectations were one of the "intervening" variables which helped in explaining the development of vote decisions. . . .

The table . . . also suggests answers to questions about the specific influences which produce changes in attitudes or behavior. Again let us focus our attention on one group, those who said in October that they did not intend to vote. It will be noted that the large majority of this group fitted their actions to their words: 59 of the 65 actually did not vote in November. But the six changers, those who shifted from an intention of inaction to an actual vote, all cast their ballots for the Republican candidates. The influences which produced this change were not hard to discover. . . . When the six changers were asked what had made them go to the polls, all stated that they had been visited at the last moment by a Republican party worker who had persuaded them to vote.

Thus, by studying the different groups which contribute to the turnover, we can analyze the influences which operate to bring about changes in behavior. This, in itself, provides a large field for investigation. We can record what people read and listen to, and relate such exposure in a twofold way to changes in mind. Some people were aware that they had been influenced by a specific reading or listening experience, and they told us so in the special interviews conducted with all changers. In other cases, a more intricate statistical analysis was necessary to trace the more unconscious influences. (These techniques have been more elaborately discussed in a recent publication.) . . . [5]

But the picture is not completed by knowledge only of who changes and in response to what influences. We also want to know the directions of the changes: Do they result in a random redistribution of opinion, or is there some discernible pattern? Turnover analysis in the present study provided preliminary, but revealing, answers to this question. For particular subgroups within the community, attitude change led to greater uniformity and *homogeneity:* individual changes brought members of specific subgroups into closer agreement with each other. For the community as a whole, however, attitude change produced greater diversity and *polarization:* individual changes brought the members of one subgroup into sharper disagreement with members of other subgroups. . . . The point to emphasize here is that, through the kind of dynamic research employed in the present study, problems such as the development of group cleavages or increasing awareness of class interests become amenable to social research. . . .

[5] Hans Zeisel, *Say It With Figures* (New York, Harper and Brothers, 1947), Chapter X.

EMILE DURKHEIM
Suicide

... Sociological method as we practice it rests wholly on the basic principle that social facts must be studied as things, that is, as realities external to the individual. There is no principle for which we have received more criticism; but none is more fundamental. Indubitably for sociology to be possible, it must above all have an object all its own. It must take cognizance of a reality which is not in the domain of other sciences. But if no reality exists outside of individual consciousness, it wholly lacks any material of its own.... On the pretext of giving the science a more solid foundation by establishing it upon the psychological constitution of the individual, it is thus robbed of the only object proper to it. *It is not realized that there can be no sociology unless societies exist, and that societies cannot exist if there are only individuals....*

It seems hardly possible to us that there will not emerge, on the contrary, from every page of this book, so to speak, the impression that the individual is dominated by a moral reality greater than himself: namely, collective reality. When each people is seen to have its own suicide-rate, more constant than that of general mortality, that its growth is in accordance with a coefficient of ac-

Reprinted in part with permission of the publisher from Emile Durkheim, *Suicide*, translated by John A. Spaulding and George Simpson, edited by George Simpson, copyright 1951 by The Free Press, a corporation, pp. 37, 38, 39, 44, 46–48, 49, 50–52, 104–06, 145–49, 151–56, 157, 158, 159–60, 171–73, 175–80, 185, 186–89, 208–09.

celeration characteristic of each society; when it appears that the variations through which it passes at different times of the day, month, year, merely reflect the rhythm of social life; and that marriage, divorce, the family, religious society, the army, etc., affect it in accordance with definite laws, some of which may even be numerically expressed—these states and institutions will no longer be regarded simply as characterless, ineffective ideological arrangements. Rather they will be felt to be real, living, active forces which, because of the way they determine the individual, prove their independence of him; which, if the individual enters as an element in the combination whence these forces ensue, at least control him once they are formed. Thus it will appear more clearly why sociology can and must be objective, since it deals with realities as definite and substantial as those of the psychologist or the biologist....[1]

Introduction

I. ... The term *suicide is applied to all cases of death resulting directly or indirectly from a positive or negative act of the victim himself, which he knows will produce this result....*

[1] Nevertheless ... we shall show that this way of looking at it, far from ruling out all liberty, is the only means of reconciling liberty with the determinism revealed by the statistical data.

II. But is the fact thus defined of interest to the sociologist? Since suicide is an individual action affecting the individual only, it must seemingly depend exclusively on individual factors, thus belonging to psychology alone. Is not the suicide's resolve usually explained by his temperament, character, antecedents and private history?

The degree and conditions under which suicides may be legitimately studied in this way need not now be considered, but that they may be viewed in an entirely different light is certain. If, instead of seeing in them only separate occurrences, unrelated and to be separately studied, the suicides committed in a given society during a given period of time are taken as a whole, it appears that this total is not simply a sum of independent units, a collective total, but is itself a new fact *sui generis,* with its own unity, individuality and consequently its own nature—a nature, furthermore, dominantly social. Indeed, provided too long a period is not considered, the statistics for one and the same society are almost invariable.... This is because the environmental circumstances attending the life of peoples remain relatively unchanged from year to year. To be sure, more considerable variations occasionally occur; but they are quite exceptional. They are also clearly always contemporaneous with some passing crisis affecting the social state. Thus, in 1848 there occurred an abrupt decline in all European states.

If a longer period of time is considered, more serious changes are observed. Then, however, they become chronic; they only prove that the structural characteristics of society have simultaneously suffered profound changes. It is interesting to note that they do not take place with the extreme slowness that quite a large number of observers

has attributed to them, but are both abrupt and progressive. After a series of years, during which these figures have varied within very narrow limits, a rise suddenly appears which, after repeated vacillation, is confirmed, grows and is at last fixed. This is because every breach of social equilibrium, though sudden in its appearance, takes time to produce all its consequences. Thus, the evolution of suicide is composed of undulating movements, distinct and successive, which occur spasmodically, develop for a time, and then stop only to begin again.... One of these waves is seen to have occurred almost throughout Europe in the wake of the events of 1848, or about the years 1850–1853, depending on the country; another began in Germany after the war of 1866, in France somewhat earlier, about 1860 at the height of the imperial government, in England about 1868, or after the commercial revolution caused by contemporary commercial treaties. Perhaps the same cause occasioned the new recrudescence observable in France about 1865. Finally, a new forward movement began after the war of 1870 which is still evident and fairly general throughout Europe.

At each moment of its history, therefore, each society has a definite aptitude for suicide. The relative intensity of this aptitude is measured by taking the proportion between the total number of voluntary deaths and the population of every age and sex. We will call this numerical datum *the rate of mortality through suicide, characteristic of the society under consideration.* It is generally calculated in proportion to a million or a hundred thousand inhabitants.

Not only is this rate constant for long periods, but its invariability is even greater than that of leading demographic data. General mortality, especially, varies much more often from year to year and the variations it undergoes are far greater. . . .

To be sure, if we compare not the successive years of a single period but the averages of different periods, the variations observed in the rate of mortality become almost negligible. The changes in one or the other direction occurring from year to year and due to temporary and accidental causes neutralize one another if a more extended unit of time is made the basis of calculation; and thus disappear from the average figures which, because of this elimination, show much more invariability. For example, in France from 1841 to 1870, it was in each successive ten-year period 23.18; 23.72; 22.87. But, first, it is already remarkable that from one year to its successor suicide is at least as stable, if not more so, than general mortality taken only from period to period. The average rate of mortality, furthermore, achieves this regularity only by being general and impersonal, and can afford only a very imperfect description of a given society. It is in fact substantially the same for all peoples of

approximately the same degree of civilization; at least, the differences are very slight. In France, for example, as we have just seen, it oscillates, from 1841 to 1870, around 23 deaths per 1,000 inhabitants; during the same period in Belgium it was successively 23.93, 22.5, 24.04; in England, 22.32, 22.21, 22.68; in Denmark, 22.65 (1845–49), 20.44 (1855–59), 20.4 (1861–68). With the exception of Russia, which is still only geographically European, the only large European countries where the incidence of mortality differs somewhat more widely from the above figures are Italy, where even between 1861 and 1867 it rose to 30.6, and Austria, where it was yet greater (32.52). On the contrary, the suicide-rate, while showing only slight annual changes, varies according to society by doubling, tripling, quadrupling, and even more. (Table 1 below.) Accordingly, to a much higher degree than the death-rate, it is peculiar to each social group where it can be considered as a characteristic index. It is even so closely related to what is most deeply constitutional in each national temperament that the order in which the differ-

Table **1**   *Rate of suicides per million inhabitants in the different European countries*

	Period			Numerical position in the		
	1866–70	1871–75	1874–78	First period	Second period	Third period
Italy	30	35	38	1	1	1
Belgium	66	69	78	2	3	4
England	67	66	69	3	2	2
Norway	76	73	71	4	4	3
Austria	78	94	130	5	7	7
Sweden	85	81	91	6	5	5
Bavaria	90	91	100	7	6	6
France	135	150	160	8	9	9
Prussia	142	134	152	9	8	8
Denmark	277	258	255	10	10	10
Saxony	293	267	334	11	11	11

ent societies appear in this respect remains almost exactly the same at very different periods. This is proved by examining this same table. During the three periods there compared, suicide has everywhere increased, but in this advance the various peoples have retained their respective distances from one another. Each has its own peculiar coefficient of acceleration.

The suicide-rate is therefore a factual order, unified and definite, as is shown by both its permanence and its variability. For this permanence would be inexplicable if it were not the result of a group of distinct characteristics, solidary one with another, and simultaneously effective in spite of different attendant circumstances; and this variability proves the concrete and individual quality of these same characteristics, since they vary with the individual character of society itself. In short, these statistical data express the suicidal tendency with which each society is collectively afflicted. We need not state the actual nature of this tendency, whether it is a state *sui generis* of the collective mind,[2] with its own reality, or represents merely a sum of individual states. Although the preceding considerations are hard to reconcile with the second hypothesis, we reserve this problem for treatment in the course of this work. Whatever one's opinion on this subject, such a tendency certainly exists under one heading or another. Each society is predisposed to contribute a definite quota of voluntary deaths. This predisposition may therefore be the subject of a special study belonging to sociology. This is the study we are going to undertake.

[2] By the use of this expression we of course do not at all intend to hypostasize the collective conscience. We do not recognize any more substantial a soul in society than in the individual. But we shall revert to this point.

We do not accordingly intend to make as nearly complete an inventory as possible of all the conditions affecting the origin of individual suicides, but merely to examine those on which the definite fact that we have called the social suicide-rate depends. The two questions are obviously quite distinct, whatever relation may nevertheless exist between them. Certainly many of the individual conditions are not general enough to affect the relation between the total number of voluntary deaths and the population. They may perhaps cause this or that separate individual to kill himself, but not give society as a whole a greater or lesser tendency to suicide. As they do not depend on a certain state of social organization, they have no social repercussions. Thus they concern the psychologist, not the sociologist. The latter studies the causes capable of affecting not separate individuals but the group. Therefore among the factors of suicide the only ones which concern him are those whose action is felt by society as a whole. The suicide-rate is the product of these factors. This is why we must limit our attention to them. . . .

Book One:
Extra-Social Factors

[Chapters omitted adduce evidence to show that the suicide rate cannot be accounted for by such factors as psychopathic states, race or heredity.]

3. SUICIDE AND COSMIC FACTORS

But if individual predispositions are not by themselves the determining causes of suicide, perhaps they are more active in combination with certain cosmic factors. Just as the material environment at times causes the appearance of diseases which, without it, would remain dormant, it might be capable of activating the general and merely potential natural aptitudes of certain persons for suicide. In that case, the suicide-rate need not be regarded as a social phenomenon; due to the cooperation between certain physical causes and an organic-psychic state, it would spring wholly or chiefly from abnormal psychology. It might, to be sure, be hard to explain how, in such cases, suicide can be so intimately typical in each social group; for the cosmic environment does not greatly differ from country to country. One important fact, however, would have been seized: that at least some of the variations connected with this phenomenon might be accounted for without reference to social causes.

Among such factors an influence on suicide has been attributed to only two: climate and seasonal temperature.

I. Suicides are distributed as follows on the map of Europe, according to the varying degrees of latitude:

Degree of latitude	Suicides per million inhabitants
36th–43rd	21.1
43rd–50th	93.3
50th–55th	172.5
Beyond 55th	88.1

Suicide is therefore at a minimum in the South and North of Europe; it is most developed in the Center. More exactly, Morselli has stated that the space between the 47th and 57th degrees of latitude, on the one hand, and the 20th and 40th of longitude on the other, was the area most favorable to suicide. This zone coincides approximately with the most temperate region of Europe. Is this coincidence to be regarded as an effect of climatic influences?

Morselli advanced this thesis, though somewhat hesitantly. Indeed, the relation is not readily discernible between temperate climate and the tendency to sui-

cide; to require such an hypothesis the facts must be in unusual agreement. Now, far from there being a relation between suicide and a given climate, we know suicide to have flourished in all climates. Italy is today relatively exempt; but it was very frequent there at the time of the Empire when Rome was the capital of civilized Europe. It has also been highly developed at certain epochs under the burning sun of India.

The very shape of this zone shows that climate is not the cause of the numerous suicides committed there. The area formed by it on the map is not a single, fairly equal and homogeneous strip, including all the countries having the same climate, but two distinct areas: one having Ile-de-France and neighboring departments as a center, the other Saxony and Prussia. They therefore coincide with the two principal centers of European civilization, not with a clearly defined climatic region. We must therefore seek the cause of the unequal inclination of peoples for suicide, not in the mysterious effects of climate but in the nature of this civilization, in the manner of its distribution among the different countries.

Another fact, already mentioned by Guerry, and confirmed through new observations by Morselli, which is fairly general though not without exceptions, may be similarly explained. In the countries outside the central zone, their regions closest to it, whether North or South, are those most stricken with suicide. Thus, it is most developed in Italy in the North, while in England and Belgium it is more so in the South. But there is no reason to ascribe these facts to the proximity to the temperate climate. Is it not more probable that the ideas and sentiments, in short, the social currents so strongly influencing the inhabitants of Northern France and of Northern Germany to suicide, reappear in the neighboring countries of a somewhat similar way of life, but with less intensity? Another fact shows the great influence of social causes upon this distribution of suicide. Until 1870 the northern provinces of Italy showed most suicides, then the center and thirdly the south. But the difference between North and Center has gradually diminished and their respective ranks have been finally reversed (See Table 2). Yet the climate of the different regions has remained the same. The change consists in the movement of the Italian capital to the center of the country as a result of the conquest of Rome in 1870. Scientific, artistic and economic activity shifted in the same manner. Suicides followed along.

One need dwell no further on an hypothesis proved by nothing and disproved by so many facts. . . .

[Omitted passages present evidence that the suicide rate depends not on seasonal temperature, but on the level of social activity.]

Book Two:
Social Causes and Social Types

1. HOW TO DETERMINE SOCIAL
   CAUSES AND SOCIAL TYPES

The results of the preceding book are not wholly negative. We have in fact shown that for each social group there is a specific tendency to suicide ex-

plained neither by the organic-psychic constitution of individuals nor the nature of the physical environment. Consequently, by elimination, it must necessarily depend upon social causes and be in itself a collective phenomenon; some of the facts examined, especially the geographic and seasonal variations of suicide, had definitely led us to this conclusion. We must now study this tendency more closely.

I. To accomplish this it would seem to be best to inquire first whether the tendency is single and indestructible or whether it does not rather consist of several different tendencies, which may be isolated by analysis and which should be separately studied. If so, we should proceed as follows. As the tendency, single or not, is observable only in its individual manifestations, we should have to begin with the latter. Thus we should observe and describe as many as possible, of course omitting those due to mental alienation. If all were found to have the same essential characteristics, they should be grouped in a single class; otherwise, which is much more likely—for they are too different not to include several varieties—a certain number of species should be determined according to their resemblances and differences. One would admit as many suicidal currents as there were distinct types, then seek to determine their causes and respective importance. . . .

Unfortunately, no classification of the suicides of sane persons can be made in

Table 2   Regional distribution of suicide in Italy

	Suicides per million inhabitants			Ratio of each region expressed in terms of the North represented by 100		
	1866–67	1864–76	1884–86	1866–67	1864–76	1884–86
North	33.8	43.6	63	100	100	100
Center	25.6	40.8	88	75	93	139
South	8.3	16.5	21	24	37	33

terms of their morphological types or characteristics, from almost complete lack of the necessary data. To be attempted, it would require good descriptions of many individual cases. One would have to know the psychological condition of the suicide at the moment of forming his resolve, how he prepared to accomplish it, how he finally performed it, whether he were agitated or depressed, calm or exalted, anxious or irritated, etc. Now we have such data practically only for some cases of insane suicide, and just such observations and descriptions by alienists have enabled us to establish the chief types of suicide where insanity is the determining cause. We have almost no such information for others. Brierre de Boismont alone has tried to do this descriptive work for 1,328 cases where the suicide left letters or other records summarized by the author in his book. But, first, this summary is much too brief. Then, the patient's revelations of his condition are usually insufficient, if not suspect. He is only too apt to be mistaken concerning himself and the state of his feelings; he may believe that he is acting calmly, though at the peak of nervous excitement. Finally, besides being insufficiently objective, these observations cover too few facts to permit definite conclusions. Some very vague dividing lines are perceptible and their suggestions may be utilized; but they are too indefinite to provide a regular classification. Furthermore, in view of the manner of execution of most suicides, proper observations are next to impossible.

But our aim may be achieved by another method. Let us reverse the order of study. Only in so far as the effective causes differ can there be different types of suicide. For each to have its own nature, it must also have special conditions of existence. The same antecedent or group of antecedents cannot some-

times produce one result and sometimes another, for, if so, the difference of the second from the first would itself be without cause, which would contradict the principle of causality. Every proved specific difference between causes therefore implies a similar difference between effects. Consequently, we shall be able to determine the social types of suicide by classifying them not directly by their preliminarily described characteristics, but by the causes which produce them. Without asking why they differ from one another, we will first seek the social conditions responsible for them; then group these conditions in a number of separate classes by their resemblances and differences, and we shall be sure that a specific type of suicide will correspond to each of these classes. In a word, instead of being morphological, our classification will from the start be aetiological. Nor is this a sign of inferiority, for the nature of a phenomenon is much more profoundly got at by knowing its cause than by knowing its characteristics only, even the essential ones. . . .

In all respects this reverse method is the only fitting one for the special problem that we have set ourselves. Indeed we must not forget that what we are studying is the social suicide-rate. The only types of interest to us, accordingly, are those contributing to its formation and influencing its variation. Now, it is not sure that all individual sorts of voluntary death have this quality. Some, though general to a certain degree, are not bound or not sufficiently bound to the moral temper of society to enter as a characteristic element into the special physiognomy of each people with respect to suicide. . . . No description, however good, of particular cases will ever tell us which ones have a sociological character. If one wants to know the several tributaries of suicide as a collective phenomenon one must regard it in its collective form, that is, through statistical data, from the start. The social rate must be taken directly as the object of analysis; progress must be from the whole to the parts. Clearly, it can only be analyzed with reference to its different causes, for in themselves the units composing it are homogeneous, without qualitative difference. We must then immediately discover its causes and later consider their repercussions among individuals.

II. But how reach these causes?

The legal establishments of fact always accompanying suicide include the motive (family trouble, physical or other pain, remorse, drunkenness, etc.), which seems to have been the determining cause, and in the statistical reports of almost all countries is found a special table containing the results of these inquiries under the title: *presumptive motives of suicides.* . . .

But as Wagner long ago remarked, what are called statistics of the motives of suicides are actually statistics of the opinions concerning such motives of officials, often of lower officials, in charge of this information service. Unfortunately, official establishments of fact are known to be often defective even when applied to obvious material facts comprehensible to any conscientious observer and leaving no room for evaluation. How suspect must they be considered when applied not simply to recording an accomplished fact but to its interpretation and explanation! To determine the cause of a phenomenon is always a difficult problem. The scholar requires all sorts of observations and experiments to solve even one question. Now, human volition is the most complex of all phenomena. The value of improvised judgments, attempting to assign a definite

origin for each special case from a few hastily collected bits of information is, therefore, obviously slight. As soon as some of the facts commonly supposed to lead to despair are thought to have been discovered in the victim's past, further search is considered useless, and his drunkenness or domestic unhappiness or business troubles are blamed, depending on whether he is supposed recently to have lost money, had home troubles or indulged a taste for liquor. Such uncertain data cannot be considered a basis of explanation for suicide.

Morover, even if more credible, such data could not be very useful, for the motives thus attributed to the suicides, whether rightly or wrongly, are not their true causes. The proof is that the proportional numbers of cases assigned by statistics to each of these presumed causes remain almost identically the same, whereas the absolute figures, on the contrary, show the greatest variations. In France, from 1856 to 1878, suicide rises about 40 per cent, and more than 100 per cent in Saxony in the period 1854–1880 (1,171 cases in place of 547). Now, in both countries each category of motives retains the same respective importance from one period to another. . . .

We therefore do not regret that certain countries like England and Austria are abandoning the collection of such supposed causes of suicide. Statistical efforts should take quite a different direction. Instead of trying to solve these insoluble problems of moral casuistry, they should notice more carefully the social concomitants of suicide. For our own part, at least, we make it a rule not to employ in our studies such uncertain and uninstructive data; no law of any interest has in fact ever been drawn from them by students of suicide. We shall thus refer to them only rarely, when they seem to have special meaning and to offer special assurance. We shall try to determine the productive causes of suicide directly, without concerning ourselves with the forms they can assume in particular individuals. Disregarding the individual as such, his motives and his ideas, we shall seek directly the states of the various social environments (religious confessions, family, political society, occupational groups, etc.), in terms of which the variations of suicide occur. Only then returning to the individual, shall we study how these general causes become individualized so as to produce the homicidal results involved.

[Three social types of suicide are formulated by Durkheim: egoistic, altruistic, anomic. The following passages deal with only the first of these types.]

2. EGOISTIC SUICIDE

First let us see how the different religious confessions affect suicide.

I. If one casts a glance at the map of European suicide, it is at once clear that in purely Catholic countries like Spain, Portugal, Italy, suicide is very little developed, while it is at its maximum in Protestant countries, in Prussia, Saxony, Denmark. The following averages compiled by Morselli confirm this first conclusion:

	Average of suicides per million inhabitants
Protestant states	190
Mixed states (Protestant and Catholic)	96
Catholic states	58
Greek Catholic states	40

The low proportion of the Greek Catholics cannot be surely attributed to religion; for as their civilization is very different from that of the other European nations, this difference of culture may be the cause of their lesser aptitude. But this is not the case with most Catholic or Protestant societies. To be sure, they are not all on the same intellectual and moral level; yet the resemblances are sufficiently essential to make it possible to ascribe to confessional differences the marked contrast they offer in respect to suicide.

Nevertheless, this first comparison is still too summary. In spite of undeniable similarities, the social environments of the inhabitants of these different countries are not identical. The civilizations of Spain and Portugal are far below that of Germany and this inferiority may conceivably be the reason for the lesser development of suicide which we have just mentioned. If one wishes to avoid this source of error and determine more definitely the influence of Catholicism and Protestantism on the suicidal tendency, the two religions must be compared in the heart of a single society.

Of all the great states of Germany, Bavaria has by far the fewest suicides. There have been barely 90 per million inhabitants yearly since 1874, while Prussia has 133 (1871–75), the duchy of Baden 156, Wurttemberg 162, Saxony 300. Now, Bavaria also has most Catholics, 713.2 to 1,000 inhabitants. On the other hand, if one compares the different provinces of Bavaria, suicides are found to be in direct proportion to the number of Protestants and in inverse proportion to that of Catholics (see Table 3). Not only the proportions of averages to one another confirm the law but all the numbers of the first column are higher than those of the second and those of the second higher than those of the third without exception.

It is the same with Prussia (see Table 4).

Table 3   Bavarian provinces (1867–75) [a]

Provinces with Catholic minority (less than 50%)	Suicides per million inhabitants	Provinces with Catholic majority (50 to 90%)	Suicides per million inhabitants	Provinces with more than 90% Catholic	Suicides per million inhabitants
Rhenish Palatinate	167	Lower Franconia	157	Upper Palatinate	64
Central Franconia	207	Swabia	118	Upper Bavaria	114
Upper Franconia	204			Lower Bavaria	19
Average	*192*	*Average*	*135*	*Average*	*75*

[a] The population below 15 years has been omitted.

Table 4   Prussian provinces (1883–90)

Provinces with more than 90% Protestant	Suicides per million inhabitants	Provinces with from 89 to 68% Protestant	Suicides per million inhabitants
Saxony	309.4	Hanover	212.3
Schleswig	312.9	Hesse	200.3
Pomerania	171.5	Brandenburg and Berlin	296.3
		East Prussia	171.3
Average	*264.6*	*Average*	*220.0*

Provinces with from 40 to 50% Protestant	Suicides per million inhabitants	Provinces with from 32 to 28% Protestant	Suicides per million inhabitants
West Prussia	123.9	Posen	96.4
Silesia	260.2	Rhineland	100.3
Westphalia	107.5	Hohenzollern	90.1
Average	*163.6*	*Average*	*95.6*

There are only two slight irregularities among the 14 provinces thus compared, so far as detail is concerned; Silesia, which because of its relatively high number of suicides should be in the second category, is only in the third, while on the contrary Pomerania would be more in its place in the second than in the first column. . . .

Besides, in a fairly large number of cases the number of suicides per million inhabitants of the population of each confession has been directly determined. The following figures were obtained by various observers:

Thus, everywhere without exception, Protestants show far more suicides than the followers of other confessions. The

Table 5   Suicides in different countries per million persons of each confession

		Protestants	Catholics	Jews	Names of observers
Austria	(1852–59)	79.5	51.3	20.7	Wagner
Prussia	(1849–55)	159.9	49.6	46.4	Wagner
Prussia	(1869–72)	187	69	96	Morselli
Prussia	(1890)	240	100	180	Prinzing
Baden	(1852–62)	139	117	87	Legoyt
Baden	(1870–74)	171	136.7	124	Morselli
Baden	(1878–88)	242	170	210	Prinzing
Bavaria	(1844–56)	135.4	49.1	105.9	Morselli
Bavaria	(1884–91)	224	94	193	Prinzing
Wurttemberg	(1846–60)	113.5	77.9	65.6	Wagner
Wurttemberg	(1873–76)	190	120	60	Durkheim
Wurttemberg	(1881–90)	170	119	142	Durkheim

difference varies between a minimum of 20 to 30 per cent and a maximum of 300 per cent. . . .

The aptitude of Jews for suicide is always less than that of Protestants; in a very general way it is also, though to a lesser degree, lower than that of Catholics. Occasionally however, the latter relation is reversed; such cases occur especially in recent times. Up to the middle of the century, Jews killed themselves less frequently than Catholics in all countries but Bavaria; [3] only towards 1870 do they begin to lose their ancient immunity. They still very rarely greatly exceed the rate for Catholics. Besides, it must be remembered that Jews live more exclusively than other confessional groups in cities and are in intellectual occupations. On this account they are more inclined to suicide than the members of other confessions, for reasons other than their religion. If therefore the rate for Judaism is so low, in spite of this aggravating circumstance, it may be assumed

[3] Bavaria is still the only exception: Jews there kill themselves twice as often as Catholics. Is there something exceptional about the position of Judaism in this country? We do not know.

that other things being equal, their religion has the fewest suicides of all.

These facts established, what is their explanation?

II. . . . We shall find these . . . causes in the nature of these two religious systems [Catholicism and Protestantism]. Yet they both prohibit suicide with equal emphasis; not only do they penalize it morally with great severity, but both teach that a new life begins beyond the tomb where men are punished for their evil actions, and Protestantism just as well as Catholicism numbers suicide among them. Finally, in both cults these prohibitions are of divine origin; they are represented not as the logical conclusion of correct reason, but God Himself is their authority. Therefore, if Protestantism is less unfavorable to the development of suicide, it is not because of a different attitude from that of Catholicism. Thus, if both religions have the same precepts with respect to this particular matter, their dissimilar influence on suicide must proceed from one of the more general characteristics differentiating them.

The only essential difference between Catholicism and Protestantism is that the second permits free inquiry to a far greater degree than the first. . . .

We thus reach our first conclusion, that the proclivity of Protestantism for suicide must relate to the spirit of free inquiry that animates this religion. . . .

If it is correct to say that free inquiry once proclaimed, multiplies schisms, it must be added that it presupposes them and derives from them, for it is claimed and instituted as a principle only in order to permit latent or half-declared schisms to develop more freely. So if Protestantism concedes a greater freedom to individual thought than Catholicism, it is because it has fewer common beliefs and practices. Now, a religious society cannot exist without a collective *credo* and the more extensive the *credo* the more unified and strong is the society. For it does not unite men by an exchange and reciprocity of services, a temporal bond of union which permits and even presupposes differences, but which a religious society cannot form. It socializes men only by attaching them completely to an identical body of doctrine and socializes them in proportion as this body of doctrine is extensive and firm. The more numerous the manners of action and thought of a religious character are, which are accordingly removed from free inquiry, the more the idea of God presents itself in all details of existence, and makes individual wills converge to one identical goal. Inversely, the greater concessions a confessional group makes to individual judgment, the less it dominates lives, the less its cohesion and vitality. We thus reach the conclusion that the superiority of Protestantism with respect to suicide results from its being a less strongly integrated church than the Catholic church.

This also explains the situation of Judaism. Indeed, the reproach to which the Jews have for so long been exposed by Christianity has created feelings of unusual solidarity among them. Their need of resisting a general hostility, the very impossibility of free communication with the rest of the population, has forced them to strict union among themselves. Consequently, each community became a small, compact and coherent society with a strong feeling of self-consciousness and unity. Everyone thought and lived alike; individual divergences were made almost impossible by the community of existence and the close and constant surveillance of all over each. The Jewish church has thus been more strongly united than any other, from its dependence on itself because of being the object of intolerance. By analogy with what has just been observed apropos of Protestantism, the same cause must therefore be assumed for the slight tendency of the Jews to suicide in spite of all sorts of circumstances which might on the contrary incline them to it. Doubtless they owe this immunity in a sense to the hostility surrounding them. But if this is its influence, it is not because it imposes a higher morality but because it obliges them to live in greater union. They are immune to this degree because their religious society is of such solidarity. Besides, the ostracism to which they are subject is only one of the causes producing this result; the very nature of Jewish beliefs must contribute largely to it. Judaism, in fact, like all early religions, consists basically of a body of practices minutely governing all the details of life and leaving little free room to individual judgment. . . .

3. EGOISTIC SUICIDE (*Continued*)

But if religion preserves men from suicide only because and in so far as it is a society, other societies probably have the same effect. From this point of view let us consider the family and political society.

I. If one consults only the absolute figures, unmarried persons seem to commit suicide less than married ones. Thus in France, during the period 1873–78, there were 16,264 suicides of married persons while unmarried persons had only 11,709. The former number is to the second as 132 to 100.[4] As the same proportion appears at other periods and in other countries, certain authors had once taught that marriage and family life multiply the chances of suicide. Certainly, if in accordance with current opinion one regards suicide primarily as an act of despair caused by the difficulties of existence, this opinion has all the appearance of probability. An unmarried person has in fact an easier life than a married one. Does not marriage entail all sorts of burdens and responsibilities? To assure the present and future of a family, are not more privations and sufferings required than to meet the needs of a single person? Nevertheless, clear as it seems, this a priori reasoning is quite false and the facts only seem to support it because of being poorly analyzed. The elder Bertillon first established this by an ingenious calculation which we shall reproduce.

Really to appreciate the figures given above, we must remember that a very large number of unmarried persons are less than 16 years old, while all married persons are older. Up to 16 years the tendency to suicide is very slight, due to age, without considering other factors. In France only one or two suicides per million inhabitants are found at this time of life; at the following period there are twenty times as many. The inclusion of many children below 16 among unmarried persons thus unduly reduces the average aptitude of the latter, since the

4 Durkheim's figure of 132 appears to be a misprint. The figure works out to 139. —G.S.

reduction is due to age, not celibacy. If they seem to contribute fewer suicides, it is not because they are unmarried but because many of them are yet immature. So, if one tries to compare the two populations to determine the influence of marital status and that alone, one must rid oneself of this disturbing element and compare with married persons only the unmarried above 16. When this subtraction is made, it appears that between 1863–68 there were on the average 173 suicides in a million unmarried persons above 16 years and 154.5 for a million married persons. The ratio of the first to the second number is that of 112 to 100.

There is thus a certain accretion due to celibacy. But it is much greater than the preceding figures show. Actually, we have assumed that all unmarried persons above 16 years and all married persons were of the same average age. This is not true. The majority of unmarried men in France, exactly 58 per cent, are between 15 and 20 years; the majority of unmarried women, exactly 57 per cent are less than 25 years. The average age of all unmarried men is 26.8, of all unmarried women 28.4. The average age of married persons, on the contrary, is between 40 and 45 years. For both sexes combined, suicide develops according to age as follows:

Years	Suicides per million inhabitants
16 to 21	45.9
21 to 30	97.9
31 to 40	114.5
41 to 50	164.4

These figures refer to the years 1848–57. If age were the only influence, the aptitude of unmarried persons for suicide could not be above 97.9 and that of married persons would be between 114.5 and 164.4, or about 140 suicides per million inhabitants. Suicides of married persons would be to those of unmarried as 100 to 69. The latter would be only two-thirds of the former whereas we know that they are actually more numerous. The effect of family life is thus to reverse the relation. Whereas without the effect of family life married persons should kill themselves half again as often as unmarried by virtue of their age, they do so perceptibly less. Thus marriage may be said to reduce the danger of suicide by about half or, more exactly, non-marriage produces an increase expressed by the proportion 112/69, or 1.6. Thus, if we represent the suicidal tendency of married persons by unity, that of unmarried persons of the same average age must be estimated as 1.6. . . .

[But] when only averages are compared, the facts and their relations to one another appear only approximately. Thus it may very well be true that married persons kill themselves in general less often than unmarried persons, and that nevertheless this proportion may be exceptionally reversed at certain ages; in fact we shall see that this is so. Now these exceptions, possibly instructive for the explanation of the phenomenon, could not be shown by the preceding method. There may also be changes from age to age, which without achieving complete inversion, have nevertheless an importance of their own and which should therefore be shown.

The only way to avoid these difficulties is to determine the rate of each group separately, at each age. Under such conditions one may, for example, compare unmarried persons of from 25 to 30 years with married and widowed persons of the same age and similarly for other periods; the influence of marital status will thus be isolated from all the other influences and all its possible variations will appear. . . . Unfortunately, official publications do not contain the necessary data for this comparison. Actually, they show the age of suicides independently of their marital status. The only publication which to our knowledge has followed a different practice is that of the grand duchy of Oldenburg (including the principalities of Lübeck and Birkenfeld). For the years 1871–85 this publication gives us the distribution of suicides by age for each category of marital status considered separately. But this little State had only 1,369 suicides during these fifteen years. As nothing certain can be concluded from so few cases, we undertook to do the work ourselves for France with the aid of unpublished documents in the possession of the Ministry of Justice. We studied the years 1889, 1890 and 1891. We classified about 25,000 suicides in this way. Not only is such a figure sufficiently important in itself to serve as a basis for induction, but we assured ourselves that there was no need to extend our observations over a longer period. From one year to another the contingent of each age remains approximately the same in each group. There is therefore no need to fix the averages for a greater number of years.

Tables 6 and 7 contain these different figures. To make their meaning clearer we have placed for each age, beside the figure expressing the rate for widowed persons and that for married persons, what we call the *coefficient of preservation,* either of the latter by comparison with the former or of both by comparison with unmarried persons. By this phrase we mean the number showing how many times less frequent suicide is in one group than in another at the same age. Thus, when we say that the coefficient of preservation of husbands of the age of 25 in relation to unmarried men is 3, we mean that if the tendency to suicide of married persons at this time of life is represented by 1, that of unmarried persons during the same period must be represented by 3. Of course, when the coefficient of preservation sinks below unity, it really becomes a coefficient of aggravation.

The laws derived from these tables may be formulated thus:

1. *Too early marriages have an aggravating influence on suicide, especially as regards men.* This result, to be sure, being calculated from a very small number of cases, should be confirmed; in France, from 15 to 20 years, in the average year barely one suicide is committed among married persons, exactly 1.33. However, as the fact is likewise observed in the grand duchy of Oldenburg,

and even for women, it is probably not accidental. Even the Swedish statistics ... show the same aggravation, at least for the male sex. If, now, for the reasons mentioned, we believe these statistics inexact for the advanced ages, we have no reason to doubt them for the first periods of life, when there are as yet no widowed persons. Besides, the mortality of very young husbands and wives is known to considerably exceed that of unmarried men and women of the same age. A thousand unmarried men between 15 and 20 give 8.9 deaths each year, a thousand married men of the same age, 51 deaths or 473 per cent more. The difference is less for the other sex, 9.9 deaths for wives, 8.3 for unmarried women; the former number is to the second only as 119 to 100. This greater

Table **6**   *Grand duchy of Oldenburg: suicides committed, by each sex, per 10,000 inhabitants of each age and marital status group throughout the period 1871–85* [a]

| | | | | Coefficients of preservation of | | |
| | | | | MARRIED | | WIDOWED |
Age	*Unmarried*	*Married*	*Widowed*	*with reference to unmarried*	*with reference to widowed*	*with reference to unmarried*
MEN						
From 0 to 20	7.2	769.2		0.09		
20 to 30	70.6	49.0	285.7	1.40	5.8	0.24
30 to 40	130.4	73.6	76.9	1.77	1.04	1.69
40 to 50	188.8	95.0	285.7	1.97	3.01	0.66
50 to 60	263.6	137.8	271.4	1.90	1.90	0.97
60 to 70	242.8	148.3	304.7	1.63	2.05	0.79
Above 70	266.6	114.2	259.0	2.30	2.26	1.02
WOMEN						
From 0 to 20	3.9	95.2		0.04		
20 to 30	39.0	17.4		2.24		
30 to 40	32.3	16.8	30.0	1.92	1.78	1.07
40 to 50	52.9	18.6	68.1	2.85	3.66	0.77
50 to 60	66.6	31.1	50.0	2.14	1.60	1.33
60 to 70	62.5	37.2	55.8	1.68	1.50	1.12
Above 70		120	91.4		1.31	

[a] These figures therefore refer not to the average year but to the total of suicides committed during these fifteen years.

mortality of young married persons is evidently due to social reasons, for if its principal cause were the immaturity of the organism this would be more marked in the female sex, due to the dangers involved in parturition. Thus everything tends to prove that premature marriages bring about a harmful moral state, especially to men.

2. *From 20 years, married persons of both sexes enjoy a coefficient of preservation in comparison with unmarried persons....*

This coefficient changes with age. It soon reaches a maximum between 25 and 30 years in France, between 30 and 40 in Oldenburg; from then on it decreases till the final period of life when a slight rise sometimes occurs.

3. *The coefficient of preservation of married persons by comparison with unmarried persons varies with the sexes.* In France it is men who are in the favorable position and the difference between the sexes is considerable; for married men the average is 2.73 while for married women it is only 1.56, or 43 per cent less. But in Oldenburg the opposite is true; the average for women is 2.16 and for men only 1.83. It is to be noted that at the same time the disproportion is less; the second number is only 16 per cent lower than the first. We shall say therefore that *the sex enjoying the higher coefficient of preservation in the state of marriage varies from society to society and that the extent of the difference between the rates of the sexes itself varies to the extent that the coefficient of preservation favors the favored*

Table **7** *France (1889–91): suicides committed per 1,000,000 inhabitants of each age and marital status group, average year*

				Coefficients of preservation of		
				MARRIED		WIDOWED
Age	*Unmarried*	*Married*	*Widowed*	*with reference to unmarried*	*with reference to widowed*	*with reference to unmarried*
MEN						
15 to 20	113	500		0.22		
20 to 25	237	97	142	2.40	1.45	1.66
25 to 30	394	122	412	3.20	3.37	0.95
30 to 40	627	226	560	2.77	2.47	1.12
40 to 50	975	340	721	2.86	2.12	1.35
50 to 60	1,434	520	979	2.75	1.88	1.46
60 to 70	1,768	635	1,166	2.78	1.83	1.51
70 to 80	1,983	704	1,288	2.81	1.82	1.54
Above 80	1,571	770	1,154	2.04	1.49	1.36
WOMEN						
15 to 20	79.4	33	333	2.39	10	0.23
20 to 25	106	53	66	2.00	1.05	1.60
25 to 30	151	68	178	2.22	2.61	0.84
30 to 40	126	82	205	1.53	2.50	0.61
40 to 50	171	106	168	1.61	1.58	1.01
50 to 60	204	151	199	1.35	1.31	1.02
60 to 70	189	158	257	1.19	1.62	0.77
70 to 80	206	209	248	0.98	1.18	0.83
Above 80	176	110	240	1.60	2.18	0.79

sex. In the course of our work we shall encounter facts confirming this law.

4. *Widowhood diminishes the coefficient of married persons of each sex, but it rarely eliminates it entirely.* Widowed persons kill themselves more often than married persons but generally less than unmarried persons. Their coefficient in certain cases even rises to 1.60 and 1.66. Like that of married persons it changes with age, but following an irregular evolution the law of which cannot be determined.

Just as for married persons, *the coefficient of preservation of widowed persons compared with unmarried persons varies with the sex.* In France men are in the favored position; their average coefficient is 1.32 while for widows it falls below unity, 0.84, or 37 per cent less. But in Oldenburg women are favored, as in marriage; they have an average coefficient of 1.07, while that of widowers is below unity, 0.89, or 17 per cent less. As in the state of marriage, when it is women who are most favored, the difference between the sexes is less than where men have the advantage. So we may say in the same terms that *the sex enjoying the higher coefficient of preservation in the state of widowhood varies from society to society, and that the extent of the difference between the rates of the sexes, itself varies to the extent that the coefficient of preservation favors the favored sex.*

Facts being thus determined, let us seek explanations. . . .

Interesting as this result is, it must be further defined; for the family environment consists of different elements. For husband and wife alike the family includes: 1. the wife or husband; 2. the children. Is the salutary effect of the family on the suicidal tendency due to the former or the latter? In other words, the family consists of two different associations: the conjugal groups and the family group proper. These two societies have not the same origin, nor the same nature, nor consequently, in all probability, the same effects. One springs from a contract and elective affinity, the other from a natural phenomenon, consanguinity; the former unites two members of the same generation, the latter unites one generation to the next; the latter is as old as humanity, the former was organized at a relatively late date. Since they are here so different it is not *a priori* certain that both combine equally to produce the fact we are studying. Anyway, if both contribute to it this cannot be in the same manner, nor probably in the same measure. Thus, we must investigate whether both take part and, if so, the share of each. . . .

We have a . . . way of measuring exactly the real influence of conjugal association upon suicide; that of observing it when reduced to its own isolated strength, or in families without children.

During the years 1887–91, a million husbands without children accounted annually for 644 suicides. To know how much the marriage status, alone and without reference to the family, insures against suicide, one has only to compare this figure with that of the unmarried men of the same average age. This comparison Table 7 permits us to make, as not the least important of its information. The average age of married men was then as now 46 years, 8 and $\frac{1}{3}$ months. A million unmarried men of this age have about 975 suicides. Now 644 is to 975 as 100 is to 150, that is, sterile husbands have a coefficient of preservation of only 1.5; they commit suicide only a third less often than unmarried of the same age. Quite otherwise when there are children. A million husbands with children annually show during this period only 336 suicides. This number is to 975 as 100 to 290; that is, when the marriage produces children the coefficient of preservation is almost doubled (2.90 instead of 1.5).

Conjugal society therefore plays only a slight role in the immunity of married men. We have in the preceding calculation even made this role somewhat larger than it really is. We have assumed that childless husbands have the same average age as husbands in general, whereas they are certainly younger. For among their ranks are all the youngest husbands, who are without children not because they are hopelessly sterile, but because they have married too recently to have any. On the average, a man has his first child not before 34 years of age, and yet he marries at about 28 or 29 years of age. The part of the married population from 28 to 34 years of age is thus almost entirely in the category of the childless, which lowers the average age of these latter; therefore we must certainly have exaggerated in estimating it at 46. But in that case the unmarried men with whom they should have been compared are not those of 46 but younger, who consequently commit suicide less often than the others. So the coefficient of 1.5 must be a little too high; if we knew exactly the average age of childless husbands, their aptitude for suicide would surely approach that of unmarried men still more than the above figures indicate.

The limited influence of marriage is well shown, moreover, in that widowers with children are in a better situation than husbands without them. The former indeed, show 937 suicides per million. Now they are 61 years, 8 and ⅓ months on the average. The rate of unmarried

men of the same age (see Table 7) is between 1,434 and 1,768, or about 1,504. This number is to 937 as 160 to 100. Widowers, when they have children, thus have a coefficient of preservation of at least 1.6, superior to that of childless husbands. Moreover, we have under- rather than overestimated this figure. For widowers with children are certainly older than widowers in general. The latter indeed include all whose marriage was without issue only because of premature end by death, that is, the youngest. Widowers with children should therefore really be compared with unmarried men above 62 years (who, because of their age, have a stronger tendency to suicide). This comparison would clearly only emphasize their immunity.

To be sure, this coefficient of 1.6 is definitely below that of husbands with children, 2.9; the difference is not quite 45 per cent. Thus, matrimonial society by itself might be thought to have more effect than we have granted it, since at its conclusion the immunity of the husband surviving is so far reduced. But this loss is only in slight degree to be ascribed to the dissolution of marriage. Proof of this is that where there are no children widowhood produces far lesser effects. A million childless widowers show 1,258 suicides, a number related to 1,504, the contingent of sixty-two-year-old unmarried men, as 100 to 119. Thus the coefficient of preservation is still about 1.2 which is little below that of husbands also childless, 1.5. The former of these figures is only 20 per cent less than the second. Accordingly, when a wife's death has no other effect than to break the conjugal bond, it has no strong repercussion on the suicidal tendency of the widower. Marriage during its existence must therefore only slightly aid in restraining this tendency, since the latter shows no greater increase with the end of marriage.

The reason why widowhood is relatively more disastrous when the union has been fruitful must be sought in the existence of the children.[5] Of course in a way the children attach the widower to life, but at the same time they make the crisis through which he is passing more intense. For not only is the conjugal relation destroyed; but precisely because a domestic society here exists, there is an impairment of its functioning too. A essential element is lacking and the whole machine is thrown out of gear. To reestablish the lost equilibrium the husband has to shoulder a double burden and perform functions for which he is unprepared. Thus he loses advantages which were his throughout the duration of the marriage. It is not because his marriage is ended but because the family which he heads is disorganized. The departure, not of the wife but of the mother, causes the disaster.

But the slight effect of marriage appears with special clarity in the woman's case when it does not find its natural fulfillment in children. A million childless wives show 221 suicides; a million unmarried women of the same age (between 42 and 43 years) only 150. The first of these numbers is to the second as 100 is to 67; the coefficient of preservation thus falls below unity and equals .67, that is, it has really become a coefficient of aggravation. *In France, then, married but childless women commit suicide half again as often as unmarried women of the same age.* We have already noticed that in general the wife profits

[5] What Durkheim seems to mean here is that widowers with children compared to husbands with children are relatively worse off than widowers without children compared to husbands without children.—G.S.

less from family life than the husband. Now we see the cause of this; in itself conjugal society is harmful to the woman and aggravates her tendency to suicide.

If most wives have, nevertheless, seemed to enjoy a coefficient of preservation, this is because childless households are the exception and consequently the presence of children in most cases corrects and reduces the evil effects of marriage. Even so these effects are only reduced. A million women having children show 79 suicides; comparing this figure with the one giving the suiciderate of unmarried woman of 42 years of age as 150, the wife is found to benefit, even when she is also a mother, only by coefficient of preservation 1.80, 35 per cent lower, therefore, than that of fathers. With respect to suicide, we must therefore disagree with the following proposition of Bertillon: "When woman enters the conjugal state she gains from the association more than man; but she necessarily suffers more than man when she leaves it."

[Passages dealing with relationship between suicide and political crises have been omitted.]

VI. We have thus successively set up the three following propositions:

Suicide varies inversely with the degree of integration of religious society.

Suicide varies inversely with the degree of integration of domestic society.

Suicide varies inversely with the degree of integration of political society.

This grouping shows that whereas these different societies have a moderating influence upon suicide, this is due not to special characteristics of each but to a characteristic common to all. Religion does not owe its efficacy to the special nature of religious sentiments, since domestic and political societies both produce the same effects when strongly integrated. This, moreover, we have already proved when studying directly the manner of action of different religions upon suicide. Inversely, it is not the specific nature of the domestic or political tie which can explain the immunity they confer, since religious society has the same advantage. The cause can only be found in a single quality possessed by all these social groups, though perhaps to varying degrees. The only quality satisfying this condition is that they are all strongly integrated social groups. So we reach the general conclusion: suicide varies inversely with the degree of integration of the social groups of which the individual forms a part.

But society cannot disintegrate without the individual simultaneously detaching himself from social life, without his own goals becoming preponderant over those of the community, in a word without his personality tending to surmount the collective personality. The more weakened the groups to which he belongs, the less he depends on them, the more he consequently depends only on himself and recognizes no other rules of conduct than what are founded on his private interests. If we agree to call this state egoism, in which the individual ego asserts itself to excess in the face of the social ego and at its expense, we may call egoistic the special type of suicide springing from excessive individualism. . . .

COMMENTARY
RELATIONSHIPS AMONG VARIABLES

We now turn from the use of data to measure single properties **(P-X)** to the *systematic* study of *relationships among properties* **(P-XI).** We shall return in Unit 9 to complex measurement and the use of interrelated *indicants*. As in all research, the analysis of relationships proceeds at two levels, the conceptual and the empirical. The conceptual model enumerates the properties of immediate research interest and postulates the nature of the relationships among them. At the empirical level, then, the analysis examines the associations (or correlations) among variables as observed in the data to see whether these observed relationships "fit" the conceptual model.

Since the data reflect an actual situation in which the properties specified in the model and countless other factors may all be at work, the analyst distinguishes between properties which he wishes to scrutinize in terms of his model—the *explanatory variables* (both "causes" and "effects")—and those which are outside of his immediate theoretical interest, but which may affect the empirical outcome —the *extraneous variables.* Whether a variable is treated as explanatory or extraneous depends upon the immediate aims of the research. For example, in the Harvard Mobility Project (Unit 6), I.Q., father's occupation, and college aspiration were considered explanatory; but in the Kahl study, which grew out of it, I.Q. and father's occupation became extraneous factors and were controlled in order to focus attention on the explanatory variables of college aspiration and its other possible determinants.

The distinction between explanatory and extraneous variables does not affect the research *operations* of multivariate analysis (as described in Manual IV-A and IV-B) so much as it affects the *interpretation* of the findings in relation to the conceptual model. When the researcher starts with a loosely defined conceptual model and an *exploratory objective,* he treats as explanatory—or potentially explanatory—*all* the variables he decides to analyze. In other words, he follows the best theory (or guess) that his vague model offers in order to discover which variables may prove relevant to the model and how they may be interrelated. From his analysis, he discovers empirical regularities, works out *ad hoc* interpretations which seem to fit his model, and uses these interpretations in the further specification of his developing theory. This is essentially the approach of Lazarsfeld and his associates in the voting study.

On the other hand, when the researcher's analytical objective is to *test a hypothesis* (or set of hypotheses) derived from theory about the nature of the relationship that he expects to find among certain variables, his primary focus is on a *limited set* of explanatory variables defined in advance. As illustrated in the analyses by Strodtbeck and by Durkheim, the researcher hopes that the data will prove consistent with such theoretically derived hypotheses, thus adding considerably to his confidence in the model. Yet, despite his preoccupation with the explanatory variables involved in the hypothesis, he must also contend with the other variables—the *extraneous* variables which may be confusing his results. Sometimes he merely assumes, as Strodtbeck does, that all these other factors are exerting little or no influence over these results. More commonly, however, as Durkheim's analysis sharply reveals, the researcher expends much effort in the attempt to *control* (or *hold constant*) such potentially confounding variables.

As we review the several analyses in this Unit, we shall see how this broad difference between exploration and hypothesis-testing helps to clarify the reasons why various investigators go through complex procedures of systematic analysis. To be sure, the distinction is a loose one, for even in hypothesis-testing—as in exploration—the model may be further elaborated, as well as tested, when clues are unexpectedly discovered as by-products of the analysis of extraneous variables.

Strodtbeck and the Testing of Two-Variable Models

The nature of an analysis designed to test hypotheses about the relationship between two variables is illustrated in Strodtbeck's study of husband-wife inter-action over revealed differences. Building upon Bales' conceptual model of small group interaction process, and upon the Bales observation procedure (Unit 3), Strodtbeck introduces the concept of balance of power or influence, and de-velops the "revealed-difference technique" for measuring each group member's influence on the development of consensus. His *substantive hypothesis* postulates a relationship between balance of power in the group (we shall call this variable Y) and the balance of decision-making activity or speaking time in the group (variable X). He also tests a *methodological hypothesis* to make sure that balance of power—as determined by his revealed-difference technique (variable Y again) —is a valid measure of the actual structure of power relationships (variable X-M). His methods of testing both hypotheses demonstrate important basic prin-ciples of analysis.

CONTROL OF VARIABLES THROUGH SAMPLING

Strodtbeck's test of his methodological hypothesis illustrates once more the method of using the sample design to control key variables in the analysis **(P-IV)**. To measure the actual structure of power relationships (X-M), he draws his sam-ple of marital couples from each of three different cultures in which "the cultural phrasing of power" is known to emphasize, in varying degree, the dominant in-fluence of the wife. Thus he uses the sample, not to represent a particular popula-tion of cases, but to reflect three categories of a variable he wants to analyze in relation to another variable (see also Strodtbeck, 1958). Note also that his sec-ond variable (Y) is handled in a special way here, since the revealed-difference procedure means that the investigator actually manipulates **(P-VI)** the decision-making process.

A Test of Validity. Let us look at Strodtbeck's Table 1 (which may be thought of as three small tables—one for each culture) to see how he handles his data in testing his methodological hypothesis. Following the usual procedure for hypothesis-testing (as in the Zelditch analysis in Unit 5), Strodtbeck states his specific assumptions (Step A)—that, according to the revealed-difference tech-nique, the Navaho wives will win more decisions than their husbands, whereas the Mormon wives will win fewer than their husbands. He next determines (in Step B) that among the ten Navaho couples, for example, since 80 decisions were contested, the "expected" wins by Navaho wives (under the research hy-pothesis) would be more than 40—or (under the null hypothesis) 40 or less. Then (Step C) he compares the observed data in Table 1 with these expected frequencies, and finds a tendency for the data to fit his research hypothesis. This gives him some assurance that his revealed-difference technique is indeed measuring family power structure.

Use of a Statistical Test. Strodtbeck goes on to a statistical test of his null hypothesis here (Step D in the use of a mathematical model). In our discussions, we shall note the use of such tests as they occur in the studies, so as to indicate where statistical testing belongs in the research process and how the test results are to be read. (We shall not consider the actual procedures for such tests until Exercise V-3.) Strodtbeck uses statistical tests in his study to determine whether the findings from these small samples might be due entirely to chance. He discovers that the Mormon finding would occur by chance in only 7 out of 1,000 imagined samples of this sort, but the Navaho finding would be expected by chance in as many as 16 samples out of 100. The conclusion, in line with the usual conventions for such tests, is that the null hypothesis is sufficiently improbable to be rejected for the Mormons, but not for the Navaho (although Strodtbeck then combines the two findings to show that their joint probability by chance would be less than .01). Incidentally, since most tests make assumptions of independence, one might question whether the 80 decisions made here by 10 couples may be assumed to be independent trials according to the rules of probability in Manual V-B.

TESTING THE ASSOCIATION BETWEEN TWO VARIABLES

Once Strodtbeck is satisfied with the validity of this measure of the balance of power in the family (variable Y), he is ready to test his substantive hypothesis of its relationship to the balance of decision-making activity (variable X). His test proceeds, as in any study of the relationship between variables, at both the conceptual and the empirical levels.

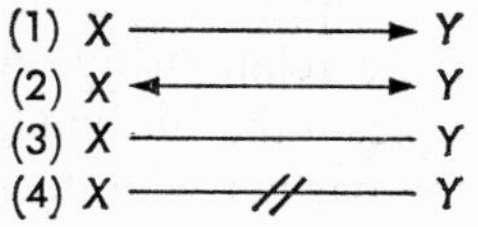

(1) $X \longrightarrow Y$
(2) $X \longleftrightarrow Y$
(3) $X \longrightarrow Y$
(4) $X \longrightarrow\!/\!/\longrightarrow Y$

Figure **8-A** *Postulated relationships between two variables, X and Y*

Conceptions of the Relationship. There are many ways in which researchers conceptualize the nature of particular relationships. For example, one of a pair of variables (X) may be viewed (see Figure 8-A) as (1) basic and antecedent to and in some sense "causing" the other (Y)—as I.Q. might be taken to "cause" the decision about college attendance (Cohen and Nagel, pp. 245–49). Or (2) each variable may be considered to affect the other—as ego's deviance and alter's deviance may successively affect each other in a vicious circle to produce ever greater deviance. Or (3) the researcher may consider the two variables as associated without having any immediate theoretical interest in whether one may influence the other—as Strodtbeck seems to associate the balance of power and the balance of talking in a family without considering the processes which may connect the two. Or (4) the two variables may be conceptualized as unrelated, i.e., as entirely independent of one another. It is often helpful to use diagrams of such postulated relationships between pairs of variables, as suggested in Figure 8-A. The presumed *direction* of association might also be shown in the diagram, i.e., whether the direction is (+) positive (so that one factor increases with the other) or (−) negative (so that it decreases with the other).

(Note that although pairs of variables are often treated at the *operational* level—Manual IV-A and Exercise IV-1—as "independent and dependent variables," or as "predictor and criterion," these operational designations do not always have meaning with reference to the conceptual model of the relationship.)

The conceptual model characteristically consists, of course, of a whole system of interrelated properties, from which we are presently selecting one pair at a time for analysis. For other studies that select several variables for analysis, we might draw larger diagrams in which the postulated relationships among several pairs of variables (as in Figure 8-A) are fitted together (see, *e.g.,* Blalock, 1961; Simon, 1957, Chapter 2).

Use of Mathematical Models in Studying Relationships. In line with his conception of the relationship between variables, the researcher looks for empirical correlations or associations in his data. We can use Strodtbeck's procedure to illustrate how the logic of mathematical models again aids the researcher in studying the fit between the observed data and the conceptual model.

Strodtbeck assumes (Step A), reasoning from previous findings of small group research, that his variables X and Y will be positively associated. At Step B, it is appropriate here to think of *alternative* mathematical models, rather than a single model, as bench marks or standards against which results may be compared. Two possible models as applied to Strodtbeck's data are suggested in Table 8-A, even though Strodtbeck merely predicts a positive relationship, saying nothing in his hypothesis about the strength or causal nature of the relationship. A *complete-association model* postulates only two types of couples—the husband-dominated and the wife-dominated—so that, in all couples, the partner who does most of the talking also wins most of the decisions. This pushes Strodtbeck's prediction to one possible extreme. Alternatively, an *independence model* represents the null hypothesis of no relationship between the two variables, so that X and Y are statistically independent—regardless of which partner dominates in talking (X), neither is more likely than the other to win decisions (Y). The expected frequencies for this model are computed by multiplying the marginal totals common to each cell, and dividing the product by 34—that is, by the number of couples. (This model is obtained by applying probability Rules 1 and 3 in Manual V-B.)

If we assume that Strodtbeck uses such alternative models in making his analysis, then we see that he compares (Step C), the respective "fit" of the two models to his *observed data* from Table 8-A(a). He finds that the data do depart

Table **8-A** *Analyses of Strodtbeck's Table 2*

Variable *X:* Number of couples in which talking is done predominantly by the husband (*H*) or the wife (*W*)

Variable *Y:* Number of couples in which decisions are won more often by the husband (*H*) or the wife (*W*)

(a) Observed data

| X—Talking | Y—Winning | | Total |
	H	W	X
H	14	5	19
W	5	10	15
Total Y	19	15	34

(c) Independence model (approximate)

| X—Talking | Y—Winning | | Total |
	H	W	X
H	11	8	19
W	8	7	15
Total Y	19	15	34

(b) Complete association model

| X—Talking | Y—Winning | | Total |
	H	W	X
H	19	0	19
W	0	15	15
Total Y	19	15	34

(d) Another association model (with fictitious marginals)

| X—Talking | Y—Winning | | Total |
	H	W	X
H	15	0	15
W	4	15	19
Total Y	19	15	34

from the independence model in the direction of the complete association model, that is, he finds a tendency toward positive association. (He might then proceed to represent this tendency by any one of various *measures of association,* which you encountered in Manual IV-A, such as epsilon, *Q,* or—particularly appropriate for this table with its similar marginals on the two variables—phi.)

The researcher who must choose one or another measure of the possible measures of association for summarizing relationships between two dichotomous variables does well to understand the implications of the possible models. Table 8-A also includes (d), *another model of association,* which adds to the two types of couples in model (b) still a third type: the wife does most of the talking but the husband wins most of the decisions. In (d), only one of the cells—the loquacious husband-wife winning type—has zero frequency. Strodtbeck could not have postulated this type of model since he found similar totals on both variables, and since model (d) is obviously possible only when the two sets of marginals differ. But the different measures of association are based on different notions as to what complete association means. For example, *Q* would be +1.00 for both (b) and (d), but phi would be +1.00 only for (b) where all the cases fall on the diagonal. (For a detailed discussion of such fourfold tables, see Francis.)

Another Statistical Test. Since such measures of association are subject to sampling variation, the researcher often carries the analysis one step further (Step D in mathematical models) to make allowances for this. The particular statistical test used here (chi square—written χ^2) estimates the likelihood of departures by chance from an *independence model* as in Table 8-A (c).

Stouffer's Simultaneous Analysis of Several Explanatory Variables

Two of Stouffer's analyses (considered in Unit 6) serve as models for exploration of the relationships among several, rather than just two, variables **(P-IX)**. In contrast to Strodtbeck, who controls his variables through sampling **(P-IV)** and through manipulation **(P-VI)** when he subjects the actors to the revealed-difference technique, Stouffer's analyses—and those in the other studies examined later in this Unit—attempt to disentangle the relationships among variables *after* the data are in hand.

CONTROL OF VARIABLES THROUGH CROSS-TABULATION

In these studies, cross-tabulation is used (as in Exercises II-3 and II-4) to classify the cases by the categories of the variables under study. The procedure for controlling variables is often called *subgroup analysis* because the punch-cards or other papers corresponding to the cases are physically sorted into piles ("subgroups" in this operational sense) having certain characteristics in common. After the data are cross-sorted and counted, the statistical computations typically follow a series of steps (demonstrated in Exercise IV-3), starting perhaps with the relationship between two variables, and then introducing a third (or a fourth or a fifth) in order to explore the original relationship further. The important operational principle is that, in order to allow a full understanding of the data, *all* of the relationships under scrutiny should be analyzed *simultaneously*— not just two variables at a time.

These complex interrelationships can yield a wide variety of statistical outcomes, which take on meaning only as they are interpreted in the light of a developing conceptual model. Although in any particular analysis the researcher may be interested only in selected sets of possible relationships of the types suggested in Figure 8-A above, a model concerned with three properties (variables) consists of three possible paired relationships; with four variables, six paired relationships are involved. (If N is the number of variables, the formula for the number of paired relationships is $\dfrac{N(N-1)}{2}$.)

THE MOBILITY ANALYSIS

The form of a three-variable analysis is illustrated in Table 1 of Kahl's report of the Harvard Mobility Project (Unit 6).

Here Stouffer and his colleagues, seeking the major determinants of boys' educational aspirations, find I.Q. and father's occupation "to be of practically equal utility as predictors." That is, they first report a positive association between one pair of variables—I.Q. and college plans; they then find a similar positive association between a second pair of variables—father's occupation and college plans. With these three explanatory variables, the next step is to examine them all simultaneously. At the conceptual level, a variety of interrelationships may have been postulated. For example, since I.Q. and social class were known to be related, either one or both of these may have been predicted to relate directly to college plans.

"Consequently," Kahl reports, "the data were arranged in the form of Table 1 to show the independent operation of these two factors." The outcome of this analysis makes clear that, indeed, both factors do contribute directly. On the one hand, the "effect" of I.Q.—with father's occupation controlled—may be seen in Table 1 by reading the cell percentages across. At each level of father's occupation, boys of higher intelligence are more likely than other boys to plan to go to college. On the other hand, the "effect" of father's occupation—with I.Q. controlled—is observed by reading down. For each quintile of I.Q. scores, boys whose fathers have higher rather than lower status occupations are more likely to have plans for college. The model used in interpreting these data is suggested in Figure 8-B, in which both I.Q. and status are thought of as contributing to educational aspiration; and in which, although I.Q. and status are themselves related, the research interest does not focus upon whether one of these two may cause the other.

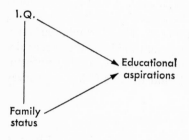

Figure **8-B** *Variables in the mobility analysis*

THE TOLERANCE ANALYSIS

The interplay between conceptual model and research operations which leads to an arrangement of data as in Kahl's table is explicated with great clarity in Stouffer's analysis (Unit 6) of age, education, and tolerance of nonconformity —another analysis which deserves careful rereading. On the basis of his finding that younger people tend to be more tolerant than older people, Stouffer asks the provocative question: Can the younger generation be expected to grow less tolerant as it ages? Proceeding with his analysis, he introduces, as a third variable, education—which is known to be related to age, and which turns out to be related also to tolerance. His reasoning is that "if education, independent of age, makes for tolerance, the present younger generation, when it reaches later years, should be more tolerant than its elders are today." His Figure 2 shows that, in fact, education is independently related to tolerance when age is controlled. For example, among people in a given age category (21 to 29 years), 77 per cent of college graduates are rated relatively tolerant as opposed to only 24 per cent of those with grade school education. But even with education controlled, age continues to exercise *some* "effect": among college graduates, for instance, the proportion of relatively tolerant individuals decreases steadily with increasing age. As Stouffer sums it up, "Although [a person] is likely to be more tolerant when he reaches 60 than were his own parents at 60, he may at the same time be less tolerant than he was in his own younger days."

Lazarsfeld's Use of Multivariate Analysis

The People's Choice is another well-known example of the exploratory study of relationships among variables at a given point of time—and also of the changes which take place over time (we shall discuss the study further in Unit 10). The researchers, Lazarsfeld, Berelson, and Gaudet, seek to study "all those conditions which determine the political behavior of people" by measuring and interrelating a considerable number of explanatory variables. Their interpretations of the findings provide the valuable beginnings of a theory of voting, and lead to a subsequent series of voting studies under Lazarsfeld's influence. And the procedures used in *The People's Choice* have since been formulated by Lazarsfeld and his collaborators (including Zeisel, Kendall, and Hyman). This formulation (see, *e.g.,* Kendall and Lazarsfeld) has served as an important guide in the recent development of multivariate analysis—especially valuable because of the unfortunate discontinuity between Durkheim's early work and the beginnings of survey research in this country.

SPECIFICATION OF THE RELATIONSHIP

A characteristic example of the elegance of the approach is given in Figure 6 of the study—which resembles the Stouffer illustrations in form, although the differing statistical result suggests an entirely different type of interpretation. Here, when three explanatory variables are interrelated, the association between age and political party preference *differs* according to religion: among Protestants, the younger are more likely than the older to favor the Democratic party; whereas among Catholics, the younger are less likely to take this position. The researchers suggest, by way of elaboration, that the younger people, generally less influenced by religion, may be the more likely to depart from the political views of their church, whatever these views may be. (Verification of this elaboration of the original relationship requires, then, further study of the relationship between religion and age.)

This type of outcome is later designated by Lazarsfeld as *specification,* since the third variable (in this instance, religion) specifies the conditions under which age and party preference are related (or, depending on the variables of principal concern, age specifies the relationship between religion and party preference). This is also sometimes referred to as *statistical interaction,* in which the "effect" of one variable is changed by the "effect" of another. Comparison of the "effects" of the two variables is often facilitated by the form of analysis shown in Table 8-B below, in which the voting study findings from Figure 6 are recapitulated. We readily see that the "effects" of religion are greater for older (epsilon, written ϵ, the difference between percentages, is —50) than for younger voters (epsilon —29). We also see that the "effects" of age change their direction depending upon religion so that the sign of epsilon shifts from + to — among Protestants as compared with Catholics.

Table **8-B** *Restatement of Figure 6 from* The People's Choice

(percentages show the proportion in each cell who are Democrats)

Age	Religion		"Effects" of religion (ϵ)
	Protestant	*Catholic*	
Below 45 years	43% (694)	72% (214)	—29
45 years and over	34% (601)	84% (150)	—50
"Effects" of age (ϵ)	+9	—12	

THE RELATIVE "STRENGTH" OF TWO RELATIONSHIPS

In another example, the analysis in the study of Figures 10 and 11 starts out as usual—but then points to an additional methodological principle. First, Figure 10 shows the association between interest in the election and the number of "cross-pressures"—an especially interesting sociological variable similar to the notion of "role conflict." Whereas persons with no cross-pressures evince most interest in the election, those with one or more cross-pressures are less likely to be interested; in other words, persons with clashes of interests are the more likely "to withdraw their interest from the field." Then, given this finding of a negative association between these two factors—i.e., between cross-pressures and degree of interest—the researchers ask whether the two may work jointly to affect the time of final decision. Figure 11, which interrelates all three, provides an affirmative answer: both cross-pressures and lack of interest tend to delay the date at which the final vote decision is made.

Lazarsfeld and his associates are not content, however, to end at this point in the analysis with such a demonstration of a joint effect. They want to discover whether one of the factors has a "more important" effect on the time of decision than the other. They attack this problem by comparing the two center bars in their chart—voters with one of the factors favorable to an early decision, but with the other factor unfavorable. As it turns out in this instance, "when the two factors— interest and cross-pressures—work in opposing directions, they are about equal in strength."

Sociologists often face this problem of assessing the relative strength of variables in producing a net association, and this study provides one useful form of analysis. Figure 8-C illustrates this form of analysis for a three-variable relationship in which comparisons are made between the (+—) and (—+) cells labeled (b) and (c). If the percentage in one of these cells is decidedly higher than in the other, the inference may be that one of the factors is in some way more closely related than the other to the dependent variable. If the data from Figure 11 of the voting study were dichotomized and entered in Figure 8-C, the two cells (+—) and (—+) would be substantially alike, reflecting the equal strength of the two relationships.

Figure **8-C**   *Analysis of relative "strength" of two relationships*

(*cells are to show proportions that are* + *on variable* Y)

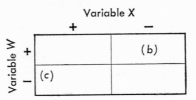

Difficulties of Interpretation.   The interpretation of the relative importance of two factors in their net association with a dependent variable presents various difficulties, however.

One difficulty arises in the comparison of (+—) and (—+) cells (as in Figure 8-C) when the two independent variables are not clearly composed of just two categories. Such variables as *number* of cross-pressures or *degree* of interest fall naturally into many categories or units which we arbitrarily dichotomize when we enter the data in Figure 8-C. What we actually compare in the analysis, then, is the relative effect of these variables as they happen to be distributed in the particular population sampled and as they are dichotomized. A different relative effect might appear in another population—not because of a difference in relative strength of given units of the variables—but merely because the variables themselves are differently distributed. (We shall see presently how Durkheim avoided this difficulty in an analysis of naturally dichotomous variables.)

More generally, of course, a full analysis by given units of each variable—degrees of interest and numbers of cross-pressures—would give more precise measures of the actual effects of the variables. But even here the meaning of the results is somewhat ambiguous, especially since the categories of the two variables are dissimilar. How can one compare degree of interest with number of cross-pressures? What increment of interest is equivalent to the addition of a single cross-pressure? Despite the ambiguities, however, Stouffer (who describes several methods for such analysis) concludes in a different example that "in trying to discover whether a raising of economic status is ultimately more important than a reduction of foreign-born in coping with juvenile delinquency" the sociologist is asking a legitimate question (Stouffer, 1962, p. 270).

Durkheim's Early Contribution to Multivariate Analysis

Before examining Durkheim's remarkable early use of statistical analysis to test his theories, let us consider the distinctive character of his conceptual model. In line with his central proposition that the suicide rate is determined by social factors, he looks upon two of his main types of suicide as manifestations of societal malintegration: Anomic suicide tends to increase as group norms and social controls break down, and egoistic suicide tends to increase as the norms prescribe excessive detachment of the individual from the group. Thus he postulates a negative association between societal integration and suicide rate, so that the less integrated the society, the higher the rate of suicide. As a major study of social phenomena that abounds with interrelated and ingeniously tested hypotheses, Durkheim's *Suicide* offers many invaluable guidelines for subsequent research.

DURKHEIM'S USE OF THE SUICIDE RATE

Since Durkheim aims to stress the sociological, not the psychological, aspects of the problem of suicide, he selects as his major research case (**P-I**) the collectivity at several levels—the society as a whole (the nation or province), the religious or ethnic segments of the society, the family, and so on. He starts by computing the suicide rate for each society by counting the number of group members per million who commit suicide at any given time. He compares societies with one another, showing that each has its characteristic rate, and then proceeds to look for factors which might account for these differing rates.

In using the suicide rate, Durkheim makes it perfectly plain that, as a sociologist, he is not directly concerned with the individual as such—with the personal reasons why one individual commits suicide and another does not. A familiar analogue is the unemployment rate, which the economist studies without attempting to explain changes in behavior or capacities of the individuals *qua* individuals. A sudden change in unemployment for the country as a whole, for example, is a problem of rate—not to be explained in terms of a sudden drop in the personal efficiency of all the individual workers—as a study focused on the individual might use personal inefficiency to explain why one person rather than another is unemployed at a given time (see Parsons, 1949-a, p. 324). As a social phenomenon, rates must be accounted for by factors outside the individual—by the complex of all individuals acting together in a system. Although such explanations are frequent, the logic behind them, as Durkheim says, often "offends common sense" (*Suicide*, p. 310). Nevertheless, neither economic depressions nor suicide rates can be fully understood by studying only discrete individuals.

Durkheim's rate is a *collective measure,* then, and some of the perplexing problems of its use are reflected in the numerous charges against Durkheim for treating the group as an entity, or for committing the fallacy of *reification* (see, *e.g.,* Selvin, 1958). Any sociologist planning to use *Suicide* as a model—or indeed to utilize any collective measure at all—should first consider this charge seriously.

Does Durkheim indeed overlook the individual, somehow attributing the suicide motivation to the group? Does he fail to take into account the psychological processes which induce certain individuals to commit suicide while other members of the same social systems refrain from doing so?

In considering these charges, one might note that Durkheim, in discarding the statistics on presumed motives of individuals, argues that such motives reflect the general social state rather than explain it. They merely indicate, he says, the weak points at which certain individuals may succumb to societal pressures. In trying to determine the causes of suicide, Durkheim says, "Disregarding the individual as such, his motives and his ideas, we shall seek directly the states of the various social environments (religious confessions, family, political society, occupational groups, etc.), in terms of which the variations of suicide occur.... Only then returning to the individual," he continues, "shall we study how these general causes become individualized so as to produce the homicidal results involved."

Thus one might argue that Durkheim does, after all, pay a great deal of attention to the individual—but to the individual in his role in the social system. He asks why individuals in some social situations are more likely to commit suicide than those in others; i.e., he divides the society into its component roles and then compares these. He shows that, within a society, individuals who are Protestants are more prone to suicide than individuals who are Catholics; divorced individuals more than married individuals; and so on. One way of formulating his thesis might be—in terms of *individuals*—that individuals who are closely knit into an integrated society are the least often motivated to kill themselves. (See the combined sociological and psychological approach to suicide and homicide as aspects of aggression in Henry and Short.)

Durkheim himself tries to banish the charges of reification, saying, "We of course do not at all intend to hypostasize the collective conscience." But whether he does commit such a fallacy—or whether, by treating the individual as part of the group, he avoids the fallacy by allowing for psychological mechanisms in interpreting his data—the argument points to a serious problem confronting any student of the group. Weber alludes to this difficulty in his discussion of *Verstehen* (see Unit 7). And whenever multiple individuals are simply aggregated to refer to the group (as in the rate) the knotty problem of possible reification seems to be raised.

TESTS OF THEORETICALLY DERIVED HYPOTHESES

Let us now turn from these larger conceptual issues to examine the form in which Durkheim casts his analysis. It is exciting to discover that Durkheim, working in the nineteenth century with few of the techniques now available for handling such data, understood the logic of multivariate analysis much as we understand it today. His inventive applications of this logic are especially impressive because he could not control the character of his data but was obliged to make use of inadequate records in whatever form they were available.

Still more remarkable is Durkheim's use of this analysis to test a whole set of theoretically based hypotheses. In Merton's restatement of Durkheim's theoretical analysis, the empirical invariance in the finding that Protestants have higher suicide rates than Catholics is predictable from a set of propositions in which Durkheim is able to substitute integration—a general property—for religious affiliation—a specific property (Merton, 1957, pp. 96–97). In this way the theory is generalized to cover a wide variety of empirical uniformities. Derivable from it are Durkheim's own hypotheses of the differential suicide rates for married as compared with widowed individuals, for example, as well as the findings of many subsequent studies in which social integration is used as a major predictor.

In testing his hypotheses, Durkheim makes use of the records available to him in a brilliant series of analyses, dealing not only with the *explanatory* variables of suicide rate and its social determinants, but also with a long series of *extraneous* variables not germane to his conceptual model. Certain extraneous variables widely presumed to be causes of suicide are demonstrated to be associated with it only indirectly, and other extraneous variables are so controlled that they will not confound the results of his theoretically based empirical tests.

ELIMINATION OF AN EXTRANEOUS FACTOR

Durkheim starts his analysis with a list of nonsocial factors as extraneous variables (such as climate, seasonal factors, temperature). Admitting that these are often apparently associated with the suicide rate, he does not believe that they can be used to account for it. His theory postulates that these are not in themselves causes. Accordingly he searches for some appropriate data and for a method of analysis which will test his hypothesis that such nonsocial factors are only spuriously related.

One example will point out the similarity between the analysis he devised and that employed in the more recent studies we have been analyzing. Durkheim starts with the statistical association between the suicide rate and—as an indicant of one extraneous factor—the geographical location of various populations in Europe. Since the two are related, with the highest rate in the central area, he admits that the difference in suicide rate might be due to differences of climate. Believing, however, that quite another factor—the intensity of social activity—contains the true causes, he sets out to find data which will allow him to examine the interrelationship of all three variables: climate, social activity, and suicide. He wants to show climate to be a spurious factor, unrelated to suicide in any direct causal sense.

In view of the paucity of data, the analysis worked out in his Table 2 seems especially ingenious. He succeeds in controlling the extraneous variable, climate, by studying the same regions at different time periods, which in turn are carefully chosen to index his explanatory variable, social activity. Thus he compares one time period when the capital of Italy, as the center of activity, was in the North, with another time period after the capital had moved to Rome in the central region. Just as he predicted, he now finds that the suicide rate changes concomitantly with the changes in intensity of social activity—with the rates highest in the North in the earlier period, but shifting to the Center at the later period. In this way, he demonstrates that climate, which of course remained constant throughout, bears no consistent relationship to suicide after all. The connection only appears to exist at certain time periods when temperate climate and intense social activity happen to coexist.

TEST OF RELIGION AS AN EXPLANATORY VARIABLE

In the foregoing example, Durkheim eliminates as causal a particular factor extraneous to his conceptual model by showing that its correlation with the suicide rate is eliminated (or reduced) when the appropriate social factor is controlled. After thus eliminating this and a number of other such *extraneous* variables, he then reverses the procedure. He is now ready to test and refine his conceptual model by examining a variety of *explanatory* variables (social factors), and he must make sure that extraneous variables are not confounding his results.

In one example, he finds a relationship between the Protestant or non-Protestant character of a country and its suicide rate. This finding indicates that *religion* (an explanatory variable in which he is interested) may be a factor in suicide. Reasoning, however, that the observed relationship may actually be due to *cultural differences,* he proceeds to introduce a third factor into the analysis in order to control for these (extraneous) differences. His first attempt is to compare within single states the suicide rates for Protestant and non-Protestant provinces whose cultures may be presumed similar. He finds, as the theory of egoistic suicide predicts, that the original relationship of suicide to religion stands, even when cultural differences are thus minimized.

A Difficulty in Analyzing Collective Measures.   But Durkheim makes a second and more definitive attempt to pin down this finding, an attempt that was necessitated by the use of collective measures. You will notice that up to this point in the analysis he has treated religious differences as characteristics of whole countries (or provinces), classifying a country as Protestant, for example, if the majority of its citizens are Protestants. His finding is then that the collective suicide rate is relatively high in collectively Protestant countries. Yet he cannot easily test his theory on the basis of this finding. To infer from it that *within* a country the Protestants are more likely to commit suicide than the non-Protestants may indeed be fallacious—the same finding could also arise from a very different situation in which all the suicides are actually committed by the minority group in each country, whether Protestant or Catholic. (We shall examine in Unit 12 this and other possible fallacies in the use of collective measures.)

Durkheim's second analysis of these same three variables (religion and suicide, with cultural differences controlled) avoids all possibility of such a fallacy. In his noteworthy Table 5, he compares suicide rates for *individuals* who are either Protestant or non-Protestant *within each country*. Here he finds as before that for every country (whatever its cultural pattern) the suicide rate is indeed higher in the Protestant segment of the population—with its characteristic institutions and values—than in the non-Protestant segments.

MARRIAGE AS AN EXPLANATORY VARIABLE

A final illustration from this complex but remarkably inventive set of analyses—in which Durkheim again, as he says, determines "the rate of each group separately"—suggests the full extent to which his work is a precurser of modern subgroup analysis. Interested in the effect of the *marriage* on the suicide rate, he begins with the observation that unmarried persons seem to commit suicide less often than married ones. Such a relationship would be consistent with a philosophy of the marital state as one of despair, but would contradict Durkheim's hypothesis that the individual's integration into groups is an impediment to suicide. And Durkheim quickly shows the relationship to be spurious, confounded by the factor of age. A large proportion of unmarried persons are under 16 years of age, and children seldom commit suicide. When he considers only those over 16 years of age, the relationship actually reverses direction. Now the married persons are found to have lower suicide rates.

A Four-Variable Analysis. Durkheim carries the analysis one step further, reasoning that, if the rates for married and unmarried were compared at each age level, the relationship might vary, even reverse itself, for different categories of age. One may, he points out (giving credit for the idea to Bertillon), "compare unmarried persons of from 25 to 30 years with married and widowed persons of the same age and similarly for other periods; the influence of marital status will then be *isolated* from all the other influences and all its possible *variations* will appear." (Italics added.) In today's language, the relationship between marital status and suicide might be *specified* by the introduction of the age variable (a variable found to specify one of the relationships in *The People's Choice*). Thus his profound analytical insight led him to perceive the sort of relationship often obscured when confounding variables have been inadequately controlled. And because data were not available in the proper form, he undertook the task himself, classifying "about 25,000" French suicides from unpublished government data.

The results of this tabulation are presented in a four-variable table (Table 7) in which the relationships of age, sex, and marital status to suicide are examined. In such a table, two variables are controlled simultaneously while the "effect" of a third on the dependent variable is examined. If we consider in addition the use he makes of Table 6, which presents the same data for another culture, he is actually examining the effect of a fifth variable, culture. By analyzing all of these together, he is able to explain a number of relationships. For example, he finds that his suspicions regarding age are confirmed—although the negative association of marriage and suicide remains for most age groups, early marriage, especially for men, seems positively associated with suicide.

Moreover, much in the manner of modern investigation, Durkheim considers himself justified in placing confidence in the finding because of the *consistency* with which the patterns are replicated in several societies. Thus he intuitively applies the logic of statistical testing when he speaks of consistent findings as "probably not accidental."

The Relative "Strength" of Two Relationships—Another Example. Finally, in relating to his conceptual model the finding that marriage has a negative effect on the suicide rate, he questions whether it is the marital bond (the "conjugal group") or the children (the "family group proper") which is actually more important, "for the family environment consists of different elements . . . and it is not *a priori* certain that both combine equally to produce the fact that we are studying." Raising a general question of current concern to many sociologists, that of the relative strength of two relationships, Durkheim again utilizes an essentially modern approach in its solution. He applies the model of our Figure 8-C above, using $(+-)$ and $(-+)$ comparisons, and finds that widowers with children have lower suicide rates than married men who are childless.

This extended discussion of *Suicide,* although it merely illustrates but does not begin to exhaust the variety and originality of Durkheim's methodological techniques and theoretical formulations, nevertheless serves to demonstrate the varied possibilities of statistical analysis of interrelationships postulated at the conceptual level. But what is perhaps even more important, it serves to demonstrate that research requires much more than the application of cut-and-dried, ready-made techniques. Research can be fully productive only to the extent that the creative aspects of the process are not ignored.

Some Methodological Implications

These studies and exercises have illustrated how the researcher combines empirical analysis—the procedures for observing and measuring concomitant regularities in data **(P-XI)**—with mathematical, logical, and imaginative methods for interpreting the empirical relationships within the context of the conceptual model. They have exemplified two broad approaches. On the one hand, the interrelationships of several *explanatory* variables may be *explored.* On the other hand, in the analysis of an *hypothesized relationship* between explanatory variables, certain *extraneous* variables may be controlled so that they will neither obscure the relationship under study, nor spuriously suggest a causal connection. Whereas both approaches afford insights and suggest additions to the conceptual model, the second aims especially to provide a more rigorous test of the hypothesis at hand. In practice, the researcher often works back and forth between the two, as

you, in the tabulation exercises (II-3 and II-4) first conducted certain exploratory analyses, and then—on the basis of your initial findings—developed hypotheses which, in turn, you tested by going back to another portion of your data.

SOME EMPIRICAL PROCEDURES

The methods of systematic analysis we have discussed have started with *subgroup comparisons*—with the actual sorting of the cases according to the categories of the variables under study. We have seen how this sorting may be accomplished by setting up a separate sample for each category (or combination of
categories) of the variables to be analyzed (see the discussion of factorial schemes
in Unit 11 below); or by cross-tabulation of the data once they are in hand. We
have also rehearsed a number of *statistical procedures* for facilitating subgroup
comparisons and for summarizing the observed correlations and associations (devoting special attention in Manual IV-A to procedures suitable for use with
nominal or ordinal measures).

There are, in addition, a great many other correlational procedures. Some
of these do not rest upon subgroup comparisons, hence do not require the inor-
dinate increases in sample size necessary when cases are actually cross-tabulated
on several variables. (Every time even a dichotomized variable is added to a cross-
tabulation the number of cells is doubled.) Some studies use electronic com-
putors to calculate literally hundreds of correlations between pairs of variables.

You should be aware of a variety of statistical measures of association in
addition to those discussed in Manual IV-A, which are widely used for studying
relationships among variables. (A statistical textbook should be consulted for the
underlying assumptions, requirements, and limitations of these procedures, as
well as for their computational details.) Some of the available procedures require that one or more of the single variables be measured on an interval (or
ratio) scale—such as the basic *correlation* and *regression* procedures for relating
two variables, *multiple correlation* for evaluation of the extent to which variation in a dependent variable is accounted for by the simultaneous effects of several
independent variables, and *partial correlation* for examination of the association
of two variables when the effects of others have been controlled. A number of
other procedures are suitable, especially for very small samples of cases such as
the Spearman and Kendall rank-order correlations.

USE OF CORRELATIONS TO DESCRIBE POPULATIONS

We are using correlational procedures in this book primarily for the systematic analysis of relationships postulated in a conceptual model. In this sense,
we use the procedures for "explanatory" or "causal" analysis in order to examine
such propositions as that one factor affects another, or varies as the consequence
of a change in another, or is associated with another in certain ways under specified conditions.

The same empirical procedures may also be used for a different purpose—

for systematic description of relationships between variables as they occur in a particular population (or empirical universe of cases). Thus a market survey may describe systematically how use of a product is related to city size or socioeconomic status within the discrete universe of United States families. Or a social survey may use statistical procedures to describe the civic and industrial conditions in a particular community—perhaps as a basis for a program of social reform (see Pauline Young, pp. 17–18).

For example, when Stouffer finds a certain correlation in his sample between age and tolerance, he might well stop his analysis at this point—*provided* he merely wants to measure the relationship between these variables *as they are distributed* in the population (universe) under study at the time of his research. But Stouffer has a further objective—he also wants to go beyond the description of this population to see what he can learn about age as a factor in (or possible cause of) tolerance. He wants to isolate particular properties (variables) to see how—apart from other properties—they may be interrelated. Accordingly, he goes on to study the effect of age on tolerance when *other associated variables* (such as education) *are controlled.*

Thus the same empirical techniques for studying relationships among variables may be used either for systematic analysis, or (as often in applied research) for systematic description.

IMPLICATIONS FOR STUDY OF THE CASE

Finally, we should note that whenever subgroup comparisons are employed for systematic analysis of *properties* (as their use has been discussed in this Unit) the findings also hold important implications for an understanding of the *cases* **(P-I)** to which these properties belong.

At the procedural level, although our concern has been with how the properties relate or whether one relationship confounds another, the consequence of the cross-tabulation procedure has been to classify cases into various types. We have, in effect, been classifying cases in terms of several variables, locating these cases in a space composed, not of *dimensions* of properties (as in Unit 7), but of the *properties* themselves. (Looking at the operations from this perspective suggests the link to Unit 9. There we shall classify cases in terms of several *indicants* of a single property, but we shall also be concerned with the relationships among these indicants, just as here we have been concerned with relationships among properties. The lines dividing indicant, dimension, and property are purely arbitrary, of course, depending upon the specific problem under study, but many analyses require dealing with all three.)

At the conceptual level, multivariate analysis adds to our understanding of the research cases—typically the actors or the social systems—by the special device of *retaining the identity* of each case throughout the analysis. For example, when Stouffer, whose case is the individual citizen, cross-tabulates age and tolerance, the cells of his table obviously tell much more about the individuals than do the marginal totals for each variable. Whereas the marginals refer at a more inclusive level to the system as a whole and merely show *how many* individuals in the American public are of a certain age or a certain degree of tolerance, the cells show to what extent the *same individuals* who are young, for example, are also tolerant. That is, individual cases are identified according to the categories of the variables under study.

A similar analysis might cross-tabulate properties of small groups as the cases. Or, to emphasize that the principle is not restricted to microscopic analyses, entire societies might be analyzed in respect to the relationship between such properties as matrilineal-patrilineal kinship structure (variable X) and expressive-instrumental role prescriptions for the husband (variable Y). As long as the properties are handled simultaneously (cross-tabulated), the analysis indicates *which* kind of case **(P-I)** contributes what to the over-all pattern of such properties in the larger system (or aggregate of cases). The procedure connects the properties—attitudes, actions, role prescriptions—to the relevant parts (levels) of the social-structural base.

Throughout much of his analysis Durkheim's research cases are of a high order of complexity—not treated as simple entities which are merely aggregated into statistical totals. In the study of religion, for example, his case is a social system (country) composed of segments within which the individuals all play homogeneous (*e.g.,* Protestant) roles. Accordingly, in his paradigmatic Table 5 he works at two levels. He not only *identifies each country* in the analysis—by handling one country at a time—but further, *within* each country, he *identifies the constituent roles* of individuals (as Protestant, Catholic, or Jew).

Although this principle of identifying each role (or each part) of a complex system under scrutiny has not yet been fully clarified in the methodological literature (it will be considered further in Unit 12), it seems to provide one key to the matching of measurement and analysis to the peculiar requirements of sociological research. As sociologists gradually learn to handle social systems as their research cases and to develop more precise instruments for measuring single variables, and as statisticians work out more appropriate statistical correlational procedures, multivariate analysis may be expected to become increasingly systematic and "hard." The essential logic and spirit of inquiry which characterizes the work of a Durkheim will no doubt remain. The changes will come in the improvement of the measurement and statistical procedures to support such analysis.

SUGGESTED READINGS FOR UNIT EIGHT

Alpert; Dornbusch and Schmid, Chapters 2 and 3; Goode and Hatt, Chapter 20; Goodman and Kruskal, 1954; Hagood and Price, Chapters 4, 20, 21; Hyman, 1955, Chapters 2, 5, 6, 7; Kendall and Lazarsfeld; Kish, 1959; Lazarsfeld and Rosenberg, pp. 115–25; Madge, Chapter 2; Mueller and Schuessler, Chapters 9 and 10; Selltiz *et al.*, pp. 406–40; Selvin, 1958; Siegel, Chapter 9; Stouffer, 1962, Chapter 13; Zeisel, Chapters 2, 4, 8, 9; Zelditch, 1959, Chapters 6, 7, 8.

QUESTIONS FOR REVIEW AND DISCUSSION

Review the following methodological terms as used in this Unit:

   causal relationship
   confounding variables
   cross-tabulation
   explanatory variables
   extraneous variables
   identification of parts of system
   independent and dependent variables
   measures of association
   model of association
   multivariate analysis
   positive or negative association
   reification
   relative "strength" of variables
   specification
   spurious factor
   statistical interaction
   test factor

1a. Set up a fictitious table, using the data from Exercise II-3, in which status is the independent variable. How would you read such a table? Set up another table using status as the dependent variable, and tell how you would read it.

   b. Formulate an hypothesis of the relationship between independent and dependent variables for each of your tables from Question 1a. For each relationship, specify the nature of the assumed *causal* relationship, if any; the *direction*, if any, of the hypothesized relationship; and the mathematical *model of association* implied by the hypothesis.

2. In order to obtain the "independence model" shown in Table 8-A(c), start by calculating the probabilities for each cell, applying Rules 1 and 3 from Manual V-B. Then apply these probabilities to the number of cases (34) in order to arrive at the estimated numbers in Table 8-A(c).

3. Why was it more important for Strodtbeck than for Bales to base his analysis on established, rather than *ad hoc,* groups?

4. How did Malinowski and Whyte handle the study of relationships among properties of the group? Considering their total research designs, might they just as well have utilized the type of analysis exemplified by Durkheim or Lazarsfeld?

5. Compare Strodtbeck's, Lazarsfeld's, and Durkheim's conceptions of the group. How do these affect the type of analyses each undertook? Illustrate your answers by reference to their studies.

6. How did Lazarsfeld and his associates develop and refine their index of socioeconomic status?

7. Examine your own findings from the analysis of one dependent and of two independent variables in Exercise II-4 (the study of adolescents and their reference groups). Do any of your findings come close to any of the ideal types of outcomes: I, II, III?

8. Contrast Weber (*The Protestant Ethic*) and Durkheim (*Suicide*) in their use of psychological data in sociological analysis.

9a. Note that Exercise II-3 makes use of a nonprobability *quota sample.* How would you assess the representativeness of such a sample?

b. Note also that the quotas for higher and lower class respondents are equal. How does this affect your handling of percentages in the analysis?

10. What methods does Strodtbeck use in extending and testing the findings of Bales' laboratory research?

a. Discuss the implications of the differences between the two studies in selection of cases.

b. Describe how Strodtbeck utilizes the Bales categories in analyzing his results.

11. Compare the use in analysis of the samples designed by Strodtbeck and by Kahl.

12. Define the methods of interpretation used in the studies by Strodtbeck; Durkheim; and Lazarsfeld, Berelson, and Gaudet. How would you formulate the interpretative processes you went through in Exercise II-3 or II-4?

UNIT NINE

MEASUREMENT AND THE CLARIFICATION OF CONCEPTS

SUGGESTED PROGRAM OF STUDY

The purpose of Unit 9 is to acquaint you with measurement procedures that test the correspondence between the actual patterns or structures in the data and the conceptual assumptions of the measurement model. Special attention is paid to the Guttman scale as one example of a procedure containing such a built-in test.

Exercises and Manual

The exercises in scale analysis (**III-4** on individual attitudes, and **III-5** on collective attitudes toward objects) will give you actual experience with the operations involved in Guttman scaling (and with the second component of the scale). The steps in these operations are fully specified in **Manual III-D.** Your detailed consideration of this one procedure as an example will provide a basic understanding of complex measurement in general.

In **Exercise III-6** (following **Manual III-E**), you will explore some of the problems and possibilities of collective measures involving multiple indicants and more than one group member.

Studies

The studies will then illustrate how these measurement operations fit into the over-all research design. Start by rereading Stouffer's description of his scale of toleration of nonconformists (Unit 6). Then examine carefully the measuring instruments used in the new studies by **Stouffer** and **Toby; Foa;** and **Riley, Toby, Cohn,** and **Riley.** Note in each instance how the G-scale aids the investigator in clarifying his definition of the property under study. The studies by **Selvin** and by Stouffer and Toby also illustrate the place in the research process of other related measurement procedures.

Commentary

The Commentary to Unit 9 discusses the problems of measuring properties of groups so as to reflect both the patterning of acts or attitudes and the structuring of the roles. It describes two partial approaches to collective measurement—a group pattern approach and an individual pattern approach—and stresses the need for improved social system measures that would combine these two partial approaches.

Questions for Review and Discussion

Use the Questions for Review and Discussion to pull together the principles of measurement you have learned from this and the foregoing Units, and to consolidate your understanding of the use of collective data.

SAMUEL A. STOUFFER
JACKSON TOBY
Role Conflict and Personality

Abstract

This paper explores operational procedures for linking the study of social norms with the study of personality. A social norm can be inferred from respondents' reports as to role obligations in a specific social situation. To the extent that an individual is consistent, in varying types of situations, in reporting one type of role obligation rather than another, this tendency is considered a personality predisposition. Data, based on a questionnaire to students on hypothetical situations, show that people can be ordered along a continuum involving the relative priority of personal and impersonal considerations in social obligations. New scaling techniques are applied, and certain kinds of discrepancies are exhibited as deserving further study.

A convenient way to examine the informal social controls operating in a given institution is through the study of role conflict. . . .

The present paper . . . seeks to provide a link between the study of social norms . . . and the study of personality. Specifically, when there is a lack of consensus in a group as to the "proper thing to do" in a morally conflicting situation, is there

Reprinted in part from *American Journal of Sociology, 56,* 1951, pp. 395–98, 399, 400, 401, 402, 403, 404–06, with permission of The University of Chicago Press.

a tendency for some individuals to have a predisposition or a personality bias toward one type of solution and for other individuals to have a predisposition toward another type of solution? If such a predisposition exists, there should be a tendency to carry over certain types of behavior from one role conflict to another with some consistency.

An especially common role conflict is that between one's institutionalized obligations of friendship and one's institutionalized obligations to a society. The obligations of friendship in Western culture, to use the terminology of Parsons, are particularistic rather than universalistic, affectively toned rather than affectively neutral, and diffuse rather than specific. A universalistic obligation is applicable to dealings with anybody (e.g., obligation to fulfil a contract); a particularistic obligation is limited to persons who stand in some special relationship to one (e.g., the obligation to help a relative or a close friend or neighbor). Diffuseness of particularistic obligations provides flexibility in the definition of these roles. That is, the content of an individual's particularistic obligations (toward a friend, a brother, a grandchild) depends in part on the intimacy of the relationship itself. The greater the affection, the greater the sense of obligation. On the other hand, universalistic obligations are defined more rigidly, for they regulate behavior toward all human beings—regardless of affective involvement. Hence, in any specific situation involving conflict between duty to a friend and duty to society, we would expect that some individuals are more prone to regard the particularistic obligation as taking precedence than others because there is variability from individual to individual in the intimacy of friendships. That is, respondents tend to project into the hypothetical situations *reference* friendships drawn from their own experience. A description of an institutionalized social norm not only must take into account, then, the beliefs and behavior of a modal member of the group but must also observe the individual variability [or "social slippage"] in the perception of obligations. . . .

In the present paper we shall deal with several situations involving conflicts between obligations to a friend and more general social obligations. If, as our conception of the intrinsic variability of particularistic obligations would lead us to expect, some people are more likely than others to choose the particularistic horn of the dilemma rather than the universalistic in a variety of situations, we should be able to devise a scale to measure such a tendency. With such a scale people should be ranked along a single dimension according to their probability of possessing the attribute or predisposition of choosing one type of solution rather than the other.

What we have to present here is only a crude beginning; indeed, only a classroom example. Yet it should prove instructive in a number of respects to those who may wish to carry on further research with needed refinements. Our data are based on a short pencil-and-paper questionnaire completed by 648 undergraduate students at Harvard and Radcliffe in February, 1950. No claim is made for the representativeness of the sample, since almost all were members of a single class, "Social Relations 1A."

Four little stories were presented, as follows:

1

You are riding in a car driven by a close friend, and he hits a pedestrian. You know he was going at least 35 miles an hour in a 20-mile-an-hour speed zone. There are no other witnesses. His lawyer says that if you testify under oath that the speed was only 20 miles an hour, it may save him from serious consequences.

What right has your friend to expect you to protect him?

Check one:

☐ My friend has a definite right as a friend to expect me to testify to the lower figure.

☐ He has some right as a friend to expect me to testify to the lower figure.

☐ He has no right as a friend to expect me to testify to the lower figure.

What do you think you'd probably do in view of the obligations of a sworn witness and the obligation to your friend?

Check one:

☐ Testify that he was going 20 miles an hour.

☐ Not testify that he was going 20 miles an hour.

2

You are a New York drama critic. A close friend of yours has sunk all his savings in a new Broadway play. You really think the play is no good.

What right does your friend have to expect you to go easy on his play in your review?

Check one:

☐ He has a definite right as a friend to expect me to go easy on his play in my review.

☐ He has some right as a friend to expect me to do this for him.

☐ He has no right as a friend to expect me to do this for him.

Would you go easy on his play in your review in view of your obligations to your readers and your obligation to your friend?

Check one:

☐ Yes
☐ No

3

You are a doctor for an insurance company. You examine a close friend who needs more insurance. You find that he is in pretty good shape, but you are doubtful on one or two minor points which are difficult to diagnose.

What right does your friend have to expect you to shade the doubts in his favor?

Check one:

☐ My friend would have a definite right as a friend to expect me to shade the doubts in his favor.

☐ He would have some right as a friend to expect me to shade the doubts in his favor.

☐ He would have no right as a friend to expect me to shade the doubts in his favor.

Would you shade the doubts in his favor in view of your obligations to the insurance company and your obligation to your friend?

Check one:

☐ Yes
☐ No

4

You have just come from a secret meeting of the board of directors of a company. You have a close friend who will be ruined unless he can get out of the market before the board's decision becomes known. You happen to be having dinner at that friend's home this same evening.

What right does your friend have to expect you to tip him off?

Check one:

☐ He has a definite right as a friend to expect me to tip him off.

☐ He has some right as a friend to expect me to tip him off.

☐ He has no right as a friend to expect me to tip him off.

Would you tip him off in view of your obligations to the company and your obligation to your friend?

Check one:

☐ Yes
☐ No

The problem is: Do the answers to these questions indicate the existence of a unidimensional scale, along which respondents can be ordered as to the degree to which they are likely to possess a trait or bias toward the particularistic solution of a dilemma? For simplicity, we label for a given item the response "My friend has a definite right ..." as particularistic, the response "He has no right ..." as universalistic. If he marks "He has some right ..." we label the response particularistic if in the second part of the question he says he would favor the friend in action; universalistic if he says he would not favor the friend.

There was a considerable spread among the four items in the percentage giving particularistic responses:

Item 1 (car accident)	26
Item 2 (drama critic)	45
Item 3 (insurance doctor)	51
Item 4 (board of directors)	70

Such frequencies suggest the hypothesis of a distance or cumulative scale.

Following Louis Guttman's scalogram method, the responses to all the items were cross-tabulated and scale patterns

Table **1** *Scalogram pattern for respondents to four items on role conflict*

Scale type	Scale pattern				Particularistic response to item number				Universalistic response to item number				"Errors"
	1	2	3	4	1	2	3	4	1	2	3	4	
5	+	+	+	+	66	66	66	66					0
	+	−	+	+	52		52	52		52			52
	+	+	−	+	15	15		15			15		15
	+	+	+	−	8	8	8					8	8
	+	−	+	−	5		5			5		5	10
	+	+	−	−	6	6					6	6	12
4	−	+	+	+		95	95	95	95				0
	−	+	+	−		16	16		16			16	16
3	−	−	+	+			80	80	80	80			0
	−	−	+	−			14		14	14		14	14
2	−	−	−	+				71	71	71	71		0
	−	+	−	+		66		66	66		66		66
	+	−	−	+	13			13		13	13		13
1	−	+	−	−		21			21		21	21	21
	+	−	−	−	6					6	6	6	6
	−	−	−	−					114	114	114	114	0
Total					*171*	*293*	*336*	*458*	*477*	*355*	*312*	*190*	*233*

$$\text{Reproducibility} = 1 - [233/(4 \times 648)] = .91$$

arranged according to nearest scale type, as shown in Table 1. While the reproducibility (.91) [1] and the distribution of cutting points suggest the admissibility of the hypothesis that these items form a Guttman scale, the items are too few in number for us to speak with confidence, especially in the presence of two sets of rather numerous nonscale responses $(+ - + +$ and $- + - +)$. Rigor would require ten or more items to start with, in order to determine scal-

ability, although we might in the end select fewer items for subsequent use.

The pure Guttman model can be viewed as the limiting case of a more general latent distance model which Paul F. Lazarsfeld has introduced.[2] It seems worth while, therefore, to examine the applicability to these data of the Lazarsfeld latent distance model, which postulates a latent continuum with as many ordered classes as there are items, plus one. The model assigns to each item a

[1] [Reproducibility measures the proportion of instances in which any given individual's response to a particular question may be correctly reproduced from his scale score. A scale with 100% reproducibility (not usually found in practice) means that each individual's scale score describes the exact pattern of his answers to all the questions.]

[2] Stouffer, Guttman, Suchman, Lazarsfeld, Star, and Clausen, *Studies in Social Psychology in World War II*, Vol. IV: *Measurement and Prediction* (Princeton: Princeton University Press, 1950). Guttman's theory and procedures are described in Chapters 2–9, Lazarsfeld's in Chapters 10 and 11. Chapter 1 provides an introduction to both methods.

probability that a positive (e.g., particularistic) response to that item assigns the respondent to a particular segment of the hypothetical continuum.[3]

For reasons of space, the arithmetic in testing the applicability of the latent distance model to our data will not be exhibited here. However, a brief technical summary of the results appears as an appendix to this paper. Although the procedure used is still too new to have developed wholly satisfactory acceptance standards, the outcome was quite encouraging.

Actually, an additional precaution was taken. Experience with projective material has taught us to expect considerable differences when we ask, "What do you think about something?" from results if we asked, "What do you think somebody else would think about something?" Especially, when we are seeking by crude question-and-answer procedures to learn something about social norms, it is very important to know what, if any, differences are produced by such shifts imposed on the point of view of the respondents. Hence, only a third of our 648 respondents were asked questions in the form exhibited above.

For a third of the subjects the stories were rewritten so that the friend of the respondent, not the respondent himself, faced the role conflict. . . .

For still another third of the respondents, a third version was presented. In this case neither the respondent nor his friend faced the dilemma but two hypothetical people, Smith and Smith's friend, Johnson. . . .

[3] Latent structure theory postulates that all the relationship between any two manifest items can be accounted for by the joint correlation of the items with the latent structure. In other words, within any segment of the latent structure the correlation between two manifest items is zero.

The different forms of the questionnaires were interleaved and handed out at random. In testing for the goodness of fit of the latent distance scale, separate tests were applied to each of the three types of items. The model seemed to fit about equally well in all three cases, and the rank order assigned to particular scale patterns was very much the same, except for a few scale types containing a negligible number of cases. As would be expected, the rank-order grouping derived from the latent distance model is very close to the rank-order grouping obtained by scoring to nearest scale type in scalogram analysis. . . .[4] It is of some interest to note that the reproducibility of each form is in the neighborhood of .90.

This is, of course, much too small a set of items about which to make any serious claims either to rigorous scalability or to generality, but the results encourage one to believe that we can develop good measures of individual predisposition to a bias in a particularistic or universalistic direction. We must note that a scale such as this is not an unequivocal measure of *particularism-universalism*. Since friendship obligations are diffuse and affectively toned as well as

[4] In scoring to nearest scale type by scalogram procedure, the objective is to arrange the scale patterns to minimize "error." Thus $+ + - +$ is grouped with $+ + + +$, on the assumption that the response to the third item only is an error. If it were grouped with $- + + +$, we should have to assume two errors, in the first and third items, respectively. However, there are some items which might be grouped in different ways with the same amount of error. For example, $- + - +$ would be grouped with $- + + +$ if we assumed that the third item was an error, but would be grouped with $- - - +$ if we assumed that the second item was an error. Such doubtful cases are resolved by the latent distance analysis, which in the present example usually gave clear and consistent information.

particularistic, and societal obligations are specific and affectively neutral as well as universalistic, we have scaled a predisposition for diffuse, affectively toned over specific, affectively neutral obligations as well as a predisposition for particularistic over universalistic obligations. But this fusion of variables in our situations *does* seem to generate a unidimensional scale, the dimension involved being the degree of strength of a latent tendency to be loyal to a friend even at the cost of other principles. The rank groupings would represent ordered degrees of probability of taking the friend's side in a role conflict.

Ideally, having assigned each of the 648 individuals to one of five scale types or rank groupings, we would like to see how these groupings relate to behavior in a new, nonverbal situation of role conflict. Such a design would be very costly and complicated but must be carried out sooner or later if we are to have full confidence that our scale is not an artifact—for example, that it does not arise merely from differences in imaginative ability, a possibility which was suggested by Leonard S. Cottrell in his discussion of the first draft of our paper. As a simple but decidedly inferior procedure, we investigated the relationship between the scale and other verbal responses relative to role conflict.

We selected some academic situations not too far removed from the experience of college students. The problem was to see whether respondents who were near the particularistic end of the scale, for example, tended to have a higher probability of giving particularistic responses in these academic situations than other respondents. (The scale itself involved no academic situations.) . . .

The following story . . . was presented and scored as were the other items quoted in the present paper.

You are proctoring an examination in a middle-group course. *You are the only proctor in the room.* About halfway through the exam you see a fellow-student, who is also your close friend, openly cheating. He is copying his answers from previously prepared crib notes. When he sees that you have seen the notes as you walked down the aisle and stopped near the seat, he whispers quietly to you, "O.K., I'm caught. That's all there is to it."

Under these circumstance, what right does he have to expect you not to turn him in?

Check one:

☐ He has a definite right as a friend to expect me not to turn him in.

☐ He has some right as a friend to expect me not to turn him in.

☐ He has no right as a friend to expect me not to turn him in.

Under these circumstances, what would you probably do in view of your obligations as a proctor and your obligation to your friend?

Check one:

☐ Report him.

☐ Not report him.

Variation was from 6 to 50 per cent, in proportions responding particularistically:

Scale type	Per cent
5	50
4	35
3	28
2	25
1	6

[Two other situations, here omitted, involve improving a friend's grade on an examination paper and holding a reserve library book for a friend. In both situations, the particularistic response tends to be associated with the scale in the predicted direction.]

These items, like the items included in the scale, were asked in three alternate forms. A respondent, for example, who had the "Smith-Johnson" form of the scale items also had a "Smith-Johnson" form of the new academic items. There was considerable variability in patterns of relationship, but the upward progression was present on all forms on each item, as is shown in Figure 1.

An important element of a friendship relationship is what Parsons calls an "other-orientation" rather than a self-orientation, such as is institutionalized in our society in a business transaction. Though other-orientation is institutionalized, it is probably not an absolute value. While the individual is supposed to subordinate his own interests to those of his friends under many circumstances, there are limits to the sacrifices which one may legitimately expect of a friend. These limits tend to be vague and undefined, perhaps so that they may vary with the intimacy of the friendship. This introduces another source of behavioral variability: The respondent's perception of the risk to himself by defying universalistic norms and coming to the friend's aid. It was of interest, therefore, to vary the cheating situation by asking the respondent to imagine an analogous setting with much greater risk to the proctor:

Consider the same cheating situation as above, with an *additional* element. Suppose now *there is another proctor (an extremely conscientious fellow!) in the examination room with you* and that you would be running a fifty-fifty risk of personal exposure by him to the authorities for failing as proctor to turn in a cheater.

(Check list the same as before)

How the increase in risk reduced the particularistic responses is shown in Table 2.

Figure **1** *Scale scores as related to the proportion "particularistic" in certain academic situations*

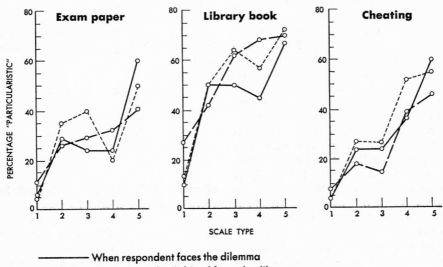

———— When respondent faces the dilemma
— — — When respondent's friend faces the dilemma
-------- When "Smith" faces the dilemma

Table **2** *Percentage "particularistic" when risk varies*

Scale type	In both situations	In situations of low risk only	In neither situation	Total
5	20	30	50	100
4	16	19	65	100
3	10	18	72	100
2	11	14	75	100
1	2	4	94	100

We hoped to make a further study of high and low risk to see how differences in predispositions might be related to other factors in this specific cheating situation, such as students' perceptions of the severity of penalties, of fellow-students' attitudes, and of the cheater's own probable reactions. Questions were designed on these points, but they were not satisfactory. The main problem which emerged, however, and which negated much further intensive cross-tabulation, was that sizable differences in response occurred depending on whether we asked the cheating question involving little risk to the proctor *prior to* or *after* the cheating question involving risk to the proctor. Actually, in a random half of the cases the little-risk situation was presented first; in the other half the risk situation was presented first.

For each form (ego as proctor, ego's friend as proctor, Smith as proctor) we have, then, two reports. There are six replications in all. . . . The form in which ego is proctor stands up well. We get about the same picture, irrespective of the order of presentation of the low-risk and high-risk situations, respectively. But the results are chaotic for the forms in which ego is the cheater or in which the actors are third persons.

The reasons for this result are not immediately obvious. Further trials and study are required before reaching a conclusion. One plausible suggestion is that a paper-and-pencil test like this re-quires a good deal of imagination on the part of a respondent and that the act of imagination is made easiest when ego himself is pictured as confronting the dilemma. By increasing the salience, one reduces the temptation for casual or careless checking. . . .

The systematic study of the extent to which identification, salience, ego defenses, etc., modify questionnaire responses is still in its infancy. Hence, the superior results . . . on the form in which ego himself faced the dilemma should not tempt us to hasty conclusions. After all, (1) . . . all three forms yielded about the same pattern of distribution of scale types, and (2), as Figure 1 shows, all three scales showed about the same general relationship in the specific academic situations, including the cheating situation.

Our study suggests that it is possible to classify people according to a predisposition to select one or the other horn of a dilemma in role conflict. As more studies are made—not only with pencil-and-paper tests, but also with role-playing in experimental and real-life situations and with other procedures—information exceedingly important to social science can be derived. We must anticipate the possibility, as Edward A. Suchman of Cornell has suggested in a letter to the writers, that tendencies of a respondent to adopt more stereotyped roles in hypothetical than in real-life situations will complicate prediction.

Studies in this field will help sociologists in developing theories of institutionalization and social psychologists in developing theories of personality and, indeed, can serve as a crucial link between the two bodies of theory. The importance of such a link, employing such variables as particularism-universalism, affectivity-neutrality, specificity-diffuseness, self-other, has been in the forefront of the thinking of Talcott Parsons and associates, who have been working on a new schema looking toward unification of social science theory.[5] The immensity of the technical task involved in making such concepts amenable to measurement in the years of patient work which lie ahead is at least suggested by the experience of our present study. Indeed, one of the most important values of this paper should be its service as a brake on the enthusiasm of those who may anticipate quick and easy progress in moving from highly abstract concepts in social science to empirical operations.

Such studies as ours can also be applied in practical research if sustained effort is devoted to technical developments. Leadership, for example, involves skill in the solution of role conflicts. Classic examples are the foreman in industry or the noncommissioned officer in the army. If such thoughtful observers as Chester I. Barnard are correct, skill in handling role conflicts is also a *sine qua non* at the high executive levels. Eventually, we may have role-playing situational tests, involving nonverbal as well as verbal behavior, which will be useful in the selection and training of leaders. The present study represents only a primitive effort to formulate some of the problems of definition and measurement.

[5] Talcott Parsons *et al., Toward a General Theory of Action,* Harvard University Press, 1951.

Note on Lazarsfeld's Latent Distance Scale as Applied to Role Conflict Data

In *Measurement and Prediction,* Chapter 11, pages 441–47, the reader will find a numerical example of a latent distance analysis carried out in full, on Research Branch data on psychoneurotic symptoms. That analysis used only one computed parameter for each item. In the present example on role-conflict data, Lazarsfeld, who kindly made the analysis, introduced more flexibility by computing two parameters for each item. The latent structure is set up as follows:

Latent class	Item 1	Item 2	Item 3	Item 4
I	a_1	a_2	a_3	a_4
II	b_1	a_2	a_3	a_4
III	b_1	b_2	a_3	a_4
IV	b_1	b_2	b_3	a_4
V	b_1	b_2	b_3	b_4

Each value of a tends to be a large fraction and each value of b tends to be small. (The example in Chapter 11 added the restriction that $a_1 = 1 - b_1$. In the perfect Guttman scale each $a = 1$ and each $b = 0$.) The algebra and arithmetical routine involved will be presented by Lazarsfeld in a separate paper. Final results, however, are shown here as Table 3, using as illustration, for reasons of space, only the form in which ego faces the dilemma. In this table, the scale patterns are ordered as in Table 1 and do not follow precisely the rank order they would have in Lazarsfeld's schema. The most serious discrepancy between the ordering indicated by the Lazarsfeld model and by the scalogram procedure of scoring to the nearest scale type is with respect to pattern $+ - - +$ based on only four cases (see Table 3). The Lazarsfeld procedure would place this pattern within the top group. By scalogram procedure, to assign this pattern to the top group would be to imply that respondents made two "errors," in both Items 2 and 3, which, indeed, may have been the case. The present assignment implies only one error, on Item 1. The reader will note that two-error patterns $+ - + -$ and $+ + - -$, with two cases and one case respectively, which could have been assigned variously by scalogram methods, belong, by the Lazarsfeld model, just where they have been put.

The picture presented in Table 3 is analogous to the picture presented in *Measurement and Prediction*, Chapter 11, Table 13, but it must be remembered

that it has involved a more flexible basic design.

The last two columns of Table 3 show good agreement between the fitted and actual totals. Approximately as good a fit was obtained with the other two forms of the questionnaire, and the rank ordering of the scale patterns on the basis of the percentage of a given pattern in each latent class is not markedly different. Much further study is needed of the latent distance model used here, especially with respect to reliability of small frequencies and, as has been mentioned earlier, to the testing of acceptance standards. The concept of a latent structure is theoretically quite appropriate to data of the type we are likely to assemble in subsequent investigations of role, and of informal social norms generally.

Table 3 *Illustrative results of fitting latent distance structure*

(*data for form in which ego faced role conflict*)

Item 1 2 3 4	Per cent of each pattern in each latent class						Totals	
	I	II	III	IV	V	Total	Fitted	Actual
$+ + + +$	95.9	4.0	0.1			100	19.1	20
$+ - + +$	94.8	3.9	0.2	0.2	0.9	100	10.0	9
$+ + - +$	91.7	3.7	3.0	0.3	1.3	100	6.5	6
$+ + + -$	95.7	4.3				100	2.5	2
$+ - + -$	96.7	3.3				100	1.3	2
$+ + - -$	92.3	5.1	2.6			100	0.8	1
$- + + +$	0.9	95.6	3.0	0.3	0.2	100	39.9	38
$- + + -$	0.8	87.7	2.7	0.4	8.4	100	5.7	7
$- - + +$	0.9	88.9	2.7	4.8	2.7	100	22.2	24
$- - + -$	0.3	34.8	1.2	1.7	62.0	100	7.4	6
$- - - +$	0.3	25.3	19.9	34.7	19.8	100	25.4	23
$- + - +$	0.5	52.3	41.2	3.8	2.2	100	23.7	25
$+ - - +$	86.2	3.6	2.4	4.8	3.0	100	3.6	4
$- + - -$	0.3	23.1	18.4	1.6	56.6	100	6.9	6
$+ - - -$	33.9	1.8		1.8	62.5	100	1.2	1
$- - - -$		2.1	1.6	2.8	93.5	100	41.0	42

URIEL G. FOA

Worker Satisfaction in Four Disciplinary Climates

I. Theoretical Introduction

Chester I. Barnard aptly expressed the feeling of many social researchers when he wrote: "... I am sure that a consideration of general purposes, 'principles', and underlying conceptions—what we may call the philosophic approach to problems—is intensely practical." Those familiar with empirical studies know only too well that abundance of observations is often a source of embarrassment; many are the possible ways of combining and splitting the data, and one may get lost in the wealth of details, unless he is helped by a guiding theory.

This paper can be considered as an exercise in applying Barnard's advice. We shall attempt to show how some of the highly generalized concepts of Parsons' theory of action were useful in observing and explaining certain group norms in a manner which is not devoid of practical significance.

One of Parsons' concepts is the *role,* that is the functional position that the actor (ego) is expected to fulfill in his interaction with another actor (alter). The role is not defined by ego alone but also by the expectation of alter with regard to behavior of ego. If ego and alter share the same values and standards, they are likely to agree on the definition of the reciprocal roles, and a stable

Prepared especially for this volume by Uriel G. Foa, the Israel Institute of Applied Social Research.

system is thus achieved. It may happen, however, that alter reacts to ego in a manner not conforming to ego's expectation and definition of alter's role; such a reaction may be serious and/or persistent enough to disrupt the equilibrium of the interaction, and to require the adjustment of ego to the newly created situation.

One source of tension between ego and alter which has received considerable attention is the conflict of roles or incompatibilities in behavior which may arise from the fact that ego may belong simultaneously to different social structures requiring from him different and even contrasting roles. Here we are interested in the *conflict of norms.* Ego and alter may have different norms either because they belong to different cultures or subcultures, because of the contrasting demands of other roles, or for any other reason.

An example of conflict of norms is given by Roethlisberger who refers to a sea-captain used to the paternalistic-authoritarian tradition. His ability to rule depends on the fact that the crew accepts the same tradition. As new people lacking this tradition join the ship, the captain finds that his leadership techniques become ineffective: a conflict develops between the captain and the crew. As a consequence, the poor captain is confronted with such ridiculous complaints as that the crew could not get "seconds on jello." Such behavior of the crew could not fit the normative frame of reference of the captain—especially since it was, after all, quite possible to obtain "seconds on jello."

Investigating norms may be of particular importance when different norms co-exist in the same culture or when inter-cultural studies are made. On the other hand, when norms are fairly uniform it may be possible to get meaningful results even if the normative aspect is not investigated directly.

Several investigations were undertaken at the Survey Research Center of the University of Michigan on the relationship between supervisory practices and workers' behavior in relation to productivity and morale. They investigated different types of workers such as railroad section gang workers, employees in an insurance company, workers in a tractor factory, and workers in several other plants. They consistently found that certain patterns of supervisory behavior are related to workers' productivity and morale. Here it is not known what kind of role workers expect and require from their supervisors, but the consistency of findings seems to indicate that such a role is fairly stable and uniform from plant to plant. At the same time, one may hypothesize that this very same supervisory behavior would arouse different and perhaps opposite worker reaction in a culture where the supervisor is expected to behave in a different manner.

II. The Empirical Setting

The data to be reported here are from a 1954 study of the seagoing personnel of an Israel shipping company, and they refer to the officers and crews of 18 ships.

Each respondent officer or crewman was interviewed by a research worker of the Israel Institute either at sea or in the home port, and asked to fill out a questionnaire which included the following two areas:

a. Need for formal discipline on board the ship.

b. Satisfaction with the officers of the ship (crews only).

The position of each respondent in each area was ascertained by means of a Guttman scale. Here are some examples of the closed questions included in each area.

Discipline:

"Do you think that a very strict discipline is always necessary on board ships?"

"Discipline on board ships requires that work should be carried out as instructed by the officers without any refusal at all. Do you think this requirement is right?"

Satisfaction with Officers:

"Are you satisfied with the attitude of the officers to seamen on your ship?"

"Do you think that the usual attitude of the officers on board your ship ensures good relations between them and the seamen?"

In each area there were three or four questions followed by four to five possible answers arranged in rank order. Pretesting showed that each area followed rather closely the Guttman scale model; it was thus possible to arrange the respondents in rank order in each area separately. The existence of a Guttman scale in a given area also suggests that the subject matter of this area is understood in the same way by the different respondents.

The intensity component was used to separate respondents in each area in an objective fashion according to positive and negative attitudes.

III. The Analysis

The first analytical step was to find out what kind of disciplinary climate prevailed in each ship. The median of the attitude toward discipline was determined separately for officers and crew in each ship. These two median values for each ship were then compared with the general median of all ships and all ranks taken together.[1] This comparison could yield four possible outcomes, and all of these occurred in practice.

[1] It was found expedient to use the general median, rather than the zero point of the intensity component, because of the strong positive skewness of distribution. Thus ship medians for both officers and crew were almost always on the positive side of the zero point. The general median, on the other hand, happened to maximize apparent differences between officers and crew.

In some ships both officers and crews wanted, on the average, a degree of formal discipline higher than the general median. In other ships both officers and crew wanted in general a degree of discipline lower than the general median. In still other ships the officers wanted a degree higher, and the crew a degree lower, than the general median. Finally in certain ships the officers wanted a degree lower and the crew a degree higher than the general median. In such a way four disciplinary climates are determined. In two of them there is on the average agreement among officers and crews about the level of discipline required: in one climate both stand for a relatively high level and in the other for a relatively low level. In the remaining two climates, officers and crew disagree, on the average, about level of discipline: in one, the officers want more discipline

Table **1** *Crew satisfaction with ship officers in different disciplinary climates*

Scale rank on satisfaction with ship officers

Disciplinary climate	Dissatisfied				Zero point	Satisfied						Total	Number of ships
	1	2	3	4	5	6	7	8	9	10	11		
Both officers and crew want discipline	1		2	4	2	8	6	*10*[a]	6	5	7	51	3
Officers want discipline more than crew	10	15	20	21	25	*13*	15	30	13	16	13	191	8
Crew want discipline more than officers					1	2	2	2	*2*	5	1	15	1
Both officers and crew do not want much discipline		1	8	2	6	*15*	12	8	3	3	2	60	6
Total frequency	*11*	*16*	*30*	*27*	*34*	*38*	*35*	*50*	*24*	*29*	*23*	*317*	*18*

[a] The entry in the cell containing the median satisfaction rank in each climate is italicized.

than the crew, and in the other, just the contrary happens—the crew comes out in favor of discipline more strongly than the officers do.

The next analytical step is to relate disciplinary climate to crew's satisfaction with the behavior of officers in their own ship. This cross tabulation is given in Table 1.

The zero point of the scale of satisfaction with ship officers, obtained by relating this scale with its intensity function, falls at score 5. It is thus possible to dichotomize this variable at the zero point, and to express in percentages the portion of the population in each disciplinary climate falling on each side of the zero point. This facilitates the analysis, as shown in Table 2.

The chi-square test indicates that the proportion of the crewmen satisfied (or dissatisfied) with their officers varies significantly with changes in disciplinary climates. The P-value is below .01.

Table 2 shows that, in a climate of agreement, there is considerable satisfaction with ships' officers, especially if there is agreement on supporting a relatively high level of discipline.

In the other two climates, where officers and crew disagree as to the desirable level of discipline, there is a substantial difference in the expressed amount of crew satisfaction with officers. Where ship officers are for a stronger discipline than the crew would like, satisfaction with officers is at its lowest: slightly more than half of the seamen are satisfied with officers' behavior. In the other group, where the crew wants more discipline than the officers do, practically all the sailors express satisfaction with officers: 14 out of 15 are satisfied, and the remaining one is not really dissatisfied, but on the borderline.

Interpretation of Results

We have a different disciplinary climate in each of the four groups. In two groups there is agreement between officers and crew about discipline. In the other two groups there is disagreement.

Let us first consider the two groups where no difference of values exists: in one of these groups, both officers and crew agree on the need for discipline; in the other group both agree that not

Table **2**   *Percentage and absolute figures of sailors satisfied and dissatisfied with ship officers in different disciplinary climates*

	Sailors' satisfaction		
Disciplinary climate	*Dissatisfied*	*Satisfied*	*Total*
Both officers and crew want discipline	16 (8) [a]	84 (43)	100 (51)
Officers want discipline more than crew	42 (81)	58 (110)	100 (191)
Crew want discipline more than officers	7 (1)	93 (14)	100 (15)
Both officers and crew do not want discipline	25 (15)	75 (45)	100 (60)
All climates	*33 (105)*	*67 (212)*	*100 (317)*

[a] Absolute figures are in parentheses.

much discipline is required. There is between these two groups *similarity* in agreement and *difference* in degree of desired discipline. Crew satisfaction with officers' behavior is higher in the agreeing group with stronger discipline, and lower in the group where officers and crew agree on a low level of discipline. This seems to indicate that discipline (when accepted) represents an efficient technique, conducive, in this situation, to a satisfactory social relationship.

We can now turn to the two remaining groups where a situation of contrast exists. In one group the officers ask for more discipline than the crews are prepared to accept; in the other one just the contrary, the crews are in favor of discipline more than the officers. In the former group crew satisfaction with officers' behavior is at its lowest; in the latter group at its highest. Thus it seems that the existence of value differences is

not always conducive to low satisfaction. Discipline imposes limitations on the behavior of the crew—and is something which restricts the seaman's freedom to act or not to act in a certain manner. When the seaman is prepared for a limitation of freedom more severe than the one actually requested by the officers, then his satisfaction is extremely high.

In both the last two groups we have a difference in norms between officers and crew, yet in the former group we found high satisfaction with officers' behavior, and in the latter low satisfaction. If the amount of satisfaction with alter's behavior can be taken as an indication of equilibrium in the social system, then we may conclude that not every difference of norms is conducive to a crisis in the system. Differences in norms may exist, yet leave the system quite unshaken.

MATILDA WHITE RILEY
JACKSON TOBY
RICHARD COHN
JOHN W. RILEY, JR.
Scale Analysis of Collective Data

Guttman scales may be used to measure, as well as to clarify, certain types of sociological variables—variables conceived as doubly complex because they involve *patterns of action* on the one hand, and *structuring of individuals* on the other. Thus task performance, as at-

Adapted from Matilda White Riley, John W. Riley, Jr., and Jackson Toby, *Sociological Studies in Scale Analysis,* New Brunswick, New Jersey: Rutgers University Press, 1954, Chapters IV and XI.

tributed to a group, may include both a sequence of steps to be performed and an organization of individuals to perform them. Similarly, status may be defined operationally as the pattern of deference accorded by the collectivity to its members—a pattern made up by individuals, themselves differentially placed in the social structure, who accord this deference in different manners and degrees.

There are therefore two aspects to the

following studies: (1) "measurement" of the variable as a pattern of action, and (2) "post-analysis" of the underlying interpersonal structure. The approach makes use of a particular kind of "collective" data. The empirical raw materials are concerned with the acts and attitudes of the individual members of a group and are fitted together in an effort to represent a synthesis for the collectivity as a whole.

Parallel Subject and Object Scales

Some simple examples from the research of the Rutgers Research Group will illustrate use of scales to measure certain concepts dealing with the interaction of members of a group. Here the focus is on uncovering *patterns in the action*. For the present, *individuals* are simply *assumed* to be acting as a group —not as unrelated individuals; then later, the post-analysis will analyze the collective action in terms of the individuals who contribute to it. These measures are based on data of a sociometric nature, and view the same individuals first as subjects, who direct action toward the group, and again as objects who receive action from the group.

The 148 girls in the 9th and 11th grades of a high school (aggregated into a single communications "group"—apart from boys) were interviewed and asked a series of questions designed to identify the patterns of their peer communications behavior. These questions ask, in effect, "Whom do you talk your problems over with?" and enumerate a list of some twenty specific problems ranging from "What to wear to a party" and "What movie to attend" to "How you get along with people" and "The fear that something terrible might happen to you." Individual

answers vary greatly, from "Nobody, I'd keep it to myself," to long lists of parents, siblings, and classmates. (No restrictions were set on the number of others who could be named.) The analysis proceeded first from the point of view of the individuals reporting, to provide a measure of the way in which the individual communicates with, or relates herself to, her peers. Each respondent was given a score, for each topic, of the number of peers to whom she talked. Thus, the collected data appear much as if the subject had merely been asked directly, "How many of your classmates do you discuss ———— with?"

One way to handle such data might have been to add up, for each girl, scores on all the twenty topics. A low total score would then have indicated a girl who communicates little with peers; a high total score, a girl who is highly communicative. In this instance, however, an alternative procedure was used. The question was raised whether talking to the same friend on ten different topics, and talking to each of ten different friends on one topic, ought both to be given the same score of 10. Moreover, there was some doubt about whether all twenty topics belonged together in the same score: perhaps some topics are perceived as more intimate than others and should be given different weights in a total score. With such problems in mind, accordingly, a scale was sought which would represent the degree of intimacy of communication.

Table 1 shows a subject scale in which four of the twenty topics were selected for scale analysis and tested for unidimensionality. Everybody, that is, who reported talking to peers on the most intimate topic, also tended to talk to peers on all the others; those who did not talk to peers on the most intimate topic, but did talk on the next most in-

Table **1** *Subject scale of communications distributed* [a,b]

Item		Right and wrong	What to wear to a party	How to get along	Boys	Nonscale types	Perfect scale types	Total
		\+ = subject talks to sufficient others about — Scale pattern				Distribution of subjects		
Minimum number of mentions required for a + rating		1	1	1	1			
Scale type of subject								
Most communicative	4	+	+	+	+	7	14	21
	3	−	+	+	+	18	13	31
	2	−	−	+	+	12	18	30
	1	−	−	−	+	6	19	25
Least communicative	0	−	−	−	−	3	38	41
Total subjects						*46*	*102*	*148*

a This table orders subjects according to the number of topics about which each subject communicates to sufficient others.

b Compare Table 8 on page 452 for further details of the scale.

timate, tended also to report peer communication on the third and fourth topics; and so on. While there is one large non-scale category (containing 13 cases —see Table 8), the tendency of the four items to approximate the cumulative scale pattern is quite apparent.

It is difficult to say whether or not such a subject scale of communications (even if it contained more items and less error) is preferable to a total subject score based on all friends talked to on all topics. Either one would serve as an index of an elusive underlying concept. Either one represents this concept by combining several topics, rather than depending upon a single topic alone. Use of the scale assumes that the concept is unidimensional, and tests whether the data fit this assumption. Use of a simple score does not raise the question of unidimensionality. Ultimately, as much further research makes use of all such tools and compares them, the rela-

tive merits of each for specific purposes may become more clearly defined.

Whatever validity may adhere to such a scale as this, its implications are clearly in terms of the individual reporting. For example, it might be interpreted as a measure of the intimacy of the orientation of the individual to his peers. Or, since the scale score goes up with the *number* of different topics of communication, it might be taken as a measure of the "diffuseness," as opposed to the "specificity," of the individual's relationship to the peer group, using the Parsonian alternatives which describe the scope of the subject's interest in the object.[1] The fact that such a scale exists at all might be interpreted as an indication that all individuals in the group become increasingly oriented to their peers by following a standard pattern of communication. Thus, it cannot be said that

[1] See Talcott Parsons, *The Social System* (The Free Press, 1951), p. 65 and *passim*.

some individuals talk to peers on one intimate topic only, others on still another intimate topic only; it must rather be said that all individuals tend to approach peers first on the same everyday topic, that all who become better acquainted go on to a slightly more intimate common topic; and so on. Thus, the data which form the scale, in this case, are individuals' reports of their communications to peers.

In the second phase of the analysis this process was reversed in order to study the same data with reference to the communications received by the peer from the collectivity of individuals. The emphasis is now on the peer as object. The data are no longer the reports of the individual about his own actions; they are the aggregated reports of the others in the group about their relationship to him. For each topic each respondent was given a score representing the number of peers who talked to him. Operation-

ally, this involved pretabulating the total communications received by each student from all other students. Each of these scores was then dichotomized, so as to distinguish between students who were talked to by at least one peer on a given topic and students who were not talked to at all on that topic.

Table 2 shows an object scale for the same four items which were used in the subject scale in Table 1. The two tables show different analyses of the same raw data. In general outline the two are closely analogous. The analogy in form between these two scales should not, however, conceal the major difference in the terms in which their implications must be stated. One measures the action or attitudes of the individual toward the group; the other measures the action or attitudes of (members of) the group toward the individual as object. Table 2, for example, classifies girls as recipients of more or less diffuse communications from

Table **2**   *Object scale of communications received* [a,b]

| | | Scale pattern | | | | Distribution of objects | | |
| | | + = object is talked to by sufficient others about | | | | | | |
Item		*Right and wrong*	*What to wear*	*How to get along*	*Boys*	*Non-scale types*	*Perfect scale types*	*Total*
Minimum number of mentions required for + rating		1	1	1	1			
Scale type of object								
Receives most communication	4	+	+	+	+	1	32	33
	3	—	+	+	+	15	18	33
	2	—	—	+	+	14	15	29
	1	—	—	—	+	4	15	19
Receives least communication	0	—	—	—	—	2	32	34
Total objects						*36*	*112*	*148*

[a] This scale orders objects according to the number of topics about which each receives communications from sufficient others.

[b] Compare Table 9 on page 453 for further details of the scale.

the group and may accordingly be interpreted on a dimension of collective acceptance. The fact that a scale was found rules out (for the present group and the four topics in question) the possibility of "experts" or "specialists," since no girl can be consulted on a highly specialized or intimate topic without first receiving communications from peers on all topics below it in the scale.

The Relation Between Subject and Object Scales

These two analyses have thus classified each girl twice: once, as subject, according to how much she communicates with peers; again, as object, according to how much others communicate with her. The two might be said to measure the two aspects of her verbal interaction with her group.

Table 3 shows a cross-tabulation of these two scales and illustrates some of the differences in their implications. While there appears to be some correlation between the scales, it is clear that the two are not necessarily related: the distribution of a high degree of communication *to* the group does not necessarily imply the reception of communication *from* the group in the same measure. Whether such asymmetry actually

exists in the communications patterns themselves, or whether it is due to individual differences in perception or reporting, its appearance in the results and the direction it takes are nonetheless fruitful of hypotheses. Thus, both subject and object scales are useful in this instance.

A Status Scale

In another example, an object scale is used to measure status. Four hundred students, comprising all the students in four grades of a New Jersey high school, were interviewed intensively, and their answers to four main questions combined in the scale: "Whom would you like to do things with?" "Who is the most popular boy (girl) in your class?" "Whom do you do things with?" and "Who is the leader of your group?" Here again the "votes" received by each student on each item were pretabulated, and the resultant scores dichotomized. The dichotomized ratings were found to form an object scale as shown in Table 4. This served, accordingly, to divide the sample into five status categories for use in further analysis. Moreover, the fact of a scale in this case indicated that no student can achieve the highest item on the status scale without also qualifying

Table **3** *Subject scale of communications related to object scale of communications*

	Subject scale types					
Object scale types	0	1	2	3	4	Total
0	20	4	3	6	1	34
1	3	5	5	5	1	19
2	7	8	5	5	4	29
3	9	5	7	8	4	33
4	2	3	10	7	11	33
Total	41	25	30	31	21	148

Table **4** *Object scale of group status* [a,b]

	Scale pattern				Distribution of Objects		
	+ = object is mentioned by sufficient others for						
Item	*Leader*	*Popular*	*Wished-for associate*	*Actual associate*	*Non-scale types*	*Perfect scale types*	*Total*
Minimum number of mentions required for + rating	1	1	4	2			
Scale type of object							
Highest status 4	+	+	+	+	8	67	75
3	−	+	+	+	7	61	68
2	−	−	+	+	15	104	119
1	−	−	−	+	6	58	64
Lowest status 0	−	−	−	−	10	64	74
Total objects					*46*	*354*	*400*

[a] This scale orders objects according to the degree of deference accorded to them by other members of the group.

[b] Compare Table 10 on page 454 for further details of the scale.

on all the other three counts, as defined; for example, a student cannot be a "leader" unless he meets a minimum requirement as also "popular," "wished for," and "associated with."

Some of the conceptual implications of such an object scale of status are noteworthy. In the first place, status is here operationally defined in terms of the acts and attitudes of others toward the object. An attempt is made to bring the measure itself as close as possible to the widely accepted definition of *status or position* which may be exemplified by William Foote Whyte's statement that "To have a position means that the individual has a customary way of interacting with other members of the group." [2]

[2] *Street Corner Society* (University of Chicago Press, 1943), p. 263. Warner similarly defines class position as related to those who "interact in the social system of a community." W. Lloyd Warner, Marchia Meeker, and Kenneth Eells, *Social Class in America* (Science Research Associates, 1949), p. 35.

There are today several widely used measures of community status. Notable among them are the famous Chapin living room scale [3] and the Warner Index of Status Characteristics. [4] As recently revised, the Chapin scale is made up of items having to do with the possession of such things as dining alcoves, venetian blinds, and television sets. The Warner index is based on four items—occupation, source of income, house type, and dwelling area—each of which is rated by the investigator on a seven-point scale. Insofar as the object scale of status selects its items directly from a universe of such interaction as that referred to in the generic definition given above by Whyte, it is to be distinguished

[3] F. Stuart Chapin, "A Quantitative Scale for Rating the Home and Social Environment of Middle Class Families in an Urban Environment: A First Approximation to the Measurement of Socio-Economic Status," *Journal of Educational Psychology,* XIX (February, 1928), pp. 99–111.

[4] Warner, *op. cit.,* p. 35 ff.

technically from such indices of the same phenomena—status—as those of Warner and Chapin which are based upon observable characteristics of the object.

The Question of Social Structure

Once the object scale has uncovered such *patterns in the collective action,* it becomes possible to study further the underlying social structure. The object scale seems to afford a peculiar opportunity for further analysis. Its data are drawn directly from the members of the group themselves, who may be further questioned and thus provide a laboratory in which to study the process by which these collective patterns are generated. Given an object scale, it thus becomes possible to observe the collective subject, to discover, for example, why certain choices are made, or which subjects contribute, or fail to contribute, the significant answers to the questionnaire items. Which students select as associates, for instance, those peers who are in the top status category? If these respondents do not also choose the same students as leaders, why do they fail to do so? What are the structure and the mechanisms of the informal "division of labor" through which a group may be said to accord deference to its individual members?

The following examples explore some possible forms of such *post-analysis.* This post-analysis starts with the cumulative pattern of acts (the scale) obtained when the answers of many respondents are treated collectively, then asks the crucial question: were we justified in our initial assumption that the individuals were acting *as a group?* (We have based the measure, in effect, upon the same group used repeatedly with reference to different objects.) But is the measure in fact derived from the integration of interdependent individual roles within a group—or from the mere aggregation of unrelated individual attitudes? In attempting to shed light on this crucial question, the post-analysis will aim to (1) challenge the relevance of the group as the research case, and (2) explore the process by which individual group members may act in concert.

Conditions Producing Object Scales

One type of post-analysis examines the ingredients of the collective measure —the attitudes of particular subjects toward particular objects (that is, the dyadic relationships) which have been collected in the scale. In principle, object scales may arise when either, or a combination of both, of the following conditions exist:

1. *Unidimensionality* within the dyads, so that each subject follows a scale pattern for each of the objects (on the scale items). Thus, in regard to status, unidimensionality would exist if each subject who names a particular object as popular also wants to associate with that *same* object.

2. *Differentiation* among the dyads, so that the object is named as an associate by one subject, as popular by another subject, and as leader by still a different subject.

When an object scale occurs under conditions of the first type, this does not necessarily reflect—although it may—a conceptual model of the individuals as members of groups. The finding might be accounted for entirely by the consistency with which *individuals* pattern their attitudes and actions toward others.

But when an object scale occurs under conditions of the second type, the scale abstracts from the idiosyncratic attitudes of particular individuals, reaching a more general level of collective attitudes. The ordering of the items depends, not on the degree of a given reaction by each subject, but on the degree of a given reception accorded to an object by the composite of all subjects taken as a group. Different subjects play different parts in the object's total reception. The existence of the object scale depends, in such an event, upon *a certain relationship among these parts,* so that certain acts are performed by some members only if certain others are performed by other members. One conceptual model that could account for this is the "organically" solidary group in Durkheim's sense—the group characterized here by a sort of informal "division of labor."

Thus one empirical test of the initial assumption that the group is relevant to the scale analysis—that the collecting of the dyadic data was indeed appropriate—seeks to discover whether any traces of such division of labor exist. In one example, the dyadic pattern for one pair of items from the object scale of status, popularity and actual association, is examined, as in Table 5. In the *object* scale (Table 4), popularity is contingent upon having associates: a person is regarded as popular by members of the group only if he is also the friend of members of the group. When we look at the dyads in Table 5, however, *no* similar cumulative pattern appears. Out of the 788 dyads in which a subject names an object as the most popular person in the class, there are only 133 in which the subject himself actually associates with this object. That is, there are 655 instances in which a student names as most popular some person who is *not* one of his own friends. This comes close to the situation in which a person names another as popular only if a *different* person associates with him. Here the dyads appear to be differentiated, so that the collective finding cannot be accounted for by the mere juxtaposition of similarly conditioned subjects and a set of objects with unidimensional properties.

(Incidentally, to be sure, we have no statistical tests to insure that the collective data do reveal a higher degree of patterning in the items than would have been predicted here if the dyad data alone had been used. A number of stubborn mathematical problems still stand in the way of answering the question: To the extent that different acts in a

Table **5** *Differentiated dyadic pattern of two selected status items*

Pattern of answers		Number of dyads in which subject names object for		Distribution of dyads
Popularity	*Actual association*	*Popularity*	*Actual association*	
+	+	133	133	133
+	−	655	—	655
−	+	—	1330	1330
Total dyads [a]		*788*	*1463*	*2118*

[a] This table includes only those dyads in which a subject names an object for either or both of the items.

collective scale of acts are performed by different individuals, are these acts related to each other in the group data to a greater extent than would be expected by chance? The dyads as units do not meet the criteria of statistical independence, since the same individual may be involved in several dyads as subject and as object. Moreover, it is difficult to determine the boundary of the "effective group" for any given dimension of action. The Rutgers analysis assumes that the outside boundary is set by the school grade, but that these large grades contain many smaller groupings. Thus the failure of *A* to name *B* as a person "talked to," for example, may mean *either* that *A* made a negative decision about talking to *B, or* that *B* simply does not come within the effective boundary of people *A* has a chance to talk with. Since there is no way in the present studies to set these boundaries—which seem unfortunately to vary from item to item—the negative answers to most of the items are overwhelmingly large. This makes it difficult to apply the usual criteria of statistical tests. For discussion of some of these problems, see Chapters X and XI by Matilda White Riley and Richard Cohn in Riley, Riley, and Toby, *Sociological Studies in Scale Analysis.*)

Once such mathematical and technical problems are solved, a finding of sufficiently differentiated dyads (as suggested by Table 5) might be used to demonstrate the *interdependence among individuals*—hence the relevance of the group to the particular analysis. To be sure, the source of this interdependence still requires further investigation. The interdependence might arise merely because the groups under study were initially made up by selecting certain (patterned) types of individuals. Or—of greater sociological interest—it might arise be-

cause of a network of role-relationships in which, even though the members themselves may be unaware of it, their actions and attitudes tend to become channeled through the expectations and sanctions of the others.

Further Study of the Nature of Interdependence

To the extent that interdependence among individuals may be demonstrable, additional support is still needed, then, for the basic assumption that such interdependence reflects a social system of action. Another example of post-analysis investigates the nature of interdependence by utilizing a peculiar feature of the object scale—the fact that the object scale, through its very nature, studies the same subjects, not once, with reference to a single object, but many times with reference to a series of objects. A simple example will suggest the value of such data. Suppose the occupants of a large sample of automobiles are questioned at a crossing at which the light is sometimes out and sometimes red. In each car there are two people, and we ask each after the car has passed the crossing:

Was the light on?

Was it green?

Was it red?

The following combinations of answers might be found in each of the several cars:

Both say the light was out.

Both say the light was red.

One says it was red and the other says it was green.

One way to account for such a finding might be to assume that in some cars there are two classes of individuals: one with normal vision (the driver) and another who is afflicted by a peculiar type of color-blindness and always sees red as green. Another suggestion might be that in some instances where the driver has not stopped for the light, the rider reports the light as green in order to protect his friend from arrest. There seems to be no basis for choice between the two hypotheses.

But now suppose that, instead of checking each car at a single crossing, we observe each over a long course on which there are many crossings. Our hypothesis is that if the answer pattern is produced entirely by two classes of subjects (normal and color-blind) who are confronted by two classes of objects (lights out or lights red), then the same subjects will always respond in the same way to the same objects. A car which reports one red and one green answer to a red light will always give this report to a red light. Whereas, if the answer pattern is due to a social situation in which one friend lies to protect another, then we should expect such a response, not invariably, but only in cases where the driver has driven through the red light and seems threatened with arrest.

For an investigation of this sort, we may use some data for an object scale of communication similar to that shown

in Table 2 above, except that here each subject named those peers with whom he would discuss each of five—rather than four—topics. In order to limit the analysis to situations in which the subject is acquainted with the object (to an "effective group"), we deal only with those dyads in which the subject names the object for at least one item. We then work with one topic at a time. We first classify each individual as subject according to whether he is the type of person who talks to peers at all on the given topic; if he talks to any peer about this, we give him a positive subject rating. We then classify each individual as object according to whether he is the sort of person to elicit conversation on this topic; if any peer talks to him about this, we give him a positive object rating. The next step, then, is to examine the dyadic data for each subject-object pair. If the characteristics of the subject and the object determine the dyadic pattern, we should expect that any combination of a positive subject with a positive object will result in conversation on this topic. If it does not, we might infer (as one explanation) that some group mechanisms are at work to

Table 6   Dyadic predictions based on qualities of subjects and objects

	Topics		
	Problems of right and wrong	What to wear to a party	How you get along with the kids
Communication predicted and occurs	20	39	39
Communication predicted but does not occur	0	5	4
Subject and object communicate with each other on this topic only	0	0	2
Subject gives and object receives only one communication on this topic	4	7	6

control who talks to whom about what, over and beyond the particular individual traits.

As it turns out, the data in this case (see Table 6) show a rather remarkable fit to the first hypothesis: no role mechanisms seem necessary to account for the pattern here. On the topic, "How you get along with kids," while there were 39 instances where the hypothesis correctly predicted that students would communicate with each other on this topic, there were only four instances where communication was predicted and did not occur. In other words, there were only four cases where a subject who spoke to some object about the topic, and an object who was spoken to about it, failed to speak to each other about it (though they did communicate on other topics).

It may be objected that if communication on this topic is sufficiently rare so that a subject ordinarily speaks about it to only one object, and the object is ordinarily spoken to by at most one subject, the hypothesis automatically will be confirmed. But this does not appear to be the case in the present data; for there were only six instances in which a subject spoke about this item to just one object who in turn received no other communications concerning it.

One might also question whether it is sufficient to use only four other items (in addition to the item under scrutiny) to determine whether the subject and the object are "acquainted." But the data show that very little error results from this procedure. There are only two cases of a subject and object who communicate on the topic "How you get along with kids" and on no other topic. These cases were not classed in Table 6 with either the 39 cases confirming the hypothesis or the four contradicting it.

Similar results with other topics are also shown in Table 6. In view of the informal nature of the process being reported on, and the rather frequent occurrence of apparent "errors" in any dyadic scale pattern for these data, it is interesting that a finding, though slight, can show as much consistency as this. This suggests that such an approach might prove rewarding in a situation where an organic structure actually does exist.

Supporting Hypotheses

Another aspect of post-analysis is the need for as much supporting data as can be obtained about the structure and operating mechanisms of the collectivity. Insofar as possible, respondents should themselves be encouraged to provide supporting information—about collective goals, group membership and boundaries, and the like. To a certain extent, of course, it may not be possible to study the loosely

Figure 1   *Diagram of a larger system of action*

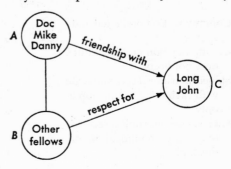

Table **7** *Popularity of objects in relation to status of the subjects who associate with them* [a]

| Number of subjects who associate with each object | Proportion of objects rated "popular" if the subjects who associate with them are primarily | | | |
| | High status | | Low status | |
	%	Total objects [b] = 100%	%	Total objects [b] = 100%
1	12	(16)	3	(31)
2	26	(27)	18	(17)
3	30	(20)	20	(25)
4	49	(35)	45	(11)
5	80	(30)	33	(9)
6 or more	73	(44)	40	(5)

[a] This analysis excludes those objects whose associates are fairly evenly divided between upper and lower status.

[b] Note that the bases for the percentages are extremely small.

The tendency of percentages in the left-hand column to exceed comparable percentages in the right-hand column suggests that popularity may be related to association with others of high status.

structured situation through such direct questioning. (The problem is often particularly difficult since we are studying, not the group, but only one dimension of action, in which the individuals may or may not be acting in their capacity as group members.) In such cases, though we must resort to inference, the aim should be to make cross-inferences which will tie into one another if possible.

Such a supporting hypothesis is suggested by William Foote Whyte's intensive analysis of a single case in which Long John's "friendship with the three top men (Doc, Mike and Danny) gave him a superior standing" in the gang. In Doc's words, " 'We give him so much attention that the rest of the fellows have to respect him.' " [5] A diagram of the interpersonal bonds might be drawn as in Figure 1. Here the respect of the "other fellows" (B), for Long John (C), is found to depend upon the fact that

[5] *Op. cit.*, p. 12.

the gang leaders, Doc, Mike and Danny (A), like Long John. Here the hypothesis is that the contingency of B's action upon A's is backed by A's high status in the group. The other fellows respect Long John, not merely because Doc likes him, but because Doc *who is the leader* likes him. It may well be that the model of the informal organic structure requires such an element of status.

What does this mean with reference to our status scale? There we have the phenomenon that one subject, A, names C as an associate and another subject, B, says C is popular. C, as a result of these supplementary acts, is pushed high up on the scale of status. But what about another person, E? He also is named as an associate by somebody called D. Yet nobody names E as popular. Why is this? If having friends leads to popularity, why is not E popular as well as C? The answer may be that A, who associated with C, is himself high-status, and therefore highly visible and influential in the group, so that B is thus influenced to call C popular. D, on the other hand, is not himself a high-status person. Accordingly, D's friendship does not have the same result for E that A's did for C. Thus status formation is conceived as an interactive process within which those who have high status tend to confer status upon others. The latter, in turn, may reinforce the status of the former, and so on.

We may set out, then, to test the following hypothesis: if the subject who associates with the object (but does not name him popular) is himself high-status, then the object is apt to be thought popular by somebody else. If the subject is low-status, then the object is less apt to be thought popular. The empirical

Table 8 *Subject scale of communications (Compare Table 1)*

Which girls *distribute* the more intimate communications to peers?

Subject scale type	Scale pattern				Subject communicates on topic number				Subject does not communicate on topic number				Errors	Total subjects
	1	2	3	4	1	2	3	4	1	2	3	4		
4	+	+	+	+	14	14	14	14	—	—	—	—	0	14
	+	+	—	+	7	7	—	7	—	—	7	—	7	7
3	—	+	+	+	—	13	13	13	13	—	—	—	0	13
	—	+	—	+	—	13	—	13	13	—	13	—	13	13
	—	+	+	—	—	5	5	—	5	—	—	5	5	5
2	—	—	+	+	—	—	18	18	18	18	—	—	0	18
	—	—	+	—	—	—	6	—	6	6	—	6	6	6
	+	—	+	+	5	—	5	5	—	5	—	—	5	5
	+	—	+	—	1	—	1	—	—	1	—	1	2	1
1	—	—	—	+	—	—	—	19	19	19	19	—	0	19
	+	—	—	+	6	—	—	6	—	6	6	—	6	6
0	—	—	—	—	—	—	—	—	38	38	38	38	0	38
	—	+	—	—	—	1	—	—	1	—	1	1	1	1
	+	—	—	—	2	—	—	—	—	2	2	2	2	2
Total					35	53	62	95	113	95	86	53	47	148

$$\text{Reproducibility} = 1 - \frac{47}{4 \times 148} = 92\% \qquad \text{Chance reproducibility} = 1 - \frac{78}{4 \times 148} = 87\%$$

Topics of conversation in order of decreasing intimacy are:	Minimum number of mentions required for a positive rating:
(1) Problems of right and wrong	1
(2) What to wear to a party	1
(3) Getting along with kids	1
(4) Boys	1

Table **9** *Object scale of communications* (*Compare Table* 2)

Which girls *receive* the more intimate communications from peers?

Object scale type	Scale pattern				Object is communicated with on topic number				Object is not communicated with on topic number				Errors	Total objects
	1	2	3	4	1	2	3	4	1	2	3	4		
4	+	+	+	+	32	32	32	32	—	—	—	—	0	32
	+	+	—	+	1	1	—	1	—	—	1	—	1	1
3	—	+	+	+	—	18	18	18	18	—	—	—	0	18
	—	+	—	+	—	9	—	9	9	—	9	—	9	9
	—	+	+	—	—	6	6	—	6	—	—	6	6	6
2	—	—	+	+	—	—	15	15	15	15	—	—	0	15
	—	—	+	—	—	—	4	—	4	4	—	4	4	4
	+	—	+	+	10	—	10	10	—	10	—	—	10	10
1	—	—	—	+	—	—	—	15	15	15	15	—	0	15
	+	—	—	+	4	—	—	4	—	4	4	—	4	4
0	—	—	—	—	—	—	—	—	32	32	32	32	0	32
	+	—	—	—	1	—	—	—	—	1	1	1	1	1
	—	+	—	—	—	1	—	—	1	—	1	1	1	1
Total					48	67	85	104	100	81	63	44	36	148

$$\text{Reproducibility} = -\frac{36}{4 \times 148} = 94\% \qquad \text{Chance reproducibility} = 1 - \frac{80}{4 \times 148} = 86\%$$

Topics of conversation in order of decreasing intimacy are:	*Minimum number of mentions required for a positive rating:*
(1) Problems of right and wrong	1
(2) What to wear to a party	1
(3) Getting along with kids	1
(4) Boys	1

problem was complicated by the fact that some objects have one associate, others have as many as six or more. Since an increasing number of associates is also a factor in popularity, this must be held constant. Accordingly, we examine at one time those objects who have the same number of associates as in Table 7.

Table 7, though based on extremely small samples, shows a tendency of the data to support such an hypothesis. An object who is associated with by five subjects, for instance, is also popular in 80 per cent of the cases if these subjects are predominantly high-status, and in only 33 per cent of the cases if the subjects are predominantly low-status.

While such fragmentary data are in no sense conclusive, they illustrate the type of supporting hypothesis which may serve to extend the understanding of collective patterns of action as uncovered by the scale.

These examples suggest how the use of models—like the Guttman scale—that uncover empirical patterns may not only measure, but also clarify, various properties of groups. Intensive studies of single social situations, as in the Whyte example above, typically reveal the complex, social-system character of much collective action. Larger studies based on statistical analysis have often failed, however, to take the system aspects of collective action into account.

We have accordingly reviewed, through simple empirical examples, the collective scale as one approach. It seems clear that a composite index that uses multiple indicants has definite advantages in uncovering the *patterns of acts and attitudes that may exist* and thus demonstrating the unidimensionality of the property being measured. In situations where the acts of individuals are differentiated and a division of labor exists, any measure based on individuals *qua* individuals may

Table **10** *Object scale of group status* (*Compare Table 4*)

Object scale type	Scale pattern				Students selected on item number				Students not selected on item number				Errors	Total objects
	1	2	3	4	1	2	3	4	1	2	3	4		
4	+	+	+	+	67	67	67	67	—	—	—	—	0	67
	+	+	—	+	6	6	—	6	—	—	6	—	6	6
	+	+	+	—	2	2	2	—	—	—	—	2	2	2
3	—	+	+	+	—	61	61	61	61	—	—	—	0	61
	—	+	—	+	—	5	—	5	5	—	5	—	5	5
	—	+	+	—	—	2	2	—	2	—	—	2	2	2
2	—	—	+	+	—	—	104	104	104	104	—	—	0	104
	—	—	+	—	—	—	7	—	7	7	—	7	7	7
	+	—	+	+	8	—	8	8	—	8	—	—	8	8
1	—	—	—	+	—	—	—	58	58	58	58	—	0	58
	+	—	—	+	6	—	—	6	—	6	6	—	6	6
0	—	—	—	—	—	—	—	—	64	64	64	64	0	64
	—	+	—	—	—	2	—	—	2	—	2	2	2	2
	+	—	—	—	7	—	—	—	—	7	7	7	7	7
	+	+	—	—	1	1	—	—	—	—	1	1	2	1
Total					97	146	251	315	303	254	149	85	47	400

$$\text{Reproducibility} = 1 - \frac{47}{4 \times 400} = 97\% \qquad \text{Chance reproducibility} = 1 - \frac{172}{4 \times 400} = 89\%$$

Items in order of decreasing difficulty are:	*Minimum number of mentions required for positive rating:*
(1) Leader	1
(2) Popular	1
(3) Wished-for associate	4
(4) Actual associate	2

conceal this pattern of collective action; and single-item measures, even though based on groups, may oversimplify its complexity.

Moreover, once a multiple-item collective measure, like the scale, has revealed the pattern of collective acts, the door is open for further analysis of the underlying *social* structure and process. Whether or not the Guttman scale is the

best approach to such post-analysis is certainly an open question. But to the extent that it can deal with the differentiated acts of individuals which are integrated in the collective action, it is *one* approach to important sociological questions which have hitherto defied precise, quantitative investigation.

Further details of scale tables are given in Tables 8, 9, and 10.

HANAN C. SELVIN
The Measurement of Leadership Climate

The development of the technique for measuring leadership climate was a long and complicated process. . . .

Although the derivation as a whole is complicated, it can be divided into four relatively simple steps:

1. . . . Leadership climate was described as the way in which an "average trainee" sees the leaders of his company. This is not altogether a figure of speech: the first step in deriving these quantitative indices is to condense the varied ratings of a given leader on a particular question into the average of the ratings given to this leader by all the trainees under him. This averaging will be explained more clearly later in this chapter, but the reader may get some idea of what is involved by keeping track of the amount of data that is dealt

Reprinted in part with permission of the publisher from Hanan C. Selvin, *The Effects of Leadership,* copyright 1960 by The Free Press, a corporation, pp. 27–44, 175, 176–83.

with in the four steps. Initially, there are almost 200,000 ratings—in each of *12* companies an average of *7* leaders is rated on *15* questions by an average of *150* trainees. The averaging process reduces the data to 1230 ratings—the means of the ratings received by each of the 82 leaders on each of the 15 questions.

2. The responses to the fifteen questions do not represent fifteen theoretically independent aspects of leader behavior. In fact, they turn out to be manifestations of only three basic dimensions. The 1230 ratings are thus reduced to 246—three ratings on these new dimensions for each of the 82 leaders.

3. Leadership climate is the way in which the average trainee sees the leaders of his company *as a group,* not as separate persons. In each company, therefore, the ratings for the individual leaders are combined into indices characterizing the "leadership corps" of the company as a whole. There are thirty-six of

these indices, three for each of the twelve companies.

4. Each company can be further classified into one or another leadership climate according to its position on the three indices—high on all three, high on one and low on the other two, and so on. Of the eight possible climates, four can be identified in the data of this study.

The procedure outlined here is *aggregative:* in effect, the leadership climates are constructed by aggregating the responses of the individual trainees into perceived characteristics of the leaders and, in turn, combining these characteristics of leaders into indices of leadership for each company. This is not, however, the only conceivable way to measure leadership climate. If one can assume that the leadership climate of a company is adequately expressed in the behavior of the Commanding Officer, then the measurement of leadership climate would be greatly simplified; one would only have to examine the behavior of a single leader in each company. Indeed, this assumption is implicit in most research on military leadership. . . . On this ground alone, this assumption is worth investigating: in addition, it will yield important information about the nature of leadership. . . .

The assumption that the leadership climate of a company can be reduced to the behavior of a single top leader, such as the commanding officer (the "C.O."), might be justified on either of two grounds: (1) that the influence of the subordinate leaders is negligible, as compared with that of the C.O., or (2) that the C.O. somehow "sets the tone" for the subordinate leaders, so that the leadership behavior they exhibit in dealing with the men is more or less a reflection of the leadership they receive from the C.O. Each of these possibilities will be explored in turn.

The first question on the leadership questionnaire asked for a rating of each officer according to his influence on the trainee's daily life. The ratings ranged from "1" for the leader who had most influence to "3" for the leader with least influence. If it is true that the influence of subordinate leaders is negligible compared to the influence of the C.O., then the average rating received by the C.O.'s of the twelve companies should be much lower than the average ratings received by other positions (since low numerical ratings correspond to high influence). But, as Table 1 shows, this is not the case.

Table **1** *Average influence scores of four company-level positions*

	Average score	Number of leaders [a]
Commanding officers	1.67	(17)
Executive officers	2.28	(20)
First sergeants	2.17	(23)
Field first sergeants	1.66	(22)

The average C.O. is thought to have had more influence than the Executive Officer or the First Sergeant, but his influence score is equal to that of the Field First Sergeant. These questionnaire scores thus agree with the reality experienced by many former soldiers: while leaders who are in direct command of troops (the C.O. and the Field First Sergeant) have more influence than leaders whose jobs are largely administrative, actual influence among the former group is not necessarily proportional to formal authority. One cannot, therefore, assume

[a] The high turnover of leaders accounts for the fact that the twelve companies have more than twelve occupants of each position. This further complicates the problem of multiple leadership over what it would have been with only one leader per position in each company.

that the C.O. exercises such a disproportionate influence on the trainees that the other leaders can be neglected.

Now what of the other possibility: does the Commanding Officer "set the tone" for his subordinate leaders, so that the measurement of leadership climate might be based on the leadership behavior of the C.O. alone? By looking ahead to a later part of this chapter it can be shown that this is not so. One of the steps in deriving measures of leadership climate is to compute for each leader a "positive-leadership score." For the moment it will suffice to say that this score measures the extent to which a leader inspires confidence in his men and enjoys their respect. If the C.O. sets the tone of a company, then where he has a high positive-leadership score, his subordinates should also have high scores, and where he is low, they should be low. But in Table 2 there is virtually

Table 2   The percentage of C.O.'s with subordinate officers of like and unlike positive leadership scores

	High scoring C.O.	Low scoring C.O.
High scoring subordinates	61	63
Low scoring subordinates	39	37
	100	*100*
Number of cases	(23)	(24)

no association between the scores of C.O.'s and their subordinates: the positive leadership exerted by the C.O. has no effect on the positive leadership of the Executive Office and the noncoms. Since the C.O. neither sets the tone for his subordinate leaders nor exercises a disproportionate influence in all companies, the measurement of leadership climate must take into account the behavior of all leaders, rather than that of the C.O. alone.

Leadership Climate as the Perceptions of an Average Trainee

When observers are called upon to make judgments, the usual result is a distribution of values, most of them clustered around some central value and a smaller number more or less extreme in either direction. If there had been only one observer, he might have given one of the values in the central cluster, but there is obviously a good chance of selecting a single observer who would have made an extreme judgment. For this reason, where one has to rely on perceived ratings, the usual practice is to take the consensus of the set of judges. In this study the judges are the trainees in each company, and their consensus about a particular leader on some question is expressed as the arithmetic mean of their ratings. Each leader is therefore described by the average ratings of the men under him—or, more vividly, by the "average trainee" in his company.

It will be easier to understand this concept of an average trainee by looking at a portion of the leadership questionnaire filled out by one trainee, Pvt. John Doe of Company X of the ——th Infantry.

15. If you were ordered into combat and you could choose the men who would be your leaders use the No. 1 for those men in your unit you would like MOST to lead you; No. 2 for those men whom you would like LESS to lead you; and the No. 3 for those men you would like LEAST to lead you if at all.

C.O.	Exec. Off.	1st Sgt.	Field 1/Sgt.
1	2	2	3
3		1	3

During his sixteen weeks of training, Doe had seven company-level leaders—two C.O.'s, one Executive Officer, two First Sergeants, and two Field First Sergeants—which is roughly the number that most trainees had. The numbers in the body of the table are Doe's ratings of each officer and noncom as a combat leader. Doe apparently thought that the first C.O. would have made a good combat leader, since he gave him the highest rating, "1." His unwillingness to follow the second C.O. into combat is indicated by the low rating of "3."

Every trainee in Doe's company rated the same company-level officers on this question. For the sake of illustration, assume that there were 100 trainees in this company and that their ratings of the first C.O. as a combat leader were:

Rating	Number of trainees
1	50
2	30
3	20
	100

The average of these ratings is 1.70. This is the rating that the first C.O. would have received from a hypothetical "average trainee." This useful procedure effects a 100:1 reduction in the data. Instead of 100 sets of ratings to analyze in each company, there is only one set. More important, however, is the fact that *the average reveals the common elements in the trainees' perceptions of their leaders;* the ratings of a trainee with deviant perceptions, from whatever cause, have an insignificant effect on the averages.

One can now disregard the trainees altogether and take each average rating as a perceived characteristic of the leader being rated. Thus the first C.O. in the illustrative example would be said to have a rating of 1.70 as a combat leader. In other words, the average ratings received by a leader may be considered, for purposes of analysis, as his perceived attributes.

Dimensions of Perceived Leadership

In the leadership questionnaire each leader was rated, as in the foregoing illustrative example, on the extent to which he:

1. Influenced the lives of the trainees. (In the following tables this is referred to simply as "influence.")
2. Commanded the respect of the trainees (respect).
3. Was a "sucker for sob stories."
4. Was a "good Joe" one minute and "mean as Hell" the next (inconsistent).
5. Could create a real fighting spirit against the enemy.
6. Acted in such a way that the trainees were afraid of him (induces fear).
7. Could not be depended on to keep his promises (breaks promises).
8. Created a feeling of confidence in the trainees.
9. Told the trainees when he thought that an order from higher headquarters was unfair or silly (comments on "silly" orders).
10. Displayed a real interest in the trainees without babying them (interested in men).
11. Treated the trainees "like dirt."
12. Gave more breaks to his favorite trainees than to others (plays favorites).
13. Seized every opportunity to punish his men.
14. Tried to have his men excused from "dirty details" ordered by

higher authorities ("goes to bat" for men).

15. Would be preferred as a leader in combat.

These perceived attributes are not independent of each other. For example, a leader who can instill a fighting spirit in his men also commands their respect; in Appendix Table 7 the correlation between these two characteristics is 0.82. Similarly, a leader who punishes at every opportunity quite naturally inspires fear; the correlation in this case is 0.84. The size of these correlations is striking: of the 105 correlations in the leadership data, forty-nine are greater than 0.50, and thirteen are greater than 0.80. This is, of course, the result of correlating averages rather than individual responses. All the idiosyncratic variability and virtually all the random errors of response and processing are eliminated; only the average perceptions remain.

The fifteen characteristics about which the trainees were questioned do not, therefore, reflect fifteen distinct traits of leaders. It seems reasonable to assume that they stem from a smaller and more fundamental set of underlying factors. Before describing how the leadership factors were identified, a more fundamental question is in order: why bother with factors anyway? Is it not equally satisfactory to deal only with the average ratings and perhaps group them according to some "logical" system, rather than to go through the complicated procedures of "factoring"? The answer is that factor analysis actually simplifies the total picture of leadership; it shows that there are patterns of consistency underneath the varied perceptions, and it provides a rational, systematic process for identifying these patterns. . . .

The techniques of factor analysis make it possible to discern groups of leadership characteristics that have some underlying uniformity. Factor analysis is not the only method for doing this, but it is one of the most useful for mapping unknown areas in an exploratory investigation. The starting point for a factor analysis is a set of correlation coefficients of each variable with every other variable—in this case the 105 coefficients measuring the extent to which high average ratings on one question are associated with high average ratings on another question (Table 7 in the Appendix). Some understanding of the patterns of association among the different ratings can be gained by a careful examination of this table, but the full implications of these correlations will become visible only after a long series of computations.

What the factor analyst hopes will result from these computations is a small number of factors that sum up the information contained in his original variables. This hope is well realized in the present study: the ratings of the leaders on fifteen questions can be replaced by their scores on only three factors with very little error. This fact not only makes possible an economical description of the leaders' behavior; it also demonstrates the existence of a meaningful structure in the trainees' ratings. Had there been no such structure, but simply haphazard guesses about the various leaders, then there might have been as many as ten factors instead of three. And these ten factors would not have the obvious cogency that our factors will be seen to display.

It is important to recognize that the isolation of factors depends only on the correlations between the original variables and not on the contents of the variables. Most factor analyses are carried out, as this one was, with the specific variables identified only by number; whatever factors emerge reflect, then, the characteristics of the data, rather than the preconceptions of the researcher. The researcher's theoretical preconceptions and his empirical knowledge do enter, however, in the interpretation of the factors.

The Interpretation of Factors

The label by which a factor is identified depends on the characteristics that enter into it and their relative importance. These relationships between the three factors and the fifteen perceived characteristics of this study are presented in Table 3. Across the top of the table are listed the three factors in the order of their power as explanatory concepts (technically, according to the vari-

ance in leadership characteristics accounted for by each factor). The entries in the body of the table measure the relative importance of each characteristic to the factor at the top of the column. For example, in the first column, the figures of 0.52 for "creates confidence" and 0.11 for "creates fighting spirit" indicate that the former is more than four times as important as the latter in determining a leader's score on this factor.

I. Positive Leadership. The entries in the first column suggest the name of "positive leadership." A leader with a high score on this factor enjoys the confidence and respect of his men; he is able to inspire them with a will to fight; and they in turn would like to have him as a leader in combat. The interest he takes in his men is manifested in his willingness to "go to bat" for them when his

Table **3**   *Structure of perceived leadership factors* [a]

	Factors		
	I	II	III
Question	*Positive*	*Tyrannical*	*Vacillating*
8. Creates confidence	.52		−.13
5. Creates fighting spirit	.11		
10. Interested in men	.08		
15. Would prefer as combat leader	.08		
2. Respect	.05		
1. Influence.	.05		
14. "Goes to bat" for men	.04	−.06	.04
13. Punishes at every opportunity		.30	.18
6. Induces fear		.28	−.06
11. Treats like dirt		.24	.09
4. Inconsistent		.06	.15
12. Plays favorites			.30
7. Breaks promises			.14
3. Sucker for sob stories			
9. Comments on "silly" orders			

[a] The figures in each column indicate relative importance of each item. All entries of 0.03 or less have been dropped for clarity....

superiors impose unpleasant duties on the company. The higher a leader's score on this dimension, the more he has escaped the "dilemma of leadership": he is able to carry out the requirements of his role and still maintain good relations with his subordinates. It is also significant that this factor is quantitatively the most important, accounting for more of the variation in leaders' ratings than either of the other two factors.

These statistically-derived scores are a long way from the raw data, the trainees' ratings of their leaders. That they make sense is indicated by some of the unsolicited comments on the questionnaires.

One trainee wrote of an officer who turned out to have a particularly high positive-leadership score:

> I think that our commanding officer, Capt. ———— was a great leader, he held the respect of all the men and was just about everyone's choice to lead them in combat if we ever saw action.

And a First Sergeant who happened to receive a conspicuously low score on this dimension elicited the remark that:

> . . . he is the most unsympathetic character that I have ever encountered in my life also sneaky. . . . I don't see how he ever earned his stripes for he has the mental capabilities of a mongoloid.

II. Tyrannical Leadership. A high score on this factor signifies harsh and oppressive leadership. The trainees report that they are punished for every minor infraction of the rules, that the leader treats them "like dirt," and that they are afraid of him. . . .

It might be thought that scores on this factor would vary inversely with "positive leadership," that a leader who treats his men "like dirt" would not be respected. But the correlation between these two factors in Table 4 is only moderately negative, -0.17. Paradoxical though it may seem, the same leader can have moderately high scores on both factors.

Table **4** *Correlations between factors*

		I	II	III
I	Positive	—		
II	Tyrannical	$-.17$	—	
III	Vacillating	$-.41$	.45	—

On closer examination of the two sets of traits, however, the paradox disappears. The leader who inspires respect as a soldier and whose men would be willing to follow him in combat is not necessarily liked; he may, in fact, be feared. This bears out Machiavelli's principle that a ruler can secure the obedience of his subjects through making himself loved or making himself feared. A military leader may be tough, or he may be gentle; as long as he knows his business, his followers will respect him. Thus the First Sergeant who received the highest tyranny score in this study *and* an above-average positive-leadership score was described by one trainee as a "tough but good cadreman."

III. Vacillating Leadership. The third factor of leadership measures the extent to which leaders depart from consistency and impartiality in their treatment of the trainees. A high score on vacillating leadership denotes a leader who breaks promises, plays favorites, and is "mean as Hell one minute and a 'good Joe' the next." On the negative side, he does not inspire confidence among the trainees.

One might even infer from the factorial structure in Table 3 that his men do not take him altogether seriously; although he punishes them "at every opportunity," they are not afraid of him. . . .

From the standpoint of the followers, a "good" leader is predictable and impersonal, as well as competent. This is corroborated by the negative correlation of −0.41 between positive leadership and vacillating leadership. Note that positive leadership is more closely related to vacillating leadership (more exactly, to *lack* of vacillation) than to tyrannical leadership.

Two of the fifteen leadership attributes do not contribute to any of these factors —the extent to which a leader is a "sucker for sob stories" and his willingness to tell the men when he thinks an order from higher headquarters is "silly." These are apparently unimportant traits which, like right-handedness or eye color, have no bearing on the factors of leadership.

Of course, no label for a factor is necessarily "correct"; intangibles of judgment always affect the factor analyst's decisions. But this arbitrariness need not lessen the precision of the subsequent analysis provided that one avoids "misplacing concreteness." Naming the factor does not thereby confer on it all that the name connotes, or make it an independently measurable entity. Exploratory factor analyses like this one, particularly when based on data gathered with other ends in mind, yield factors that may best be interpreted as empirical constructs—i.e., as useful indices to summarize a group of related characteristics.

The analysis to this point has dealt with individual leaders. The ratings of a given leader by the individual trainees were combined into the ratings of an "average trainee." In turn, these average ratings can be considered as manifestations of three more fundamental aspects of leadership, the factors of positive, tyrannical, and vacillating leadership. Now it is time to combine the ratings of all the leaders in each company to get a single set of leadership characteristics.

Indices of Leadership Climate

The task here is to describe the leadership of each company as a whole, rather than the individual leaders. Just as there are three factor scores for each leader, so there will be three indices of leadership climate for each company. The simplest procedure would be to average the scores of all the leaders in a company on each factor. For example, the "index of positive leadership" for a company might be computed by simply averaging the positive-leadership scores of all the officers and noncoms. However, this procedure would be open to two serious objections. First, all leaders do not affect the trainees' behavior to the same extent. In one company the C.O. may be the dominant figure, while in another the first sergeant may "run" the company with little interference from the officers. What is needed here is some measure of each leader's relative impact on the trainees. This is supplied by the question on influence (Question 1 on the leadership questionnaire). The mean influence rating accorded to a leader can be used to weight his scores on the three factors in computing the leadership indices for each company.

The second objection to averaging the leadership scores is that many leaders did not serve the full sixteen weeks of the training cycle. The eighty-two officers and noncoms on whom the leadership factor analysis was based occupied only forty-eight positions, an average of almost two occupants per position. Obviously, it will not do to give the same weight to the scores of a first sergeant who served four weeks and his successor who was with the company for twelve weeks. The solution to this problem is to weight the scores of each leader by his relative length of service with the company during the training cycle.

In other words, the indices of leadership climate are based on *weighted* means of the factor scores of each leader, the weights taking into account his relative influence on the trainees and the proportion of the total training cycle during which he was with the company. The resulting three indices of company leadership climate are presented in Table 5. The companies are listed in the order of their ranking on the index of positive leadership.

Types of Leadership Climate

The ultimate aim in developing these indices is to relate leadership climate to the behavior of the trainees. It might seem that this task could be accomplished by studying the association of

each index with some form of behavior —for example, comparing the rates of drinking in companies with high and low indices of positive leadership. But closer inspection of Table 5 reveals that one index of leadership cannot be considered apart from the others. Some companies have high indices of positive leadership and low indices of tyrannical leadership; some display the reverse combination; and others are low on both indices or high on both. To describe the leadership climate of a company adequately, one must use both the positive and the tyrannical indices; if each index is divided into "high" and "low," this yields four distinct types of leadership climate.

But should not the vacillating-leadership indices also be included, thus making eight combinations instead of four? Actually, the vacillating and tyrannical indices are so highly correlated that, with only a single exception, companies high on one are high on the other. With the small number of companies in this study, it is impossible to separate tyranny from vacillation. Consequently,

Table **5** *Indices of perceived leadership climate*

	I		II		III	
	Positive		Tyrannical		Vacillating	
Company	Score	Rank	Score	Rank	Score	Rank
1	.96	(1)	−.26	(7)	−.54	(8)
2	.82	(2)	−1.35	(12)	−1.16	(11)
3	.62	(3)	−.17	(6)	−.36	(7)
4	.58	(4)	.56	(3)	.14	(4)
5	.53	(5)	−.47	(10)	−.68	(9)
6	.52	(6)	−.37	(8)	−.35	(6)
7	.48	(7)	−1.02	(11)	−1.39	(12)
8	.12	(8)	−.43	(9)	−.78	(10)
9	−.01	(9)	−.12	(5)	.13	(5)
10	−.01	(10)	1.41	(1)	.72	(3)
11	−.10	(11)	.81	(2)	.88	(2)
12	−.72	(12)	.23	(4)	1.06	(1)

Table **6** *Types of leadership climate*

Indices of Leadership		Leadership Climates	Number of Companies	
Positive	Tyrannical and Vacillating		Total	Analyzed
High	High	"Paternal"	1	0
High	Low	"Persuasive"	6	3
Low	High	"Arbitrary"	3	2
Low	Low	"Weak"	2	2
			12	7

only the four combinations of indices in Table 6 are considered.

Table 6 contains the results toward which this chapter has been building: a set of leadership climates derived from ratings of individual leaders by trainees. [These] leadership climates will be central to [later] analyses. . . .

Appendix. The Derivation of Leadership Climates: Notes on Methods and Techniques

. . . The derivation of the leadership indices . . . began with the ratings of each leader by all the men in his company. These ratings were then averaged, to give one figure for each leader on each question—the "average perception" of this leader by his trainees. The correlations between each pair of average ratings were computed, and these correlations were factored to get the three dimensions of perceived leadership.

The important point here is that *the correlations are based on group or aggregate data,* the averages of the trainees' ratings, *and not on the individual ratings themselves.* Instead of computing the group averages and correlating them, we could have correlated the original ratings (and, indeed, we did compute

many such correlations in developing the method actually used). For example, we could have computed the correlation between the trainees' ratings of the C.O. in Company X on "influence" and "respect," the first two questions on the leadership questionnaire. This correlation would have been based on pairs of responses from the questionnaires of each trainee in that company. What we actually did, however, was to compute the correlation between the mean ratings on "influence" and the mean ratings on "respect" of all the eighty-two company-level leaders. This correlation, to repeat, is based on aggregate data, rather than on individual responses. . . .

THE FACTOR ANALYSIS OF
AVERAGE RATINGS

Table 7 depicts the correlations between the average ratings for the eighty-two leaders. The extent to which the use of averages eliminates individual variation and enhances central tendencies in leadership perception (as is implied in the use of an average) is striking. . . .

This correlation matrix was factored by Thurstone's "complete centroid method," yielding three factors as shown in Table 8. Then this factor matrix was rotated by the matrix of Table 9 to the oblique simple structure shown in Table

Table **7** *Intercorrelations of average leadership ratings*
(82 company-level leaders)

	1	2	3	4	5	6	7	8	9	10	11	12	13	14	15
1 Influence	—														
2 Respect	72	—													
3 Sucker	28	32	—												
4 Inconsist-ent	−05	−41	−30	—											
5 Fighting spirit	80	82	24	−11	—										
6 Fear	−08	−28	−41	74	−01	—									
7 Breaks promises	−19	−56	−21	69	−35	54	—								
8 Confidence	78	86	23	−20	95	−04	−44	—							
9 Passes buck	56	45	37	12	57	−11	−20	52	—						
10 Interested	66	82	26	−22	85	−10	−54	88	57	—					
11 Like dirt	−32	−66	−37	80	−40	77	80	−45	−22	−52	—				
12 Plays fa-vorites	04	−39	04	68	−24	36	74	−33	13	−41	66	—			
13 Punishes	−11	−45	−30	85	−16	84	74	−24	00	−29	90	67	—		
14 Sticks up for men	67	79	42	−36	74	−40	−53	75	62	76	−64	−28	−47	—	
15 Combat leader	78	86	28	−31	85	−17	−55	91	49	81	−57	−38	−38	74	—

Table **8** *Unrotated matrix of correlations of leadership items*
with reference vectors

		R_1	R_2	R_3	h^2
1	Influence	64	56	19	76
2	Respect	88	26	−09	85
3	Sucker	42	−05	42	36
4	Inconsistent	−61	66	12	82
5	Fighting spirit	77	56	−10	92
6	Fear	−54	63	−41	86
7	Breaks promises	−75	38	25	77
8	Confidence	81	52	−21	97
9	Passes buck	48	45	37	57
10	Interested	82	40	−19	87
11	Like dirt	−85	45	−04	93
12	Plays favorites	−54	43	56	79
13	Punishes	−69	66	−03	91
14	Sticks up for men	85	22	23	83
15	Combat leader	86	36	−12	88

10. It seemed desirable to carry out the tedious process of oblique rotation, rather than impose the artificiality of an orthogonal structure on the data.

Table **9** *Transformation matrix* [a]

	R′₁	R′₂	R′₃
R₁	71	−37	−08
R₂	68	53	43
R₃	16	−76	90

[a] Entries are direction cosines of angles between unrotated reference vector system in Table 8 and final reference vector system in Table 10.

Table **10** *Final reference-vector matrix* [a]

		R′₁	R′₂	R′₃
1	Influence	87	−08	36
2	Respect	79	−12	−04
3	Sucker	33	−50	32
4	Inconsistent	03	48	44
5	Fighting spirit	91	09	09
6	Fear	−02	85	−05
7	Breaks promises	−23	29	45
8	Confidence	90	14	−03
9	Passes buck	71	−22	49
10	Interested	84	05	−06
11	Like dirt	−30	58	23
12	Plays favorites	00	00	73
13	Punishes	−05	63	31
14	Sticks up for men	79	−37	23
15	Combat leader	84	−04	−02

[a] This is the original set of reference vectors in Table 8 rotated to oblique simple structure.

In interpreting the meaning of uncorrelated factors one has only to consider the relationship between each item and the factor. However, in dealing with correlated factors, as in this study, each item makes two contributions to each factor—a "direct contribution" resulting from its correlation with the factor and an "indirect contribution" resulting from its correlation with other factors which, in turn, are correlated with the factor being interpreted. The sum of these two contributions is the "total contribution" of the item to the factor, as reported in Table 3. . . .

The next step was to compute scores for each of the eighty-two leaders on the three factors. The estimating equations for these scores were derived by means of Holzinger and Harman's "Shortened Method." It was possible to simplify the estimation without appreciable loss of accuracy so that none of the estimating equations has more than six items. Chapter II describes how these factor scores were combined into indices of leadership climate for each company; the factor scores of each leader were weighted by his relative influence and the proportion of the total training cycle that he served.

In retrospect, this procedure was unnecessarily complicated. For the kinds of analysis that ultimately were undertaken in this study, it would have been equally satisfactory to select one or two highly discriminating items from each of the three factors in Table 3 and combine them into simple indices of leadership. Even the weighting for the relative influence of the different leaders probably required more work than was justified by the crude typology that was finally used: had the various leaders been assumed to be equally influential, the results would not have been much different. With an average of seven leaders per company, the variations in influence weights would have had to be much greater than they were to have a significant effect on a company's score, as compared with what would have been obtained with equal weights.

This is not to say, of course, that such rough-and-ready methods should have been used in this study. When one is exploring a relatively unknown area, uncertain even as to the kinds of analyses that ultimately will be done, it is best to retain as much precision as possible. However, once an exploratory study like this one has indicated some fruitful directions for analysis, the less technical complexity the analyst has to cope with, the more time he will have for theoretical and substantive questions.

"POOLED" AND "SEPARATE" FACTOR ANALYSES

The outcome of a factor analysis depends on two sets of variables—the content of the tests or questions and the population to which the tests are given. In this study three clear factors of leadership have been identified for the population consisting of all eighty-two company-level leaders. Alternatively, the factorial composition of the leadership ratings could have been determined separately in each of the twelve companies by means of twelve separate factor analyses. Should this have been done? Apart from the expense, which would be multiplied at least eight or ten times, there is a good reason for using only one "pooled" factor analysis instead of twelve separate ones. The factors are simply composite variables synthesized from the perceived characteristics of each leader. Using one "pooled" factor analysis ensures that all twelve companies are described with the "same" variables. Had we factored the leadership correlations in each company separately, it would have been impossible to compare the leadership climates of different companies, since dimensions of leadership would have been different in each company.

"BIMODALITY" OF RATINGS

The problem of bimodality arose in connection with the use of average ratings. Arithmetic means or other measures of central tendency are satisfactory only with distributions that are unimodal (single-peaked). If half of the men in a company gave a leader the rating of "1" on some question and the other half gave him the rating of "3," it would be meaningless to say that the average rating was "2." If such bimodal distributions had occurred frequently, it would mean that there was little consensus on the ratings of the officers; the entire approach to leadership climates would have had to be different.

Each of the 1230 distributions (82 leaders times 15 questions) was examined to see how many exhibited even a slight degree of bimodality. A distribution was judged bimodal if the proportion of "2" ratings was 10 percentage points or more below either of the other two proportions—for example, a leader's ratings on some question would be considered bimodal if 40 per cent of the men gave him a "1" rating; 25 per cent, "2"; and 35 per cent, "3." This occurred for less than 3 per cent of the 1230 distributions. Only four leaders had more than one bimodal distribution out of fifteen, and only one leader had as many as three. Bimodality thus occurs so rarely and is so thinly spread across the total set of leaders that it is not a serious problem.

It is noteworthy that there were no cases of bimodality in the influence ratings. This is important because of the central position of influence in the computation of leadership indices. Question 11 ("treats trainees 'like dirt'") had the greatest number of bimodal distributions, six out of a possible eighty-two, perhaps indicating some ambiguity in the wording of this question.

"HALO" EFFECT

This problem is basic to the whole technique of measuring leadership climates. We have assumed that the ratings of the different leaders in a company are psychologically independent, that the men were able to discriminate between the leaders on all questions. But it is also possible that some sort of "halo" effect operated, that the personality of the most influential leader in a company so dominated the minds of the trainees that they tended to rate the other leaders in the same way.

To test the hypothesis of a halo effect it is necessary to examine the distribution of responses for an average of seven leaders in twelve companies on either the fifteen original questions or the three factors—a minimum of 246 distributions. Both of these distributions were examined minutely in the course of developing the leadership ratings, and virtually no evidence of a halo effect was found. Within each company the variation between leaders on either the factor scores or the original questions is so large that the halo hypothesis is not substantiated.

COMMENTARY

MEASUREMENT AND THE
CLARIFICATION OF CONCEPTS

Measuring procedures can be designed to clarify the meanings of properties as well as to measure them. Part of the clarification occurs *before* the measurements are actually made; as we saw in Unit 7, the property must be defined as clearly as possible in advance, and rules established for translating it into concrete indicants. Still further clarification is possible *after* the measurements have been made and the data are in hand.

In this Unit we are examining measurement procedures **(P-X)** that use the data for this additional purpose of exploring the meaning of properties. In these procedures the investigator scrutinizes the data to see whether they fit the advance assumptions of correspondence between property and indicants—the procedures themselves contain an empirical test of the measurement model. Our consideration of procedures with a built-in test focuses upon the Guttman scale (G-scale) as one comparatively simple example. In using the G-scale, the researcher hypothesizes in advance a particular patterning in the data, and then observes whether or not the data fit this pattern. We shall also examine studies that employ two of the many other possible procedures—latent structure analysis and factor analysis.

Throughout the discussion we shall keep in mind the important distinction drawn in Unit 7 between *composite measures*—which combine indicants of several aspects or units of properties, and *collective measures*—which combine indicants referring to several constituent parts of a social system (dyads, roles, subgroups) in order to refer to a more inclusive level of the system. Thus in our scrutiny of the measurement data, we shall seek, on the one hand, reflections of underlying patterning of *properties* in which specific acts, attitudes, or characteristics fit together—as in Stouffer's scale of toleration of nonconformists, or in Exercises III-4 and III-5. We shall also begin to search for any latent structure in the *social system* in which group members may play complementary and interdependent roles—as in the Rutgers post-analysis of the status scale, or in Exercise III-6.

As sociologists, we often seek combined procedures that fit together both types of measures—those referring to collective acts or attitudes and their meanings, and those referring to the actors as parts of the group. A combined measure might classify symphony orchestras, for example, according to both the pattern of notes they play (the collective acts and their meanings) and the organization of the players of the several instruments (the actors as parts of the group). A great danger of such complex measures, however, is that the different kinds of indicants may become so confused that action and actors are no longer distinguishable, and all traces of patterns and structure are lost, as you saw in Exercise III-6. We shall accordingly explore the possibilities of reflecting the sociological variable more adequately, avoiding indiscriminate aggregations of data, and seeking measuring instruments that may perhaps reveal and index the empirical patterning of acts and structuring of roles.

The Nature of Guttman Scaling

The G-scale, as illustrated in the exercises and three of the studies in this Unit, is a procedure (1) for ordering cases in terms of a property conceived as unidimensional, which (2) combines multiple indicants (or items) into a composite measure, and which at the same time (3) tests the assumption that these indicants do "hang together" to represent a single dimension (or unitary concept).

Guttman and his colleagues have used the procedure widely for studying individual attitudes. Thus they typically employ as indicants a series of statements that are successively harder to endorse. The procedure itself is general, however, and may be used in many applications. The cases may be individuals, dyads, or groups. The indicants may be responses to attitude questions, answers to questions on a mental test, or observed acts. As employed by sociologists, the procedure affords one means for measuring complex variables and exploring various patterns in which specific acts and orientations may fit together.

We shall first examine the G-scale as a special kind of *composite measure,* and then consider how it may sometimes be applied to *collective* as well as to unitary properties. Its distinctive character as a measurement model with a built-in test will become clearer in comparison with the procedure used in *arbitrary* scores that are based entirely on the judgment of the investigator.

THE REDUCTION OF A CLASSIFICATION SPACE

Both the G-scale and the arbitrary score may be viewed as forms of reduction of a property-space—a matter already introduced in Unit 7. Consider a simple example drawn from your earlier analysis of adolescents and their reference groups (Exercise II-4) in which you used a score based on the number of topics each adolescent would discuss with his friends. Let us now think of using this score to measure the *intimacy* of an adolescent's relations to these friends. To keep the example simple, we shall examine only two of the topics, moral problems and movies, though the logic may easily be extended to include all ten. Each adolescent can then be classified in the space in Figure 9-A, according to whether he talks to his friends about movies and about moral problems (as indicants).

Figure **9-A** *A space for measuring intimacy*

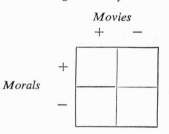

Note that our interest here is not in all four types of intimacy, because we are not now thinking of intimacy as including different dimensions of communication. We are not concerned with the specific topics that make up the patterns of communication. We are seeking a unifying measure to tap a general underlying property—intimacy—not a multidimensional measure like that of deviance discussed in Unit 7. Thus we assume that individuals differ in *degree of intimacy,* and that we can arrange them along a single dimension using these indicants. To accomplish this, we need some procedure for reducing the space in Figure 9-A—converting it to a continuum.

In the score of peer intimacy used in the exercise, we accomplish this reduction by arbitrarily assigning weights to each of the topics. In effect—by counting the topics discussed—we assign a weight of 1 for discussing a given topic, and a weight of 0 for not discussing it. Accordingly, those individuals in the upper left-hand cell score 2, because they talk on both topics, while those in the lower right-hand cell score 0, because they do not talk on either. And those in each of the other cells, who talk on either one of the topics alone, score 1.

This reduction greatly enhances the utility of the measure. First, we can now arrange all the individuals along a *single dimension* from low intimacy (score 0) to high intimacy (score 2). We have succeeded in classifying them according to how intimate their peer relationships are. And second, we have also *collapsed the cells* in the space so that there are now only three (2, 1, 0) instead of the original four. Three types of cases ranked on an ordinal scale are, of course, easier to use in further analysis (as in Unit 8) than four types on two different dimensions. (Note, incidentally, how the mathematical character of the measure changes as the indicants are combined to form a composite measure: a nominal measure—the individual either talks or does not talk about a topic— becomes an ordinal measure as the individual is ranked along the single dimension.)

The advantage of reduction is still more striking when all ten topics are used. The ten-topic score you used in Exercise II-4 classifies the cases on an ordinal scale into eleven types—with scores from 0 through 10. But, if we tried to build a multidimensional measure using all possible combinations of topics— and showing *which* topics are discussed—this would produce 1,024 different types (2^{10}).

ARBITRARY MEASURES

Although such reduction of a space is always convenient in these respects, the assumption that there is an underlying single dimension is not always justified. In this score of peer intimacy, we do not test the assumption, but use arbitrary measurement—measurement by *fiat*. Such an arbitrary score has one distinguishing characteristic which must be kept in mind whenever it is employed. The score of 1, for example, does not in itself tell us *which* topic is involved. In Figure 9-A, we have put together two different types of individuals from two different cells, and given them all the same score of 1; that is, we have arbitrarily assumed that certain cells in the space are equivalent. In assuming such equivalence, the researcher must always question the reasonableness of the assumption for the particular research problem. Does it seem appropriate here, for example, in the light of our knowledge of adolescent relationships, to equate talking on movies and talking on morals as indicants of intimacy? Some investigators might argue that talking about morals indicates a higher degree of intimacy, and should be given a greater weight in the score, than talking about movies. Different investigators may make different judgments about the appropriate weights for the items, or even about which items should be included at all. Thus the characteristic feature of an arbitrary measure is that it makes no attempt to test any of these underlying assumptions—that the model rests entirely upon the researcher's judgment.

A G-SCALE OF INTIMACY

By contrast, the G-scale—which also arranges the cases along a single dimension—is one of several procedures that *do* enable the investigator to examine the data for their fit to the model used as a guide in the selection of indicants and the assignment of numerical values. The G-scale model has its distinctive definition of unidimensionality which implies that the data will be arranged in the cells in a special way. For example, in Figure 9-A, the *expected finding* if a G-scale exists is that the upper right-hand cell in the figure will tend to be empty. The G-scale procedure then tests to see whether this pattern in fact occurs.

Suppose that we actually classify a sample of adolescents in Figure 9-A, and find that nearly all of them are fairly evenly divided among three of the boxes, thus leaving the *zero cell,* as predicted by the model; that is, we find hardly any individuals who talk to friends about morals but not about movies. The scale pattern (with no $+-$ types) would be written, following the Guttman convention, as in Table 9-A. Some adolescents talk to their friends about *neither* of these

Table **9-A** *A G-scale of intimacy*

Scale type	Morals	Movies
2	+	+
1	−	+
0	−	−

topics $(--)$; others about just *one* topic—movies $(-+)$; and still others about morals, but *only* if they also talk about movies. The model is like a ladder: you have to climb the movies rung before you can go on to the morals rung. (Of course, in most scales, the ladder has more than two rungs, as you already know.)

What, then, is the conception of unidimensionality that corresponds to such an arrangement of the data according to the special G-scale pattern? The notion might be in this instance that the adolescent enters into the discussion of more intimate topics (such as morals) only after he has passed through a phase of discussing matters involving less intimacy and privacy (such as movies). Scaling is used to see whether such provisional notions may be supported or negated by the data themselves.

The Spelling Test Example.   Stouffer uses a simple and instructive example of a scale with three items (Stouffer, 1955, p. 262 ff.). Each student has to spell three words: cat, cattle, catastrophe. Some get none of them right, and get a score of 0. Some get just one right, but in most instances this one word is not just any one of the three, but the easiest word, cat. Some get two right; but these are almost always the same two, cat and cattle. (Of course, there are a few exceptions, but we think of these as scaling *errors*—the student knew the word but was careless in writing it down, for example, or the teacher misread his writing.) Usually, then, the student has to pass on cat before he can pass on cattle, and on cattle before he can pass the hardest word, catastrophe (see Table 9-B). Here

Table **9-B**   *A scale of spelling ability*

Scale type	Catastrophe	Cattle	Cat
3	+	+	+
2	−	+	+
1	−	−	+
0	−	−	−

the words form the rungs of the ladder. The steps (the answers to the several test questions) themselves belong in an order—and we say that these answer categories are cumulative or transitive.

Here again the G-scale achieves the same purpose as the arbitrary score: it orders individuals along a single dimension of spelling ability. In addition, unlike the score, which is not concerned with possible patterning in the items, it uncovers the cumulative arrangement of the answers. Since the spelling examination had assumed in advance that only the perfect scale patterns of answers (as in Table 9-B) would occur (and not any of the other possible combinations of answers such as $+-+$, or $++-$), the actual performance of the students serves as an empirical test that confirms this assumption.

Scale of Toleration of Nonconformists.   In another example, which you examined in Unit 6, Stouffer describes the utility of such a scale in his cross-section study of *Communism, Conformity, and Civil Liberties.* Pointing out that "a scale of opinions based on a series of related questions is usually more stable than a single item," he looks for a scale to summarize each individual's relative degree of tolerance. He finds a "remarkable consistency in *patterns* of response" and is able to put together fifteen questions that hang together in a way that is consistent with the G-scale model. Such patterning assures him not only, as he says, of question reliability—i.e., that different respondents will interpret the questions in the same way—but also of the internal validity or consistency with which the several items all tap the same dimension.

Stouffer further emphasizes the "economy of presentation" which, as we have noted, is afforded by the G-scale. In order to use conformity as a variable in analysis, he is not obliged to work with the multiplicity of possible combinations of answers to the fifteen questions. Since these answers fall into simple patterns, he is able to arrange respondents along a single ordinal scale, then to subdivide them into the three broad rank groupings called "relatively more tolerant," "relatively less tolerant," and "in-between." Thus he can easily compare the tolerance scores of leaders and the rank and file, or of the national cross section at the several interview periods.

Stouffer and Toby and the G-Scale Procedure

The role conflict study by Stouffer and Toby has provided a detailed and realistic example of what can be accomplished with the G-scale as a measure. Let us review your analysis of this study by asking: *What* are these researchers using the scale to measure? The property to be measured, as they define it, is the individual's tendency toward particularism or universalism, that is, toward meeting the obligations of particular friendships or those of society in general. Their case **(P-I)** is the individual in several different group roles; their research focus is on "personality bias"—toward one or the other horn of the particularistic-universalistic dilemma—as this bias may cut across the several roles the individual plays.

Why do the researchers in measuring the dimension make use of more than one item (or question)? Their decision hinges, of course, upon the *general* character of the tendency they are studying. It would be difficult to frame a question asking the respondent about his particularistic, as compared with his universalistic, bias; but even if this dimension could be communicated to him, he would find it difficult to generalize about the many different concrete situations in which he makes such a choice. Therefore each scale item refers to a specific situation (the car accident, the drama criticism, etc.) which the respondent can consider on its own merits. Only after the researchers have obtained answers about a variety of such specific situations are they in a position to see whether some general tendency underlies them all.

Finally (to review one further question), why do the researchers use a scale—instead of an arbitrary score—for combining the answers and abstracting the underlying general tendency? Why not just count the number of items on which the respondent gives a particularistic answer, for example? Here it is clear, of course, that the researchers want to *test* their hypothesis that the same *kind* of predisposition is being measured in all the situations. The G-scale is designed especially to provide such a test.

TESTING THE G-SCALE MODEL

Let us rehearse the logic of such a test applied to scaling individual attitudes, before going on to the more complicated problems of scaling collective data. You are already familiar with the steps in the procedure from your scaling of the attitudes of students toward their undergraduate college (in Exercise III-4 following Manual III-D). And you have undoubtedly noticed that the procedure is essentially that of testing any mathematical model, as we have discussed this in Units 3 and 5 in connection with the models used by Bales and by Zelditch.

In formulating the assumptions to be tested, Stouffer and Toby ask, "Do the answers . . . indicate the existence of a unidimensional scale, along which respondents can be ordered as to the degree to which they are likely to possess a trait or bias toward the particularistic solution of a dilemma?" Guttman's more general formulation is, "A universe of items comprises but a single factor [dimension] in the sense that from but a single set of scores . . . the responses to each of the items can be reproduced" (Guttman, 1950-b, p. 181). The scale model itself, which translates the assumption of unidimensionality into simple mathematical terms, is then tested against the data obtained by questioning respondents on a set of items—a sample from Guttman's "universe" of items (Guttman, *op. cit.,* p. 172).

If the data turn out to fit the model, this not only serves to order the cases, but also shows that the predicted pattern of responses exists. It provides some assurance that there is indeed a kind of self-consistency in the data. Thus not only will any individual with a higher scale score than another be just as high as or higher than the other person on *every* item, but all individuals with the same score will have the same pattern of responses. And the scale score itself will show just which responses went together to make it up. In this sense, the score has a definite meaning in terms of the actual items, so that the pattern of responses is *reproducible* from the scale score.

THE PROBLEM OF ERROR

Guttman uses the coefficient of reproducibility as one of the major criteria of fit to the model (as you already know from the exercises). A reproducibility coefficient of 100 per cent would mean that *each individual's scale score describes the exact pattern of his answers for all the questions.* Because the perfect scale model with 100 per cent reproducibility is not usually found in practice, however, the question arises of how far the distribution of the data in a given study may depart from this perfect scale model and still be judged to "scale." Guttman uses an arbitrary criterion of 90 per cent (combining this criterion with other requirements on the number of items and the size of the marginals) so as to prevent misreading as a G-scale a finding that might actually be generated by statistically independent items. Since these requirements—set by Guttman as practical rules of thumb—are sometimes difficult to meet, we have substituted a somewhat different criterion (found in principle in Guttman's writings and used in the Rutgers study): a coefficient of *reproducibility by chance,* which helps to determine whether or not a G-scale furnishes a reasonably close model for a given set of data.

This chance model is based on the assumption that the items are not related in a cumulative pattern, but are statistically independent. As a multi-item model, it is comparable to the two-item independence model used in analyzing the

Strodtbeck study (see Table 8-C). The chance reproducibility is obtained, as shown in Table 9-C, by multiplying the respective marginal frequencies on the items in order to compute the probability of each perfect scale type, and by then adding the probabilities of all perfect scale types. (You will see that this chance model is obtained by applying probability Rules 1, 2, and 3 in Manual V-B.) The chance reproducibility found in the fictitious example in Table 9-C is 75 per cent.

Table **9-C**   *An example of the computation of chance reproducibility*

Marginal proportions (in per cent)	*Item 1*	*Item 2*	*Item 3*	*Probabilities*
+	25	50	75	
−	75	50	25	

	Item 1	*Item 2*	*Item 3*	*Probabilities*
	+	+	+	
	.25	.50	.75	.0938
Probability	−	+	+	
of perfect	.75	.50	.75	.2812
scale	−	−	+	
types	.75	.50	.75	.2812
	−	−	−	
	.75	.50	.25	.0938

Total probability of
perfect scale types
= chance reproducibility   .7500

The coefficient of reproducibility for the actual data is then compared with this chance reproducibility to see whether the actual is higher, that is, whether the data depart from the independence model in the direction of a closer approach to scalability. Edgar F. Borgatta (in a lecture at New York University, 1956) proposed that this comparison be stated in the form of an *error ratio* of found errors divided by chance errors. (The proportion of chance errors may be obtained by subtracting chance reproducibility from 1.00. If the error ratio is small —perhaps less than .5—this provides intuitive confidence in the scale.)

Whenever the set of items fails to fit the scale model, the investigator must decide upon next steps. Sometimes he may be able to trace the errors to one or two items, which may perhaps scale if they are dichotomized differently, or which may have to be dropped entirely from the scale. If, after such revisions, the data still fail to fit the G-scale model, it is clear that some pattern other than the G-scale, or no discernible pattern at all, characterizes the data at hand. Sometimes the investigator tries other measurement procedures based on other models that might uncover the actual pattern. (We shall mention some of these models later.) Or, failing to find any pattern, he may nevertheless sometimes decide to combine the items into an arbitrary score—i.e., to assume a pattern which he does not know how to test. Here (as with all arbitrary scores) he must carefully weigh the conceptual model he uses in deciding what items to select and how to combine them, since he no longer has any empirical check.

If, on the other hand, the data are judged to fit the scale model, there will still be some nonscale cases that reflect errors. Because the aim is to order *all* the cases in terms of the common element running through the series of items, these *nonscale* cases must, in some way, be *assigned* to perfect scale categories after the scale analysis has been made. A procedure of arbitrary assignment (such as that in the Ford method in Manual III-D) is often used. Stouffer and Toby use a different procedure here—a latent distance analysis (conducted by Lazarsfeld) which, as they say, "in the present example usually gave clear and consistent information."

The Use of Latent Structure Analysis.   We are interested in the application of the latent distance model here because—quite apart from its specific utility in the assignment of nonscale cases—it serves as an illustration of the use of Lazarsfeld's latent structure analysis. Stouffer and Toby report that this analysis shows good agreement between the fitted and the actual totals. Although the computational problems prove generally stubborn, the latent structure approach constitutes another important attack on measurement of which you should be aware. Stouffer states its basic postulate: "There exists a set of latent classes, such that the manifest relationship between any two or more items on a test can be accounted for by the existence of these basic classes and by these alone" (Stouffer, 1950, p. 6). Thus it grapples with the special problems of applying to qualitative data the principles of factor analysis as illustrated in the Selvin study. (See, *e.g.,* Lazarsfeld, 1950; Stouffer, 1951, pp. 691–705.)

Foa's Group Measures

Foa's use of G-scales is especially interesting because he analyzes groups, rather than individuals, as the research case **(P-I)**. In order to investigate conflict of norms within the social system, he questions both officers and crew members (as subsystems) in a sample of eighteen ships. His aim is to measure and interrelate two variables: attitudes toward the need for formal discipline, and crew satisfaction with officers. But the research problem is not: Is an *individual's* attitude about discipline related to his satisfaction with officers? Instead the problem is, in effect: Is the climate of *group* opinion about discipline related to the group rate of satisfaction with officers? Thus Foa wants to generate measures, not of individual attitudes, but of the collective attitudes within each of the ships. Accordingly, he follows Guttman's use of the scale to combine multiple indicants of properties, but he also adapts the procedure for use with a collective measure. (Scales may also be used, of course, to combine indicants which consist of *unitary* rather than collective measures of group properties. See, *e.g.,* the cumulative pattern of such community characteristics as having a public square, an official, access to electric power, and a doctor in residence, as reported in Young and Young.)

INDIVIDUAL PATTERN APPROACH

In the procedure for preparing a collective measure, we have (in Unit 7 and Manual III-A) distinguished three steps, repeated here in Figure 9-B. When the collective measure also requires the combining of multiple indicants, the researcher must decide, as you know from your experience with Exercise III-6, where in this procedure the combining should take place. The Foa study illustrates the decision to combine the indicants in Step 1—that is, at the stage of assigning constituent measures to individuals (which, in later steps, will be collected for the groups). When indicants are combined in Step 1, we speak of the *individual pattern approach*. Let us see exactly what Foa's procedure is, so that we may begin to formulate the principles of this approach.

Figure **9-B**   *Combining indicants of properties in* (*arbitrary*) *collective measurement*

Basic procedure for (arbitrary) collective measurement (Manual III-A)

Steps at which indicants of properties may be combined

Individual pattern approach / Group pattern approach

Step 1
Assign a constituent measure to each individual (or subgroup or dyad)

e.g., Foa's group scales

Step 2
Collect these constituent measures for each group (or role)

Step 3
Assign a collective measure to each group (or role) on the basis of Step 2

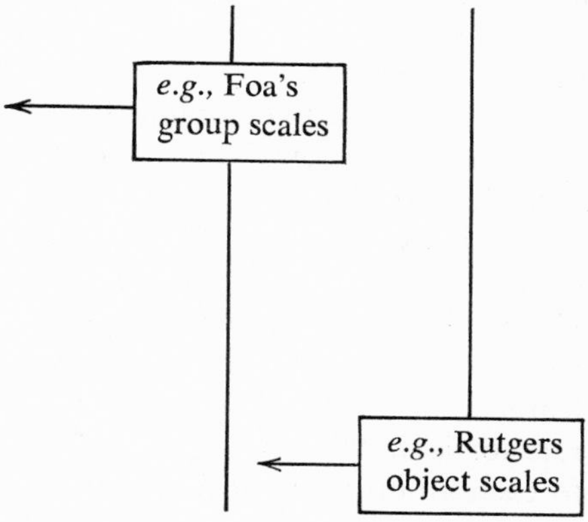

e.g., Rutgers object scales

Since Foa uses the G-scale for the combining of indicants, he starts out, as in the foregoing Stouffer examples, by seeking a scale pattern of unidimensionality in the attitudes of the *individuals* in all the ships. (Incidentally, you will notice that he does not dichotomize the answers to each question as in the short Ford method of G-scaling we have been using in Manual III-D, but combines *multiple category answers* to the three or four questions in each scale. See, *e.g.,* Ford, p. 298 ff.) In this way, he arranges the individuals in rank order according to attitude toward discipline, and again (for crew members only) according to satisfaction with officers. Thus at Step 1 in the collective measurement procedure, he succeeds in combining the several attitudinal indicants (answers to questions) at the same time that he assigns appropriate scale scores (constituent measures) to individual group members.

OBTAINING THE COLLECTIVE MEASURE

The subsequent steps in Foa's measurement procedure—which make no further use of G-scaling—suggest some ingenious ways of handling the group as the research case. His first variable, disciplinary climate, requires preliminary preparation of two collective measures for each ship, one for officers and one for crew. Accordingly, at Step 2, the number of officers—and the number of men—in each scale type (from Step 1) are counted for each ship. These yield a total of thirty-six (two per ship) distributions by scale scores (comparable in form to the distributions by income Bogue obtained for the several segments of the United States population).

At Step 3, Foa finds the median attitude toward discipline for the officers and for the crew of each ship, and then compares each of these group medians with the general median for all respondents together. By rating each ship twice in this way—according to whether officers and crew each want a degree of discipline above or below the over-all median—he obtains the four types of ships' climates shown (as the independent variable) in his two tables. Thus he classifies the personnel of each ship according to the degree of discipline desired, and also according to the agreement (or conflict) between the norms of officers and men. He has succeeded in using the group as a case, while retaining the identity of its two main parts.

Aiming now to determine how these four climates relate to rates of satisfaction among the crew, he proceeds to develop a collective measure of this second variable. Again (at Step 2) he counts the number of men in each scale type, as shown in his Table 1. He then summarizes these distributions (Step 3) by simply showing the percentages of satisfied, as compared with dissatisfied, men (in his Table 2). You will notice, however, that he prepares these collective measures for each of the four *types* of ships—although he might perhaps have learned still more from his data had he dealt separately with the satisfaction rate for *each ship* (within these four types) so as to assign a collective measure to each group (see our Step 3).

HIGHER COMPONENTS OF THE GUTTMAN SCALE

In dividing individuals into the two categories of satisfied and dissatisfied here, Foa illustrates the use of the *zero point* of the *intensity component* in order, as he says, "to separate respondents . . . in an objective fashion according to positive and negative attitudes." Guttman defines the second component of a scale of individual attitudes as the intensity with which the attitude is held. As you know from the procedure in scale Exercise III-4, each individual is given an intensity score (often an arbitrary score comprising answers to several intensity questions). The intensity scores are then cross-tabulated against the attitude (or content) scale. Guttman's hypothesis is that this cross-tabulation will suggest a U-curve, with those who are most extreme (at either end) on the attitude scale holding the attitude with the highest degree of intensity. Those with neutral attitudes, he predicts, will show least intensity, and the low point in the U-curve will suggest where (toward the center of the attitude scale) the indifferent individuals may be said to separate those with positive, from those with negative, views (see Manual III-D). Foa's use of this zero point of indifference allows him to dichotomize his attitude scale in a meaningful way.

In developing this notion of a second component, Guttman, after working out the mathematical properties of the scale model, says that the model has many functions or components. His mathematical analysis shows as a first component the scale model itself, which is a straight line; the second takes the form of a curve with one bend; the third has two bends; and so on. Guttman has sought psychological equivalents of the first four components; you are already familiar with the first two of these. His first component, which corresponds to the simple rank order along one dimension, Guttman calls the "content" of the attitude. The second component is the "intensity" or strength with which the individual holds the attitude; the intensity measure forms a U-shaped curve when related to content. He gives the names "closure" and "involution" to the third and fourth components (see Guttman, 1954-a; Foa, 1954). Following this lead, the Rutgers Research Group has sought *sociological* equivalents of the components of the status scale reported in the Rutgers study. They find a second component, "consensus," which measures the extent to which group members coincide in the same attitude, and which tends to form a U-curve when related to the object scale of the content of the collective attitudes (see Riley, Riley, Toby, and Cohn). Their data also provide clues to a possible third component, "vividness," or variety of characteristics for which an individual is noted. This component tends to form a curve with two bends when related to the object scale of content (see Bredemeier, Toby, and Riley).

LIMITATIONS OF THE APPROACH

Summarizing Foa's approach in developing a group measure, we emphasize once again that his use of the G-scale model and the second component occurs at Step 1 in our procedural outline (Figure 9-B). That is, he uses his measurement model to seek—and in this instance to find—patterning in the attitudes of the constituent *individuals*. There are other types of empirical situations, however, as we shall see, where the pattern of acts or attitudes can only emerge at Step 3 where the research case is no longer the individual, but the group. Such special types of group patterns cannot be uncovered by the individual pattern approach.

The Rutgers Object Scales

Let us now turn to the Rutgers approach which, since it looks for patterning of acts or attitudes at the group level (Step 3) rather than the individual level (Step 1), serves as the complement to the Foa approach.

In the scale of status, to take one example from the Rutgers studies, the definition of the property is based upon the assumption that there is a process of interaction within the group which includes certain acts of liking and deference among individuals. This process is thought to result in a sort of deference hierarchy, in which some individuals (as objects) receive more liking and deference than others. At any given time, then, it may be possible to measure the positions of individuals within this hierarchy. The researchers use more than one question in such a measure, because they believe that status may depend upon different kinds of acts and attitudes of the subjects, such as actually associating with a person, wishing to associate with him, and following him as a leader. They use a G-scale to test the assumption that these different acts cumulate, or hang together, so as to produce a unified dimension of status.

*Figure **9-C** Research cases used in collective measurement*

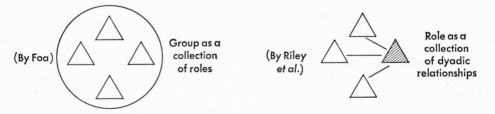

Here the research case **(P-I)** is the individual role—conceived, not as a simple undifferentiated entity, but as a structure of constituent dyadic relationships. The measurement problem is to deal with the individual as he relates to each of the other individuals in the group. Figure 9-C illustrates the nature of this case, as compared with the group as a structure of individual roles in the Foa study. If Foa's group measures are obtained by collecting individual information, the Rutgers object (and subject) role measures are obtained by collecting dyadic information. Thus the *cases* used in the two studies parallel one another, but at different system levels. Another way to think of the object measure is that (members of) the same group are questioned repeatedly—and their answers collected—

with reference to a whole series of objects (each of the group members in turn). The case is parallel to that used in Merton's study of influentials in a community, where, in effect, the members collectively rate various individuals according to their influence. (The difference between the two studies is, of course, that Merton uses overall ratings on one indicant, whereas the Rutgers researchers combine several indicants into a composite measure.)

THE GROUP PATTERN APPROACH

Both the Foa study and the Rutgers study go through the three steps for collective measurement of the properties of these cases, but they combine indicants at entirely different stages in this process. Foa seeks, and tests for, patterning in the attitudes of individuals; the Rutgers researchers seek such patterning in the collective attitudes of the group (toward one of their members).

If you review the Rutgers procedure (with which you are familiar through your analyses of the study selection and your own experience with obtaining a status scale in Exercise III-5), you will notice that Step 1 in the collective measurement (Figure 9-B above) does *not* consist of G-scale analysis of the constituent dyads. The researchers do not look at the dyads at this step to see whether *A*'s naming *B* as popular depends, for example, upon *A*'s also naming *B* as an associate. Step 1 consists merely of coding each dyad on each of the separate items: one person, *A,* may or may not name another, *B,* as an associate, or as a wished-for associate, or as popular, or as a leader. Step 2 consists of collecting for each object the dyadic information—again on each of the separate items—counting how many times the object is named as an associate, for example, or as a leader. Only in Step 3 are the several items finally combined and a G-scale pattern of unidimensionality found. Here the assignment of a collective measure to each object role requires that the scale analysis be carried out—as in your use of the group pattern approach in Exercise III-6.

The group pattern approach is quite different, then, from the individual pattern approach of the Foa study. (This contrast is unrelated, however, to the differing levels at which the two sets of measures are developed. Foa might equally well have first counted the number of individuals in each group who gave the various answers to each of the questions, and then combined the questions at Step 3. Or the Rutgers Group might have sought a dyad scale at Step 1, only then collecting the dyads.)

LIMITATIONS OF THE APPROACH

Our analysis of these two studies shows that both of these different approaches are possible. The analysis also reveals that neither approach is in itself sufficient to clarify the concept being measured, a fact that we shall presently examine further. The individual pattern approach can uncover patterning only if it occurs in the *constituent* data (for individuals). Similarly, the group pattern approach may uncover patterning in the *collective* data (for the group), but it does not in itself provide any assurance that the group is, after all, relevant to the analysis. The finding of the status scale in the collective data might mean, for example, that individuals who are *not* in interaction with one another at all merely tend to organize their personal attitudes toward objects with a similar consistency.

Selvin's Use of a Related Measurement Procedure

Before considering the differing implications of the group pattern and the individual pattern approaches, we shall examine the Selvin study as a sociological application of one of the many other available measurement procedures— factor analysis.

You should be aware of the wide variety of possible measuring devices, in addition to the arbitrary scores and the G-scales we have been examining in detail and the latent structure analysis used by Stouffer and Toby. Many specific sets of measurement rules have been developed during the past several decades; although they were first applied in psychophysics and mental testing, they have recently been used with increasing frequency both to clarify and to measure sociological variables. In psychophysics, Fechner, attempting to specify the relationship between sensation and the physical stimulus, developed basic techniques which, together with their various elaborations, form the basis of many modern methods. Such men as Guilford and Thurstone, combining knowledge of various fields, did much to codify and create interest in measurement techniques; Thurstone himself is identified with rating scales, paired comparisons, equal-appearing interval scales, and multiple-factor analysis. Much research on attitude measurement, which builds upon these foundations, has resulted in the work (as described in Bert Green) of Guttman and Lazarsfeld, and in such procedures as Likert-type scales, Coombs' unfolding technique, and item analysis (in which the scores on each item are tested for their correlation with the total scores on the set of items). Thus, for example, Stouffer's scale of tolerance (Unit 6) actually employs a modification, called the H-technique or the contrived-item scale, which reduces error in the G-scale procedure (see Stouffer *et al.*, 1954). The G-scales in the Foa study utilize image analysis—another innovation for isolating the common element running through a set of items (see Guttman, 1954-c). Both the contrived-item scale and image analysis have been applied at Rutgers to measurement of status (see Toby *et al.*, 1954).

Another important procedure, multiple-factor analysis, is a method for reducing a large number of items to the set of common factors (dimensions) to which they are all mutually related. The underlying dimensions are defined in terms of these interrelationships or consistencies among the items. When the effects of these factors are held constant in the computations, there should no longer be any relationship among the items. Once the factors have been abstracted, a factor loading is used to designate the correlation between an item and each of the factors (see, *e.g.,* Blalock, 1960, Chapter 21). Thus the G-scale and factor analysis may both be regarded as instruments for uncovering patterning in the data; an important difference between them is, however, that the G-scale hypothesizes and tests for a single dimension, whereas multiple-factor analysis examines the correlations to determine how many and what the dimensions are.

Although you cannot, in a single program of study, master the procedures involved in the many complicated and rapidly developing forms of measurement, your intensive experience with the comparatively simple G-scale should enable you to approach new procedures with greater understanding and imagination. In the meantime, through careful reading of studies (like Selvin's or the study by Sewell and Haller) that utilize factor analysis or other complex procedures, you can learn a good deal about their nature and use.

SELVIN'S USE OF COLLECTIVE MEASURES

If we analyze Selvin's procedure for measuring leadership climate, we find that it consists of a sequence of two collective measures, in which the factor analysis is just one step. In terms of our framework for collective measurement, Selvin's first set of two steps involves collecting dyadic relationships in order to measure the (object) roles of military leaders; his second set of two steps goes on to collect these individual roles in order to yield group measures (of climate).

Thus his first steps are formally parallel to the steps in the Rutgers object scale—except, of course, that the details of Selvin's procedure are very different, and that his objects are measured, not on one dimension, but on three. He starts by *collecting* leader-trainee *dyads* for each item, assembling for each leader the ratings of all the trainees under him. (He uses the mean of these ratings for each leader, checking them later for any bimodal distribution of the ratings.) Thus, he collects the dyads on each of the fifteen items *before* combining the items—as in the group pattern approach used in the Rutgers status scale. It is at this point that he uses the factor analysis to deal with the fifteen items combined, computing object scores for each of the eighty-two leaders—not on one—but on the three dimensions (factors) of "positive," "tyrannical," and "vacillating" leadership.

Once Selvin has obtained these three-dimensional object ratings, his last set of steps is formally parallel to Foa's analysis. In these steps he collects individual measures (objects rather than subjects, to be sure) into group measures—and, as in the Foa study, collects these measures *after* the items have been combined for individuals and the individual (object) pattern established through the factor analysis. For each company, Selvin collects the individual object ratings of its seven leaders on each of the three dimensions. (Here he also uses weights to take into account the leader's relative influence and his length of service.) What he thus derives for the group (the company) is an index of leadership climate for each dimension—a multidimensional measure—which he treats in a property-space. (See his Table 6 for which he shows only two of the dimensions, dichotomizing each of these.)

Through this step-by-step procedure, Selvin finally classifies his companies into four types—quite a reduction from the 200,000 ratings with which he started. Yet, he says that "in retrospect" the procedure for accomplishing the reduction was "unnecessarily complicated"—and we might agree that, despite the desirable simplicity of the final measure, its meaning is difficult to trace through the complexities of its derivation. The utility of the procedure depends of course upon whether it will lead, as Selvin points out, to "fruitful directions for analysis," as he finds that it does in the later portions of his volume on the effects of leadership (Selvin, 1960).

Utility of the Factor Analysis.   Thus Selvin makes use of factor analysis, as one part of his multi-stage procedure, to measure the "average trainee's" perceptions of the leaders of his company. He introduces the factor analysis at Step 3 of a group pattern approach to collective measurement, and demonstrates how the method may be used for determining the relevant number of dimensions (factors), and for combining and weighting the items as they apply to each dimension. Despite its utility, the computations required by the method (see Thurstone; Cattell; or Fruchter), starting with the matrix of correlations between pairs of items (Selvin's Table 7), and proceeding through the extraction of factors and the necessary rotations, are extensive (though they can be greatly facilitated by the use of computers).

Although there are numerous controversies about the implications of this complex procedure (see Guttman, 1954-b), Selvin explains the rationale by saying that "factor analysis actually simplifies the total picture of leadership; it shows that there are patterns of consistency underneath the varied perceptions, and it provides a rational, systematic process for identifying these patterns." Even though the researcher may start with diverse data not held together in advance by any unifying theory, the factor analysis itself may uncover empirical regularities, or, as Selvin puts it, "useful indices to summarize a group of related characteristics." It is then up to the researcher to interpret such empirical patterns, to give names to the resultant factors, and perhaps in this way to use research findings for the clarification of concepts. Unlike G-scaling, which starts with conceptual definitions and tests them against the facts, factor analysis starts with a search for empirical patterning that may suggest clues to new conceptual formulations.

Patterns of Collective Acts

In summary, then, the studies and exercises in this Unit have begun to show the nature of the measurement problem when the researcher wants to deal both with several individual members of groups, and with multiple indicants of properties. Here he must accomplish two quite different types of combining. First, he wants to *combine the indicants,* as this is commonly done in measuring acts (or attitudes) of individuals; and second, he wants to *collect the individuals* in order to obtain an over-all measure for each group. Since, in measuring a collective property, he is concerned as well with the individuals who do the thinking or the acting, he works with both individual and group; in one approach, as we saw in Figure 9-B, he may combine indicants at the individual level before obtaining the collective measure; in another approach, he may go directly to the group level to combine his indicants.

In any such approach to measurement, there are two broad *types of outcomes.* First, the researcher may discover *patterns* (or structures) in the data. This is the more desirable outcome, since it allows him to combine or collect the indicants (to reduce the complex space) in a form consistent with the empirical situation under study; i.e., it produces manageable measures that correspond to reality. Moreover, the discovery of patterns in itself adds to his understanding of the concept. Second, there are also many outcomes that do *not* show any patterning. Either the patterns do not exist in the given situation; or the researcher does not employ procedures appropriate for uncovering the particular patterns that do exist—for example, he may fail to discover an actual multidimensional pattern. An alternative, then (if he still wishes to measure the property), is to use judgment in assigning arbitrary scores.

A FICTITIOUS EXAMPLE

The possibilities and limitations of such attempts to abstract patterns of collective action may become clearer if we consider a fictitious, and highly simplified, example. Suppose that we observe a large number of maintenance laborers in a railroad marshaling yard working on the job of replacing all the worn-out ties. The measurement problem is to classify the section gangs according to the stage in the operation at which each has arrived. We start with some conceptual definition of the process, assuming that it includes inspection, spike removal, digging, laying of new ties, rock replacement, rail alignment, spike driving, and other operations. But we are not sure in advance whether there is any fixed pattern in these operations, whether, for example, they necessarily occur in a particular order. And we are also not sure whether the laborers may be organized in some way within each gang, or whether each laborer replaces his "own" ties—whether he performs the various operations as an individual without reference to what the other laborers are doing.

Whatever the pattern of activities and the social organization may be, it happens in this instance that no one laborer is completely aware of them—he cannot act as an "expert" in informing us; it also happens that we cannot observe the total interaction directly since the marshaling yard extends over many acres and is characterized by a high degree of activity. Our illustration, then, though stylized, represents many research situations in which inferences must be made from partial clues obtained from the several group members. What we do here is to select certain items as indicants, check each laborer on each indicant, then imagine what might be learned from these indicants alone.

Let us consider only two of the indicants: each laborer is asked whether he has replaced rocks, and whether he has engaged in any digging. The aim now is to combine these data in order to classify section gangs. That is, we must combine items and we must collect individuals.

A PATTERN FOR INDIVIDUALS

If we start with the individual pattern approach, we first deal (much as Foa does) with all the laborers as individuals. We combine the two indicants for each laborer (Step 1), and look at the data to see whether any underlying pattern may be found. If, for instance, we seek a G-scale of individuals, one possible outcome is that we will, indeed, find a unidimensional pattern (in these two indicants and all the others selected), as in Table 9-D.

Table **9-D** *A G-scale pattern for individuals*

Scale type of individual	Replacing rocks	Digging
2	+	+
1	−	+
0	−	−

Let us restate the implications of such a patterned finding. We can now assign a scale score to each laborer that tells exactly which acts he has performed. We can also arrange all the laborers along a single dimension of maintenance operations. Moreover, the finding of a scale suggests the nature of the process—apparently each laborer goes through these acts in a particular pattern, so that no one of them replaces rocks unless he has also dug. If this is so, then we have found *within-role patterning*—a designation we use to mean that an individual's acts or attitudes are not just random relative to each other, but fit together within his own role.

Now, given this outcome at Step 1, it is a simple matter to go on to the remaining steps in collective measurement so as to classify each gang according to its stage in the operation. Since, with the indicants combined, we now have to manage only one measure for each individual, we can simply count the number of individuals in each scale type for each group (Step 2), and then (Step 3) classify each group according to its median scale type, for example, or (by dichotomizing the scale) according to the proportion of laborers with a given scale score or higher. The collective measurement is thus clearly facilitated by the finding of a simple pattern for the individuals, as Foa's analysis has already shown.

No Pattern for Individuals.   But suppose that the outcome of Step 1 is quite different and *no* within-role patterning appears; we find all the individual laborers fairly equally divided among four types as in Table 9-E. Here there is no indication that replacing rocks and digging are integral parts of the same procedure, or that one step may be contingent upon another. The data merely show that some laborers replace rocks, others dig, others do both or neither. The items are independent at the individual level. What are the next steps in obtaining the collective measure (unless we are willing to resort to arbitrary scores at this early stage of the measurement procedure)? It is patently more complicated to handle four types of laborers—a nominal multicategory measure—than scale types arranged in rank order. At Step 2, we might count for each gang the number of laborers in each of the four types. This would utilize all of the available information (without making arbitrary reductions); but it would be hard to handle and compre-

Table **9-E**   *Four types of individuals*

Type of individual	Replacing rocks	Digging
a	+	+
b	+	−
c	−	+
d	−	−

hend comparisons among all the groups at Step 3—as you know from the examples in Manual III-A(2). And the difficulties are greatly compounded, of course, when all the scale items are used instead of just these two. Alternatively, we might dichotomize each group measure, so that (at Step 3) we classify groups according to the proportions of their members who are in just one of the types (the percentage of members who have performed both functions, for example), but this excludes the information about the other types.

A General Principle.   So far these illustrations suggest that, in general, the individual pattern approach to collective measurement may be useful whenever the researcher does in fact discover patterning within the roles (as in the Foa study). He has then learned something about the process; he has, at the same time, simplified the research task by reducing the classification space to fit the simpler (in this instance, cumulative) patterning. On the other hand, if he does not find any within-role patterning at Step 1, he runs into complications which may well encourage him to start over again and try the group pattern approach. Accordingly, before we attempt to evaluate the individual pattern approach further, let us now apply the group pattern approach in our fictitious example.

A PATTERN FOR GROUPS

Suppose that we had originally started the collective measurement by the group pattern approach, looking for a G-scale at the group level rather than at the individual level. Step 1 now consists merely of the coding of each individual (as + or—) on each item. We then go on to Step 2, counting the individuals in each gang who are + on each of the items; that is, we think of the laborers together in the groups to which they belong, we classify each group on an ordinal scale for each item, but we do not combine items until Step 3. At Step 3, we employ the familiar G-scale analysis—with the groups as the cases. We choose an arbitrary cutting point for each item (if the Ford short method is to be used), so that, for example, a group might be rated + on the item if at least three laborers had engaged in digging, or if at least one laborer had replaced rocks. After next combining these items in the usual way, we may perhaps find that the group data do not fit the scale model—that we must try other cutting points, use another model, or resort to arbitrary group scores. Alternatively, however, we may find a G-scale pattern for the groups, as in Table 9-F.

Table **9-F** *A G-scale pattern for groups*

Scale type of group	Replacing rocks	Digging
2	+	+
1	−	+
0	−	−

The implications of this group scale pattern are somewhat different, of course, from the implications of an individual pattern. It is now the groups to which the scale scores are assigned, which are ordered along a single dimension, and about which inferences are drawn. Thus it appears that a group (or some of its members) has engaged in replacing rocks only if the group (or some of its members) has also engaged in digging.

POST-ANALYSIS

We have now completed the collective measurement by the group pattern approach; even if we find a group scale, however, we have not yet learned all we might about the patterning of these items. Because this group approach does not deal directly with any possible *individual* patterning, we have not yet utilized the data fully to clarify our conception of the property under study. This shortcoming will be clearer if we now imagine still another step—a post-analysis—in which we go back and look at the individual data used in the collective measurement.

In post-analysis, there arises the interesting possibility of discrepancy between individual and group findings: we might find a scale pattern for the groups (as in Table 9-F) in a situation where no such pattern occurs for the individuals; the individuals might be evenly divided among all four possible types (as in Table 9-E), although only the three perfect scale types of groups occur. Thus, we find that a consistent relationship between replacing rocks and digging emerges only when the collectivity, not the individual, is taken as the point of reference. Replacing rocks, which appears at the individual level to be unrelated to digging, appears at the group level to be contingent upon it.

The exciting aspect of any such discrepancy in individual vs. group findings is the clue it affords to a possible social organization of the group members for the action under study. How could these findings come about? What might they mean? The *individual* data (Table 9-E) show some laborers $(+-)$ who have performed one act, and other laborers $(-+)$ who have performed a different act. The *group* scale makes plain that, within the concerted action pattern, the acts of $+-$ laborers are contingent upon the acts of $-+$ laborers or $++$ laborers; that is, there can be no gang in which there are $+-$ laborers (who replace rocks but do not dig) unless there are other laborers in the same gang who are $++$ or $-+$ (who dig). Here we say that *patterning between or among roles* exists. This patterning rests upon some kind of structure of individuals within the group. One conceptual model that obviously could account for these findings is that of an organized division of labor, with individual laborers of types $+-$ and $-+$ playing differentiated roles which are integrated into the collective pattern of action. (Further information would be required, though, to ensure that the findings do not merely arise because laborers with certain individual tendencies to replace rocks or to dig belong together in groups, but *without* interacting to establish a division of labor.)

We shall return presently to post-analysis as one means of uncovering possible role structures from apparently random individual acts or attitudes. Post-analysis is potentially valuable in the study of informal group situations where the roles are not clearly defined, where the group structure tends to develop on an *ad hoc* basis, and where there is often no single group member who is completely aware of and able to report on, the over-all pattern.

THE TWO APPROACHES COMPARED

How, then, does the researcher choose between the group pattern approach and the individual pattern approach? Which approach is more likely to uncover patterning in the acts when such patterning actually exists? Although at first glance both approaches appear to be equally useful, the group approach actually has an advantage over the other for most sociological investigations.

The advantage of the group approach is suggested in Figure 9-D, which classifies the possible alternative situations that might actually exist in the data. The group approach seems more appropriate for discovering the collective patterns in situations I and III, and the individual approach for discovering the individual patterns in situations I and II. When G-scaling is used, however, situation II (which is shown in parentheses) is rather unlikely to exist, because if the indicants form a cumulative pattern for individuals, these same indicants will tend automatically to form a cumulative pattern for the groups also. (There are, of course, exceptions. See, for example, Riley and Riley, 1954, p. 172, for a discussion of the conditions under which a scale for the dyads will result only in a "degenerate" scale for the objects in which all the objects fall into a single category. Thus, when the objects or groups appear to be all alike, the researcher will know that the individual pattern should be examined.) Accordingly, the group pattern approach seems the more useful, since it will uncover group patterning of type I as well as group patterning of type III (the division of labor)—though it cannot in itself distinguish between them.

Figure **9-D**   *Approaches to situations of varied types*

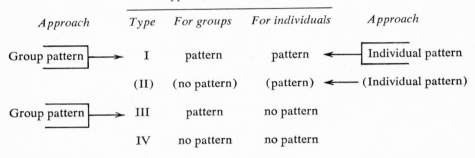

| | | Types of actual situations | | |
Approach	Type	For groups	For individuals	Approach
Group pattern —→	I	pattern	pattern	←— Individual pattern
	(II)	(no pattern)	(pattern)	←— (Individual pattern)
Group pattern —→	III	pattern	no pattern	
	IV	no pattern	no pattern	

The Structuring of Roles

These fictitious examples have helped us to evaluate two approaches in measuring the patterning of acts; in addition they have pointed to the possibilities of investigating the structuring of roles. So far we have seen that a clear division of labor, if it exists within the groups, may be discovered—not from the group pattern approach alone (which cannot distinguish between situations I and III in Figure 9-D), but from the group approach combined with a post-analysis of the data.

POST-ANALYSIS OF THE OBJECT SCALE

An actual search for such an underlying division of labor has been described in the Rutgers study. Having found a pattern in the collective data on status, the researchers wanted to learn whether this pattern tended to arise from situation I or situation III. Accordingly, they went back (to Step 1 of the procedure) to see whether the collective pattern (found at Step 3) also exists in the dyads.

The interpretations placed upon these differing situations I and III would obviously be quite different. On the one hand, the discovery of situation III—a collective pattern *without* a comparable dyadic pattern—would reveal a phenomenon that definitely refers in some way to the group, for which the group is the relevant research case, and which the investigators would interpret by postulating a division of labor in the peer group perhaps (as in the fictitious railroad maintenance crews) or some other *group* process.

On the other hand, the discovery of situation I—in which the collective pattern merely repeats itself in the dyads—would reveal little about whether the group or the individual is the relevant research case. Situation I could be interpreted in two quite different ways. First, it could mean that individuals are indeed interacting with one another in collateral *group roles* to produce the collective status pattern for objects—*e.g.,* by reinforcing one another's feelings of liking or deference for particular objects. Or second, the finding could merely reflect purely *individual* patterns. Perhaps the feelings and attitudes of all the individuals (as subjects) fit into consistent patterns because the individuals—even though they are *not* in interaction—have been socialized within a common culture. Or perhaps the characteristics of all the individuals (as objects) are so patterned that nobody elicits feelings of deference from others unless he also elicits feelings of friendship. Since such purely individual patterns were of less interest than the group patterns to the Rutgers researchers, the discovery of situation I would have contributed little to their understanding of status. They hoped to find the crucial instance—situation III.

And, as you know from your reading of the Rutgers study, the post-analysis of the object scale actually reveals that the collective pattern of status is *not* repeated in the dyads: A's naming B as popular does not depend upon A's naming B as an associate. There is the suggestion then (though not clearly demonstrated in this instance), that the actual situation approximates the pure type of situation III. Dyads which tend to be differentiated are structured in such a way that certain individuals think of someone (the object) as popular (or follow him as a leader) only if still other individuals regard him as a friend. Thus the group does seem relevant to the measurement here. Indeed—and this is generally true when measurement is applied to a *situation of type III*—the patterning of attitudes (or acts) tends to be obscured in the dyadic (individual) data, emerging only when the data are collected for the group.

This post-analysis illustrates the possibility of revealing latent patterns of collective action or orientation which depend upon the fitting together of individual acts or attitudes. (Procedures for such post-analysis will be illustrated in the future Exercise II-5.) By studying possible patterning at *both* the group level and the individual level, we can uncover, if it exists, a clearly marked differentiation and structuring of the roles.

To be sure, when the researcher finds that situation III exists, he would require additional information to make sure that the source of such structuring is the *interaction* and reciprocal *role expectations* postulated in the social system model. He would want to rule out the alternative possibility that situation III arises from some *special combination of individual* characteristics that may occur in the groups without any interaction or mutual expectations. Take an obvious example of boy-girl couples in which one member (the boy) always says yes and the other says no to the question, "Are you taller than your partner?" The patterning between the roles of the partners here would scarcely mean that the answers are a *necessary* part of an established role relationship, since the pattern might occur through random selection from populations which differ in height. Or, in a sociometric test, if *A* says he would like to sit beside *B* and *B* says the same about *A*, this might merely reflect the similar characteristics of the two individuals whose private definitions and opinions *happen to coincide*. In such instances, further assurance that the differentiated individual patterns are organized as parts of a social system may require the testing of supporting hypotheses—as suggested by the attempts reported in the Rutgers study (see also Riley and Cohn, 1954-b).

SCALE ANALYSIS AND THE STRUCTURING OF ROLES

In addition to this type of post-analysis—which is used here to make inferences only indirectly from the juxtaposition of group data and individual data—it seems likely that G-scaling might be used to discover certain role structures directly. You might have found in your study of marriage pairs in Exercise III-6,

Figure **9-E**   *A space for measuring disciplinary climate*

	Ships in which officers	
Ships in which crew	Want discipline	Do not want discipline
Want discipline		(0)
Do not want discipline		

for example, that only these three situations occurred: (1) both husband and wife, or (2) wife only, or (3) neither one took an equalitarian position—that is, there were no couples in which only the husband took such a position. Would not such a finding indicate a structuring of *roles* in regard to this collective pattern of orientations?

Or consider a fictitious extension of the Foa study. Suppose that, when Foa rates each ship according to the disciplinary attitudes of officers and crew, he discovers only three types of disciplinary climate, as in Figure 9-E. The finding of a zero cell here (Foa actually finds one case in this cell) might have suggested a special structuring of officers and crew in regard to disciplinary norms. (It would also have allowed Foa to classify groups on a single dimension of disciplinary climate.)

Figure **9-F** *Combining indicants of properties in collective measurement*

Basic procedure for collective measurement (*Manual III-A*)	Steps at which indicants of properties may be combined		Steps at which structure of roles may be observed
	Individual pattern approach	*Group pattern approach*	
Step 1 Assign a constituent measure to each individual (or subgroup or dyad)	←		
Step 2 Collect these constituent measures for each group (or role)			←
Step 3 Assign a collective measure to each group (or role) on the basis of Step 2		←	
(*Post-analysis*)			←

The distinguishing characteristic of these examples is that the items designate, not different acts or attitudes, but the relevant parts of the social system—the roles of husband and wife, or of officers and crew. In contrast, the studies we have been analyzing in this Unit all use the measurement model to test for patterning in acts or attitudes—in the *properties* of systems. But the *cases* in these studies have been handled by collecting parts of systems (individuals, dyads, subgroups) into *arbitrary aggregates.* These arbitrary aggregates have been used much like the arbitrary scores for combining indicants of acts or attitudes. Just as the arbitrary score assumes without testing that certain acts belong together and should be given certain weights, so the arbitrary collective measure aggregates roles without making any tests. And just as the arbitrary score fails to tell *which* acts are contributing to it, the arbitrary aggregate measure does not (except through post-analysis) identify *who* contributes *what* to the over-all pattern of action or attitudes.

Nevertheless, although little work has so far been done on this, it seems quite possible to apply measurement models so that they will test for the structuring of roles in a fashion similar to the more usual tests for the patterning of acts. Such tests are applied, as your experience with Exercise III-6 demonstrates, at Step 2 of the procedure for collective measurement (see Figure 9-F).

Beyond these simple examples, many modifications and elaborations are of course possible. For instance, more than two items representing several roles might fit together in an extension of the cumulative model suggested in Figure 9-E. Or in a two-role group the G-scale based on several items might attack simultaneously the pattern of collective action and the relation of group members in the performance of this action, as suggested in the fictitious example in Table 9-G. An actual example of empirical patterning of acts that is also consistent with the

Table **9-G** *A G-scale reflecting both patterned acts and structured roles*

	Scale pattern [a]					
Scale type of dyad	B performs act 6	A performs act 5	B performs act 4	A performs act 3	B performs act 2	A performs act 1
6	+	+	+	+	+	+
5	−	+	+	+	+	+
4	−	−	+	+	+	+
3	−	−	−	+	+	+
2	−	−	−	−	+	+
1	−	−	−	−	−	+
0	−	−	−	−	−	−

[a] + = act has been performed in dyad; − = act has not been performed in dyad.

assumption of simple structuring of roles is afforded in Table 9-H. Here the role partners, *A* and *B,* alternate in the performance of a cumulative series of acts. (For a further discussion of such specialized cases of the countless possible structures that might be reflected in measurement, see Riley and Cohn, 1954-a, pp. 218–23.)

Various other measurement models may be more appropriate than the G-scale for uncovering many of the role structures of sociological interest. In informal groups, role definitions are often not as rigid as those suggested in, for example, Table 9-G. The greater flexibility allows the set of acts defined as belonging to one role to be readily rearranged and partially redistributed to other roles. Such alternative procedures as image analysis or the contrived item scale seem better adapted than the G-scale for the measurement of these flexible role structures.

THE NEED FOR A SOCIAL SYSTEM APPROACH

Such examples point to the possibility of studying the patterns of group properties, on the one hand, and the structuring of group roles, on the other. Group *patterns* may be uncovered, as we have seen, by dealing with the *group* as the research case **(P-I)**. And the general principle underlying measures of group *structure* is that the *roles within* each group must be named or somehow identified in terms of the action under study. (This principle of *role identification* has already been suggested in Unit 8.) What seem to be needed, then, are methods which will combine the study of patterned properties with the study of social structures.

Table **9-H**   *An interactive dyad scale of intimacy* [a]

| | | Scale pattern | | | | | Distribution of dyads | | |
| | | + = designated partner names the other for item | | | | | | | |
Scale type of dyads		*B guesses A will confide in him*	*B confides in A*	*B likes A*	*A guesses B likes him*	*A likes B*	*Nonscale types*	*Perfect scale types*	*Total*
Most intimate	5	+	+	+	+	+	12	42	54
	4	−	+	+	+	+	3	9	12
	3	−	−	+	+	+	10	18	28
	2	−	−	−	+	+	36	50	86
	1	−	−	−	−	+	1	58	59
Least intimate	0 [b]	−	−	−	−	−	3	[b]	3
Total dyads [b]							65	177 [b]	242 [b]

[a] This table orders dyads in terms of the degree of intimacy with which each subject perceives each relationship. (Riley and Cohn, 1954-a, p. 221.)
[b] The table excludes dyads in which a subject names an object on none of the items.

Although much ground-breaking work still remains to be done here, Unit 12 will explore further these dual possibilities, seeking methods—which we shall call a social system approach—for studying simultaneously the patterns and the underlying social-structural base. The key to this approach, as we shall see, is that, when the focus is on the group, the groups must be used as the cases **(P-I)**, but they must be classified in such a way as to retain the role identifications *within* each group. Only then will it become possible to examine simultaneously the patterns among acts and the questions about who contributes what to these patterns.

The Clarification of Concepts

Each of the examples we have examined illustrates the point that measurement is not only a means of classifying cases—designed to meet increasingly high criteria of precision and reliability. Measurement may also be used to shed light on the conceptual scheme.

Thus the Rutgers researchers, for example, developed a clearer understanding of peer group status, in part through post-analysis of the data, but in part from the measurement experience itself. Much of the clarification occurred, of course, prior to the research operations, when the investigators attempted to draw up a property-space and to find indicants, and were thereby forced to specify their conception of status by defining the items postulated to fit together in the scale. But in addition, they learned a great deal more about the concept (for the given sample of adolescents) after they had obtained the data and were able to study actual distributions within the property-space—when they learned, for example, that being a leader seems to depend upon having *some* friends, but not necessarily *many* friends.

Of course, the data might have been distributed in various ways throughout the cells; any resultant distribution would have been useful in showing how leadership, popularity, and friendship interrelate with one another. The fact that the actual distribution happened to fit the G-scale (as hypothesized) gave support to the hunch that all these items belong together in the same dimension and that they are arranged in a cumulative pattern. But entirely different distributions might well have been found. A large number of individuals, for instance, might have been chosen as leaders but not liked or thought popular. In such an event, the researchers might have been led to the inference that a second dimension is present in this population. Perhaps people can achieve status in the school grade whether or not they also achieve it in intimate friendship groups. Such a finding might have suggested a revision of the original conception of status, a subdivision perhaps into two different concepts of status in the intimate group and status in the larger system.

Such conceptual clarification occurs when the measurement process is used to confirm (or reject) the investigator's advance hypotheses about the nature of the sociological variable—peer status or disposition toward universalism-particularism or crew satisfaction with officers or tolerance of nonconformists. The measuring instrument itself is used to analyze the relationships among the various indicants, and to illuminate, rather than obscure, the contributions of each in-dicant to the total pattern or structure. It uncovers the consistencies beneath the diversity of the data, the One within the Many. For, as Sorokin writes in his *Social and Cultural Dynamics:* "Hidden behind the empirically different, seemingly un-related fragments of the cultural complex lies an identity of meaning, which brings them together into consistent *styles,* typical *forms,* and significant *pat-terns."* (Sorokin, Vol. I, p. 23.)

Thus the process of measurement may itself clarify sociological concepts (see Merton, 1957, pp. 114–17) and bring them more nearly into line with the facts. A number of measuring instruments are now being used effectively to discover the facts about patterning of acts or attitudes, hence to revise the researcher's defini-tions of many specific collective properties (group opinion about formal dis-cipline or peer group communications or railroad maintenance operations). Fur-ther extensions and adaptations of these instruments are needed, however, to reflect the underlying social-structural base—to identify which members of the group contribute what aspects to the collective patterns. As instruments are de-veloped and improved to meet these needs, measures will come more nearly into the desired one-to-one alignment with the concepts of sociological interest, and will serve as more powerful devices for enlarging sociological knowledge.

SUGGESTED READINGS FOR UNIT NINE

Coombs; Goode and Hatt, Chapter 17; Bert F. Green; Hagood and Price, Chap-ters 10, 26; Peak; Selltiz *et al.,* Chapters 5, 10; Stouffer, 1950.

QUESTIONS FOR REVIEW AND DISCUSSION

Review the following methodological terms as used in this Unit:
  arbitrary score
  between-role patterning
  continuum
  factor analysis
  flexible (rigid) role structures
  group pattern approach

Guttman scale
  coefficient of chance reproducibility
  coefficient of reproducibility
  cumulative or transitive items
  intensity component
  object scale
  zero point
individual pattern approach

post-analysis of a scale
reduction of a property space
unidimensionality
within-role patterning

1. Describe in detail the conception of the research case (**P-I**) used in the studies by (a) Stouffer and Toby, (b) Foa and (c) Riley *et al.* What is the relevance of this conception to the measurement approach used in (1) combining multiple indicants? (2) collecting multiple individuals?

2a. Study the scalogram pattern in Table 1 of the study by Stouffer and Toby. How do you interpret the tendency of these items to form a Guttman scale? How would you define the dimension being measured?

b. Note that there are two sets of rather numerous nonscale responses, $+ - + +$ and $- + - +$. Study these two nonscale patterns to see whether they suggest any possible additional dimensions in the data.

3. Compute the chance reproducibility for Table 1 of the Stouffer and Toby study, working from the marginal percentages and applying Rules 1, 2, and 3 from Manual V-B.

4. What is the utility of the notions of intensity and a zero point in the measurement of attitudes? If attitude intensity fits the model of a second component in a subject scale, what notion might operate as a second component in an object scale?

5. Discuss the procedures used in the study by Stouffer and Toby to increase the validity and reliability of measurement.

6. We have used two procedures for collective measurement which seek patterning in the properties at either the individual level or the group level.

a. Now imagine that Foa had used the group (rather than the individual)

pattern approach. Exactly what would he have done at each of the steps in the procedure? How and why might his findings have been affected by this change in approach?

b. Now imagine that the Rutgers researchers had used the individual (rather than the group) pattern approach in seeking a collective (object) measure of status. Exactly what would they have done at each of the steps in the procedure? How and why might the findings have been affected by this change in approach?

7. How do you assess the possibilities of representing structuring of roles in sociological measurement, in place of measures that aggregate constituent data in a purely arbitrary fashion? What might Foa have done to test for possible role structuring? What did the Rutgers researchers attempt, and how might they have carried this further?

8. The Rutgers researchers examine the hypothesis that the characteristics of subjects and objects as individuals determine the dyadic pattern of communication (in their Table 6). Compare this with the test of a similar model from Bales' Table 2 discussed in Unit 3.

9. How is the self-administered questionnaire used in the studies by (a) Stouffer and Toby, (b) Foa and (c) Riley *et al.* to facilitate study of many members of the same group?

10. The method of construction of an "index of political predisposition" is explained by the appendix note in the study by Lazarsfeld, Berelson, and Gaudet. Study this note and consider the following:

a. Can you figure out what weights were used in order to obtain the index (or crude score)?

b. How is this score methodologically similar to (or different from) the communication scores in Exercise

II-4?

Consider in your answer the difference between combining indicants to reflect internal consistency and combining indicants to predict an outside criterion.

c. What are the advantages of such a score? (See, for example, its use in Figure 7 of the study.)

d. What are the disadvantages?

e. State the assumptions on which such a score is based.

UNIT TEN
DYNAMIC STUDIES

SUGGESTED PROGRAM OF STUDY

This Unit deals with dynamic analysis—methods of studying process or change in social systems over time (P-V), in contrast to static studies made at a single point in time.

Exercises and Manual

Exercise IV-4 demonstrates the procedures, and illustrates some problems and possibilities, of panel analysis (which is based on data obtained from the same sample at two or more periods of time). Review the use of panel analysis in the study by Lazarsfeld, Berelson, and Gaudet (Unit 8) and in your own investigation in **Exercise II-4.**

Studies

Examine carefully the studies by **Ogburn** and **Thomas; Lazarsfeld** and **Merton; Coleman, Katz,** and **Menzel;** and **Hare** in this Unit to determine exactly what methods of dynamic analysis these researchers use. Compare these studies with those in earlier Units that also study the system over time. Review the earlier use of mathematical models (in Units 3 and 5, for example) as a basis for understanding how various dynamic models may be applied.

Commentary

In the Commentary, we distinguish three dynamic approaches (in contrast to the static cross-section approach): panel analysis, trend studies, and a combined approach that relates trends to a sequence of cross-section studies.

Questions for Review and Discussion

In reviewing this Unit, try to organize and consolidate the principles of dynamic analysis with the methods of measuring variables and studying their relationships as you have learned these in previous Units.

WILLIAM F. OGBURN
DOROTHY S. THOMAS

The Influence of the Business Cycle on Certain Social Conditions

The influence of economic changes on social conditions has for a long time been a subject of study for historians, economists, and sociologists. We know that changes in the economic system of a people are accompanied by profound social changes. Thus, the industrial revolution of the past century brought changes in political organization, in the family, the position of women, industrial classes, education, etc. Such effects are the materials back of the theory of the economic interpretation of history.

There is, however, another type of economic changes which also occasions social modifications. These changes are not the lasting changes in the economic order but are oscillatory changes of short duration. Thus, while time brings enduring change, there are also brief swings in economic conditions through prosperity and depression, around the line of general economic change. These fluctuations in business conditions occur over short intervals with some regularity and are usually referred to as business cycles. Do these fluctuations in business produce fluctuations in social conditions? Do we find relatively more births, deaths, marriages, and divorces in periods of business depression? Does crime and do other social phenomena fluctuate with the business cycle? Of course the fact that social statistics fluctuate simultaneously with indexes of the

business cycle does not necessarily prove a causal influence, that is, that the economic changes produce the social changes. For instance, if the birth-rate is correlated with the business cycle, such a change in the birth-rate may not be due directly to the business cycle but may perhaps be due to the changes in the marriage-rate which may correspond to changes in the business cycle. Our first problem, however, is to determine the amount of concurrence in the fluctuations of certain social conditions with the fluctuations of business.

It is possible to measure the amount of this concurrence in several social phenomena, for in some cases we have series of statistics going back a number of years. Furthermore, during the last few years, a great deal of success has been achieved in describing the business cycle, and there also exists the technique for measuring quantitatively the concurrence in fluctuations in time series. In the following pages, therefore, we shall inquire to what extent certain data of marriages, divorces, births, deaths, and crime vary with the indexes of the business cycle. Our first step is to measure the cycles of business during recent years.

I

One difficulty in getting a measure of the business cycles to correlate with social statistics for so large and varied an area as the United States is the diversity of our economic life. Our economic life

Reprinted in part from Dorothy S. Thomas, *Social Aspects of the Business Cycle,* New York: Alfred A. Knopf, 1927, pp. 53–74, with permission of Routledge & Kegan Paul Ltd.

consists in the main of agriculture on the one hand, and of manufacturing, mining, and trade on the other. The products of agriculture are affected in large part by rainfall and climate; oscillations in crops were in early times referred to as good years and lean years, famines being the extremes of the lean period. The business cycle is a phenomenon more characteristic of the period of great manufacturing development. However, during the last half-century in the United States there has been a fairly close relationship between economic welfare in agriculture and in manufacturing. Prosperity and depression in business affect the profits from agriculture, if not so much the volume of agricultural production.

The problem of procuring data which are representative of the state of manufacturing and commerce has been already satisfactorily met. Business failures, prices, volume of production, banking data, and employment are sufficiently widely representative.

Representative indexes must also have one other attribute. They must fluctuate concurrently. The analyses, particularly of Persons and of Mitchell, show that there are a number of economic series that reach their maximum when general prosperity is at its greatest height and reach their minimum when business depression is at its lowest depth. There are also various other series which, when measured in months, reach their maximum at various intervals preceding or following the peak of general business prosperity. Years of research by various economists have resulted in an excellent description in quantitative terms of the cycle of business based on a combination of these representative synchronous series.

We wished to take a curve of the business cycle already constructed but could find none covering a sufficient number of years. Most of the curves of business cycles are for very recent years. . . . Since it was desirable to have as long a period as possible, we have constructed a curve from 1870 to 1920. In working out a single series to describe the business cycle we have chosen to combine the following series:

1. Wholesale prices, 1870–1915.
2. Commercial failures, 1870–1920.
3. Bituminous coal production, 1870–1920.
4. Pig iron production, 1870–1920.
5. Railroad freight ton mileage, 1882–1920.
6. Bank clearings outside New York, 1881–1915.
7. Employment in Massachusetts, 1889–1920.
8. Railroad mileage constructed, 1870–88.
9. Imports, 1870–88.

. . . The next step was to determine the cycles for each series. The data for most of these nine series when plotted showed a general upward movement for the whole period, with small fluctuations up and down around the line of the general upward movement. (A similar upward movement is seen in the curve of divorce-rates shown in Figure 3.) To each series lines were then fitted which appeared to describe the general movement. These lines are called the trend lines. The actual data deviated in each year above or below these trend lines. (In Figure 3, showing divorce-rates, similar trend lines and deviations of the data from the trend lines are shown.) These deviations of the actual data from the trend for each year were computed in percentages of the trend data for the respective years. Then each percentage deviation was divided by the standard deviation of these percentage deviations for the particular series. The results were the cycles for the particular series in terms of their respective standard deviations as units. The arithmetic mean, unweighted, was then found for the cycles of the nine series. The result is a single series describing the business cycle for the period and is seen plotted as curve A in Figure 1.

In constructing this curve showing the fluctuations of business for the past fifty years, the chief methodological difficulty was in selecting the equations of the trend lines that seemed to describe best the general movement of the particular series. As there was no mechanical test to show which particular line best described the true trend of the data, it was largely a matter of judgment of the eye. For instance, one investigator might think that the trend of wholesale prices from 1870 to 1896 was that best described by a straight line, and another investigator might prefer a parabola.

In order to get around this difficulty of individual bias, which as a source of error, however, may be limited, we decided

to check our results by constructing another curve of the business cycle by computing the cycles of each series from trend lines consisting of nine-year moving averages. This was done and the result is curve B in Figure 1. It is seen to be remarkably similar to curve A, the coefficient of correlation of the two curves being +0.95.

Because of the fact that there may be a variation in preference on the part of different investigators in choosing equations to describe trends, it is of value to compare our curve of business cycles, curve A in the chart, with the curve constructed by Axe. Axe's curve is not constructed from identically the same series, and it is for intervals of a month.... It is quite similar to curve A, the coefficient of correlation being +0.92.

From the foregoing considerations, then, we think that the cycle series in curve A is a sufficiently satisfactory measure of the business fluctuations from 1870 to 1920 to use in correlation with the data of certain social phenomena.

Figure **1** *Curves of business cycles*

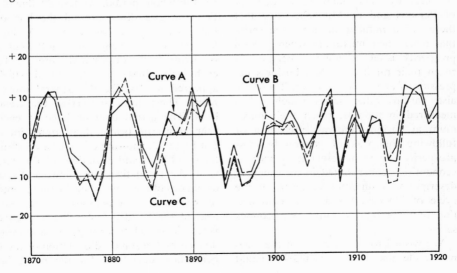

II

For a study of the variations in marriage-rates the only data that have been collected for the United States as a whole are from 1866 to 1906. Since it was desirable to have a longer record, we have collected the figures for the number of persons married during the year for the period 1870–1920 for the States for which satisfactory statistics were available. These States are Connecticut, Massachusetts, Michigan, New Hampshire, Rhode Island, and Vermont. A parabola seems to describe the general movement of the marriage-rates as seen in Figure 2. The fluctuation of these marriage-rates around the trend appears to be, in general, concurrent with the cycles of business indexes, the coefficient of correlation being +0.66. Although in general the marriage-rate increases in prosperity and diminishes in depression, this is rather noticeably not true in the year 1918. The marked drop in the marriage-rate in this very prosperous year is thought to be due to the extraordinary conditions of war time. If we omit from the correlation table the data for the year 1918, the correlation becomes +0.87. When the cycles of

marriage-rates are computed from a trend of nine-year moving averages, their correlation with the business cycles for 1874–1916 is +0.81. . . .

That the marriage-rate should be greater when business is good, and less when business is bad appears to be what one would expect. Yule thinks that one reason for the very large degree of correlation is probably the fact that the non-occurrence of the event in a business depression means in many cases only a postponement until business prosperity returns. The changes in the marriage-rate seem to be practically simultaneous with changes in the business cycle. When the correlation is made between the indexes of the business cycle and changes in the marriage-rates, not of the same year but of the following year, the coefficient of correlation (omitting the data for 1918) is +0.62, smaller than the coefficient when the correlation is made without the assumption of a one-year lag. Hooker finds that the correlation is a maximum with a lag of about a third of a year. The correspondence in the fluctuations of the marriage-rate and the business cycle seem to be a little closer for the earlier years than for the later year, from both the British and the American data.

Figure **2** *Marriage rates*

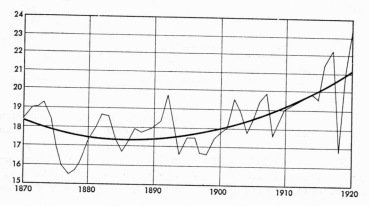

Figure **3**   *Divorce rates*

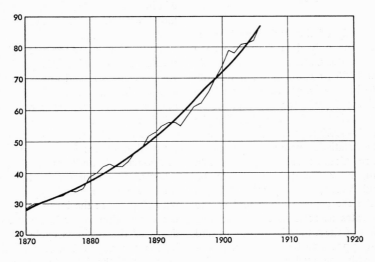

Figure **4**   *Birth rates*

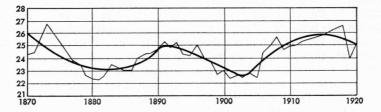

Figure **5**   *Death rates*

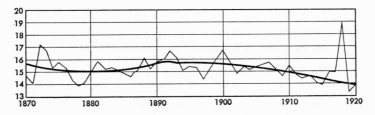

III

That the divorce-rate is influenced by business conditions was noted by Willcox as early as 1893. The curve of di-

vorce-rates for the United States from 1866 to 1886, showed low divorce-rates in the periods 1873–9 and 1884–6, which Willcox observed were periods of depression in trade. The similarity in the drops in the curve of divorce-rates and the curve of trade was so close as to lead to the conclusion of a causal relationship.

Since the publication of Willcox's article, the divorce statistics for the United States have been extended to 1906. There has been a marked increase in the divorce-rate, as is seen in the Figure 3. Figure 3 also shows the trend line describing the upward movement. The fluctuations around this trend line correspond quite closely to the fluctuations of the business cycles, the correlation for the forty years, 1867–1906, being +0.70.

The tendency to secure more divorces in prosperity and fewer divorces in business depression is quite marked, and this conclusion is perhaps surprising. The reason is not clear, although the economic argument is clearer than the psychological. The fact that divorces are expensive, involving lawyers' and court fees and perhaps alimony, may be the reason for relatively more divorces in times of business prosperity. It would be interesting to know whether there are also more desertions in periods of prosperity. It would also be interesting to know what psychological factors are involved in decreasing the divorce-rate in times of business depression.

On account of the fact that time is involved in the court procedure of granting divorces, we might be led to expect a lag in the variations in the divorce rate corresponding to the business cycle. The correlation is, however, lower with a one-year lag in the divorce-rates, being +0.58.

We have been able to procure the divorce-rates for thirteen States through 1920. The correlation between the business cycles for the United States and the divorce cycles for the thirteen States is lower (+0.33) than the correlation between the former and the divorce cycles

of the United States as a whole for the shorter period. The lack of correspondence between the divorce cycles of the thirteen States and the business cycles appears to be greater for the earlier years, however, than for the later years. Also, from an inspection of the curves of divorce-rates as published in the census volumes for separate sections of the United States, such as the South Atlantic States and the North Central States, it appears that there is a less close correspondence in fluctuations with the business cycle than there is for the nation as a whole. Just why these samples should show lower correspondences than the whole, we do not know. Possible causes may be changes in laws, migrations, changes in residence, or the influence of crop cycles.

IV

Statistics of the annual death-rate for the registration area go back only to 1900. We were able to obtain the death-rates from 1870 to 1920, however, for the same States for which we secured marriage-rates [see Figure 5]. The fluctuations in the curve of these death-rates seem to correspond somewhat with the business cycles. The correlation is found to be positive and fairly high, $r = +0.57$, and with cycles from nine-year moving averages, $r = +0.63$. This is a surprising result, as one would guess that if there were any correlation at all between business conditions and death-rates it would be negative, that is, there would be relatively more deaths in business depression and fewer in business prosperity. Such an inference would be drawn, for instance, from the studies of the Children's Bureau, Washington, D.C., which have shown that when the earnings of the father are low, the infant death-rates are high. We are also told that pulmonary tuberculosis is a disease of poverty. The impression that disease is more prevalent in conditions of poverty would lead one to expect more deaths in business depression.

Assumptions of lags do not clarify the matter. With a one-year lag in the death-rate the correlation is +0.49, and with a two-year lag it is +0.03. If we assumed a four- or five-year lag or longer in the influence of the business cycle on the death-rate, we should probably get a negative correlation. But what basis is there for such an assumption? Such an assumption would be quite unjustified in the case of infant death-rates. Yet the curve of infant death-rates for these States is quite similar to the curve of general death-rates. Yule has found a correlation of +0.77 between the general death-rates in England and Wales and the infant death-rates.

The infant mortality-rate [see Figure 7] shows about the same positive correlation with the business cycle as does the general death-rate, +0.42, for the same States and for the same period. The correlation, when the trend is nine-year moving averages, is +0.37. And with a one-year lag in the infant mortality rates the correlations are, for these types of trends, +0.43 and +0.29. The infant mortality rates, then, like the general death-rates, show the strange result of increasing in prosperity and decreasing in depression.

If the registration bureaus were in the habit of collecting and registering more records in good times and fewer in bad times, this positive correlation would be explained; but persons familiar with the administration of vital statistics assure us that there is no such variation in the registration of death records.

*Figure **6** Death rate from tuberculosis*

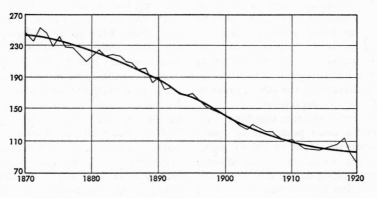

*Figure **7** Infant mortality rates*

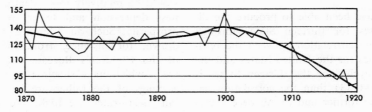

Figure **8**   *Suicide rates*

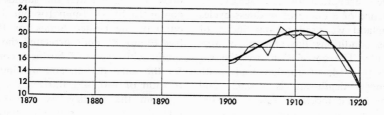

Figure **9**   *Convictions for crime in New York*

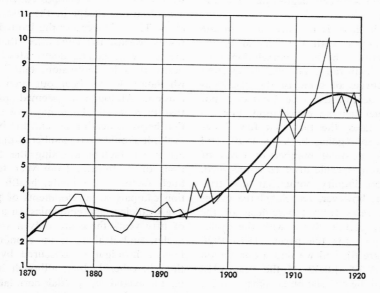

We know that the filing of death records for all deaths does not occur. . . . But even if the statistics of deaths are much less than 100 per cent complete, the partial records might quite conceivably show much the same cyclical fluctuation around a trend that they would if the records were complete. On the other hand, errors in the record may be due to various causes.

It may be that the death-rates for the registration area since 1900 are more accurate than the death-rates for the selected group of States from 1870 to 1900.

We have therefore correlated the death-rate for the United States registration area, 1900–20, with the business cycle for that period with the same results, +0.44 ± .12 for the general rates, and +0.41 for the infant mortality rates.

On account of these unexpected results it is desirable to see if they are borne out by statistics for other countries. We have not found any published results of correlations by other investigators of death-rates and business conditions. We did, however, examine the mortality rates in England and Wales where the registration of vital statistics has been exceptionally satisfactory. In the absence of a curve of business cycles for England we used as our index of business conditions the amount of foreign trade. The correlation, for the period 1870–1914, of foreign trade with the general death-rate is +0.02, and with the infant mortality rate is −0.09. These results increase our scepticism regarding the existence of a significant correlation between death-rates and the business cycle.

Even if there is no correlation of the business cycle with the general death-rate, there might be a correlation with specific death-rates, although inspection of the curves of some of the classifications of death-rates since 1900 does not encourage such an expectation. For the United States, the fact that few States have records going back to 1870, and that only a small number of cases of deaths from specific diseases is recorded, makes an inquiry somewhat doubtful. We have, however, correlated the cycles of death-rates from tuberculosis of the lungs for certain States with the cycles of business, for the period 1870–1920 [see Figure 6], and we find a correlation coefficient of +0.32. If the year 1918 is omitted the correlation becomes +0.24, and with a one-year lag it is +0.16. For the United States registration area, 1900–20, the correlation is +0.193; omitting 1918, it is −0.05. The relationship of death-rates from pulmonary tuberculosis to the business cycle is much the same as that of the general death-rate.

The suicide-rate would be expected, we think, to vary with business prosperity and business depression, and so it does. We have taken the suicide-rate as computed by Hoffman for one hundred cities of the United States for 1900–20 [see Figure 8], and correlated the suicide cycles with cycles of business conditions for the same period, and we find a correlation of −0.74 ± 0.07.

From the inquiry, as thus far conducted, into a possible correlation between death-rates and business cycles, we do not draw a definite conclusion of a correlation, except in the case of suicides. The evidence for the United States points toward the conclusion that there are somewhat greater death-rates in prosperity than in depression; but the British data [1] do not bear out such a conclusion. Although it seemed probable that there would be a negative correlation between death-rates and the business cycle, it should be remembered that there are other factors affecting the fluctuations of death-rates from year to year. Such factors are climate, health education campaigns, developments of preventive medicine, and epidemics. In a period of fifty years there are only a very few cycles, and if there is an economic influence it might be obscured by variations in other factors, although it could be uncovered by partial correlations if we could procure series of data for the other factors.

[Similar analyses of birth rates, see Figure 4, and crime statistics, see Figure 9, are here omitted.]

---

[1] Author's note: The result of a careful study of the British data show that they *do* bear out such a conclusion. . . .

PAUL F. LAZARSFELD
ROBERT K. MERTON
Friendship as Social Process:
A Substantive and Methodological Analysis

Part I. Substantive Analysis (Merton)

This analysis of friendship as social process is drawn from a study, begun some years ago, of social organization and interpersonal relations in two housing communities: Craftown, a project of some seven hundred families in New Jersey, and Hilltown, a bi-racial, low-rent project of about eight hundred families in western Pennsylvania.

Among other things, we sought to identify the networks of intimate social relationships in these communities. As a first step, Hilltowners and Craftowners were asked to designate their "three closest friends, whether they live in Hilltown (Craftown) or not." In both communities, about 10 per cent reported that they did not know as many as three persons whom they could properly describe as really close friends. But the rest had no such difficulty. This resulted in the identification of a cumulative total of almost two thousand friends by Hilltowners and Craftowners, with roughly half of these living in the same community as the informants.

From data of this kind, it was a short further step to search out patterns in

Reprinted in part from Monroe Berger, Theodore Abel, and Charles H. Page, *Freedom and Control in Modern Society,* New York: D. Van Nostrand Company, Inc., 1954, pp. 21–54, with permission of the editors.

the selection of close friends with respect to likeness or difference of attitudes and values or of social status (for example, of sex, race and age, social class, organizational affiliation and standing in the local community). Although this is not the place to present these findings in detail, a short general summary is needed as context for our discussion of friendship as social process. Within each community, it was found that the degree of similarity of status-attributes of close friends varied greatly for different attributes, running a gamut from the almost complete limitation of intimate friendships among those of the same race and sex, to entirely negligible selectivity in terms of educational status. We found, further, that for some of the *same* social attributes, the degree of selectivity differed widely between the two communities. There was, for example, a relatively high degree of selectivity in terms of religious affiliation in Hilltown, and relatively little in Craftown. The social and cultural context provided by the community went far toward determining both the general extent of selecting status-similars as close friends and the particular statuses for which such selectivity was most marked. Thus, the more cohesive community of Craftown consistently exhibited a lower degree of selection of status-similars as friends; but when such selectivity did occur, it was as likely to be in terms of *acquired* statuses—those resulting from

513

the individual's own choice or achievement—as in terms of *ascribed* statuses such as nativity and age, which are fixed or predetermined at birth. In Hilltown, on the contrary, selectivity was much more marked in terms of ascribed status, since there was less by way of overarching community purposes to focus the attention of residents on locally achieved or acquired statuses.

From these and comparable findings, it soon became evident that the problem of selection was not adequately formulated by the familiar and egregiously misleading question: When it comes to close friendships, do birds of a feather actually flock together? Rather, it is a more complex problem of determining the degree to which such selectivity varies for different kinds of social attributes, how it varies within different kinds of social structure, and how such selective patterns come about. Our efforts to deal with the first two questions must be left to the complete report of the study; part of the effort to deal with the third question is described in this paper.

Before turning to the analysis of friendship as a social process, however, we must consider a note on terminology.

A Terminological Note. Oddly enough, the English language lacks a word to signify a tendency for friendships to form between people of "the same kind" just as it lacks a word to signify a tendency for friendships to form between those of differing kinds. . . . Perhaps we shall be allowed, therefore, to summarize the fifteen-word phrase, "a tendency for friendships to form between those who are alike in some designated respect" by the single word *homophily,* and to summarize the complementary phrase, "a tendency for friendships to form between those who differ in some designated respect," by the correlative word *heterophily* (thus following the comparable terminological practice long since established for types of marriage). . . .

Selective and Adjustive Processes in Value-Homophily. . . . This section will consider selective and adjustive processes in friendship, the discussion being rooted in our empirical materials but branching out to report inferences drawn from these materials. . . .

By selective and adjustive processes in friendship we mean patterned sequences of social interaction between friends in which each phase generates and regulates the subsequent phase in such manner as to give rise to the observed patterns of friendship between people of designated kinds. In principle, one phase is said to "generate" the next when the conditions obtaining at one time prove to be both necessary and sufficient for the relationship obtaining at the next time of observation. We say that this is so "in principle" because, at the still-primitive stage reached by sociological analyses of social processes, it must be considered adequate if, in actual practice, we can identify the sufficient antecedent conditions without being able to show that they are also necessary.

Throughout our studies of friendship, it has been provisionally assumed that the observed patterns of status-homophily —the positive correlation between the statuses of close friends—are, to some significant but unknown extent, the products of an underlying agreement between the values harbored by friends. The dynamic role of similarities and differences of these values in forming, maintaining, or disrupting friendships therefore requires notice in its own right.

Racial Attitudes. As a case in point, we consider the racial attitudes and values of Hilltowners, and their dynamic role in local patterns of friendship. These values are singled out because in Hilltown, with its equal number of Negro and white families, they have great meaning for residents. They may therefore affect patterns of intimate association among those who held these values (just as our studies have found that political values affect personal association in the intensely political atmosphere of Craftown). These attitudes toward race vary in many, sometimes minute, respects, and no single classification can do justice to their every nuance of detail. For our present purposes, however, it is enough to divide Hilltowners roughly into three types, in terms of their racial values and perceptions.

The first type embraces the Hilltowners who believe that "colored and white people should live together in housing projects" and who support this belief by saying that the two racial groups "get along pretty well" in Hilltown itself. Since their values and their perception of local experience are both consistent with a liberal turn of mind in matters of race relations, these will be called the "liberals." At the other end is the second type, made up of those residents who maintain that the races should be residentially segregated and who justify this view by claiming that, in Hilltown, where the two races do live in the same project, they fail to get along. This kind of consistency between belief and appraisal of the local situation qualifies these residents to be called racial "illiberals." Between these two types is a third, holding an ambivalent position: these residents believe that the races should not be allowed to live in the same project, even though it must be admitted that they have managed

to get along in Hilltown. In describing this type as "ambivalent," we mean only that they cannot buttress their opposition to co-residence of Negroes and whites, as the illiberals do, by saying that it inevitably leads to interracial conflict. The logically possible fourth type, comprised by those advocating interracial projects and reporting unsatisfactory race relations in Hilltown, is an empirically empty class and is therefore omitted from further consideration.

With these types before us, we can now ask: do close friends in Hilltown tend to share the same values and further, what is the bearing of similarity or difference of values upon the formation, maintenance and disruption of friendship? Is there, in other words, a pattern of value-homophily and if so, how does it come about?

To answer these questions, it is obviously necessary to devise appropriate indices of homophily and heterophily. We can develop such indices by tracing out the logic of what is ordinarily meant by saying that particular kinds of people usually choose friends of the same kind in their community. This means, presumably, that the proportion of their friends having the designated similar characteristic (of social status or, in this instance, of racial values) is appreciably greater than the proportion of people with this characteristic in the local population. That is to say, they tend to *over-select* similars as friends and, at the extreme, to confine their friendships to individuals of like kind. Thus, if value-homophily does obtain among Hilltowners, then the proportion of friendships involving liberals will be significantly larger than the proportion of liberals in the Hilltown population at large. They will have more liberal friends than "would be expected" under the hypothesis that they choose their friends without regard to their racial values (or without regard to the statuses correlated with these values). Correlatively, if heterophily obtains, they will have fewer liberal friends than would be expected. . . .

Among the white residents of Hilltown, there are definite patterns of friendship in terms of racial values. What is more, these patterns take the shape to be expected, if the similarity of values does indeed make for the formation and continuance of close friendships. First of all, we find that the residents having consistent racial values— the liberals, at one pole, and the illiberals, at the other—tend to over-select friends among those having the same values. The liberals over-select other liberals by 43 per cent; the illiberals, other illiberals, by 30 per cent. Correlatively, liberals under-select illiberals as close friends by 53 per cent, and illiberals under-select liberals by 39 per cent.

But these patterns of value-homophily contrast notably with the pattern exhibited by white Hilltowners with *ambivalent* racial attitudes. These residents truly reflect their ambivalence in their interpersonal relations: they manifest neither homophily nor heterophily. . . .

These general findings provide a point of departure for discussing the chief problem in hand: What are the dynamic processes through which the similarity or opposition of values shape the formation, maintenance, and disruption of close friendships? On this matter, the very limitations of these data prove instructive. True, we deal here with only one set of values, and, to this extent, we abstract greatly from the many values which find expression in social interaction. But these simplified findings carry further implications: for if some degree of value-homophily—as we call the selection of friends on the basis of common values—occurs when even a single set of values is held in common, then it would presumably be all the greater if several sets of values were held in common. In a sense, we are exploring the limiting case and what holds for it should hold, *a fortiori,* for those cases which better approximate the hypothesis that common values promote the formation or maintenance of close friendship. This study is a first approximation and, manifestly, there is need for extension and further empirical testing of the hypothesis.

The Dynamics of Value-Homophily. These statistical indices simply represent the patterns of friendship as they existed *at a particular moment*—in this case, as they were observed at the time of our field-interviews. But, of course, these friendships are in fact continually in process of change—some being only in the early stages of formation, others long and firmly established, and still others, for one reason or another, being well along toward dissolution. Static observations, made at a given instant, tempt one to drop this obvious fact from view. Yet we cannot afford to become imprisoned in the framework of fact that happens to be at hand, even if breaking out of this narrow framework means leaving demonstrated fact for acknowledged conjecture.

In other words, we must form a picture or a model of the dynamic processes, both social and psychological, of which the observed patterns of friendship are merely the resultants. And since our explorations provide scanty and scattered rather than systematic evidence bearing on such processes, this model must remain, for the time being, largely a matter of supposition. Nevertheless, it may be useful to report our conjectures, growing out of these limited materials, since little enough is known about the dynamic processes that give rise to the observed patterns of an over-representation of friends among those with common values, and an under-representation among those with discordant values.

In picturing the processes leading to value-homophily, let us consider first the early social contacts between people having identical or compatible values. To the extent that these values are given expression, first contacts will be mutually gratifying and, in some proportion of cases, will motivate persons to seek future contact (or, at the least, not to avoid future contact).... In some proportion of cases, this early series of gratifying experiences will motivate them to seek continued contact and gradually result in a strong personal attachment....

For those with similar values, then—whether they both be liberals or illiberals—social contact, because it is rewarding, will motivate them to seek further contact. In due course, the proportion of these repeated contacts eventuating in close friendships will be sufficient to produce a pattern of value-homophily along the lines observed in our data on the over-selection of like-minded friends....

But if this model accounts roughly for the dominant pattern of value-homophily, can it also account for the further fact that some close friendships have developed among Hilltowners having diametrically opposed racial values?... How shall we picture the social interaction of persons holding contradictory values, significant to each of them?

In a substantial proportion, perhaps most, of these cases, the fragile beginnings of a social relationship between liberals and illiberals will be broken almost before they have developed. The possible beginnings of friendship are nipped in the bud. Thus, take the case of Mrs. Marsh, a white Hilltowner, firmly liberal in her racial attitudes, who believes that "here anyway, Negroes are a lot nicer than the whites. The main thing is that they are friendlier, and want to be nicer to you." She happens to express her views to other white residents, living in her own apartment house. "When I talk to them about it they just call me an 'old nigger-lover.' It doesn't bother me. I just say to them, 'Well, they're better friends to me than you,' and let it go at that. That happened once when I had some Negroes to my house for a supper. Some neighbor said, 'What do you mean having niggers in your house?' But I don't care what anyone thinks of me, as long as I know I'm doing right." Mrs. Marsh "may not be bothered" by this exchange of sentiments, but the fact remains that she has not formed a close personal relationship with any of her neighbors who harbor illiberal attitudes. This episode might stand almost as a prototype of the consequences that follow the expression of diametrically opposed values by both parties to an incipient social relationship: each individual provides punitive experience for the other and, under such circumstances, it is not strange that a warm personal attachment does not develop between them. The expression of conflicting values, even of a single value, motivates both parties to avoid future contact....

However, it is not always the case that *both* parties to an incipient relationship will express their opposed values. Not infrequently, either because of personal timidity, or an ingrained sense of courtesy or fear of losing status, one party may respond to the unpalatable views of the other by preserving an expedient silence. But to inhibit expressions of one's values, because their expression would only "irritate" one's associates, is itself a frustrating experience. Under such conditions, further contact with the acquaintance, rather than being rewarding, becomes an occasion for self-defeat and, at times, an occasion for self-contempt. The silent partner is, to this degree, motivated to avoid further contact, lest this lead to open conflict. The partner who has freely expressed his views and has no inkling of the punitive experience he has thus provided for his associate may continue to seek opportunities for further contact which, in an appreciable proportion of cases, will meet with no success, as his timid but aggrieved acquaintance sedulously avoids him. This type of interactive process, generating motivated avoidance, again results in an underselection of unlike-minded associates as friends, in the manner we have found to be the case.

There is, however, a third pattern of interaction between those holding disparate values which does allow close friendships to develop between them. As we noted in the case of social contact between like-minded individuals, it is not at all inevitable that a particular value will be expressed, by one or the other, in the *early* stages of a developing relationship. In some proportion of cases, personal attachments will form in the course of repeated contact long before either partner to the relationship is aware that they are sharply at odds in this one particular respect—say, with respect to racial values. Once the relationship has become firmly established —which means only that the partners have experienced separate and mutual gratifications from their repeated interaction—it can, in some instances, tolerate a larger load of disagreement over

certain values than is possible during the early phases, when the relationship is still fragile. . . .

The implication of this hypothetical pattern for further research is clear: it means that the degree and kind of value-conflict between friends must be examined within the distinctly different contexts of firm, established friendships, and of tenuous, early friendships. The same degree and kind of divergence in values would, on the average, have very different consequences in the two contexts. In any case, this part of our provisional model helps account for the minor statistical pattern of a modicum of close friendships among those holding sharply opposed racial values. . . .

In the cumulative give-and-take of the friendship, initial divergences of value tend to be reduced. If the friends have an approximately equal emotional stake in the relationship, this is likely to occur through mutual accommodation of their values. If one is more deeply involved in the relationship than the other, his values are more likely to be modified to accord with the values of the less deeply involved. Presumably, if this self-corrective process did not occur, then close friendships would be even harder to come by and to maintain than they apparently are. As processes of mutual or unilateral accommodation of originally conflicting values run their course, these cases also contribute to the pattern of value-homophily rather than to that of heterophily. This has direct bearing on research, such as ours, which observes patterns of friendship at a particular instant: for some of the cases of close friendship between liberals and illiberals which turn up in our statistical tables will, at a later time, appear as cases of friendship between like-minded individuals, as one or the other or both revise their values in the interest of preserving the relationship. . . .

This conversion of disparate into common values will not, of course, inevitably take place. The original values may be so deep-seated that neither individual finds it possible to modify or to abandon them. . . . When closely interacting persons have strongly opposed values, continuance of the relationship involves a series of reciprocally induced crises, in which the actions of each often evoke hostility in the other. However, not all such open conflict of values is destructive of the friendship. The kind of conflict which clarifies the sources of previously obscure mutual irritation may actually solidify the relationship, by making it clear to both that the relationship means more to them than their clashing values. In any event, we see once again why value-homophily prevails: for if the close relationship remains intact, this phase of unstable compromise will in general give way to accordant, rather than discordant, values.

But it is not always the case, of course, that the friendship does remain intact. When the contradictory values are so deep-rooted as to be unyielding, the social contacts of friends are likely to irritate rather than to satisfy. Continued social interaction then involves progressive alienation from one another. As the friendship cools, the estranged friends look elsewhere for like-minded companions, and these newfound attachments hasten the final dissolution of the relationship. Once more, we see that this model of dynamic interplay between values and friendship anticipates the prevailing pattern of value-homophily among current relationships, because the opposition of deeply-held values tends to disrupt the friendship.

It is now apparent that the static observation of the values of friends at a particular instant too easily loses sight of one class of friendships altogether: the class of disrupted or broken friendships. This oversight is not inherent in the procedure of cross-sectional interviews and is readily overcome by the use of panel-interviews: it would have been possible, for example, to ask Craftowners and Hilltowners to designate their recently broken friendships and to carry on the inquiry from there, much along the lines we followed for current and still viable friendships. But if the oversight is not inherent, it is, surely, prevalent. Few systematic studies of the formation of friendship also incorporate materials on the disruption of friendship. And candor compels us to insist that such materials do not appear in our own quantitative data simply because the need for these materials was not foreseen during our field work. Yet it is the data on broken friendships which may provide the most critical evidence testing this provisional model of the interplay of values and friendship; for these disrupted friendships set a definite analytical task: they should be accounted for by the same model that seeks to account for the prevailing pattern of value-homophily among still-current relationships. . . .

In spite of these limitations of data, the model we have sketched out does move a certain distance toward a tentative formulation of the processes which give rise to the observed dominant pattern of value-homophily and the observed subsidiary pattern of a few friendships among those with opposed values. At bottom, the model represents merely an extended application to the special case of friendship of the hard-won sociological commonplace that, in non-coerced social relations, common values and strong personal attachments act both as cause and effect, modifying and in turn being modified by one another. Common values make social interaction a rewarding experience, and the gratifying experience promotes the formation of common values. And just as close association and common values go hand in hand, so do dissociation and alienation from one another's values. For when the partners to the friendship develop opposed values, their initial close relations are subjected to strain and some may deteriorate to the final point of dissolution. . . .

Part II. Methodological Analysis (Lazarsfeld)

The foregoing discussion of value-homophily affords an occasion for examining, specifically and concretely, the interplay between substantive analysis and methodological formalization.

The substantive analysis begins with the finding that friends in Hilltown tend to hold similar values concerning race relations and proceeds to develop a model of social process which might account for this fact. The logical and other analytical operations in this account remain implicit. We can, however, specify the major "operations"—the logical arrangement of data into categories having specified interrelations—implied in the substantive analysis. That is what is meant by "methodological formalization." This formal analysis [1] has two

---

[1] . . . We shall use hypothetical figures rather than algebraic or other symbolic terminology.

---

useful purposes. It will bring out, first of all, a logical scheme for the further analysis of processes involved in the formation of friendship. Secondly, it will bring out the respects in which such a scheme of analysis can apply, not only to friendship, but to other studies of social process. . . .

Reformulation of the Problem. We will assume that all the members of a community have been classified as liberals or illiberals in terms of their racial attitudes. We will assume, further, that by some kind of chance procedure members of the community have been formed into pairs, which have then been classified as friendship-pairs or as nonfriendship-pairs. . . . Later on we shall amply rectify this original simplification; provisions will be made for people being neutral in their attitudes, for the existence of one-sided attachments between pairs and for many other more realistic situations.

Our schematic starting point, then, will be a large number of pairs, each of which has been characterized by the two dimensions of agreement-disagreement, on the one hand, and the presence or absence of friendship, on the other. These pairs can be arranged in a fourfold table, so that the relationship between agreement and friendship can be studied. A set of hypothetical figures which reproduce the finding with which the substantive analysis began might look somewhat like the following:

Table **1**

	Friends	*Not friends*
Agree	150	50
Disagree	50	150

The empirical finding about value-homophily is of the type represented in these hypothetical figures. Here, as in the actual data, there is definite relationship between the two variables. Among the pairs characterized by the presence of friendship, a majority are also characterized by agreement of values. But among the pairs which have no friendship, a majority are in disagreement.

Table 1 represents the type of result which is obtained in a so-called cross-sectional survey taken at one specific period of time. The purpose of the interpretative analysis was to specify, on a hypothetical basis, some of the main processes resulting in an observed correlation between friendship and a similarity of values. But conjectures about processes, of course, require the introduction of a *time dimension*. In order to study the development of a particular pattern one must be able to observe the units of analysis at successive points in time. The first finding is enlarged by the assumption that at some previous period friendship and opinion were not, or not as clearly, related. The static result is replaced by a more complicated one, implying a change; it is this change which then has to be explained. Again we resort to schematic figures. And now an additional element is added to the schematization: in actuality, only one survey was made; but the existence and probable results of an earlier survey are implied in the analysis given in the first part of this paper.

To keep the demonstration as simple as possible, we shall assume that the preceding survey, done at Time I, resulted in the findings of Table 2[a]; Table 2[b] repeats the results of the original survey which was carried out at what is now labeled Time II.

Table **2**

	[a] Time I	
	Friends	*Not friends*
Agree	100	100
Disagree	100	100

	[b] Time II	
Agree	150	50
Disagree	50	150

According to these figures there was no discernible relationship between friendship and agreement at the time of the first observation, when, say, the residents had been in the community for only a short time. But by the time of the second observation, after a six months' interval, the relationship between these variables had become marked. This change in the degree of relationship is exactly of the kind hypothesized in the substantive section.

We shall find it useful to talk of the contact-value combinations which are represented in the four cells of each of the tables. The frequencies of these contact-value combinations have changed from Time I to Time II. And to add one final bit of terminology: the "harmonious" combinations have become more frequent. By "harmonious" we shall mean either pairs who are friends and agree, or pairs who are not friends and do not hold the same value. The main issue is now restated in more formal terms: the increasing number of harmonious contact-value combinations through time is to be analyzed.

Now such a formal restatement can be useful only if it contains elements which can be further developed without recourse, at least at first, to additional ideas or assumptions. This is indeed possible in the present case because Table 2 tells only part of the story which would be available to us as a result of observations made at two periods of time with the same set of pairs. The reader is invited to study Table 3, which is sometimes called a sixteen-fold table, with care; it contains all combinations of friendship and agreement at two time periods. Again we introduce hypothetical figures which, as we shall see, reproduce the substantive discussion we are attempting to analyze. They might be of the following sort:

Table **3** [a]

Time I	Time II			
FA	FA	FA	FA	FA
	++	+−	−+	−−
++	50	20	10	20	100
+−	30	20	0	50	100
−+	50	0	40	10	100
−−	20	10	0	70	100
	150	50	50	150	

[a] The first symbol in each designation refers to the presence or absence of friendship in the pair; the second to agreement or disagreement.

Note that the marginals of this sixteen-fold table reproduce the fourfold tables of Table 2. And they indicate the same fact observed previously, namely, that the relationship between agreement and friendship becomes more marked with the passage of time.

It is the purpose of this discussion to show that the proper analysis of this sixteen-fold table, taken in conjunction with other materials which we shall specify, makes it possible to organize profitably all statements about the phenomenon of value-homophily and the processes leading to it contained in the substantive section. It is our contention, in other words, that a sixteen-fold table of this kind provides a formal scheme for statements of process. In order to demonstrate this we must indicate the various analytic operations which can be carried out through use of a sixteen-fold table. We shall then consider whether we have omitted essential parts of the substantive discussion.

The Analysis of Sequence Rules (*1*). The analysis of what we shall call sequence rules is perhaps the basic operation in this kind of formalization. We mean by a sequence any particular cell in the sixteen-fold table presented above. (We call these cells sequences, because each represents a shift in the state of friendship and agreement from one time to another. Thus, the cell, [(+−) to (−−)], represents a change, between the first and second times of observation, from the state of friendship-and-disagreement to that of absence-of-friendship-and-disagreement.) And we mean by a sequence rule any statement about the frequency of a single sequence or the comparative size of two or more sequences.

Clearly, sequence rules will be of varying complexity, depending on the number of sequences involved. The simplest ones are those referring to a single cell in the sixteen-fold table. ... Thus the substantive account refers to the "fact that some close friendships have developed among Hilltowners having diametrically opposed racial values." This states, in other words, that, perhaps contrary to expectations, some pairs can be found in the cell characterized by the (−−) pattern at the time of the first interview, but by the (+−) pattern by the time of the second. ...

In still another part of the substantive discussion we read that:

> ... some of the cases of close friendship between liberals and illiberals which turn up in our statistical tables will, at a later time, appear as cases of friendship between like-minded individuals, as one or the other or both revise their values in the interest of preserving the relationship.

A reformulation of part of this statement indicates that the analyst expects to find a number of pairs characterized by the $[(+ -)$ to $(+ +)]$ sequence.

In general, then, sequence rules involving single cells in the sixteen-fold table are usually concerned with the generality or rarity of particular kinds of shifts. They indicate which patterns of change or stability are expected, and which are unexpected.

A somewhat more complex kind of sequence rule is that involving the comparison of two or more cells in a row of the table. ... The usual purpose of this type of comparison is to show that one kind of shift—one sequence—is more frequent than others. For example, we find the following comment in the substantive section:

> ... let us begin by considering those early contacts in which residents express in words or in behavior a value to which the others are radically opposed. In a substantial proportion, perhaps most, of these cases, the fragile beginnings of a social relationship between liberals and illiberals will be broken almost before they have developed. The possible beginnings of friendship are nipped in the bud.

Because this is an extended comment, let us analyze it in some detail. The passage starts out by focusing attention on the pairs of friends who were initially in disagreement. In terms of our sixteen-fold table these are the pairs characterized by a $(+ -)$ combination of characteristics at the time of the first interview; they will be found in the second row of the table. The analysis then considers the most likely outcome for pairs characterized in this way. It is assumed that "in a substantial proportion, perhaps most, of these cases" the early contacts will not be continued and no firm friendship will develop. It is assumed, in other words, that the sequence $[(+ -)$ to $(- -)]$ is more likely than any others for pairs starting out with this combination of characteristics. ...

The Heuristic Value of Schematic Presentation. ... One distinct use of such a formal scheme ... is that it enables one to bring out specifically and systematically the points which are being stressed in a substantive analysis and, more importantly perhaps, the points which are being disregarded. Another application consists in pointing to alternative options of analysis, to additional ways in which the same material could be analyzed. Our previous distinction between harmonious and disharmonious friendship-value combinations permits us to exemplify such an elaboration.

Looking at Table 3, we may concentrate on the second and third rows; these contain all the pairs which were disharmonious at the first observation, and indicate what has become of them at the time of the second observation. As a direct consequence of our definition of the process of homophily, we find that 140 of these 200 pairs had become "harmonious," meaning that they either were now friends in agreement $(+ +)$, or people holding different values and not friendly $(- -)$. But how has this progress toward homophily been achieved?

Did the value configuration more often determine the fate of friendships, or did friendship more often affect the constancy of attitudes? The theory under analysis is silent on this point, but our formalization has forced us to make some assumptions, if only because the cells of the sixteen-fold table, Table 3, had to be filled in. Its most pertinent part is reproduced as Table 4:

Table **4**

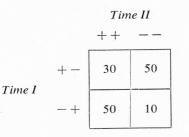

Time II

Two kinds of sequences can be distinguished. In $(+ -)$ to $(- -)$ and in $(- +)$ to $(+ +)$ the second sign, designating the values, remains the same, and the first sign, symbolizing friendship, changes; there are 100 such cases. In the other 40 cases the values at Time II become adjusted to the friendship patterns as they existed at (and persisted from) Time I. In somewhat loose language we can therefore say that the values are "stronger" than the friendships; if there is disharmony between the two, the social system, represented by our hypothetical community, increases homophily by changing the distribution of attitudes. This set of figures is probably more in the spirit of the general theory than a different set implying the opposite assumption. It is important to realize, however, that the homophily result, the shift in marginals, would have remained the same if the entries in Table 4 had been made to read 60 and 20 in the first line and 20 and 40 in the second. In this case, the implied assumption

would have been that friendships are "stronger" than attitudes in their mutual effect.

A second heuristic value of such formalization, then, is to bring out assumptions which have not been made explicit by the original analyst, or those on which he chose not to take a stand.... So far, we have confined ourselves to those rules that can be derived from one sixteen-fold table. This is the simplest scheme relating two variables at two times. Various extensions of this notion result in new, and more complicated, rules. With these elaborations we can begin to restore the complexity of the substantive conceptions which our simplification has necessarily eliminated for the time being.

The Analysis of Chains (2). A first elaboration to be considered is that of the time dimension. So far we have assumed that we have only two observations of the pairs of individuals. We can now study what develops when these observations are increased to three or more. In order to do this, we shall introduce the notion of "chains," sequences which are extended in time. That is, a pair which, in terms of friendship and agreement, is characterized as $(- +)$ at Time I, $(+ +)$ at Time II, and $(+ -)$ at Time III represents one of the many chains which can be distinguished.

The substantive section of this paper does refer to some of these chains.... Perhaps the most clearcut of these references is:

... when the partners to the friendship develop opposed values, their initial close relations are subjected to strain and some may deteriorate to the final point of dissolution.

This, as we can see, describes the processes accounting for the chain $[(+ +)$ to $(+ -)$ to $(- -)]$.

The special importance of an extended time dimension is that it permits us to explore new problems. Specifically, we can study whether the future shifts of pairs characterized in a particular way depend on their past history. We note in our original sixteen-fold table, for example, that at the time of the second interview there are 50 pairs characterized by the $(+-)$ combination of friendship and agreement. But these 50 pairs have quite different histories: 20 of them were originally friends sharing similar values; another 20 have a past history, as well as a present pattern, of friendship but disagreement; and the final 10 pairs were characterized at Time I both by the absence of friendship and the absence of agreement. The question is how these past histories will influence future courses of development among these 50 pairs. Operationally, what can we expect from a third observation? Will the 20 pairs characterized by the stable sequence, $[(+-)$ to $(+-)]$, manifest a different development in the future than those who have shifted to the $(+-)$ pattern from either the $(++)$ or the $(--)$ states? That is, will disagreeing friends who have exhibited both friendship and disagreement in the past differ, in their future patterns, from disagreeing friends who previously agreed? There is reason to believe that they will.

The importance of this kind of analysis is that it leads to the development of more refined and specific rules of change, which, in turn, permit more accurate predictions of the ways in which particular types of pairs will behave in the future. One aspect of this deserves special attention.

The Idea of Equilibrium. So far we have dealt with two major elements of a process: (a) an initial distribution of the friendship-value combinations, represented by Table 2[a]; (b) a set of sequence rules telling how these combinations change over a designated period of time, represented by Table 3.[2]

With the help of these two elements we can describe how the system under study changes from a first to a second stage. And Table 3 tells us what the social theorist has to do: he must make plausible assumptions about the frequencies in each cell; and, in the light of other knowledge, he must state why he makes these assumptions.

But the idea of observations repeated more than twice brings out certain additional matters that have to be considered. One is characteristic for all theory formation: we have to assume that no extraneous factors will disturb the system. Suppose, for example, that as a result of some wave of terror, the community comes to believe that liberal values are dangerous; it might then develop that people who hold liberal values avoid each other, in order to deflect suspicion. This would obviously change the sequence rules exemplified in Table 3, and consequently change the future distribution of the friendship-value combinations.

The present discussion implies, then, that *ceteris paribus,* the sequence rules remain unaffected by outside influences for a reasonable period of time. But this still leaves two possibilities open: the rules may remain completely constant or may change as a result of intrinsic developments.

Let us first assume that we deal with what is sometimes called a stationary process: the sequence rules controlling the change from one time period to the next remain about the same.

Under these circumstances, it is possible to "compute" the equilibrium posi-

[2] To the statistician, these are known as transition probabilities; but we wish to avoid technical language here. Appendix I gives a more precise formulation.

tion of the system. Our scheme showed that in the first time step, the marginal distribution 100–100–100–100 of Table 2[a] changed to 150–50–50–150 of Table 2[b]; as a matter of fact, this shift turned out to be the essence of value-homophily as a process. We now could predict what would happen in another time step by applying the same sequence rules to this new distribution: without elaborating the arithmetic, we should find a Table 2[c] (not given here) showing frequencies of 145–55–35–165 for the 4 friendship-value combinations, respectively.

A somewhat more complicated computation would tell us that the equilibrium distribution would be 133–57–24–186. This distribution can easily be defined in non-mathematical terms: it is the one which does not change if the sequence rules of Table 3 are applied to it. This kind of equilibrium is well known to social research from many empirical studies. Repeated interviews on such diversified topics as race attitudes, opinions on the role of labor unions, etc., often show the following characteristics: many individual respondents change their positions; but these individual shifts concel each other out and the so-called marginal distributions for the whole group remain fairly constant over time.

Now let us briefly consider the idea of a process where the sequence rules do not remain constant but are still unaffected by extraneous factors. The sequence rules could depend upon the distribution of friendship-value combinations reached at a certain moment. If, for example, value-homophily has become very strong in a community, a counter-tendency might develop with the view that different kinds of people ought to become associated. The homophily trend described in the text might weaken until a lower degree of correlation between friendship and value has

been reached; then the reverse tendency might set in. The result would be an oscillation of the value-friendship distributions around an average. This would be quite different from the introduction of extraneous elements, mentioned above. The whole process would still go on within the system; however, the sequence rules exemplified in Table 3 would not be constant, but would be dependent upon the "marginal" distribution reached at a given moment. . . .

The assumption of a stationary process is probably more in keeping with the spirit of the main analysis than is the assumption of intrinsic oscillations. But even then it can be seen that, for a full understanding of the phenomenon, one more topic needs explication. If one were to apply the notion of homophily loosely, one could ask why the system does not end in complete homogeneity. Why does it not happen that all the people with like values, and only these, are friends? Actually, Table 3 shows that "counter-tendencies" are provided for: there are sequences like $[(++)$ to $(-+)]$ which tell us that, in spite of agreement, friendships will break off and refill the reservoir of "disharmonious" pairs. At least three kinds of speculations can be attached to these counter-sequences. One has to do with extraneous elements, often ascribed to chance: accidental feuds, the conversion of one partner, etc. A second possibility is that other values—those not specifically concerned with racial problems—play a part in the formation and dissolution of friendships. The third possibility is perhaps the most interesting: there could be a phenomenon of satiation, a desire for new challenges when agreement has lasted too long. Whether such tendencies actually play a role can only be discovered by empirical research. . . . At this point, our only purpose has been to indicate what problems derive from the notion of equilibrium, which, in turn, derives from formalization of the idea of an explanatory process. . . .

The Elaboration of Variables (3). So far we have confined ourselves exclusively to the two variables of friendship and agreement. But this represents an oversimplification of the foregoing model of processes leading to value-homophily. At numerous points in the discussion, the analyst indicates that other variables need to be considered if the various processes are to be specified adequately. The introduction of these new variables provides another kind of elaboration.

What kinds of additional variables are brought into the discussion? . . . The analyst contrasts the situations which exist when members of a pair express or fail to express their values. . . . He points to timidity, courtesy, or fear of losing status as variables which might explain why some individuals do not express disagreement. . . . He indicates that awareness of agreement or disagreement may affect the development of friendship. . . . And he suggests that a "conflict [of values] which clarifies the sources of previously obscure mutual irritation may actually solidify the relationship, by making it clear to both that the relationship means more to them than their clashing values. . . ."

The introduction of these new variables has the effect, basically, of increasing the number of patterns with which we deal and of adding to the sequence rules which can be specified. Let us consider how this comes about. Suppose that we start with pairs which are friendly, but in disagreement, the $(+ -)$ cases; and suppose that we introduce as our third variable the notion that some of these pairs express their

conflicting views while others do not. The first step in analyzing the role of this third variable is to divide the total number of $(+ -)$ pairs into those which express their values and those which do not. By then studying the most likely sequences within these two groups, we can determine the influence of such overt expression on friendship. The hypothetical table below indicates that dissolution of friendship is more likely to take place within pairs which give voice to their conflicting values.

Table 5

Time I $(+ -)$	*Time II*				
cases	FA $+ +$	FA $+ -$	FA $- +$	FA $- -$	
Express views	10	5	0	30	45
Do not express views	20	15	0	20	55
	30	20	0	50	

A sequence . . . can be derived from these hypothetical figures. The most frequent sequence for those who express their views is $[(+ -)$ to $(- -)]$; 30 out of the 45 pairs made this shift. Among those who do not express their conflicting values, however, no single sequence is numerically outstanding.

There are two further points to be noted in connection with this kind of elaboration. The first is that the same variable may have different consequences with different kinds of pairs. That is, the effect of a third variable will depend, in general, on the configuration of the first two variables. For example, as the analyst suggests, the expression of values will, in all probability, serve to reinforce the friendship of individuals who are in agreement to start with. In other words, we assume that this variable, expression of values, has a different effect on the (+ +) pairs than it does on those characterized as (+ −).

A second point is that the substantive contribution made by the introduction of a third variable will depend partly on how that variable is defined. For example, the "expression of values" can mean anything from casual references to those values to incessant discussions of them. Also, the conversations can take place early in the friendship, or at a time when it is well established. The observed effects of these expressions, then, depend partly on how they have been defined and to what stages of the friendship they refer.

The Elaboration of Categories (4). This last point suggests another type of elaboration, namely, a refinement of the variables so that they are no longer simply dichotomous attributes. Throughout our discussion we have dealt with the dichotomies, agreement-disagreement and friends–not friends. It is clear, however, that both of these variables can be defined differently, as was indeed done in the substantive text. Each might be classified as a trichotomy, for example. In that case, agreement might be divided into complete, partial and no agreement. Similarly, the attribute of friendship might be converted into a trichotomy. One might then distinguish pairs involving mutual friendship, those in which only one person claims friendly relations with the other, and those in which neither considers the other a friend. Or, different aspects of the variables might be considered. For example, the substantive formulation refers to different phases of friendships—those which are incipient, those which are firmly established, those which are in one stage or another of dissolution...

These refinements of our variables have the same effect, in general, as the addition of a new one—an increase in the number of patterns to be distinguished and a multiplication of possible sequence rules. If our dichotomies are converted into trichotomies, then our original fourfold tables are transformed into ninefold tables, and the original sixteen-fold table, relating the information from two interviews, becomes a somewhat unwieldy table with 81 cells.

We have now reviewed the basic operations involved in this kind of analysis. And, except for one type of statement to be considered presently, the substantive part of the text now seems to have been wholly analyzed in formal terms.

"Mechanism" vs. Sequence Rules. We started out with a sixteen-fold table reporting personal relations and agreement for all pairs of individuals at two points of time. We then introduced three kinds of elaboration: an extension of the time dimension, an increase in the number of variables considered, and finer subdivisions for some of these variables. This permitted us to classify our pairs in an increasingly discriminating way, or, to put it in different terms, the state in which any pair was at a particular moment became progressively more specific. But the propositions with which we dealt were all of the same kind. They were sequence rules indicating the relative frequencies with which transitions from one state to another took place.

It turned out that a considerable number of the pages under examination could be translated into such "time-series language." An effort was made to show that such translation clarified the interrelation between different parts of a more discursive language, that it brought out assumptions implied in the original analysis, and that it pointed to further problems—not by adding new questions, but by exploiting systematically the operations introduced by the original author.

This does not mean at all that the reflections under scrutiny were obvious to begin with. As a matter of fact, a formalism highlights a substantive contribution. This can be shown in many ways; but two points deserve special mention. It is possible to develop a theory which assumes that people have a tendency to change friends frequently and are eager for varying intellectual experiences; therefore, they prefer their new friends to have different opinions than did their old ones. Under this assumption we also would find homophily in the sense of increasing correlation of friendship and attitudes from one observation to the next. Appendix II gives an example of a sixteen-fold table where the two marginal value-friendship distributions are exactly the same as in Table 3, while the sequence rules within the table are completely different; the reader is invited to study this table in some detail and to see what its behavioral implications are. The formalism, then, only brings out that one aspect of a process analysis is the existence of certain sequence rules and chains; the actual content of the rules is a theoretical contribution, made in the light of general knowledge and susceptible to further empirical test—a test, incidentally, which is often facilitated by a more formal restatement.

The introduction of additional variables points to a second aspect of the substantive contribution. It obviously makes a difference which specifications are introduced. Under some conditions, changes will come about much more rapidly or frequently than under others; some developments will gather momentum over time, whereas others will stimulate counter-tendencies and be arrested. All this can be put into formal language after someone has thought about such alternatives; and some of these hypotheses will later be corroborated by actual findings, while others will remain stillborn speculations. Behind the formal notion of variables is the hidden hope that those variables which alone can make the formalism productive will be selected.

It would be possible to close our discussion on this note. But there is one final matter to be brought to the fore, even if it must remain in the form of an unanswered question. We have now translated almost all the main passages in the pages under scrutiny—but only almost. A careful reader will have noticed that certain terms were not covered by our formalization. The language used in our formalization always took the form: often (or seldom) people move from one kind of state (however specified) to another kind. But at a score of points the document described these movements in a specific kind of language. When pairs moved away from a state it was because of a "frustrating, punitive experience," because the individual was "irritated, subject to strain," etc. Conversely, if pairs maintained a state or moved toward it, this state was described as "mutually gratifying," "rewarding," etc. . . .

There are three ways of looking at these comments. They could be stylistic devices, making the sequence rules more vivid by referring to common experiences and observations; in that case, they would be outside the province of the present endeavor. Or they could be short-hand expressions for the introduction of new variables. Earlier sequence rules regarding friends in disagreement, the $(+ -)$ pairs, differed according to whether or not they assumed that the members expressed their conflicting views. Similarly, we might distinguish $(+ -)$ pairs according to whether or not they experience irritation as a result of their disagreement. Thus, if these comments about reward-frustration refer to additional specifying conditions or to intermediate steps to be covered in additional observations, then we have dealt with them before and they do not offer a new problem. But it could be, finally, that we are faced with an additional notion: mechanisms which are supposed to account for the observed sequence rules in a way not analyzed before.

If this third alternative is the appropriate one, then a whole new area of formal inquiry opens up. Obviously, the introduction of new variables is itself one form of accounting. How does it differ, then, from these proposed mechanisms? Is it that we are moving here to an underlying psychological level, just as, in the field of thermodynamics, we move from consideration of the heat of bodies to consideration of the velocity of their molecules? Or do we have to introduce new concepts, like Lewin's vectors and barriers, operating in the "field" in which we make our observations?

Within the frame of the task which we set for ourselves, these questions cannot be answered. We meet here residual elements in the text which, in their present form, have not been formalized. If we were told a great deal more about at least some of these mechanisms, it might be possible to explicate the role they play in the total analysis. As it stands, our formalization renders its final service by pointing to a next step in the continuity of inquiry.

Appendix 1. The equilibrium is obviously obtained if the contact-value distribution of the 400 pairs satisfies the following condition:

$$A = .5A + .3B + .5C + .2D$$
$$B = .2A + .2B \qquad\quad + .1D$$
$$C = .1A \qquad\qquad + .4C$$
$$D = .2A + .5B + .1C + .7D$$

The coefficients in each of these equations correspond to the columns of Table 3 in the text. The four frequences add up to $A + B + C + D = 400$. The terminal turnover table is approximately:

Table **6**

Time I F A	Time II				
	F A + +	F A + −	F A − +	F A − −	
+ +	66	27	14	26	133
+ −	18	11	0	28	57
− +	12	0	10	2	24
− −	37	19	0	130	186
	133	57	24	186	400

Appendix II. A 16-fold table which would correspond to the scheme of such a restless and novelty-seeking community is exemplified in Table 7. The reader should interpret both tables in terms of the substantive discussion in the text.

Table **7**

Time I F A	Time II				
	F A + +	F A + −	F A − +	F A − −	
+ +	10	20	10	60	100
+ −	60	5	15	20	100
− +	20	15	5	60	100
− −	60	10	20	10	100
	150	50	50	150	

JAMES COLEMAN
ELIHU KATZ
HERBERT MENZEL

The Diffusion of an Innovation Among Physicians

Anthropologists and sociologists have long been concerned with the processes through which customs, practices, attitudes, or messages spread. Traditionally, these processes have been studied by examining the ecological distribution of the trait at successive points in time. In a few cases, the actual transmission of messages from person to person has been traced out. . . . A still different approach to the study of this problem is reported in this paper. The population is physicians in four cities; the item whose use was spreading was a new drug; and the study focused on the ongoing social processes which finally led to widespread adoption of the drug by these physicians.

Data were collected fifteen months after a new drug with wide potential use, here called "gammanym," had been placed on the market. By this time almost all the doctors in relevant specialties in the four cities studied had used the drug, some almost immediately, others only after a considerable interval of time. The research problem, stated most concretely, is this: What were the social processes which intervened between the initial trials of the drug by a few local innovators and its final use by virtually the whole medical community? The results

Reprinted in part from *Sociometry, 20,* 1957, pp. 253–69, with permission of the American Sociological Association and the authors.

reported below concern the effectiveness of networks of interpersonal relations at each stage of the diffusion process. . . .

Methods. I

The method of survey research, involving structured interviews with a sample of physicians, was used. But since the problem as defined concerned the social structure which linked these doctors together, it was necessary to deviate in two important ways from the customary survey design which, in effect, treats individuals as so many independent units of observation. (a) Each doctor interviewed was asked three sociometric questions: To whom did he most often turn for advice and information? With whom did he most often discuss his cases in the course of an ordinary week? Who were the friends, among his colleagues, whom he saw most often socially? In response to each of these questions, the names of three doctors were requested. This made it possible to trace out the links by which each doctor was connected with the rest of the medical community. (b) It was decided to include in the sample, as nearly as possible, *all* the local doctors in whose specialties the new drug was of major potential significance. This assured that the "others" named by each

531

doctor in answer to the sociometric questions were included in the sample, so that it became possible to characterize pairs or chains of socially connected doctors. Accordingly, 125 general practitioners, internists, and pediatricians were interviewed; they constituted 85 per cent of the doctors practicing in these fields in four Midwestern cities, ranging in population from 30,000 to 110,000.

The dependent variable of the analysis which follows is the month during which each doctor first used the drug. This information was *not* obtained in the interviews; it was obtained through a search of the prescription records of the local pharmacies for three-day sampling periods at approximately monthly intervals over the fifteen months following the release date of gammanym. In this way, the month during which each doctor first used the drug was ascer-

tained. The research is thus based on three kinds of data: the month of each doctor's first prescription for the new drug, obtained through a search of pharmacists' files; data about the informal social structure of the medical community, derived from doctors' replies to sociometric questions in an interview; and many individual attributes of each doctor, likewise obtained by interview.

Results. I

Before presenting the results concerning interpersonal relations, the results concerning other ("individual") determinants will be briefly characterized. As expected, the date on which a doctor first prescribed the new drug was related to a large number of his *individual* attributes, e.g., his age, the number of medi-

Figure **1**   *Cumulative proportion of doctors introducing gammanym: profession-oriented* vs. *patient-oriented*

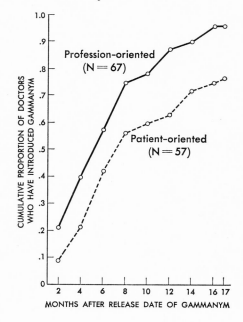

cal journals he subscribed to, his attachments to medical institutions outside his community, and certain attitudinal characteristics. To illustrate the relationship of drug introduction date to such individual attributes, one of the latter will be singled out: the doctor's relative orientation to his professional colleagues and to patients. . . .

Figure 1 shows the relationship of the resulting classification to the date of introduction of the new drug. The solid curve represents those doctors who were classified as profession-oriented, and shows the cumulative proportion of gammanym users among them for each month. Thus, for example, by the fourth month 40 per cent of these doctors had used gammanym; by the sixth month over 50 per cent. The lower curve similarly represents the doctors who were classified as patient-oriented; by the sixth month only 42 per cent had used the drug. Thus the more profession-oriented doctors in these cities generally used the drug earlier than the less profession-oriented ones.[1] Similar results were obtained for many other individual attributes—i.e., attributes describing individuals without reference to their social relations with one another.

But even stronger relations were found when we turned to *social* attributes—those characterizing a doctor's ties to his local colleagues. Doctors who were

mentioned by many of their colleagues in answer to any of the three sociometric questions used the drug, on the average, earlier than those who were named by few or none of their colleagues. More generally speaking, the degree of a doctor's integration among his local colleagues was strongly and positively related to the date of his first use of the new drug. Figure 2 shows, for example, the results with regard to the network of friendships. The "integrated" doctors —those named as "friends" by three or more of their colleagues—were much faster to introduce gammanym into their practices than the rest. The networks of discussion and of advisorship yielded similar findings.

Two important contrasts differentiate Figure 2 from Figure 1, and, more generally, social attributes from individual ones, in their relation to gammanym introduction. First, the relationship in Figure 2 (as measured, for example, by the difference between the mean drug introduction dates of the extreme groups) is greater than that in Figure 1; greater, in fact, than the relationship of the introduction date of gammanym to all but one of the many individual characteristics which were examined. . . . This emphasizes the importance of social contacts among doctors as a crucial determinant of their early use of the new drug.

But it may reasonably be questioned whether the relationship shown in Figure 2 may not arise merely because the measures of social integration are themselves associated with some personality or other individual differences which predispose a doctor to early introduction. It is in answer to this question that a second contrast between Figures 1 and 2 is relevant.

Notice that the two curves in Figure 1 are roughly parallel, differing from one another only in vertical displacement.

[1] The difference between the mean adoption dates of the two groups in Figure 1 is 2.8 months, which is significant at the .01 level, using a standard two-tailed test of difference between means of normally distributed variables. It should be pointed out, however, that the argument of this report does not rest on the statistical significance of isolated findings so much as on the consistency of the results of several diverse approaches with one another and with prior theoretical notions. It is doubtful that significance tests in the usual sense are meaningful in situations like the present. . . .

Figure **2**   *Cumulative proportion of doctors introducing gammanym: differences in integration on friendship criterion*

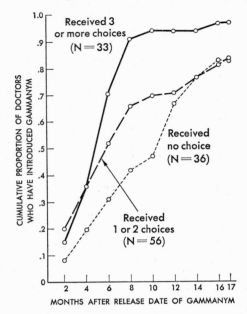

MONTHS AFTER RELEASE DATE OF GAMMANYM

This is true as well in most of the remaining charts (not shown) which relate individual characteristics to gammanym introduction. The curves in Figure 2, by contrast, differ from each other in shape as well as location: the curve for the more integrated doctors, although not starting out much higher than the other curves, rises steeply upward with a slight gain in slope at the fourth month, while the curve for the more isolated doctors rises at a moderate and almost constant slope. To put it differently, the integrated doctors were little different from their isolated colleagues at the very beginning; but then their rate accelerated to produce an increasing gap between the curves. In contrast, the profession-oriented doctors in Figure 1 differed from the patient-oriented from the very start almost as much as later on.

The constant difference between the profession-oriented and patient-oriented doctors suggests that they differ individually in their receptivity to new developments in medicine. On the other hand, the accelerating difference between the integrated and isolated doctors suggests a kind of "snowball" or "chain-reaction" process for the integrated: They are individually little different in receptivity from their more isolated colleagues, but as their fellows come to use the drug, they pick it up from these doctors themselves; and as more of their fellows come to use it, their chances of picking it up are greater.

The difference between the two kinds of relationship to drug introduction is also shown by Table 1, which compares the individual variables and the social variables in their relation to gammanym introduction at two points in time: one month and seven months after the drug

Table **1**   *The average relation of twelve "individual" variables and of three measures of social integration to the rate of gammanym introduction at two points in time*

| | Average difference in per cent of gammanym users between high and low groups | | Ratio of differences |
	After 1 month	After 7 months	
Individual variables	9.2	27.4	2.98
Social integration	8.7	40.3	4.64

was introduced. For each of these dates, the table shows the average difference in per cent of gammanym users (a) between those measuring "high" and "low" on each of twelve individual variables and (b) between those measuring "high" and "low" on three measures of social integration. The latter are based on choices received in response to the three sociometric questions mentioned earlier. The twelve individual variables include all those examined which showed a difference of two or more months in mean date of introduction between the high and the low groups.

The size of these differences measures the size of the relationship at the two times. As is evident, the social integration measures show a slightly *smaller* relationship than do the individual variables after one month, but a much *larger* relationship after seven months. Thus, as exemplified by the comparison between Figures 1 and 2, the socially integrated doctors "pull away" from their isolated colleagues, while the doctors differing in some individual attribute simply maintain their intrinsically different receptivity as time goes on.

Figures 3 and 4 show the difference between two corresponding theoretical "models" of the introduction process. In Figure 3, the upper and lower curves both express a model of "individual innovation"; the difference between the

two is simply that the receptivity is greater for the upper. This difference in individual innovation rate or receptivity corresponds, we suggest, to the difference between profession-oriented and patient-oriented doctors (and between doctors who differ in other individual attributes as well). In contrast, in Figure 4 the upper curve (which is roughly similar in shape to the curve for the integrated doctors) represents a snowball process in which those who have been introduced pass on the innovation to their colleagues. (This curve is described by an equation which has been used to characterize rates of population growth, certain chemical reactions, and other phenomena which obey a chain-reaction process.) The lower curve in Figure 4 is still the individual innovation process. (Technically, the individual and snowball processes are described by equations on the graphs, which can be paraphrased as follows: *Individual process*—the number of doctors introducing the new drug each month would remain a constant percentage of those who have not already adopted the drug. *Snowball process*—the number of doctors introducing the new drug each month would increase in proportion to those who have already been converted.)

In short, these comparisons suggest that the process of introduction for those doctors who were deeply embedded in

Figure **3**   *Model of individual innovation, showing effects of differences in individual receptivity k*

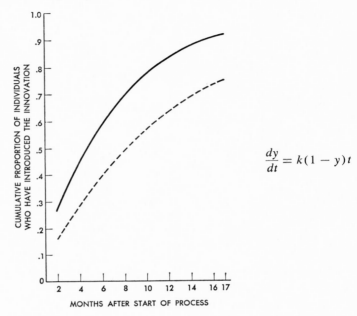

$$\frac{dy}{dt} = k(1 - y)t$$

their professional community was in fact different from the process for those who were relatively isolated from it. The highly integrated doctors seem to have learned from *one another,* while the less integrated ones, it seems, had each to learn afresh from the journals, the detail man (drug salesman), and other media of information.

Methods. II

This result called for a more detailed investigation into the ways in which the networks of relations among the doctors affected their introduction of the new drug. Such an investigation required a shift of focus from doctors to relationships among doctors or to the networks

themselves as the units of analysis. Various methods could have been devised to do this. We chose to record the behavior of *pairs* of doctors who were sociometrically related to one another, reasoning that if the networks of relations were effective, then pairs of doctors who were in contact must have been more *alike* in their behavior than pairs assorted at random. That is, if there was a snowball or chain-reaction process of drug introduction from one doctor to another, then adjacent links in the chain—pairs of socially related doctors—should have introduced the drug about the same time.

In order to test this hypothesis for the discussion network, Figure 5 was constructed. (Similar figures were constructed for the networks of friendship and advisorship.) Each sociometric pair was assigned to a column of this matrix according to the gammanym introduction date of the chooser, and to a row according to the gammanym introduction date of the doctor chosen. (A mutual choice constitutes two pairs in this tabulation, since any chooser and his choice constitute a pair.) Pairs of doctors who introduced the drug during the same month (interval zero) fall in the main diagonal; pairs of doctors who differed in introducing the drug by an interval of one month fall into cells adjoining the diagonal; and so on.

The resulting distribution of these intervals for the sociometric pairs was then compared to the corresponding distribution of intervals for a set of "random pairs" which has the following characteristics. If a pair is selected at random: (a) the probability that the chooser-member

of the pair introduced gammanym during a particular month is the same as in the actual sample but is independent of the introduction date of the doctor chosen; (b) the probability that the chosen member introduced gammanym during a particular month is the same as in the actual sample but is independent of the introduction date of the doctor making the choice. Thus, for example, among the random pairs, those who introduced gammanym in the first month and those who did so in the seventh gave equal portions of their choices to other first-month introducers. Similarly, those who introduced gammanym in the first month and those who introduced it in the seventh *received* equal portions of their choices from first-month introducers. Operationally, a set of "chance" frequencies satisfying these criteria can easily be obtained by computing

Figure **4**   *Comparison of model of "chain-reaction" innovation with model of individual innovation*

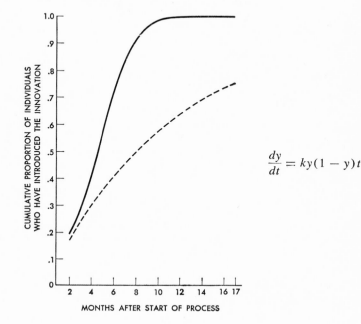

$$\frac{dy}{dt} = ky(1 - y)t$$

CUMULATIVE PROPORTION OF INDIVIDUALS WHO HAVE INTRODUCED THE INNOVATION

MONTHS AFTER START OF PROCESS

Figure **5**   *Chart showing dates of adoption of each member of discussion pairs*

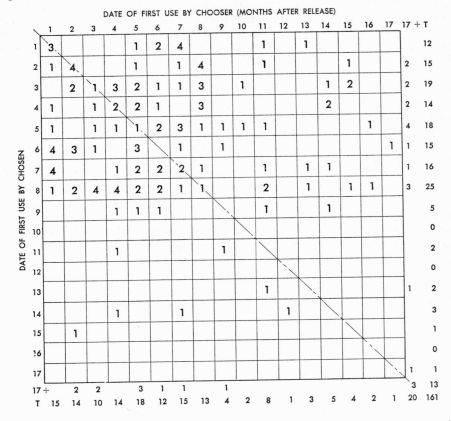

DATE OF FIRST USE BY CHOOSER (MONTHS AFTER RELEASE)

DATE OF FIRST USE BY CHOSEN

for each cell of Figure 5 the product of the associated marginal totals, divided, for convenience, by the grand total.[2]

Contrary to expectations, the proportion of pairs whose members had introduced gammanym during the same month, one month apart, two months apart, and so on, according to the chance model proved to be almost identical to the proportion of actual discussion pairs who had introduced gammanym simultaneously or with varying intervals. The results for pairs of friends and for advisor-advisee pairs were similarly disappointing. This meant the rejection of our original hypothesis that pairs of doctors in contact would introduce the drug more nearly simultaneously than pairs of doctors assorted at random.

There was, on the other hand, the earlier evidence that the doctor's integration was important to his introduction of

[2] A complication arose from the fact that the study was carried on in four different cities, with sociometric choices between cities excluded. This could spuriously raise any measure of pair-wise similarity of behavior, if there are large differences in behavior between the cities.... In order to avoid such a spurious relation, "chance" frequencies, as above described, were calculated separately from the marginal totals for each city, and only then summed over the cities.

gammanym. This dictated a more intensive look at the behavior of pairs of doctors. Accordingly, we raised the question whether the networks, though ineffective for the *whole* period studied, may have been effective for the *early* period, immediately after the drug was marketed. An inspection of Figure 5 suggests that this could easily be the case. If only the upper left-hand portion of the matrix, representing the first two, three, or four months, is considered, then there appears to be a tendency for both members of a pair to introduce the drug in the same month.

In order to describe this tendency more precisely, it was decided to eliminate from consideration those associates of each doctor who used the drug only after *he* did. That is to say, the following question was now asked of the data: How closely did the drug introduction of each doctor follow upon the drug introductions of those of his associates who had introduced the drug before

him? The answer is: very closely, for early introducers of the drug; not at all closely, for late introducers of the drug.

This result is based on a measure for each month, obtained by dividing up the total matrix of pairs of doctors as shown in Figure 6. The single cell in the upper left-hand corner represents those pairs both of whose members introduced the drug in the first month. The L-shaped section next to it contains the pairs which consist of one doctor who introduced the drug in the second month and one who introduced it in the first *or* second. The next L-shaped section contains all pairs which consist of one third-month adopter and one third-month-or-earlier adopter, and so on. It was now possible to determine the average interval for the sociometric pairs in each L-shaped section; likewise the average interval for the corresponding random pairs. On this basis, a measure of simultaneity was computed for each section, according to the formula:

Measure of simultaneity (positive)

$$= \frac{(\text{average interval for random pairs}) - (\text{average interval for sociometric pairs})}{\text{average interval for random pairs}}$$

This measure expresses the difference between the random and actual intervals as a fraction of the difference between the random interval and complete simultaneity (i.e., an interval of zero). The measure thus has a maximum of 1, and

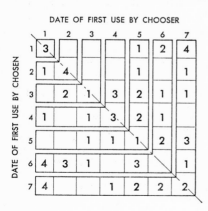

DATE OF FIRST USE BY CHOOSER

Figure 6   Exploded view of portion of Figure 5, showing monthly segments

Figure **7** *Index of pair-simultaneity for three networks at different times*

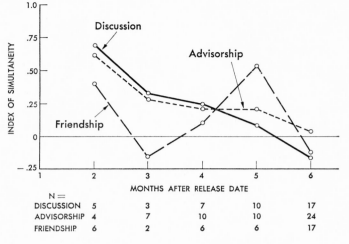

N =				
DISCUSSION	5	3	7	10	17
ADVISORSHIP	4	7	10	10	24
FRIENDSHIP	6	2	6	6	17

is zero when pairs are no closer than chance. In those cases where the actual interval exceeded the random interval, a different denominator was used.[3]

Results. II

The values of the index are plotted in Figure 7 for the second through the sixth months. Separate curves are plotted for pairs of friends, discussion pairs, and advisor-advisee pairs. The interpretation of these results must be tentative because of the small numbers of cases; on the other hand, the patterns which emerge are rather consistent.

Figure 7 suggests, first of all, that the networks of doctor-to-doctor contacts operated most powerfully during the first five months after the release of the new drug: such influence as any doctor's drug introduction had upon his immediate associates evidently occurred soon after the drug became available. (Figure 7 omits the later months during which the index is negative or very small.) Second, the three networks did not behave identically.[4] The discussion network and the advisor network showed most pair-simultaneity at the very beginning and then progressively declined. The friendship network shows initially less pair-simul-

[3] Measure of simultaneity (negative)

$$= \frac{\text{(average interval for random pairs)} - \text{(average interval for sociometric pairs)}}{(s - 1) - \text{(average interval for random pairs)}}$$

s being defined as the number of the latest month included in the particular L-shaped section. (E.g., $s = 4$ in the case of pairs consisting of one fourth-month adopter and one fourth-month-or-earlier adopter.) When the index has a negative value, it therefore expresses the difference between the random and actual intervals as a fraction of the difference between the random interval and the maximum interval that is possible.

[4] Many of the sociometric ties reappear in two or three of the networks. The three sociometric questions yielded a total of 958 "pairs" within the sample of 125 doctors; but since some of these pairs were identical in answer to two or all three of the questions, there were only 704 *different* pairs. This overlap is still small enough to allow differences in patterns to emerge, as shown in the text.

taneity than the other two, but—with some instability—appears to reach its maximum effectiveness later. Finally, after the fifth or sixth month following the release of the new drug, none of the networks any longer showed pair-simultaneity beyond chance.

These results, however tentative, suggest that there may be successive stages in the diffusion of this innovation through the community of doctors. The first networks to be operative as chains of influence appear to be those which connect the doctors in the professional relationships of advisors and discussion partners. Only then, it seems, does the friendship network become operative— among those doctors who are influenced in their decisions more by the colleagues they meet as friends than by those whom they look to as advisors or engage in discussion during working hours. Finally, for those doctors who have not yet introduced the drug by about six months after the drug's release these networks seem completely *inoperative* as chains of influence. The social structure seems to have exhausted its effect; those doctors

who have not responded to its influence by this time are apparently unresponsive to it. When they finally use gammanym, they presumably do so in response to influences outside the social network, such as detail men, ads, journal articles, and so on, and not in response to their relations with other doctors.

But one further phase in the social diffusion of gammanym can be discerned by examining separately the sociometrically integrated and the relatively isolated doctors. One would expect the networks of doctor-to-doctor contact to show their effectiveness first among the more integrated doctors and only then among those who are less integrated in their medical community. It has already been seen (Figure 2 and text) that the more isolated doctors, on the average, introduced gammanym considerably later than the socially more integrated doctors. We now propose, however, that when more isolated doctors *did* introduce the drug early, it was not with the help of the social networks. While the networks were operative as channels of influence *early* for the integrated doctors, they were operative

Figure 8   Index of pair-simultaneity at different times for doctors differing in integration

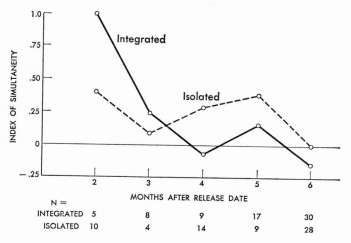

only later for the more isolated ones. This is what seems to have occurred. Figure 8 plots the index of simultaneity separately for more and less integrated doctors. (The graphs show weighted averages for all three networks; separately the numbers of cases would be so small as to produce erratic trends.)

The peak of effectiveness of doctor-to-doctor contacts for the well-integrated doctors appeared in the earliest month for which it can be plotted—the second month—after which effectiveness sharply declined. For the relatively isolated doctors, by contrast, the networks were not so effective at first as were those for the integrated doctors, but they maintained their effectiveness longer. Thus it appears that the networks of relations were effective not only for the more integrated doctors but also for the relatively isolated doctors who introduced the drug during the first five months of the drug's availability.

Conclusion

The above results, taken together, suggest a process which may be summarized as follows: At first the influence of these social networks operated only among the doctors who were integrated into the community of their colleagues through ties of a professional nature—as advisors or as discussion partners. Then it spread through the friendship network to doctors who were closely tied to the medical community through their friendship relations. By this time, social influence had also become operative in the more "open" parts of the social structure—

i.e., among the relatively isolated doctors. Finally, there came a phase during which most of the remaining doctors introduced gammanym but did so in complete independence of the time at which their associates had introduced it: the networks now showed no effect. For the integrated doctors, this phase began about four months after the drug's release; for the isolated doctors, it began about six months after the drug's release. This picture is of course a tentative one, for the small size of the sample introduces variability, and there may be factors which produce spurious results.

There remains the question: Why should these sociometric ties to colleagues who have used the drug be influential during the first months of the drug's availability, but not later? One possible answer lies in the greater uncertainty about the drug that must have prevailed when it was new. (Data not reported here show that those doctors who introduced gammanym early did so far more tentatively than those who introduced it later.) We know from work in the tradition of Sherif that it is precisely in situations which are objectively unclear that social validation of judgments becomes most important.

More generally, this explanation implies that a doctor will be influenced more by what his colleagues say and do in uncertain situations, whenever and wherever they may occur, than in clear-cut situations. This explanation was confirmed by further data from the study which show that doctors influence each other more in treatments whose effects are unclear than in treatments whose effects are clear-cut. . . .

A. PAUL HARE

Computer Simulation of Interaction in Small Groups

For the past few years, the . . . persons who have worked with . . . Bales on various research projects at the Laboratory of Social Relations at Harvard have had an interest in computer simulation of interaction in small groups. Bales, . . . following the development of the Newell-Shaw-Simon IPL-V Programming Language [1] . . . has suggested that the goal of naturalistic prediction of behavior in small groups may only be possible through the use of computer simulation.[2] To this end, Bales has been developing a comprehensive outline for a program for simulation that he has called the "Interaction Simulator." The goal of the Interaction Simulator is to reproduce the actual content and process of small group discussion once the personality characteristics of the members and the discussion topic have been specified. That is, the output of the computer will be a series of statements each indicating who is speaking, to whom he is making his comment, and the task and social-emotional content of the comment. A series of statements representing 40 minutes of interaction could then be compared with the interaction of real people holding a discussion on the same topic. This is a long-range goal, a goal that has only appeared to be attainable through the use of high-speed computers. . . .

In relation to this goal, Bales' master program, the Interaction Simulator, is well underway. A. S. Couch . . . has made a major contribution on the side of content by doing a series of factor analyses to discover the personality and interaction factors that must be considered in the simplest model of social interaction.[3] On the side of method, Couch has written computer programs which cover all the data-processing steps necessary to monitor and analyze the output from a five-man discussion group.

Over the past two years while we were waiting for IPL-V . . . I decided to try out some of the smaller pieces of the puzzle on the IBM 650. Although it lacks the storage capacity of the large machines, the 650 nevertheless performs all the basic operations and has the added advantage that one can deal directly with the machine as programmer and operator. My programs are written in machine language. I decided to begin writing programs for the task activities of individuals, then of groups, and then to begin adding programs to simulate the social-emotional behavior which goes on concurrently with the task behavior. The group to be simulated is a five-man group of college undergraduates with a discussion task, the "standard" laboratory group.

Reprinted in part from *Behavioral Science*, 6, 1961, pp. 261–65, with permission of the Mental Health Research Institute and the author.

[1] B. F. Green, Jr., IPL-V: The Newell-Shaw-Simon Programming Language, *Behavioral Science*, 5, 1960, pp. 94–98.

[2] R. F. Bales, "Small-Group Theory and Research," in R. K. Merton, L. Broom, and L. S. Cottrell, Jr., eds., *Sociology Today: Problems and Prospects*, New York: Basic Books, 1959, pp. 293–305.

[3] A. S. Couch, "Psychological Determinants of Interpersonal Behavior," unpublished doctoral dissertation, Harvard University, 1960.

Task Aspects of Interaction

One task which has been developed for use with five-man laboratory groups requires the subjects to predict the responses of an unknown student on the Bales-Couch Value Profile.[4] Group members are given the answers to five items from the value profile and then asked to predict the responses of an unknown student to ten or more additional items. The possible responses are: strongly disagree, disagree, slightly disagree, slightly agree, agree, and strongly agree. Among the five items might be: "Each one should get what he needs—the things we have belong to all of us" which the unknown student answered "Strongly agree"; and "You have to respect authority, and when you stop respecting authority, your situation isn't worth much" which the unknown student answered "Disagree." After the five group members discuss the answers to the five initial items, they are given a new set of items and asked to predict the responses. After each prediction, the actual answer to the item is revealed. An item to predict might be "Obedience and respect for authority are the most important virtues children should learn." Those of you who are familiar with the "F" Scale will recognize this as an item representing the value "Authoritarianism." Knowing this, you would probably predict that the unknown student answered this item "Disagree," as he did the "Authoritarian" item in the example above. Actually, he answered "Strongly disagree" and you would have an absolute discrepancy of one point on the first item.

The particular unknown student in the example above was a graduate student in clinical psychology who was chosen because he held strong and rather inconsistent opinions. If you are a person who is familiar with the Value Profile, or if you are a properly programmed computer, you know that the four principal value factors are: (I) Acceptance of authority, (II) Need-determined expression vs. value-determined restraint, (III) Equalitarianism, and (IV) Individualism, and that the test items represent these factors or combinations of them. With this knowledge you would be able to do fairly well in predicting responses. If you are a Harvard undergraduate, you will probably not be able to do as well but you will find it an interesting task.

The task of simulation began with an attempt to reproduce the process each group member would use in reaching his own individual decision on an item before he announced his prediction to the other group members. This program could also be used to simulate his performance as an individual on the same task since for some groups we have used individual performance on this task as a premeasure of the subject's task ability. The question is, by what process does the subject make his predictions? One possibility is that the subject looks for the previous item most similar in content to the new item and predicts that the unknown student will answer in a consistent fashion. In the machine, the content of an item can be represented by the four factor loadings on the major value factors. P. Stone of this group has written a program which, by correlating the four factor loadings for a new item with the factor loadings of all previous items in turn, identifies the item having the highest correlation with the new item. This approach is fairly successful but it does not take into account response tendency, since it

[4] R. F. Bales, and A. S. Couch, "The Value Profile: A Factor Analytic Study of Value Statements," Harvard University: Laboratory of Social Relations, 1960.

considers only one item at a time, and it slows down rapidly as the number of items to be considered is increased.

Another possibility for which I have written a 650 program is that the subject first identifies a new item as belonging to one of a limited number of categories which include the four principal value factors and their major combinations, and then predicts that the unknown student will answer the new item as he has answered similar items "on the average" in the past. (The average of the previous items was first calculated by taking the median. This was later changed to the mean when I found that the mean gave a more accurate representation of real subjects.) Since the machine—as well as the group—is given initial items which cover only the four major factors on the Value Profile, new items representing combinations of these factors are not contained in its memory. In such a case, for example an item which is highly loaded on both (I), Authoritarianism, and (III), Equalitarianism, the machine is programmed to take the mean of all previous I and III responses. Since there is no zero point in the response form for each item the machine is not allowed to guess "zero." If the mean of all previous responses happens to be zero, the machine looks at the unknown student's response set to see whether he has a tendency to agree or disagree and then predicts accordingly. With a "predictable" unknown student, the machine makes an average error of about .71 over a typical run of a dozen predictions. The program takes about 400 words of storage. The input is one card for each item giving the four factor loadings for that item and the true answer. The output is a card giving the category the item is guessed to be, the guessed answer, the discrepancy, the average discrepancy for all items up to that point,

and the response set. At present, this program does not allow for individual differences in problem solving, although we have some ideas for possibilities to try.

A second piece of the puzzle is a program for the IBM 650 to simulate the decision reached by the group on the prediction for each item. This program, written with Elizabeth Borland, begins with the five individual predictions as inputs. The program assumes that the group members typically reach a decision that represents an average of the individual members' judgments. As before, if the mean of the individual judgments is zero, the program checks the response set. If the response set is also zero, the machine determines whether the majority of the group members thought the unknown student would answer on the agree side or the disagree side of the scale. This is a smaller program than the first, about 100 words. The input consists of a card with the five individual predictions and the true answer for each item. The output consists of a card with the true answer, the guess, the averaged discrepancy, the response set, and a note if the "majority opinion" loop was used.

As a test of the effectiveness of these two "simulations," the predictions generated by the machine program were compared with actual predictions of individuals and decisions . . . of 20 laboratory groups of five Harvard undergraduates. These data were collected by Lindsey Churchill. The group members met for one 70-minute discussion. Most of the members were unknown to each other before the experiment began. Each member was given a card with one item from the Value Profile and the answer given by the unknown student (the clinical psychologist). After a short discussion of about 10 minutes, during which the members pooled their information about the unknown subject, they predicted his responses to an average of about 10 items, depending upon the speed of the group. Before each group decision was made, each subject recorded privately his own prediction.

The average discrepancy between the guess and the true answer for the 100 experimental subjects was 2.40. The average discrepancy for the computer making the same predictions was 2.00. Although better than the average subject, this is still not very good. Recall that the unknown student was chosen because he was thought to hold strong opinions and to be somewhat unpredictable. This hypothesis is confirmed. He was indeed unpredictable. The average discrepancy score for the 20 men who were the most accurate in their groups was 1.85, slightly better than the machine. Apparently the machine still has something to learn.

A comparison of the group decision on each item with the true answer indicates an average discrepancy of 2.38, about the same as that for the average individual. This means that the results of group discussion do not differ significantly from the accuracy obtained by simply pooling the individual guesses. Since in every group the subject who was most accurate was not the one whose answers were closest to the group decision (in two groups the most accurate man was tied with another), it is evident that the groups were not making full use of their most insightful members. The groups which were the most accurate were the ones which contained, on the average, the most accurate individuals. These groups also completed the largest number of predictions in the allotted time. . . .

The members of the 20 groups made a total of 180 group predictions. Of these, 112, or about two-thirds, were reproduced exactly by machine simulation that took the mean of the five individual predictions. In those cases where the mean was different from the actual group decision, the machine was closer to the correct answer about half of the time. During the analysis of the data, it appeared that a program which took the majority opinion when there was a clear majority might be closer to the actual group decision than one simply taking the mean. If the majority opinion has been considered first, the simulation of the group prediction would have reproduced the actual group prediction in an additional nine instances (or about 5 per cent). However, the "majority" routine would have been less accurate than a routine which always took the mean in predicting the true answer by almost the same amount, in eight instances. One concludes that a routine that took the majority opinion first and took the mean of the individual guesses when there was no clear majority would have improved the simulation only slightly.

Since one-third of the group predictions are not reproduced by the present simulation, it would be desirable to find some other source of unaccounted-for variance. Is it possible that these groups have leaders who are influencing group opinion? In nine of the groups, we would have done better to use the guesses of the subject who was closest to the group prediction than to use the mean of all the individual guesses. If we could identify these men before the experiment, we might be able to improve our predictions. Unfortunately, with only nine such persons in our sample it is difficult to draw any definite conclusions. Although seating position and pretested personality measures have been found to be related to amount of talk and amount of influence in other experiments, these nine subjects do not show distinct preferences in seating or distinct personality characteristics for the dimensions of anxiety, warmth, and aggression. There is one possible exception in that five of the nine rank lowest in their groups on the dimension of aggression. However, this does not fit our impression of a very influential type. In any event, this is only the beginning; we will continue to try to improve the simulation. . . .

And so we proceed. . . . In my experience, the computer is a hard master since it forces one to be specific about the variables in interpersonal behavior and the exact relations between them. But its special value lies in its ability to make predictions by considering in a systematic way far more variables and relationships than an individual could hope to handle in the short run. Thus it becomes possible to make real predictions in real time about social interaction in small groups.

COMMENTARY
DYNAMIC STUDIES

Many of the studies discussed in previous chapters have dealt with social systems, present or past, as they exist not merely at a single point in time, but *over* time. Bales observes interaction as it progresses through phases in a laboratory session. Lazarsfeld, Berelson, and Gaudet analyze changes in political predispositions over a period of several months. Thomas and Znanieski assess the impact on the Polish family of societal changes at the end of the nineteenth century. Weber focuses on a change in the institutionalization of one set of values as this change may create a psychological readiness to accept other related changes. Sorokin plots the trends in systems of truth over the broad sweep of centuries.

How does this dimension of time enter into the working model of a social system and its translation into research operations? The conceptual model always involves time—but with varying degrees of emphasis (see, *e.g.,* Parsons, 1951, Chapter 11). Some models are relatively static. Here the researcher thinks of the system as if it were a stable structure, and conducts a cross-section study at a single point of time. Yet even such static models usually involve certain assumptions about the time order in which changes in the variables occur; the researcher typically interprets the cross-section finding of a correlation (between education and tolerance, or between socioeconomic status and voting intention) by postulating a connecting process that takes place over time. Other models are clearly dynamic. Here the researcher in defining the system focuses attention upon its processes of interaction and change—upon the development or the dissolution of friendships, for example, upon cyclical societal trends or societal decay.

By introducing time, what may appear to be a static model becomes a dynamic one, with time as the axis along which process and change occur. The place of time is suggested even in Henderson's rubber band example. At Time 1, a given arrangement of the rubber bands—a certain organization or structure among the parts—may be observed. Then the position of one of the rubber bands is changed—Henderson introduces a disturbance from outside the system, and notes that this change in one part affects all of the other parts; at Time 2, then, a new organization or structure of the rubber bands is observed. Thus, Henderson makes observations at two different time periods and compares the two sets of observations. It is from this comparison over time that he is able to learn something about the interdependence of the parts—about the nature of the system.

Or consider Malinowski's canoe, where again the understanding of the system depends upon the notion of time. At Time 1 the watcher for fish performs his task; he is followed at Time 2 by the caster of the nets performing his task; and at Time 3 by the master of the canoe dividing the catch. The actual process is still more complex; in a motion picture of everything that went on from Time 1 through Time 2 to Time 3, each of the individuals would be seen more or less continually in motion. Each is performing a different task; yet all of these tasks fit together over time to constitute the total social process of fishing.

Thus some kind of process or change is always going on in a social system; and process or change occurs over time—one cannot think of change as belonging only to a single instant in time. At the research level, the sociologist may hope ultimately to find means of understanding the entire process. An ideal design might study over time the complex actions and thoughts of each of the individual role incumbents (or the changing characteristics of the subgroups or other parts of the system), and then fit together all these interdependent actions and orientations as they make up the social process as a whole. But the sociologist often finds that such ideal research objectives and his immediately feasible objectives are poles apart. (Compare Kurt Lewin's discussion of the difficulties of reconstructing the group as a whole from the miniature "biographies" of group members secured through careful observation of each role incumbent separately. Lewin, 1939.) In reducing the social process to manageable terms, he often restricts the research focus, as we have repeatedly noticed, selecting for study just one part or level of the case **(P-I),** or just one or a few properties **(P-IX).** We shall now consider still further means of designing research on social process or social change through the additional selection of the *periods of time* to be encompassed in the study.

The time factor **(P-V)** may be handled in research in a variety of ways. In this and the following Unit, we shall discuss studies that suggest—in addition to the *static* cross-section approach—at least three *dynamic* approaches which simplify the researcher's task and make it more practicable. We shall compare the dynamic approaches with the static *cross-section study,* which attempts to eliminate time from the research procedure altogether (depending upon assumptions about the time order of the variables). This approach produces a snapshot of the system. As the first dynamic approach, *panel analysis* may be viewed as a sequence of cross-section studies, a series of snapshots at successive points in time which are then compared. Using time as a variable in a highly controlled fashion, the researcher draws inferences about the intervening processes without actually having observed them—like studying the process of aging by comparing the photographs of a boy, the same person in middle age, and then as an old man. The second dynamic approach, the *trend study,* or study of partial process, does not restrict its selection of time periods so rigidly, but deals with a few selected properties or aspects of the system continually, over time.

Figure **10-A** *Selected focuses of dynamic studies*

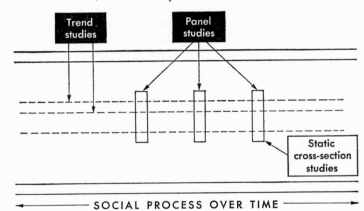

Such research approaches are, of course, arbitrary abstractions that attempt to simplify the process. If the social process undergone by any system is viewed as a band extending across time, as in Figure 10-A, then the cross-section study or the panel analysis of cross sections cuts across parts of this process at given points in time, whereas the trend study traces parts of the process over time. Many dynamic studies reach beyond either of these pure types of approaches, merging into the third dynamic approach, the *combined approach,* which ties together in various ways the trends and the cross-section states of the system.

Ogburn and Thomas and the Trend Study

As the dynamic approach forming the opposite extreme to the familiar cross-section study (as in the previous selections by Merton or Kahl, for example, or in Exercise II-3), let us first consider the trend study. Ogburn and Thomas, whose objective is to find out for the country as a whole "the amount of concurrence in the fluctuations of certain social conditions with the fluctuations of business," plot trends and compare them over a fifty-year period. Recognizing that the causes for long-range increase (secular trends) in prosperity may be quite different from the causes of (short-term changes in) business cycles, they first disentangle the business cycles from the secular trend. Then they examine the relationship between business cycles and short-term fluctuations of various social factors.

FORM OF THE ANALYSIS

Treating the United States as the research case **(P-I)** and its economic and social conditions as its changing properties, these researchers employ two different types of measures discussed in Unit 7: (1) To study the economic state of the country as a whole, they combine nine different sets of indicants (such as wholesale prices, commercial failures, pig iron production). Here they form a *composite measure* by putting together indicants of several aspects of a property (economic prosperity and depression). (2) To study the social conditions, they use *collective measures* (such as marriage rates, suicide rates, divorce rates), which they obtain by counting individuals in order to characterize the society. Here they are measuring properties of the society by combining indicants that refer initially to constituent parts of the social system. (For a methodological discussion of marriage rates, see Glick, *e.g., p.* 586 ff.)

Each of these measures is obtained for each year over the period from 1870 to 1920, and its trends are then examined. Their Figure 2 shows, for instance, the two lines representing the short-term and the secular trends in marriage rates. The rapidly fluctuating line shows the year-by-year changes in the proportions of individuals married, while the smooth curve has been fitted to these data to reflect the main tendency over the half-century. By taking the deviations of the annual fluctuations from the major secular trend in marriages, the researchers are then in a position to test their hypothesis that these are concurrent with the (similarly obtained) economic oscillations between prosperity and depression. They test this hypothesis by finding the coefficient of correlation between these two sets of cyclical deviations from their respective base lines. The correlation between marriage-rate fluctuations (Figure 2) and the business cycle turns out to be +0.66, indicating a general tendency for the marriage rate to increase in prosperity and diminish in depression. In this fashion, the researchers control (or hold constant) the secular trends in order to measure the relationship between annual fluctuations in business and in each of the social factors in turn.

ADVANTAGES OF SUCH TREND STUDIES

The procedures of this study provide an important guide to systematic research covering long periods of time. By revealing the parallelism between trends in selected properties, the method suggests clues to possible relationships between aspects of the over-all process. For example, it tells something about the relationship between changes in prosperity and changes in various social phenomena, showing which changes go on together, and which operate at cross-purposes with one another.

Since understanding of causal relationships often depends upon knowledge of the time sequence of variables, it is important to note that these researchers are observing, not just one or two fluctuations or oscillations in the pair of variables under study, but a long sequence of fluctuations over a fifty-year period. Thus they are in a position to check the *consistency* with which the two trends coincide, or with which one of the trends may lag behind the other. They examine the data for such possible lags. Noting, for example, that changes in the marriage rate "seem to be practically simultaneous with changes in the business cycle" they speculate about the possible consequences: Does *not* getting married during a depression merely mean postponement until prosperity returns? To test this hypothesis, they compute a second correlation coefficient to allow for a possible one-year lag of marriage rates behind the business cycle. Their findings show a lower relationship than before, however, thus failing to support such a notion of the process.

CONTROL OF CONFOUNDING FACTORS

Two sets of difficulties which may arise in interpreting such trend data become clear if we compare trend studies with the cross-section analysis of variables discussed in Unit 8. In the Ogburn and Thomas study, there is no attempt, on the one hand, to *control* extraneous variables (except for the secular trend itself) or, on the other hand, to *identify* the parts of the system which may be contributing to the particular processes. Nevertheless, consideration of two further examples suggests that either control or identification *may* be built into trend studies, if the research objective requires it.

Standardization. One procedure for holding constant extraneous variables is called *standardization* (see, *e.g.,* Petersen, p. 627). The Census demographers may want to observe, for example, changes in the proportions of the population who are married. Age distribution is a potentially confounding factor, however, because age affects the marriage rate and there has been a steadily increasing proportion of persons in the United States who are of marriageable age. Therefore, the objective is to examine changes in marriage when changes in age are held constant. The Census procedure, which is equivalent to the cross-tabulation discussed in Unit 8, results in detailed data on the changes in marriage rates for each of the categories of age (with their changing relative frequencies). These data are too complex to be fully presented, however, or to facilitate inspection of changes over time. Therefore the demographers recombine the several age categories by using as weights the population distribution for a year selected as a standard. Thus, to find the standardized marriage rate for each particular year, they multiply the rate in each age category by the number of persons in that category in the standard year and then take the total of all age categories. As Hawley puts it, "the age composition of a 'standard population' is substituted for the actual age composition, and the age-specific frequencies observed in the actual population are applied to the 'standard' age distribution to obtain an adjusted or standardized total rate." (Hawley, 1959, p. 376; see also Hawley's discussion of cohort analysis as another important tool for studying trends over time. *Ibid.*)

Table **10-A**   *Changes in marital status with age distribution standardized* [a]

| Year | Selected figures for males | |
	Crude percentage married	Percentage married based on 1950 age distribution as standard
1890	52.1	61.2
1930	58.4	62.1
1950	68.0	68.0

[a] Data adapted from United States Census Abstracts, 1960, Table 36, p. 38.

For example, the selected trend figures in Table 10-A compare the crude changes in the proportion of married males in the population with the changes when these proportions are standardized for age. You will see that the age-specific rates—which treat the 1950 age distribution as if it had obtained throughout the period—show a change in the marital status of the population of the United States; whereas the change is far less pronounced in the comparable unadjusted figures.

Although standardization may be most useful in trend analysis (or in cross-cultural analysis) where many time periods (or countries) are to be compared, it is similarly applied in cross-section studies. Here its virtue is to focus attention on the relationships between the explanatory variables, while holding constant (standardizing) the effects of extraneous variables. For example, in a cross-section study of a community, the investigators tested the hypothesis that mental health varies inversely with the number of generations the individual's family had lived in the United States, and they found the predicted negative correlation in the data. They wanted to take the precaution, however, of inquiring into the potential play of other demographic factors—for the generation categories in the sample differed by age and family socioeconomic status (SES), and frequency of mental impairment was known to vary positively with age and negatively with SES. Accordingly, they standardized the generation categories, recomputing the mental health distributions that would result if all generation categories were identical in age and SES with a population accepted as a standard. On this standardized basis, they found no differences, after all, among generation categories—the original support for the hypothesis was seen to be largely spurious (Srole *et al.,* pp. 257–58).

IDENTIFICATION OF PARTS OF THE SYSTEM

Besides using standardization or similar controls in analyzing changes in the *properties* of a system (of a country, for example), sociological researchers often want to see how these trends are tied to the parts of the research *case*— to the social-structural base. They may want to know *who,* or what parts of the system, contribute to the changes which are occurring. For example, what structural changes might underlie the finding that the suicides in a population tend to increase during periods of economic depressions, and homicides during periods of economic prosperity? What segments of the population are involved in such concomitant trends? Is the tendency to self-destruction aggravated among those individuals whose own status has declined, while the tendency to kill is heightened among the other individuals who remain in low status although their erstwhile peers have achieved economic success? (See Henry and Short.) Such researchers face the familiar problem of identifying the relevant parts of the system under study, and following these parts through the analysis.

Although Ogburn and Thomas are not concerned with this matter of identification, they do make brief reference to separate trend analyses for population segments located in different regions of the countries. Moreover, they comment that it would be "interesting to know what psychological factors are involved in decreasing the divorce rate in time of business depressions." Thus they implicitly raise questions as to how such macroscopic processes might be tied—not merely to regions or classes of societies—but to the psychological factors operating within the component roles.

An analysis which does illustrate this principle of analyzing societal trends in such fashion that the parts of the society are identified is included in Sorokin's study of social and cultural dynamics (a portion of which you read in Unit 5). In an examination of the economic well-being of countries, Sorokin maps the secular trends for each country *as a whole* (much as he plots the trends for great thinkers). Then he breaks these trends down further to show changes in the prosperity ratings for each of the main *classes* within each country. Figure 10-B illustrates his procedure for a single country in which the over-all changes appear as the composite of the separate changes for the aristocracy, the clergy, the peasants, and each of the other sectors of the class structure. Obviously, the trends for the classes do not all follow the over-all trend exactly; and Sorokin attaches particular importance to "those classes, like the aristocracy, the clergy, the intelligentsia, governmental officials, and—especially in the Sensate culture —the bourgeoisie, which are the main bearers of the given culture." (1937, Volume III, p. 230.)

To be sure, Sorokin's procedure does not fully utilize in the trend analysis

Figure **10-B** *Sorokin's identification of classes in trend analysis of economic situations in France, 800–1926* [a]

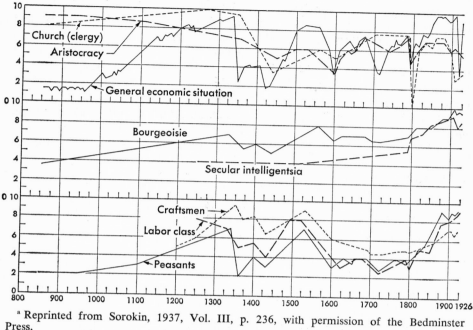

[a] Reprinted from Sorokin, 1937, Vol. III, p. 236, with permission of the Bedminster Press.

the method of multivariate analysis possible in a cross-section study (Unit 8). That is, he does not attempt to classify cases in terms of two (or more) interrelated variables *both* (or all) of which are changing. What he does achieve is identification of the parts of the system in terms of class status—a property which he does not treat as changing over time. He is then able to relate the various parts to a second property that does change—to trends in prosperity.

Panel Study of Individual Voting Behavior

Exactly such an analysis of interrelationships between trends may be achieved by the panel design—a design in which the same sample is examined at two or more periods of time. Panel design, with which Exercise II-4 (the analysis of changing adolescent reference groups) has previously provided experience, is exemplified in the classic study of voting behavior by Lazarsfeld, Berelson, and Gaudet (Unit 8). Further examination of this study will indicate the principles of panel analysis. With the aim of discovering the *process* by which voting decisions are formed, these researchers utilize data obtained by repeatedly interviewing the *same* individuals every month for seven months, asking each how he plans to vote in the coming election.

NATURE OF PANEL ANALYSIS

The procedures for analyzing such data, as initially formulated by Lazarsfeld, Zeisel, and their colleagues, have been demonstrated in the problems and examples of correct answers in Exercise IV-4. The appearance of the tables and the operations performed are similar to the subgroup comparisons made in the cross-section analysis of interrelated variables discussed in Unit 8—but, since time now enters into the definitions of the variables, the meaning of the data is quite different.

One characteristic feature of panel analysis, *turnover,* in contrast to the *net shift* in the totals between any two time periods, is illustrated in the fictitious data of Table 10-B (compare Exercise IV-4, Problem 1). In this table the re-

Table **10-B** *Panel analysis based on individuals* [a]

| | Time 2: In August | | |
Time 1: In June	Republican	Democratic	Total in June
Republican	30	25	55
Democratic	20	25	45
Total in August	50	50	100

[a] Figures, which are fictitious, show number of individuals planning to vote either Republican or Democratic.

searchers have simply dichotomized individuals at each of two time periods according to their voting intentions. At Time 1, 55 per cent planned to vote Republican in contrast to only 50 per cent at Time 2. Thus the difference of 5 percentage points measures net shift. In addition, the table also shows whether the *same* people who planned to vote one way at Time 1 still plan to vote this way at Time 2. Of the 45 who planned to vote Democratic at Time 1, for example, 20 switched to Republican at Time 2. The turnover, then, consists of these 20 from the Democratic camp plus the 25 former Republicans who shifted to the Democratic camp. Such an outcome would indicate important shifts in both directions during the intervening period, but since these shifts tend to counteract one another, there is only the slight *net* shift toward the Democrats of 5 percentage points. Note that this outcome could not be predicted from the marginal total figures alone for each of the time periods. Indeed, one could predict from the same marginals quite a different turnover pattern in which only five people altogether switched.

Use of the Case in Panel Analysis. What are the implications of such turnover analysis for understanding the research case **(P-I)?** Clearly, the panel study *identifies* each case, following it through the analysis—just as in the cross-tabulations of Unit 8; but here in addition the case is followed *over time.* When the case is the individual in a (political) role, as in the voting study, special interest may focus on "the processes of attitude formation and change" which characterize the changers and shifters. The fact that this analysis is at the role level facilitates, as these researchers say, inferences about the "psychological mediators which connect the social situation and the individual decision."

Moreover, these cases—the roles of individuals—fit together in this study to form the larger system of the community. Here, then, as in many sociological studies, the analysis focuses on *two levels* of the system, with the concrete cases under scrutiny treated as the *parts* or elements comprising the system as a whole. Viewed from the system (community) level, the panel analysis compares the voting structure of the group at one time with its structure at another time. In the example of high turnover, a major internal change and rearrangement in the roles is revealed. Thus the turnover analysis provides information both about the changing *structure* of voting in the community, and about the changes in individual types of *roles* identified within this structure.

Of course, although these students of voting behavior are dealing with particular role incumbents, researchers using panel analysis are often not so much interested in the individual as in the roles as parts of the social structure. Thus, Stouffer, if he were to conduct a long-range panel study of community leaders, might follow through the analysis the leadership *roles* he identified in his concrete sample of communities (Unit 6), even though the *individual* leaders themselves might shift periodically. Moreover, the structural elements of interest in a given study are by no means always roles. In Sorokin's trend analysis (Figure 10-B above), for example, the social system elements were classes of the society. In summary, then, the more general form of panel analysis may include any sequence of cross-section studies of the same system or set of roles—or set of individuals (as in the definition used in *The People's Choice*).

Use of Properties in Panel Analysis. We should consider the value of panel analysis as it contributes to our understanding, not only of internal rearrangements of system parts, but also of the changing patterns of properties. The method is especially useful in sociological research because it shows how changing properties of individuals (roles, subsystems, or other parts of the system) fit together into the changing collective patterns for the system as a whole.

Since the full pattern of change is only apparent from the cells of Table 10-B above, for example—not from the collective group properties alone as these are shown in the marginals of the table—a striking distinction appears between panel analysis and the trend study as illustrated by Ogburn and Thomas. Both show changes in collective system properties. But the data in the trend study consist only of what would be the marginal totals in the voting study. Trend analysis would record the information, for example, that the percentage of persons planning to vote Democratic has gone up from 45 at one time period to 50 at another; it would *not* show to what extent the *same* people may have remained Democratic in their intentions. On the other hand, whereas trend studies may utilize marginal total information over extended periods of time, panel analysis of the full turnover pattern (in contrast to study of transition probabilities over extended time periods, as discussed below) is rarely applied to more than two or three time periods, because of the very large sample required for—and the difficulties of interpreting—more complex subgroup comparisons. Thus the two methods furnish quite different information about the changing properties of systems.

A COMBINED APPROACH

One aspect of the voting study utilizes a combination of *panel analysis* and a procedure for examining certain of the *trends* which connect the cross-section periods. The researchers were not fully satisfied with the turnover analysis alone. They were not satisfied by knowing only that, between the beginning of the month and the end of the month, great shifts of opinion had occurred which showed a slight preponderance in favor of the Democrats. They wanted to know what had taken place between the first of the month and the end of the month which might have influenced some people to change one way or the other. In short, they wanted to know more about the intervening process.

To study this intervening process, they used an exploratory approach (since they had few definite hypotheses); and (since they had no systematic procedure for measuring trends), they developed an interesting descriptive procedure for learning as much as possible about what had taken place. One device they used was to isolate individuals who had switched their intentions either way (those characterized by "turnover"), and subsequently to observe who these people were, where they fitted into the social structure, or what pressures might have been brought upon their voting intentions by others. Another device was to note particular events, such as radio appeals, to which these people were exposed between the two time periods, and which might have caused them to change. Finally, they asked respondents directly about their reasons for change.

In such ways, Lazarsfeld and his associates used their ingenuity to explore the process of change. They were able to do this particularly effectively because they did not, like Ogburn and Thomas, focus exclusively upon the trends as such. Instead, they were able to tie their analysis into the structural picture within which such trends were taking place.

SAMPLES FOR PANEL ANALYSIS

Two procedural difficulties should be noted which arise in repeated interviewing of the same sample—"control effect" (with which you are familiar) and "sample mortality." Repeated interviewing is often found to have an undesired and confusing effect **(P-VI)** on the action or attitudes under study—perhaps influencing the behavior of respondents, sensitizing them to formerly unnoticed matters, or stimulating communication with others on unwonted topics.

(Control effect from repeated interviewing is sometimes called "measurement effect"—but this term may be used loosely without specific reference to the action or attitudes under study.) The voting study utilizes an important device for testing—and, if necessary, making allowances for—control effect. The researchers set up four matched samples of 600 persons each. They focused major attention on one of these samples, interviewing each of the others only once as a control group, or *control sample,* to ensure that their findings were not the mere artifact of control effect. (The use of control samples will be considered in further detail in Unit 11 on experiments.)

A problem which is generally more difficult to solve is that of "sample mortality," which arises because some panel members refuse to be reinterviewed, move away, or are unavailable at an interview period. As in any sample (Unit 6), the loss of respondents through self-selection introduces a potential sampling bias. These researchers held the losses down to 14 per cent and report that analysis of the characteristics of missing cases shows a "practically unnoticeable" influence on the total trends. (Compare Stouffer's analysis of the "fish which were not caught" in his study of conformity in Unit 6.) Substitutions, which are generally undesirable in any sample, are particularly useless in a panel analysis where the same individuals are to be followed throughout the period under study.

Panel Study of Friendship as Social Process

Following the early study of voting (for which the data were collected in 1940), the procedure for panel analysis has undergone a continual development under Lazarsfeld's leadership. A more recent formulation appears in the methodological conversation between Merton and Lazarsfeld about the study of friendship process. Merton describes (although he does not present the actual data) the research finding of "homophily"—the sharing of similar values by close friends —and then discusses the further problem of discovering "the *dynamic processes* through which the similarity or opposition of values shape the formation, maintenance, and disruption of close friendships" (italics added). He sets forth a detailed conceptual model of "selective and adjustive processes," describing "the patterned sequences of social interaction between friends in which each phase generates and regulates the subsequent phase in such manner as to give rise to the observed patterns of friendship between people of designated kinds."

LAZARSFELD'S SCHEME FOR ANALYSIS

Lazarsfeld then sets forth an operational scheme for panel analysis of such processes, as in his table which we reproduce as Table 10-C (in which "F+" designates the presence of friendship in a dyad, and "A+" the presence of agreement). Here the research case **(P-I)** is the dyadic relationship—the friendship

Table **10-C** *Panel analysis based on groups* [a]

Time 1	Time 2				
FA	FA ++	FA +−	FA −+	FA −−	
++	50	20	10	20	100
+−	(30)	20	0	(50)	100
−+	(50)	0	40	(10)	100
−−	20	10	0	70	100
	150	50	50	150	

[a] Adapted from Lazarsfeld and Merton, Table 3.

pair—with the marginals representing all possible dyads under study. (The form of the analysis is demonstrated, using Lazarsfeld's figures but using individuals as the research unit, in Problem 2 of Exercise IV-4.) This sixteenfold table can handle two variables at each of two time periods—in contrast to the fourfold Table 10-B above, based on a single variable at the two periods; the distinctive features of the larger scheme deserve your careful consideration. As discussed by Lazarsfeld, three types of results may be obtained from three different analyses of such a table, as you know from Problem 2:

> *Static correlations,* between the two variables at each time period;
> *Turnover* on each of the variables over time and on the combination of the two variables;
> *Measures of relative "strength"* of the two variables (by examination of the circled figures in Table 10-C).

Moreover, like all panel tables, these analyses succeed in retaining the identity of the cases **(P-I)**—in this instance, of the particular dyads as they move through the friendship process.

POSSIBLE ELABORATIONS AND PREDICTIONS

Lazarsfeld goes on to suggest how the analysis might become more complex (through extensions of Table 10-C) in order to take care of further refinements of the conceptual model. For instance, he claims—and we illustrate the possibilities later—that more than two variables might be studied, or each variable might be subdivided into several categories rather than into just two. Especially interesting are the possibilities of adding to the number of time periods. Not only can the researcher observe in the data the frequencies with which certain patterns of change occur, but he can make predictions based on the specific rules assumed to govern such change.

Use of Mathematical Models. Let us see how Lazarsfeld makes such predictions by using a mathematical model (as in Unit 5, for example) and applying principles of probability with which you are already familiar (from Manual V-B). Like a great many of the mathematical models used in sociology, Lazarsfeld's stochastic (that is, probabilistic) model rests on the assumption that the process under study follows the rules of chance. Lazarsfeld defines the "transition probabilities" by which given types of pairs move from one state of friendship-agreement to another state; and treats them as a "Markov chain process," which means he assumes that the state of the pair at any given period in some way depends upon its "past history" (Step A).

The underlying logic of the mathematical procedure (Step B) may be understood by the simple exercise (following Rule 1 of Manual V-B) of applying the probabilities shown in Lazarsfeld's Appendix I to the marginal frequencies at Time 2. (Lazarsfeld obtains these probabilities from the cell frequencies across in Table 10-C.) The result of this exercise, which we show in Table 10-D, is

Table **10-D** *Turnover table predicted from transition probabilities*

Time 2		Time 3			
F A	F A	F A	F A	F A	
	+ +	+ −	− +	− −	
+ +	75	30	15	30	150
+ −	15	10	0	25	50
− +	25	0	20	5	50
− −	30	15	0	105	150
	145	55	35	165	

the predicted turnover table showing the shifts from Time 2 to Time 3—making the assumption of a "stationary process" in which the sequence rules controlling the change from one time period to the next remain constant. By a series of repetitions of such computations—always using only the marginals of the latest time period for computing the subsequent turnover table—Lazarsfeld obtains the "equilibrium table" in his Appendix I; that is, further computations beyond this point will no longer change the table.

If data were actually available for a series of time periods, such predictions for the later periods might be tested against the facts (Step C). Such empirical tests, followed by strategic exploratory analyses of the data, would undoubtedly add greatly to the clarification and refinement of the various assumptions underlying this model (and other possible models)—that extraneous factors do not disturb the friendship process, for example, or that other values not specifically concerned with racial problems play no major part. Although no such empirical tests are reported here, similar models have been applied by Anderson (1954) and by Goodman (1962) to the data from *The People's Choice*. Because these original data were obtained for seven time periods, models can be developed from two or three early periods and then tested against the real situation at later periods, resulting in increased understanding of the voting process.

It is interesting to speculate about whether this simple stationary process model is as applicable to the friendship dyads as to the individual voters. Within the dyadic network of a community, each individual belongs in many dyads. Thus if, within one of his dyadic relationships, an individual changes his values to agree with one friend, he may thereby come into disagreement with another friend in another dyad. The sequence rules are, accordingly, not specific to the discrete dyads. The changing patterns in which the many dyads may fit together are taken into account more explicitly in the snowball process model used by Coleman, Katz, and Menzel (as discussed below).

THE PROBLEM OF ROLE IDENTIFICATION

Thus Lazarsfeld's scheme affords a highly important general model that may prove useful in analyzing many of the processes studied through panels. The provocative remaining problem, raised by Lazarsfeld himself at the end of the study, concerns the "psychological mechanisms" underlying homophily. This problem again concerns the levels at which the social system as the research case **(P-I)** is being analyzed. Just as in the voting study, two levels are involved—in this instance, the dyadic pairs are the parts which fit together into the system of the larger community. The turnover analysis shows, as we have noted, the shifts and realignments of these parts from one time period to the next. But Lazarsfeld's analysis does *not* extend further to the level of the role. It shows *how many* members of the pair (two, one, or none) evince feelings of friendship, for example, but not *which* members. You should consider carefully the possibilities of extending such analysis further in order to identify the characteristics of the role; we shall examine some of these possibilities in Unit 12.

A Combined Approach in the Drug Diffusion Study

The brilliant analysis by Coleman, Katz, and Menzel illustrates a procedure for combining many of the assets of both trend studies and cross-section sequences. Designed to study the flow of influence through the social structure of a medical community, it measures changes over time and also ties these changes to individuals and to dyads within the network of relationships among doctors, tracing the "social processes which intervened between the initial trials of the drug by a few local innovators and its final use by virtually the whole medical community." The conceptual model is based on earlier work on personal influence as the channel for mass-communicated messages (see Katz and Lazarsfeld, 1956), and relates more generally to the diffusion of innovations, as Katz shows in his reanalysis of the parallel process (see Ryan and Gross) by which hybrid seed corn gained acceptance among Iowa farmers (Elihu Katz, 1961).

Treating the social structure of the community of doctors as setting the boundaries within which innovations spread, the researchers study *all* (or nearly all) of the doctors (see the discussion of the sampling of social structures in Unit 6) in order to locate the "pairs or chains of socially connected doctors." The analysis then proceeds to identify several levels within this structure: the individual roles, the dyadic pairs, the networks of pairs. (A difficulty arises, however, in dealing with the community as the larger system, since—presumably in order to obtain enough cases for the several analyses—data for four communities are aggregated. Thus the larger system itself is not identified. This is a frequent difficulty in studies of groups, as in the aggregations of several groups by Bales, for example, or by Riley, Toby, Cohn, and Riley. Both panel studies we have examined—by Lazarsfeld, Berelson, and Gaudet, and by Lazarsfeld and Merton —are able to work at the system level since each deals with just one community consisting respectively of large numbers of individual roles or of large numbers of dyads. And Durkheim's famous Table 5 in Unit 8—to which you should refer once again—succeeds in identifying roles within each of several identified systems by studying the individual correlation between religion and suicide within each of the countries separately.)

THEORETICALLY BASED TREND MODELS

The trend analyses in the drug study are especially interesting because the researchers set up alternative hypotheses as to the possible underlying processes, and then develop appropriate probability models as an aid to testing these hypotheses (compare the uses of alternative models in Units 8 and 9). Ogburn and Thomas also use models to interpret trends by fitting curves to the data on prosperity or on marriage rates, for example. Their curves, however, are simplified descriptions of empirical generalizations developed from the *data*. The models are not worked out in advance as an aid in testing a theory. By contrast, the curves in the drug study (Figures 3 and 4) are based upon *theoretical* assumptions. Here the investigators use the mathematical models to derive the curves that would be expected if their two sets of conceptual assumptions are correct—and then compare the expected curves with the data to see how well they fit. One curve is based on the assumption of a snowball process in which doctors learn through communication with one another. The probability formula translates the idea that the innovation is diffused through the social structure, with the early innovators first influencing their friends, the adoptions increasing rapidly as more and more doctors learn of the drug, until finally—within the boundaries of the structure—only the few die-hards remain to be converted (cf. Dodd). The alternative curve is based on the assumption of individualistic adoptions, in which doctors are uninfluenced by personal contacts, but respond directly to advertising and sales pressures.

When the researchers then compare the observed data with these alternative models, it turns out that the actual cumulative trend curves for two different types of doctors correspond respectively to these two models. That is, the researchers plot two separate curves—for the socially integrated doctors and for the isolated doctors (much as Sorokin plots separate curves for different classes within the society). And the result is that the shape of the adoption curve for the *integrated* doctors comes close, as one would predict from the theory, to the snowball process model, whereas the actual curve for the *isolated* doctors approximates the individualistic model. Such an analysis gives confidence in the original conceptions of the impact of personal influence upon those doctors "who were deeply embedded in their professional community."

Coleman, in his monograph on a number of different models used in the mathematical study of small groups, points out that theoretically based models are useful not only in testing hypotheses, but in the derivation of additional hypotheses which may subsequently be tested. Because the number of variables which may easily be handled mathematically at one time (through simultaneous equations) is restricted, however, the utility of mathematical models is somewhat limited (Coleman, 1960).

IDENTIFICATION OF DYADS AND ROLES

The trends in drug adoption seem to be explainable in terms of the models employed; the researchers, accordingly, proceed to investigate the underlying social-relational networks. Since the doctor's social integration appeared from the trend analysis to be important to his introduction of the drug, they want to discover how influence flows within the system. They first use *pairs of doctors* as the research case. And you have seen how they make use of an independence model of "random choices," and the interesting device of indexing the "simultaneity" with which one doctor and his sociometric colleague adopted the drug. Here the researchers are able to demonstrate especially high simultaneity for early adopters—thus manifesting the effect of interpersonal influence.

The researchers then carry this analysis to still another social system level, identifying the *roles* of different types of doctors within the *networks*. Each dyad is classified (in their Figure 8), not merely according to its (collective) index of simultaneity, but also in terms of the social integration of the individual doctors. The procedure at this point does not seem quite clear in the study; but Coleman says (in a personal communication) that "the pair was characterized by the isolation or integration of the chooser; this is not as good as if we had considered only pairs in which both were isolated or both integrated, but we would have lost too many cases that way." This analysis brings the researchers to the further finding that "the networks of doctor-to-doctor contact . . . show their effectiveness first among the more integrated doctors and only then among those who are less integrated in their medical community."

Thus the details of this design deserve careful study as one model of dynamic research (and also as an illustration of the many special devices required for the analysis of social system data; see the further discussion in Unit 12). The trends uncovered in the research are tied into the changing social-structural base from which they arise.

Use of Computers To Simulate Behavior

In addition to the drug study design, there are various types of studies which attempt a combined approach—which attempt to overcome the restrictions of trend studies alone or panel studies alone by observing the trends which connect the series of cross-sections. We have seen how the panel study of voting behavior added a supplementary *descriptive analysis* of the intervening processes. Unit 11 will suggest the highly systematic fashion in which the *experimental design,* in effect, examines process, in line with an hypothesis, by controlling the independent variable and the conditions under which it operates and then observing the consequences for the dependent variable. Still another type of study makes use of the rapidly developing high-speed *computers* (which are also used, of course, for other purposes, as in the analysis of cross-section studies).

Apart from their obvious utility in making cross-tabulations and computations with massive data (see, *e.g.,* Pool and Abelson), computers perform a function related to that of the mathematical model—with the added advantage that many more variables may be interrelated because of the high speed of computation. To make full use of these machines, the sociologist must be able (Step A) to state assumptions (for testing or further exploration) which include precise definitions (to which numerical values may be attached) of several relevant variables and their interrelationships. He must also have access to empirical data against which he can later (in Step C) compare the output of the machine in order to see how closely his assumptions fit the real situation. Only then does it become worthwhile to program the computer to produce this output—to determine the expected findings based on the assumptions (Step B). There are at present relatively few sociological topics—such as voting behavior (as in McPhee, or Coleman, 1961-a) or small group interaction (as outlined in advance by Bales, 1959)—on which these requirements for computer simulation can be approximated. The study by Hare outlines one early attempt.

HARE'S SIMULATION OF SMALL GROUP PREDICTIONS

As Hare makes plain, his work is part of Bales' comprehensive plan for an "interaction simulator" program which aims eventually to start with known personality characteristics of group members and an assigned discussion topic; the program will then make predictions—for subsequent testing against the interactions of real people—about who says what to whom (in the Bales categories) over a 40-minute period. The materials for this program build upon the store of Balesian theory and data, adding certain personality factors and value profiles derived from a series of factor analyses. In order for the machine to operate upon such materials, the program must be translated into a special machine "language" (just as in a simpler machine language, the countersorter is programed to sort and count the punch cards which represent the cases and their properties).

As Hare describes his own procedure (giving much of the flavor of the talk *about* computers), it corresponds to the steps in the use of mathematical models (as in Units 3 and 5 above)—except that many more variables may be used. He and his co-workers start with certain assumptions (corresponding to our Step A) about, first, the process by which each group member makes his own individual prediction about the responses of an unknown (but actual) student to a values question; and second, the process by which a prediction is finally agreed upon by the group. They then translate these assumptions into machine language and feed them into an I.B.M. 650, so that the machine (our Step B) can compute what predictions the individuals and the group would make if these assumptions about the process are correct. Then, as Step C, they test the predictions generated by the machine simulation against actual predictions made by real groups in the laboratory and against the actual answers of the student himself. Using twenty groups of five men each, they obtain 180 actual group predictions, for example, on a set of items. About two-thirds of these actual predictions correspond exactly with the predictions generated by the machine.

The researchers then proceed to use such results as a basis for improving their assumptions, for seeking additions to the model (such as finding a possible leader who is influencing group opinion), and for refining their mathematical statements of the prediction process.

Despite the rudimentary character of many such early studies—and warnings from varied sources that fruitful developments may occur slowly—the ultimate potential of the use of computers seems very great indeed. A constant restriction upon sociological research has been the difficulty of handling—in the practical operations of cross-tabulation, for example, or the verbal, statistical, or mathematical operations of analysis and interpretation—the large number of variables in their complex interrelationships which constitute even the simplest social system. This restriction has continually narrowed the research focus to few properties, to selected aspects of the case, or to limited time periods. There is reason to believe that imaginative use of these new technological developments may, perhaps, enable sociologists to widen the scope of their research and to synthesize the many partial findings (see, *e.g.,* Borko).

Some Methodological Implications

What implications for dynamic studies in general are suggested by these varied analyses? The panel analysis obviously inherits certain of its distinctive features from the cross-section study. And the cross-section study as a pure type, as discussed in Unit 8, might be characterized as follows:

1. It is made at a single point in time. In this sense, it is a static study—although the dynamic character of the system is recognized in the full conceptual model.
2. Its focus is chiefly on the *structure* of the system—on the patterns of system properties and the arrangement of system parts. (Of course, although the model typically assumes that each part contributes in certain ways to the ongoing process within the system, the research focus is not on this processual aspect.)

The *panel study* uses a single cross-section study as its base or starting point for subsequent cross-section studies of the same system, proceeding then to trace the changes and departures from this initial structure. Once a second study has been added to the first, it becomes possible, not only to repeat the full original analysis for the later data, but to compare the two states of the system, and to infer the processes which may have gone on in the interim. The characteristic features of the panel study can be listed as follows:

1. It is made at a series of points in time.
2. It is focused on *changes in the structure* of the system—on the shifting sets of patterns in the system properties and in the arrangements of system parts. (Turnover analysis seems feasible for two or three variables at two or three periods of time.)

The *trend study* is quite different from the other two types of studies. To illustrate this difference, let us use an analogy of an exploratory investigation of a gasoline engine by a person not trained in automotive engineering. The cross-section study might achieve a truly static picture by examining the engine while it is turned off. The panel study compares this static picture with another static picture by allowing the engine to run for a while after the first cross-section study, then re-examining the gasoline supply, *e.g.,* the temperature of the water, and the positions of pistons in the cylinders—and making inferences about the way the engine probably runs. The trend study, on the other hand, studies the engine only while it is running. Since the trend study, by definition, selects from the entire process, its focus might be on the coordinate operation of only two or three of the parts—perhaps discovering a certain synchronization between gasoline flow and the action of the spark plugs, for example. But this approach does not locate such partial processes within the total structure of the other parts of the engine. In a similar sense, then, the characteristic features of the trend study are:

1. The study is made, not at a few isolated points in time, but continually over time.
2. Its focus is chiefly on certain *selected processes,* rather than on the structure within which these processes occur.

Finally, the various combinations of panels and trend studies provide a *combined approach.* Here the investigator starts with the cross-section study, and only then attempts to observe the trends which develop out of the social structure and, in turn, react upon the structure. Such a combined approach might be defined as follows:

1. It combines cross-section studies at isolated points in time with certain continuous observations over time.
2. Like the panel study, it focuses on shifts in structure, but also, like the trend study, it focuses on the processes intervening.

Thus it succeeds in tying process into its social-structural base. Because of the complexity of such a combined approach, original designs may be needed to fit each particular research objective. Perhaps the increasing mastery of electronic computers will allow the development of special new designs for studies of social process and change.

SUGGESTED READINGS FOR UNIT TEN

Bales, 1959; Browning; Coleman, 1960; Dorn; Glick; Glock; Hagood and Price, Chapter 11; Hawley, 1959; Jaffe; Lazarsfeld and Rosenberg, pp. 203–12, 228–30; Moore, 1959; Ryder; Zeisel, Chapter 10.

QUESTIONS FOR REVIEW AND DISCUSSION

Review the following methodological terms as used in this Unit:

computer simulation
cross-section study
dynamic studies
equilibrium table
panel analysis
sample mortality
secular trend
standardization
trend study
turnover

1. The data for Exercise II-4 were obtained by questioning each respondent twice, at two different time periods. From your own experience in analyzing these data, what seem to be the methodological implications of questioning the *same* respondents twice, rather than questioning two comparable but *different* samples at two time periods?

2a. Compute the series of turnover tables which result in equilibrium in the study of friendship process. Start with Table 3 in that study and use the transition probabilities in Lazarsfeld's Appendix I. Test the notion of equilibrium by applying these probabilities again to your final table (which should be approximately the same as Lazarsfeld's Table 6 in his Appendix I).

b. What assumptions underlie such an equilibrium model, and how might the model help to test these in research?

3a. Compute the "chance frequencies" of the "random pairs" for a block of cells in the upper left-hand corner of Figure 5 in the drug study by Coleman, Katz, and Menzel. (Assume that the entire study was conducted in a single community.)

b. How would you state in words the meaning of such chance frequencies? What is their utility in research?

4. Analyze Table 1 of the drug study, stating exactly how the epsilons are calculated and used.

5. Compare in detail the trend analyses presented by Ogburn and Thomas and the two panel analyses presented by Lazarsfeld and his associates. State the advantages and limitations of each method.

6a. Study Table 3 in the study of friendship process, as the simplest example of Lazarsfeld's formalization. What conception of the group seems to be implied here? How do psychological processes or properties of the individual seem to fit into this conception?

b. Lazarsfeld's Table 3 may be thought of as a reduction of a more complete scheme, which utilizes more of the available information about the relationship between (1) liking another person or not, and (2) holding liberal or illiberal values. Can you draw a diagram of the full scheme? What kinds of information may be concealed by the reduction?

c. How would you resolve Lazarsfeld's dilemma (as he states it near the

end of his study) that his scheme for formal analysis of process in two-person groups does not take care of situations reported as "gratifying," "frustrating," and the like? Would the information obtainable from your answer to Question 6b be useful in solving this dilemma?

7. How does Bales handle "phase movement" in the study of interaction process?

8. Contrast the collective measures used by Bogue, Durkheim, and Ogburn and Thomas. What assumptions are made in developing and interpreting each of these measures?

9. Discuss the possible advantages and difficulties of using available data to study social process and change.

10. Suppose you were going to conduct a study of friendship process with objectives similar to those in the study by Lazarsfeld and Merton. Would you choose a descriptive method by which concepts are discursively analyzed or a formal procedure as suggested by Lazarsfeld? State your reasons, giving special attention to the handling of time as an element in the analysis.

11. Compare the analyses of dyads—in which each role is in some way identified—in the studies by Coleman, Katz, and Menzel, and by Lundberg and Lawsing.

12. What do Lazarsfeld, Berelson, and Gaudet learn from their use of control samples (or control groups)? What in general is the value of such control samples in a panel analysis?

13. Describe the relationship between the empirical phase and the interpretative phase in the study of trends by Ogburn and Thomas, on the one hand, and by Coleman, Katz, and Menzel, on the other hand.

UNIT ELEVEN
EXPERIMENTAL DESIGN

SUGGESTED PROGRAM OF STUDY

Rigorous designs for testing causal hypotheses are discussed in this Unit. In these designs, the investigator "experiments" by controlling systematically the independent variable as well as the extraneous variables.

Exercises and Manual

Since statistical tests of hypotheses are widely used, both in experiments and in cross-section studies, **Exercise V-3** will illustrate the nature of such tests, and show how tests fit into the research process.

You should review Step D in the use of mathematical models in Units 5 and 8, and reread Appendix D to the Stouffer study of conformity in Unit 6. **Manual V-C** gives instructions for some simple test procedures selected to exemplify the wide variety of tests available for particular purposes.

Studies

Analyze the studies by **Powers, Sherif, Homans,** and **Chapin** to see whether and how their objectives and research designs differ from the previous studies not classified as experiments. Consider in each instance how the investigator attempts to manipulate or control the experimental conditions in order to focus research attention directly upon the explanatory variables of immediate concern.

Commentary

The discussion outlines the classical experimental design and various possible elaborations as illustrated in these studies. It shows how the cross-section approach and other designs used in testing causal hypotheses may be viewed as modifications of the experimental design.

Questions for Review and Discussion

Consider carefully the advantages and disadvantages of experimentation in sociology today. State some specific research objectives for which an experimental design might be suitable, and then formulate and evaluate the design decisions and other considerations you would take into account in planning an experiment for each objective.

EDWIN POWERS
An Experiment in Prevention of Delinquency

Numerous statistical studies have demonstrated the close association of overt delinquent behavior with specific personal and environmental factors. Relatively few reports, however, have highlighted the effectiveness or ineffectiveness of methods of prevention. Such reports as have been written are generally based on nothing more than faith or bold assertion, buttressed by illustrative cases.

The Cambridge-Somerville Youth Study

Dr. Richard C. Cabot relatively early in life won a reputation in medical research as the "greatest contributor to cardiology in our generation." In his later years he was equally well known and respected in the fields of social service and social ethics. He was keenly aware of the discrepancy in method between the laboratory technician and the social scientist who seldom had available adequate measures of evaluation by which to check his practice. . . .

Dr. Cabot established a ten-year research project in delinquency prevention utilizing, perhaps for the first time in history, a carefully constructed control group.[1] To each of six men and four women, trained in social work or allied

professional fields, were assigned a number of boys, usually 30 to 35, all under the age of 12 (with an average age of $10\frac{1}{2}$), in the hope that by wise and friendly counsel supplemented by social case work techniques, these young children might be encouraged to make the most of their potential assets and become useful, law-abiding citizens. About half of the group were already showing definite signs that pointed to a delinquent career.

The plan called for an evaluation by comparing 325 T boys at the end of a contemplated ten-year program with a C-group[2] similar in numbers and in all other relevant respects but receiving no help or guidance from the study, the hypothesis being that if the two groups were similar at the outset, then any significant behavioral differences between

Reprinted in part from *The Annals of the American Academy of Political and Social Science, 261*, 1949, pp. 77, 78, 79, 80, 81, 82, 83, 84, 85–87, 88, with permission of The American Academy of Political and Social Science.

[1] This project, located in Cambridge, Massachusetts, was called the Cambridge-Somerville Youth Study, as it embraced in its operations the city of Cambridge and the adjacent city of Somerville. It was supported entirely by funds contributed by the Ella Lyman Cabot Foundation, a charity incorporated in Massachusetts in 1935. Dr. Richard C. Cabot and Dr. P. Sidney de Q. Cabot were the original codirectors of the project until the death of the former in May 1939, when Dr. P. Sidney de Q. Cabot became the sole director. On his resignation on January 1, 1941, the author became the director of the project until its termination. During the course of the treatment program a total of approximately 75 people were employed, half of them on a part-time schedule. Approximately 22,000 pages of records have been compiled relating the story of what happened in the lives of these boys over a crucial period of their existence.

[2] T and C in this article refer to the treatment and control groups.

them at the end of the program could reasonably be attributed to the major variable in the picture—the counselors' treatment.

Length of Program

Work was started at the end of 1937 with five selected boys. Seventy-one additional boys were placed in the program in 1938, and work with the remainder was commenced during the first half of 1939. After two or three experimental years, 65 boys, or 20 per cent of the total group, were dropped from the program because they presented no special problems and were definitely nondelinquent.

The remaining 260 boys, including both the delinquency-prone and the nondelinquent, were retained for varying periods of time. Death of a few, removal of some of the boys from the local area, the loss of staff due to the demands of World War II, and the departure of some of the older boys for war service or enlistment in the Merchant Marine made it impossible for the counselors to continue with all of the 260 boys. Close associations were maintained and case work continued with 113 boys for an average period of 4 years and 2 months; with 72 boys for an average of 5 years and 11 months; and with 75 boys for an average of 6 years and 9 months. For none did the treatment program, which closed on December 31, 1945, last more than 8 years and 1 month, although many of the counselors still keep in touch with the boys assigned to them.

The Experimental Design

As the project was essentially a study in the prevention of boy delinquency, it called for the selection of boys under 12 who had not yet become delinquent but who might some day constitute part of the prison population. . . . Secondly, it was necessary to balance this group of predelinquents with boys who showed no such signs of early delinquency, for one aspect of the project was to study a wide variety of boys and to note later what kind became delinquent and what kind did not. Furthermore, for practical reasons it was necessary to include a group of presumed nondelinquents, for to deal solely with boys who would be labeled "predelinquent" would be unfair to the boys and impractical of accomplishment.

Teachers in the Cambridge and Somerville public schools and the Cambridge parochial schools submitted on request the names of many boys whom they regarded as "difficult" (in the study's scheme this meant "probably predelinquent") and many others whom they considered normal or "average" boys. All referrals were subsequently classified in accordance with the delinquency prognostic scale as described below. Approximately 1,500 names of boys under 12 were submitted by the schools. At this point neither the boy nor his family knew that his name had been submitted.

Social agencies in the locality were also requested to submit names of "difficult" boys known to them. Court records were examined and police and probation officers were interviewed in order to include all boys in both cities who at an early age were considered troublesome or likely to become delinquent. From these supplementary sources 450 names (with some duplications) were received.

Thus, at the end of a two-year search, there were on file at the study the names of all boys in both cities (with the exception of boys attending the private schools or the Somerville parochial schools) who were believed destined to become delinquent, plus an equal number who were thought to be non-predelinquent.

How Each Boy Was Studied

A comprehensive picture of the boy, his family, and his social environment was obtained from a variety of sources. Social workers were sent to the homes for interviews with one or both of the boy's parents. Information concerning the boy's developmental history, his habits, his recreation, his attitudes toward school, his religion, and his personality was obtained and recorded. Basic information relating to the parents' education, employment history, social activities, and so on was also sought. The boy's potentialities as well as the total impact of forces upon him were described by the social workers with their own interpretations and numerous rating scales. Although they went to the boys' homes unannounced and without previous notification to the parents, they were, in most cases, cordially received. . . . In only eight cases out of 839 homes visited did the parents definitely refuse to be interviewed in the first instance.

Extensive information was then obtained from each boy's teacher through long personal interviews conducted by a member of the staff, supplemented by the checking by the teacher of rating scales and cards listing personality traits. The teacher was also asked to give a brief personality description of the boy.

Staff psychologists gave each boy tests to measure his mental ability and school achievement, and the boy's grade placement was recorded. Dr. Richard C. Cabot himself gave the physical examinations, noting at the same time the general impressions made upon him by the child. He was assisted by a staff nurse who independently recorded her own impressions and interviews with the boys. Official reports about delinquency or criminality of boys or parents were obtained from the State Board of Probation, from the local courts, and from the police and probation officers of the two cities, all of whom were very co-operative. Information was also obtained from those agencies listed in a central Social Service Index as acquainted with the families. The neighborhoods in which the boys lived were studied and rated in terms of the probable good or bad influences on a boy living in each locality. Delinquency "spot maps" constructed on the basis of a survey of all official court records for the two cities over a four-year period assisted in establishing the neighborhood ratings. A small school photograph of each boy was also available.

Separating Good from Bad Prognoses

The plan called for 650 boys to be divided equally into an experimental and a control group. Almost three times that number had been referred. A selection and screening process was necessary to assure the study a group of boys about equally balanced between the predelinquent and the non-predelinquent. The policy was adopted of not eliminating any boy who showed obvious predelinquent traits, provided he met the other necessary requirements of age, residence, and school attendance.

To determine which boys might reasonably be labeled predelinquent and which non-predelinquent was the next problem. Reliance could not be placed on the teachers' referral alone, for the teachers were not acquainted with the great variety of facts pertaining to the boy and his family that were available to the study. A committee of three individuals experienced in dealing with both youthful and adult delinquents made a thorough study of the comprehensive data assembled in each case, although they had no opportunity for personal interviews with the boys.

This committee consisted of one psychiatrist and two prison case workers. With a prognostic scale that ranged from plus five, indicating the greatest probability that the boy would *not* develop a delinquent career, through zero, the mid point, to minus five, indicating the greatest probability that the boy *would* develop a delinquent career, they were able to classify the 782 boys who had survived the preliminary screening process. Judgments of committee members were independently arrived at, group judgments being invoked in cases of initial disagreement. Thus, all 782 boys were finally scored on an eleven-point scale for probable delinquency.

Creation of Two Matched Groups

Out of the 782 cases available, two staff psychologists created two matched groups consisting of 325 boys each. A method of matching boy with boy, combining a statistical study of more than 100 relevant variables with a clinical interpretation of the personality as a whole, divided the 650 boys into two similar groups. Two boys were considered a well-matched pair if the configurational pattern of the most important variables showed them to be psychologically similar. A coin was tossed to determine which boy of a given pair was to be placed in the treatment group and which in the control group, thus eliminating any possible "constant error" after a pairing had been made.

The most important variables, in addition to age and prediction rating (which within each pair showed little, if any, variation), were health, intelligence and educational achievement, personality, family factors, and environment. Emphasis was placed on the relationship of the variables, on the profile or "contour" of the personality, rather than on the presence or absence of a large number of independent factors. It was subsequently found that the T-C group differences in the arithmetic means of 20 selected variables were extremely small—so small as to be almost negligible. Thus, the study was provided with controls that adequately served the purpose of comparing quantitative data later ascertained for each group.

The Treatment Program

The 325 T boys were then assigned to ten counselors. The younger boys, as a rule, were assigned to the four women counselors. During the course of the program nine additional counselors were engaged to meet the unanticipated turnover of personnel due to the war demands.

Treatment consisted of the application of whatever skills each counselor was capable of applying. The essence of the relationship between the boy and his counselor was personal intimacy and friendship. . . .

Each counselor was left largely to his own resources. . . . To social workers the "friendship" emphasis may have seemed old-fashioned and paternalistic; in practice, counselors were permitted and encouraged to utilize any of the modern techniques of social work with which they were familiar.

Although some counselors considered the job to be that of an orthodox social case worker, others did not. One counselor, for example, believed that genuine, personal friendship was of greater value to a boy than all the technical skills that a more objective social worker could bring to the case. . . . Others believed that the skill of the psychiatric social worker was indispensable in treating delinquency as a symptom of the boy's maladjustment. Certainly no one point of view prevailed, either as to therapy or as to the interpretation of the concepts used.

Attention was given to each boy individually. Many visits were made to his home and to his school. Group work was seldom used. Sometimes the boy was taken on trips or to the counselor's home, or (particularly in the later years of the study) to the office of the study for scheduled interviews with the counselor. Some boys were seen two or three times a week for long periods of time; most of them at less frequent intervals. An important feature of the program was its co-ordination with available resources and agencies in the community.

AREAS OF EMPHASIS

Treatment comprised a wide variety of activities. An analysis of the records at the end of the program showed that major emphasis had been placed on the boy's adjustment to school. The co-operation of the school officials was good throughout the history of the study. Counselors continually visited each school to seek information or to enlist the co-operative efforts of the teachers in treatment planning. Frequently it was important to interpret to the teachers the boy's difficulties and to acquaint them with the conditions in the boy's home which so frequently were unknown to them.

So many of the boys in trouble were retarded in school that the staff employed special tutors, who had had public school teaching experience, to give individual attention to 93 of the boys during or after school. Special attention was given to reading difficulties commonly found among retarded children.

Another area of treatment constantly receiving the attention of the counselors was the boy's health. The counselors arranged for more thoroughgoing physical examinations for the boys, and many of them were taken to clinics or hospitals or were treated by the staff pediatricians. For eight summers camping was made available through local camping associations or other youth organizations. Two hundred and four boys were sent to camps for two-week periods or longer. Counselors, too, frequently took the boys on overnight or week-end camping trips. They guided them to recreational opportunities and in some cases obtained for them scholarships or memberships in various organized youth groups. Boys were encouraged to develop their own religious ties.

The study initiated the placement of twenty-four boys in foster homes; sent ten to private schools, the expenses being underwritten by the study if the families could not meet all the costs. Much family case work was called for to gain the co-operation and understanding of the parents and to assist them in dealing with their own or their children's problems. In fact, the counselors realized that winning and retaining the friendship and confidence of the parents was essential. . . .

In brief, it can be said that the treatment program, utilizing some of the best professional advice obtainable, comprised an unusually wide diversity of special services to boys and their families, from removing nits from boys' heads (and their siblings' heads, too!) to preparing them for higher education.

Distinguishing Features of the Study

It is so unusual for one to carry on research with boys with whom one is at the same time attempting treatment that the project was faced with a number of unprecedented situations. As there has not been, to the writer's knowledge, any other research project comparable to the study, some of its unique aspects may be pointed out.

Aid Unsought. Boys receiving guidance from the study had not asked for it. The counselor's first visit to the boy and his family occasioned surprise in some cases, while in others it was taken as a matter of course, the assumption being that the counselor came from the school. Would a boy or his family profit by help if they were not motivated to seek it in the first place? The answer was "yes" and "no." Experience showed that in a few cases the offer of help was received with polite tolerance. In these instances case work was not possible. In a great majority of cases, however, a friendly relationship was very easily and early established. The personality of the worker seemed to be the determining factor. . . .

Not Linked to Special Need. The closing of a case did not follow upon the solution of a specific problem, as is usually true in social agencies. Most boys, in fact, had not been referred because of the existence of an acute problem. The case work relationship was, then, generally maintained beyond or in disregard of any special need, and in this respect was more akin to friendship than to conventional social work. The counselor stood by the boy "for better or for worse."

Before the Act. Most studies of delinquents are made only after a boy has been in court or committed to an institution. The study was in the unusual position of observing the development of delinquent behavior in boys who, when first known, were not overt delinquents and in some cases not even considered predelinquents.

Nonproblem Boys. The facilities of the study were not limited to those who were in need, but included a wide variety of boys, both "good" and "bad." The inclusion within the T group of boys whose problems were the normal problems of an average boy (or whose parents were adequate to meet any problem that arose) occasionally left the counselors in a state of confusion. It was frequently stated in case conferences that "the boys without problems are our greatest problems." Although there were obvious research advantages in including within the T group, for observation at least, all kinds of boys, the trained social workers were not eager to develop a relationship that seemed, from a professional point of view, to have no point. Nevertheless, the project probably would not have been able to develop good public relations if it had not included "all kinds of boys." However, 18.7 per cent of the "nonproblem" boys were carried through the entire treatment period.

Objectivity. Ordinarily, the very existence of an agency depends upon convincing a board of directors that its money has been well spent. Under such circumstances one is sometimes blinded to failure and is thus denied the benefit of searching self-criticism. The study, on the other hand, had ten years to go—and no longer—regardless of its effectiveness in preventing delinquency. It was trying to test, not to prove, the hypothesis that delinquency might be prevented by an intensive, enduring, personal, friendly relationship. It insisted only on doing what was best for the boy, on the keeping of accurate records, and on a fair evaluation. It is now in a position to give its first report on its successes and failures.

Did the C.S.Y.S. Prevent Delinquency?

Looking at the record at the end of the treatment program, *without reference to the C group,* the counselors could point to several very satisfying reports:

THE TREATMENT GROUP

1. There are 70 T boys who are now well past the age of 17 whose careers have been closely followed and who, as boys under 12, appeared to the predictors to be more likely than not to develop delinquent careers. That is, they had been rated on the "minus" side of the prediction scale. After these boys had been through the treatment program, not more than one-third (23 boys) committed serious or repeated delinquent acts, while 31 of them proved not to be delinquent at all.

2. There are 163 T boys who, when under 12, were rated on the "minus" side of the prediction scale as "probable" predelinquents. How many of these boys in the ensuing years committed delinquent acts that led to their commitment to a correctional institution? Inspection of the registers of the two Massachusetts correctional institutions for juveniles, the reformatory for older offenders and the House of Correction for the county in which Cambridge is located, shows that only 23 had been committed as of March 1, 1948. This rate, of 14.1 per cent, seems a surprisingly low figure in view of the fact that the study, it was believed, included practically all boys in the two cities, with a combined population of 213,000, who showed early signs of future delinquency.

3. Counselors' opinions were sought— an unusual research procedure, and yet who would be in a better position to know the effect of their own treatment on their own boys? Each counselor, dur-

ing the middle period of the program, was asked on three or four different occasions to list all T boys who he or she thought had been "substantially benefited by their contact with the study." Of the 255 boys then in the program, 166, or about two-thirds, were so listed. About half of the 166 were recorded by the counselors as having been "outstanding" in respect to benefit received.

4. Let us turn to the T boys themselves. They are much older now. They are in a position to look back upon their years of association with the study and to evaluate the experience with some insight. One hundred and twenty-five boys who in 1946 and 1947 were still in the Cambridge-Somerville area and who were available for a personal interview were questioned by special (nonstaff) investigators who had had no prior information about the study. The boys were asked direct questions concerning the part the study may have played in their lives. More than half (62 per cent) of this large, unselected sample stated that the study had been of value to them. Jim's declaration that "they helped me keep out of trouble" was typical of many of the replies. Henry summed up the impact of the study upon his life by saying, "I used to be backward but they snapped me out of it and got me interested in so many different things and finally I got to college."

By such evidence alone, one might reasonably conclude that the study had been successful in preventing delinquency. Many illustrative cases could be given to "prove" the point in the traditional manner. Such evaluation, though of the customary type, is inconclusive.

THE CONTROL GROUP

At the core of the plan was the *control group.* What had happened to boys who had received *no* help at all from the study during the years in question? Had they become delinquent with greater or less frequency and seriousness than the T boys? We now look at the record.

1. The records of the Crime Prevention Bureau, established in 1938 by the police department in the city of Cambridge, reveal some interesting facts relating to the T and C boys who lived in Cambridge. Practically all boys who are reported by citizens or officials for minor offenses come to the attention of this bureau. Some recorded offenses were relatively trivial, such as "upsetting bags of ashes" or "taking rope from a flagpole"; others were serious enough to be referred to the local court for disposition. Without differentiating degrees of seriousness, a tabulation of offenses from 1938 to 1945 (while treatment was in progress) lists the names of 267 T boys but only 246 C boys. It appears, at first sight, that treatment was ineffectual.

2. Two evaluations were made, also while treatment was in progress, by comparing samples of T boys with their paired controls. Comparisons of scores on a wide variety of tests, questionnaires, and rating scales pertaining to character, personality, social behavior, and achievements showed that while, as a general rule, the T boys excelled the C boys, the group differences were uniformly so small that they could be attributed to chance.

3. Studying the records of the 68 C boys who have passed the age of 17 and who were characterized as predelinquents in their early years (that is, they had been rated "minus" on the prediction scale in the same manner as the 70 T boys above referred to) but who were not subjected to the study program, we find that an almost equal proportion had refrained from serious delinquency. The record shows that 27, or 39.7 per cent, of the older C boys had become more or less

serious delinquents, compared to 23, or 32.9 per cent, of the comparable group of T boys. The difference of 6.8 per cent in favor of the T boys is obviously not great.

4. Taking the 165 C boys who had been predicted on the "minus" side (in the same manner as the 163 T boys above referred to), we find on an inspection of the registers of the same correctional institutions where we sought the names of our T boys, that 22, or 13.3 per cent, of the C boys had been committed for delinquent behavior—about 1 per cent *less* than the percentage of committed T boys.

5. A comparison can also be made of the frequency of delinquent offenses that brought the T or the C boy to the attention of the court (although court appearance may not have led to an institutional commitment). The State Board of Probation that compiles data recording the appearance of boys in any court of the state discloses the following facts:

Of the 325 T boys, 76 are listed as having a court appearance for a relatively serious offense, compared to 67 of the 325 C boys.

If we include minor offenses along with the serious, the score stands: 90 T boys, 85 C boys.[3]

First Conclusion

A T-C comparison of official records made within a few years after the termination of the treatment program shows that the special work of the counselors was no more effective than the usual forces

---

[3] By "minor offense" is meant: traffic violations, breaking glass, using profane language, hopping a ride on a streetcar, or the like. The Board of Probation records were cleared as of July 1, 1947.

in the community in preventing boys from committing delinquent acts.

The utilization of a control group thus casts a sharply revealing beam of light on the record. The effectiveness of the professional staff in preventing delinquency was clearly below anticipations, although it must be conceded that the difficulties of carrying out a well-planned and consistent program were considerable, in view of the impact of the war and the resulting turnover of personnel.

Before we conclude that the treatment program was completely ineffectual, let us look deeper. There is evidence to suggest that, given a further lapse of time, greater differences between T and C groups in the seriousness of official offenses may appear in favor of the T boys. It begins to look as though the C boys are the more serious and the more persistent offenders. We find, for example:

1. The Crime Prevention Bureau statistics show that the C boys are more frequently brought in for repeated violations.

2. The records of correctional institutions show that more C boys (8 in number) have been sent to more than one institution than T boys (4 in number).

3. Eight of the more serious offenders were committed to the Massachusetts Reformatory, an institution for older male criminals between the ages of 17 and 30. Seven of these were C boys.

4. Again, in comparing the number of boys who had committed more than four serious offenses (known to the authorities), we find the names of five T boys and nine C boys.

5. In a list of the 108 relatively serious offenses (arson, sex offenses, burglary, assault with a dangerous weapon, robbery, and manslaughter), 46 were committed by T boys, 62 by C boys.

Second Conclusion

Though the counselors were unable to stop the rapid advance of young boys into delinquency with any greater success than the usual deterrent forces in the community, some of the boys were evidently deflected from delinquent careers which, without the counselors' help, might have resulted in continued or more serious violations. Thus, the evidence seems to point to the fact that though the first stages of delinquency are not wholly averted when starting treatment at the 8-to-11-year level, the later and more serious stages are to some degree curtailed.

This conclusion must, of course, be subject to a further check at a later time.

These facts, based on group statistics, do not necessarily imply that the counselors were not helpful in individual cases. Furthermore, delinquency was not the whole story. The making of good citizens —"social adjustment" in the language of the social worker—was the broader objective on which the study was based. An examination of the records and interviews with the boys themselves offer evidence that in many cases, even in the lives of many of the delinquent boys, emotional conflicts were alleviated, practical problems were dealt with successfully and boys were given greater confidence to face life's problems.

MUZAFER SHERIF

A Preliminary Experimental Study of Inter-group Relations

This study of group relations was conducted in a camp in Northern Connecticut during the summer of 1949 with the active and generous backing of Professor Carl I. Hovland, chairman of the Department of Psychology, Yale University. It was carried out in the conviction that experimental study of the essential variables underlying group tension will contribute effectively to a more realistic approach to problems of inter-group tensions in actual life situations. The study represents an attempt to include within a single experimental design the study of in-group properties and of inter-group relations. The dominant idea in its conception was to create controlled situations which would make possible (1) the formation and functioning of in-groups, and (2) inter-group relations between these experimentally produced in-groups.

On the basis of lessons learned from the sociological and psychological study of the properties of small in-groups and functional relationships between in-groups, the following hypotheses were formulated:

1. When individuals having no established relationships are brought together in a group situation to interact in group activities with common goals, they produce a group structure with hierarchical positions and roles within it. The group

structure tends in time to generate by-products or *norms* peculiar to the group, such as common attitudes, positive in-group identifications, nicknames, catchwords, etc.

2. The second part of the hypothesis is related directly to inter-group relations. If two in-groups thus formed are brought into functional relationship, positive or negative out-group attitudes and appropriate friendly or hostile actions in relation to the out-group and its members will arise, depending upon the harmony or friction between the goals of the two groups. The testing of this hypothesis also involves in prototype form the process of the rise of group stereotypes. . . .

Subjects

In order to test these hypotheses, it was necessary to eliminate, insofar as possible, group formation and positive or negative relations between groups on the basis of background factors such as ethnic differences and differences in class, religion, education, age, sex, etc. In short, the subject had to be *homogeneous* in as many background and individual respects as possible.

Interviews were held with parents of prospective subjects in their homes and with the ministers of their church groups. Information sheets were filled in for each subject, including the relevant background material as well as the

Reprinted in part with permission of the publisher from John H. Rohrer and Muzafer Sherif, eds., *Social Psychology at the Crossroads,* copyright 1951 by Harper & Row, Publishers, Incorporated, pp. 397–406, 407, 408, 409, 410–19, 420–21.

subject's interests, play-group activities, school experiences, etc.

The possibility of grouping together on the basis of previous acquaintance was minimized by selecting subjects from different neighborhoods and towns of the New Haven area, such as West Haven and Hamden. There were thus no definitely established friendship bonds among the subjects.

Prior to the experiment, several tests were administered to the subjects by Professor Richard Wittenborn and Dr. Elmer Potter at the Yale Psychology Department. The tests were deliberately administered prior to the appearance of the subjects at the experimental situation. In order to prevent any suspicion on the part of the subjects that these tests would be related to observations of their behavior in the main experimental situation, the test administrators never appeared on the scene while the experiment was in progress. The tests given included an intelligence test, the Rosenzweig Picture-Frustration test, and selected pictures of the TAT.

In attempting to satisfy this criterion of *homogeneity* of subjects, we selected 24 boys of about twelve years of age, all coming from settled American families of the lower middle-class income group in the New Haven area. All of the boys were Protestants. In fact, 19 came from the same denomination, and the other 5 from highly similar denominations. The educational opportunities and backgrounds of the boys were similar. The group had a mean I.Q. of 104.8. All the boys might be called more or less "normal"; none were "behavior problems."

With these factors equated as much as possible, the kind of groupings, statuses within groups, and attitudes which were to be produced between groups could not be attributed to such cultural

and social background factors as ethnic, religious, or class differences, or to existing friendship bonds.

The possibility remained that the formation of a particular in-group might be determined chiefly by personal preferences or attractions among the boys, or by their common personal interests. It was necessary, therefore, to plan the experiment in such a way that the weight of personal preferences and interests and personality factors between the experimental groups could be neutralized.

Design and Procedure

Stage I was planned as the period of spontaneous groupings on the basis of personal inclinations and interests. All activities were camp-wide, with a maximum of freedom and "mixing up" of the boys in various games and camp duties. Thus, it became possible to ascertain budding friendship groups and, more or less, to equate the weight of personal factors in the two experimental groups of *Stage II*.

Stage II was designed as the *stage of in-group formation* of two experimental groups as similar in composition as possible. Each experimental group would participate separately in activities involving all of the members of the group. Activities were chosen on the basis of their motivational appeal and their involvement of the whole group. Different activities afforded varied situations in which all members of a group could find opportunity to participate and "shine." All rewards given in this stage were made on a group-unit basis, not to particular individuals.

Stage III was planned to study *intergroup relations* between the two experimental in-groups thus produced when brought into contact (a) in a series of competitive activities and situations, and (b) in mildly frustrating situations caused by one group to the other. The frustrating situations were arranged in such a way that the blame or responsibility for the frustration would be placed on the experimental groups and not on the adults in the situation. . . .

The experiment was conducted at an isolated camp site near the Massachusetts state line and lasted for eighteen days. The nearest town was eight miles away, and there was no bus service in the neighborhood; consequently there were no distractions from neighborhood soda fountains, movies, townspeople, etc. Neither boys nor staff members were permitted to have any visitors during the course of the study.

The site consisted of about 125 acres of land, largely hills and timber, with a stream suitable for swimming and fishing running through it. There were two bunk-houses, a mess hall, kitchen, infirmary, administration building, latrines, etc., and broad level areas for athletic events.

Before giving a more detailed description of the three stages of the experiment and the main results, it is necessary to emphasize the techniques of observation and the role of adults in the camp. Of course, it is well known that individuals behave differently when they know they are being observed or studied, especially by psychologists. The consideration cannot be "allowed for" or explained away. Therefore, all those associated with the study were strongly urged to prevent the boys' suspecting that their behavior was being observed or that various periods of camp activities were planned. The parents and boys were simply told that new methods in camping were being tried out.

The bulk of observational data was obtained by two participant observers who were graduate students. They acted as counselors to the two experimental groups. Each participant observer had the assistance of a junior counselor who was under his direct control and was instructed to follow his lead. Since the junior counselors were experienced in camping activities, the participant observers were comparatively free to observe their groups and to stay with them throughout the camp period. However, the participant observers were instructed not to make notes in the boys' presence unless the situation clearly called for writing something, such as a cabin discussion in which "minutes" could be taken down. Otherwise, the participant observers withdrew or surreptitiously jotted down short notes which they expanded each evening after their boys were asleep.

The other staff members, including an official camp director, activities director, and nurse, were instructed to perform their duties in the camp in strict accordance with the planned activities and stages. The specific demands of the experiment for the next day were discussed in detail each night after the boys' bedtime and after the main observations for the day were obtained from the participant observers.

As far as the boys were concerned, therefore, the situation was as natural and attractive as the usual summer-camp situation. For this reason, and to satisfy the criterion of homogeneity among subjects and staff members, the author appeared on the premises as a caretaker with the name of "Mr. Mussee." This gave me freedom to be at crucial places at crucial times doing odd jobs without attracting the boys' attention. In addition, it was sometimes possible to make naïve statements to the boys and ask naïve questions about matters which every other staff member was expected to know as a matter of course. For example, I usually pretended not to know what group a particular boy belonged to, and I was sometimes able to elicit information that might not have been easily available otherwise.

According to the participant observers and other staff members, who were instructed to watch carefully for any sign to the contrary, this role of caretaker was never suspected. . . .

In addition to observational data, charts of seating arrangements at meals, of bunk choices, of athletic teams chosen, of partners or buddies in various activities and situations were made for each day throughout the camp. A record was kept of all outgoing and incoming mail. Postcards were recorded.

One more point related to group technique is fundamental in understanding the results which will follow. This point concerns the counselors and other members of the staff. The counselors (i.e., participant observers) were in the camp primarily to observe. They and other staff members were *not* to be leaders in the usual sense at boys' camps. They were instructed, rather, to look after the safety of the boys, and to set things right if behavior went too far out of bounds. Neither the counselors nor the boy leaders were asked to exercise any particular kind of leadership technique, democratic or authoritarian. Nor was authority to be delegated or suggested to the boys by the staff members. The tendency to depart from the observance of these instructions on the part of any staff member was forcefully called to his attention so that it might be corrected. The boy leaders and their lieutenants emerged from the ranks of the two experimental groups in the course of group interaction, especially during the stage of in-group formation (i.e., Stage II).

The daily camp program was made up of the activities for which the boys themselves expressed preference. If a hike was scheduled, the boys were left to their own devices in organizing it. Of course, they were given tents, canteens, food, equipment, etc. as they asked for them and were given any necessary help. The boys were not preached to or organized from above to discuss among themselves the manner in which they would execute their activities. It was their affair and their discussion and their action. On the whole, the demands of the situations, not adult leadership, led the groups to discuss their affairs collectively. For example, the participant observer at one time gave his group a whole watermelon, leaving the division strictly to them. On another occasion, four large chocolate bars were given to each group of 12 boys as a reward in their collective Treasure Hunts. The ways in which the watermelon and chocolate were distributed were up to the boys.

Results

From this study, several types of data were obtained:

1. The main data related to group relations, that is, to in-group formation; the rise of group structure with relative positions and leader-follower relations; the development of in-group products, including in-group and out-group attitudes; and the development of intergroup tension, with rudimentary stereotypes and attitudes of prejudice.

2. Data were also collected concerning individual factors determining particular statuses and roles within the group. Groups are necessarily hierarchical, and it is such individual factors

which largely determine the position which each member occupies. For example, when we classify our data, it will be possible to relate intelligence and certain measures from the TAT and Rosenzweig Picture-Frustration test to statuses attained and behavior in the actual group situations.

3. Finally, a special study was made of two boys in the camp, one in each experimental group, who were lowest in their groups in participation in group activities and inconsistent in their identifications. From these data, we will develop some valuable hints for the study of *marginality* and *social isolates*.

Since the principal problem of the study concerns inter-group relations, our concern here will be only with those results most directly related to group relations. Within the limitations of this paper, we shall have to concentrate on the main trend in formation of in-group and inter-group relations without going into details other than those necessary to make this trend clear.

Stage I, which lasted three days, was the stage of "natural" groupings based on personal likes and dislikes and common interests. As mentioned before, the main purpose of Stage I was to rule out, or at least to minimize, the possibility of interpreting results of the experimentally induced in-group formations and inter-group relations of later stages on the basis of personal inclinations of the individual members for one another. Therefore, during Stage I, all of the 24 boys were put in one large bunkhouse.

It should be emphasized that the boys were free to select their own bunks, seats at meals, buddies for play activities, athletic teams, etc. All activities were camp-wide, i.e. potentially including all boys.

At this stage, an informal poll of preferred activities was taken with the promise that activities would be scheduled which the boys liked best. The main results of this poll were as follows:

Softball and hiking—20 choices each
Football—14 choices
Swimming—13 choices
Soccer—12 choices
Fishing—9 choices
Ping-pong—7 choices
Horseshoes and volleyball—5 choices each
A number of other activities were given choices of 4 or less.

At the end of Stage I, popularity ratings (sociograms) were obtained during informal interviews held on the pretext of getting suggestions for favored activities and for improving the camp. As other such studies have found, the sociograms showed the boys clustering in budding friendship groups of two, three, or four boys. These sociograms served as the most important criterion in assigning the boys to the two experimental groups for the period of experimental in-group formation of Stage II. In addition, the two experimental groups were equated in other respects insofar as possible without violating the requirements of the sociogram results. Chief among these other characteristics were size, strength, ability in games, intelligence and personality ratings previously made on the basis of the tests by Professor Wittenborn and Dr. Potter.

The division of the subjects into the two experimental groups was deliberately done to split the budding friendship groups which had developed. For example, if two boys showed preference for one another, one was put in one group and the other boy in the second group. If more than one friendship choice was made, we attempted to put the boy in that group holding the *fewest* of his friendship choices. Therefore, at the start of Stage II—the stage of experimental in-group formation—the number of friendship choices given to members of the experimental in-group was fewer than the number of friendship choices given to members of the experimental out-group.

Table **1** *Total choices of friends, end of Stage I*

	Choices received by:	
Choices made by:	Eventual Red Devils	Eventual Bull Dogs
Eventual Red Devils	35.1%	64.9%
Eventual Bull Dogs	65.0%	35.0%

One of these experimental groups came to be known as the Red Devils, the other as the Bull Dogs. Therefore, it will be helpful to refer to them by these names although at this point in the experiment the groups had existence only on paper. As Table 1 shows, of the total friendship choices made by boys who were to become Red Devils, only 35.1 percent were choices of other boys assigned to their group. The remainder, almost two-thirds, of the friendship choices made by future Red Devils were directed to boys who were placed in the Bull Dog group, that is, the out-group. Similarly, only 35 percent of the total friendship preferences of boys who were to become Bull Dogs were for other future Bull Dogs. Sixty-five percent of their friendship choices were for boys who were placed in the Red Devil group.

Stage II, which lasted five days, was the stage of experimental in-group formation. The subjects were divided into two groups as described. The groups lived in separate bunkhouses. As it happened, the Red Devils, as they were to be known, voted to remain in the old bunkhouse, while the Bull Dogs voted to move to the new bunkhouse.

It had been anticipated that this split into two groups might not be taken easily by some of the boys. In fact, one boy cried for ten minutes at his separation from another camper with whom he had struck up a friendship in the preceding days at camp. For this reason, immediately after the bunkhouse change was made, cars took each group separately from the camp for a hike and cook-out. . . .

During Stage II, the two experimental groups were separated as much as possible. They lived separately, ate at separate tables, served on K.P. on alternate days, and engaged separately in frequent hikes, overnight camping trips, etc. Swimming was scheduled separately for the two groups, and each very soon found their own special places some distance apart. One of these swimming places, the Bull Dogs', was secret from the other group.

Each group chose its own special hide-out in the woods in opposite directions from each other. When leaving their hide-out, one group devised an elaborate plan of departure in groups of 2 or 3 designed to camouflage the direction of their hide-out.

The activities of Stage II required that members of each group cooperate collectively in achieving their ends. In addition to hiking, overnight camping trips, and swimming, each group had a "Treasure Hunt" and engaged in group games such as fox and hounds, or bean toss, in which each member had to collect a certain number of beans to win a group reward. A small sum of money ($10.00) was given to each group to spend as they chose. Considerable group effort went to improving their cabins, stenciling insignia on T-shirts, making standards, etc. In addition, one of the groups sometimes chose to engage in craftwork, collecting wildlife, and the like. . . .

One of the major findings of the study in line with the hypothesis was the formation of a well-defined in-group organization or structure. By in-group structure is meant simply the development of relative hierarchical positions within the group unit ranging from highest to lowest position. In addition to evidence from the sociograms, the hierarchical roles were manifested in terms of successful or unsuccessful initiation of group activities, the greater or lesser responsibility taken in their planning and execution, the degree of adherence to the line of activity taken by the group, the source and effectiveness of group sanctions, etc. . . .

The Bull Dog group was . . . focalized around C.'s leadership. However, he did not lead in every situation. For example, he was not as good in athletic events or those requiring muscular skill as a boy named H. H. took over the lead in such situations with C.'s approval. However, C. would occasionally overrule a decision of H.'s in such a situation, telling him, for example, not to put in a substitute player in a game; and H. would comply. A third popular boy, E., was delegated authority by C. in other tasks, such as camping or hiking.

In some contrast to the Bull Dog group, the boy who became recognized as leader of the Red Devils, S., won his position chiefly by virtue of his daring, athletic skill, and "toughness." He is noted as successfully leading the group in games and in daring expeditions. He was overtly recognized as "the captain" by other Red Devils. Yet S. tended to be "cliquish," confining his favors and most of his attention on the whole to a few other boys high in status, and preferring to be with them. He sometimes enforced his decisions by threats or actual physical encounters. On some later occasion, he even encouraged and participated in an attack on two members low in status in his own group. For this reason, S.'s leadership position was sometimes shaky. In fact, on the basis of popularity ratings at the end of Stage II, another boy, L., received one more choice from the group than did S. . . . As it happened, S. retained power over his lieutenants, including L., and these boys in turn had effective and consistent influence over the rest of the group. It was the consensus of the staff that L. could have taken over the leadership of the group if he had wished to. For some reason, he remained subordinate to S. personally and in the group. S. once announced to the group: "My first successor is L." Later, at a time when his leadership was very shaky, he referred to L. as "the co-captain." Actually L. at no time asserted leadership over S. . . .

Along with the formation of a more or less definite group structure, with which we have dealt only sketchily here, each group developed strong in-group feelings of *loyalty* and *solidarity* within the group and of identification of varying degrees with its activities and products. This in-group identification is illustrated by the reaction of the in-groups to those members who continued to mingle with boys in the experimental out-groups several days after the division into two groups at the end of Stage I. For example, three members of the Red Devil group, all low in the status hierarchy, were branded as "traitors" and even threatened with beatings until they saw less of the boys with whom they had been friendly in Stage I and who became Bull Dogs. When one of the counselors returned from a necessary trip to the cabin of the other group, he was greeted with cries of "Traitor!"

Even the most retiring and ambivalent members were *at times* caught in the in-group. For example, one boy who was lowest in the Bull Dog group for participation, and was caught between loyalty to the group and waves of homesickness, was observed driving a long stick into a piece of red paper, saying, "That's what we'd do to the Red Devils."

An example of in-group identification is a boy's reference to his cabin as "home." He asked the boy leader if he had some equipment "at home." The leader asked, "Which home?" and the boy replied, "Our cabin, I mean."

Along with the group structure, products were standardized by the group, which in turn served to further solidify the in-groups. Obviously one example of such standardization was the names for the groups. The choice of these names was without doubt influenced by the larger setting—Bull Dogs, for example, being a symbol of Yale. Most of the boys were quickly given nicknames in their group. . . .

Each group came to prefer certain songs. In some of them they inserted their own group's name in a glorifying fashion and the names of the other group in a less complimentary way.

Both groups standardized methods of punishment. In the case of the Red Devils, as we have mentioned, sanctions were imposed by S., the leader, through threats or actual encounters. Wayward Bull Dogs, on the other hand, were kept in line with a system of sanctions suggested and always imposed by C., the leader. Although he once was observed verbally threatening a boy, C. relied on the method of sanctions rather consistently. A Bull Dog who got out of line, had to remove a certain number of heavy stones, usually ten, from the Bull

Dog Pond. This method started when the boys were improving their secret swimming place by damming it and removing rocks. They actually succeeded in raising the water level six inches.

One of the *crucial tests* of the study was whether or not these experimentally introduced in-group relationships would bring shifts or reversals in the friendship ties which began to form in Stage I on the basis of personal likes or affinities. At the end of Stage II, sociograms were obtained through informal talks with each boy. In obtaining these sociograms, it should be emphasized that the boys were free to mention those boys they liked to be with best *in the whole camp,* i.e., from the other group as well as their own.

The results indicating that such reversals were indeed found can be summarized as shown in the following table:

Table **2**   *Total choices of friends, end of Stage II*

	Choices received by:	
Choices made by:	Red Devils	Bull Dogs
Red Devils	95.0%	5.0%
Bull Dogs	12.3%	87.7%

For comparison purposes the reversals of friendship choices obtained at the end of Stage I, the stage of natural groupings, and at the end of Stage II, the stage of experimental in-group formation, are presented together in Table 3. It becomes sharply evident from this comparison that the friendship preferences of these boys were at first predominantly for members of the experimental out-groups. During Stage II, shifts in friendship choices occurred which were definitely in the direction of the members of the developing in-groups.

It is evident from these tables that after

Table **3** *Total choices of friends at the end of Stage I and end of Stage II, composite table* [a]

	Choices made by:	Choices received by:	
		Eventual in-group	Eventual out-group
End of Stage I	Eventual Red Devils	35.1%	64.9%
	Eventual Bull Dogs	35.0%	65.0%
End of Stage II	Red Devils	95.0%	5.0%
	Bull Dogs	87.7%	12.3%

[a] Note the reversals.

the stage of in-group formation was completed, the members of each experimental group predominantly preferred to associate with members of their own in-group.

Very briefly, we will summarize the results of Stage II. In line with the first part of our hypothesis, it was found that when the two experimentally produced groups were brought together in situations and activities calling for group coöperation toward common goals, an unmistakable in-group structure developed with hierarchical positions and roles within it. The structure was not static, changing with situations within certain limits. As the group formed, the members achieved positive in-group identifications and common attitudes toward the group. By-products or *norms* peculiar to the group were standardized —nicknames, catchwords, ways of doing things, sanctions, preferred songs, etc.

Before going on to the results of Stage III, the period of inter-group relations, it is necessary to emphasize one more finding of Stage II which is related to in-group formation and *specifically related to the cultural background of the subjects.* Along with the delineation of the "we" or in-group, the two experimental groups referred to the "they" or out-group frequently and in a

clear-cut way, even though there was comparatively little functional contact between the groups.

More than this, these groups of boys immediately and spontaneously began to make *comparisons,* not just in terms of "what *we* have or do, and what *they* have or do," but in terms of "their lousy cabin," "our pond is better," and even "those low kind." They began to express a desire to each other and to the staff to compete with the other group in games, with considerable assurance that their own group would win. In fact, on the second day of Stage II which followed the rather strenuous hike and cook-out for each group separately on the first day, signs of competitive attitudes between the two groups were mounting. The groups devoted a good share of this second day to the more leisurely activity of improving their respective bunkhouses and surroundings with the help of their counselors. During this activity, comparisons between the efforts of the groups cropped up and boundaries were drawn around the bunkhouse areas. The boundary questions led to disputes between some members of the two groups and some raiding of each other's cabins. This raiding was carried on in a rather playful and adventurous spirit and had the effect of intensifying the developing in-group demarcations. Since the main aim of Stage II was to produce in-group formations through coöperative group interaction rather than through opposition or competition in relation to an out-group, possible contact between the two experimental groups was further reduced during the following days of Stage II by keeping their activities farther apart through overnight hiking, swimming separately, and cook-outs in their respective hide-outs.

This rather strong desire to compete and the spontaneous derogation of the other group in *specific* respects probably *stems from the cultural background and specific socialization of these boys in a competitive society.* However, these instances of competitive feelings and, in some cases, of derogation, were *not* at this stage *standardized* in the sense that they were consistent modes of response to the out-group and its members. They were confined chiefly to the urgent desire to participate in the most attractive of all pastimes for American boys of this age—competition in sports. There was no consistent day-to-day tension or hostility between the groups at this stage.

In Stage III, the stage of inter-group relations which formally lasted nearly five days, the two experimental groups —each with varying degrees of in-group structure and strengthening friendships within the in-group—were brought into functional relationship with each other in competitive and mildly frustrating situations. The frustrating situations were planned in such a way that *on the whole* they seemed to one group to have been caused by the other.

At the beginning of Stage III, a series of competitive games was announced as though giving in to the boys' requests. The plan was for each group to receive a certain number of points or credits for winning athletic events during the coming days and for the excellence of performance in camp duties, such as cabin cleaning, K.P., etc. This point system, which was explained and given to each group orally and on typed sheets, was simple and clear. However, it allowed for some manipulation by the staff in the points given at cabin inspection, K.P., etc. It was possible, therefore, to keep the number of points attained by each group within a surmountable range until near the end of the contest, thus keeping up the strivings of both groups to win. For example, victory in athletic events brought about 15 points, whereas 1 to 10 points could be given for K.P. duties. Since such duties were performed separately, this manipulation did not arouse too much suspicion. The staff agreed that both sides were evenly matched in sports in terms of the size and skill of individual members.

A poster with two thermometers was placed on the bulletin board and the rising score of each group filled in. This poster became a center of attention for the competing groups. The prize to the winning group, which was displayed and much admired, was twelve four-bladed knives—one knife for each member of the winning group.

The effects of competitive games were not immediate. Observers all noted considerable "good sportsmanship" on the part of the two groups at the start. For example, after the first contest, the winning group spontaneously gave a cheer for the losers; and the losers, though still scattered around the field, responded as a group with a cheer for the winners. However, as the contest series progressed, this cheer changed. It started out as "2–4–6–8, who do we appreciate," followed by the name of the other team. It changed to "2–4–6–8, who do we appreci*hate.*"

Each day of Stage III began with a

Tug of War between the two groups. . . . In this contest, the group members organized themselves and exhorted each other in the intense common effort. As it happened, the Red Devils lost the first contest. Their reaction to the loss represents one of many *perceptual distortions occurring in the group situations*. . . . All Red Devils were convinced that the "ground was against us." They spent most of the morning discussing this and their strategy for the next Tug of War. The following day, this group was on the verge of winning the Tug of War when the Bull Dogs' leader began a series of shouts and encouragement to his boys. This apparently made possible a "second wind" in which the Bull Dogs regained their lost ground and finally defeated the Red Devils again. This time, the Red Devils rationalized their defeat by agreeing that the Bull Dogs "must have done something to the rope."

The series of games also included softball, soccer and touch football. These contests tended to solidify further the in-group structure and loyalty. For example, one of the Bull Dogs became ill and was unable to participate in one of the games. He and other members of his group cried. The boy who was ill said that if the Bull Dogs won the series, he would not accept a knife because he had "let them down." But the other boys shouted down this sacrifice, gave him a cheer, and loudly proclaimed that he was "one of them."

In the Red Devil group, one of the members low in status, a boy named F., revealed increasing identification with the group during this period. When the Red Devils were trailing the Bull Dogs with two outs, and no one on the bases, F. came to bat and was tagged out with a ground ball. He sobbed for some time and went off by himself, saying to a counselor, "I lost the game for us." He was almost afraid to show his face in the Red Devil cabin; but his group never mentioned the incident and were, in fact, kind to him. This incident typifies the manner in which *group efforts and goals* became intensely *personal* ones for the individual members.

As mentioned earlier, inter-group rivalry and hostility increased rapidly during the days of the competitive contest. During one game when the boys were becoming overheated, a staff member cautioned a Red Devil not to drink too much water, because he might get sick. At this, a Bull Dog called out in a nasty tone, "Let him drink all he can. He's a Red Devil." Such expressions of hostility became increasingly frequent.

As the contest progressed, the Bull Dog group pulled out in the lead, probably because of their highly effective organization directed by C. and, in athletic events, led by H. The Red Devils responded to their increasingly apparent losing position by labeling the Bull Dogs as "dirty players." They were sure that they could win if the Bull Dogs were not "such cheaters." They said, "At least we play fair." By the contest's end, the words "dirty players" and "cheats" were almost synonymous with Bull Dogs as far as the Red Devils were concerned. Of course, the Bull Dogs denied such charges and even recognized the role of their more integrated group structure in their performance with such remarks as "We win because we have an organization."

The cumulative effect of the competitive games caused considerable group friction and, to the Red Devils, considerable frustration. The common expression of the winning Bull Dogs and the losing Red Devils in pictures taken immediately following the victory of the Bull Dogs in the athletic series convey an objective glimpse of this fact.

The winning Bull Dogs were tremendously elated at their victory. The reward of knives was distributed by C.'s suggested method—each boy was blindfolded and chose a knife from a bucket. Thus, not even the high-status members had advantage in choosing preferred colors, etc.

The losing group, the Red Devils, was by this time weakened. In their case, the group failure was conducive to disintegration. S., the leader and athletic captain, was bitter and began blaming and ridiculing members of his own group. At the same time he retired more and more to the company of his lieutenants. This was resented by Red Devils lower in status. Until the Red Devil group experienced an attack from the Bull Dogs and even fought with them at a later time, there was considerable disorganization.

In addition to this competition in Stage III, there were also arranged situations in which it seemed that one group interfered with or frustrated the other. Several such incidents were planned by the staff, but they could not all be carried out because of the extreme effectiveness of the first ones. The examples given were carefully recorded and, with the background of the two crystallized but hostile in-groups, constitute a little experiment in themselves. Unfortunately, many fascinating details must be omitted in this presentation.

On the evening of the victory of the Bull Dogs over the Red Devils in the athletic series and camp competition, both groups were asked to attend a party in the mess hall. By careful timing and by indirectly interesting one group in something else momentarily, the participant observers were able to see to it that the Red Devils got to the mess hall a short time before the Bull Dogs. None of the subjects in either group suspected that this timing was deliberate.

The refreshments of ice cream, cake, etc. were on a table. Half of them had been battered, broken, or crushed; the other half remained whole and delectable. When the first group (the Red Devils) arrived, they were told to go ahead and take their share of the refreshments, leaving half of it for the Bull Dogs, who were late. As we know, the Red Devils were the defeated group and had expressed in no uncertain terms their frustration and envy of the Bull Dogs for winning the prize.

Faced with the refreshments, half fresh and appetizing and half broken and crushed, the Red Devils chose the good portion and carried it to their own table. At this point the Bull Dogs arrived. Upon seeing the sorry-looking refreshments left for them, and the feasting Red Devils, they immediately protested by sulking and by remarks of hostility against the Red Devils. The Red Devils were quick to justify their actions in terms of "first come, first served," which became the standardized justification for all Red Devil members.

The Bull Dogs discussed the possibility of throwing their beaten-up cake at the Red Devils, but decided against it on the grounds that, after all, it would taste good. They went to the far corner of the mess hall and proceeded to hurl insults and names at the Red Devils. The names were by now standardized, among them being "dirty bums," "rotten jerks," "pukes," and several more objectionable terms.

The Red Devils ate their refreshments in righteous indignation, referring to the Bull Dogs as "dirty players," "cheats," etc. The most vociferous Red Devils were four boys at the bottom status level in their group. The leaders remained more sullen and resentful to the "unjustified" attack. L., the leader's chief lieutenant, told the group to "ignore it."

When they finished, the Red Devils left the mess hall, but one of the stragglers caught sight of the Bull Dogs dumping their dirty plates and ice cream cartons on the Red Devil table. He became involved in a physical altercation which was stopped by the counselor when one Bull Dog pulled out his knife, opened the blade, and had to be restrained from brandishing it.

This event, which the Bull Dogs saw as the doings of the Red Devils, set off a series of raids and fights which soon had to be stopped by all means. The next morning, the Red Devils deliberately dirtied up their table at breakfast to make the clean-up work hard for the Bull Dogs, who were on K.P. that day. When the Bull Dogs saw the messy table, they decided to mess up the table further and leave it. C., their leader, was against this action, but the group went ahead and he joined in. They smeared the table with cocoa, sugar, syrup, etc., and left it. It was soon alive with bees and wasps. The group hung the walls with threatening and derogatory posters against the Red Devils.

The upshot of this was that at lunch that day the two groups lined up across the mess hall from each other and began to fight—shouting, throwing knives, cups, etc., and becoming so excited that intervention became necessary.

No one of either group knew who started the fight. Each was sure it was someone in the other group.

At this point, it was quickly decided by the staff to stop Stage III of the experiment immediately and to concentrate on breaking down the in-groups. The decision was to stop the intense inter-group conflict by any means necessary and then to initiate a camp program in which all boys would participate on a camp-wide basis. The experiment, from

the point of view of controlling the situation, was over at this point. There was no systematic attempt at integration after Stage III. The instructions to all the staff members were to do away with the hostility as much as possible in order to send everyone home feeling good. In this period, a great deal of information and significant leads were gained for the future study of integration of hostile groups and elimination of hostility, which is certainly the pressing problem to be tackled.

In spite of the genuine efforts of the participant observers and junior counselors to stop the fighting, the acts and words of hostility continued. . . .

The degree of hostility between the two groups can be clearly seen in the posters which were made by the boys and hung in the mess hall and in each others' cabins. These posters were made in every case by boys low in status in their respective groups. This, along with other evidence which has been touched upon, suggests that manifestations of inter-group hostility and rivalry of group members low in status may at times be more intense than the manifestations of members higher in status. It seems likely that the members low in status, having greater strivings for status within the group, may go to greater lengths in trying to gain recognition by showing their identification and loyalty to the in-group. . . .

In brief, the consequences of the inter-group relations in competitive situations and in frustrating situations which members of one group perceived as coming from the other group were: (1) to solidify the in-group belongingness and solidarity, to enhance in-group democracy, and to strengthen in-group friendships; (2) to generate and increase out-group hostility, to produce derogatory *name-calling* which came close to standardizing of negative stereotypes in relation to the out-group (i.e., *rudiments of prejudice*).

Thus we see in a concrete way that in-group democracy and coöperation does not necessarily mean democracy and coöperation with the out-group and its members, if the directions and interests of the groups are in conflict.

In dealing with inter-group relations, the vital interests and directions of the groups in their day-to-day living have to be given their due weights. The attempts to bring people into contact in a group situation and to change their perceptions and attitudes without giving proper weight to the *vital interests* of group members is hardly more than playing with shadows. *The facts of structuring and re-structuring perceptions and attitudes are not arbitrary affairs.* They are organically related to the motives sanctioned and regulated by actual group memberships.

It is not possible here to deal at any length with other aftermaths of this experiment. After Stage III, the boys were brought together once more. Their tables were separated so that all boys would "mix up," and they were encouraged to do so by the counselors. With some persuasion, the groups attended birthday parties, camp fires, and other activities together. Individual competitions, track meets, a stunt night, etc. were held.

Probably the most effective event for the breaking up of the in-groups was a camp-wide softball game in which a team chosen by the boys from the entire camp competed with an outside group of boys from the neighboring town. In this, the boys participated *as campers*, not as in-group members. However, it should be recognized that any future experiment designed to study the process of integration between two such hostile in-groups should hardly be started by uniting the in-groups against still another in-group.

The postexperimental period did relieve a good deal of the generated tension, in that there were no more collective fights. However, the evidences of the in-group lines developed during the experimental period were observed on subsequent days. Seating arrangements, friendship preferences, etc. continued to follow group lines on the whole. On the last night of camp, the boys of the two experimental groups insisted that they wanted separate campfires because they wanted to be "by themselves" for the last time. In spite of their mixing, the old names and songs for the opposite group cropped up occasionally at these gatherings.

GEORGE CASPAR HOMANS
Group Factors in Worker Productivity

In April, 1927, six girls were selected from a large shop department of the Hawthorne works. They were chosen as

Reprinted in part from George Caspar Homans, "Group Factors in Worker Productivity," in Committee on Work in Industry of the National Research Council, *Fatigue of Workers: Its Relation to Industrial Pro-*

average workers, neither inexperienced nor expert, and their work consisted of the assembling of telephone relays. A coil, armature, contact springs, and in-

duction, New York: Reinhold Publishing Corp., 1941, pp. 58–62, 63–65, 77, 78, 79, 80–82, 85–86, with permission of Reinhold Publishing Corp.

sulators were put together on a fixture and secured in position by means of four machine screws. The operation at that time was being completed at the rate of about five relays in six minutes. This particular operation was chosen for the experiment because the relays were being assembled often enough so that even slight changes in output rate would show themselves at once on the output record. Five of the girls were to do the actual assembly work; the duty of the sixth was to keep the others supplied with parts.

The test room itself was an area divided from the main department by a wooden partition eight feet high. The girls sat in a row on one side of a long workbench. The bench and assembly equipment were identical with those used in the regular department, except in one respect. At the right of each girl's place was a hole in the bench, and into this hole she dropped completed relays. It was the entrance to a chute, in which there was a flapper gate opened by the relay in its passage downward. The opening of the gate closed an electrical circuit which controlled a perforating device, and this in turn recorded the completion of the relay by punching a hole in a tape. The tape moved at the rate of one-quarter of an inch a minute and had space for a separate row of holes for each operator. When punched, it thus constituted a complete output record for each girl for each instant of the day. Such records were kept for five years.

In this experiment, then, as in the earlier illumination experiments, great emphasis was laid on the rate of output. A word of caution is needed here. The Western Electric Company was not immediately interested in increasing output. The experiments were not designed for that purpose. On the other hand, output is easily measured, i.e., it yields

precise quantitative data, and experience suggested that it was sensitive to at least some of the conditions under which the employees worked. Output was treated as an index. In short, the nature of the experimental conditions made the emphasis on output inevitable.

From their experience in the illumination experiments, the investigators were well aware that factors other than those experimentally varied might affect the output rate. Therefore arrangements were made that a number of other records should be kept. Unsuitable parts supplied by the firm were noted down, as were assemblies rejected for any reason upon inspection. In this way the type of defect could be known and related to the time of day at which it occurred. Records were kept of weather conditions in general and of temperature and humidity in the test room. Every six weeks each operator was given a medical examination by the company doctor. Every day she was asked to tell how many hours she had spent in bed the night before and, during a part of the experiment, what food she had eaten. Besides all these records, which concerned the physical condition of the operators, a log was kept in which were recorded the principal events in the test room hour by hour, including among the entries snatches of conversation between the workers. At first these entries related largely to the physical condition of the operators: how they felt as they worked. Later the ground they covered somewhat widened, and the log ultimately became one of the most important of the test room records. Finally, when the so-called Interviewing Program was instituted at Hawthorne, each of the operators was interviewed several times by an experienced interviewer.

The girls had no supervisor in the ordinary sense, such as they would have had in a regular shop department, but a "test room observer" was placed in the room, whose duty it was to maintain the records, arrange the work, and secure a cooperative spirit on the part of the girls. Later, when the complexity of his work increased, several assistants were assigned to help him.

When the arrangements had been made for the test room, the operators who had been chosen to take part were called in for an interview in the office of the superintendent of the Inspection Branch, who was in general charge of the experiment and of the researches which grew out of it. The superintendent described this interview as follows: "The nature of the test was carefully explained to these girls and they readily consented to take part in it, although they were very shy at the first conference. An invitation to six shop girls to come up to a superintendent's office was naturally rather startling. They were assured that the object of the test was to determine the effect of certain changes in working conditions, such as rest periods, midmorning lunches, and shorter working hours. They were expressly cautioned to work at a comfortable pace, and under no circumstances to try and make a race out of the test." This conference was only the first of many. Whenever any experimental change was planned, the girls were called in, the purpose of the change was explained to them, and their comments were requested. Certain suggested changes which did not meet with their approval were abandoned. They were repeatedly asked, as they were asked in the first interview, not to strain but to work "as they felt."

The experiment was now ready to begin. Put in its simplest terms, the idea of those directing the experiment was that if an output curve was studied for a long enough time under various changes in working conditions, it would be pos-

sible to determine which conditions were the most satisfactory. Accordingly, a number of so-called "experimental periods" were arranged. For two weeks before the operators were placed in the test room, a record was kept of the production of each one without her knowledge. In this way the investigators secured a measure of her productive ability while working in the regular department under the usual conditions. This constituted the first experimental period. And for five weeks after the girls entered the test room no change was made in working conditions. Hours remained what they had been before. The investigators felt that this period would be long enough to reveal any changes in output incidental merely to the transfer. This constituted the second experimental period.

The third period involved a change in the method of payment. In the regular department, the girls had been paid according to a scheme of group piecework, the group consisting of a hundred or more employees. Under these circumstances, variations in an individual's total output would not be immediately reflected in her pay, since such variations tended to cancel one another in such a large group. In the test room, the six operators were made a group by themselves. In this way each girl received an amount more nearly in proportion to her individual effort, and her interests became more closely centered on the experiment. Eight weeks later, the directly experimental changes began. An outline will reveal their general character: Period IV: two rest pauses, each five minutes in length, were established, one occurring in midmorning and the other in the early afternoon. Period V: these rest pauses were lengthened to ten minutes each. Period VI: six five-minute rests were established. Period

VII: the company provided each member of the group with a light lunch in the midmorning and another in the midafternoon, accompanied by rest pauses. This arrangement became standard for subsequent Periods VIII through XI. Period VIII: work stopped a half-hour earlier every day—at 4:30 P.M. Period IX: work stopped at 4 P.M. Period X: conditions returned to what they were in Period VII. Period XI: a five-day work week was established. Each of these experimental periods lasted several weeks.

Period XI ran through the summer of 1928, a year after the beginning of the experiment. Already the results were not what had been expected. The output curve, which had risen on the whole slowly and steadily throughout the year, was obviously reflecting something other than the responses of the group to the imposed experimental conditions. Even when the total weekly output had fallen off, as it could hardly fail to do in such a period as Period XI, when the group was working only five days a week, daily output continued to rise. Therefore, in accordance with a sound experimental procedure, as a control on what had been done, it was agreed with the consent of the operators that in experimental Period XII a return should be made to the original conditions of work, with no rest pauses, no special lunches, and a full-length working week. This period lasted for twelve weeks. Both daily and weekly output rose to a higher point than ever before: the working day and the working week were both longer. The hourly output rate declined somewhat but it did not approach the level of Period III, when similar conditions were in effect.

The conclusions reached after Period XII may be expressed in terms of another observation. Identical conditions of work were repeated in three different experimental periods: Periods VII, X, and XIII. If the assumptions on which the study was based had been correct, that is to say, if the output rate were directly related to the physical conditions of work, the expectation would be that in these three experimental periods there would be some similarity in output. Such was not the case. The only apparent uniformity was that in each experimental period output was higher than in the preceding one. In the Relay Assembly Test Room, as in the previous illumination experiments, something was happening which could not be explained by the experimentally controlled conditions of work.

The question remains:

With what facts, if any, can the changes in the output rate of the operators in the test room be correlated? Here the statements of the girls themselves are of the first importance. Each girl knew that she was producing more in the test room than she ever had in the regular department, and each said that the increase had come about without any conscious effort on her part. It seemed easier to produce at the faster rate in the test room than at the slower rate in the regular department. When questioned further, each girl stated her reasons in slightly different words, but there was uniformity in the answers in two respects. First, the girls liked to work in the test room; "it was fun." Secondly, the new supervisory relation or, as they put it, the absence of the old supervisory control, made it possible for them to work freely without anxiety.

For instance, there was the matter of conversation. In the regular department, conversation was in principle not allowed. In practice it was tolerated if it was carried on in a low tone and did not interfere with work. In the test room an effort was made in the beginning to discourage conversation, though it was soon abandoned. The observer in charge of the experiment was afraid of losing the cooperation of the girls if he insisted too strongly on this point. Talk became common and was often loud and general. Indeed, the conversation of the operators came to occupy an important place in the log. T. N. Whitehead has pointed out that the girls in the test room were far more thoroughly supervised than they ever had been in the regular department. They were watched by an observer of their own, an interested management, and outside experts. The point is that the character and purpose of the supervision were different and were felt to be so.

The operators knew that they were taking part in what was considered an important and interesting experiment. They knew that their work was expected to produce results—they were not sure what results—which would lead to the improvement of the working conditions of their fellow employees. They knew that the eyes of the company were upon them. Whitehead has further pointed out that although the experimental changes might turn out to have no physical significance, their social significance was always favorable. They showed that the management of the company was still interested, that the girls were still part of a valuable piece of research. In the regular department, the girls, like the other employees, were in the position of responding to changes the source and purpose of which were beyond their knowledge. In the test room, they had frequent interviews with the superintendent, a high officer of the company. The reasons for the contemplated experimental changes were explained to them. Their views were consulted and in some instances they were allowed to veto what had been proposed.

Professor Mayo has argued that it is idle to speak of an experimental period like Period XII as being in any sense what it purported to be—a return to the original conditions of work. In the meantime, the entire industrial situation of the girls had been reconstructed.

Another factor in what occurred can only be spoken of as the social development of the group itself. When the girls went for the first time to be given a physical examination by the company doctor, someone suggested as a joke that ice cream and cake ought to be served. The company provided them at the next examination, and the custom was kept up for the duration of the experiment. When one of the girls had a birthday, each of the others would bring her a present, and she would respond by offering the group a box of chocolates. Often one of the girls would have some good reason for feeling tired. Then the others would "carry" her. That is, they would agree to work especially fast to make up for the low output expected from her. It is doubtful whether this "carrying" did have any effect, but the important point is the existence of the practice, not its effectiveness. The girls made friends in the test room and went together socially after hours. One of the interesting facts which has appeared from Whitehead's analysis of the output records is that there were times when variations in the output rates of two friends were correlated to a high degree. Their rates varied simultaneously and in the same direction—something, of course, which the girls were not aware of and could not have planned. Also, these correlations were destroyed by such apparently trivial events as a change in the order in which the girls sat at the workbench.

Finally, the group developed leadership and a common purpose. The leader, self-appointed, was an ambitious young

Italian girl who entered the test room as a replacement after two of the original members had left. She saw in the experiment a chance for personal distinction and advancement. The common purpose was an increase in the output rate. The girls had been told in the beginning and repeatedly thereafter that they were to work without straining, without trying to make a race of the test, and all the evidence shows that they kept this rule. In fact, they felt that they were working under less pressure than in the regular department. Nevertheless, they knew that the output record was considered the most important of the records of the experiment and was always closely scrutinized. Before long they had committed themselves to a continuous increase in production. In the long run, of course, this ideal was an impossible one, and when the girls found out that it was, the realization was an important element of the change of tone which was noticeable in the second half of the experiment. But for a time they felt that they could achieve the impossible. In brief, the increase in the output rate of the girls in the Relay Assembly Test Room could not be related to any changes in their physical conditions of work, whether experimentally induced or not. It could, however, be related to what can only be spoken of as the development of an organized social group in a peculiar and effective relation with its supervisors. . . .

In order to study this kind of problem further, to make a more detailed investigation of social relations in a working group, and to supplement interview material with direct observation of the behavior of employees, the Division of Industrial Research decided to set up a new test room. But the investigators remembered what happened in the former test room and tried to devise an experiment which would not be radically al-

tered by the process of experimentation itself. They chose a group of men—nine wiremen, three soldermen, and two inspectors—engaged in the assembly of terminal banks for use in telephone exchanges, took them out of their regular department and placed them in a special room. Otherwise no change was made in their conditions of work, except than an investigator was installed in the room, whose duty was simply to observe the behavior of the men. In the Relay Assembly Test Room a log had been kept of the principal events of the test. At the beginning it consisted largely of comments made by the workers in answer to questions about their physical condition. Later it came to include a much wider range of entries, which were found to be extremely useful in interpreting the changes in the output rate of the different workers. The work of the observer in the new test room was in effect an expansion of the work of keeping the log in the old one. Finally, an interviewer was assigned to the test room; he was not, however, one of the population of the room but remained outside and interviewed the employees from time to time in the usual manner. No effort was made to get output records other than the ones ordinarily kept in the department from which the group came, since the investigators felt that such a procedure would introduce too large a change from a regular shop situation. In this way the experiment was set up which is referred to as the Bank Wiring Observation Room. It was in existence seven months, from November 1931 to May 1932.

The method of payment is the first aspect of this group which must be described. It was a complicated form of group piecework. . . .

An individual's earnings would be affected by changes in his rate or in his output and by changes in the output of the group as a whole. The only way in which the group as a whole could increase its earnings was by increasing its total output.... The experts who designed the system made certain implicit assumptions about the behavior of human beings, or at least the behavior of workers in a large American factory. They assumed that every employee would pursue his economic interest by trying to increase not only his own output but the output of every other person in the group. The group as a whole would act to prevent slacking by any of its members. One possibility, for instance, was that by a few weeks' hard work an employee could establish a high rate for himself. Then he could slack up and be paid out of all proportion with the amount he actually contributed to the wages of the group. Under these circumstances, the other employees were expected to bring pressure to bear to make him work harder.

Such was the way in which the wage incentive scheme ought to have worked. The next question is how it actually did work. At first the workers were naturally suspicious of the observer, but when they got used to him and and found that nothing out of the ordinary happened as a result of his presence in the room, they came to take him for granted. The best evidence that the employees were not distrustful of the observer is that they were willing to talk freely to him about what they were doing, even when what they were doing was not strictly in accord with what the company expected. Conversation would die down when the group chief entered the room, and when the foreman or the assistant foreman entered everyone became serious. But no embarrassment was felt at the presence of the observer. To avoid misunderstanding, it is important to point out that the observer

was in no sense a spy. The employees were deliberately and obviously separated from their regular department. The observer did not, and could not, pass himself off as one of them. And if only from the fact that a special interviewer was assigned to them, the members of the group knew they were under investigation.

The findings reached by the observer were more detailed but in general character the same as those which had emerged from the early interviews of other groups. Among the employees in the observation room there was a notion of a proper day's work. They felt that if they had wired two equipments a day they had done about the right amount. Most of the work was done in the morning. As soon as the employees felt sure of being able to finish what they considered enough for the day, they slacked off. This slacking off was naturally more marked among the faster than among the slower workmen.

As a result, the output graph from week to week tended to be a straight line.... At the end of the day, the observer would make an actual count of the number of connections wired—something which was not done by the supervisors—and he found that the men would report to the group chief sometimes more and sometimes less work than they actually had accomplished. At the end of the period of observation, two men had completed more than they ever had reported, but on the whole the error was in the opposite direction. The theory of the employees was that excess work produced on one day should be saved and applied to a deficiency on another day....

The findings of the observer were confirmed by tests which were made as a part of the investigation. Tests of intelligence, finger dexterity, and other skills were given to the workers in the room, and the results of the tests were studied in order to discover whether there was any correlation between output on the one hand and earnings, intelligence, or finger dexterity on the other. The studies showed that there was not. The output was apparently not reflecting the native intelligence or dexterity of the members of the group.

Obviously the wage incentive scheme was not working in the way it was expected to work. The next question is why it was not working. In this connection, the observer reported that the group had developed an informal social organization, such as had been revealed by earlier investigations. The foreman who selected the employees taking part in the Bank Wiring Observation Room was cooperative and had worked with the investigators before. They asked him to produce a normal group. The men he chose all came out of the same regular shop department, but they had not been closely associated in their work there. Nevertheless, as soon as they were thrown together in the observation, friendships sprang up and soon two well-defined cliques were formed. The division into cliques showed itself in a number of ways: in mutual exclusiveness, in differences in the games played during off-hours, and so forth.

What is important here is not what divided the men in the observation room but what they had in common. They shared a common body of sentiments. A person should not turn out too much work. If he did, he was a "rate-buster." The theory was that if an excessive amount of work was turned out, the management would lower the piecework rate so that the employees would be in the position of doing more work for approximately the same pay. On the other hand, a person should not turn out too little work. If he did, he was a "chiseler"; that is, he was getting paid for work he did not do. A person should say nothing which would injure a fellow member of the group. If he did, he was a "squealer." Finally, no member of the group should act officiously.

The working group had also developed methods of enforcing respect for its attitudes. The experts who devised the wage incentive scheme assumed that the group would bring pressure to bear upon the slower workers to make them work faster and so increase the earnings of the group. In point of fact, something like the opposite occurred. The employees brought pressure to bear not upon the slower workers but upon the faster ones, the very ones who contributed most to the earnings of the group. The pressure was brought to bear in various ways. One of them was "binging." If one of the employees did something which was not considered quite proper, one of his fellow workers had the right to "bing" him. Binging consisted of hitting him a stiff blow on the upper arm. The person who was struck usually took the blow without protest and did not strike back. Obviously the virtue of binging as punishment did not lie in the physical hurt given to the worker but in the mental hurt that came from knowing that the group disapproved of what he had done. Other practices which naturally served the same end were sarcasm and the use of invectives. If a person turned out too much work, he was called names, such as "Speed King" or "The Slave."

It is worth while pointing out that the output of the group was not considered low. If it had been, some action might have been taken, but in point of fact it was perfectly satisfactory to the management. It was simply not so high as it would have been if fatigue and skill had been the only limiting factors.

In the matter of wage incentives, the actual situation was quite different from the assumptions made by the experts.

Other activities were out of line in the same way. The wiremen and the soldermen did not stick to their jobs; they frequently traded them. This was forbidden, on the theory that each employee ought to do his own work because he was more skilled in that work. There was also much informal helping of one man by others. In fact, the observation of this practice was one means of determining the cliques into which the group was divided. A great many things, in short, were going on in the observation room which ought not to have been going on. For this reason it was important that no one should "squeal" on the men. . . .

The Bank Wiring Observation Room seemed to show that action taken in accordance with the technical organization tended to break up, through continual change, the routines and human associations which gave work its value. The behavior of the employees could be described as an effort to protect themselves against such changes, to give management the least possible opportunity of interfering with them. When they said that if they increased their output, "something" was likely to happen, a process of this sort was going on in their minds. But the process was not a conscious one. It is important to point out that the protective function of informal organization was not a product of deliberate planning. It was more in the nature of an automatic response. The curious thing is that, as Professor Mayo pointed out to the Commit-

tee, these informal organizations much resembled formally organized labor unions, although the employees would not have recognized the fact. . . .

It is curious how, at all points, the Relay Assembly Test Room and the Bank Wiring Observation Room form a contrast. In the former, the girls said that they felt free from the pressure of supervision, although as a matter of fact they were far more thoroughly supervised than they ever had been in their regular department. In the latter, the men were afraid of supervision and acted so as to nullify it. The Bank Wiremen were in the position of having to respond to technical changes which they did not originate. The Relay Assemblers had periodic conferences with the superintendent. They were told what experimental changes were contemplated; their views were canvassed, and in some instances they were allowed to veto what had been proposed. They were part of an experiment which they felt was interesting and important. Both groups developed an informal social organization, but while the Bank Wiremen were organized in opposition to management, the Relay Assemblers were organized in cooperation with management in the pursuit of a common purpose. Finally, the responses of the two groups to their industrial situation were, on the one hand, restriction of output and, on the other, steady and welcome increase of output. These contrasts carry their own lesson.

F. STUART CHAPIN

The Social Effects of Public Housing in Minneapolis

This study is an effort to measure the effects of good housing upon former slum families rehoused in Sumner Field Homes of Minneapolis, originally a project of the Housing Division of the PWA and since 1937 under the management of the FPHA.

The most interesting findings of this study are: (1) No significant change in morale or in general adjustment was found in 1940 as compared to 1939, either for the 44 experimental families resident in the project, or for the control group of 38 families residing in the slum; (2) both the resident and control groups gained in social participation from 1939 to 1940, but the resident families gained twice as much in absolute score as the control group; (3) both resident and control groups gained in social status from 1939 to 1940, but the residents showed a gain of greater magnitude; (4) a score made on the "condition of the furnishings of the living room" showed for the residents a striking gain but for the control group a real loss for the 12-month period; and (5) both residents and control group had improved in the percentage of families "use-crowded" in 1940 over 1939, but the gain of the residents was about three times that of the control group.

Thus the improvements in condition accrue in much larger degree to the residents of the project, and seem to justify

the housing program in so far as the facts of this single study are concerned.

Before examining the evidence that supports the foregoing conclusions, it may be helpful to analyze the causal components in the complex of factors which operate in the social situation of slum dwelling compared with public housing, as well as to consider the factors chosen to measure the patterns of response to these differences in housing. . . .

The assertion has been made that housing per se, the intrinsic housing factor, cannot be defined or measured. It may be submitted that housing per se is a combination of many factors, such as adequate space and light, reduced noise, room-crowding prevention, and provision for indoor entertainment and recreation, safety and sanitation. The response of tenants to different degrees of this pattern of intrinsic housing factors may be observed and measured by the score on the condition of living rooms, the score on social participation, and the percentage use-crowded, all three showing differences before and after public housing, as compared with continuous slum dwelling.

But these specific factors . . . do not exhaust the list of influences at work. There are always present status factors such as the state of unemployment, differences in education and in income, various occupational groups, etc.; and biological factors, such as the size of family and racial differences (which operate not as intrinsic biological differences but as biological variations which

Reprinted in part with permission of the publisher from F. Stuart Chapin, *Experimental Designs in Sociological Research*, copyright 1947, 1955 by Harper & Row, Publishers, Incorporated, pp. 58–69, 70, 71–74.

lead to social factors such as exclusion and segregation). Then, too, there are known but unmeasured factors such as differences in the state of health and in habits of household economy. Last of all there are many unknown factors. All of these may operate to obscure the real effect of differences in the causal pattern of intrinsic housing factors. . . .

Measures of Results

In studies by experimental design of the social effects of housing, we need to decide in advance of the investigation upon some measures of effect or some means of appraising the degree to which the desired end has been achieved. In this connection it is advisable to meet certain conditions as follows:

1. Scales used to measure effect should be reliable and valid instruments of observation and numerical description. . . .
2. Scales that have been used in previous studies of the same problem or a similar problem and have yielded norms on the same kind of population to be studied are valuable for comparisons, and should be chosen for use.
3. These scales should, of course, measure traits or responses that will be accepted as indices of effect or as indices of the degree to which the desired end has been achieved. The scales should, in short, measure traits or responses that are relevant to the problem.
4. Such scales will be even more useful if we have prior knowledge of whether they are correlated with certain known causal variables—variables other than the complex of factors which have been selected as the means to the end desired, or the assumed cause of the effect to be studied—because this facilitates control

of these disturbing factors by matching on measurements. . . .

5. Finally, the scales will be still more serviceable if it can be shown that they measure a *bundle* of interrelated traits that emerge as a *pattern of response* to the particular treatment or program which is the causal complex to be evaluated in terms of its results.

All these conditions are met in some degree for an experimental study of the social effects of housing if the three following measures are used: scale on the condition of the living room [see below]; percentage of dwelling units that are use-crowded; and the social participation scale. . . . The evidence for this assertion will now be considered.

1. The scale on *the condition of the living room* of a dwelling unit has shown reliability coefficients as high as $r = .95$, despite its appearance of subjectivity of estimate, and validity coefficients of bis. $r = .45$ with use-crowding, and of $r = .52$ with deficiency rating obtained by use of the *Appraisal Form* of the Committee on Hygiene of Housing (condition 1); it is a scale that has been used in several studies of many low-income families living in slum areas of the Twin Cities (condition 2); it supplies an objective measure of such qualitative traits as cleanliness, orderliness, and condition of repair of articles and furnishings in a living room (condition 3); it shows different mean scores for different income classes and different occupational groups in an urban community, and rises from 3.9 for unskilled and semi-skilled occupational groups to 6.4 for managerial and professional groups, of a representative sample of an urban community, so that, by matching on income and occupation, that part of its variation not due to housing, but due to status

factors, may be partially controlled (condition 4); and finally, it has been found related to use-crowding by bis. $r = .45$. Scores on the condition of the living room of a dwelling are obtained from part II of the *Social Status Scale* cited below.

2. The percentage of dwelling units that are *use-crowded* is a measure of the multiple use of the rooms of a dwelling. When a bedroom (BR) is used also as a dining room (DR), or a kitchen (K) is used also as a living room (LR), the situation is called use-crowded. The following multiple uses of rooms originally designed to serve only one function represent degrees of use-crowding with appropriate penalties expressed numerically for purposes of measurement: LR and DR (-6); LR and K (-9); LR and BR (-12) or DR and K (-12); LR and BR and DR and K (-15). Such situational uses distort and confuse the functions of living. Thus the incidence and degree of use-crowding is taken as an index of undesirable housing and is an index quite different from, but related to, room-crowding, or the number of persons per room in the dwelling unit. Use-crowding is a sensitive measure of housing adequacy.

3. *Social participation,* or the number of clubs, formal social groups, organizations, or societies, that the persons in the family are active in, or members of, is related to provisions for indoor entertainment of visitors and to the recreation of individuals in the home. Social participation has been measured by a simple scale which obtains a total score on any person as follows: one point counted for each group membership; two points counted for each group that is attended; three points counted for each group to which some financial contribution is made; four points counted

for each committee membership held; and five points counted for each official position held, such as secretary, treasurer, president, etc. This social participation scale has shown reliability coefficients of from $r = .88$ to $r = .95$, and validity coefficients of from $r = .52$ to $r = .62$ (condition 1); it has been used to measure the social activities in formal groups of the community in urban areas of both low social status and high social status, and tentative norms are available to show the mean scores obtained for different income classes and occupational groups . . . , and for both sexes (condition 2); social participation is relevant to housing since most public housing programs encourage clubs and social activities (condition 3); social participation scores have been found to be correlated with income, $r = .36$ to $.49$, with occupational group, $r = .31$ to $.56$, and with years of formal education, $r = .33$ to $.44$. For these reasons it is evident that by matching on education, income, and occupation, that part of any change in social participation score due to such non-housing factors as education, income, and occupation may be partially controlled (condition 4); finally, an attractive living room, not used also for eating, or cooking, or sleeping purposes, is a place in which club meetings may be comfortably held, and so social participation in the home may be related to measures of use-crowding and the condition of the living room.

Since the three measures just described were shown to be interrelated in ways expressed as correlation coefficients or by other empirical evidence, they satisfy condition 5. Furthermore, the use of the multiple critical ratio, which combines critical ratios on each of the separate measures, yields results that have high statistical significance for the results in the housing study herein described—additional evidence that condition 5 has been met.

The study was planned in 1938 to test the hypothesis: the rehousing of slum families in a public housing project results in improvement of the living conditions and the social life of these families. Sumner Field Homes was selected as the test case.... To test the hypothesis of improvement, we selected 108 project families (1939) as the experimental group and 131 families in slum neighborhoods as the control group.

The experimental group of resident families were those admitted to the project after December 16, 1938. The families in the control group were living in the slum and were chosen from the "waiting list," i.e., from the group of applicants fully investigated by the USHA agents but not immediately accepted as residents because they lived in poor housing not definitely sub-standard, or their income was uncertain, or there was some question of economic or social stability. They remained as eligible rejects or deferred cases for later reconsideration provided subsequent applicants did not meet the requirements in sufficient numbers to fill up the project. There were about 603 families on the waiting list. For the reasons given, they were a group comparable to residents. The control group of slum families was 21.3 per cent larger than the experimental group of residents to allow for shrinkage due to moving away, refusals, or other reasons.

How can we measure the effects of good housing? Are residents of the project better adjusted than slum residents? The attempt to measure the effects of good housing utilized four sociometric scales that have been applied successfully in other previous studies: a slum family study in Minneapolis in 1935–1936, and a WPA relief study in St. Paul in 1939.

The scales measure: (1) *morale,* or the degree that the individual *feels* competent to cope with the future and to achieve his desired goals; (2) *general adjustment,* or the *feelings* about his relationship to other persons, toward present or future social conditions, and toward present social institutions; (3) *social participation,* or the degree to which an individual *actually* engages in the organized activities of his community in terms of membership, attendance, contributions, committees, and offices; and (4) *social status,* or the position the family occupies with reference to the average prevailing household possessions of other families in the community.

Interviewing of residents and non-residents began in February, 1939, and continued intermittently through July, 1939, when a total of 239 had been interviewed, 108 residents and 131 non-residents. A group of 12 interviewers, graduate students in sociology and social work at the University of Minnesota, made the interviews. Only two were paid; the remainder were volunteers. The visitors were instructed in a group meeting and each was provided with sheets of typed directions before going into the field. Entree to the families was obtained by the visitor's stating that he was collecting information about people's opinions as part of a wider study being made under the direction of a university scientist. No mention was made of any connection of this study with the USHA. In this way it was felt that a more spontaneous response would be obtained. The interview furnished the following data.

Minnesota Survey of Opinions, two sheets with 31 questions about the individual's attitudes, to be filled in by the subject. After the interview, the *morale score* and the *general adjustment score* may be extracted from the subject's marked response by a simple system of weighting and scoring. It takes the subject from 20 to 30 minutes to fill this in.[1]

Social Participation Scale, one sheet for entries on each group affiliation of subjects recorded in five entries under five columns by the visitor in reply to questions answered by the subject. It takes 10 or 15 minutes to fill in the subject's answers.[2]

Social Status Scale, one sheet containing 21 entries filled in as observations made by the visitor, with perhaps one or two non-inquisitorial questions. Can be completed in 5 minutes' observation.[2]

The flow chart illustrates the actual shrinkage from the initial group of 108 resident families to the final group of 44 resident families, and from the initial group of 131 slum families not resident in the project (called the control group) to the final group of 38 families. At each step in the study, the elimination of families is shown in the flow chart with the reason for this.

The 103 resident families and the 88 non-resident families that were interviewed in 1939 were matched on the following factors:

1. Race or cultural class of husband (Negro, Jew, mixed white)
2. Employment of husband (private, unemployed, OAA, WPA)
3. Occupational class of husband (I-professional, II-managerial, III-

[1] These scales and their norms will be found in E. A. Rundquist and R. F. Sletto, *Personality in the Depression,* University of Minnesota Press, 1936.
[2] These scales and their norms will be found in F. S. Chapin, *Contemporary American Institutions,* Harper & Brothers, 1935, and W. C. Brown, 1946, pp. 373–97; and F. S. Chapin, "Social Participation and Social Intelligence," *American Sociological Review,* April, 1939, pp. 157–66.

clerical, etc., using the Minnesota Rating Scale of occupations)
4. Number of persons in the family (2, 2–3, 3–5, etc.)
5. Income of the family ($690–814, 815–939, etc.)

When so matched, the results of interviewing to obtain scores on morale and on general adjustment, as well as scores on social participation and social status, showed the two groups to be very much alike. In fact, none of the critical ratios of the absolute differences in scores were statistically significant and in all cases were −1.01 or less. This result establishes the fact that the initial experimental group and the initial control group matched on five factors began the experiment in 1939 (visiting was from February 1 to July 31) with a common base or zero point from which to measure change or gains.

Five additional matching factors were then added because it was found that the responses on the morale and general adjustment scales were made chiefly by housewives. These five factors were:

6. Race or cultural class of wife
7. Employment of wife
8. Occupational class of wife
9. Age of wife (16–20, 21–30, etc.)
10. Years education of wife (1–4, 5–8, etc.)

This process eliminated 47 cases from the experimental group of residents, and 12 cases from the control group of non-residents for the reasons shown on the flow chart. This brought us to the end of the 1939 study with measurements on 56 cases of residents and 76 cases of non-residents or controls.

The next step was taken a year later (February 1 to May 31, 1940), when the follow-up eliminated 12 more cases from the resident group and 38 more

Figure **1**   *Flow chart of effects of good housing in Minneapolis, 1939–1940*

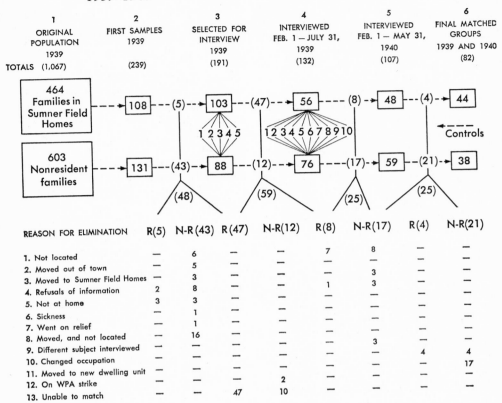

	1	2	3	4	5	6
	ORIGINAL POPULATION 1939	FIRST SAMPLES 1939	SELECTED FOR INTERVIEW 1939	INTERVIEWED FEB. 1 – JULY 31, 1939	INTERVIEWED FEB. 1 – MAY 31, 1940	FINAL MATCHED GROUPS 1939 AND 1940
TOTALS	(1,067)	(239)	(191)	(132)	(107)	(82)

REASON FOR ELIMINATION   R(5)   N-R(43)   R(47)   N-R(12)   R(8)   N-R(17)   R(4)   N-R(21)

	R(5)	N-R(43)	R(47)	N-R(12)	R(8)	N-R(17)	R(4)	N-R(21)
1. Not located	—	6	—	—	7	8	—	—
2. Moved out of town	—	5	—	—	—	—	—	—
3. Moved to Sumner Field Homes	—	3	—	—	—	3	—	—
4. Refusals of information	2	8	—	—	1	3	—	—
5. Not at home	3	3	—	—	—	—	—	—
6. Sickness	—	1	—	—	—	—	—	—
7. Went on relief	—	1	—	—	—	—	—	—
8. Moved, and not located	—	16	—	—	—	3	—	—
9. Different subject interviewed	—	—	—	—	—	—	4	4
10. Changed occupation	—	—	—	—	—	—	—	17
11. Moved to new dwelling unit	—	—	—	—	—	—	—	—
12. On WPA strike	—	—	—	2	—	—	—	—
13. Unable to match	—	—	47	10	—	—	—	—

cases from the non-resident group for the reasons listed on the flow chart. This left final groups of 44 resident families and 38 non-resident families matched on 10 factors. The 38 families were *occupants of the same dwelling unit in 1939 and in 1940.* This also added one more constant matching factor.

The mean scores were then calculated for these two matched groups and the 1939 values were compared with the 1940 values. The differences or gains are shown in Table 1, together with the critical ratios of these changes.

It will be observed that the changes in morale and in general adjustment were very small, absolutely and relatively, and that the critical ratios of these changes show them to be not statistically significant (that is, less than 2). On the other hand, the measured changes in social participation and in social status were large in absolute magnitude and were statistically significant. This observation applies with special emphasis to the residents, who gained more in magnitude and with statistically significant gains. . . .

Since the changes measured on morale and general adjustment were so indeterminate, our remaining argument will be based upon the substantial changes in (a) social participation, (b) condition of furnishings in the living room, and

Table **1** *Measured changes associated with housing*

	Means of measures of effect			
Groups compared	*Morale* [a] *scores*	*General* [a] *adjustment scores*	*Social participation scores*	*Social status scores*
Residents ($N = 44$)				
1939	60.1	45.0	1.73	60.5
1940	60.2	44.0	6.34	86.7
Change	0.1	−1.0	4.61	26.2
Critical ratio of change	0.12	−0.97	3.69	4.27
Non-residents ($N = 38$)				
1939	58.0	42.4	2.76	61.1
1940	56.6	41.2	4.87	82.2
Change	−1.4	−1.2	2.11	21.1
Critical ratio of change	−1.28	−1.34	2.88	3.82

[a] Reverse scales, hence minus change interpreted as a gain.

(c) percentage of families in each group use-crowded.

Let us now turn to a systematic consideration of the factual evidence to discover how far it supports our original hypothesis. As stated [above], this hypothesis was: "The rehousing of slum families in a public housing project results in improvement of the living conditions and the social life of these families."

This positive form of the hypothesis has certain disadvantages for social science research which are not always apparent to the casual reader of such statements, but which may be overcome by the null statement. . . . Let us now transform the single and positively stated hypothesis into a series of three null hypotheses and examine the factual evidence which supports them or which may lead us to reject them.

1. There are *no changes* in social participation, condition of the living room, and percentage use-crowded, if differences in composition of the experimental group and the control group are held constant in respect to the 10

matching factors, race of husband, employment of husband, occupation of husband, number of persons in the family, income of family, race of wife, employment of wife, occupation of wife, age of wife, and years education of wife.

The evidence: Table 2 shows in rows 3 and 8 for all columns that *changes were obtained* as a result of the experiment. Hence the evidence fails to support, or conversely it disproves, the first null hypothesis.

2. The observed changes in social participation, condition of the living room, and percentage use-crowded are *not greater* than those that could occur between two groups selected by random sampling from the same population.

The evidence: Table 2 shows in row 4 that all of these changes are statistically significant for the experimental group of residents, thus disproving the second null hypothesis in this respect. But for the control group of non-residents only column (1) of row 9 shows a statistically significant difference. But when the multiple critical ratio is calculated it will be observed that for a pattern of response (combining all three

Table **2** *Changes in measures of social effects of housing, 1939 to 1940*

	Measures of social effect		
Groups compared	Mean social participation scores (1)	Mean scores on condition of the living room (2)	Percentage use-crowded [a] (3)	
Residents (N = 44)				
1939	1.73	−0.20	50.00	1
1940	6.34	+3.00	6.00	2
Changes	+4.61	+3.20	−44.00	3
Critical ratios	+3.69	+2.28	−4.44	4
Multiple critical ratio		+6.01		5
Non-residents (N = 38)				
1939	2.76	+3.50	44.70	6
1940	4.87	+2.20	28.90	7
Changes	+2.11	−1.30	−15.80	8
Critical ratios	+2.88	−1.14	−1.43	9
Multiple critical ratio		+1.82		10
Differences in changes [b]	+4.50	+4.50	28.20	11
Critical ratios	+1.90	+2.60	+4.11	12
Multiple critical ratio		+4.97		13

[a] In column (3) a negative sign (−) is interpreted as a gain, since it expressed a decline in percentage use-crowded.
[b] Changes in favor of residents, i.e., changes of residents in excess of gains of non-residents.

measures of social effect), the *pattern of change,* row 5, is 6.01 in statistical significance for the experimental group of residents, whereas for the control group of non-residents in row 10 it is only 1.82, or not statistically significant. Thus the evidence of Table 2 disproves the second null hypothesis.

3. The observed differences between changes in social participation, condition of the living room, and percentage use-crowded are *not greater than* those that could occur frequently between two groups selected by random sampling from the same population.

The evidence: The differences in changes between the two groups are all substantial, as shown in row 11, but taken individually they are statistically significant only for measures on condition of the living room and percentage use-crowded, columns (2) and (3) of row 12. But again, when the *pattern of change* in response (combining all three measures) is taken as the criteria of significance, we note in row 13 that the multiple critical ratio is 4.97, or of high statistical significance. Thus this evidence disproves the third null hypothesis.

Where does this leave us? How can we state the net result? It leaves us with the conclusion that all three null hypotheses are not supported by the factual evidence, and this is not a process of setting up straw men to be knocked down. Our net conclusion is that the residents did change significantly in the social pattern of their response to a change in housing from slum living to a public housing project, whereas the control group of families which remained in the same slum dwellings throughout the experimental period of one year changed only to a degree which could occur so frequently as a fluctuation of random sampling as to be insignificant of any real change in their condition.

It will be observed that one of the conditions of the first null hypothesis is the constancy of the ten matching factors. These factors were held constant throughout the period of the experiment. A further word is relevant, however, as to the procedure in matching. The matching process when carried out in strict manner involves identical individual matching, that is, each individual in the experimental group is matched against another individual in the control group exactly similar in respect to the ten matching factors. Since this rigorous process of matching inevitably leads to heavy eliminations of cases that cannot be paired on all factors, we resorted to the expedient of pairing two or more from the experimental group against one case of the control group within a stated range. To put the matter in different phraseology, the families in the non-resident group were paired against the families in the resident group when one or more non-resident families had the same classification according to the list of matching factors as one or more of the resident families. As indicated, this procedure was less rigorous than identical individual matching but gave us greater freedom in the pairing process, prevented excessive elimination of cases, yielded terminal groups of larger size, and was followed by determinate results.

Final proof that the gains of the residents are *due solely to their improved housing* would require that we had listed all the community and personal influences that operated in the period studied and then controlled, by matching, all of these differences *excepting only* the fact that the resident group were in the project and the non-resident group were in the slum. Obviously such a task would have been impossible to perform. We did, however, control by matching ten factors of a personal and social nature, which, if not controlled, might have explained the differences eventually found. With these ten factors controlled or held constant throughout the experiment, we found by application of probability formulas that the differences measured could not have been due to chance in any reasonable expectation that reasonable persons would insist upon.

COMMENTARY

EXPERIMENTAL DESIGN

The controlled experiment is a powerful design for testing hypotheses of causal relationships among variables. Ideally, in the experimental design the investigator throws into sharp relief the explanatory variables in which he is interested, controlling or manipulating the independent variable (X), observing its effect on the dependent variable (Y), and minimizing the effects of the extraneous variables which might confound his result. The classical form of the design is often diagramed as in Figure 11-A (see Stouffer, 1962, p. 292). Its characteristic features (which together distinguish it from the cross-section studies

Figure **11-A**   *Diagram of the classical experimental design*

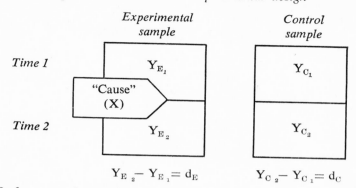

$$Y_{E_2} - Y_{E_1} = d_E \qquad Y_{C_2} - Y_{C_1} = d_C$$

in Unit 8, for example, or the dynamic studies in Unit 10) may be listed as follows:

> Two samples—an experimental sample (E) and a control sample (C)—are drawn in such a way that they will be as nearly alike as possible at Time 1 in regard to all factors potentially affecting the results.
>
> The presumed causal factor X is introduced into the experimental sample, but withheld from the control sample.
>
> The dependent variable Y is observed in both samples at both Time 1 and Time 2.
>
> The changes occurring in the experimental sample (d_E) are then compared with the changes occurring in the control sample (d_C), and any difference attributed to the causal factor.

As Stouffer puts it, "the test of whether a difference [d_E] is attributable to what we think it is attributable to is whether [d_E] is significantly larger than [d_C]" (Stouffer, 1962, p. 292).

In terms of our Paradigm, then, the classical experiment in its pure form is a dynamic study **(P-V)** in which the time sequence of the variables can be established. It controls systematically the action or attitudes under study **(P-VI)** by manipulating both the independent (causal) variable and those experimental conditions that might otherwise allow extraneous factors (W) to interfere with the results of the study. And it utilizes a set of experimental and control samples designed especially for purposes of analyzing **(P-IV)** the relationship between the explanatory variables.

Although experiments are widely used in the physical sciences, they have only begun to be effectively and precisely applied in sociology—partly because of the cost, the difficulty, and sometimes the questionable morality of experimenting with human beings; and partly because theoretical developments in sociology at the present stage do not often warrant such precise design. An experimental design, to be effective for hypothesis-testing, presupposes that the investigator can specify his conceptual model before starting the research—that he can identify and define the explanatory and extraneous variables with reference to a body of theoretical and empirical knowledge, and state how the results of his experiment will relate to some more inclusive model. When the investigator cannot formulate such hypotheses, he will frequently learn more from a looser, more exploratory type of design that will allow interpretation and development of the conceptual model to follow, rather than to precede, the empirical operations.

The studies you have analyzed in this Unit illustrate the difficulties to be overcome and the compromises often made when the researcher attempts to devise and carry out an experimental design. At the same time, they point to the potential of this design as a powerful tool for empirical verification of theoretically derived hypotheses.

The Cambridge-Somerville Youth Study and the Classical Experimental Design

Let us examine, as an illustration of the experimental design, the ten-year research project reported by Powers. We shall note the utility of a *control sample* and distinguish various *interim factors* and *characteristics of the cases themselves* which may (unless properly controlled) confound the results of an experiment.

This study, which deals with the problem of delinquency among pre-adolescent and adolescent boys, has the practical objective of evaluating a potential technique for social workers and others actively involved in the prevention of juvenile delinquency.

Dr. Richard C. Cabot and the other originators of the Cambridge-Somerville project began with the hypothesis that "delinquency might be prevented by an intensive, enduring, personal, friendly relationship" between a counselor and a potentially delinquent boy. The implication of the hypothesis is that delinquency is a problem to be treated on the individual level through "wise and friendly counsel supplemented by social case work techniques"; the research case **(P-I)** is accordingly the individual boy.

OUTLINE OF THE DESIGN

The researchers attempted to approximate the classical experimental design here because they wanted to test a hypothesis of pressing practical significance, and no alternative research design seemed suitable for such a test. Their design, an ambitious one, was made possible by adequate research funds that provided a wide range of special services by a large staff over an extended period of time. We can abstract some general principles of experimental design by investigating the difficulties of conceptualization and execution that beset these researchers. Their design may be outlined as follows:

> Experimental and control samples were set up that were "similar in numbers and in all other relevant respects," and equal numbers of boys adjudged "predelinquent" and "non-predelinquent" were assigned to experimental and control samples respectively.

Over a period of from four to eight years, the independent variable X of adult counsel (which, partly because of the counselors' varying definitions of appropriate treatment, encompassed a wide variety of activities) was applied to all the boys in the experimental sample, but to none in the control sample;

The dependent variable was measured at Time 1 on an eleven-point scale for probable delinquency; and at Time 2 through official records of offenses.

Comparisons were made between the two samples.

FUNCTION OF A CONTROL SAMPLE

Powers and his colleagues emphasize the importance of a "carefully constructed control group," stating that "if the two groups were similar at the outset, then any significant differences between them at the end of the program could reasonably be attributed to the major variable in the picture—the counselors' treatment." The researchers demonstrate the importance of this aspect of experimental design in their frank discussion of the disappointing results. If there had been no control sample, they might well have concluded that there was a positive relationship between this type of treatment and the checking of delinquency, because there were successful outcomes in a number of individual cases in the experimental sample. A comparison of the experimental sample with the control sample reveals, however, substantially the *same* extent of delinquency in the two sets of boys. It is this comparison which casts doubt upon the effectiveness of the treatment. Their comparison of the official delinquency records of boys in the two samples, as Powers sums it up, shows that "the special work of the counselors" did not add to the effectiveness of "the usual forces in the community in preventing boys from committing delinquent acts."

There are many extraneous factors which, like the "usual forces in the community," may impinge upon the dependent variable once the experiment is under way. Thus, from the experimental sample alone, the researcher cannot usually distinguish between the effects of the extraneous variables and the effects of the explanatory variable X (the treatment). Comparison with the control sample *does* ideally facilitate such a distinction, because the control sample—which might better be called the *comparison sample*—is presumably exposed to all the same interfering forces and events as the experimental sample—*except* for the causal factor X. Hence (despite many practical difficulties in particular studies) comparison helps to focus attention on the effects of X.

TYPES OF INTERIM FACTORS

The Cambridge-Somerville study illustrates some main types of extraneous factors which may be at least partly offset through comparison with the control sample (see Figure 11-B). Since these are all extraneous factors that may operate upon the dependent variable (or on the relationship between dependent and independent variables) *after* the experiment is under way (after the treatment X has been introduced), we shall speak of them as *interim factors*. Such interim factors may interfere with the results of any experiment (see, *e.g.,* Donald Campbell), but they become exacerbated when the experiment, like this one, extends over a long period of time. We shall now examine such interim factors in some detail before going on to consider how they may be minimized through sample design or through control of experimental conditions.

Figure **11-B**   *Types of interim factors that may confound experimental results*

Coincidental changes (apart from the research) that affect Y (in the XY relationship)	Procedures for offsetting such *confounding effects:*
Type 1. History	⎱ Minimizing by manipulation of experimental conditions
Type 2. Development	⎰ Offsetting by comparison with control sample(s)
Extraneous *effects of the research itself* on Y (in the XY relationship)	
Type 3. Control effect	⎱ Minimizing by careful research design
Type 4. Biased-viewpoint effect	⎰ Offsetting by comparison with control sample(s)

The *coincidental changes* that occur apart from the experiment proper, but that may nevertheless impinge upon it, comprise one whole complex of interim factors. *History* or the course of outside events—ranging in the Cambridge-Somerville study from the broad changes related to the War to the specific processes serving to socialize youths in the community—is one of these potentially confounding factors. Historical changes have their unknown impact upon the delinquent tendencies of boys in both experimental and control samples. Another type of coincidental change is the *developmental change* that may take place within the cases themselves independent of the experiment. For example, in this study, the individual boys went through the developmental change of maturation and growth.

One factor frequently associated with coincidental changes is *sample mortality*, which we encountered in the panel studies in Unit 10. Sample mortality was obviously an important factor in the Cambridge-Somerville experiment: many boys became unavailable during the ten-year period because of death, removal from the local area, or departure for service in World War II. Sample mortality is sometimes a result of the individual's becoming bored or annoyed with a study and deciding to withdraw, or of the researchers' deciding, as in the Cambridge-Somerville study, to drop 65 boys from the program "because they presented no special problems." In such instances the mortality results, not from coincidental changes in history or development occurring apart from the research, but from the research process itself.

This brings us to another main set of interim factors, the *extraneous effects of the research procedures.* Although the research design aims to control systematically the independent variable, it also involves various measurements and various manipulations of the experimental conditions. Such procedures often have indirect consequences that may confound the results. These additional interim factors will be treated as either control effects, or biased-viewpoint effects, as we discussed these in Unit 2.

Control effect, or the unplanned *effect* of the research *on the action* or attitudes under study **(P-VI),** may perhaps have occurred in the Cambridge-Somerville study as the result of *testing.* The social workers' interviews with parents and the varied tests, questionnaires, and rating scales administered to the boys during the course of the treatment may have sensitized the boys to their status as guinea pigs, thus possibly exerting an unintended and unmeasured control effect on their development into law-abiding citizens. To be sure, the researchers made an effort to reduce any specific control effect by diverting attention from their real interest in the predelinquents through the inclusion of other boys presumed to be nondelinquents.

Biased-viewpoint effect may also occur—and develop over time—as the experimental design imposes various changing restrictions on the *researcher's understanding* of the action he is studying. Thus his observations may become less accurate as he suffers from fatigue in a long investigation, or as increasing immersion in the system may reduce his objectivity. Also, the measuring instruments employed may change or deteriorate over time. In Powers' report, for instance, the instruments used in the successive measurements of delinquency appear so diffuse, and the necessary changes in staffing so pronounced, that it is hard to determine how greatly the measuring procedure may have changed from the beginning to the end of the experiment.

Incidentally, you should also be aware of a specific technical difficulty, *regression effect,* which sometimes interferes with the researcher's understanding of the results of an experiment (see R. L. Thorndike, 1942). Regression effect may operate when the sample consists of the *extreme* examples of the phenomenon measured at Time 1. At any given time that a population is measured (such as Time 1), some of the cases will give the appearance of being unusually extreme only because of random errors in the measurements, or random instability of the people themselves. Consequently, a selected extreme sample will tend, on the average, to appear less extreme at any other measurement period (such as Time 2)— a tendency which is entirely independent of any changes in experimental or other conditions. In the Cambridge-Somerville study, a regression effect might occur if only extreme predelinquents had been chosen for the experiment.

Offsetting the Effects of Interim Factors. There are several devices for counteracting the effects of these various interim factors (see Figure 11-B). The main device used in the study reported by Powers is the single control sample. To the extent, then, that all these interim factors actually affect the delinquent tendencies of both samples of boys *alike,* the extraneous effects may be eliminated from the analysis through the comparison between experimental and control samples (as in Figure 11-A). This was clearly the hope of Cabot and his colleagues. Yet, some critics may feel this was an unrealistic hope. Consequently, many other designs are planned more tightly—conducted in laboratory settings, for example, or over shorter periods of time—so as to prevent any differential impact of the interim factors by bringing under experimental supervision and control some of the extraneous factors that were beyond the reach of the Cambridge-Somerville investigators.

THE SELECTION OF EQUIVALENT SAMPLES

In addition to these types of interim factors which may beset the experiment once it is under way, another major set of potentially confounding factors is associated with the *nature of the cases* themselves and the process by which the cases were *initially selected* at Time 1. Because the analysis will depend upon comparison of experimental and control samples after X has been introduced, the two samples must start out as nearly alike as possible. Systematic bias must be minimized through appropriate sampling procedures so that—within the limits of chance error that we shall presently discuss—all extraneous factors will operate in the two samples in the same way.

In effect, an extra phase is added to the sampling procedure discussed in Unit 6: after a main sample or reservoir of cases is drawn (as in the usual sampling Phases I and II in Table 6-A), this main sample is then subdivided into the experimental and control samples. Let us consider Powers' account of how this subdivision of the main sample is accomplished here (dealing later with the implications of the Phase I and II procedure for selecting the main sample itself). Starting with 782 boys rated as either predelinquent or not, the researchers attempted to create two similar samples of 325 each, with equal numbers of pre- and nondelinquent boys in each sample. In assigning cases to the two samples, they might well have used simple random sampling (as in Manual V-A). But they actually employed a more efficient procedure, which holds constant certain variables before making the random assignment.

Matching or Stratification. Their first step is *matching.* Individual boys were put together in pairs according to similarity on predelinquency rating and on many other variables considered relevant to delinquency. Two boys were considered a well-matched pair if their personality "profiles" (the combination of, and relationships among, personality factors) were similar; Powers reports that certain of the variables—age, delinquency-prediction rating, health, intelligence, educational achievement, personality, family factors, and environment—were weighted more heavily than others. This matching produced comparable mean scores for the experimental sample and the control sample on twenty selected variables.

In principle, then, the objective of matching is to control—by holding them constant—certain potentially confounding factors that may be associated with crucial characteristics of the cases themselves (see Greenwood). A similar procedure, stratified sampling (as discussed in Unit 6), might alternatively have been used here in place of case-by-case matching. Such matching (or stratification), though not necessary to the selection of equivalent samples in the experimental design, may greatly increase the efficiency of the design by reducing—for a sample of a given size—the error due to chance alone. The more variables are controlled, the fewer variables there are on which differences in the experimental result can occur through chance. With this reduced chance error, the matched sample design becomes more sensitive; it can detect even relatively slight differences which may appear in the dependent variable as a result of the change in the independent variable.

Randomization. The sociological researcher cannot depend upon matching or stratification alone, however, to equate the experimental and control samples. He can never be sure he has recognized and been able to hold constant *all* the extraneous factors that may be associated with Y or with the XY relationship. Even though the Cambridge-Somerville researchers used in their matching procedure over 100 variables (far more than the number ordinarily deemed useful), they could not be certain that the two samples were distributed alike on all the potentially confounding factors. Indeed, as Sir Ronald Fisher says in his classic work, *The Design of Experiments,* to insist that the samples be totally alike in every respect except that to be tested is "a totally impossible requirement in . . . all . . . forms of experimentation" (Fisher, p. 21). Hence the essential step in the design of the two samples is not matching, but randomization, or the *random assignment* of X (the treatment)—following procedures which Fisher has specified for various research situations (Fisher, pp. 20–24 and *passim*).

The random element in the Cambridge-Somerville procedure is introduced when "a coin was tossed to determine which boy of a given pair was to be placed in the treatment group and which in the control group." This random assignment eliminates, as Powers puts it, "any possible 'constant error.' " The researcher is thereby prevented from (consciously or unconsciously) selecting for the experimental sample those boys apparently most likely to improve under treatment. In addition, the effects of all those potentially confounding variables on which the researcher does not attempt to match—or on which his matching is erroneous or imperfect—are thus *randomized* at the outset. Since both experimental and control samples are selected at random from the same reservoir of cases, the two samples differ only by chance.

This powerful feature of the experimental procedure is indicated in Figure 11-C, which compares this type of sample design with that used in the cross-section study as discussed in Unit 8 (see Wold; Kish, 1959). The research focus of both is on the relationship between the explanatory variables X and Y. For im-

Figure **11-C** *Reduction of the confounding effects associated with initial char-*
acteristics of cases themselves

Handling of effects of extraneous variables	*In ideal experimental design*	*In cross-section study of causal relationships*
Held constant	By stratified (matched) sampling	By cross-tabulation (subgroup comparisons)
Randomized	By random assignment to experimental and control samples (chance error estimated through statistical testing)	(merely assumed)
Allowed to confound relationships of explanatory variables		Always possible that influential variables are not held constant

mediate research purposes, all other potentially related variables W are considered extraneous; the objective is to minimize the effects of all extraneous variables that might confound the results by influencing Y directly or by indirectly conditioning the effect of X on Y. Yet cross-section studies and experiments attack the analysis of causal relationships differently, as our further discussions will show in some detail. In the cross-section study, the effects of those extraneous variables which are not held constant by cross-tabulation are merely *assumed* to be randomized. (More precisely, each subgroup of cases is a sample—it may or may not be a probability sample—of a different population, and the extraneous variables do not necessarily have the same distributions in these populations. Yet the researcher, in drawing his conclusions, assumes the identity of these distributions.) Actually the extraneous variables may be very unevenly distributed in the subgroups being compared—although the researcher cannot know this—thus operating to confound the apparent results.

In the samples used in experiments, on the other hand, the effects of all variables not held constant through some kind of matching are, ideally at least, randomized before the experiment starts. In this sense, then, there are no *unsuspected* confounding variables in the ideal experimental design. Although many experimental designs fall short of this ideal, of course, we shall see how the principle of randomization is a very important one, sufficing—apart from other avoidable errors of design—to guarantee, as Fisher states it, "the validity of the test of significance by which the result of the experiment is to be judged" (Fisher, p. 24).

THE ESTIMATION OF CHANCE ERROR

To be sure, the random assignment to experimental and control samples also results in errors—differences between the two samples which may confound the results. But these errors are not unsuspected. They are the errors due to chance variation; it is exactly these chance errors which the statistical tests (as in Exercise V-3) are designed to estimate. Thus the difference between the two samples found in the dependent variable at the end of the *ideal* experiment is produced by just two factors—by the independent variable X and by the errors due to chance variation—for the attempt has been made to equalize, hold constant, or randomize the effects of all other factors. The statistical test, then, by estimating the probability of obtaining the observed differences on the basis of chance alone, aids the investigator in disentangling the effects of X from the effects of chance. The Cambridge-Somerville investigators decided on the basis of statistical tests that there was a high probability that the small differences they observed could be explained by chance variation—hence, that *no* significant differences could be attributed to the treatment.

PROBLEMS OF INTERPRETATION

Before inspecting further examples of sample designs and control of interim factors in experiments, we should note how the attempt to *interpret* a set of experimental findings, like those from the Cambridge-Somerville study, brings us again to the close linkage between theory and research. For, even if the investigators' hypothesis had been confirmed by a positive finding (as it was not), replications of the experiment under varying conditions and further testing of the implications of the theory would still be desirable. Such replications would serve to eliminate alternative theories which might better explain the findings, or to establish a more inclusive theory into which the specific findings could be incorporated (see Westie). But a *negative* finding, as in this study, presents a special problem in interpretation since it is a sure sign that either (a) the research design was faulty or was not carried out properly, or (b) the conceptual model was incorrect or inadequate.

We consider first some of the possible flaws in the research procedure which might account for the negative finding. Such flaws are not peculiar to experiments, of course, but the potential for hypothesis-testing that characterizes this design requires a special rigor in execution. We shall then reconsider the conceptual framework for possible defects of theory.

Problems of Empirical Procedure. In addition to the problems of minimizing interferences from extraneous factors, as we have already discussed these, difficulties often arise in the attempts to represent the explanatory variables themselves in the research. Thus the causal or *independent variable* certainly requires consistent and *uniform manipulation* and application as a treatment. Yet, in the

Cambridge-Somerville study, the treatment comprised a wide and loosely defined variety of activities, from help in reading to medical attention to summer camp. Furthermore, "Each counselor was left largely to his own resources," and treatment thus consisted of "the application of whatever skills each counselor was capable of applying." The fact that during the course of the study some of the counselors were drafted into the armed services frequently resulted in considerable changes in the treatment of individual boys.

Thus it is difficult to know just what the treatment was or whether it was applied uniformly. Even if the results had shown a significant difference between the two sets of boys, the researchers would have been able to conclude only that "treatment" was somehow effective in combatting juvenile delinquency, without knowing exactly which aspects of the treatment were responsible. Indeed, a full awareness of the importance of a clear conceptual model as the basis for any rigorous research design might have shown in advance that such a construct as "warm and friendly counsel" is altogether too vague to be translated into precise empirical operations, or interpreted as part of a clearly defined theory of causation or method of treatment.

An additional methodological difficulty which complicates the interpretation of many experimental results lies in inadequate *measurement of the dependent variable*. Accurate measurement is important, of course, in any research; but the controlled experiment requires a special precision.

Powers describes a great variety of materials and techniques utilized in measuring "predelinquency" (Y) at Time 1. Available records from school and agency files were combined with data gathered from personal interviews, psychological tests, teacher ratings, ecological ratings of neighborhoods, and so on. A committee of "experts" or judges then rated the boys from all the materials assembled on each case, using an eleven-point scale of probable delinquency. At Time 2, the dependent variable, which had changed from predelinquency to delinquency, was again measured by a variety of data, ranging from Crime Prevention Bureau statistics to counselors' personal opinions. Although great effort was made to obtain all potentially relevant materials and to deal with them as systematically as possible, it is very difficult, as we have seen, to develop truly systematic measures by combining such diffuse and varied materials as official statistics on delinquency and the personal opinions of counselors. And comparisons of inadequate measures can scarcely yield useful results.

In general, then, proper conduct of an experiment must meet consistently high standards throughout the research process. Rigor in the designing of equivalent samples or in control of interim factors, for example, cannot guarantee valid results unless the same rigor is used in manipulation of the independent variable and measurement of the dependent variable.

Conceptual Problems. The disappointing results of the Cambridge-Somerville study do more than raise questions about appropriate design. They also point to a possible need for re-examination and clarification of the original conceptualization of the problem. If we scrutinize the present negative findings, we note, for example, that the conceptual model (vague though it perhaps is) focuses clearly on treatment of the boy as a discrete individual. Thus the research results might cast doubt upon the assumption that delinquency may be effectively treated apart from the roles of the individual boy in the many social systems of which he is a member (his family, his gang or clique, his school). Incorporation of an additional explanatory variable—such as adolescent gang membership—into the conceptual model and the design of the experiment might perhaps have produced more clear-cut findings (see, for example, the reanalysis of these data reported by Jackson Toby, 1961).

In sum, the negative findings of an experiment do not constitute in any sense a research "failure." They may suggest improvements in the future design of similar studies. And they may provide important clues to sociological knowledge. The Cambridge-Somerville study, despite its shortcomings in contrast to the ideal experiment, points to the great advantages of the experimental design over the cross-section study for analyzing possible causal relationships, and for evaluating broad programs of social intervention and treatment.

Sherif and the Manipulation of Experimental Conditions

In contrast to the Cambridge-Somerville study, which attempted to minimize the effects of confounding factors entirely through the design and the relatively large size of its *sample,* the study by Sherif shows how the investigator may *manipulate the conditions* of the experiment in order to reduce certain effects of these factors.

Stating that his objective is to "include within a single experimental design the study of in-group properties and inter-group relations," Sherif formulates two hypotheses. His first is that unrelated individuals, when brought together to interact in a group situation with common goals (independent variables X), will form a hierarchical group structure with common norms (dependent variables Y). His second hypothesis refers to the out-group hostility and group stereotyping (Y) which is generated when competition arises between groups and one group perceives another as a source of frustration (X).

SHERIF'S EXPLANATORY VARIABLES

Sherif describes in detail the ingenious translation of these two sets of concepts into the terms of his experiment. In testing the first hypothesis, he manipulates the independent variable by using such devices as group housing and group funds of spending money, in order to stimulate interaction and produce common goals for each group. Then he proceeds to measure the dependent variable. He observes the development of hierarchical structure, using sociometric measures of popularity, and he determines power positions by observing the initiation of action and the taking of responsibility. He further notes the development of solidarity symbols such as names for the groups, nicknames for the boys, and standardized group sanctions.

Proceeding then to his second hypothesis, he stimulates competition by announcing competitive games—at first controlling the scoring so as to keep the competition fairly even, then noting the group friction and frustration produced as the Red Devils lose several contests. He even deliberately provokes frustration by contriving the party plans in such a way that the Red Devils get the better food for themselves. Here he indexes the dependent variable, out-group hostility, through the observed fights and name-calling, which developed far beyond the point planned by the investigators.

MANIPULATING THE EXPERIMENTAL CONDITIONS

In addition to such control of the independent variable—which characterizes all experimental designs—the researcher frequently manipulates a number of other conditions of the experiment. Thus Sherif manipulates the environment in which the research takes place. Unlike Dr. Cabot and his colleagues, who left the boys to develop within the natural environment of their own homes, Sherif (although he does not move his boys into a laboratory as Bales does) contrives a special setting (a summer camp).

Now consider the consequences of such a contrived setting. Not only does it make possible the necessary control of the independent variables, but it protects the experiment from the contamination of outside influences. The boys were effectively held in isolation for eighteen days, without visitors or neighborhood distractions. Thus Sherif succeeds in virtually eliminating that set of extraneous factors that we have called coincidental changes of history (Type 1 in Figure 11-B), as well as sample mortality (since all the boys presumably stayed for the full 18 days). The comparatively short duration of the experiment and the possibilities of controlling the social environment both enable Sherif to avoid the intrusion of certain interim factors which, in such an extended experiment as the Cambridge-Somerville study, could merely be offset through comparison between experimental and control samples.

Sherif is also able to create, for the purposes of his experiment, the groups he wishes to use as his cases. This special opportunity for experimental control over the internal composition of the case itself—as we saw in the Bales study (Unit 3)—arises because the research case **(P-I)** is the group (rather than an individual). Starting with twenty-four boys chosen for their similarity in various background and personality respects, Sherif wants to fulfill the condition that they have "no established relationships." Furthermore, suspecting that there may be some tendencies for spontaneous groupings to form, he allows an initial expression of personal likes, dislikes, and common interests; then he takes pains to separate the budding friendships when he divides the boys into two similar groups.

ONE MODIFICATION OF THE EXPERIMENTAL DESIGN

Once he has set up these two groups, which is the control group and which the experimental? Clearly, he treats neither the Red Devils nor the Bull Dogs as a control. For the first hypothesis, he stimulates interaction and common goals (X) in both groups. Here, that is, Sherif uses an experimental sample which consists of two cases. For the second hypothesis, he requires, as part of his conception, "two in-groups" in "functional relationships." Accordingly (just as the case may often consist of dyads) Sherif uses as his case a single pair of interacting groups. What he does is to study intensively and to describe in detail the process that goes on in a single pair of groups after the experimenters have manipulated independent variables and other conditions. He uncovers many clues and insights. But he does not employ any control group.

This experimental design with no control group is one of many possible modifications of the classical design (see Selltiz *et al.,* p. 115 ff.). If we compare it with the diagram in Figure 11-A, only two of the original cells—E_1 and E_2—are retained, as shown in Figure 11-D.

Figure **11-D** *Modified experimental design with no control sample*

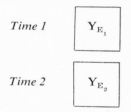

The implications of this modification are suggested if we speculate about what Sherif might have found had he run a second summer camp in which no competitive games and no ruined party plans were introduced. Would no name-calling and no fights have ensued, in line with his hypothesis? Or would competition and derogation of the out-group have developed spontaneously as a by-product of in-group formation—without experimental intervention? (Sherif reports that such tendencies did appear anyway in his experimental groups, in advance of the researchers' planned controls.) The point is, of course, that without the control sample, Sherif cannot really be sure whether or how the presumed effects are related to the presumed causes, or whether the various dependent variables would simply have arisen in the normal course of events uninfluenced by the kinds of factors in which he is interested. The uncontrolled factors here relate to *development* of the groups—a set of factors (Type 2 in Figure 11-B) which cannot be accounted for in the single sample design that Sherif used.

Sherif's modification emphasizes again the importance of the control sample as one of the fundamental characteristics of the full experimental design.

The Hawthorne Studies and Problems of Control Effect

If the Powers report demonstrates the utility of a comparison sample, and the Sherif study suggests some potentialities of controlling experimental conditions, the Hawthorne studies illustrate certain of the difficulties of such experimental control. These studies constitute a long-term research program carried out between 1927 and 1932 at the Western Electric Company's Hawthorne works in Chicago by Elton Mayo and his associates. They have become widely known through Roethlisberger and Dickson's book *Management and the Worker*. The particular studies described in the excerpt by George Homans have long been discussed and debated in the literature, and the findings have had wide implications for the sociological use of experimental design.

TIME PERIODS IN A SINGLE-SAMPLE DESIGN

In line with the research objective of studying the relationship between the physical conditions of work (X) and the productivity of the workers (Y), the researchers use the "precise quantitative data" of output rate as the measure of the dependent variable. The idea of one experiment—that in the Relay Assembly Room—is, then, that "if an output curve was studied for a long enough time under various changes in working conditions, it would be possible to determine which conditions were the most satisfactory." Thus, the independent variable here is not the simple presence or absence of a treatment, for example, but a whole series of variations in the conditions of work in the plant (affecting rest pauses, lunches, length of the workweek, etc.)

Figure **11-E**   *Extension of time periods in a single-sample design*

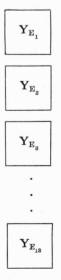

All these variations in the independent variable (sometimes studied in other designs by multiplying the number of samples, as discussed below) are made possible in this research by adding to the number of time periods (see Figure 11-E). Again, as in the Sherif study, the researchers do not use a control sample. Instead they use the sample—the group of girls **(P-I)**—as its *own control* in the following fashion. When they noted that the ouput rate was rising steadily throughout the year as the conditions were manipulated in different ways, they decided that, "as a control on what had been done . . . a return should be made to the original conditions of work, with no rest pauses, no special lunches, and a full-length working week." Indeed, they repeated these identical conditions of work in three of the thirteen different time periods. And, as they say, "if the output rate were directly related to the physical conditions of work [as hypothesized], the expectation would be that in these three experimental periods there would be similarity in output."

In fact, however, this was not the case. The output rate continued to go up and up, regardless of the manipulated conditions. (In the light of modern sociological and psychological theory, the investigators might have expected that the behavior of the group at the later time periods would be partly a function of its intervening experiences—not a simple return to the *status quo ante*. Indeed, the difficulty of assessing the effect of intervening experiences presents itself whenever a researcher attempts to use a sample as its own control, as well as in other more elaborate experimental designs which we shall discuss.) In this instance, the investigators deduced from the unexpectedly consistent increases that the output curve was reflecting "something other than the responses of the group to the imposed experimental conditions." That is, the research design enabled the researchers to discover that some extraneous factors must be at work.

But what kind of factors? Clearly, the enduring characteristics of the case itself—and its component individuals—can be ruled out because of the sample design. A strong feature of using the sample as its own control is that there can be no error in the results due to imperfect matching of two samples since, by definition, the sample is always composed of the same individuals. Among the interim factors, the effects of history and outside events (Types 1 and 2 in Figure 11-B above)—including sample mortality—can be largely ruled out or measured, because these girls worked in a contrived setting under isolated, carefully controlled conditions, and because various supplementary records were kept on factors "other than those experimentally varied that might affect the output rate."

CONTROL EFFECTS

After the elimination of such types of factors, the researchers discovered another set that were confounding the results of their study. Although the girls had been expressly cautioned in advance that they were to work at their normal pace, nevertheless the "fun" of working in the test room and enjoying the personal interest of the management had the indirect consequence that "before long they had committed themselves to a continuous increase in production." The confounding factor proved to be the "social development of the group itself," a factor involving leadership, a common purpose, and "a peculiar and effective relation with its supervisors." This was not the pure type of coincidental development (Type 2 in Figure 11-B) which might be expected to occur anyway apart from the conditions imposed by the research. This development occurred, rather, as a special control effect of the research itself (Type 3).

Thus the Hawthorne researchers, by isolating the Relay Assembly group from the rest of the factory in order to control the experimental situation closely, thereby created a new problem which has come to be thought of more generally as the "Hawthorne effect." The example indicates how any investigator, in making a decision under **P-VI**, must weigh the disadvantages of unsystematic control against the possible indirect, and often unrecognized, disadvantages of systematic control. For, by removing the actors from the environment they regard as normal, or by intruding into the research situation himself, or by heightening the actors' awareness that they are under study, he often runs the risk of *changing* the very action he wishes to observe.

A similar control effect also operated in the Bank Wiring Room study, although an explicit attempt was made here, on the basis of the earlier experience, "to devise an experiment which would not be radically altered by the process of experimentation itself." Here too an informal social organization developed which had its influence upon the dependent variable—though here the common sentiments that "a person should not turn out too much work" affected the output rate quite differently.

As it turned out, of course, this fortuitous discovery of the relationship between informal group structure and group productivity was to become one of the major findings of the research. Control effect, so often a defect in the research, is in this rare instance itself the substance of the discovery. This is a further example of serendipity. As in the Merton study of influentials (Unit 4), skillful researchers were able to utilize an unanticipated result to reformulate their entire theoretical framework and suggest new hypotheses.

THE LOG

The Hawthorne researchers were aided in interpreting these findings by a device which was not an integral part of the experimental design per se, but which provided the first clues to the nature of the Relay Assembly's group structure and norms and to their effect on the group's behavior. This was the log, a collection of detailed though unsystematic notes kept by the investigators as they observed the group throughout the course of the experiment. As Homans describes this document, it recorded:

> the principal events in the test room hour by hour, including among the entries snatches of conversation between the workers. At first these entries related largely to the physical condition of the operators: how they felt as they worked. Later the ground they covered somewhat widened, and the log ultimately became one of the most important of the test room records.

The value of the log illustrates the wisdom of balancing or supplementing a rigorous, structured research design, such as the experiment, with some instrument for adding qualitative data which may aid in explaining quantitative results—much as Le Play used his explanatory supplements. Even the most carefully designed quantitative study may benefit from some qualitative clues, and in the Hawthorne study, this little extra helped to prevent a costly and lengthy piece of research from being a waste of time.

Chapin and the Problem of Equivalent Samples

The Chapin study, although not an experiment according to our definition, emphasizes through its departures the special features of experimental design. Chapin aims to test the hypothesis that "the rehousing of slum families in a public housing project results in improvement of the living conditions and the social life of these families." If Chapin had been able to make the housing assignments himself, he might have divided families at random into equivalent samples, only one of which is to be rehoused. Unable to manipulate the experimental variable in this way, however, he makes use of a "natural" change in his independent variable, building his analysis around a sample of families who had already been rehoused in the usual course of events, and a control sample of families who remained on the waiting list (see Figure 11-F). The pioneering procedures which he evolves, and calls the *ex post facto design,* merit careful examination as a compromise method of studying the many sociologically important variables which cannot be manipulated in the ideal experimental fashion.

Figure **11-F**   *The ex post facto study*

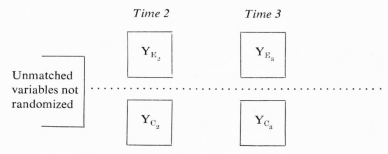

PROBLEMS OF THE NONRANDOM SAMPLE

Consider how Chapin proceeds to set up his two samples. In addition to the independent variable X—rehousing—which differentiates the two, Chapin takes into account various other "influences at work" upon the family's living conditions and social life (*Y*). Thus, starting with 103 families resident in the housing project and 88 "comparable" nonresident families, he selects the samples by matching, first on five, and later on five additional, factors. As a result, he finds in his initial interview, conducted soon after the move, a high degree of comparability between the samples on the dependent variables. He reports that "scores on morale and on general adjustment, as well as scores on social participation and social status, showed the two groups to be very much alike." This gives him some assurance that the study began "with a common base . . . from which to measure change or gains." Accordingly, when he reinterviews the same families a year later—and interprets the data as showing a relatively greater pattern of change for the residents—he wants to infer that the improved housing is the causal factor.

The critical question for our understanding of experimental design is whether he is justified in such an inference. He himself expresses considerable doubt. He suggests, for example, that "final proof that the gains of the residents are *due solely to their improved housing*" would have required the impossible task of controlling by matching *all* the differences between the two samples, except for the difference in housing. He also admits that "many unknown factors . . . may operate to obscure the real effect of differences in the causal pattern of intrinsic housing factors." He uses statistical tests to discover how much of the differences measured might have been due to chance (although he fails to apply these to differences between residents and nonresidents so as to compare d_E and d_C in our Figure 11-A). Yet he does not—indeed cannot—allow chance to operate in the design of his sample as it does in the experimental design because, as in the subgroup comparisons used in cross-section studies, he is unable to randomize the effects of uncontrolled variables (see Figure 11-C above).

As a consequence, Chapin cannot rule out the possible interference of confounding factors. He cannot be sure that people admitted to the housing project were not different kinds of people from those still on the waiting list. Even though the test scores were comparable immediately after the move, there may have been other factors correlated with moving (the presumed cause) which might themselves be operating as the actual cause. Indeed, Chapin reports that the income of the nonresidents was uncertain, or there was some question of their economic or social stability, suggesting that there may have been a systematic bias in the samples at the outset.

The ex post facto design cannot, as a consequence, provide the same kind of assurance as the experiment. Moreover, there seem to be other difficulties in the design, because it does not use a representative sample of the nonresidents, but only of those nonresidents who match the residents. Easily matched families may give different results from difficult-to-match families, for example, or regression effect may set in, or investigation of additional factors through cross-tabulation may prove abortive (see, *e.g.,* Edwards, pp. 281–82, and the related discussion by Strodtbeck, 1958, pp. 159–61).

UTILITY OF THE EX POST FACTO DESIGN

Despite its shortcoming as compared with the full experiment, however, the ex post facto study has certain definite assets as compared with a cross-section study (or even a panel study that starts with a cross section). First, the sample is set up **(P-IV)** to reflect the categories of the independent variable (see the Strodtbeck sample in Unit 8), and also to hold constant certain extraneous variables. Thus, because of its control of a large number of factors, it has a sharper sensitivity to a possible relationship between the explanatory variables than a cross-section sample of its size. Second, the observations are extended over time, so that the researcher can trace the dynamic processes; Chapin, for example, has the opportunity to determine what changes in the dependent variables take place after—rather than before—the rehousing.

Thus this design, although it cannot detect the possible effects of uncontrolled variables, is nevertheless a valuable means of studying causal relationships where experimentation is impossible or impractical. In research on the social isolation of schizophrenics, to cite one further example, the investigators can scarcely manipulate the variables; but use of an ex post facto design may enable them to contrast schizophrenics with controls who, at a time many years before the onset of their illness (see Kohn and Clausen), were similar in certain crucial respects.

PREMATURE RIGOR OF DESIGN

Apart from the inherent limitations of the design itself, Chapin seems to attempt here, as in the Cambridge-Somerville study, to apply a tight design to a vague conceptual model. Chapin has little to say about the "better adjustment" hypothesized to follow upon rehousing, and about the process through which the change might take place. His apparent preoccupation is more with the performance of his various scores and scales in previous research than with their correspondence to any properties of immediate theoretical interest. Moreover, he pays little heed to the nature of his research case **(P-I)**, using some measures that refer to the family as a *group* (rehousing, use-crowding, status), but also using other measures that seem to apply to just one *individual* in each family (*e.g.,* morale, general adjustment, and social participation as he describes these). Is he not really interested in examining the effects of better housing on the family? And if so, why does he not consider the social participation, for example, of all members of the family? Until such basic questions are answered, an elaborate design and standardized measurements can yield little useful information.

Accordingly, this study is of interest, not as a model of how research should be done, but as an early suggestion of one way to examine hypotheses about the effects of "natural" causes, and as an illustration of the difficulties to be coped with in such a study.

Some Implications for Sociological Research

These studies have thus isolated as essential requirements of the ideal experimental design (1) the control over the independent variable and (2) the randomization of the effects of extraneous variables. By definition, then, in an experiment it must be possible to manipulate the independent variable so as to hold within the limits of random error those extraneous factors—both interim changes and factors associated with the characteristics of the cases themselves—that might otherwise confound the results.

ELABORATIONS OF THE CLASSICAL DESIGN

Although we have been discussing as a prototype the design with a single dichotomized independent variable—X or no X—many elaborations are possible to fit particular research objectives and experimental conditions. Such elaborations often consist in multiplying the number of experimental and control samples to take care of more complex independent variables.

For example, the design often calls for more than one explanatory variable, because, as Fisher puts it, "We are usually ignorant which, out of innumerable possible factors, may prove ultimately to be the most important," and "We have usually no knowledge that any one factor will exert its effects independently of all others" (Fisher, p. 101). According to Fisher's *factorial scheme,* a separate sample is set up for each possible combination of the factors to be examined. Thus a design using two independent variables, each of which is varied in only two ways, might appear as in Figure 11-G. (In its simpler form, no measurements are used at Time 1 and direct comparisons are made among the four cells at Time 2.)

Figure **11-G**　*Diagram of a factorial design*

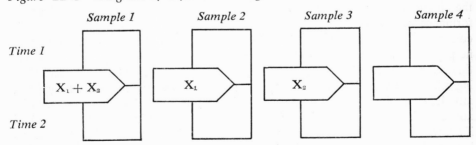

Consider the nature of such comparisons at Time 2, if the two independent variables were two different kinds of treatments, for example, and the dependent variable were delinquency scores. The mean scores (or the percentages of boys with low scores) in the four samples might then be arranged as in Figure 11-H. Here we use for experiments the familiar fourfold table showing the interrelationship among three variables—as discussed for cross-section studies in Unit 8 and Manual IV-B. The analysis is used in the experimental design (with the effects of all other factors randomized) to show the joint effects of X_1 and X_2. Various outcomes are possible, similar to the pure Types I, II, and III in Manual IV-B. Sometimes, as in the present imaginary example, the epsilon—or the difference in the means—for one of the partials may differ markedly from the other, indicating a *statistical interaction* between the effects of the two independent variables, as in the circled figure in Figure 11-H. (In this example, statistical interaction means that treatment X_2 appears to deter delinquency only if X_1 is also administered; for, among individuals *not* receiving X_1, the proportion of delinquents actually increases with receipt of X_2.)

Figure **11-H** *Analysis of joint effects of two treatments*

	Treatment X_1	No Treatment X_1	"Effect" of X_1 ϵ
Treatment X_2	70	20	+50
No Treatment X_2	40	30	+10
"Effect" of X_2 ϵ	+30	−10	(40)

Figures in cells are the percentages of individuals in each sample with low delinquency scores at Time 2.

Additional samples may sometimes be used in experiments for handling the effects of certain *extraneous* factors. Solomon has worked out special designs, for example, that correct for the unsystematic control effects of pre-testing. Respondents who have been pre-tested on the problem under study (who have been questioned, for example, about a given set of values) may—*because* they thereby become sensitized to this problem—respond differently from those not pre-tested to the treatment X (to a mass communication designed to change these particular values, for instance). Thus if boy scouts are questioned about their adherence to scout norms before and after being exposed to propaganda against these norms, the after-measure might show no decrease, or even an increase, in adherence (despite the propaganda) if the pre-test stimulates the boys to discuss their views and reinforce one another's loyalties (see Kelley and Volkart). You will recognize such control effects of pre-testing as related to the control effects of repeated experimentation with the same sample we observed in the Hawthorne studies. In order to take care of control effects of this kind, Solomon adds to the classical design control samples which have *not* been exposed to the pre-test (or to earlier experimentation) as a potentially confounding factor (see Solomon).

These examples merely suggest the possibilities for elaboration that would allow analysis of complex interrelationships of several variables wherever such experimentation proves feasible. Moreover, by testing several factors simultaneously in this way, the design may be made more efficient, if "by more efficient," as Fisher says, "we mean that more knowledge and a higher degree of precision are obtainable by the same number of observations" (Fisher, p. 102).

NONEXPERIMENTAL DESIGNS AS MODIFIED EXPERIMENTS

Against this background of the experimental design, the more commonly used sociological designs considered in previous chapters take on a new clarity (see Stouffer, 1962, Chapter 15). In one aspect, the matter of proof, they may be less effective than experiments. (In another aspect—representativeness—they sometimes have a comparative advantage, as we shall see later.)

The *panel study* (Unit 10), for example, studies and restudies the same cases, using the sample as its own control, as in the Hawthorne experiment (Figure 11-E above). But the panel study departs from the experimental design because, in the first place, the investigator does not attempt to manipulate the independent variable. Thus the panel may be thought of as more similar to the control sample than to the experimental sample, as suggested in Figure 11-I. In the second place, the panel study, though it uses cross-tabulation (or matched control samples as in the voting study) to study relationships between the dependent variable(s) Y and various independent and extraneous variables (X and W), cannot ensure that the effects of still other uncontrolled extraneous variables are randomized. It has great advantages, as we have seen, in establishing time sequence of variables and in providing important information about relationships among these variables for the given sample under study. But its limitation lies in the indirect inferences which must be made about causal relationships—about which factors are responsible for the changes observed in the dependent variable.

Figure **11-I**   *Panel study*

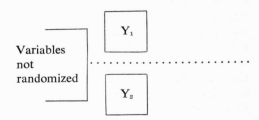

The character of this limitation is easier to see (as in Figure 11-C above) in the *cross-section study* (which adds the further disadvantage, of course, that the time order of the variables is difficult to establish). We saw in Unit 8 how the investigator, after finding that X is associated with (or seems to make a difference in) Y, wants to determine how much of this difference can actually be attributed to X, the independent variable in which he is interested. In order to rule out various possibly confounding factors, he makes cross-tabulations which hold these constant. In this way, he is able to study the XY relationship within subsamples that are homogeneous on such variables as sex, *e.g.*, marital status, or degree of political interest. This corresponds to the matching used in experimental designs. Nevertheless, he cannot be sure that some other variable may not, after all, be the true "cause" (see Wold). There is too often, as Stouffer puts it, "a wide-open gate through which other uncontrolled variables can march" (Stouffer, 1962, p. 294).

The experiment and the cross-section study can also be compared in terms of the distribution within the sample of all possible extraneous variables. In the ideal experimental design, the X sample and the not-X sample are distributed alike (except for chance error) on all these extraneous variables. Even after cross-tabulation in the cross-section study, however, the X subsample and the not-X subsample may be distributed quite differently on some uncontrolled extraneous variable W. And it may be this uneven distribution of W, rather than X or not-X, which accounts for the differences in Y. Chapin, of course, encounters a similar difficulty with the distributions in the *ex post facto design* he uses in the housing study.

GENERALIZING FROM EXPERIMENTAL FINDINGS

In this Unit we have been evaluating experiments and various alternative designs as *methods of proof of causal hypotheses*. We have seen that experimentation cannot afford absolute proof; but that the logic of experimentation—to the extent that it is in fact closely approximated in an investigation—can provide a highly reasonable basis for inferring that X is (or is not) related to Y under the particular conditions studied. In this respect the experimental design has an advantage over cross-section studies, panel analyses, or ex post facto designs.

In addition to the testing of causal hypotheses as the experiment's main reason for being, the researcher typically hopes to generalize his findings to a conceptual universe of theoretical concern. Donald Campbell defines these two aspects of research as the *internal validity* ("Did in fact the experimental stimulus make some significant difference in this specific instance?"); and the *external validity* ("To what populations, settings, and variables can this effect be generalized?"). (See Donald Campbell, p. 1.) The optimal design of *any* piece of research has *both* types of validity. But we shall see how the procedures used to secure internal validity sometimes interfere with the generalizability of results—a difficulty which may be especially acute in the designing of particular experiments.

In examining the research problems of generalizing from experimental findings, we shall consider first how the sampling procedure affects the representativeness of the *cases* which are selected for the experiment. Then later we shall turn to *other aspects* of the design of particular experiments that may restrict the possibilities of generalizing from the findings.

Representativeness of the Equivalent Sample Design.   The necessity for equivalent samples in the experimental design raises some interesting questions about the representativeness **(P-IV)** of the particular sample, in line with our discussion in Unit 6. The use of control samples in experiments imposes a special requirement, as we have seen, upon the sampling procedure, which must yield, not a single sample, but (at least) two samples as nearly alike as possible. By drawing a main sample, and then subdividing it at random (usually holding certain variables constant through stratification or matching), the investigator designs the sample properly for purposes of *analyzing* the relationships between the explanatory variables. But although he may have designed a sample that is internally valid, he may be ignoring the further—and quite separate—question: Was the procedure for selecting the main sample designed to represent the population of theoretical concern? In other words, to what extent is the researcher justified in generalizing from the cases in his sample in terms of his conceptual model?

Let us examine the representational character of the sample used in the Cambridge-Somerville study, as one example. The question of representativeness arises, as usual (see Table 6-A above) in Phases I and II of the sampling procedure when the main sample is drawn from the larger population or frame. Powers tells us that the population of interest includes "a wide variety of boys," since the researchers wanted to "note later what kind became delinquent and what kind did not." A frame was obtained, by using the judgment of teachers, social agencies, and police and probation officers, to secure the names of "all boys" (of the required age, residence, and school attendance) "who were believed destined to become delinquent, plus an equal number who were thought to be nondelinquent." By a further "selection and screening process" the original list of some 1,950 names was reduced to 782; here the policy was not to eliminate "any boy who showed obvious predelinquent traits," and to balance the boys about equally between predelinquents and nonpredelinquents. The number was further reduced to the 650 finally used in the two samples. If generalizing to a particular population is of interest, it is impossible to assess the representativeness of such a sample, of course, as is often the case when nonprobability selection methods are used.

Yet, if there are difficulties in generalizing from such a painstakingly chosen sample (requiring a "two-year search"), what alternative might there be? The researchers might perhaps consider a main sample drawn at random from all boys of the proper age and in suitable cities. This main sample might then be pre-tested, stratified (or matched as nearly as possible case-by-case) on delinquency prediction ratings and other relevant variables, and then divided at random into the experimental and control samples. Since the "average" boys in this main sample would undoubtedly greatly outnumber the "predelinquents," the nondelinquents might be subsampled; this could again be done on a random basis (and the final results corrected by the appropriate weighting). *All* the boys so chosen would then be used in the experiment, as in Phase III of representational sampling—without elimination of some boys because of difficulties in matching, self-selection, or the judgment of the investigator.

Some such representational procedure would have the *advantage* that the investigators would be in a better position to generalize from their findings to a clearly defined larger population of boys. But it would have attendant *disadvantages* unless very considerable time and funds were available for the random drawing of the main sample and for the pre-testing of a large enough main sample to uncover as many as 325 "predelinquents." Moreover, the requirement of representational sampling that *all* the cases selected must be covered in the research would complicate the matching procedure, sometimes reducing the precision when hard-to-match cases are dropped from the sample, and hence restricting the efficiency and sensitivity of the design.

Thus, the Cambridge-Somerville study suggests that if the researchers were to design the sample not only for purposes of analysis but to represent the population of research interest, they might have to divert resources from the experiment itself. Still other types of difficulties (as noted in Unit 6) arise in experimental designs where the investigator, in order to secure the necessary cases for experimentation, must resort to volunteers or to captive populations (in prisons or schools, for example) or to artificially formed groups which may be quite atypical of the population to which he would like to generalize.

Other Restrictions on Generalization. There are, of course, other types of restrictions imposed by many experimental designs upon the representativeness of the findings, in addition to those of sampling. The *experimental arrangements* and controls set certain limitations. The investigator cannot be sure whether the responses of groups in a laboratory, for example, or of individuals reacting to a communicated message after they have been alerted through a pre-test, bear much resemblance to the responses of such groups or individuals under more natural conditions. To some extent, as we have seen, elaborate designs may be used to reduce the control effect of the research itself.

Another important type of restriction springs from the limited and *rigid selection* for study of just two or—in the more elaborate designs—*just a few of the properties* in the conceptual model **(P-IX).** In studying hypothesized relationships between two (or more) selected variables, researchers deliberately select from a whole system of interdependent relationships among many variables (as discussed in Unit 1—see Turner); in the classical experiment, all these other variables are accounted for, since they are held constant. Yet the removal of the effects of these other variables may sometimes eliminate the very conditions which, *outside* of the experiment, determine *Y*—or the *XY* relationships. (For a discussion of the artificial "tying" or "untying" of variables in experiments, and a proposal for extension of representative sampling from the cases themselves to the "stimulus situations and tests" used in the design, see Brunswik, p. 58 and *passim.*) To some extent, as we have seen, factorial schemes may be used to reduce these difficulties by taking into account several—or multidimensional— independent variables. Furthermore, replications of the experiment under widely varied conditions will test the broader applicability of the findings.

Nevertheless, the experiment per se, by definition selectively focused on a few variables, may sometimes fail to include the very factors which are crucial in the situations of theoretical concern. Hence, as Festinger puts it, "experiments . . . must derive their direction from studies of real-life situations, and results must continually be checked against real-life situations" (Festinger, 1953, pp. 169–70). Experiments may be used to verify or refine our conceptual model of social system processes and relationships; the results of experiments cannot be applied to the model directly, however, but must be further tested within the fuller complex of variables which have not been artificially controlled.

STATISTICAL TESTS OF HYPOTHESES

Before attempting to assess the utility of experiments at the present stage of development of sociology, let us note the use of hypothesis tests. As in the previous illustration of Zelditch's hypothesis (Unit 5), the experimenter states his research hypothesis (Step A in the use of mathematical models)—that the treatment will have a positive effect, for example; then (Step B), he translates this into an "expected" result—*e.g.,* a difference between the experimental and the control groups; and (Step C), he compares the observed findings against the expected result.

In making this comparison between observed and expected findings, he wants to make allowances for chance variation, and so he proceeds to use an appropriate statistical test (Step D). He assumes that his hypotheses as incorporated in his mathematical model are correct, and imagines that a very large number of experiments like the present one have been made; then he computes the theoretical distribution of the results of all these experiments (following probability principles as illustrated in Manual V-B).

You have seen in Exercise V-3 how such tests are applied when the indirect method of using the null hypothesis (in place of the research hypothesis) is used. By locating the observed finding in the theoretical distribution of all possible findings, the investigator determines the probability of obtaining the finding by chance if the null hypothesis is actually correct. If this probability turns out to be small enough (less than a predetermined level such as .05 or .01), he then decides to reject the null hypothesis.

A wide variety of statistical tests are available—for use both in experiments and in cross-section studies—to meet particular research requirements, including the binomial and chi-square tests illustrated in Exercise V-3, the analysis of variance often used for multiple-sample experimental designs, and many other tests described in statistical textbooks. Statistical methods may be used in hypothesis-testing (as in Exercise V-3), or in setting *confidence limits* around estimates from the sample to parameters of the population. (The use of confidence limits was illustrated earlier in Exercise V-1.)

In general, a statistical test may thus be viewed as an adjunct to the use of a mathematical model. The mathematical model is the tool necessary for comparing the findings of research with the sociological processes and relationships postulated in the conceptual model (as we saw in the mathematical models used in Units 3, 5, 8, 9, and 10). The statistical test is a supplementary tool which helps to rule out a finding so small that it may be due to chance alone. Failure to "pass" a statistical test often alerts the researcher to the need for a larger sample which will be more effective or sensitive in discriminating small differences, or it may encourage him to search for possible consistencies within a whole set of comparable findings. Thus the value of such tests (as Stouffer formulates it in the Appendix to the study of conformity, which you analyzed in Unit 6) lies in the avoidance of two dangers of misinterpreting the findings of research:

1. taking seriously small differences that are mostly the result of chance in the sampling and minor variations of the . . . work [Type I errors];
2. ignoring differences which may be indicative of important contrasts between two or more kinds of people [Type II errors].

Two Uses of Statistical Tests. It is interesting to note, in connection with the earlier distinction between external and internal validity, that the research hypothesis being tested may refer either to the question (1) How likely is it that this result will occur by chance, if all other factors are held constant? or to the question (2) How likely is it that this result will occur by chance, if all other factors are distributed "naturally" as they actually exist in the empirical population from which the sample is drawn? The statistical tests as used in experiments are usually applied to hypotheses of form (1), whereas the tests in cross-section studies tend to apply to hypotheses of form (2).

At any rate, in any statistical testing it is essential to use a test which fits the research problem as closely as possible. (A recent controversy in the sociological literature has discussed problems of using inappropriate tests, or of naïvely confusing "statistical significance" with the substantive importance of the hypothesis under study. See Selvin, 1957; McGinnis; Gold; Kish, 1959; T. A. Ryan; and Camilleri.)

ETHICAL PROBLEMS

The technical and statistical refinements possible in experimentation often outrun the practical opportunities and conceptual formulations necessary for their use in sociological applications. In experiments which involve human beings, of course, ethical questions may frequently become so salient as to challenge the very existence of the procedure. On what authority, for example, does the medical researcher withhold a promising drug or therapy from afflicted patients simply because they happened to fall into a control sample? Indeed, with what justification did the researchers in the Cambridge-Somerville study give individual attention to some "predelinquent" boys and deny it to others? On what basis would those in charge of a public housing project have provided improved housing to some families while leaving others to continue living in slum conditions, so as to assist Chapin in an experimental investigation? Or under what circumstances would social researchers be justified in creating conditions designed to produce divorce, mental illness, suicide, or crime? Would not the answer to all these questions, in terms of ethical considerations, be approximately the same?

Fortunately, many experiments pose no such ethical problems. The coffee breaks, improved lighting, paid vacations, and other experimental variables of the Western Electric studies proved to be delightful changes in an otherwise routine factory situation. Yet the good intention of the researcher does not always prevent *indirect* control effects which could have serious consequences. Acute embarrassment, for example, frequently occurs in small group experiments when individuals are seduced by stooges to report judgments which fly in the face of actual experience—to deny, for example, that the longer of two lines is the longer simply because all the other members (have been primed to) deny it. Or, to take another instance, was not Sherif aware that emotional disturbances in his young campers were likely to result from the breaking up of friendships or from the contrived frustrations at the group level?

In all social experiments, of course, the dignity, privacy, and safety of the involved individuals must be kept constantly in mind. The researcher who proposes to carry out an experiment requiring manipulation of people must always be sensitive to the ethical implications of his design and techniques, and under all conditions must ensure that the individuals involved in the experiment agree to its terms and are aware of what this agreement entails. Sometimes he may feel that his plans should be governed by the extent to which the new knowledge derived will, in the long run, be beneficial for all. But in making such decisions he must be sure that his personal ethical principles are congruent with the values of the society in which he conducts his experiments, and are not mere rationalizations of his desire to conduct the research.

THEORY AND EXPERIMENTAL DESIGN

Apart from the ethical issues which frequently make social experimentation difficult, it is predictable that, as both sociological theory and appropriate research methods advance, experiments will come to be more widely used. Many improvements are already being made over the early attempts we have examined in this Unit. More elaborate designs are being more thoughtfully applied to sociological problems, which use many samples to handle complex independent variables, to control the disturbing effects of pre-testing, and the like.

Yet, there is still considerable danger that the right designs will not be applied to the right problems and at the right time, either because the relevant theory lags behind methods and techniques, or because methods are not applied to fit the theory. The essence of the experiment lies in its testing of hypotheses derived from a model. Thus, on the one hand, it would be wasteful to experiment prematurely before the model is specified clearly enough to yield testable hypotheses. A bevy of tightly designed experiments at this time might overly restrict our conceptualizations, shutting us away from the broader view. On the other hand, exclusive reliance upon descriptive studies and exploratory surveys, with no experimental testing of the preliminary findings, would only retard the progress of the science.

The Importance of Flexibility. One means of seeking a balance between these extremes is to conduct experiments, wherever they seem appropriate—but to build an added element of flexibility into the design. A good example of such flexibility is supplied by the log that was kept during the Hawthorne experiment. Without this informal account, which recorded miscellaneous and presumably unrelated incidents as they occurred, the results of the experiment proper would have been unintelligible, and the major serendipitous finding of the study might never have emerged.

Even when the conceptual model has been clearly defined in advance, and a more elaborate design is used, such safeguards may also be valuable. In a sophisticated experiment dealing with the effects of group norms on individual opinions, and of group sanctions on the expression of opinions, several troops of boy scouts were exposed to antiscout propaganda and were individually questioned (Kelley and Volkart). When some of the findings of the study showed negative results, the researchers, although they came up with ingenious ex post facto explanations, had gathered no data on which to test such alternative explanations. Yet, in such instances, a few questions on some possible alternatives may often be included in the original questionnaire; or one or two unstructured questions may throw further light on the underlying processes which often turn out—as they did in this study—to be more complex than the investigators had anticipated.

A wide variety of such devices is available for supplementing highly structured experimental designs with a modicum of opportunity for *further exploration* of other potentially related factors and conditions.

The Importance of Planned Design. Another means of benefiting from some of the virtues of the experiment, without full commitment at this stage to experimental designs, is to keep the experimental model in mind in using other, more flexible, methods. Stouffer, in advocating such an approach, has written: "We must be clear in our minds what proof consists of. . . . The heart of our problem lies in study designs *in advance,* such that the evidence is not capable of a dozen alternative explanations." (Stouffer, 1962, p. 262.) In planning any kind of study, we may learn from the experiment to sense the difference between the promising idea and proof, to train ourselves to use theory in advance of setting particular problems, and to narrow the number of measurable variables so that they become manageable within an appropriate design.

Eventually, of course, the hope is that many theoretically based hypotheses will be appropriately tested through experiment. Ideally, these will not be isolated hypotheses, but will be interrelated, so that testing can provide mutually supporting evidence. Ideally too, each hypothesis will not be a single statement of a null hypothesis to be tested against the whole range of possible alternatives, but will be a prediction of the magnitude of the relationship; or it will be a statement of alternative hypotheses deduced from theory, so that elimination of the one affords some confidence in the other.

SUGGESTED READINGS FOR UNIT ELEVEN

Donald Campbell; Edwards, 1954; Festinger, 1953; Fisher; French; Goode and Hatt, Chapters 7 and 8; Hagood and Price, Chapters 12–16, 19; Hyman, 1955, pp. 242–47; Kish, 1959; Madge, Chapter 6; Moser, Chapter 1; Mosteller and Bush; Mosteller, Rourke, and Thomas, Chapter 8; Mueller and Schuessler, Chapter 12; Selltiz *et al.,* Chapter 4; Siegel, pp. 36–42, 68–82, 104–11; Solomon; Stouffer, 1962, Chapter 15; Zelditch and Hopkins.

QUESTIONS FOR REVIEW AND DISCUSSION

Review the following methodological terms as used in this Unit:

classical experimental design
ex post facto design
interim factors
statistical interaction

statistics of inference:
binomial test
chi-square test
sign test
Type I error
Type II error

terms defining samples:
control sample
equivalent samples
experimental sample
random assignment

1. Contrast the conceptions of the group held by Sherif and by the Hawthorne researchers in the Relay Assembly experiment. How do differences in these conceptions help account for differing research designs?

2. Compare the methods of data-collection and analysis of Sherif with those of Whyte. How are they similar? How do they differ?

3. Study Table 3 in the Sherif study. State in words what the table shows. Compare Sherif's concept of in-group formation with Lundberg and Lawsing's concept of nucleation.

4. Sherif specifies several hypotheses in advance of data-collection. Is this advance specification a requirement of experimental design? What are the implications of the Hawthorne studies for the answer to this question?

5. Compare the use of the production rate as a measure in the Hawthorne studies with Le Play's use of the budget.

6. What aspects of the studies by Bales and by Strodtbeck come closest to approximating the experimental design? In what sense is Strodtbeck's Table 2 based on cross-section analysis? How does it differ from the model of a classical experiment?

7. Compare the focused sample used by Kahl with the sample in Chapin's ex post facto design.

8. Chapin's hypothesis is that "the re-housing of slum families in a public housing project results in improvement of the living conditions and the social life of these families."

    a. Which are the dependent variables?

    b. Describe the measures Chapin used as indicants of the dependent variables.

    c. What is Chapin's research unit (P-I) as stated in the hypothesis?

    d. Was Chapin's research unit the same on both the theoretical and the operational levels? Explain.

    e. State the findings shown in his Tables 1 and 2. Do they seem to support Chapin's hypothesis?

9. How might the studies by Sherif, by the Hawthorne investigators, and by Chapin have retained the full structure of the experimental design? Would a classical design be better suited to the research objective in each of these studies?

10. How might you design an experiment in prevention of delinquency which would utilize theoretical assumptions other than those implicit in the Cambridge-Somerville project?

11. Suppose you wished to test the hypothesis that the total amount of group interaction decreases as the heterogeneity of the group increases (birds of unlike feather have little to say to one another).

    a. How would you design an experiment to test this hypothesis?

    b. Which would be your dependent and which your experimental variable?

    c. How would you define and manipulate your experimental variable?

    d. What kinds of indicants would be suitable in measuring your dependent variable? How would you use these to reflect the property you wish to study?

    e. How would you control for extraneous factors?

UNIT TWELVE
SPECIAL PROBLEMS OF SOCIOLOGICAL ANALYSIS

SUGGESTED PROGRAM OF STUDY

Unit 12 reviews some of the problems of studying the social system at various levels as the research case **(P-I)**, particularly when collective measures **(P-XII)** combine data about parts of the system to refer to the system as a whole.

Exercises and Manual

Exercise II-5 furnishes experience in analyzing data (to be obtained from the class) on dyadic role relationships among the members of a group. After completing your own plans for this analysis, study the designs suggested in the notes on checking the exercise. **Manual II-D** contains instructions for handling dyadic data by hand (or through the use of I.B.M. equipment).

Exercise I-4 (which extends over several weeks) asks you to design and test a data-collection instrument (a questionnaire) for research on social systems; it serves as an operational review of decisions made in planning a study. You should review **Manual I-B** on questioning and questionnaire development.

Studies

Analyze the studies in this Unit by **Davis** and **Golden; Faris** and **Dunham; James Davis;** and **Riley** and **Cohn.** Notice how each deals with two or more levels of the social system. You should define, for each study, what systems and parts are under investigation, what properties are being measured, and how the cross-level relationships among these properties are analyzed. Review Durkheim's study of religion and suicide (Unit 8) as another analysis of the cross-level relationship between individual acts (suicides) and a characteristic (institutionalized values) of the social system as a whole. Review also the study of friendship process by Lazarsfeld and Merton in Unit 10; note especially the ideas you developed under the Questions for Review and Discussion 6a, 6b, and 6c in that Unit.

Commentary

The Commentary outlines several pitfalls that beset the researcher who attempts research on social systems, and formulates a number of possible research approaches that avoid such pitfalls. Some of these approaches (individual analysis, contextual analysis, group analysis, and structural analysis) are partial approaches useful for particular research objectives. A full analysis (called a social system analysis) is also illustrated. It attempts to study the full set of cross-level relationships among selected properties of individual members and their groups.

Questions for Review and Discussion

Use the Questions for Review and Discussion to bring the special problems discussed in this Unit into the general context of the process of sociological research.

KINGSLEY DAVIS
HILDA HERTZ GOLDEN
Urbanization and the Development of Pre-Industrial Areas

The process of urbanization, known to be intimately associated with economic development, deserves close attention if we are to understand the recent and future mechanisms of change in pre-industrial areas. Yet up to the present our comparative knowledge of cities and of urbanization is slight, particularly for underdeveloped areas. . . .

This does not mean that there has been no interest in cities. On the contrary, the literature on cities and city problems is enormous. But most of this material deals with a particular town or at most with a single province or country. Conspicuously absent are systematic comparative analyses putting together and interpreting data on the cities of different countries and different cultures.

Indeed, the study of cities and of urbanization has been heavily confined to countries of European culture. As a result many of our generalizations about urban phenomena, though treated as if they were universal, are actually limited to Western (and often to American or West European) experience and are wrong when applied to most of the rest of the world. In other words, there is as yet no general science of cities. Without such a general science, one cannot get far

Reprinted in part from Kingsley Davis and Hilda Hertz Golden, "Urbanization and the Development of Pre-Industrial Areas," *Economic Development and Cultural Change,* 3, 1954, pp. 6–20, 23–24, with permission of the Research Center in Economic Development and Cultural Change, the University of Chicago.

in analyzing and documenting the interrelations between urbanization and economic development.

The claim may be made that a comparative science of urban phenomena is impossible because the data are lacking for most of the world. But this view is hardly justified. In the first place, if we always waited for perfect information before attempting to build a comparative social science we would wait forever. In the second place, the data on cities are more numerous, more accurate, and more accessible than most people who have not looked into the matter seem to believe. The fact that the statistical materials are often lacking or inaccurate in a given country or for a given time, is not a signal for defeat. It is rather a challenge to ingenuity to make the best use of what is available and to supplement this with systematic estimates wherever necessary. . . .

Urbanization vs. the Presence of Cities

At the outset a distinction must be made between urbanization and the mere presence of cities. Urbanization as the term is used here refers to a ratio—the urban people divided by the total population. It is therefore as much a function of the rural as of the urban population, the formula being as follows:

$$u = \frac{P_c}{P_t}$$

where u is urbanization, P_c is city population, and P_t is total population.

Obviously the degree of urbanization in a given country or region can vary independently of the absolute number of people living in cities. India has more people in cities than the Netherlands, but it is far less urbanized than the latter. In other words, by transposing in the preceding equation, we find

$$P_c = uP_t$$

Since the two values u and P_c can vary independently, they have to be kept separate in any comparative analysis. Also, the sheer number of cities in a given country may be as much a function of total population as of degree of urbanization. The distribution of urbanization over the globe, in short, is not equivalent to either the distribution of cities or the distribution of urban inhabitants.

With respect to urbanization, there can be no doubt that the underdeveloped areas of the world have less of it than the advanced areas. If we take as underdeveloped, or pre-industrial, all areas with more than 50 per cent of their occupied males engaged in agriculture, we find that only 9 per cent of their combined population lives in cities of 100,000 or over, whereas for the other countries (industrial) the proportion is 27 per cent. Table 1 gives the indices of urbanization for the

world's countries and territories classified by degree of agriculturalism. It can be seen that the degree of urbanization increases sharply as industrialism increases.

It follows that those parts of the world still mainly in the peasant-agrarian stage of economic development manifest the least urbanization. . . .

These results are of course what one would expect, but it is worth having figures to show the precise extent of the association between economic development and urbanization. Another method of showing the relationship is by a correlation coefficient. As of 1950, the (Pearsonian) correlation between degree of industrialization and degree of urbanization, as measured by our indices, was .86, taking the countries and territories of the world as our units.

It is plain, then, that urbanization is unequally distributed in the world. The achievement of high levels of urbanization anywhere in the world had to wait for the industrial revolution. This remarkable transformation had its rise in one part of the world, western Europe, and thence spread to other parts as industrialism spread. With the exception of Japan, the centers of urbanization today are the places where industrialization has gone hand-in-hand with the expansion of European civilization. In many instances, the spread of this kind of civilization has em-

Table 1   Degree of urbanization in world's countries and territories classified by degree of agriculturalism

Per cent of gainfully occupied males in agriculture	Number of countries	Per cent of population in cities of 100,000–plus
0–19	11	32.3
20–29	11	23.6
30–39	7	23.2
40–49	7	21.9
50–59	16	17.7
60–69	17	8.9
70–plus	86	6.3

braced "new" areas of vast extent and sparse native populations, such as North and South America and Australia. The urbanism of Europe was directly transplanted to these new areas, so that they became highly urbanized without acquiring overall dense populations. They were not hampered by the necessity of a slow evolution from densely settled peasant-agrarianism to modern industrialism. Thus we find that some of the most urbanized regions of the world are among the most sparsely settled, whereas some of the least urbanized are among the most densely settled.

The Share of Cities and City People in Underdeveloped Areas

The concentration of urbanization in industrial areas should not lead us to believe that most of the cities and most of the city people are found in those areas, as is commonly thought. The truth is that three-fourths of the world's population lives in pre-industrial countries. Although these countries are mainly rural, they are all urbanized to some degree because of the commercial impact of the industrial nations. Consequently, we find that the underdeveloped countries contain as many cities as do the industrial countries, as Table 2 shows. The countries having more than half of their occupied males in

agriculture, forestry and fishing (the underdeveloped nations), contain 463 large cities. From the last column of Table 2 it can be seen that the underdeveloped countries have more people (160 million) living in cities of 100,000 or more than do the industrialized nations (155 million).

The same general finding can be shown in another way. If instead of grouping countries according to their degree of agriculturalism, we group them according to their degree of urbanization, it turns out that the more rural countries have as many large cities and as many dwellers in large cities as the more urbanized ones.

It becomes clear that the science of cities must concern itself just as much with underdeveloped countries as with advanced countries. Too much of the past study and interpretation of cities has ignored this simple fact. Deductions concerning "the city" have been made principally on the basis of American and European cases, embracing at best less than half of the universe being discussed.

Urbanization and Agricultural Density

The point has already been made that no relation exists between degree of urbanization and average density of population. Some of the underdeveloped and

*Table **2** Distribution of world's large cities and city population by degree of agriculturalism of countries*

Per cent of active males in agriculture	Number of countries	Number of cities	Per cent of all cities	Population in cities (000's)	Per cent of total city population
0–29	22	286	31.9	101,438	32.2
30–49	14	148	16.5	53,721	17.1
50–69	33	287	32.0	97,429	30.9
70–plus	86	176	19.6	62,478	19.8
Total	155	897	100.0	315,067	100.0

hence least urbanized countries are among the most densely settled, and some of the most highly developed are among the most sparsely settled; and vice versa. There is, however, a relationship—a negative one—between urbanization and what we call agricultural density (the number of males occupied with agriculture, hunting and forestry per square mile of cultivated land), exhibited in Table 3.

Table 3   Agricultural density according to degree of urbanism

Per cent of population in cities 100,000–plus	Agricultural males per square mile of agricultural land
0–9.9	136
10–19.9	72
20–29.9	67
30–plus	13

Although this negative relationship seems to affront common sense (for we might think that cities demand more agricultural products and hence require a dense population in rural areas), the reason for it is apparent upon reflection. As economic development and hence urbanization occur, agriculture tends to become more efficient. Capital equipment, science and better organization replace manpower. Less labor is required per unit of land to produce the same or even a higher agricultural output. The growing cities, in addition to furnishing a market for commercial crops and supplying manufactured goods and services for improving the per-man productivity of agriculture, absorb people from the countryside. As a consequence, the farming population may diminish not only as a proportion of the total population but also in absolute terms (as it has done in the United States and several other industrial countries in recent decades).

The oft-condemned "depopulation" of rural areas is therefore a sign of economic modernization, the growth of cities a boon to progress. This statement is not only true of densely settled agrarian countries such as those of southeast Asia but also true of sparsely settled ones such as those of central and east Africa. The latter, despite a low overall density, have a high ratio of people to land under cultivation. Their main advantage often lies in the fact that an increase in the land under cultivation is possible on a big scale, so that rural-urban migration does not have to absorb the entire surplus population released by the modernization of agriculture.

The Growth of Urbanization in Underdeveloped Areas

The facts of the current situation—the positive correlation between urbanization and industrialization and the negative association between urbanization and agricultural density—suggest what one might expect to find historically. The present concentration of urbanization (as distinct from cities) in the advanced nations is almost wholly a product of the last 150 years. In 1800 the population in large cities was distributed over the earth in much the same fashion as the general population. With the rise and spread of industrialism in the nineteenth century, the European peoples, as we noted, rapidly and markedly increased their degree of urbanization. This hiatus between the advanced and non-advanced parts of the world, however, is but a temporary phenomenon—a lag due to the time required for the geographical and cross-cultural spread of a radically new type of economic and social organization. As the great transformation has been completed in the most advanced countries, as these countries have achieved a high degree of urbanization, the rate of growth of their cities has begun to slacken. Indeed, this

has noticeably happened in the twentieth
century in countries such as Britain,
Switzerland, the Netherlands, and the
United States (see Figures 1 and 2).
It is bound to happen, because as the
proportion of the population living in
cities becomes greater and greater, the
chance of maintaining the *rate* of increase in that proportion becomes less
and less. Furthermore, we know that the
growth of cities has been mainly a result
of rural-urban migration, which has contributed at times far more to urban numbers than the natural increase in cities
could ever contribute. As the rural proportion declines to a small fraction of the
total population, the cities have an ever
smaller pool of people to draw on for the
maintenance of growth rates.

The figures show the steady decline in
the rate of urbanization in the most advanced countries in recent decades. But
at the same time that this has been hap-

pening in industrial areas, the rate of
urbanization has been increasing in most
underdeveloped regions, as the figures
also show. There is thus going on today a
balancing of accounts, an incipient evening out of urbanization throughout the
world. As a result the next fifty or one
hundred years may find the city population once again distributed roughly in
proportion to the world's total population.
If so, it will mark the end of a gigantic
cycle—the urbanization of the world.

The rapidity of urbanization in most
of the pre-industrial areas is surprising.
Only in such out-of-the-way places as
Saudi Arabia, Yemen, and some African
territories has urban expansion failed to
make much headway, and these countries
are few in number and small in total population. As a group, the underdeveloped
countries, with 7 per cent of their people
in 100,000–plus cities and 11 per cent in
20,000–plus cities in 1950, have moved

Figure **1**   *Growth of the proportion of population in cities of 100,000–
plus for the world and for selected countries, 1800–1951*

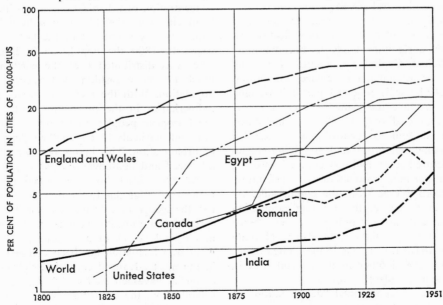

*Figure 2   Growth of the proportion of population in cities of 20,000–
plus for the world and for selected countries, 1800–1951*

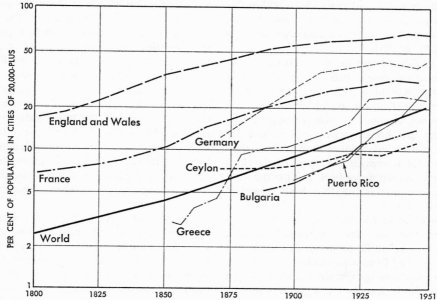

some distance toward a high degree of urbanization. The general picture is therefore one of fast urbanization comparable to that experienced at earlier periods in the now industrialized nations. Since the more recently industrialized countries have tended to urbanize faster once they started than the older countries did, there is reason to believe that the future pace of the currently underdeveloped regions may be fast indeed. Should these regions achieve the rapid rate of urbanization experienced either by Germany or Japan, they will as a group become highly urbanized (with more than 15 per cent of their population in large cities) within the next fifty years.

The pace of urbanization in the backward areas shows that they are anything but static. Sometimes, when one looks at the myriad difficulties and inefficiencies in the pre-industrial countries, when it appears that immemorial customs still pre-

vail and that there is a vicious circle of poverty breeding poverty, one is tempted to think that these societies are static. But the data on trends of city growth and urbanization show them to possess highly dynamic attributes. Since urbanization is not an isolated culture trait but is a function of the total economy, its rapid growth indicates that fundamental changes are occurring at a rate sufficient to transform these pre-industrial societies within a few decades.

These generalizations concerning the underdeveloped countries as a whole seem well worth pondering. They can be documented by statistical analysis of a comparative kind. At the same time, anyone will recognize that the pre-industrial countries are not all alike. Some are more urbanized than others. Some differ in demography, economy, and society from others. It therefore becomes instructive to consider particular countries which represent types of cases—types that may recur in various underdeveloped countries but are not found everywhere within the pre-industrial category. Accordingly, we have picked out a few countries for particular analysis.

In this attempt to analyze briefly some particular cases, two things should be borne in mind. First, as one would expect, our statistics for underdeveloped areas are not as good as those for other areas. They are, however, as good as those we have for industrial nations when they were at a comparable stage of development. As we move back in time the data become poorer, so that long historical series on the underdeveloped countries are quite scarce and our selection of illustrative countries is narrowed. Second, from a scientific point of view little can be learned from a particular case without the benefit of comparative analysis. When a nation is described as a "type" with reference to urbanization it can be so described only in terms of its similarities and contrasts to other countries. Our case analyses are therefore undertaken with comparative statistical analysis in the background, as will become evident.

The particular areas selected for brief presentation below are India, an old agrarian country with a moderate rate of urbanization; Egypt, an over-urbanized and disorganized agrarian country; and central and west Africa, a region of revolutionary new urbanization. The study of these regions in comparative terms raises some fundamental questions about the dynamics of urbanization.

The Case of India

Since pre-industrial countries are not all "underdeveloped" to the same degree, one of the first questions to be asked about any one of them is how its situation compares with that of other countries. India, with respect to our index of industrialization, stands at about the midpoint of the array. Fifty-one per cent of the rest of the world's population lives in countries more industrialized than India and 49 per cent in countries less industrialized. When each country is treated as a unit regardless of population, only 43 per cent of the countries and colonies of the world are more industrialized than India. With 68.9 per cent of her male population dependent on agriculture in 1951, India is definitely in the underdeveloped category, but she is somewhat more advanced than the average country in that category.

But now an interesting question arises. Modernization has different aspects, and if indices can be found which approximately measure these aspects, we can find in what ways a country is more developed and in what ways less developed than its general position would indicate. In other words, in addition to comparing different countries with reference to a particular index, we can compare several indices within the same country. By way of illustration, Table 4 shows that India seems far behind on literacy and considerably behind on per capita income and the reduction of agricultural density. She is best off in terms of occupational structure (our measure of industrialization) and in terms of urbanization. Thus we may say that there is some tendency for urbanization to run ahead of other aspects of development in India, but not noticeably except with respect to educational development.

Without attempting here to explain the particular character of India's situation which these indices point up—which is a significant problem in understanding economic change in pre-industrial countries —let us say that even though urbanization tends to be slightly more advanced than

Table **4** *India's relative position on selected indices*

	Per cent of world's population in countries ahead of India	Per cent of countries ahead of India
Non-agricultural employment	51	43
Agricultural density	57	69
Urbanization	59	51
Literacy	92	68
Per capita income	57	73

her total economy and society would lead us to estimate, it is still modest in world terms. In 1951, the country had 6.8 per cent of its population in cities of 100,000 or more, as compared to 13.1 per cent for the world as a whole. India manifests less than half the urbanization found in Brazil (13.9 per cent in 100,000–plus cities in 1950) and only one-fourth that found in Chile (26.0 per cent in 1950).

The present percentage of India's population living in large cities is about the same as that of the United States in 1855. But urbanization is proceeding somewhat more slowly in India than in the United States at that time, and it went much more slowly in the early periods. From 1820 to 1860 in the United States the average gain per decade in the proportion living in large cities was 63 per cent. In India from 1891 to 1951 it was 22 per cent. In spite of the fact that progress can be faster the more recently it occurs, this is not proving true in India, at least so far as urbanization is concerned. This suggests that there have been dampers on India's development which did not operate in America in its early history. As a result of the unequal rates of development at similar stages of urbanization, India has fallen further behind than it was. Whereas in 1891 India was about 55 years behind the United States in this matter, by 1931 she was over 90 years behind. After 1931, however, India's rate of urbanization increased markedly, al-

most equalling the United States gain at similar levels. How long she will continue to do so is hard to say, and if she does, it may be a consequence of "over-urbanization" such as seems to occur occasionally in other densely peopled agrarian countries. This possibility is suggested by the apparently static character of India's occupational structure, for the proportion of occupied males in agriculture has shown virtually no sign of change for several decades.

Egypt: An Over-Urbanized Country

That there is, on a world-wide basis, a high correlation (.86) between urbanization and our index of economic development has already been mentioned. About one-fourth of the variation in urbanization from one country to another, however, cannot be explained by variation in the degree of non-agriculturalism. If the relationship between the two variables is represented in the form of a regression curve, certain countries are found to be off the line to a significant extent. One of these is Egypt, which has far more urbanization than its degree of economic development would lead us to expect. In this sense Egypt is "over-urbanized," and since this is a condition found also in certain [other] underdeveloped areas (notably Greece and Korea, and probably Lebanon), an examination of the case

offers some clues to the dynamics of urbanization in underdeveloped areas under
certain conditions. [This section is drawn
heavily from the work of Robert Parke,
Jr.]

How far out of line Egypt is can be
seen from the following figures:

	Per cent of population in cities	
	100,000–plus	20,000–plus
Switzerland, 1950	20.6	31.2
Egypt, 1947	19.3	28.5
Sweden, 1945	17.4	29.2
France, 1946	16.6	31.9

By no stretch of the imagination is Egypt
as industrialized as the other three countries in the list, yet she is nearly as urbanized as Switzerland and is more urbanized
on the 100,000 level than Sweden or
France. Indeed, the proportion urban in
the 1947 Egyptian census is so high that
some suspicion attaches to the figure, but
even if a correction factor is introduced
to compensate for overenumeration of the
large city population, Egypt is far more
urbanized than its industrial position
would require. Furthermore, this condition is not of recent origin (i.e., not found
in the 1947 census alone) but has characterized the country for at least forty years,
as Table 5 shows. The overurbanization
is therefore real, and it has increased
with time.

In looking for an explanation of this
situation, one has to take into account
the fact that Egypt's cultivated rural area
is, to an extraordinary degree, densely
settled and impoverished. The density is
a product of rapid population growth for
a century and a half and the inability of
the economy to expand its non-agricultural sector proportionately. The poverty
is due to the same factors, plus the familiar pattern of tenancy associated with

large landholdings whose absentee owners
live in the cities. As the result of the im-
poverishment of the rural masses and the
absence from the countryside of those
who utilize the agricultural surplus, a curious thing has happened: nearly everybody who is not actually farming the
land has gotten out and gone to the cities.
Mr. Parke, on the basis of the 1947 census, has estimated that only 10 per cent of
the occupied males living in rural places
—i.e., villages and towns of less than
5,000—are engaged in non-agricultural
pursuits. For 1950 in Puerto Rico the
figure is 23 per cent (except that rural is
there defined as places of less than 2,500,
which makes the contrast sharper), and
in France the figure is estimated at 50
per cent. One cannot avoid feeling that
in Egypt the social and economic structure has so deprived the cultivator that
he has little or nothing beyond bare subsistence. He cannot command much by
way of services or handicraft products,

Table **5**   *Expected and actual*
urbanization in Egypt, 1907–1947

	Per cent of oc-cupied males in non-agricultural activities	Per cent of population in cities 100,000–plus	
		Expected [a]	Actual
1907	27	6.6	8.7
1917	30	7.9	9.7
1927	34	9.7	12.2
1937	31	8.4	13.3
1947	38	11.4	19.3 [b]

[a] The expected figure is derived from the
regression equation in which the proportion
of non-agricultural male employment is the
independent variable and the proportion in
large cities is the dependent variable. The
compilation of the necessary data and the
derivation of the equation are mainly the
work of Hilda Hertz.

[b] If a correction is made for overenumeration, the figure comes out to 17.6 per cent.

and consequently the people who furnish such goods and services have gone to the cities. In the cities the non-agricultural producer can at least find the people—landowners, government workers, and middle classes—who drain the countryside of its surplus; and it is to them that he looks for support. The city therefore gathers to itself practically everybody who does not actually have to work the land to get a living.

Not only do productive non-agriculturalists come to the cities in Egypt, but also a great many unproductive people. Whereas the cities in industrial countries normally have a disproportionate share of people in the working ages, the Egyptian cities fail to exhibit this characteristic. They have, to an astonishing degree, the same age-sex structure as the total population. This is particularly strange since normally in an oriental city the sex ratio is heavily distorted in favor of males. Since Muslim-culture women do not participate in non-agricultural economic activities, the normal city sex ratio in Egypt, along with an unusually high proportion of children, means that the inactive population in the cities is extremely high. The data indicate, according to Parke, that about 92 per cent of women aged 15 and over in Cairo and Alexandria are economically inactive.

Such facts show that the densely settled and impoverished countryside in Egypt is pushing people into the cities because they have no other alternative. When they get into the cities it is perhaps harder for the government to let them starve, and they run some chance of picking up some crumbs from the wealthy who inhabit only the cities. . . . Much of the migration to the cities seems therefore to be a refugee migration from the countryside where increased population, diminished size of holdings, and absentee landlord exactions have gradually squeezed out families by the thousands.

These facts are sufficient to account for the overurbanization which we found to characterize Egypt. That they do so was found by certain calculations performed by Parke. He first assumed that the non-agriculturalists in Egypt were distributed as between the urban and rural sectors in the same ratio as in Puerto Rico. The effect of this assumption was to reduce the population in large cities by 13 per cent. Hence, the concentration of non-agriculturalists and of the inactive population in cities would virtually account for the observed overurbanization in Egypt. . . .

A similar tendency toward overurbanization seems to have occurred in Greece and may occur in the future in India and some other underdeveloped areas if the underlying conditions arise. One must therefore raise the question of what its significance is for economic development.

One's first tendency is to condemn such overurbanization as artificial and perhaps harmful to economic growth. One frequently hears the old plaint that people are being turned off the land and are drifting unhappily to the metropolis, and the temptation is to say that the process should be stopped. The use of the word "overurbanization" may connote such an evaluative interpretation. But the term as used here has only a statistical meaning, with no overtone of evaluation intended. From the standpoint of future economic growth, three considerations stand out. First, overurbanization surely has its limits. It is possible for city growth to get ahead of general modernization, but not very far ahead for very long. If there is economic stagnation, urban growth itself must ultimately cease. In Egypt we can expect, then, that either the rate of urbanization will fall off sharply or industrialization will gain a new impetus. Second, overurbanization may have some effect in stimulating economic growth. Insofar as the city represents an efficient locale for non-agricultural production (as we believe it does), the accumulation of people in cities represents at least a potential setting for enhanced output. Also, in the process of modernizing agriculture, the more people who can be moved off the land, the better. Third, it is primarily in the cities that the leadership and the mobile following for revolutionary activities are to be found. Overurbanization, as we have analyzed it, is well calculated to provoke the maximum discontent in the population. Faced with idle, impoverished, and rootless urban masses, the government is forced to take drastic action or to allow itself to be displaced by a new revolutionary group. Since economic development is often hindered by outmoded institutional and political arrangements, the role of urbanization in fostering revolutionary activity (whether communist or not) can be said to be potentially favorable to change. It should be emphasized, however, that we are speaking of potentialities. Whether or not these potentialities are in fact realized depends on other factors in the situation. Urbanization, and particularly overurbanization, is only one of several major variables in industrial change, and so it is wise to avoid the appearance of determinism with reference to its role.

Revolutionary New Urbanization in Africa

In cases such as India, Egypt, Korea and Greece, we are confronted with countries that have long experienced the phenomenon of cities and which have old and complex civilizations. In central and west Africa, on the other hand, we find ourselves in a totally different kind of underdeveloped region—one in which primitive tribal life, completely rural in character, has been the dominant mode of existence until very recently. It is still a region of unlettered rurality, its people getting their subsistence mainly by hoe agriculture, by herding, or by hunting and fishing.

Yet into this still heavily primitive region is now being thrust an extremely rapid and patently modern city development. The urbanization that is rapidly taking place is not the urbanization of the late medieval period in Europe, not the urbanization of the 18th and 19th centuries; it is rather the urbanization of the 20th century. This sudden juxtaposition of 20th-century cities and extremely primitive cultures (virtually stone-age in their organization and technology) gives rise in some respects to a sharper rural-urban contrast than can be found anywhere else in the world. It is the contrast between Neolithic cultures on the one hand and industrial culture on the other, not mitigated by intervening centuries of sociocultural evolution but juxtaposed and mixed all at once.

It follows that the flow of migrants from countryside to city in Africa corresponds to a rapid transition telescoping several millennia into a short span. The social disorganization to which it gives rise is probably greater than that ever before experienced by urban populations. The native coming to the city cannot immediately divest himself of his tribal customs and allegiances, his superstitions and taboos; yet these are fantastically inappropriate to a modern urban milieu. Nor can he acquire suddenly the knowledge and habitudes necessary to make city life reasonable and workable. The result is a weird and chaotic mixture which gives to the average African city an unreal, tense, jangling quality. . . .

Most of Negro Africa, the world's most

rural region, is yielding rapidly to urbanization, and that in spite of (perhaps because of) the disorganization of this twentieth-century intrusion into Neolithic culture, the region stands a chance of shortcircuiting much of the painful evolution that the older partially urbanized civilizations will have to go through before they achieve an urban-industrial society with a commensurate level of living.

Conclusion: The Role of Cities in Economic Development

Behind much of our reasoning is the assumption that urbanization is not only an excellent index of economic development and social modernization but also itself a stimulus to such change. This assumption should not be taken for granted. It should be examined, and in comparative urban research we have an opportunity to do so. Space does not permit a full treatment of the matter here, but the line of reasoning may be briefly intimated as a fitting conclusion to this paper.

Basically, the city is an efficient mode of human settlement because, with great numbers concentrated in a small area, it minimizes one of the greatest obstacles to human production—what Haig has called "the friction of space." This achievement is not possible without a high degree of urbanization (i.e., not possible in a predominantly agricultural or nonindustrial economy) because by their very nature such activities as hunting and tillage require a large area in relation to number of workers. In non-agricultural production, however, land is not a factor in production but merely a site. Consequently, production can be concentrated in small space; and when this is done in a city, a great variety of goods and services can be supplied by numerous special-

ized producers whose mutual interdependence is facilitated by the possibility of ready and cheap transport and communication within the city. The city thus becomes, in essence, one great factory.

The gain in efficiency thus achieved, though enormous, is not without its limits. The main limitation is that the city is not self-contained. It must export and import to live. It must export either goods or services, or both, to its rural hinterland, and it must usually export to other cities as well. It therefore requires other means of overcoming friction of space than the sheer fact of close settlement within its own boundaries. This is why adequate transportation is indispensable to a high degree of urbanization. Insofar as the technology of rural-urban and of interurban transport and communication is itself an urban product, the city becomes something of a self-generating system, for it is producing the means for ever greater urbanization. The steamboat, railroad, and airplane, by facilitating long-distance transport, made it possible for individual cities to become larger and for a greater proportion of a country's population to live in them. Improved transport made it easier for rural people to migrate to the cities; and the cities, by removing excess rural manpower, by stimulating the demand for agricultural products, and by furnishing capital and new organizational principles and techniques for rural enterprise, contributed to the modernization of agriculture itself.

The efficiency of the city is not limited to the economic sphere. It also makes possible a greater accumulation of capital and personnel for purposes of formal education, public health, science, art, etc. Doubtless much is wasted on excrescences of religious superstition and frivolous fashion and display, but the possibility of specialization in different branches of knowledge, of the accumulation of libraries and the exchange of ideas, exists because of the character of the city. . . .

All told, then, the city makes its own peculiar contribution to the process of economic development. It is no accident that urbanization and industrialization have gone hand-in-hand. The appearance of rapid urbanization in underdeveloped areas is therefore both a sign of change already under way and an augury of future change. Its stimulating role is possibly more hampered in well-established agrarian civilizations such as those of India and Egypt and least hampered in primitive but potentially rich areas such as central and west Africa, but its effect in any case would seem to be substantial.

As yet only a small part of the world has become highly urbanized, but that small part is dominant over the rest and is diffusing its urban pattern widely. As the whole world begins to become highly urbanized, human society can be expected to become more dynamic than in the past. The process of urbanization itself must come to an end when nearly all people live in urban aggregations, but the forms of life and the ecological patterns within these aggregates will doubtless continue to change and the innovating force of urbanism will continue to modify culture and society.

ROBERT E. L. FARIS
H. WARREN DUNHAM
Mental Disorders in Urban Areas

Natural Areas of the City

A relationship between urbanism and social disorganization has long been recognized and demonstrated. Crude rural-urban comparisons of rates of dependency, crime, divorce and desertion, suicide, and vice have shown these problems to be more severe in the cities, especially the large rapidly expanding industrial cities. But as the study of urban sociology advanced, even more striking comparisons between the different sections of a city were discovered. Some parts were found to be as stable and peaceful as any well-organized rural neighborhood while other parts were found to be in the extreme stages of social disorganization. Extreme disorganization is confined to certain areas and is not characteristic of all sections of the city.

Out of the interaction of social and economic forces that cause city growth a pattern is formed in these large expanding American cities which is the same for all the cities, with local variations due to topographical and other differences. This pattern is not planned or intended, and to a certain extent resists control by planning. The understanding of this order is necessary to the understanding of the social disorganization that characterizes urban life.

Reprinted in part from Robert E. L. Faris and H. Warren Dunham, *Mental Disorders in Urban Areas,* Chicago, Illinois: University of Chicago Press, 1939, pp. 1–10, 20–21, 23, 25, 28, 35–42, 48–57, 63, 71–72, 75–76, 80, 160, with permission of The University of Chicago Press.

The most striking characteristics of this urban pattern, as described by Professor Burgess, may be represented by a system of concentric zones, shown in Figure 1. Zone I, at the center, is the central business district. The space is occupied by stores, business offices, places of amusement, light industry, and other business establishments. There are few residents in this area, except for transients inhabiting the large hotels, and the homeless men of the "hobohemia" section which is usually located on the fringe of the business district.

Zone II is called the zone in transi-

Figure 1   Natural areas and urban zones [a]

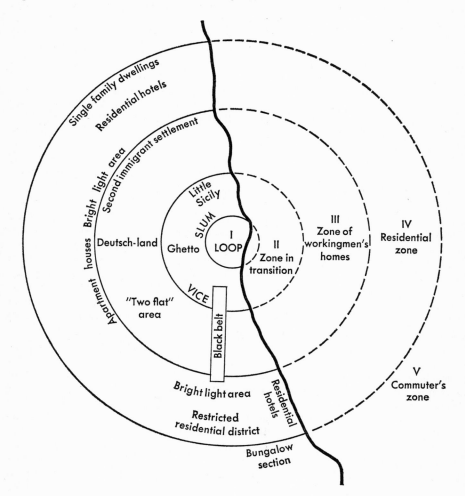

tion. This designation refers to the fact that the expanding industrial region encroaches on the inner edge. Land values are high because of the expectation of sale for industrial purposes, and since residential buildings are not expected to occupy the land permanently, they are not kept in an improved state. Therefore, residential buildings are in a deteriorated state and rents are low. These slums are inhabited largely by unskilled laborers and their families. All the settlements of foreign populations as well as the rooming-house areas are located in this zone.

Zone III, the zone of workingmen's homes, is inhabited by a somewhat more stable population with a higher percentage of skilled laborers and fewer foreign-born and unskilled. It is intermediate in many respects between the slum areas and the residential areas. In it is located the "Deutschlands," or second immigrant settlement colonies, representing the second generation of those families who have migrated from Zone II.

Zones IV and V, the apartment-house and commuters' zones, are inhabited principally by upper-middle-class families. A high percentage own their homes and reside for long periods at the same address. In these areas stability is the rule and social disorganization exceptional or absent.

The characteristics of the populations in these zones appear to be produced by the nature of the life within the zones rather than the reverse. This is shown by the striking fact that the zones retain all their characteristics as different populations flow through them. The large part of the population migration into the city consists of the influx of unskilled labor into the second zone, the zone in transition. These new arrivals displace the populations already there, forcing them to move farther out into the next zone. In general, the flow of population in the city is of this character, from the inner zones

toward the outer ones. Each zone, however, retains its characteristics whether its inhabitants be native-born, white, foreign-born, or Negro. Also each racial or national group changes its character as it moves from one zone to the next.

Within this system of zones, there is further sifting and sorting of economic and social institutions and of populations. In the competition for land values at the center of the city, each type of business finds the place in which it can survive. The finding of the place is not infrequently by trial and error, those locating in the wrong place failing. There emerge from this competition financial sections, retail department store sections, theater sections, sections for physicians' and dentists' offices, for specialized shops, for light industry, for warehouses, etc.

Similarly, there are specialized regions for homeless men, for rooming-houses, for apartment hotels, and for single homes. The location of each of these is determined ecologically and the characteristics also result from the interaction of unplanned forces. They maintain their characteristics in spite of the flow of various racial and national groups through them and invariably impress their effects on each of these groups. These have been called "natural areas" by Professor Park, because they result from the interaction of natural forces and are not the result of human intentions.

Fortunately, the city of Chicago has been studied somewhat more intensively than most cities of its size. Certain of these areas are significant in relation to social disorganization. It is possible to define and describe these areas with certain kinds of objective data. . . . Extending outward from the central business district are the principal industrial and railroad properties. The rooming-house sections extend along three arms radiating from the center to the north, west, and south. The slum areas are roughly defined by the regions containing over 50 per cent foreign-born and native-born of foreign parentage and over 50 per cent Negro. Beyond these areas is the residential section. In the Lake Calumet section at the southeastern corner of the city is another industrial region inhabited by a foreign-born population.

Too small to be shown on [a] map are the areas of homeless men—the "hobohemia" areas. These are located on three main radial streets and are just outside the central business district. Their inhabitants are the most unstable in the city. The mobility and anonymity of their existence produce a lack of sociability and in many cases deterioration of the personality. Although spending their time in the most crowded parts of the city, these homeless men are actually extremely isolated. For the most part they represent persons unable to obtain an economic foothold in society, and so they maintain themselves by occasional labor, by petty thievery, by begging, and by receiving charity. As they have no opportunity for normal married life, their sexual activities are limited to relations with the lowest type of prostitutes and to homosexuals. The rate of venereal infection is high among these men. Chronic alcoholism is also a common characteristic of the members of this group. Their lives are without goal or plan, and they drift aimlessly and alone, always farther from the conventional and normal ways of living.

Another area of importance is the rooming-house area. This is usually located along main arteries of transportation and a little farther from the center of the city. In Chicago there are several rooming-house sections, the three largest consisting of arms radiating to the north, west, and south, just beyond the hobohemia areas, each extending for something over two miles in length and from a half-mile to over a mile in width. The populations of these areas are principally young, unmarried white-collar workers, who are employed in the central business district during the day and live in low-priced rented rooms within walking distance or a short ride from their work. Within the area the population is constantly shifting, turning over entirely about once each four months. Anonymity and isolation also characterize the social relations in this area; no one knows his neighbors and no one cares what they might think or say. Consequently the social control of primary group relations is absent, and the result is a breakdown of standards of personal behavior and a drifting into unconventionality and into dissipations and excesses of various sorts. The rates of venereal diseases and of alcoholism are high in this area, and the suicide rate is higher than for any other area of the city.

The foreign-born slum areas occupy a large zone surrounding the central business and industrial area. Within this zone there are a number of segregated ethnic communities, such as the Italian, Polish, Jewish, Russian, and Mexican districts. The newly arrived immigrants of any nationality settle in these communities with their fellow-countrymen. In these groups the language, customs, and many institutions of their former culture are at least partly preserved. In some of the most successfully isolated of these, such as the Russian-Jewish "ghetto," the Old-World cultures are preserved almost intact. Where this is the case, there may be a very successful social control and little social disorganization, especially in the first generation. But as soon as the isolation of these first-settlement communities begins to break down, the disorganization is severe. Extreme poverty is the rule; high rates of juvenile delinquency, family disorganization, and alcoholism reflect the various stresses in the lives of these populations.

Two distinct types of disorganizing factors can be seen in the foreign-born slum areas. The first is the isolation of the older generation, the foreign-born who speak English with difficulty or not at all and who are never quite able to become assimilated to the point of establishing intimate friendships with anyone other than their native countrymen. Within the segregated ethnic communities these persons are well adapted to their surroundings, but as soon as they move away or are deserted by their neighbors, they suffer from social isolation. The second type of disorganizing factor operates among the members of the second and third generations. The very high delinquency rate among the second-generation children has been shown by Shaw. This disorganization can be shown to develop from the nature of the child's social situation. Also growing out of the peculiar social situation of the second generation is the mental conflict of the person who is in process of transition between two cultures—the culture of his ancestors and the culture of the new world in which he lives. As he attends American schools and plays with children of other than his own nationality, the child soon finds himself separated from the world of his parents. He loses respect for their customs and traditions and in many cases becomes ashamed of his own nationality, while at the same time he often fails to gain complete acceptance into the American group of his own generation. This is particularly true if he is distinguished by color or by features which betray his racial or national origin. This person is then a "man without a culture," for though he participates to some extent in two cultures, he rejects the one and is not entirely accepted by the other.

The Negro areas are, in general, similar in character to the foreign-born slum areas. The principal Negro district in Chicago extends for several miles southward from the business district. Two smaller Negro districts are located on the Near West side, as well as one on the Near North Side. In the larger area on the South Side, the social disorganization is extreme only at the part nearest the business district. In the parts farther to the south live the Negroes who have resided longer in the city and who have become more successful economically. These communities have much the same character as the nearby apartment-house areas inhabited by native-born whites.

For some miles along the Lake Front in Chicago a long strip of apartment-hotel districts has grown up. These districts occupy a very pleasant and favorable location and attract residents who are able to pay high rentals. The rates of various indices of social disorganization are in general low in these sections.

[In] outlying residential districts [the] middle-class and upper-middle-class native-born white population live in apartments, two-flat homes, and single homes. In these districts, and especially the single home areas in which there is a large percentage of homes owned by the inhabitants, the population is stable and there is little or no social disorganization in comparison with those areas near the center of the city. . . .

The natural areas . . . can be identified by the use of certain mathematical indices for different types of social phenomena. Such indices as the percentage of foreign-born, the percentage of homes owned, the sex ratio, the median rentals paid, the density of population, the rate of mobility, the educational rate, the percentage of rooming-houses and hotels, and the percentage of condemned buildings, roughly tend to identify these areas and to differentiate between them. These indices might be regarded as ones which measure the extent of social disorganization between the different communities and the natural areas of the city. Other types of objective data, representing such social problems as juvenile delinquency, illegitimacy, suicide, crime, and family disorganization, might be considered as indices representing effects or results of certain types of social processes. As in the research of Clifford Shaw . . . the rates for these different social problems tend to fit rather closely into the ecological structure of the city as described by Park, Burgess, and others. In other words, in all of these social problems there is the concentration of high rates close to the center of the city, with the rates declining in magnitude as one travels in any direction toward the city's periphery. Shaw's study of juvenile delinquency gives one of the most complete pictures of this pattern. The other studies, in general, show the same pattern with certain variations which develop because of the location of certain ethnic groups in certain parts of the city.

The problem of mental disorder has been for the first time approached by the utilizing of this ecological technique. It is the attempt to examine the spatial character of the relations between persons who have different kinds of mental breakdowns. While this type of approach is used in this study, the authors wish to emphasize that they regard it as having definite limitations in understanding the entire problem of mental disorder. It can be looked upon as a purely cultural approach and as such does not tend to conflict with any understanding of this problem which may come from biological, physiological, or psychological approaches. However, in the light of these

previous studies of social problems utilizing this method it does seem particularly desirable to study the distribution of the different types of mental disorders. . . .

Urban Distribution of Insanity Rates

All cases of mental disorder in Chicago that are cared for in public institutions are first brought to the Cook County Psychopathic Hospital, where they are held for a week or more for examination and a tentative diagnosis. The number of new cases brought here average over 3,000 each year. Some are judged not insane; some cases are mild enough to be allowed to live at home or with relatives. Those needing hospital care are committed to one of several state institutions in the vicinity of Chicago. . . .

DISTRIBUTION OF RATES FOR STATE HOSPITALS

The [28,763] cases used are from four state institutions, and consist of all those committed to those institutions from Chicago during the years 1922–34. [These are supplemented by 6,101 private hospital cases, representing] all the cases for the years 1922–34 from eight of the largest private hospitals in Chicago or vicinity. . . . [The rates are expressed per 100,000 population age 15 or over. . . .]

INSANITY RATES BY URBAN ZONES

A clearer understanding of the actual ecology of insanity in Chicago may be obtained by an examination of the rates by zones in Map 1. . . . On this map the city is divided into five sections, each containing four or more zones within a two-mile radius of each other, with the exception of Zone I, the central business district, constructed on a one-mile radius. On ex-

Map **1**   *Insanity average rates, 1922–1934, for Chicago, by zones and divisions of the city* [a]

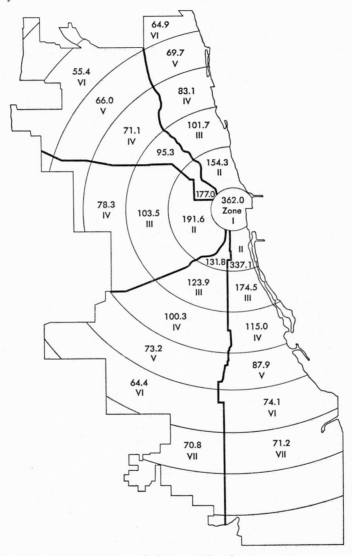

[a] Rates based on 100,000, 1930 population, age 15 and over.

amination of Map 1 it is clearly shown that by far the highest rate for insanity in the city occurs in the central business district or Zone I. In every zone, in every section of the city, with the exception of the southwest side, there is a steady decline in rates as one travels from the center of the city to the periphery. On the southwest side there is a slight rise in Zone VII.

This presentation definitely establishes the fact that insanity, like other social problems, fits into the ecological structure of the city. As such the distribution of insanity appears to be a function of the city's growth and expansion, and more specifically of certain undetermined types of social processes. With this fact well established the question immediately arises whether the different psychoses are distributed in the same manner throughout the city. In the following chapters the various psychoses will be examined to see whether they fit into the configuration which has been established for all types of mental disorder. . . .

The Typical Pattern in the Distribution of Schizophrenia

The symptomatology of schizophrenia is varied but certain symptoms appear to be somewhat common to all forms. The text books of psychiatry generally include the following symptoms: apathy and indifference, lack of contact with reality, disharmony between mood and thought, stereotyped attitudes, ideas of reference, delusions, illusions, hallucinations, impaired judgment, lack of attention . . . lack of insight, defects of interest, seclusive makeup, hypochondriacal notions, negativism, and autistic thinking. . . .

Between 1922 and 1931, 7,253 persons admitted to the state hospitals from Chicago for the first time were given a

diagnosis of schizophrenia. . . . The distribution of rates . . . follows the same general pattern as the rates for the general insanity series. The high rates are in and near the center of the city and the low rates consistently occur at the city's periphery. The characteristic rise in the Lake Calumet region in South Chicago is also shown. The highest rates occur in the hobohemia communities.[1] The central rooming-house districts . . . also have very high rates. The rates above the average are also found in first-settlement immigrant communities near the center of the city and in the deteriorated parts of the Negro area immediately south of the central business district. The three Negro communities, 35, 38, and 40, in the column extending to the south of the loop have rates of 662, 470, and 410, respectively. Since all three communities are populated almost entirely by Negroes, the gradation of rates would require an explanation in terms of some other factor or factors than racial tendency toward this psychosis. . . .

From the pattern of rates it appears possible that much of the variation might be explained on the basis of the varying proportions of the foreign-born in the different parts of the city. A useful test of this possibility is found in the following foreign-born rates. These are computed on the basis of the eleven groupings of subcommunities based on housing . . . and are formed by dividing the number of foreign-born cases of schizophrenia in each housing area by the foreign-born population of the area. Table 1 shows the rates and the range of variability.

The high rates in the Negro and the rooming-house areas stand out in con-

[1] Many of the maps shown in this study are based on subdivisions of the zones of Map 1 into 120 subcommunities of the city, which are referred to by number or otherwise described in the text.

Table **1**   *Foreign-born schizophrenic rates . . . for housing areas in Chicago, 1922–1934* [a]

Area	Description	Cases	Foreign-born population as of 1930 × 13	Rate [b]
1.	Single home and two-flat, over $50	210	997,347	21.06
2.	Single home and two-flat, under $50	235	717,691	32.74
3.	Two-flat and single home, over $50	189	665,743	28.39
4.	Two-flat and single home, under $50	684	1,952,795	35.03
5.	Apartment house (native-born)	356	1,507,441	23.62
6.	Hotel and apartment hotel	134	427,986	31.31
7.	Apartment and two-flat	622	1,449,188	42.92
8.	Apartment house (foreign-born)	361	890,474	40.54
9.	Apartment house (Negro)	125	95,732	130.57
10.	Tenement and rooming house	460	711,893	64.62
11.	Rooming house	309	245,427	125.90
	City total	3,685	9,661,717	38.14

[a] [Data on potential variability have been omitted.]
[b] Rates computed on the basis of 100,000, 1930 foreign-born population, ages 15–64: total.

trast to all others. This high rate for the foreign-born in the Negro area indicates that this district contains high rates for other races which, as will be shown [see Table 1], are significantly higher than the rate for Negroes within their own area. The foreign-born have low rates in those areas inhabited by the native-born, although even here the rates are somewhat higher than the rates for the native-born themselves. This variation of rates in the different areas definitely appears to be caused by other factors than the varying proportions of races or nationalities. Table 2 shows that similar results hold for both the male and female foreign-born rates.

ZONE RATES FOR SCHIZOPHRENIA

The closeness with which the configuration of schizophrenia rates follow a typical ecological pattern for Chicago can be seen by an examination of the rates for the different urban zones shown in Map 2. The rates for schizophrenia in the dif-

erent zones follow very closely the zone rates for all types of mental disorder. In every section of the city with the exception of the Southwest and South sides there is a steady decline in rates as one travels from the center of the city to its periphery. On the Southwest and South sides there is a slight rise in the rate of Zone VII. The extremely high rate in the central business district, or Zone I, is quite significant in comparison with the much lower rate in Zone II in the various sections of the city. This configuration of schizophrenic rates would appear to indicate that the distribution of this psychosis is a function of the differentiation of urban areas resulting from the growth of the city. The rates reflect the vast differences which are found in the various urban areas.

AREA RATES FOR SCHIZOPHRENIA

In addition to the zone rates for schizophrenia, rates according to the nativity and racial classification were also com-

Map **2** *Schizophrenia average rates for Chicago, 1922–1934, by zones and divisions of the city* [a]

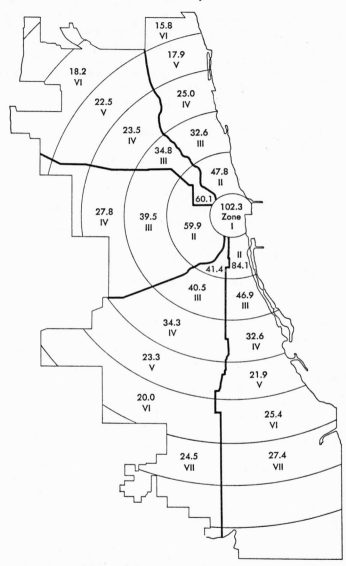

[a] Rates based on 100,000, 1930 population, age 15–64.

puted for the eleven housing areas of the city. The number of cases in relation to the population of these various areas is large enough so that practically all the rates are statistically reliable. Table 2 shows the schizophrenic rate for each of these housing areas according to the race and nativity classification.

It is significant that although the rate for the Negroes in Area 9, the apartment-house (Negro) district, is extremely low as compared to the rates for Negroes in the other areas of the city, the rates for the native white of native parentage and the foreign-born white for this area are the highest rates within these classifications as compared to any of the other areas of the city. It is apparent that the schizophrenic rate is significantly higher for those races residing in areas not pri-

Table **2**   *Area rates for schizophrenia according to nativity and race, 1922–1934* [a, b]

Area	Native white of native parentage		Native white of foreign or mixed parentage		Foreign-born white		Total white [c]		Negro	
	Number	Rate	Number	Rate	Number	Rate	Number	Rate	Number	Rate
1. Single home, over $50	191	18.7	331	19.1	210	21.1	767	20.5	14	35.7
2. Single home, under $50	90	24.2	153	19.6	235	32.7	490	26.2	5	37.3
3. Two-flat, over $50	137	22.0	242	24.9	189	28.4	605	26.8	2	58.1
4. Two-flat, under $50	270	27.1	706	29.4	684	35.0	1,732	32.4	22	37.9
5. Apartment house (native-born)	454	19.8	505	21.8	356	23.6	1,422	23.3	8	67.1
6. Hotel and apartment hotel	195	20.4	149	23.5	134	31.3	539	26.7	12	62.0
7. Apartment and two-flat	194	33.2	428	31.1	622	42.9	1,302	38.2	24	68.5
8. Apartment house (foreign-born)	35	35.6	243	45.1	361	40.5	680	44.5	2	34.0
9. Apartment house (Negro)	125	137.4	77	88.2	125	130.6	359	131.0	821	39.4
10. Tenement and rooming house	99	35.1	267	44.6	460	64.6	867	54.5	25	63.8
11. Rooming house	202	64.1	157	72.2	309	125.9	697	89.6	38	95.5
City total	*1,992*	*26.1*	*3,258*	*28.0*	*3,685*	*38.1*	*9,460*	*32.7*	*973*	*41.4*

[a] The rates here presented are based upon the distribution into the 120 subcommunities of total schizophrenic cases admitted during the period 1922–34 inclusive.... The rates have been refined by both age and nativity and are expressed per 100,000 of the population of the respective age and nativity group....

[b] [Data on "other races" and totals have been omitted.]

[c] Includes "Whites of unknown parentage," and this accounts for corrected figures in total cases. The difference between the number of "Total white" and the sum of the three columns to the left equals the number of white of unknown parentage.

marily populated by members of their own groups. For the entire city the rates, as has been indicated, are highest in the foreign-born and Negro groups. For all classes in the city, Area 11, the rooming-house section, has the highest rate, with the tenement and rooming-house area (10) having the next highest rate and the Negro area (9) following next in order. The highest rates for all classes in these three areas emphasize again the close correspondence and relationship of the high rates of schizophrenia with the disorganized and deteriorated areas of the city. All of the other areas of the city, it should be noted, have rates considerably lower than these three urban areas.

The objective findings in connection with the ecology of schizophrenia can be stated as follows: (1) the high rates for schizophrenia are concentrated in communities of extreme social disorganization in Chicago; (2) the distribution for male and female schizophrenic cases separately shows the same concentration in the disorganized areas of the city; (3) the distribution of rates shows the same pattern and concentration by both local and subcommunities; (4) all distributions of schizophrenic rates show a skewed frequency distribution with the bulk of the communities having low rates and a few of the communities having high rates; (5) the rates of schizophrenia for the foreign-born by total number and by sex in the different housing areas of the city indicate that the variation between rates is due to other factors than the varying proportions of foreign-born; (6) not only are the high rates near the center of the city but the upper quartile of the communities contains 40 per cent of the cases and only 24 per cent of the population; (7) the rates according to race and nativity in the different housing areas of the city show constant high rates in the extremely disorganized parts of the city;

(8) the rate for each white group is the highest in the Negro area, although the rate for Negroes in their own area is low. . . .

The Random Pattern in the Distribution of the Manic-Depressive Psychoses

The distributions of schizophrenic rates attain an additional significance when compared with the other main functional psychosis, manic-depressive. This latter term describes superficially the type of behavior of those persons affected on the one hand by an extremely elated mood, and on the other hand, by an extremely depressed mood. . . . In contrast to the schizophrenia series the absence of the typical ecological pattern is . . . noticeable in the manic-depressive series when the rates are computed for the different zones and the various sections of the city. The zone rates for the various sections of the city are shown in Map 3. While the first zone or central business district still has the highest rate in the city, the rates do not decline in magnitude as a function of the distance traveled from the center of the city. In all the other zones of the city the difference between rates is so small that they have hardly any statistical significance. On the North, Northwest, West, and Southwest sides it appears significant to note the low rates in Zones II and III, the inner zones, as contrasted to the higher rates in the outer zones in these sections of the city. Again, the difference in comparison with the schizophrenic series is observed with the absence of a rise in Zone VII on the South and Southwest sides of the city. . . .

The objective findings in connection with the ecology of the manic-depressive psychosis can be stated as follows: (1) The pattern formed by the states is a random one. Neither high nor low rates are

Map **3**   *Manic-depressive average rates for Chicago, 1922–1934, by zones and divisions of the city* [a]

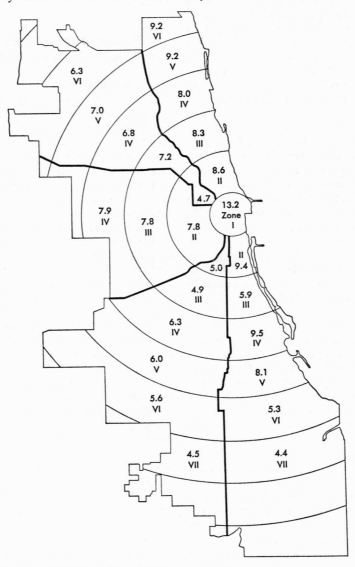

[a] Rates based on 100,000, 1930 population, age 15–64.

distributed in any systematic fashion throughout the city. (2) The distribution for male and female manic-depressive cases separately show the same typical random and unsystematic distribution. (3) The distribution of rates for private and state hospitals exhibits the same random pattern for both local communities and subcommunities. (4) The rates for the separate types, both manic and depressed, are also extremely random in their distribution.... (5) Both distributions of manic-depressive rates show an absence of skewness in their frequency distributions, with approximately the same number of communities having high rates as have low rates. (6) The percentages of cases in each quartile is approximately the same for each of the two main types of the manic-depressive psychoses. This indicates the absence of any definite concentration of cases. However, the percentages of cases in each quartile for the complete series is similar to the concentration of schizophrenic cases. (7) The rates for nativity and race by housing areas show the same lack of consistency and absence of pattern....

From the comparative analysis of the distribution of the schizophrenic and manic-depressive psychoses and their relation to certain indices of social life, the following conclusions might be briefly stated: (1) A comparison of the distribution of the rates of the schizophrenic and manic-depressive psychoses shows them to be unlike each other in almost every respect. (2) The schizophrenic rates show the typical ecological pattern and are concentrated in the disorganized areas of the city, while the manic-depressive psychoses do not show a typical pattern nor any definite concentration in the disorganized and poverty-stricken areas of the city. (3) There is a tendency, although not clearly defined, for the manic-depressive cases to come from a higher

cultural and economic level than the schizophrenic cases. (4) The manic-depressive rates according to race and nativity within the different housing areas of the city show a lack of consistency and pattern while the schizophrenic rates tend to show that a rate for a given nativity group increases in areas not primarily populated by members of that group....

Hypotheses and Interpretations of Distributions

The establishment of the fact that there are great differences in the patterns of rates for different psychoses in the natural areas of the city is in itself a complicated task. The interpretation of the meaning of these facts is a separate problem; different methods of study are necessary for this part of the research. The distributions of certain psychoses can be fairly successfully explained; others are more difficult and explanations can only be suggested.

It is necessary before discussing the meaning of the configuration of rates for the different psychoses to examine certain possible flaws in the method. It may be possible that insanity is not concentrated, and that it appears to be so only because of some statistical illusion. Several possible explanations for the appearance of concentration are discussed below.

An obvious possibility is that the concentration of cases in certain areas of the city may be due to chance. This suggestion has been made by Professor Frank Alexander Ross, with reference to the computation of rates based on data for a single year. Using a formula to test the chance variation of a rate, he tested whether each rate was significantly different from the rate in an adjacent community. In some cases he found differences were not significant and in other cases they were. By combining two communities and computing a rate he was able to show more definitely that the concentration of rates could not be due to chance alone. The logic of this procedure has been questioned by Charles C. Peters, who pointed out the fact that many rates combined into a pattern greatly increased the statistical significance of the pattern itself, and that the possibility that chance variation alone could produce such a pattern is too small to be considered. Since this preliminary study was made, much larger numbers have been used, further decreasing the possibility that the patterns could be due to chance. . . . In those maps which show a clear pattern of distribution, the conclusions are drawn from the pattern and not from differences between adjacent communities. It seems permissible to dismiss the possibility that these patterns are due to chance variation.

A second possibility is that the patterns of rate distribution represent only a concentration of cases of mental disorder which have been institutionalized because of poverty. If the actual incidence of mental disorder is equal in all parts of the city and if those in the higher-income classes are more frequently cared for at home or sent out of the state, the hospitalized cases would show a bias toward the lower-income classes and therefore toward the slum section of the city. An attempt is made to minimize this bias by including in the rates all the cases from the regional private hospitals as well as from public hospitals. Because of the small number of patients in the private hospitals, the rates were only slightly affected by the addition of these cases. No way has been found to estimate the amount of bias in the rates caused by the practice of caring for some patients in the homes. It is possible that there is an income selection in such cases. But it appears unlikely that such an effect dominates the patterns of distribution, because of the fact that different psychoses show different patterns of distribution. If a poverty concentration were the only, or the principal, factor in producing these patterns, they should be reasonably similar for all psychoses.

Another possibility is that the apparent concentration of cases is due to a statistical error or failure to adjust the rates for transiency. That is, if the cases from an area taken during the period of a year are divided by the population taken as of a single day, the rate may be regarded as too high if the population during the year had turned over enough to make a significantly larger population than was present on the one census enumeration day. Professor Ross made this point in the discussion previously mentioned. No satisfactory method was found to make a direct adjustment for this criticism. It is known, however, that in the hobo and rooming-house areas, which show very high rates for several types of mental disorder, the population is transient enough to turn over, perhaps two or three times or more. Ross made the suggestion that in such cases the rate be reduced to one-half or one-third. To justify this, however, it would be necessary to know where the excess population was the rest of the year and what the chances of hospitalization were wherever the people were. Only if it is true that the other cities and towns in which this transient population spends a part of the year do not take their quota in their hospitals, should the rate be adjusted. It seems significant, here, to point out that if the rates in the hobohemia communities for all types of mental disorders were divided by three, the resulting rates would still be two of the highest in the distribution of the rates. These considerations appear to be important in the statistical criticism presented by the factor of mobility.

An interpretation frequently made of the concentration in the center of the city of insanity rates, and the schizophrenia rates particularly, is that persons who are mentally abnormal fail in their economic life and consequently drift down into the slum areas because they are not able to compete satisfactorily with others. Such a process is, of course, possible, although the explanation does not appear to be valid in the case of the manic-depressive patterns. Many of the cases of schizophrenia consist of persons who were born in and have always lived in deteriorated areas. These did not drift into the high-rate areas. There are also cases that are hospitalized from high-income areas, persons who developed a mental disorder before their failure had caused them to drift to the slums. It is a question whether this drift process, which undoubtedly contributes something to the apparent concentration of rates, is anything more than an insignificant factor in causing the concentration. No decisive material on this point was obtained in this study. Some relevant findings should be stated, however.

One method of testing this drift hypothesis is the comparison of the distribution of young and old cases. For this purpose the paranoid and catatonic types of schizophrenia were selected because of the radical difference in both the pattern of the rates and the age distribution. Since those who are first committed at an advanced age have had a longer time in which to fail in their economic life and consequently to drift toward the slums, the distribution of the older cases should show a sharper concentration than the younger cases. . . . The younger cases, mostly too young to have had much time to drift, are [found to be] concentrated in the central areas in much the same pattern as the older cases. . . .

A somewhat similar result emerges from a comparison of young and old catatonic cases. . . . Both young and old cases are [found to be] concentrated, although in this instance there is an indication of some possible drift. The central business district, which has a low rate of younger cases, has a high rate of older cases. . . . Except for this, however, the main pattern does not appear to be the product of drift.

A possible interpretation of the concentration of rates in the central areas might be that this measures the racial tendency to mental disorders of the foreign-born populations that inhabit these areas. It is pointed out above, however (chap. iii), that rates for foreign-born cases divided by foreign-born populations are distributed similarly to the rates for all cases. Likewise, rates for Negroes show a variation, being high in the central disorganized areas not populated primarily by members of their own race and low in the actual Negro areas. Some factors other than being foreign-born or Negro are necessary to explain these patterns that are the same no matter which race or nationality inhabits the area. Furthermore, not all psychoses are concentrated in foreign-born areas. Although the correlation of several psychoses with percentages of foreign-born and Negro population is high or medium, such as catatonic schizophrenia (0.86), epilepsy (0.53), and alcoholic psychoses (0.48), others such as paranoid schizophrenia (0.11), manic-depressive psychoses (0.14), general paralysis (0.15), and senile psychoses (0.17), show little or no correlation. The supposed tendency to mental disorders of the foreign-born populations, then, does not appear to explain the rate patterns.

The last possibility to be discussed is that the patterns of rates reveal that the nature of the social life and conditions in certain areas of the city is in some way a cause of high rates of mental disorder. If there is any truth in this hypothesis, it will be necessary to find separate explanations for each psychosis, since the distributions of rates differ both to a large and to a small degree for each psychosis.

Although the distributions are not exactly alike, the explanations of the concentration of general paralysis, drug addiction, and alcoholic psychoses rates according to this hypothesis are roughly similar. Different combinations of social factors, however, are no doubt functioning in the case of each of these psychoses. The general paralysis rates are highest in the hobo and rooming-house areas and in the Negro areas. These are the areas in which there is little family life, and in which the sex experience of the men is in large part with casual contacts and with prostitutes, who are relatively numerous in these districts. These conditions make for the spread of syphilitic infection and hence for general paralysis. The dispensing and the use of drugs is very much of an underworld activity and this is reflected by the high rates in the zone of transition. Lack of normal social life may underlie the dissatisfactions which cause the use of drugs to be felt as a release, hence the slight rise in rates in the upper-income hotel and rooming-house districts. Also, for the use of alcohol to become an appealing habit, basic dissatisfactions are often essential. High rates of alcohol consumption and of alcoholic psychoses are in the foreign-born and rooming-house areas and may be caused by such conditions of life as monotony, insecurity, and other problems difficult to solve, from which alcohol may be a temporary relief. The significant variations of rates according to nativity and race in the different housing areas of the city indicate the greater chances for mental breakdown and personality disorganization in relation to these psychoses es-

pecially when a person is living in an area not primarily populated by members of his own group. This fact alone would appear to be the beginning for further research in these mental disorders. In the case of the alcoholic psychoses it would seem to indicate the presence of other important factors in addition to the use of alcohol. . . .

Perhaps the most provocative finding in this study resulted from a comparison of the distribution of the manic-depressive and schizophrenic rates. The great contrast between these two patterns seems to imply that some valid distinction has been made in classification. The absence of any pattern in the manic-depressive series makes the interpretation of this distribution extremely difficult, although certain leads for further research might be definitely indicated. The absence of any pattern combined with the absence of skewness in the manic-depressive distribution might suggest that social factors are unimportant in relation to this disorder. If such proved to be the case, there would be a certain justification for asserting the priority of the hereditary and constitutional factors. This of course would be in line with the statistical studies of heredity in the functional psychoses which universally show that biological inheritance is more significant in manic-depressive psychoses than in schizophrenia.

While the ecological and statistical evidence does not bring out any relationship between this disorder and the social milieu, it does not follow that there is no such relationship. Manic-depressive psychoses may be connected with a different type of social process than is the case with the schizophrenic disorders. A possible sociological explanation of the manic-depressive pattern might be found in the suggestion that precipitating factors are causal in relation to these psychoses. Such precipitating factors occur in all social and economic levels of life and consequently are not so likely to have a definite connection with the community situation but rather with the interplay of personality and psychological factors of family relationships and intimate personal contacts. Such a theory tends to connect the manic-depressive disorder with extremely intimate and intense social contacts. This apparently is just the opposite from the situation of the schizophrenic, where isolation from such contacts appears to be an associated condition.

In contrast the schizophrenic rates are arranged into very definite patterns which follow closely the ecological structure of the city and the concentration of all types is very marked. With the exception of the catatonic type, which differs from the others in several respects, the high rates appear to be related to areas of high mobility and, in somewhat less degree, to foreign-born and Negro areas. In the following paragraphs is suggested a possible explanation of the relation between the social life of these areas and the abnormal behavior of the schizophrenic. The hypothesis is that extended isolation of the person produces the abnormal traits of behavior and mentality.

If the various types of unconventional behavior observed in different schizophrenic patients can be said to result from one condition, it appears that extreme seclusiveness may be that condition. . . .

If seclusiveness is the key trait of the schizophrenic, the explanation of the disorder lies in the cause of the development of this trait. It is important to determine whether the seclusiveness is due to an innate lack of sociability or to experiences which destroyed the sociability. An examination of one hundred and one consecutive cases of schizophrenia in an eastern state hospital by one of the authors

revealed that twenty-seven were definitely reported to have been normally sociable in their childhood. Only twenty-one were reported never to have been sociable. In the remaining fifty-three cases, there was not enough evidence to decide. The cases reported as formerly sociable showed three typical stages in the development of their seclusive personality: (1) sociably inclined, making attempts to get the companionship of others; (2) being excluded by the others, but continuing to make the effort to establish intimate social relationships; (3) accepting defeat, changing the interests, and building up a system of rationalization. After this third stage, a sort of "vicious circle" process begins to operate. The acceptance of failure to mix with others and the development of a certain profile of personality traits makes the person less acceptable to others than before and more than ever liable to exclusion and, in the case of boys especially, more liable to actual persecution. The treatment in turn furthers the development of the schizophrenic traits. Of the one hundred and one cases included in this study forty-eight contained sufficient data to reveal the isolating factors. Twenty-nine of these persons were reported to have been "spoiled children." Many of these became the victims of practical jokes at school, and were subject to a considerable amount of persecution. Four cases were discovered with no evidence of being spoiled but with very strict moral and religious training. Each of these four had a strong sense of guilt because of sex experiences and had delusions referring to them.

In addition, there were four cases which showed hallucinations and delusions due to the isolation brought on by deafness. Other cases showed such isolating factors as the inability to speak English, not being allowed by strict parents to play with other children, and sensitivity because of disfiguring physical deformities.

Any factor which interferes with social contacts with other persons produces isolation. The role of an outcast has tremendous effects on the development of the personality. Lack of sufficient self-confidence and the consciousness that others do not desire one's company may act as a serious barrier to intimate social relations. The individual who feels that he is conspicuously ugly, inferior, or in disgrace may be isolated through this conception of himself.

The hypothesis that such forms of isolation are significant factors to account for the high rates of schizophrenia in certain parts of the city is strengthened by the studies which have shown that the conditions producing isolation are much more frequent in the disorganized communities. Especially significant is the connection between the rates of schizophrenia, excepting the catatonic type, and indices of mobility. . . . In addition, the fact that rates for Negro, foreign-born, and native-born are all significantly higher in areas not primarily populated by their own members tends to support this isolation hypothesis. When the harmony of all these facts bearing on the isolation hypothesis is considered, the result is sufficiently impressive to make further pursuit of this lead appear to be worth while.

JAMES A. DAVIS
Compositional Effects, Role Systems, and the Survival of Small Discussion Groups

The Great Books Program

One of the more interesting phenomena in American cultural life is the Great Books program, one of the most successful organizations for the liberal education of educated adults. The program itself consists of some 2,000 discussion groups in the United States, and a few in Canada and Europe. Each group meets every other week from September to June, and at each meeting the members discuss specific selections that they have read before the meetings. The readings are either complete works or excerpts from such

Reprinted in part from *Public Opinion Quarterly*, 25, 1961, pp. 575–84, with permission of Princeton University Press.

writers as Aristotle, Virgil, St. Francis, Melville, Shakespeare, Hume, Darwin, and Aeschylus. The readings are organized into blocks of one year each, and, in theory, groups proceed from the first-year readings through the second, third, and so on, in a never-ending progression.

From the viewpoint of the social scientist, the groups are as interesting as the books they read. They vary in size, around an average of eleven, and in sponsorship—most are affiliated with public libraries, but some are sponsored by churches and business firms and some are unsponsored. The participants tend to be upper-middle-class professional men and wives of businessmen. They have high education (84 per cent have some college training) and they are concentrated in the thirties and early forties in terms of age. They split 50-50 between Republicans and Democrats; 62 per cent are Protestants. The participants are very active in community organizations, and, interestingly, they are *less* upwardly mobile than comparable people in the general population. Thus, the program is not a self-help movement but an outlet for intellectual and social motivations among a population with high educational achievement.

To a social scientist, however, the most striking characteristic of the groups is the things they don't have. The leaders are not professional teachers but volunteers who receive no pay. Members pay no tuition and receive no diplomas, promotions, or merit badges. In fact, no one can complete the program, as additional readings are always available, currently up to the fourteenth year. The national Great Books Foundation makes up the curriculum and sells the readings, although purchase of the readings is not required, but the foundation has little or no contact with a given group.

The upshot of all this is that there are very few institutionalized pressures for a member to continue, since he has invested no money and has no diploma as a reward. Although it is dangerous to compare "live" groups with laboratory ones, Great Books come pretty close to being "pure" discussion groups in which very few variables other than the books, the members' characteristics, and the discussion process can affect the results.

The Study

In December 1957 NORC interviewers attended the meetings of 172 Great Books groups, sampled on a national basis. Members had not been informed before the meeting that they were going to participate in the research that night. Each member of the sampled groups was asked to fill out a rather lengthy self-administered questionnaire, netting us 1,909 completed schedules.

A year later an additional grant from the Fund for Adult Education, our sponsors, enabled us to determine the continuation status of all the groups and 92 per cent of the respondents in our original sample.

It turned out that 64 per cent of the members had continued with the same group, 3 per cent had transferred to other groups, and 33 per cent had left the program. In terms of groups, 3 per cent kept all their members; 60 per cent lost some, but less than half, of their members; 20 per cent lost a majority of their members; and 17 per cent were defunct.

The aim of our research was to find out what variables explained attrition and differences in attrition among these groups. In particular, we wanted to know how much of the process could be explained by individual characteristics of the members, and how much by characteristics of the groups themselves.

ROLE STRUCTURES AND DROP-OUT

Detailed analyses of these data turned up some dozen and a half variables that influence program retention, but the most important of these is the role structure of the discussion group. That roles are important for groups can hardly come as a surprise to sociologists, but the precise nature of the relationship turns out to be one which is rather unexpected.

Through a large number of sociological writings runs an implicit or explicit thread which we can call the functional hypothesis. Bales, for example, writes:

> A basic assumption here is that what we call the "social structure" of groups

can be understood primarily as a system of solutions to the functional problems of interaction which become institutionalized in order to reduce the tensions growing out of uncertainty and unpredictability in the actions of others. (Bales, 1950, pp. 15–16.)

It seemed to us that if role structures arise to meet functional needs and if small groups have similar needs, then groups with different role structures might show differences in survival rates, since loss of members is a reasonable index of inability to meet needs.

In order to assess role structures, it is necessary to begin by assessing roles. Our procedures were as follows. In the questionnaire, five discussion roles were listed:

1. Providing "fuel" for the discussion by introducing ideas and opinions for the rest of the group to discuss (fuel).
2. Getting the discussion to the point by getting terms defined and pointing out logical problems (clarification).
3. Pulling the threads of the discussion together and getting different viewpoints reconciled (threads).
4. Making tactful comments to heal any hurt feelings which might arise in the discussion (tact).
5. Joking and kidding, finding the potentially humorous implications in the discussion (joking).

Role 1, "Fuel," is a "proactive" task role; roles 2 and 3, "Clarification" and

"Threads," are "reactive" task roles; and roles 4 and 5, "Tact" and "Joking," are socioemotional roles.

Each respondent was asked to rate himself on activity in these areas and then to list the other members of his group who "tend to perform this role frequently." The associations between self-ratings and designations by others indicated fair agreement. (Q coefficients for the associations run from .51 on Fuel to .73 on Joking.)

Granted then that the groups have these roles, what do we mean when we talk about role structure? It seems to us that by role structure we mean role differentiation and that a set of roles has a structure to the degree that they are not randomly related to each other, that playing a given role affects the probability of playing another role. If this convention is satisfactory, role structure can be assessed by the intercorrelations of roles. In Table 1, we see Q coefficients for the associations between our roles, using as our dichotomy two or more mentions by other members versus zero or one.

What kind of role structure does Table 1 suggest? First, since all the relationships are positive, Great Books groups apparently do not have a highly differentiated role system. If we had taken roles such as mother, father, son, daughter, we would have gotten a matrix of strong negative correlations, but here people who play one role also tend to play another. This, of course, suggests some gen-

Table **1** *Interrelations of roles* (*Yule's Q*)

Role	Joking	Fuel	Clarification	Threads	Tact
Joking		.68	.45	.51	.16
Fuel	.68		.83	.84	.55
Clarification	.45	.83		.88	.60
Threads	.51	.84	.88		.72
Tact	.16	.55	.60	.72	

Table **2** *Role differentiation, role volume, and drop-out: percentage dropping out of their discussion group between 1957 and 1958*

		Per cent named as active		
Differentiation		Less than 20	20–49	50 or more
TASK ROLES:				
Fuel [a]	Clarification or threads [b]			
+	+	49 (102)	36 (616)	23 (514)
+	−	58 (89)	15 (20)	(0)
−	+	37 (79)	30 (56)	37 (16)
−	−	55 (232)	(6)	(0)
SOCIO-EMOTIONAL ROLES:				
Joking [a]	Tact [a]			
+	+	67 (39)	35 (349)	24 (423)
+	−	48 (136)	28 (171)	25 (64)
−	+	69 (35)	16 (73)	13 (37)
−	−	49 (292)	58 (105)	(6)

[a] + means one or more members were named as playing that role; — means none.
[b] + means one or more people were named as playing one role or the other or both; — means none were named for either.

eral dimension of role activity per se underlying the data.

On the other hand, the associations are not 1.00, and the pattern of relationships suggests that the system is not unidimensional. Without subjecting the data to sophisticated analytical techniques that are unsuited to these measures, we can assume that there is some qualitive differentiation of role performance along with a general tendency for persons active in one role to be active in others.

Because the associations are moderate, we can expect that some roles and combinations of roles will be present in some groups and not in others. This enables us to see whether the presence or absence of specific roles is related to the success or failure of a group. Thus, if joking serves to express the tensions of the members, and if the expression of tension helps maintain the social system, then groups with jokers should have greater retention.

The reasoning involves two steps, so negative findings would be difficult to interpret. If, for instance, the presence or absence of a joker is not related to retention, it could be because either (1) joking is not necessary for the expression of tension or (2) expression of tension is not necessary for membership retention, or both.[1] Our test of the functionalist hypothesis will be pretty weak but, because it is seldom tested at all, it will be worth a try.

Table 2 arrays members according to characteristics of the role systems of their groups. The rows refer to members in groups characterized by the presence or absence of members playing specific roles, the columns refer to members in groups

[1] It could also be that our measures do not tap the right functions or measure them unreliably. All the conclusions in this paper should carry the implicit qualification, "roles, as we have measured them."

characterized by various proportions of the group named as playing any one or more of the five roles. Thus, the group context is varied simultaneously in terms of role quality and role quantity.

There are no consistent differences among the drop-out rates in the different rows of Table 2. We do not have enough cases to examine all combinations of all five roles simultaneously, but every combination we have examined gives results much like Table 2: the presence or absence of a given role has no consistent effect on drop-out when role volume is controlled. At the same time, although there are exceptions and a number of cells with too few cases to percentage, in most of the comparisons drop-out is inverse to role volume. Thus, in groups with both types of task roles, drop-out declines from 49 to 36 to 23 per cent as the proportion of members playing some role increases.

Table 2 suggests that there is a rela-

tionship between roles and survival of small discussion groups, but the relationship is not due to variation in role content, but rather to variation in the role volume.

ROLE VOLUME AND DROP-OUT

Let us then pursue the volume idea a little. To begin with, we are curious whether it is a true contextual effect, or whether it is a reversed ecological correlation fallacy. Groups with many members named as active role players do very well in terms of holding their members, but we do not know—from that—whether role volume creates a favorable group climate or whether individuals who play roles tend to stick with Great Books and the success of the high-volume groups is due merely to the fact that they have lots of people who are good risks. An answer to this problem is to examine the loss

Figure **1** *Discussion activity and drop-out* [a]

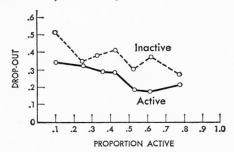

[a] The N's for this chart were:

	Proportion active in the discussion						
Members	*0–.19*	*.2–.29*	*.3–.39*	*.4–.49*	*.5–.59*	*.6–.69*	*.7–1.00*
Active:							
Drop-out	16	14	31	31	25	18	22
Stay	31	30	74	77	108	82	80
Total	*47*	*44*	*105*	*108*	*133*	*100*	*102*
Inactive:							
Drop-out	241	56	72	56	35	21	8
Stay	214	69	108	80	78	36	17
Total	*455*	*125*	*180*	*136*	*113*	*57*	*25*

rates for role players and non-role players in groups which vary in the proportion of role players.

The accompanying Figure 1 gives the results. Each respondent is classified according to whether he is named as a role player or not, and also in terms of the proportion of his group who are named as role players. Two kinds of effects are apparent. At each level of volume, active members (role players) have lower drop-out rates than inactive members. This is an individual-level effect. At the same time, drop-out rates for both actives and inactives decline with the proportion active in a group. This is a group-level or compositional effect, since the group characteristic shows a difference when the individual characteristic is held constant. Both effects are fairly important. The individual-level difference averages about 12 per cent but at the same time active members in low-volume groups have higher drop-out rates than inactive members in high-volume groups.

OUTSIDE CONTACTS AND DROP-OUT

We began by asking whether sociologists are correct in claiming that roles are important for the survival of small social systems. We found that Great Books groups do have roles, in the sense that members' claims about their role performance are in accordance with their group's perception. Next we found that there is a role structure, although not a highly differentiated one. Then we found that, while *content* of the role structure had little to do with membership retention, the *volume* of role performance goes with higher membership retention in a way that cannot be explained by individual-level risks. Thus, roles in these groups seem to affect their survival by creating climates of activity and participation, rather than by the content of their contribution.

What are the sources of these role climates? Why do some groups have many active participants and some very few? Interestingly, group size and age have very little to do with it, but to a degree role volume is a function of another climate, the climate of interpersonal relationships outside the group discussions.

Each respondent was asked, "How many members of your group (excluding your spouse) do you see regularly outside the group discussion?" When respondents are divided into those who see one or more vs. those who see none, and groups are arrayed in terms of the proportion with one or more outside contacts, we can see the relationship between outside contacts and role volume, at the group level and at the individual level. Groups

Table 3 *Outside contacts, activity, educational composition, and role volume: percentage named as active in discussion roles*

Per cent of college graduates	Individual contacts	Per cent with one or more outside contacts	
		Less than 60	60 or more
50 or more	Yes	31 (277)	45 (506)
	No	28 (368)	43 (123)
	Total	30 (645)	45 (629)
Less than 50	Yes	37 (118)	31 (164)
	No	40 (158)	38 (50)
	Total	39 (276)	33 (214)

are divided into those with 50 per cent or more college graduates and those with less than half college graduates. Table 3 gives the results.

Table 3 gives us the percentage named as active role players for individuals with and without extragroup contacts, in four types of groups: high education, high contacts; high education, low contacts; low education, high contacts; and low education, low contacts. We can begin with the groups with a majority of college graduates. We see that regardless of whether the individual himself has social relationships with the members outside of the meetings, role activity is greater where the proportion with such relationships is higher. There is very little individual-level difference. Thus, among highly educated groups there appears to be a climate effect such that high volumes of outside interaction produce high volumes of role participation in the discussion. This stands to reason, as we would expect role relationships developed outside the program to carry over into Great Books.

When, however, we consider the less educated groups, the climate effect reverses. Among individuals with and without outside contacts, role activity is, if anything, lower in groups with high outside interaction, and there is some tendency for the active role players to be people with no outside contacts, whereas among the highly educated groups the actives, if anything, had more contacts.

With cross-sectional survey data it is impossible to draw firm conclusions about these relationships. However, one line of interpretation is as follows: Among highly educated people, the cultural climate of extragroup interaction is probably more intellectual and leads to a set of interpersonal relationships that are highly consonant with group discussion of intellectual matters. Among the less educated (remembering, however, that in our sample the less educated are typically part college rather than high school graduates or less), however, the outside culture is probably less intellectual and the role patterns which exist are less transferable to active group discussion of ideas. Thus, depending on the value climate of the extragroup social relationships, they either facilitate or inhibit role volume in the discussions.

The net result is that there is a relationship between outside contacts and role volume, but the relationship varies with the educational level of the group. Table 4 shows these differences.

*Table **4**   Outside contacts, role volume, and education: Q association between outside contacts and role activity (group level)*

Per cent of college graduates in group	Q	Number of groups
70 or more	.76	58
50–69	.43	68
40–49	−.38	20
0–39	−.33	26

Since most Great Books groups are composed of a majority of college graduates, over-all outside contacts are associated with lower drop-out rates. Common sense suggests that people who are knit together by high outside contacts would be more cohesive. Perhaps, then, people who see each other a lot stick together, and the high rate of role performance is merely a side effect.

In order to check this hypothesis, let us consider the simultaneous effects on group retention of role volume and outside contacts, controlling for educational level. Table 5 suggests that the effect of role volume is not spurious. Regardless of educational level and volume of outside interaction, groups with higher role volume keep more of their members. Out-

Table 5 Role volume, outside contacts, educational composition, and drop-out: percentage dropping out

Per cent of college graduates	Per cent with outside contacts	Per cent of active role performers		
		40 or more	*0–39*	*Total*
50 or more	60 or more	21 (414)	31 (214)	24 (628)
	Less than 60	34 (164)	42 (462)	40 (626)
Less than 50	60 or more	39 (59)	67 (136)	58 (195)
	Less than 60	32 (137)	41 (143)	37 (28)

side contacts, however, show different effects in the two educational levels. Among the highly educated groups, high outside contacts go with high membership retention. Among the less educated, however, high outside contacts go with greater loss of members, a reversal similar to the one we saw in the relationship between outside contacts and role volume.

Conclusion

Now, let us see whether we can piece all of this together.

We began by wondering whether role structures were related to membership retention in Great Books discussion groups. Applying ideas from laboratory studies of small groups, we asked whether the *kind* of role played in the group affected the group's ability to keep its members. It turned out that role quality is unimportant but that role quantity is a major factor. Our analysis showed not only that active role participants are more likely to stay with the program but that, for both active and nonactive members, retention increases with the volume of role performance in the group. In short, it appears that heavy participation in the discussions creates a climate favorable for group survival.

Further analysis suggested a second climatic or contextual factor, and that is the volume of interaction outside the discussion meetings. This climate appears more catalytic than anything else, and it has two different effects: (1) Among groups with high education, high rates of outside contact lead to greater role volume and also contribute independently to membership retention. (2) Among groups with lower educational levels, high rates of outside interaction inhibit role volume and also contribute independently to membership loss. Thus, among highly educated people the climate of outside interaction is a double benefit to the group, and for less educated people the climate of outside interaction is a double drawback.

We began with a theory which essentially assumes that the process of interaction in small groups is determined by the content of the immediate interpersonal relationships and the problems they present. We have ended, however, with a rather different conception of role processes in these—admittedly rather different —groups. Great Books groups appear heavily affected, not by role quality, but by the quantitative climate of role participation. This in turn is heavily influenced by the content of interpersonal relations outside of the immediate situation. As contrasted with laboratory groups, these natural groups appear strongly affected by their degree of fit or abrasion with role patterns and cultural values in the larger social world.

MATILDA WHITE RILEY
RICHARD COHN
Control Networks in Informal Groups

A group is often conceived as controlling the actions and attitudes of its members so that they will conform to the group norms. A system of expectations, definitions, and sanctions is involved. That is, first, any member is expected by the others to hold certain values and to behave in certain ways; and, at the same time, he is expected *not* to hold certain other values or to behave in certain other ways. Second, the member's expressed attitudes and actions are defined or judged by the others as either conforming to these expectations or deviating from them. And third, the member's conformity is rewarded with positive sanctions, while his deviance is punished with negative sanctions. Even after many of the members have in large part learned the norms and developed dispositions toward conformity, this combination of positive and negative sanctions continues to channel motivation in a generally conformist direction. . . .

In some types of groups there is a clear-cut social organization for carrying out these control processes. In formal groups, for instance, the several norm-enforcement roles (such as policeman, foreman, judge) are often highly differentiated and organized according to a definite division of labor. In certain less formally structured groups, some one person may assume the over-all norm-enforcement role. Durkheim talks of the parent and the teacher as the intermediaries through

Reprinted in part from *Sociometry, 21,* 1958, pp. 30–48, with permission of the American Sociological Association.

whom the child is subjected to the "pressure of the social milieu which tends to fashion him in its own image." Students of the gang describe the emergence of the leader and his lieutenants. But what happens in still more loosely knit groups—of factory workers, hospital ward patients, friends, children at play, and the like— where the norm-enforcement functions are often not explicitly allocated, and where no over-all leader assumes entire responsibility for social control? Who is responsible for the control processes in such informal groups? Who adjudges the conformity or deviance of the others? Who metes out approval for conformity and disapproval for deviance? Is this manipulation of sanctions left haphazardly to the discrete acts of the several members acting without reference to one another? Or does some form of organization develop in such groups also?

On this point existing theory is often vague, and little detailed research has been conducted. Indeed, organization for social control is difficult to study in group situations where the control process itself is not explicit. In informal groups, as contrasted with more highly structured systems, the expectations are usually not clearly stated as laws, rules of the game, or job descriptions. The character of the rewards and of the punishments is not ordinarily openly stipulated; the sanctions often seem to be highly subtle, consisting mainly of symbols of approval or disapproval. Durkheim, for instance, speaks of social isolation, LaPiere of alternate scolding and smiling, Parsons of tactful disagreement, silence, or humor. Under such conditions, the members themselves may be quite unable to describe the mechanisms through which shared expectations may lead them to conformity. They may be quite unaware of any underlying organization through which sanctions may be imposed.

The purpose of this paper is, first, to propose the "social control network" as one possible type of organization for control in such loosely knit informal groups; and second, to report briefly on some research which seems to support certain of the assumptions implicit in this idea of social control networks.

Working Model of a Social Control Network

We start with the familiar network of interpersonal relationships which bind each member to the group. The networks of the several members overlap or mesh with one another to form the system of the group as a whole. Such networks have presumably developed over time through a complex process in which each member interacts with other members, these others become oriented to him in various ways, and their orientations in turn affect the course of the interaction. If we cut through the ongoing process at a given point in time, we may find that any given member has, on the one hand, friends, confidantes, admirers—other members with preponderantly positive feelings toward him. On the other hand, he may have enemies—other members with predominantly negative feelings toward him. And now we go on to suggest that this network of affective or cathectic relationships, once it has become established, may serve not merely to tie the member into the structure of the group. It may also

have a further consequence—though perhaps an unintended one. We suggest that the network serves to bind the member to the group norms as well.

This occurs, we assume, because of a special kind of *cognitive differentiation* which develops within the network of cathectic relationships. This differentiation takes the following form. The object's friends and others in his network who feel positively toward him, however they may have perceived him upon first acquaintance, have come to think of him in generally positive terms. Their definitions of him emphasize his "nice" characteristics and his desirable acts, at the same time tending to ignore any less attractive traits which he may display. Meanwhile, those other subjects in his network who feel negatively toward him are relatively apt to define him negatively. Whatever they may have thought of him in the formative stages of the relationship, once their aversion has become somewhat stabilized they pay special heed to the less pleasant aspects of his personality and behavior. Moreover—and this is the aspect of the differentiation which seems crucial for social control—individual subjects do not have entirely idiosyncratic notions about what is "nice" or "not nice." Indeed, to the extent that certain values are widely shared or institutionalized in the group as a whole, members tend to agree that given traits are desirable which embody such values; they come to some consensus that other traits are unacceptable which conflict with these values. To this extent, then, the friend's positive view of the object tends to define him as *conforming* to group expectations; while the enemy's negative view tends to define him as *deviant*.

For example, let us consider any two members of the group, designating one *S* (the subject) and the other *O* (the object). If *S* likes *O,* he will be apt to note his conformist acts and to overlook his deviance. But if *S* dislikes *O,* he will be especially alert to his deviant actions and largely unmindful of any conformity which he may evince. That differentiation of definition actually occurs in some such form as this is the *first assumption* which will be examined below through some research on informal groupings among adolescents.

There is much in the literature of social psychology which might account for any such differences in the way likers and dislikers define an object. Heider in particular points out the readiness of the perceiver to attribute a positively valued act to a liked person, and a negatively valued act to a disliked person. Citing as one example the Zillig experiment, in which the mistakes of liked classmates are erroneously perceived as emanating from *dis*liked classmates, he comments that "a bad act is easily connected with a bad person." Beyond this, he suggests that various changes, including cognitive reorganization, may occur to redress the balance in the event that the subject's attitudes toward the person and his actions are *not* both positive, or both negative, in this way.

Here we look at these disparate definitions of likers and dislikers from quite a different point of view, however. We are concerned now with only those selected acts or personal traits which reflect the institutionalized values of the group. And, rather than examining those intrapersonal processes which might explain why subjects differ in their definitions of the object, we now devote attention to the possible effects upon the object. We ask whether the liker's conformist view of him and the disliker's deviant view may not have special consequences in terms of social control. We introduce the possibility that the object, as Simmel suggests, may "modify its behavior in view

of the fact that it is recognized"—may modify it in the direction of conformity because of the special structuring of this recognition within the network.

That is, we place a particular interpretation upon the differentiation of definition which is assumed in our model: We suggest that there may be a *differentiation of control function* between positive and negative relationships within the network of any given object. That subject who feels generally positive toward an object, at the same time that he tends to define him as conformist, may in effect be setting an indirect stamp of approval upon him. This may well serve to reward the object for his conformity, and we shall refer to such a relationship as a "conformity-approving relationship." Another subject who feels generally negative toward an object, and at the same time defines him as deviant, may well be indicating disapproval. This may act as a punishment for deviance, and we shall accordingly speak of a "deviance-disapproving relationship."

In other words, such positive and negative cathexes may serve respectively as positive and negative sanctions. The object's conformity may be noted by his friend, who in general is disposed to reward him for it; while, at the same time, enemies may be at hand to rebuke him at some other point where he seems to step over the line in the deviant direction.

According to this interpretation, such differentiated approval and disapproval relationships tend to be mutually supporting when they are directed in combination toward the same object. (Cf. Merton's notion of articulating the "role-set.") Both may operate to reinforce the norms of the group, but in different ways: one by selecting and rewarding conformist aspects of the object's behavior, the other by directing critical attention to any apparently deviant aspects. Thus a composite of other persons may tend to divide among them the labor of imposing the positive and negative sanctions which support the individual's conformity.

Finally, our proposal is that this *combination* of approval and disapproval relationships in an object's network may be *functionally important* for social control. If this proposal is correct, we might expect—as the *second assumption* which we select for testing below—that such combinations would occur most often in the networks of the highly successful and acceptable members of the group. An individual's conformity or deviance is often believed to be roughly commensurate with his status in the informal group. That is, members who embody the group norms tend to be widely accepted; while the deviant members tend to be widely rejected, even ostracized, often driven into affiliation with outside deviant groups. The notion of social control networks affords a possible basis for such structuring of conformity by status. It suggests that high status members may be surrounded, not only by conformity-approving, but also by deviance-disapproving, relationships; and that such combined relationships may be more effective for social control than the networks of low status members which tend to be made up exclusively of deviance-disapproving relationships.

The Matching of Cathexes and Cognitions

These two selected assumptions, which are essential parts of such a theory of social control networks, will now be examined empirically in the light of data drawn from a panel study of 2,500 ninth- and tenth-grade students from 15 different high-school grades.

As a preliminary to the later phases of the analysis, a *list of personal traits* was drawn up, each of which was felt by most members of these grades to be either conformist or deviant. For this purpose, a series of vignettes or models was first used, consisting of brief descriptions of high-school boys and girls as they embody particular attributes, skills, activity patterns, or tendencies to elicit various responses from others in the group. Each model was originally prepared to represent certain values which were believed, on the basis of preliminary intensive interviewing, to be of central concern to adolescents. Some of these values were given several expressions in line with the deviance paradigms of Parsons and Merton; and each model was classified a priori as presumably either conforming to, or deviating from, the norms of the group.

Respondents were then asked two questions at an early questioning period about each of these models. One question, which aimed to discover which traits were generally institutionalized, was: "Do the well-liked kids in your grade want their friends to be like this?" The second question, which aimed to discover which traits had been widely internalized as either conformist or deviant, was: "Do I want to be just like this?" Each answer was recorded on a rating scale from extreme "yes" to extreme "no." The analysis of both sets of answers showed that, as predicted, the "yes" response is the largest for each of the conformist models, and the "no" response the largest for each of the deviant models. In this sense, the underlying values are taken to be generally institutionalized in the group, and internalized by large majorities of the individual members.

On the basis of this preliminary research, a list of 18 characteristics was developed for use two years later in obtaining the data which are presented here. This list is shown in full detail in Table 1 below. Nine of the characteristics are

Table **1**   *Relation between liking or disliking and the attribution of conformist or deviant traits*

| | | Per cent of dyads in which *S* says *O* has the characteristic | | | | | |
| | | Male dyads in which | | | Female dyads in which | | |
Characteristic	*Classification*	*S* likes *O*	*S* dislikes *O*	Dif-fer-ence	*S* likes *O*	*S* dislikes *O*	Dif-fer-ence
0 Likes to be with *older* friends or relatives	Deviant	6	16	−10	10	17	− 7
1 Fits in with anybody he (she) is with at the time	Conformist	44	9	+35	53	9	+44
2 Pretty much all-round; not out-standing in any *one* way	Conformist	45	16	+29	43	23	+20
3 Expert on popular music or sports news	Conformist	11	10	+ 1	5	3	+ 2
4 Cares most about having fun with friends	Conformist	52	22	+30	58	28	+30
5 Looks for excitement (smok-ing, petting, etc.)	Deviant	23	42	−19	8	37	−29
6 Not too interested in teen-age fun	Deviant	9	25	−16	7	19	−12
7 Is liked by important people in the grade	Conformist	34	10	+24	31	10	+21
8 His (her) ideas are respected by others in the grade	Conformist	26	6	+20	32	8	+24
9 Doesn't stand too well with others in the grade	Deviant	7	61	−54	7	57	−50
10 Exclusive; sticks to his (her) own group	Deviant	20	50	−30	20	59	−39
11 Friendly to *everyone* in grade; not exclusive	Conformist	46	6	+40	53	5	+48
12 Always trying to get other people to like him (her)	Deviant	11	18	− 7	12	21	− 9
13 Cares about top grades most of all	Deviant	11	14	− 3	12	15	− 3
14 Always trying to get on good side of teacher	Deviant	5	23	−18	3	27	−24
15 Good student, but not a book-worm	Conformist	34	9	+25	36	12	+24
16 Studies hard, but doesn't al-ways hope for top grades	Conformist	13	5	+ 8	15	5	+10
17 Not too interested in school work	Deviant	24	46	−22	15	25	−10
Total dyads = 100%		2,626	1,141		4,069	1,658	

conformist, the other nine deviant, in terms of the original models.

Following this initial classification of traits, the analysis then proceeds to an investigation of one of the basic assumptions stated in our working model: the assumption of cognitive differentiation in the networks, so that likers and dislikers tend to define the object's conformity or deviance quite differently. For purposes of analysis, the assumption is broken down into two hypotheses. The first deals with the simple dyadic relationship between an object and any one subject; the second, which will be examined in the next section of this paper, then goes on to the network of dyadic relationships in which any object potentially participates as he interacts, not merely with one subject, but with a number of different subjects.

The first of these hypotheses is concerned with the idea that *in general* a positive cathexis tends to coincide with the definition of the object as conforming to group norms, a negative cathexis with the definition of him as deviant. The two types of cathexes are represented respectively by dyads in which one person says he likes another, and dyads in which one person says he dislikes another. We state this hypothesis then in the following form:

Hypothesis 1. The attribution of conformist traits is *more* likely to go with liking than with disliking; and conversely, the attribution of deviant traits is *less* likely to go with liking than with disliking.

For this purpose, two sets of questions were asked at the later questioning period. First, each respondent was asked (among other sociometric choice questions) which people in the grade he personally liked and which he disliked. Since space for several names was provided beside each of these questions, this produced about 6,500 dyads in which one person named another as liked, and about 2,500 dyads in which one named another as disliked. (Cross-sex choices are omitted throughout this analysis, since they are very few and may be different in character from same-sex choices.)

The second set of questions asked the respondent to describe each of these others whom he had named by selecting from the prepared list the three or four characteristics which described him best. Thus, it should be noted, the definitions obtained require a selection of the most salient traits, not a rating of each person on each one of the traits. (A special effort was made in the questioning procedure to separate this attribution of traits from the earlier sociometric choice questions, so that one would bias the other as little as possible.)

In terms of these data, the hypothesis is that any one of these conformist characteristics will be attributed to an object more often by a person who likes than by one who dislikes him; but that any given deviant characteristic will be attributed relatively more often by a disliker. Table 1 shows the outcome of this analysis. Here the male dyads, for example, are divided into two sets: first, the 2,626 in which one boy, S, names another boy, O, as somebody he likes; and second, those 1,141 in which one boy names another as somebody he *dis*likes. Then these two sets of dyads are examined to see whether the liker is relatively more apt than the disliker to describe the object as having any given one of the characteristics. Consider characteristic 2, "Pretty much all-round; not outstanding in any *one* way." As it turns out for male dyads, S says O is all-round in 45 per cent of the dyads in which S likes O. By contrast, S says O is all-round in only 16 per cent of the dyads in which S dislikes O. The difference between 45 and 16 is in the predicted direction, since all-round was classified initially as a conformist trait.

In similar fashion, each of the 18 characteristics is examined in turn, for each sex separately. In every instance, the difference is in the predicted direction, as Table 1 shows. This difference proved significant for 17 out of 18 characteristics at the .025 level (one-sided), based on the Wilcoxon test as described in the Appendix. Thus this analysis lends support to the notion that, in any given peer group relationship of this kind, liking tends to be associated with a definition of the object as conforming to institutionalized expectations, whereas disliking tends to coincide with the definition of him as deviant. Likers and dislikers, that is, are apt to emphasize definitions of objects which fall on different sides of the expectations of the group.

Cognitively Differentiated Networks

This step in the analysis does not carry us far enough, however. Hypothesis 1 says only that likers tend to define their friends as conformist, while dislikers define as deviant the objects of their aversion. We want to go beyond this, to make sure that likers and dislikers within the same network will show this differentiation when they define the *same* object.

Actually, two quite different situations might underlie the matching between cathectic and cognitive orientations found under Hypothesis 1. On the one hand, the networks themselves may in fact tend to be "cognitively differentiated," as suggested in our working model. Any given object, that is, may not have exactly the same general reputation with all the subjects in his network, but may have different reputations in each of his several relationships corresponding to the direction of the cathexis. Those who like an object, for instance, may define him as a good student, or as caring about having fun with friends; by contrast, those who dislike him may take note of his exclusiveness, or his attempts to get on the good side of the teacher—thus tending to overlook those characteristics which were emphasized by the likers. (Perhaps such cognitive differentiation tends to occur because the object actually behaves differently toward those who like and those who dislike him. Or perhaps selective perception is at work so that subjects with different feelings pick up different cues from the object's behavior.)

On the other hand, the finding under Hypothesis 1 does not necessarily reflect any such differentiation of definition within the networks. It might arise from quite another set of circumstances in which certain objects, especially those who are widely liked, tend to have *general* reputations for conformity; while other objects, especially the widely disliked ones, tend to have *general* reputations for deviance. That is, all the subjects who relate to any given object, whether they like or dislike him, might tend to define him in the same way. In this situation, the networks would tend to be "cognitively *un*differentiated," thus precluding the possible combination of conformity-approving and deviance-disapproving relationships postulated in our model. (Perhaps such consensus of definition might arise because the object has inherent properties which elicit similar cognitive responses from the various others around him; or perhaps some form of interaction among these others results in a consensus about him.)

Our assumption is that the actual situation falls somewhere between these two extremes. While there is undoubtedly some tendency toward consensus, there is also a contrary tendency toward differentiation in the definitions placed upon any given object in positively oriented, as contrasted with negatively oriented, relationships. This implies that any subject's definition of an object, although it may be in part tied to the object's general reputation, is also in part specific to the character of the interpersonal relationship between the subject and the object.

Two different analyses were designed, accordingly, to test the following hypothesis:

Hypothesis 2. When some subjects like and others dislike the *same* object, the likers will be more apt than the dislikers to select conformist characteristics in describing him, while the dislikers will be relatively more apt to describe him in deviant terms.

As one test of this, we arbitrarily selected objects whose networks contained a considerable number of both positive and negative relationships, so that we could compare directly likers and dislikers of the same object. The form of the analysis is comparable to that used in Table 1 for Hypothesis 1, except that in Table 1 all the objects are thrown together, whereas now we deal with just one object at a time. The question now becomes: given this particular person, whatever his inherent qualities may be, do the likers in his network stress his conformist characteristics, while the dislikers stress his deviant ones? This question was asked for each of the 18 characteristics in turn. The results appeared to be generally in the predicted direction for both sexes; but, because of the small number of male objects (only 46) who met the selection criteria, the Wilcoxon test was applied to the data for girls only, as described in the Appendix. Results for 13 of the 18 characteristics proved significant at the .025 level (one-sided test).

This particular test of Hypothesis 2 seemed inadequate in itself, however, because it was based on a few selected objects who might, after all, be quite atypical. A further means of examining the hypothesis was sought, which would utilize all the objects, and which would attempt to extricate the tendency toward differentiation from any contrary tendencies toward consensus in the definitions of widely liked or widely disliked objects. For this purpose (as suggested by both F. Mosteller and E. F. Borgatta in personal communications), each of the 2,500 objects was classified along two dimensions: first, by his "likability," or the number of others who said they liked him; and again further by his "dislikability," or the number of others who said they disliked him. This classification resulted in a matrix which divided male objects into 96 cells, and another matrix dividing female objects into 112 cells. The dyads belonging to the objects in each of these cells were then examined to see how the likers and the dislikers define the object respectively.

To the extent that the networks are differentiated, we should then expect that, for any given degree of the object's likability and of his dislikability, the likers will be more apt than the dislikers to call him conformist, and less apt to call him deviant. That is, Hypothesis 2 should hold true for similar objects when their likability and dislikability are both controlled. Consequently, comparisons were made between the definitions made by likers and by dislikers for each of the cells in the likability-dislikability matrix for each sex. The majority of these comparisons came out in the predicted direction for each of the 18 characteristics for females, and for all but one of the characteristics for males.

Thus these two separate analyses of Hypothesis 2 combine to point to certain rather consistently patterned differences in the definitions of the same object by those who like and those who dislike him. They are consistent with our (first) assumption of cognitive differentiation which is basic to our working model.

Some Tendencies Toward Consensus

Before considering the implications of such a finding, let us take note of any contrary tendencies toward lack of differentiation in the networks. As we have said, the existence of a certain amount of differentiation by no means precludes the further possibility that subjects may also show a degree of consensus in their definitions of an object. If some agreement does exist, this would mean that the definition of the object is not entirely specific to the dyadic relationship. It cannot be a mere fiction conjured up by the individual subject. It receives some validation, either from the supporting views of other subjects, or from some inherent properties of the object himself.

Let us first examine the notion that people may tend to agree that the more popular members are also the more conformist. We state this as follows:

Hypothesis 3. The more widely an object is *liked,* the more likely he is to be described by either likers or dislikers as having conformist traits; the less likely he is to be described as having deviant traits.

For this purpose, the likability-dislikability matrix for each sex as described above was employed again (except that here the full set of cells was collapsed considerably so as to increase the number

of dyads per cell). We now ask whether the attribution of traits by likers or dislikers will vary as predicted according to the object's over-all likability (when his dislikability is held constant). The analysis was made separately for likers and for dislikers. Thus, the question in regard to any conformist trait is: as *O*'s likability increases (for any given degree of his dislikability), does *S*'s tendency to attribute the characteristic to him also increase? Each pair of adjacent cells on the likability dimension was inspected to see whether, in fact, such an increase occurred. The number of such increases was counted for all the pairs of cells, and compared with the number of decreases and ties, in order to determine whether the increases were the more numerous. Conversely, the per cent of dyads in which *S* attributes a *deviant* trait was predicted to *de*crease with *O*'s likability; and the analysis counted the relative number of decreases. By applying the Wilcoxon test at the .025 level (one-sided) to the proportions of increases and decreases, the null hypothesis was rejected for nine of the characteristics among likers, and for eight among dislikers.

This seems to provide assurance that a degree of consensus does exist within the networks. Moreover, there appears to be a tendency here, in respect to many characteristics at least, for an object's likability to coincide with a general reputation for conformity. This would be consistent, for instance, with such a very simple notion as that some objects are more conformist in their behavior than others, that this behavior is directly reflected in the definitions of the subjects, and that subjects are at the same time more apt to like the conformist members than the deviant ones.

Let us now turn to the dislikability dimension. Is it also the case that objects who arouse widespread feelings of aversion tend to have general reputations for deviance? We state this as follows:

> *Hypothesis 4.* The more widely an object is *disliked*, the more likely he is to be described by either likers or dislikers as having deviant traits; the less likely he is to be described as having conformist traits.

At first glance, Hypothesis 4 might appear to be merely a restatement of Hypothesis 3. That is, one might perhaps expect that the likability and the dislikability of the object are simple opposites of each other, so that objects who are widely disliked (and widely defined as deviant) are quite different people from those who are widely liked (and widely defined as conformist). On further consideration, however, it seems clear that likability and dislikability may not be simple opposites, after all. Indeed, one of the assumptions of our working model is that the networks of high status objects contain, not friends alone, but enemies as well. Such objects, that is, are assumed to be both likable and dislikable. Moreover, such objects are further assumed to be the relatively conformist members of the group. Such assumptions, which will be examined and discussed in further detail in the last section of this paper, would lead us to expect a looser relationship between dislikability and deviant reputation (Hypothesis 4) than between likability and a conformist reputation (Hypothesis 3).

Accordingly, Hypothesis 4 was examined by a procedure parallel to that used for Hypothesis 3. As it turned out, somewhat less evidence was found to support Hypothesis 4—the null hypothesis for dislikability was rejected for only 2 out of the 18 characteristics among likers, and for 3 among dislikers.

Networks for Social Control

What are the possible consequences of such networks, in which cognitive orientations show only a partial consensus, and beyond this tend to vary with cathectic orientations? What effect may be exerted upon the object by these tendencies for friends to stress his conformity while enemies stress his deviance, even though there may be a modicum of underlying agreement between friends and enemies about the kind of person he seems to be?

Our present research cannot establish empirically which are the antecedents and which the consequences. It seems likely that the ongoing process may consist of (1) actions by the object; which in turn (2) are defined in certain ways by the subjects and which arouse certain feelings in them; and (3) the expression of these definitions and feelings then indicates to the object that he is approved or disapproved for being the kind of person he seems to be; so that (4) subsequent actions by the object may be modified in line with the preceding chain of events. It seems clear, however, that, within such a process, different subjects take note of his conformist, or his deviant actions. Perhaps he is a fun-loving person, for instance, who neglects his schoolwork. Then his friends may openly admire him for the former, while his enemies criticize him for the latter. Or perhaps both friend and enemy observe the same general characteristic in him; but each notices differing manifestations of it, so that their differing definitions may serve complementary functions. Both may consider that he studies hard, for instance; but his friends, who define him as a good student, may have the effect of patting him on the back for this; while his enemies, who complain about any indication that he is an apple-polisher and cares only for top grades, serve thereby as a check on any perceived tendencies toward deviance (or compulsive conformity). That is, friends and enemies may divide between them the functions of noting the object's success and failure in meeting group expectations.

Any such division of functions might have interesting implications in terms of Parsons' paradigm of social control. Parsons describes the therapist as the prototype, who self-consciously evaluates the patient's behavior and manipulates both the rewards and the punishments, alternately giving support to the patient and withdrawing it, permitting a certain amount of deviance but setting limits to this amount. In the peer group, the full therapist role may tend to be divided between at least two different people. The friend's selective emphasis may serve not only to reward the object's conformity but also to provide the requisite permissiveness, allowing the object to get away with a degree of deviance without disturbing the friendship. At the same time, the major emphasis on deviance may be left to the enemy, who is apt to overlook, rather than to encourage, any conformist tendencies which the disliked object may display.

Thus liking and disliking are considered here as general dispositions to approve or to disapprove. On occasions, to be sure, the friend may punish, the enemy may reward. Our study does not investigate this. There may well be, however, a degree of incompatibility in the peer relationship between praising and blaming. A degree of strain would undoubtedly devolve upon the friend who attempted to play the full therapist role. Not only is the friend less detached than the therapist, less able to evaluate behavior objectively; he may also be less willing to express criticism because of the

consequent risk of losing reciprocal approval from the liked object. Such strain may be obviated to the extent that, as our data suggest, the task of judging the object's deviance is relegated to quite a different person, who in any case feels generally negatively disposed toward him.

If approval and disapproval relationships are actually to operate in some such fashion as controls within an informal social system, certain conditions must of course be met. The subject must in some way communicate to the object both his definition of him and his positive or negative feelings toward him. Even though this communication may often occur through vague cues, O must interpret such cues correctly. Moreover, S's approval or disapproval must be significant to O, if O is to make any effort to meet S's expectations. No systematic effort has been made here to determine the extent to which such necessary conditions may actually be met. It seems likely, however, that they are often at least approximated, especially since all the subjects in an object's network are members of the same larger group, and hence potentially related to one another. This means that communication of approval-disapproval may often flow from one subject through other subjects before it finally reaches the object. The disapproval of one subject, for instance, may act, not directly upon O, but indirectly through some third person whose attitudes O understands and whose good opinion matters to O. O may refrain from deviance, not so much to avoid the disfavor of the disliker, as to prevent the disliker from pointing out this deviance to others in the network. To cite an example from another situation, the son's radical behavior may be censured, not by his parents who love him and are permissive, but by his neighbors whose feelings toward him are neutral or negative. The son, knowing that these neighbors are significant to his parents, may modify his behavior in order to protect his parents from their adverse views. In this way, the impact of disapproval may often tend to operate circuitously through the network of the several interdependent relationships.

Possible Functional Importance of Combined Approval and Disapproval Relationships

We have thus suggested a possible functional differentiation between conformity-approving and deviance-disapproving relationships. Likers take note when the object lives up to group expectations; dislikers note his tendencies to deviate. Beyond this, if *combined* approval and disapproval are indeed functional for social control, in line with our model, then we should look for a special kind of structuring of the networks of objects who are differently placed in the social system as a whole. We should expect that the more approval *O* receives the more likely he will also be to receive some disapproval too. (This is the *second* of the assumptions stated in our model which is examined in the present analysis.)

In order to bring our data to bear on this final point, we first arrange the objects according to the extent to which they attract positive orientations of various kinds, such as friendship, deference, confidence. We refer to this dimension as "status," and measure it by a contrived item object scale. The networks of objects at the low end of the status continuum contain by definition very few positive relationships, while those at the high end contain a great many. (Status so defined is, of course, closely related to the likability dimension employed above, but includes a wider variety of positive orienta-

tions which may be drawn, not merely from the object's circle of friends, but from the group as a whole. Being liked is one of ten different items used in the status scale.)

We now ask about the disapproval relationships of these objects. Our theory leads us to expect that high status objects are more likely than others both to be disliked and to have their deviance noticed. Table 2 shows the outcome of this analysis. Dislikers are indeed found to be relatively numerous in the networks of high status objects. (They also focus especially upon objects near the bottom of the status scale, though not at the very bottom because of the obscurity of extremely low status objects.) In roughly parallel fashion, as the object's status increases, there is a generally upward trend in the number of deviant characteristics ascribed to him by likers and dislikers combined. That is, high status objects seem to be hedged about by a combination of approval and disapproval relationships, while the networks of low status objects tend to consist exclusively of disapproval relationships. Such a structuring is consistent with our theory of the functional importance of combined networks.

At the same time, this finding suggests that the underlying process may be fairly complex. What simple process might produce such an apparent paradox in which high status persons are at once the most liked and the most disliked, the most widely adjudged both conformist and deviant? This is not consistent with any notion that likability and dislikability are merely opposite ends of the same continuum. It does not fit any simple theory that objects are ranged along a single continuum of conformity-deviance which tends to coincide with another single continuum of likability-dislikability. To be sure, the apparent paradox occurs only in the *absolute numbers* of dislikers and

Table **2** *Networks of objects of differing status*

	Low 0	1	2	3	4	High 5
			Status of object			
MALES						
Number of relationships per object in which subject:						
(1) Likes	.28	.96	1.84	3.15	4.71	7.13
(2) Dislikes	.91	2.10	1.18	1.31	1.53	2.16
Ratio of (1) to (2)	.31	.45	1.56	2.40	3.12	3.30
Number of attributions per object of traits classified as:						
(3) Conformist	.68	2.59	3.94	7.27	11.78	17.17
(4) Deviant	1.94	4.62	3.73	5.57	6.62	7.31
Ratio of (3) to (4)	.35	.56	1.06	1.31	1.78	2.35
Number of objects	179	221	272	201	265	159
FEMALES						
Number of relationships per object in which subject:						
(1) Likes	.20	1.09	1.82	3.25	4.58	7.75
(2) Dislikes	.74	1.57	1.14	1.16	1.51	2.60
Ratio of (1) to (2)	.27	.70	1.60	2.80	3.04	2.98
Number of attributions per object of traits classified as:						
(3) Conformist	.61	3.05	4.41	9.07	13.10	22.50
(4) Deviant	1.90	4.62	4.28	5.31	6.54	9.17
Ratio of (3) to (4)	.32	.66	1.03	1.71	2.00	2.45
Number of objects	86	144	251	261	511	192

deviant definitions in the networks of high status objects. There is nothing in Table 2 to negate the usual proposition that high status goes with a *preponderantly* conformist reputation, and low status with a *preponderantly* deviant reputation. The process may well consist of a kind of exchange of high status for conformity, of low status for deviance. Thus the *ratios* in the table show that as O's status goes up —and as he tends to have relatively more friends than enemies—there is also an increasing relative emphasis on the conformist traits in his reputation. Nevertheless, as his status goes up, the absolute numbers of dislikers in his network tend also to go up, rather than down; and as his

reputation becomes relatively more conformist, the absolute numbers of deviant definitions of him likewise tend to increase. What accounts for this?

Bales, who finds a somewhat similar structuring of hostile relationships in small laboratory groups, provides a possible explanation for it. He suggests that the very success of high status individuals may in itself provoke ambivalent responses. Some of this hostility is drained off on the "scapegoat" at the bottom of the status structure; but the greater part of it is focused directly on the leaders themselves. A comparable process may well take place in our adolescent groupings as well, even though high status adolescents are not required, as in the Bales groups, to guide the others in the performance of a specified task. Here too the aggression against the successful members of the group may be evoked in part because other members envy them or feel excluded from their circle of intimates. It may not, that is, be entirely the result of the deviant reputations of these successful members—a speculation which is in line with the rather meager support adduced for the dislikability Hypothesis 4 above. Thus the Bales findings and ours in Table 2 may perhaps both be special instances of a more general group process in which the high status object's receipt of positive and of negative orientations may arise in entirely different ways. His success in eliciting positive orientations may be closely related to his conformity; perhaps the conformity itself elicits high status, and the status in turn gives the object a continuing stake in conformity. In quite a different fashion, however, his receipt of negative orientations may arise less from any actual deviance on his part than from his high position in the status structure.

We are concerned here, however, not with such possible processes which may lead to the structuring of friendly and hostile relationships, but with the possible consequences for social control. Although our research does not bear directly upon such consequences, the present peer group findings seem compatible with a situation in which high status objects, surrounded as they are by both friends and enemies, are especially rigidly controlled. Meanwhile, low status members, even when they do conform, are apt to be quite unnoticed in this conformity, since they have enemies but few friends. They receive little of the support which would make them feel secure in the group. Few friendly opportunities are provided to

them for acting out their tensions or their deviant impulses. Their main response from the other group members is that of criticism and disapproval.

Under such circumstances, it might not seem strange if many low status members were motivated either to active deviance or to withdrawal from the group. Negative sanctions alone may fail to discourage further transgressions on the part of the object, or to re-integrate him into the group. . . . Some such asymmetry in the informal structure of social controls may be in part responsible for the tendencies of many low status members to align themselves with outside groups which support their deviant norms, or to drop out of school entirely.

What happens in such a situation, in which an object belongs also to an outside deviant group? His case seems very different from those we have been studying, in which likers and dislikers belong to the same group and tend to share the same norms. He may have out-group friends who support the very behavior which is negatively sanctioned by his in-group enemies. The ineffectual controls of his exclusively negative network in the school grade are thus coupled with outside approval relationships which merely reinforce his deviance. Such reverse control mechanisms may well be at work in many types of deviant groups, as well as in correctional situations where the approval roles are played by the object's unregenerated peers while the authorities express mainly disapproval.

If further research were to establish the functional importance of combined approval and disapproval relationships (as well as the possible reverse control effects of approval from outside deviant groups), this would seem to have important implications for a fuller understanding of social controls. For example, various studies of extreme deviance, such as delinquency or severe neurosis in children, might be reanalyzed with reference to the total interpersonal control structure. In the family, as in the peer group, conformity or deviance in the child may depend upon the combined roles of all the other members. Thus, a crucial question which is not always asked in such studies might be—not merely whether or not any *one* parent is excessively punitive (or overprotective)—but whether the child is receiving in the combination of all his relationships an appropriate admixture of attention paid both to his successes and to his failures in meeting expectations.

Conclusion

This paper develops a theory of social control networks, proposing that the dyadic relationships in informal groups may be differentiated and organized in such a way as to channel the motivations of some members in conformist, others in deviant, directions.

It has demonstrated a tendency toward cognitive differentiation, so that subjects who feel positively toward another person emphasize his conformity, while those who feel negatively toward this same person emphasize his deviance. It has suggested that these differentiated relationships may serve the complementary functions of rewarding conformity and punishing deviance. Accordingly, to the extent that rewarding and punitive relationships may be differentiated in this way, the social controls which converge upon any given member of the group derive, not from a single subject, but from a composite of all the subjects in his network. Some individuals participate as objects in both types of relationships—are both liked and disliked and hence presumably receive both rewards for con-

formity and punishments for deviance. Other individuals participate primarily in relationships where they are disliked, so that their deviance tends to be observed far more than their conformity. This leads to the question for further research whether participation in combined rewarding and punitive relationships may tend to produce conformity, while participation in exclusively punitive relationships may merely foster deviance.

Appendix

FURTHER DETAILS OF THE ANALYSIS

The statistical significance of the dyadic differences shown here cannot be tested directly, since any given individual may be involved as subject and, in some instances, as object, in a number of different dyads. Furthermore, the answers on the 18 characteristics are, of course, not independent of one another. Therefore, the usual procedure has been to break the dyads down into independent groups according to school, grade, and sex.

For *Hypothesis 1,* 16 groups were used. For each group the difference was obtained between the per cent of likers and the per cent of dislikers who attribute the given trait to the object as in Table 1. Under the null hypothesis, roughly equal numbers of groups exhibiting plus and minus differences would be expected.

For the first test of *Hypothesis 2,* those 98 girls who had sufficient likers and dislikers were divided into 7 independent groups. Two scores were computed for each of the groups: score *a*, representing the tendency for likers to ascribe the characteristic to the object, and score *b*, representing the tendency for dislikers to ascribe it. These scores were designed to be treated as matched pairs for the group and to be tested by the Wilcoxon signed rank procedure. In order to obtain these two scores for any one group, tabulations had been made for each of the individual objects, indicating the per cent of the likers and the per cent of the dislikers who attribute the trait to him. Here too the Wilcoxon procedure was then used, this time in a modified form. We first ranked the differences in the two percentages for each object according to their absolute values. We then computed the sum of the ranks for those objects where the per cent for likers exceeded that for dislikers; and divided this by the sum of all the ranks. This furnishes score *a* for the group, measuring the tendency for likers to ascribe the characteristic. The sum of the remaining ranks divided by the total sum furnishes score *b*, measuring the tendency for dislikers to ascribe the characteristic. (These scores will always add to 1 for any group.) Using these two scores, the Wilcoxon statistic was then obtained for the seven subsamples.

For *Hypotheses 3 and 4*, eight groups were used for each sex.

COMMENTARY

SPECIAL PROBLEMS OF SOCIOLOGICAL ANALYSIS

This Unit brings together one set of problems we have encountered throughout this book in investigating human societies and groups as systems of interdependent parts: how to deal in research with different levels of the social system. We have been reading studies that treat the lower-level parts of the collectivity—the subgroups or the roles played by individual members—as fitting together to form the more inclusive, higher-level system of the collectivity as a whole. And we have seen repeatedly what a complex task the sociologist faces when he attempts to translate this notion of system into research. Since each level has its characteristic properties, he often has difficulty in handling or understanding cross-level relationships between individual properties such as attitudes and group properties such as societal values or population density.

700

Yet, in order to understand the full nature of social systems, the sociologist must deal with properties of two or more levels of the system—with the constituent parts (at a lower level) as they combine to form the more inclusive (higher-level) system. It is only through combined analysis of these levels that he is able to investigate the interactions and interdependence of the parts and to determine functional or dysfunctional consequences for the system as a whole.

Let us consider a typical example. Suppose that a researcher wants to examine the occupational and rural-urban characteristics of societies at both the individual role and the total society level. His conceptual model, then, might specify the nature of the society's occupational structure, describing how individuals (as the parts) are employed in various roles in agriculture or industry. It might also describe the distribution of the total population over the land, indicating how some individuals and families settle together in urban concentrations, while others are widely dispersed in outlying areas. How, then, is the sociologist to translate into empirical research the relationships he postulates between occupation and residence?

An ideal analysis might observe for a sample of societies the full set of interrelationships among these characteristics as properties of both system levels. Such an analysis—we should call it a *social system analysis*—would start by identifying each individual (in terms of the role properties under study) as engaged in industry or agriculture, for example, and as dwelling in an urban or a rural area. Then it would determine how these types of individuals are arranged to form the internal structure of roles within each of the societies under study. Finally, it would compare the several societies in terms of their internal role structures and their over-all patterns of urbanism and industrialism.

In practice, however, a full social system analysis of this sort is rarely used at the present stage of sociological research development. A good deal of confusion over the conceptual definitions of the levels and their relationships still exists, and few appropriate research methods have been worked out. For many purposes, too, the full analysis is not necessary. Therefore most studies are selective in their focus. Some deal exclusively with a single level—group or individual. Others focus upon one level, but take another level into account. Many such selective approaches are possible, but in this Unit we shall cut through these complex possibilities by suggesting—and beginning to evaluate—four types of partial analysis that seem useful to meet particular research objectives, as outlined in Table 12-A. Before we examine in detail the uses of these four types of analysis in the study selections, let us illustrate their objectives as selections from the conceptual model in our example.

First, an *individual analysis* deals exclusively with individuals in roles—disregarding the groups to which the individuals belong. Here the researcher might ask, for instance, whether (and to what extent) urban individuals are more likely than rural individuals to work in industry. This approach is useful for describing and comparing individuals (as in the individual pattern approach to measurement discussed in Unit 9) and for analyzing the interrelated properties of individuals.

Second, a *contextual analysis* also focuses on the individual, but it locates and explains the individual's role with reference to its group context. Theories of the individual in relation to the social system may be concerned with what the individual gets out of the system that induces him to engage in certain occupational pursuits and to dwell in certain locations; or with how the societal norms of occupational and geographic mobility affect the individual in furthering his own interests, or with how the individual relates to and is influenced by other individuals and groups within the economic and demographic structure. A contextual analysis might extend an individual analysis by asking, for example, whether rural individuals are more likely to engage in industrial occupations in the context of a highly urbanized—rather than in the context of a predominantly rural—society.

Table **12-A**   *Some types of partial analysis of social systems*

Type of analysis	Selective focus of model	Research case **(P-I)**
Individual	Individual-in-role	Individuals
Contextual	Individual with reference to group context	Individuals characterized by properties of the groups to which they belong
Group	Group (collectivity)	Groups
Structural	Group with reference to internal arrangement of parts	Group segments characterized by properties of individual members

Third, a *group analysis* deals exclusively with the higher-level systems (groups)—disregarding the individuals who compose each group. It might ask whether countries that are highly industrialized are necessarily also highly urbanized. Here the value of the research lies in describing and comparing groups or societies (as in the group pattern approach to measurement) and in studying relationships among the properties of groups.

Fourth, a *structural analysis* focuses on the group but with some reference to the differentiated roles that interrelate to form the group's internal structure. Here the actions and motivations of the individual actors are viewed as mechanisms in the operation of the collectivity, and the norms and rules governing individuals are viewed as the conditions under which the processes of urbanization and industrialization can be carried out without disturbing the integration of the system. One form of structural analysis (*within-group analysis*) might ask, for example, how the several types of individuals (rural or urban, agricultural or industrial) are arranged within each of the several societies—thus focusing on the internal structure *within* each group. Another form (*segmental comparisons*) might make comparisons among the rural inhabitants of many societies to see, for example, whether the degree of industrialization of the total society affects the industrialization of even its rural segments.

We use the term "structural analysis" to mean that this too is only a *partial* approach to the study of systems, even though it comes closer to social system analysis than the three other types. Unlike the preferable (but little understood) approach that we call social system analysis, we shall see how structural analysis does not *fully* delineate the internal structure of each group *at the same time* that it makes systematic comparisons among groups. It is designed to *test specific hypotheses* about group differences in internal structure, whereas a social system analysis would organize all the data to facilitate *exploration* of the nature of group differences and similarities. Only the social system analysis seems adequate to explore fully, for example, the consequences of societal urbanization and in-dustrialization for the internal integration of each system.

In considering such forms of analysis in this Unit, we shall deal mainly with studies that focus either on the role (as the part) or on the collectivity (as the higher-level system), because these two levels in particular highlight some of the possibilities, as well as the difficulties, of treating psychological and personal processes as mechanisms of the social system. Much of the discussion will have more general implications, however, for studies focused on other levels of the system—on dyadic relationships as parts as opposed to roles as higher-level sys-tems, or on subgroups as opposed to more inclusive groups, or on more than just two levels of the system. We shall also pay special attention to the use of collective measures **(P-XII).** Such measures, since they always pull together information about lower-level parts, may, even in a group analysis, raise questions about the possible relevance of these parts to the research problem.

Some Possible Fallacies

Unfortunately no complete set of methodological principles is available to guide the researcher who attempts to use one or another of such approaches in the study of social systems. He faces a host of empirical and interpretative problems which have not yet been fully formulated—and of which he may even be unaware. We shall therefore begin by suggesting a few of the more obvious pitfalls that beset him before going on to examine the study selections for possible clues to the developing solutions to such problems.

Some of the difficulties confronting the researcher arise because he fails to translate his conceptual model into operations at the appropriate social system level; others because the single level to which he restricts his empirical analysis is by itself insufficient to uncover the relevant facts. Such difficulties potentially result in fallacious, inadequate, or misleading findings or interpretations. We shall

Table **12-B**   *Some possible fallacies*

(1) *Fallacies arising because methods fail to fit model*

Type of fallacy	Selective focus of model	Type of research case (P-I)	Appropriate forms of partial analysis (to prevent fallacies)
Aggregative (ecological)	Individual	Group	Individual or contextual
Atomistic	Group	Individual	Group or structural

(2) *Fallacies arising because methods fail to fit facts*

Type of fallacy	Type of research case (P-I)	Implications of the facts	Appropriate forms of partial analysis (to prevent fallacies)
Psychologistic	Individual	Interpretation of individual findings affected by group context	Contextual
Sociologistic	Group	Interpretation of group findings affected by internal structure	Structural

illustrate some broad types of fallacies (see Table 12-B) through simple examples in which two properties, X and Y—each of which may pertain to either or both levels—are to be related. The basic dilemmas involved may occur much more generally, however—they may occur in measurement **(P-X)** as well as in statistical analysis **(P-XI),** and in the study of any number of interrelated variables or indicants.

FROM MODEL TO METHOD

One set of fallacies endangers the researcher who chooses his research case **(P-I)** from a social system level that does not fit his conceptual model. If his model refers to individuals in roles, but his analysis is based on groups (small or large collectivities or aggregates), we shall speak of a possible aggregative fallacy. Conversely, if his model refers to the group, but his analysis is based on individuals, we shall speak of a possible atomistic fallacy. Strange as it may at first appear, such misuses of one level for another are still rather widespread, and must be recognized to be avoided.

Aggregative Fallacies.   One type of fallacy was originally defined by W. S. Robinson in a widely quoted article (Robinson, 1950). Although he called it "ecological fallacy," we give it another name (*aggregative fallacy*) because the difficulty is not limited to ecological analysis, and many ecological studies (such as the one by Faris and Dunham) avoid it entirely. In Robinson's example, the research hypothesis refers to *individuals*. It postulates that, since educational standards are lower for the foreign-born than for the native-born, there ought to be a positive relationship between foreign birth and illiteracy. In order to test this, the researcher looks at data (see Figure 12-A) for *groups* of individuals in Census areas. These data, as it turns out in this particular example, show a *negative* correlation ($-.619$) between the proportions of foreign-born inhabitants and the proportions of illiterates.

Figure **12-A** *Robinson's group correlation between nativity and illiteracy in the United States* [a]

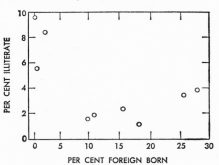

(*each dot represents a Census area*)

[a] Robinson, 1950, p. 354.

Now, do such group data negate the hypothesis? Do they support the contrary inference that the same individuals who are foreign-born tend necessarily to be literate? Certainly not! Indeed, if the analysis were based on individuals instead of groups, there might be no correlation at all, or even a positive correlation, between being foreign-born and being illiterate. Robinson emphasizes this point by showing an actual rearrangement of the same Census data now based on individuals (see Table 12-C)—where the correlation is, after all, positive. The percentage of illiterates is now *higher* among the foreign-born than among the native-born.

In our terms, then, a group analysis is inappropriate if the hypothesis refers to the individual. Thus a positive correlation for cities between suicide rates and transiency rates would not in itself support the hypothesis that transient *individuals* are more apt to commit suicide than stationary individuals. Nor would the finding of a high negative relationship for correctional institutions between recidivism rates and the proportions of delinquents learning new values indicate any necessary relationship between these variables for individuals; here again the group finding does not bear directly on the hypothesis that the same individuals who learn new attitudes in a correctional institution are less apt to commit new offenses after release. In all such instances, the researcher who uses group data runs into the danger of the aggregative fallacy.

Table **12-C**   *Robinson's individual correlation between nativity and illiteracy in the United States* [a]

	Foreign-born	Native-born	*Total*
Illiterate	1,304	2,614	3,918
Literate	11,913	81,441	93,354
Total	*13,217*	*84,055*	*97,272*

[a] Robinson, 1950, p. 354 (000 omitted).

Aggregative fallacies may be prevented by using individuals as the research case whenever the conceptual model focuses on the individual. A suitable individual analysis is illustrated in Robinson's table, for example, and we shall discuss contextual analyses which are also based on individuals as cases.

Atomistic Fallacies.   Although Robinson (who is mainly concerned with models focused on individuals) does not speak of the converse atomistic fallacy, it too is suggested by his data. If the researcher's hypothesis were that the foreign-born tend to predominate in those ecological groupings where illiteracy rates are low, he could scarcely draw any accurate inferences from the individual data in Table 12-C. A conclusion about groups of individuals in Census areas drawn from the individual data is subject to a possible atomistic fallacy. Or, suppose the hypothesis were that transiency and suicide are both manifestations of social disorganization, and tend to appear together in the same neighborhoods. This again could not properly be tested by a study of individuals—which merely attempts to discover whether the same individuals who commit suicide have also been transients. The finding of a positive correlation for individuals (as in Table 12-C), for example, does not ordinarily tell whether for a sample of neighborhoods there will be a positive or negative correlation, or no correlation at all. Similarly, studies of individual husbands and wives might be misleading whenever the theoretical focus is on the married pair (as we discussed this in Unit 4).

In general, then, if the hypothesis refers to the group, an analysis based on individuals can often lead to an atomistic fallacy by obscuring the social processes of interest. This type of fallacy may be avoided by analysis based on groups. Appropriate group analyses are illustrated in Figure 12-A (compare your earlier interpretation of another Robinson figure in Exercise IV-2, Problem 9) and in the study by Davis and Golden. We shall also discuss structural analyses as another group procedure that obviates atomistic fallacies.

The researcher who fails in such ways to match his research operations to his conceptual model is not always acting inadvertently, however; he may be unable to find the appropriate data or methods for handling them. If he is obliged to work at the wrong level—choosing, because no other data or methods are available, individual data to refer to groups or group data to refer to individuals —he should at least be on the alert for a possible atomistic or aggregative fallacy so as to interpret his findings with the necessary caution. (See the further discussion of Robinson's article in Duncan and Davis; Goodman, 1953; Menzel.)

FROM METHOD TO FACTS

Another set of fallacies may occur, even when the research case does fit the level emphasized in the model, when the exclusive focus on a single level conceals some of the information important to an understanding of the findings. Here the method, though it fits the *model,* fails to discover the relevant *facts.* Group data *alone* may not be enough to prevent a sociologistic fallacy even when the focus is on the group. By the same token, individual data *alone* may fail to prevent a psychologistic fallacy even when the focus is on the individual.

Psychologistic Fallacies. In one example, an individual analysis of older women might show that married women have more friends than widows have. But suppose that this relationship holds true, in fact, only for communities where married women are in the majority—whereas, in communities with widows in the majority, the widows have more friends than do the married women. (Compare your analysis of Problem 6 in Exercise IV-1.) And suppose the (imaginary) researcher does not discover this because he looks only at the facts about each discrete individual, disregarding the character of the community context. Using individual data alone, he develops an elaborate explanation of friendship patterns in terms of the marital status of the individual. This explanation would constitute a psychologistic fallacy that overemphasizes the personal or psychological factors because an understanding of the individual property (having friends) also requires knowledge of a group property (the marital structure of each community).

The form of analysis designed to prevent such fallacies seeks the relevant group factors that may impinge upon the individual phenomenon under study. This is the contextual analysis we shall consider in connection with the study by James Davis.

Sociologistic Fallacies. In a different example, a group analysis for the neighborhoods in a city might show a positive correlation between transiency rates and suicide rates. Here the (imaginary) researcher explains the neighborhood differences in suicide rates in terms of a social process. He postulates that transiency produces social disorganization in the area which, in turn, weakens social controls and reduces social rewards, and thereby operates to encourage suicide. According to such a theory, those individuals in the neighborhood who are transients have an effect upon other individuals who are not transients themselves, but whose social ties are weakened by the general disorganization of the neighborhood.

But now suppose that, in this fictitious example, the facts are that the *individual* relationship between transiency and suicide is the same for all of the neighborhoods. That is, the relatively high proportions who commit suicide among the transient individuals are approximately the same for all the different neighborhoods; and the relatively low proportions who commit suicide among the stationary individuals are approximately the same for all the different neighborhoods. Such facts would refute the theory that the group (or neighborhood) is in some way necessary to an understanding of the process connecting the two variables. The explanation involving interaction and between-role patterning (so that what other transient individuals do and think affects what the nontransient individuals do and think) would constitute a sociologistic fallacy. Indeed, the facts in this example—that within each neighborhood the transient individuals are consistently more disposed to suicide than the nontransient individuals—would point to the need for a personal explanation of the individual correlation in psychological terms, or in terms of the cultural norms that foster tendencies toward both suicide and transiency in the same individuals. (Here too the sociologist must explain why some neighborhoods have more transients than others.)

A partial approach designed to forestall such arbitrary attribution to the group of individual-level processes is *structural analysis*. In the above example of the correlation between suicide and transiency, structural analysis would go beyond group analysis to examine the individuals within each of the neighborhoods. Thus it would discover the crucial fact: that the neighborhood transiency rate is not correlated with the suicide rate when we consider only the stationary segment of individuals in each neighborhood. The study by Faris and Dunham illustrates and clarifies the nature of such a structural analysis.

(The researcher will often be warned of a sociologistic or psychologistic fallacy if he compares a group analysis with an individual analysis of the same data. The juxtaposition of Robinson's Figure 12-A with his Table 12-C, for example, would show the researcher that he cannot rely upon a single-level explanation of the relationship between birthplace and literacy. The nature of the relationship between the variables is rarely clear, however, without the more detailed structural or contextual analysis.)

The use of partial methods that do not reflect the full patterning of the facts applies to *measurement* as well as to analysis, as you will have recognized from your experience in Exercise III-6. The problems of using either an individual analysis or a group analysis alone are closely related to the problems of collective measurement discussed in Unit 9. In measuring a single variable, we saw in Figure 9-D that neither the individual pattern approach nor the group pattern approach is necessarily sufficient in itself to uncover the patterns of acts and structuring of roles that exist in the social system under study. In classifying railroad repair gangs according to their stage of operations, for example, the contingency of one act (replacing rocks) upon another act (digging) appeared at the group level (Table 9-F) but was completely obscured at the individual level (Table 9-E). It was only through post-analysis (or, in this extreme example, by contrasting the individual-level data with the group-level data) that the fact of division of labor within the gangs could be discovered. Our experience with post-analysis of the group pattern approach led to the idea of a social system approach to measurement which would study simultaneously both the patterns and their underlying social-structural base. The key to such an approach is that it deals with *two levels* of the system at once—*identifying* the patterned properties of both the inclusive *system* (the group) and its constituent *roles* (the individuals). We shall now find this key useful in a more general consideration of social system analysis and its possible modifications.

THE DATA FOR SOCIAL SYSTEM ANALYSIS

In considering the problems posed by the fallacies and their solutions, we shall first try out the various partial analyses that should avoid the aggregative and atomistic fallacies of studying the wrong level, as well as the psychologistic fallacy of focusing exclusively on the individual level of a social system, and the sociologistic fallacy of focusing exclusively on the group level. Then we shall turn to some incipient possibilities of social system analysis that deals with systems and with the fitting together of the parts within each system.

Ultimate development of general methods of social system analysis and measurement will rest upon an understanding, not only of the theory of social systems, but of the formal character of the necessary data. For example, the full data for Robinson's analysis (although Robinson himself is concerned only with avoiding one type of fallacy in order to analyze individuals as cases) consist of a whole series of group tables, one for each area in the country, in which individuals are cross-tabulated by nativity and literacy. Each of these group tables is similar in form to the total Table 12-C. More generally, we shall think of the data necessary for a social system analysis of any two-level, two-variable problem as consisting of a set of group tables (one for each group) within which the relevant individual variables are cross-tabulated.

We shall see how each partial analysis of social systems (Table 12-A) is a selection from a full set of data of this sort—with each partial analysis yielding a particular type of result for particular research objectives, and each encountering possible fallacies (Table 12-B). It is clear in advance, for example, that the data for an *individual analysis* (illustrated in Table 12-C) are selected and aggregated from all the group tables by adding together the information in the *cells*. And the data for a *group analysis* (as in Figure 12-A) are selected from the *marginals* of all the group tables. These two sets of selections from the same data may give quite different results, since, for any given set of marginal frequencies, a great many arrangements of cell information are possible, as you know. (Robinson's article develops the mathematical connections between individual analysis and group analysis.) We shall also examine contextual analysis and structural analysis as different types of selections from the full set of social system data.

Davis and Golden and Group Analysis

The value of an analysis made at the *single level of the group* as a whole is evidenced by the far-flung demographic research of Kingsley Davis and Hilda Golden. In order "to understand the recent and future mechanisms of change in pre-industrial areas," these researchers examine the relationship between the process of urbanization and economic development. Using as their cases the countries and territories of the world, they succeed in measuring a number of important societal properties, despite the inadequacies and inaccuracies of the sta-

Figure **12-B**   *Analysis of agriculturalism and urbanization of countries*

(*each dot represents a country or territory*) [a]

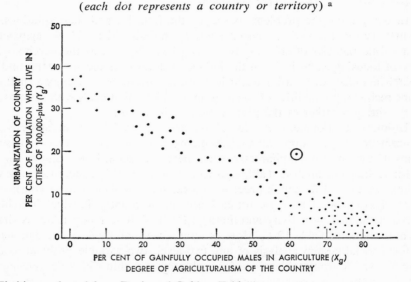

[a] Fictitious, adapted from Davis and Golden, Table 1.

tistical materials available for many of the countries (see Gibbs and Davis). They look upon urbanization, not as an "isolated culture trait," but as "a function of the total economy"; and undertake a systematic comparative study leading to assumptions about the impact of urbanization throughout the total range of pre-industrial and industrial areas.

FORM OF THE GROUP ANALYSIS

Davis and Golden's method of uncovering the pattern of group properties (see Figure 12-B) is to measure as collective variables two properties of each country or territory: the economic development or industrialization of a country is indexed by the percentage of gainfully occupied males engaged in industry rather than agriculture, and the country's urbanization is indexed by the proportion of the total population living in cities. (We shall refer to these collective properties as X_g and Y_g respectively—with the subscript g indicating that the measure is taken to refer to the group rather than the individual.) Then the correlation between these properties is obtained, based on the group **(P-I)** as the case. If we imagined a scatter diagram of Davis and Golden's group analysis, it would look approximately like our (fictitious) Figure 12-B. Each dot represents a country, and all the dots tend to fit a line that slopes downward to the right. The researchers report a —.86 correlation between agriculturalism and urbanization.

Figure **12-C** *Data used in the Davis-Golden analysis*

(*for each country*)

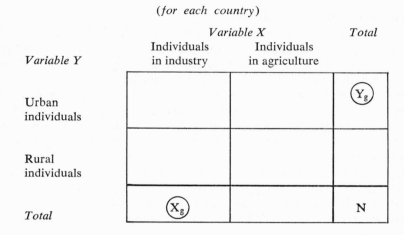

| Variable Y | Variable X | | Total |
	Individuals in industry	Individuals in agriculture	
Urban individuals			Y_g
Rural individuals			
Total	X_g		N

Nature of the Data.   Since we have claimed that a group analysis is a partial approach that selects from the data for a full social system analysis, let us now examine the selective character of the Davis and Golden data. The underlying set of facts for each country is suggested in Figure 12-C. Here each individual is first coded (in the simplest terms) as urban or rural, and again as engaged in industry or in agriculture. Then these individual data are cross-tabulated for the country, so that the frequencies in the cells of Figure 12-C show the *within-group* arrangement of *individuals*. The marginal totals of the table become the collective measures for the *group*. (Now you may want to review the steps in collective measurement in Manual III-A.) Thus Davis and Golden use, as their collective measures for each country, the two circled figures from the marginals of Figure 12-C— taken as proportions of the total number (N) of individuals in the group.

This type of analysis, then, does not make use of any individual information from the cells of such a table. Such exclusive use of marginal data distinguishes the single-level group analysis from a structural analysis, which might also take into account certain cell information for each group.

Of course, demographers are also frequently interested in the internal arrangements of individuals within groups or areas (see, *e.g.,* Casis and Davis). Hawley has codified the variety of studies of "population composition" that deal with the "various internal differentials which influence the comparability of populations or of demographic phenomena" (Hawley, 1959, p. 361). The age-sex pyramid that graphs the distribution by age categories of the males and females within each country, as well as the numerical indexes for summarizing such distributions, are examples of demographic tools that are generally useful for studying more complex within-group arrangements that correspond to the cell information in Figure 12-C (see, *e.g.,* Browning; Peterson, p. 628).

UTILITY OF THE GROUP ANALYSIS

Davis and Golden are not immediately concerned here with questions of group composition or structure, however, even if the necessary individual information were available for each country. The group analysis bears directly upon their research objective, which regards the collective measures as indexes of fundamental traits of the societies themselves (see Gibbs and Davis, p. 419). This form of single-level analysis is perfectly adequate for the research objective of classifying and comparing societies, and explaining (in terms of agriculturalism-industrialism) why some countries and areas rather than others may be characterized by a high degree of urbanization.

Moreover, since this analysis is based on groups as the cases, it results in a classification of countries into types, allowing the researchers to locate each particular country in relation to the others, and to select certain countries for intensive case study. It is against this background of "comparative statistical analysis" that India, for example, emerges as an "agrarian country with a moderate rate of urbanization" (see also the further intensive analysis in Kingsley Davis, 1962, pp. 3–26); or that our (adapted) Figure 12-B shows the position of Egypt as an "over-urbanized" deviant case (see the circled dot). The figure also suggests how a freehand line drawn to fit these dots would indicate the "expected" degree of urbanization of Egypt (as in Davis and Golden's Table 5).

THE COMBINING OF GROUPS

Davis and Golden also analyze the same data in another way, which, although it does not correspond exactly to any of the pure types of partial analysis we are discussing, is interesting because it combines inhabitants of the countries of the world to refer to the single higher-level system of the world as a whole. In Table 12-D (a rearrangement of their Table 1), one of the measures (of agriculturalism) still shows how each country is classified according to its percentage of males engaged in agriculture (with these percentages collapsed into seven categories). The second measure (of urbanization) no longer refers to the country as the case, however, but to the combined individuals in all countries with a given degree of agriculturalism. Thus, for example, the individuals in all eleven countries having 0–19 per cent of the males in agriculture have been added together; the single figure 32.3 per cent shows what proportion of these combined populations live in cities.

Table **12-D** *Analysis of agriculturalism and urbanization of the world* [a]

	Degree of *agriculturalism* of the country						
	Per cent of gainfully occupied males in agriculture (X_g)						
Urbanization	*0–19*	*20–29*	*30–39*	*40–49*	*50–59*	*60–69*	*70–plus*
Per cent of population who live in cities of 100,000–plus	32.3	23.6	23.2	21.9	17.7	8.9	6.3
Total individuals in each category = 100 per cent (not shown)							
Number of countries in each category	(11)	(11)	(7)	(7)	(16)	(17)	(86)

[a] Adapted from Davis and Golden, Table 1.

Does this shift in the level mean that the researchers are now focusing on the individual rather than the group? Do they now treat dwelling in cities as an *individual* property, with the objective of explaining why some individuals rather than others reside in cities? In this particular study, obviously not. Their discussion makes clear that the shift is not to a microscopic but to a more macroscopic level. Urbanization is now treated as a property of *segments of the world population*—with each segment living in countries or territories of a given degree of agriculturalism. The focus is now on explaining (in terms of agriculturalism or industrialization) how the population of the world is distributed between urban and rural places.

These two types of analysis used by Davis and Golden—one based on countries as groups (as in Figure 12-B), and the other on countries combined into a single world group (Table 12-D)—can produce quite different results. The researchers provide an illustration of the differences by contrasting India's position in the world when the index of industrialization is figured both ways: When *each* country is treated as the case in the group analysis (Figure 12-B), only 43 per cent of the countries are more industrialized than India. But when *all* the countries are combined (Table 12-D), 51 per cent of the world's population lives in countries more industrialized than India.

We shall demonstrate later how such differences come about. But let us note here what procedure we follow in order to combine groups, as in Table 12-D. First, to arrive at the world data in Table 12-D, we add together the data from many group tables as in Figure 12-C. Although these tables for the several groups may differ markedly from one another in their proportions of urban inhabitants, their differences become concealed when all the groups are combined. Moreover, if the groups vary greatly in size (as the countries and territories of the world vary), the patterns of the larger groups will be more heavily weighted when the groups are aggregated. Thus the combined group data may obscure differences among the groups themselves, but they are useful in yielding answers to questions about a different level of the system—in this instance, about the world.

AMBIGUITY OF COLLECTIVE MEASURES

It is significant, too, in connection with Table 12-D, that we can question whether the researcher is using the dependent variable, urbanization, to refer to the individual or to a segment of the larger social system. Urbanization might refer to the individual's probability of living in a city, explained in terms of some individual process; or to the proportion of the group—or of a particular segment of the group—living in cities, explained in terms of some social process. This dilemma often arises in interpreting a collective measure. The proper interpretation depends in part, as in the Davis and Golden study, upon the system-level reference defined in the conceptual model. Sometimes, also, as in the study we are about to examine, the researcher tests his model against the facts to determine whether he is justified in assuming that the property under investigation does refer to the group as a whole, or whether it refers to segments composed of similar individuals within the group.

Faris and Dunham and Structural Analysis

Faris and Dunham illustrate how *structural analysis* may be used to extend and refine the results of a group analysis. They attempt to determine whether the rate of mental breakdown is indeed partly "a function of . . . certain undetermined types of social processes" within the city, or whether it is due merely to the distribution within areas of individuals with certain personal characteristics.

The study is an example of the ecological approach widely used in sociological investigation, and defined by Amos Hawley as the "study of the morphology of collective life in both its static and dynamic aspects" (Hawley, 1950, p. 67). Faris and Dunham suggest in their report the nature of much of the early work of Park, Burgess, and other scholars at the University of Chicago in observing and analyzing populations and community structures with reference to their territorial location. An immense research literature has been produced on such diverse topics as delinquent gangs, taxi dance halls, the journey to work, suicide, family disorganization, and mental disorders—all based on the population in the region or area as the research case (P-I). A region, as Bogue defines it, is "a unique cluster of interrelated conditions, traits, or forces present in an area at a given time" (Bogue, 1959-a, p. 396). Despite the difficulty that the ecological boundary sometimes marks off a mere population aggregate, the ecologist typically assumes that, as Duncan puts it, "at least some spatially delimited population aggregates have unit character," and that "there are significant properties of such an aggregate which differ from the properties of its component elements" (Duncan, 1959, p. 681).

THE INITIAL GROUP ANALYSIS

The Faris and Dunham study begins with a group analysis that examines the relationship between two variables, "differentiation of urban areas resulting from the growth of the city," and insanity rates. Faris and Dunham, as human ecologists, plot these rates on a map of Chicago, treating the "natural areas" or "communities" within the city as the cases **(P-I).**

Their conceptual model states that "the characteristics of the populations in [the various city] zones appear to be produced by the nature of the life within the zones rather than the reverse." Several zone or area indexes, such as the percentage of foreign-born, rate of mobility, or median rental paid are together assumed to "measure the extent of social disorganization between the different communities and the natural areas of the city." These area differences in disorganization—with the accompanying differences in social control, primary group relationships, and standards of personal behavior—have been found to fit a pattern of concentric zones within the city.

The research objective is, then, "to examine the spatial character of the relations between persons who have different kinds of mental breakdowns." If these patterns of mental illness and personality disorganization (Y) are found to fit into patterns of social disorganization (X), this would suggest the importance of social as well as biological, physiological, and psychological factors as possible causes of mental disorder. Inspection of the completed map shows that, indeed, the insanity rate "fits into the ecological structure of the city," with the highest rates in the central zone, and "a steady decline in rates as one travels from the center of the city to the periphery."

Thus the initial form of the analysis is somewhat similar to that used by Davis and Golden in Figure 12-B—though much cruder because the independent variable in this study is not clearly measured along a single dimension (but laid out in a complex pattern on a map); also, it is not a collective variable.

SEGMENTAL COMPARISONS

Faris and Dunham do not end their analysis at this point, however, since they want to avoid what we call a sociologistic fallacy. They want to make sure that their group-level finding cannot be ascribed solely to characteristics of the individuals themselves, but rather to social disorganization as a characteristic of the area. They want to hold constant *within* each area a series of extraneous individual characteristics that might account for the differing insanity rates. They see that, if schizophrenia were a function of the *individual's* birth place, for example, then the *area* differences in schizophrenia might "be explained on the basis of the varying proportions of the foreign-born in the different parts of the city." Accordingly, they make use of one form of structural analysis—segmental comparisons—by comparing segments of the several areas (groups) in which *individuals are alike* in respect to an individual characteristic, country of birth.

Figure **12-D**   *Data used in the Faris-Dunham analysis* [a]

(for selected areas)

Degree of disorganization of the area (X_g)

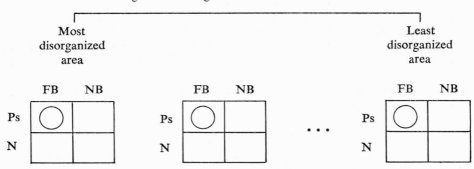

[a] Classification of individuals in each group: FB = foreign-born $(X+)$, NB = native-born $(X-)$, Ps = psychotic, and N = normal.

Nature of the Data.   We can see the principle of segmental comparisons by rearranging Faris and Dunham's data, as in Figure 12-D. Here we imagine that the ecological investigation makes it possible, first, to classify and arrange the areas (groups) according to degree of disorganization. Next, within each area, individuals in the population are divided into native-born and foreign-born segments, and a separate insanity rate is obtained for each segment. Then, by *comparing similar segments of the several areas* (the circled numbers in Figure 12-D), the researcher can control for the possible effects of the extraneous variable (the property of individuals in the segment) and make sure that the original finding holds—i.e., that there is indeed a group correlation between disorganization and rate of schizophrenia. Faris and Dunham, although they do not describe their analyses in these terms, report that they are convinced—by this and similar efforts to control for a possible "racial tendency toward psychosis" or for a "drift down into the slum areas" of the mentally abnormal—that "some factors" other than these "are necessary to explain these patterns [of psychosis] that are the same no matter which race or nationality inhabits the area."

Segmental comparisons among groups are useful, then, in testing whether a dependent variable is associated with a group property even within similar group segments--that is, even when certain relevant characteristics of the constituent individuals are held constant. This method is somewhat similar to the familiar multivariate procedure of holding constant through cross-tabulation a property of the cases (Unit 8), *except* that here the analysis actually subdivides each case (group) according to the properties of its parts. Each group is split into segments consisting of homogeneous individuals (parts).

DURKHEIM AND WITHIN-GROUP ANALYSIS

If Faris and Dunham want to make sure that the broad character of the group is related to the dependent variable (insanity rate) even when a segmental characteristic (nativity) is controlled, Durkheim uses a second form of structural analysis (within-group analysis) to test a converse hypothesis. Having found in a group analysis that a country's suicide rate is associated with its religious composition (see Unit 8), Durkheim wants to make sure that religion is not a spurious factor, that the Protestant and Catholic segments of the population do differ in suicide rate even when the whole "social environment" of the country (its religion, family composition, politics, and the like) is controlled.

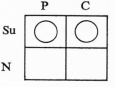
Country A

Figure **12-E**   *Data used in the Durkheim analysis* [a]

(for selected countries)

Country B

Country C

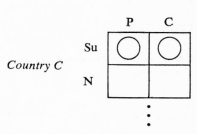

[a] Classification of individuals in each group: P = Protestant (X+), C = Catholic (X−), Su = commits suicide, and N = does not commit suicide.

Nature of the Data.   We have schematized the form of Durkheim's analysis in Figure 12-E. He does not attempt, as Faris and Dunham do, to measure or map the group variable of "social environment." He does not arrange the groups in any order, or make segmental comparisons *among* groups. But, working with one group at a time, he divides each, much as they do, into a segment composed of

Protestant individuals and a segment composed of Catholic individuals—for, as he says, in order to hold constant the effects of broad differences among groups, "two religions must be compared in the heart of a single society." By then comparing the Protestant segment with the Catholic segment *within* each of the groups, he is able to demonstrate his point that those segments characterized by Protestant values and institutions are indeed the ones with the consistently higher suicide rates. His within-group analysis shows *for every country* that Protestant individuals are more likely to commit suicide than Catholic individuals regardless of the character of the country.

TWO FORMS OF STRUCTURAL ANALYSIS

These examples begin to suggest the distinctive meaning of each form of structural analysis. The Faris and Dunham study illustrates how segmental comparisons may focus on the effects of a group factor (such as area disorganization) by holding constant the effect of a segmental characteristic (such as country of birth of individuals composing the group segments). The Durkheim analysis demonstrates how within-group analysis may focus on the effects of segmental factors (such as the religious institutions impinging upon individuals in different segments of the group) by holding constant any effect of the over-all characteristics of the groups (countries) themselves.

You can imagine how the two forms of structural analysis might fit together in a single study. Faris and Dunham might have undertaken a supplementary within-group analysis. By comparing the cell percentages within each group, they could learn whether the individual's country of birth—in addition to group disorganization—might be related to insanity rates. Conversely, Durkheim might have supplemented his within-group analysis with segmental comparisons to see whether, even among Protestants, the suicide rate varies with the religious composition of the country (the proportion of its inhabitants who are Protestant). The two forms of structural analysis combined may yield a variety of possible outcomes which help the researcher disentangle the joint effects of the independent variable as it refers, on the one hand, to the group, and, on the other hand, to the individual—or more properly, to similar individuals as they form segments of the group.

James Davis and Contextual Analysis

James Davis' study of small discussion groups exemplifies a different partial approach to the study of social systems—contextual analysis—which focuses on the individual rather than on the group (see Table 12-A). Davis uses data from questionnaires filled out by the 2,000 members of 172 Great Books discussion groups, in order to learn "what variables explained attrition and differences in attrition among these groups." In particular, his aim is to discover "how much of the process could be explained by individual characteristics of the members, and how much by characteristics of the groups themselves."

We shall review the formal procedure for contextual analysis as Davis uses it, and then consider what differences might occur in his findings if he were to use a structural analysis instead. We shall see how contextual analysis, like structural analysis, aims to separate the group effects from the individual effects of an independent variable. Both forms of analysis are also alike in the data with which they start. Yet the two handle these data quite differently, and may sometimes produce very different results. In structural analysis, *groups* are the research case **(P-I),** and properties of individuals refer to homogeneous segments of individuals within each group. In contextual analysis, on the other hand, *individuals aggregated* from many groups are the research case, and properties of groups are treated as contextual characteristics of discrete individuals.

AN INDIVIDUAL ANALYSIS

In principle, just as structural analysis clarifies and specifies a group analysis, contextual analysis clarifies and specifies an individual analysis. Although Davis does not present an individual analysis, we can imagine one designed to discover why it is that some individuals rather than others drop out of study groups. Each individual is coded as active or inactive in his group (X_i), and as dropping out or remaining a member of his group during the period under study (Y_i)—here the subscript i indicates the reference to individual, rather than to group, properties. For each group these individual data are cross-tabulated and entered in the cells of a group table in the usual manner. The cell data from all the group tables are then added together to provide an aggregate individual table— exactly comparable in form to Robinson's individual analysis in Table 12-C above. This analysis (presumably) shows that individuals who are active role players are more likely than inactive individuals to stick with the study groups.

INTRODUCTION OF THE CONTEXTUAL VARIABLE

But Davis, obviously not content with any such single-level analysis of individuals, wants also to take into account the composition of the group to which each individual belongs. He believes that the "role volume" of the *group* (the proportion of group members who are active role players) may have a further contextual effect on the individual's tendency to drop out when the effect of the individual's own activity-inactivity is held constant.

Now notice how Davis handles role volume of the group as a variable to be added to his analysis. He does not change the research case **(P-I)**—the case remains the individual, not the group. What he does do is to characterize (code) each individual to show the kind of group he belongs to. A property (role-volume) of the higher-level system now becomes a contextual characteristic of the individual member (for a discussion of contextual characteristics, see Kendall and Lazarsfeld, p. 215; Lazarsfeld and Barton, p. 190).

THE CONTEXTUAL ANALYSIS

Then Davis uses this additional variable in a further cross-tabulation of individuals. As in any multivariate analysis, he now interrelates all three variables—the original pair (X_i and Y_i) and the new contextual characteristic (X_c). In order to avoid excessive collapsing of the contextual variable, which theoretically can range from 0 to 100 per cent active in the group, he presents the data graphically in his Figure 1. This analysis helps him to disentangle two types of effects—the "group-level effect" of the contextual characteristic (when the individual characteristic X_i is held constant), and the "individual-level effect" of X_i (when the contextual characteristic is held constant).

Because of the obvious importance of this form of contextual analysis, considerable attention is paid to it in the sociological literature. The procedure has been formally stated by Peter Blau (1960), for example, and more recently by James Davis and some of his associates, who discuss several types of possible outcomes and their mathematical and sociological implications. (Davis, Spaeth, and Huson; see also the demographic analysis of rural and urban populations by the proximity of the area to the influence of an urban center, Duncan, 1961-b.) This procedure (variously said to study the "climate of opinion," "structural effects," or "compositional effects") involves, as David Sills defines it in a symposium on the subject, "characterizing individuals by some characteristic of the group to which they belong (the context), and then noting how individuals who are similar in other ways differ in their opinions or behavior in accordance with the group context in which they are located" (Sills, p. 572). It aims to assess "the effects of a given attribute, both as a characteristic of individuals and as a characteristic of the aggregates to which the individuals belong" (Davis, Spaeth, and Huson, p. 224).

Nature of the Data.   Let us now see how this procedure relates to our full set of data involved in any social system analysis. Figure 12-F is an imaginary rearrangement of Davis' materials, showing a few of the group tables in which individuals are cross-tabulated according to their activity-inactivity (X_i) and their readiness to drop out (Y_i). The marginal totals of X provide a collective measure (X_g) of the degree of activity (role volume) of the various groups. We have circled the marginal percentages of $X+$ because Davis uses these in indexing the contextual characteristic of each individual. The group tables are also arranged in columns in Figure 12-F according to the degree of group activity (X_g).

Now, Davis' only direct use of these group tables is in measuring the contextual variable. His main data are obtained by adding together for each column the cell information for all the group tables in the column, to give the aggregate individual tables for each column shown at the bottom of Figure 12-F. The circled figures in these aggregate tables are the percentages that Davis uses in his analysis (compare his Figure 1).

Figure **12-F**   *Data for the James Davis analysis* [a, b]

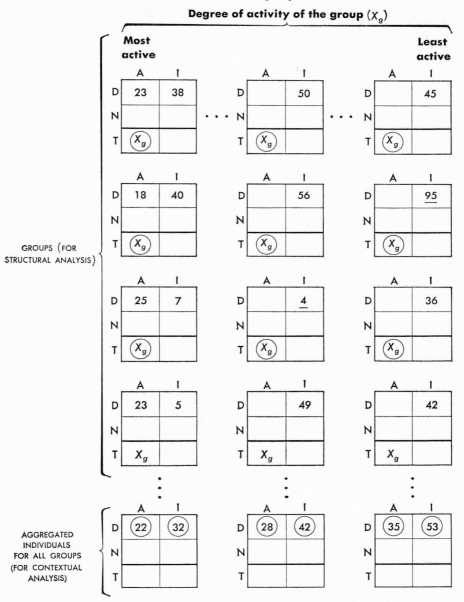

(*for selected small groups*)

[a] Classification of individuals: A = active (X+), I = inactive (X−), D = drops out of group, N = does not drop out of group, and T = marginal total of individuals.
[b] Numbers in cells are percentages.

COMPARISON WITH A STRUCTURAL ANALYSIS

Aggregating the group tables in this way directs major attention to the individuals rather than to the groups; hence, it may change the character of the group findings, as we noted but did not investigate in the study by Davis and Golden. Thus it will be instructive to consider what might be learned from a different analysis of these same data—a structural analysis, that does not aggregate the groups.

Let us now suppose that the primary research focus is not on the individual **(P-I),** but on the small group; and the dependent variable to be explained is the survival rate of the group. Indeed, we might question why Davis did not use a structural analysis—his own conceptual model seems to demand the use of the group as the research case, by assuming that role structures arise to meet the functional needs of small group interaction, so that "groups with different role structures might show differences in survival rates, since loss of members is a reasonable index of inability to meet needs." (In practice, to be sure, the chance variability would be high in an analysis based on Davis' small eleven-man groups. For an important discussion of a similar procedure for studying larger population distributions, see Bogue, 1959-a.) If Davis actually wants to explain the survival rate of groups (the proportion of members who do not drop out) rather than the staying powers of individuals, use of a contextual (rather than a structural) analysis might lead to possible atomistic fallacies. Let us explore the conditions under which such fallacies could occur.

Segmental Comparisons.   Once the researcher has established through a group analysis that groups with high proportions of active members do comparatively well at holding onto their members, he wants to make sure that this relationship is not explainable entirely in terms of an extraneous factor, a tendency for the inactive individuals in each group to drop out. Accordingly, he divides each group (as in the top portion of Figure 12-F) into an active segment and an inactive segment, and examines the survival rates for each of these group segments. He wants to determine whether the total activity of each group affects its survival rate among both its active and its inactive members. This is, of course, the same problem that Faris and Dunham faced (compare Figure 12-D above), although they had fewer groups and did not attempt to measure the group property systematically.

If the researcher wants to test the hypothesis that the more active the group is generally, the better its chances of survival—even among its inactive members—he should examine, as James Davis puts it, "the loss rates for . . . non-role players in groups which vary in the proportion of role players." In Figure 12-F, he uses the percentage in the upper right-hand cell of each group table, which shows the proportion of the inactive members who drop out. He would expect to find these percentages generally lower for groups in the left-hand column of the figure (the most active groups) than for groups in the center column, and lower in the center column than in the right-hand column (since the groups become less active as we read across the figure from left to right).

In order to demonstrate how segmental comparisons might differ from a contextual analysis of the same data, we have shown fictitious drop-out rates for the groups in Figure 12-F like this:

center column: 50, 56, *4*, 49 . . .
right column: 45, *95*, 36, 42. . . .

This extreme example tends to run counter to the hypothesis: except for the two italicized percentages, the range of drop-out rates is *higher* in the center column than in the right column. Here the general tendency observed from segmental comparisons of *groups* would be just the opposite of the finding of the contextual analysis, which shows for *aggregated individuals* (in the bottom row of Figure 12-F) that the drop-out percentage is indeed *lower* in the center column (42 per cent) than in the right-hand column (53 per cent). Such a distorted individual finding, which might lead to an atomistic fallacy in inferences drawn about groups, could occur if the (italicized) groups which are out of line with all the others happened to be unusually large.

Within-Group Analysis.   Or suppose that the researcher wants to test the hypothesis that the active members in a group are less likely than the inactive members to drop out, regardless of the character of the group (much as in Durkheim's analysis in Figure 12-E above). Here a test based on aggregated individuals might produce a different result from a test based on within-group analysis. Davis finds, looking at the aggregated individual data for any given column in our Figure 12-F, that this hypothesis is true. But we could again imagine pairs of drop-out percentages for the segments of each group (as suggested in the left column of group tables in the figure) that would read like this:

23, 38
18, 40
25, 7
23, 5

That is, instead of the right-hand percentage (for the inactive segment) being *consistently* higher than the comparable left-hand percentage (for the active segment), the hypothesis holds true in some groups but not in others. Such a result might lead the investigator to look for some additional factor that distinguishes between two such different types of groups. In a more complete social system analysis, the within-group arrangements might be found to vary with X_g (the proportion of active members in the group).

These examples show that, in principle, structural analysis, which is aimed to study groups, and contextual analysis, which is aimed to study individuals, are quite distinct. Each aims to study a set of questions that the other cannot, and the results of the two may lead to quite different interpretations. The differences arise, not because the two sets of data are actually incompatible, but because the researcher looks at only one set—and fails, in making his interpretations, to consider the possible implications of the alternative set.

An important principle, then, in using either contextual analysis or structural analysis is to recognize that each is a partial approach. It is important to understand fully what kinds of hypotheses each can test, what each can accomplish and what it cannot accomplish.

Ultimately, a social system analysis might uncover the full set of relationships, showing how the findings of the partial approaches fit together. Before considering what might be meant by such a social system analysis, let us take note of another scheme that is formally similar to contextual analysis—but applied at a different level of the social system.

The Analysis of Dyadic Networks

The study by Riley and Cohn demonstrates the viability for research based on dyadic relationships of the analytical schemes we are discussing, and illustrates the use of a contextual analysis and a structural (within-group) analysis of the same data. In this study, the conceptual model starts with the interpersonal relationships in adolescent peer groups within which control is effected through expectations, definitions, and sanctions, and from there goes on to postulate what the control process may be in such informal groups. Two sets of assumptions are selected from the model for empirical testing. The first of these, which we shall consider briefly here, deals with each group member as an object (O) surrounded by a network of other members as subjects (S's) who either like or dislike him. Cognitive differentiation is assumed to occur within each network, so that likers tend to note O's conformist traits, while dislikers tend to note his deviant characteristics. Such differentiated networks, the model further postulates, operate at the social system level as sanctions, with likers tending to reward O's conformity by approving it, and dislikers to punish O's deviance through disapproval.

The second assumption tested in the research states that, if combinations of approval and disapproval relationships are indeed functionally important for social control, such combinations would be expected to occur most often in the networks of objects who are successful and acceptable (high-status) members of the group. Here the model requires that the research procedures go beyond the level of the object as he is surrounded by his network of subjects—to fit together the many dyadic networks into the status structure of the school grade as a whole.

THE CONTEXTUAL ANALYSIS

One form of analysis used here in testing the assumption of cognitive differentiation in the networks is exactly parallel to the contextual analysis used by James Davis—though Riley and Cohn work at a different social system level, studying the role relationships of the object as the higher-level system (comparable to the group), and the individual subjects as the parts of the system. (Compare the two levels of the case with those used in the Rutgers object scale of status in Unit 9.) Davis studies the joint effects on an individual characteristic of two independent variables—one an individual characteristic, and the other a collective (contextual) characteristic of the group. Riley and Cohn study the joint effects on an individual (or dyadic) characteristic (how S defines O) of two independent variables—one an individual characteristic (whether or not S likes O), and the other a collective characteristic of the object (how many people like him). The aims of this particular analysis are stated in the study as Hypotheses 2 and 3.

Nature of the Data. You will see this parallelism if you study Figure 12-G and compare it with Figure 12-F for the Davis analysis. Figure 12-G shows the nature of the data used for a conformist characteristic (in this example), and for each of the sixteen other characteristics. In figure 12-G, each dyad is classified twice, according to whether or not S likes O, and again according to whether S thinks O has the particular conformist characteristic. These dyadic data are cross-tabulated in tables for each object—comparable to our usual group tables. These *object tables* are arranged in columns according to the collective characteristic (X_g)—O's likability. (Actually, the figure refers to only one category of dislikability of the object—since dislikability was employed as a second object-level variable.)

Here, as in the Davis analysis, these object tables are not used directly (except to determine X_g for each object). The cell data for all objects in a column are added together to give aggregate tables for the combined objects (at the bottom of Figure 12-G), and these data are used to test the two hypotheses. First, likers and dislikers (in adjacent pairs of cells) are compared (with likability controlled) to make sure the likers are the more apt to attribute the conformist trait. Then the effect of the object's likability is examined (in the cells for likers, and again in the cells for dislikers) to make sure that the more likable O is, the more apt he is to be regarded as a person who conforms.

SUPPLEMENTARY STRUCTURAL ANALYSIS

We have seen, however, that a contextual analysis sometimes conceals certain information—in particular, it might conceal very different patterns in the object (group) tables that are simply averaged out when the several groups are combined. These researchers feared some such possibility, thinking that there

Figure **12-G**   *Data used in the Riley-Cohn analysis* [a]

(*for networks of selected objects*)

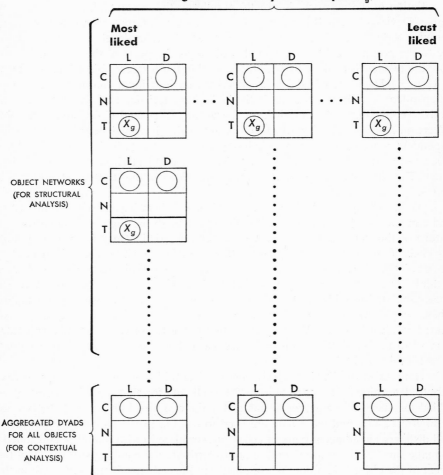

[a] Classification of dyads: L = S likes O (X+), D = S does not like O (X−), C = S attributes conformist trait to O, N = S does not attribute conformist trait to O, and T = marginal total for dyad.

might be hidden types of objects whose networks did not fit the hypothesis of cognitive differentiation.

Accordingly, they conducted another analysis—a within-group analysis— that studies *each object separately*. They wanted to make sure that for each particular person, "whatever his inherent qualities may be," the likers in his network stress his conformist characteristics, while the dislikers stress his deviant ones. Working with object tables similar to those in the top portion of Figure 12-G, they inspected the pairs of cells for consistency among the several object tables. (In practice, only a few of the objects—98 girls and 46 boys—had large enough networks to permit such an analysis.) This method exactly parallels Durkheim's use of separate analysis of each country, in which he holds constant the characteristics of the higher-level system (the country) in order to make sure of a consistency in the within-group patterns (of religion related to suicide).

Clearly, then, it is possible to supplement a contextual analysis by a further structural analysis, which will provide greater understanding of the nature of the data.

USE OF DATA BASED ON DYADS

Let us interrupt our general discussion of cross-level analysis to notice some of the special problems and possibilities of studying dyads—the smallest relational unit in the social system—and the variety of structures which they compose (see also Foa, 1962). Careful examination of the study of control networks illustrates the procedural details (as you have worked with these in Exercise II-5) which are involved in handling the two points of view for each dyad, and in collecting dyads to represent the total subject and object role of each individual. Comparison with the procedures used in the drug diffusion study by Coleman *et al.* (in Unit 10) shows again the importance of studying *all* the members of a group in order to determine its structure.

The experience of the study of control networks resulted in some generally useful devices for studying dyads with respect to both data-gathering and statistical testing. When each member of a large group is to be questioned about each other member, respondents tend to become confused, as well as bored. Therefore, Riley and Cohn used a "blue-card technique": after a respondent had recorded long lists of names in answer to many sociometric choice questions, he was given a blue card containing a list of teen-age characteristics. He then checked off the appropriate characteristics for each sociometric choice object while matching the name to each card—a device that held his interest and provided a great deal of necessary information.

After all these data had been analyzed, the problem of statistical testing arose. How is it possible to apply the usual tests, which assume statistical independence, to dyads which are in no sense independent of one another (since the same individual participates in many dyads both as subject and as object)? As you know from your experience in Exercise V-3, this difficulty was resolved here by basing the tests on aggregates of dyads which were clearly separated from one another—as relationships among boys in one school, for example, are independent of relationships among boys in a different school.

A Social System Analysis

What is the special feature of the social system analysis that distinguishes it from the partial analyses we have been considering? We have said that it classifies and analyzes groups, but that it also identifies the parts within each group, taking into account the internal arrangements of these parts. Thus it interrelates the group comparisons of a group analysis with the within-group and segmental comparisons of a structural analysis. Such full analyses, though generally rare, are entirely feasible when the research deals with very small groups. There is no example of a full social system analysis in the study selections in this book; but the study of friendship process by Lazarsfeld and Merton that we discussed in Unit 10—though it does not go beyond a group analysis—sets the stage for us to consider a social system analysis of two-person groups.

Table **12-E**   *Panel scheme for group analysis* [a]

Like (Xg)	Hold liberal views (Yg)	Observation II — Like(Xg) — Both — Hold liberal views (Yg) Both	One	Neither	One — Both	One	Neither	Neither — Both	One	Neither
Both — Both										
Both — One										
Both — Neither										
One — Both										
One — One	AB CD									
One — Neither										
Neither — Both										
Neither — One										
Neither — Neither										

(Left margin: Observation I)

[a] Adapted from Lazarsfeld and Merton, Table 3.

You will remember that Lazarsfeld's analytical scheme for this study deals with two group variables (X_g and Y_g) at two different periods of time. It shows (as in Table 12-E) how many members of each pair (two, one, or none) evince feelings of friendship. But it *does not show which* members. Thus, in our terms, it is a group analysis. Its data are similar to those in the Davis and Golden analysis, for example, except that more variables are interrelated.

In concluding his statement of this scheme, Lazarsfeld points to the very problem we call the danger of a sociologistic fallacy. His formalization, he says, does not take care of situations reported as "gratifying," "frustrating," and the like. He speculates that such situations may possibly belong on quite another level of inquiry, on a "psychological" level.

LIMITATIONS OF THE GROUP ANALYSIS

Let us now explore the character of Lazarsfeld's dilemma (see Riley and Moore, 1959) by examining Lazarsfeld's own form of analysis. It is our contention that the group scheme does not identify individual roles, and that some information is thereby lost. To maximize the usefulness of his scheme, we do not limit the measures to the simple dichotomies shown in his Table 3, but follow his suggestions for elaborating it, as in Table 12-E. Thus, on the friendship variable, for instance, the groups (pairs) are classified—not simply into friendship vs. nonfriendship—but further according to whether one, both, or neither of the partners claims friendship with the other. If this full group scheme is inadequate, then, it will fail to reflect the facts about those interpersonal processes which are described in Merton's conceptual model.

An Example. Let us, accordingly, see what will happen if we try to use the group scheme to classify some of the substantive information analyzed by Merton in his dialogue with Lazarsfeld, and set forth in the conceptual scheme. Take a particular fictitious couple, *AB*. At Time 1, *A* is liberal in his views, and also reports no particular liking for *B*. On the other hand, *B* is illiberal but likes *A*. Thus at Time 1, only *A* is liberal, and only *B* likes. When the researchers return at Time 2, however, a considerable change has taken place. At Time 2, both partners are liberal, and both like. *B* has shifted his views; he has become liberal so that he now agrees with *A*. And *A* is now found to reciprocate *B*'s friendship.

Where will this *AB* case be located in Lazarsfeld's scheme? At Time 1 (headings down the side of Table 12-E) it clearly belongs in the middle row, where only one of the partners likes and only one is liberal. At Time 2 (headings across the top) it belongs in the column where both like and both hold liberal views. Thus it is located in the cell marked *AB*.

Now that we have applied the scheme, let us ask the crucial question: To what extent does the scheme reflect *all* the original information? It certainly reflects the fact that two people came to agree in values and to reciprocate each other's friendship. But where does the table reflect the fact that the person *who* shifted his views is the same one who felt friendship for the other? Or, to put it another way, how can we determine from this table who shifted his views, as this was indicated in the original data? Obviously, this important element is missing.

The nature of this omission may become clearer if we consider the instance of another couple, *CD*. In many respects, the *CD* case is similar to the *AB* case. Both couples start out with only one partner liberal and only one partner liking the other. And at Time 2 both agree on liberalism and reciprocate each other's liking. But this *CD* couple is different in one crucial respect: this time it is not the friendly partner, but the indifferent partner, who shifts his views. Here, it is *D* who starts out as illiberal and as a nonliker, and it is *D* who makes both shifts—to liberalism and to liking *C* (while *C* does not change at all: he is still liberal and still likes *D*).

Obviously, the processes of internal shifting which occur in these two groups are quite different. The theorist might speculate about two quite different sets of explanations. In the *AB* case, *B* who likes *A* may well be motivated to learn to accept *A*'s values in the hope that *A* will approve and will come to reciprocate his liking. This seems to fit Merton's postulate that if one of the friends "is more deeply involved in the relationship than the other, his values are more likely to be modified to accord with the values of the less deeply involved." In the *CD* case, however, since *D* does not originally like *C,* he presumably is not motivated by the desire for reciprocal liking in this way. Some inducement of quite a different character may encourage *D* to shift his values (perhaps *C* is a powerful member of the group who can control its resources, thereby succeeding in superimposing his values upon other members like *D*). Whatever the underlying explanations, the *AB* process is clearly different from the *CD* process. And now let us ask: Is this difference reflected in the Table 12-E? We answer this by locating the *CD* observations in the table and find that *CD* belongs in exactly the same box as *AB*. That is, although *AB* and *CD* go through different processes, they seem in the group analysis to be exactly alike.

In other words, this group scheme fails to reveal the way the variables are patterned within and between the individual roles. The categories—"one likes" or "one is liberal"—do not tell us *who* likes, or *who* is liberal. Thus it fails to distinguish one group (*AB*) from another group (*CD*) in which the role patterning is different. In this sense it treats the group as an undifferentiated whole, and deals with each variable only as a collective property of the group.

A SOCIAL SYSTEM SCHEME FOR TWO-PERSON GROUPS

What seems to be needed is an analytical scheme that identifies and classifies groups as the group scheme does, but one that goes beyond the group scheme by identifying the individual roles and following them through the analysis. A scheme of this sort is necessarily much larger and more complex, since it represents the group not as an entity but as a system of individual roles. Such a scheme for social system analysis of two-person groups (which we shall call the *S*-scheme), as it might be used for the friendship-agreement data, is suggested in Table 12-F.

The *S*-scheme—and it can do this successfully with such small groups—deals simultaneously with the group and with its parts (the respective roles are arbitrarily labeled *M* and *N* to help us identify them). Each variable is measured —as friendship is measured, for example—both as a property of the group (which has a given number of likers) and as a property of the individual (who likes or

Table **12-F** *Scheme for panel analysis of two-person groups*

Observation II

Like (Xgi)	Hold liberal views (Ygi)	Like(Xgi)															
		Both				Only M				Only N				Neither			
		Hold liberal views (Ygi)															
		Both	M	N	Neither	Both	M	N	Neither	Both	M	N	Neither	Both	M	N	Neither
Both	Both																
	Only M	CD															
	Only N																
	Neither																
Only M	Both																
	Only M																
	Only N																
	Neither																
Only N	Both																
	Only M	AB															
	Only N																
	Neither																
Neither	Both																
	Only M																
	Only N																
	Neither																

Observation I

731

not). The subscript *gi* is used to indicate this dual reference to group and individual. Then each group is classified in the table in terms of the patterning of its constituent roles on the several interrelated variables.

Let us examine the potential use of the scheme, before assessing its characteristics more generally. We now classify *AB* and *CD* in order to see whether the scheme can in fact reflect the essential difference between the two couples. We identify as *M* one member of each couple—*A* and *C;* we identify *B* and *D* as *N*. Then, at Time 1, the *AB* group belongs in the row in which "only *N* likes" and "only *M* is liberal." The *CD* group belongs in a different row, in which "only *M* likes" and "only *M* is liberal." At Time 2 both groups belong in the column in which both like and both are liberal. Thus these two situations, which looked alike in the group scheme, are now seen in the *S*-scheme to be quite different. Here the important distinction between the two processes is recorded.

In practice, the *S*-scheme as applied here is not quite so unwieldy as Table 12-F implies. Although the form of the table helps to visualize the analysis, you can see that certain cells are similar because the arbitrary identifications *M* and *N* have no meaning here (as they might if *M* were always a husband, for instance, and *N* always a wife); thus the 256 cells of the table are actually reducible to 136. (For a full discussion of the *S*-scheme, see M. W. Riley, 1957.) Even 136 cells may be too many to handle, of course—which shows why the 81 cells of the group analysis (Table 12-E) or some other form of partial analysis are often used.

SOME ADVANTAGES OF SOCIAL SYSTEM ANALYSIS

Partial analyses serve only to examine selected relationships or to test specific hypotheses. They do not classify the full set of data. Thus, as this example begins to suggest, social system analysis is useful in delineating the system—or, to state it differently, in avoiding the fallacies that we listed at the outset. We have just seen how it avoids the possible sociologistic fallacies of an exclusive group analysis that may (Table 12-E) obscure the roles played by individual members as these fit together to constitute the over-all pattern of social change. Similarly, since the *S*-scheme identifies groups as well as roles, it forestalls the danger of going too far toward the psychologistic extreme of studying a social process as if it were contained entirely within the individual. And because the scheme does not focus exclusively on either system level, it is not subject to aggregative or atomistic fallacies.

A Simpler Example.   In order to see how such a social system analysis relates to the partial analyses we have been considering in this Unit, let us take a more comparable example that uses two variables at only a single time period. Table 12-G, which shows schematically the results of a study of liking and status (similar to the findings in Table 4-D above), is another *S*-scheme in which both groups and individuals are simultaneously identified on both variables. Here the groups (dyads) are again composed of only two individuals (the subject and the object in each dyadic pair). Incidentally, you can see here more easily than in Table 12-F the basis on which certain cells of the *S*-scheme may be combined when the role designations, such as *M* and *N,* have no intrinsic meaning. In dyads where only one member likes the other, it makes no difference whether this one is called *M* or *N* (we arbitrarily designate the liker as *M*); and in cells where both like (or neither like), it again makes no difference which partner is called *M* or *N.*

Table **12-G**   *Use of the S-scheme at a single time period* [a]

(*the figures in the cells represent numbers of groups*)

Liking (Y_{gi})	Both are high	Only *M* is high	Only *N* is high	Neither is high	Total groups
			10		
Both like	60	5	5	30	100
Only one					
(*M*) likes	30	2	18	50	100
Neither likes	10	5	5	80	100
			10		
Total groups	100	12	28	160	300

Status (X_{gi})

[a] Adapted from Riley, Cohn, Toby, and Riley, 1954.

A Complete Tabulation of the Data.   We now want to see how this *S*-scheme is obtained from the data we should use for the various partial analyses —to make sure that it is, as we have claimed, a complete tabulation of all the original data. We arrange these data in the familiar series of group tables, as in Figure 12-H. Imagine that we start our table by laying out every group *separately,* as we did in considering the partial analyses (Figures 12-D and 12-E). We now introduce the added feature of the social system analysis: we classify the groups into *all the possible relevant types* to permit us to tabulate and analyze these types.

First we classify the groups (by arranging them across and down in Figure 12-H) according to both group properties—the number of high status members in the group (X_g) and the number of likers in the group (Y_g). This *group analysis* shows the relationship between collective status and collective liking for the group. Thus reciprocal liking occurs in 60 out of the 100 groups in which both have high status, in 10 out of the 40 groups (in the combined center column) in which one has high status, and in only 30 of the 160 groups in which neither has high status.

Then we classify the groups further according to the possible types of internal arrangements. That means that we can now proceed with both types of structural analysis. If you study Figure 12-H, you will see how to make the

Figure **12-H**   *Data used in the status analysis* [a]

(*complete tabulation of dyads*)

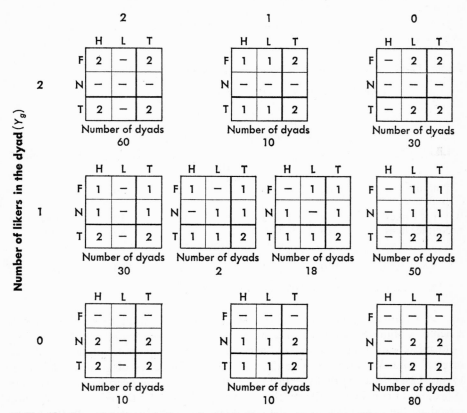

Number of high status members (X_g) **in the dyad**

[a] Classification of individuals in each dyad: H = S is high status (X+), L = S is low status (X−), F = S chooses O as a friend, N = S does not choose O as a friend, and T = marginal total for dyads.

segmental comparisons of a structural analysis in order to test the hypothesis that the proportion of likers is associated with the proportion of high status members even when the status of the individual members is controlled. We can, for example, compare the low status segments of groups in the center column of the figure (where one member is low status) and in the right column (where both members are low status). In the right column, there are 19 per cent of the groups (30 out of 160) in which all of the low status members like, 31 per cent (50 groups) in which half of the low status members like, and 50 per cent (80 groups) in which none like. In the center column, there are 70 per cent (10 + 18 of the 40 groups) in which all of the low status members like, and 30 per cent (10 + 2 groups) in which none like. Of course, in these small groups, to say that "all" of the low status members like means either that two of them like, or that one of them likes; but even here the segmental analysis shows the *range* of liking in the different segments. Similarly, we can compare the high status segments of groups in the left and the center columns, again with a result consistent with the hypothesis.

We can also make a structural *within-group analysis* to test the hypothesis that, within each group, individuals who are high status are more apt to like than individuals who are low status. Although, in these small groups, no comparisons are possible in the left or the right columns of Figure 12-H, we can see that out of the 40 groups in the center column, 20 groups show no relationship between status and liking, that only 2 groups support the hypothesis, whereas 18 display the opposite tendency. That is, the analysis shows that unreciprocated liking is more apt to be upward-directed than downward-directed, that the non-liker is the high status member more often than the liker. Note that this finding would not be discernible in a group analysis, which would not differentiate between the types of group tables in the center of Figure 12-H (nor between the identified roles "only *M*" and "only *N*" in Table 12-G).

We could also, if we wished, extract from Figure 12-H the materials for an individual or contextual analysis, although we have seen how the aggregating of groups may conceal the ranges and complexity of the group data.

This example for two-person groups thus demonstrates again the additional advantage of social system analysis over group analysis, and suggests some of the possibilities of simultaneous analysis of group-level and segmental variables. The full advantages of social system analysis cannot be seen in these very small groups, however, but will come into play only as appropriate methods are developed for handling larger groups. It should then be possible to overcome many of the limitations of the partial contextual and structural analyses, to discover the ranges of variation among group segments, to relate within-group arrangements to the over-all properties of groups, and to deal with many other complexities of cross-level relationships.

Some Methodological Implications

We have reserved for discussion in the last Unit the important questions of analyzing the levels of the social system because the appropriate procedures are only now developing. The studies we have examined have illustrated four types of partial analysis. We have seen how all four types complement each other, and are merely different ways of selecting from the same set of data. The *individual* and the *contextual analyses* aggregate information from the cells of the group tables. The *group analysis* utilizes only the marginal information from these tables. And the *structural analysis* may either use the full cell information for within-group comparison, or select one set of marginal data and one set of cell data for segmental comparison.

We have also considered in detail a possible *social system analysis* that will utilize this full set of data by classifying all possible types of groups (and their component individual members). This discussion suggests the potential value for many sociological studies of a social system analysis that identifies in respect to the variables under study both the groups and the individual members within each group. But the practical procedures discussed here apply only to the very simple instance of two-person groups.

PROBLEMS OF HANDLING LARGER GROUPS

How then can the methodologist of the future conduct social system analyses of larger groups? In simple situations involving relatively small samples of groups, we may often learn a good deal merely by laying out the group tables and inspecting them—as we did in considering fictitious examples of James Davis' small study groups (Figure 12-F). Davis' group tables might be ordered across and down according to the marginal percentages (the proportions of members active X_g, and the proportions dropping out Y_g). A thorough inspection—in addition to a structural analysis—would doubtless show more than the separate structural tests of specific hypotheses without any examination of the rest of the data.

Mathematically, the percentage data for each of Davis' study groups (as in Figure 12-G) might be represented by a dot in a three-dimensional space. We have seen how Kingsley Davis and Golden base a *group analysis* on societies located as dots in a *two-dimensional* space (Figure 12-B); and how the additional segmented information in the James Davis study could be handled by adding a *third dimension*. For some purposes, it may be worthwhile to develop methods of handling such a space by using partial or multiple correlation procedures. As more variables are added, the formulation rapidly becomes more complex; three collective measures for groups and the corresponding individual measures, for example, would require a seven-dimensional space.

Extensions of Partial Analyses. As long as the full procedures seem impractical or problematical, however, sociologists will continue to utilize—and to formulate more clearly—a variety of partial approaches, which will doubtless go far beyond the types we have been discussing. They will deal with more than two levels of the social system. They will work with a wide range of social system properties (as these have been classified, for example, in Barton, 1961; Merton, 1957, p. 309 ff.; or Borgatta and Cottrell). They will examine changes in system patterns over time (as in Newcomb, 1961, for example; or in Festinger, Schachter, and Back). New types of statistical tests will perhaps be developed which would help to rule out the possibility that apparent group effects might be accounted for merely by the fact that the individual members were originally selected from populations with different characteristics (see the incipient approach by Cohn *et al.,* 1960). And computers will be used to simulate the social system processes —even though these may not be fully formulated.

The discussions of this Unit have suggested certain principles that seem to apply to any partial analysis: the analysis should locate the selected data within the complete framework of the relevant information, and it should interpret the specific finding with reference to the model of a system as composed of inter-dependent parts.

IMPORTANCE OF THESE PROBLEMS

Immediate approaches to the problems of social system analysis must be worked out—and optimum resolutions ultimately found—if research is to bear upon many of the central problems of sociology—on how, for example, the relationship between two individual properties is affected by the kinds of groups to which the individuals belong; or how the relationship between two group properties is affected by the kinds of individuals of which the groups are composed.

Such problems become especially challenging whenever the researcher attempts to work back and forth between the social system and the individual actors who supply the motivations, attitudes, and actions that constitute the social process (see, *e.g.,* Heider; Lewin; Festinger, 1957; Newcomb, 1953-b). Many of the studies we have discussed give evidence of the need for methods of treating the individual's role as a link between the group to which he belongs and his own personality. The researcher may want to focus, for example, on the individual's feelings of gratification and deprivation both as part of the individual process of learning new values and developing new attachments, and as part of the group process of maintaining equilibrium or moving from one state of value-homophily to another. As sociologists, our emphasis is usually on the latter. But as Parsons and Shils state, while "all motivational processes of action are processes *in the individual personality,"* they may be viewed in terms of their functional significance for the social system as well as for the personality system (Parsons and Shils, 1951, p. 227). As Merton suggests, interpersonal relations in general may be studied so as to "deal with the consequences of these relations for those directly involved in them *and* for the larger group. . . ." (Merton, 1957, pp. 57–58. Italics added.) A dual research focus on individual and group will often result in a fuller understanding of personal and psychological processes as the basic mechanisms of the social system.

In short, as we solve the various special problems of social system analysis, we shall comply with Parsons' caveat that "it is essential to be able to follow [the] analysis from the level of ascertaining uniformities in the process of change in the structure of the social system, to that of analyzing the relevant motivational processes in the personalities of the individual actors" (Parsons, 1951, p. 50). Appropriate procedures will encompass societies and groups as systems of interacting and interrelated parts. They will refute charges of hypostatization brought against the use of societal rates by a Durkheim, and provide answers to the demand of a Weber for elucidation of the subjective aspects of group uniformities. They will deal with groups in terms of the relevant motivational processes that go on within the individual members, in terms of the overt acts and personal characteristics of these individuals as participants in the social process, and in terms of the functions of differentiated subsystems as these fit together into the macroscopic whole.

SUGGESTED READINGS FOR UNIT TWELVE

Barton, 1961; Peter Blau, 1960; Bogue, 1959-a; Davis, Spaeth, and Huson; Duncan, 1959; Durkheim, *The Rules of Sociological Method;* Kendall and Lazarsfeld, pp. 187–97; Lazarsfeld and Menzel; Merton, 1957, Chapter 9; Robinson, 1950.

QUESTIONS FOR REVIEW AND DISCUSSION

Review the following methodological terms as used in this Unit:

  aggregative fallacy
  atomistic fallacy
  psychologistic fallacy
  sociologistic fallacy

  contextual analysis
  group analysis
  individual analysis
  structural analysis
    segmental comparisons
    within-group analysis

1. Discuss the advantages and disadvantages of self-administered questionnaires in research on social systems. Cite examples from your own experience.

2. Describe and evaluate the use of the dyad as the research case in the drug diffusion study by Coleman, Katz, and Menzel (Unit 10), in the study of the friendship process by Lazarsfeld and Merton (Unit 10), and in the study of control networks by Riley and Cohn (Unit 12).

3a. Explain why James Davis, in studying the effect of a group variable (X_g) in a contextual analysis, holds constant the individual variable (X_i).

b. Consider Table D in Problem 5 of Exercise IV-1, which relates a collective variable (X_g) directly to a dependent variable (Y). Why is X_i not controlled in this table? In answering this question, take into account the particular character of the findings shown in the table.

4. Why do Durkheim and Faris and Dunham use different forms of structural

analysis? Consider for each of their studies whether and how the two forms of structural analysis might have been combined.

5. The forms of the Davis and Golden analysis (our Figure 12-B), and the James Davis analysis in Figure 1 of his study are somewhat similar in appearance, but have different meanings. Describe the formal similarity (and difference) and explain why the interpretations are on different levels.

6. Selvin's measure of leadership climate (Unit 9) uses an object measure of each leader obtained by collecting the answers of many individual trainees as subjects. Does Selvin run into any danger of a fallacy here? Discuss your reasoning in detail.

7. In Strodtbeck's analysis of certain properties of married couples (in Unit 8), how does he identify the roles of husband and wife? How does his analysis relate to the analytical schemes discussed in Unit 12?

8. In Exercise III-5 you derived a status scale from the Rutgers practice scale cards. Exactly how does the suggested Analysis B in Exercise II-5 (on the use of the dyad in analysis) relate to such a status scale?

9. How do the suggested analyses C and D in Exercise II-5 compare with the dyad analyses in the study by Riley and Cohn?

10. What use can you make of your experience from Exercise II-5 in handling the data for your research design in Exercise I-4?

11. Why does James Davis question all the members of his small groups, rather than a sample from each group?

12. How does James Davis study the relationship between "role volume within the group" and "the climate of interpersonal relationships outside the group?"

13. What research procedures do Riley and Cohn use to locate the "networks" of particular individuals in the larger structure of the school grade?

14. What *major* similarities and differences do you see in the conceptual models used by Davis and Golden and by Faris and Dunham? How do these similarities and differences affect the two research designs?

FINAL PROGRAM
DESIGNING A STUDY

In order to organize the principles of sociological research you have learned from the foregoing Units, you are to design (though not necessarily to carry out in full) a study of your own, to conduct some actual "pilot" operations making use of data, and to submit a brief report.

Preliminary statement of plans
Prepare in advance a brief statement of your objective and the nature of the project you propose to design.

Tentative report
Prepare a brief report (for final revision later) of your design and your "pilot" study experience. Your report should include:
(1) A short written statement of:
the objective of your project;
the theoretical framework within which you are defining the concepts you use;
the broad design, covering all the relevant items from the Paradigm of research design and the reasons for your choice of particular alternatives.
(2) Detailed exhibits of any actual or proposed instruments or worksheets for data-collection, coding, tabulation, or analysis. You should have tested at least one of these research instruments using actual data.

Class advisory sessions
Present your project (or a few selected projects) to the class, so that the class may acquire experience in evaluating actual research designs, and so that you may receive the questions, criticisms, and suggestions of others. Prepare for advance distribution to the class a brief summary of your report, and a paragraph stating the specific problem or aspect of work on which you want class advice.

Final report
Revise your tentative report, making full use of the class advisory sessions on your own and related projects. In preparing your final report, make specific reference to all the relevant materials you have learned from the studies, exercises, manual notes, commentaries, and class discussions throughout this program of study.

LIST OF WORKS CITED

Abel, Theodore, 1947. "The Nature and Use of Biograms," *American Journal of Sociology,* **53,** pp. 111–18.

Abel, Theodore, 1948. "The Operation Called Verstehen," *American Journal of Sociology,* **54,** pp. 211–18.

Ackoff, Russell L., 1953. *The Design of Social Research,* Chicago: University of Chicago Press.

Alpert, Harry, 1939. *Emile Durkheim and His Sociology,* New York: Columbia University Press.

Anderson, T. W., 1954. "Probability Models for Analyzing Time Changes in Attitudes," in Paul F. Lazarsfeld (ed.), *Mathematical Thinking in the Social Sciences,* Glencoe, Illinois: The Free Press.

Angell, Robert C., 1945. "A Critical Review of the Development of the Personal Document Method in Sociology 1920–1940," in L. Gottschalk, C. Kluckhohn, and R. C. Angell, *The Use of Personal Documents in History, Anthropology, and Sociology,* Bulletin 53, Social Science Research Council.

Angell, Robert C., and Ronald Freedman, 1953. "The Use of Documents, Records, Census Materials, and Indices," in Leon Festinger and Daniel Katz (eds.), *Research Methods in the Behavioral Sciences,* New York: The Dryden Press.

Bales, Robert F., 1950. *Interaction Process Analysis: A Method for the Study of Small Groups,* Cambridge, Massachusetts: Addison-Wesley Publishing Company, Inc.

Bales, Robert F., 1959. "Small-Group Theory and Research," in Robert K. Merton, Leonard Broom, and Leonard S. Cottrell, Jr. (eds.), *Sociology Today,* New York: Basic Books, Inc.

Barton, Allen H., 1955. "The Concept of Property-Space in Social Research," in Paul F. Lazarsfeld and Morris Rosenberg (eds.), *The Language of Social Research,* Glencoe, Illinois: The Free Press, pp. 40–53.

Barton, Allen H., 1961. *Organizational Measurement,* College Entrance Examination Board, New York.

Becker, Howard S., 1958. "Problems of Inference and Proof in Participant Observation," *American Sociological Review,* **23,** pp. 652–60.

Bell, Earl H., 1961. *Social Foundations of Human Behavior,* New York: Harper & Row.

Bendix, Reinhard, 1956. *Work and Authority in Industry,* New York: John Wiley & Sons, Inc.

Bendix, Reinhard, 1961. "The Image of Man in the Social Sciences: The Basic Assumptions of Present-Day Research," in Seymour Martin Lipset and Neil J. Smelser (eds.), *Sociology: The Progress of a Decade.* Englewood Cliffs, New Jersey: Prentice-Hall, Inc.

Berelson, Bernard, 1952. *Content Analysis in Communication Research,* Glencoe, Illinois: The Free Press.

Berelson, Bernard, 1954. "Content Analysis," in Gardner Lindzey (ed.), *Handbook of Social Psychology,* Reading, Massachusetts: Addison-Wesley Publishing Company, Inc.

Berger, Joseph, Bernard P. Cohen, J. Laurie Snell, and Morris Zelditch, Jr., 1962. *Types of Formalization in Small-Group Research,* Boston: Houghton Mifflin Company.

Beshers, James M., 1957. "Models and Theory Construction," *American Sociological Review,* **22,** pp. 32–38.

Bierstedt, Robert, 1957. *The Social Order: An Introduction to Sociology,* New York: McGraw-Hill Book Company, Inc.

Blalock, Hubert M., Jr., 1960. *Social Statistics,* New York: McGraw-Hill Book Company, Inc.

Blalock, Hubert M., Jr., 1961. "Evaluating the Relative Importance of Variables," *American Sociological Review,* **26,** pp. 866–74.

Blau, Peter, 1956. *Bureaucracy in Modern Society,* New York: Random House, Inc.

Blau, Peter, 1960. "Structural Effect," *American Sociological Review,* **25,** pp. 178–93.

Blau, Zena Smith, 1961. "Structural Constraints on Friendship in Old Age," *American Sociological Review,* **26,** pp. 429–39.

Blumer, Herbert, 1939. *An Appraisal of Thomas and Znaniecki's "The Polish Peasant in Europe and America,"* New York: Social Science Research Council.

Bogue, Donald J., 1959-a. "Population Distribution," in Philip M. Hauser and Otis

Dudley Duncan (eds.), *The Study of Population*, Chicago: University of Chicago Press, pp. 383–99.

Bogue, Donald J., 1959-b. *Population of the United States*, Glencoe, Illinois: The Free Press.

Boocock, Sarane Spence, 1961. "Perceived Family Value Congruency as Related to the Adolescent Girl's Future Self Image and Other Selected Factors," M.A. thesis, Rutgers University.

Borgatta, Edgar F., and Robert F. Bales, 1953. "The Consistency of Subject Behavior and the Reliability of Scoring in Interaction Process Analysis," *American Sociological Review*, 18, pp. 566–69.

Borgatta, Edgar F., and Leonard S. Cottrell, Jr., 1955. "On the Classification of Groups," *Sociometry and the Science of Man*, 18, pp. 409–22.

Borko, Harold (ed.), 1962. *Computer Applications in the Behavioral Sciences*, Englewood Cliffs, New Jersey: Prentice-Hall, Inc.

Braithwaite, R. B., 1960. *Scientific Explanation*, New York: Harper Torchbooks, Harper & Brothers.

Bredemeier, Harry C., Marcia L. Toby, and Matilda White Riley, 1954. "Reputation," in Matilda White Riley, John W. Riley, Jr., and Jackson Toby, *Sociological Studies in Scale Analysis*, New Brunswick, New Jersey: Rutgers University Press, pp. 126–44.

Bredemeier, Harry C., and Richard M. Stephenson, 1962. *The Analysis of Social Systems*, New York: Holt, Rinehart & Winston, Inc.

Bridgman, P. W., 1928. *The Logic of Modern Physics*, New York: The Macmillan Company.

Broom, Leonard, and Philip Selznick, 1958. *Sociology: A Text with Adapted Readings*, New York: Row Peterson and Company.

Browning, Harley L., 1961. "Methods for Describing the Age-Sex Structure of Cities," in Jack P. Gibbs (ed.), *Urban Research Methods*, Princeton, New Jersey: D. Van Nostrand Company, Inc., pp. 129–39.

Brunswik, Egon, 1956. *Perception and the Representative Design of Psychological Experiments*, Berkeley and Los Angeles: University of California Press.

Burgess, Ernest W., and Leonard S. Cottrell, Jr., 1939. *Predicting Success or Failure in Marriage*, Englewood Cliffs, New Jersey, Prentice-Hall, Inc.

Camilleri, Santo F., 1962. "Theory, Probability, and Induction in Social Research," *American Sociological Review*, 27, pp. 170–78.

Campbell, Angus, and George Katona, 1946. "A National Survey of Wartime Savings," *Public Opinion Quarterly*, 10, pp. 373–83.

Campbell, Donald T., 1957. "Factors Relevant to the Validity of Experiments in Social Settings," *Psychological Bulletin*, 54, pp. 297–312.

Campbell, Norman, 1956. "Measurement," in James R. Newman (ed.), *The World of Mathematics*, New York: Simon and Schuster, Inc., pp. 1,797–1,823.

Cannell, Charles F., and Robert L. Kahn, 1953. "The Collection of Data by Interviewing," in Leon Festinger and Daniel Katz (eds.), *Research Methods in the Behavioral Sciences*, New York: The Dryden Press.

Cannon, Walter B., 1939. *The Wisdom of the Body*, New York: W. W. Norton and Company, Inc.

Cartwright, Dorwin P., 1953. "Analysis of Qualitative Material," in Leon Festinger and Daniel Katz (eds.), *Research Methods in the Behavioral Sciences*, New York: The Dryden Press.

Casis, Ana, and Kingsley Davis, 1961. "Traits of the Urban and Rural Populations of Latin America," in Jack P. Gibbs (ed.), *Urban Research Methods*, Princeton, New Jersey: D. Van Nostrand Company, Inc., pp. 505–25.

Cattell, R. B., 1952. *Factor Analysis: an Introduction and Manual for the Psychologist and Social Scientist*, New York: Harper & Brothers.

Chein, Isidor, 1959. "An Introduction to Sampling," in Claire Selltiz, Marie Jahoda, Morton Deutsch, and Stuart W. Cook, *Research Methods in Social Relations*, Appendix B, New York: Henry Holt and Company, Inc.

Chinoy, Eli S., 1961. *Society: An Introduction to Sociology*, New York: Random House, Inc.

Clausen, John A., and Robert N. Ford, 1947. "Controlling Bias in Mail Questionnaires," *Journal of the American Statistical Association*, 42, pp. 497–511.

Cochran, William G., Frederick Mosteller, and John W. Tukey, 1953. "Statistical Problems of the Kinsey Report," *Journal of the American Statistical Association*, 48, pp. 673–716.

Cohen, Morris R., and Ernest Nagel,

1934. *An Introduction to Logic and Scientific Method,* New York: Harcourt, Brace & World, Inc.

Cohn, Richard, Frederick Mosteller, John W. Pratt, and Maurice Tatsuoka, 1960. "Maximizing the Probability that Adjacent Order Statistics of Samples from Several Populations Form Overlapping Intervals," *The Annals of Mathematical Statistics,* **31,** pp. 1,095–1,104.

Coleman, James S., 1960. "The Mathematical Study of Small Groups," in Herbert Solomon (ed.), *Mathematical Thinking in the Measurement of Behavior,* Glencoe, Illinois: The Free Press.

Coleman, James S., 1961-a. "Computer Simulation of Electoral Behavior." Paper delivered at the annual meeting of the American Sociological Association.

Coleman, James S., 1961-b. "Relational Analysis: The Study of Social Organizations with Survey Methods," in Amitai Etzioni (ed.), *Complex Organizations,* New York: Holt, Rinehart & Winston, Inc.

Coleman, James S., and Duncan MacRae, Jr., 1960. "Electronic Processing of Sociometric Data for Groups up to 1,000 in Size," *American Sociological Review,* **25,** pp. 722–27.

College Entrance Examination Board, Commission on Mathematics, 1959. *Introductory Probability and Statistical Inference.*

Conant, James B., 1952. *Modern Science and Modern Man,* Garden City, New York: Doubleday Anchor Books, Doubleday & Company, Inc.

Coombs, Clyde H., 1953. "Theory and Methods of Social Measurement," in Leon Festinger and Daniel Katz (eds.), *Research Methods in the Behavioral Sciences,* New York: The Dryden Press.

Cuber, John F., 1959. *Sociology: A Synopsis of Principles,* New York: Appleton-Century-Crofts, Inc.

Davis, James A., 1961. *Great Books and Small Groups,* Glencoe, Illinois: The Free Press.

Davis, James A., Joe L. Spaeth, and Carolyn Huson, 1961. "Analyzing Effects of Group Composition," *American Sociological Review,* **26,** pp. 215–25.

Davis, Kingsley, 1949. *Human Society,* New York: The Macmillan Company.

Davis, Kingsley, 1959. "The Myth of Functional Analysis as a Special Method in Sociology and Anthropology," *American Sociological Review,* **24,** pp. 757–72.

Davis, Kingsley, 1962. "Urbanization in India: Past and Future," in Roy Turner (ed.), *India's Urban Future,* Berkeley and Los Angeles: University of California Press.

Dean, J. P., 1954. "Participant Observation and Interviewing," in J. T. Doby (ed.), *An Introduction to Social Research,* New York: Stackpole.

Deming, W. Edwards, 1950. *Some Theory of Sampling,* New York: John Wiley & Sons, Inc.

Dodd, Stuart C., 1955. "Diffusion Is Predictable: Testing Probability Models for Laws of Interaction," *American Sociological Review,* **20,** pp. 392–401.

Dorn, Harold F., 1959. "Mortality," in Philip M. Hauser and Otis Dudley Duncan (eds.), *The Study of Population,* Chicago: University of Chicago Press, pp. 437–71.

Dornbusch, Sanford M., and Calvin F. Schmid, 1955. *A Primer of Social Statistics,* New York: McGraw-Hill Book Company, Inc.

Duncan, Otis Dudley, 1959. "Human Ecology and Population Studies," in Philip M. Hauser and Otis Dudley Duncan (eds.), *The Study of Population,* Chicago: University of Chicago Press.

Duncan, Otis Dudley, 1961-a. "Community Size and the Rural-Urban Continuum," in Jack P. Gibbs (ed.), *Urban Research Methods,* Princeton, New Jersey: D. Van Nostrand Company, Inc., pp. 490–504.

Duncan, Otis Dudley, 1961-b. "Gradients of Urban Influence on the Rural Population," in Jack P. Gibbs (ed.), *Urban Research Methods,* Princeton, New Jersey: D. Van Nostrand Company, Inc., pp. 550–55.

Duncan, Otis Dudley, and Beverly Davis, 1953. "An Alternative to Ecological Correlation," *American Sociological Review,* **18,** pp. 665–66.

Durkheim, Emile, 1933. *The Division of Labor in Society* (George Simpson, trans.), Glencoe, Illinois: The Free Press.

Durkheim, Emile, 1950. *The Rules of Sociological Method* (George E. G. Catlin, trans.), Glencoe, Illinois: The Free Press.

Durkheim, Emile, 1951. *Suicide* (John A. Spaulding and George Simpson, trans.), Glencoe, Illinois: The Free Press.

Edwards, Allen L., 1954. "Experiments: Their Planning and Execution," in Gardner Lindzey (ed.), *Handbook of Social Psychology,* Reading, Massachusetts: Addison-Wesley Publishing Company, Inc., pp. 259–89.

Eldridge, Hope, 1959. *The Materials of Demography: A Selected and Annotated Bibliography,* New York: Columbia University Press.

Festinger, Leon, 1953. "Laboratory Experiments," in Leon Festinger and Daniel Katz (eds.), *Research Methods in the Behavioral Sciences,* New York: The Dryden Press.

Festinger, Leon, 1957. *A Theory of Cognitive Dissonance,* Evanston, Illinois: Row, Peterson and Company.

Festinger, Leon, Stanley Schachter, and Kurt Back, 1950. *Social Pressures in Informal Groups,* New York: Harper & Brothers.

Fisher, R. A., 1937. *The Design of Experiments,* Edinburgh: Oliver and Boyd.

Foa, Uriel G., 1954. "Higher Components of Dyadic Relationships," in Matilda White Riley, John W. Riley, Jr., and Jackson Toby, *Sociological Studies in Scale Analysis,* New Brunswick, New Jersey; Rutgers University Press, pp. 181–87.

Foa, Uriel G., 1957. "Relation of Workers' Expectation to Satisfaction with Supervisor," *Personnel Psychology,* **10,** pp. 161–68.

Foa, Uriel G., 1962. "The Structure of Interpersonal Behavior in the Dyad," in Joan H. Criswell, Herbert Solomon, and Patrick Suppes (eds.), *Mathematical Methods in Small Group Process,* Stanford, California: Stanford University Press.

Ford, Robert N., 1954. "A Rapid Scoring Procedure for Scaling Attitude Questions," in Matilda White Riley, John W. Riley, Jr., and Jackson Toby, *Sociological Studies in Scale Analysis,* New Brunswick, New Jersey: Rutgers University Press.

Francis, Roy G., 1961. *The Rhetoric of Science: A Methodological Discussion of the Two-By-Two Table,* Minneapolis: University of Minnesota Press.

Franzen, Raymond, and Darwin Teilhet, 1940. "A Method for Measuring Product Acceptance," *The Journal of Marketing,* Vol. 5, No. 2, pp. 156–61.

Freedman, Ronald, Amos H. Hawley, Werner S. Landecker, Horace M. Miner, and Guy E. Swanson, 1952. *Principles of Sociology: A Text with Readings,* New York: Henry Holt and Company, Inc.

French, John R. P., Jr., 1953. "Experiments in Field Settings," in Leon Festinger and Daniel Katz (eds.), *Research Methods in the Behavioral Sciences,* New York: The Dryden Press.

Fruchter, Benjamin, 1954. *Introduction to Factor Analysis.* New York: D. Van Nostrand Company, Inc.

Furfey, Paul Hanly, 1953. *The Scope and Method of Sociology,* New York: Harper & Brothers.

Gaudet, Hazel, and E. C. Wilson, 1940. "Who Escapes the Personal Investigator?" *The Journal of Applied Psychology,* **24,** pp. 773–77.

Gendell, Murray, and Hans L. Zetterberg (eds.), 1961. *A Sociological Almanac for the United States,* New York: The Bedminster Press.

Gibbs, Jack P., and Kingsley Davis, 1961. "Conventional Versus Metropolitan Data in the International Study of Urbanization," in Jack P. Gibbs (ed.), *Urban Research Methods,* Princeton, New Jersey: D. Van Nostrand Company, Inc., pp. 419–36.

Glick, Paul C., 1959. "Family Statistics," in Philip M. Hauser and Otis Dudley Duncan (eds.), *The Study of Population,* Chicago: University of Chicago Press, pp. 576–603.

Glock, Charles Y., 1955. "Some Applications of the Panel Method to the Study of Change," in Paul F. Lazarsfeld and Morris Rosenberg (eds.), *The Language of Social Research,* Glencoe, Illinois: The Free Press, pp. 242–50.

Glueck, Sheldon, and Eleanor Glueck, 1950. *Unravelling Juvenile Delinquency,* New York: Commonwealth Fund.

Gold, David, 1958. "Comment on 'A Critique of Tests of Significance,'" *American Sociological Review,* **23,** pp. 85–86.

Goode, William J., and Paul K. Hatt, 1952. *Methods in Social Research,* New York: McGraw-Hill Book Company, Inc.

Goodman, Leo A., 1953. "Ecological Regressions and Behavior of Individuals," *American Sociological Review,* **18,** pp. 663–64.

Goodman, Leo A., 1962. "Statistical Methods for Analyzing Process of Change," *American Journal of Sociology,* **68,** pp. 57–87.

Goodman, Leo A., and W. H. Kruskal, 1954. "Measures of Association for Cross-Classifications," *Journal of the American Statistical Association,* **49,** pp. 732–64.

Gouldner, Alvin W., 1954. *Patterns of Industrial Bureaucracy,* Glencoe, Illinois: The Free Press.

Green, Arnold W., 1960. *Sociology: An Analysis of Life in Modern Society,* New York: McGraw-Hill Book Company, Inc.

Green, Bert F., 1954. "Attitude Measurement," in Gardner Lindzey (ed.), *Handbook of Social Psychology,* Reading, Massachusetts: Addison-Wesley Publishing Company, Inc., pp. 335–69.

Greenwood, Ernest, 1945. *Experimental Sociology,* New York: King's Crown Press.

Guilford, J. P., 1936. *Psychometric Methods,* New York: McGraw-Hill Book Company, Inc.

Guttman, Louis, 1950-a. "The Basis for Scalogram Analysis," in Samuel A. Stouffer, *et al., Measurement and Prediction,* Princeton, New Jersey: Princeton University Press, pp. 60–90.

Guttman, Louis, 1950-b. "Relation of Scalogram Analysis to Other Techniques," in Samuel A. Stouffer, *et al., Measurement and Prediction,* Princeton, New Jersey: Princeton University Press, pp. 172–212.

Guttman, Louis, 1954-a. "The Principal Components of Scalable Attitudes," in Paul F. Lazarsfeld (ed.), *Mathematical Thinking in the Social Sciences,* Glencoe, Illinois: The Free Press, pp. 216–57.

Guttman, Louis, 1954-b. "A New Approach to Factor Analysis: The Radex," in Paul F. Lazarsfeld (ed.), *Mathematical Thinking in the Social Sciences,* Glencoe, Illinois: The Free Press, pp. 258–348.

Guttman, Louis, 1954-c. "The Israel Alpha Technique for Scale Analysis," in Matilda White Riley, John W. Riley, Jr., and Jackson Toby, *Sociological Studies in Scale Analysis,* New Brunswick, New Jersey: Rutgers University Press, pp. 410–15.

Hagood, Margaret Jarman, and Daniel O. Price, 1952. *Statistics for Sociologists,* New York: Henry Holt and Company, Inc.

Hansen, Morris H., William N. Hurwitz, and William G. Madow, 1953. *Sample Survey Methods and Theory,* New York: John Wiley & Sons.

Hare, A. Paul, 1962. *Handbook of Small Group Research,* Glencoe, Illinois: The Free Press.

Hauser, Philip M., and Otis Dudley Duncan, 1959. "The Data and Methods," in Philip M. Hauser and Otis Dudley Duncan (eds.), *The Study of Population,* Chicago: University of Chicago Press, pp. 45–74.

Hawley, Amos H., 1950. *Human Ecology: A Theory of Community Structure,* New York: The Ronald Press Company.

Hawley, Amos H., 1959. "Population Composition," in Philip M. Hauser and Otis Dudley Duncan (eds.), *The Study of Population,* Chicago: University of Chicago Press, pp. 361–82.

Heider, Fritz, 1958. *The Psychology of Interpersonal Relations,* New York: John Wiley & Sons, Inc.

Hempel, Carl G., 1952. *Fundamentals of Concept Formation in Empirical Science,* Vol. 2, No. 7 of Otto Neurath, Rudolf Carnap, and Charles Morris (eds.), *International Encyclopedia of Unified Science,* Chicago: University of Chicago Press.

Henderson, L. J., 1937. *Pareto's General Sociology,* Cambridge, Massachusetts: Harvard University Press.

Henry, Andrew F., and James F. Short, Jr., 1954. *Suicide and Homicide,* Glencoe, Illinois: The Free Press.

Heyns, Roger W., and Ronald Lippitt, 1954. "Systematic Observational Techniques," in Gardner Lindzey (ed.), *Handbook of Social Psychology,* Reading, Massachusetts: Addison-Wesley Publishing Company, Inc., pp. 370–404.

Heyns, Roger W., and Alvin F. Zander, 1953. "Observation of Group Behavior," in Leon Festinger and Daniel Katz (eds.), *Research Methods in the Behavioral Sciences,* New York: The Dryden Press, pp. 381–417.

Hollingshead, A. B., 1949. *Elmtown's Youth,* New York: John Wiley & Sons, Inc.

Homans, George Caspar, 1950. *The Human Group,* New York: Harcourt, Brace & World, Inc.

Homans, George Caspar, 1961. *Social Behavior: Its Elementary Forms,* New York: Harcourt, Brace & World, Inc.

Hughes, Everett C., 1960. "The Place of Field Work in Social Science," Introduction to Buford H. Junker, *Field Work: An Introduction to the Social Sciences,* Chicago: University of Chicago Press.

Hyman, Herbert H., 1953. "The Value Systems of Different Classes: A Social Psychological Contribution to the Analysis of Stratification," in Reinhard Bendix and Seymour Martin Lipset (eds.), *Class, Status and Power: A Reader in Social Stratification,* Glencoe, Illinois: The Free Press, pp. 426–42.

Hyman, Herbert H., 1955. *Survey Design and Analysis,* Glencoe, Illinois: The Free Press.

Hyman, Herbert H., 1959. *Political Socialization,* Glencoe, Illinois: The Free Press.

Hyman, Herbert H., William J. Cobb, Jacob J. Feldman, Clyde W. Hart, and Charles H. Stember, 1954. *Interviewing in Social Research,* Chicago: University of Chicago Press.

Inkeles, Alex, and Peter H. Rossi, 1956. "National Comparisons of Occupational Prestige," *American Journal of Sociology*, **61**, pp. 329–39.

Jacobson, Allvar H., 1952. "Conflict of Attitudes Toward the Roles of the Husband and Wife in Marriage," *American Sociological Review*, **17**, pp. 146–50.

Jaffe, A. J., 1959. "Working Force," in Philip M. Hauser and Otis Dudley Duncan (eds.), *The Study of Population*, Chicago: University of Chicago Press, pp. 604–20.

Johnson, Harry M., 1960. *Sociology: A Systematic Introduction*, New York: Harcourt, Brace & World, Inc.

Kahn, Robert L., and Charles F. Cannell, 1957. *The Dynamics of Interviewing*, New York: John Wiley & Sons, Inc.

Katz, Daniel, 1953. "Field Studies," in Leon Festinger and Daniel Katz (eds.), *Research Methods in the Behavioral Sciences*, New York: The Dryden Press, pp. 56–97.

Katz, Elihu, 1961. "The Social Itinerary of Technical Change: Two Studies on the Diffusion of Innovation," *Human Organization*, **20**, pp. 70–82.

Katz, Elihu, and Paul F. Lazarsfeld, 1956. *Personal Influence: The Part Played by People in the Flow of Mass Communication*, Glencoe, Illinois: The Free Press.

Kelley, Harold H., and Edmund H. Volkart, 1952. "The Resistance to Change of Group-Anchored Attitudes," *American Sociological Review*, **17**, pp. 453–65.

Kendall, Patricia L., and Paul F. Lazarsfeld, 1950. "Problems of Survey Analysis," in Robert K. Merton and Paul F. Lazarsfeld (eds.), *Continuities in Social Research: Studies in the Scope and Method of "The American Soldier,"* Glencoe, Illinois: The Free Press.

Kendall, Patricia L., and Katherine M. Wolf, 1955. "The Two Purposes of Deviant Case Analysis," in Paul F. Lazarsfeld and Morris Rosenberg (eds.), *The Language of Social Research,* Glencoe, Illinois: The Free Press.

Kish, Leslie, 1949. "A Procedure for Objective Respondent Selection Within the Household," *Journal of the American Statistical Association*, **44**, pp. 380–87.

Kish, Leslie, 1952. "A Two-Stage Sample of a City," *American Sociological Review*, **17**, pp. 761–69.

Kish, Leslie, 1953. "Selection of the Sample," in Leon Festinger and Daniel Katz (eds.), *Research Methods in the Behavioral Sciences*, New York: The Dryden Press.

Kish, Leslie, 1959. "Statistical Problems in Research Design," *American Sociological Review*, **24**, pp. 328–38.

Kohn, Melvin L., and John A. Clausen, 1955. "Social Isolation and Schizophrenia," *American Sociological Review*, **20**, pp. 265–73.

Kornhauser, Arthur, and Paul B. Sheatsley, 1959. "Questionnaire Construction and Interview Procedure," in Claire Selltiz, Marie Jahoda, Morton Deutsch, and Stuart W. Cook, *Research Methods in Social Relations*, New York: Henry Holt and Company, Inc., pp. 546–87.

Landis, Benson Y., 1959. "A Guide to the Literature of Statistics of Religious Affiliation with References to Related Social Studies," *Journal of the American Statistical Association*, **54**, pp. 335–57.

Landis, Paul H., 1958. *Introductory Sociology*, New York: The Ronald Press.

Lazarsfeld, Paul F., 1944. "The Controversy Over Detailed Interviews: An Offer for Negotiation," *Public Opinion Quarterly*, **8**, pp. 38–60.

Lazarsfeld, Paul F., 1950. "The Logical and Mathematical Foundation of Latent Structure Analysis," in Samuel A. Stouffer, *et al., Measurement and Prediction*, Princeton, New Jersey: Princeton University Press, pp. 362–412.

Lazarsfeld, Paul F., 1954. "A Conceptual Introduction to Latent Structure Analysis," in Paul F. Lazarsfeld (ed.), *Mathematical Thinking in the Social Sciences*, Glencoe, Illinois: The Free Press, pp. 349–87.

Lazarsfeld, Paul F., 1959. "Problems in Methodology," in Robert K. Merton, Leonard Broom, and Leonard S. Cottrell, Jr. (eds.), *Sociology Today: Problems and Prospects*, New York: Basic Books, Inc., pp. 39–78.

Lazarsfeld, Paul F., 1962. "The Sociology of Empirical Social Research," *American Sociological Review*, **27**, pp. 757–67.

Lazarsfeld, Paul F., and Allen H. Barton, 1955. "Some General Principles of Questionnaire Classification," in Paul F. Lazarsfeld and Morris Rosenberg (eds.), *The Language of Social Research*, Glencoe, Illinois: The Free Press, pp. 83–92.

Lazarsfeld, Paul F., and Herbert Menzel, 1961. "On the Relation Between Individual and Collective Properties," in Amitai Etzioni (ed.), *Complex Organizations*, New York: Holt, Rinehart & Winston, Inc.

Lazarsfeld, Paul F., and Morris Rosenberg (eds.), 1955. *The Language of Social*

Research, Glencoe, Illinois: The Free Press.

Lazarsfeld, Paul F., and Wagner Thielens, Jr., 1958. *The Academic Mind,* Glencoe, Illinois: The Free Press, p. 147.

Lewin, Kurt, 1939. "Field Theory and Experiment in Social Psychology: Concepts and Methods," *American Journal of Sociology,* **44,** pp. 868–95.

Lewis, Oscar, 1951. *Life in a Mexican Village: Tepoztlan Restudied,* Urbana, Illinois: University of Illinois Press.

Liebman, Arthur, 1961. "Institutional Affiliations of Sociologists: 1950–1959," M.A. thesis, Rutgers University.

Lindzey, Gardner, and Edgar F. Borgatta, 1954. "Sociometric Measurement," in Gardner Lindzey (ed.), *Handbook of Social Psychology,* Reading, Massachusetts: Addison-Wesley Publishing Company, Inc., pp. 405–48.

Lipset, Seymour Martin, and Reinhard Bendix, 1959. *Social Mobility in Industrial Society,* Berkeley and Los Angeles: University of California Press.

Loomis, Charles P., 1960. *Social Systems: Essays on Their Persistence and Change,* Princeton, New Jersey: D. Van Nostrand Company.

Lundberg, George A., C. C. Schrag, and O. N. Larsen, 1958. *Sociology,* New York: Harper and Row.

Lynd, Robert S., and Helen M. Lynd, 1929. *Middletown,* New York: Harcourt, Brace & World, Inc.

Maccoby, Eleanor E., and Nathan Maccoby, 1954. "The Interview: A Tool of Social Science," in Gardner Lindzey (ed.), *Handbook of Social Psychology,* Reading, Massachusetts: Addison-Wesley Publishing Company, Inc., pp. 449–87.

MacIver, R. M., and C. H. Page, 1937. *Society: An Introductory Analysis,* New York: Rinehart and Company.

Mack, Raymond W., 1951. "The Need for Replication Research in Sociology," *American Sociological Review,* **16,** pp. 93–94.

Madge, John, 1962. *The Origins of Scientific Sociology,* New York: The Free Press of Glencoe.

McCarthy, Philip J., 1951. "Sample Design," in Marie Jahoda, Morton Deutsch, and Stuart W. Cook (eds.), *Research Methods in Social Relations,* New York: The Dryden Press.

McGinnis, Robert, 1958. "Randomization and Inference in Sociological Research," *American Sociological Review,* **23,** pp. 408–14.

McPhee, William N., 1961. "Note on a Campaign Simulator," *Public Opinion Quarterly,* **25,** pp. 184–93.

Meadows, Paul, 1957. "Models, Systems, and Science," *American Sociological Review,* **22,** pp. 3–9.

Menzel, Herbert, 1950. "Comment on Robinson's Ecological Correlations and the Behavior of Individuals," *American Sociological Review,* **15,** p. 674.

Mercer, Blaine E., 1958. *The Study of Society,* New York: Harcourt, Brace & World, Inc.

Merrill, Francis E., 1961. *Society and Culture* (2d. ed.), Englewood Cliffs, New Jersey: Prentice-Hall, Inc.

Merton, Robert K., 1947. "Selected Properties of Field Work in the Planned Community," *American Sociological Review,* **12,** pp. 304–12.

Merton, Robert K., 1957. *Social Theory and Social Structure* (rev. ed.), Glencoe, Illinois: The Free Press.

Merton, Robert K., 1959. "Notes on Problem-Finding in Sociology," in Robert K. Merton, Leonard Broom, and Leonard S. Cottrell, Jr. (eds.), *Sociology Today,* New York: Basic Books, Inc., pp. ix–xxxiv.

Merton, Robert K., Marjorie Fiske, and Patricia L. Kendall, 1956. *The Focused Interview,* Glencoe, Illinois: The Free Press.

Moore, Wilbert, 1959. "Sociology and Demography," in Philip M. Hauser and Otis Dudley Duncan (eds.), *The Study of Population,* Chicago: University of Chicago Press, pp. 832–51.

Moroney, M. J., 1956. *Facts from Figures,* Baltimore, Maryland: Penguin Books.

Moser, C. A., 1958. *Survey Methods in Social Investigation,* New York: The Macmillan Company.

Mosteller, Frederick, and Robert R. Bush, 1954. "Selected Quantitative Techniques," in Gardner Lindzey (ed.), *Handbook of Social Psychology,* Reading, Massachusetts: Addison-Wesley Publishing Company, Inc., pp. 289–334.

Mosteller, Frederick, Robert Rourke, and George Thomas, Jr., 1961. *Probability and Statistics,* Reading, Massachusetts: Addison-Wesley Publishing Company, Inc., pp. 285–313.

Mueller, John H., and Karl F. Schuessler, 1961. *Statistical Reasoning in Sociology,* Boston: Houghton Mifflin Company.

Murdock, George P., 1949. *Social Structure,* New York: The Macmillan Company.

Nagel, Ernest, 1955. *Principles of the Theory of Probability*, Vol. I, No. 6 of Otto Neurath, Rudolf Carnap, Charles W. Morris (eds.), *International Encyclopedia of Unified Science*, Chicago: University of Chicago Press.

Nagel, Ernest, 1961. *The Structure of Science*, New York: Harcourt, Brace & World, Inc.

Newcomb, Theodore M., 1953-a. "The Interdependence of Social-Psychological Theory and Methods: A Brief Overview," in Leon Festinger and Daniel Katz (eds.), *Research Methods in the Behavioral Sciences*, New York: The Dryden Press, pp. 1–12.

Newcomb, Theodore M., 1953-b. "Motivation in Social Behavior," in *Current Theory and Research in Motivation*, Lincoln, Nebraska: University of Nebraska Press.

Newcomb, Theodore M., 1961. *The Acquaintance Process*, New York: Holt, Rinehart & Winston, Inc.

Ogburn, William F., and Meyer F. Nimkoff, 1958. *Sociology*, Boston: Houghton Mifflin Company.

Parsons, Talcott, 1949-a. *The Structure of Social Action*, Glencoe, Illinois: The Free Press.

Parsons, Talcott, 1949-b. *Essays in Sociological Theory, Pure and Applied*, Glencoe, Illinois: The Free Press.

Parsons, Talcott, 1951. *The Social System*, Glencoe, Illinois: The Free Press.

Parsons, Talcott, 1961. "An Outline of the Social System" in Talcott Parsons, Edward Shils, Kaspar D. Naegele, Jesse R. Pitts (eds.), *Theories of Society*, Glencoe, Illinois: The Free Press, Vol. I, pp. 30–79.

Parsons, Talcott, and Robert F. Bales, 1953. "The Dimensions of Action-Space," in Talcott Parsons, Robert F. Bales, and Edward A. Shils, *Working Papers in the Theory of Action*, Glencoe, Illinois: The Free Press.

Parsons, Talcott, and Edward A. Shils, 1951. "Values, Motives and Systems of Action," in Talcott Parsons and Edward A. Shils (eds.), *Toward a General Theory of Action*, Cambridge, Massachusetts: Harvard University Press, pp. 45–275.

Parsons, Talcott, *et al.*, 1951. "Some Fundamental Categories of the Theory of Action: A General Statement," in Talcott Parsons and Edward A. Shils (eds.), *Toward a General Theory of Action*, Cambridge, Massachusetts: Harvard University Press, pp. 3–29.

Parsons, Talcott, Edward Shils, Kaspar D. Naegele, and Jesse R. Pitts (eds.), 1961. *Theories of Society*, Glencoe, Illinois: The Free Press.

Parten, Mildred, 1950. *Surveys, Polls, and Samples: Practical Procedures*, New York: Harper & Brothers.

Peak, Helen, 1953. "Problems of Objective Observation," in Leon Festinger and Daniel Katz (eds.), *Research Methods in the Behavioral Sciences*, New York: The Dryden Press.

Petersen, William, 1961. *Population*, New York: The Macmillan Company.

Pool, Ithiel de Sola (ed.), 1959. *Trends in Content Analysis*, Urbana, Illinois: University of Illinois Press.

Pool, Ithiel de Sola, and Robert Abelson, 1961. "The Simulmatics Project," *Public Opinion Quarterly*, **25**, pp. 167–83.

Proctor, Charles H., and Charles P. Loomis, 1951. "Analysis of Sociometric Data," in Marie Jahoda, Morton Deutsch, and Stuart W. Cook, *Research Methods in Social Relations*, New York: The Dryden Press.

RAND Corporation, 1955. *A Million Random Digits*, Glencoe, Illinois: The Free Press.

Riesman, David, and Nathan Glazer, 1954. "The Meaning of Opinion," in David Riesman, *Individualism Reconsidered and Other Essays*, Glencoe, Illinois: The Free Press.

Riley, John W., Jr., 1962. "Reflections on Data Sources in Opinion Research," *Public Opinion Quarterly*, **26**, pp. 313–22.

Riley, Matilda White, 1957. "Panel Analysis of Groups: Some Notes on Lazarsfeld's Formalization," New Brunswick, New Jersey: Rutgers Department of Sociology (mimeographed).

Riley, Matilda White, and Richard Cohn, 1954-a. "Problems in the Analysis of Two-Person Action Systems," in Matilda White Riley, John W. Riley, Jr., and Jackson Toby, *Sociological Studies in Scale Analysis*, New Brunswick, New Jersey: Rutgers University Press, pp. 210–37.

Riley, Matilda White, and Richard Cohn, 1954-b. "Problems in the Analysis of Larger Action Systems," in Matilda White Riley, John W. Riley, Jr., and Jackson Toby, *Sociological Studies in Scale Analysis*, New Brunswick, New Jersey: Rutgers University Press, pp. 238–67.

Riley, Matilda White, Richard Cohn, Jackson Toby, and John W. Riley, Jr., 1954. "Interpersonal Orientations in Small Groups:

A Consideration of the Questionnaire Approach," *American Sociological Review,* **19,** pp. 715–24.

Riley, Matilda White, Marilyn E. Johnson, and Sarane S. Boocock, 1963. "Women's Changing Occupational Role," *American Behavioral Scientist,* Vol. VI, No. 9.

Riley, Matilda White, and Mary E. Moore, 1959. "Analysis of Two-Person Groups: Some Notes on Lazarsfeld's Formalization." Paper delivered at the annual meetings of the American Sociological Association.

Riley, Matilda White, and Mary E. Moore, 1963. "Sorokin's Use of Sociological Measurement," in Philip J. Allen (ed.), *Pitirim A. Sorokin in Review,* Durham, North Carolina: Duke University Press, pp. 206–24.

Riley, Matilda White, and John W. Riley, Jr., 1951. "A Sociological Approach to Communications Research," *Public Opinion Quarterly,* **15,** p. 452.

Riley, Matilda White, and John W. Riley, Jr., 1954. "The Dyad, or Subject-Object Pair," in Matilda White Riley, John W. Riley, Jr., and Jackson Toby, *Sociological Studies in Scale Analysis,* New Brunswick, New Jersey: Rutgers University Press, pp. 150–80.

Riley, Matilda White, John W. Riley, Jr., Marcia L. Toby, and Richard Cohn, 1954. "Consensus," in Matilda White Riley, John W. Riley, Jr., and Jackson Toby, *Sociological Studies in Scale Analysis,* New Brunswick, New Jersey: Rutgers University Press, pp. 93–125.

Robinson, W. S., 1950. "Ecological Correlations and Behavior of Individuals," *American Sociological Review,* **15,** pp. 351–57.

Roethlisberger, F. J., and William J. Dickson, 1940. *Management and the Worker,* Cambridge, Massachusetts: Harvard University Press.

Rogoff, Natalie, 1953. "Social Stratification in France and in the United States," *American Journal of Sociology,* **58,** pp. 347–57.

Rose, Arnold M., 1953. "Generalizations in the Social Sciences," *American Journal of Sociology,* **59,** pp. 49–58.

Rose, Arnold M., 1956. *Sociology: The Study of Human Relations,* New York: Alfred A. Knopf, Inc.

Ryan, Bryce, and Neal Gross, 1950. *Acceptance and Diffusion of Hybrid Seed Corn in Two Iowa Communities,* Iowa State College of Agriculture and Mechanic Arts, Bulletin 372.

Ryan, T. A., 1959. "Multiple Comparisons in Psychological Research," *Psychological Bulletin,* **56,** pp. 26–47.

Ryder, N. B., 1959. "Fertility," in Philip M. Hauser and Otis Dudley Duncan (eds.), *The Study of Population,* Chicago: University of Chicago Press, pp. 400–36.

Selltiz, Claire, Marie Jahoda, Morton Deutsch, and Stuart W. Cook, 1959. *Research Methods in Social Relations,* New York: Henry Holt and Company, Inc.

Selvin, Hanan C., 1957. "A Critique of Tests of Significance in Survey Research," *American Sociological Review,* **22,** pp. 519–27.

Selvin, Hanan C., 1958. "Durkheim's *Suicide* and Problems of Empirical Research," *American Journal of Sociology,* **63,** pp. 607–19.

Selvin, Hanan C., 1960. *The Effects of Leadership,* Glencoe, Illinois: The Free Press.

Selznick, Philip, 1957. *Leadership in Administration,* Evanston, Illinois: Row, Peterson and Company.

Sewell, William H., and A. O. Haller, 1959. "Factors in the Relationship Between Social Status and the Personality Adjustment of the Child," *American Sociological Review,* **24,** pp. 511–20.

Shils, Edward, 1961. "The Calling of Sociology," in Talcott Parsons, Edward Shils, Kaspar D. Naegele, Jesse R. Pitts (eds.), *Theories of Society,* Glencoe, Illinois: The Free Press, Vol. II, pp. 1,405–48.

Siegel, Sidney, 1956. *Nonparametric Statistics,* New York: McGraw-Hill Book Company, Inc.

Sills, David L., 1961. "Three 'Climate of Opinion' Studies," *Public Opinion Quarterly,* **25,** pp. 571–73.

Simmel, Georg (Kurt H. Wolff, trans.), 1950. *The Sociology of Georg Simmel,* Glencoe, Illinois: The Free Press.

Simon, Herbert A., 1952. "A Formal Theory of Interaction in Social Groups," *American Sociological Review,* **17,** pp. 202–11.

Simon, Herbert A., 1957. *Models of Man,* New York: John Wiley & Sons, Inc.

Solomon, R. L., 1949. "Extension of Control Group Design," *Psychological Bulletin,* **46,** pp. 137–50.

Sorokin, Pitirim A., 1928. *Contemporary Sociological Theories,* New York: Harper & Brothers.

Sorokin, Pitirim A., 1937. *Social and Cultural Dynamics,* Vols. I and III, New York: American Book Company.

Srole, Leo, Thomas S. Langner, Stanley

T. Michael, Marvin K. Opler, and Thomas A. C. Rennie, 1962. *Mental Health in the Metropolis: The Midtown Manhattan Study,* New York: McGraw-Hill Book Company, Inc.

Stanton, Howard, Kurt W. Back, and Eugene Litwak, 1956. "Role-Playing in Survey Research," *American Journal of Sociology,* **62,** pp. 172–76.

Stephan, Frederick F., and Philip J. McCarthy, 1958. *Sampling Opinions: An Analysis of Survey Procedures,* New York: John Wiley & Sons, Inc.

Stevens, Stanley S., 1951. "Mathematics, Measurement and Psycho-physics," in Stanley S. Stevens (ed.), *Handbook of Experimental Psychology,* New York: John Wiley & Sons, Inc.

Stinchcombe, Arthur L., 1961. "On the Use of Matrix Algebra in the Analysis of Formal Organization," in Amitai Etzioni (ed.), *Complex Organizations,* New York: Holt, Rinehart & Winston, Inc.

Stouffer, Samuel A., 1930. *"An Experimental Comparison of Statistical and Case History Methods of Attitude Research,* University of Chicago Ph.D. dissertation.

Stouffer, Samuel A., 1934. "Sociology and Sampling," in L. L. Bernard (ed.), *Fields and Methods of Sociology,* New York: Long and Smith, pp. 476–87.

Stouffer, Samuel A., 1950. "An Overview of the Contributions to Scaling and Scale Theory," in Samuel A. Stouffer, *et al., Measurement and Prediction,* Princeton, New Jersey: Princeton University Press, pp. 3–45.

Stouffer, Samuel A., 1951. "Scaling Concepts and Scaling Theory," in Marie Jahoda, Morton Deutsch, and Stuart W. Cook (eds.), *Research Methods in Social Relations,* New York: The Dryden Press, pp. 681–711.

Stouffer, Samuel A., 1955. *Communism, Conformity, and Civil Liberties,* Garden City, New York: Doubleday & Company, Inc.

Stouffer, Samuel A., 1957. "Quantitative Methods," in Joseph B. Gittler (ed.), *Review of Sociology: Analysis of a Decade,* New York: John Wiley & Sons, Inc., pp. 25–55.

Stouffer, Samuel A., 1962. *Social Research To Test Ideas,* New York: The Free Press of Glencoe.

Stouffer, Samuel A., Edgar F. Borgatta, David G. Hays, and Andrew F. Henry, 1954. "A Technique for Improving Cumulative Scales," in Matilda White Riley, John

W. Riley, Jr., and Jackson Toby, *Sociological Studies in Scale Analysis,* New Brunswick, New Jersey: Rutgers University Press, pp. 372–89.

Strodtbeck, Fred L., 1958. "Family Interaction, Values, and Achievement," in David C. McClelland, *et al., Talent and Society,* Princeton, New Jersey: D. Van Nostrand Company, Inc.

Strodtbeck, Fred L., Rita M. James, and Charles Hawkins, 1957. "Social Status in Jury Deliberations," *American Sociological Review,* **22,** pp. 713–19.

Strodtbeck, Fred L., and R. D. Mann, 1956. "Sex Role Differentiation in Jury Deliberations," *Sociometry,* **19,** pp. 3–11.

Suchman, E. A., and Boyd McCandless, 1940. "Who Answers Questionnaires?" *Journal of Applied Psychology,* **24,** pp. 758–69.

Sussman, Leila, 1956. "F.D.R. and the White House Mail," *Public Opinion Quarterly,* **20,** pp. 5–16.

Sutherland, Robert F., Julian Woodward, and Milton A. Maxwell, 1956. *Introductory Sociology,* Philadelphia: J. B. Lippincott Co.

Swanson, Guy E., 1951. "Some Problems of Laboratory Experiments with Small Populations," *American Sociological Review,* **16,** pp. 349–58.

Taeuber, Conrad, and Irene Taeuber, 1958. *The Changing Population of the United States,* New York: John Wiley & Sons, Inc.

Thorndike, Edward L., 1910. "Handwriting," *Teachers College Record,* **11,** pp. 1–93.

Thorndike, R. L., 1942. "Regression Fallacies in the Matched Groups Experiment," in *Psychometrika,* **7,** pp. 85–102.

Thurstone, L. L., 1947. *Multiple-Factor Analysis: A Development and Expansion of the Vectors of the Mind,* Chicago: University of Chicago Press.

Thurstone, L. L., and Ernest J. Chave, 1948. *The Measurement of Attitudes,* Chicago: University of Chicago Press.

Timasheff, Nicholas B., 1957. *Sociological Theory: Its Nature and Growth,* New York: Random House, Inc.

Tippett, L. C. H., 1956. "Sampling and Standard Error," in James R. Newman (ed.), *The World of Mathematics,* New York: Simon and Schuster, Inc., pp. 1,459–86.

Toby, Jackson, 1961. "Early Identification and Intensive Treatment of Predelinquents: A Negative View," *Social Work,* Vol. 6, No. 3, pp. 3–13.

Toby, Jackson, and Marcia L. Toby, 1954. "A Method of Selecting Dichotomous Items by Cross-Tabulation," in Matilda White Riley, John W. Riley, Jr., and Jackson Toby, *Sociological Studies in Scale Analysis,* New Brunswick, New Jersey: Rutgers University Press.

Toby, Jackson, Matilda White Riley, Paul Fine, and Mary Moore, 1954. "Techniques for the Improvement of Object Scales," in Matilda White Riley, John W. Riley, Jr., and Jackson Toby, *Sociological Studies in Scale Analysis,* New Brunswick, New Jersey: Rutgers University Press, pp. 390–409.

Toby, Marcia L., and Mary Moore, 1954. "Object Scale Procedure: Using Hand Tabulation," in Matilda White Riley, John W. Riley, Jr., and Jackson Toby, *Sociological Studies in Scale Analysis,* New Brunswick, New Jersey: Rutgers University Press.

Tolman, Edward C., 1951. "A Psychological Model," in Talcott Parsons and Edward A. Shils (eds.), *Toward a General Theory of Action,* Cambridge, Massachusetts: Harvard University Press, pp. 279–361.

Turner, Ralph H., 1953. "The Quest for Universals in Sociological Research," *American Sociological Review,* **18,** pp. 604–11.

United Nations. Economic and Social Affairs Department, *Demographic Yearbook.*

U.S. Bureau of the Census, 1960-a. *Statistical Abstract of the United States: 1960,* Washington, D.C.: U.S.G.P.O.

U.S. Bureau of the Census, 1960-b. *Historical Statistics of the United States: Colonial Times to 1957,* Washington, D.C.: U.S.G.P.O.

U.S. Bureau of the Census, 1961. *Eighteenth Census of the United States: 1960,* Vol. I, Part A, Washington, D.C.: U.S.G.P.O.

U.S. Department of Health, Education and Welfare (annual). *Health, Education, and Welfare Trends,* Washington, D.C.: U.S.G.P.O.

Wallace, David, 1954. "A Case For—and Against—Mail Questionnaires," *Public Opinion Quarterly,* **18,** pp. 40–52.

Weber, Max, 1947. *The Theory of Social and Economic Organization* (A. M. Henderson and Talcott Parsons, trans.), Glencoe, Illinois: The Free Press.

Weiss, Robert S., and Eugene Jacobsen, 1961. "A Method for the Analysis of the Structure of Complex Organizations," in Amitai Etzioni (ed.), *Complex Organizations,* New York: Holt, Rinehart & Winston, Inc.

Westie, Frank R., 1957. "Toward Closer Relations Between Theory and Research: A Procedure and an Example," *American Sociological Review,* **22,** pp. 149–54.

Whiting, John M., 1954. "The Cross-Cultural Method," in Gardner Lindzey (ed.), *Handbook of Social Psychology,* Reading, Massachusetts: Addison-Wesley Publishing Company, Inc.

Whyte, William Foote, 1941. "Corner Boys: A Study of Clique Behavior," *American Journal of Sociology,* **46,** pp. 647–64.

Whyte, William Foote, 1951. "Observational Field-Work Methods," in Marie Jahoda, Morton Deutsch, and Stuart W. Cook (eds.), *Research Methods in Social Relations,* New York: The Dryden Press.

Whyte, William Foote, 1955. *Street Corner Society,* Chicago: University of Chicago Press.

Williams, Robin M., Jr., 1960. *American Society,* New York: Alfred A. Knopf, Inc.

Wilson, Logan, and William L. Kolb, 1949. *Sociological Analysis,* New York: Harcourt, Brace & World, Inc.

Winch, Robert F., 1952. *The Modern Family,* New York: Henry Holt and Company, Inc.

Wold, Herman, 1956. "Causal Inference from Observational Data," in *Journal of the Royal Statistical Society,* **119,** pp. 28–50.

Young, Frank W., and Ruth C. Young, 1963. "Toward a Theory of Community Development," in *Social Problems of Development and Urbanization,* Vol. VII of *Science, Technology, and Development,* United States Papers Prepared for the United Nations Conference on the Application of Science and Technology for the Benefit of the Less Developed Areas, U.S.G.P.O.

Young, Kimball, and Raymond W. Mack, 1959. *Sociology and Social Life,* New York: American Book Company.

Young, Pauline V., 1949. *Scientific Social Surveys and Research,* Englewood Cliffs, New Jersey, Prentice-Hall, Inc.

Zeisel, Hans, 1957. *Say It with Figures,* New York: Harper & Brothers.

Zelditch, Morris, Jr., 1959. *Sociological Statistics,* New York: Henry Holt and Company, Inc.

Zelditch, Morris, Jr., and Terence K. Hopkins, 1961. "Laboratory Experiments with Organizations," in Amitai Etzioni (ed.), *Complex Organizations,* New York: Holt, Rinehart & Winston, Inc.

Zetterberg, Hans L., 1954. *On Theory and Verification in Sociology,* New York: The Tressler Press.

NAME INDEX

(Page numbers from Volume II appear in *italics*.)

SUBJECT INDEX

(Page numbers from Volume II appear in *italics*.)